D1430060

# Quality Time for Students

## LEARNING IN AND OUT OF SCHOOL

OECD

LB
1060
.Q35
2011

HARVARD UNIVERSITY
GRADUATE SCHOOL OF EDUCATION
MONROE C. GUTMAN LIBRARY

This work is published on the responsibility of the Secretary-General of the OECD. The opinions expressed and arguments employed herein do not necessarily reflect the official views of the Organisation or of the governments of its member countries.

**Please cite this publication as:**
OECD (2011), *Quality Time for Students: Learning In and Out of School*, OECD Publishing.
*http://dx.doi.org/10.1787/9789264087057-en*


ISBN 978-92-64-08754-5 (print)
ISBN 978-92-64-08705-7 (PDF)

The statistical data for Israel are supplied by and under the responsibility of the relevant Israeli authorities. The use of such data by the OECD is without prejudice to the status of the Golan Heights, East Jerusalem and Israeli settlements in the West Bank under the terms of international law.

**Photo credits:**
Getty Images © Ariel Skelley
Getty Images © Geostock
Getty Images © Jack Hollingsworth
Stocklib Image Bank © Yuri Arcurs

Corrigenda to OECD publications may be found on line at: *www.oecd.org/publishing/corrigenda*.
PISA™, OECD/PISA™ and the PISA logo are trademaks of the Organisation for Economic Co-operation and Development (OECD). All use of OECD trademarks is prohibited without written permission from the OECD.

© OECD 2011

You can copy, download or print OECD content for your own use, and you can include excerpts from OECD publications, databases and multimedia products in your own documents, presentations, blogs, websites and teaching materials, provided that suitable acknowledgment of OECD as source and copyright owner is given. All requests for public or commercial use and translation rights should be submitted to *rights@oecd.org*. Requests for permission to photocopy portions of this material for public or commercial use shall be addressed directly to the Copyright Clearance Center (CCC) at *info@copyright.com* or the Centre français d'exploitation du droit de copie (CFC) at *contact@cfcopies.com*.

# Foreword

The OECD's Programme for International Student Assessment (PISA) represents a commitment by governments to monitor student achievement within an internationally agreed framework. In the decade since its first report was issued, PISA has become the most comprehensive and rigorous student assessment programme in the world. The countries participating in PISA together make up close to 90% of the global economy.

PISA 2006 focused on science literacy, although students' skills in mathematics and reading were also assessed. This report uses data from PISA 2006 to investigate the relationship between time spent in deliberate learning activities and student performance in school. While students acquire knowledge in myriad ways, the activities studied in this report are limited to school classes, after-school classes, and independent study or homework. As the report ultimately shows, the number of hours spent learning only partly influences performance in school; the quality of learning time is just as, if not more, important than the quantity.

This report was prepared and written by Francesca Borgonovi, Miyako Ikeda and Soojin Park, with editorial support from Marilyn Achiron, Simone Bloem, Marika Boiron, Niccolina Clements and Elisabeth Villoutreix. David Kaplan provided important analytical guidance in the developing of the report.

This report is published on the responsibility of the Secretary-General of the OECD.

**Lorna Bertrand**
*Chair of the PISA Governing Board*

**Barbara Ischinger**
*Director for Education, OECD*

# Table of Contents

**BOXES**

© OECD 2011  Quality Time for Students: Learning In and Out of School

## FIGURES

## TABLES

# Reader's Guide

### Data underlying the figures

The data referred to in this volume are presented in Annex B and, in greater detail, on the PISA website (*www.pisa.oecd.org*).

Five symbols are used to denote missing data:

a   The category does not apply in the country concerned. Data are therefore missing.

c   There are too few observations or no observation to provide reliable estimates (*i.e.* there are fewer than 30 students or less than five schools with valid data).

m   Data are not available. These data were not submitted by the country or were collected but subsequently removed from the publication for technical reasons.

w   Data have been withdrawn or have not been collected at the request of the country concerned.

x   Data are included in another category or column of the table.

### Country coverage

The statistical data for Israel are supplied by and under the responsibility of the relevant Israeli authorities. The use of such data by the OECD is without prejudice to the status of the Golan Heights, East Jerusalem and Israeli settlements in the West Bank under the terms of international law.

### Calculating international averages

An OECD average was calculated for most indicators presented in this report. The OECD average corresponds to the arithmetic mean of the respective country estimates.

### Rounding figures

Because of rounding, some figures in tables may not exactly add up to the totals. Totals, differences and averages are always calculated on the basis of exact numbers and are rounded only after calculation.

All standard errors in this publication have been rounded to one or two decimal places. Where the value 0.00 is shown, this does not imply that the standard error is zero, but that it is smaller than 0.005.

### Reporting student data

The report uses "15-year-olds" as shorthand for the PISA target population. PISA covers students who are aged between 15 years 3 months and 16 years 2 months at the time of assessment and who have completed at least 6 years of formal schooling, regardless of the type of institution in which they are enrolled and of whether they are in full-time or part-time education, of whether they attend academic or vocational programmes, and of whether they attend public or private schools or foreign schools within the country.

### Reporting school data

The principals of the schools in which students were assessed provided information on their schools' characteristics by completing a school questionnaire. Where responses from school principals are presented in this publication, they are weighted so that they are proportionate to the number of 15-year-olds enrolled in the school.

### Focusing on statistically significant differences

This volume discusses only statistically significant differences or changes. These are denoted in darker colours in figures and in bold font in tables.

### *Abbreviations used in this report*

ESCS   PISA index of economic, social and cultural status

GDP    Gross domestic product

ISCED  International Standard Classification of Education (OECD, 1999)

S.D.   Standard deviation

S.E.   Standard error

### *Further documentation*

For further information on the PISA assessment instruments and the methods used in PISA, see the *PISA 2006 Technical Report* (OECD, 2009a) and the PISA website (*www.pisa.oecd.org*).

# Executive Summary

At a time when the OECD and partner countries are trying to figure out how to reduce burgeoning debt and make the most of shrinking public budgets, spending on education, which averages slightly more than 6% of GDP among OECD countries, is an obvious target for scrutiny. Education officials, teachers, policy makers, parents and students are discussing the merits of shorter or longer school days or school years, how much time should be allotted to various subjects, and the usefulness of after-school lessons and independent study. This report, which draws on data from the 2006 cycle of the Programme of International Student Assessment (PISA), describes differences across and within countries in how much time students spend studying different subjects, how much time they spend in different types of learning activities, how they allocate their learning time and how they perform academically.

> **Across countries, the country average of learning time in regular school lessons is positively, but weakly, related to country average performance, while learning time in out-of-school-time lessons and individual study is negatively related to performance.**

Some 97% of students across OECD countries report participating in regular school lessons in mathematics and in the language of instruction, while 90% report participating in regular school lessons in science. Not only is the share of students studying mathematics and the language of instruction in school greater than that of those studying science, but students also report spending more time in regular school lessons learning mathematics and the language of instruction than they do learning science. Meanwhile, students spend more time in out-of-school-time lessons on mathematics and the language of instruction than on science, and students in partner countries and economies spend more time in out-of-school-time lessons than students in OECD countries.

> **Across countries, findings show that students tend to perform better if a high percentage of their total learning time, including regular school lessons, out-of-school-time lessons and individual study, is dedicated to regular school lessons.**

In both learning time spent in regular school lessons and in individual study, females spend more time than males, socio-economically advantaged students spend more time than disadvantaged students, students in private schools tend to spend more time than students in public schools, students in academic schools tend to spend more time than students in vocational schools, and students in urban schools tend to spend more time than students in schools in rural areas. However, students' socio-economic backgrounds may have a greater influence on learning than the individual characteristics of the schools. Across most countries, students with an immigrant background spend more time than native students in individual study.

> **Students who spend up to four additional hours a week doing homework or studying by themselves tend to perform better than those who spend less time in those activities; but beyond four hours per week, they do not necessarily perform better in proportion to the time they spend.**

Given that out-of-school-time lessons have different meanings and functions, both across and within countries, there are differences in students' involvement in these kinds of lessons, depending on student characteristics and the particular type of lesson. For example, out-of-school-time lessons with school teachers are favoured by males, socio-economically disadvantaged students, students in lower secondary schools,

and, especially in partner countries and economies, students in schools in rural areas. Meanwhile, one-to-one, out-of-school-time lessons with non-school teachers are favoured by females, socio-economically advantaged students, students in academic schools, students in private schools and students in urban schools.

While out-of-school-time lessons can enhance learning, these lessons could also reinforce inequalities, since they vary across socio-economic groups. Group lessons led by a school teacher tend to reduce the impact of socio-economic background on performance, since socio-economically disadvantaged students are more likely to attend this type of lesson and are, in turn, more likely to achieve higher scores than students who do not participate in any out-of-school-time lessons. In contrast, group lessons with a non-school teacher tend to reinforce the impact of socio-economic background on performance, since socio-economically advantaged students are more likely to attend this type of lesson and are then more likely to achieve higher scores than students who do not participate in any out-of-school-time lesson.

Students in countries that perform well in PISA spend less time, on average, in out-of-school-time lessons and individual study, and more time in regular school lessons than students in low-performing countries. The evidence implies that it is the quality of regular school lessons, not the quantity of learning hours, that makes the most impact on student performance across countries. This positive relationship between learning time in regular school lessons and performance is even more pronounced when the time students spend in regular school lessons is considered as a share of total learning time. Countries with low relative learning time in these lessons also share some educational system characteristics that are related to low overall performance: less human and material resources, less school autonomy, and fewer standardised external examinations of student performance.

**If a country wants to improve its average performance, it should encourage students from socio-economically disadvantaged backgrounds, male students, students in rural schools, students in public schools and students in vocational schools to spend more time learning science in regular school lessons.**

In general, students who spend more time learning science in regular school lessons tend to achieve higher scores, yet in many countries, students who spend a long time learning mathematics and the language of instruction in regular school lessons perform less well than students who spend a moderate amount of time learning in regular school lessons. This might be because students who spend a long time in regular school lessons in science are those who choose to do so in optional courses, because they are interested in science, while students who spend a long time in regular school lessons in mathematics and in the language of instruction are obliged to do so for remedial purposes. It is crucial, then, to make the most of learning time, since students have a limited amount of it in school, and to enhance students' understanding of why it is important to learn a particular subject.

**When students believe that doing well in science is very important, spending more time learning science in regular school lessons is an efficient way of improving their performance.**

# Students' Learning Time

## INTRODUCTION

At a time when OECD and partner countries are trying to figure out how to reduce burgeoning debt and make the most of shrinking public budgets, spending on education, which averages slightly more than 6% of GDP among OECD countries, is an obvious target for scrutiny. Education officials, teachers, policy makers, parents and students are discussing the merits of shorter or longer school days or school years, how much time should be allotted to various subjects, and the usefulness of lessons outside of school and independent study.

This report focuses on how learning time is used, both in and out of school. What are the ideal conditions to ensure that students use their learning time efficiently? What can schools do to maximise the learning that occurs during the limited amount of time students spend in class? In what kinds of lessons does learning time reap the most benefits?

To answer these questions, this report draws on data from the 2006 cycle of the Programme of International Student Assessment (PISA) to describe differences across and within countries in how much time students spend studying different subjects, how much time students spend in different types of learning activities, how students allocate their learning time and how they perform academically. PISA contains information on student performance and deliberate learning time in three specific subjects – science, mathematics and the language of instruction – and three specific settings – regular lessons at school (referred to as "regular school lessons" for the remainder of this report), out-of-school-time lessons, and individual study and homework (referred to as "individual study" for the remainder of this report). While learning may occur while students interact with friends, speak with neighbours, read magazines or go to the supermarket, this report examines the amount of time students spend on activities specifically intended for learning. These kinds of activities are defined as "deliberate learning" and include the amount of time, per week, that students report spending in regular school lessons, out-of-school-time lessons and individual study.

Other terms in this report are used to denote specific measures of students' learning time. "Absolute learning time" refers to the amount of deliberate learning time that students spend in each subject of science, mathematics or the language of instruction. "Relative learning time" refers to the proportion of total deliberate learning time in a given subject, either science, mathematics or the language of instruction, that is allocated to one of the three types of learning activities discussed in this report – regular school lessons, out-of-school-time lessons or individual study.

This report focuses strictly on students' deliberate learning activities and measures allocation of time for learning and for the opportunity to learn. Other constructs related to deliberate learning activities, such as engaged time (time when students are actively absorbing information) and quality of instruction time, were not captured in PISA 2006 data.

## OECD PROGRAMME FOR INTERNATIONAL STUDENT ASSESSMENT (PISA)

The Programme for International Student Assessment (PISA) is one of the most rigorous and comprehensive international studies assessing students' competencies in science, mathematics and reading. PISA measures to what extent students have acquired the knowledge and skills necessary for full participation in today's knowledge-based society. The programme also explores why students perform differently in different contexts by collecting a wealth of data on individual student characteristics, students' family backgrounds and the characteristics of schools and education systems. PISA also identifies which countries are successful in achieving both high student performance and an equitable distribution of learning opportunities and, in so doing, signals sound educational policies and practices.

PISA surveys assess the performance of 15-year-old students in reading, mathematics and science (the term "student" used in the rest of this report denotes a 15-year-old student unless otherwise specified). Since these students are nearing the end of their compulsory education in most countries, PISA offers an invaluable opportunity to map the skills and competencies of young people as they enter the job market for the first time.

The first PISA survey in 2000, took place in 32 countries and focused on the domain of reading. The second survey, in 2003, was carried out in 41 countries and focused on mathematics. In 2006, PISA assessed more than 400 000 students in 30 OECD countries and 27 partner countries and economies and focused on science. Each assessment covers the other two domains, albeit as minor subjects.

### Figure 1.1
### A map of PISA countries and economies

**OECD countries***

| | |
|---|---|
| Australia | Korea |
| Austria | Luxembourg |
| Belgium | Mexico |
| Canada | Netherlands |
| Czech Republic | New Zealand |
| Denmark | Norway |
| Finland | Poland |
| France | Portugal |
| Germany | Slovak Republic |
| Greece | Spain |
| Hungary | Sweden |
| Iceland | Switzerland |
| Ireland | Turkey |
| Italy | United Kingdom |
| Japan | United States |

*\* These are the countries that were members of the OECD at the time of the PISA 2006 main data collection in 2006*

**Partner countries and economies in PISA 2006**

| | |
|---|---|
| Argentina | Liechtenstein |
| Azerbaijan | Lithuania |
| Brazil | Macao-China |
| Bulgaria | Montenegro |
| Chile | Qatar |
| Colombia | Romania |
| Croatia | Russian Federation |
| Estonia | Serbia |
| Hong Kong-China | Slovenia |
| Indonesia | Chinese Taipei |
| Israel | Thailand |
| Jordan | Tunisia |
| Kyrgyzstan | Uruguay |
| Latvia | |

**Partner countries and economies in previous PISA surveys or in PISA 2009**

| | |
|---|---|
| Albania | Moldova |
| Costa Rica | Netherlands-Antilles |
| Dominican Republic | Panama |
| Georgia | Peru |
| Himachal Pradesh-India | Shanghai-China |
| Kazakhstan | Singapore |
| Macedonia | Tamil Nadu-India |
| Malaysia | Trinidad and Tobago |
| Malta | United Arab Emirates |
| Mauritius | Viet Nam |
| Miranda-Venezuela | |

## HOW PISA MEASURES STUDENTS' LEARNING TIME

In addition to assessment instruments, detailed student and school principal questionnaires are included in PISA, thereby ensuring that information about the students, their families and the schools they attend is collected. The questionnaires also gather information on students' attitudes, motivation levels and use of learning time. This report focuses on the part of the questionnaires that seek to find out how much time students spend learning science, mathematics and reading in deliberate learning activities, and how students allocate their learning time across different subjects.

In PISA 2006, the student questionnaire asked students to identify how many hours they spent learning different subjects in different settings. More specifically, questions probed students on the amount of time, per week, they spent studying science, mathematics, the language of instruction and other subjects in regular school lessons, out-of-school-time lessons, and individual study. Students indicated their learning time by ticking one of five possible categories: "No time", "Less than 2 hours per week", "2 or more but less than 4 hours per week", "4 or more but less than 6 hours per week", and "6 or more hours per week". The exact wording of the questions is displayed in Box 1.1.

---

### Box 1.1 **Student questionnaire items for learning time**

**Q31** **How much time do you typically spend per week studying the following subjects?**
For each subject, please indicate separately:
- the time spent attending regular lessons at your school;
- the time spent attending out-of-school-time lessons (at school, at home or somewhere else);
- the time spent studying or doing homework by yourself.

*<An hour here refers to 60 minutes, not to a class period>*
*(Please tick only one box in each row)*

| | | No time | Less than 2 hours a week | 2 or more but less than 4 hours a week | 4 or more but less than 6 hours a week | 6 or more hours a week |
|---|---|---|---|---|---|---|
| | **Science** | | | | | |
| a) | Regular lessons in science at my school | □₁ | □₂ | □₃ | □₄ | □₅ |
| b) | Out-of school-time lessons in science | □₁ | □₂ | □₃ | □₄ | □₅ |
| c) | Study or homework in science by myself | □₁ | □₂ | □₃ | □₄ | □₅ |
| | **Mathematics** | | | | | |
| d) | Regular lessons in mathematics at my school | □₁ | □₂ | □₃ | □₄ | □₅ |
| e) | Out-of school-time lessons in mathematics | □₁ | □₂ | □₃ | □₄ | □₅ |
| f) | Study or homework in mathematics by myself | □₁ | □₂ | □₃ | □₄ | □₅ |
| | **Test Language** | | | | | |
| g) | Regular lessons in *test language* at my school | □₁ | □₂ | □₃ | □₄ | □₅ |
| h) | Out-of school-time lessons in *test language* | □₁ | □₂ | □₃ | □₄ | □₅ |
| i) | Study or homework in *test language* by myself | □₁ | □₂ | □₃ | □₄ | □₅ |

---

© OECD 2011 *Quality Time for Students: Learning In and Out of School*

Students taking part in PISA 2006 not only reported the amount of time they spent in deliberate learning activities, they also reported the type of activities they participated in, including the type of out-of-school-time lessons. These included lessons in school-related subjects that were held outside normal school hours. Lessons could be held at school, at home or elsewhere and could be taught by either school or non-school teachers, tutors or staff. Students were asked to report whether they participated in the following activities: one-to-one out-of-school-time lessons, small group out-of-school-time lessons (lessons attended by fewer than eight students) or large group out-of-school-time lessons (lessons attended by eight students or more). They were also asked to report who (school teachers or non-school teachers) oversaw them during these lessons. The exact wording of the questions is displayed in Box 1.2.

---

### Box 1.2 **Student questionnaire items for out-of-school-time lessons**

**Q32**  **What type of out-of-school-time lessons do you attend currently (if any)?**
These are lessons in subjects that you are learning at school, that you spend extra time learning outside of normal school hours. The lessons might be held at your school, at your home or somewhere else. These are only lessons in subjects that you also learn at school.
*(Please tick only one box in each row)*

| | | Yes | No |
|---|---|---|---|
| a) | *One to one* lessons with a *teacher* who is also a teacher at your school | ☐₁ | ☐₂ |
| b) | *One to one* lessons with a *teacher* who is not a teacher at your school | ☐₁ | ☐₂ |
| c) | Lessons in small groups (less than 8 students) with a *teacher* who is also a teacher at your school | ☐₁ | ☐₂ |
| d) | Lessons in small groups (less than 8 students) with a *teacher* who is not a teacher at your school | ☐₁ | ☐₂ |
| e) | Lessons in larger groups (8 students or more) with a *teacher* who is also a teacher at your school | ☐₁ | ☐₂ |
| f) | Lessons in larger groups (8 students or more) with a *teacher* who is not a teacher at your school | ☐₁ | ☐₂ |

---

## WHY LEARNING TIME IS STUDIED

The strong association between learning time and academic performance is widely acknowledged in the literature. Not surprisingly, the more time students spend learning, on average, the higher their grades are (Fisher *et al.*, 1980; Clark and Linn, 2003; Smith, 2002). Over the years, PISA has consistently indicated that the competency levels of 15-year-old students in reading, mathematics and science differ greatly both across and within countries (OECD, 2001; OECD, 2004; OECD, 2007). One of the factors repeatedly found to be associated with students' academic performance is students' learning time. For example, students who spend more time in regular school lessons achieve higher scores in the PISA reading, science and mathematics assessment than those who devote less time to learning.

Ever since the seminal study by John B. Carroll (1963) on the degree of learning as a function of the time a student spent learning in relation to the time the student needed, educators and policy makers have attempted to understand how students' learning activities should be organised to maximise learning (Bloom, 1968). The literature suggests that optimising academic learning time is one of the key factors to improving academic achievement (Carroll, 1989; Hawley and Rosenholtz, 1984; Sheerens and Bosker, 1997; Marzano, 2003).

Thus, the length of time one spends participating in deliberate learning activities may be important, but not necessarily the most important factor in learning.

The basic premise of Carroll's model is that under fixed-time conditions, individual characteristics, such as inherent ability, motivation, social environment and schooling, work together with circumstantial factors, such as the quality of teaching, and translate into various degrees of learning and achievement. Learning time is thus necessary, but not sufficient, for acquiring knowledge. Effective learning ultimately depends on the way in which time is organised, the proportion of time dedicated to students' perseverance, or full engagement, in learning and the time students with varying aptitudes and motivation levels require to internalise concepts and elaborate ideas (Carroll, 1989).

Factors such as ability and motivation differ greatly among students (OECD, 2007) and are likely to have a strong influence on the rate of learning that occurs per hour to acquire knowledge and eventually mastery (Anderson, 1984). In other words, the learner plays a fundamental role in determining how well learning time is used.

In practice, not all time spent learning is the same, and Carroll points out that the association between learning time and achievement is likely to depend on the circumstances in which learning occurs. Individuals are constantly exposed to a multitude of stimuli. While learning takes place in a variety of formal and informal settings, not all learning is of equal value; young adults are endowed with different skills and competencies in a variety of specific domains, such as reading, mathematics and science. Research indicates that structured lesson time at school (referred to as "regular school lessons" in this report) is an important pre-requisite for students to develop the competencies that are assessed in the PISA science framework (Scheerens and Bosker, 1997; Seidel and Shavelson, 2007).

School-level factors, such as teaching practices, can also have an impact on academic performance across schools and classrooms as well as on subjects within the same classroom (Aaronson *et al.*, 2007; Hanushek, 1986). Less is known about how out-of-school-time lessons and individual study can promote academic achievement or be better organised to develop students' skills and impart knowledge.

Since deliberate learning activities, such as regular school lessons, are more apt to create a level playing field for students, it is valuable to comprehensively map students' involvement in them. Both the quantity and quality of opportunities that young people have to learn in informal situations are likely to vary significantly across social groups. Indirect evidence of this comes from studies examining possible causes for the social gradient in the cognitive skills of young children entering school (Hart and Risley, 1995; Natriello *et al.*, 1990; Huttenlocher *et al.*, 1991; Jencks and Phillips, 1998). In these studies, differences in informal learning opportunities can be attributed to: more restricted vocabulary used by adults in the social networks of children coming from disadvantaged backgrounds; lower participation rates in pre-school education among children from disadvantaged backgrounds; the lack of educational resources available to parents with little education; and the fact that the achievement gap between social groups tends to grow during school breaks, reflecting differences in what children are exposed to while outside of school and formal learning environments.

## AIMS AND ORGANISATION OF THE REPORT

This report contains a comprehensive and rigorous description of learning time in a comparative context and draws on data from 57 countries and economies. Its aim is to examine cross-country and within-country variations in students' participation in deliberate learning activities and links to academic performance in science, mathematics and reading. When interpreting the results, it is important to keep in mind the limitations of the PISA data as described in Box 1.3.

The report investigates how students organise their learning time and what effect this has on their academic performance. The questions posed by the report include:

## Do students from different countries organise their learning time and activities differently?

Chapter 2 responds to this question by examining whether the time students spend learning different subjects in different settings varies by country. The report provides a detailed overview of cross-country differences in how students organise their learning time across three subjects – science, mathematics and the language of instruction – and three types of activities – regular school lessons, out-of-school-time lessons and individual study. The latter half of Chapter 2 focuses on different types of out-of-school-time lessons and describes patterns of students' learning time spent in these different types of lessons across countries.

## Do students from different population sub-groups within countries organise their learning time and activities differently?

Chapter 3 investigates within-country variations in deliberate learning time and activities by comparing differences in the amount of learning time, patterns of learning time allocation across different settings, and participation rates in the different types of out-of-school-time lessons for various student sub-groups. First, the chapter focuses on individual characteristics of students, such as gender, socio-economic background and immigrant background. Then it examines the structural characteristics of schools and assesses whether students' deliberate learning time and activities are related to the characteristics of the schools themselves, such as upper secondary or lower secondary, public or private, academic or vocational and school location.

## What are the cross-country and within-country relationships between learning time and performance?

Chapter 4 begins by examining the relationship across countries and then looks at the relationship within countries. While how much time students spend in deliberate learning activities is important in relation to performance, how students spend their time learning is also important. This chapter also closely examines the use of learning time in regular school lessons and out-of-school-time lessons.

Chapters 2 and 3 also present detailed descriptive statistics on the time students spend learning, which will help highlight the relationship between students' learning time and their academic performance.

### Box 1.3 **Interpreting the data on students' learning time**

The data on students' learning time used in this report are based on 15-year-old students' self-reports on their "typical" use of time per week at the time of the PISA data collection. The time students spend learning each subject might vary according to the week. The number of instruction weeks per year may also vary across education systems, depending on the length of the school year and vacation time. The scatter plot below presents the relationship between the numbers of hours per week and the number of hours per year spent in regular school lessons in science. The system-level data on the number of weeks of instruction time, as part of the teachers' working time (*Education at a Glance 2009*, OECD), is used as a proxy for the number of instruction weeks per year in each education system. This is then multiplied by the number of school lessons per week, taken from the students' reports in PISA. This linear relationship between two indicators, as seen in the scatter plot, confirms that the numbers of hours per week spent in regular school lessons could be a good proxy for the numbers of hours per year spent in regular school lessons.

**The relationship between learning hours per week and learning hours per year**

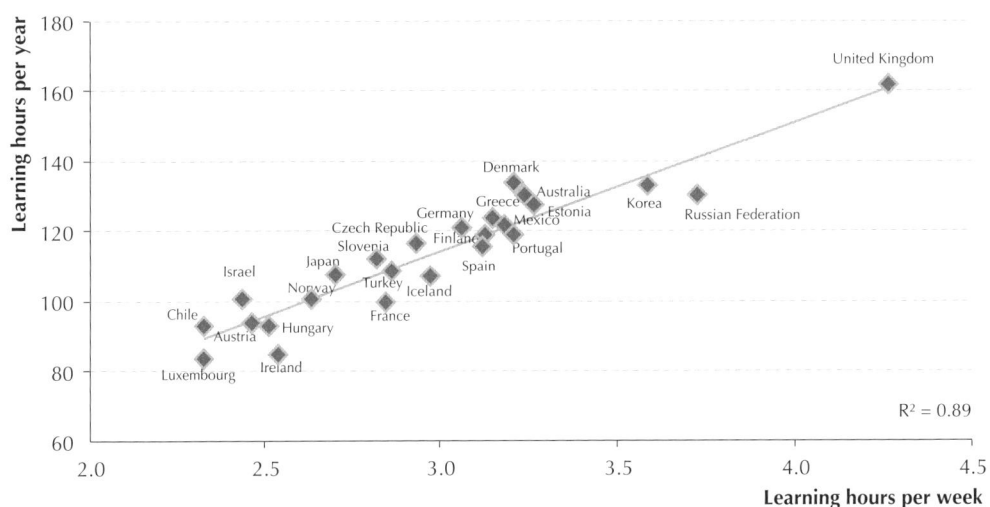

Source: *OECD PISA Database 2006*, Table 2.2a, *EAG Database 2009*, Table D4.2.

There are several reasons to be careful when interpreting the data. The deliberate learning time that students report in PISA may be only partially indicative of the learning time that shapes students' educational experiences. Earlier schooling experiences should be considered to develop a complete picture of a student's learning time. For example, students might spend more time in out-of-school-time lessons or individual study during a year when they have an entrance or exit examination.

In addition, the nature of out-of-school-time lessons is not necessarily the same across countries and even within countries. Even when students report attending the same type of out-of-school-time lessons, they might attend a lesson with different incentives and objectives. For example, some schools offer additional lessons to students who need remedial education, while other schools offer them to students who seek further enrichment. In some countries, out-of-school-time lessons with school teachers are systematic and standardised across schools, while in other countries these are organised by individual schools and the quality of lessons varies greatly from school to school.

...

© OECD 2011 Quality Time for Students: Learning In and Out of School

...

As practice varies among and within countries, it is difficult to generalise about the differences between out-of-school-time lessons with school teachers and those with non-school teachers. In some countries, tuition fees are charged for out-of-school-time lessons with non-school teachers, but fees are not charged for lessons with school teachers. In other countries, the opposite is true, or the setup of out-of-school-time lessons with any kind of teacher may be entirely different. Since socio-economically disadvantaged families may have difficulties paying additional tuition fees, out-of-school-time lessons could contribute to an inequality in educational opportunities. Given that out-of-school-time lessons across and within countries vary so much, and because this variability is not captured in the data in this report, it is impossible to generalise about the effects of out-of-school-time lessons.

Other factors related to out-of-school-time lessons must also be considered, such as the cost of lessons, quality of teaching, resources (textbooks, school materials, etc.) used during lessons and motivation of students to participate in lessons.

Examining the relationship between learning time and performance discussed in Chapter 4 is especially complex. Because the analysis is based on cross-sectional data, it is difficult to determine the causality of the relationships. For example, students may spend more time in out-of-school-time lessons because their parents, their teachers or they themselves might think that they need to catch up with other students by attending extra classes. On the other hand, students may spend more time engaging in individual study because they require more time than other students to complete a certain number of tasks.

# References

**Aaronson, D., L. Barrow** and **W. Sander** (2007), "Teachers and student achievement in the Chicago Public High Schools," *Journal of Labor Economics*, Vol. 25, No. 1, pp. 95-135.

**Carroll, J.B.** (1963), *A model of school learning*, Teachers College Record, Vol. 64, pp. 723-733.

**Carroll, J.B.** (1989), "The Carroll Model: A 25-Year Retrospective and Prospective View," *Educational Researcher*, Vol. 18, No. 1, pp. 26-31.

**Clark, D. and M.C. Linn** (2003), Designing for Knowledge Integration: The Impact of Instructional Time, *Journal of the Learning Sciences*, Vol. 12, No. 4, pp. 451-493.

**Fisher, C.W.,** *et al.* (1980), "Teaching behaviors, academic learning time and student achievement: An Overview," in D. Denham and A. Lieberman (eds.), *Time to Learn*, National Institutes of Education, California, pp. 7-32.

**Hanushek, E.A.** (1986), "The economics of schooling: Production and efficiency in public schools," *Journal of Economic Literature*, Vol. 24, No. 3, pp. 1141-1178.

**Hart, B.** and **T. Risley** (1995), *Meaningful Differences in Everyday Parenting and Intellectual Development in Young American Children*, Brookes, Baltimore.

**Hawley, W.D.** and **S.J. Rosenholtz** (1984), Effective teaching, *Peabody Journal of Education*, Vol. 61, No. 4, pp. 15-52.

**Huttenlocher, J.** *et al.* (1991), "Early Vocabulary Growth: Relation to Language Input and Gender", *Developmental Psychology*, Vol. 27, No. 2, pp. 236-248.

**Jencks, C.** and **M. Phillips,** (1998), *The Black-White Test Score Gap*, Brookings Institution Press, Washington, D.C.

**Marzano, R.J.** (2003), *What works in schools: Translating research into action*, Association for Supervision and Curriculum Development, Alexandria, Virginia.

**Natriello, G., E.L. McDill** and **A.M. Pallas** (1990), *Schooling Disadvantaged Children: Racing Against Catastrophe*, Teachers College Press, New York.

**OECD** (1999), *Classifying Educational Programmes: Manual for ISCED-97 Implementation in OECD Countries,* OECD Publishing.

**OECD** (2001), *Knowledge and Skills for Life: First Results from PISA 2000,* OECD Publishing.

**OECD** (2004), *Learning for Tomorrow's World: First Results from PISA 2003*, OECD Publishing.

**OECD** (2007), *PISA 2006 Science Competencies for Tomorrow's World*, OECD Publishing.

**OECD** (2009), *Education at a Glance 2009: OECD Indicators*, OECD Publishing.

**Seidel, T.** and **R. Shavelson** (2007), "Teaching Effectiveness Research in the Past Decade: The Role of Theory and Research Design in Disentangling Meta-Analysis Results," *Review of Educational Research*, Vol. 77, No. 4, pp. 454-499.

**Sheerens, J.** and **R.J. Bosker** (1997), "The Foundations of Educational Effectiveness," *International Review of Education*, Vol. 45, No. 1, pp. 113-120.

**Smith, B.** (2002), "Quantity Matters: Annual Instructional Time in an Urban School System," *Educational Administration Quarterly*, Vol. 36, No. 5, pp. 652-682.

# Patterns of Students' Learning Time

## INTRODUCTION

How much time do students spend learning science, mathematics and the language of instruction through deliberate learning activities? In PISA 2006, students were asked to report how much time they typically spent per week studying these three subjects in deliberate learning activities, such as regular school lessons, out-of-school-time lessons, or individual study. Students could report one of the following five options: "No time", "Less than 2 hours per week", "2 or more but less than 4 hours per week", "4 or more but less than 6 hours per week" or "6 or more hours per week".

## LEARNING TIME IN REGULAR SCHOOL LESSONS

Virtually all students from countries and economies that participated in PISA 2006 report being involved in regular school lessons in mathematics and the language of instruction. However, not all students are involved in regular school lessons in science. For example, around 97% of students across OECD countries report participating in regular school lessons in mathematics and on the language of instruction, while 90% report participating in regular school lessons in science (Tables 2.1a, 2.1b and 2.1c). This confirms the idea that most countries place a great emphasis on the study of mathematics and the language of instruction at school.

Not only is the share of students studying mathematics and the language of instruction in lessons at school greater, students also report spending more time in regular school lessons learning mathematics and the language of instruction than they do learning science. Two-thirds of students report spending two hours or more per week learning science in regular school lessons and only one third spends as much as four hours or more per week. However, at least 85% of students report spending two hours or more per week learning mathematics and their language of instruction in regular school lessons; almost half of them spend four hours or more per week in regular school lessons on mathematics and the language of instruction.

Students' participation rates in regular school lessons vary substantially not only across subjects but also across countries. The variation across countries is greatest in science. For example in Norway, Sweden, Poland, the United Kingdom, Korea, Finland, Denmark, Iceland and Japan, and the partner countries Estonia and Lithuania, over 95% of students take part in regular school lessons in science. In Turkey and the Netherlands, and the partner countries and economies Hong Kong-China, Croatia, Kyrgyzstan and Israel, only around three-quarters of students take part in regular school lessons in science.

Few students are exposed to science lessons during their regular school hours; when they are, many of them may only have a limited number of learning hours. In two-thirds of all OECD countries and in 25 out of 27 partner countries and economies, over one-quarter of students spend less than two hours per week studying science in regular school lessons. In one-third of OECD countries and in four partner countries and economies, less than 5% of students have six or more hours per week of science lessons at school. Conversely, the large majority of students in all OECD countries and in all partner countries and economies spend between two and six hours per week studying mathematics and the language of instruction, and sizeable proportions spend six hours or more.

In sum, countries vary widely in how they provide regular school lessons in science, both in terms of how many students attend such lessons and the amount of time students spend engaged in lessons. In some countries, science learning time at school is minimal. This could mean that some students do not receive the necessary training for them to be sufficiently equipped for an increasingly science-oriented world. An alternative explanation could be that in some countries, science learning has already taken place in previous grades and by the age of 15, students have already progressed to a level at which science is no longer compulsory.

## LEARNING TIME IN OUT-OF-SCHOOL-TIME LESSONS

In many countries, sizeable proportions of students attend out-of-school-time lessons, especially in mathematics and the language of instruction (Tables 2.1a, 2.1b and 2.1c). Across OECD countries, 35% of students attend these kinds of lessons for science, while the proportion reaches 48% for mathematics and 41% for the language of instruction. The higher proportion of students attending out-of-school-time classes in mathematics as compared to science is only partly due to the lower proportion of students taking regular science classes. Some 38% of students who take regular classes in science attend out-of-school-time lessons for science and 48% of students who take regular classes in mathematics attend out-of-school-time lessons in mathematics. Students not only attend more mathematics and language of instruction classes in regular hours when compared to science, they are also more likely to attend classes in mathemathics and the language of instruction after school.

On average, students in OECD countries are less likely to attend out-of-school-time lessons than students in the partner countries and economies, but cross-country variations in attendance rates are wide. For example, at least 70% of students are involved in out-of-school-time lessons in science in Greece and the partner country Tunisia, while at least 70% of students in Austria, Japan, Iceland, Belgium, Ireland, Australia, Finland, Switzerland, New Zealand, Germany, Luxembourg, Spain and the partner countries Croatia and Argentina are not involved in these types of lessons at all. In mathematics, 70% of students or more are involved in out-of-school-time lessons in Turkey, Korea, Greece and the partner countries Qatar, Israel and Tunisia, while at least 70% of students in Finland and Austria are not involved in these kinds of lessons. In the language of instruction, at least 70% of students are involved in out-of-school-time lessons in Turkey, Denmark and the partner countries Kyrgyzstan and Tunisia, while at least 70% of students in Austria, Finland, Belgium, Japan, Spain, Iceland, Switzerland and the partner countries Croatia, Liechtenstein and Argentina do not attend these kinds of lessons.

The difference across subjects is manifested not only in the proportion of the student population that engages in out-of-school-time lessons, but also in the amount of time students devote to such activities. Generally, students spend more time in out-of-school-time lessons in mathematics and the language of instruction than in science, and students in partner countries and economies spend more time in out-of-school-time lessons than students in OECD countries.

The majority of students who attend out-of-school-time lessons, particularly among OECD countries, do so on a limited basis in terms of learning hours. For example, in more than one-third of OECD countries, at least 70% of students who are involved in out-of-school-time lessons in science spend less than two hours per week in such activities. Similarly, many students attend out-of-school-time lessons in mathematics and the language of instruction, but most of them attend such lessons for less than two hours per week (notable exceptions in the OECD include Greece, Korea, Spain and Turkey). Students in the partner countries and economies make a slightly greater use of out-of-school-time lessons: while the majority of students engage in these kinds of lessons in the three subjects for less than two hours per week, large fractions of the student population in some partner countries and economies attend similar kinds of lessons for more than two hours.

## LEARNING TIME IN INDIVIDUAL STUDY

Across OECD and partner countries and economies, around 75% of students report spending time engaged in individual study learning science; around 85% do so for mathematics and the language of instruction (Tables 2.1a, 2.1b and 2.1c). This difference in participation rates across subjects could be partly explained by the different participation rates in regular school lessons in these subjects.

There is no major difference between OECD countries and partner countries and economies in participation rates in individual study. Most students who engage in individual study in PISA participating countries and economies spend less than two hours per week studying each of the three subjects. However, significant proportions of students both in OECD and partner countries and economies spend two hours or more per week per subject, especially on mathematics.

The amount of time, if any, that students spend on individual study varies across countries, especially in science, although variations are not as great as they are in relation to participation in out-of-school-time lessons. In general, engagement in individual study in mathematics and the language of instruction varies little across countries while variations are more pronounced in relation to science. In 18 out of 30 OECD countries and in 17 out of 27 partner countries and economies, over 85% of students spend at least some time learning mathematics through individual study. Individual study of the language of instruction is marginally less common since, in only about half of the OECD and partner countries and economies, over 85% of students spend some time engaged in individual study. In contrast, the proportion of students engaged in learning science through individual study varies significantly across countries. For example, in Japan, 54% of students engage in some kind of individual study each week, while 90% of Polish students study science individually. Among the partner countries and economies, around 60% of students in Israel and Hong Kong-China engage in individual study in science, while over 90% of students in Indonesia, Jordan, Thailand and Tunisia do so.

In most countries, the majority of students spend two hours or less per week in individual study in science, mathematics and the language of instruction. Across OECD countries, 51% of students spend some time, but less than two hours per week, doing homework or studying by themselves in science and mathematics; 54% spend similar amounts of time studying the language of instruction. These percentages vary widely among countries. For example, in science, over 50% of students in the partner countries the Russian Federation, Jordan, Tunisia and Azerbaijan spend two hours or more per week doing homework or studying by themselves, while only 15% or less of students in Japan, Finland, Denmark, Sweden and partner country Lichtenstein do so.

## ALLOCATION OF LEARNING TIME AND DIFFERENT FORMS OF DELIBERATE LEARNING ACTIVITIES

To obtain the results for this section, the original categorical variable, which described time spent in learning science, mathematics and the language of instruction, was recoded into the number of hours individual students reported spending on different deliberate learning activities. Students who reported spending "no time" in any given activity were assumed to have spent 0 hours in that activity. Similarly, students were assumed to have spent 1 hour per week on an activity if they reported having spent "less than 2 hours per week", 3 hours if they reported having spent "2 or more but less than 4 hours per week", 5 hours if they had reported "4 or more but less than 6 hours per week", and 7 hours if they had reported "6 or more hours per week". Although it creates a risk of introducing measurement errors in the estimates, the recoding of categorical variables into continuous variables enables more direct comparisons across countries in the average number of organised learning hours in which students participate, and in the relative share of time students spend in lessons at school, out-of-school-time lessons and individual study out of total learning time. The comparisons should thus be interpreted with caution.

Students spend more time in deliberate learning activities studying mathematics and the language of instruction than studying science (Tables 2.2a, 2.2b and 2.2c). Across OECD countries, total learning time in school lessons, out-of-school-time lessons and individual study, includes at least 6 hours and 30 minutes per week for the study of mathematics, around 6 hours and 20 minutes for the study of the language of instruction, and 5 hours for the study of science. Students in partner countries and economies also spend more time in learning activities focused on mathematics: in all but seven partner countries and economies,

students allocate significantly more time to mathematics than to the language of instruction and science. In general, students spend more time in activities related to mathematics than the language of instruction or science. However, in five OECD countries – Sweden, Norway, Poland, Italy and Denmark – and four partner countries – Azerbaijan, Kyrgyzstan, Lithuania and Romania – learning activities related to the language of instruction take up more time than activities related to science and mathematics. Science takes up the most time among students in the Russian Federation.

Figures 2.1a, 2.1b and 2.1c highlight the total number of hours students spend in various learning activities (*i.e.* school lessons, out-of-school-time lessons and individual study in science, mathematics and the language of instruction). In science, the total number of learning hours ranges from less than 4 hours per week in Japan, Switzerland, the Netherlands, Austria and the partner country Croatia, to over 7 hours per week in Greece and the partner countries the Russian Federation, Jordan and Tunisia. In mathematics, the total amount of time ranges from 5 hours or less per week in Sweden, the Netherlands and Finland, to over 9 hours per week in Korea. In the language of instruction, the total number of learning hours ranges from 5 hours or less per week in Finland, Austria, the Netherlands, Sweden and the partner countries the Russian Federation, Argentina and Uruguay, to over nine hours per week in Denmark.

Across OECD countries, the total amount of time students spend in deliberate learning activities is 6 hours and 30 minutes in mathematics, 6 hours and 20 minutes in the language of instruction and 5 hours in science (Tables 2.2a, 2.2b and 2.2c). In some countries, these differences were more pronounced, especially between mathematics and science. For example, the difference between mathematics and science learning time is half an hour or less in Finland, Portugal and Sweden, but over two-and-a-half hours in Iceland, Japan and Korea, among OECD countries, and Macao-China, Hong Kong-China, Chinese Taipei, Latvia and Israel, among partner countries and economies (Tables 2.2a and 2.2b). Although the difference in learning time devoted to mathematics and to the language of instruction is small in most countries, it is over an hour in three OECD countries – Austria, Japan and Korea – and in eight partner countries and economies.

Figures 2.1a, 2.1b and 2.1c present the total number of learning hours broken down into various activities – school lessons, out-of-school-time lessons and individual study – by subjects. While students in two countries may spend the same total amount of time in an activity studying a particular subject, the share of the overall time they dedicate to learning may differ greatly. For example, while students in both Finland and Greece spend three-and-a-half hours per week learning mathematics in regular school lessons, mathematics school lessons represent approximately 70% of total mathematics learning time in Finland and 50% in Greece.

Across OECD countries, the distribution of deliberate learning time in regular school lessons, out-of-school-time lessons and individual study is similar across the three different subjects (Tables 2.2a, 2.2b and 2.2c). This section primarily describes cross-country variations in the allocation of overall deliberate learning time, combining science, mathematics and the language of instruction, across different activities. Students in OECD countries are engaged in regular school lessons for 62% of their overall learning time, individual study for 26% of their time and out-of-school-time lessons for the remaining 12% of their time (Table 2.2d). How students allocate their overall time of engagement in deliberate learning activities varies greatly across countries. For example, Finnish and Japanese students spent about 70% or more of their overall learning time in school lessons, while the corresponding percentage is 50% or less in Greece and in seven partner countries and economies: Azerbaijan, Bulgaria, Jordan, Kyrgyzstan, Qatar, Romania and Tunisia. Participation in out-of-school-time lessons accounts for over 20% of students' overall learning time in Greece, Turkey and in six partner countries and economies: Romania, Israel, Jordan, Kyrgyzstan, Qatar and Tunisia. In 12 OECD countries and in partner countries Croatia and Liechtenstein, out-of-school-time lessons account for 10% or less of overall time that students spend on learning science, mathematics and the language of instruction.

Figure 2.1a

# Mean learning hours and allocation of learning hours out of total time in science

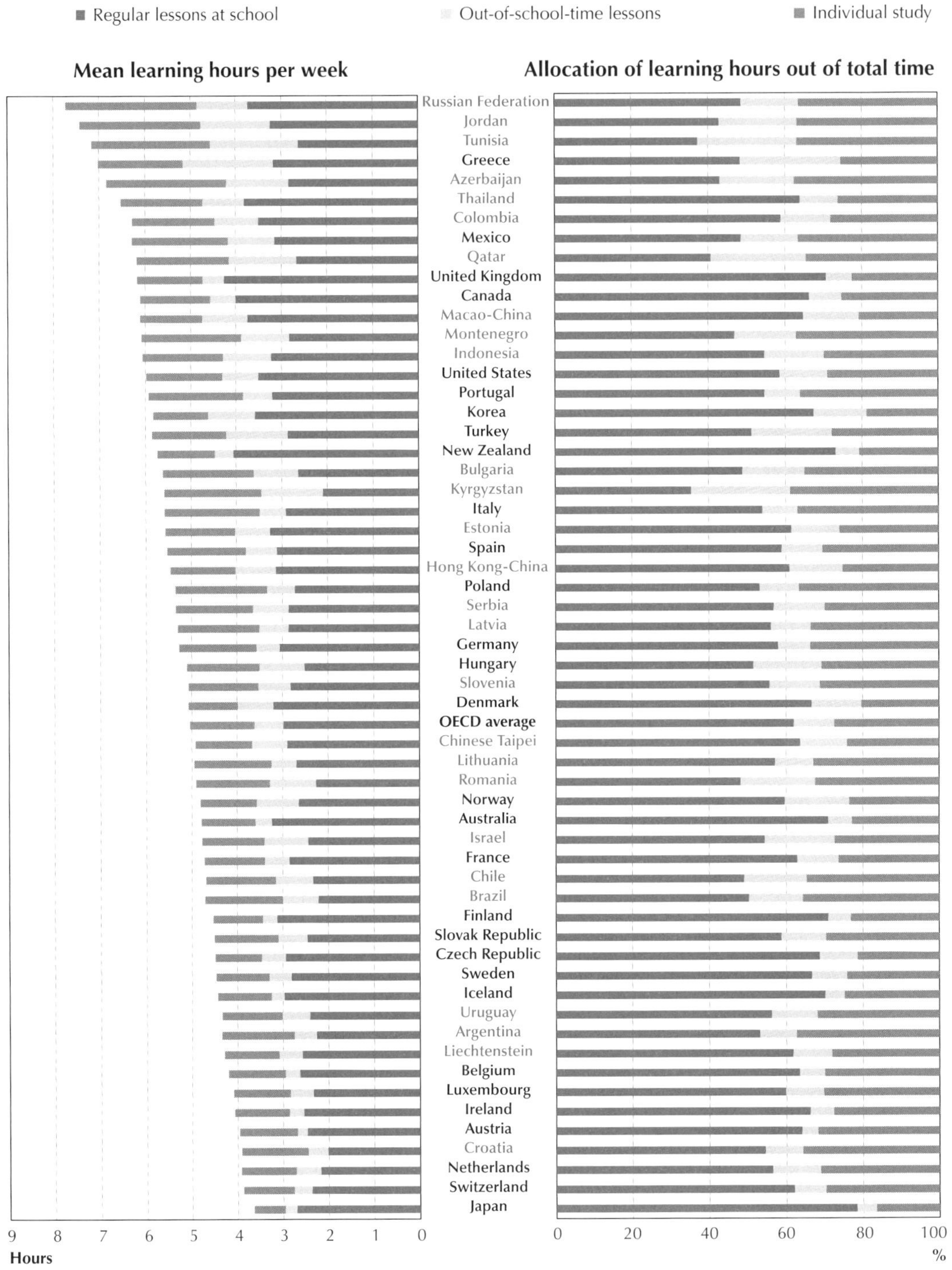

■ Regular lessons at school　　■ Out-of-school-time lessons　　■ Individual study

## Mean learning hours per week　　Allocation of learning hours out of total time

| | | |
|---|---|---|
| Russian Federation | | |
| Jordan | | |
| Tunisia | | |
| Greece | | |
| Azerbaijan | | |
| Thailand | | |
| Colombia | | |
| Mexico | | |
| Qatar | | |
| United Kingdom | | |
| Canada | | |
| Macao-China | | |
| Montenegro | | |
| Indonesia | | |
| United States | | |
| Portugal | | |
| Korea | | |
| Turkey | | |
| New Zealand | | |
| Bulgaria | | |
| Kyrgyzstan | | |
| Italy | | |
| Estonia | | |
| Spain | | |
| Hong Kong-China | | |
| Poland | | |
| Serbia | | |
| Latvia | | |
| Germany | | |
| Hungary | | |
| Slovenia | | |
| Denmark | | |
| OECD average | | |
| Chinese Taipei | | |
| Lithuania | | |
| Romania | | |
| Norway | | |
| Australia | | |
| Israel | | |
| France | | |
| Chile | | |
| Brazil | | |
| Finland | | |
| Slovak Republic | | |
| Czech Republic | | |
| Sweden | | |
| Iceland | | |
| Uruguay | | |
| Argentina | | |
| Liechtenstein | | |
| Belgium | | |
| Luxembourg | | |
| Ireland | | |
| Austria | | |
| Croatia | | |
| Netherlands | | |
| Switzerland | | |
| Japan | | |

9　8　7　6　5　4　3　2　1　0　　　　0　　20　　40　　60　　80　　100
**Hours**　　　　　　　　　　　　　　　　　　　　　　　　　　　　　%

Countries are ranked in descending order of the total learning hours in science.
*Source*: *OECD PISA Database 2006*, Table 2.2a.

© OECD 2011 Quality Time for Students: Learning In and Out of School

## Figure 2.1b
# Mean learning hours and allocation of learning hours out of total time in mathematics

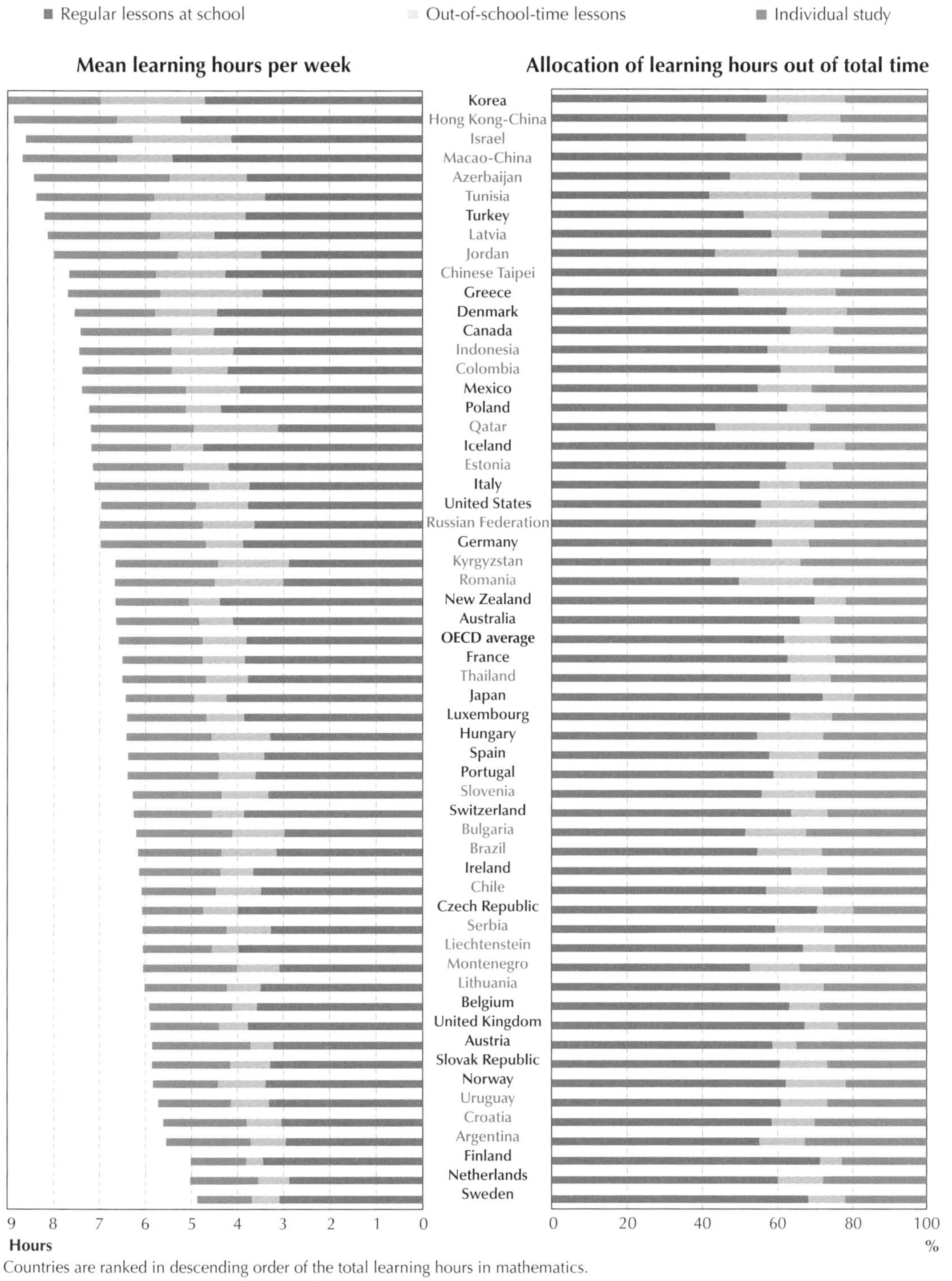

■ Regular lessons at school      ▢ Out-of-school-time lessons      ■ Individual study

| Mean learning hours per week | Allocation of learning hours out of total time |

Korea
Hong Kong-China
Israel
Macao-China
Azerbaijan
Tunisia
Turkey
Latvia
Jordan
Chinese Taipei
Greece
Denmark
Canada
Indonesia
Colombia
Mexico
Poland
Qatar
Iceland
Estonia
Italy
United States
Russian Federation
Germany
Kyrgyzstan
Romania
New Zealand
Australia
OECD average
France
Thailand
Japan
Luxembourg
Hungary
Spain
Portugal
Slovenia
Switzerland
Bulgaria
Brazil
Ireland
Chile
Czech Republic
Serbia
Liechtenstein
Montenegro
Lithuania
Belgium
United Kingdom
Austria
Slovak Republic
Norway
Uruguay
Croatia
Argentina
Finland
Netherlands
Sweden

9  8  7  6  5  4  3  2  1  0
**Hours**

0  20  40  60  80  100
%

Countries are ranked in descending order of the total learning hours in mathematics.

*Source*: *OECD PISA Database 2006*, Table 2.2b.

### Figure 2.1c
### Mean learning hours and allocation of learning hours out of total time on the language of instruction

■ Regular lessons at school          ■ Out-of-school-time lessons          ■ Individual study

**Mean learning hours per week**          **Allocation of learning hours out of total time**

Denmark
Azerbaijan
Italy
Turkey
Jordan
Macao-China
Hong Kong-China
Poland
Korea
Canada
Tunisia
Romania
Colombia
Mexico
Chinese Taipei
Kyrgyzstan
Greece
Indonesia
United States
New Zealand
Latvia
Iceland
Qatar
Australia
Hungary
France
OECD average
Norway
Germany
Lithuania
Spain
United Kingdom
Bulgaria
Israel
Chile
Brazil
Estonia
Ireland
Serbia
Slovak Republic
Montenegro
Portugal
Switzerland
Czech Republic
Luxembourg
Slovenia
Thailand
Croatia
Belgium
Liechtenstein
Japan
Sweden
Netherlands
Uruguay
Austria
Finland
Argentina
Russian Federation

9   8   7   6   5   4   3   2   1   0                    0    20    40    60    80    100
**Hours**                                                                              **%**

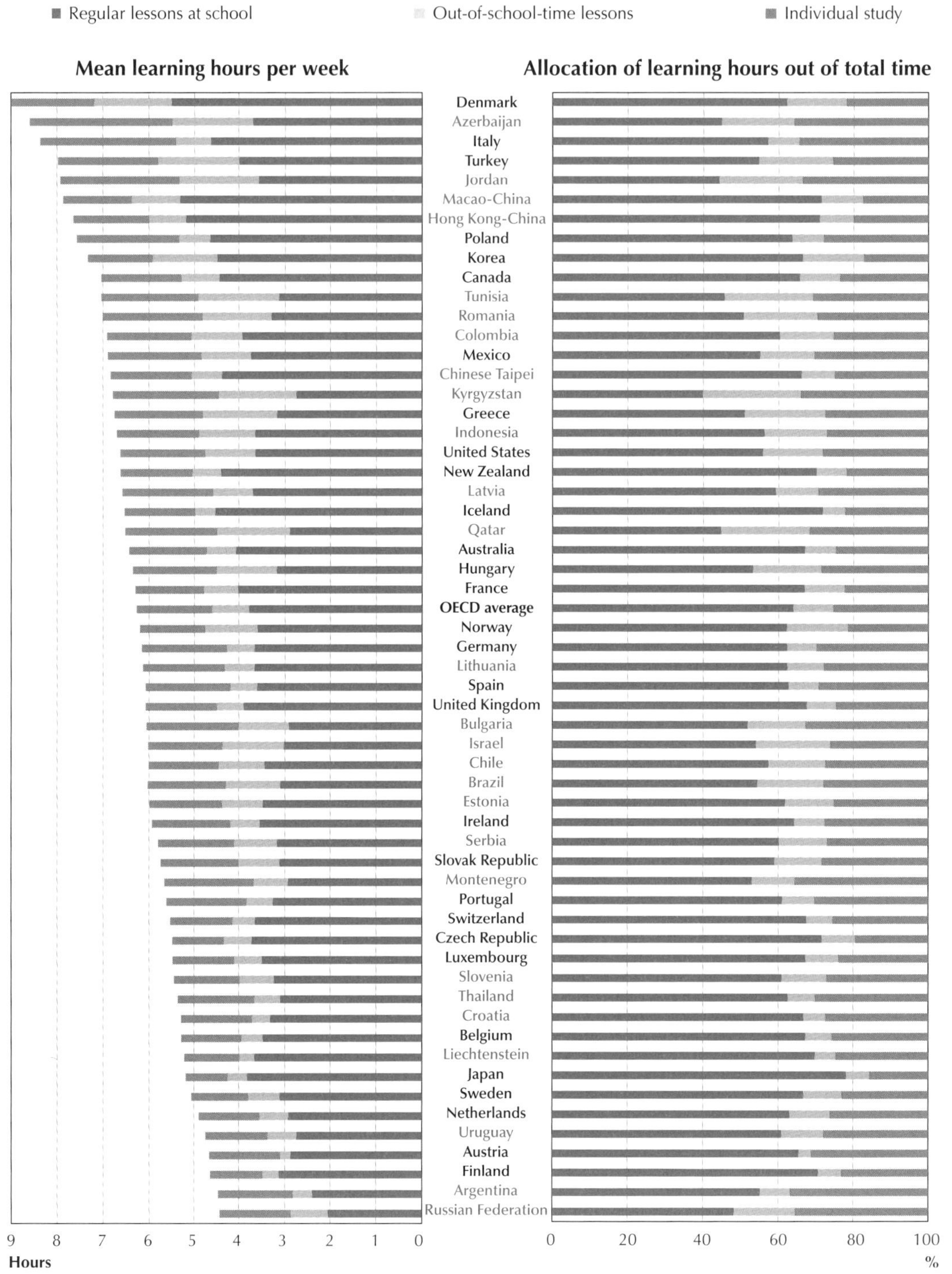

Countries are ranked in descending order of the total learning hours on the language of instruction.
*Source*: *OECD PISA Database 2006*, Table 2.2c.

© OECD 2011  Quality Time for Students: Learning In and Out of School

## TO WHAT EXTENT ARE STUDENTS INVOLVED IN OUT-OF-SCHOOL-TIME LESSONS?

In PISA 2006, students were asked to report their engagement in each of the following six types of out-of-school-time lessons: one-to-one lessons with a school teacher; one-to-one lessons with a teacher not from the school; lessons in small groups with a school teacher; lessons in small groups with a teacher not from the school; lessons in large groups with a school teacher; or lessons in large groups with a teacher not from the school.

Across OECD countries, 43% of students are engaged in out-of-school-time lessons on school subjects (Table 2.3). About one-quarter of students are involved in at least one type of out-of-school-time lessons with teachers from their own school and another quarter are involved in out-of-school-time lessons with instructors who are not the teachers in the schools the students attend. Figures 2.2a and 2.2b illustrate the differences across OECD countries in the proportions of students taking different types of out-of-school-time lessons from teachers who teach in the schools they attend or from those who don't. The differences in proportions between these two groups are generally small, except for Greece, Spain and the partner countries Kyrgyzstan and the Russian Federation. In general, students who engage in out-of-school-time lessons with teachers who are not teachers in their schools (referred to as "non-school teachers" for the rest of this report) also tend to show extensive engagement in out-of-school-time lessons with school teachers.

Previous sections in this chapter suggest that student attendance in out-of-school-time lessons varies greatly from country to country. Figures 2.2a and 2.2b show that the type of out-of-school-time lessons students attend also varies across countries. Less than 15% of students in Finland, Norway, Denmark, the Netherlands and Sweden attend at least one type of out-of-school-time lessons with non-school teachers, while over 50% of students do so in Greece, Korea and partner countries and economies Azerbaijan, Chinese Taipei, Israel and Hong Kong-China. Similarly, around 15% or less of students in Australia, Denmark, Belgium and the Netherlands attend at least one type of out-of-school-time lesson with school teachers, but that proportion exceeds 50% in Korea and the partner countries Kyrgyzstan, Azerbaijan, the Russian Federation, Jordan, Tunisia, Indonesia and Latvia.

### Figure 2.2a
**Percentage of students taking out-of-school-time lessons with non-school teachers, by type of out-of-school-time lessons**

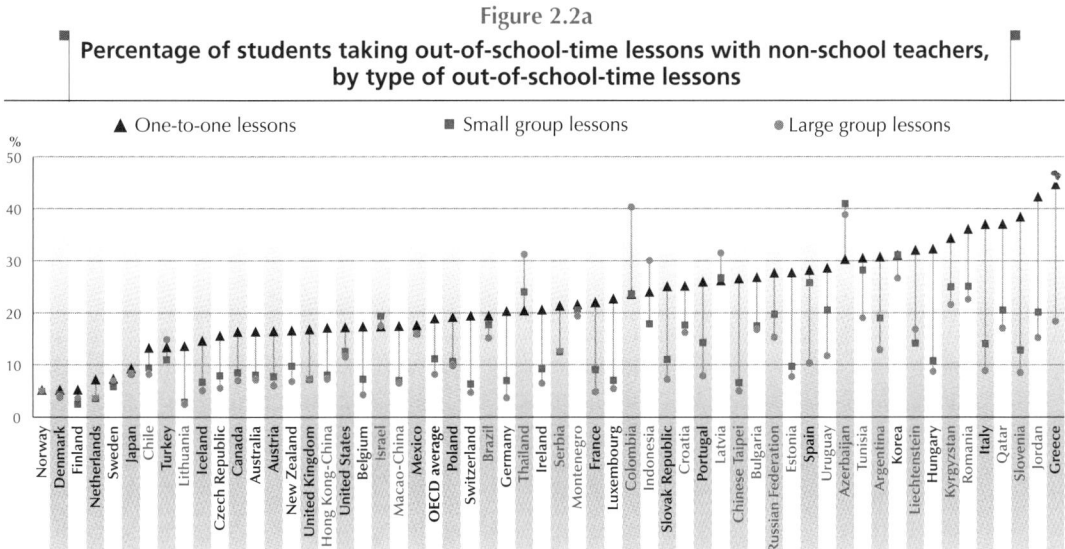

Countries are ranked in ascending order of the percentage of students taking out-of-school-time one-to-one lessons.
*Source*: OECD PISA Database 2006, Table 2.3.

### Figure 2.2b
### Percentage of students taking out-of-school-time lessons with school teachers, by type of out-of-school-time lessons

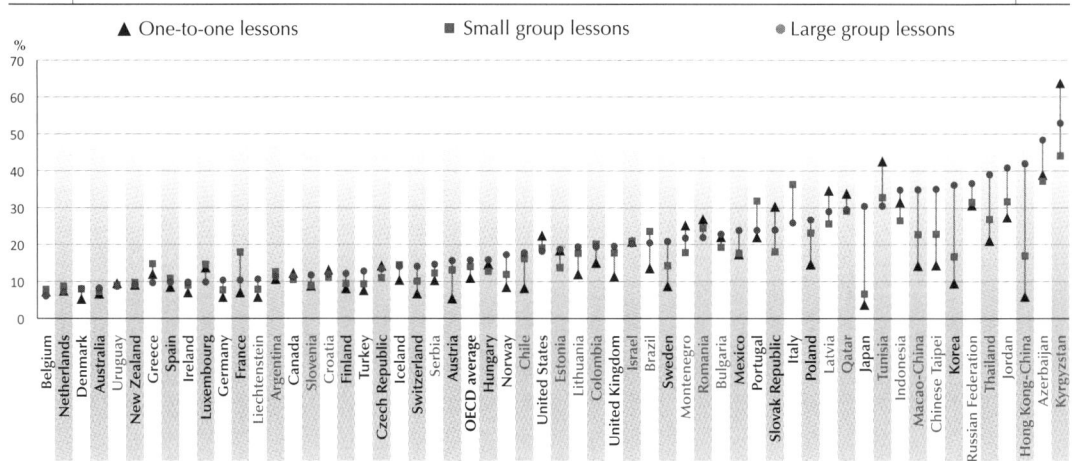

Countries are ranked in ascending order of the percentage of students taking out-of-school-time large group lessons.
*Source: OECD PISA Database 2006, Table 2.3.*

Differences in the size of lessons for out-of-school-time activities appear to be primarily determined by whether students in a particular country attend out-of-school-time lessons with school or non-school teachers. One-to-one lessons seem to be the most prevalent type of out-of-school-time lessons with non-school teachers, while large group lessons are the most prevalent type of these kinds of lessons when they are led by school teachers.

## PATTERNS OF STUDENTS' ABSOLUTE AND RELATIVE LEARNING TIME

In order to summarise the differences and similarities in the patterns of students' learning time, countries are grouped according to two factors. The first is absolute learning time in regular school lessons, which is equivalent to the length of learning time spent in regular school lessons in science, mathematics and the language of instruction altogether. The second is relative learning time in regular school lessons, which is equivalent to the proportion of total learning time (*i.e.* the time spent in regular school lessons, out-of-school-time lessons and individual study combined) allocated to regular school lessons out of total learning time in all three subjects. This grouping of countries shows both the amount of time students spend in regular school lessons and the way they allocate learning time across countries[1]. The relationship between absolute learning time or relative learning time in regular school lessons and performance is examined in detail in Chapter 4.

As shown in Figure 2.3, four groups were identified: "high absolute learning time in regular school lessons, and high relative learning time in regular school lessons","low absolute learning time in regular school lessons, but high relative learning time in regular school lessons","high absolute learning time in regular school lessons, but low relative learning time in regular school lessons" and "low absolute learning time in regular school lessons, and low relative learning time in regular school lessons".

Box 2.1 shows the lists of countries in the four groups identified in Figure 2.3. The "high absolute and high relative learning time in regular school lessons" group includes 12 OECD countries and 6 partner countries and economies. Interestingly, it includes five Asian countries and economies (Japan, Korea, Chinese Taipei, Hong Kong-China and Macao-China). In this group of countries and economies, more time is spent in regular school lessons and the proportion of time spent in regular school lessons is higher than the average across all participating countries and economies.

© OECD 2011 Quality Time for Students: Learning In and Out of School

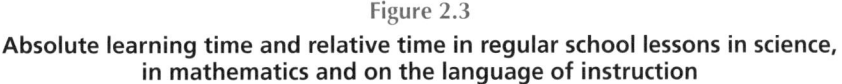

Figure 2.3
**Absolute learning time and relative time in regular school lessons in science,
in mathematics and on the language of instruction**

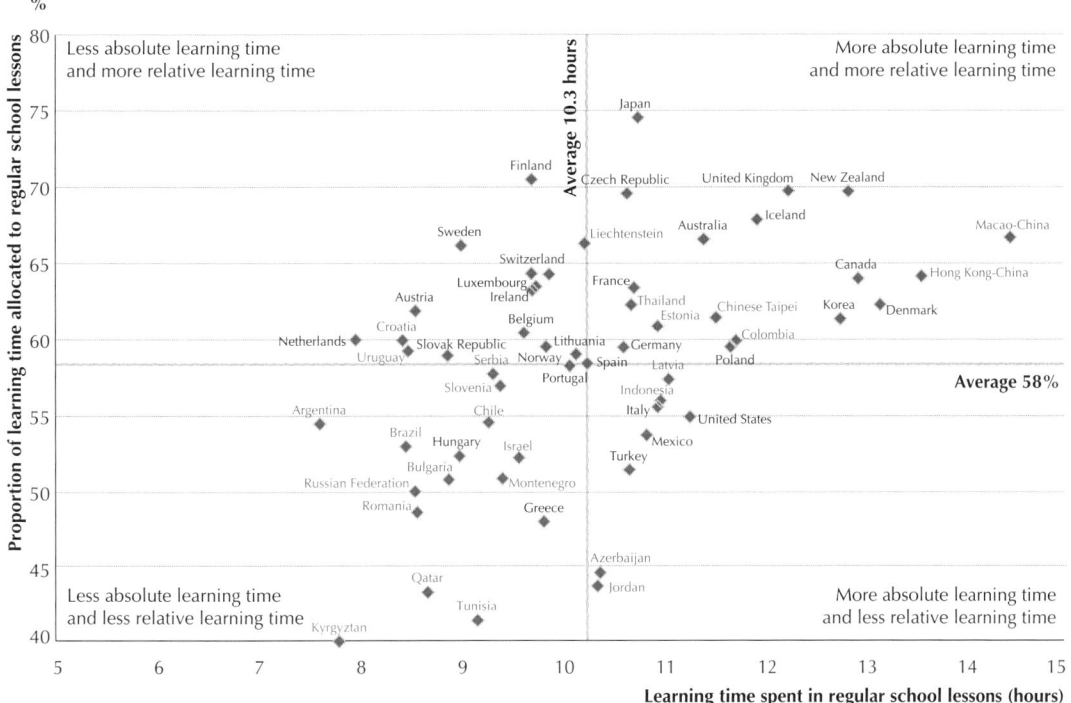

Source: OECD PISA Database 2006, Table 2.2d.

The "less absolute but more relative learning time in regular school lessons" group includes 11 OECD countries and 4 partner countries, including 3 Nordic countries (Norway, Sweden and Finland). This group is characterised by a shorter amount of learning time in regular school lessons, but a higher proportion of hours spent in regular school lessons than the average across all participating countries and economies. As students spend a small amount of time in regular school lessons and outside regular school lessons, the total learning time is the shortest among these four groups of countries.

The "more absolute but less relative learning time in regular school lessons" group includes four OECD countries and four partner countries. In this group, the amount of time spent in regular school lessons is higher, but the proportion of time spent in regular school lessons is lower than the average across all participating countries and economies. In this group, the total learning time tends to be long since students spend larger amounts of time in regular school lessons and in out-of-school-time lessons and individual study.

The "less absolute and less relative learning time in regular school lessons" group includes 3 OECD countries and 13 partner countries. This group is characterised by smaller amounts of learning time in regular school lessons and a lower proportion of learning hours in regular school lessons than the average across all participating countries. One could infer that students' learning in regular school lessons is limited because the students tend to spend a small amount of time in those lessons, but a large amount of learning time outside of those lessons.

## Box 2.1. **Patterns of learning time in regular school lessons, by country**

| More absolute learning time and more relative learning time | | Less absolute learning time and more relative learning time | | More absolute learning time and less relative learning time | | Less absolute learning time and less relative learning time | |
|---|---|---|---|---|---|---|---|
| OECD | Partner | OECD | Partner | OECD | Partner | OECD | Partner |
| Germany | Thailand | Norway | Croatia | Turkey | Jordan | Hungary | Argentina |
| Czech Republic | Estonia | Austria | Uruguay | Mexico | Azerbaijan | Greece | Kyrgyzstan |
| France | Chinese Taipei | Slovak Republic | Lithuania | United States | Indonesia | Portugal | Brazil |
| Japan | Colombia | Sweden | Liechtenstein | Italy | Latvia | | Bulgaria |
| Australia | Hong Kong-China | Netherlands | | | | | Romania |
| Poland | Macao-China | Belgium | | | | | Qatar |
| United Kingdom | | Finland | | | | | Montenegro |
| Iceland | | Luxembourg | | | | | Tunisia |
| Korea | | Ireland | | | | | Chile |
| New Zealand | | Switzerland | | | | | Serbia |
| Canada | | Spain | | | | | Slovenia |
| Denmark | | | | | | | Russian Federation |
| | | | | | | | Israel |

*Source*: *OECD PISA Database 2006*, Table 2.2d.

## *Note*

1. As no difference is observed across subjects, the three subjects – science, mathematics and the language of instruction – are combined and reported together.

© OECD 2011 Quality Time for Students: Learning In and Out of School

3

# Patterns of Students' Learning Time by Population Sub-Groups

## INTRODUCTION

In general, the findings in this chapter show that students' learning time patterns differ according to individual and school characteristics within countries. The individual characteristics examined are gender, socio-economic status and immigrant status; the school characteristics studied involve lower and upper secondary schools, academic and vocational schools, public and private schools, and schools in urban and rural areas.

## STUDENT BACKGROUND CHARACTERISTICS

PISA assessments have consistently shown that across countries, females are more interested in reading than males, and males are more interested in mathematics than females (OECD, 2004; OECD, 2007; OECD, 2009a). This chapter looks at whether or not these gender differences are also reflected in how students allocate time for learning.

PISA results have also shown that students' socio-economic backgrounds are related to performance, such that socio-economically advantaged students tend to achieve higher scores in mathematics, science and the language of instruction (OECD, 2002; OECD, 2004; OECD, 2007). This chapter seeks to understand how the patterns of learning time differ according to students' socio-economic backgrounds, as the time spent learning might be one of the major factors that reinforces the relationship between socio-economic background and performance. The PISA index of economic, social and cultural status provides a comprehensive measure of students' socio-economic background. This index is derived from information about the highest educational level of parents, the highest occupational status of parents, and possessions in the home (OECD, 2009b).

Examining participation rates in out-of-school-time lessons according to students' socio-economic background is also interesting since it could be suggested that socio-economically advantaged students have more opportunities to attend out-of-school-time lessons and, consequently, achieve higher scores in PISA. Chapter 4 examines the relationship between socio-economic background and performance, through participation in out-of-school-time lessons, in more detail.

This chapter also examines how learning time differs according to students' immigrant status. Students with immigrant backgrounds are defined as those whose parents were born in a foreign country. This group includes both first- and second-generation students. First-generation students are those born outside of the country of assessment whose parents are also foreign-born. Second-generation students are those born in the country of assessment with both parents foreign-born. Native students are defined as students who were born in the country of assessment and have at least one parent who was also born in the country of assessment. Analysis is only conducted for countries with a sufficient number of sampled students and schools in relevant sub-groups: *i.e.* statistics should be based on at least 30 students in 5 schools.

Given the increase in international migration, in some countries, a significant proportion of students were born in another country. For example, the proportion of students who are foreign-born or who have foreign-born parents now exceeds 10% in Germany, Belgium, Austria, France, the Netherlands and Sweden, as well as the partner countries Croatia, Estonia and Slovenia. That proportion is: 15% in the United States; 17% in Jordan; between 21% and 23% in Switzerland, Australia, New Zealand, Canada and the partner country Israel; 36% in Luxembourg; 37% in Liechtenstein; and over 40% in the partner countries and economies Macao-China, Hong Kong-China and Qatar (Table 3.1).

The differences in deliberate learning time by immigrant status are also examined in relation to the socio-economic background of the students and schools. In some countries, the socio-economic status of students with immigrant backgrounds could differ significantly because of immigration policies and practices, and the criteria used to decide who will be admitted into a country. If the socio-economic status of these students differs significantly, the observed differences in learning hours according to immigrant status could be due

© OECD 2011 Quality Time for Students: Learning In and Out of School

to their different socio-economic backgrounds and not to their immigrant status. Thus, this chapter also examines differences in learning hours between natives and immigrants who share similar socio-economic status, by adjusting the estimates to differences in the socio-economic background of students and schools.

## SCHOOL CHARACTERISTICS

This chapter also looks at how patterns of students' learning time may differ according to school structural and geographical characteristics. Specifically, it compares patterns in students' learning time in lower and upper secondary schools, academic and vocational schools, public and private schools, and schools in city and rural areas. Analysis of school characteristics is only conducted for countries with a sufficient number of sampled students and schools in relevant sub-groups: *i.e.* statistics should be based on at least 30 students in 5 schools.

PISA assesses students who are aged between 15 years 3 months and 16 years 2 months at the time of assessment, regardless of whether they are in lower secondary or upper secondary schools. In some countries, PISA target populations are all in upper secondary or all in lower secondary schools, while in other countries the students are in both lower secondary and upper secondary schools (Table 3.2).

In countries with a sufficient proportion of students in both academic and vocational schools, patterns of students' learning time are also compared between those of students in academic programmes and those of students in vocational programmes. Academic schools are defined as schools offering a study programme with a general curriculum. Vocational schools are defined as schools offering a study programme with a pre-vocational or vocational curriculum. The proportion of students in academic and vocational schools varies across countries (Table 3.4).

Institutional characteristics, such as lower or upper secondary schools and academic or vocational schools, are often related to each other. This also varies greatly across countries. In some countries, vocational schools are mainly at the upper secondary level, while in other countries this is not the case.

This chapter also examines how patterns in learning time differ between students in public schools and students in private schools. PISA assessments ask school principals whether their schools are managed directly or indirectly by a public education authority, government agency, or governing board appointed by government or elected by or public franchise (*i.e.* public schools); or by a non-government organisation, such as a church trade union, business, or other private institution (*i.e.* private schools) (Table 3.3).

Since the location of schools could also affect patterns in students' learning time, this chapter also looks at whether the time students spend in various learning activities differs between schools in urban areas and those in rural areas. Cities are defined as communities with 100 000 or more people; rural areas are defined as communities with fewer than 100 000 people. The proportion of 15-year-old students in schools in urban *versus* rural areas varies across countries (Table 3.5).

Among these school characteristics, the differences in deliberate learning time between students in public and private schools, academic and vocational schools, and schools in urban and rural areas are also explored by taking into consideration the socio-economic background of the students and schools. Since in many countries the socio-economic status of students and schools differs significantly according to these school characteristics, the observed differences could be due to their different socio-economic backgrounds rather than to the characteristics of schools.

## CHARACTERISTICS OF LEARNING TIME

Differences in the time spent in regular school lessons, according to students' and schools' characteristics, tend to look similar to those spent in individual study. This finding is largely consistent across countries. However, the same is not true for the time spent in out-of-school-time lessons. Because the nature, meaning and function of out-of-school-time lessons are not necessarily the same across countries, differences in the time spent in out-of-school-time lessons, according to students' and schools' characteristics, are more complex and the results vary across countries.

## Characteristics of learning time in regular school lessons and individual study

### Gender

In most countries, females spend more time in regular school lessons and individual study in science, mathematics and the language of instruction than males, but the gender difference is greater in the language of instruction than in science and mathematics (Tables 3.6a, 3.6b and 3.6c). Across OECD countries, females spend around 40 minutes more per week than males in regular school lessons and individual study on the language of instruction, while females spend around 18 to 23 minutes more per week than males in regular school lessons and individual study in science and mathematics. In Greece, Hungary, Poland and Italy, and in the partner countries Jordan, Kyrgyzstan, Tunisia, Lithuania, Slovenia and Uruguay, females spend an additional 30 minutes or more per week than males in regular school lessons on the language of instruction. In Poland, Italy, Greece, Canada, the Slovak Republic, the United States, Hungary, Turkey and Spain, and partner countries Kyrgyzstan, Romania and Bulgaria, females spend at least 30 minutes per week more than males in individual study on the language of instruction.

The gender difference in time spent in regular school lessons in mathematics is small compared to time spent in regular school lessons in science and the language of instruction. Across OECD countries, females spend only five minutes more per week than males on regular school lessons in mathematics. Females spend an additional 30 minutes or more per week than males in regular school lessons in mathematics in Poland and the partner countries Slovenia, Lithuania and Jordan, while in 12 other OECD countries and 10 partner countries and economies this difference varies from an additional 6 to 28 minutes. In Austria, the Czech Republic and the Netherlands, males spend more time in regular school lessons in mathematics than females.

### Socio-economic status

In most countries, socio-economically advantaged students spend much more time in regular school lessons and individual study in science, mathematics and the language of instruction than disadvantaged students (Tables 3.7a, 3.7b and 3.7c). Across OECD countries, socio-economically advantaged students spend 11.5 hours per week studying those 3 subjects in regular school lessons, while disadvantaged students spend 9.8 hours per week in regular school lessons (Table 3.7d). This difference of 1 hour and 42 minutes per week in regular school lessons reflects a difference of around 50 minutes per week in science, around 30 minutes per week in mathematics and around 20 minutes in the language of instruction. Socio-economically advantaged students have more opportunities to learn and acquire knowledge and skills than disadvantaged students, particularly in science.

### Immigrant status

When students' immigrant status is taken into account, the results for time spent in regular school lessons are more complex and vary across countries. In about a half of the countries, there is no significant difference between native students and students with an immigrant background in the time spent in regular school lessons in science, mathematics and the language of instruction, while in other countries the results vary significantly across countries as well as by subject. For example, in the United States and the partner

© OECD 2011 Quality Time for Students: Learning In and Out of School

economy Chinese Taipei, native students spend more time than students with an immigrant background on regular school lessons in the three subjects, while in Australia and the partner country Qatar, students with an immigrant background spend more time than native students. In Austria and Germany, the results are different by subject: native students spend more time in regular school lessons in science while students with an immigrant background spend more time in regular school lessons on the language of instruction.

Students with immigrant backgrounds tend to spend more time in individual study in science, mathematics and the language of instruction than native students (Table 3.8a, 3.8b and 3.8c). Across OECD countries, students with immigrant backgrounds spend 12 minutes more per week than native students on mathematics and the language of instruction. Students with an immigrant background spend ten minutes less per week in individual study in science than native students. In Australia, New Zealand, Canada, Sweden and the United Kingdom, students with immigrant backgrounds spend an additional 31 minutes or more in mathematics than native students.

After adjusting for the difference in socio-economic background of students and schools, students with an immigrant background still tend to spend more time on individual study, while the difference in time spent in regular school lessons varies according to countries (Table 3.8d). On average across OECD countries, and after adjusting for differences in socio-economic background, students with an immigrant background spend 40 minutes more than native students on individual study in science, mathematics and the language of instruction combined. Differences in time spent in regular school lessons between native students and those with immigrant backgrounds are insignificant in half the countries. However, students with an immigrant background spend more time in regular school lessons in Belgium, Australia, Austria, Luxembourg and in partner countries and economies Qatar, Macao-China, Hong Kong-China and Israel.

### School-level variation

In general, the amount of hours students spend in regular school lessons varies within as well as between schools. Across OECD countries, 15% of variation in students' learning time in regular school lessons can be attributed to differences between schools (Table 3.9d). There is a 17% variation in science, 12% in mathematics and 11% in the language of instruction (Tables 3.9a, 3.9b and 3.9c). These differences vary considerably from country to country. As shown in Figure 3.1, in Japan, the Slovak Republic, France, Turkey, Korea, Belgium and the partner countries and economies Thailand and Chinese Taipei, 25% or more of the variation of students' learning time in regular school lessons on the three subjects combined is due to the difference between schools. But differences between schools account for only 5% of the variation in Ireland, Poland, the United States and partner countries Liechtenstein and Estonia (Table 3.9d). This shows that in most countries, variation in the learning time in regular school lessons is mostly due to differences between students within schools, and only partly due to differences between schools.

By contrast, learning time spent in individual study does not vary much between schools. Across OECD countries, 7% of variation in individual study can be attributed to the difference between schools (Table 3.9d). School-level variation in learning time through individual study is only 10% or less in all countries and economies except Japan, Korea, Italy, France and the partner countries and economies Chinese Taipei, Bulgaria, the Russian Federation, Macao-China and Thailand.

Figure 3.1

**Percentage of between school variance out of total variance in regular school lessons, out-of-school-time lessons, and individual study**

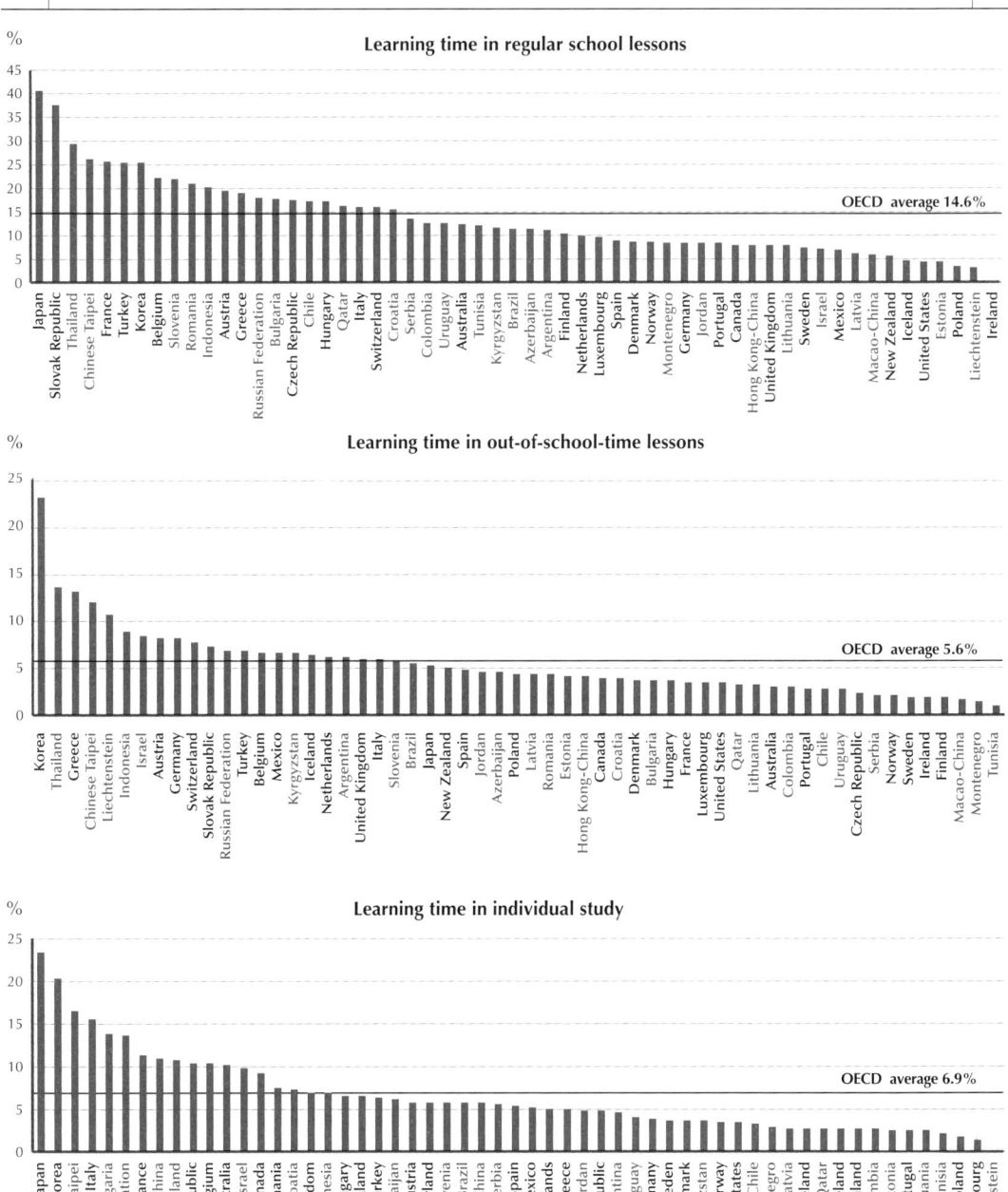

Countries are ranked in descending order of the percentage of between-school variance out of total variance.

*Source: OECD PISA Database 2006*, Table 3.9d.

© OECD 2011 Quality Time for Students: Learning In and Out of School

### Lower secondary and upper secondary schools

In general, students in upper secondary schools spend more time in regular school lessons in science than students in lower secondary schools. Students in upper secondary schools also spend more time in regular school lessons in mathematics than students in lower secondary schools, but the difference is small. For example, across OECD countries, students in upper secondary schools spend an additional 35 minutes per week in regular school lessons in science and an additional 7 minutes per week in regular school lessons in mathematics compared with students in lower secondary schools (Tables 3.10a and 3.10b). The biggest differences are found in France and Poland, where students in upper secondary schools spend an additional 90 minutes per week or more in regular school lessons in science compared with students in lower secondary schools.

Results comparing differences between lower and upper secondary schools in time spent in regular school lessons on the language of instruction vary across countries (Table 3.10c). In 9 OECD countries and 11 partner countries and economies, students in upper secondary spend more time in regular school lessons on the language of instruction than students in lower secondary schools, while in 8 OECD countries and 5 partner countries and economies, students in lower secondary schools spend more time than students in upper secondary schools.

Similarly, students in upper secondary schools tend to spend more time in individual study in science and mathematics than students in lower secondary schools, although the results vary across countries in the language of instruction (Tables 3.10a, 3.10b and 3.10c). Across OECD countries, students in upper secondary schools spend an additional eight minutes per week in individual study in both science and mathematics compared with students in lower secondary schools. In five OECD countries and four partner countries and economies, students in upper secondary spend more time in individual study in the language of instruction than students in lower secondary schools, while in five OECD countries and eight partner countries and economies, students in lower secondary schools spend more time than students in upper secondary schools.

### Public and private schools

In general, students attending private schools tend to spend more time in regular school lessons in science, mathematics and the language of instruction than those who attend public schools. Across OECD countries, students in private schools spend an additional 30 minutes per week in regular school lessons in the 3 subjects compared with students in public schools (Table 3.11d). However, in Italy, the Czech Republic, Sweden and the partner countries and economies Tunisia, Thailand, Indonesia, Chinese Taipei and Estonia, students in public schools spend more time than those in private schools in regular school lessons in at least one of the three subjects (Tables 3.11a, 3.11b and 3.11c).

The difference in time spent in regular school lessons between students in public and private schools varies across countries. In some of the partner countries and economies, the difference is remarkable. For example, in Greece and partner countries Slovenia, Qatar and Brazil, students in private schools spend an additional 2 hours and 30 minutes or more in regular school lessons in science, mathematics and the language of instruction than students in public schools (Table 3.11d).

Taking into account differences in the socio-economic status of students, the variation in hours spent in regular school lessons in favour of students in private schools no longer exists in the majority of countries and economies. Across OECD countries, once socio-economic background is accounted for, students in public schools spend an average of ten minutes more in regular school lessons than students in private schools. The difference in hours spent in regular school lessons, favouring students from private schools, is statistically significant in only three OECD countries and five partner countries and economy: Iceland,

Norway, Spain, Luxembourg, Qatar, Macao-China, Slovenia, Uruguay and Brazil. The difference is larger in countries where students in public schools spend more time in regular lessons than students in private schools (Table 3.11d). This implies that the difference between public and private schools in the number of hours students spend in school regular lessons is not attributable only to school characteristics, but is largely driven by the socio-economic level of schools' student population.

Students attending private schools spend more time in individual study than students in public schools in many countries, including nine OECD countries and six partner countries and economies; but, the difference is smaller or insignificant in two-thirds of countries after accounting for socio-economic status (Table 3.11d). Across OECD countries, students attending private schools spend an additional 15 minutes per week in individual study of science, mathematics and the language of instruction compared with students in public schools.

### Academic and vocational schools

In almost every country, students attending academic schools spend more time in learning science, mathematics and the language of instruction in regular school lessons and individual study than students in vocational schools (Tables 3.12a, 3.12b and 3.12c). For example, across OECD countries, students attending academic schools spend an additional 1 hour per week in regular school lessons in science, an additional 50 minutes per week in regular school lessons in mathematics and an additional 45 minutes per week in regular school lessons on the language of instruction compared with students attending vocational schools.

Even after adjusting for the socio-economic status of students and schools, students attending academic schools spend more time learning the three subjects in regular school lessons and individual study (Table 3.12d). Although the difference in learning hours is smaller, it remains considerable. For example, students attending academic schools spend 2 hours and 37 minutes more in regular school lessons, 28 minutes more in out-of-school-time lessons and 41 minutes more on individual study, on average across OECD countries, compared with students of similar socio-economic backgrounds who attend vocational schools.

### Schools in urban and rural areas

In general, students in urban schools tend to spend more time in regular school lessons than students in schools in rural areas. The differences are large in some countries, but relatively small in others. In most countries, the difference is one hour per week or less in regular school lessons in science, mathematics and the language of instruction (Table 3.13d). However, in the United States, students in schools in rural areas spend more time in regular school lessons in all three subjects than students in urban schools.

In eight OECD countries and four partner countries and economies, students in urban schools also spend more time engaged in individual study in science, mathematics and the language of instruction than students in schools in rural areas (Table 3.13d). In some partner countries and economies, however, students in schools in rural areas spend more time in individual study than students in urban schools.

However, after the socio-economic status of students and schools is taken into account, the difference in hours spent in regular school lessons and individual study practically disappears in some countries. On average across OECD countries, students in urban schools spend eight minutes more in regular school lessons than students in schools in rural areas (Table 3.13d). Students in schools in urban areas spend more time in regular school lessons in only one OECD country and two partner countries and economies: Belgium, Qatar and Macao-China. The pattern regarding hours spent in individual study is mixed. In eight OECD countries and one partner country, students in urban schools spend more time on individual study than students in schools in rural areas, while in four OECD countries and eight partner countries, students in schools in rural areas spend more time on individual study than students in urban schools.

© OECD 2011 Quality Time for Students: Learning In and Out of School

## Characteristics of learning time in out-of-school-time lessons

This section considers how students' backgrounds and school characteristics are related to patterns of learning time in out-of-school-time lessons. Students' gender, socio-economic background and immigrant status are considered, as are differences between lower and upper secondary schools, academic and vocational schools, public and private schools, and schools in urban and in rural areas.

### Gender

In out-of-school-time lessons, the pattern of gender difference varies across countries (Tables 3.6a, 3.6b and 3.6c). In 3 OECD countries and 1 partner country, females spend more time than males in out-of-school-time lessons in science, while males spend more time than females in 16 OECD countries and 10 partner countries and economies. In five OECD countries and one partner country, females spend more time than males in out-of-school-time lessons in mathematics, while males spend more time than females in ten OECD countries and five partner countries and economies. In ten OECD countries and six partner countries and economies, females spend more time than males in out-of-school-time lessons on the language of instruction, while males spend more time than females in nine OECD countries and seven partner countries and economies.

### Figure 3.2
**Participation rates in out-of-school-time lessons with school teachers, by gender**

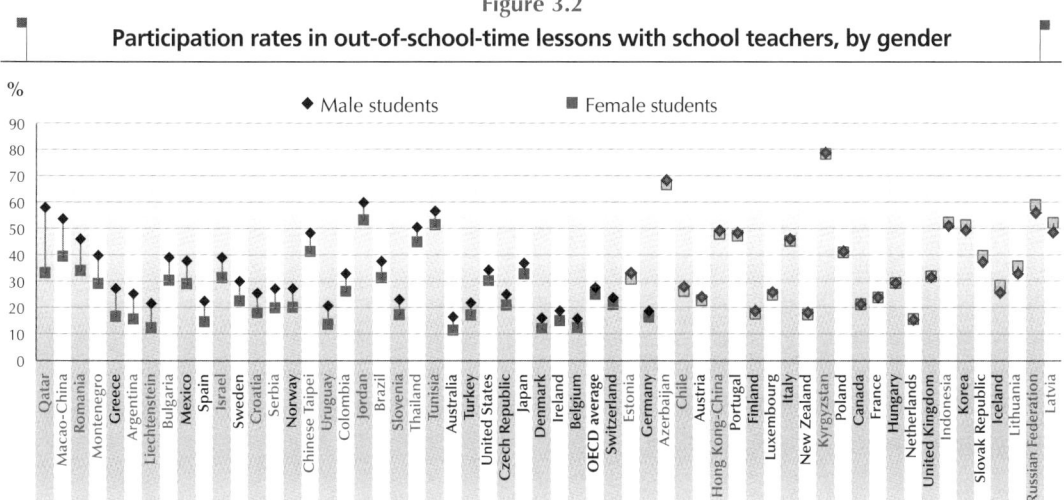

*Note*: Gender differences that are statistically significant are marked in a darker tone.
Countries are ranked in descending order of the difference in rates of participation in out-of-school-time lessons with school teachers between male and female students.
*Source*: OECD PISA 2006 Database, Table 3.14.

Are males and females involved in the same types of out-of-school-time lessons? Females tend to be more involved in one-to-one out-of-school-time lessons with non-school teachers than males, while males are more involved in large group, out-of-school-time lessons with non-school teachers (Table 3.14). Males are also more involved in out-of-school-time lessons of any size with school teachers, including one-to-one, small group and large group lessons. Interestingly, the gender differences favouring males in these types of out-of-school-time lessons are greater in the partner countries and economies than in OECD countries. Among OECD countries, Greece has the highest gender difference – 9% favouring males – in the enrolment rate in one-to-one, out-of-school-time lessons with school teachers. In the partner countries and economies, the gender difference in the enrolment rate in this type of out-of-school-time lesson is greater than 10%, favouring males in Qatar, Jordan, Romania and Montenegro.

### Socio-economic background

The pattern of difference in hours spent in out-of-school-time lessons between socio-economically advantaged and disadvantaged students is not consistent across countries (Tables 3.7a, 3.7b and 3.7c). For example, advantaged students spend more time than disadvantaged students in out-of-school-time lessons in science in five OECD countries and eight partner countries and economies, while disadvantaged students spend more time than advantaged students in five OECD countries and three partner countries and economies. In mathematics, advantaged students spend more time in these kinds of lessons than disadvantaged students in 9 OECD countries and 15 partner countries and economies, while disadvantaged students spend more time than disadvantaged students in eight OECD countries and only one partner country, Slovenia. In the language of instruction, advantaged students spend more time in these kinds of lessons than disadvantaged students in two OECD countries and two partner countries and economies, while disadvantaged students spend more time than advantaged students in 14 OECD countries and 10 partner countries and economies.

How does student participation in different types of out-of-school-time lessons vary according to socio-economic background? Students' involvement differs greatly according to who is teaching out-of-school-time lessons. In general, as shown in Figures 3.3b and 3.3c, socio-economically advantaged students are more likely than disadvantaged students to attend out-of-school-time lessons taught by someone who is not a teacher in the school that the students attend (*i.e.* a non-school teacher) (Table 3.15). For example, across OECD countries, 35% of advantaged students attend out-of-school-time lessons with non-school teachers, while only 21% of disadvantaged students do so. However, socio-economically disadvantaged students are more likely than advantaged students to attend out-of-school-time lessons taught by teachers from the school that the students attend (*i.e.* school teachers). For example, across OECD countries, 30% of disadvantaged students attend out-of-school-time lessons with school teachers, while 23% of advantaged students do so.

While it is important to be careful when interpreting results and deriving certain ideas about out-of-school-time lessons across countries and cultures, in general, the purpose of out-of-school-time lessons with school teachers is different from those with non-school teachers. Out-of-school-time lessons given by school teachers are often organised for remedial purposes, to help underperforming students keep up with the rest of the class. Out-of-school-time lessons instructed by non-school teachers are often for enrichment purposes. In addition, while out-of-school-time lessons with school teachers often do not require additional fees, those with non-school teachers often do. Students from disadvantaged socio-economic backgrounds are thus less likely to be involved in out-of-school-time lessons with non-school teachers. This is in line with previous research that shows that private tutoring is more readily available to the rich than to the poor (Bray, 1999).

### Figure 3.3a
## Difference in learning time in science, by quarters of the PISA index of economic, social and cultural status (ESCS)

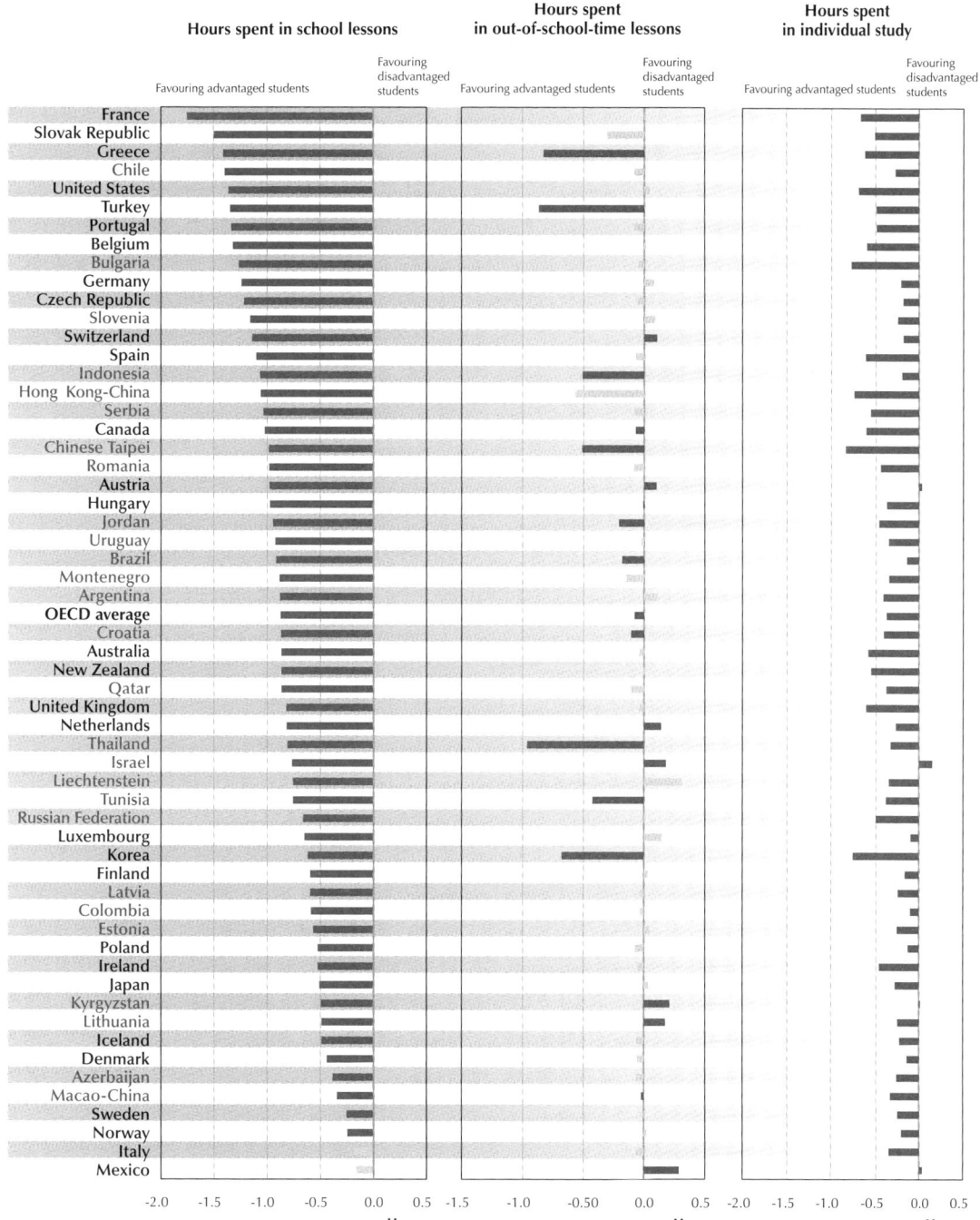

*Note:* Difference in learning time in science, by quarters of PISA index of economic, social and cultural status (ESCS).

Countries are ranked in descending order of the difference in learning hours in school lessons between the top and bottom quarters of ESCS students.

*Source: OECD PISA 2006 Database,* Table 3.7a.

### Figure 3.3b
### Participation rates in out-of-school-time lessons with non-school teachers, by quarters of the PISA index of economic, social and cultural status (ESCS)

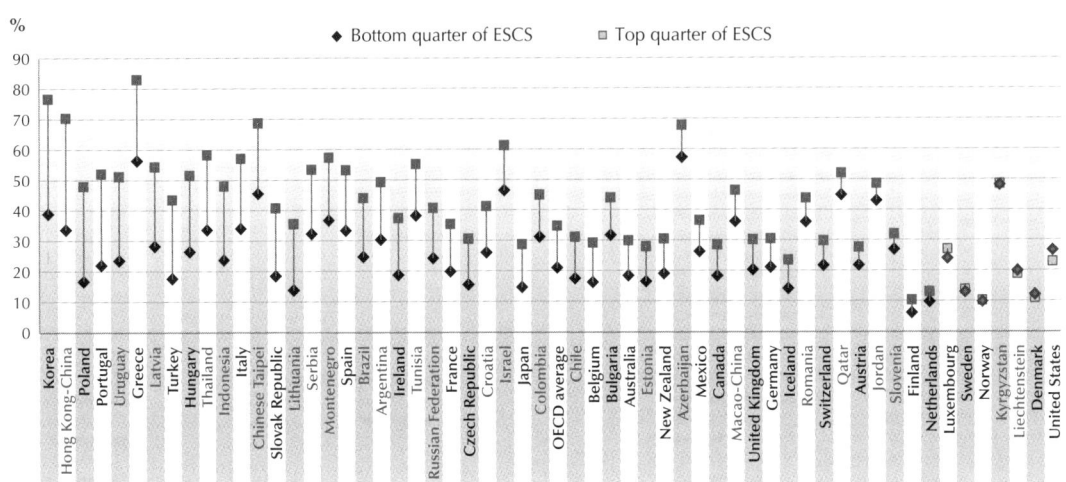

*Note:* Differences that are statistically significant are marked in a darker tone.

Countries are ranked in descending order of the difference in rates of participation in out-of-school-time lessons with non-school teachers between the top and bottom quarters of ESCS students.

*Source: OECD PISA 2006 Database*, Table 3.15.

### Figure 3.3c
### Participation rates in out-of-school-time lessons with school teachers, by quarters of PISA index of economic, social and cultural status (ESCS)

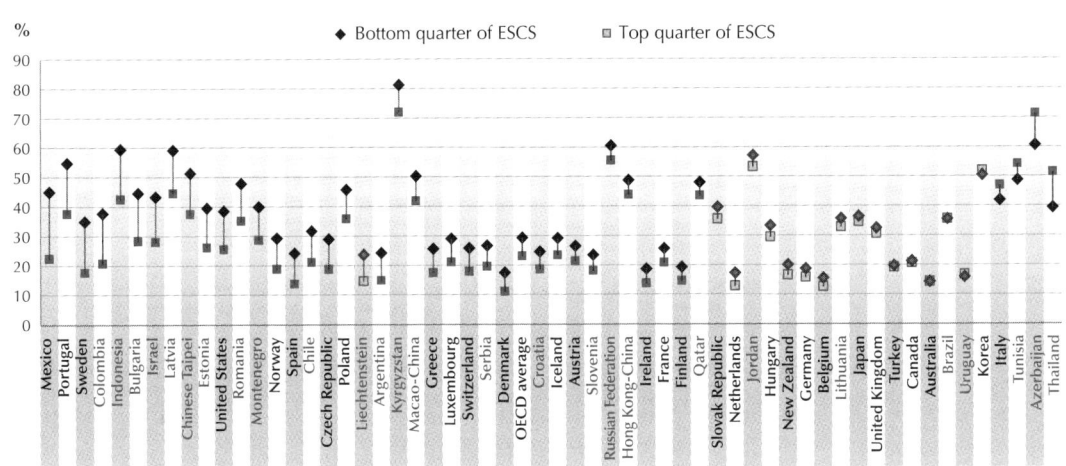

*Note:* Differences that are statistically significant are marked in a darker tone.

Countries are ranked in descending order of the difference in rates of participation in out-of-school-time lessons with school teachers between the bottom and top quarters of ESCS students.

*Source: OECD PISA 2006 Database*, Table 3.15.

© OECD 2011 Quality Time for Students: Learning In and Out of School

### Immigrant status

In most countries, students with an immigrant background tend to spend more time in out-of-school-time lessons regardless of subject (Tables 3.8a, 3.8b and 3.8c). Across OECD countries, students with an immigrant background spend an additional 42 minutes per week in out-of-school-time lessons in all 3 subjects combined compared with native students (Table 3.8d). After adjusting for the difference in socio-economic status of students and schools, students with an immigrant background still tend to spend more time in out-of-school-time lessons than native students. On average across OECD countries, and after adjusting for differences in socio-economic background, students with an immigrant background spend 40 minutes per week more in out-of-school-time lessons than native students.

Students with an immigrant background tend to be more involved in out-of-school-time lessons than native students in most countries except Greece and the partner countries and economies Qatar, Hong Kong-China, Kyrgyzstan and Macao-China (Table 3.16). In most countries, students with an immigrant background tend to be more involved in any type of out-of-school-time lessons than native students. However, there is no consistent pattern across countries concerning one-to-one out-of-school-time lessons with non-school teachers. The difference in the proportion of students participating in out-of-school-time lessons according to immigrant status varies according to the type of out-of-school-time lesson. The difference between out-of-school-time lessons with school teachers and those with non-school teachers is great. In Mexico, for example, 71% of students with an immigrant background participate in out-of-school-time lessons with a school teacher while only 31% of native students do so. In Denmark, Sweden, Spain, Norway, Portugal, the United States and the partner countries Tunisia, Liechtenstein and Brazil, the difference is 10% or more, favouring students with an immigrant background.

### School-level variation

Learning time spent in out-of-school-time lessons does not vary much between schools. Across OECD countries, 6% of variation in learning time in out-of-school-time lessons can be attributed to the difference between schools (Table 3.9d). School-level variation in learning time in out-of-school-time lessons is small in almost all countries: it is 5% or less in about half of the participating countries and economies, and 10% or less in all countries and economies except Korea, Greece and the partner countries and economies Thailand, Chinese Taipei and Liechtenstein.

### Lower secondary and upper secondary schools

Students in lower secondary schools tend to spend more time in out-of-school-time lessons than students in upper secondary schools. This might be because the end of lower secondary education in some countries marks the time for important examinations that determine entry into upper secondary schools (Dang, 2007; Tan, 2009). These students are also more likely to attend any type of out-of-school-time lessons, except one-to-one lessons taught by a non-school teacher (Table 3.17). Meanwhile, students in upper secondary schools in Greece, Portugal, Hungary, Poland, Switzerland, France and the partner countries and economies Slovenia, Uruguay, Bulgaria, Azerbaijan, Argentina and Hong Kong-China generally attend more one-to-one lessons with non-school teachers than students in lower secondary schools.

### Public and private schools

Students in public schools tend to spend more time in out-of-school-time lessons than students in private schools in seven OECD countries and nine partner countries and economies (Table 3.11d). In Greece and Mexico, and the partner countries Israel and Estonia, students in public schools tend to spend an additional one hour or more per week in out-of-school-time lessons in science, mathematics and the language of instruction compared with students in private schools.

There is a significant difference in some type of out-of-school-time lessons students in public and private schools attend (Table 3.18). In 14 OECD countries and 5 partner countries and economies, students in private schools generally attend more one-to-one, out-of-school-time lessons taught by a non-school teacher than students in public schools. Meanwhile, in 11 OECD countries and 6 partner countries and economies, students in public schools attend more large group, out-of-school-time lessons taught by school teachers than students in private schools; but in four OECD countries and two partner countries and economies, students in private schools attend these types of lessons more than public school students.

### Academic and vocational schools

In almost every country, students attending academic schools spend more time in learning science and mathematics in out-of-school-time lessons; but the results are mixed across countries in the language of instruction (Tables 3.12a, 3.12b and 3.12c). Across OECD countries, students attending academic schools spend an additional 13 minutes per week in out-of-school-time lessons in science and an additional 17 minutes in mathematics. In seven OECD countries and five partner countries, students in academic schools spend more time in out-of-school-time lessons in the language of instruction than students in vocational schools, but in five OECD countries and three partner countries, students in vocational schools spend more time in these lessons than students in academic schools.

Even after accounting for the socio-economic status of students and schools, students attending academic schools spend more time in learning science, mathematics and the language of instruction in out-of-school-time lessons in most countries (Table 3.12d). Although the difference in learning hours is smaller, it remains considerable. For example, on average across OECD countries, students attending academic schools spend 28 minutes more in out-of-school-time lessons than students with a similar socio-economic background who attend vocational schools.

Students in academic schools spend more time in out-of-school-time lessons, especially for science and mathematics. In most countries, students in academic schools are more likely to attend any type of out-of-school-time lesson than students in vocational schools, but the difference in participation is remarkable for the one-to-one, out-of-school-time lessons taught by someone who is not a teacher in the school the student attends (*i.e.* one-to-one lessons with non-school teachers) (Table 3.19). For example, in Greece, 48% of students in academic schools, but only 24% of students in vocational schools, attend out-of-school-time lessons. This means that the difference in participation rates between students in academic and vocational schools is 24 percentage points. Across OECD countries, there is a difference of more than eight percentage points between students in academic schools who attend this type of out-of-school-time lesson and students in vocational schools who do so. The difference in the participation rate is ten percentage points or higher in Greece, Korea, France, Italy, Hungary, Austria and in the partner country and economy Macao-China and Serbia. In most countries, this difference does not change much after adjusting for socio-economic background: on average across OECD countries, the difference between students in academic schools and students in vocational schools who attend this type of out-of-school-time lesson is five percentage points or greater.

### Schools in urban and rural areas

The results for out-of-school-time lessons according to school location vary across countries. Earlier studies have shown that tutoring is more common in cities (UNESCO, 2009). PISA 2006 data show that, in most countries, students in urban schools are more involved in out-of-school-time lessons taught by non-school teachers. This is especially true in one-to-one, out-of-school-time lessons with non-school teachers (Table 3.20). Across OECD countries, 22% of students in urban schools attend this type of out-of-school-time lesson, while 18% of students in schools in rural areas do so. This means that the difference in participation rates between students in urban and rural areas is four percentage points. As shown in Figure 3.4b, the difference in the attendance rate for this type of out-of-school-time lessons is ten percentage points or

© OECD 2011 Quality Time for Students: Learning In and Out of School

higher in Switzerland, New Zealand and the partner countries Tunisia, Estonia, Lithuania and Serbia. The difference in this participation rate, favouring students in urban schools, is significant in half the countries, after adjusting for the socio-economic status of students and schools (Table 3.20).

### Figure 3.4a
## Participation rates in out-of-school-time lessons with school teachers, by school location

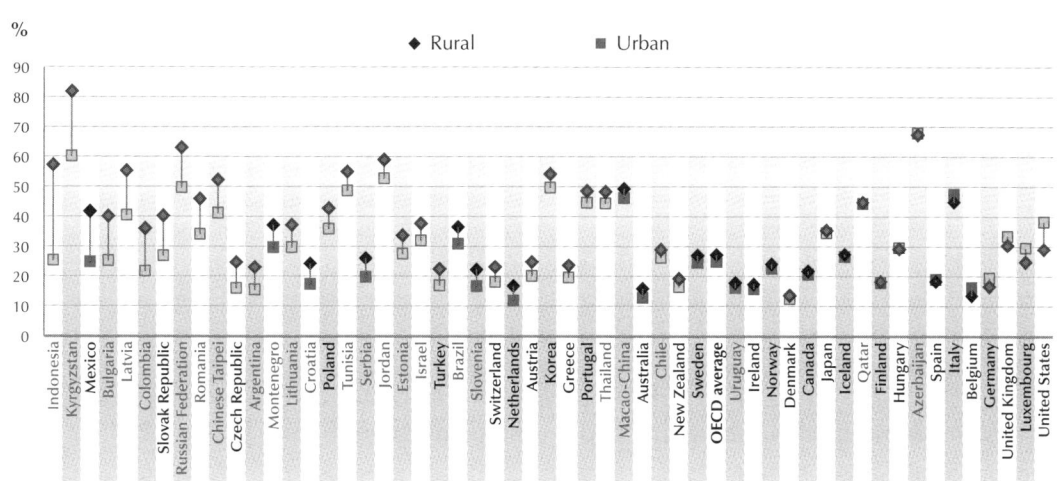

*Note:* Differences that are statistically significant are marked in a darker tone.
Countries are ranked in descending order of the difference in rates of participation in out-of-school-time lessons with school teachers between rural and urban schools.
*Source*: OECD PISA 2006 Database, Table 3.20.

### Figure 3.4b
## Participation rates in out-of-school-time lessons with non-school teachers, by school location

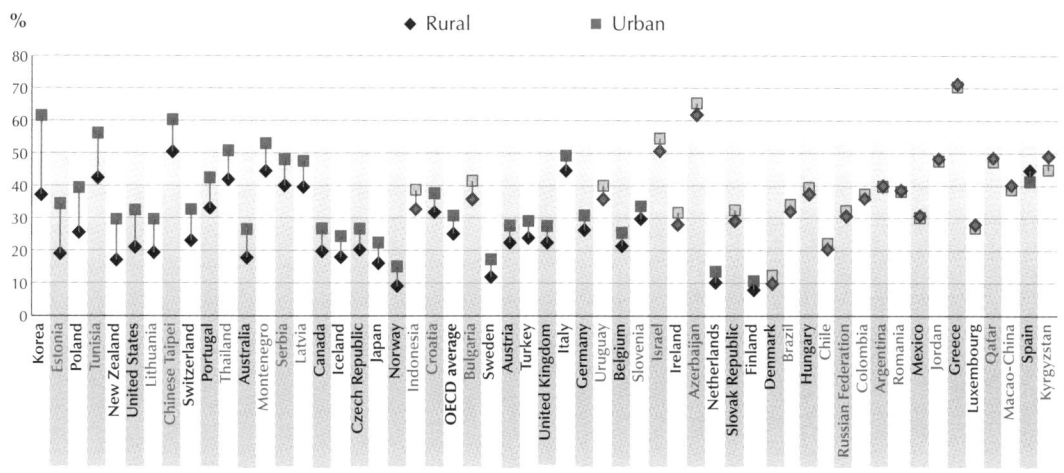

*Note:* Differences that are statistically significant are marked in a darker tone.
Countries are ranked in descending order of the difference in rates of participation in out-of-school-time lessons with non-school teachers between urban and rural schools.
*Source*: OECD PISA 2006 Database, Table 3.20.

In most countries, students in schools in rural areas are more likely than students in urban schools to attend out-of-school-time lessons that are taught by teachers from the schools the students attend, but this pattern disappears in two-thirds of countries once the difference in socio-economic status of students and schools

is taken into account (Table 3.20). The difference in the attendance rates for this type of out-of-school-time lessons is ten percentage points or more in Mexico, the Slovak Republic and the partner countries and economies Indonesia, Kyrgyzstan, Bulgaria, Latvia, Colombia, the Russian Federation, Romania and Chinese Taipei. However, after adjusting for the socio-economic status of students and schools, only in the Russian Federation and Indonesia is the difference ten percentage points or more.

## Who spends more time in regular school lessons and individual study?

In both learning time spent in regular school lessons and in individual study, females spend more time than males, socio-economically advantaged students spend more time than disadvantaged students, students in private schools spend more time than students in public schools, students in academic schools spend more time than students in vocational schools, and students in urban schools spend more time than students in schools in rural areas. However, the difference in hours spent in regular school lessons and individual study favours students in private schools or in schools in urban areas; but once the socio-economic background of the students and schools is accounted for, there is no appreciable difference. Students with an immigrant background spend more time than native students in individual study across most countries, and students in upper secondary schools spend more time in individual study in science and mathematics, but there is no consistent pattern for individual study in the language of instruction.

## Who spends more time in which types of out-of-school-time lessons?

Given that out-of-school-time lessons are not necessarily the same across countries, or even within countries, since different types of out-of-school-time lessons have different meanings and functions, there are differences in students' involvement in out-of-school-time lessons according to student subgroups and to the different types of out-of-school-time lessons. For example, out-of-school-time lessons with school teachers are favoured by males, socio-economically disadvantaged students, students in lower secondary schools, and, especially in partner countries and economies, students in schools in rural areas. However, the difference in attendance rates in this type of out-of-school-time lesson between rural and urban schools disappears after adjustments are made for the socio-economic backgrounds of the students and schools.

Meanwhile, one-to-one, out-of-school-time lessons with non-school teachers are favoured by females, socio-economically advantaged students, students in academic schools, students in private schools and students in urban schools. The pattern does not change much even after the socio-economic backgrounds of students and schools are adjusted for. The patterns of involvement differ, as the purpose and organisation of these two types of out-of-school-time lessons are different.

## Box 3.1 **Summary of observed learning patterns by student and school characteristics**

The table below presents the overview of patterns in the deliberate learning time among population sub-groups. The population sub-group, which is shown consistently to spend more time in each learning activity across countries in three subject domains, is presented in a darker tone. The number of countries is presented only in science, as the pattern does not differ greatly across subject domains. Any significant difference in pattern across subject domains is explained in a footnote. The number of OECD countries is indicated in brackets. For example, female students spend more time in regular school lessons than male students in 27 OECD countries and 42 partner countries and economies.

| | | Regular school lessons | Out-of-school-time lessons | Individual study |
|---|---|---|---|---|
| **Gender** | Female | 42(27) | 4(3) | 43(20) |
| | Male | 3(1) | 26(16)[1] | 3(1) |
| **ESCS** | Advantaged | 55(28) | 13(5) | 50(26) |
| | Disadvantaged | 0(0) | 8(5) | 0(0) |
| **Immigrant background** | Native | 15(11) | 3(1) | 3(1) |
| | Immigrant | 3(1) | 22(19) | 14(10) |
| **Lower/Upper secondary school** | Upper secondary | 35(15) | 3(1) | 23(12)[2] |
| | Lower secondary | 5(3) | 18(12) | 7(5) |
| **Private/Public school** | Private | 23(11) | 4(0) | 13(8) |
| | Public | 7(3) | 13(7) | 9(3) |
| **Academic/Vocational school** | Academic | 30(17) | 17(11) | 31(17) |
| | Vocational | 2(1) | 2(1) | 1(1) |
| **Region** | City | 21(8) | 9(7) | 12(10) |
| | Rural | 3(3) | 10(4) | 5(1) |

*Note:* These results are based on the observed differences in deliberate learning hours by population sub-group. For those who are interested in the results after accounting for socio-economic background of students and schools, please refer to the previous text in corresponding sections.
1. Mathematics and the language of instruction showed a different pattern from science. In mathematics, the difference is in favour of male students in 15(10) countries and it is in favour of female students in 6(5) countries. In the language of instruction, the difference is in favour of male students in 16(9) countries and it is in favour of female students in 16(11) countries.
2. Unlike science and mathematics, there is no consistent pattern in the language of instruction.

*Source:* *OECD PISA 2006 Database,* Tables 3.6a, 3.7a, 3.8a, 3.9a, 3.10a, 3.11a, 3.12a and 3.13a.

...

**...**

The following table shows attendance in out-of-school-time lessons. The population sub-group, which is shown consistently to be more likely to attend a particular type of out-of-school-time lessons across countries, is presented in a darker tone.

| | | Out-of-school-time lessons with school teachers | One-to-one out-of-school-time lessons with non-school teachers |
|---|---|---|---|
| **Gender** | Female | 0(0) | 24(13) |
| | Male | 32(15) | 5(1) |
| **ESCS** | Advantaged | 4(1) | 53(27) |
| | Disadvantaged | 37(18) | 0(0) |
| **Immigrant background** | Native | 2(0) | 5(2) |
| | Immigrant | 23(16) | 9(8) |
| **Lower/Upper secondary school** | Upper secondary | 2(1) | 12(6) |
| | Lower secondary | 30(17) | 8(7) |
| **Private/Public school** | Private | 8(6) | 19(14) |
| | Public | 13(8) | 1(1) |
| **Academic/ Vocational school** | Academic | 13(8) | 28(13) |
| | Vocational | 12(5) | 1(0) |
| **Region** | Urban | 2(2) | 32(16) |
| | Rural | 28(10) | 0(0) |

*Note:* These results are based on the observed differences in deliberate learning hours by population sub-group. For those who are interested in the results after accounting for socio-economic background of students and schools, please refer to the previous text in corresponding sections.

*Source: OECD PISA 2006 Database,* Tables 3.14 - 3.20.

© OECD 2011 Quality Time for Students: Learning In and Out of School

# References

**Bray, M.** (1999), "The Shadow Education System: Private Tutoring and its Implications for Planners", *Fundamentals of Educational Planning*, No. 61, UNESCO International Institute for Educational Planning, Paris.

**Bray, M.** (2009), *Confronting the Shadow Education System: What Government Policies for What Private Tutoring?*, UNESCO, Paris.

**OECD** (2002), *PISA 2000 Technical Report*, OECD Publishing.

**OECD** (2004), *Learning for Tomorrow's World: First Results from PISA 2003*, OECD Publishing.

**OECD** (2007), *PISA 2006: Science Competencies for Tomorrow's World*, OECD Publishing.

**OECD** (2009a), *Equally Prepared for Life? How 15-year-old Boys and Girls Perform in School*, OECD Publishing.

**OECD** (2009b), *PISA 2006 Technical Report*, OECD Publishing.

4

# Relationships between Students' Learning Time and Performance

## INTRODUCTION

This chapter examines the relationship between students' learning time and students' academic performance in PISA, both across and within countries. Do students who spend more time learning achieve higher scores? Is the amount of time spent learning more important than how that time is spent? In other words, is the quality of learning time as important as the quantity of learning time?

The section on regular school lessons examines how students' perceptions of the importance of subjects play a role in their performance. These perceptions are used as an indirect proxy for "perseverance", which was identified as one of the factors related to students' learning in Carroll's seminal model on school learning (Carroll, 1963). Other factors identified in Carroll's model, such as "aptitude", "quality of instruction" and "ability to understand instruction", are not examined, as the PISA 2006 data do not provide indicators for these factors. The section on out-of-school-time lessons analyses what types of lessons enhance learning without introducing inequities.

Since the analysis is based on cross-sectional data, it is difficult to determine the causality of the relationships. For example, students may spend more time in out-of-school-time lessons because these students themselves or their parents or teachers conclude that they need to attend extra classes to catch up with other students; and students may spend more time engaging in individual study because they need more time than other students to complete a certain number of tasks. Given the complexity of the relationship, the results in this chapter are carefully examined and interpreted, using relatively neutral terms such as "relationship" or "association". Terms such as "effect" or "impact", which imply a causal relationship, are generally avoided for the same reasons.

## LEARNING TIME AND PERFORMANCE ACROSS COUNTRIES

What are the relationships between the average time students spend learning science, mathematics and the language of instruction and the country average performance in PISA 2006? Do countries where students spend more time learning tend to achieve higher scores? The time that students spend in regular school lessons is positively related to performance across countries in all three subjects (Tables 4.1a, 4.1b and 4.1c). Countries with longer average learning time in regular school lessons tend to achieve higher scores. This relationship is stronger in mathematics and reading than in science. About 25% of variation in performance in mathematics and reading across countries is explained by learning time in regular school lessons, while only 7% of the variation in science scores is explained in that way (Table 4.1b).

The time students spend in out-of-school-time lessons and the time spent in individual study are both negatively related to performance in science, mathematics and reading across countries. These relationships are strong, especially in science, as 41% of the cross-country variation in science performance can be explained by the country average learning time in out-of-school time lessons in science. That proportion is 23% in mathematics and 29% in reading. Meanwhile, 42% of the variation in science performance between learning time in individual study and performance can be explained by the country average learning time in individual study. That proportion is 14% in mathematics and 28% in reading (Table 4.1b).

© OECD 2011 Quality Time for Students: Learning In and Out of School

### Figure 4.1a
### Cross-country relationship between performance in science and learning time in regular school lessons in science

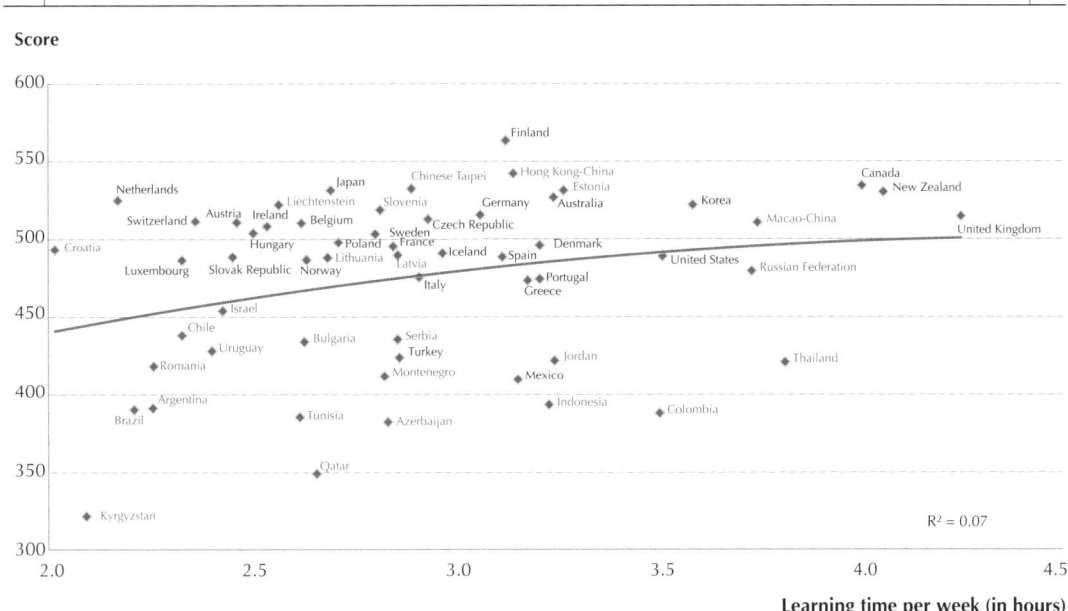

*Source*: *OECD PISA 2006 Database*, Table 4.1a.

### Figure 4.1b
### Cross-country relationship between performance in science and learning time in out-of-school-time lessons in science

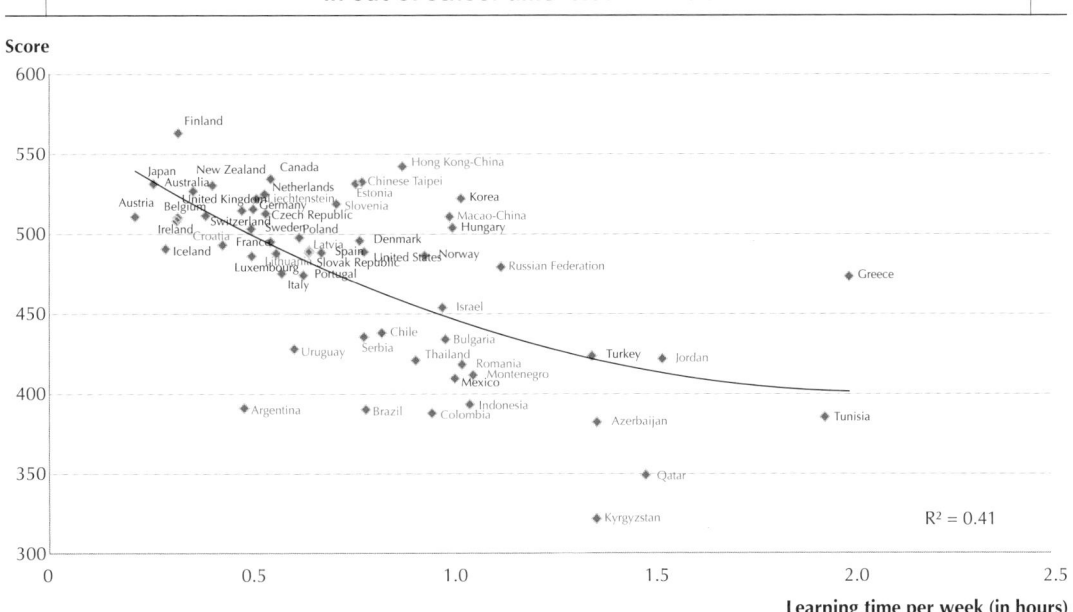

*Source*: *OECD PISA 2006 Database*, Table 4.1a.

## Figure 4.1c
## Cross-country relationship between performance in science and learning time in individual study in science

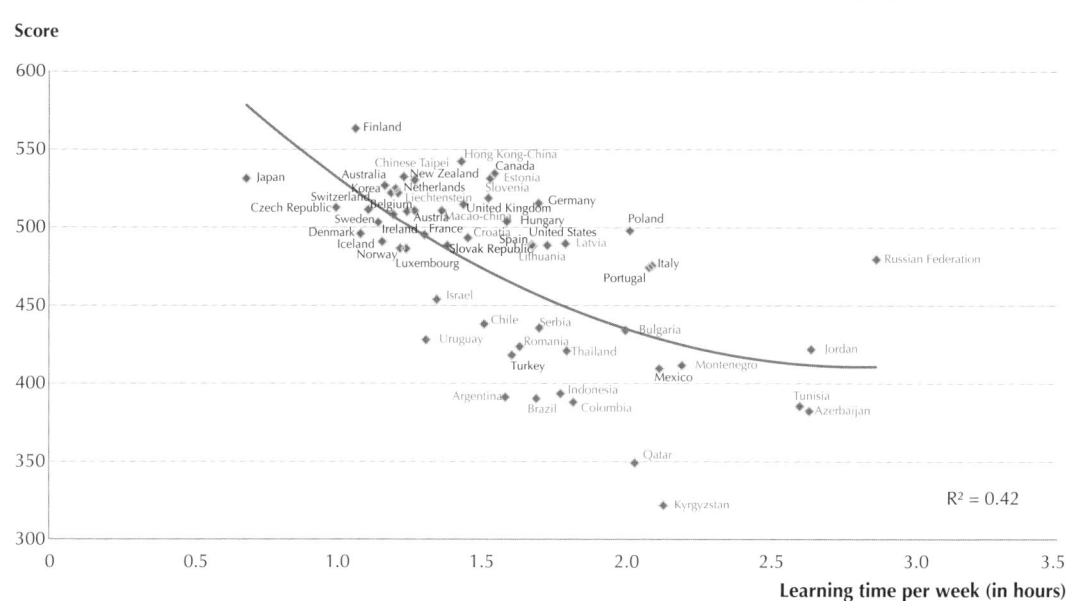

*Source: OECD PISA 2006 Database*, Table 4.1a.

Across countries, relative learning time in regular school lessons, which is equivalent to the proportion of absolute learning time in regular school lessons out of absolute total learning time (*i.e.* the time spent in regular school lessons, out-of-school-time lessons and individual study combined), is strongly related to performance. For example, 63% of the variation in science performance across countries can be explained by the proportion of learning time in regular school lessons in science out of total science learning time (Table 4.1c). Countries with a higher proportion of time allocated to regular school lessons tend to perform better. Countries with the lowest proportions of regular school lessons in science out of total science learning time – from 35% to 43% – including the partner countries Kyrgyzstan, Tunisia, Qatar, Jordan and Azerbaijan, perform between 322 to 422 score points in science, while countries with the highest proportions of science regular school lessons – from 71% to 78% – including the OECD countries Japan, New Zealand, Australia, Finland and the United Kingdom, perform between 515 to 563 score points in science (Table 4.1a). Similar relationships are observed in mathematics and reading.

In summary, students in high-performing countries spend less time, on average, in out-of-school-time lessons and individual study, and more time in regular school lessons than students in low-performing countries. This positive relationship between learning time in regular school lessons and performance is even more pronounced when the time students spend in regular school lessons is considered as a relative term, *i.e.* a share out of total time spent learning.

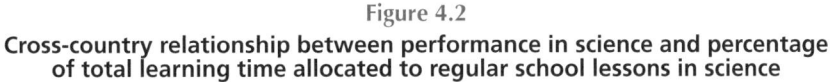

### Figure 4.2
### Cross-country relationship between performance in science and percentage of total learning time allocated to regular school lessons in science

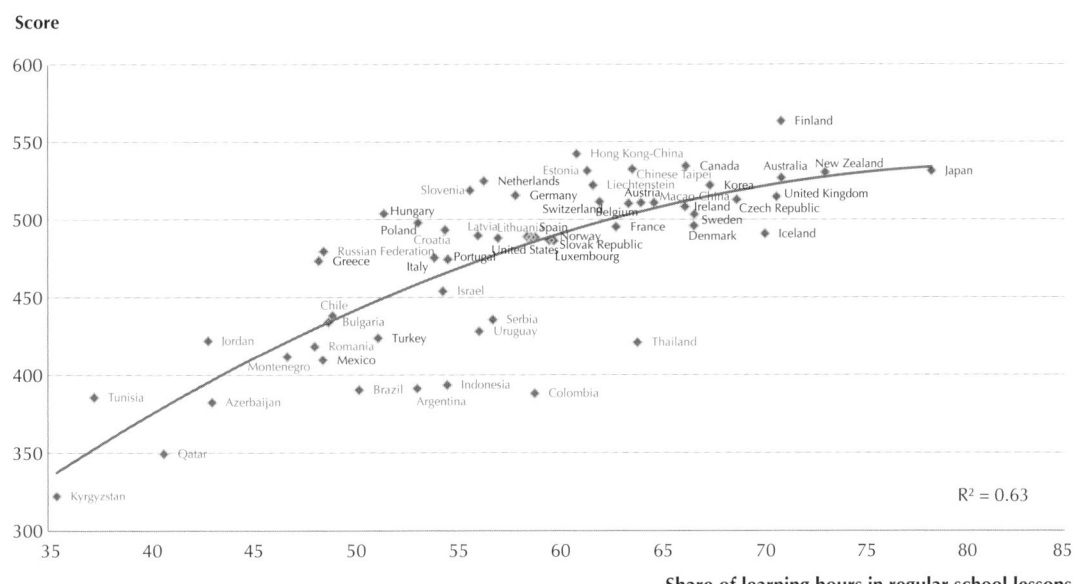

Source: OECD PISA 2006 Database, Table 4.1a.

To explain the difference in performance across countries, the relative learning time in regular school lessons – a higher proportion of time spent in regular school lessons – is more important than the absolute learning time, or the overall length of learning time. This is true for each of three subjects as well as for the three subjects combined. For instance, Finland's absolute learning time in regular school lessons for science is 3.1 hours, which is equivalent to relative learning time of 71% of total learning time. In 10 OECD countries and 8 partner countries, the absolute learning time of regular school lessons for science is more than that of Finland. In all of these countries, except New Zealand, relative learning time is 71% or less. Although the absolute learning time spent in regular school lessons is longer in these countries, Finland achieves the highest scores in science among 57 countries (Table 4.1a). A possible explanation is that, even if countries have the same absolute length of learning time in schools, there is no guarantee that the same quality of education is provided to students across countries, particularly since factors such as the way schools and teaching are organised, student motivation levels, and schools' socio-economic status vary widely across countries. In high-performing countries, the biggest proportion of students' learning time – 70% to 80% of their learning time – happens within regular school lessons. In these countries, students may not need to spend more time in out-of-school-time lessons or studying by themselves if they receive sufficient education during regular school lessons. In low-performing countries, 50% or more of students' learning time happens outside regular school lessons. Students in these countries may need to supplement their learning by attending out-of-school-time lessons or studying by themselves. As learning outside regular school lessons tends to be less structured and less regulated, quality varies. Consequently, the large number of hours spent learning in out-of-school-time lessons or individual study do not necessarily lead to high performance.

In order to determine the relationship between quality of regular school lessons and countries' relative learning time, some characteristics of the school system that have an impact on educational quality are compared between countries with a high or low proportion of hours spent in regular school lessons. Countries were divided into two groups: those that spend a higher proportion of hours in regular school lessons in

61

science, mathematics and the language of instruction than the average across all participating countries (58%), and those that spend a lower proportion of hours (Figure 2.3). The system characteristics, such as the level of school resources, the level of school autonomy and accountability policies are examined, because an earlier PISA study identified them as having a significant positive relationship with students' performance (OECD, 2007). The indicators of school resources include human resources (*i.e.* the index of teacher shortage) and material resources (*i.e.* the index of the school's educational resources) reported by school principals. Higher values on these indices indicate higher rates of teacher shortage at a school and higher levels of educational resources. A school's autonomy is measured by the responsibility for tasks regarding resource allocation (*i.e.* the index of resource autonomy) and curriculum and assessment (*i.e.* the index of curricular autonomy) reported by school principals. Higher values indicate relatively higher levels of school responsibility and autonomy in these domains. These indices were standardised so that at the OECD level they have a mean of zero and a standard deviation of one. When standardised external examinations exist in some parts of the system, but not throughout the system (*e.g.* regional variations or variations between different types of education programmes), the proportion of students who are affected by such examinations are indicated by a value between 0 and 1. Higher values indicate a relatively higher proportion of standardised external examinations.

The analysis show that in countries where the proportion of hours spent in regular school lessons is low, schools tend to struggle more with teacher shortages and low quality of educational resources, compared with countries with a high proportion of hours spent in regular school lessons. Box 4.1 shows the average difference in the index of teacher shortage and the index of the quality of educational resources between countries where students spend less than 58% of their learning time in regular school lessons and countries where students spend 58% or more of their learning time in regular school lessons. Countries with a low proportion of hours spent in regular school lessons have higher levels of teacher shortage: their score on the index of teacher shortage is 0.35 standard deviation higher than countries with a high proportion of hours spent in regular school lessons. The difference in the index of the quality of educational resources is 0.76 standard deviation, so that, on average, schools in countries with a high proportion of hours in regular school lessons have better school resources than schools in countries where students spend less of their learning time in regular school lessons.

In addition, in countries where the proportion of regular school lessons is low, schools tend to have less autonomy on the allocation of resources, curriculum and assessment compared with countries with a high proportion of hours spent in regular school lessons. The difference in the index of resource autonomy and the index of curricular autonomy is 0.55 and 0.91 standard deviations, favouring countries with a high proportion of hours in regular school lessons. It could be inferred that teachers or principals in countries with a low proportion of hours spent in regular school lessons may be less motivated than countries with a high proportion of hours spent in regular school lessons, as principals and teachers are less likely to be involved in decision making in the areas of staffing, budgeting and instructional content.

Countries where the proportion of hours spent in regular school lessons is low tend to have fewer standardised external examinations than countries where the proportion of hours spent in regular school lessons is high. For example, the proportion of this type of examination is 0.46 in countries where students spend fewer hours in regular school lessons, while it is 0.60 in countries where students spend more hours in those kinds of lessons. This result may not provide enough evidence to determine whether the schools' quality of education is regulated systemically or not, but it shows, to a limited extent, that countries where the proportion of hours spent in regular school lessons is low tend to be less regulated in assessing students' performance compared with countries where a high proportion of time spent in regular school lessons.

In short, compared with the countries with high relative learning time in regular school lessons, the countries with low relative learning time in these lessons turn out to have system characteristics that are related to low overall performance: lower levels of school materials and human resources, less school autonomy and lower proportions of standardised external examinations. Students in these countries may have to spend more time in out-of-school-time lessons or in individual study to compensate for any shortfalls in learning during regular school lessons.

The comparison between Figure 4.1a and Figure 4.2 and the results in Box 4.1 implies that it is the quality of regular school lessons, not the quantity of learning hours, that would explain more of the difference in performance across countries. A simple intervention to increase the number of school hours or to encourage students to spend more hours learning outside of regular school lessons would not be an effective way to improve performance in low-performing countries, especially for those countries that already have long hours of absolute learning time in regular school lessons. Instead, these countries including Italy, Mexico, Turkey, the Unites States, Azerbaijan, Indonesia, Jordan and Latvia (Figure 2.3) may need to consider improving the quality of education and providing an environment that is conducive to learning.

As the comparison in system characteristics shows, one way to improve the quality of education would be to reduce the levels of teacher shortage by employing more qualified teachers and increase schools' educational resources. Countries might consider encouraging principals and teachers to be more involved in decision making in the areas of staffing, budgeting and instructional content. In countries with insufficient accountability arrangements, greater use of standardised external examinations of student performance could be another way to improve the quality of learning time in regular school lessons.

---

Box 4.1. **Mean indices of teacher shortage and the school's educational resources, by share of learning time in regular school lessons out of the total learning time in science**

| | | Countries where students spend less than 58% of their learning time in regular school lessons in science (A) | | Countries where students spend 58% or more of their learning time in regular school lessons in science (B) | | Difference (A-B) | |
|---|---|---|---|---|---|---|---|
| | | Mean | S.E. | Mean | S.E. | Mean | S.E. |
| Performance | Science | 431.9 | (0.7) | 503.3 | (0.5) | **-71.4** | (0.8) |
| | Mathematics | 423.3 | (0.8) | 502.3 | (0.5) | **-79.0** | (0.9) |
| | Reading | 413.7 | (0.9) | 491.5 | (0.6) | **-77.7** | (1.0) |
| School material | Teacher shortage | 0.32 | -(0.03) | -0.03 | -(0.01) | **0.35** | -(0.03) |
| | Quality of educational resource | -0.88 | -(0.02) | -0.12 | -(0.01) | **-0.76** | -(0.02) |
| School autonomy | Responsibility for resource allocation | -0.59 | -(0.01) | -0.04 | -(0.01) | **-0.55** | -(0.02 |
| | Responsibility for curriculum and assessment | -0.89 | -(0.01) | 0.02 | -(0.01) | **-0.91** | -(0.01) |
| Accountability policies | Standards-based external examinations (ratio of existence) | 0.46 | (0.00) | 0.6 | (0.00) | **-0.14** | (0.00) |

*Source*: OECD PISA 2006 Database, Table 4.1a.

## LEARNING TIME AND PERFORMANCE WITHIN COUNTRIES

Cross-country analysis in the previous section has shown the importance of relative learning time in regular school lessons, but the relationship between learning time and performance within countries is different from the relationship between countries: within countries, the absolute length in learning time is more strongly related to performance than the relative learning time in regular school lessons. This may be because the quality of regular school lessons within countries does not vary as much as across countries.

This section compares average performance scores for the following six categories of students' learning time: "no time", "less than 2 hours per week", "2 to less than 4 hours per week", "4 to less than 6 hours per week", and "6 or more hours per week". Students who spend a moderate amount of hours learning are defined as those who spend two to six hours per week studying. Students who spend long hours learning are defined as those who spend six or more hours per week studying. Differences in performance among students who spend different amounts of time learning are also compared, with adjustments made for the socio-economic background of students and schools, and for learning time in out-of-school-time lessons and individual study.

## LEARNING TIME IN REGULAR SCHOOL LESSONS AND PERFORMANCE

### Science

In general, students who spend more time learning science in regular school lessons tend to achieve higher scores, as shown in Figure 4.3. Across OECD countries, students who spend less than two hours per week in regular school lessons in science tend to perform 15 score points higher in science than students who do not spend any time learning science in regular school lessons; students who spend two to less than four hours per week tend to perform 59 score points higher; students who spend four to less than six hours per week tend to perform 89 score points higher; and students who spend six or more hours per week tend to perform 104 score points higher (Table 4.2a).

Adjusting for the socio-economic background of students and schools, and for students' learning time in out-of-school lessons and individual study in science, the relationship between learning time in regular school lessons in science and performance in science is still positive. However, differences in scores are smaller when these other factors are taken into account (Table 4.2a).

The positive relationship between learning time in regular school lessons in science and performance in science is more evident in countries where students spend two or more hours per week in regular school lessons in science. In most countries, science performance improves steadily as learning time in regular school lessons increases beyond two hours per week. However, this improvement in science performance varies greatly across countries; in a few countries, the improvement is not steady. In France, the United Kingdom, Switzerland, the Slovak Republic, Belgium and Greece, a significant improvement in science performance goes hand-in-hand with an increase in learning time: students who spend six or more hours per week learning perform at least 140 score points higher than students who do not spend any time in regular school lessons in science. However, in a few countries, students who spend six or more hours per week learning science in regular school lessons perform lower than students who spend a moderate amount of hours. For example, in Norway and Mexico, students who spend six or more hours per week in regular school lessons tend to perform lower than students who spend a moderate amount of time learning (from four to less than six hours per week), and they perform at the same level as students who do not spend any time learning science in regular school lessons (Table 4.2a).

© OECD 2011 Quality Time for Students: Learning In and Out of School

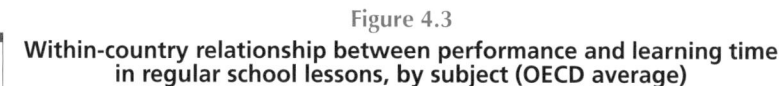

Figure 4.3
**Within-country relationship between performance and learning time
in regular school lessons, by subject (OECD average)**

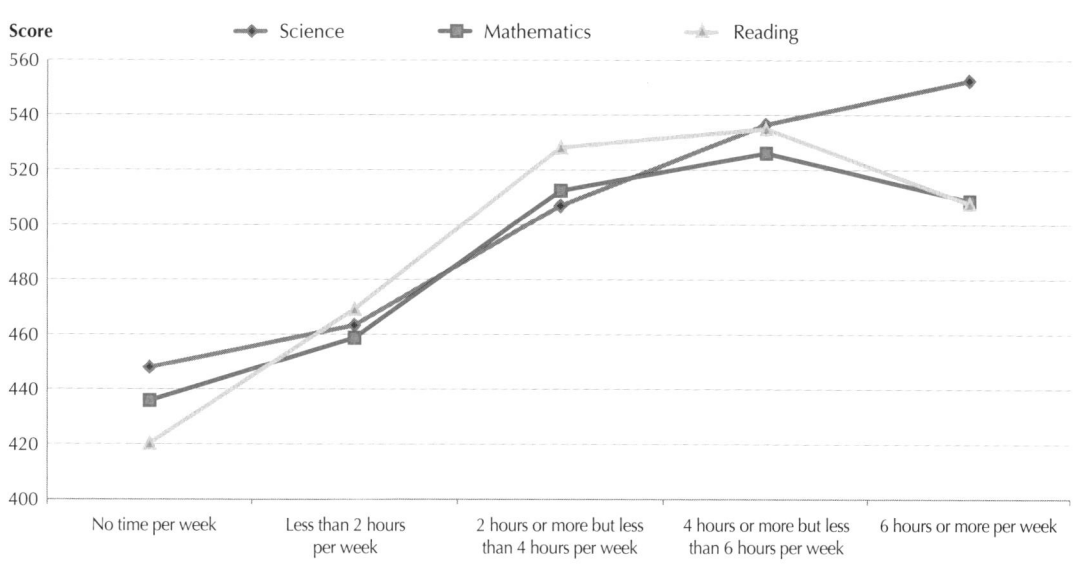

*Source*: *OECD PISA 2006 Database*, Tables 4.2a, 4.2b and 4.2c.

## Mathematics

In general, there is a curvilinear relationship between learning time in regular school lessons and performance in mathematics, as shown in Figure 4.3. When students spend less than six hours per week in regular school lessons, there is a positive relationship between learning time and performance; but beyond six hours per week, students tend to perform lower than students who spend from two hours to less than four hours per week in regular school lessons. Across OECD countries, students who spend between 2 and 4 hours per week learning mathematics tend to perform 64 score points higher than students who do not spend any time learning mathematics in regular school lessons; students who spend between 4 and 6 hours per week tend to perform 78 score points higher; and students who spend more than 6 hours per week tend to perform 61 score points higher. This curvilinear relationship can be also observed after adjusting for the socio-economic background of students and schools, and for students' learning time in mathematics in out-of-school-time lessons and individual study (Table 4.2b).

The general pattern observed in many countries indicates that students who spend long hours in mathematics in regular school lessons perform much lower than students who spend a moderate amount of hours. For example, in Spain, Norway, Luxembourg, Germany, the Netherlands and the partner country Croatia, students who spend 6 or more hours per week in regular school lessons in mathematics perform at least 44 score points lower than students who spend from 4 to less than 6 hours per week in lessons.

In only a few countries do students who spend a long time learning mathematics in regular schools lessons perform significantly better in mathematics than other students. For example, in Korea and the partner economies Chinese Taipei and Hong Kong-China, students who spend 6 or more hours per week in regular school lessons in mathematics perform at least 140 score points higher than students who do not spend any time in regular school lessons in mathematics.

## Language of instruction

The relationship between the time students spend in regular school lessons and their performance in the language of instruction is generally curvilinear, as well, as shown in Figure 4.3. Reading performance increases steadily as learning time in regular school lessons increases up to six hours per week, but beyond six hours per week, the relationship becomes negative. For example, across OECD countries, students who spend two to less than four hours per week in lessons tend to perform 80 score points higher than students who do not spend any time learning the language of instruction in regular school lessons; students who spend four to less than six hours per week tend to perform 87 score points higher; and students who spend six or more hours per week in lessons tend to perform 60 score points higher. This relationship can also be observed when adjusting for the socio-economic background of students and schools, and for students' learning time in the language of instruction in out-of-school-time lessons and individual study (Table 4.2c).

When country-by-country data are examined, the results show that students in many OECD countries who spend long hours learning the language of instruction in regular school lessons achieve lower scores in reading than students who spend a moderate number of hours. In the Netherlands, Belgium, Austria and the partner country Croatia, students who spend six or more hours a week perform lower than students who spend from four to less than six hours per week by at least 50 score points. In the Netherlands and Austria, students who spend six or more hours per week perform lower than students who do not spend any time learning the language of instruction in regular school lessons (Table 4.2b).

However, in a few countries, including Greece, Hungary, Japan, Korea, Norway, Poland and the partner economy Chinese Taipei, students who spend a long time learning the language of instruction in school lessons achieve substantially higher scores in reading. In these countries, students who spend six or more hours per week in regular school lessons on the language of instruction perform at least 100 scores higher than students who do not spend any time in regular school lessons on the language of instruction.

Surprisingly, it appears that in many countries, students who spend a long time learning mathematics and the language of instruction in regular school lessons perform lower than students who spend a moderate amount of time learning in regular school lessons. One might argue that as the proportion of students spending a long time in regular school lessons in science is smaller than that of students who spend a long time in regular school lessons in mathematics and the language of instruction, the former are the students who are especially keen to study science. However, the results show that across OECD countries, about the same average proportion of students spend six hours or more per week in regular school lessons in all three subjects: 8% for regular school lessons in science and mathematics, and 9% for regular school lessons on the language of instruction (Tables 2.1a, 2.1b and 2.1c), although these percentages vary across countries. In Iceland and the partner economies Macao-China, Hong Kong-China and Chinese Taipei, the proportion of students spending six hours or more per week in regular school lessons in science is at least 12% less than the proportions of students spending six hours or more per week in regular school lessons in mathematics and in the language of instruction. But in Portugal and the partner country the Russian Federation, around 20% of students spend six hours or more per week in regular school lessons in science, while 10% or less spend six hours or more per week in regular school lessons in mathematics and in the language of instruction.

It is possible that students who spend a long time in regular school lessons in science do so for different reasons than students who spend a long time in regular school lessons in mathematics and in the language of instruction. One hypothesis is that the students who spend a long time in regular school lessons in science are those who choose to do so in optional courses, because they are interested in science, while students who spend a long time in regular school lessons in mathematics and in the language of instruction are obliged to do so for remedial purposes.

To investigate this hypothesis, students' interest in each subject domain and the types of courses they took were examined. The differences in the proportion of students who believe that to do well in each subject is "very important" were recorded between students who spend six hours or more per week and other students who spend less than six hours per week in regular school lessons. Results show that, in many countries, differences in proportions are consistently greater in science than in the other two subjects. This, in turn, indicates higher levels of commitment towards the subject among those students who spend more hours in science lessons compared with those who spend more hours on the language of instruction or mathematics. For example, in Iceland, the difference in proportion is 34 percentage points in science, while it is 6 percentage points for mathematics and 7 percentage points for the language of instruction (Table 4.3).

Differences in the proportion of students taking optional courses were also recorded between those who spend six hours or more per week and those who spend four to six hours per week in regular school lessons in science. This was done only for science, since students were asked whether they attended optional courses in science, such as optional biology, physics, chemistry courses, but not for mathematics and the language of instruction. Figure 4.4 shows that students who spend six hours or more tend to take more optional science courses, while students who spend four to six hours tend to take more compulsory science courses. This pattern is prominent especially in the OECD countries. On average across OECD countries, the difference in proportion of students who take optional courses is 11%, favouring students who spend 6 hours or more in regular school lessons. In New Zealand and Sweden, the difference in the proportion of students taking optional courses favouring students who spend 6 hours or more in regular school lessons is more than 30%, while in France and the partner country Colombia the difference is less than 5%.

This suggests that students who spend a long time in regular science classes believe that doing well in science is important, and tend to take more optional courses than students who spent a moderate amount of time in school lessons. These findings partly support the hypothesis that students who spend more time studying science are those who choose to spend more time in regular school lessons as optional courses. However, this conclusion is limited, given that the data concerning the proportion of students who take optional courses in regular school lessons is only available for the subject of science and not for mathematics or the language of instruction.

In many countries, schools typically tend to offer classes in mathematics and in the language of instruction as compulsory courses. Thus, students may be obliged to attend classes in mathematics and the language of instruction, and those students who are underperforming in mathematics or reading may be required to take more classes to catch up with other students. In turn, students who are obliged to spend a long time in regular school lessons perform lower than students who spend a moderate amount of time in regular school lessons in mathematics and the language of instruction.

It is, thus, somewhat misleading to conclude that spending a long time in regular school lessons is an inefficient way to achieve better performance if that conclusion is only based on the results for mathematics and reading shown in Figure 4.3. Educational curricula vary across countries, and the amount of time allocated to each subject across different grade levels differs greatly among countries. Rules and practices on how much choice students have in taking various regular school lessons vary across subjects and across education systems. In order to determine who are the students spending a long time in regular school lessons in mathematics and the language of instruction, and how students' choice of classes and their interest in subjects play a role in the relationship between learning time and performance, it is essential to conduct further study and collect relevant information on school curricula and practices.

Figure 4.4

**Difference in percentage of students who take optional science courses, by learning time in regular school lessons in science**

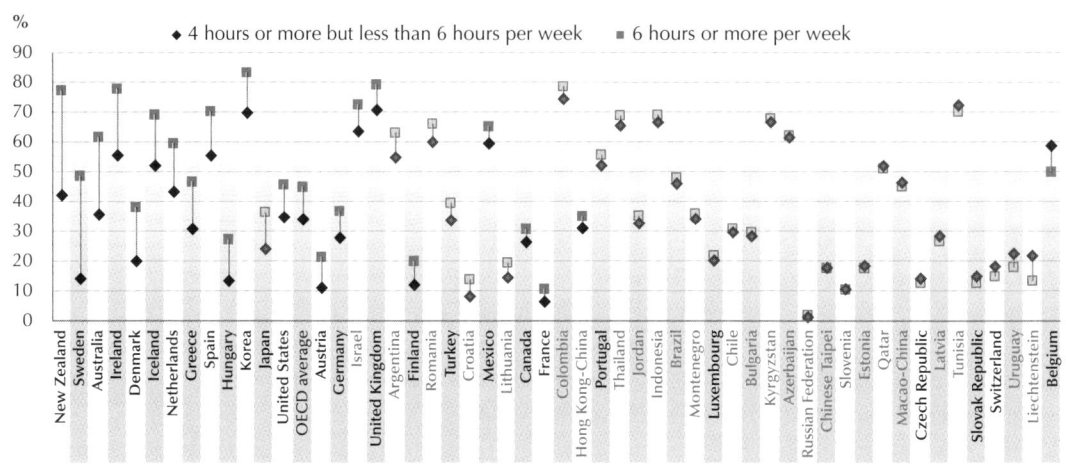

*Note:* Differences that are statistically significant are marked in a darker tone.
Countries are ranked in descending order of the difference in percentage of students who take optional courses between students who spend 6 hours or more a week in school lessons and 4 to 6 hours a week in school lessons in science.
*Source: OECD PISA 2009 Database,* Table 4.4.

## The role of students' motivation

When students can choose whether or not to participate in more science lessons in school, how does their motivation to learn science influence the relationship between learning time and performance? In PISA 2006, students were asked to report whether doing well in the subject of science was "very important", "important", "of little importance" or "not important at all" to them. The relationships between learning time in regular school lessons in science and performance in science are compared between students who reported that doing well in science was very important and other students who reported that doing well in science was not very important.

Figure 4.5 provides a comparison of students with different views on the importance of doing well in science. It shows that the relationship between learning time in regular school lessons in science and performance in science is similar when students spend less time learning, but the difference increases when students spend a long time learning. On average across OECD countries, among students who reported that doing well in science was very important, an increase of one hour in regular school lessons in science corresponds to an increase of around 26 score points in performance. Among students who reported that doing well in science was not very important, an increase of one hour in regular school lessons in science corresponds to an increase of around 22 score points in performance, after the socio-economic background of students and schools was taken into account. This means that when these two groups of students with different views on the importance of doing well in science are compared, the difference in performance increases by four score points for every additional hour a student spends learning science in regular school lessons. Consequently, there is a substantial difference in performance – 20 score points or more – between these students when they spend five hours or more per week in regular school lessons in science (Table 4.5a).

A similar pattern is observed in 19 OECD countries and 14 partner countries and economies. In France, Iceland, Portugal, Spain, New Zealand, Greece, the Czech Republic and the partner country Romania, the difference in performance between students with different views on science increases by six score points or more for every additional hour in regular school lessons in science.

© OECD 2011 *Quality Time for Students: Learning In and Out of School*

When students in academic and vocational schools are analysed separately (Table 4.5b), the same kind of pattern appears, showing an increase in score points for every additional hour a student is in school. One might argue that this pattern could be the result of students' various motivations and reasons for attending each school type (academic or vocational), rather than students' different views on the importance of doing well in science. For example, students in vocational schools may be less likely to believe that doing well in science is important, while students in academic schools may be more likely to prioritise science in their lives. Perhaps students' different attitudes towards science were influenced by tracking. If so, then the resulting pattern would have strongly favoured academic students. However, when students with different views on the importance of doing well in science were compared, the difference in performance increased by four points in academic schools and by two points in vocational schools for every additional hour a student spent learning science in regular school lessons. Tracking was thus eliminated as a possible explanation for the different views of importance of science and science performance.

The resulting patterns imply that when students believe that doing well in science is very important, spending more time learning science in regular school lessons is a more efficient way of improving their performance. This result confirms what Carroll propounded: students' full engagement is one of the key factors for learning (Carroll, 1963). Thus, it is crucial to make the most of learning time and of students' quality of learning per hour, since it is not often feasible to increase the absolute number of learning hours because students have a limited amount of learning time in school. The more important task would be to enhance students' understanding of why it is important to learn a particular subject. That could help make learning time more efficient.

### Figure 4.5
### Relationship between performance in science and learning time in regular school lessons in science, by students' perception of doing well in science

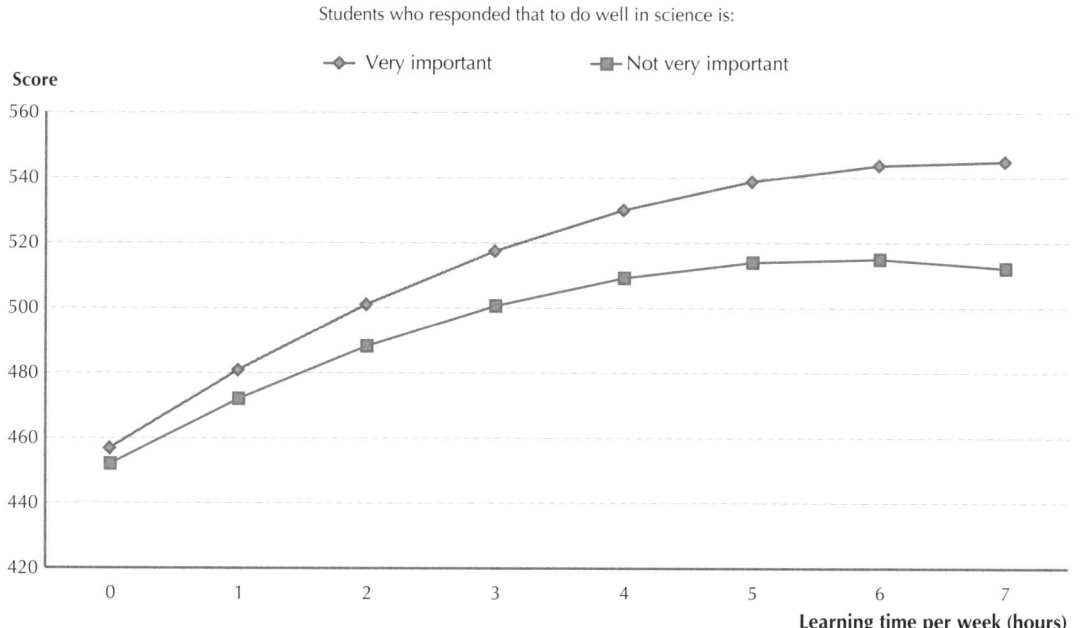

Students who responded that to do well in science is:

◆ Very important　　■ Not very important

*Source: OECD PISA 2006 Database, Table 4.5a.*

## LEARNING TIME IN OUT-OF-SCHOOL-TIME LESSONS AND PERFORMANCE

### Science

The patterns reflecting the relationship between the out-of-school-time lessons and science performance are vastly different from those concerning regular school lessons. In science, there is a consistently negative relationship between learning time in out-of-school-time lessons and performance in most countries. In general, students who spend more time learning science in out-of-school-time lessons tend to perform lower in science, as shown in Figure 4.6. Across OECD countries, students who spend less than two hours per week in out-of-school-time lessons in science tend to perform 19 score points lower in science than students who do not spend any time learning science in out-of-school-time lessons; students who spend between two and six hours tend to perform 28 score points lower; students who spend six or more hours per week show little difference in performance from students who do not spend any time learning science. A similar relationship is observed even when adjusting for the socio-economic background of students and schools, and for students' science learning time in regular school lessons and individual study (Table 4.6a).

However, in Greece, Turkey and the partner countries and economies Azerbaijan, Hong Kong-China, Chinese Taipei, Thailand and Tunisia, students who spend time learning science in out-of-school-time lessons tend to achieve higher scores than students who do not spend any time learning science in out-of-school-time lessons. The relationship remains positive after adjusting for the socio-economic background of students and schools in all of these countries, except for Azerbaijan and Chinese Taipei, even though the positive differences become smaller. The relationship disappears in all countries except Turkey, however, when adjusting for learning time in regular school lessons and learning time in individual study, and for the socio-economic background of students and schools (Table 4.6a).

### Figure 4.6
**Within-country relationship between performance and learning time in out-of-school-time lessons, by subject (OECD average)**

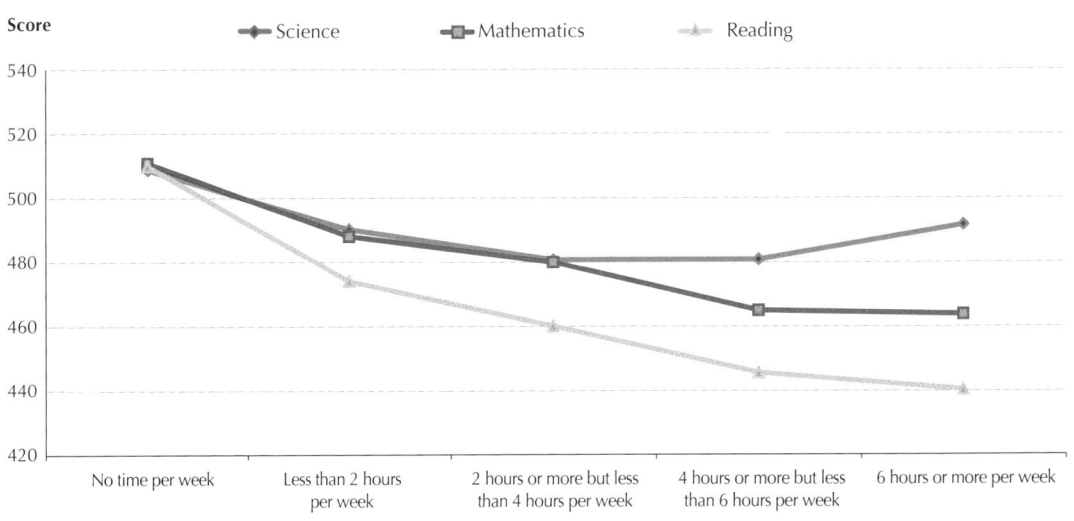

*Source: OECD PISA 2006 Database, Tables 4.6a, 4.6b and 4.6c.*

## Mathematics

In mathematics as in science there is a consistently negative relationship between learning time in out-of-school-time lessons and performance in most countries. In general, students who spend more time learning mathematics in out-of-school-time lessons tend to perform less well in mathematics, as shown in Figure 4.6. Across OECD countries, students who spend less than 2 hours per week in out-of-school-time lessons in mathematics tend to perform 23 score points lower in mathematics than students who do not spend any time learning mathematics in out-of-school-time lessons; students who spend 2 to less than 4 hours per week tend to perform 31 score points lower; students who spend 4 to less than 6 hours per week tend to perform 46 score points lower; and students who spend 6 or more hours per week tend to perform 47 score points lower. A similar relationship is observed even when adjusting for the socio-economic background of students and schools, and for students' mathematics learning time in regular school lessons and individual study (Table 4.6b).

Some positive relationships between learning time in out-of-school-time lessons in mathematics and performance in mathematics are found in a few countries, including Greece, Korea, the Slovak Republic, Turkey and the partner countries and economies Chinese Taipei and Tunisia. After adjusting for learning time in regular school lessons and individual study, in addition to the socio-economic background of students and schools, only a slight positive relationship can be observed in Korea, Turkey and the partner economy Chinese Taipei.

## Language of instruction

In most countries, there is also a consistently negative relationship between learning time in out-of-school-time lessons and performance in the language of instruction. In general, students who spend more time learning the language of instruction in out-of-school-time lessons tend to perform lower in reading, as shown in Figure 4.6. Across OECD countries, students who spend less than 2 hours per week in out-of-school-time lessons in the language of instruction tend to perform 36 score points lower in reading than students who do not spend any time learning the language of instruction in out-of-school-time lessons; students who spend 2 to less than 4 hours per week tend to perform 50 score points lower; students who spend 4 to less than 6 hours per week tend to perform 64 score points lower; and students who spend 6 or more hours per week tend to perform 69 score points lower. A similar relationship is observed even when adjusting for the socio-economic background of students and schools, and for students' learning time on the language of instruction in regular school lessons and individual study (Table 4.6c).

However, there are some positive relationships between learning time in out-of-school-time lessons in the language of instruction and performance in reading in Korea and the Slovak Republic, even after the socio-economic background of students and schools are adjusted for. After adjusting for learning time in regular school lessons and individual study, and for the socio-economic background of students and schools, only a slight positive relationship can be observed: in Korea, students who spend 2 to less than 4 hours per week tend to perform 12 score points higher than students who do not spend any time learning the language of instruction in out-of-school-time lessons, while in the Slovak Republic, students who spend less than 2 hours per week in out-of-school-time lessons on the language of instruction tend to perform 7 score points higher than students who do not spend any time learning the language of instruction in out-of-school-time lessons.

## Performance by different types of out-of-school-time lessons

Since PISA is a cross-sectional study, it is difficult to determine the causality of the relationships. Thus the results of this examination of the relationship between the specific types of out-of-school-time lessons and performance should be interpreted with caution. The difference in performance between students who do not take any out-of-school-time lessons and those who attend one type of out-of-school-time lesson cannot be conclusively attributed to the effectiveness of the out-of-school-time lessons.

Seven types of out-of-school-time lessons are defined according to two factors: size of lessons and affiliation of instructors. Students are thus grouped into one of the following three categories: those who attend one-to-one lessons only, group lessons only, or both one-to-one and group lessons. Students are also grouped into one of the following three categories: those who attend out-of-school-time lessons with an instructor who is a teacher at the students' schools (*i.e.* with a school teacher) only, out-of-school-time lessons with an instructor who is not a teacher at the students' schools (*i.e.* with a non-school teacher) only, or both out-of-school-time lessons with school and non-school teachers. Consequently, students are grouped into nine mutually exclusive types. As in many countries, there are very few students who attend the type of "one-to-one lessons only with a school teacher only" and the type of "one-to-one-lessons only with both school and non-school teachers", these two types are merged and labelled as "others". For the rest of seven types of out-of-school-time lessons, student's average performance is computed and compared with the performance score for students who do not attend any of these types of out-of-school-time lessons.

Below are the seven different types of out-of-school-time lessons with the variable names presented in brackets:

- one-to-one lesson with a non-school teacher [TYPE1];

- group lesson with a school teacher [TYPE2];

- group lesson with a non-school teacher [TYPE3];

- group lesson with both school and non-school teachers [TYPE4];

- both one-to-one lessons and group lessons with school teachers [TYPE5];

- both one-to-one lessons and group lessons with non-school teachers [TYPE6]; or

- both one-to-one lessons and group lessons with both school and non-school teachers [TYPE7].

Students' performance in science, mathematics and reading are considered simultaneously, since the questions regarding the different types of out-of-school-time lessons were not asked separately by subject, but for subjects that students were learning at school in general. A structural equation model developed for this analysis is presented in the annex.

As shown in Figure 4.7, students who attend out-of-school-time lessons generally perform less well than students who do not attend out-of-school-time lessons in all types of out-of-school-time lessons, except students who attend "group lesson with a non-school teacher" and "group lesson with a school teacher".

As presented in Box 4.2, among these seven different types of out-of-school-time lessons, the type of "group lesson only with a non-school teacher" shows the most consistent positive relationship with performance across countries, after holding constant the socio-economic background of students and schools. Suppose that there are two students from families with similar socio-economic backgrounds in schools with similar socio-economic backgrounds. One of the students does not take any types of out-of-school-time lessons, while the other student is involved in a "group lesson with a non-school teacher". The latter student performs

© OECD 2011  Quality Time for Students: Learning In and Out of School

better than the former in seven OECD countries and nine partner countries and economies (Table 4.7). Students who are involved in "group lessons only with a non-school teacher only" perform around 20 score points or higher in Turkey, Greece, Korea, Australia, Poland and in the partner countries and economies Chinese Taipei, Bulgaria, Hong Kong-China and Kyrgyzstan.

Students who are involved in a "group lesson with a school teacher" also tend to achieve higher scores than students who do not take any type of out-of-school-time lessons, after adjusting for the socio-economic background of students and schools. This positive relationship can be observed in five OECD countries and five partner countries and economies: Korea, the United Kingdom, Poland, Italy, Turkey and the partner countries and economies Kyrgyzstan, the Russian Federation, Lithuania, Bulgaria and Chinese Taipei (Table 4.7).

---

### Box 4.2. **Summary of performance difference by seven types of out-of-school-time lessons**

The table below presents the number of countries that show a significant difference, either negative or positive, between the average performance of students who attend a certain type of out-of-school-time lesson and the average performance of students who do not attend any type of out-of-school-time lesson. The number of OECD countries is indicated in brackets. For example, regarding "one-to-one lessons only with non-school teacher only", in 32 countries (of which 20 are OECD countries), students who attend this type of out-of-school-time lesson tend to perform lower than students who do not attend any type of out-of-school-time lesson. However, in three countries (of which two are OECD countries), students who attend this type of out-of-school-time lesson tend to achieve higher scores than students who do not attend any type of these lessons.

| | | Affiliation of instructors | | | | | |
| | | School teacher | | Non-school teacher | | Both school and non-school teachers | |
| | | Negative | Positive | Negative | Positive | Negative | Positive |
|---|---|---|---|---|---|---|---|
| Size of lessons | One-to-one lesson | | | 32(20) | 3 (2) | | |
| | Group lesson | 22 (15) | 10 (5) | 5(3) | 16 (7) | 47 (27) | 2(1) |
| | Both one-to-one and group lessons | 46 (25) | 1 (0) | 30 (20) | 6 (4) | 55 (29) | 1(1) |

*Source*: *OECD PISA 2006 Database*, Table 4.7.

---

Figure 4.7

## Difference in students' latent performance, by different types of out-of-school-time lessons

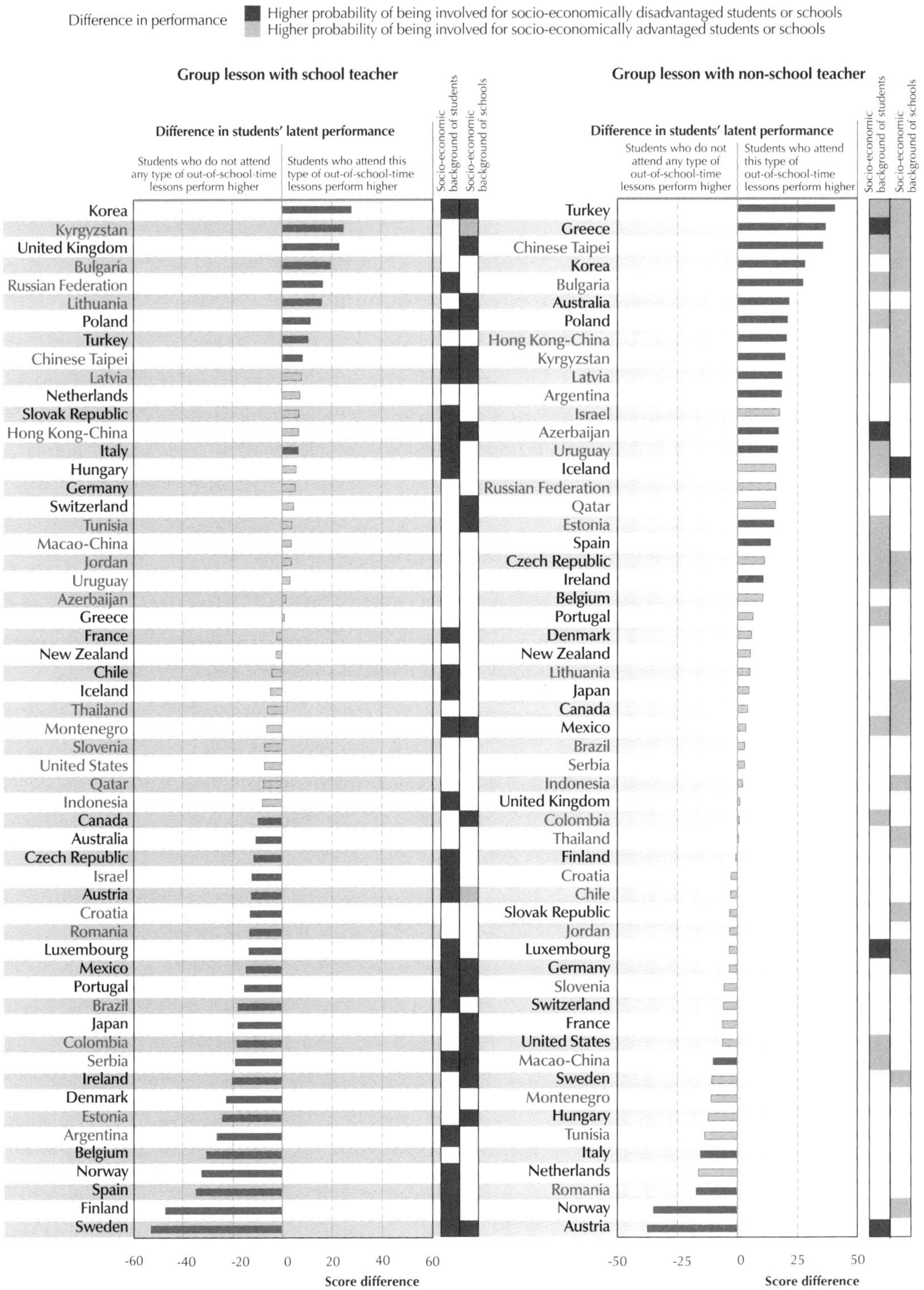

Difference in performance    ■ Higher probability of being involved for socio-economically disadvantaged students or schools
   □ Higher probability of being involved for socio-economically advantaged students or schools

*Note:* Differences that are statistically significant are marked in a darker tone.
Countries are ranked in descending order of the difference in students' latent performance.
*Source:* OECD PISA 2006 Database, Table 4.7.

© OECD 2011 Quality Time for Students: Learning In and Out of School

While out-of-school-time lessons can enhance learning, these lessons could also reinforce inequalities, since they vary across socio-economic groups. Which types of out-of-school-time lessons enhance learning without introducing inequities? And in which countries are they found?

When focusing on the countries where the "group lesson with a school teacher" or "group lesson with a non-school teacher" types are related to better performance, different patterns emerge in the way these lessons mediate the relationship between students' socio-economic background and performance. The "group lesson with a school teacher" tends to reduce the impact of socio-economic background on performance, since socio-economically disadvantaged students are more likely to attend this type of lesson (*i.e.* negative logit scores in Table 4.7) and are, in turn, more likely to achieve higher scores than students who do not participate any out-of-school-time lesson. The results show that, out of ten countries in which there are positive relationships between performance and the "group lesson with a school teacher", socio-economically disadvantaged students and/or schools tend to be more involved in this type of lesson than socio-economically advantaged students and/or schools in seven of these countries: Korea, the United Kingdom, Poland, Italy and the partner countries and economies the Russian Federation, Lithuania and Chinese Taipei. Only in Kyrgyzstan does this type of out-of-school-time lesson reinforce inequity, as socio-economically advantaged schools tend to be more involved in these lessons and tend to achieve higher scores (Table 4.7).

In contrast, the "group lesson with a non-school teacher" tends to reinforce the impact of socio-economic background on performance, since socio-economically advantaged students are more likely to attend this type of lesson (*i.e.* positive logit scores in Table 4.7) and are, in turn, more likely to achieve higher scores than those students who do not participate in any out-of-school-time lessons. Consequently, the difference in performance between socio-economically advantaged and disadvantaged students and/or schools is magnified by this type of out-of-school lesson. The results show that out of 16 countries that show a positive relationship between performance and "group lesson with a non-school teacher", more advantaged students and/or schools tend to be involved in this type of out-of-school-time lessons in 12 countries and economies.

## LEARNING TIME IN INDIVIDUAL STUDY AND PERFORMANCE

### Science

In most countries, students who spend more time engaged in individual study of science achieve higher scores than students who do not spend any time in individual study of science. As shown in Figure 4.8, across OECD countries, students who spend less than 2 hours per week in individual study of science tend to perform 34 score points higher in science than students who do not spend any time in individual study of science; students who spend 2 to less than 4 hours per week tend to perform 41 score points higher; students who spend 4 to less than 6 hours per week tend to perform 38 score points higher; and students who spend six or more hours per week tend to perform 40 score points higher (Table 4.8a).

Even though students who spend time in individual study of science outperform those who do not, in some countries, spending more time in individual study is not necessarily related to better performance. The relationship between learning time in individual study of science and performance in science is not linear; often the relationship shows a steep increase up to four hours per week, but then decreases slightly. Students who spend a moderate amount of time, around two to four hours per week, tend to achieve the highest scores and perform better than students who spend six hours or more per week.

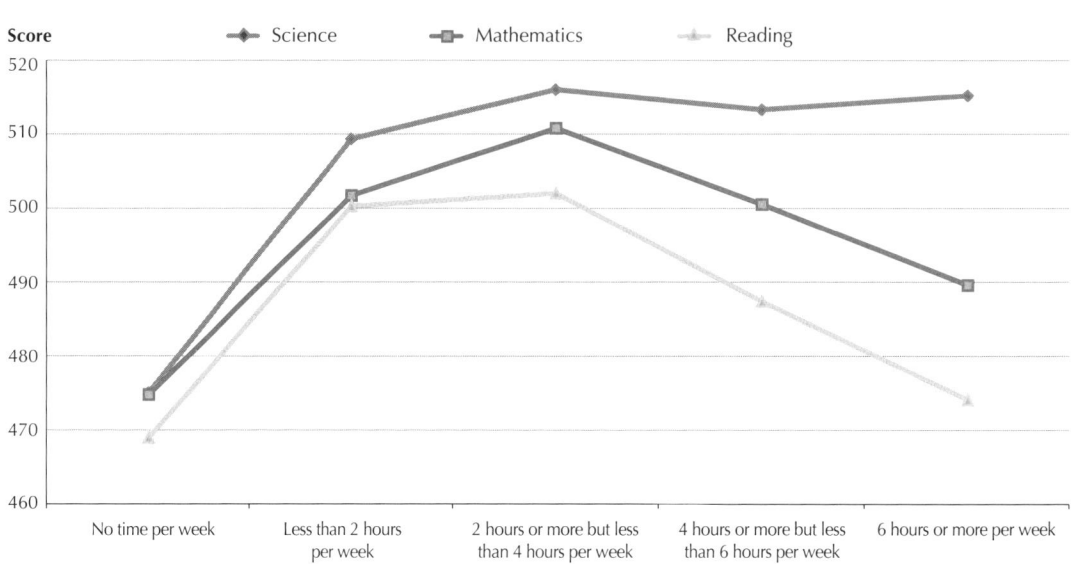

Figure 4.8
**Within-country relationship between performance
and learning time in individual study, by subject (OECD average)**

*Source: OECD PISA 2006 Database*, Tables 4.8a, 4.8b, and 4.8c.

## Mathematics

As with the study of science, students who spend a moderate amount of time in individual study in mathematics tend to achieve the highest scores, while students who spend a long time in individual study in mathematics do not perform as well as those who spend a moderate amount of time. This pattern is more prominent for individual study in mathematics than for individual study of science. As shown in Figure 4.8, across OECD countries, students who spend less than two hours per week in individual study in mathematics tend to perform 27 score points higher in mathematics than students who do not spend any time in individual study in mathematics; students who spend two to less than four hours per week tend to perform 36 score points higher; and students who spend four to less than six hours per week tend to perform 26 score points higher. But students who spend six or more hours per week do not tend to achieve higher scores (Table 4.8b).

In some countries, students who spend a long time in individual study in mathematics tend to perform even lower than students who do not spend any individual study time. For example, in Switzerland, Austria, Luxembourg, the Czech Republic and Iceland, students who spend six or more hours per week in individual study in mathematics tend to perform lower, by 28 to 72 score points, in mathematics than students who do not spend any time in individual study. In Switzerland, the Czech Republic, Sweden and the partner country Israel, students who spend from four to less than six hours per week in individual study in mathematics tend to perform lower, by 24 to 40 score points than students who do not spend any time in individual study.

## Language of instruction

Students who spend a moderate amount of time in individual study in the language of instruction achieve higher scores than students who spend a long time in individual study. In general, the relationship between learning time in individual study in reading and performance in reading show a mountain shape, as shown in Figure 4.8. Across OECD countries, students who spend less than two hours per week in individual study in the language of instruction tend to perform 31 score points higher in reading than students who do not

© OECD 2011 *Quality Time for Students: Learning In and Out of School*

spend any time in individual study on the language of instruction; and students who spend from 2 to less than 4 hours per week tend to perform 33 score points higher. But students who spend four or more hours per week do not tend to achieve higher scores (Table 4.8c).

In ten OECD countries and nine partner countries and economies, students who spend six or more hours per week in individual study in the language of instruction achieve higher scores than students who do not spend any time in individual study. However, in Austria, Switzerland, Germany, Luxembourg, Ireland and the partner countries Israel and Argentina, students who spend 6 or more hours per week in individual study in the language of instruction tend to perform lower than students who do not spend any time in individual study, by 24 to 105 score points.

In all three subjects, students who spend up to four hours per week more in individual study tend to achieve higher scores, but beyond four hours per week, students do not necessarily achieve higher scores in proportion to the time they spend. This may be because of differences in characteristics between students who spend a long time in individual study and those who spend a moderate amount of time. For example, students who spend long hours in individual study are often the students who need more time than other students to complete a certain number of tasks. Students may also spend a long time in individual study because their teachers give them additional assignments in order to catch up with other classmates. Thus, there is not enough evidence to conclude that the efficiency of learning time diminishes after a certain amount of time dedicated to individual study.

## DO STUDENTS WHO STUDY LONGER PERFORM BETTER?

Across countries, relative learning time in regular school lessons, which is equivalent to the proportion of absolute learning time in regular school lessons out of absolute total learning time, which includes time spent in regular school lessons, out-of-school-time lessons and individual study, is strongly related to performance. Countries with a higher proportion of time allocated to regular school lessons tend to perform better. Students in high-performing countries spend less relative time, on average, in out-of-school-time lessons and individual study, and more relative time in regular school lessons than students in low-performing countries.

Compared with the countries with high relative learning time in regular school lessons, the countries with low relative learning time in these lessons turn out to have system characteristics that are related to low overall performance: less human and material resources, less school autonomy and lower proportions of standardised external examinations. The evidence implies that it is the quality of regular school lessons, not the quantity of learning hours, that explains more of the difference in performance across countries.

Within countries, the absolute length of learning time in regular school lessons is more strongly related to performance than relative learning time in regular school lessons. This is because the quality of learning time in regular school lessons within countries does not vary as much as across countries.

Students who spend a long time in regular school lessons in science do better than those who spend a shorter amount of time in regular science classes, but the same is not true in mathematics and the language of instruction: students who spend a long time learning these two subjects in regular school lessons perform less well than students who spend a moderate amount of time in regular school lessons. One hypothesis for this difference among the three subjects is that the students who spend a long time in regular school lessons in science are those who choose to do so in optional courses, because they are interested in science, while students who spend a long time in regular school lessons in mathematics and in the language of instruction are obliged to do so for remedial purposes. In addition, when students in regular school science lessons believe that it is very important to do well in science, they use their time in school classes more efficiently to

perform better. These results imply that when students believe that doing well in science is very important, spending more time learning science in regular school lessons is a more efficient way of improving their performance.

Students who spend a long time in out-of-school-time lessons tend to perform lower in all three subjects. However, in the two specific types of out-of-school-time lessons, "group lesson with a non-school teacher" and "group lesson with a school teacher", students in several countries tend to achieve higher scores than students who do not attend any out-of-school-time lessons.

While "group lessons with a non-school teacher" seem to lead to better student performance, these types of out-of-school-time lessons sometimes reinforce educational inequity. "Group lessons with a school teacher", however, seem to provide both quality and equity in some countries. Socio-economically disadvantaged students are more likely to be involved in these types of lessons and tend to achieve higher scores than students who do not take any type of out-of-school-time lessons.

Students who spend up to four hours per week more in individual study in science, mathematics and reading tend to achieve higher scores, but beyond four hours per week, students do not necessarily achieve higher scores in proportion to the time they spend. This may be because of differences in characteristics between students who spend a long time in individual study and those who spend a moderate amount of time. For example, students who spend long hours in individual study are often the students who need more time than other students to complete a certain number of tasks.

## POLICY IMPLICATIONS

## For policy makers

### *Improve quality of in-school lessons*

Across countries, absolute learning time in schools is positively, but weakly, related to performance, but relative learning time in schools – the proportion of time spent in school classes relative to other learning activities – is more strongly related to performance. The implication of this finding is that the quality of school lessons leads to better overall student performance.

Given these findings, simply adding hours to the school day or encouraging students to spend more time in after-school lessons or individual study would not automatically help low-performing countries improve their test scores. Instead, these countries should explore ways to improve the quality of school lessons. One way of doing so would be to improve the quality of teachers. Training to at least a minimum standard of subject knowledge and confidence in working with students should be required of all teachers. Resources for education should be bolstered to the greatest extent possible to ensure the quality of education. Countries could also consider giving schools more autonomy in staffing, budget and curriculum decisions. This will give school officials greater incentive to make the most of the resources available to them. In addition, developing an independent system to assess student performance would improve accountability in individual schools and help raise the quality of education among all schools within the country.

An in-depth study of how regular school lessons are structured – including when in the day classes are held, class size, length of school day and school term, the length and frequency of vacation time – could assist policy makers in developing a schedule of school lesson time that is most effective for learning.

### *Promote learning activities that foster equity*

In several countries, students who attend after-school group lessons tend to achieve higher scores than students who do not attend any out-of-school-time lessons.

But there is a difference in equity between those out-of-school-time lessons taught by a school teacher and those taught by a non-school teacher. While group lessons with a non-school teacher seem to be related to high performance, they could reinforce educational inequity, since socio-economically advantaged students are more involved in this type of out-of-school-time lesson and consequently achieve higher scores. Group lessons with a school teacher, however, offer both quality and equity. Socio-economically disadvantaged students are more likely to be involved in this type of out-of-school-time lesson and tend to achieve higher scores than students who do not take any type of out-of-school-time lesson. This is the case in Korea, the United Kingdom, Poland, Italy and the partner countries and economies the Russian Federation, Lithuania and Chinese Taipei. An in-depth study of how these lessons with a school teacher are organised in these countries would help policy makers develop recommendations on offering similar kinds of lessons in other countries.

...

## For school administrators, teachers, parents and students

### *Motivate students*

The relationship between learning time and performance within countries is different from that between countries. Here, the absolute length of learning time in regular school lessons is more strongly related to performance than relative learning time in school, probably because the quality of learning time in regular school lessons does not vary much between schools within countries.

In many countries, students who spend more time in regular school lessons in science tend to achieve higher scores, while students who spend more time in regular school lessons in mathematics and the language of instruction achieve lower scores than students who spend a moderate amount of time. One possible explanation for these different relationships is that students tend to have the flexibility to choose whether they spend more time in science classes, while they tend to be obliged to attend mathematics classes and classes on the language of instruction.

Students who have more freedom to choose optional courses tend to take classes in subjects that interest them. The study shows that when students believe it is very important to do well in science, they use their learning time in school more efficiently and effectively, and so achieve higher scores. Teachers, schools, and policy makers could not only encourage students to spend more time in learning, but also develop measures to help change attitudes. As resources permit, schools could offer more optional courses for those students who show an interest in exploring their required subjects more deeply or in broadening the range of subjects they study. Parents could emphasise the importance of learning each subject, perhaps by explaining how mastery of those subjects will broaden their children's future job opportunities, enable them to participate fully in society and enrich their lives.

The importance of learning science should be emphasised to all students, but particularly to boys, students from socio-economically disadvantaged backgrounds, those in rural schools, in public schools and in vocational schools, as these students tend to spend less time in school science classes.

© OECD 2011 Quality Time for Students: Learning In and Out of School

# Annex

**Annex A1:** Questionnaire indices

**Annex A2:** Data tables

## ANNEX A1: QUESTIONNAIRE INDICES

This annex describes the indices derived from student and school questionnaires that are used in this report. This report uses five distinctive indices reflecting population sub-groups. Population sub-groups at the individual level include gender, socio-economic status and immigrant status; population sub-groups at the school level comprise lower or upper secondary schools, academic or vocational schools, public or private school and school location. Among these, gender and school location are recoded from single questionnaire items. For further information on constructing indices, see Chapter 16 in the *PISA 2006 Technical Report*.

## Student-level indices

### Economic, social and cultural status

The PISA index of economic, social and cultural status (ESCS) was derived from the following three indices: highest occupational status of parents (HISEI), highest educational level of parents in years of education according to ISCED (PARED), and home possessions (HOMEPOS). The index of home possessions (HOMEPOS) comprises all items on the indices of WEALTH, CULTPOSS and HEDRES, as well as books in the home recoded into a three-level categorical variable (less than 25, 25-100 books, or more than 100 books).

The PISA index of economic, social and cultural status (ESCS) was derived from a principal component analysis of standardised variables (each variable has an OECD mean of zero and a standard deviation of one), taking the factor scores for the first principal component as measures of the index of economic, social and cultural status.

Principal component analysis was also performed for each participating country to determine to what extent the components of the index operate in similar ways across countries. The analysis revealed that all three components contribute more or less equally to this index with factor loadings ranging from 0.55 to 0.87 except only in a few countries. Internal consistency ranges between 0.52 and 0.80, the median scale reliability for the pooled OECD countries is 0.67.

The imputation of components for students missing data on one component was done on the basis of a regression on the other two variables, with an additional random error component. The final values on the PISA index of economic, social and cultural status (ESCS) have an OECD mean of zero and a standard deviation of one.

### Immigrant background

As in PISA 2000 and PISA 2003, information on the country of birth of the students and their parents was collected in PISA 2006. Included in the database are three country-specific variables relating to the country of birth of the student, mother, and father (COBN_S, COBN_M and COBN_F). Also, the items ST11Q01, ST11Q02 and ST11Q03 have been re-coded for the database into the following categories: (1) country of birth is same as country of assessment; and (2) otherwise.

The index on immigrant background (IMMIG) is calculated from these variables, and has the following categories: (1) native students (those students who had at least one parent born in the country of assessment); (2) second-generation students (those born in the country of assessment but whose parent(s) were born in another country); and (3) first-generation students (those students born outside the country of assessment and whose parents were also born in another country). Students with missing responses for either the student or both parents have been given missing values for this variable.

© OECD 2011 Quality Time for Students: Learning In and Out of School

# School-level indices

### Study programme

PISA 2006 collected data on study programmes available to 15-year-old students in each country. This information was obtained through the student tracking form and the student questionnaire. All study programmes were classified using the international standard classification of education (ISCED). In the PISA international database, all national programmes is included in a separate variable (PROGN) where the first three digits are the ISO code for a country, the next two digits are the sub-national category, and the last two digits are the nationally specific programme code.

The following indices are derived from the data on study programmes:

▪ Programme level (ISCEDL) indicates whether students are in lower secondary education level (ISCED 2) or upper secondary level (ISCED 3).

▪ Programme designation (ISCEDD) indicates the designation of the study programme (A = general programmes designed to give access to the next programme level, B = programmes designed to give access to vocational studies at the next programme level, C = programmes designed to give direct access to the labour market, M = modular programmes that combine any or all of these characteristics).

▪ Programme orientation (ISCEDO) indicates whether the programme's curricular content is (1) general, (2) pre-vocational or (3) vocational.

### School type

Schools are classified as either public or private according to whether a private entity or a public agency has the ultimate power to make decisions concerning each school's affairs. The index on school type (SCHLTYPE) has three categories: (1) public schools controlled and managed by a public education authority or agency; (2) government-dependent private schools, controlled by a non-government organisation or with a governing board not selected by a government agency, which receive more than 50% of their core funding from government agencies; or (3) government-independent private schools, controlled by a non-government organisation or with a governing board not selected by a government agency, which receive less than 50% of their core funding from government agencies.

## ANNEX A2: DATA TABLES

[Part 1/2]

### Table 2.1a  Percentage of students, by time spent learning science

| | Regular school lessons | | | | | | | | | | Out-of-school-time lessons | | | | | | | | | |
| | No time per week | | Less than 2 hours per week | | 2 hours or more but less than 4 hours per week | | 4 hours or more but less than 6 hours per week | | 6 hours or more per week | | No time per week | | Less than 2 hours per week | | 2 hours or more but less than 4 hours per week | | 4 hours or more but less than 6 hours per week | | 6 hours or more per week | |
| | % | S.E. | % | S.E. | % | S.E. | % | S.E. | % | S.E. | % | S.E. | % | S.E. | % | S.E. | % | S.E. | % | S.E. |
|---|---|---|---|---|---|---|---|---|---|---|---|---|---|---|---|---|---|---|---|---|
| **OECD** | | | | | | | | | | | | | | | | | | | | |
| Australia | 14.3 | (0.6) | 10.1 | (0.3) | 38.5 | (0.8) | 30.6 | (0.7) | 6.5 | (0.3) | 77.0 | (0.5) | 17.7 | (0.4) | 4.3 | (0.2) | 0.8 | (0.1) | 0.2 | (0.1) |
| Austria | 17.3 | (0.8) | 27.3 | (0.9) | 35.0 | (0.9) | 14.3 | (0.8) | 6.1 | (0.8) | 88.2 | (0.6) | 8.1 | (0.5) | 2.8 | (0.2) | 0.7 | (0.1) | 0.3 | (0.1) |
| Belgium | 15.1 | (0.8) | 27.1 | (0.7) | 33.9 | (0.7) | 16.6 | (0.7) | 7.2 | (0.5) | 80.8 | (0.5) | 14.2 | (0.4) | 3.9 | (0.2) | 0.8 | (0.1) | 0.3 | (0.1) |
| Canada | 9.3 | (0.4) | 14.3 | (0.5) | 19.6 | (0.9) | 35.4 | (0.6) | 21.5 | (0.8) | 66.4 | (0.7) | 24.9 | (0.6) | 6.9 | (0.3) | 1.4 | (0.1) | 0.4 | (0.1) |
| Czech Republic | 11.1 | (1.0) | 29.3 | (1.0) | 31.6 | (1.2) | 13.1 | (0.6) | 14.8 | (1.0) | 67.8 | (0.9) | 23.7 | (0.8) | 6.9 | (0.4) | 1.1 | (0.2) | 0.6 | (0.1) |
| Denmark | 3.5 | (0.6) | 14.0 | (0.7) | 55.3 | (1.1) | 24.9 | (0.9) | 2.4 | (0.4) | 46.8 | (1.1) | 43.3 | (0.9) | 8.1 | (0.5) | 1.5 | (0.2) | 0.4 | (0.1) |
| Finland | 3.4 | (0.3) | 19.6 | (0.8) | 49.9 | (1.2) | 23.2 | (1.3) | 3.9 | (0.4) | 76.9 | (0.7) | 19.1 | (0.6) | 3.5 | (0.3) | 0.4 | (0.1) | 0.1 | (0.0) |
| France | 7.7 | (0.6) | 30.2 | (0.8) | 36.3 | (0.8) | 17.5 | (0.9) | 8.3 | (0.6) | 62.7 | (0.8) | 29.7 | (0.9) | 6.6 | (0.4) | 0.9 | (0.1) | 0.2 | (0.1) |
| Germany | 9.3 | (0.7) | 25.3 | (0.9) | 33.1 | (0.9) | 22.3 | (0.8) | 10.0 | (0.5) | 70.6 | (0.8) | 20.8 | (0.7) | 7.0 | (0.4) | 1.1 | (0.2) | 0.5 | (0.1) |
| Greece | 8.7 | (0.6) | 19.3 | (0.8) | 38.5 | (0.9) | 25.8 | (0.9) | 7.8 | (0.5) | 27.0 | (0.9) | 28.7 | (0.7) | 29.4 | (0.8) | 10.9 | (0.6) | 3.9 | (0.3) |
| Hungary | 10.3 | (1.0) | 31.8 | (1.0) | 39.6 | (1.0) | 14.2 | (0.7) | 4.2 | (0.4) | 44.9 | (1.0) | 36.9 | (0.9) | 14.5 | (0.7) | 3.3 | (0.3) | 0.5 | (0.1) |
| Iceland | 3.6 | (0.3) | 19.7 | (0.6) | 55.2 | (0.8) | 19.3 | (0.6) | 2.2 | (0.3) | 81.5 | (0.6) | 14.0 | (0.6) | 3.8 | (0.3) | 0.5 | (0.1) | 0.2 | (0.1) |
| Ireland | 14.6 | (1.0) | 18.9 | (0.8) | 50.8 | (1.0) | 13.6 | (0.6) | 2.1 | (0.3) | 79.0 | (0.7) | 16.6 | (0.6) | 3.7 | (0.3) | 0.6 | (0.1) | 0.2 | (0.1) |
| Italy | 11.1 | (1.1) | 23.2 | (0.6) | 40.8 | (1.0) | 14.3 | (0.6) | 10.6 | (0.7) | 69.9 | (0.9) | 19.6 | (0.4) | 7.7 | (0.3) | 2.1 | (0.1) | 0.7 | (0.1) |
| Japan | 3.9 | (1.1) | 22.7 | (1.4) | 61.2 | (1.5) | 10.9 | (1.1) | 1.3 | (0.3) | 82.4 | (0.7) | 13.8 | (0.6) | 3.4 | (0.3) | 0.3 | (0.1) | 0.1 | (0.0) |
| Korea | 3.4 | (1.1) | 5.9 | (0.4) | 55.0 | (1.8) | 31.2 | (1.6) | 4.5 | (1.2) | 50.0 | (1.3) | 27.8 | (1.0) | 18.8 | (0.8) | 2.6 | (0.2) | 0.7 | (0.1) |
| Luxembourg | 11.0 | (0.5) | 39.5 | (0.7) | 31.6 | (0.7) | 13.0 | (0.5) | 4.8 | (0.3) | 70.5 | (0.7) | 21.1 | (0.6) | 6.7 | (0.4) | 1.3 | (0.2) | 0.4 | (0.1) |
| Mexico | 14.2 | (0.5) | 26.8 | (0.5) | 22.3 | (0.5) | 17.6 | (0.6) | 19.1 | (0.5) | 50.0 | (0.9) | 31.5 | (0.7) | 13.3 | (0.6) | 3.7 | (0.2) | 1.5 | (0.2) |
| Netherlands | 23.3 | (0.9) | 28.1 | (0.9) | 32.2 | (0.8) | 11.0 | (0.5) | 5.4 | (0.4) | 66.2 | (0.8) | 25.6 | (0.7) | 6.7 | (0.4) | 1.3 | (0.2) | 0.2 | (0.1) |
| New Zealand | 8.9 | (0.7) | 7.7 | (0.5) | 18.7 | (0.8) | 55.8 | (1.1) | 9.0 | (0.6) | 74.5 | (0.8) | 19.5 | (0.7) | 4.7 | (0.3) | 1.0 | (0.2) | 0.3 | (0.1) |
| Norway | 2.8 | (0.3) | 21.9 | (1.0) | 68.4 | (1.0) | 5.8 | (0.5) | 1.1 | (0.2) | 39.4 | (1.0) | 46.9 | (0.9) | 11.5 | (0.5) | 1.7 | (0.2) | 0.5 | (0.1) |
| Poland | 3.0 | (0.3) | 33.7 | (1.0) | 42.5 | (0.8) | 17.6 | (0.7) | 3.2 | (0.3) | 59.6 | (1.1) | 31.4 | (0.9) | 7.4 | (0.5) | 1.1 | (0.1) | 0.4 | (0.1) |
| Portugal | 13.0 | (0.7) | 24.6 | (1.1) | 27.0 | (1.0) | 16.2 | (0.7) | 19.2 | (0.7) | 66.8 | (0.8) | 21.7 | (0.8) | 8.6 | (0.4) | 2.5 | (0.2) | 0.5 | (0.1) |
| Slovak Republic | 11.2 | (0.8) | 44.6 | (1.3) | 19.5 | (0.8) | 15.1 | (0.9) | 9.6 | (0.9) | 61.3 | (1.3) | 29.1 | (1.1) | 7.1 | (0.5) | 1.7 | (0.2) | 0.8 | (0.1) |
| Spain | 9.9 | (0.4) | 17.7 | (0.6) | 45.4 | (0.9) | 15.4 | (0.7) | 11.5 | (0.5) | 70.1 | (0.8) | 16.0 | (0.5) | 9.9 | (0.4) | 3.1 | (0.3) | 1.0 | (0.1) |
| Sweden | 2.9 | (0.3) | 17.1 | (1.0) | 69.3 | (0.9) | 9.6 | (0.5) | 1.1 | (0.2) | 64.4 | (0.9) | 29.2 | (0.8) | 5.6 | (0.3) | 0.6 | (0.1) | 0.2 | (0.1) |
| Switzerland | 13.9 | (0.6) | 34.7 | (0.8) | 32.7 | (0.7) | 13.5 | (0.6) | 5.1 | (0.5) | 75.8 | (0.5) | 18.1 | (0.5) | 5.0 | (0.2) | 0.9 | (0.1) | 0.2 | (0.1) |
| Turkey | 26.8 | (1.3) | 16.2 | (0.9) | 26.1 | (1.0) | 12.4 | (0.5) | 18.6 | (1.3) | 48.4 | (1.2) | 25.0 | (0.7) | 15.3 | (0.7) | 7.5 | (0.6) | 3.8 | (0.4) |
| United Kingdom | 3.1 | (0.3) | 7.0 | (0.4) | 28.0 | (0.9) | 49.8 | (1.1) | 12.1 | (0.7) | 67.5 | (0.8) | 25.9 | (0.7) | 5.5 | (0.3) | 0.7 | (0.1) | 0.3 | (0.1) |
| United States | 7.8 | (0.5) | 25.2 | (0.9) | 17.9 | (0.8) | 35.8 | (1.2) | 13.3 | (0.8) | 56.0 | (0.8) | 30.9 | (0.7) | 9.8 | (0.5) | 2.6 | (0.3) | 0.7 | (0.1) |
| **OECD average** | 9.9 | (0.1) | 22.8 | (0.2) | 38.5 | (0.2) | 20.5 | (0.2) | 8.2 | (0.1) | 64.7 | (0.2) | 24.4 | (0.1) | 8.3 | (0.1) | 2.0 | (0.0) | 0.7 | (0.0) |
| **Partners** | | | | | | | | | | | | | | | | | | | | |
| Argentina | 14.5 | (1.1) | 36.8 | (1.1) | 32.3 | (1.2) | 11.3 | (0.8) | 5.1 | (0.5) | 72.8 | (0.9) | 18.7 | (0.8) | 6.7 | (0.4) | 1.4 | (0.2) | 0.4 | (0.1) |
| Azerbaijan | 9.1 | (0.6) | 29.4 | (1.1) | 37.5 | (1.4) | 13.1 | (0.8) | 10.9 | (0.8) | 39.0 | (1.1) | 34.5 | (0.9) | 18.5 | (0.9) | 5.0 | (0.4) | 3.0 | (0.3) |
| Brazil | 8.1 | (0.4) | 41.7 | (0.9) | 38.8 | (0.7) | 8.1 | (0.5) | 3.2 | (0.4) | 54.6 | (0.9) | 32.0 | (0.7) | 10.8 | (0.5) | 1.7 | (0.2) | 0.8 | (0.2) |
| Bulgaria | 13.9 | (0.9) | 32.6 | (1.1) | 29.3 | (1.0) | 13.3 | (0.9) | 10.8 | (0.8) | 50.2 | (1.0) | 31.2 | (0.7) | 14.2 | (0.6) | 3.1 | (0.3) | 1.3 | (0.2) |
| Chile | 15.4 | (0.8) | 37.4 | (0.9) | 27.4 | (0.8) | 12.6 | (0.7) | 7.2 | (0.5) | 50.9 | (0.9) | 35.6 | (0.8) | 10.9 | (0.5) | 1.9 | (0.2) | 0.7 | (0.1) |
| Colombia | 5.3 | (0.9) | 18.7 | (1.7) | 33.8 | (1.9) | 32.9 | (1.5) | 9.4 | (1.8) | 49.2 | (1.2) | 34.2 | (1.2) | 11.7 | (0.6) | 4.2 | (0.4) | 0.7 | (0.2) |
| Croatia | 24.3 | (1.1) | 25.6 | (0.8) | 39.8 | (1.0) | 7.8 | (0.5) | 2.6 | (0.3) | 75.2 | (0.9) | 17.2 | (0.7) | 6.1 | (0.4) | 1.2 | (0.2) | 0.2 | (0.1) |
| Estonia | 3.0 | (0.3) | 25.2 | (0.9) | 40.2 | (1.0) | 20.0 | (0.7) | 11.6 | (0.6) | 55.3 | (0.9) | 31.8 | (0.8) | 10.7 | (0.5) | 1.7 | (0.2) | 0.6 | (0.1) |
| Hong Kong-China | 32.8 | (1.0) | 10.0 | (0.5) | 17.0 | (0.8) | 14.1 | (0.5) | 26.2 | (0.7) | 61.2 | (1.0) | 21.0 | (0.8) | 12.4 | (0.7) | 4.0 | (0.3) | 1.4 | (0.2) |
| Indonesia | 5.9 | (0.8) | 20.7 | (1.4) | 44.5 | (1.1) | 16.5 | (1.2) | 12.4 | (0.9) | 42.6 | (1.6) | 38.8 | (0.9) | 14.3 | (0.9) | 3.3 | (0.3) | 0.9 | (0.1) |
| Israel | 24.0 | (1.1) | 24.5 | (0.9) | 28.2 | (0.9) | 14.5 | (0.7) | 8.8 | (0.6) | 50.4 | (0.9) | 31.5 | (0.6) | 13.1 | (0.6) | 4.0 | (0.3) | 1.0 | (0.2) |
| Jordan | 10.4 | (0.7) | 26.0 | (0.8) | 25.3 | (0.8) | 22.7 | (1.3) | 15.6 | (0.6) | 35.1 | (1.1) | 32.9 | (0.8) | 22.3 | (0.7) | 7.6 | (0.5) | 2.1 | (0.2) |
| Kyrgyzstan | 22.7 | (0.8) | 38.7 | (1.0) | 20.6 | (0.7) | 8.7 | (0.5) | 9.3 | (0.9) | 33.7 | (1.0) | 41.1 | (0.8) | 18.2 | (0.6) | 4.4 | (0.2) | 2.6 | (0.2) |
| Latvia | 6.7 | (0.5) | 29.0 | (0.9) | 39.9 | (1.2) | 16.5 | (1.0) | 7.8 | (0.6) | 61.3 | (1.0) | 28.3 | (0.8) | 8.4 | (0.5) | 1.5 | (0.2) | 0.6 | (0.1) |
| Liechtenstein | 5.3 | (1.1) | 33.9 | (2.3) | 45.3 | (2.5) | 10.6 | (1.5) | 4.9 | (1.1) | 69.1 | (2.8) | 21.9 | (2.5) | 7.4 | (1.5) | 1.5 | (0.7) | a | a |
| Lithuania | 3.8 | (0.3) | 37.4 | (1.0) | 35.9 | (0.7) | 18.4 | (0.6) | 4.5 | (0.4) | 64.8 | (1.0) | 26.6 | (0.9) | 6.9 | (0.4) | 1.4 | (0.2) | 0.3 | (0.1) |
| Macao-China | 11.3 | (0.4) | 14.7 | (0.5) | 28.4 | (0.7) | 22.3 | (0.6) | 23.3 | (0.7) | 52.6 | (0.8) | 30.2 | (0.8) | 10.8 | (0.5) | 3.7 | (0.3) | 2.6 | (0.3) |
| Montenegro | 10.9 | (0.4) | 32.3 | (0.8) | 28.8 | (0.8) | 15.8 | (0.6) | 12.2 | (0.6) | 48.9 | (0.8) | 31.5 | (0.8) | 13.8 | (0.5) | 4.1 | (0.3) | 1.7 | (0.2) |
| Qatar | 16.6 | (0.5) | 30.6 | (0.5) | 25.6 | (0.6) | 15.6 | (0.5) | 11.5 | (0.4) | 31.3 | (0.7) | 38.8 | (0.6) | 21.6 | (0.6) | 6.5 | (0.3) | 1.7 | (0.2) |
| Romania | 17.5 | (1.0) | 37.0 | (1.8) | 27.8 | (1.8) | 9.3 | (0.6) | 8.5 | (0.7) | 44.6 | (1.1) | 37.4 | (1.1) | 13.5 | (0.7) | 3.3 | (0.4) | 1.2 | (0.3) |
| Russian Federation | 6.7 | (0.6) | 22.6 | (0.9) | 25.7 | (0.8) | 21.2 | (1.1) | 23.9 | (1.4) | 41.4 | (1.3) | 38.7 | (1.1) | 14.5 | (0.6) | 3.6 | (0.3) | 1.7 | (0.2) |
| Serbia | 12.4 | (0.7) | 25.5 | (0.9) | 36.5 | (0.8) | 13.9 | (0.6) | 11.6 | (0.7) | 57.8 | (0.8) | 28.2 | (0.7) | 11.0 | (0.6) | 2.0 | (0.2) | 1.0 | (0.1) |
| Slovenia | 9.3 | (0.4) | 33.6 | (0.7) | 29.8 | (0.7) | 16.2 | (0.6) | 11.1 | (0.5) | 55.2 | (0.8) | 33.8 | (0.8) | 9.1 | (0.5) | 1.4 | (0.2) | 0.5 | (0.1) |
| Chinese Taipei | 11.5 | (0.9) | 23.5 | (0.9) | 38.0 | (0.9) | 18.5 | (0.8) | 8.4 | (0.5) | 64.8 | (0.7) | 17.9 | (0.6) | 14.0 | (0.5) | 2.5 | (0.2) | 0.8 | (0.1) |
| Thailand | a | a | 6.7 | (0.6) | 61.3 | (1.2) | 16.8 | (0.8) | 15.2 | (0.6) | 59.6 | (1.2) | 21.6 | (0.9) | 13.6 | (0.6) | 3.8 | (0.3) | 1.4 | (0.2) |
| Tunisia | 10.6 | (0.8) | 34.8 | (0.9) | 33.2 | (0.9) | 11.2 | (0.5) | 10.2 | (0.7) | 19.9 | (0.7) | 40.3 | (0.9) | 26.9 | (0.7) | 9.4 | (0.5) | 3.6 | (0.3) |
| Uruguay | 16.4 | (0.9) | 33.2 | (0.9) | 30.3 | (1.0) | 12.3 | (0.6) | 7.8 | (0.5) | 66.3 | (0.8) | 23.2 | (0.7) | 7.9 | (0.4) | 2.1 | (0.3) | 0.5 | (0.1) |

© OECD 2011  Quality Time for Students: Learning In and Out of School

[Part 2/2]
## Table 2.1a  Percentage of students, by time spent learning science

| | Individual study | | | | | | | | | |
| | No time per week | | Less than 2 hours per week | | 2 hours or more but less than 4 hours per week | | 4 hours or more but less than 6 hours per week | | 6 hours or more per week | |
| | % | S.E. | % | S.E. | % | S.E. | % | S.E. | % | S.E. |
|---|---|---|---|---|---|---|---|---|---|---|
| **OECD** | | | | | | | | | | |
| Australia | 30.5 | (0.6) | 50.5 | (0.7) | 14.9 | (0.5) | 3.2 | (0.2) | 0.9 | (0.1) |
| Austria | 31.8 | (1.0) | 46.8 | (0.8) | 14.9 | (0.6) | 4.6 | (0.3) | 1.9 | (0.2) |
| Belgium | 25.5 | (0.8) | 53.6 | (0.7) | 17.1 | (0.6) | 3.0 | (0.2) | 0.7 | (0.1) |
| Canada | 22.0 | (0.6) | 48.7 | (0.6) | 21.7 | (0.6) | 5.9 | (0.3) | 1.7 | (0.2) |
| Czech Republic | 39.5 | (0.9) | 44.7 | (0.8) | 12.4 | (0.7) | 2.5 | (0.3) | 0.8 | (0.2) |
| Denmark | 22.8 | (1.2) | 63.9 | (1.1) | 11.1 | (0.6) | 1.7 | (0.2) | 0.5 | (0.1) |
| Finland | 21.3 | (0.7) | 66.2 | (0.8) | 10.8 | (0.6) | 1.4 | (0.2) | 0.2 | (0.1) |
| France | 23.1 | (1.0) | 55.2 | (0.9) | 17.2 | (0.7) | 3.5 | (0.4) | 1.0 | (0.2) |
| Germany | 13.8 | (0.7) | 54.7 | (0.8) | 23.4 | (0.7) | 5.7 | (0.4) | 2.4 | (0.2) |
| Greece | 21.7 | (0.8) | 40.2 | (1.0) | 26.3 | (0.6) | 8.6 | (0.5) | 3.2 | (0.3) |
| Hungary | 19.0 | (1.0) | 50.7 | (0.9) | 23.0 | (0.8) | 5.5 | (0.3) | 1.8 | (0.2) |
| Iceland | 22.3 | (0.7) | 61.4 | (0.8) | 13.8 | (0.6) | 1.9 | (0.2) | 0.6 | (0.1) |
| Ireland | 29.7 | (1.0) | 50.5 | (0.9) | 15.4 | (0.7) | 3.4 | (0.3) | 0.9 | (0.1) |
| Italy | 15.9 | (1.2) | 40.1 | (0.9) | 29.2 | (0.8) | 11.0 | (0.5) | 3.8 | (0.3) |
| Japan | 46.0 | (1.3) | 47.7 | (1.2) | 5.4 | (0.3) | 0.8 | (0.1) | 0.1 | (0.1) |
| Korea | 28.5 | (1.1) | 52.1 | (1.2) | 14.9 | (0.6) | 3.0 | (0.3) | 1.4 | (0.6) |
| Luxembourg | 26.7 | (0.6) | 53.9 | (0.7) | 14.4 | (0.5) | 3.5 | (0.3) | 1.4 | (0.2) |
| Mexico | 12.0 | (0.5) | 46.3 | (0.6) | 26.4 | (0.6) | 10.2 | (0.4) | 5.1 | (0.3) |
| Netherlands | 29.9 | (1.0) | 49.5 | (0.9) | 16.4 | (0.6) | 3.6 | (0.3) | 0.6 | (0.1) |
| New Zealand | 25.4 | (0.9) | 53.3 | (0.8) | 17.1 | (0.6) | 3.1 | (0.3) | 1.1 | (0.2) |
| Norway | 20.5 | (0.8) | 61.0 | (0.8) | 16.0 | (0.8) | 2.0 | (0.2) | 0.6 | (0.1) |
| Poland | 9.7 | (0.4) | 49.3 | (0.8) | 29.2 | (0.7) | 8.9 | (0.4) | 2.9 | (0.2) |
| Portugal | 15.8 | (0.8) | 41.1 | (0.9) | 28.3 | (0.7) | 10.4 | (0.5) | 4.4 | (0.3) |
| Slovak Republic | 30.4 | (1.2) | 43.1 | (0.8) | 19.9 | (0.8) | 5.0 | (0.4) | 1.6 | (0.3) |
| Spain | 20.1 | (0.7) | 45.1 | (0.7) | 25.2 | (0.7) | 7.3 | (0.3) | 2.3 | (0.2) |
| Sweden | 19.3 | (1.6) | 66.6 | (1.7) | 11.3 | (0.6) | 2.1 | (0.3) | 0.5 | (0.1) |
| Switzerland | 26.0 | (0.8) | 58.8 | (0.8) | 12.0 | (0.5) | 2.7 | (0.2) | 0.5 | (0.1) |
| Turkey | 34.3 | (1.3) | 32.0 | (0.9) | 21.7 | (0.8) | 8.5 | (0.6) | 3.5 | (0.3) |
| United Kingdom | 14.0 | (0.6) | 61.1 | (0.8) | 21.2 | (0.8) | 3.0 | (0.2) | 0.7 | (0.1) |
| United States | 17.6 | (0.8) | 50.3 | (0.9) | 23.3 | (0.6) | 6.8 | (0.4) | 2.1 | (0.2) |
| **OECD average** | 23.8 | (0.2) | 51.3 | (0.2) | 18.5 | (0.1) | 4.8 | (0.1) | 1.7 | (0.0) |
| **Partners** | | | | | | | | | | |
| Argentina | 20.2 | (0.9) | 50.7 | (1.0) | 20.8 | (0.8) | 5.8 | (0.5) | 2.4 | (0.3) |
| Azerbaijan | 12.7 | (0.7) | 34.5 | (0.9) | 28.3 | (1.0) | 13.3 | (0.7) | 11.2 | (0.7) |
| Brazil | 16.3 | (0.6) | 52.0 | (0.8) | 23.2 | (0.7) | 5.7 | (0.3) | 2.8 | (0.2) |
| Bulgaria | 22.1 | (1.0) | 37.3 | (0.8) | 25.2 | (1.0) | 10.2 | (0.7) | 5.2 | (0.4) |
| Chile | 20.9 | (0.9) | 51.1 | (0.8) | 21.2 | (0.6) | 5.0 | (0.3) | 1.7 | (0.2) |
| Colombia | 16.2 | (0.9) | 49.2 | (1.0) | 22.6 | (0.8) | 9.3 | (0.8) | 2.7 | (0.2) |
| Croatia | 34.3 | (1.1) | 35.0 | (0.7) | 22.8 | (0.8) | 6.0 | (0.4) | 1.8 | (0.2) |
| Estonia | 21.2 | (0.7) | 49.7 | (0.8) | 22.0 | (0.6) | 5.8 | (0.3) | 1.3 | (0.2) |
| Hong Kong-China | 41.6 | (0.9) | 29.8 | (0.7) | 18.3 | (0.6) | 6.2 | (0.4) | 4.0 | (0.4) |
| Indonesia | 9.2 | (0.7) | 58.0 | (0.9) | 23.9 | (0.8) | 6.8 | (0.5) | 2.1 | (0.2) |
| Israel | 38.5 | (1.1) | 34.2 | (0.9) | 19.4 | (0.8) | 5.9 | (0.4) | 1.9 | (0.2) |
| Jordan | 10.0 | (0.5) | 34.9 | (0.9) | 31.3 | (0.8) | 15.3 | (0.6) | 8.5 | (0.6) |
| Kyrgyzstan | 22.0 | (0.7) | 37.3 | (0.9) | 21.9 | (0.5) | 10.4 | (0.5) | 8.4 | (0.4) |
| Latvia | 14.0 | (0.7) | 50.4 | (1.0) | 26.6 | (0.9) | 6.7 | (0.4) | 2.3 | (0.2) |
| Liechtenstein | 19.8 | (2.5) | 65.7 | (2.8) | 10.7 | (1.5) | 2.7 | (0.9) | 1.2 | (0.6) |
| Lithuania | 15.7 | (0.6) | 52.3 | (0.8) | 23.9 | (0.7) | 6.2 | (0.4) | 1.9 | (0.2) |
| Macao-China | 30.8 | (0.7) | 44.6 | (0.8) | 17.4 | (0.7) | 4.9 | (0.4) | 2.3 | (0.3) |
| Montenegro | 13.4 | (0.6) | 43.8 | (0.8) | 25.4 | (0.7) | 10.9 | (0.5) | 6.5 | (0.4) |
| Qatar | 16.3 | (0.5) | 40.1 | (0.6) | 30.8 | (0.6) | 9.4 | (0.4) | 3.5 | (0.3) |
| Romania | 26.1 | (1.1) | 44.1 | (0.9) | 19.5 | (0.8) | 6.9 | (0.5) | 3.5 | (0.4) |
| Russian Federation | 10.9 | (1.0) | 29.1 | (0.7) | 32.5 | (1.1) | 16.2 | (0.6) | 11.4 | (0.5) |
| Serbia | 28.2 | (0.9) | 37.1 | (0.7) | 23.6 | (0.8) | 7.5 | (0.5) | 3.7 | (0.3) |
| Slovenia | 18.2 | (0.5) | 53.8 | (0.7) | 21.9 | (0.5) | 4.7 | (0.3) | 1.5 | (0.2) |
| Chinese Taipei | 32.8 | (1.2) | 44.7 | (0.8) | 17.6 | (0.6) | 3.7 | (0.3) | 1.1 | (0.1) |
| Thailand | 9.5 | (0.5) | 56.6 | (0.8) | 25.3 | (0.6) | 6.1 | (0.4) | 2.5 | (0.2) |
| Tunisia | 9.9 | (0.6) | 36.2 | (0.8) | 30.7 | (0.7) | 15.3 | (0.6) | 8.1 | (0.4) |
| Uruguay | 26.5 | (1.1) | 51.0 | (1.0) | 17.1 | (0.6) | 4.2 | (0.4) | 1.2 | (0.2) |

[Part 1/2]
## Table 2.1b Percentage of students, by time spent learning mathematics

| | Regular school lessons | | | | | | | | | | Out-of-school-time lessons | | | | | | | | | |
| | No time per week | | Less than 2 hours per week | | 2 hours or more but less than 4 hours per week | | 4 hours or more but less than 6 hours per week | | 6 hours or more per week | | No time per week | | Less than 2 hours per week | | 2 hours or more but less than 4 hours per week | | 4 hours or more but less than 6 hours per week | | 6 hours or more per week | |
| | % | S.E. | % | S.E. | % | S.E. | % | S.E. | % | S.E. | % | S.E. | % | S.E. | % | S.E. | % | S.E. | % | S.E. |
|---|---|---|---|---|---|---|---|---|---|---|---|---|---|---|---|---|---|---|---|---|
| **OECD Australia** | 1.9 | (0.1) | 6.9 | (0.3) | 36.8 | (0.9) | 44.1 | (0.9) | 10.3 | (0.4) | 60.6 | (0.6) | 25.8 | (0.5) | 10.4 | (0.4) | 2.5 | (0.1) | 0.8 | (0.1) |
| Austria | 4.0 | (0.4) | 13.9 | (0.9) | 54.8 | (1.2) | 23.6 | (1.1) | 3.7 | (0.5) | 73.6 | (0.9) | 17.5 | (0.8) | 6.4 | (0.4) | 1.9 | (0.2) | 0.6 | (0.1) |
| Belgium | 4.1 | (0.4) | 18.1 | (0.6) | 29.0 | (0.8) | 44.8 | (0.9) | 4.1 | (0.5) | 69.5 | (0.7) | 21.1 | (0.6) | 7.2 | (0.3) | 1.7 | (0.2) | 0.5 | (0.1) |
| Canada | 3.7 | (0.2) | 11.5 | (0.5) | 17.9 | (0.8) | 41.5 | (0.7) | 25.4 | (0.9) | 52.8 | (0.7) | 29.9 | (0.5) | 12.6 | (0.5) | 3.4 | (0.2) | 1.3 | (0.1) |
| Czech Republic | 1.1 | (0.2) | 8.9 | (0.6) | 36.0 | (1.4) | 47.5 | (1.4) | 6.5 | (0.5) | 57.4 | (0.9) | 30.0 | (0.8) | 9.8 | (0.5) | 2.0 | (0.2) | 0.9 | (0.2) |
| Denmark | 0.7 | (0.2) | 3.4 | (0.3) | 29.8 | (1.1) | 56.2 | (1.0) | 9.9 | (0.6) | 30.5 | (0.9) | 41.8 | (0.9) | 22.7 | (0.6) | 4.3 | (0.4) | 0.7 | (0.1) |
| Finland | 1.3 | (0.2) | 9.4 | (0.6) | 58.0 | (1.6) | 28.9 | (1.5) | 2.4 | (0.4) | 74.9 | (0.7) | 20.4 | (0.6) | 3.8 | (0.3) | 0.6 | (0.1) | 0.3 | (0.1) |
| France | 1.8 | (0.3) | 9.1 | (0.5) | 37.4 | (0.9) | 49.6 | (1.0) | 2.1 | (0.3) | 46.2 | (0.7) | 37.5 | (0.8) | 13.6 | (0.5) | 2.1 | (0.2) | 0.5 | (0.1) |
| Germany | 2.2 | (0.2) | 8.9 | (0.5) | 39.5 | (1.0) | 42.7 | (1.1) | 6.7 | (0.6) | 59.1 | (1.0) | 25.5 | (0.8) | 11.3 | (0.6) | 3.2 | (0.3) | 0.9 | (0.2) |
| Greece | 4.5 | (0.4) | 14.1 | (0.7) | 44.4 | (1.1) | 30.6 | (1.2) | 6.4 | (0.4) | 26.3 | (0.9) | 23.3 | (0.7) | 31.0 | (0.8) | 14.3 | (0.7) | 5.1 | (0.4) |
| Hungary | 2.8 | (0.3) | 19.3 | (0.8) | 44.6 | (1.3) | 28.9 | (1.3) | 4.5 | (0.4) | 33.8 | (0.9) | 42.3 | (0.8) | 17.7 | (0.7) | 4.8 | (0.4) | 1.3 | (0.2) |
| Iceland | 0.6 | (0.1) | 4.2 | (0.3) | 21.5 | (0.7) | 55.1 | (0.9) | 18.6 | (0.6) | 60.8 | (0.9) | 26.3 | (0.8) | 10.2 | (0.5) | 1.9 | (0.2) | 0.7 | (0.2) |
| Ireland | 1.6 | (0.2) | 11.9 | (0.6) | 46.8 | (1.0) | 32.4 | (0.8) | 7.3 | (0.5) | 60.8 | (0.8) | 26.8 | (0.7) | 9.6 | (0.5) | 2.0 | (0.2) | 0.9 | (0.2) |
| Italy | 3.0 | (0.2) | 14.3 | (0.6) | 33.9 | (0.9) | 42.0 | (0.9) | 6.8 | (0.4) | 57.7 | (0.5) | 24.9 | (0.5) | 12.8 | (0.4) | 3.2 | (0.2) | 1.3 | (0.1) |
| Japan | 0.2 | (0.1) | 8.1 | (1.0) | 35.5 | (1.4) | 42.3 | (1.5) | 14.0 | (1.3) | 62.5 | (1.4) | 24.2 | (1.0) | 10.5 | (0.7) | 1.9 | (0.2) | 0.9 | (0.1) |
| Korea | 1.3 | (0.2) | 3.2 | (0.4) | 21.3 | (0.9) | 58.2 | (1.2) | 15.9 | (1.1) | 27.4 | (0.9) | 21.1 | (0.8) | 31.6 | (0.9) | 13.7 | (0.6) | 6.2 | (0.5) |
| Luxembourg | 2.8 | (0.3) | 10.6 | (0.4) | 34.2 | (0.8) | 47.1 | (0.8) | 5.3 | (0.3) | 56.3 | (0.8) | 28.5 | (0.7) | 11.5 | (0.5) | 2.8 | (0.2) | 0.9 | (0.1) |
| Mexico | 2.7 | (0.2) | 23.3 | (0.7) | 19.7 | (0.6) | 33.9 | (0.7) | 20.3 | (0.6) | 45.3 | (0.9) | 32.2 | (0.7) | 15.1 | (0.4) | 5.5 | (0.4) | 1.9 | (0.2) |
| Netherlands | 7.8 | (0.8) | 15.8 | (0.9) | 56.7 | (1.2) | 18.3 | (0.8) | 1.4 | (0.2) | 57.1 | (0.9) | 32.2 | (0.7) | 8.6 | (0.5) | 1.8 | (0.2) | 0.2 | (0.1) |
| New Zealand | 1.5 | (0.2) | 7.3 | (0.5) | 19.4 | (0.8) | 65.0 | (1.0) | 6.8 | (0.4) | 62.3 | (0.9) | 26.1 | (0.7) | 8.5 | (0.4) | 2.3 | (0.2) | 0.8 | (0.1) |
| Norway | 2.1 | (0.2) | 10.8 | (0.5) | 56.3 | (0.9) | 28.0 | (1.0) | 2.8 | (0.3) | 36.4 | (1.0) | 46.8 | (0.9) | 13.8 | (0.6) | 2.1 | (0.2) | 0.8 | (0.1) |
| Poland | 2.0 | (0.2) | 11.1 | (0.5) | 17.5 | (0.6) | 56.7 | (0.8) | 12.6 | (0.7) | 49.4 | (1.3) | 40.2 | (1.2) | 7.8 | (0.4) | 1.9 | (0.2) | 0.6 | (0.1) |
| Portugal | 7.4 | (0.5) | 12.2 | (0.8) | 36.3 | (1.1) | 34.5 | (0.9) | 9.6 | (0.5) | 53.3 | (1.1) | 32.7 | (1.1) | 11.2 | (0.5) | 2.3 | (0.2) | 0.5 | (0.1) |
| Slovak Republic | 1.9 | (0.2) | 18.6 | (1.3) | 45.6 | (1.6) | 31.9 | (1.7) | 2.0 | (0.3) | 45.5 | (1.3) | 40.9 | (1.0) | 10.8 | (0.5) | 2.3 | (0.3) | 0.5 | (0.1) |
| Spain | 2.8 | (0.2) | 10.1 | (0.5) | 55.2 | (1.0) | 28.3 | (1.0) | 3.5 | (0.3) | 57.6 | (0.7) | 21.5 | (0.5) | 14.7 | (0.4) | 4.8 | (0.3) | 1.4 | (0.1) |
| Sweden | 1.0 | (0.1) | 10.7 | (0.6) | 73.1 | (0.8) | 13.8 | (0.8) | 1.4 | (0.2) | 30.9 | (0.9) | 31.7 | (0.8) | 6.8 | (0.4) | 1.4 | (0.2) | 0.3 | (0.1) |
| Switzerland | 1.9 | (0.3) | 11.7 | (0.6) | 36.1 | (0.8) | 43.0 | (0.8) | 7.3 | (0.5) | 59.1 | (0.9) | 29.4 | (0.7) | 9.0 | (0.4) | 1.9 | (0.2) | 0.6 | (0.1) |
| Turkey | 9.3 | (0.9) | 10.4 | (0.8) | 25.6 | (1.1) | 44.3 | (1.3) | 10.5 | (0.7) | 29.6 | (1.0) | 26.4 | (0.7) | 25.2 | (0.8) | 13.1 | (0.6) | 5.8 | (0.4) |
| United Kingdom | 1.1 | (0.1) | 6.6 | (0.4) | 49.8 | (1.3) | 37.8 | (1.2) | 4.6 | (0.3) | 60.3 | (0.9) | 30.1 | (0.7) | 7.8 | (0.3) | 1.5 | (0.2) | 0.3 | (0.1) |
| United States | 4.7 | (0.4) | 22.8 | (0.8) | 19.5 | (1.1) | 37.8 | (1.3) | 15.3 | (0.8) | 45.0 | (1.2) | 33.2 | (1.0) | 15.5 | (0.5) | 4.5 | (0.3) | 1.8 | (0.2) |
| **OECD average** | 2.8 | (0.1) | 11.6 | (0.1) | 37.7 | (0.2) | 39.6 | (0.2) | 8.3 | (0.1) | 52.4 | (0.2) | 29.7 | (0.1) | 12.9 | (0.1) | 3.7 | (0.1) | 1.3 | (0.0) |
| **Partners Argentina** | 7.0 | (0.5) | 27.7 | (1.2) | 35.0 | (1.0) | 24.7 | (1.3) | 5.5 | (0.7) | 60.8 | (1.3) | 25.5 | (1.0) | 9.6 | (0.6) | 2.7 | (0.3) | 1.4 | (0.2) |
| Azerbaijan | 7.8 | (0.5) | 19.1 | (0.8) | 25.2 | (1.0) | 25.5 | (1.2) | 22.4 | (1.1) | 37.8 | (1.1) | 28.7 | (1.0) | 18.7 | (0.8) | 9.5 | (0.8) | 5.3 | (0.4) |
| Brazil | 3.8 | (0.3) | 26.2 | (0.7) | 37.6 | (0.8) | 25.7 | (0.8) | 6.8 | (0.4) | 41.0 | (0.9) | 35.9 | (0.8) | 16.9 | (0.6) | 4.4 | (0.3) | 1.8 | (0.2) |
| Bulgaria | 7.4 | (0.6) | 26.1 | (1.1) | 40.2 | (1.3) | 16.3 | (1.0) | 10.0 | (0.8) | 46.6 | (1.1) | 31.7 | (0.6) | 15.3 | (0.6) | 4.4 | (0.4) | 2.0 | (0.3) |
| Chile | 7.7 | (0.5) | 24.2 | (0.8) | 23.8 | (0.8) | 28.2 | (0.9) | 16.0 | (1.0) | 45.9 | (1.0) | 36.7 | (0.9) | 13.3 | (0.6) | 3.3 | (0.3) | 0.9 | (0.1) |
| Colombia | 3.1 | (0.3) | 10.7 | (0.9) | 25.0 | (1.3) | 46.2 | (1.6) | 14.9 | (1.2) | 41.7 | (1.0) | 34.5 | (0.9) | 16.9 | (0.7) | 5.5 | (0.5) | 1.4 | (0.2) |
| Croatia | 3.9 | (0.3) | 17.5 | (0.8) | 54.3 | (0.9) | 22.7 | (1.0) | 1.5 | (0.2) | 60.5 | (0.8) | 24.9 | (0.6) | 11.3 | (0.5) | 2.6 | (0.3) | 0.7 | (0.1) |
| Estonia | 2.3 | (0.3) | 11.2 | (0.6) | 21.8 | (0.8) | 55.3 | (1.0) | 9.5 | (0.5) | 46.9 | (0.9) | 35.4 | (0.8) | 13.2 | (0.6) | 3.7 | (0.3) | 0.8 | (0.1) |
| Hong Kong-China | 1.4 | (0.2) | 6.3 | (0.4) | 13.9 | (0.8) | 36.8 | (0.9) | 41.6 | (1.0) | 38.0 | (1.1) | 34.5 | (0.9) | 18.8 | (0.7) | 6.3 | (0.4) | 2.4 | (0.3) |
| Indonesia | 1.3 | (0.3) | 13.1 | (1.1) | 33.6 | (1.0) | 34.5 | (1.3) | 17.5 | (1.1) | 32.5 | (1.3) | 41.2 | (0.9) | 19.7 | (1.1) | 5.4 | (0.4) | 1.3 | (0.2) |
| Israel | 5.0 | (0.5) | 11.7 | (0.6) | 24.6 | (1.0) | 41.8 | (1.1) | 16.8 | (0.8) | 23.4 | (0.9) | 31.4 | (0.9) | 27.5 | (0.8) | 11.5 | (0.6) | 6.3 | (0.4) |
| Jordan | 8.6 | (0.5) | 24.8 | (0.9) | 23.3 | (0.9) | 25.2 | (0.9) | 18.2 | (0.7) | 32.1 | (1.1) | 28.7 | (0.8) | 25.2 | (0.7) | 10.2 | (0.5) | 3.9 | (0.3) |
| Kyrgyzstan | 14.3 | (0.7) | 29.9 | (0.8) | 23.6 | (0.7) | 18.8 | (0.7) | 13.4 | (0.8) | 31.3 | (1.1) | 39.9 | (0.9) | 18.0 | (0.6) | 6.9 | (0.5) | 3.9 | (0.3) |
| Latvia | 0.8 | (0.1) | 7.3 | (0.6) | 25.7 | (0.8) | 49.2 | (0.9) | 16.9 | (0.8) | 37.5 | (1.3) | 39.9 | (1.2) | 17.8 | (0.9) | 3.6 | (0.3) | 1.2 | (0.2) |
| Liechtenstein | 0.6 | (0.4) | 13.6 | (1.7) | 31.0 | (2.2) | 46.3 | (2.3) | 8.6 | (1.3) | 63.3 | (2.2) | 27.5 | (2.2) | 7.8 | (1.4) | 1.5 | (0.7) | 0.0 | c |
| Lithuania | 2.9 | (0.3) | 20.2 | (1.0) | 34.6 | (0.9) | 35.1 | (0.9) | 7.2 | (0.4) | 53.3 | (1.0) | 35.9 | (1.0) | 8.3 | (0.5) | 2.0 | (0.2) | 0.4 | (0.1) |
| Macao-China | 1.1 | (0.1) | 5.7 | (0.4) | 10.8 | (0.5) | 37.1 | (0.8) | 45.3 | (0.9) | 47.9 | (0.8) | 30.6 | (0.8) | 12.5 | (0.6) | 5.3 | (0.4) | 3.6 | (0.3) |
| Montenegro | 7.2 | (0.5) | 28.3 | (0.7) | 32.5 | (0.8) | 20.7 | (0.7) | 11.4 | (0.5) | 58.3 | (0.8) | 24.5 | (0.8) | 11.1 | (0.5) | 4.0 | (0.3) | 2.1 | (0.2) |
| Qatar | 7.8 | (0.3) | 30.4 | (0.6) | 26.5 | (0.6) | 22.8 | (0.6) | 12.5 | (0.5) | 29.1 | (0.6) | 32.6 | (0.6) | 24.5 | (0.5) | 9.2 | (0.4) | 4.7 | (0.3) |
| Romania | 5.2 | (0.4) | 26.8 | (1.2) | 39.5 | (2.2) | 21.9 | (1.6) | 6.5 | (0.8) | 33.6 | (0.9) | 36.7 | (0.8) | 20.3 | (1.0) | 6.7 | (0.8) | 2.7 | (0.3) |
| Russian Federation | 2.7 | (0.4) | 16.3 | (1.0) | 38.1 | (1.2) | 33.7 | (1.1) | 9.2 | (0.6) | 33.7 | (1.4) | 48.1 | (1.2) | 14.3 | (0.7) | 2.7 | (0.3) | 1.2 | (0.2) |
| Serbia | 3.6 | (0.4) | 16.3 | (0.7) | 49.7 | (1.0) | 25.5 | (1.0) | 4.9 | (0.4) | 51.9 | (0.8) | 30.5 | (0.7) | 12.2 | (0.5) | 3.8 | (0.3) | 1.6 | (0.2) |
| Slovenia | 3.5 | (0.3) | 18.7 | (0.6) | 41.5 | (0.8) | 32.4 | (0.7) | 4.0 | (0.3) | 45.7 | (0.7) | 35.8 | (0.8) | 14.0 | (0.5) | 3.3 | (0.3) | 1.1 | (0.2) |
| Chinese Taipei | 3.1 | (0.3) | 14.2 | (0.7) | 23.5 | (0.9) | 36.8 | (0.9) | 22.4 | (0.9) | 44.4 | (0.9) | 17.8 | (0.6) | 29.1 | (0.9) | 6.8 | (0.4) | 2.0 | (0.2) |
| Thailand | a | a | 5.4 | (0.3) | 58.8 | (1.1) | 27.4 | (1.0) | 8.4 | (0.7) | 56.2 | (1.1) | 24.9 | (0.8) | 14.5 | (0.6) | 3.5 | (0.3) | 0.9 | (0.2) |
| Tunisia | 9.2 | (0.5) | 20.1 | (0.8) | 26.3 | (0.7) | 35.4 | (0.9) | 9.0 | (0.5) | 19.8 | (0.3) | 29.9 | (0.7) | 28.0 | (0.9) | 13.9 | (0.5) | 8.4 | (0.4) |
| Uruguay | 4.2 | (0.3) | 19.5 | (0.7) | 41.3 | (1.0) | 28.5 | (0.9) | 6.5 | (0.5) | 57.6 | (0.8) | 26.9 | (0.6) | 11.3 | (0.5) | 3.2 | (0.3) | 1.0 | (0.2) |

© OECD 2011  Quality Time for Students: Learning In and Out of School

[Part 2/2]
## Table 2.1b  Percentage of students, by time spent learning mathematics

| | | No time per week | | Less than 2 hours per week | | 2 hours or more but less than 4 hours per week | | 4 hours or more but less than 6 hours per week | | 6 hours or more per week | |
|---|---|---|---|---|---|---|---|---|---|---|---|
| | | % | S.E. | % | S.E. | % | S.E. | % | S.E. | % | S.E. |
| OECD | Australia | 13.2 | (0.4) | 51.7 | (0.6) | 26.0 | (0.6) | 6.9 | (0.3) | 2.1 | (0.2) |
| | Austria | 9.7 | (0.5) | 46.7 | (0.8) | 30.0 | (0.7) | 9.6 | (0.5) | 4.0 | (0.3) |
| | Belgium | 13.8 | (0.6) | 49.8 | (0.8) | 28.2 | (0.7) | 6.3 | (0.3) | 1.8 | (0.2) |
| | Canada | 15.9 | (0.5) | 44.3 | (0.7) | 26.7 | (0.5) | 9.4 | (0.3) | 3.7 | (0.3) |
| | Czech Republic | 22.8 | (1.1) | 57.0 | (1.1) | 14.9 | (0.6) | 3.5 | (0.3) | 1.8 | (0.3) |
| | Denmark | 9.6 | (0.5) | 55.6 | (0.9) | 28.8 | (0.7) | 4.7 | (0.4) | 1.2 | (0.2) |
| | Finland | 15.3 | (0.6) | 68.9 | (0.8) | 13.9 | (0.7) | 1.6 | (0.2) | 0.2 | (0.1) |
| | France | 12.3 | (0.8) | 53.6 | (0.8) | 26.6 | (0.7) | 5.9 | (0.4) | 1.5 | (0.2) |
| | Germany | 6.3 | (0.5) | 44.8 | (1.0) | 34.5 | (0.8) | 10.7 | (0.6) | 3.6 | (0.3) |
| | Greece | 19.4 | (0.6) | 39.0 | (0.8) | 27.5 | (0.8) | 9.9 | (0.4) | 4.2 | (0.3) |
| | Hungary | 11.1 | (0.6) | 53.2 | (0.9) | 26.2 | (0.8) | 7.4 | (0.5) | 2.2 | (0.2) |
| | Iceland | 13.1 | (0.6) | 53.9 | (0.8) | 25.4 | (0.8) | 5.9 | (0.3) | 1.7 | (0.2) |
| | Ireland | 13.8 | (0.7) | 51.8 | (0.7) | 25.7 | (0.8) | 6.6 | (0.4) | 2.1 | (0.2) |
| | Italy | 7.4 | (0.3) | 39.1 | (0.8) | 34.3 | (0.7) | 14.1 | (0.5) | 5.1 | (0.3) |
| | Japan | 25.4 | (1.2) | 48.2 | (1.2) | 18.8 | (0.9) | 4.9 | (0.4) | 2.7 | (0.4) |
| | Korea | 16.5 | (1.0) | 37.3 | (0.9) | 27.5 | (0.8) | 10.0 | (0.5) | 8.8 | (0.9) |
| | Luxembourg | 12.7 | (0.6) | 55.3 | (0.7) | 24.1 | (0.6) | 5.9 | (0.3) | 2.0 | (0.2) |
| | Mexico | 5.9 | (0.4) | 50.3 | (0.8) | 27.3 | (0.6) | 10.7 | (0.5) | 5.7 | (0.4) |
| | Netherlands | 16.7 | (0.8) | 56.8 | (0.8) | 22.0 | (0.9) | 3.7 | (0.3) | 0.9 | (0.2) |
| | New Zealand | 15.8 | (0.7) | 55.5 | (0.9) | 21.8 | (0.7) | 5.1 | (0.4) | 1.7 | (0.2) |
| | Norway | 20.0 | (0.9) | 55.9 | (0.9) | 19.4 | (0.8) | 3.7 | (0.3) | 1.0 | (0.2) |
| | Poland | 9.4 | (0.5) | 48.1 | (0.8) | 29.2 | (0.7) | 10.1 | (0.5) | 3.3 | (0.3) |
| | Portugal | 13.3 | (0.7) | 46.6 | (0.9) | 28.2 | (0.8) | 8.8 | (0.5) | 3.0 | (0.3) |
| | Slovak Republic | 17.9 | (0.8) | 48.4 | (0.9) | 25.7 | (0.8) | 6.6 | (0.4) | 1.4 | (0.2) |
| | Spain | 12.8 | (0.5) | 46.7 | (0.8) | 29.0 | (0.6) | 9.0 | (0.4) | 2.5 | (0.2) |
| | Sweden | 20.2 | (1.1) | 64.7 | (1.0) | 11.9 | (0.6) | 2.5 | (0.3) | 0.7 | (0.1) |
| | Switzerland | 8.4 | (0.4) | 60.1 | (0.8) | 25.8 | (0.6) | 4.5 | (0.2) | 1.3 | (0.2) |
| | Turkey | 16.1 | (1.1) | 35.7 | (1.0) | 28.9 | (0.8) | 13.5 | (0.6) | 5.8 | (0.4) |
| | United Kingdom | 10.7 | (0.5) | 64.1 | (0.7) | 21.1 | (0.6) | 3.3 | (0.2) | 0.6 | (0.1) |
| | United States | 13.7 | (0.6) | 44.8 | (0.8) | 27.6 | (0.8) | 10.0 | (0.4) | 3.9 | (0.3) |
| | **OECD average** | 14.0 | (0.1) | 50.9 | (0.2) | 25.2 | (0.1) | 7.2 | (0.1) | 2.7 | (0.1) |
| Partners | Argentina | 15.1 | (0.7) | 51.2 | (1.2) | 22.3 | (1.0) | 7.5 | (0.5) | 3.8 | (0.4) |
| | Azerbaijan | 12.8 | (0.8) | 30.6 | (0.8) | 25.5 | (0.9) | 14.9 | (0.8) | 16.1 | (0.8) |
| | Brazil | 14.4 | (0.7) | 52.2 | (0.8) | 22.9 | (0.7) | 7.2 | (0.4) | 3.3 | (0.3) |
| | Bulgaria | 17.9 | (1.1) | 41.1 | (0.9) | 24.7 | (0.9) | 10.7 | (0.6) | 5.7 | (0.6) |
| | Chile | 17.5 | (0.7) | 53.3 | (0.7) | 21.9 | (0.8) | 5.0 | (0.4) | 2.3 | (0.2) |
| | Colombia | 13.5 | (0.8) | 49.5 | (1.2) | 24.2 | (0.7) | 9.6 | (0.6) | 3.3 | (0.3) |
| | Croatia | 18.0 | (0.6) | 45.2 | (0.8) | 26.9 | (0.6) | 7.5 | (0.4) | 2.4 | (0.3) |
| | Estonia | 14.9 | (0.6) | 45.3 | (0.8) | 27.3 | (0.8) | 9.4 | (0.5) | 3.1 | (0.3) |
| | Hong Kong-China | 12.0 | (1.0) | 42.4 | (1.1) | 28.8 | (0.8) | 11.3 | (0.6) | 5.5 | (0.4) |
| | Indonesia | 5.2 | (0.4) | 56.2 | (0.8) | 27.6 | (0.6) | 8.1 | (0.5) | 2.8 | (0.2) |
| | Israel | 17.7 | (0.8) | 34.2 | (0.9) | 27.6 | (1.0) | 13.7 | (0.6) | 6.8 | (0.5) |
| | Jordan | 10.1 | (0.6) | 35.0 | (0.8) | 29.8 | (0.7) | 15.5 | (0.5) | 9.6 | (0.5) |
| | Kyrgyzstan | 19.6 | (0.7) | 38.9 | (0.7) | 21.1 | (0.8) | 11.4 | (0.6) | 8.8 | (0.4) |
| | Latvia | 5.8 | (0.6) | 41.9 | (1.0) | 34.0 | (1.0) | 13.7 | (0.7) | 4.5 | (0.3) |
| | Liechtenstein | 9.1 | (1.8) | 65.7 | (2.5) | 21.7 | (2.4) | 3.3 | (0.8) | 0.3 | (0.3) |
| | Lithuania | 15.4 | (0.6) | 49.7 | (0.7) | 25.4 | (0.7) | 7.0 | (0.4) | 2.5 | (0.2) |
| | Macao-China | 14.7 | (0.7) | 44.6 | (0.8) | 25.7 | (0.7) | 9.9 | (0.5) | 5.1 | (0.3) |
| | Montenegro | 13.3 | (0.6) | 49.6 | (0.8) | 22.4 | (0.7) | 8.3 | (0.5) | 6.4 | (0.4) |
| | Qatar | 14.5 | (0.5) | 39.3 | (0.7) | 28.7 | (0.6) | 12.8 | (0.4) | 4.7 | (0.2) |
| | Romania | 13.3 | (0.7) | 45.4 | (0.8) | 24.1 | (0.9) | 11.1 | (0.9) | 6.1 | (0.5) |
| | Russian Federation | 8.1 | (0.8) | 46.3 | (1.0) | 30.5 | (0.9) | 10.3 | (0.5) | 4.7 | (0.4) |
| | Serbia | 19.1 | (0.8) | 44.8 | (0.8) | 25.2 | (0.7) | 7.3 | (0.4) | 3.5 | (0.3) |
| | Slovenia | 10.9 | (0.5) | 51.0 | (0.7) | 27.2 | (0.7) | 8.2 | (0.4) | 2.7 | (0.2) |
| | Chinese Taipei | 18.8 | (1.0) | 42.1 | (0.7) | 28.1 | (0.7) | 7.6 | (0.3) | 3.3 | (0.2) |
| | Thailand | 9.0 | (0.5) | 57.3 | (0.7) | 24.9 | (0.8) | 6.5 | (0.4) | 2.4 | (0.2) |
| | Tunisia | 12.6 | (0.8) | 36.5 | (0.9) | 26.8 | (0.9) | 14.4 | (0.5) | 9.7 | (0.5) |
| | Uruguay | 16.4 | (0.7) | 57.0 | (0.9) | 18.9 | (0.7) | 5.3 | (0.4) | 2.5 | (0.3) |

[Part 1/2]
## Table 2.1c Percentage of students, by time spent learning the language of instruction

| | Regular school lessons | | | | | | | | | | Out-of-school-time lessons | | | | | | | | | |
|---|---|---|---|---|---|---|---|---|---|---|---|---|---|---|---|---|---|---|---|---|
| | No time per week | | Less than 2 hours per week | | 2 hours or more but less than 4 hours per week | | 4 hours or more but less than 6 hours per week | | 6 hours or more per week | | No time per week | | Less than 2 hours per week | | 2 hours or more but less than 4 hours per week | | 4 hours or more but less than 6 hours per week | | 6 hours or more per week | |
| | % | S.E. | % | S.E. | % | S.E. | % | S.E. | % | S.E. | % | S.E. | % | S.E. | % | S.E. | % | S.E. | % | S.E. |
| **OECD** | | | | | | | | | | | | | | | | | | | | |
| Australia | 1.2 | (0.1) | 7.5 | (0.3) | 38.1 | (0.8) | 44.1 | (0.8) | 9.1 | (0.3) | 65.7 | (0.6) | 22.4 | (0.5) | 8.7 | (0.3) | 2.6 | (0.2) | 0.6 | (0.1) |
| Austria | 4.5 | (0.4) | 17.5 | (0.8) | 62.0 | (1.2) | 14.3 | (0.8) | 1.7 | (0.3) | 87.3 | (0.8) | 8.6 | (0.6) | 2.8 | (0.4) | 1.0 | (0.1) | 0.2 | (0.1) |
| Belgium | 4.2 | (0.3) | 17.6 | (0.5) | 32.2 | (0.9) | 43.9 | (0.9) | 2.1 | (0.2) | 75.0 | (0.5) | 17.3 | (0.5) | 5.7 | (0.3) | 1.6 | (0.2) | 0.5 | (0.1) |
| Canada | 5.0 | (0.2) | 11.6 | (0.5) | 18.1 | (0.8) | 40.0 | (0.6) | 25.3 | (0.8) | 58.7 | (0.7) | 25.7 | (0.6) | 10.2 | (0.4) | 3.9 | (0.2) | 1.6 | (0.2) |
| Czech Republic | 1.3 | (0.2) | 8.5 | (0.5) | 47.0 | (1.2) | 39.8 | (1.2) | 3.3 | (0.3) | 62.5 | (0.8) | 27.8 | (0.8) | 8.0 | (0.4) | 1.1 | (0.2) | 0.6 | (0.1) |
| Denmark | 0.2 | (0.1) | 2.7 | (0.3) | 11.6 | (0.7) | 42.9 | (0.9) | 42.6 | (1.1) | 28.5 | (0.9) | 34.9 | (0.8) | 26.8 | (0.8) | 7.8 | (0.4) | 2.0 | (0.3) |
| Finland | 1.6 | (0.2) | 13.0 | (0.9) | 64.9 | (1.8) | 18.8 | (1.6) | 1.7 | (0.4) | 75.5 | (0.7) | 19.7 | (0.6) | 3.9 | (0.3) | 0.4 | (0.1) | 0.4 | (0.1) |
| France | 2.0 | (0.3) | 7.9 | (0.5) | 31.5 | (0.7) | 55.6 | (0.9) | 3.0 | (0.3) | 54.4 | (0.9) | 32.6 | (0.8) | 10.7 | (0.5) | 1.8 | (0.3) | 0.4 | (0.1) |
| Germany | 2.7 | (0.3) | 11.2 | (0.6) | 42.9 | (1.0) | 38.6 | (0.9) | 4.7 | (0.5) | 69.5 | (0.9) | 19.2 | (0.7) | 8.1 | (0.5) | 2.5 | (0.3) | 0.7 | (0.2) |
| Greece | 6.4 | (0.4) | 19.8 | (0.8) | 45.6 | (0.8) | 18.4 | (0.7) | 9.9 | (0.5) | 33.7 | (0.8) | 31.1 | (0.7) | 24.8 | (0.7) | 7.6 | (0.5) | 2.8 | (0.3) |
| Hungary | 3.0 | (0.3) | 21.2 | (0.8) | 44.7 | (1.1) | 27.5 | (1.1) | 3.7 | (0.3) | 36.2 | (0.9) | 38.6 | (0.8) | 18.2 | (0.6) | 5.7 | (0.3) | 1.3 | (0.2) |
| Iceland | 0.7 | (0.1) | 5.0 | (0.3) | 26.8 | (0.6) | 52.6 | (0.8) | 14.8 | (0.6) | 72.7 | (0.8) | 20.2 | (0.7) | 5.2 | (0.4) | 1.4 | (0.2) | 0.5 | (0.1) |
| Ireland | 2.0 | (0.2) | 13.1 | (0.6) | 48.5 | (1.1) | 29.4 | (0.8) | 7.1 | (0.4) | 69.4 | (0.9) | 19.3 | (0.7) | 7.3 | (0.4) | 2.8 | (0.3) | 1.1 | (0.2) |
| Italy | 1.8 | (0.2) | 10.9 | (0.4) | 20.2 | (0.6) | 39.7 | (0.6) | 27.4 | (0.7) | 68.2 | (0.6) | 15.9 | (0.4) | 9.8 | (0.3) | 4.4 | (0.2) | 1.7 | (0.2) |
| Japan | 0.3 | (0.1) | 7.2 | (0.7) | 49.3 | (1.1) | 37.7 | (1.1) | 5.4 | (0.7) | 73.6 | (1.1) | 19.6 | (0.9) | 5.5 | (0.4) | 1.1 | (0.2) | 0.2 | (0.1) |
| Korea | 0.9 | (0.2) | 3.8 | (0.4) | 27.4 | (1.1) | 56.6 | (1.2) | 11.2 | (0.7) | 38.5 | (1.3) | 28.1 | (0.8) | 26.5 | (1.1) | 5.7 | (0.4) | 1.2 | (0.2) |
| Luxembourg | 5.3 | (0.3) | 11.0 | (0.5) | 43.3 | (0.7) | 36.7 | (0.8) | 3.8 | (0.3) | 68.5 | (0.7) | 21.5 | (0.7) | 7.0 | (0.4) | 2.1 | (0.2) | 1.0 | (0.1) |
| Mexico | 3.6 | (0.3) | 24.5 | (0.6) | 23.2 | (0.6) | 30.8 | (0.7) | 17.8 | (0.6) | 47.5 | (0.9) | 31.1 | (0.6) | 15.2 | (0.6) | 4.7 | (0.4) | 1.4 | (0.2) |
| Netherlands | 2.4 | (0.2) | 17.4 | (0.8) | 64.3 | (0.9) | 14.8 | (0.7) | 1.1 | (0.2) | 59.9 | (1.0) | 30.2 | (0.8) | 8.1 | (0.5) | 1.3 | (0.2) | 0.4 | (0.1) |
| New Zealand | 1.6 | (0.2) | 6.9 | (0.5) | 19.4 | (0.8) | 65.3 | (0.9) | 6.8 | (0.4) | 66.0 | (0.9) | 22.6 | (0.7) | 8.0 | (0.4) | 2.4 | (0.3) | 1.0 | (0.2) |
| Norway | 2.1 | (0.3) | 10.8 | (0.6) | 48.5 | (1.1) | 33.5 | (1.1) | 5.1 | (0.4) | 35.7 | (0.9) | 44.3 | (0.8) | 15.7 | (0.6) | 2.8 | (0.2) | 1.5 | (0.2) |
| Poland | 1.6 | (0.2) | 9.3 | (0.5) | 13.6 | (0.5) | 57.3 | (0.9) | 18.2 | (0.8) | 56.1 | (1.4) | 33.8 | (1.2) | 7.4 | (0.5) | 2.0 | (0.2) | 0.6 | (0.1) |
| Portugal | 1.9 | (0.3) | 14.7 | (0.7) | 57.4 | (0.9) | 21.2 | (0.7) | 4.8 | (0.3) | 65.8 | (1.1) | 25.1 | (1.0) | 7.3 | (0.5) | 1.6 | (0.2) | 0.2 | (0.1) |
| Slovak Republic | 1.1 | (0.2) | 21.4 | (1.5) | 49.8 | (1.4) | 26.4 | (1.4) | 1.3 | (0.2) | 46.2 | (1.2) | 39.6 | (0.9) | 11.4 | (0.6) | 2.5 | (0.3) | 0.3 | (0.1) |
| Spain | 2.5 | (0.3) | 10.9 | (0.5) | 45.1 | (0.7) | 38.2 | (0.9) | 3.3 | (0.2) | 73.2 | (0.8) | 15.5 | (0.6) | 7.7 | (0.3) | 2.7 | (0.2) | 0.9 | (0.1) |
| Sweden | 0.7 | (0.1) | 11.8 | (0.8) | 70.8 | (1.0) | 14.6 | (0.8) | 2.1 | (0.4) | 59.6 | (0.9) | 30.3 | (0.9) | 7.4 | (0.5) | 1.8 | (0.2) | 1.0 | (0.2) |
| Switzerland | 2.8 | (0.4) | 12.6 | (0.6) | 40.6 | (0.8) | 38.5 | (0.9) | 5.4 | (0.3) | 72.0 | (0.9) | 20.2 | (0.7) | 5.6 | (0.3) | 1.6 | (0.2) | 0.5 | (0.1) |
| Turkey | 2.2 | (0.3) | 11.6 | (0.8) | 32.6 | (1.0) | 42.8 | (1.3) | 10.8 | (0.7) | 28.5 | (1.0) | 33.8 | (0.9) | 24.1 | (0.8) | 9.9 | (0.7) | 3.6 | (0.4) |
| United Kingdom | 1.1 | (0.1) | 6.4 | (0.4) | 45.2 | (1.4) | 42.2 | (1.3) | 5.2 | (0.4) | 65.2 | (0.8) | 25.1 | (0.6) | 7.5 | (0.4) | 1.9 | (0.2) | 0.3 | (0.1) |
| United States | 5.3 | (0.4) | 25.2 | (1.0) | 18.8 | (1.2) | 36.5 | (1.3) | 14.3 | (0.8) | 46.8 | (1.1) | 31.8 | (0.7) | 15.3 | (0.5) | 4.4 | (0.3) | 1.7 | (0.2) |
| **OECD average** | 2.4 | (0.0) | 12.4 | (0.1) | 39.4 | (0.2) | 36.6 | (0.2) | 9.1 | (0.1) | 58.7 | (0.2) | 26.2 | (0.1) | 11.0 | (0.1) | 3.1 | (0.0) | 1.0 | (0.0) |
| **Partners** | | | | | | | | | | | | | | | | | | | | |
| Argentina | 7.3 | (0.6) | 37.6 | (1.3) | 40.1 | (1.3) | 11.9 | (0.7) | 3.1 | (0.7) | 75.7 | (1.2) | 16.9 | (0.9) | 5.9 | (0.5) | 1.3 | (0.2) | 0.2 | (0.1) |
| Azerbaijan | 5.8 | (0.4) | 18.4 | (0.7) | 31.0 | (1.0) | 28.0 | (1.3) | 16.8 | (0.9) | 35.2 | (1.2) | 28.8 | (1.1) | 20.2 | (0.7) | 10.0 | (0.6) | 5.8 | (0.4) |
| Brazil | 3.7 | (0.3) | 28.4 | (1.0) | 36.4 | (0.9) | 23.9 | (0.8) | 7.6 | (0.5) | 41.3 | (0.8) | 36.2 | (0.8) | 16.6 | (0.6) | 4.7 | (0.3) | 1.3 | (0.2) |
| Bulgaria | 5.7 | (0.5) | 26.7 | (1.1) | 43.8 | (1.1) | 16.4 | (0.8) | 7.3 | (0.4) | 49.4 | (1.1) | 29.4 | (0.9) | 14.6 | (0.6) | 4.9 | (0.4) | 1.6 | (0.2) |
| Chile | 6.3 | (0.4) | 25.6 | (0.9) | 25.2 | (0.8) | 28.2 | (0.9) | 14.6 | (1.0) | 47.7 | (1.2) | 34.2 | (0.8) | 13.5 | (0.7) | 3.7 | (0.3) | 0.9 | (0.1) |
| Colombia | 2.7 | (0.4) | 11.9 | (0.8) | 30.6 | (1.5) | 47.6 | (2.0) | 7.2 | (0.6) | 42.8 | (1.0) | 35.1 | (1.2) | 16.2 | (0.7) | 5.0 | (0.3) | 0.9 | (0.2) |
| Croatia | 3.4 | (0.2) | 11.2 | (0.6) | 54.6 | (1.1) | 28.7 | (1.0) | 2.0 | (0.3) | 79.7 | (0.7) | 12.8 | (0.5) | 6.0 | (0.4) | 1.1 | (0.2) | 0.4 | (0.1) |
| Estonia | 2.5 | (0.3) | 14.0 | (0.8) | 45.6 | (1.0) | 33.9 | (1.0) | 4.0 | (0.3) | 50.5 | (1.1) | 33.6 | (0.8) | 12.5 | (0.6) | 3.1 | (0.3) | 0.3 | (0.1) |
| Hong Kong-China | 1.4 | (0.2) | 6.5 | (0.4) | 13.9 | (0.8) | 38.2 | (0.9) | 40.0 | (1.1) | 57.4 | (1.2) | 28.8 | (1.0) | 9.7 | (0.5) | 3.0 | (0.3) | 1.1 | (0.2) |
| Indonesia | 0.9 | (0.2) | 17.5 | (1.3) | 42.2 | (1.8) | 27.8 | (1.0) | 11.5 | (0.8) | 32.8 | (1.9) | 44.4 | (1.2) | 17.7 | (0.9) | 3.9 | (0.3) | 1.2 | (0.1) |
| Israel | 12.8 | (0.7) | 20.9 | (0.7) | 33.3 | (0.9) | 24.6 | (0.9) | 8.4 | (0.5) | 42.6 | (1.0) | 30.6 | (0.9) | 18.0 | (0.7) | 6.4 | (0.5) | 2.4 | (0.2) |
| Jordan | 8.3 | (0.7) | 25.1 | (0.8) | 21.3 | (0.7) | 24.9 | (1.1) | 20.4 | (0.7) | 31.1 | (1.0) | 31.0 | (0.7) | 24.4 | (0.7) | 10.6 | (0.5) | 2.9 | (0.3) |
| Kyrgyzstan | 13.6 | (0.7) | 30.5 | (0.9) | 28.4 | (0.7) | 16.8 | (0.8) | 10.7 | (0.7) | 28.1 | (0.9) | 39.3 | (0.7) | 21.0 | (0.7) | 6.7 | (0.4) | 4.9 | (0.3) |
| Latvia | 1.0 | (0.1) | 11.6 | (0.7) | 44.7 | (0.9) | 37.7 | (0.9) | 5.0 | (0.5) | 50.0 | (1.3) | 35.0 | (0.9) | 11.7 | (0.8) | 2.8 | (0.3) | 0.5 | (0.1) |
| Liechtenstein | 3.4 | (1.0) | 13.2 | (1.6) | 35.9 | (2.3) | 43.7 | (2.3) | 3.9 | (1.0) | 77.8 | (2.3) | 17.8 | (2.0) | 3.9 | (1.0) | 0.6 | (0.4) | 0.0 | c |
| Lithuania | 2.1 | (0.3) | 20.0 | (0.7) | 30.7 | (1.0) | 38.4 | (0.9) | 8.8 | (0.5) | 61.7 | (1.1) | 28.0 | (1.1) | 7.7 | (0.4) | 1.9 | (0.2) | 0.7 | (0.1) |
| Macao-China | 0.8 | (0.2) | 6.2 | (0.4) | 13.2 | (0.5) | 36.4 | (0.9) | 43.4 | (0.9) | 51.6 | (0.8) | 30.2 | (0.7) | 10.6 | (0.6) | 4.8 | (0.4) | 2.8 | (0.3) |
| Montenegro | 12.8 | (0.5) | 25.0 | (0.8) | 32.0 | (0.8) | 19.7 | (0.6) | 10.5 | (0.5) | 65.9 | (0.8) | 20.4 | (0.7) | 9.1 | (0.5) | 2.7 | (0.3) | 1.9 | (0.2) |
| Qatar | 8.0 | (0.3) | 33.8 | (0.6) | 28.4 | (0.6) | 19.0 | (0.5) | 10.8 | (0.4) | 32.2 | (0.6) | 35.8 | (0.6) | 21.1 | (0.6) | 8.2 | (0.4) | 2.6 | (0.2) |
| Romania | 4.0 | (0.5) | 19.5 | (1.2) | 41.7 | (1.6) | 29.0 | (1.1) | 5.8 | (0.7) | 31.8 | (1.1) | 37.4 | (1.1) | 22.1 | (0.9) | 6.6 | (0.5) | 2.1 | (0.4) |
| Russian Federation | 3.5 | (0.5) | 53.4 | (1.5) | 34.0 | (1.2) | 7.2 | (0.4) | 1.8 | (0.2) | 46.6 | (1.4) | 42.0 | (1.4) | 9.1 | (0.5) | 1.7 | (0.2) | 0.6 | (0.1) |
| Serbia | 3.9 | (0.4) | 16.5 | (0.7) | 52.9 | (1.0) | 22.2 | (0.8) | 4.4 | (0.3) | 55.0 | (0.7) | 27.5 | (0.7) | 12.6 | (0.5) | 3.2 | (0.2) | 1.7 | (0.2) |
| Slovenia | 4.2 | (0.3) | 21.8 | (0.7) | 35.8 | (0.8) | 35.9 | (0.7) | 2.3 | (0.2) | 55.8 | (0.8) | 32.0 | (0.8) | 10.2 | (0.5) | 1.8 | (0.2) | 0.2 | (0.1) |
| Chinese Taipei | 1.6 | (0.2) | 12.0 | (0.6) | 25.3 | (0.8) | 39.7 | (0.8) | 21.6 | (0.9) | 66.7 | (0.8) | 19.3 | (0.6) | 10.9 | (0.4) | 2.5 | (0.2) | 0.7 | (0.1) |
| Thailand | a | a | 13.4 | (0.6) | 69.7 | (0.9) | 15.4 | (0.8) | 1.5 | (0.2) | 69.5 | (0.9) | 20.4 | (0.7) | 7.8 | (0.5) | 2.0 | (0.3) | 0.4 | (0.1) |
| Tunisia | 11.8 | (0.8) | 22.1 | (0.6) | 26.6 | (0.8) | 32.5 | (1.1) | 7.0 | (0.5) | 25.5 | (1.0) | 39.0 | (0.9) | 22.9 | (0.8) | 8.8 | (0.5) | 3.8 | (0.4) |
| Uruguay | 8.6 | (0.5) | 24.2 | (0.8) | 46.3 | (1.0) | 17.6 | (0.9) | 3.3 | (0.3) | 65.1 | (0.9) | 23.9 | (0.9) | 8.2 | (0.5) | 1.9 | (0.3) | 0.9 | (0.2) |

© OECD 2011 Quality Time for Students: Learning In and Out of School

[Part 2/2]
## Table 2.1c Percentage of students, by time spent learning the language of instruction

| | | Individual study | | | | | | | | |
|---|---|---|---|---|---|---|---|---|---|---|
| | | No time per week | | Less than 2 hours per week | | 2 hours or more but less than 4 hours per week | | 4 hours or more but less than 6 hours per week | | 6 hours or more per week | |
| | | % | S.E. | % | S.E. | % | S.E. | % | S.E. | % | S.E. |
| **OECD** | Australia | 13.1 | (0.5) | 54.8 | (0.6) | 24.1 | (0.5) | 6.2 | (0.2) | 1.9 | (0.2) |
| | Austria | 16.7 | (0.9) | 57.4 | (0.9) | 18.2 | (0.8) | 5.7 | (0.4) | 2.0 | (0.3) |
| | Belgium | 15.5 | (0.6) | 63.5 | (0.5) | 17.4 | (0.5) | 2.8 | (0.2) | 0.7 | (0.1) |
| | Canada | 19.8 | (0.4) | 47.2 | (0.7) | 22.1 | (0.5) | 7.8 | (0.4) | 3.1 | (0.3) |
| | Czech Republic | 24.8 | (1.1) | 58.9 | (1.0) | 13.3 | (0.6) | 2.1 | (0.3) | 0.9 | (0.2) |
| | Denmark | 5.5 | (0.4) | 47.4 | (0.9) | 35.6 | (0.8) | 9.3 | (0.4) | 2.3 | (0.2) |
| | Finland | 18.1 | (0.8) | 68.9 | (0.7) | 10.9 | (0.6) | 1.5 | (0.2) | 0.7 | (0.1) |
| | France | 15.8 | (0.8) | 56.7 | (0.8) | 22.1 | (0.7) | 4.6 | (0.3) | 0.8 | (0.1) |
| | Germany | 10.1 | (0.4) | 52.7 | (0.8) | 27.2 | (0.8) | 7.9 | (0.5) | 2.2 | (0.3) |
| | Greece | 18.2 | (0.6) | 42.0 | (0.8) | 27.1 | (0.6) | 9.2 | (0.5) | 3.5 | (0.3) |
| | Hungary | 10.5 | (0.6) | 53.1 | (0.9) | 26.9 | (0.8) | 7.2 | (0.4) | 2.3 | (0.2) |
| | Iceland | 13.3 | (0.6) | 59.0 | (0.8) | 22.5 | (0.7) | 4.4 | (0.3) | 0.8 | (0.1) |
| | Ireland | 15.0 | (0.7) | 52.2 | (0.8) | 23.3 | (0.8) | 6.9 | (0.4) | 2.7 | (0.3) |
| | Italy | 5.4 | (0.3) | 31.0 | (0.7) | 35.9 | (0.7) | 19.0 | (0.5) | 8.8 | (0.5) |
| | Japan | 36.7 | (1.3) | 50.5 | (1.0) | 10.4 | (0.6) | 1.8 | (0.2) | 0.5 | (0.1) |
| | Korea | 23.5 | (0.9) | 52.2 | (0.8) | 18.3 | (0.6) | 4.4 | (0.3) | 1.6 | (0.2) |
| | Luxembourg | 19.4 | (0.6) | 59.0 | (0.6) | 16.1 | (0.5) | 3.8 | (0.3) | 1.7 | (0.2) |
| | Mexico | 7.4 | (0.4) | 53.6 | (0.8) | 25.5 | (0.6) | 9.6 | (0.5) | 4.0 | (0.3) |
| | Netherlands | 14.0 | (0.7) | 66.6 | (0.9) | 16.3 | (0.7) | 2.2 | (0.2) | 0.9 | (0.2) |
| | New Zealand | 16.6 | (0.7) | 55.1 | (0.8) | 21.3 | (0.7) | 5.1 | (0.4) | 1.8 | (0.2) |
| | Norway | 19.1 | (0.8) | 55.6 | (0.9) | 20.0 | (0.7) | 4.0 | (0.3) | 1.3 | (0.2) |
| | Poland | 7.6 | (0.4) | 45.9 | (0.9) | 31.6 | (0.8) | 11.5 | (0.4) | 3.4 | (0.2) |
| | Portugal | 8.6 | (0.4) | 58.1 | (0.8) | 24.7 | (0.8) | 6.7 | (0.4) | 1.9 | (0.2) |
| | Slovak Republic | 16.1 | (0.7) | 48.5 | (0.9) | 27.1 | (0.8) | 6.8 | (0.4) | 1.4 | (0.2) |
| | Spain | 12.5 | (0.6) | 49.5 | (0.8) | 27.6 | (0.6) | 8.2 | (0.4) | 2.2 | (0.2) |
| | Sweden | 18.7 | (1.4) | 63.8 | (1.6) | 13.5 | (0.5) | 3.0 | (0.3) | 0.9 | (0.2) |
| | Switzerland | 10.9 | (0.5) | 68.0 | (0.6) | 17.5 | (0.5) | 2.9 | (0.2) | 0.8 | (0.1) |
| | Turkey | 11.5 | (0.7) | 44.5 | (0.9) | 28.0 | (1.0) | 11.4 | (0.6) | 4.6 | (0.4) |
| | United Kingdom | 11.4 | (0.5) | 59.9 | (0.8) | 23.3 | (0.7) | 4.3 | (0.3) | 1.0 | (0.1) |
| | United States | 16.0 | (0.8) | 47.3 | (0.9) | 25.2 | (0.8) | 8.4 | (0.4) | 3.1 | (0.2) |
| | **OECD average** | 15.1 | (0.1) | 54.1 | (0.2) | 22.4 | (0.1) | 6.3 | (0.1) | 2.1 | (0.0) |
| **Partners** | Argentina | 13.6 | (0.7) | 58.3 | (1.2) | 20.5 | (0.9) | 5.0 | (0.6) | 2.7 | (0.4) |
| | Azerbaijan | 8.9 | (0.5) | 30.4 | (0.9) | 28.2 | (0.7) | 15.9 | (0.7) | 16.6 | (0.7) |
| | Brazil | 15.1 | (0.6) | 53.2 | (0.7) | 22.0 | (0.6) | 6.5 | (0.4) | 3.2 | (0.3) |
| | Bulgaria | 16.9 | (1.0) | 41.5 | (0.9) | 26.5 | (0.8) | 10.7 | (0.6) | 4.4 | (0.4) |
| | Chile | 17.3 | (0.6) | 55.5 | (0.7) | 19.3 | (0.7) | 5.9 | (0.4) | 1.9 | (0.2) |
| | Colombia | 13.1 | (0.7) | 52.3 | (0.9) | 23.4 | (0.6) | 8.8 | (0.6) | 2.5 | (0.3) |
| | Croatia | 20.1 | (0.7) | 49.4 | (0.7) | 23.4 | (0.8) | 5.7 | (0.4) | 1.4 | (0.2) |
| | Estonia | 16.4 | (0.8) | 53.1 | (1.0) | 23.4 | (0.8) | 5.7 | (0.3) | 1.4 | (0.2) |
| | Hong Kong-China | 18.2 | (1.0) | 51.3 | (0.8) | 22.2 | (0.6) | 6.2 | (0.5) | 2.2 | (0.2) |
| | Indonesia | 3.8 | (0.3) | 64.6 | (1.0) | 23.3 | (0.6) | 6.1 | (0.4) | 2.2 | (0.4) |
| | Israel | 28.0 | (0.9) | 40.4 | (0.8) | 20.0 | (0.7) | 8.0 | (0.5) | 3.7 | (0.3) |
| | Jordan | 8.9 | (0.6) | 37.8 | (0.8) | 30.4 | (0.9) | 15.1 | (0.6) | 7.8 | (0.5) |
| | Kyrgyzstan | 18.0 | (0.6) | 36.8 | (0.7) | 23.9 | (0.7) | 12.0 | (0.5) | 9.3 | (0.5) |
| | Latvia | 6.1 | (0.6) | 52.3 | (0.9) | 31.4 | (0.9) | 8.3 | (0.4) | 1.8 | (0.2) |
| | Liechtenstein | 12.9 | (2.0) | 72.7 | (2.4) | 11.4 | (1.6) | 2.1 | (0.8) | 0.9 | (0.5) |
| | Lithuania | 14.3 | (0.6) | 49.9 | (0.7) | 26.0 | (0.7) | 7.3 | (0.4) | 2.5 | (0.2) |
| | Macao-China | 20.1 | (0.7) | 55.0 | (0.9) | 17.5 | (0.6) | 5.3 | (0.4) | 2.2 | (0.2) |
| | Montenegro | 15.9 | (0.6) | 46.8 | (0.8) | 23.3 | (0.6) | 8.0 | (0.4) | 6.0 | (0.4) |
| | Qatar | 16.0 | (0.6) | 43.5 | (0.8) | 25.8 | (0.5) | 10.0 | (0.4) | 4.7 | (0.3) |
| | Romania | 10.4 | (0.7) | 45.7 | (0.9) | 28.5 | (0.8) | 10.1 | (0.6) | 5.4 | (0.4) |
| | Russian Federation | 10.3 | (0.9) | 64.4 | (1.2) | 19.2 | (0.8) | 4.7 | (0.4) | 1.4 | (0.2) |
| | Serbia | 20.8 | (0.7) | 46.5 | (0.8) | 22.9 | (0.7) | 7.1 | (0.4) | 2.8 | (0.3) |
| | Slovenia | 14.8 | (0.6) | 60.0 | (0.7) | 20.0 | (0.6) | 4.5 | (0.3) | 0.8 | (0.1) |
| | Chinese Taipei | 14.3 | (0.8) | 50.3 | (0.7) | 27.3 | (0.7) | 5.8 | (0.3) | 2.2 | (0.2) |
| | Thailand | 7.8 | (0.4) | 62.5 | (0.8) | 22.0 | (0.7) | 5.8 | (0.4) | 1.9 | (0.2) |
| | Tunisia | 13.2 | (0.6) | 45.0 | (1.0) | 26.8 | (0.7) | 9.4 | (0.6) | 5.6 | (0.4) |
| | Uruguay | 21.9 | (0.8) | 56.1 | (0.9) | 16.9 | (0.6) | 3.7 | (0.3) | 1.4 | (0.2) |

Table 2.1d **Percentage of students who spend no time in out-of-school-time lessons, among those who take regular lessons at school**

| | Science | | Mathematics | | Language of instruction | |
|---|---|---|---|---|---|---|
| | % | S.E. | % | S.E. | % | S.E. |
| **OECD** Australia | 73.7 | (0.6) | 60.2 | (0.6) | 65.5 | (0.6) |
| Austria | 87.1 | (0.7) | 73.0 | (0.9) | 87.0 | (0.8) |
| Belgium | 79.0 | (0.6) | 69.0 | (0.7) | 75.0 | (0.5) |
| Canada | 64.0 | (0.7) | 51.6 | (0.7) | 57.3 | (0.7) |
| Czech Republic | 65.5 | (1.0) | 57.0 | (0.9) | 62.4 | (0.8) |
| Denmark | 45.3 | (1.0) | 30.2 | (0.9) | 28.4 | (0.9) |
| Finland | 76.4 | (0.7) | 74.8 | (0.7) | 75.3 | (0.7) |
| France | 61.0 | (0.9) | 45.8 | (0.7) | 54.5 | (0.9) |
| Germany | 69.3 | (0.9) | 58.7 | (1.0) | 69.3 | (0.9) |
| Greece | 24.8 | (0.9) | 24.8 | (0.9) | 32.8 | (0.8) |
| Hungary | 41.3 | (1.0) | 32.9 | (0.9) | 35.4 | (1.0) |
| Iceland | 81.4 | (0.6) | 60.8 | (0.9) | 72.9 | (0.8) |
| Ireland | 76.4 | (0.7) | 60.5 | (0.8) | 69.3 | (0.9) |
| Italy | 68.1 | (0.6) | 57.1 | (0.5) | 68.2 | (0.6) |
| Japan | 81.8 | (0.7) | 62.5 | (1.4) | 73.6 | (1.1) |
| Korea | 48.6 | (1.4) | 26.6 | (0.9) | 38.1 | (1.3) |
| Luxembourg | 69.0 | (0.7) | 55.9 | (0.8) | 67.9 | (0.7) |
| Mexico | 45.8 | (0.9) | 45.1 | (0.9) | 47.1 | (0.9) |
| Netherlands | 58.4 | (1.1) | 54.6 | (1.0) | 59.8 | (1.0) |
| New Zealand | 72.7 | (0.9) | 62.0 | (1.0) | 65.9 | (1.0) |
| Norway | 38.7 | (1.0) | 35.3 | (1.0) | 34.9 | (0.9) |
| Poland | 59.0 | (1.1) | 48.8 | (1.3) | 55.8 | (1.4) |
| Portugal | 62.4 | (0.9) | 50.0 | (1.2) | 65.6 | (1.1) |
| Slovak Republic | 58.1 | (1.3) | 44.9 | (1.4) | 45.9 | (1.2) |
| Spain | 68.3 | (0.8) | 57.1 | (0.7) | 73.3 | (0.8) |
| Sweden | 63.5 | (0.9) | 59.8 | (0.9) | 59.5 | (0.9) |
| Switzerland | 73.7 | (0.6) | 58.6 | (1.0) | 71.6 | (0.9) |
| Turkey | 35.4 | (1.1) | 25.2 | (0.9) | 28.2 | (1.0) |
| United Kingdom | 67.0 | (0.8) | 60.3 | (0.9) | 65.2 | (0.8) |
| United States | 53.7 | (0.9) | 43.4 | (1.1) | 45.2 | (1.1) |
| **OECD average** | **62.3** | **(0.2)** | **51.6** | **(0.2)** | **58.4** | **(0.2)** |
| **Partners** Argentina | 72.3 | (0.9) | 60.4 | (1.3) | 76.3 | (1.2) |
| Azerbaijan | 39.0 | (1.2) | 36.3 | (1.2) | 34.2 | (1.3) |
| Brazil | 53.6 | (0.9) | 40.8 | (0.9) | 41.2 | (0.9) |
| Bulgaria | 47.6 | (1.0) | 45.4 | (1.0) | 48.3 | (1.1) |
| Chile | 46.1 | (0.9) | 43.3 | (1.0) | 45.8 | (1.3) |
| Colombia | 48.3 | (1.3) | 41.0 | (1.0) | 42.7 | (1.1) |
| Croatia | 70.0 | (1.0) | 59.9 | (0.8) | 79.7 | (0.7) |
| Estonia | 54.9 | (0.9) | 46.3 | (1.0) | 50.4 | (1.2) |
| Hong Kong-China | 42.8 | (1.1) | 37.2 | (1.1) | 57.0 | (1.0) |
| Indonesia | 41.1 | (1.6) | 32.4 | (1.4) | 32.9 | (1.9) |
| Israel | 43.0 | (1.0) | 21.8 | (0.8) | 38.6 | (1.0) |
| Jordan | 34.5 | (1.2) | 30.7 | (1.1) | 30.4 | (1.1) |
| Kyrgyzstan | 31.2 | (1.1) | 28.6 | (1.2) | 26.2 | (0.8) |
| Latvia | 60.2 | (1.1) | 37.4 | (1.3) | 50.1 | (1.3) |
| Liechtenstein | 68.7 | (2.8) | 63.0 | (2.1) | 77.4 | (2.3) |
| Lithuania | 64.7 | (1.0) | 52.8 | (1.0) | 61.8 | (1.1) |
| Macao-China | 48.3 | (0.9) | 47.6 | (0.9) | 51.5 | (0.8) |
| Montenegro | 46.4 | (0.8) | 57.1 | (0.8) | 63.6 | (0.8) |
| Qatar | 30.4 | (0.7) | 27.5 | (0.6) | 30.7 | (0.6) |
| Romania | 40.3 | (1.2) | 32.2 | (1.1) | 31.3 | (1.1) |
| Russian Federation | 40.2 | (1.3) | 33.4 | (1.3) | 46.4 | (1.4) |
| Serbia | 54.6 | (0.9) | 51.1 | (0.9) | 54.8 | (0.9) |
| Slovenia | 53.0 | (0.9) | 44.5 | (0.7) | 54.9 | (0.8) |
| Chinese Taipei | 60.9 | (0.7) | 43.0 | (0.9) | 66.5 | (0.8) |
| Thailand | 59.6 | (1.2) | 56.2 | (1.1) | 69.5 | (0.9) |
| Tunisia | 19.0 | (0.7) | 16.4 | (0.7) | 23.1 | (1.0) |
| Uruguay | 62.7 | (0.8) | 56.9 | (0.8) | 63.9 | (0.9) |

© OECD 2011  Quality Time for Students: Learning In and Out of School

## Table 2.2a Mean learning hours and allocation of total learning time in science

| | | Mean learning hours per week[1] | | | | | | | Allocation of total leaning time in science for | | | | | |
| | Regular school lessons | | Out-of-school-time lessons | | Individual study | | Total learning hours | | Regular school lessons | | Out-of-school-time lessons | | Individual study | |
| | Mean | S.E. | Mean | S.E. | Mean | S.E. | Mean | S.E. | % | S.E. | % | S.E. | % | S.E. |
|---|---|---|---|---|---|---|---|---|---|---|---|---|---|---|
| **OECD** | | | | | | | | | | | | | | |
| Australia | 3.24 | (0.03) | 0.36 | (0.01) | 1.17 | (0.02) | 4.77 | (0.05) | 70.9 | (0.3) | 6.2 | (0.2) | 22.8 | (0.2) |
| Austria | 2.47 | (0.07) | 0.21 | (0.01) | 1.28 | (0.03) | 3.96 | (0.09) | 64.1 | (0.6) | 4.2 | (0.2) | 31.7 | (0.5) |
| Belgium | 2.63 | (0.04) | 0.32 | (0.01) | 1.25 | (0.02) | 4.20 | (0.07) | 63.5 | (0.4) | 6.6 | (0.2) | 29.9 | (0.3) |
| Canada | 4.00 | (0.04) | 0.55 | (0.01) | 1.55 | (0.02) | 6.13 | (0.06) | 66.3 | (0.4) | 8.5 | (0.2) | 25.2 | (0.3) |
| Czech Republic | 2.93 | (0.07) | 0.54 | (0.02) | 1.00 | (0.03) | 4.47 | (0.10) | 68.7 | (0.6) | 9.9 | (0.3) | 21.4 | (0.4) |
| Denmark | 3.21 | (0.04) | 0.77 | (0.02) | 1.09 | (0.02) | 5.06 | (0.07) | 66.7 | (0.5) | 13.0 | (0.3) | 20.3 | (0.3) |
| Finland | 3.13 | (0.04) | 0.32 | (0.01) | 1.07 | (0.02) | 4.52 | (0.06) | 70.9 | (0.4) | 5.9 | (0.2) | 23.1 | (0.3) |
| France | 2.85 | (0.05) | 0.55 | (0.02) | 1.31 | (0.03) | 4.72 | (0.08) | 62.9 | (0.5) | 10.8 | (0.3) | 26.3 | (0.4) |
| Germany | 3.06 | (0.05) | 0.51 | (0.02) | 1.71 | (0.03) | 5.28 | (0.07) | 58.0 | (0.5) | 8.5 | (0.3) | 33.6 | (0.3) |
| Greece | 3.18 | (0.05) | 1.99 | (0.04) | 1.85 | (0.04) | 7.02 | (0.10) | 48.3 | (0.6) | 26.2 | (0.4) | 25.4 | (0.4) |
| Hungary | 2.51 | (0.04) | 1.00 | (0.03) | 1.60 | (0.03) | 5.10 | (0.08) | 51.5 | (0.5) | 17.8 | (0.4) | 30.6 | (0.4) |
| Iceland | 2.97 | (0.02) | 0.29 | (0.01) | 1.16 | (0.02) | 4.42 | (0.04) | 70.1 | (0.4) | 5.1 | (0.2) | 24.8 | (0.3) |
| Ireland | 2.54 | (0.04) | 0.32 | (0.01) | 1.20 | (0.03) | 4.05 | (0.07) | 66.2 | (0.4) | 6.1 | (0.2) | 27.6 | (0.4) |
| Italy | 2.91 | (0.05) | 0.58 | (0.01) | 2.10 | (0.04) | 5.58 | (0.10) | 54.0 | (0.3) | 9.2 | (0.2) | 36.9 | (0.2) |
| Japan | 2.70 | (0.05) | 0.26 | (0.01) | 0.69 | (0.02) | 3.65 | (0.07) | 78.4 | (0.4) | 5.2 | (0.2) | 16.4 | (0.4) |
| Korea | 3.58 | (0.06) | 1.02 | (0.04) | 1.22 | (0.06) | 5.84 | (0.14) | 67.4 | (0.6) | 13.8 | (0.4) | 18.7 | (0.4) |
| Luxembourg | 2.33 | (0.03) | 0.50 | (0.02) | 1.25 | (0.02) | 4.09 | (0.05) | 59.8 | (0.4) | 10.0 | (0.3) | 30.2 | (0.4) |
| Mexico | 3.15 | (0.04) | 1.01 | (0.03) | 2.12 | (0.03) | 6.24 | (0.07) | 48.5 | (0.4) | 14.9 | (0.3) | 36.5 | (0.4) |
| Netherlands | 2.17 | (0.04) | 0.54 | (0.02) | 1.21 | (0.03) | 3.90 | (0.06) | 56.4 | (0.6) | 12.6 | (0.4) | 31.0 | (0.4) |
| New Zealand | 4.06 | (0.04) | 0.41 | (0.02) | 1.28 | (0.02) | 5.74 | (0.06) | 73.1 | (0.4) | 6.2 | (0.2) | 20.7 | (0.3) |
| Norway | 2.64 | (0.03) | 0.93 | (0.02) | 1.23 | (0.02) | 4.80 | (0.05) | 59.6 | (0.5) | 16.9 | (0.3) | 23.5 | (0.3) |
| Poland | 2.72 | (0.04) | 0.62 | (0.02) | 2.02 | (0.03) | 5.36 | (0.07) | 53.2 | (0.4) | 10.3 | (0.3) | 36.5 | (0.4) |
| Portugal | 3.21 | (0.04) | 0.63 | (0.02) | 2.09 | (0.04) | 5.93 | (0.08) | 54.6 | (0.5) | 9.3 | (0.3) | 36.0 | (0.4) |
| Slovak Republic | 2.46 | (0.07) | 0.65 | (0.03) | 1.39 | (0.04) | 4.51 | (0.12) | 58.7 | (0.6) | 11.7 | (0.4) | 29.6 | (0.4) |
| Spain | 3.12 | (0.04) | 0.68 | (0.02) | 1.74 | (0.03) | 5.56 | (0.07) | 58.9 | (0.3) | 10.7 | (0.3) | 30.4 | (0.3) |
| Sweden | 2.81 | (0.03) | 0.50 | (0.01) | 1.15 | (0.02) | 4.45 | (0.04) | 66.7 | (0.6) | 9.2 | (0.2) | 24.1 | (0.5) |
| Switzerland | 2.36 | (0.04) | 0.39 | (0.01) | 1.12 | (0.02) | 3.87 | (0.06) | 62.1 | (0.4) | 8.3 | (0.2) | 29.6 | (0.3) |
| Turkey | 2.86 | (0.09) | 1.35 | (0.05) | 1.64 | (0.05) | 5.81 | (0.18) | 51.2 | (0.5) | 20.9 | (0.4) | 27.8 | (0.4) |
| United Kingdom | 4.25 | (0.04) | 0.48 | (0.02) | 1.45 | (0.02) | 6.18 | (0.05) | 70.7 | (0.3) | 6.8 | (0.2) | 22.5 | (0.3) |
| United States | 3.51 | (0.05) | 0.78 | (0.02) | 1.68 | (0.03) | 6.01 | (0.06) | 58.5 | (0.5) | 12.5 | (0.4) | 28.9 | (0.3) |
| **OECD average** | 2.99 | (0.01) | 0.64 | (0.00) | 1.42 | (0.01) | 5.04 | (0.01) | 62.0 | (0.1) | 10.6 | (0.1) | 27.4 | (0.1) |
| **Partners** | | | | | | | | | | | | | | |
| Argentina | 2.26 | (0.06) | 0.49 | (0.02) | 1.59 | (0.04) | 4.32 | (0.09) | 53.1 | (0.8) | 9.6 | (0.4) | 37.2 | (0.6) |
| Azerbaijan | 2.84 | (0.05) | 1.36 | (0.03) | 2.64 | (0.05) | 6.83 | (0.10) | 43.1 | (0.6) | 19.3 | (0.5) | 37.6 | (0.4) |
| Brazil | 2.21 | (0.03) | 0.79 | (0.02) | 1.70 | (0.02) | 4.70 | (0.06) | 50.3 | (0.4) | 14.1 | (0.3) | 35.6 | (0.3) |
| Bulgaria | 2.63 | (0.08) | 0.98 | (0.03) | 2.00 | (0.06) | 5.65 | (0.13) | 48.8 | (0.7) | 16.3 | (0.6) | 34.9 | (0.4) |
| Chile | 2.33 | (0.05) | 0.83 | (0.02) | 1.52 | (0.03) | 4.70 | (0.07) | 49.0 | (0.6) | 16.4 | (0.4) | 34.6 | (0.4) |
| Colombia | 3.50 | (0.11) | 0.95 | (0.03) | 1.83 | (0.04) | 6.28 | (0.17) | 58.9 | (0.6) | 13.1 | (0.3) | 28.0 | (0.4) |
| Croatia | 2.02 | (0.04) | 0.43 | (0.02) | 1.46 | (0.04) | 3.93 | (0.09) | 54.5 | (0.5) | 9.8 | (0.4) | 35.6 | (0.5) |
| Estonia | 3.27 | (0.04) | 0.76 | (0.02) | 1.54 | (0.03) | 5.57 | (0.06) | 61.5 | (0.5) | 12.6 | (0.4) | 25.9 | (0.3) |
| Hong Kong-China | 3.14 | (0.05) | 0.88 | (0.03) | 1.44 | (0.03) | 5.45 | (0.10) | 61.0 | (0.5) | 13.9 | (0.4) | 25.2 | (0.4) |
| Indonesia | 3.23 | (0.07) | 1.04 | (0.04) | 1.78 | (0.03) | 6.04 | (0.11) | 54.6 | (1.0) | 15.6 | (0.7) | 29.8 | (0.4) |
| Israel | 2.43 | (0.05) | 0.98 | (0.03) | 1.35 | (0.04) | 4.75 | (0.10) | 54.4 | (0.7) | 18.3 | (0.4) | 27.3 | (0.5) |
| Jordan | 3.25 | (0.06) | 1.52 | (0.03) | 2.65 | (0.04) | 7.40 | (0.09) | 42.9 | (0.6) | 20.3 | (0.4) | 36.8 | (0.4) |
| Kyrgyzstan | 2.09 | (0.06) | 1.36 | (0.03) | 2.14 | (0.03) | 5.63 | (0.09) | 35.4 | (0.6) | 25.8 | (0.6) | 38.7 | (0.4) |
| Latvia | 2.86 | (0.06) | 0.65 | (0.02) | 1.80 | (0.03) | 5.30 | (0.09) | 56.1 | (0.5) | 10.4 | (0.3) | 33.5 | (0.4) |
| Liechtenstein | 2.57 | (0.08) | 0.52 | (0.06) | 1.20 | (0.06) | 4.29 | (0.10) | 61.8 | (1.4) | 10.2 | (1.0) | 28.1 | (1.3) |
| Lithuania | 2.69 | (0.04) | 0.57 | (0.02) | 1.69 | (0.03) | 4.94 | (0.06) | 57.1 | (0.5) | 10.1 | (0.3) | 32.8 | (0.3) |
| Macao-China | 3.74 | (0.03) | 1.00 | (0.03) | 1.37 | (0.03) | 6.11 | (0.06) | 64.7 | (0.4) | 14.5 | (0.3) | 20.7 | (0.3) |
| Montenegro | 2.83 | (0.04) | 1.05 | (0.02) | 2.20 | (0.03) | 6.08 | (0.07) | 46.8 | (0.4) | 16.1 | (0.3) | 37.1 | (0.5) |
| Qatar | 2.66 | (0.03) | 1.48 | (0.02) | 2.04 | (0.02) | 6.21 | (0.06) | 40.7 | (0.3) | 24.8 | (0.3) | 34.5 | (0.3) |
| Romania | 2.26 | (0.07) | 1.03 | (0.02) | 1.61 | (0.05) | 4.88 | (0.11) | 48.1 | (0.6) | 19.5 | (0.5) | 32.4 | (0.5) |
| Russian Federation | 3.73 | (0.08) | 1.12 | (0.03) | 2.87 | (0.06) | 7.72 | (0.13) | 48.6 | (0.5) | 15.0 | (0.5) | 36.4 | (0.5) |
| Serbia | 2.86 | (0.06) | 0.78 | (0.02) | 1.71 | (0.04) | 5.35 | (0.10) | 56.8 | (0.5) | 13.4 | (0.4) | 29.8 | (0.4) |
| Slovenia | 2.82 | (0.03) | 0.72 | (0.02) | 1.53 | (0.02) | 5.08 | (0.05) | 55.7 | (0.4) | 13.2 | (0.3) | 31.1 | (0.4) |
| Chinese Taipei | 2.89 | (0.05) | 0.78 | (0.02) | 1.24 | (0.03) | 4.94 | (0.10) | 63.7 | (0.4) | 12.3 | (0.2) | 24.1 | (0.3) |
| Thailand | 3.81 | (0.04) | 0.91 | (0.03) | 1.80 | (0.03) | 6.52 | (0.07) | 63.9 | (0.4) | 9.9 | (0.3) | 26.2 | (0.3) |
| Tunisia | 2.62 | (0.05) | 1.93 | (0.03) | 2.61 | (0.04) | 7.14 | (0.10) | 37.3 | (0.4) | 25.9 | (0.4) | 36.9 | (0.4) |
| Uruguay | 2.40 | (0.05) | 0.61 | (0.02) | 1.32 | (0.03) | 4.35 | (0.07) | 56.2 | (0.5) | 12.0 | (0.3) | 31.8 | (0.4) |

1. "No time" in any given activity is recoded to 0 hours per week in that activity, "less than 2 hours per week" is recoded to 1 hour per week, "2 or more but less than 4 hours per week" is recoded to 3 hours per week, "4 or more but less than 6 hours per week" is recoded to 5 hours per week and "6 or more hours per week" is recoded to 7 hours per week.

## Table 2.2b  Mean learning hours and allocation of total learning time in mathematics

| | Mean learning hours per week[1] | | | | | | | | Allocation of total learning time in mathematics for | | | | | |
| | Regular school lessons | | Out-of-school-time lessons | | Individual study | | Total learning hours | | Regular school lessons | | Out-of-school-time lessons | | Individual study | |
| | Mean | S.E. | Mean | S.E. | Mean | S.E. | Mean | S.E. | % | S.E. | % | S.E. | % | S.E. |
|---|---|---|---|---|---|---|---|---|---|---|---|---|---|---|
| Australia | 4.10 | (0.03) | 0.75 | (0.02) | 1.79 | (0.02) | 6.65 | (0.05) | 65.8 | (0.3) | 9.3 | (0.2) | 25.0 | (0.2) |
| Austria | 3.22 | (0.05) | 0.51 | (0.02) | 2.13 | (0.04) | 5.88 | (0.08) | 58.5 | (0.5) | 6.6 | (0.3) | 34.9 | (0.4) |
| Belgium | 3.58 | (0.04) | 0.55 | (0.01) | 1.79 | (0.03) | 5.93 | (0.06) | 63.1 | (0.3) | 8.0 | (0.2) | 28.9 | (0.3) |
| Canada | 4.50 | (0.04) | 0.94 | (0.02) | 1.97 | (0.03) | 7.45 | (0.07) | 63.3 | (0.3) | 11.4 | (0.2) | 25.2 | (0.2) |
| Czech Republic | 4.00 | (0.05) | 0.76 | (0.02) | 1.32 | (0.03) | 6.06 | (0.08) | 70.3 | (0.4) | 9.8 | (0.2) | 19.8 | (0.3) |
| Denmark | 4.44 | (0.03) | 1.36 | (0.03) | 1.74 | (0.02) | 7.52 | (0.06) | 62.3 | (0.3) | 16.0 | (0.3) | 21.6 | (0.2) |
| Finland | 3.45 | (0.04) | 0.37 | (0.02) | 1.20 | (0.02) | 5.02 | (0.06) | 71.1 | (0.3) | 6.0 | (0.2) | 22.9 | (0.2) |
| France | 3.84 | (0.03) | 0.93 | (0.02) | 1.74 | (0.03) | 6.50 | (0.06) | 62.6 | (0.3) | 12.6 | (0.2) | 24.8 | (0.3) |
| Germany | 3.88 | (0.04) | 0.82 | (0.03) | 2.27 | (0.03) | 6.99 | (0.07) | 58.4 | (0.3) | 9.8 | (0.3) | 31.8 | (0.3) |
| Greece | 3.45 | (0.04) | 2.23 | (0.05) | 2.01 | (0.03) | 7.71 | (0.10) | 49.4 | (0.5) | 26.0 | (0.5) | 24.7 | (0.4) |
| Hungary | 3.29 | (0.04) | 1.29 | (0.03) | 1.84 | (0.03) | 6.42 | (0.09) | 54.3 | (0.4) | 17.7 | (0.3) | 28.0 | (0.3) |
| Iceland | 4.74 | (0.02) | 0.72 | (0.02) | 1.71 | (0.02) | 7.18 | (0.05) | 69.4 | (0.3) | 8.5 | (0.2) | 22.1 | (0.2) |
| Ireland | 3.66 | (0.03) | 0.72 | (0.02) | 1.76 | (0.03) | 6.14 | (0.06) | 63.6 | (0.4) | 9.5 | (0.3) | 26.9 | (0.3) |
| Italy | 3.74 | (0.03) | 0.89 | (0.02) | 2.48 | (0.03) | 7.12 | (0.07) | 55.0 | (0.2) | 10.8 | (0.2) | 34.2 | (0.2) |
| Japan | 4.24 | (0.07) | 0.71 | (0.03) | 1.48 | (0.06) | 6.43 | (0.13) | 71.7 | (0.5) | 8.7 | (0.3) | 19.6 | (0.4) |
| Korea | 4.70 | (0.04) | 2.28 | (0.04) | 2.31 | (0.06) | 9.32 | (0.13) | 57.0 | (0.5) | 20.9 | (0.3) | 22.1 | (0.4) |
| Luxembourg | 3.86 | (0.03) | 0.83 | (0.02) | 1.71 | (0.02) | 6.42 | (0.05) | 63.3 | (0.3) | 11.1 | (0.2) | 25.6 | (0.3) |
| Mexico | 3.94 | (0.03) | 1.18 | (0.03) | 2.26 | (0.03) | 7.35 | (0.07) | 54.5 | (0.4) | 14.4 | (0.3) | 31.1 | (0.3) |
| Netherlands | 2.87 | (0.03) | 0.69 | (0.02) | 1.47 | (0.03) | 5.02 | (0.07) | 60.0 | (0.4) | 12.0 | (0.3) | 27.9 | (0.4) |
| New Zealand | 4.38 | (0.03) | 0.68 | (0.02) | 1.59 | (0.03) | 6.66 | (0.05) | 69.6 | (0.4) | 8.5 | (0.3) | 21.9 | (0.3) |
| Norway | 3.39 | (0.03) | 1.05 | (0.02) | 1.40 | (0.03) | 5.84 | (0.06) | 62.2 | (0.4) | 15.9 | (0.3) | 21.9 | (0.3) |
| Poland | 4.36 | (0.04) | 0.78 | (0.02) | 2.09 | (0.03) | 7.23 | (0.06) | 62.5 | (0.3) | 10.1 | (0.3) | 27.4 | (0.3) |
| Portugal | 3.61 | (0.04) | 0.81 | (0.02) | 1.96 | (0.03) | 6.38 | (0.07) | 58.9 | (0.4) | 11.6 | (0.3) | 29.6 | (0.3) |
| Slovak Republic | 3.29 | (0.05) | 0.88 | (0.03) | 1.69 | (0.03) | 5.87 | (0.10) | 60.6 | (0.5) | 12.6 | (0.3) | 26.8 | (0.3) |
| Spain | 3.42 | (0.03) | 0.99 | (0.02) | 1.96 | (0.03) | 6.41 | (0.06) | 57.7 | (0.3) | 13.1 | (0.2) | 29.3 | (0.3) |
| Sweden | 3.09 | (0.03) | 0.61 | (0.02) | 1.18 | (0.02) | 4.88 | (0.04) | 68.1 | (0.5) | 9.9 | (0.2) | 22.0 | (0.4) |
| Switzerland | 3.86 | (0.04) | 0.70 | (0.02) | 1.69 | (0.02) | 6.26 | (0.06) | 63.6 | (0.4) | 9.6 | (0.3) | 26.8 | (0.2) |
| Turkey | 3.82 | (0.06) | 2.08 | (0.05) | 2.31 | (0.05) | 8.17 | (0.14) | 50.8 | (0.4) | 22.7 | (0.4) | 26.6 | (0.3) |
| United Kingdom | 3.78 | (0.03) | 0.63 | (0.02) | 1.49 | (0.02) | 5.90 | (0.05) | 67.1 | (0.3) | 8.9 | (0.2) | 24.0 | (0.2) |
| United States | 3.77 | (0.05) | 1.15 | (0.03) | 2.05 | (0.03) | 7.01 | (0.07) | 55.4 | (0.5) | 15.4 | (0.4) | 29.2 | (0.5) |
| **OECD average** | 3.81 | (0.01) | 0.96 | (0.00) | 1.81 | (0.01) | 6.59 | (0.01) | 61.7 | (0.1) | 12.2 | (0.1) | 26.1 | (0.1) |
| Argentina | 2.95 | (0.06) | 0.78 | (0.04) | 1.82 | (0.04) | 5.56 | (0.10) | 55.0 | (0.6) | 12.4 | (0.5) | 32.7 | (0.4) |
| Azerbaijan | 3.79 | (0.06) | 1.70 | (0.05) | 2.95 | (0.06) | 8.49 | (0.13) | 47.1 | (0.5) | 18.6 | (0.4) | 34.3 | (0.5) |
| Brazil | 3.15 | (0.04) | 1.21 | (0.03) | 1.80 | (0.03) | 6.14 | (0.07) | 54.4 | (0.5) | 17.3 | (0.4) | 28.3 | (0.4) |
| Bulgaria | 2.98 | (0.07) | 1.14 | (0.04) | 2.08 | (0.06) | 6.23 | (0.15) | 51.2 | (0.5) | 16.4 | (0.5) | 32.4 | (0.4) |
| Chile | 3.49 | (0.06) | 0.99 | (0.03) | 1.60 | (0.03) | 6.12 | (0.10) | 56.8 | (0.5) | 15.1 | (0.3) | 28.0 | (0.4) |
| Colombia | 4.21 | (0.06) | 1.23 | (0.03) | 1.93 | (0.03) | 7.37 | (0.08) | 60.7 | (0.6) | 14.2 | (0.3) | 25.0 | (0.3) |
| Croatia | 3.05 | (0.04) | 0.77 | (0.02) | 1.80 | (0.03) | 5.66 | (0.06) | 58.3 | (0.5) | 11.5 | (0.3) | 30.2 | (0.4) |
| Estonia | 4.19 | (0.04) | 0.99 | (0.03) | 1.96 | (0.03) | 7.15 | (0.07) | 62.2 | (0.4) | 12.3 | (0.3) | 25.5 | (0.3) |
| Hong Kong-China | 5.23 | (0.04) | 1.39 | (0.04) | 2.24 | (0.04) | 8.87 | (0.08) | 62.6 | (0.4) | 14.0 | (0.3) | 23.4 | (0.3) |
| Indonesia | 4.09 | (0.07) | 1.36 | (0.05) | 1.99 | (0.03) | 7.44 | (0.10) | 57.2 | (0.6) | 16.4 | (0.5) | 26.5 | (0.3) |
| Israel | 4.12 | (0.04) | 2.15 | (0.04) | 2.33 | (0.05) | 8.69 | (0.11) | 51.4 | (0.6) | 23.1 | (0.3) | 25.5 | (0.4) |
| Jordan | 3.48 | (0.05) | 1.82 | (0.04) | 2.69 | (0.04) | 7.96 | (0.08) | 43.2 | (0.5) | 22.3 | (0.5) | 34.5 | (0.4) |
| Kyrgyzstan | 2.88 | (0.05) | 1.55 | (0.04) | 2.22 | (0.03) | 6.71 | (0.09) | 42.0 | (0.5) | 24.1 | (0.5) | 33.9 | (0.4) |
| Latvia | 4.49 | (0.04) | 1.20 | (0.04) | 2.44 | (0.04) | 8.14 | (0.09) | 58.2 | (0.3) | 13.3 | (0.4) | 28.4 | (0.3) |
| Liechtenstein | 3.98 | (0.08) | 0.58 | (0.05) | 1.49 | (0.06) | 6.04 | (0.12) | 66.7 | (1.2) | 8.5 | (0.6) | 24.8 | (1.0) |
| Lithuania | 3.50 | (0.04) | 0.74 | (0.02) | 1.78 | (0.03) | 6.02 | (0.06) | 60.7 | (0.4) | 11.5 | (0.3) | 27.8 | (0.3) |
| Macao-China | 5.41 | (0.03) | 1.20 | (0.03) | 2.07 | (0.03) | 8.68 | (0.06) | 66.2 | (0.4) | 11.8 | (0.2) | 21.9 | (0.3) |
| Montenegro | 3.09 | (0.04) | 0.93 | (0.04) | 2.03 | (0.03) | 6.03 | (0.07) | 52.5 | (0.4) | 13.4 | (0.3) | 34.1 | (0.4) |
| Qatar | 3.11 | (0.03) | 1.85 | (0.03) | 2.22 | (0.02) | 7.21 | (0.06) | 43.3 | (0.3) | 25.2 | (0.3) | 31.6 | (0.3) |
| Romania | 3.01 | (0.07) | 1.50 | (0.03) | 2.16 | (0.04) | 6.67 | (0.11) | 49.5 | (0.6) | 19.7 | (0.4) | 30.7 | (0.4) |
| Russian Federation | 3.63 | (0.06) | 1.13 | (0.03) | 2.23 | (0.05) | 6.99 | (0.10) | 53.9 | (0.5) | 15.7 | (0.6) | 30.4 | (0.4) |
| Serbia | 3.27 | (0.04) | 0.97 | (0.02) | 1.82 | (0.03) | 6.06 | (0.07) | 59.3 | (0.5) | 13.0 | (0.3) | 27.7 | (0.4) |
| Slovenia | 3.33 | (0.03) | 1.02 | (0.02) | 1.92 | (0.02) | 6.30 | (0.05) | 55.6 | (0.3) | 14.4 | (0.2) | 30.1 | (0.3) |
| Chinese Taipei | 4.26 | (0.05) | 1.53 | (0.04) | 1.88 | (0.04) | 7.72 | (0.12) | 59.7 | (0.4) | 16.9 | (0.3) | 23.4 | (0.2) |
| Thailand | 3.77 | (0.03) | 0.92 | (0.03) | 1.81 | (0.03) | 6.50 | (0.07) | 63.4 | (0.4) | 10.6 | (0.3) | 26.0 | (0.3) |
| Tunisia | 3.39 | (0.04) | 2.42 | (0.03) | 2.57 | (0.04) | 8.38 | (0.10) | 41.7 | (0.4) | 27.1 | (0.3) | 31.2 | (0.4) |
| Uruguay | 3.31 | (0.03) | 0.84 | (0.03) | 1.57 | (0.03) | 5.74 | (0.07) | 60.8 | (0.4) | 12.4 | (0.3) | 26.8 | (0.3) |

1. "No time" in any given activity is recoded to 0 hours per week in that activity, "less than 2 hours per week" is recoded to 1 hour per week, "2 or more but less than 4 hours per week" is recoded to 3 hours per week, "4 or more but less than 6 hours per week" is recoded to 5 hours per week and "6 or more hours per week" is recoded to 7 hours per week.

© OECD 2011  Quality Time for Students: Learning In and Out of School

### Table 2.2c Mean learning hours and allocation of total learning time on the language of instruction

| | Mean learning hours per week[1] | | | | | | | | Allocation of total learning time on the language of instruction for | | | | | |
| | Regular school lessons | | Out-of-school-time lessons | | Individual study | | Total learning hours | | Regular school lessons | | Out-of-school-time lessons | | Individual study | |
| | Mean | S.E. | Mean | S.E. | Mean | S.E. | Mean | S.E. | % | S.E. | % | S.E. | % | S.E. |
|---|---|---|---|---|---|---|---|---|---|---|---|---|---|---|
| **OECD** | | | | | | | | | | | | | | |
| Australia | 4.06 | (0.03) | 0.66 | (0.02) | 1.71 | (0.02) | 6.43 | (0.04) | 67.1 | (0.3) | 8.3 | (0.2) | 24.7 | (0.2) |
| Austria | 2.87 | (0.03) | 0.24 | (0.02) | 1.55 | (0.04) | 4.66 | (0.07) | 65.5 | (0.4) | 3.3 | (0.2) | 31.2 | (0.4) |
| Belgium | 3.49 | (0.03) | 0.46 | (0.01) | 1.35 | (0.02) | 5.30 | (0.04) | 67.3 | (0.3) | 7.1 | (0.2) | 25.7 | (0.2) |
| Canada | 4.43 | (0.04) | 0.86 | (0.02) | 1.74 | (0.03) | 7.06 | (0.06) | 65.6 | (0.3) | 10.8 | (0.2) | 23.6 | (0.2) |
| Czech Republic | 3.72 | (0.03) | 0.61 | (0.01) | 1.16 | (0.02) | 5.49 | (0.05) | 71.6 | (0.4) | 9.0 | (0.2) | 19.4 | (0.4) |
| Denmark | 5.50 | (0.03) | 1.68 | (0.03) | 2.16 | (0.03) | 9.34 | (0.07) | 62.2 | (0.3) | 16.0 | (0.2) | 21.9 | (0.2) |
| Finland | 3.13 | (0.05) | 0.36 | (0.01) | 1.13 | (0.02) | 4.63 | (0.07) | 70.7 | (0.4) | 6.2 | (0.2) | 23.1 | (0.3) |
| France | 4.01 | (0.03) | 0.77 | (0.02) | 1.51 | (0.02) | 6.30 | (0.04) | 67.0 | (0.4) | 10.7 | (0.3) | 22.3 | (0.3) |
| Germany | 3.66 | (0.03) | 0.61 | (0.02) | 1.89 | (0.03) | 6.17 | (0.05) | 62.3 | (0.4) | 7.9 | (0.3) | 29.8 | (0.3) |
| Greece | 3.18 | (0.04) | 1.63 | (0.03) | 1.94 | (0.03) | 6.75 | (0.08) | 51.0 | (0.5) | 21.6 | (0.4) | 27.5 | (0.3) |
| Hungary | 3.18 | (0.04) | 1.31 | (0.03) | 1.86 | (0.03) | 6.36 | (0.08) | 53.2 | (0.4) | 18.3 | (0.3) | 28.5 | (0.3) |
| Iceland | 4.52 | (0.02) | 0.46 | (0.02) | 1.54 | (0.02) | 6.54 | (0.04) | 71.8 | (0.3) | 6.0 | (0.2) | 22.2 | (0.2) |
| Ireland | 3.55 | (0.03) | 0.63 | (0.02) | 1.75 | (0.03) | 5.94 | (0.07) | 64.3 | (0.4) | 8.1 | (0.3) | 27.6 | (0.3) |
| Italy | 4.62 | (0.03) | 0.79 | (0.02) | 2.95 | (0.04) | 8.37 | (0.07) | 57.2 | (0.2) | 8.3 | (0.2) | 34.5 | (0.2) |
| Japan | 3.82 | (0.04) | 0.43 | (0.02) | 0.94 | (0.03) | 5.19 | (0.07) | 78.1 | (0.5) | 6.3 | (0.3) | 15.5 | (0.4) |
| Korea | 4.48 | (0.04) | 1.45 | (0.04) | 1.40 | (0.03) | 7.34 | (0.09) | 66.4 | (0.5) | 16.5 | (0.4) | 17.2 | (0.2) |
| Luxembourg | 3.50 | (0.03) | 0.60 | (0.02) | 1.38 | (0.02) | 5.48 | (0.04) | 67.3 | (0.3) | 8.8 | (0.2) | 23.9 | (0.3) |
| Mexico | 3.73 | (0.04) | 1.10 | (0.03) | 2.06 | (0.03) | 6.87 | (0.07) | 55.1 | (0.4) | 14.6 | (0.3) | 30.4 | (0.3) |
| Netherlands | 2.92 | (0.03) | 0.64 | (0.02) | 1.33 | (0.02) | 4.89 | (0.05) | 63.0 | (0.4) | 10.8 | (0.3) | 26.2 | (0.3) |
| New Zealand | 4.39 | (0.03) | 0.65 | (0.03) | 1.57 | (0.03) | 6.62 | (0.06) | 70.2 | (0.4) | 8.0 | (0.3) | 21.9 | (0.4) |
| Norway | 3.60 | (0.04) | 1.16 | (0.03) | 1.44 | (0.03) | 6.19 | (0.06) | 62.2 | (0.5) | 16.4 | (0.3) | 21.4 | (0.3) |
| Poland | 4.64 | (0.03) | 0.70 | (0.03) | 2.22 | (0.03) | 7.56 | (0.05) | 63.5 | (0.3) | 8.5 | (0.3) | 27.9 | (0.3) |
| Portugal | 3.27 | (0.03) | 0.57 | (0.02) | 1.79 | (0.03) | 5.63 | (0.05) | 61.0 | (0.4) | 8.7 | (0.3) | 30.3 | (0.3) |
| Slovak Republic | 3.12 | (0.05) | 0.89 | (0.03) | 1.74 | (0.03) | 5.75 | (0.08) | 59.0 | (0.5) | 12.7 | (0.3) | 28.3 | (0.5) |
| Spain | 3.60 | (0.03) | 0.58 | (0.02) | 1.89 | (0.03) | 6.10 | (0.05) | 62.7 | (0.3) | 8.1 | (0.3) | 29.2 | (0.3) |
| Sweden | 3.12 | (0.03) | 0.68 | (0.02) | 1.26 | (0.02) | 5.06 | (0.06) | 66.7 | (0.5) | 10.3 | (0.2) | 23.0 | (0.4) |
| Switzerland | 3.65 | (0.04) | 0.49 | (0.02) | 1.40 | (0.02) | 5.54 | (0.05) | 67.5 | (0.4) | 7.1 | (0.3) | 25.4 | (0.2) |
| Turkey | 3.99 | (0.05) | 1.81 | (0.05) | 2.18 | (0.05) | 7.96 | (0.12) | 54.7 | (0.6) | 19.8 | (0.4) | 25.5 | (0.3) |
| United Kingdom | 3.89 | (0.04) | 0.59 | (0.02) | 1.59 | (0.02) | 6.08 | (0.06) | 67.6 | (0.3) | 7.8 | (0.2) | 24.6 | (0.3) |
| United States | 3.64 | (0.04) | 1.11 | (0.03) | 1.87 | (0.03) | 6.65 | (0.06) | 55.8 | (0.6) | 16.0 | (0.4) | 28.2 | (0.3) |
| **OECD average** | 3.78 | (0.01) | 0.82 | (0.00) | 1.68 | (0.01) | 6.28 | (0.01) | 63.9 | (0.1) | 10.7 | (0.1) | 25.4 | (0.1) |
| **Partners** | | | | | | | | | | | | | | |
| Argentina | 2.39 | (0.05) | 0.43 | (0.03) | 1.64 | (0.04) | 4.45 | (0.08) | 55.2 | (0.6) | 8.0 | (0.5) | 36.8 | (0.5) |
| Azerbaijan | 3.69 | (0.05) | 1.80 | (0.05) | 3.10 | (0.05) | 8.66 | (0.11) | 44.9 | (0.6) | 19.3 | (0.5) | 35.8 | (0.5) |
| Brazil | 3.10 | (0.04) | 1.18 | (0.03) | 1.74 | (0.03) | 6.01 | (0.06) | 54.4 | (0.4) | 17.7 | (0.4) | 27.8 | (0.3) |
| Bulgaria | 2.91 | (0.05) | 1.09 | (0.04) | 2.05 | (0.05) | 6.08 | (0.11) | 51.8 | (0.5) | 15.4 | (0.4) | 32.7 | (0.4) |
| Chile | 3.45 | (0.06) | 1.00 | (0.03) | 1.56 | (0.03) | 6.03 | (0.08) | 57.4 | (0.6) | 15.2 | (0.5) | 27.4 | (0.4) |
| Colombia | 3.92 | (0.05) | 1.15 | (0.03) | 1.84 | (0.04) | 6.92 | (0.08) | 60.2 | (0.6) | 14.5 | (0.4) | 25.3 | (0.4) |
| Croatia | 3.33 | (0.03) | 0.39 | (0.02) | 1.58 | (0.03) | 5.32 | (0.06) | 66.8 | (0.4) | 5.9 | (0.2) | 27.4 | (0.4) |
| Estonia | 3.48 | (0.04) | 0.88 | (0.03) | 1.62 | (0.03) | 5.99 | (0.06) | 61.8 | (0.5) | 13.1 | (0.4) | 25.2 | (0.3) |
| Hong Kong-China | 5.19 | (0.04) | 0.81 | (0.03) | 1.64 | (0.03) | 7.64 | (0.08) | 70.9 | (0.4) | 9.1 | (0.3) | 20.0 | (0.3) |
| Indonesia | 3.64 | (0.05) | 1.25 | (0.04) | 1.80 | (0.03) | 6.68 | (0.10) | 56.3 | (0.7) | 16.7 | (0.6) | 27.1 | (0.3) |
| Israel | 3.03 | (0.04) | 1.33 | (0.03) | 1.66 | (0.04) | 6.04 | (0.09) | 54.0 | (0.5) | 19.8 | (0.4) | 26.1 | (0.4) |
| Jordan | 3.56 | (0.05) | 1.77 | (0.04) | 2.59 | (0.04) | 7.92 | (0.09) | 44.2 | (0.6) | 22.2 | (0.5) | 33.6 | (0.4) |
| Kyrgyzstan | 2.74 | (0.06) | 1.70 | (0.03) | 2.34 | (0.04) | 6.85 | (0.09) | 39.9 | (0.5) | 26.1 | (0.4) | 34.0 | (0.4) |
| Latvia | 3.69 | (0.04) | 0.88 | (0.03) | 2.01 | (0.03) | 6.58 | (0.07) | 59.2 | (0.4) | 11.4 | (0.4) | 29.3 | (0.3) |
| Liechtenstein | 3.66 | (0.08) | 0.32 | (0.04) | 1.24 | (0.06) | 5.21 | (0.10) | 69.8 | (1.2) | 5.6 | (0.7) | 24.6 | (0.9) |
| Lithuania | 3.66 | (0.04) | 0.66 | (0.02) | 1.82 | (0.03) | 6.13 | (0.06) | 62.3 | (0.4) | 9.9 | (0.3) | 27.8 | (0.3) |
| Macao-China | 5.32 | (0.03) | 1.06 | (0.03) | 1.49 | (0.03) | 7.86 | (0.06) | 71.4 | (0.3) | 11.1 | (0.2) | 17.5 | (0.2) |
| Montenegro | 2.93 | (0.04) | 0.75 | (0.02) | 1.99 | (0.03) | 5.66 | (0.07) | 53.0 | (0.4) | 11.4 | (0.3) | 35.6 | (0.4) |
| Qatar | 2.90 | (0.03) | 1.59 | (0.03) | 2.04 | (0.02) | 6.51 | (0.06) | 44.7 | (0.3) | 23.6 | (0.3) | 31.7 | (0.3) |
| Romania | 3.30 | (0.06) | 1.52 | (0.03) | 2.19 | (0.04) | 7.02 | (0.10) | 50.6 | (0.6) | 19.7 | (0.4) | 29.6 | (0.3) |
| Russian Federation | 2.04 | (0.04) | 0.82 | (0.03) | 1.55 | (0.04) | 4.40 | (0.07) | 48.2 | (0.6) | 16.4 | (0.6) | 35.4 | (0.5) |
| Serbia | 3.17 | (0.04) | 0.93 | (0.03) | 1.70 | (0.03) | 5.80 | (0.07) | 60.2 | (0.5) | 12.9 | (0.4) | 26.9 | (0.3) |
| Slovenia | 3.25 | (0.03) | 0.73 | (0.02) | 1.48 | (0.02) | 5.47 | (0.04) | 60.9 | (0.4) | 12.1 | (0.2) | 27.1 | (0.3) |
| Chinese Taipei | 4.37 | (0.05) | 0.69 | (0.03) | 1.77 | (0.03) | 6.87 | (0.08) | 66.1 | (0.4) | 8.9 | (0.3) | 25.0 | (0.2) |
| Thailand | 3.10 | (0.02) | 0.56 | (0.02) | 1.71 | (0.03) | 5.36 | (0.05) | 62.5 | (0.4) | 7.4 | (0.3) | 30.1 | (0.3) |
| Tunisia | 3.14 | (0.05) | 1.78 | (0.04) | 2.12 | (0.04) | 7.05 | (0.10) | 45.6 | (0.7) | 23.6 | (0.5) | 30.8 | (0.5) |
| Uruguay | 2.74 | (0.04) | 0.65 | (0.02) | 1.35 | (0.02) | 4.76 | (0.06) | 60.8 | (0.5) | 11.3 | (0.4) | 27.9 | (0.3) |

1. "No time" in any given activity is recoded to 0 hours per week in that activity, "less than 2 hours per week" is recoded to 1 hour per week, "2 or more but less than 4 hours per week" is recoded to 3 hours per week, "4 or more but less than 6 hours per week" is recoded to 5 hours per week and "6 or more hours per week" is recoded to 7 hours per week.

## Table 2.2d Mean learning hours and allocation of total learning time in science, in mathematics and on the language of instruction

| | Science, mathematics and language of instruction | | | | | | | | | | | | | |
| | Mean learning hours per week[1] | | | | | | | | Allocation of total learning time in science, in mathematics and on the language of instruction for | | | | | |
| | Regular school lessons | | Out-of-school-time lessons | | Individual study | | Total learning hours | | Regular school lessons | | Out-of-school-time lessons | | Individual study | |
| | Mean | S.E. | Mean | S.E. | Mean | S.E. | Mean | S.E. | % | S.E. | % | S.E. | % | S.E. |
|---|---|---|---|---|---|---|---|---|---|---|---|---|---|---|
| Australia | 11.40 | (0.07) | 1.76 | (0.04) | 4.67 | (0.06) | 17.85 | (0.12) | 66.5 | (0.2) | 8.7 | (0.2) | 24.8 | (0.2) |
| Austria | 8.56 | (0.09) | 0.94 | (0.04) | 4.95 | (0.08) | 14.49 | (0.16) | 61.9 | (0.4) | 5.4 | (0.2) | 32.8 | (0.3) |
| Belgium | 9.70 | (0.10) | 1.32 | (0.03) | 4.39 | (0.06) | 15.43 | (0.14) | 64.3 | (0.3) | 7.8 | (0.2) | 27.9 | (0.2) |
| Canada | 12.93 | (0.11) | 2.35 | (0.05) | 5.26 | (0.07) | 20.63 | (0.17) | 64.0 | (0.3) | 11.0 | (0.2) | 25.1 | (0.2) |
| Czech Republic | 10.65 | (0.11) | 1.89 | (0.04) | 3.47 | (0.05) | 15.98 | (0.15) | 69.5 | (0.4) | 10.2 | (0.2) | 20.2 | (0.3) |
| Denmark | 13.16 | (0.07) | 3.83 | (0.07) | 5.00 | (0.06) | 21.94 | (0.15) | 62.3 | (0.3) | 15.9 | (0.2) | 21.8 | (0.2) |
| Finland | 9.71 | (0.11) | 1.06 | (0.04) | 3.41 | (0.05) | 14.16 | (0.16) | 70.5 | (0.3) | 6.4 | (0.2) | 23.1 | (0.2) |
| France | 10.71 | (0.10) | 2.24 | (0.04) | 4.56 | (0.07) | 17.55 | (0.15) | 63.4 | (0.3) | 12.1 | (0.2) | 24.5 | (0.3) |
| Germany | 10.61 | (0.08) | 1.92 | (0.06) | 5.87 | (0.08) | 18.44 | (0.15) | 59.5 | (0.3) | 9.3 | (0.3) | 31.2 | (0.2) |
| Greece | 9.82 | (0.12) | 5.84 | (0.11) | 5.79 | (0.08) | 21.48 | (0.24) | 48.1 | (0.5) | 25.7 | (0.3) | 26.2 | (0.3) |
| Hungary | 8.99 | (0.10) | 3.59 | (0.06) | 5.29 | (0.08) | 17.89 | (0.19) | 52.4 | (0.4) | 18.7 | (0.3) | 28.9 | (0.2) |
| Iceland | 12.24 | (0.06) | 1.46 | (0.04) | 4.42 | (0.05) | 18.14 | (0.09) | 69.7 | (0.3) | 7.2 | (0.2) | 23.1 | (0.2) |
| Ireland | 9.75 | (0.08) | 1.65 | (0.05) | 4.70 | (0.08) | 16.08 | (0.15) | 63.5 | (0.4) | 8.7 | (0.2) | 27.8 | (0.3) |
| Italy | 11.27 | (0.09) | 2.25 | (0.04) | 7.53 | (0.07) | 21.07 | (0.17) | 54.9 | (0.2) | 9.9 | (0.2) | 35.2 | (0.2) |
| Japan | 10.75 | (0.13) | 1.40 | (0.05) | 3.11 | (0.10) | 15.26 | (0.22) | 74.5 | (0.5) | 7.5 | (0.3) | 18.0 | (0.4) |
| Korea | 12.76 | (0.11) | 4.74 | (0.08) | 4.93 | (0.12) | 22.49 | (0.25) | 61.4 | (0.4) | 18.4 | (0.3) | 20.3 | (0.3) |
| Luxembourg | 9.71 | (0.06) | 1.93 | (0.04) | 4.33 | (0.05) | 15.98 | (0.10) | 63.2 | (0.3) | 10.7 | (0.2) | 26.1 | (0.2) |
| Mexico | 10.84 | (0.09) | 3.28 | (0.08) | 6.42 | (0.08) | 20.41 | (0.19) | 53.7 | (0.4) | 14.7 | (0.3) | 31.6 | (0.3) |
| Netherlands | 7.97 | (0.07) | 1.88 | (0.05) | 3.99 | (0.06) | 13.82 | (0.12) | 60.0 | (0.4) | 12.3 | (0.3) | 27.8 | (0.3) |
| New Zealand | 12.84 | (0.09) | 1.74 | (0.06) | 4.42 | (0.07) | 19.02 | (0.14) | 69.7 | (0.4) | 8.2 | (0.3) | 22.1 | (0.2) |
| Norway | 9.63 | (0.08) | 3.13 | (0.05) | 4.06 | (0.06) | 16.79 | (0.12) | 60.4 | (0.4) | 17.0 | (0.3) | 22.6 | (0.3) |
| Poland | 11.71 | (0.09) | 2.11 | (0.05) | 6.34 | (0.07) | 20.19 | (0.14) | 59.9 | (0.3) | 10.1 | (0.3) | 30.0 | (0.3) |
| Portugal | 10.08 | (0.10) | 1.99 | (0.05) | 5.83 | (0.08) | 17.94 | (0.16) | 58.3 | (0.4) | 10.2 | (0.2) | 31.5 | (0.3) |
| Slovak Republic | 8.88 | (0.14) | 2.40 | (0.07) | 4.81 | (0.09) | 16.11 | (0.25) | 58.9 | (0.4) | 12.7 | (0.3) | 28.3 | (0.3) |
| Spain | 10.15 | (0.09) | 2.24 | (0.05) | 5.58 | (0.08) | 18.08 | (0.16) | 59.0 | (0.3) | 11.2 | (0.2) | 29.7 | (0.3) |
| Sweden | 9.01 | (0.07) | 1.79 | (0.04) | 3.58 | (0.05) | 14.37 | (0.12) | 66.1 | (0.5) | 10.3 | (0.2) | 23.6 | (0.4) |
| Switzerland | 9.88 | (0.09) | 1.57 | (0.04) | 4.20 | (0.04) | 15.66 | (0.13) | 64.3 | (0.3) | 8.9 | (0.2) | 26.8 | (0.2) |
| Turkey | 10.67 | (0.16) | 5.22 | (0.09) | 6.11 | (0.09) | 21.88 | (0.29) | 51.4 | (0.4) | 21.6 | (0.3) | 26.9 | (0.3) |
| United Kingdom | 11.92 | (0.09) | 1.70 | (0.05) | 4.52 | (0.06) | 18.16 | (0.14) | 67.8 | (0.3) | 8.2 | (0.2) | 24.0 | (0.2) |
| United States | 10.95 | (0.13) | 3.04 | (0.07) | 5.59 | (0.07) | 19.69 | (0.15) | 55.6 | (0.5) | 15.3 | (0.4) | 29.1 | (0.2) |
| **OECD average** | **10.58** | **(0.02)** | **2.41** | **(0.01)** | **4.90** | **(0.01)** | **17.90** | **(0.03)** | **61.8** | **(0.1)** | **11.8** | **(0.0)** | **26.4** | **(0.0)** |
| Argentina | 7.62 | (0.16) | 1.66 | (0.07) | 5.04 | (0.10) | 14.32 | (0.23) | 54.5 | (0.6) | 10.6 | (0.4) | 35.0 | (0.4) |
| Azerbaijan | 10.37 | (0.12) | 4.86 | (0.10) | 8.71 | (0.13) | 24.10 | (0.27) | 44.4 | (0.5) | 19.7 | (0.4) | 35.8 | (0.3) |
| Brazil | 8.46 | (0.09) | 3.15 | (0.06) | 5.21 | (0.07) | 16.78 | (0.17) | 53.0 | (0.4) | 17.1 | (0.3) | 29.9 | (0.3) |
| Bulgaria | 8.55 | (0.17) | 3.20 | (0.08) | 6.15 | (0.16) | 17.98 | (0.33) | 50.0 | (0.5) | 16.8 | (0.4) | 33.1 | (0.4) |
| Chile | 9.28 | (0.17) | 2.81 | (0.06) | 4.69 | (0.08) | 16.86 | (0.23) | 54.6 | (0.5) | 16.3 | (0.3) | 29.1 | (0.3) |
| Colombia | 11.66 | (0.20) | 3.31 | (0.07) | 5.58 | (0.09) | 20.55 | (0.27) | 59.5 | (0.6) | 14.5 | (0.3) | 26.0 | (0.4) |
| Croatia | 8.43 | (0.09) | 1.58 | (0.05) | 4.85 | (0.07) | 14.94 | (0.15) | 59.9 | (0.4) | 9.6 | (0.3) | 30.5 | (0.3) |
| Estonia | 10.95 | (0.09) | 2.63 | (0.06) | 5.11 | (0.06) | 18.71 | (0.14) | 60.9 | (0.4) | 13.3 | (0.3) | 25.9 | (0.2) |
| Hong Kong-China | 13.57 | (0.11) | 3.08 | (0.08) | 5.33 | (0.08) | 21.98 | (0.21) | 64.1 | (0.4) | 12.9 | (0.3) | 22.9 | (0.2) |
| Indonesia | 10.98 | (0.17) | 3.66 | (0.11) | 5.58 | (0.08) | 20.17 | (0.25) | 56.0 | (0.7) | 16.6 | (0.5) | 27.5 | (0.3) |
| Israel | 9.58 | (0.11) | 4.44 | (0.08) | 5.34 | (0.11) | 19.44 | (0.24) | 52.3 | (0.4) | 21.7 | (0.2) | 26.1 | (0.3) |
| Jordan | 10.36 | (0.14) | 5.10 | (0.10) | 7.90 | (0.11) | 23.35 | (0.22) | 43.6 | (0.5) | 21.9 | (0.4) | 34.5 | (0.3) |
| Kyrgyzstan | 7.80 | (0.16) | 4.60 | (0.09) | 6.70 | (0.09) | 19.24 | (0.25) | 40.0 | (0.5) | 25.2 | (0.4) | 34.8 | (0.3) |
| Latvia | 11.06 | (0.11) | 2.72 | (0.08) | 6.25 | (0.08) | 20.03 | (0.19) | 57.4 | (0.3) | 12.7 | (0.3) | 30.0 | (0.3) |
| Liechtenstein | 10.23 | (0.19) | 1.37 | (0.08) | 3.93 | (0.15) | 15.51 | (0.23) | 66.3 | (1.1) | 8.4 | (0.6) | 25.4 | (0.9) |
| Lithuania | 9.85 | (0.10) | 1.93 | (0.05) | 5.27 | (0.07) | 17.04 | (0.14) | 59.5 | (0.3) | 11.1 | (0.3) | 29.4 | (0.2) |
| Macao-China | 14.46 | (0.07) | 3.25 | (0.07) | 4.93 | (0.07) | 22.63 | (0.15) | 66.7 | (0.3) | 12.8 | (0.2) | 20.5 | (0.2) |
| Montenegro | 8.89 | (0.09) | 2.68 | (0.05) | 6.20 | (0.08) | 17.73 | (0.16) | 50.8 | (0.3) | 14.6 | (0.3) | 34.7 | (0.3) |
| Qatar | 8.68 | (0.08) | 4.90 | (0.07) | 6.27 | (0.06) | 19.89 | (0.16) | 43.2 | (0.2) | 24.6 | (0.2) | 32.2 | (0.2) |
| Romania | 8.58 | (0.15) | 4.04 | (0.07) | 5.96 | (0.10) | 18.57 | (0.26) | 48.7 | (0.4) | 20.5 | (0.3) | 30.9 | (0.2) |
| Russian Federation | 9.41 | (0.13) | 3.07 | (0.07) | 6.65 | (0.12) | 19.13 | (0.24) | 50.9 | (0.5) | 15.7 | (0.5) | 33.5 | (0.4) |
| Serbia | 9.32 | (0.11) | 2.66 | (0.06) | 5.22 | (0.08) | 17.19 | (0.18) | 57.7 | (0.4) | 13.8 | (0.3) | 28.4 | (0.3) |
| Slovenia | 9.39 | (0.07) | 2.47 | (0.04) | 4.93 | (0.05) | 16.84 | (0.12) | 56.9 | (0.3) | 13.9 | (0.2) | 29.1 | (0.2) |
| Chinese Taipei | 11.52 | (0.15) | 3.00 | (0.06) | 4.88 | (0.09) | 19.53 | (0.27) | 61.4 | (0.3) | 14.0 | (0.2) | 24.6 | (0.2) |
| Thailand | 10.69 | (0.08) | 2.40 | (0.07) | 5.31 | (0.08) | 18.37 | (0.16) | 62.3 | (0.4) | 10.3 | (0.3) | 27.5 | (0.3) |
| Tunisia | 9.17 | (0.12) | 6.10 | (0.06) | 7.29 | (0.08) | 22.60 | (0.21) | 41.4 | (0.3) | 26.4 | (0.2) | 32.2 | (0.3) |
| Uruguay | 8.49 | (0.08) | 2.08 | (0.06) | 4.23 | (0.06) | 14.84 | (0.15) | 59.2 | (0.3) | 12.6 | (0.3) | 28.2 | (0.3) |

1. "No time" in any given activity is recoded to 0 hours per week in that activity, "less than 2 hours per week" is recoded to 1 hour per week, "2 or more but less than 4 hours per week" is recoded to 3 hours per week, "4 or more but less than 6 hours per week" is recoded to 5 hours per week and "6 or more hours per week" is recoded to 7 hours per week.

© OECD 2011 Quality Time for Students: Learning In and Out of School

**Table 2.3** Percentage of students participating in out-of-school-time lessons, by different types of out-of-school-time lessons

| | Proportion of students participating in out-of-school-time lessons | | Proportion of students participating in out-of-school-time lessons with non-school teachers | | | | | | | | Proportion of students participating in out-of-school-time lessons with school teachers | | | | | | | |
| | | | One-to-one lessons | | Small group lessons | | Large group lessons | | At least one of these types of out-of-school-time lessons | | One-to-one lessons | | Small group lessons | | Large group lessons | | At least one of these types of out-of-school-time lessons | |
| | % | S.E. | % | S.E. | % | S.E. | % | S.E. | % | S.E. | % | S.E. | % | S.E. | % | S.E. | % | S.E. |
|---|---|---|---|---|---|---|---|---|---|---|---|---|---|---|---|---|---|---|
| **OECD** Australia | 31.2 | (0.6) | 16.4 | (0.4) | 8.0 | (0.4) | 7.2 | (0.3) | 23.1 | (0.6) | 6.7 | (0.3) | 7.3 | (0.4) | 8.2 | (0.4) | 14.1 | (0.5) |
| Austria | 36.3 | (1.1) | 16.5 | (0.8) | 7.7 | (0.6) | 6.1 | (0.5) | 24.2 | (0.9) | 5.4 | (0.5) | 13.1 | (0.8) | 15.6 | (0.9) | 23.4 | (1.1) |
| Belgium | 30.4 | (0.6) | 17.4 | (0.6) | 7.2 | (0.3) | 4.3 | (0.4) | 22.5 | (0.6) | 7.3 | (0.4) | 7.8 | (0.4) | 6.0 | (0.3) | 14.2 | (0.5) |
| Canada | 35.8 | (0.7) | 16.4 | (0.5) | 8.4 | (0.4) | 7.1 | (0.3) | 22.8 | (0.6) | 12.3 | (0.4) | 10.5 | (0.4) | 11.3 | (0.4) | 21.3 | (0.6) |
| Czech Republic | 37.3 | (0.9) | 15.6 | (0.7) | 7.8 | (0.6) | 5.6 | (0.5) | 21.8 | (0.8) | 14.3 | (0.7) | 10.9 | (0.6) | 13.4 | (0.8) | 23.3 | (1.0) |
| Denmark | 20.6 | (0.8) | 5.3 | (0.4) | 4.4 | (0.3) | 3.8 | (0.4) | 10.4 | (0.6) | 5.3 | (0.4) | 8.0 | (0.5) | 8.0 | (0.5) | 14.1 | (0.7) |
| Finland | 23.5 | (0.7) | 5.3 | (0.4) | 2.4 | (0.2) | 3.6 | (0.2) | 8.5 | (0.4) | 8.1 | (0.5) | 9.4 | (0.5) | 12.1 | (0.6) | 18.2 | (0.7) |
| France | 41.6 | (0.9) | 22.1 | (0.9) | 9.0 | (0.5) | 4.9 | (0.4) | 26.4 | (1.0) | 7.0 | (0.6) | 17.9 | (0.7) | 10.4 | (0.5) | 23.9 | (0.8) |
| Germany | 37.0 | (0.7) | 20.4 | (0.6) | 6.9 | (0.4) | 3.7 | (0.4) | 27.3 | (0.6) | 5.8 | (0.5) | 7.7 | (0.5) | 10.4 | (0.6) | 17.6 | (0.7) |
| Greece | 76.4 | (0.9) | 44.7 | (1.1) | 45.7 | (1.3) | 18.4 | (0.9) | 70.7 | (1.0) | 12.0 | (0.8) | 14.8 | (0.8) | 9.6 | (0.7) | 22.0 | (1.0) |
| Hungary | 54.2 | (1.1) | 32.3 | (1.0) | 10.7 | (0.6) | 8.7 | (0.5) | 38.3 | (1.0) | 14.7 | (0.7) | 12.7 | (0.7) | 15.9 | (0.7) | 29.4 | (1.1) |
| Iceland | 40.4 | (0.8) | 14.7 | (0.6) | 6.6 | (0.5) | 5.1 | (0.4) | 19.8 | (0.7) | 10.4 | (0.5) | 14.5 | (0.6) | 14.1 | (0.6) | 27.0 | (0.7) |
| Ireland | 38.1 | (0.9) | 20.7 | (0.6) | 9.2 | (0.5) | 6.5 | (0.5) | 28.9 | (0.8) | 7.0 | (0.5) | 9.0 | (0.6) | 9.8 | (0.6) | 16.9 | (0.8) |
| Italy | 66.4 | (0.6) | 37.1 | (0.6) | 14.0 | (0.5) | 8.9 | (0.4) | 45.9 | (0.7) | a | a | 36.3 | (0.8) | 25.8 | (0.6) | 45.7 | (0.8) |
| Japan | 45.6 | (1.4) | 9.4 | (0.6) | 8.4 | (0.6) | 8.2 | (0.6) | 20.2 | (1.0) | 3.7 | (0.3) | 6.6 | (0.3) | 30.5 | (1.2) | 34.9 | (1.2) |
| Korea | 79.2 | (0.9) | 31.1 | (0.8) | 31.1 | (0.9) | 26.7 | (0.8) | 57.8 | (1.0) | 9.5 | (0.5) | 16.7 | (0.6) | 36.2 | (1.3) | 50.4 | (1.2) |
| Luxembourg | 43.8 | (0.7) | 22.8 | (0.6) | 7.0 | (0.5) | 5.5 | (0.3) | 28.0 | (0.7) | 13.8 | (0.5) | 14.6 | (0.5) | 9.9 | (0.4) | 25.3 | (0.6) |
| Mexico | 47.7 | (0.9) | 17.7 | (0.6) | 16.0 | (0.6) | 15.9 | (0.6) | 30.5 | (0.8) | 17.4 | (0.8) | 17.6 | (0.7) | 23.8 | (0.8) | 33.3 | (0.9) |
| Netherlands | 22.1 | (0.9) | 7.2 | (0.5) | 3.5 | (0.4) | 3.6 | (0.3) | 11.1 | (0.6) | 7.5 | (0.5) | 8.7 | (0.5) | 7.2 | (0.5) | 15.5 | (0.8) |
| New Zealand | 33.7 | (0.9) | 16.6 | (0.6) | 9.7 | (0.5) | 6.9 | (0.4) | 23.9 | (0.7) | 9.1 | (0.8) | 9.7 | (0.6) | 9.1 | (0.6) | 17.7 | (0.9) |
| Norway | 27.3 | (0.8) | 5.2 | (0.4) | 4.9 | (0.4) | 5.0 | (0.4) | 9.9 | (0.6) | 8.5 | (0.5) | 11.9 | (0.6) | 17.2 | (0.7) | 23.8 | (0.8) |
| Poland | 56.2 | (1.0) | 19.2 | (0.8) | 10.6 | (0.6) | 9.9 | (0.4) | 28.9 | (0.9) | 14.7 | (0.6) | 23.1 | (0.8) | 26.7 | (0.9) | 41.2 | (1.0) |
| Portugal | 68.8 | (1.0) | 26.0 | (0.9) | 14.2 | (0.7) | 7.9 | (0.6) | 35.3 | (1.0) | 22.0 | (0.9) | 31.8 | (1.1) | 23.9 | (1.1) | 47.8 | (1.3) |
| Slovak Republic | 55.7 | (1.2) | 25.2 | (1.0) | 11.0 | (0.5) | 7.3 | (0.6) | 29.7 | (1.0) | 30.4 | (1.3) | 18.0 | (1.0) | 23.9 | (1.2) | 38.6 | (1.4) |
| Spain | 53.8 | (0.7) | 28.3 | (0.8) | 25.7 | (0.7) | 10.4 | (0.5) | 43.4 | (0.8) | 8.5 | (0.5) | 10.8 | (0.4) | 9.8 | (0.5) | 18.6 | (0.6) |
| Sweden | 31.9 | (0.8) | 7.4 | (0.4) | 5.8 | (0.4) | 7.0 | (0.4) | 13.1 | (0.6) | 8.8 | (0.6) | 14.3 | (0.6) | 20.8 | (0.7) | 26.4 | (0.8) |
| Switzerland | 40.0 | (0.7) | 19.5 | (0.6) | 6.3 | (0.4) | 4.7 | (0.3) | 24.6 | (0.6) | 6.8 | (0.3) | 10.1 | (0.4) | 14.1 | (0.6) | 22.5 | (0.7) |
| Turkey | 36.9 | (1.1) | 13.4 | (0.7) | 10.9 | (0.6) | 14.9 | (1.0) | 26.5 | (1.2) | 7.6 | (0.6) | 9.3 | (0.6) | 12.8 | (0.7) | 19.7 | (0.9) |
| United Kingdom | 45.5 | (0.9) | 16.9 | (0.5) | 7.2 | (0.4) | 7.3 | (0.4) | 24.1 | (0.7) | 11.3 | (0.4) | 17.7 | (0.6) | 19.5 | (0.7) | 31.8 | (0.9) |
| United States | 42.3 | (1.2) | 17.3 | (0.8) | 12.5 | (0.9) | 11.6 | (0.8) | 25.2 | (1.1) | 22.4 | (1.0) | 19.1 | (0.9) | 18.1 | (1.0) | 32.4 | (1.2) |
| **OECD average** | 43.3 | (0.2) | 18.9 | (0.1) | 11.1 | (0.1) | 8.2 | (0.1) | 27.4 | (0.1) | 11.0 | (0.1) | 14.0 | (0.1) | 15.8 | (0.1) | 26.4 | (0.2) |
| **Partners** Argentina | 48.5 | (1.2) | 30.8 | (1.3) | 18.9 | (0.9) | 12.9 | (0.8) | 39.9 | (1.2) | 10.7 | (0.9) | 12.6 | (1.0) | 11.3 | (1.0) | 20.2 | (1.3) |
| Azerbaijan | 79.5 | (1.1) | 30.3 | (1.2) | 40.9 | (1.0) | 38.9 | (1.0) | 62.7 | (1.0) | 39.0 | (1.2) | 37.2 | (1.3) | 48.4 | (1.4) | 67.6 | (1.4) |
| Brazil | 48.4 | (0.9) | 19.5 | (0.6) | 17.6 | (0.5) | 15.2 | (0.5) | 33.1 | (0.7) | 13.6 | (0.6) | 23.5 | (0.8) | 20.4 | (0.7) | 34.3 | (0.9) |
| Bulgaria | 54.2 | (1.4) | 26.9 | (0.9) | 17.4 | (1.0) | 16.8 | (1.1) | 38.1 | (1.1) | 22.0 | (1.4) | 19.2 | (1.1) | 22.8 | (1.2) | 34.9 | (1.6) |
| Chile | 38.2 | (1.2) | 13.3 | (0.8) | 9.4 | (0.5) | 8.2 | (0.5) | 21.4 | (0.9) | 8.2 | (0.5) | 16.2 | (0.8) | 17.7 | (0.7) | 27.2 | (1.1) |
| Colombia | 51.0 | (1.1) | 23.7 | (0.5) | 23.6 | (0.5) | 40.3 | (0.9) | 36.7 | (0.8) | 15.0 | (1.1) | 20.1 | (1.2) | 19.4 | (1.1) | 29.3 | (1.3) |
| Croatia | 45.4 | (0.9) | 25.2 | (0.7) | 17.6 | (0.8) | 16.2 | (0.7) | 34.0 | (0.9) | 13.2 | (0.5) | 11.2 | (0.6) | 12.0 | (0.7) | 21.8 | (0.9) |
| Estonia | 46.0 | (0.9) | 27.8 | (0.9) | 9.7 | (0.5) | 7.8 | (0.5) | 23.4 | (0.7) | 18.4 | (0.9) | 13.7 | (0.7) | 18.6 | (0.7) | 32.1 | (1.0) |
| Hong Kong-China | 75.4 | (0.9) | 17.2 | (0.6) | 8.0 | (0.5) | 7.3 | (0.5) | 52.1 | (1.2) | 5.9 | (0.4) | 16.9 | (0.8) | 42.0 | (1.3) | 48.6 | (1.3) |
| Indonesia | 65.8 | (2.3) | 24.1 | (1.3) | 17.8 | (0.8) | 30.1 | (1.1) | 34.0 | (1.0) | 31.6 | (2.3) | 26.5 | (2.0) | 34.9 | (2.3) | 51.8 | (3.0) |
| Israel | 64.4 | (1.1) | 17.4 | (0.8) | 19.4 | (0.8) | 17.5 | (0.9) | 52.7 | (1.3) | 20.8 | (1.0) | 20.9 | (0.9) | 20.2 | (0.8) | 35.2 | (1.1) |
| Jordan | 72.6 | (0.9) | 42.3 | (1.1) | 20.1 | (0.8) | 15.2 | (0.8) | 48.0 | (0.9) | 27.4 | (1.0) | 31.7 | (0.9) | 40.9 | (0.9) | 56.6 | (1.1) |
| Kyrgyzstan | 85.2 | (1.0) | 34.4 | (0.8) | 24.9 | (0.8) | 21.6 | (0.8) | 48.6 | (1.0) | 63.8 | (1.0) | 44.1 | (1.1) | 52.9 | (1.2) | 78.5 | (1.1) |
| Latvia | 71.5 | (1.1) | 26.3 | (0.8) | 26.7 | (0.9) | 31.5 | (1.0) | 42.3 | (1.1) | 34.7 | (1.2) | 25.6 | (1.1) | 29.0 | (1.2) | 50.5 | (1.3) |
| Liechtenstein | 27.8 | (2.4) | 32.1 | (1.2) | 14.1 | (0.5) | 16.9 | (0.7) | 16.1 | (2.0) | 5.8 | (1.2) | 7.9 | (1.3) | 10.6 | (1.6) | 16.7 | (1.9) |
| Lithuania | 48.8 | (1.1) | 13.6 | (1.8) | 2.8 | (1.0) | 2.5 | (0.9) | 23.4 | (0.8) | 12.0 | (0.6) | 17.6 | (0.8) | 19.4 | (0.8) | 34.4 | (1.0) |
| Macao-China | 62.3 | (0.8) | 17.5 | (0.8) | 6.9 | (0.4) | 6.5 | (0.5) | 39.1 | (0.8) | 14.3 | (0.6) | 22.7 | (0.6) | 34.9 | (0.7) | 46.7 | (0.8) |
| Montenegro | 62.1 | (0.7) | 21.7 | (0.7) | 20.6 | (0.7) | 19.4 | (0.7) | 47.5 | (0.8) | 25.2 | (0.6) | 17.8 | (0.6) | 21.7 | (0.6) | 34.7 | (0.8) |
| Qatar | 63.6 | (0.5) | 37.1 | (0.8) | 20.5 | (0.6) | 17.1 | (0.6) | 48.5 | (0.7) | 33.9 | (0.6) | 29.1 | (0.5) | 29.5 | (0.6) | 45.3 | (0.6) |
| Romania | 56.8 | (1.5) | 36.1 | (0.7) | 25.1 | (0.6) | 22.6 | (0.5) | 38.5 | (1.3) | 26.9 | (1.3) | 24.4 | (1.1) | 21.9 | (1.5) | 40.1 | (1.6) |
| Russian Federation | 69.4 | (1.4) | 27.8 | (1.3) | 19.7 | (1.2) | 15.3 | (1.2) | 31.2 | (1.1) | 30.7 | (0.9) | 31.6 | (1.2) | 36.7 | (1.3) | 57.6 | (1.3) |
| Serbia | 53.9 | (1.0) | 21.4 | (0.8) | 12.5 | (0.8) | 12.7 | (0.6) | 43.3 | (1.1) | 10.3 | (0.7) | 12.3 | (0.6) | 14.6 | (0.8) | 23.7 | (0.9) |
| Slovenia | 41.6 | (0.6) | 38.5 | (1.1) | 12.8 | (0.6) | 8.6 | (0.5) | 31.2 | (0.6) | 8.9 | (0.4) | 8.9 | (0.5) | 11.7 | (0.5) | 20.2 | (0.6) |
| Chinese Taipei | 75.0 | (0.5) | 26.7 | (0.6) | 6.5 | (0.4) | 5.0 | (0.3) | 56.9 | (0.8) | 14.4 | (0.6) | 22.8 | (0.7) | 35.1 | (0.8) | 45.1 | (0.9) |
| Thailand | 63.5 | (1.2) | 20.5 | (0.8) | 24.0 | (0.9) | 31.3 | (1.2) | 44.3 | (1.3) | 21.0 | (0.7) | 26.9 | (0.9) | 39.0 | (1.2) | 47.4 | (1.2) |
| Tunisia | 70.4 | (1.0) | 30.6 | (1.4) | 28.2 | (1.1) | 19.0 | (0.9) | 44.9 | (1.4) | 42.6 | (1.3) | 32.8 | (1.2) | 30.5 | (0.9) | 54.0 | (1.2) |
| Uruguay | 44.6 | (1.0) | 28.7 | (0.8) | 20.5 | (0.7) | 11.7 | (0.6) | 37.6 | (1.0) | 9.5 | (0.8) | 9.0 | (0.6) | 8.7 | (0.5) | 17.1 | (0.9) |

95

## Table 3.1 Percentage of students, by immigrant status

| | Native students | | Students with an immigrant background | |
|---|---|---|---|---|
| | % | S.E. | % | S.E. |
| **OECD** Australia | 78.1 | (1.2) | 21.9 | (1.2) |
| Austria | 86.8 | (1.2) | 13.2 | (1.2) |
| Belgium | 86.7 | (1.0) | 13.3 | (1.0) |
| Canada | 78.9 | (1.2) | 21.1 | (1.2) |
| Czech Republic | 98.1 | (0.2) | 1.9 | (0.2) |
| Denmark | 92.4 | (0.8) | 7.6 | (0.8) |
| Finland | 98.5 | (0.3) | 1.5 | (0.3) |
| France | 87.0 | (1.0) | 13.0 | (1.0) |
| Germany | 85.8 | (1.0) | 14.2 | (1.0) |
| Greece | 92.4 | (0.7) | 7.6 | (0.7) |
| Hungary | 98.3 | (0.3) | 1.7 | (0.3) |
| Iceland | 98.2 | (0.2) | 1.8 | (0.2) |
| Ireland | 94.4 | (0.5) | 5.6 | (0.5) |
| Italy | 96.2 | (0.3) | 3.8 | (0.3) |
| Japan | 99.6 | (0.1) | 0.4 | (0.1) |
| Korea | 100.0 | (0.0) | 0.0 | (0.0) |
| Luxembourg | 63.9 | (0.6) | 36.1 | (0.6) |
| Mexico | 97.6 | (0.3) | 2.4 | (0.3) |
| Netherlands | 88.7 | (1.1) | 11.3 | (1.1) |
| New Zealand | 78.7 | (1.0) | 21.3 | (1.0) |
| Norway | 93.9 | (0.7) | 6.1 | (0.7) |
| Poland | 99.8 | (0.1) | 0.2 | (0.1) |
| Portugal | 94.1 | (0.8) | 5.9 | (0.8) |
| Slovak Republic | 99.5 | (0.1) | 0.5 | (0.1) |
| Spain | 93.1 | (0.7) | 6.9 | (0.7) |
| Sweden | 89.2 | (0.9) | 10.8 | (0.9) |
| Switzerland | 77.6 | (0.7) | 22.4 | (0.7) |
| Turkey | 98.5 | (0.4) | 1.5 | (0.4) |
| United Kingdom | 91.4 | (0.9) | 8.6 | (0.9) |
| United States | 84.8 | (1.2) | 15.2 | (1.2) |
| **OECD average** | 90.7 | (0.1) | 9.3 | (0.1) |
| **Partners** Argentina | 97.3 | (0.3) | 2.7 | (0.3) |
| Azerbaijan | 97.6 | (0.5) | 2.4 | (0.5) |
| Brazil | 97.6 | (0.2) | 2.4 | (0.2) |
| Bulgaria | 99.8 | (0.1) | 0.2 | (0.1) |
| Chile | 99.4 | (0.1) | 0.6 | (0.1) |
| Colombia | 99.6 | (0.1) | 0.4 | (0.1) |
| Croatia | 88.0 | (0.7) | 12.0 | (0.7) |
| Estonia | 88.4 | (0.6) | 11.6 | (0.6) |
| Hong Kong-China | 56.2 | (1.4) | 43.8 | (1.4) |
| Indonesia | 99.8 | (0.1) | 0.2 | (0.1) |
| Israel | 77.0 | (1.2) | 23.0 | (1.2) |
| Jordan | 83.2 | (0.9) | 16.8 | (0.9) |
| Kyrgyzstan | 97.4 | (0.4) | 2.6 | (0.4) |
| Latvia | 92.9 | (0.6) | 7.1 | (0.6) |
| Liechtenstein | 63.2 | (2.7) | 36.8 | (2.7) |
| Lithuania | 97.9 | (0.4) | 2.1 | (0.4) |
| Macao-China | 26.4 | (0.6) | 73.6 | (0.6) |
| Montenegro | 92.8 | (0.5) | 7.2 | (0.5) |
| Qatar | 59.5 | (0.5) | 40.5 | (0.5) |
| Romania | 99.9 | (0.0) | 0.1 | (0.0) |
| Russian Federation | 91.3 | (0.5) | 8.7 | (0.5) |
| Serbia | 91.0 | (0.5) | 9.0 | (0.5) |
| Slovenia | 89.7 | (0.5) | 10.3 | (0.5) |
| Chinese Taipei | 99.4 | (0.1) | 0.6 | (0.1) |
| Thailand | 99.7 | (0.1) | 0.3 | (0.1) |
| Tunisia | 99.2 | (0.1) | 0.8 | (0.1) |
| Uruguay | 99.6 | (0.1) | 0.4 | (0.1) |

© OECD 2011  Quality Time for Students: Learning In and Out of School

## Table 3.2 Percentage of students, by lower and upper secondary schools

| | Lower secondary school students | | Upper secondary school students | |
|---|---|---|---|---|
| | % | S.E. | % | S.E. |
| **OECD** | | | | |
| Australia | 80.1 | (0.6) | 19.9 | (0.6) |
| Austria | 6.7 | (0.7) | 93.3 | (0.7) |
| Belgium | 6.8 | (0.5) | 93.2 | (0.5) |
| Canada | 15.0 | (0.6) | 85.0 | (0.6) |
| Czech Republic | 50.4 | (1.5) | 49.6 | (1.5) |
| Denmark | 98.9 | (0.4) | 1.1 | (0.4) |
| Finland | 100.0 | (0.0) | 0.0 | (0.0) |
| France | 40.0 | (1.2) | 60.0 | (1.2) |
| Germany | 97.3 | (0.5) | 2.7 | (0.5) |
| Greece | 8.0 | (1.0) | 92.0 | (1.0) |
| Hungary | 7.7 | (0.9) | 92.3 | (0.9) |
| Iceland | 99.4 | (0.1) | 0.6 | (0.1) |
| Ireland | 61.3 | (0.9) | 38.7 | (0.9) |
| Italy | 1.7 | (0.5) | 98.3 | (0.5) |
| Japan | 0.0 | c | 100.0 | c |
| Korea | 2.0 | (0.6) | 98.0 | (0.6) |
| Luxembourg | 64.2 | (0.4) | 35.8 | (0.4) |
| Mexico | 44.5 | (2.1) | 55.5 | (2.1) |
| Netherlands | 73.5 | (1.0) | 26.5 | (1.0) |
| New Zealand | 6.2 | (0.4) | 93.8 | (0.4) |
| Norway | 99.5 | (0.3) | 0.5 | (0.3) |
| Poland | 99.4 | (0.1) | 0.6 | (0.1) |
| Portugal | 50.2 | (1.5) | 49.8 | (1.5) |
| Slovak Republic | 38.6 | (2.2) | 61.4 | (2.2) |
| Spain | 100.0 | (0.0) | 0.0 | (0.0) |
| Sweden | 97.8 | (0.3) | 2.2 | (0.3) |
| Switzerland | 82.8 | (1.3) | 17.2 | (1.3) |
| Turkey | 5.3 | (1.2) | 94.7 | (1.2) |
| United Kingdom | 0.5 | (0.1) | 99.5 | (0.1) |
| United States | 12.4 | (1.7) | 87.6 | (1.7) |
| **OECD average** | **50.0** | **(0.2)** | **51.7** | **(0.2)** |
| **Partners** | | | | |
| Argentina | 31.2 | (2.1) | 68.8 | (2.1) |
| Azerbaijan | 59.4 | (1.6) | 40.6 | (1.6) |
| Brazil | 33.6 | (1.7) | 66.4 | (1.7) |
| Bulgaria | 7.4 | (1.0) | 92.6 | (1.0) |
| Chile | 4.3 | (0.7) | 95.7 | (0.7) |
| Colombia | 40.8 | (1.9) | 59.2 | (1.9) |
| Croatia | 0.4 | (0.3) | 99.6 | (0.3) |
| Estonia | 98.2 | (0.2) | 1.8 | (0.2) |
| Hong Kong-China | 36.9 | (0.9) | 63.1 | (0.9) |
| Indonesia | 52.0 | (4.1) | 48.0 | (4.1) |
| Israel | 13.1 | (1.2) | 86.9 | (1.2) |
| Jordan | 100.0 | c | 0.0 | c |
| Kyrgyzstan | 75.5 | (1.4) | 24.5 | (1.4) |
| Latvia | 96.6 | (0.4) | 3.4 | (0.4) |
| Liechtenstein | 88.7 | (0.5) | 11.3 | (0.5) |
| Lithuania | 100.0 | (0.0) | 0.0 | (0.0) |
| Macao-China | 62.9 | (0.1) | 37.1 | (0.1) |
| Montenegro | 0.3 | (0.2) | 99.7 | (0.2) |
| Qatar | 21.6 | (0.1) | 78.4 | (0.1) |
| Romania | 100.0 | c | 0.0 | c |
| Russian Federation | 37.3 | (2.0) | 62.7 | (2.0) |
| Serbia | 1.9 | (0.6) | 98.1 | (0.6) |
| Slovenia | 3.7 | (0.3) | 96.3 | (0.3) |
| Chinese Taipei | 33.4 | (1.1) | 66.6 | (1.1) |
| Thailand | 31.8 | (1.1) | 68.2 | (1.1) |
| Tunisia | 49.2 | (1.7) | 50.8 | (1.7) |
| Uruguay | 34.6 | (1.5) | 65.4 | (1.5) |

## Table 3.3 Percentage of students, by public and private schools

| | | Public schools[1] | | Private schools[2] | |
|---|---|---|---|---|---|
| | | % | S.E. | % | S.E. |
| OECD | Australia | w | w | w | w |
| | Austria | 90.7 | (2.2) | 9.3 | (2.2) |
| | Belgium | w | w | w | w |
| | Canada | 92.7 | (0.6) | 7.3 | (0.6) |
| | Czech Republic | 93.4 | (2.7) | 6.6 | (2.7) |
| | Denmark | 76.0 | (3.1) | 24.0 | (3.1) |
| | Finland | 97.0 | (1.2) | 3.0 | (1.2) |
| | France | w | w | w | w |
| | Germany | 94.3 | (1.8) | 5.7 | (1.8) |
| | Greece | 94.8 | (1.2) | 5.2 | (1.2) |
| | Hungary | 83.7 | (3.3) | 16.3 | (3.3) |
| | Iceland | 98.9 | (0.1) | 1.1 | (0.1) |
| | Ireland | 39.7 | (1.3) | 60.3 | (1.3) |
| | Italy | 96.1 | (0.7) | 3.9 | (0.7) |
| | Japan | 69.1 | (1.3) | 30.9 | (1.3) |
| | Korea | 53.7 | (3.9) | 46.3 | (3.9) |
| | Luxembourg | 85.6 | (0.0) | 14.4 | (0.0) |
| | Mexico | 85.0 | (2.1) | 15.0 | (2.1) |
| | Netherlands | 32.3 | (4.3) | 67.7 | (4.3) |
| | New Zealand | 94.3 | (0.3) | 5.7 | (0.3) |
| | Norway | 98.1 | (0.9) | 1.9 | (0.9) |
| | Poland | 98.4 | (0.1) | 1.6 | (0.1) |
| | Portugal | 89.8 | (1.3) | 10.2 | (1.3) |
| | Slovak Republic | 92.3 | (1.9) | 7.7 | (1.9) |
| | Spain | 64.6 | (0.9) | 35.4 | (0.9) |
| | Sweden | 91.7 | (0.8) | 8.3 | (0.8) |
| | Switzerland | 95.0 | (0.6) | 5.0 | (0.6) |
| | Turkey | 97.7 | (1.4) | 2.3 | (1.4) |
| | United Kingdom | 92.4 | (0.7) | 7.6 | (0.7) |
| | United States | 92.2 | (1.1) | 7.8 | (1.1) |
| | **OECD average** | 82.9 | (0.3) | 17.1 | (0.3) |
| Partners | Argentina | 65.9 | (3.7) | 34.1 | (3.7) |
| | Azerbaijan | 99.1 | (0.4) | 0.9 | (0.4) |
| | Brazil | 86.4 | (1.2) | 13.6 | (1.2) |
| | Bulgaria | m | m | m | m |
| | Chile | 43.4 | (2.4) | 56.6 | (2.4) |
| | Colombia | 80.7 | (2.6) | 19.3 | (2.6) |
| | Croatia | 98.6 | (1.0) | 1.4 | (1.0) |
| | Estonia | 98.1 | (0.9) | 1.9 | (0.9) |
| | Hong Kong-China | 7.5 | (0.2) | 92.5 | (0.2) |
| | Indonesia | 60.1 | (3.5) | 39.9 | (3.5) |
| | Israel | 69.4 | (3.7) | 30.6 | (3.7) |
| | Jordan | 80.0 | (1.6) | 20.0 | (1.6) |
| | Kyrgyzstan | 98.5 | (0.7) | 1.5 | (0.7) |
| | Latvia | 100.0 | c | 0.0 | c |
| | Liechtenstein | 92.9 | (0.4) | 7.1 | (0.4) |
| | Lithuania | 99.3 | (0.7) | 0.7 | (0.7) |
| | Macao-China | 3.8 | (0.0) | 96.2 | (0.0) |
| | Montenegro | 99.8 | (0.0) | 0.2 | (0.0) |
| | Qatar | 83.5 | (0.1) | 16.5 | (0.1) |
| | Romania | 100.0 | c | 0.0 | c |
| | Russian Federation | 100.0 | c | 0.0 | c |
| | Serbia | 99.4 | (0.7) | 0.6 | (0.7) |
| | Slovenia | 97.7 | (0.0) | 2.3 | (0.0) |
| | Chinese Taipei | 64.9 | (2.4) | 35.1 | (2.4) |
| | Thailand | 83.5 | (0.7) | 16.5 | (0.7) |
| | Tunisia | 97.7 | (1.0) | 2.3 | (1.0) |
| | Uruguay | 84.9 | (0.8) | 15.1 | (0.8) |

1. Schools which are managed directly or indirectly by a public education authority, government agency, or governing board appointed by government or elected by public franchise.
2. Schools which are managed directly or indirectly by a non-government organisation.

© OECD 2011 Quality Time for Students: Learning In and Out of School

## Table 3.4 Percentage of students, by academic and vocational orientation of schools

| | Academic schools | | Vocational schools | |
|---|---|---|---|---|
| | % | S.E. | % | S.E. |
| Australia | 89.4 | (0.8) | 10.6 | (0.8) |
| Austria | 29.6 | (1.4) | 70.4 | (1.4) |
| Belgium | 52.6 | (1.4) | 47.4 | (1.4) |
| Canada | 100.0 | c | 0.0 | c |
| Czech Republic | 58.8 | (1.7) | 41.2 | (1.7) |
| Denmark | 100.0 | c | 0.0 | c |
| Finland | 100.0 | (0.0) | a | a |
| France | 90.7 | (0.8) | 9.3 | (0.8) |
| Germany | 97.6 | (0.5) | 2.4 | (0.5) |
| Greece | 86.3 | (1.5) | 13.7 | (1.5) |
| Hungary | 43.0 | (1.6) | 57.0 | (1.6) |
| Iceland | 99.9 | (0.0) | 0.1 | (0.0) |
| Ireland | 98.7 | (0.2) | 1.3 | (0.2) |
| Italy | 44.0 | (0.8) | 56.0 | (0.8) |
| Japan | 75.3 | (1.6) | 24.7 | (1.6) |
| Korea | 76.8 | (1.0) | 23.2 | (1.0) |
| Luxembourg | 87.0 | (0.3) | 13.0 | (0.3) |
| Mexico | 68.1 | (2.0) | 31.9 | (2.0) |
| Netherlands | 69.4 | (1.4) | 30.6 | (1.4) |
| New Zealand | 100.0 | c | 0.0 | c |
| Norway | 100.0 | c | 0.0 | c |
| Poland | 100.0 | c | 0.0 | c |
| Portugal | 86.0 | (1.1) | 14.0 | (1.1) |
| Slovak Republic | 56.9 | (2.4) | 43.1 | (2.4) |
| Spain | 100.0 | c | 0.0 | c |
| Sweden | 99.2 | (0.2) | 0.8 | (0.2) |
| Switzerland | 93.3 | (1.3) | 6.7 | (1.3) |
| Turkey | 59.4 | (2.0) | 40.6 | (2.0) |
| United Kingdom | 100.0 | c | 0.0 | c |
| United States | 100.0 | c | 0.0 | c |
| **OECD average** | **82.1** | **(0.2)** | **25.6** | **(0.3)** |
| Argentina | 97.6 | (0.8) | 2.4 | (0.8) |
| Azerbaijan | 99.0 | (0.5) | 1.0 | (0.5) |
| Brazil | 100.0 | c | 0.0 | c |
| Bulgaria | 52.9 | (2.6) | 47.1 | (2.6) |
| Chile | 97.1 | (0.3) | 2.9 | (0.3) |
| Colombia | 83.3 | (2.5) | 16.7 | (2.5) |
| Croatia | 27.8 | (0.8) | 72.2 | (0.8) |
| Estonia | 100.0 | c | 0.0 | c |
| Hong Kong-China | 92.8 | (2.1) | 7.2 | (2.1) |
| Indonesia | 82.6 | (4.2) | 17.4 | (4.2) |
| Israel | 81.7 | (3.0) | 18.3 | (3.0) |
| Jordan | 100.0 | c | 0.0 | c |
| Kyrgyzstan | 98.2 | (0.6) | 1.8 | (0.6) |
| Latvia | 96.6 | (0.4) | 3.4 | (0.4) |
| Liechtenstein | 100.0 | c | 0.0 | c |
| Lithuania | 99.8 | (0.2) | 0.2 | (0.2) |
| Macao-China | 98.7 | (0.0) | 1.3 | (0.0) |
| Montenegro | 32.0 | (0.2) | 68.0 | (0.2) |
| Qatar | 100.0 | c | 0.0 | c |
| Romania | 76.6 | (2.6) | 23.4 | (2.6) |
| Russian Federation | 86.4 | (2.2) | 13.6 | (2.2) |
| Serbia | 26.2 | (1.7) | 73.8 | (1.7) |
| Slovenia | 47.9 | (0.2) | 52.1 | (0.2) |
| Chinese Taipei | 64.5 | (1.9) | 35.5 | (1.9) |
| Thailand | 85.2 | (0.7) | 14.8 | (0.7) |
| Tunisia | 100.0 | c | 0.0 | c |
| Uruguay | 87.7 | (1.8) | 12.3 | (1.8) |

## Table 3.5  Percentage of students, by school location

| | Village (fewer than 3 000 people) | | Small town (3 000 to about 15 000 people) | | Town (15 000 to about 100 000 people) | | City (100 000 to about 1000 000 people) | | Large city (over 1 000 000 people) | |
|---|---|---|---|---|---|---|---|---|---|---|
| | % | S.E. | % | S.E. | % | S.E. | % | S.E. | % | S.E. |
| **OECD** | | | | | | | | | | |
| Australia | 6.7 | (1.4) | 9.5 | (1.6) | 23.2 | (2.4) | 21.8 | (2.1) | 38.7 | (2.4) |
| Austria | 12.2 | (2.1) | 33.2 | (3.3) | 22.3 | (3.1) | 16.0 | (2.5) | 16.4 | (2.3) |
| Belgium | 2.1 | (1.1) | 24.2 | (2.8) | 52.8 | (3.5) | 20.5 | (2.9) | 0.4 | (0.4) |
| Canada | 7.4 | (0.5) | 19.0 | (1.7) | 28.7 | (2.1) | 30.3 | (2.5) | 14.6 | (2.1) |
| Czech Republic | 12.0 | (1.9) | 28.1 | (3.7) | 40.8 | (4.3) | 11.7 | (2.7) | 7.5 | (1.7) |
| Denmark | 22.5 | (2.6) | 29.6 | (3.2) | 35.5 | (3.8) | 8.8 | (2.3) | 3.6 | (1.5) |
| Finland | 15.4 | (2.3) | 30.5 | (3.7) | 33.4 | (3.1) | 20.8 | (3.0) | 0.0 | c |
| France | w | w | w | w | w | w | w | w | w | w |
| Germany | 3.8 | (1.1) | 27.6 | (2.9) | 45.0 | (3.5) | 15.7 | (2.6) | 7.9 | (1.6) |
| Greece | 6.4 | (1.6) | 18.4 | (3.1) | 40.9 | (3.4) | 21.2 | (3.2) | 13.1 | (2.0) |
| Hungary | 2.6 | (0.6) | 16.8 | (2.8) | 37.3 | (3.6) | 24.6 | (3.4) | 18.7 | (2.2) |
| Iceland | 23.1 | (0.2) | 19.0 | (0.1) | 24.4 | (0.1) | 33.5 | (0.1) | 0.0 | c |
| Ireland | 26.8 | (3.2) | 27.2 | (3.4) | 18.9 | (3.0) | 9.1 | (2.6) | 18.0 | (2.8) |
| Italy | 1.1 | (0.4) | 20.2 | (2.1) | 50.2 | (3.3) | 19.6 | (2.1) | 8.9 | (1.6) |
| Japan | 0.0 | c | 5.8 | (1.7) | 29.1 | (3.4) | 40.6 | (3.6) | 24.5 | (3.3) |
| Korea | 2.8 | (1.3) | 2.0 | (0.9) | 10.2 | (1.5) | 35.4 | (2.8) | 49.6 | (2.4) |
| Luxembourg | 0.0 | c | 33.9 | (0.1) | 56.8 | (0.1) | 9.3 | (0.0) | 0.0 | c |
| Mexico | 16.6 | (1.9) | 16.7 | (2.0) | 17.8 | (1.4) | 26.3 | (1.9) | 22.6 | (2.3) |
| Netherlands | 2.3 | (1.0) | 16.3 | (3.0) | 55.6 | (3.8) | 25.9 | (3.4) | 0.0 | c |
| New Zealand | 6.6 | (1.5) | 13.0 | (2.3) | 26.9 | (3.1) | 26.2 | (2.9) | 27.3 | (2.3) |
| Norway | 30.6 | (3.0) | 35.5 | (3.7) | 22.3 | (3.2) | 11.6 | (2.3) | 0.0 | c |
| Poland | 29.9 | (2.3) | 25.9 | (2.8) | 20.3 | (2.1) | 22.5 | (1.1) | 1.3 | (0.9) |
| Portugal | 7.6 | (1.8) | 34.9 | (3.6) | 35.9 | (3.7) | 14.9 | (2.3) | 6.7 | (2.1) |
| Slovak Republic | 10.2 | (2.0) | 24.6 | (3.3) | 51.6 | (3.7) | 13.7 | (2.5) | 0.0 | c |
| Spain | 3.7 | (1.1) | 25.9 | (2.7) | 31.4 | (2.9) | 30.0 | (3.2) | 9.0 | (1.0) |
| Sweden | 15.0 | (2.8) | 28.0 | (2.8) | 35.4 | (3.4) | 16.7 | (2.1) | 4.9 | (0.9) |
| Switzerland | 12.6 | (1.9) | 44.6 | (2.8) | 30.0 | (2.6) | 12.9 | (1.5) | 0.0 | c |
| Turkey | 2.6 | (0.9) | 11.2 | (2.2) | 36.5 | (3.9) | 29.0 | (3.2) | 20.7 | (3.0) |
| United Kingdom | 5.0 | (1.4) | 22.9 | (2.8) | 40.5 | (3.6) | 18.5 | (2.5) | 13.0 | (2.8) |
| United States | 13.8 | (2.5) | 19.8 | (2.8) | 32.1 | (3.6) | 23.8 | (3.4) | 10.5 | (2.3) |
| **OECD average** | 45.5 | (0.2) | 35.9 | (0.7) | 45.5 | (0.2) | 35.9 | (0.7) | 35.9 | (0.7) |
| **Partners** | | | | | | | | | | |
| Argentina | 7.3 | (2.3) | 19.4 | (3.0) | 32.6 | (3.9) | 26.8 | (3.3) | 13.9 | (3.1) |
| Azerbaijan | 39.1 | (2.9) | 25.8 | (3.7) | 14.0 | (2.4) | 9.6 | (1.9) | 11.5 | (2.1) |
| Brazil | 6.8 | (1.3) | 19.2 | (1.8) | 33.4 | (2.9) | 23.9 | (2.1) | 16.6 | (2.0) |
| Bulgaria | 8.8 | (2.3) | 18.5 | (3.2) | 38.0 | (2.7) | 21.0 | (1.8) | 13.7 | (0.9) |
| Chile | 1.7 | (0.7) | 14.9 | (3.5) | 24.2 | (3.7) | 32.5 | (4.0) | 26.8 | (3.6) |
| Colombia | 6.2 | (1.7) | 23.4 | (4.8) | 21.7 | (4.9) | 22.7 | (3.5) | 26.0 | (3.8) |
| Croatia | 0.8 | (0.8) | 20.4 | (2.8) | 42.3 | (2.8) | 17.1 | (1.8) | 19.3 | (1.7) |
| Estonia | 27.4 | (2.4) | 17.9 | (2.2) | 26.6 | (2.3) | 28.1 | (1.9) | 0.0 | c |
| Hong Kong-China | a | a | a | a | a | a | a | a | a | a |
| Indonesia | 26.4 | (3.8) | 43.5 | (3.8) | 11.7 | (2.8) | 14.6 | (4.4) | 3.8 | (1.6) |
| Israel | 11.5 | (2.7) | 15.6 | (2.9) | 28.4 | (3.6) | 39.6 | (4.5) | 4.9 | (1.9) |
| Jordan | 13.4 | (2.4) | 24.3 | (3.0) | 22.6 | (3.3) | 21.3 | (3.0) | 18.4 | (2.7) |
| Kyrgyzstan | 56.2 | (2.2) | 20.6 | (1.9) | 9.6 | (1.6) | 11.9 | (1.6) | 1.8 | (1.0) |
| Latvia | 31.5 | (1.7) | 18.2 | (1.9) | 17.5 | (2.3) | 32.9 | (2.1) | 0.0 | c |
| Liechtenstein | 11.3 | (0.5) | 88.7 | (0.5) | 0.0 | c | 0.0 | c | 0.0 | c |
| Lithuania | 18.7 | (1.5) | 22.3 | (2.5) | 20.3 | (2.4) | 36.0 | (1.7) | 2.7 | (1.2) |
| Macao-China | 4.3 | (0.0) | 3.5 | (0.0) | 9.0 | (0.1) | 83.2 | (0.1) | 0.0 | c |
| Montenegro | 0.1 | (0.0) | 15.8 | (0.1) | 50.4 | (0.1) | 33.7 | (0.1) | 0.0 | c |
| Qatar | 9.6 | (0.1) | 35.9 | (0.1) | 28.6 | (0.1) | 25.1 | (0.1) | 0.8 | (0.0) |
| Romania | 3.7 | (1.0) | 16.8 | (2.5) | 29.4 | (4.0) | 41.8 | (5.7) | 8.3 | (2.3) |
| Russian Federation | 19.4 | (2.0) | 15.3 | (2.6) | 25.2 | (2.9) | 27.6 | (2.8) | 12.6 | (1.9) |
| Serbia | 0.4 | (0.2) | 10.7 | (1.8) | 49.9 | (3.4) | 20.2 | (2.4) | 18.9 | (1.4) |
| Slovenia | 1.9 | (0.3) | 11.7 | (0.4) | 49.1 | (0.3) | 37.2 | (0.2) | 0.0 | c |
| Chinese Taipei | 0.6 | (0.4) | 7.3 | (2.5) | 26.5 | (2.9) | 43.5 | (3.3) | 22.1 | (2.0) |
| Thailand | 25.0 | (2.9) | 22.0 | (3.4) | 27.5 | (3.3) | 20.6 | (2.9) | 4.9 | (1.5) |
| Tunisia | 10.3 | (2.7) | 17.8 | (3.4) | 55.0 | (3.9) | 13.5 | (3.2) | 3.3 | (1.3) |
| Uruguay | 7.1 | (1.7) | 15.7 | (2.0) | 36.5 | (2.3) | 7.7 | (1.5) | 33.0 | (2.0) |

© OECD 2011  Quality Time for Students: Learning In and Out of School

[Part 1/3]
## Table 3.6a Mean learning hours and allocation of total learning time in science, by gender

| | | Mean learning hours per week | | | | | | | | | | |
| | | Regular school lessons | | | | | | Out-of-school-time lessons | | | | |
| | | Male students | | Female students | | Difference (male-female) | | Male students | | Female students | | Difference (male-female) |
| | | Mean | S.E. | Mean | S.E. | Dif. | S.E. | Mean | S.E. | Mean | S.E. | Dif. | S.E. |
|---|---|---|---|---|---|---|---|---|---|---|---|---|---|
| OECD | Australia | 3.17 | (0.04) | 3.32 | (0.04) | **-0.15** | (0.05) | 0.41 | (0.01) | 0.31 | (0.01) | **0.12** | (0.02) |
| | Austria | 2.34 | (0.10) | 2.60 | (0.07) | **-0.26** | (0.10) | 0.26 | (0.02) | 0.17 | (0.02) | **0.12** | (0.03) |
| | Belgium | 2.49 | (0.06) | 2.76 | (0.05) | **-0.27** | (0.07) | 0.36 | (0.02) | 0.28 | (0.01) | **0.10** | (0.02) |
| | Canada | 3.82 | (0.05) | 4.18 | (0.05) | **-0.36** | (0.05) | 0.55 | (0.02) | 0.56 | (0.02) | -0.00 | (0.02) |
| | Czech Republic | 2.67 | (0.08) | 3.29 | (0.11) | **-0.62** | (0.14) | 0.49 | (0.02) | 0.60 | (0.03) | **-0.10** | (0.04) |
| | Denmark | 3.10 | (0.05) | 3.32 | (0.05) | **-0.22** | (0.05) | 0.80 | (0.03) | 0.74 | (0.03) | **0.07** | (0.03) |
| | Finland | 2.88 | (0.05) | 3.36 | (0.05) | **-0.48** | (0.06) | 0.36 | (0.02) | 0.29 | (0.01) | **0.08** | (0.02) |
| | France | 2.77 | (0.06) | 2.93 | (0.06) | **-0.16** | (0.07) | 0.54 | (0.02) | 0.56 | (0.02) | -0.01 | (0.03) |
| | Germany | 2.90 | (0.06) | 3.23 | (0.06) | **-0.34** | (0.07) | 0.55 | (0.03) | 0.46 | (0.02) | **0.09** | (0.03) |
| | Greece | 2.95 | (0.07) | 3.41 | (0.05) | **-0.46** | (0.08) | 1.99 | (0.05) | 1.99 | (0.05) | 0.06 | (0.06) |
| | Hungary | 2.38 | (0.05) | 2.64 | (0.05) | **-0.26** | (0.06) | 1.01 | (0.03) | 1.00 | (0.04) | 0.00 | (0.04) |
| | Iceland | 2.88 | (0.04) | 3.06 | (0.04) | **-0.19** | (0.05) | 0.33 | (0.02) | 0.25 | (0.01) | **0.09** | (0.03) |
| | Ireland | 2.53 | (0.05) | 2.55 | (0.05) | -0.03 | (0.06) | 0.36 | (0.02) | 0.28 | (0.02) | **0.09** | (0.03) |
| | Italy | 2.98 | (0.05) | 2.85 | (0.08) | **0.13** | (0.07) | 0.67 | (0.02) | 0.49 | (0.02) | **0.17** | (0.03) |
| | Japan | 2.74 | (0.06) | 2.66 | (0.07) | 0.08 | (0.07) | 0.32 | (0.02) | 0.20 | (0.01) | **0.13** | (0.02) |
| | Korea | 3.59 | (0.07) | 3.57 | (0.09) | 0.02 | (0.10) | 1.09 | (0.06) | 0.95 | (0.05) | 0.13 | (0.07) |
| | Luxembourg | 2.11 | (0.04) | 2.55 | (0.04) | **-0.44** | (0.06) | 0.56 | (0.02) | 0.45 | (0.02) | **0.14** | (0.03) |
| | Mexico | 3.14 | (0.05) | 3.17 | (0.04) | -0.02 | (0.06) | 1.07 | (0.03) | 0.95 | (0.03) | **0.12** | (0.04) |
| | Netherlands | 2.16 | (0.05) | 2.18 | (0.04) | -0.02 | (0.06) | 0.60 | (0.03) | 0.48 | (0.02) | **0.13** | (0.04) |
| | New Zealand | 3.96 | (0.06) | 4.14 | (0.05) | **-0.17** | (0.06) | 0.42 | (0.02) | 0.39 | (0.02) | 0.04 | (0.03) |
| | Norway | 2.59 | (0.03) | 2.69 | (0.03) | **-0.10** | (0.04) | 0.98 | (0.02) | 0.89 | (0.03) | **0.11** | (0.03) |
| | Poland | 2.43 | (0.04) | 3.00 | (0.05) | **-0.58** | (0.05) | 0.62 | (0.03) | 0.63 | (0.03) | 0.00 | (0.03) |
| | Portugal | 3.10 | (0.06) | 3.31 | (0.05) | **-0.21** | (0.07) | 0.61 | (0.02) | 0.65 | (0.03) | **-0.08** | (0.04) |
| | Slovak Republic | 2.22 | (0.09) | 2.70 | (0.08) | **-0.48** | (0.09) | 0.55 | (0.03) | 0.75 | (0.04) | **-0.18** | (0.04) |
| | Spain | 2.97 | (0.04) | 3.26 | (0.05) | **-0.28** | (0.05) | 0.67 | (0.03) | 0.69 | (0.03) | -0.03 | (0.03) |
| | Sweden | 2.76 | (0.04) | 2.85 | (0.03) | **-0.09** | (0.04) | 0.53 | (0.02) | 0.48 | (0.02) | 0.06 | (0.03) |
| | Switzerland | 2.19 | (0.04) | 2.55 | (0.06) | **-0.36** | (0.06) | 0.44 | (0.02) | 0.34 | (0.01) | **0.12** | (0.03) |
| | Turkey | 2.85 | (0.10) | 2.88 | (0.10) | -0.03 | (0.09) | 1.34 | (0.06) | 1.36 | (0.07) | -0.13 | (0.08) |
| | United Kingdom | 4.23 | (0.04) | 4.27 | (0.05) | -0.04 | (0.06) | 0.53 | (0.02) | 0.44 | (0.02) | **0.09** | (0.02) |
| | United States | 3.39 | (0.06) | 3.62 | (0.05) | **-0.23** | (0.06) | 0.82 | (0.03) | 0.75 | (0.03) | 0.09 | (0.05) |
| | **OECD average** | 2.88 | (0.01) | 3.10 | (0.01) | **-0.22** | (0.01) | 0.66 | (0.01) | 0.61 | (0.01) | **0.05** | (0.01) |
| Partners | Argentina | 2.08 | (0.06) | 2.42 | (0.10) | **-0.34** | (0.10) | 0.53 | (0.03) | 0.45 | (0.02) | **0.09** | (0.04) |
| | Azerbaijan | 2.76 | (0.07) | 2.92 | (0.06) | **-0.16** | (0.08) | 1.45 | (0.04) | 1.27 | (0.05) | **0.19** | (0.06) |
| | Brazil | 2.28 | (0.04) | 2.16 | (0.04) | **0.12** | (0.06) | 0.76 | (0.03) | 0.81 | (0.03) | -0.05 | (0.04) |
| | Bulgaria | 2.30 | (0.08) | 2.98 | (0.10) | **-0.68** | (0.08) | 1.00 | (0.03) | 0.96 | (0.04) | 0.08 | (0.06) |
| | Chile | 2.24 | (0.06) | 2.44 | (0.08) | **-0.20** | (0.08) | 0.80 | (0.02) | 0.86 | (0.02) | -0.05 | (0.03) |
| | Colombia | 3.47 | (0.10) | 3.53 | (0.15) | -0.07 | (0.12) | 0.91 | (0.04) | 0.99 | (0.05) | -0.08 | (0.07) |
| | Croatia | 1.83 | (0.05) | 2.20 | (0.06) | **-0.36** | (0.06) | 0.43 | (0.03) | 0.43 | (0.02) | 0.06 | (0.04) |
| | Estonia | 2.97 | (0.05) | 3.58 | (0.06) | **-0.61** | (0.06) | 0.79 | (0.03) | 0.73 | (0.03) | 0.07 | (0.04) |
| | Hong Kong-China | 3.39 | (0.08) | 2.91 | (0.06) | **0.48** | (0.09) | 0.99 | (0.04) | 0.77 | (0.03) | **0.14** | (0.06) |
| | Indonesia | 3.22 | (0.10) | 3.24 | (0.09) | -0.02 | (0.11) | 1.01 | (0.05) | 1.08 | (0.04) | -0.11 | (0.06) |
| | Israel | 2.23 | (0.07) | 2.62 | (0.08) | **-0.39** | (0.10) | 1.01 | (0.04) | 0.94 | (0.04) | 0.11 | (0.06) |
| | Jordan | 2.86 | (0.07) | 3.61 | (0.07) | **-0.75** | (0.10) | 1.68 | (0.05) | 1.37 | (0.05) | **0.33** | (0.07) |
| | Kyrgyzstan | 1.87 | (0.07) | 2.27 | (0.08) | **-0.40** | (0.07) | 1.27 | (0.04) | 1.44 | (0.04) | **-0.14** | (0.05) |
| | Latvia | 2.58 | (0.07) | 3.12 | (0.06) | **-0.55** | (0.06) | 0.70 | (0.03) | 0.60 | (0.03) | **0.13** | (0.04) |
| | Liechtenstein | 2.50 | (0.14) | 2.62 | (0.11) | -0.12 | (0.20) | 0.59 | (0.10) | 0.45 | (0.06) | 0.13 | (0.11) |
| | Lithuania | 2.37 | (0.05) | 3.02 | (0.05) | **-0.65** | (0.06) | 0.57 | (0.02) | 0.56 | (0.02) | 0.02 | (0.03) |
| | Macao-China | 3.68 | (0.05) | 3.81 | (0.05) | -0.13 | (0.07) | 1.07 | (0.04) | 0.92 | (0.04) | **0.16** | (0.06) |
| | Montenegro | 2.60 | (0.06) | 3.06 | (0.05) | **-0.46** | (0.08) | 1.05 | (0.03) | 1.06 | (0.03) | 0.04 | (0.05) |
| | Qatar | 2.52 | (0.05) | 2.80 | (0.04) | **-0.28** | (0.06) | 1.62 | (0.03) | 1.35 | (0.03) | **0.27** | (0.05) |
| | Romania | 2.14 | (0.07) | 2.38 | (0.06) | **-0.25** | (0.06) | 1.08 | (0.04) | 0.98 | (0.04) | **0.14** | (0.06) |
| | Russian Federation | 3.46 | (0.08) | 3.97 | (0.10) | **-0.51** | (0.07) | 1.13 | (0.04) | 1.11 | (0.04) | 0.02 | (0.05) |
| | Serbia | 2.55 | (0.07) | 3.18 | (0.06) | **-0.63** | (0.08) | 0.81 | (0.03) | 0.76 | (0.03) | **0.11** | (0.04) |
| | Slovenia | 2.34 | (0.05) | 3.27 | (0.04) | **-0.92** | (0.07) | 0.73 | (0.03) | 0.70 | (0.03) | 0.07 | (0.04) |
| | Chinese Taipei | 2.94 | (0.06) | 2.84 | (0.07) | 0.10 | (0.08) | 0.83 | (0.03) | 0.72 | (0.03) | **0.09** | (0.03) |
| | Thailand | 3.64 | (0.06) | 3.93 | (0.06) | **-0.29** | (0.09) | 0.96 | (0.05) | 0.87 | (0.04) | 0.09 | (0.06) |
| | Tunisia | 2.48 | (0.07) | 2.75 | (0.06) | **-0.26** | (0.07) | 1.89 | (0.04) | 1.96 | (0.04) | -0.06 | (0.06) |
| | Uruguay | 2.21 | (0.06) | 2.58 | (0.05) | **-0.37** | (0.07) | 0.59 | (0.02) | 0.63 | (0.03) | -0.02 | (0.04) |

*Note*: Values that are statistically significant at the 5% level (p < 0.05) are indicated in bold.

[Part 2/3]
## Table 3.6a   Mean learning hours and allocation of total learning time in science, by gender

| | | Mean learning hours per week | | | | | | | | | |
| | **Individual study** | | | | | | **Total learning hours** | | | | |
| | Male students | | Female students | | Difference (male-female) | | Male students | | Female students | | Difference (male-female) |
| | Mean | S.E. | Mean | S.E. | Dif. | S.E. | Mean | S.E. | Mean | S.E. | Dif. | S.E. |
|---|---|---|---|---|---|---|---|---|---|---|---|---|
| Australia | 1.17 | (0.03) | 1.18 | (0.03) | -0.02 | (0.03) | 4.74 | (0.06) | 4.80 | (0.06) | -0.06 | (0.08) |
| Austria | 1.27 | (0.05) | 1.28 | (0.04) | -0.01 | (0.05) | 3.88 | (0.14) | 4.05 | (0.09) | -0.16 | (0.14) |
| Belgium | 1.14 | (0.03) | 1.37 | (0.03) | **-0.24** | (0.04) | 3.99 | (0.09) | 4.41 | (0.07) | **-0.42** | (0.11) |
| Canada | 1.35 | (0.03) | 1.76 | (0.03) | **-0.41** | (0.04) | 5.75 | (0.07) | 6.50 | (0.07) | **-0.75** | (0.09) |
| Czech Republic | 0.89 | (0.03) | 1.15 | (0.05) | **-0.26** | (0.05) | 4.03 | (0.11) | 5.03 | (0.17) | **-1.00** | (0.20) |
| Denmark | 1.07 | (0.03) | 1.11 | (0.03) | -0.04 | (0.03) | 4.96 | (0.08) | 5.16 | (0.08) | **-0.20** | (0.09) |
| Finland | 0.97 | (0.02) | 1.17 | (0.03) | **-0.19** | (0.03) | 4.22 | (0.07) | 4.81 | (0.08) | **-0.60** | (0.08) |
| France | 1.22 | (0.05) | 1.39 | (0.04) | **-0.17** | (0.05) | 4.54 | (0.11) | 4.89 | (0.09) | **-0.35** | (0.13) |
| Germany | 1.61 | (0.04) | 1.80 | (0.03) | **-0.19** | (0.04) | 5.07 | (0.09) | 5.50 | (0.08) | **-0.43** | (0.10) |
| Greece | 1.85 | (0.05) | 1.84 | (0.04) | 0.01 | (0.06) | 6.81 | (0.13) | 7.22 | (0.12) | **-0.41** | (0.14) |
| Hungary | 1.49 | (0.04) | 1.72 | (0.04) | **-0.23** | (0.05) | 4.87 | (0.10) | 5.35 | (0.10) | **-0.48** | (0.11) |
| Iceland | 1.14 | (0.03) | 1.19 | (0.02) | -0.06 | (0.04) | 4.34 | (0.06) | 4.51 | (0.05) | -0.16 | (0.09) |
| Ireland | 1.20 | (0.03) | 1.21 | (0.04) | -0.02 | (0.05) | 4.08 | (0.09) | 4.03 | (0.09) | 0.05 | (0.11) |
| Italy | 2.04 | (0.04) | 2.15 | (0.05) | **-0.11** | (0.04) | 5.70 | (0.09) | 5.47 | (0.13) | **0.23** | (0.11) |
| Japan | 0.72 | (0.02) | 0.66 | (0.03) | **0.07** | (0.03) | 3.78 | (0.08) | 3.51 | (0.09) | **0.27** | (0.09) |
| Korea | 1.23 | (0.09) | 1.21 | (0.04) | 0.01 | (0.08) | 5.93 | (0.20) | 5.74 | (0.15) | 0.19 | (0.22) |
| Luxembourg | 1.16 | (0.03) | 1.33 | (0.03) | **-0.17** | (0.05) | 3.85 | (0.07) | 4.32 | (0.06) | **-0.47** | (0.10) |
| Mexico | 2.05 | (0.04) | 2.19 | (0.03) | **-0.14** | (0.05) | 6.21 | (0.10) | 6.27 | (0.07) | -0.06 | (0.10) |
| Netherlands | 1.18 | (0.03) | 1.24 | (0.03) | -0.06 | (0.04) | 3.93 | (0.08) | 3.87 | (0.08) | 0.06 | (0.10) |
| New Zealand | 1.20 | (0.03) | 1.35 | (0.04) | **-0.16** | (0.05) | 5.60 | (0.09) | 5.87 | (0.08) | **-0.27** | (0.11) |
| Norway | 1.20 | (0.02) | 1.25 | (0.03) | -0.05 | (0.03) | 4.76 | (0.06) | 4.83 | (0.07) | -0.08 | (0.08) |
| Poland | 1.66 | (0.03) | 2.37 | (0.03) | **-0.71** | (0.04) | 4.71 | (0.07) | 6.00 | (0.09) | **-1.29** | (0.09) |
| Portugal | 1.85 | (0.05) | 2.31 | (0.04) | **-0.46** | (0.06) | 5.57 | (0.10) | 6.26 | (0.09) | **-0.69** | (0.12) |
| Slovak Republic | 1.22 | (0.04) | 1.57 | (0.06) | **-0.36** | (0.06) | 4.00 | (0.13) | 5.04 | (0.15) | **-1.04** | (0.15) |
| Spain | 1.53 | (0.03) | 1.95 | (0.04) | **-0.42** | (0.03) | 5.20 | (0.08) | 5.91 | (0.09) | **-0.71** | (0.09) |
| Sweden | 1.09 | (0.03) | 1.21 | (0.03) | **-0.12** | (0.03) | 4.37 | (0.06) | 4.53 | (0.06) | **-0.16** | (0.07) |
| Switzerland | 1.06 | (0.02) | 1.18 | (0.03) | **-0.12** | (0.04) | 3.69 | (0.07) | 4.05 | (0.08) | **-0.36** | (0.10) |
| Turkey | 1.55 | (0.05) | 1.75 | (0.07) | **-0.19** | (0.06) | 5.68 | (0.19) | 5.96 | (0.21) | -0.27 | (0.18) |
| United Kingdom | 1.40 | (0.03) | 1.49 | (0.03) | **-0.09** | (0.03) | 6.16 | (0.06) | 6.20 | (0.07) | -0.04 | (0.08) |
| United States | 1.56 | (0.03) | 1.81 | (0.04) | **-0.25** | (0.05) | 5.83 | (0.08) | 6.18 | (0.08) | **-0.35** | (0.10) |
| **OECD average** | 1.34 | (0.01) | 1.51 | (0.01) | **-0.17** | (0.01) | 4.88 | (0.02) | 5.21 | (0.02) | **-0.33** | (0.02) |
| Argentina | 1.40 | (0.05) | 1.76 | (0.05) | **-0.37** | (0.05) | 3.98 | (0.10) | 4.61 | (0.13) | **-0.63** | (0.15) |
| Azerbaijan | 2.48 | (0.05) | 2.80 | (0.06) | **-0.32** | (0.06) | 6.64 | (0.11) | 7.03 | (0.14) | **-0.39** | (0.15) |
| Brazil | 1.60 | (0.03) | 1.79 | (0.04) | **-0.19** | (0.05) | 4.64 | (0.07) | 4.75 | (0.08) | -0.11 | (0.10) |
| Bulgaria | 1.76 | (0.06) | 2.26 | (0.08) | **-0.50** | (0.07) | 5.09 | (0.12) | 6.22 | (0.18) | **-1.13** | (0.16) |
| Chile | 1.43 | (0.03) | 1.63 | (0.04) | **-0.20** | (0.05) | 4.50 | (0.08) | 4.93 | (0.12) | **-0.44** | (0.14) |
| Colombia | 1.68 | (0.05) | 1.95 | (0.05) | **-0.28** | (0.07) | 6.05 | (0.15) | 6.48 | (0.24) | -0.43 | (0.23) |
| Croatia | 1.25 | (0.04) | 1.67 | (0.05) | **-0.43** | (0.05) | 3.53 | (0.10) | 4.31 | (0.11) | **-0.78** | (0.11) |
| Estonia | 1.36 | (0.04) | 1.73 | (0.03) | **-0.37** | (0.05) | 5.12 | (0.09) | 6.04 | (0.08) | **-0.92** | (0.12) |
| Hong Kong-China | 1.54 | (0.04) | 1.35 | (0.05) | **0.19** | (0.07) | 5.91 | (0.13) | 5.01 | (0.13) | **0.90** | (0.18) |
| Indonesia | 1.64 | (0.04) | 1.93 | (0.04) | **-0.30** | (0.05) | 5.86 | (0.12) | 6.24 | (0.15) | **-0.38** | (0.15) |
| Israel | 1.36 | (0.06) | 1.35 | (0.04) | 0.01 | (0.07) | 4.60 | (0.14) | 4.89 | (0.13) | -0.29 | (0.18) |
| Jordan | 2.43 | (0.04) | 2.85 | (0.07) | **-0.42** | (0.08) | 6.95 | (0.11) | 7.82 | (0.13) | **-0.87** | (0.16) |
| Kyrgyzstan | 1.88 | (0.05) | 2.35 | (0.05) | **-0.47** | (0.07) | 5.15 | (0.11) | 6.03 | (0.11) | **-0.88** | (0.13) |
| Latvia | 1.57 | (0.04) | 2.02 | (0.05) | **-0.45** | (0.06) | 4.84 | (0.10) | 5.73 | (0.11) | **-0.88** | (0.12) |
| Liechtenstein | 1.19 | (0.11) | 1.20 | (0.08) | -0.01 | (0.14) | 4.30 | (0.21) | 4.27 | (0.16) | 0.03 | (0.31) |
| Lithuania | 1.47 | (0.04) | 1.91 | (0.04) | **-0.43** | (0.05) | 4.41 | (0.08) | 5.47 | (0.08) | **-1.05** | (0.10) |
| Macao-China | 1.33 | (0.03) | 1.42 | (0.03) | **-0.09** | (0.04) | 6.07 | (0.08) | 6.14 | (0.09) | -0.06 | (0.12) |
| Montenegro | 2.01 | (0.04) | 2.40 | (0.04) | **-0.38** | (0.06) | 5.68 | (0.10) | 6.49 | (0.10) | **-0.82** | (0.15) |
| Qatar | 2.01 | (0.04) | 2.06 | (0.03) | -0.04 | (0.05) | 6.19 | (0.09) | 6.22 | (0.08) | -0.03 | (0.12) |
| Romania | 1.53 | (0.05) | 1.70 | (0.07) | -0.17 | (0.07) | 4.74 | (0.11) | 5.01 | (0.15) | -0.27 | (0.14) |
| Russian Federation | 2.57 | (0.07) | 3.14 | (0.06) | **-0.57** | (0.06) | 7.15 | (0.15) | 8.25 | (0.15) | **-1.10** | (0.13) |
| Serbia | 1.49 | (0.05) | 1.93 | (0.05) | **-0.44** | (0.06) | 4.85 | (0.11) | 5.86 | (0.10) | **-1.01** | (0.13) |
| Slovenia | 1.34 | (0.03) | 1.72 | (0.03) | **-0.38** | (0.04) | 4.44 | (0.08) | 5.68 | (0.06) | **-1.24** | (0.11) |
| Chinese Taipei | 1.30 | (0.04) | 1.18 | (0.04) | **0.12** | (0.04) | 5.11 | (0.10) | 4.75 | (0.13) | **0.36** | (0.13) |
| Thailand | 1.64 | (0.05) | 1.92 | (0.04) | **-0.28** | (0.06) | 6.24 | (0.11) | 6.73 | (0.11) | **-0.49** | (0.18) |
| Tunisia | 2.48 | (0.06) | 2.73 | (0.04) | **-0.25** | (0.07) | 6.83 | (0.14) | 7.42 | (0.11) | **-0.59** | (0.16) |
| Uruguay | 1.11 | (0.04) | 1.51 | (0.04) | **-0.40** | (0.05) | 3.94 | (0.09) | 4.73 | (0.10) | **-0.79** | (0.12) |

*Note:* Values that are statistically significant at the 5% level (p < 0.05) are indicated in bold.

© OECD 2011  Quality Time for Students: Learning In and Out of School

[Part 3/3]
## Table 3.6a Mean learning hours and allocation of total learning time in science, by gender

| | Allocation of total learning time in science for | | | | | | | | | | | | | | | | | |
| | Regular school lessons | | | | | | Out-of-school-time lessons | | | | | | Individual study | | | | | |
| | Male students | | Female students | | Difference (male-female) | | Male students | | Female students | | Difference (male-female) | | Male students | | Female students | | Difference (male-female) | |
| | % | S.E. | % | S.E. | Dif. | S.E. | % | S.E. | % | S.E. | Dif. | S.E. | % | S.E. | % | S.E. | Dif. | S.E. |
|---|---|---|---|---|---|---|---|---|---|---|---|---|---|---|---|---|---|---|
| Australia | 70.3 | (0.4) | 71.6 | (0.3) | -1.4 | (0.5) | 7.2 | (0.2) | 5.3 | (0.2) | 1.9 | (0.2) | 22.6 | (0.3) | 23.1 | (0.3) | -0.5 | (0.4) |
| Austria | 63.0 | (0.9) | 65.1 | (0.8) | -2.0 | (1.1) | 5.2 | (0.3) | 3.3 | (0.3) | 1.8 | (0.4) | 31.8 | (0.8) | 31.6 | (0.7) | 0.2 | (0.9) |
| Belgium | 63.3 | (0.5) | 63.7 | (0.4) | -0.4 | (0.6) | 7.8 | (0.3) | 5.4 | (0.2) | 2.5 | (0.4) | 28.9 | (0.4) | 31.0 | (0.4) | -2.1 | (0.5) |
| Canada | 67.3 | (0.4) | 65.3 | (0.5) | 1.9 | (0.6) | 9.0 | (0.3) | 8.0 | (0.2) | 1.0 | (0.3) | 23.7 | (0.4) | 26.7 | (0.4) | -2.9 | (0.5) |
| Czech Republic | 70.1 | (1.0) | 67.1 | (0.6) | 3.0 | (1.1) | 9.6 | (0.6) | 10.3 | (0.4) | -0.7 | (0.8) | 20.4 | (0.6) | 22.7 | (0.6) | -2.3 | (0.7) |
| Denmark | 66.2 | (0.6) | 67.1 | (0.6) | -0.9 | (0.7) | 13.9 | (0.3) | 12.2 | (0.3) | 1.6 | (0.4) | 19.9 | (0.5) | 20.6 | (0.4) | -0.7 | (0.5) |
| Finland | 70.8 | (0.6) | 71.1 | (0.4) | -0.3 | (0.7) | 6.9 | (0.3) | 5.0 | (0.2) | 2.0 | (0.3) | 22.3 | (0.4) | 23.9 | (0.3) | -1.6 | (0.5) |
| France | 63.9 | (0.6) | 61.9 | (0.6) | 2.0 | (0.8) | 11.1 | (0.4) | 10.5 | (0.4) | 0.7 | (0.5) | 24.9 | (0.6) | 27.6 | (0.5) | -2.6 | (0.7) |
| Germany | 57.3 | (0.8) | 58.6 | (0.6) | -1.3 | (0.9) | 9.5 | (0.5) | 7.5 | (0.3) | 2.1 | (0.5) | 33.2 | (0.6) | 33.9 | (0.4) | -0.8 | (0.7) |
| Greece | 45.6 | (0.8) | 50.9 | (0.6) | -5.3 | (0.9) | 27.5 | (0.6) | 25.0 | (0.5) | 2.5 | (0.7) | 26.9 | (0.6) | 24.0 | (0.5) | 2.9 | (0.7) |
| Hungary | 51.4 | (0.7) | 51.7 | (0.7) | -0.3 | (0.8) | 18.9 | (0.6) | 16.8 | (0.5) | 2.1 | (0.6) | 29.8 | (0.6) | 31.5 | (0.4) | -1.8 | (0.8) |
| Iceland | 69.2 | (0.5) | 71.0 | (0.5) | -1.8 | (0.7) | 6.0 | (0.3) | 4.2 | (0.2) | 1.8 | (0.4) | 24.8 | (0.4) | 24.8 | (0.4) | -0.0 | (0.5) |
| Ireland | 65.5 | (0.6) | 66.9 | (0.6) | -1.4 | (0.8) | 6.9 | (0.4) | 5.4 | (0.3) | 1.4 | (0.5) | 27.6 | (0.5) | 27.6 | (0.5) | -0.0 | (0.7) |
| Italy | 53.9 | (0.4) | 54.1 | (0.4) | -0.1 | (0.6) | 10.7 | (0.3) | 7.6 | (0.2) | 3.1 | (0.4) | 35.4 | (0.4) | 38.3 | (0.3) | -2.9 | (0.5) |
| Japan | 77.6 | (0.5) | 79.2 | (0.6) | -1.6 | (0.6) | 6.2 | (0.3) | 4.2 | (0.3) | 2.0 | (0.4) | 16.2 | (0.4) | 16.6 | (0.4) | -0.4 | (0.6) |
| Korea | 67.2 | (0.9) | 67.7 | (0.8) | -0.5 | (1.1) | 14.6 | (0.5) | 13.0 | (0.6) | 1.6 | (0.8) | 18.2 | (0.6) | 19.3 | (0.5) | -1.1 | (0.7) |
| Luxembourg | 58.7 | (0.5) | 61.0 | (0.6) | -2.3 | (0.8) | 11.8 | (0.4) | 8.2 | (0.3) | 3.6 | (0.5) | 29.5 | (0.5) | 30.8 | (0.5) | -1.3 | (0.8) |
| Mexico | 48.6 | (0.5) | 48.4 | (0.5) | 0.2 | (0.6) | 16.1 | (0.4) | 13.9 | (0.4) | 2.2 | (0.5) | 35.3 | (0.5) | 37.7 | (0.4) | -2.4 | (0.5) |
| Netherlands | 55.8 | (0.8) | 57.0 | (0.7) | -1.2 | (0.9) | 14.0 | (0.5) | 11.0 | (0.4) | 3.0 | (0.7) | 30.1 | (0.5) | 32.0 | (0.5) | -1.8 | (0.7) |
| New Zealand | 73.7 | (0.5) | 72.6 | (0.5) | 1.1 | (0.7) | 6.4 | (0.3) | 6.0 | (0.3) | 0.4 | (0.4) | 19.9 | (0.3) | 21.4 | (0.4) | -1.5 | (0.5) |
| Norway | 58.9 | (0.6) | 60.3 | (0.7) | -1.4 | (0.8) | 18.0 | (0.4) | 15.7 | (0.4) | 2.2 | (0.5) | 23.1 | (0.3) | 23.9 | (0.4) | -0.8 | (0.5) |
| Poland | 54.1 | (0.6) | 52.3 | (0.4) | 1.8 | (0.6) | 11.5 | (0.4) | 9.1 | (0.3) | 2.5 | (0.4) | 34.3 | (0.5) | 38.7 | (0.4) | -4.3 | (0.5) |
| Portugal | 56.1 | (0.6) | 53.2 | (0.6) | 2.9 | (0.7) | 9.6 | (0.4) | 9.0 | (0.4) | 0.6 | (0.5) | 34.3 | (0.6) | 37.8 | (0.5) | -3.5 | (0.7) |
| Slovak Republic | 60.2 | (0.8) | 57.3 | (0.7) | 2.9 | (0.9) | 11.1 | (0.6) | 12.3 | (0.5) | -1.1 | (0.6) | 28.7 | (0.6) | 30.4 | (0.6) | -1.8 | (0.8) |
| Spain | 59.5 | (0.5) | 58.4 | (0.4) | 1.1 | (0.6) | 11.5 | (0.4) | 9.8 | (0.4) | 1.7 | (0.4) | 29.0 | (0.4) | 31.8 | (0.4) | -2.8 | (0.5) |
| Sweden | 67.0 | (0.8) | 66.3 | (0.5) | 0.7 | (0.8) | 9.7 | (0.3) | 8.6 | (0.4) | 1.1 | (0.6) | 23.3 | (0.6) | 25.0 | (0.5) | -1.8 | (0.5) |
| Switzerland | 61.1 | (0.5) | 63.0 | (0.5) | -1.9 | (0.7) | 9.5 | (0.3) | 7.0 | (0.3) | 2.5 | (0.4) | 29.3 | (0.4) | 29.9 | (0.4) | -0.6 | (0.6) |
| Turkey | 52.4 | (0.7) | 49.8 | (0.9) | 2.6 | (1.2) | 20.9 | (0.5) | 21.0 | (0.7) | -0.2 | (0.9) | 26.8 | (0.5) | 29.2 | (0.7) | -2.4 | (0.9) |
| United Kingdom | 70.7 | (0.4) | 70.7 | (0.4) | -0.0 | (0.5) | 7.4 | (0.3) | 6.1 | (0.2) | 1.3 | (0.3) | 21.9 | (0.4) | 23.2 | (0.4) | -1.2 | (0.4) |
| United States | 58.4 | (0.7) | 58.7 | (0.6) | -0.2 | (0.7) | 13.6 | (0.7) | 11.5 | (0.4) | 2.1 | (0.7) | 28.0 | (0.4) | 29.9 | (0.5) | -1.9 | (0.6) |
| **OECD average** | 61.9 | (0.1) | 62.1 | (0.1) | -0.1 | (0.1) | 11.4 | (0.1) | 9.8 | (0.1) | 1.6 | (0.1) | 26.7 | (0.1) | 28.2 | (0.1) | -1.5 | (0.1) |
| Argentina | 53.2 | (1.0) | 53.1 | (1.0) | 0.1 | (1.2) | 11.6 | (0.7) | 7.9 | (0.5) | 3.7 | (0.9) | 35.2 | (0.8) | 39.0 | (0.9) | -3.8 | (1.1) |
| Azerbaijan | 41.6 | (0.8) | 44.6 | (0.7) | -2.9 | (1.0) | 21.8 | (0.6) | 16.8 | (0.5) | 5.0 | (0.7) | 36.6 | (0.5) | 38.6 | (0.6) | -2.0 | (0.7) |
| Brazil | 52.9 | (0.6) | 48.1 | (0.6) | 4.8 | (0.8) | 13.6 | (0.5) | 14.5 | (0.5) | -0.9 | (0.7) | 33.5 | (0.5) | 37.4 | (0.5) | -3.9 | (0.7) |
| Bulgaria | 47.4 | (1.0) | 50.2 | (0.7) | -2.8 | (1.1) | 18.5 | (0.8) | 14.0 | (0.6) | 4.5 | (0.8) | 34.1 | (0.6) | 35.8 | (0.5) | -1.7 | (0.8) |
| Chile | 49.0 | (0.6) | 49.1 | (0.7) | -0.1 | (0.7) | 16.6 | (0.5) | 16.2 | (0.5) | 0.4 | (0.6) | 34.5 | (0.5) | 34.8 | (0.5) | -0.3 | (0.7) |
| Colombia | 59.6 | (0.8) | 58.3 | (0.7) | 1.3 | (1.0) | 13.3 | (0.5) | 12.9 | (0.4) | 0.4 | (0.6) | 27.1 | (0.6) | 28.8 | (0.6) | -1.7 | (0.8) |
| Croatia | 55.1 | (0.8) | 54.0 | (0.6) | 1.1 | (0.9) | 11.1 | (0.6) | 8.8 | (0.4) | 2.3 | (0.7) | 33.8 | (0.6) | 37.2 | (0.6) | -3.4 | (0.8) |
| Estonia | 61.1 | (0.6) | 61.9 | (0.6) | -0.8 | (0.7) | 14.1 | (0.5) | 11.1 | (0.4) | 3.0 | (0.6) | 24.9 | (0.5) | 27.0 | (0.3) | -2.1 | (0.6) |
| Hong Kong-China | 60.3 | (0.8) | 61.7 | (0.6) | -1.5 | (0.9) | 14.9 | (0.5) | 12.8 | (0.5) | 2.1 | (0.6) | 24.9 | (0.5) | 25.5 | (0.5) | -0.6 | (0.7) |
| Indonesia | 56.4 | (1.3) | 52.7 | (0.7) | 3.7 | (1.2) | 15.3 | (1.0) | 15.9 | (0.5) | -0.6 | (0.8) | 28.4 | (0.5) | 31.4 | (0.5) | -3.1 | (0.6) |
| Israel | 49.4 | (1.1) | 58.8 | (0.8) | -9.4 | (1.4) | 20.6 | (0.6) | 16.2 | (0.5) | 4.4 | (0.8) | 30.0 | (0.8) | 25.0 | (0.6) | 5.0 | (1.0) |
| Jordan | 39.0 | (0.9) | 46.4 | (0.7) | -7.5 | (1.1) | 24.5 | (0.7) | 16.5 | (0.5) | 8.1 | (0.8) | 36.5 | (0.6) | 37.1 | (0.6) | -0.6 | (0.8) |
| Kyrgyzstan | 35.2 | (0.8) | 35.6 | (0.7) | -0.5 | (0.9) | 27.0 | (0.8) | 24.9 | (0.6) | 2.1 | (0.9) | 37.8 | (0.7) | 39.5 | (0.6) | -1.6 | (1.1) |
| Latvia | 56.1 | (0.8) | 56.1 | (0.6) | 0.0 | (1.0) | 12.1 | (0.5) | 8.9 | (0.4) | 3.3 | (0.6) | 31.7 | (0.6) | 35.0 | (0.5) | -3.3 | (0.8) |
| Liechtenstein | 61.9 | (2.4) | 61.7 | (1.4) | 0.2 | (2.7) | 11.2 | (1.6) | 9.3 | (1.2) | 1.9 | (2.0) | 26.9 | (1.9) | 29.0 | (1.4) | -2.1 | (2.0) |
| Lithuania | 56.9 | (0.7) | 57.3 | (0.5) | -0.4 | (0.9) | 11.5 | (0.4) | 8.7 | (0.3) | 2.8 | (0.5) | 31.6 | (0.5) | 34.0 | (0.4) | -2.4 | (0.7) |
| Macao-China | 64.2 | (0.6) | 65.2 | (0.5) | -1.0 | (0.8) | 15.9 | (0.4) | 13.1 | (0.5) | 2.8 | (0.6) | 19.9 | (0.5) | 21.6 | (0.4) | -1.8 | (0.6) |
| Montenegro | 46.1 | (0.7) | 47.5 | (0.5) | -1.5 | (0.8) | 17.6 | (0.5) | 14.6 | (0.4) | 3.0 | (0.7) | 36.3 | (0.6) | 37.9 | (0.6) | -1.6 | (0.8) |
| Qatar | 36.9 | (0.5) | 44.2 | (0.5) | -7.2 | (0.7) | 28.2 | (0.5) | 21.7 | (0.4) | 6.5 | (0.6) | 34.9 | (0.5) | 34.1 | (0.4) | 0.8 | (0.6) |
| Romania | 46.6 | (0.9) | 49.6 | (0.8) | -3.0 | (1.2) | 21.5 | (0.7) | 17.7 | (0.7) | 3.8 | (0.9) | 31.9 | (0.7) | 32.8 | (0.6) | -0.8 | (0.8) |
| Russian Federation | 48.6 | (0.6) | 48.6 | (0.6) | -0.0 | (0.8) | 15.9 | (0.6) | 14.2 | (0.6) | 1.8 | (0.7) | 35.5 | (0.7) | 37.3 | (0.5) | -1.8 | (0.7) |
| Serbia | 55.4 | (0.7) | 58.2 | (0.6) | -2.7 | (0.8) | 15.6 | (0.5) | 11.3 | (0.5) | 4.2 | (0.6) | 29.0 | (0.6) | 30.5 | (0.5) | -1.5 | (0.7) |
| Slovenia | 53.2 | (0.7) | 58.0 | (0.5) | -4.8 | (0.8) | 15.3 | (0.5) | 11.3 | (0.4) | 4.1 | (0.6) | 31.5 | (0.5) | 30.8 | (0.4) | 0.7 | (0.6) |
| Chinese Taipei | 63.0 | (0.5) | 64.4 | (0.5) | -1.4 | (0.6) | 12.9 | (0.3) | 11.5 | (0.3) | 1.5 | (0.4) | 24.0 | (0.5) | 24.1 | (0.4) | -0.1 | (0.5) |
| Thailand | 64.5 | (0.7) | 63.5 | (0.4) | 0.9 | (0.7) | 11.2 | (0.5) | 9.0 | (0.4) | 2.2 | (0.6) | 24.3 | (0.5) | 27.5 | (0.3) | -3.1 | (0.6) |
| Tunisia | 35.9 | (0.7) | 38.5 | (0.4) | -2.6 | (0.8) | 26.8 | (0.5) | 25.1 | (0.5) | 1.7 | (0.7) | 37.3 | (0.6) | 36.4 | (0.5) | 0.9 | (0.7) |
| Uruguay | 56.5 | (0.8) | 55.9 | (0.6) | 0.6 | (1.0) | 13.0 | (0.5) | 11.2 | (0.5) | 1.8 | (0.7) | 30.5 | (0.6) | 32.9 | (0.6) | -2.4 | (0.8) |

*Note:* Values that are statistically significant at the 5% level (p < 0.05) are indicated in bold.

[Part 1/3]
## Table 3.6b  Mean learning hours and allocation of total learning time in mathematics, by gender

| | | Mean learning hours per week | | | | | | | | | |
| | Regular school lessons | | | | | | Out-of-school-time lessons | | | | |
| | Male students | | Female students | | Difference (male-female) | | Male students | | Female students | | Difference (male-female) |
| | Mean | S.E. | Mean | S.E. | Dif. | S.E. | Mean | S.E. | Mean | S.E. | Dif. | S.E. |
|---|---|---|---|---|---|---|---|---|---|---|---|---|
| Australia | 4.08 | (0.04) | 4.12 | (0.03) | **-0.04** | (0.05) | 0.83 | (0.02) | 0.66 | (0.02) | **0.16** | (0.03) |
| Austria | 3.36 | (0.07) | 3.07 | (0.04) | 0.29 | (0.08) | 0.51 | (0.03) | 0.50 | (0.03) | 0.01 | (0.04) |
| Belgium | 3.56 | (0.05) | 3.60 | (0.05) | -0.03 | (0.06) | 0.59 | (0.02) | 0.51 | (0.02) | **0.08** | (0.03) |
| Canada | 4.35 | (0.04) | 4.65 | (0.05) | **-0.29** | (0.05) | 0.91 | (0.03) | 0.96 | (0.02) | -0.06 | (0.04) |
| Czech Republic | 4.11 | (0.04) | 3.85 | (0.07) | **0.26** | (0.06) | 0.79 | (0.03) | 0.72 | (0.03) | 0.05 | (0.04) |
| Denmark | 4.41 | (0.05) | 4.46 | (0.04) | -0.04 | (0.05) | 1.37 | (0.04) | 1.36 | (0.04) | 0.01 | (0.05) |
| Finland | 3.34 | (0.04) | 3.55 | (0.05) | **-0.21** | (0.04) | 0.42 | (0.02) | 0.32 | (0.02) | **0.11** | (0.02) |
| France | 3.79 | (0.04) | 3.89 | (0.04) | -0.11 | (0.05) | 0.88 | (0.03) | 0.97 | (0.03) | **-0.10** | (0.04) |
| Germany | 3.79 | (0.04) | 3.97 | (0.04) | **-0.18** | (0.05) | 0.83 | (0.03) | 0.81 | (0.03) | 0.01 | (0.04) |
| Greece | 3.39 | (0.06) | 3.51 | (0.05) | -0.12 | (0.06) | 2.21 | (0.07) | 2.25 | (0.06) | -0.01 | (0.07) |
| Hungary | 3.19 | (0.05) | 3.39 | (0.05) | **-0.20** | (0.06) | 1.25 | (0.03) | 1.32 | (0.04) | -0.09 | (0.05) |
| Iceland | 4.60 | (0.04) | 4.89 | (0.03) | **-0.29** | (0.05) | 0.68 | (0.03) | 0.75 | (0.03) | -0.07 | (0.04) |
| Ireland | 3.63 | (0.04) | 3.68 | (0.04) | -0.05 | (0.05) | 0.75 | (0.03) | 0.68 | (0.03) | **0.08** | (0.04) |
| Italy | 3.75 | (0.04) | 3.73 | (0.04) | 0.02 | (0.04) | 0.93 | (0.03) | 0.84 | (0.02) | **0.09** | (0.04) |
| Japan | 4.24 | (0.08) | 4.23 | (0.11) | 0.01 | (0.13) | 0.76 | (0.03) | 0.66 | (0.04) | **0.09** | (0.04) |
| Korea | 4.65 | (0.06) | 4.75 | (0.07) | -0.10 | (0.09) | 2.30 | (0.08) | 2.25 | (0.07) | 0.02 | (0.12) |
| Luxembourg | 3.81 | (0.04) | 3.90 | (0.03) | -0.09 | (0.05) | 0.84 | (0.03) | 0.82 | (0.03) | 0.00 | (0.04) |
| Mexico | 3.94 | (0.05) | 3.95 | (0.05) | -0.02 | (0.08) | 1.25 | (0.04) | 1.11 | (0.04) | **0.13** | (0.04) |
| Netherlands | 2.94 | (0.04) | 2.81 | (0.05) | **0.13** | (0.06) | 0.71 | (0.03) | 0.66 | (0.02) | 0.06 | (0.03) |
| New Zealand | 4.28 | (0.04) | 4.47 | (0.03) | **-0.19** | (0.05) | 0.71 | (0.03) | 0.66 | (0.03) | 0.03 | (0.04) |
| Norway | 3.35 | (0.04) | 3.43 | (0.04) | -0.07 | (0.04) | 1.11 | (0.03) | 0.98 | (0.03) | **0.14** | (0.04) |
| Poland | 4.10 | (0.05) | 4.60 | (0.04) | **-0.50** | (0.05) | 0.80 | (0.03) | 0.76 | (0.03) | 0.04 | (0.03) |
| Portugal | 3.53 | (0.05) | 3.68 | (0.05) | **-0.15** | (0.06) | 0.77 | (0.03) | 0.86 | (0.03) | **-0.11** | (0.04) |
| Slovak Republic | 3.33 | (0.06) | 3.24 | (0.06) | 0.08 | (0.06) | 0.78 | (0.03) | 0.99 | (0.04) | **-0.20** | (0.04) |
| Spain | 3.32 | (0.03) | 3.52 | (0.04) | **-0.20** | (0.04) | 0.93 | (0.03) | 1.06 | (0.03) | **-0.13** | (0.04) |
| Sweden | 3.09 | (0.03) | 3.09 | (0.03) | 0.00 | (0.04) | 0.63 | (0.02) | 0.59 | (0.02) | 0.03 | (0.03) |
| Switzerland | 3.79 | (0.04) | 3.93 | (0.05) | **-0.13** | (0.05) | 0.76 | (0.03) | 0.64 | (0.03) | **0.13** | (0.03) |
| Turkey | 3.74 | (0.06) | 3.92 | (0.09) | -0.18 | (0.10) | 1.96 | (0.05) | 2.21 | (0.07) | **-0.24** | (0.08) |
| United Kingdom | 3.77 | (0.03) | 3.79 | (0.04) | -0.02 | (0.03) | 0.67 | (0.02) | 0.59 | (0.02) | **0.09** | (0.03) |
| United States | 3.66 | (0.06) | 3.88 | (0.05) | **-0.21** | (0.06) | 1.17 | (0.04) | 1.12 | (0.04) | 0.05 | (0.05) |
| **OECD average** | 3.76 | (0.01) | 3.85 | (0.01) | **-0.09** | (0.01) | 0.97 | (0.01) | 0.95 | (0.01) | 0.01 | (0.01) |
| Argentina | 2.81 | (0.07) | 3.07 | (0.08) | **-0.26** | (0.09) | 0.77 | (0.04) | 0.78 | (0.04) | 0.01 | (0.05) |
| Azerbaijan | 3.77 | (0.07) | 3.81 | (0.07) | -0.05 | (0.09) | 1.94 | (0.06) | 1.44 | (0.06) | **0.49** | (0.08) |
| Brazil | 3.12 | (0.05) | 3.18 | (0.04) | -0.06 | (0.05) | 1.15 | (0.04) | 1.26 | (0.04) | -0.11 | (0.06) |
| Bulgaria | 2.79 | (0.08) | 3.17 | (0.08) | **-0.38** | (0.08) | 1.12 | (0.05) | 1.16 | (0.05) | -0.02 | (0.06) |
| Chile | 3.43 | (0.08) | 3.55 | (0.09) | -0.12 | (0.11) | 0.96 | (0.03) | 1.03 | (0.04) | -0.07 | (0.04) |
| Colombia | 4.16 | (0.09) | 4.25 | (0.06) | -0.09 | (0.09) | 1.26 | (0.05) | 1.20 | (0.04) | 0.04 | (0.08) |
| Croatia | 3.00 | (0.05) | 3.09 | (0.05) | -0.09 | (0.06) | 0.74 | (0.03) | 0.79 | (0.04) | -0.03 | (0.05) |
| Estonia | 3.97 | (0.05) | 4.43 | (0.04) | **-0.46** | (0.05) | 0.98 | (0.05) | 1.00 | (0.04) | -0.02 | (0.07) |
| Hong Kong-China | 5.18 | (0.05) | 5.27 | (0.06) | -0.09 | (0.07) | 1.44 | (0.05) | 1.35 | (0.04) | 0.08 | (0.07) |
| Indonesia | 4.05 | (0.10) | 4.12 | (0.07) | -0.07 | (0.08) | 1.31 | (0.05) | 1.42 | (0.05) | **-0.15** | (0.05) |
| Israel | 3.89 | (0.06) | 4.34 | (0.05) | **-0.44** | (0.08) | 2.07 | (0.06) | 2.23 | (0.06) | -0.11 | (0.08) |
| Jordan | 3.22 | (0.07) | 3.72 | (0.06) | **-0.50** | (0.10) | 1.97 | (0.06) | 1.68 | (0.05) | **0.29** | (0.09) |
| Kyrgyzstan | 2.61 | (0.06) | 3.10 | (0.07) | **-0.50** | (0.07) | 1.48 | (0.05) | 1.61 | (0.05) | -0.12 | (0.06) |
| Latvia | 4.34 | (0.05) | 4.63 | (0.05) | **-0.29** | (0.05) | 1.20 | (0.05) | 1.19 | (0.05) | 0.02 | (0.05) |
| Liechtenstein | 3.84 | (0.14) | 4.10 | (0.10) | -0.26 | (0.18) | 0.65 | (0.08) | 0.52 | (0.05) | 0.16 | (0.11) |
| Lithuania | 3.25 | (0.05) | 3.76 | (0.04) | **-0.51** | (0.05) | 0.73 | (0.03) | 0.74 | (0.03) | -0.01 | (0.04) |
| Macao-China | 5.25 | (0.05) | 5.56 | (0.04) | **-0.31** | (0.06) | 1.26 | (0.04) | 1.15 | (0.05) | 0.13 | (0.07) |
| Montenegro | 3.09 | (0.05) | 3.09 | (0.05) | -0.00 | (0.06) | 0.98 | (0.04) | 0.87 | (0.03) | **0.14** | (0.06) |
| Qatar | 3.10 | (0.04) | 3.13 | (0.04) | -0.03 | (0.06) | 2.07 | (0.04) | 1.65 | (0.03) | **0.43** | (0.06) |
| Romania | 2.96 | (0.08) | 3.05 | (0.08) | -0.10 | (0.08) | 1.47 | (0.04) | 1.53 | (0.04) | -0.05 | (0.05) |
| Russian Federation | 3.50 | (0.05) | 3.75 | (0.07) | **-0.25** | (0.06) | 1.13 | (0.05) | 1.13 | (0.03) | 0.01 | (0.05) |
| Serbia | 3.23 | (0.05) | 3.32 | (0.04) | **-0.10** | (0.05) | 1.02 | (0.03) | 0.92 | (0.03) | **0.10** | (0.04) |
| Slovenia | 3.04 | (0.04) | 3.60 | (0.04) | **-0.55** | (0.06) | 1.00 | (0.03) | 1.05 | (0.03) | -0.03 | (0.05) |
| Chinese Taipei | 4.25 | (0.06) | 4.26 | (0.08) | -0.00 | (0.09) | 1.57 | (0.04) | 1.48 | (0.05) | 0.04 | (0.06) |
| Thailand | 3.60 | (0.06) | 3.91 | (0.05) | **-0.31** | (0.09) | 0.94 | (0.05) | 0.91 | (0.04) | 0.04 | (0.06) |
| Tunisia | 3.32 | (0.06) | 3.46 | (0.07) | -0.14 | (0.09) | 2.44 | (0.05) | 2.40 | (0.05) | 0.04 | (0.08) |
| Uruguay | 3.18 | (0.05) | 3.44 | (0.04) | **-0.26** | (0.06) | 0.86 | (0.04) | 0.81 | (0.03) | 0.06 | (0.05) |

OECD — Partners

*Note:* Values that are statistically significant at the 5% level (p < 0.05) are indicated in bold.

© OECD 2011  Quality Time for Students: Learning In and Out of School

[Part 2/3]
## Table 3.6b  Mean learning hours and allocation of total learning time in mathematics, by gender

| | | Mean learning hours per week | | | | | | | | | |
|---|---|---|---|---|---|---|---|---|---|---|---|
| | | Individual study | | | | | | Total learning hours | | | |
| | | Male students | | Female students | | Difference (male-female) | | Male students | | Female students | | Difference (male-female) |
| | | Mean | S.E. | Mean | S.E. | Dif. | S.E. | Mean | S.E. | Mean | S.E. | Dif. | S.E. |

| | | Mean | S.E. | Mean | S.E. | Dif. | S.E. | Mean | S.E. | Mean | S.E. | Dif. | S.E. |
|---|---|---|---|---|---|---|---|---|---|---|---|---|---|
| OECD | Australia | 1.77 | (0.03) | 1.81 | (0.03) | **-0.04** | (0.04) | 6.69 | (0.07) | 6.60 | (0.06) | 0.09 | (0.09) |
| | Austria | 2.07 | (0.05) | 2.19 | (0.05) | **-0.12** | (0.06) | 5.97 | (0.12) | 5.79 | (0.08) | 0.18 | (0.14) |
| | Belgium | 1.64 | (0.03) | 1.94 | (0.04) | **-0.30** | (0.05) | 5.82 | (0.08) | 6.05 | (0.08) | **-0.23** | (0.10) |
| | Canada | 1.73 | (0.04) | 2.21 | (0.04) | **-0.48** | (0.05) | 7.04 | (0.08) | 7.84 | (0.08) | **-0.80** | (0.10) |
| | Czech Republic | 1.31 | (0.03) | 1.32 | (0.04) | **-0.01** | (0.04) | 6.19 | (0.07) | 5.88 | (0.10) | **0.31** | (0.09) |
| | Denmark | 1.68 | (0.03) | 1.81 | (0.03) | **-0.13** | (0.04) | 7.42 | (0.09) | 7.62 | (0.08) | -0.20 | (0.11) |
| | Finland | 1.12 | (0.02) | 1.29 | (0.02) | **-0.17** | (0.03) | 4.89 | (0.06) | 5.15 | (0.07) | **-0.26** | (0.06) |
| | France | 1.57 | (0.05) | 1.89 | (0.03) | **-0.32** | (0.05) | 6.25 | (0.09) | 6.74 | (0.07) | **-0.50** | (0.11) |
| | Germany | 2.09 | (0.04) | 2.47 | (0.04) | **-0.38** | (0.04) | 6.75 | (0.08) | 7.23 | (0.09) | **-0.48** | (0.09) |
| | Greece | 2.07 | (0.05) | 1.94 | (0.04) | 0.13 | (0.06) | 7.71 | (0.14) | 7.70 | (0.10) | 0.01 | (0.14) |
| | Hungary | 1.73 | (0.04) | 1.96 | (0.04) | **-0.24** | (0.05) | 6.19 | (0.10) | 6.67 | (0.11) | **-0.48** | (0.12) |
| | Iceland | 1.61 | (0.03) | 1.81 | (0.03) | **-0.20** | (0.05) | 6.88 | (0.07) | 7.46 | (0.06) | **-0.58** | (0.09) |
| | Ireland | 1.68 | (0.04) | 1.84 | (0.04) | **-0.16** | (0.06) | 6.08 | (0.08) | 6.19 | (0.09) | -0.12 | (0.11) |
| | Italy | 2.36 | (0.04) | 2.60 | (0.04) | **-0.24** | (0.04) | 7.07 | (0.07) | 7.16 | (0.09) | -0.08 | (0.09) |
| | Japan | 1.42 | (0.06) | 1.53 | (0.08) | -0.11 | (0.08) | 6.43 | (0.15) | 6.43 | (0.20) | -0.01 | (0.23) |
| | Korea | 2.29 | (0.10) | 2.33 | (0.07) | -0.04 | (0.11) | 9.29 | (0.20) | 9.34 | (0.17) | -0.05 | (0.27) |
| | Luxembourg | 1.61 | (0.04) | 1.82 | (0.03) | **-0.21** | (0.05) | 6.31 | (0.07) | 6.54 | (0.06) | **-0.23** | (0.09) |
| | Mexico | 2.21 | (0.04) | 2.31 | (0.04) | **-0.10** | (0.05) | 7.35 | (0.10) | 7.35 | (0.08) | -0.00 | (0.12) |
| | Netherlands | 1.42 | (0.03) | 1.53 | (0.04) | **-0.11** | (0.04) | 5.07 | (0.08) | 4.97 | (0.09) | 0.10 | (0.10) |
| | New Zealand | 1.52 | (0.04) | 1.65 | (0.04) | **-0.13** | (0.06) | 6.53 | (0.08) | 6.77 | (0.07) | **-0.24** | (0.11) |
| | Norway | 1.35 | (0.03) | 1.45 | (0.04) | **-0.10** | (0.05) | 5.80 | (0.07) | 5.87 | (0.08) | -0.07 | (0.08) |
| | Poland | 1.81 | (0.03) | 2.37 | (0.04) | **-0.56** | (0.04) | 6.70 | (0.08) | 7.74 | (0.07) | **-1.04** | (0.08) |
| | Portugal | 1.74 | (0.05) | 2.18 | (0.04) | **-0.44** | (0.06) | 6.04 | (0.10) | 6.70 | (0.08) | **-0.66** | (0.12) |
| | Slovak Republic | 1.57 | (0.05) | 1.81 | (0.04) | **-0.25** | (0.06) | 5.69 | (0.12) | 6.06 | (0.12) | **-0.36** | (0.13) |
| | Spain | 1.74 | (0.03) | 2.18 | (0.04) | **-0.44** | (0.04) | 6.05 | (0.07) | 6.77 | (0.06) | **-0.72** | (0.07) |
| | Sweden | 1.12 | (0.03) | 1.25 | (0.03) | **-0.13** | (0.03) | 4.84 | (0.06) | 4.92 | (0.05) | -0.08 | (0.07) |
| | Switzerland | 1.61 | (0.03) | 1.77 | (0.03) | **-0.16** | (0.04) | 6.19 | (0.07) | 6.34 | (0.08) | **-0.16** | (0.09) |
| | Turkey | 2.15 | (0.05) | 2.49 | (0.07) | **-0.35** | (0.07) | 7.81 | (0.14) | 8.59 | (0.21) | **-0.78** | (0.21) |
| | United Kingdom | 1.45 | (0.02) | 1.53 | (0.03) | **-0.08** | (0.03) | 5.89 | (0.06) | 5.90 | (0.06) | -0.01 | (0.06) |
| | United States | 1.88 | (0.04) | 2.22 | (0.04) | **-0.34** | (0.05) | 6.80 | (0.08) | 7.21 | (0.08) | **-0.40** | (0.10) |
| | **OECD average** | 1.71 | (0.01) | 1.92 | (0.01) | **-0.21** | (0.01) | 6.46 | (0.02) | 6.72 | (0.02) | **-0.26** | (0.02) |
| Partners | Argentina | 1.70 | (0.06) | 1.93 | (0.05) | **-0.23** | (0.07) | 5.29 | (0.13) | 5.78 | (0.13) | **-0.49** | (0.15) |
| | Azerbaijan | 3.00 | (0.07) | 2.88 | (0.07) | 0.12 | (0.08) | 8.74 | (0.18) | 8.23 | (0.15) | **0.51** | (0.19) |
| | Brazil | 1.65 | (0.04) | 1.92 | (0.04) | **-0.27** | (0.05) | 5.91 | (0.09) | 6.34 | (0.09) | **-0.43** | (0.11) |
| | Bulgaria | 1.87 | (0.07) | 2.31 | (0.08) | **-0.44** | (0.08) | 5.83 | (0.16) | 6.64 | (0.18) | **-0.81** | (0.17) |
| | Chile | 1.60 | (0.04) | 1.61 | (0.05) | **-0.01** | (0.05) | 6.05 | (0.11) | 6.20 | (0.14) | -0.15 | (0.16) |
| | Colombia | 1.91 | (0.04) | 1.95 | (0.05) | -0.04 | (0.07) | 7.33 | (0.13) | 7.41 | (0.11) | -0.08 | (0.17) |
| | Croatia | 1.65 | (0.04) | 1.96 | (0.04) | **-0.31** | (0.05) | 5.45 | (0.08) | 5.86 | (0.08) | **-0.41** | (0.11) |
| | Estonia | 1.70 | (0.04) | 2.23 | (0.04) | **-0.53** | (0.06) | 6.65 | (0.09) | 7.66 | (0.09) | **-1.01** | (0.12) |
| | Hong Kong-China | 2.17 | (0.05) | 2.30 | (0.05) | -0.13 | (0.07) | 8.81 | (0.11) | 8.92 | (0.11) | -0.12 | (0.14) |
| | Indonesia | 1.80 | (0.04) | 2.19 | (0.04) | **-0.39** | (0.05) | 7.16 | (0.13) | 7.73 | (0.11) | **-0.58** | (0.11) |
| | Israel | 2.26 | (0.08) | 2.39 | (0.07) | -0.13 | (0.10) | 8.40 | (0.17) | 8.96 | (0.13) | **-0.55** | (0.21) |
| | Jordan | 2.56 | (0.05) | 2.81 | (0.06) | **-0.25** | (0.08) | 7.72 | (0.12) | 8.18 | (0.12) | **-0.46** | (0.18) |
| | Kyrgyzstan | 1.96 | (0.05) | 2.43 | (0.05) | **-0.47** | (0.07) | 6.19 | (0.12) | 7.14 | (0.13) | **-0.95** | (0.16) |
| | Latvia | 2.25 | (0.05) | 2.62 | (0.05) | **-0.37** | (0.06) | 7.80 | (0.11) | 8.46 | (0.10) | **-0.66** | (0.12) |
| | Liechtenstein | 1.41 | (0.11) | 1.56 | (0.08) | -0.15 | (0.14) | 5.94 | (0.23) | 6.14 | (0.13) | -0.20 | (0.28) |
| | Lithuania | 1.56 | (0.04) | 2.01 | (0.04) | **-0.44** | (0.06) | 5.55 | (0.08) | 6.49 | (0.07) | **-0.94** | (0.10) |
| | Macao-China | 1.87 | (0.04) | 2.27 | (0.04) | **-0.40** | (0.06) | 8.38 | (0.08) | 8.98 | (0.09) | **-0.60** | (0.12) |
| | Montenegro | 2.02 | (0.05) | 2.05 | (0.04) | -0.03 | (0.06) | 6.07 | (0.10) | 5.98 | (0.09) | 0.09 | (0.13) |
| | Qatar | 2.24 | (0.04) | 2.21 | (0.03) | 0.03 | (0.05) | 7.44 | (0.09) | 7.00 | (0.08) | **0.44** | (0.13) |
| | Romania | 2.08 | (0.05) | 2.24 | (0.05) | -0.16 | (0.07) | 6.53 | (0.15) | 6.81 | (0.13) | -0.28 | (0.16) |
| | Russian Federation | 2.06 | (0.06) | 2.38 | (0.05) | **-0.31** | (0.06) | 6.70 | (0.11) | 7.26 | (0.11) | **-0.55** | (0.11) |
| | Serbia | 1.72 | (0.04) | 1.92 | (0.04) | **-0.20** | (0.06) | 5.96 | (0.09) | 6.16 | (0.09) | -0.20 | (0.11) |
| | Slovenia | 1.74 | (0.03) | 2.10 | (0.03) | **-0.37** | (0.04) | 5.81 | (0.08) | 6.76 | (0.06) | **-0.95** | (0.10) |
| | Chinese Taipei | 1.85 | (0.05) | 1.90 | (0.05) | -0.05 | (0.06) | 7.76 | (0.13) | 7.67 | (0.16) | 0.09 | (0.18) |
| | Thailand | 1.61 | (0.05) | 1.95 | (0.03) | **-0.34** | (0.06) | 6.14 | (0.11) | 6.76 | (0.11) | **-0.62** | (0.18) |
| | Tunisia | 2.48 | (0.06) | 2.65 | (0.05) | -0.17 | (0.07) | 8.24 | (0.14) | 8.50 | (0.14) | -0.27 | (0.19) |
| | Uruguay | 1.43 | (0.04) | 1.70 | (0.04) | **-0.27** | (0.06) | 5.50 | (0.11) | 5.97 | (0.08) | **-0.47** | (0.13) |

*Note:* Values that are statistically significant at the 5% level (p < 0.05) are indicated in bold.

[Part 3/3]
## Table 3.6b Mean learning hours and allocation of total learning time in mathematics, by gender

| | Allocation of total learning time in mathematics for | | | | | | | | | | | | | | | | |
| | Regular school lessons | | | | | | Out-of-school-time lessons | | | | | | Individual study | | | | | |
| | Male students | | Female students | | Difference (male-female) | | Male students | | Female students | | Difference (male-female) | | Male students | | Female students | | Difference (male-female) | |
| | % | S.E. | % | S.E. | Dif. | S.E. | % | S.E. | % | S.E. | Dif. | S.E. | % | S.E. | % | S.E. | Dif. | S.E. |
|---|---|---|---|---|---|---|---|---|---|---|---|---|---|---|---|---|---|---|
| **OECD** Australia | 65.5 | (0.4) | 66.1 | (0.3) | **-0.6** | (0.5) | 10.2 | (0.3) | 8.3 | (0.2) | **1.8** | (0.3) | 24.4 | (0.3) | 25.6 | (0.3) | **-1.2** | (0.4) |
| Austria | 60.2 | (0.6) | 56.8 | (0.6) | **3.4** | (0.7) | 6.6 | (0.3) | 6.7 | (0.4) | -0.1 | (0.5) | 33.2 | (0.5) | 36.6 | (0.5) | **-3.3** | (0.6) |
| Belgium | 64.2 | (0.4) | 62.0 | (0.4) | **2.2** | (0.5) | 8.6 | (0.3) | 7.3 | (0.3) | **1.3** | (0.3) | 27.2 | (0.3) | 30.7 | (0.4) | **-3.5** | (0.5) |
| Canada | 64.8 | (0.4) | 62.0 | (0.4) | **2.8** | (0.5) | 11.7 | (0.2) | 11.2 | (0.3) | 0.5 | (0.3) | 23.6 | (0.3) | 26.9 | (0.3) | **-3.3** | (0.4) |
| Czech Republic | 71.3 | (0.5) | 69.1 | (0.6) | **2.2** | (0.7) | 9.9 | (0.3) | 9.7 | (0.3) | 0.3 | (0.5) | 18.8 | (0.4) | 21.2 | (0.5) | **-2.4** | (0.6) |
| Denmark | 62.7 | (0.4) | 62.0 | (0.4) | 0.6 | (0.5) | 16.4 | (0.3) | 15.6 | (0.3) | 0.7 | (0.4) | 21.0 | (0.2) | 22.3 | (0.3) | **-1.3** | (0.4) |
| Finland | 71.0 | (0.5) | 71.2 | (0.4) | -0.2 | (0.6) | 7.0 | (0.3) | 4.9 | (0.2) | **2.1** | (0.3) | 22.0 | (0.4) | 23.9 | (0.3) | **-1.9** | (0.4) |
| France | 64.3 | (0.5) | 61.0 | (0.4) | **3.3** | (0.7) | 12.6 | (0.3) | 12.7 | (0.3) | -0.1 | (0.5) | 23.1 | (0.5) | 26.4 | (0.3) | **-3.3** | (0.5) |
| Germany | 59.0 | (0.5) | 57.8 | (0.4) | **1.3** | (0.6) | 10.4 | (0.4) | 9.2 | (0.3) | **1.2** | (0.5) | 30.6 | (0.4) | 33.1 | (0.3) | **-2.5** | (0.5) |
| Greece | 48.4 | (0.7) | 50.3 | (0.6) | **-1.9** | (0.8) | 25.7 | (0.6) | 26.2 | (0.6) | -0.5 | (0.7) | 25.9 | (0.5) | 23.4 | (0.4) | **2.5** | (0.6) |
| Hungary | 54.6 | (0.6) | 54.0 | (0.5) | 0.6 | (0.7) | 17.9 | (0.4) | 17.6 | (0.4) | 0.3 | (0.5) | 27.5 | (0.4) | 28.4 | (0.4) | -0.9 | (0.5) |
| Iceland | 70.0 | (0.5) | 68.8 | (0.3) | **1.2** | (0.5) | 8.4 | (0.3) | 8.5 | (0.3) | -0.1 | (0.4) | 21.5 | (0.3) | 22.7 | (0.3) | **-1.1** | (0.4) |
| Ireland | 63.7 | (0.6) | 63.6 | (0.5) | 0.1 | (0.8) | 10.2 | (0.3) | 8.7 | (0.4) | **1.5** | (0.5) | 26.1 | (0.4) | 27.7 | (0.4) | **-1.6** | (0.7) |
| Italy | 55.2 | (0.4) | 54.9 | (0.3) | 0.3 | (0.5) | 11.8 | (0.3) | 9.7 | (0.2) | **2.1** | (0.4) | 33.0 | (0.3) | 35.4 | (0.2) | **-2.4** | (0.4) |
| Japan | 72.2 | (0.6) | 71.2 | (0.7) | 1.1 | (0.7) | 9.2 | (0.4) | 8.1 | (0.4) | **1.2** | (0.4) | 18.5 | (0.5) | 20.7 | (0.5) | **-2.2** | (0.5) |
| Korea | 57.0 | (0.8) | 57.0 | (0.6) | 0.0 | (1.2) | 21.2 | (0.5) | 20.6 | (0.5) | 0.6 | (0.8) | 21.8 | (0.6) | 22.4 | (0.4) | -0.6 | (0.7) |
| Luxembourg | 64.1 | (0.5) | 62.5 | (0.4) | **1.6** | (0.6) | 11.4 | (0.4) | 10.9 | (0.3) | 0.5 | (0.5) | 24.5 | (0.4) | 26.7 | (0.4) | **-2.2** | (0.5) |
| Mexico | 54.1 | (0.5) | 54.8 | (0.5) | -0.7 | (0.6) | 15.5 | (0.4) | 13.4 | (0.4) | **2.1** | (0.4) | 30.4 | (0.4) | 31.8 | (0.4) | **-1.4** | (0.5) |
| Netherlands | 61.2 | (0.6) | 58.7 | (0.5) | **2.5** | (0.7) | 12.2 | (0.4) | 11.9 | (0.4) | 0.3 | (0.5) | 26.6 | (0.4) | 29.4 | (0.5) | **-2.8** | (0.5) |
| New Zealand | 69.7 | (0.6) | 69.5 | (0.5) | 0.2 | (0.7) | 8.9 | (0.4) | 8.1 | (0.3) | 0.8 | (0.4) | 21.4 | (0.4) | 22.4 | (0.4) | -1.0 | (0.5) |
| Norway | 61.8 | (0.6) | 62.6 | (0.6) | -0.8 | (0.7) | 17.1 | (0.4) | 14.7 | (0.4) | **2.4** | (0.4) | 21.1 | (0.4) | 22.7 | (0.4) | **-1.6** | (0.6) |
| Poland | 62.9 | (0.4) | 62.1 | (0.4) | 0.8 | (0.5) | 11.2 | (0.4) | 9.0 | (0.3) | **2.2** | (0.4) | 25.9 | (0.3) | 28.9 | (0.3) | **-3.0** | (0.5) |
| Portugal | 60.8 | (0.5) | 57.0 | (0.6) | **3.8** | (0.7) | 11.6 | (0.4) | 11.6 | (0.4) | -0.1 | (0.5) | 27.6 | (0.4) | 31.4 | (0.5) | **-3.8** | (0.6) |
| Slovak Republic | 63.6 | (0.7) | 57.5 | (0.7) | **6.0** | (0.9) | 11.3 | (0.4) | 13.9 | (0.4) | **-2.6** | (0.5) | 25.1 | (0.5) | 28.6 | (0.5) | **-3.5** | (0.7) |
| Spain | 59.1 | (0.4) | 56.3 | (0.4) | **2.9** | (0.5) | 13.1 | (0.3) | 13.0 | (0.4) | 0.1 | (0.4) | 27.8 | (0.4) | 30.7 | (0.4) | **-2.9** | (0.4) |
| Sweden | 69.1 | (0.8) | 67.1 | (0.4) | **2.0** | (0.8) | 10.1 | (0.4) | 9.7 | (0.3) | 0.4 | (0.5) | 20.8 | (0.5) | 23.2 | (0.4) | **-2.4** | (0.5) |
| Switzerland | 63.1 | (0.4) | 64.1 | (0.4) | **-1.0** | (0.5) | 10.6 | (0.4) | 8.6 | (0.3) | **2.0** | (0.4) | 26.3 | (0.3) | 27.4 | (0.3) | **-1.1** | (0.4) |
| Turkey | 52.4 | (0.6) | 48.8 | (0.6) | **3.6** | (0.8) | 21.9 | (0.5) | 23.6 | (0.6) | -1.7 | (0.8) | 25.7 | (0.4) | 27.6 | (0.4) | **-1.9** | (0.5) |
| United Kingdom | 67.1 | (0.4) | 67.2 | (0.4) | -0.1 | (0.5) | 9.6 | (0.3) | 8.2 | (0.3) | **1.4** | (0.4) | 23.3 | (0.3) | 24.6 | (0.3) | **-1.3** | (0.3) |
| United States | 55.8 | (0.6) | 55.0 | (0.5) | 0.7 | (0.6) | 16.3 | (0.6) | 14.4 | (0.4) | **1.9** | (0.5) | 27.9 | (0.4) | 30.5 | (0.3) | **-2.6** | (0.5) |
| **OECD average** | 62.3 | (0.1) | 61.0 | (0.1) | **1.3** | (0.1) | 12.6 | (0.1) | 11.9 | (0.1) | **0.8** | (0.1) | 25.1 | (0.1) | 27.1 | (0.1) | **-2.0** | (0.1) |
| **Partners** Argentina | 55.0 | (0.9) | 54.9 | (0.8) | 0.1 | (1.2) | 12.8 | (0.6) | 12.0 | (0.6) | 0.7 | (0.7) | 32.2 | (0.8) | 33.0 | (0.7) | -0.8 | (1.3) |
| Azerbaijan | 44.9 | (0.7) | 49.5 | (0.8) | -4.7 | (1.0) | 21.0 | (0.5) | 16.0 | (0.5) | 5.0 | (0.7) | 34.1 | (0.6) | 34.4 | (0.6) | -0.3 | (0.7) |
| Brazil | 56.0 | (0.7) | 53.1 | (0.6) | **3.0** | (0.8) | 17.1 | (0.6) | 17.5 | (0.4) | -0.5 | (0.7) | 26.9 | (0.5) | 29.4 | (0.5) | **-2.5** | (0.6) |
| Bulgaria | 51.3 | (0.9) | 51.1 | (0.6) | 0.2 | (1.0) | 17.5 | (0.8) | 15.3 | (0.4) | 2.2 | (0.8) | 31.2 | (0.6) | 33.6 | (0.5) | **-2.3** | (0.7) |
| Chile | 56.4 | (0.6) | 57.4 | (0.7) | -1.0 | (0.8) | 15.1 | (0.4) | 15.1 | (0.4) | -0.1 | (0.5) | 28.5 | (0.4) | 27.5 | (0.6) | 1.1 | (0.7) |
| Colombia | 59.7 | (0.7) | 61.6 | (0.7) | -1.9 | (0.9) | 14.9 | (0.4) | 13.7 | (0.5) | 1.2 | (0.6) | 25.4 | (0.5) | 24.7 | (0.4) | 0.7 | (0.6) |
| Croatia | 59.4 | (0.6) | 57.3 | (0.6) | 2.1 | (0.8) | 11.9 | (0.4) | 11.1 | (0.4) | 0.8 | (0.5) | 28.7 | (0.5) | 31.6 | (0.5) | **-2.9** | (0.6) |
| Estonia | 63.1 | (0.6) | 61.3 | (0.5) | 1.8 | (0.7) | 13.1 | (0.5) | 11.6 | (0.4) | 1.5 | (0.7) | 23.8 | (0.4) | 27.1 | (0.4) | **-3.3** | (0.6) |
| Hong Kong-China | 62.5 | (0.7) | 62.6 | (0.5) | -0.1 | (0.8) | 14.6 | (0.4) | 13.5 | (0.4) | 1.1 | (0.5) | 22.8 | (0.4) | 23.8 | (0.4) | -1.0 | (0.5) |
| Indonesia | 58.9 | (0.7) | 55.4 | (0.7) | 3.5 | (0.9) | 16.2 | (0.6) | 16.5 | (0.5) | -0.3 | (0.6) | 24.9 | (0.3) | 28.1 | (0.4) | **-3.1** | (0.5) |
| Israel | 49.6 | (0.9) | 53.1 | (0.8) | -3.5 | (1.2) | 24.0 | (0.5) | 22.3 | (0.4) | 1.7 | (0.7) | 26.5 | (0.6) | 24.6 | (0.6) | 1.8 | (0.8) |
| Jordan | 40.4 | (0.8) | 45.7 | (0.5) | -5.3 | (1.1) | 25.5 | (0.5) | 19.5 | (0.6) | 5.9 | (0.9) | 34.2 | (0.5) | 34.8 | (0.6) | -0.6 | (0.8) |
| Kyrgyzstan | 41.9 | (0.7) | 42.1 | (0.6) | -0.2 | (0.8) | 25.2 | (0.7) | 23.1 | (0.6) | 2.1 | (0.7) | 32.9 | (0.6) | 34.8 | (0.5) | **-1.9** | (0.7) |
| Latvia | 58.8 | (0.5) | 57.8 | (0.4) | 1.0 | (0.6) | 13.9 | (0.5) | 12.8 | (0.4) | 1.2 | (0.5) | 27.3 | (0.4) | 29.5 | (0.4) | **-2.2** | (0.6) |
| Liechtenstein | 65.9 | (1.9) | 67.4 | (1.2) | -1.6 | (2.1) | 10.1 | (1.1) | 7.2 | (0.7) | 2.9 | (1.4) | 24.1 | (1.5) | 25.4 | (1.1) | -1.3 | (1.7) |
| Lithuania | 61.1 | (0.5) | 60.3 | (0.5) | 0.9 | (0.7) | 12.5 | (0.4) | 10.5 | (0.4) | 2.1 | (0.4) | 26.3 | (0.4) | 29.3 | (0.4) | **-3.0** | (0.6) |
| Macao-China | 66.9 | (0.5) | 65.5 | (0.5) | 1.4 | (0.7) | 12.6 | (0.4) | 11.1 | (0.4) | 1.5 | (0.6) | 20.5 | (0.4) | 23.4 | (0.4) | **-2.9** | (0.5) |
| Montenegro | 52.2 | (0.5) | 52.7 | (0.6) | -0.5 | (0.9) | 14.0 | (0.5) | 12.9 | (0.5) | 1.1 | (0.7) | 33.8 | (0.5) | 34.4 | (0.6) | -0.6 | (0.8) |
| Qatar | 41.2 | (0.5) | 45.1 | (0.4) | -3.9 | (0.6) | 27.8 | (0.5) | 22.8 | (0.4) | 5.1 | (0.6) | 31.0 | (0.4) | 32.1 | (0.4) | -1.1 | (0.6) |
| Romania | 49.3 | (0.7) | 49.7 | (0.7) | -0.4 | (0.9) | 20.3 | (0.5) | 19.2 | (0.4) | 1.1 | (0.6) | 30.4 | (0.5) | 31.1 | (0.5) | -0.7 | (0.7) |
| Russian Federation | 54.1 | (0.8) | 53.8 | (0.5) | 0.2 | (0.8) | 16.6 | (0.7) | 14.9 | (0.7) | 1.7 | (0.7) | 29.3 | (0.6) | 31.3 | (0.4) | **-2.0** | (0.6) |
| Serbia | 59.5 | (0.6) | 59.1 | (0.5) | 0.4 | (0.7) | 14.1 | (0.4) | 11.9 | (0.4) | 2.2 | (0.5) | 26.5 | (0.5) | 29.0 | (0.4) | **-2.6** | (0.6) |
| Slovenia | 55.0 | (0.6) | 56.1 | (0.4) | -1.1 | (0.8) | 15.2 | (0.3) | 13.5 | (0.4) | 1.7 | (0.6) | 29.7 | (0.5) | 30.4 | (0.3) | -0.6 | (0.6) |
| Chinese Taipei | 59.3 | (0.5) | 60.2 | (0.5) | -0.9 | (0.7) | 17.6 | (0.3) | 16.1 | (0.4) | 1.6 | (0.5) | 23.1 | (0.3) | 23.7 | (0.3) | -0.6 | (0.5) |
| Thailand | 64.5 | (0.8) | 62.6 | (0.4) | 1.9 | (0.8) | 11.5 | (0.5) | 10.0 | (0.4) | 1.5 | (0.6) | 24.0 | (0.5) | 27.4 | (0.3) | **-3.4** | (0.5) |
| Tunisia | 41.6 | (0.5) | 41.8 | (0.6) | -0.2 | (0.7) | 27.9 | (0.4) | 26.3 | (0.4) | 1.6 | (0.6) | 30.5 | (0.6) | 31.8 | (0.5) | -1.3 | (0.9) |
| Uruguay | 60.7 | (0.6) | 60.9 | (0.5) | -0.2 | (0.8) | 13.6 | (0.5) | 11.3 | (0.4) | 2.3 | (0.7) | 25.7 | (0.5) | 27.8 | (0.4) | **-2.1** | (0.6) |

*Note:* Values that are statistically significant at the 5% level (p < 0.05) are indicated in bold.

© OECD 2011 Quality Time for Students: Learning In and Out of School

## Table 3.6c  Mean learning hours and allocation of total learning time on
[Part 1/3] the language of instruction, by gender

| | | Mean learning hours per week | | | | | | | | | | |
| | | Regular school lessons | | | | | | Out-of-school-time lessons | | | | | |
| | | Male students | | Female students | | Difference (male-female) | | Male students | | Female students | | Difference (male-female) | |
| | | Mean | S.E. | Mean | S.E. | Dif. | S.E. | Mean | S.E. | Mean | S.E. | Dif. | S.E. |
|---|---|---|---|---|---|---|---|---|---|---|---|---|---|
| OECD | Australia | 3.96 | (0.03) | 4.17 | (0.03) | **-0.21** | (0.04) | 0.69 | (0.02) | 0.63 | (0.02) | **0.07** | (0.03) |
| | Austria | 2.77 | (0.04) | 2.97 | (0.05) | **-0.20** | (0.06) | 0.29 | (0.02) | 0.18 | (0.02) | **0.10** | (0.03) |
| | Belgium | 3.35 | (0.04) | 3.63 | (0.04) | **-0.28** | (0.05) | 0.48 | (0.02) | 0.43 | (0.02) | 0.04 | (0.03) |
| | Canada | 4.24 | (0.04) | 4.62 | (0.05) | **-0.38** | (0.04) | 0.78 | (0.02) | 0.95 | (0.03) | **-0.15** | (0.03) |
| | Czech Republic | 3.67 | (0.04) | 3.79 | (0.06) | -0.12 | (0.07) | 0.55 | (0.02) | 0.69 | (0.02) | **-0.15** | (0.03) |
| | Denmark | 5.39 | (0.04) | 5.61 | (0.04) | **-0.22** | (0.05) | 1.52 | (0.04) | 1.85 | (0.04) | **-0.34** | (0.05) |
| | Finland | 2.98 | (0.05) | 3.28 | (0.05) | **-0.30** | (0.04) | 0.36 | (0.02) | 0.36 | (0.02) | 0.00 | (0.03) |
| | France | 3.91 | (0.04) | 4.11 | (0.04) | **-0.19** | (0.05) | 0.70 | (0.03) | 0.83 | (0.03) | **-0.13** | (0.04) |
| | Germany | 3.50 | (0.04) | 3.82 | (0.04) | **-0.32** | (0.05) | 0.65 | (0.03) | 0.57 | (0.03) | 0.07 | (0.04) |
| | Greece | 2.74 | (0.06) | 3.60 | (0.04) | **-0.86** | (0.07) | 1.42 | (0.04) | 1.83 | (0.04) | **-0.42** | (0.05) |
| | Hungary | 2.91 | (0.05) | 3.48 | (0.05) | **-0.57** | (0.06) | 1.15 | (0.03) | 1.48 | (0.04) | **-0.35** | (0.05) |
| | Iceland | 4.37 | (0.04) | 4.68 | (0.03) | **-0.31** | (0.06) | 0.53 | (0.03) | 0.40 | (0.02) | **0.14** | (0.03) |
| | Ireland | 3.47 | (0.04) | 3.62 | (0.04) | **-0.15** | (0.05) | 0.69 | (0.03) | 0.58 | (0.03) | **0.10** | (0.04) |
| | Italy | 4.36 | (0.04) | 4.87 | (0.04) | **-0.51** | (0.05) | 0.82 | (0.03) | 0.77 | (0.02) | 0.03 | (0.04) |
| | Japan | 3.73 | (0.06) | 3.90 | (0.05) | -0.17 | (0.08) | 0.47 | (0.02) | 0.38 | (0.02) | **0.08** | (0.03) |
| | Korea | 4.43 | (0.06) | 4.52 | (0.06) | -0.09 | (0.09) | 1.49 | (0.06) | 1.40 | (0.05) | 0.07 | (0.08) |
| | Luxembourg | 3.32 | (0.04) | 3.69 | (0.03) | **-0.37** | (0.04) | 0.64 | (0.03) | 0.55 | (0.02) | **0.09** | (0.04) |
| | Mexico | 3.67 | (0.05) | 3.79 | (0.04) | -0.11 | (0.06) | 1.15 | (0.03) | 1.06 | (0.04) | **0.09** | (0.04) |
| | Netherlands | 2.83 | (0.03) | 3.01 | (0.03) | **-0.18** | (0.04) | 0.65 | (0.02) | 0.64 | (0.03) | 0.02 | (0.04) |
| | New Zealand | 4.27 | (0.04) | 4.50 | (0.04) | **-0.23** | (0.05) | 0.67 | (0.05) | 0.64 | (0.02) | 0.00 | (0.04) |
| | Norway | 3.46 | (0.05) | 3.74 | (0.05) | **-0.28** | (0.05) | 1.11 | (0.03) | 1.20 | (0.03) | -0.09 | (0.05) |
| | Poland | 4.35 | (0.05) | 4.92 | (0.03) | **-0.57** | (0.05) | 0.69 | (0.03) | 0.72 | (0.03) | -0.03 | (0.03) |
| | Portugal | 3.16 | (0.04) | 3.36 | (0.03) | **-0.20** | (0.04) | 0.56 | (0.02) | 0.57 | (0.03) | -0.03 | (0.03) |
| | Slovak Republic | 3.07 | (0.06) | 3.17 | (0.06) | -0.10 | (0.06) | 0.70 | (0.03) | 1.08 | (0.04) | **-0.36** | (0.04) |
| | Spain | 3.46 | (0.04) | 3.75 | (0.03) | **-0.29** | (0.04) | 0.63 | (0.03) | 0.53 | (0.02) | **0.09** | (0.04) |
| | Sweden | 3.07 | (0.04) | 3.16 | (0.03) | **-0.09** | (0.04) | 0.64 | (0.03) | 0.72 | (0.03) | -0.09 | (0.04) |
| | Switzerland | 3.50 | (0.05) | 3.81 | (0.04) | **-0.31** | (0.05) | 0.51 | (0.02) | 0.46 | (0.02) | **0.06** | (0.03) |
| | Turkey | 3.81 | (0.07) | 4.20 | (0.08) | **-0.39** | (0.09) | 1.64 | (0.05) | 2.02 | (0.06) | **-0.30** | (0.06) |
| | United Kingdom | 3.87 | (0.04) | 3.92 | (0.05) | -0.05 | (0.04) | 0.62 | (0.02) | 0.57 | (0.02) | 0.04 | (0.03) |
| | United States | 3.47 | (0.06) | 3.80 | (0.05) | **-0.33** | (0.07) | 1.01 | (0.04) | 1.22 | (0.03) | **-0.19** | (0.05) |
| | **OECD average** | **3.64** | **(0.01)** | **3.92** | **(0.01)** | **-0.28** | **(0.01)** | **0.79** | **(0.01)** | **0.84** | **(0.01)** | **-0.05** | **(0.01)** |
| Partners | Argentina | 2.22 | (0.05) | 2.54 | (0.07) | **-0.32** | (0.08) | 0.50 | (0.03) | 0.36 | (0.03) | **0.14** | (0.03) |
| | Azerbaijan | 3.59 | (0.05) | 3.79 | (0.06) | **-0.20** | (0.07) | 1.89 | (0.06) | 1.70 | (0.06) | **0.15** | (0.07) |
| | Brazil | 3.08 | (0.05) | 3.12 | (0.04) | -0.04 | (0.05) | 1.08 | (0.03) | 1.26 | (0.03) | **-0.17** | (0.05) |
| | Bulgaria | 2.67 | (0.05) | 3.16 | (0.06) | **-0.49** | (0.08) | 1.07 | (0.04) | 1.11 | (0.05) | -0.05 | (0.06) |
| | Chile | 3.38 | (0.07) | 3.52 | (0.09) | -0.15 | (0.10) | 0.94 | (0.04) | 1.06 | (0.04) | **-0.11** | (0.04) |
| | Colombia | 3.83 | (0.06) | 3.99 | (0.06) | -0.16 | (0.07) | 1.11 | (0.04) | 1.18 | (0.04) | -0.08 | (0.06) |
| | Croatia | 3.14 | (0.04) | 3.51 | (0.05) | **-0.37** | (0.06) | 0.43 | (0.03) | 0.35 | (0.02) | **0.09** | (0.03) |
| | Estonia | 3.24 | (0.05) | 3.73 | (0.04) | **-0.49** | (0.05) | 0.87 | (0.04) | 0.91 | (0.04) | -0.04 | (0.05) |
| | Hong Kong-China | 5.08 | (0.06) | 5.29 | (0.05) | **-0.21** | (0.07) | 0.87 | (0.04) | 0.75 | (0.04) | 0.10 | (0.06) |
| | Indonesia | 3.57 | (0.07) | 3.71 | (0.07) | -0.15 | (0.09) | 1.26 | (0.06) | 1.25 | (0.05) | -0.04 | (0.06) |
| | Israel | 2.77 | (0.06) | 3.26 | (0.06) | **-0.49** | (0.08) | 1.31 | (0.05) | 1.36 | (0.04) | -0.03 | (0.06) |
| | Jordan | 3.16 | (0.08) | 3.94 | (0.06) | **-0.77** | (0.10) | 1.87 | (0.06) | 1.68 | (0.06) | **0.21** | (0.09) |
| | Kyrgyzstan | 2.36 | (0.06) | 3.05 | (0.07) | **-0.69** | (0.07) | 1.50 | (0.04) | 1.87 | (0.05) | **-0.38** | (0.06) |
| | Latvia | 3.59 | (0.05) | 3.80 | (0.04) | **-0.21** | (0.05) | 0.92 | (0.04) | 0.83 | (0.04) | **0.10** | (0.04) |
| | Liechtenstein | 3.45 | (0.15) | 3.85 | (0.10) | **-0.40** | (0.18) | 0.36 | (0.07) | 0.29 | (0.04) | 0.13 | (0.08) |
| | Lithuania | 3.33 | (0.05) | 3.99 | (0.05) | **-0.66** | (0.06) | 0.67 | (0.03) | 0.64 | (0.03) | 0.01 | (0.03) |
| | Macao-China | 5.15 | (0.04) | 5.49 | (0.04) | **-0.34** | (0.06) | 1.09 | (0.04) | 1.02 | (0.04) | 0.07 | (0.06) |
| | Montenegro | 2.75 | (0.05) | 3.12 | (0.05) | **-0.36** | (0.07) | 0.73 | (0.03) | 0.76 | (0.03) | -0.04 | (0.05) |
| | Qatar | 2.95 | (0.04) | 2.85 | (0.04) | 0.10 | (0.06) | 1.76 | (0.04) | 1.42 | (0.03) | **0.37** | (0.05) |
| | Romania | 3.05 | (0.06) | 3.54 | (0.07) | **-0.50** | (0.07) | 1.34 | (0.05) | 1.69 | (0.04) | **-0.33** | (0.07) |
| | Russian Federation | 2.07 | (0.04) | 2.02 | (0.04) | 0.04 | (0.04) | 0.81 | (0.03) | 0.83 | (0.03) | -0.01 | (0.03) |
| | Serbia | 3.02 | (0.04) | 3.34 | (0.04) | **-0.32** | (0.04) | 0.94 | (0.03) | 0.92 | (0.03) | -0.02 | (0.04) |
| | Slovenia | 2.93 | (0.04) | 3.55 | (0.04) | **-0.62** | (0.06) | 0.76 | (0.02) | 0.71 | (0.02) | 0.05 | (0.04) |
| | Chinese Taipei | 4.29 | (0.06) | 4.45 | (0.07) | -0.16 | (0.08) | 0.65 | (0.03) | 0.74 | (0.03) | **-0.11** | (0.04) |
| | Thailand | 3.07 | (0.05) | 3.13 | (0.03) | -0.06 | (0.07) | 0.71 | (0.04) | 0.45 | (0.02) | **0.25** | (0.04) |
| | Tunisia | 2.78 | (0.07) | 3.46 | (0.06) | **-0.68** | (0.08) | 1.66 | (0.05) | 1.89 | (0.06) | **-0.22** | (0.07) |
| | Uruguay | 2.48 | (0.04) | 2.98 | (0.04) | **-0.51** | (0.05) | 0.63 | (0.04) | 0.66 | (0.03) | -0.04 | (0.04) |

*Note:* Values that are statistically significant at the 5% level ($p < 0.05$) are indicated in bold.

### Table 3.6c [Part 2/3] Mean learning hours and allocation of total learning time on the language of instruction, by gender

| | | Mean learning hours per week | | | | | | | | | | |
| | | Individual study | | | | | | Total learning hours | | | | |
| | | Male students | | Female students | | Difference (male-female) | | Male students | | Female students | | Difference (male-female) |
| | | Mean | S.E. | Mean | S.E. | Dif. | S.E. | Mean | S.E. | Mean | S.E. | Dif. | S.E. |
|---|---|---|---|---|---|---|---|---|---|---|---|---|---|
| OECD | Australia | 1.59 | (0.03) | 1.83 | (0.02) | **-0.24** | (0.04) | 6.24 | (0.06) | 6.63 | (0.06) | **-0.39** | (0.09) |
| | Austria | 1.45 | (0.04) | 1.65 | (0.05) | **-0.20** | (0.05) | 4.53 | (0.08) | 4.79 | (0.09) | **-0.27** | (0.11) |
| | Belgium | 1.23 | (0.02) | 1.48 | (0.02) | **-0.26** | (0.03) | 5.07 | (0.06) | 5.54 | (0.05) | **-0.47** | (0.07) |
| | Canada | 1.47 | (0.03) | 2.01 | (0.03) | **-0.54** | (0.04) | 6.53 | (0.07) | 7.58 | (0.08) | **-1.05** | (0.08) |
| | Czech Republic | 1.06 | (0.03) | 1.29 | (0.04) | **-0.22** | (0.05) | 5.28 | (0.05) | 5.77 | (0.08) | **-0.49** | (0.10) |
| | Denmark | 1.94 | (0.03) | 2.39 | (0.04) | **-0.45** | (0.05) | 8.83 | (0.08) | 9.85 | (0.09) | **-1.02** | (0.10) |
| | Finland | 0.95 | (0.02) | 1.32 | (0.03) | **-0.37** | (0.03) | 4.29 | (0.07) | 4.96 | (0.08) | **-0.66** | (0.06) |
| | France | 1.26 | (0.03) | 1.75 | (0.03) | **-0.50** | (0.04) | 5.88 | (0.07) | 6.70 | (0.06) | **-0.82** | (0.09) |
| | Germany | 1.74 | (0.03) | 2.05 | (0.04) | **-0.31** | (0.04) | 5.92 | (0.07) | 6.43 | (0.08) | **-0.51** | (0.09) |
| | Greece | 1.64 | (0.04) | 2.24 | (0.04) | **-0.59** | (0.05) | 5.82 | (0.10) | 7.67 | (0.09) | **-1.85** | (0.13) |
| | Hungary | 1.61 | (0.03) | 2.13 | (0.04) | **-0.53** | (0.05) | 5.69 | (0.10) | 7.08 | (0.11) | **-1.39** | (0.13) |
| | Iceland | 1.43 | (0.03) | 1.65 | (0.02) | **-0.22** | (0.04) | 6.33 | (0.06) | 6.73 | (0.05) | **-0.40** | (0.08) |
| | Ireland | 1.61 | (0.04) | 1.89 | (0.04) | **-0.28** | (0.05) | 5.78 | (0.08) | 6.10 | (0.08) | **-0.32** | (0.10) |
| | Italy | 2.57 | (0.04) | 3.33 | (0.05) | **-0.76** | (0.05) | 7.77 | (0.08) | 8.96 | (0.08) | **-1.19** | (0.09) |
| | Japan | 0.91 | (0.04) | 0.97 | (0.04) | -0.06 | (0.04) | 5.12 | (0.09) | 5.26 | (0.10) | -0.14 | (0.12) |
| | Korea | 1.37 | (0.04) | 1.44 | (0.04) | -0.07 | (0.05) | 7.32 | (0.13) | 7.36 | (0.13) | -0.04 | (0.18) |
| | Luxembourg | 1.28 | (0.03) | 1.49 | (0.03) | **-0.21** | (0.04) | 5.25 | (0.06) | 5.71 | (0.05) | **-0.46** | (0.07) |
| | Mexico | 1.96 | (0.04) | 2.14 | (0.03) | **-0.18** | (0.04) | 6.76 | (0.10) | 6.97 | (0.08) | **-0.21** | (0.10) |
| | Netherlands | 1.25 | (0.03) | 1.41 | (0.03) | **-0.16** | (0.04) | 4.73 | (0.06) | 5.04 | (0.06) | **-0.31** | (0.07) |
| | New Zealand | 1.42 | (0.05) | 1.72 | (0.03) | **-0.30** | (0.06) | 6.38 | (0.11) | 6.85 | (0.06) | **-0.47** | (0.13) |
| | Norway | 1.29 | (0.03) | 1.60 | (0.04) | **-0.31** | (0.05) | 5.84 | (0.08) | 6.55 | (0.09) | **-0.72** | (0.11) |
| | Poland | 1.83 | (0.04) | 2.61 | (0.03) | **-0.78** | (0.05) | 6.86 | (0.08) | 8.24 | (0.06) | **-1.38** | (0.09) |
| | Portugal | 1.54 | (0.03) | 2.02 | (0.04) | **-0.48** | (0.05) | 5.28 | (0.07) | 5.95 | (0.07) | **-0.67** | (0.09) |
| | Slovak Republic | 1.48 | (0.03) | 2.02 | (0.05) | **-0.54** | (0.05) | 5.26 | (0.08) | 6.26 | (0.11) | **-1.00** | (0.10) |
| | Spain | 1.64 | (0.04) | 2.14 | (0.04) | **-0.50** | (0.04) | 5.77 | (0.08) | 6.43 | (0.06) | **-0.67** | (0.09) |
| | Sweden | 1.14 | (0.03) | 1.39 | (0.03) | **-0.25** | (0.04) | 4.84 | (0.07) | 5.28 | (0.07) | **-0.43** | (0.08) |
| | Switzerland | 1.32 | (0.02) | 1.48 | (0.02) | **-0.16** | (0.03) | 5.35 | (0.07) | 5.75 | (0.06) | **-0.41** | (0.08) |
| | Turkey | 1.94 | (0.04) | 2.45 | (0.07) | **-0.51** | (0.07) | 7.37 | (0.12) | 8.66 | (0.17) | **-1.28** | (0.17) |
| | United Kingdom | 1.47 | (0.03) | 1.70 | (0.03) | **-0.22** | (0.04) | 5.96 | (0.07) | 6.19 | (0.08) | **-0.23** | (0.09) |
| | United States | 1.60 | (0.04) | 2.14 | (0.04) | **-0.54** | (0.05) | 6.14 | (0.09) | 7.16 | (0.09) | **-1.02** | (0.12) |
| | **OECD average** | 1.50 | (0.01) | 1.86 | (0.01) | **-0.36** | (0.01) | 5.94 | (0.01) | 6.62 | (0.02) | **-0.68** | (0.02) |
| Partners | Argentina | 1.47 | (0.05) | 1.78 | (0.05) | **-0.32** | (0.07) | 4.18 | (0.11) | 4.68 | (0.10) | **-0.50** | (0.13) |
| | Azerbaijan | 2.94 | (0.05) | 3.28 | (0.07) | **-0.34** | (0.08) | 8.48 | (0.12) | 8.84 | (0.15) | **-0.36** | (0.14) |
| | Brazil | 1.61 | (0.04) | 1.86 | (0.03) | **-0.25** | (0.05) | 5.76 | (0.09) | 6.22 | (0.08) | **-0.46** | (0.10) |
| | Bulgaria | 1.79 | (0.06) | 2.33 | (0.07) | **-0.53** | (0.07) | 5.56 | (0.10) | 6.61 | (0.15) | **-1.05** | (0.16) |
| | Chile | 1.47 | (0.03) | 1.68 | (0.05) | **-0.21** | (0.05) | 5.83 | (0.09) | 6.26 | (0.14) | **-0.43** | (0.16) |
| | Colombia | 1.69 | (0.04) | 1.96 | (0.06) | **-0.27** | (0.08) | 6.65 | (0.08) | 7.15 | (0.12) | **-0.50** | (0.13) |
| | Croatia | 1.38 | (0.03) | 1.77 | (0.04) | **-0.39** | (0.04) | 4.99 | (0.07) | 5.64 | (0.08) | **-0.65** | (0.10) |
| | Estonia | 1.45 | (0.04) | 1.80 | (0.04) | **-0.35** | (0.05) | 5.57 | (0.08) | 6.43 | (0.08) | **-0.87** | (0.10) |
| | Hong Kong-China | 1.52 | (0.05) | 1.76 | (0.04) | **-0.25** | (0.06) | 7.47 | (0.10) | 7.80 | (0.10) | **-0.33** | (0.12) |
| | Indonesia | 1.68 | (0.05) | 1.93 | (0.03) | **-0.25** | (0.06) | 6.49 | (0.14) | 6.89 | (0.10) | **-0.40** | (0.17) |
| | Israel | 1.59 | (0.06) | 1.72 | (0.05) | -0.14 | (0.08) | 5.73 | (0.14) | 6.32 | (0.11) | **-0.60** | (0.18) |
| | Jordan | 2.45 | (0.06) | 2.72 | (0.06) | **-0.28** | (0.08) | 7.48 | (0.14) | 8.32 | (0.11) | **-0.84** | (0.18) |
| | Kyrgyzstan | 1.94 | (0.04) | 2.67 | (0.06) | **-0.74** | (0.07) | 5.93 | (0.10) | 7.61 | (0.13) | **-1.68** | (0.14) |
| | Latvia | 1.86 | (0.04) | 2.15 | (0.04) | **-0.29** | (0.04) | 6.37 | (0.09) | 6.78 | (0.08) | **-0.41** | (0.09) |
| | Liechtenstein | 1.15 | (0.09) | 1.31 | (0.08) | -0.17 | (0.13) | 4.97 | (0.18) | 5.42 | (0.14) | -0.44 | (0.24) |
| | Lithuania | 1.57 | (0.04) | 2.07 | (0.04) | **-0.50** | (0.05) | 5.57 | (0.08) | 6.71 | (0.08) | **-1.14** | (0.11) |
| | Macao-China | 1.41 | (0.04) | 1.57 | (0.04) | **-0.16** | (0.05) | 7.65 | (0.08) | 8.08 | (0.08) | **-0.43** | (0.11) |
| | Montenegro | 1.79 | (0.05) | 2.19 | (0.05) | **-0.40** | (0.07) | 5.27 | (0.10) | 6.06 | (0.10) | **-0.79** | (0.15) |
| | Qatar | 2.06 | (0.04) | 2.02 | (0.03) | 0.04 | (0.04) | 6.77 | (0.09) | 6.28 | (0.07) | **0.48** | (0.11) |
| | Romania | 1.87 | (0.04) | 2.51 | (0.06) | **-0.64** | (0.08) | 6.29 | (0.12) | 7.73 | (0.12) | **-1.44** | (0.16) |
| | Russian Federation | 1.48 | (0.05) | 1.62 | (0.03) | -0.14 | (0.04) | 4.33 | (0.08) | 4.45 | (0.08) | -0.12 | (0.07) |
| | Serbia | 1.51 | (0.04) | 1.89 | (0.04) | **-0.38** | (0.05) | 5.46 | (0.07) | 6.13 | (0.09) | **-0.67** | (0.10) |
| | Slovenia | 1.35 | (0.03) | 1.60 | (0.03) | **-0.24** | (0.04) | 5.07 | (0.06) | 5.86 | (0.06) | **-0.79** | (0.08) |
| | Chinese Taipei | 1.60 | (0.03) | 1.95 | (0.04) | **-0.34** | (0.04) | 6.60 | (0.08) | 7.16 | (0.10) | **-0.56** | (0.10) |
| | Thailand | 1.59 | (0.05) | 1.79 | (0.04) | **-0.21** | (0.05) | 5.35 | (0.10) | 5.37 | (0.07) | -0.02 | (0.13) |
| | Tunisia | 1.95 | (0.05) | 2.27 | (0.06) | **-0.33** | (0.07) | 6.42 | (0.13) | 7.62 | (0.15) | **-1.20** | (0.19) |
| | Uruguay | 1.14 | (0.03) | 1.55 | (0.03) | **-0.41** | (0.04) | 4.27 | (0.09) | 5.20 | (0.07) | **-0.93** | (0.10) |

*Note*: Values that are statistically significant at the 5% level (p < 0.05) are indicated in bold.

© OECD 2011  Quality Time for Students: Learning In and Out of School

## Table 3.6c [Part 3/3] Mean learning hours and allocation of total learning time on the language of instruction, by gender

| | Allocation of total learning time on the language of instruction for | | | | | | | | | | | | | | | | |
| | Regular school lessons | | | | | | Out-of-school-time lessons | | | | | | Individual study | | | | | |
| | Male students | | Female students | | Difference (male-female) | | Male students | | Female students | | Difference (male-female) | | Male students | | Female students | | Difference (male-female) | |
| | % | S.E. | % | S.E. | Dif. | S.E. | % | S.E. | % | S.E. | Dif. | S.E. | % | S.E. | % | S.E. | Dif. | S.E. |
|---|---|---|---|---|---|---|---|---|---|---|---|---|---|---|---|---|---|---|
| Australia | 67.5 | (0.4) | 66.6 | (0.3) | **1.0** | (0.4) | 9.0 | (0.2) | 7.6 | (0.2) | **1.8** | (0.3) | 23.4 | (0.3) | 25.9 | (0.2) | **-2.4** | (0.4) |
| Austria | 65.4 | (0.6) | 65.6 | (0.6) | -0.1 | (0.8) | 4.3 | (0.4) | 2.4 | (0.2) | -0.1 | (0.5) | 30.3 | (0.5) | 32.0 | (0.5) | **-1.7** | (0.7) |
| Belgium | 67.6 | (0.4) | 66.9 | (0.4) | 0.7 | (0.6) | 7.8 | (0.3) | 6.3 | (0.2) | **1.3** | (0.3) | 24.6 | (0.3) | 26.8 | (0.3) | **-2.2** | (0.4) |
| Canada | 67.3 | (0.4) | 64.0 | (0.4) | **3.3** | (0.5) | 10.8 | (0.2) | 10.8 | (0.3) | 0.5 | (0.3) | 21.9 | (0.3) | 25.2 | (0.3) | **-3.3** | (0.4) |
| Czech Republic | 73.4 | (0.5) | 69.3 | (0.6) | **4.1** | (0.8) | 8.3 | (0.3) | 9.8 | (0.3) | 0.3 | (0.5) | 18.3 | (0.4) | 20.9 | (0.5) | **-2.6** | (0.6) |
| Denmark | 63.9 | (0.4) | 60.4 | (0.4) | **3.5** | (0.5) | 15.3 | (0.3) | 16.6 | (0.3) | 0.7 | (0.4) | 20.8 | (0.2) | 23.0 | (0.3) | **-2.2** | (0.4) |
| Finland | 72.4 | (0.5) | 69.0 | (0.5) | **3.4** | (0.6) | 6.6 | (0.3) | 5.8 | (0.3) | **2.1** | (0.3) | 20.9 | (0.4) | 25.2 | (0.4) | **-4.3** | (0.5) |
| France | 69.5 | (0.5) | 64.6 | (0.4) | **5.0** | (0.6) | 10.5 | (0.3) | 10.9 | (0.3) | -0.1 | (0.4) | 20.0 | (0.4) | 24.5 | (0.3) | **-4.6** | (0.5) |
| Germany | 62.3 | (0.4) | 62.3 | (0.4) | -0.0 | (0.6) | 8.7 | (0.4) | 7.1 | (0.3) | **1.2** | (0.5) | 29.0 | (0.4) | 30.6 | (0.4) | **-1.6** | (0.5) |
| Greece | 50.9 | (0.9) | 51.0 | (0.5) | -0.1 | (0.9) | 22.1 | (0.5) | 21.1 | (0.4) | -0.5 | (0.7) | 27.0 | (0.6) | 27.9 | (0.4) | -0.9 | (0.7) |
| Hungary | 53.9 | (0.6) | 52.5 | (0.5) | 1.4 | (0.7) | 18.2 | (0.4) | 18.3 | (0.4) | 0.3 | (0.5) | 27.9 | (0.4) | 29.2 | (0.3) | **-1.3** | (0.5) |
| Iceland | 71.8 | (0.5) | 71.8 | (0.4) | 0.1 | (0.6) | 6.9 | (0.3) | 5.1 | (0.3) | -0.1 | (0.4) | 21.3 | (0.3) | 23.1 | (0.3) | **-1.8** | (0.4) |
| Ireland | 64.5 | (0.6) | 64.0 | (0.6) | 0.6 | (0.8) | 9.2 | (0.4) | 7.2 | (0.3) | **1.5** | (0.5) | 26.3 | (0.4) | 28.8 | (0.5) | **-2.5** | (0.6) |
| Italy | 57.6 | (0.4) | 56.8 | (0.3) | 0.9 | (0.5) | 9.5 | (0.3) | 7.1 | (0.2) | **2.1** | (0.4) | 32.8 | (0.3) | 36.1 | (0.2) | **-3.3** | (0.4) |
| Japan | 77.8 | (0.6) | 78.5 | (0.6) | -0.7 | (0.6) | 7.1 | (0.3) | 5.5 | (0.3) | **1.2** | (0.4) | 15.1 | (0.5) | 16.0 | (0.5) | -0.8 | (0.5) |
| Korea | 66.0 | (0.7) | 66.7 | (0.6) | -0.7 | (0.9) | 17.3 | (0.6) | 15.6 | (0.5) | 0.6 | (0.8) | 16.7 | (0.3) | 17.7 | (0.3) | **-1.0** | (0.4) |
| Luxembourg | 67.4 | (0.5) | 67.2 | (0.4) | 0.1 | (0.6) | 9.7 | (0.4) | 8.0 | (0.3) | 0.5 | (0.5) | 22.9 | (0.4) | 24.8 | (0.3) | **-1.9** | (0.5) |
| Mexico | 54.9 | (0.5) | 55.2 | (0.5) | -0.3 | (0.6) | 15.7 | (0.4) | 13.6 | (0.4) | **2.1** | (0.4) | 29.4 | (0.4) | 31.2 | (0.3) | **-1.8** | (0.4) |
| Netherlands | 63.4 | (0.6) | 62.7 | (0.5) | 0.7 | (0.7) | 11.3 | (0.3) | 10.3 | (0.4) | 0.3 | (0.5) | 25.3 | (0.4) | 27.0 | (0.4) | **-1.6** | (0.5) |
| New Zealand | 71.2 | (0.7) | 69.2 | (0.4) | **2.0** | (0.7) | 8.4 | (0.4) | 7.6 | (0.3) | 0.8 | (0.4) | 20.3 | (0.4) | 23.2 | (0.3) | **-2.9** | (0.5) |
| Norway | 63.1 | (0.6) | 61.2 | (0.6) | **1.9** | (0.8) | 16.9 | (0.4) | 16.0 | (0.4) | **2.4** | (0.4) | 20.0 | (0.4) | 22.8 | (0.5) | **-2.7** | (0.5) |
| Poland | 65.0 | (0.5) | 62.1 | (0.3) | **2.9** | (0.5) | 9.3 | (0.4) | 7.8 | (0.3) | **2.2** | (0.4) | 25.7 | (0.4) | 30.2 | (0.3) | **-4.5** | (0.4) |
| Portugal | 62.7 | (0.5) | 59.4 | (0.6) | **3.3** | (0.7) | 9.3 | (0.4) | 8.1 | (0.4) | -0.1 | (0.5) | 27.9 | (0.4) | 32.5 | (0.5) | **-4.6** | (0.6) |
| Slovak Republic | 63.2 | (0.7) | 54.5 | (0.7) | **8.7** | (1.0) | 10.8 | (0.4) | 14.6 | (0.4) | **-2.6** | (0.5) | 25.9 | (0.6) | 30.8 | (0.7) | **-4.9** | (0.8) |
| Spain | 63.6 | (0.5) | 61.7 | (0.4) | **1.9** | (0.5) | 9.5 | (0.3) | 6.8 | (0.3) | 0.1 | (0.4) | 26.9 | (0.3) | 31.5 | (0.4) | **-4.5** | (0.4) |
| Sweden | 68.0 | (0.8) | 65.4 | (0.4) | **2.6** | (0.8) | 10.1 | (0.4) | 10.4 | (0.3) | 0.4 | (0.5) | 21.9 | (0.6) | 24.2 | (0.4) | **-2.3** | (0.5) |
| Switzerland | 67.0 | (0.4) | 68.0 | (0.5) | **-1.0** | (0.5) | 7.9 | (0.3) | 6.2 | (0.3) | **2.0** | (0.4) | 25.0 | (0.3) | 25.8 | (0.3) | -0.8 | (0.4) |
| Turkey | 56.0 | (0.7) | 53.2 | (0.8) | **2.8** | (0.8) | 19.5 | (0.5) | 20.2 | (0.5) | -1.7 | (0.8) | 24.5 | (0.4) | 26.6 | (0.5) | **-2.1** | (0.6) |
| United Kingdom | 68.5 | (0.4) | 66.7 | (0.4) | **1.9** | (0.5) | 8.3 | (0.3) | 7.4 | (0.2) | **1.4** | (0.3) | 23.2 | (0.3) | 26.0 | (0.3) | **-2.8** | (0.4) |
| United States | 57.5 | (0.8) | 54.2 | (0.5) | **3.3** | (0.7) | 15.9 | (0.6) | 16.0 | (0.4) | **1.9** | (0.5) | 26.5 | (0.4) | 29.8 | (0.4) | **-3.2** | (0.5) |
| **OECD average** | **64.8** | **(0.1)** | **63.0** | **(0.1)** | **1.8** | **(0.1)** | **64.8** | **(0.1)** | **63.0** | **(0.1)** | **1.8** | **(0.1)** | **24.1** | **(0.1)** | **26.6** | **(0.1)** | **-2.6** | **(0.1)** |
| Argentina | 55.3 | (1.0) | 55.1 | (0.7) | 0.2 | (1.2) | 9.8 | (0.6) | 6.5 | (0.5) | 0.7 | (0.7) | 34.9 | (0.8) | 38.3 | (0.7) | **-3.4** | (1.2) |
| Azerbaijan | 44.2 | (0.7) | 45.6 | (0.8) | -1.4 | (0.8) | 21.4 | (0.6) | 17.1 | (0.5) | **5.0** | (0.7) | 34.4 | (0.5) | 37.3 | (0.6) | **-2.9** | (0.7) |
| Brazil | 56.4 | (0.6) | 52.8 | (0.5) | **3.6** | (0.7) | 17.0 | (0.5) | 18.4 | (0.5) | -0.5 | (0.7) | 26.7 | (0.4) | 28.9 | (0.5) | **-2.2** | (0.6) |
| Bulgaria | 52.0 | (1.0) | 51.6 | (0.6) | 0.5 | (1.0) | 16.6 | (0.6) | 14.3 | (0.5) | **2.2** | (0.8) | 31.4 | (0.6) | 34.1 | (0.5) | **-2.7** | (0.7) |
| Chile | 58.1 | (0.7) | 56.6 | (0.9) | 1.5 | (0.9) | 14.9 | (0.5) | 15.6 | (0.6) | -0.1 | (0.5) | 27.1 | (0.4) | 27.8 | (0.5) | -0.7 | (0.6) |
| Colombia | 60.2 | (1.0) | 60.3 | (0.7) | -0.1 | (1.2) | 15.0 | (0.7) | 14.0 | (0.4) | 1.2 | (0.6) | 24.8 | (0.6) | 25.7 | (0.5) | -1.0 | (0.7) |
| Croatia | 67.6 | (0.6) | 66.0 | (0.5) | **1.6** | (0.7) | 6.9 | (0.4) | 4.9 | (0.3) | 0.8 | (0.5) | 25.5 | (0.4) | 29.1 | (0.4) | **-3.5** | (0.5) |
| Estonia | 62.1 | (0.7) | 61.5 | (0.5) | 0.6 | (0.8) | 13.8 | (0.6) | 12.4 | (0.5) | **1.5** | (0.7) | 24.2 | (0.4) | 26.2 | (0.4) | **-2.0** | (0.6) |
| Hong Kong-China | 71.2 | (0.7) | 70.7 | (0.5) | 0.6 | (0.8) | 10.0 | (0.4) | 8.2 | (0.3) | **1.1** | (0.5) | 18.8 | (0.5) | 21.1 | (0.3) | **-2.3** | (0.5) |
| Indonesia | 56.8 | (0.8) | 55.6 | (0.7) | 1.2 | (0.8) | 17.3 | (0.7) | 16.0 | (0.7) | -0.3 | (0.6) | 25.9 | (0.5) | 28.3 | (0.5) | **-2.4** | (0.6) |
| Israel | 52.3 | (0.8) | 55.6 | (0.7) | **-3.3** | (1.1) | 20.8 | (0.6) | 18.9 | (0.5) | **1.7** | (0.7) | 26.9 | (0.6) | 25.5 | (0.6) | 1.4 | (0.9) |
| Jordan | 40.6 | (1.0) | 47.4 | (0.7) | **-6.8** | (1.2) | 25.6 | (0.6) | 19.1 | (0.6) | **5.9** | (0.9) | 33.8 | (0.6) | 33.5 | (0.5) | 0.3 | (0.8) |
| Kyrgyzstan | 39.5 | (0.7) | 40.1 | (0.6) | -0.6 | (0.9) | 27.1 | (0.7) | 25.3 | (0.5) | **2.1** | (0.7) | 33.4 | (0.6) | 34.5 | (0.5) | -1.1 | (0.8) |
| Latvia | 59.8 | (0.5) | 58.7 | (0.5) | 1.1 | (0.6) | 12.3 | (0.5) | 10.6 | (0.4) | **1.2** | (0.5) | 27.9 | (0.4) | 30.7 | (0.4) | **-2.7** | (0.4) |
| Liechtenstein | 67.5 | (2.3) | 71.7 | (1.1) | -4.2 | (2.6) | 7.0 | (1.2) | 4.4 | (0.6) | **2.9** | (1.4) | 25.5 | (1.8) | 23.9 | (1.0) | 1.6 | (2.0) |
| Lithuania | 62.4 | (0.7) | 62.2 | (0.5) | 0.2 | (0.8) | 11.1 | (0.4) | 8.6 | (0.3) | **2.1** | (0.4) | 26.5 | (0.5) | 29.2 | (0.4) | **-2.7** | (0.6) |
| Macao-China | 71.3 | (0.5) | 71.5 | (0.5) | -0.3 | (0.7) | 12.0 | (0.3) | 10.3 | (0.4) | **1.5** | (0.6) | 16.8 | (0.4) | 18.2 | (0.3) | **-1.4** | (0.5) |
| Montenegro | 53.0 | (0.6) | 52.9 | (0.6) | 0.1 | (1.0) | 12.1 | (0.4) | 10.9 | (0.4) | 1.1 | (0.7) | 34.9 | (0.6) | 36.2 | (0.6) | -1.3 | (0.9) |
| Qatar | 43.0 | (0.4) | 46.2 | (0.3) | **-3.2** | (0.7) | 26.0 | (0.4) | 21.5 | (0.4) | **5.1** | (0.6) | 30.9 | (0.4) | 32.3 | (0.4) | **-1.4** | (0.6) |
| Romania | 51.6 | (0.8) | 49.7 | (0.7) | **1.9** | (0.9) | 19.7 | (0.6) | 19.7 | (0.5) | 1.1 | (0.6) | 28.6 | (0.5) | 30.6 | (0.5) | **-1.9** | (0.8) |
| Russian Federation | 49.5 | (0.8) | 47.1 | (0.6) | **2.5** | (0.8) | 16.6 | (0.6) | 16.2 | (0.7) | **1.7** | (0.7) | 33.9 | (0.6) | 36.7 | (0.5) | **-2.8** | (0.5) |
| Serbia | 60.5 | (0.7) | 59.9 | (0.5) | 0.6 | (0.7) | 14.2 | (0.5) | 11.6 | (0.4) | **2.2** | (0.5) | 25.4 | (0.5) | 28.5 | (0.4) | **-3.1** | (0.6) |
| Slovenia | 59.5 | (0.6) | 62.2 | (0.5) | **-2.7** | (0.8) | 13.4 | (0.4) | 10.9 | (0.3) | **1.7** | (0.6) | 27.2 | (0.4) | 27.0 | (0.4) | 0.2 | (0.6) |
| Chinese Taipei | 67.4 | (0.5) | 64.7 | (0.4) | **2.7** | (0.6) | 9.1 | (0.3) | 8.8 | (0.3) | **1.6** | (0.5) | 23.5 | (0.4) | 26.5 | (0.3) | **-3.0** | (0.5) |
| Thailand | 63.0 | (0.7) | 62.1 | (0.4) | 0.9 | (0.8) | 9.2 | (0.4) | 6.0 | (0.3) | **1.5** | (0.6) | 27.7 | (0.6) | 31.9 | (0.3) | **-4.1** | (0.6) |
| Tunisia | 44.0 | (0.9) | 47.0 | (0.7) | **-3.0** | (0.9) | 24.8 | (0.6) | 22.6 | (0.6) | **1.6** | (0.6) | 31.2 | (0.6) | 30.4 | (0.5) | 0.8 | (0.7) |
| Uruguay | 61.2 | (0.7) | 60.5 | (0.6) | 0.6 | (0.9) | 12.3 | (0.6) | 10.4 | (0.5) | **2.3** | (0.7) | 26.5 | (0.5) | 29.1 | (0.4) | **-2.6** | (0.7) |

*Note:* Values that are statistically significant at the 5% level (p < 0.05) are indicated in bold.

**Table 3.6d** [Part 1/3] **Mean learning hours and allocation of total learning time in science, in mathematics and on the language of instruction, by gender**

| | Mean learning hours per week | | | | | | | | | | | |
| | Regular school lessons | | | | | | Out-of-school-time lessons | | | | | |
| | Male students | | Female students | | Difference (male-female) | | Male students | | Female students | | Difference (male-female) | |
| | Mean | S.E. | Mean | S.E. | Dif. | S.E. | Mean | S.E. | Mean | S.E. | Dif. | S.E. |
|---|---|---|---|---|---|---|---|---|---|---|---|---|
| **OECD** Australia | 11.21 | (0.10) | 11.60 | (0.10) | **-0.39** | (0.13) | 1.92 | (0.05) | 1.60 | (0.04) | **0.33** | (0.07) |
| Austria | 8.47 | (0.13) | 8.65 | (0.10) | -0.18 | (0.15) | 1.04 | (0.06) | 0.84 | (0.05) | **0.20** | (0.07) |
| Belgium | 9.41 | (0.13) | 10.01 | (0.11) | **-0.59** | (0.14) | 1.41 | (0.05) | 1.21 | (0.04) | **0.20** | (0.06) |
| Canada | 12.41 | (0.12) | 13.44 | (0.13) | **-1.04** | (0.13) | 2.23 | (0.06) | 2.47 | (0.06) | **-0.23** | (0.08) |
| Czech Republic | 10.43 | (0.12) | 10.92 | (0.18) | **-0.49** | (0.21) | 1.81 | (0.06) | 2.00 | (0.06) | **-0.20** | (0.08) |
| Denmark | 12.92 | (0.10) | 13.39 | (0.09) | **-0.47** | (0.11) | 3.70 | (0.08) | 3.97 | (0.08) | **-0.27** | (0.11) |
| Finland | 9.21 | (0.11) | 10.19 | (0.13) | **-0.99** | (0.11) | 1.15 | (0.05) | 0.97 | (0.04) | **0.18** | (0.06) |
| France | 10.46 | (0.13) | 10.95 | (0.12) | **-0.49** | (0.15) | 2.12 | (0.06) | 2.36 | (0.06) | **-0.23** | (0.09) |
| Germany | 10.20 | (0.10) | 11.03 | (0.10) | **-0.83** | (0.12) | 2.02 | (0.08) | 1.82 | (0.06) | **0.19** | (0.08) |
| Greece | 9.10 | (0.17) | 10.53 | (0.12) | **-1.43** | (0.18) | 5.62 | (0.13) | 6.07 | (0.12) | **-0.45** | (0.14) |
| Hungary | 8.50 | (0.12) | 9.52 | (0.12) | **-1.02** | (0.14) | 3.39 | (0.06) | 3.80 | (0.10) | **-0.41** | (0.10) |
| Iceland | 11.84 | (0.10) | 12.64 | (0.08) | **-0.79** | (0.13) | 1.53 | (0.06) | 1.40 | (0.05) | 0.13 | (0.08) |
| Ireland | 9.63 | (0.11) | 9.86 | (0.11) | -0.23 | (0.13) | 1.78 | (0.07) | 1.53 | (0.06) | **0.26** | (0.09) |
| Italy | 11.09 | (0.10) | 11.45 | (0.11) | **-0.36** | (0.12) | 2.41 | (0.06) | 2.09 | (0.05) | **0.31** | (0.08) |
| Japan | 10.71 | (0.17) | 10.80 | (0.20) | -0.09 | (0.25) | 1.56 | (0.06) | 1.24 | (0.07) | **0.32** | (0.07) |
| Korea | 12.67 | (0.16) | 12.84 | (0.17) | -0.17 | (0.24) | 4.89 | (0.15) | 4.59 | (0.14) | 0.30 | (0.24) |
| Luxembourg | 9.26 | (0.09) | 10.17 | (0.07) | **-0.91** | (0.12) | 2.04 | (0.06) | 1.82 | (0.05) | **0.22** | (0.08) |
| Mexico | 10.76 | (0.14) | 10.91 | (0.12) | -0.15 | (0.17) | 3.47 | (0.09) | 3.10 | (0.10) | **0.37** | (0.10) |
| Netherlands | 7.93 | (0.10) | 8.01 | (0.08) | -0.08 | (0.12) | 1.97 | (0.06) | 1.78 | (0.06) | **0.19** | (0.07) |
| New Zealand | 12.53 | (0.11) | 13.11 | (0.10) | **-0.58** | (0.14) | 1.80 | (0.09) | 1.69 | (0.07) | 0.11 | (0.11) |
| Norway | 9.40 | (0.10) | 9.86 | (0.10) | **-0.46** | (0.11) | 3.19 | (0.06) | 3.07 | (0.08) | 0.12 | (0.10) |
| Poland | 10.88 | (0.11) | 12.53 | (0.09) | **-1.65** | (0.10) | 2.11 | (0.07) | 2.11 | (0.06) | -0.00 | (0.07) |
| Portugal | 9.80 | (0.13) | 10.34 | (0.11) | **-0.54** | (0.13) | 1.92 | (0.05) | 2.07 | (0.07) | -0.15 | (0.08) |
| Slovak Republic | 8.63 | (0.17) | 9.13 | (0.16) | **-0.50** | (0.17) | 2.02 | (0.07) | 2.81 | (0.10) | **-0.80** | (0.09) |
| Spain | 9.76 | (0.09) | 10.53 | (0.11) | **-0.77** | (0.09) | 2.22 | (0.07) | 2.26 | (0.07) | -0.05 | (0.09) |
| Sweden | 8.93 | (0.09) | 9.10 | (0.08) | -0.18 | (0.09) | 1.79 | (0.06) | 1.79 | (0.06) | 0.01 | (0.08) |
| Switzerland | 9.49 | (0.11) | 10.29 | (0.12) | **-0.81** | (0.13) | 1.72 | (0.06) | 1.42 | (0.05) | **0.30** | (0.07) |
| Turkey | 10.39 | (0.19) | 11.01 | (0.22) | **-0.62** | (0.25) | 4.90 | (0.10) | 5.60 | (0.13) | **-0.70** | (0.16) |
| United Kingdom | 11.88 | (0.10) | 11.97 | (0.11) | -0.09 | (0.12) | 1.80 | (0.06) | 1.60 | (0.06) | **0.21** | (0.07) |
| United States | 10.57 | (0.17) | 11.31 | (0.14) | **-0.74** | (0.17) | 2.99 | (0.10) | 3.08 | (0.08) | -0.08 | (0.11) |
| **OECD average** | 10.28 | (0.02) | 10.87 | (0.02) | **-0.59** | (0.03) | 2.42 | (0.01) | 2.40 | (0.01) | 0.01 | (0.02) |
| **Partners** Argentina | 7.13 | (0.15) | 8.03 | (0.23) | **-0.90** | (0.25) | 1.75 | (0.09) | 1.58 | (0.08) | 0.17 | (0.09) |
| Azerbaijan | 10.17 | (0.16) | 10.59 | (0.15) | **-0.42** | (0.20) | 5.26 | (0.12) | 4.44 | (0.13) | **0.82** | (0.16) |
| Brazil | 8.48 | (0.12) | 8.45 | (0.10) | 0.03 | (0.13) | 2.96 | (0.09) | 3.31 | (0.09) | **-0.35** | (0.11) |
| Bulgaria | 7.78 | (0.18) | 9.34 | (0.21) | **-1.56** | (0.21) | 3.17 | (0.10) | 3.23 | (0.11) | -0.06 | (0.14) |
| Chile | 9.05 | (0.19) | 9.53 | (0.23) | -0.48 | (0.27) | 2.68 | (0.06) | 2.96 | (0.08) | **-0.28** | (0.08) |
| Colombia | 11.48 | (0.23) | 11.82 | (0.21) | -0.34 | (0.21) | 3.26 | (0.12) | 3.36 | (0.09) | -0.10 | (0.16) |
| Croatia | 8.02 | (0.10) | 8.84 | (0.12) | **-0.82** | (0.14) | 1.59 | (0.07) | 1.56 | (0.06) | 0.02 | (0.08) |
| Estonia | 10.17 | (0.11) | 11.74 | (0.11) | **-1.57** | (0.13) | 2.61 | (0.11) | 2.64 | (0.08) | -0.03 | (0.14) |
| Hong Kong-China | 13.66 | (0.15) | 13.48 | (0.12) | 0.19 | (0.16) | 3.29 | (0.11) | 2.88 | (0.09) | **0.42** | (0.12) |
| Indonesia | 10.86 | (0.22) | 11.10 | (0.18) | -0.24 | (0.20) | 3.56 | (0.15) | 3.77 | (0.12) | -0.21 | (0.15) |
| Israel | 8.89 | (0.15) | 10.22 | (0.14) | **-1.33** | (0.20) | 4.37 | (0.12) | 4.51 | (0.11) | -0.14 | (0.15) |
| Jordan | 9.34 | (0.20) | 11.31 | (0.16) | **-1.98** | (0.25) | 5.50 | (0.15) | 4.72 | (0.14) | **0.77** | (0.21) |
| Kyrgyzstan | 6.92 | (0.16) | 8.50 | (0.20) | **-1.58** | (0.18) | 4.24 | (0.11) | 4.90 | (0.11) | **-0.66** | (0.14) |
| Latvia | 10.52 | (0.13) | 11.56 | (0.11) | **-1.05** | (0.12) | 2.82 | (0.09) | 2.62 | (0.09) | 0.20 | (0.10) |
| Liechtenstein | 9.77 | (0.34) | 10.62 | (0.23) | **-0.85** | (0.42) | 1.60 | (0.19) | 1.17 | (0.09) | **0.43** | (0.22) |
| Lithuania | 8.95 | (0.12) | 10.77 | (0.12) | **-1.82** | (0.14) | 1.94 | (0.06) | 1.92 | (0.06) | 0.02 | (0.08) |
| Macao-China | 14.08 | (0.11) | 14.86 | (0.10) | **-0.78** | (0.16) | 3.42 | (0.10) | 3.08 | (0.11) | **0.34** | (0.16) |
| Montenegro | 8.45 | (0.13) | 9.33 | (0.12) | **-0.88** | (0.17) | 2.73 | (0.08) | 2.64 | (0.08) | 0.09 | (0.12) |
| Qatar | 8.57 | (0.11) | 8.79 | (0.11) | -0.21 | (0.16) | 5.43 | (0.09) | 4.41 | (0.09) | **1.02** | (0.12) |
| Romania | 8.16 | (0.17) | 8.99 | (0.18) | **-0.83** | (0.18) | 3.89 | (0.09) | 4.19 | (0.09) | **-0.30** | (0.12) |
| Russian Federation | 9.04 | (0.13) | 9.76 | (0.16) | **-0.71** | (0.11) | 3.07 | (0.09) | 3.06 | (0.09) | 0.01 | (0.11) |
| Serbia | 8.80 | (0.13) | 9.86 | (0.11) | **-1.06** | (0.13) | 2.75 | (0.07) | 2.57 | (0.07) | 0.17 | (0.08) |
| Slovenia | 8.31 | (0.11) | 10.41 | (0.09) | **-2.10** | (0.16) | 2.48 | (0.06) | 2.46 | (0.07) | 0.02 | (0.10) |
| Chinese Taipei | 11.49 | (0.17) | 11.56 | (0.21) | -0.07 | (0.23) | 3.05 | (0.07) | 2.94 | (0.07) | 0.12 | (0.09) |
| Thailand | 10.31 | (0.14) | 10.97 | (0.13) | **-0.66** | (0.22) | 2.62 | (0.12) | 2.23 | (0.09) | **0.38** | (0.15) |
| Tunisia | 8.58 | (0.16) | 9.71 | (0.13) | **-1.13** | (0.18) | 5.96 | (0.09) | 6.23 | (0.09) | **-0.27** | (0.13) |
| Uruguay | 7.92 | (0.12) | 9.00 | (0.10) | **-1.08** | (0.13) | 2.08 | (0.08) | 2.08 | (0.07) | 0.01 | (0.10) |

*Note:* Values that are statistically significant at the 5% level (p < 0.05) are indicated in bold.

© OECD 2011 Quality Time for Students: Learning In and Out of School

**Table 3.6d** Mean learning hours and allocation of total learning time in science, in mathematics
[Part 2/3] and on the language of instruction, by gender

| | | Mean learning hours per week | | | | | | | | | | |
|---|---|---|---|---|---|---|---|---|---|---|---|---|
| | | Individual study | | | | | | Total learning hours | | | | |
| | | Male students | | Female students | | Difference (male-female) | | Male students | | Female students | | Difference (male-female) |
| | | Mean | S.E. | Mean | S.E. | Dif. | S.E. | Mean | S.E. | Mean | S.E. | Dif. | S.E. |
| OECD | Australia | 4.53 | (0.08) | 4.82 | (0.07) | **-0.30** | (0.10) | 17.68 | (0.17) | 18.02 | (0.16) | -0.35 | (0.22) |
| | Austria | 4.77 | (0.10) | 5.13 | (0.09) | **-0.35** | (0.12) | 14.36 | (0.23) | 14.62 | (0.17) | -0.26 | (0.25) |
| | Belgium | 4.00 | (0.07) | 4.80 | (0.07) | **-0.80** | (0.09) | 14.87 | (0.19) | 16.02 | (0.16) | **-1.15** | (0.22) |
| | Canada | 4.54 | (0.08) | 5.98 | (0.09) | **-1.43** | (0.11) | 19.30 | (0.20) | 21.92 | (0.20) | **-2.62** | (0.23) |
| | Czech Republic | 3.25 | (0.06) | 3.75 | (0.08) | **-0.50** | (0.10) | 15.47 | (0.15) | 16.65 | (0.26) | **-1.19** | (0.28) |
| | Denmark | 4.69 | (0.07) | 5.30 | (0.08) | **-0.62** | (0.09) | 21.23 | (0.19) | 22.65 | (0.18) | **-1.41** | (0.22) |
| | Finland | 3.04 | (0.06) | 3.77 | (0.06) | **-0.73** | (0.06) | 13.40 | (0.16) | 14.91 | (0.19) | **-1.51** | (0.16) |
| | France | 4.06 | (0.11) | 5.04 | (0.08) | **-0.98** | (0.13) | 16.68 | (0.23) | 18.35 | (0.18) | **-1.67** | (0.28) |
| | Germany | 5.43 | (0.08) | 6.33 | (0.10) | **-0.90** | (0.09) | 17.72 | (0.15) | 19.18 | (0.20) | **-1.46** | (0.19) |
| | Greece | 5.56 | (0.11) | 6.02 | (0.10) | **-0.46** | (0.13) | 20.32 | (0.32) | 22.61 | (0.26) | **-2.29** | (0.33) |
| | Hungary | 4.80 | (0.08) | 5.82 | (0.10) | **-1.02** | (0.12) | 16.73 | (0.20) | 19.12 | (0.26) | **-2.40** | (0.29) |
| | Iceland | 4.18 | (0.07) | 4.67 | (0.06) | **-0.49** | (0.10) | 17.54 | (0.16) | 18.73 | (0.12) | **-1.19** | (0.21) |
| | Ireland | 4.47 | (0.09) | 4.93 | (0.10) | **-0.46** | (0.12) | 15.85 | (0.19) | 16.30 | (0.20) | -0.45 | (0.24) |
| | Italy | 6.96 | (0.09) | 8.08 | (0.09) | **-1.12** | (0.10) | 20.54 | (0.18) | 21.58 | (0.20) | **-1.04** | (0.19) |
| | Japan | 3.06 | (0.10) | 3.16 | (0.13) | -0.10 | (0.13) | 15.32 | (0.26) | 15.19 | (0.33) | 0.13 | (0.39) |
| | Korea | 4.89 | (0.19) | 4.98 | (0.11) | -0.10 | (0.21) | 22.54 | (0.42) | 22.44 | (0.35) | 0.10 | (0.59) |
| | Luxembourg | 4.03 | (0.08) | 4.63 | (0.06) | **-0.60** | (0.11) | 15.38 | (0.15) | 16.57 | (0.12) | **-1.19** | (0.19) |
| | Mexico | 6.19 | (0.10) | 6.62 | (0.09) | **-0.43** | (0.11) | 20.24 | (0.25) | 20.56 | (0.21) | -0.32 | (0.25) |
| | Netherlands | 3.83 | (0.07) | 4.16 | (0.07) | **-0.33** | (0.09) | 13.75 | (0.17) | 13.89 | (0.15) | -0.15 | (0.22) |
| | New Zealand | 4.11 | (0.10) | 4.72 | (0.09) | **-0.61** | (0.14) | 18.50 | (0.22) | 19.50 | (0.18) | **-1.01** | (0.29) |
| | Norway | 3.84 | (0.07) | 4.30 | (0.10) | **-0.46** | (0.12) | 16.34 | (0.15) | 17.26 | (0.19) | **-0.93** | (0.24) |
| | Poland | 5.30 | (0.08) | 7.35 | (0.08) | **-2.05** | (0.10) | 18.30 | (0.18) | 22.03 | (0.15) | **-3.72** | (0.20) |
| | Portugal | 5.12 | (0.11) | 6.51 | (0.11) | **-1.39** | (0.15) | 16.90 | (0.23) | 18.92 | (0.18) | **-2.03** | (0.26) |
| | Slovak Republic | 4.25 | (0.10) | 5.40 | (0.12) | **-1.15** | (0.15) | 14.91 | (0.27) | 17.36 | (0.31) | **-2.44** | (0.31) |
| | Spain | 4.90 | (0.09) | 6.26 | (0.10) | **-1.36** | (0.09) | 17.03 | (0.20) | 19.12 | (0.18) | **-2.09** | (0.18) |
| | Sweden | 3.33 | (0.08) | 3.84 | (0.06) | **-0.51** | (0.09) | 14.04 | (0.15) | 14.72 | (0.14) | **-0.68** | (0.17) |
| | Switzerland | 3.99 | (0.05) | 4.42 | (0.06) | **-0.43** | (0.07) | 15.23 | (0.17) | 16.11 | (0.16) | **-0.89** | (0.22) |
| | Turkey | 5.61 | (0.09) | 6.70 | (0.14) | **-1.09** | (0.15) | 20.74 | (0.32) | 23.24 | (0.43) | **-2.49** | (0.45) |
| | United Kingdom | 4.31 | (0.07) | 4.72 | (0.07) | **-0.41** | (0.08) | 18.00 | (0.16) | 18.32 | (0.18) | -0.32 | (0.20) |
| | United States | 5.03 | (0.09) | 6.15 | (0.09) | **-1.12** | (0.12) | 18.82 | (0.21) | 20.53 | (0.20) | **-1.72** | (0.27) |
| | **OECD average** | 4.54 | (0.02) | 5.28 | (0.02) | **-0.74** | (0.02) | 17.26 | (0.04) | 18.55 | (0.04) | **-1.29** | (0.05) |
| Partners | Argentina | 4.55 | (0.13) | 5.47 | (0.12) | **-0.92** | (0.15) | 13.37 | (0.28) | 15.13 | (0.30) | **-1.76** | (0.37) |
| | Azerbaijan | 8.44 | (0.15) | 8.98 | (0.17) | **-0.54** | (0.18) | 23.95 | (0.31) | 24.26 | (0.36) | -0.31 | (0.40) |
| | Brazil | 4.81 | (0.09) | 5.54 | (0.10) | **-0.73** | (0.13) | 16.24 | (0.22) | 17.24 | (0.21) | **-1.00** | (0.26) |
| | Bulgaria | 5.42 | (0.15) | 6.91 | (0.20) | **-1.49** | (0.18) | 16.49 | (0.31) | 19.49 | (0.44) | **-3.01** | (0.40) |
| | Chile | 4.49 | (0.08) | 4.92 | (0.12) | **-0.43** | (0.13) | 16.37 | (0.26) | 17.43 | (0.35) | **-1.06** | (0.41) |
| | Colombia | 5.26 | (0.11) | 5.85 | (0.14) | **-0.59** | (0.18) | 20.00 | (0.30) | 21.01 | (0.35) | **-1.00** | (0.39) |
| | Croatia | 4.28 | (0.09) | 5.42 | (0.08) | **-1.13** | (0.10) | 14.00 | (0.18) | 15.85 | (0.20) | **-1.85** | (0.24) |
| | Estonia | 4.50 | (0.09) | 5.75 | (0.09) | **-1.25** | (0.13) | 17.29 | (0.20) | 20.16 | (0.20) | **-2.87** | (0.29) |
| | Hong Kong-China | 5.23 | (0.12) | 5.43 | (0.11) | -0.20 | (0.15) | 22.20 | (0.28) | 21.76 | (0.24) | 0.44 | (0.31) |
| | Indonesia | 5.12 | (0.11) | 6.06 | (0.09) | **-0.94** | (0.14) | 19.50 | (0.32) | 20.87 | (0.29) | **-1.37** | (0.34) |
| | Israel | 5.20 | (0.17) | 5.47 | (0.13) | -0.27 | (0.21) | 18.70 | (0.38) | 20.11 | (0.28) | **-1.41** | (0.46) |
| | Jordan | 7.40 | (0.11) | 8.37 | (0.17) | **-0.97** | (0.19) | 22.18 | (0.31) | 24.39 | (0.29) | **-2.21** | (0.42) |
| | Kyrgyzstan | 5.79 | (0.11) | 7.47 | (0.14) | **-1.68** | (0.18) | 17.25 | (0.28) | 20.87 | (0.34) | **-3.62** | (0.39) |
| | Latvia | 5.67 | (0.09) | 6.78 | (0.11) | **-1.11** | (0.13) | 19.03 | (0.24) | 20.95 | (0.21) | **-1.92** | (0.26) |
| | Liechtenstein | 3.77 | (0.26) | 4.07 | (0.19) | -0.30 | (0.34) | 15.22 | (0.46) | 15.75 | (0.31) | -0.53 | (0.62) |
| | Lithuania | 4.59 | (0.09) | 5.98 | (0.10) | **-1.39** | (0.14) | 15.47 | (0.20) | 18.63 | (0.19) | **-3.16** | (0.26) |
| | Macao-China | 4.61 | (0.09) | 5.26 | (0.09) | **-0.65** | (0.13) | 22.11 | (0.19) | 23.17 | (0.21) | **-1.06** | (0.28) |
| | Montenegro | 5.78 | (0.11) | 6.65 | (0.11) | **-0.87** | (0.16) | 16.93 | (0.25) | 18.57 | (0.23) | **-1.63** | (0.36) |
| | Qatar | 6.27 | (0.08) | 6.27 | (0.08) | 0.00 | (0.12) | 20.35 | (0.22) | 19.49 | (0.21) | **0.85** | (0.29) |
| | Romania | 5.48 | (0.10) | 6.44 | (0.15) | **-0.97** | (0.18) | 17.57 | (0.29) | 19.55 | (0.33) | **-1.98** | (0.37) |
| | Russian Federation | 6.10 | (0.14) | 7.15 | (0.12) | **-1.04** | (0.11) | 18.21 | (0.26) | 19.96 | (0.26) | **-1.75** | (0.23) |
| | Serbia | 4.70 | (0.10) | 5.75 | (0.09) | **-1.05** | (0.13) | 16.23 | (0.22) | 18.16 | (0.20) | **-1.93** | (0.26) |
| | Slovenia | 4.43 | (0.08) | 5.42 | (0.07) | **-0.99** | (0.10) | 15.29 | (0.19) | 18.29 | (0.15) | **-3.01** | (0.25) |
| | Chinese Taipei | 4.75 | (0.11) | 5.02 | (0.11) | **-0.27** | (0.12) | 19.49 | (0.30) | 19.58 | (0.36) | -0.08 | (0.37) |
| | Thailand | 4.83 | (0.12) | 5.67 | (0.09) | **-0.85** | (0.15) | 17.71 | (0.28) | 18.86 | (0.26) | **-1.15** | (0.43) |
| | Tunisia | 6.89 | (0.12) | 7.65 | (0.10) | **-0.76** | (0.15) | 21.54 | (0.30) | 23.55 | (0.24) | **-2.01** | (0.35) |
| | Uruguay | 3.66 | (0.09) | 4.77 | (0.08) | **-1.11** | (0.11) | 13.70 | (0.22) | 15.87 | (0.17) | **-2.18** | (0.25) |

*Note*: Values that are statistically significant at the 5% level (p < 0.05) are indicated in bold.

### Table 3.6d [Part 3/3] Mean learning hours and allocation of total learning time in science, in mathematics and on the language of instruction, by gender

| | Allocation of total learning time in science, in mathematics and on the language of instruction for | | | | | | | | | | | | | | | | | |
| | Regular school lessons | | | | | | Out-of-school-time lessons | | | | | | Individual study | | | | | |
| | Male students | | Female students | | Difference (male-female) | | Male students | | Female students | | Difference (male-female) | | Male students | | Female students | | Difference (male-female) | |
| | % | S.E. | % | S.E. | Dif. | S.E. | % | S.E. | % | S.E. | Dif. | S.E. | % | S.E. | % | S.E. | Dif. | S.E. |
|---|---|---|---|---|---|---|---|---|---|---|---|---|---|---|---|---|---|---|
| **OECD** | | | | | | | | | | | | | | | | | | |
| Australia | 66.5 | (0.4) | 66.6 | (0.3) | -0.1 | (0.4) | 9.5 | (0.2) | 7.8 | (0.2) | **1.7** | (0.3) | 24.0 | (0.3) | 25.6 | (0.2) | **-1.6** | (0.3) |
| Austria | 62.2 | (0.5) | 61.5 | (0.5) | 0.7 | (0.6) | 6.0 | (0.3) | 4.8 | (0.2) | **1.2** | (0.3) | 31.8 | (0.4) | 33.7 | (0.4) | **-1.9** | (0.5) |
| Belgium | 64.9 | (0.3) | 63.6 | (0.3) | **1.3** | (0.5) | 8.6 | (0.3) | 6.9 | (0.2) | **1.7** | (0.3) | 26.5 | (0.3) | 29.4 | (0.3) | **-3.0** | (0.4) |
| Canada | 65.5 | (0.4) | 62.5 | (0.4) | **3.0** | (0.5) | 11.2 | (0.2) | 10.8 | (0.3) | 0.4 | (0.3) | 23.3 | (0.3) | 26.7 | (0.3) | **-3.4** | (0.3) |
| Czech Republic | 70.8 | (0.5) | 67.9 | (0.5) | **2.9** | (0.7) | 9.9 | (0.3) | 10.5 | (0.2) | -0.6 | (0.4) | 19.2 | (0.3) | 21.6 | (0.4) | **-2.4** | (0.5) |
| Denmark | 63.0 | (0.4) | 61.6 | (0.4) | **1.4** | (0.5) | 16.0 | (0.3) | 15.9 | (0.3) | 0.0 | (0.4) | 21.0 | (0.2) | 22.5 | (0.3) | **-1.5** | (0.3) |
| Finland | 70.9 | (0.4) | 70.1 | (0.4) | 0.8 | (0.5) | 7.4 | (0.3) | 5.5 | (0.3) | **1.8** | (0.3) | 21.8 | (0.3) | 24.4 | (0.2) | **-2.6** | (0.3) |
| France | 65.1 | (0.5) | 61.8 | (0.4) | 3.3 | (0.6) | 12.1 | (0.3) | 12.1 | (0.3) | 0.0 | (0.4) | 22.8 | (0.4) | 26.1 | (0.3) | **-3.3** | (0.4) |
| Germany | 59.6 | (0.4) | 59.3 | (0.4) | 0.3 | (0.5) | 10.1 | (0.4) | 8.6 | (0.3) | **1.5** | (0.4) | 30.3 | (0.3) | 32.1 | (0.3) | **-1.8** | (0.4) |
| Greece | 47.1 | (0.7) | 49.0 | (0.4) | **-1.9** | (0.6) | 26.2 | (0.4) | 25.2 | (0.4) | 0.9 | (0.4) | 26.7 | (0.5) | 25.8 | (0.3) | 1.0 | (0.5) |
| Hungary | 52.8 | (0.5) | 51.8 | (0.4) | 1.0 | (0.6) | 19.0 | (0.4) | 18.4 | (0.4) | 0.6 | (0.4) | 28.1 | (0.4) | 29.7 | (0.3) | **-1.6** | (0.4) |
| Iceland | 69.9 | (0.4) | 69.5 | (0.3) | 0.4 | (0.5) | 7.6 | (0.3) | 6.8 | (0.2) | **0.8** | (0.4) | 22.5 | (0.3) | 23.7 | (0.2) | **-1.2** | (0.4) |
| Ireland | 63.5 | (0.6) | 63.4 | (0.5) | 0.0 | (0.7) | 9.6 | (0.3) | 7.8 | (0.3) | **1.8** | (0.4) | 26.9 | (0.4) | 28.7 | (0.4) | **-1.8** | (0.6) |
| Italy | 55.1 | (0.3) | 54.7 | (0.4) | 0.4 | (0.4) | 11.2 | (0.3) | 8.7 | (0.2) | **2.5** | (0.3) | 33.7 | (0.2) | 36.6 | (0.2) | **-2.9** | (0.3) |
| Japan | 74.4 | (0.7) | 74.7 | (0.6) | -0.3 | (0.6) | 8.2 | (0.3) | 6.7 | (0.3) | **1.5** | (0.3) | 17.4 | (0.4) | 18.6 | (0.5) | **-1.2** | (0.4) |
| Korea | 61.1 | (0.7) | 61.6 | (0.5) | -0.4 | (1.0) | 19.0 | (0.5) | 17.8 | (0.4) | 1.2 | (0.7) | 19.9 | (0.5) | 20.7 | (0.3) | -0.8 | (0.5) |
| Luxembourg | 63.1 | (0.4) | 63.3 | (0.3) | -0.2 | (0.6) | 11.6 | (0.3) | 9.8 | (0.2) | **1.8** | (0.4) | 25.3 | (0.3) | 26.9 | (0.3) | **-1.6** | (0.4) |
| Mexico | 53.6 | (0.4) | 53.9 | (0.5) | -0.3 | (0.5) | 15.8 | (0.3) | 13.7 | (0.3) | **2.0** | (0.4) | 30.6 | (0.3) | 32.4 | (0.3) | **-1.7** | (0.4) |
| Netherlands | 60.1 | (0.5) | 59.8 | (0.4) | 0.4 | (0.6) | 13.0 | (0.4) | 11.5 | (0.3) | **1.4** | (0.4) | 26.9 | (0.3) | 28.7 | (0.3) | **-1.8** | (0.4) |
| New Zealand | 70.2 | (0.6) | 69.2 | (0.4) | 1.0 | (0.6) | 8.6 | (0.3) | 7.8 | (0.3) | 0.8 | (0.4) | 21.1 | (0.3) | 23.0 | (0.3) | **-1.8** | (0.4) |
| Norway | 60.6 | (0.5) | 60.3 | (0.6) | 0.3 | (0.7) | 17.8 | (0.3) | 16.1 | (0.3) | **1.6** | (0.4) | 21.7 | (0.3) | 23.6 | (0.4) | **-1.9** | (0.5) |
| Poland | 60.9 | (0.4) | 59.0 | (0.3) | **1.9** | (0.4) | 11.1 | (0.3) | 9.1 | (0.3) | **2.0** | (0.3) | 28.0 | (0.3) | 32.0 | (0.3) | **-3.9** | (0.4) |
| Portugal | 60.0 | (0.4) | 56.7 | (0.5) | **3.3** | (0.6) | 10.7 | (0.3) | 9.8 | (0.3) | 0.8 | (0.4) | 29.4 | (0.4) | 33.5 | (0.4) | **-4.1** | (0.5) |
| Slovak Republic | 62.1 | (0.6) | 55.7 | (0.6) | **6.4** | (0.8) | 11.4 | (0.4) | 14.1 | (0.4) | **-2.8** | (0.4) | 26.5 | (0.4) | 30.2 | (0.5) | **-3.6** | (0.7) |
| Spain | 60.1 | (0.4) | 58.0 | (0.3) | **2.2** | (0.4) | 11.9 | (0.3) | 10.6 | (0.3) | **1.3** | (0.4) | 28.0 | (0.3) | 31.5 | (0.3) | **-3.5** | (0.3) |
| Sweden | 67.1 | (0.8) | 65.1 | (0.4) | **2.1** | (0.8) | 10.5 | (0.3) | 10.1 | (0.3) | 0.3 | (0.5) | 22.4 | (0.5) | 24.8 | (0.3) | **-2.4** | (0.5) |
| Switzerland | 63.7 | (0.3) | 64.9 | (0.4) | **-1.2** | (0.4) | 10.0 | (0.3) | 7.8 | (0.3) | **2.2** | (0.3) | 26.3 | (0.3) | 27.3 | (0.2) | **-1.0** | (0.4) |
| Turkey | 53.1 | (0.5) | 49.5 | (0.4) | **3.6** | (0.6) | 21.1 | (0.3) | 22.3 | (0.4) | **-1.2** | (0.5) | 25.8 | (0.3) | 28.2 | (0.3) | **-2.4** | (0.5) |
| United Kingdom | 68.2 | (0.4) | 67.5 | (0.4) | 0.7 | (0.4) | 8.7 | (0.2) | 7.7 | (0.2) | **1.0** | (0.3) | 23.1 | (0.3) | 24.8 | (0.3) | **-1.7** | (0.4) |
| United States | 56.3 | (0.4) | 54.8 | (0.4) | **1.5** | (0.6) | 15.8 | (0.3) | 14.8 | (0.3) | **1.1** | (0.5) | 27.8 | (0.3) | 30.4 | (0.3) | **-2.6** | (0.4) |
| **OECD average** | 62.4 | (0.1) | 61.2 | (0.1) | **1.1** | (0.1) | 12.3 | (0.1) | 11.3 | (0.1) | **1.0** | (0.1) | 25.3 | (0.1) | 27.4 | (0.1) | **-2.1** | (0.1) |
| **Partners** | | | | | | | | | | | | | | | | | | |
| Argentina | 54.6 | (0.8) | 54.4 | (0.7) | 0.2 | (1.0) | 11.6 | (0.5) | 9.6 | (0.4) | **2.0** | (0.5) | 33.8 | (0.6) | 36.0 | (0.6) | **-2.2** | (0.9) |
| Azerbaijan | 43.4 | (0.6) | 45.6 | (0.6) | **-2.2** | (0.7) | 21.7 | (0.5) | 17.6 | (0.4) | **4.1** | (0.5) | 34.9 | (0.4) | 36.8 | (0.4) | **-1.9** | (0.5) |
| Brazil | 54.9 | (0.6) | 51.3 | (0.5) | **3.6** | (0.6) | 16.6 | (0.4) | 17.6 | (0.4) | -1.0 | (0.6) | 28.5 | (0.4) | 31.0 | (0.4) | **-2.5** | (0.6) |
| Bulgaria | 49.8 | (0.8) | 50.3 | (0.5) | -0.5 | (0.9) | 18.2 | (0.6) | 15.5 | (0.4) | **2.7** | (0.6) | 32.0 | (0.5) | 34.3 | (0.5) | **-2.2** | (0.6) |
| Chile | 54.9 | (0.6) | 54.2 | (0.7) | 0.7 | (0.7) | 16.2 | (0.4) | 16.5 | (0.4) | -0.3 | (0.4) | 28.9 | (0.3) | 29.3 | (0.4) | -0.4 | (0.5) |
| Colombia | 59.2 | (0.8) | 59.8 | (0.7) | -0.5 | (0.9) | 15.0 | (0.5) | 14.1 | (0.3) | 0.9 | (0.6) | 25.8 | (0.5) | 26.2 | (0.4) | -0.4 | (0.5) |
| Croatia | 61.1 | (0.6) | 58.8 | (0.4) | **2.3** | (0.6) | 10.3 | (0.4) | 8.9 | (0.3) | **1.4** | (0.4) | 28.6 | (0.4) | 32.3 | (0.4) | **-3.8** | (0.4) |
| Estonia | 61.2 | (0.6) | 60.5 | (0.4) | 0.6 | (0.6) | 14.2 | (0.5) | 12.3 | (0.4) | **1.9** | (0.5) | 24.7 | (0.4) | 27.1 | (0.3) | **-2.5** | (0.4) |
| Hong Kong-China | 64.0 | (0.6) | 64.3 | (0.4) | -0.3 | (0.7) | 13.7 | (0.4) | 12.2 | (0.4) | **1.5** | (0.4) | 22.3 | (0.4) | 23.5 | (0.3) | **-1.2** | (0.5) |
| Indonesia | 57.2 | (0.9) | 54.7 | (0.7) | **2.5** | (0.8) | 16.7 | (0.7) | 16.4 | (0.5) | 0.3 | (0.6) | 26.1 | (0.3) | 28.9 | (0.4) | **-2.8** | (0.4) |
| Israel | 50.0 | (0.8) | 54.3 | (0.6) | **-4.2** | (0.9) | 22.9 | (0.4) | 20.6 | (0.4) | **2.3** | (0.5) | 27.1 | (0.5) | 25.2 | (0.5) | **1.9** | (0.7) |
| Jordan | 40.6 | (0.8) | 46.3 | (0.6) | **-5.7** | (1.0) | 25.1 | (0.6) | 18.9 | (0.5) | **6.2** | (0.8) | 34.2 | (0.4) | 34.7 | (0.5) | -0.5 | (0.6) |
| Kyrgyzstan | 40.0 | (0.6) | 40.1 | (0.5) | -0.1 | (0.6) | 26.1 | (0.6) | 24.4 | (0.4) | **1.8** | (0.6) | 33.9 | (0.5) | 35.6 | (0.4) | **-1.7** | (0.6) |
| Latvia | 57.7 | (0.4) | 57.1 | (0.4) | 0.6 | (0.6) | 13.7 | (0.4) | 11.7 | (0.4) | **2.0** | (0.4) | 28.6 | (0.3) | 31.2 | (0.3) | **-2.6** | (0.4) |
| Liechtenstein | 64.8 | (2.0) | 67.6 | (0.9) | -2.8 | (2.1) | 10.0 | (1.1) | 6.9 | (0.6) | **3.1** | (1.3) | 25.2 | (1.4) | 25.5 | (0.9) | -0.3 | (1.5) |
| Lithuania | 59.6 | (0.5) | 59.4 | (0.4) | 0.2 | (0.6) | 12.4 | (0.3) | 9.9 | (0.3) | **2.5** | (0.4) | 28.0 | (0.4) | 30.7 | (0.3) | **-2.7** | (0.5) |
| Macao-China | 66.7 | (0.4) | 66.7 | (0.4) | 0.0 | (0.6) | 13.9 | (0.3) | 11.8 | (0.4) | **2.1** | (0.5) | 19.4 | (0.3) | 21.6 | (0.3) | **-2.1** | (0.4) |
| Montenegro | 50.5 | (0.5) | 51.1 | (0.5) | -0.5 | (0.7) | 15.5 | (0.4) | 13.6 | (0.3) | **2.0** | (0.5) | 34.0 | (0.4) | 35.4 | (0.4) | **-1.4** | (0.5) |
| Qatar | 40.9 | (0.3) | 45.2 | (0.4) | **-4.3** | (0.5) | 27.2 | (0.3) | 22.3 | (0.3) | **4.9** | (0.4) | 31.9 | (0.3) | 32.5 | (0.3) | -0.6 | (0.4) |
| Romania | 48.9 | (0.5) | 48.5 | (0.6) | 0.4 | (0.7) | 20.9 | (0.4) | 20.1 | (0.4) | 0.8 | (0.4) | 30.2 | (0.3) | 31.5 | (0.4) | -1.3 | (0.5) |
| Russian Federation | 51.3 | (0.6) | 50.5 | (0.5) | 0.8 | (0.6) | 16.5 | (0.5) | 14.9 | (0.6) | **1.6** | (0.5) | 32.3 | (0.6) | 34.6 | (0.3) | **-2.3** | (0.5) |
| Serbia | 57.6 | (0.5) | 57.8 | (0.4) | -0.2 | (0.5) | 15.3 | (0.3) | 12.3 | (0.3) | **3.0** | (0.3) | 27.0 | (0.4) | 29.8 | (0.3) | **-2.8** | (0.5) |
| Slovenia | 55.8 | (0.5) | 58.0 | (0.4) | **-2.3** | (0.6) | 15.3 | (0.3) | 12.6 | (0.3) | **2.6** | (0.5) | 29.0 | (0.3) | 29.3 | (0.3) | -0.4 | (0.4) |
| Chinese Taipei | 61.6 | (0.5) | 61.3 | (0.3) | 0.3 | (0.5) | 14.6 | (0.2) | 13.3 | (0.3) | **1.2** | (0.3) | 23.9 | (0.3) | 25.4 | (0.3) | **-1.5** | (0.4) |
| Thailand | 63.0 | (0.6) | 61.8 | (0.3) | **1.2** | (0.7) | 11.5 | (0.4) | 9.4 | (0.3) | **2.2** | (0.5) | 25.5 | (0.4) | 28.9 | (0.4) | **-3.4** | (0.5) |
| Tunisia | 40.8 | (0.4) | 41.9 | (0.4) | -1.2 | (0.6) | 27.1 | (0.4) | 25.9 | (0.3) | **1.2** | (0.4) | 32.1 | (0.4) | 32.2 | (0.3) | -0.1 | (0.5) |
| Uruguay | 59.8 | (0.5) | 58.7 | (0.5) | 1.1 | (0.7) | 13.7 | (0.4) | 11.6 | (0.4) | **2.1** | (0.6) | 26.5 | (0.4) | 29.7 | (0.3) | **-3.2** | (0.5) |

*Note:* Values that are statistically significant at the 5% level (p < 0.05) are indicated in bold.

© OECD 2011 Quality Time for Students: Learning In and Out of School

Table 3.7a Mean learning hours and allocation of total learning time in science,
[Part 1/7] by quarters of the PISA index of economic, social and cultural status (ESCS)

| | | Mean learning hours per week | | | | | | | | |
| --- | --- | --- | --- | --- | --- | --- | --- | --- | --- | --- |
| | | Regular school lessons | | | | | | | | |
| | | Bottom quarter of ESCS | | Second quarter of ESCS | | Third quarter of ESCS | | Top quarter of ESCS | | Difference (bottom-top) | |
| | | Mean | S.E. | Mean | S.E. | Mean | S.E. | Mean | S.E. | Dif. | S.E. |
| OECD | Australia | 2.83 | (0.05) | 3.16 | (0.04) | 3.31 | (0.05) | 3.69 | (0.05) | **-0.87** | (0.06) |
| | Austria | 2.02 | (0.07) | 2.26 | (0.08) | 2.59 | (0.09) | 3.00 | (0.09) | **-0.98** | (0.11) |
| | Belgium | 1.95 | (0.07) | 2.47 | (0.06) | 2.83 | (0.07) | 3.28 | (0.05) | **-1.32** | (0.09) |
| | Canada | 3.45 | (0.06) | 3.90 | (0.06) | 4.20 | (0.06) | 4.46 | (0.07) | **-1.02** | (0.07) |
| | Czech Republic | 2.44 | (0.07) | 2.70 | (0.08) | 2.95 | (0.11) | 3.66 | (0.11) | **-1.22** | (0.11) |
| | Denmark | 3.00 | (0.06) | 3.17 | (0.06) | 3.22 | (0.06) | 3.45 | (0.06) | **-0.44** | (0.08) |
| | Finland | 2.87 | (0.07) | 3.03 | (0.05) | 3.16 | (0.06) | 3.46 | (0.06) | **-0.60** | (0.08) |
| | France | 2.07 | (0.06) | 2.54 | (0.07) | 3.00 | (0.07) | 3.82 | (0.08) | **-1.75** | (0.10) |
| | Germany | 2.39 | (0.08) | 2.98 | (0.07) | 3.29 | (0.07) | 3.61 | (0.07) | **-1.24** | (0.11) |
| | Greece | 2.54 | (0.07) | 3.00 | (0.08) | 3.23 | (0.07) | 3.95 | (0.09) | **-1.41** | (0.11) |
| | Hungary | 2.10 | (0.06) | 2.35 | (0.06) | 2.51 | (0.07) | 3.08 | (0.11) | **-0.97** | (0.12) |
| | Iceland | 2.73 | (0.05) | 2.88 | (0.05) | 3.06 | (0.05) | 3.22 | (0.05) | **-0.49** | (0.07) |
| | Ireland | 2.30 | (0.07) | 2.46 | (0.06) | 2.57 | (0.06) | 2.83 | (0.06) | **-0.53** | (0.09) |
| | Italy | 2.72 | (0.06) | 2.94 | (0.06) | 3.09 | (0.06) | 2.89 | (0.10) | -0.18 | (0.10) |
| | Japan | 2.43 | (0.05) | 2.61 | (0.06) | 2.81 | (0.07) | 2.94 | (0.08) | **-0.51** | (0.08) |
| | Korea | 3.26 | (0.07) | 3.55 | (0.07) | 3.65 | (0.07) | 3.88 | (0.13) | **-0.62** | (0.15) |
| | Luxembourg | 2.01 | (0.05) | 2.24 | (0.05) | 2.46 | (0.06) | 2.65 | (0.06) | **-0.65** | (0.08) |
| | Mexico | 3.18 | (0.10) | 3.02 | (0.06) | 3.05 | (0.06) | 3.37 | (0.06) | -0.16 | (0.12) |
| | Netherlands | 1.84 | (0.08) | 1.98 | (0.06) | 2.23 | (0.07) | 2.66 | (0.07) | **-0.82** | (0.10) |
| | New Zealand | 3.58 | (0.08) | 3.98 | (0.07) | 4.23 | (0.06) | 4.46 | (0.06) | **-0.87** | (0.10) |
| | Norway | 2.49 | (0.05) | 2.63 | (0.04) | 2.71 | (0.04) | 2.74 | (0.05) | **-0.25** | (0.06) |
| | Poland | 2.51 | (0.06) | 2.56 | (0.05) | 2.76 | (0.05) | 3.04 | (0.05) | **-0.53** | (0.07) |
| | Portugal | 2.56 | (0.07) | 3.06 | (0.08) | 3.33 | (0.08) | 3.90 | (0.09) | **-1.33** | (0.12) |
| | Slovak Republic | 1.81 | (0.07) | 2.20 | (0.09) | 2.51 | (0.09) | 3.30 | (0.12) | **-1.50** | (0.12) |
| | Spain | 2.65 | (0.05) | 2.88 | (0.05) | 3.20 | (0.06) | 3.74 | (0.08) | **-1.10** | (0.09) |
| | Sweden | 2.66 | (0.04) | 2.77 | (0.05) | 2.89 | (0.04) | 2.91 | (0.04) | **-0.25** | (0.05) |
| | Switzerland | 1.89 | (0.05) | 2.14 | (0.05) | 2.41 | (0.07) | 3.04 | (0.07) | **-1.14** | (0.07) |
| | Turkey | 2.38 | (0.11) | 2.58 | (0.08) | 2.77 | (0.10) | 3.73 | (0.19) | **-1.34** | (0.20) |
| | United Kingdom | 3.85 | (0.06) | 4.16 | (0.05) | 4.35 | (0.04) | 4.67 | (0.05) | **-0.82** | (0.07) |
| | United States | 2.85 | (0.12) | 3.33 | (0.08) | 3.68 | (0.06) | 4.20 | (0.07) | **-1.36** | (0.15) |
| | **OECD average** | 2.58 | (0.01) | 2.85 | (0.01) | 3.07 | (0.01) | 3.45 | (0.02) | **-0.88** | (0.02) |
| Partners | Argentina | 1.89 | (0.08) | 2.06 | (0.07) | 2.33 | (0.08) | 2.76 | (0.09) | **-0.88** | (0.13) |
| | Azerbaijan | 2.63 | (0.07) | 2.79 | (0.09) | 2.90 | (0.09) | 3.03 | (0.08) | **-0.39** | (0.09) |
| | Brazil | 1.91 | (0.06) | 1.97 | (0.05) | 2.15 | (0.05) | 2.83 | (0.07) | **-0.92** | (0.09) |
| | Bulgaria | 2.07 | (0.11) | 2.35 | (0.08) | 2.78 | (0.09) | 3.33 | (0.12) | **-1.26** | (0.15) |
| | Chile | 1.74 | (0.06) | 2.05 | (0.06) | 2.39 | (0.07) | 3.14 | (0.08) | **-1.40** | (0.10) |
| | Colombia | 3.36 | (0.13) | 3.41 | (0.15) | 3.27 | (0.08) | 3.96 | (0.17) | **-0.59** | (0.15) |
| | Croatia | 1.58 | (0.06) | 1.98 | (0.06) | 2.04 | (0.07) | 2.46 | (0.06) | **-0.87** | (0.08) |
| | Estonia | 3.06 | (0.08) | 3.13 | (0.06) | 3.27 | (0.07) | 3.63 | (0.07) | **-0.57** | (0.10) |
| | Hong Kong-China | 2.69 | (0.09) | 3.03 | (0.09) | 3.10 | (0.09) | 3.75 | (0.11) | **-1.06** | (0.15) |
| | Indonesia | 2.87 | (0.08) | 2.99 | (0.08) | 3.13 | (0.09) | 3.94 | (0.11) | **-1.07** | (0.14) |
| | Israel | 2.05 | (0.07) | 2.43 | (0.08) | 2.42 | (0.09) | 2.85 | (0.09) | **-0.77** | (0.12) |
| | Jordan | 2.81 | (0.09) | 3.08 | (0.08) | 3.34 | (0.08) | 3.75 | (0.09) | **-0.95** | (0.12) |
| | Kyrgyzstan | 1.94 | (0.15) | 1.87 | (0.07) | 2.10 | (0.08) | 2.45 | (0.08) | **-0.50** | (0.17) |
| | Latvia | 2.58 | (0.08) | 2.78 | (0.09) | 2.91 | (0.08) | 3.17 | (0.10) | **-0.60** | (0.11) |
| | Liechtenstein | 2.36 | (0.17) | 2.28 | (0.16) | 2.57 | (0.17) | 3.12 | (0.19) | -0.76 | (0.22) |
| | Lithuania | 2.45 | (0.07) | 2.63 | (0.06) | 2.74 | (0.06) | 2.94 | (0.06) | **-0.49** | (0.08) |
| | Macao-China | 3.48 | (0.07) | 4.00 | (0.09) | 3.69 | (0.07) | 3.81 | (0.07) | **-0.34** | (0.09) |
| | Montenegro | 2.45 | (0.07) | 2.72 | (0.08) | 2.82 | (0.08) | 3.33 | (0.08) | **-0.89** | (0.11) |
| | Qatar | 2.18 | (0.06) | 2.45 | (0.07) | 2.95 | (0.08) | 3.06 | (0.06) | **-0.87** | (0.09) |
| | Romania | 1.89 | (0.08) | 2.03 | (0.11) | 2.27 | (0.10) | 2.86 | (0.12) | **-0.98** | (0.13) |
| | Russian Federation | 3.43 | (0.12) | 3.58 | (0.11) | 3.82 | (0.09) | 4.09 | (0.08) | **-0.66** | (0.12) |
| | Serbia | 2.42 | (0.07) | 2.65 | (0.08) | 2.91 | (0.09) | 3.46 | (0.07) | **-1.04** | (0.09) |
| | Slovenia | 2.29 | (0.07) | 2.70 | (0.06) | 2.82 | (0.05) | 3.46 | (0.06) | **-1.16** | (0.09) |
| | Chinese Taipei | 2.45 | (0.08) | 2.70 | (0.07) | 3.01 | (0.07) | 3.43 | (0.07) | **-0.98** | (0.09) |
| | Thailand | 3.59 | (0.05) | 3.68 | (0.05) | 3.59 | (0.06) | 4.39 | (0.08) | **-0.81** | (0.09) |
| | Tunisia | 2.34 | (0.07) | 2.45 | (0.06) | 2.60 | (0.07) | 3.10 | (0.12) | **-0.76** | (0.13) |
| | Uruguay | 1.98 | (0.08) | 2.21 | (0.07) | 2.53 | (0.08) | 2.90 | (0.08) | **-0.92** | (0.09) |

*Note*: Values that are statistically significant at the 5% level (p < 0.05) are indicated in bold.

Table 3.7a Mean learning hours and allocation of total learning time in science,
[Part 2/7] by quarters of the PISA index of economic, social and cultural status (ESCS)

| | Mean learning hours per week | | | | | | | | | |
| | Out-of-school-time lessons | | | | | | | | | |
| | Bottom quarter of ESCS | | Second quarter of ESCS | | Third quarter of ESCS | | Top quarter of ESCS | | Difference (bottom-top) | |
| | Mean | S.E. | Mean | S.E. | Mean | S.E. | Mean | S.E. | Dif. | S.E. |
|---|---|---|---|---|---|---|---|---|---|---|
| Australia | 0.35 | (0.02) | 0.35 | (0.02) | 0.36 | (0.02) | 0.38 | (0.02) | -0.04 | (0.03) |
| Austria | 0.28 | (0.03) | 0.21 | (0.03) | 0.19 | (0.02) | 0.18 | (0.03) | **0.10** | (0.04) |
| Belgium | 0.32 | (0.02) | 0.34 | (0.02) | 0.30 | (0.02) | 0.32 | (0.02) | 0.01 | (0.03) |
| Canada | 0.52 | (0.02) | 0.52 | (0.02) | 0.59 | (0.03) | 0.59 | (0.03) | **-0.07** | (0.03) |
| Czech Republic | 0.53 | (0.03) | 0.50 | (0.04) | 0.56 | (0.04) | 0.57 | (0.03) | -0.05 | (0.04) |
| Denmark | 0.78 | (0.04) | 0.71 | (0.04) | 0.75 | (0.04) | 0.84 | (0.03) | -0.05 | (0.05) |
| Finland | 0.33 | (0.02) | 0.34 | (0.03) | 0.32 | (0.02) | 0.30 | (0.02) | 0.03 | (0.03) |
| France | 0.53 | (0.03) | 0.56 | (0.03) | 0.59 | (0.03) | 0.52 | (0.03) | -0.00 | (0.05) |
| Germany | 0.55 | (0.04) | 0.49 | (0.03) | 0.52 | (0.04) | 0.47 | (0.03) | 0.08 | (0.05) |
| Greece | 1.54 | (0.07) | 1.90 | (0.07) | 2.15 | (0.07) | 2.37 | (0.09) | **-0.83** | (0.12) |
| Hungary | 1.01 | (0.04) | 0.94 | (0.04) | 1.03 | (0.05) | 1.02 | (0.06) | -0.01 | (0.07) |
| Iceland | 0.26 | (0.03) | 0.23 | (0.02) | 0.36 | (0.03) | 0.32 | (0.03) | -0.06 | (0.04) |
| Ireland | 0.28 | (0.02) | 0.30 | (0.02) | 0.36 | (0.02) | 0.33 | (0.02) | -0.05 | (0.03) |
| Italy | 0.54 | (0.03) | 0.57 | (0.03) | 0.60 | (0.03) | 0.61 | (0.03) | -0.07 | (0.04) |
| Japan | 0.29 | (0.02) | 0.24 | (0.02) | 0.24 | (0.02) | 0.25 | (0.02) | 0.04 | (0.03) |
| Korea | 0.69 | (0.04) | 0.87 | (0.04) | 1.16 | (0.05) | 1.37 | (0.12) | **-0.68** | (0.13) |
| Luxembourg | 0.56 | (0.03) | 0.56 | (0.03) | 0.49 | (0.03) | 0.42 | (0.03) | **0.15** | (0.05) |
| Mexico | 1.17 | (0.06) | 0.96 | (0.03) | 1.01 | (0.04) | 0.89 | (0.05) | **0.29** | (0.09) |
| Netherlands | 0.60 | (0.04) | 0.54 | (0.03) | 0.53 | (0.03) | 0.47 | (0.03) | **0.14** | (0.05) |
| New Zealand | 0.41 | (0.03) | 0.39 | (0.03) | 0.41 | (0.03) | 0.42 | (0.03) | -0.01 | (0.05) |
| Norway | 0.96 | (0.03) | 0.97 | (0.04) | 0.86 | (0.04) | 0.94 | (0.04) | 0.02 | (0.05) |
| Poland | 0.60 | (0.04) | 0.59 | (0.03) | 0.62 | (0.03) | 0.67 | (0.03) | -0.07 | (0.05) |
| Portugal | 0.59 | (0.04) | 0.62 | (0.04) | 0.65 | (0.04) | 0.68 | (0.04) | -0.09 | (0.06) |
| Slovak Republic | 0.57 | (0.03) | 0.54 | (0.04) | 0.62 | (0.04) | 0.86 | (0.04) | **-0.30** | (0.05) |
| Spain | 0.63 | (0.03) | 0.67 | (0.04) | 0.71 | (0.04) | 0.70 | (0.05) | -0.07 | (0.07) |
| Sweden | 0.50 | (0.03) | 0.50 | (0.03) | 0.49 | (0.03) | 0.50 | (0.03) | 0.00 | (0.05) |
| Switzerland | 0.45 | (0.02) | 0.39 | (0.02) | 0.37 | (0.02) | 0.35 | (0.02) | **0.10** | (0.03) |
| Turkey | 1.11 | (0.07) | 1.05 | (0.06) | 1.28 | (0.06) | 1.97 | (0.10) | **-0.87** | (0.11) |
| United Kingdom | 0.45 | (0.03) | 0.48 | (0.03) | 0.51 | (0.02) | 0.49 | (0.03) | -0.04 | (0.04) |
| United States | 0.78 | (0.06) | 0.77 | (0.03) | 0.84 | (0.03) | 0.74 | (0.04) | 0.04 | (0.07) |
| **OECD average** | 0.61 | (0.01) | 0.60 | (0.01) | 0.65 | (0.01) | 0.68 | (0.01) | **-0.08** | (0.01) |
| Argentina | 0.54 | (0.05) | 0.51 | (0.04) | 0.47 | (0.04) | 0.42 | (0.04) | 0.11 | (0.06) |
| Azerbaijan | 1.36 | (0.08) | 1.33 | (0.05) | 1.33 | (0.05) | 1.42 | (0.05) | -0.07 | (0.09) |
| Brazil | 0.75 | (0.04) | 0.67 | (0.04) | 0.79 | (0.04) | 0.94 | (0.05) | **-0.18** | (0.07) |
| Bulgaria | 0.95 | (0.05) | 1.02 | (0.05) | 0.96 | (0.05) | 1.01 | (0.05) | -0.05 | (0.06) |
| Chile | 0.81 | (0.04) | 0.79 | (0.04) | 0.83 | (0.04) | 0.89 | (0.04) | -0.08 | (0.05) |
| Colombia | 0.97 | (0.05) | 0.98 | (0.09) | 0.86 | (0.04) | 1.00 | (0.07) | -0.03 | (0.10) |
| Croatia | 0.41 | (0.03) | 0.39 | (0.03) | 0.42 | (0.03) | 0.51 | (0.04) | **-0.11** | (0.05) |
| Estonia | 0.79 | (0.04) | 0.77 | (0.03) | 0.75 | (0.05) | 0.74 | (0.04) | 0.05 | (0.05) |
| Hong Kong-China | 0.63 | (0.04) | 0.80 | (0.05) | 0.88 | (0.04) | 1.20 | (0.05) | **-0.57** | (0.06) |
| Indonesia | 0.84 | (0.04) | 0.94 | (0.04) | 1.04 | (0.06) | 1.35 | (0.11) | **-0.51** | (0.10) |
| Israel | 1.11 | (0.06) | 1.03 | (0.06) | 0.85 | (0.04) | 0.93 | (0.05) | **0.18** | (0.08) |
| Jordan | 1.43 | (0.06) | 1.46 | (0.06) | 1.56 | (0.05) | 1.64 | (0.06) | **-0.21** | (0.08) |
| Kyrgyzstan | 1.41 | (0.05) | 1.46 | (0.06) | 1.36 | (0.06) | 1.20 | (0.05) | **0.21** | (0.07) |
| Latvia | 0.63 | (0.04) | 0.67 | (0.04) | 0.64 | (0.03) | 0.66 | (0.04) | -0.03 | (0.06) |
| Liechtenstein | 0.83 | (0.15) | 0.28 | (0.07) | 0.45 | (0.11) | 0.50 | (0.13) | 0.31 | (0.19) |
| Lithuania | 0.66 | (0.03) | 0.56 | (0.03) | 0.55 | (0.03) | 0.49 | (0.04) | **0.17** | (0.05) |
| Macao-China | 1.01 | (0.05) | 1.00 | (0.04) | 0.95 | (0.05) | 1.03 | (0.06) | -0.02 | (0.08) |
| Montenegro | 0.98 | (0.05) | 1.08 | (0.06) | 1.02 | (0.05) | 1.13 | (0.05) | -0.15 | (0.08) |
| Qatar | 1.45 | (0.04) | 1.40 | (0.05) | 1.53 | (0.05) | 1.56 | (0.05) | -0.11 | (0.06) |
| Romania | 1.03 | (0.08) | 0.93 | (0.05) | 1.02 | (0.04) | 1.12 | (0.04) | -0.08 | (0.11) |
| Russian Federation | 1.13 | (0.05) | 1.13 | (0.05) | 1.12 | (0.06) | 1.11 | (0.04) | 0.01 | (0.07) |
| Serbia | 0.72 | (0.04) | 0.82 | (0.04) | 0.78 | (0.04) | 0.80 | (0.04) | -0.08 | (0.06) |
| Slovenia | 0.75 | (0.04) | 0.73 | (0.04) | 0.71 | (0.03) | 0.67 | (0.03) | 0.09 | (0.05) |
| Chinese Taipei | 0.55 | (0.03) | 0.69 | (0.03) | 0.83 | (0.04) | 1.06 | (0.05) | **-0.51** | (0.06) |
| Thailand | 0.56 | (0.05) | 0.75 | (0.05) | 0.81 | (0.04) | 1.53 | (0.08) | **-0.96** | (0.10) |
| Tunisia | 1.80 | (0.06) | 1.85 | (0.06) | 1.84 | (0.06) | 2.23 | (0.08) | **-0.43** | (0.10) |
| Uruguay | 0.58 | (0.05) | 0.58 | (0.04) | 0.68 | (0.04) | 0.60 | (0.03) | -0.02 | (0.07) |

*Note:* Values that are statistically significant at the 5% level (p < 0.05) are indicated in bold.

© OECD 2011 Quality Time for Students: Learning In and Out of School

**Table 3.7a**
[Part 3/7]
**Mean learning hours and allocation of total learning time in science, by quarters of the PISA index of economic, social and cultural status (ESCS)**

| | | Mean learning hours per week | | | | | | | | |
| | | Individual study | | | | | | | | |
| | | Bottom quarter of ESCS | | Second quarter of ESCS | | Third quarter of ESCS | | Top quarter of ESCS | | Difference (bottom-top) | |
| | | Mean | S.E. | Mean | S.E. | Mean | S.E. | Mean | S.E. | Dif. | S.E. |
|---|---|---|---|---|---|---|---|---|---|---|---|
| **OECD** | Australia | 0.91 | (0.03) | 1.09 | (0.03) | 1.21 | (0.04) | 1.49 | (0.03) | **-0.59** | (0.04) |
| | Austria | 1.30 | (0.05) | 1.26 | (0.05) | 1.29 | (0.06) | 1.25 | (0.06) | 0.03 | (0.06) |
| | Belgium | 0.96 | (0.04) | 1.13 | (0.03) | 1.35 | (0.04) | 1.57 | (0.03) | **-0.60** | (0.05) |
| | Canada | 1.25 | (0.04) | 1.42 | (0.04) | 1.70 | (0.04) | 1.85 | (0.05) | **-0.61** | (0.05) |
| | Czech Republic | 0.92 | (0.04) | 1.03 | (0.06) | 0.97 | (0.06) | 1.09 | (0.04) | **-0.18** | (0.05) |
| | Denmark | 1.04 | (0.04) | 1.03 | (0.04) | 1.10 | (0.03) | 1.18 | (0.04) | **-0.14** | (0.06) |
| | Finland | 0.99 | (0.04) | 1.06 | (0.03) | 1.09 | (0.03) | 1.15 | (0.03) | **-0.16** | (0.04) |
| | France | 1.03 | (0.04) | 1.18 | (0.05) | 1.35 | (0.05) | 1.71 | (0.05) | **-0.67** | (0.07) |
| | Germany | 1.58 | (0.05) | 1.70 | (0.05) | 1.79 | (0.05) | 1.77 | (0.05) | **-0.20** | (0.08) |
| | Greece | 1.60 | (0.06) | 1.67 | (0.06) | 1.88 | (0.06) | 2.23 | (0.06) | **-0.62** | (0.08) |
| | Hungary | 1.43 | (0.04) | 1.56 | (0.06) | 1.59 | (0.05) | 1.80 | (0.07) | **-0.37** | (0.08) |
| | Iceland | 1.07 | (0.04) | 1.12 | (0.03) | 1.18 | (0.04) | 1.30 | (0.04) | **-0.23** | (0.05) |
| | Ireland | 0.97 | (0.05) | 1.11 | (0.04) | 1.29 | (0.04) | 1.43 | (0.05) | **-0.46** | (0.06) |
| | Italy | 1.86 | (0.04) | 2.05 | (0.05) | 2.26 | (0.05) | 2.21 | (0.08) | **-0.36** | (0.08) |
| | Japan | 0.54 | (0.02) | 0.64 | (0.03) | 0.75 | (0.03) | 0.82 | (0.03) | **-0.28** | (0.03) |
| | Korea | 0.91 | (0.04) | 1.03 | (0.04) | 1.27 | (0.05) | 1.67 | (0.15) | **-0.76** | (0.16) |
| | Luxembourg | 1.17 | (0.04) | 1.31 | (0.04) | 1.26 | (0.04) | 1.27 | (0.04) | **-0.10** | (0.06) |
| | Mexico | 2.16 | (0.07) | 2.10 | (0.04) | 2.11 | (0.04) | 2.13 | (0.04) | 0.04 | (0.08) |
| | Netherlands | 1.11 | (0.04) | 1.10 | (0.04) | 1.26 | (0.05) | 1.38 | (0.04) | **-0.27** | (0.05) |
| | New Zealand | 1.02 | (0.04) | 1.19 | (0.05) | 1.35 | (0.04) | 1.57 | (0.05) | **-0.56** | (0.06) |
| | Norway | 1.15 | (0.04) | 1.22 | (0.04) | 1.18 | (0.04) | 1.36 | (0.04) | **-0.21** | (0.05) |
| | Poland | 2.01 | (0.05) | 1.91 | (0.05) | 2.02 | (0.05) | 2.14 | (0.06) | -0.13 | (0.08) |
| | Portugal | 1.83 | (0.06) | 2.07 | (0.06) | 2.13 | (0.06) | 2.31 | (0.06) | **-0.49** | (0.09) |
| | Slovak Republic | 1.18 | (0.05) | 1.28 | (0.06) | 1.42 | (0.07) | 1.68 | (0.07) | **-0.51** | (0.08) |
| | Spain | 1.45 | (0.05) | 1.63 | (0.04) | 1.81 | (0.05) | 2.06 | (0.05) | **-0.61** | (0.07) |
| | Sweden | 1.02 | (0.04) | 1.11 | (0.03) | 1.21 | (0.04) | 1.27 | (0.04) | **-0.26** | (0.06) |
| | Switzerland | 1.06 | (0.03) | 1.07 | (0.03) | 1.09 | (0.03) | 1.24 | (0.03) | **-0.18** | (0.04) |
| | Turkey | 1.47 | (0.05) | 1.51 | (0.06) | 1.62 | (0.07) | 1.96 | (0.11) | **-0.49** | (0.12) |
| | United Kingdom | 1.15 | (0.03) | 1.38 | (0.03) | 1.52 | (0.04) | 1.77 | (0.04) | **-0.61** | (0.05) |
| | United States | 1.40 | (0.05) | 1.48 | (0.04) | 1.77 | (0.05) | 2.08 | (0.06) | **-0.69** | (0.08) |
| | **OECD average** | **1.25** | **(0.01)** | **1.35** | **(0.01)** | **1.46** | **(0.01)** | **1.63** | **(0.01)** | **-0.38** | **(0.01)** |
| **Partners** | Argentina | 1.35 | (0.06) | 1.57 | (0.05) | 1.67 | (0.06) | 1.77 | (0.07) | **-0.41** | (0.09) |
| | Azerbaijan | 2.48 | (0.09) | 2.60 | (0.07) | 2.71 | (0.07) | 2.78 | (0.08) | **-0.27** | (0.12) |
| | Brazil | 1.69 | (0.05) | 1.54 | (0.04) | 1.74 | (0.05) | 1.83 | (0.03) | **-0.14** | (0.07) |
| | Bulgaria | 1.65 | (0.08) | 1.81 | (0.06) | 2.13 | (0.08) | 2.44 | (0.09) | **-0.78** | (0.11) |
| | Chile | 1.37 | (0.04) | 1.42 | (0.04) | 1.66 | (0.06) | 1.63 | (0.05) | **-0.27** | (0.06) |
| | Colombia | 1.83 | (0.07) | 1.85 | (0.07) | 1.68 | (0.06) | 1.95 | (0.09) | -0.10 | (0.13) |
| | Croatia | 1.26 | (0.06) | 1.42 | (0.06) | 1.49 | (0.06) | 1.68 | (0.05) | **-0.41** | (0.07) |
| | Estonia | 1.41 | (0.04) | 1.50 | (0.05) | 1.58 | (0.04) | 1.67 | (0.05) | **-0.26** | (0.07) |
| | Hong Kong-China | 1.14 | (0.05) | 1.34 | (0.05) | 1.40 | (0.06) | 1.88 | (0.08) | **-0.75** | (0.09) |
| | Indonesia | 1.73 | (0.05) | 1.69 | (0.04) | 1.80 | (0.06) | 1.91 | (0.09) | **-0.19** | (0.10) |
| | Israel | 1.46 | (0.06) | 1.42 | (0.07) | 1.22 | (0.06) | 1.33 | (0.06) | 0.15 | (0.08) |
| | Jordan | 2.42 | (0.08) | 2.58 | (0.07) | 2.71 | (0.06) | 2.88 | (0.08) | **-0.46** | (0.10) |
| | Kyrgyzstan | 2.13 | (0.09) | 2.17 | (0.06) | 2.13 | (0.06) | 2.12 | (0.06) | 0.00 | (0.10) |
| | Latvia | 1.66 | (0.06) | 1.80 | (0.06) | 1.83 | (0.05) | 1.91 | (0.06) | **-0.25** | (0.08) |
| | Liechtenstein | 1.14 | (0.11) | 0.98 | (0.11) | 1.14 | (0.14) | 1.49 | (0.13) | **-0.35** | (0.18) |
| | Lithuania | 1.62 | (0.05) | 1.57 | (0.05) | 1.69 | (0.05) | 1.87 | (0.05) | **-0.25** | (0.07) |
| | Macao-China | 1.21 | (0.04) | 1.34 | (0.05) | 1.38 | (0.05) | 1.56 | (0.06) | **-0.34** | (0.07) |
| | Montenegro | 2.03 | (0.06) | 2.17 | (0.06) | 2.24 | (0.07) | 2.37 | (0.06) | **-0.35** | (0.09) |
| | Qatar | 1.84 | (0.05) | 1.96 | (0.05) | 2.14 | (0.05) | 2.21 | (0.05) | **-0.38** | (0.06) |
| | Romania | 1.44 | (0.09) | 1.46 | (0.08) | 1.68 | (0.07) | 1.88 | (0.06) | **-0.44** | (0.12) |
| | Russian Federation | 2.62 | (0.09) | 2.82 | (0.09) | 2.93 | (0.07) | 3.11 | (0.06) | **-0.50** | (0.10) |
| | Serbia | 1.47 | (0.06) | 1.66 | (0.06) | 1.68 | (0.07) | 2.03 | (0.07) | **-0.56** | (0.08) |
| | Slovenia | 1.40 | (0.05) | 1.58 | (0.05) | 1.51 | (0.05) | 1.64 | (0.05) | **-0.24** | (0.07) |
| | Chinese Taipei | 0.86 | (0.03) | 1.11 | (0.04) | 1.31 | (0.04) | 1.69 | (0.05) | **-0.84** | (0.06) |
| | Thailand | 1.70 | (0.07) | 1.75 | (0.05) | 1.74 | (0.05) | 2.03 | (0.05) | **-0.33** | (0.09) |
| | Tunisia | 2.48 | (0.07) | 2.53 | (0.07) | 2.55 | (0.06) | 2.87 | (0.07) | **-0.39** | (0.11) |
| | Uruguay | 1.12 | (0.06) | 1.29 | (0.05) | 1.40 | (0.05) | 1.47 | (0.05) | **-0.35** | (0.07) |

*Note:* Values that are statistically significant at the 5% level (p < 0.05) are indicated in bold.

115

Table 3.7a Mean learning hours and allocation of total learning time in science,
[Part 4/7] by quarters of the PISA index of economic, social and cultural status (ESCS)

| | Mean learning hours per week | | | | | | | | | |
| | Total learning hours | | | | | | | | | |
| | Bottom quarter of ESCS | | Second quarter of ESCS | | Third quarter of ESCS | | Top quarter of ESCS | | Difference (bottom-top) | |
| | Mean | S.E. | Mean | S.E. | Mean | S.E. | Mean | S.E. | Dif. | S.E. |
|---|---|---|---|---|---|---|---|---|---|---|
| Australia | 4.10 | (0.08) | 4.58 | (0.06) | 4.88 | (0.08) | 5.56 | (0.08) | **-1.47** | (0.10) |
| Austria | 3.63 | (0.11) | 3.72 | (0.11) | 4.08 | (0.14) | 4.42 | (0.14) | **-0.81** | (0.14) |
| Belgium | 3.26 | (0.12) | 3.94 | (0.11) | 4.48 | (0.10) | 5.16 | (0.07) | **-1.86** | (0.14) |
| Canada | 5.26 | (0.09) | 5.87 | (0.09) | 6.50 | (0.09) | 6.91 | (0.11) | **-1.68** | (0.11) |
| Czech Republic | 3.87 | (0.10) | 4.21 | (0.14) | 4.48 | (0.18) | 5.32 | (0.14) | **-1.48** | (0.15) |
| Denmark | 4.82 | (0.12) | 4.91 | (0.11) | 5.05 | (0.08) | 5.46 | (0.10) | **-0.64** | (0.14) |
| Finland | 4.18 | (0.10) | 4.42 | (0.08) | 4.57 | (0.08) | 4.91 | (0.07) | **-0.74** | (0.11) |
| France | 3.63 | (0.11) | 4.32 | (0.11) | 4.93 | (0.12) | 6.05 | (0.12) | **-2.43** | (0.16) |
| Germany | 4.54 | (0.13) | 5.17 | (0.11) | 5.62 | (0.12) | 5.84 | (0.10) | **-1.33** | (0.16) |
| Greece | 5.66 | (0.16) | 6.61 | (0.16) | 7.24 | (0.15) | 8.56 | (0.16) | **-2.92** | (0.23) |
| Hungary | 4.53 | (0.11) | 4.87 | (0.13) | 5.13 | (0.12) | 5.89 | (0.21) | **-1.35** | (0.23) |
| Iceland | 4.04 | (0.08) | 4.21 | (0.07) | 4.61 | (0.08) | 4.83 | (0.08) | **-0.79** | (0.11) |
| Ireland | 3.55 | (0.12) | 3.86 | (0.10) | 4.22 | (0.10) | 4.58 | (0.10) | **-1.03** | (0.15) |
| Italy | 5.12 | (0.10) | 5.57 | (0.11) | 5.95 | (0.12) | 5.68 | (0.19) | **-0.56** | (0.18) |
| Japan | 3.26 | (0.07) | 3.49 | (0.08) | 3.81 | (0.09) | 4.01 | (0.10) | **-0.76** | (0.09) |
| Korea | 4.89 | (0.11) | 5.47 | (0.11) | 6.10 | (0.14) | 6.89 | (0.39) | **-2.01** | (0.42) |
| Luxembourg | 3.73 | (0.09) | 4.14 | (0.09) | 4.19 | (0.10) | 4.34 | (0.08) | **-0.61** | (0.12) |
| Mexico | 6.43 | (0.17) | 6.05 | (0.09) | 6.13 | (0.10) | 6.36 | (0.11) | 0.10 | (0.20) |
| Netherlands | 3.55 | (0.12) | 3.60 | (0.10) | 4.00 | (0.12) | 4.47 | (0.10) | **-0.91** | (0.14) |
| New Zealand | 5.01 | (0.12) | 5.57 | (0.11) | 5.99 | (0.09) | 6.46 | (0.10) | **-1.44** | (0.15) |
| Norway | 4.61 | (0.09) | 4.82 | (0.09) | 4.74 | (0.09) | 5.03 | (0.10) | **-0.41** | (0.13) |
| Poland | 5.14 | (0.10) | 5.07 | (0.10) | 5.40 | (0.10) | 5.83 | (0.11) | **-0.71** | (0.15) |
| Portugal | 5.01 | (0.13) | 5.75 | (0.14) | 6.10 | (0.13) | 6.86 | (0.16) | **-1.87** | (0.21) |
| Slovak Republic | 3.60 | (0.13) | 4.02 | (0.17) | 4.54 | (0.16) | 5.88 | (0.18) | **-2.29** | (0.20) |
| Spain | 4.78 | (0.10) | 5.20 | (0.10) | 5.73 | (0.10) | 6.52 | (0.13) | **-1.74** | (0.16) |
| Sweden | 4.18 | (0.09) | 4.36 | (0.06) | 4.59 | (0.07) | 4.67 | (0.08) | **-0.50** | (0.12) |
| Switzerland | 3.41 | (0.07) | 3.61 | (0.08) | 3.85 | (0.09) | 4.62 | (0.10) | **-1.20** | (0.11) |
| Turkey | 4.89 | (0.20) | 5.12 | (0.17) | 5.61 | (0.20) | 7.63 | (0.38) | **-2.74** | (0.41) |
| United Kingdom | 5.47 | (0.09) | 6.02 | (0.08) | 6.38 | (0.07) | 6.92 | (0.09) | **-1.44** | (0.11) |
| United States | 5.07 | (0.14) | 5.63 | (0.11) | 6.31 | (0.10) | 7.04 | (0.11) | **-1.98** | (0.20) |
| **OECD average** | 4.44 | (0.02) | 4.81 | (0.02) | 5.17 | (0.02) | 5.76 | (0.03) | **-1.32** | (0.03) |
| Argentina | 3.76 | (0.13) | 4.13 | (0.11) | 4.46 | (0.13) | 4.94 | (0.13) | **-1.18** | (0.18) |
| Azerbaijan | 6.52 | (0.18) | 6.72 | (0.16) | 6.91 | (0.16) | 7.17 | (0.16) | **-0.60** | (0.23) |
| Brazil | 4.33 | (0.11) | 4.21 | (0.10) | 4.65 | (0.10) | 5.60 | (0.12) | **-1.23** | (0.16) |
| Bulgaria | 4.73 | (0.18) | 5.21 | (0.14) | 5.91 | (0.16) | 6.75 | (0.22) | **-2.04** | (0.25) |
| Chile | 3.93 | (0.10) | 4.28 | (0.10) | 4.91 | (0.13) | 5.69 | (0.12) | **-1.75** | (0.15) |
| Colombia | 6.12 | (0.14) | 6.28 | (0.27) | 5.80 | (0.14) | 6.93 | (0.30) | **-0.78** | (0.33) |
| Croatia | 3.27 | (0.13) | 3.80 | (0.12) | 3.97 | (0.13) | 4.68 | (0.10) | **-1.40** | (0.14) |
| Estonia | 5.28 | (0.10) | 5.39 | (0.10) | 5.61 | (0.12) | 6.02 | (0.10) | **-0.75** | (0.13) |
| Hong Kong-China | 4.45 | (0.15) | 5.18 | (0.15) | 5.34 | (0.16) | 6.84 | (0.20) | **-2.38** | (0.27) |
| Indonesia | 5.41 | (0.12) | 5.60 | (0.11) | 5.95 | (0.14) | 7.22 | (0.25) | **-1.80** | (0.28) |
| Israel | 4.63 | (0.16) | 4.88 | (0.17) | 4.45 | (0.16) | 5.11 | (0.16) | **-0.42** | (0.23) |
| Jordan | 6.70 | (0.15) | 7.10 | (0.15) | 7.58 | (0.10) | 8.24 | (0.14) | **-1.55** | (0.19) |
| Kyrgyzstan | 5.64 | (0.22) | 5.49 | (0.13) | 5.58 | (0.13) | 5.79 | (0.14) | -0.15 | (0.26) |
| Latvia | 4.86 | (0.14) | 5.22 | (0.13) | 5.40 | (0.11) | 5.73 | (0.16) | **-0.88** | (0.21) |
| Liechtenstein | 4.22 | (0.31) | 3.59 | (0.22) | 4.16 | (0.26) | 5.20 | (0.28) | **-0.96** | (0.44) |
| Lithuania | 4.72 | (0.12) | 4.78 | (0.11) | 4.97 | (0.09) | 5.30 | (0.11) | **-0.59** | (0.15) |
| Macao-China | 5.70 | (0.11) | 6.33 | (0.13) | 6.01 | (0.12) | 6.39 | (0.13) | **-0.70** | (0.16) |
| Montenegro | 5.48 | (0.13) | 5.95 | (0.14) | 6.08 | (0.16) | 6.82 | (0.14) | **-1.35** | (0.20) |
| Qatar | 5.48 | (0.09) | 5.84 | (0.13) | 6.66 | (0.14) | 6.84 | (0.13) | **-1.35** | (0.16) |
| Romania | 4.37 | (0.21) | 4.40 | (0.16) | 4.94 | (0.16) | 5.80 | (0.19) | **-1.46** | (0.31) |
| Russian Federation | 7.15 | (0.19) | 7.55 | (0.19) | 7.88 | (0.18) | 8.32 | (0.13) | **-1.19** | (0.21) |
| Serbia | 4.59 | (0.12) | 5.16 | (0.13) | 5.38 | (0.16) | 6.28 | (0.14) | **-1.67** | (0.17) |
| Slovenia | 4.45 | (0.12) | 5.02 | (0.11) | 5.06 | (0.10) | 5.77 | (0.10) | **-1.32** | (0.16) |
| Chinese Taipei | 3.90 | (0.13) | 4.52 | (0.12) | 5.19 | (0.12) | 6.18 | (0.13) | **-2.30** | (0.17) |
| Thailand | 5.84 | (0.13) | 6.18 | (0.10) | 6.14 | (0.13) | 7.94 | (0.17) | **-2.11** | (0.24) |
| Tunisia | 6.57 | (0.14) | 6.78 | (0.15) | 7.02 | (0.13) | 8.20 | (0.24) | **-1.61** | (0.28) |
| Uruguay | 3.71 | (0.16) | 4.10 | (0.11) | 4.62 | (0.14) | 4.97 | (0.13) | **-1.27** | (0.17) |

*Note:* Values that are statistically significant at the 5% level (p < 0.05) are indicated in bold.

© OECD 2011  Quality Time for Students: Learning In and Out of School

**Table 3.7a** **Mean learning hours and allocation of total learning time in science,**
[Part 5/7] **by quarters of the PISA index of economic, social and cultural status (ESCS)**

| | Allocation of total learning time in science for | | | | | | | | | |
|---|---|---|---|---|---|---|---|---|---|---|
| | Regular school lessons | | | | | | | | | |
| | Bottom quarter of ESCS | | Second quarter of ESCS | | Third quarter of ESCS | | Top quarter of ESCS | | Difference (bottom-top) | |
| | % | S.E. | % | S.E. | % | S.E. | % | S.E. | Dif. | S.E. |
| **OECD** Australia | 72.1 | (0.6) | 71.9 | (0.5) | 70.6 | (0.5) | 69.2 | (0.5) | **2.6** | (0.8) |
| Austria | 58.3 | (1.0) | 62.7 | (1.0) | 65.5 | (1.0) | 70.0 | (0.9) | **-11.5** | (1.3) |
| Belgium | 62.2 | (0.8) | 63.4 | (0.8) | 63.7 | (0.6) | 64.9 | (0.5) | **-3.0** | (1.1) |
| Canada | 66.2 | (0.7) | 67.1 | (0.6) | 65.6 | (0.6) | 66.1 | (0.5) | -0.0 | (0.8) |
| Czech Republic | 66.2 | (1.2) | 67.4 | (1.3) | 69.8 | (0.9) | 71.5 | (0.7) | **-4.8** | (1.3) |
| Denmark | 66.5 | (1.0) | 67.5 | (0.8) | 66.6 | (0.8) | 66.3 | (0.6) | 0.2 | (1.1) |
| Finland | 70.7 | (0.7) | 70.3 | (0.6) | 70.5 | (0.7) | 72.2 | (0.6) | -1.6 | (0.9) |
| France | 61.9 | (1.0) | 62.1 | (0.9) | 62.9 | (0.8) | 65.1 | (0.7) | **-3.5** | (1.1) |
| Germany | 52.4 | (0.9) | 58.3 | (0.8) | 59.0 | (1.0) | 62.2 | (0.8) | **-9.9** | (1.2) |
| Greece | 48.7 | (0.8) | 48.0 | (0.9) | 47.1 | (0.9) | 49.5 | (0.9) | -1.0 | (1.2) |
| Hungary | 48.5 | (0.9) | 51.0 | (0.9) | 52.0 | (0.9) | 54.7 | (0.7) | **-6.2** | (1.2) |
| Iceland | 70.3 | (0.7) | 70.9 | (0.7) | 70.1 | (0.8) | 69.3 | (0.7) | 0.9 | (1.0) |
| Ireland | 68.0 | (0.9) | 66.8 | (1.0) | 64.9 | (0.7) | 65.4 | (0.8) | **2.6** | (1.2) |
| Italy | 54.9 | (0.6) | 54.3 | (0.5) | 53.9 | (0.5) | 52.9 | (0.5) | **2.0** | (0.8) |
| Japan | 79.8 | (0.7) | 79.2 | (0.7) | 77.8 | (0.8) | 77.0 | (0.6) | **2.9** | (0.8) |
| Korea | 72.4 | (0.8) | 70.3 | (0.7) | 65.2 | (0.8) | 61.8 | (1.1) | **10.7** | (1.3) |
| Luxembourg | 57.2 | (0.9) | 57.9 | (1.0) | 61.6 | (0.8) | 62.6 | (0.8) | **-6.1** | (1.3) |
| Mexico | 47.6 | (1.1) | 46.8 | (0.6) | 47.7 | (0.6) | 52.1 | (0.8) | **-4.4** | (1.4) |
| Netherlands | 53.4 | (1.0) | 55.6 | (0.9) | 56.1 | (1.3) | 60.7 | (0.9) | **-7.5** | (1.2) |
| New Zealand | 73.7 | (0.8) | 73.6 | (0.7) | 73.2 | (0.7) | 71.7 | (0.6) | **2.2** | (1.0) |
| Norway | 59.3 | (0.8) | 59.4 | (0.9) | 61.1 | (0.8) | 58.7 | (0.8) | 0.4 | (1.1) |
| Poland | 51.7 | (0.7) | 52.9 | (0.7) | 53.6 | (0.7) | 54.4 | (0.6) | **-2.6** | (0.9) |
| Portugal | 52.2 | (1.0) | 53.4 | (0.8) | 55.4 | (0.7) | 57.6 | (0.7) | **-5.4** | (1.2) |
| Slovak Republic | 56.1 | (0.9) | 59.7 | (1.2) | 59.2 | (1.1) | 60.0 | (0.9) | **-3.9** | (1.3) |
| Spain | 58.9 | (0.8) | 57.9 | (0.6) | 59.1 | (0.7) | 59.8 | (0.5) | -0.8 | (1.0) |
| Sweden | 67.5 | (0.9) | 66.4 | (0.9) | 66.4 | (0.7) | 66.6 | (0.7) | 1.0 | (1.0) |
| Switzerland | 58.0 | (0.9) | 61.1 | (0.8) | 63.3 | (0.8) | 65.9 | (0.5) | **-8.2** | (1.1) |
| Turkey | 49.0 | (0.9) | 52.6 | (1.1) | 51.4 | (1.0) | 51.7 | (0.9) | -2.5 | (1.4) |
| United Kingdom | 72.4 | (0.7) | 70.9 | (0.5) | 69.8 | (0.5) | 69.7 | (0.5) | **2.8** | (0.8) |
| United States | 56.2 | (1.4) | 58.4 | (0.8) | 59.1 | (0.8) | 60.8 | (0.7) | **-4.6** | (1.6) |
| **OECD average** | 61.1 | (0.2) | 61.9 | (0.2) | 62.1 | (0.1) | 63.0 | (0.1) | **-2.0** | (0.2) |
| **Partners** Argentina | 52.4 | (1.3) | 50.4 | (1.4) | 52.8 | (1.2) | 57.0 | (1.2) | **-4.9** | (1.8) |
| Azerbaijan | 41.9 | (1.1) | 41.7 | (0.9) | 44.0 | (0.9) | 44.9 | (0.9) | **-3.1** | (1.3) |
| Brazil | 48.2 | (0.9) | 50.9 | (0.9) | 49.1 | (0.9) | 53.0 | (0.8) | **-4.9** | (1.2) |
| Bulgaria | 46.4 | (1.2) | 47.8 | (1.2) | 49.6 | (1.0) | 51.5 | (0.8) | **-5.5** | (1.5) |
| Chile | 44.5 | (0.9) | 47.6 | (0.9) | 47.5 | (0.9) | 56.5 | (0.7) | **-11.4** | (1.1) |
| Colombia | 58.2 | (1.5) | 57.8 | (1.1) | 59.2 | (1.0) | 60.3 | (0.9) | -2.4 | (1.9) |
| Croatia | 51.1 | (1.0) | 55.5 | (0.8) | 54.9 | (0.9) | 56.5 | (1.1) | **-5.6** | (1.3) |
| Estonia | 61.2 | (1.0) | 60.5 | (0.9) | 61.1 | (0.8) | 63.2 | (0.9) | -2.0 | (1.2) |
| Hong Kong-China | 63.3 | (1.0) | 62.5 | (0.9) | 60.3 | (0.8) | 57.9 | (0.8) | **5.3** | (1.3) |
| Indonesia | 54.4 | (1.0) | 54.2 | (0.8) | 53.6 | (1.4) | 56.2 | (1.5) | -1.9 | (1.3) |
| Israel | 47.4 | (1.5) | 54.1 | (1.3) | 56.8 | (1.2) | 59.4 | (1.1) | **-11.9** | (1.8) |
| Jordan | 40.9 | (1.0) | 42.3 | (0.8) | 43.5 | (0.8) | 45.0 | (0.9) | **-4.2** | (1.2) |
| Kyrgyzstan | 32.8 | (1.3) | 33.0 | (0.9) | 35.0 | (1.0) | 40.9 | (1.0) | **-7.9** | (1.5) |
| Latvia | 54.9 | (0.8) | 55.1 | (1.0) | 56.5 | (0.8) | 57.9 | (0.7) | **-3.0** | (1.0) |
| Liechtenstein | 57.0 | (2.7) | 64.0 | (2.7) | 65.4 | (2.8) | 61.0 | (2.4) | -4.3 | (3.7) |
| Lithuania | 55.0 | (1.0) | 58.3 | (0.7) | 57.9 | (0.7) | 57.2 | (0.9) | -2.1 | (1.2) |
| Macao-China | 64.7 | (0.9) | 66.3 | (0.8) | 64.7 | (0.9) | 63.4 | (0.8) | 1.2 | (1.1) |
| Montenegro | 44.4 | (0.8) | 46.4 | (0.9) | 47.0 | (0.9) | 49.5 | (0.8) | **-5.2** | (1.1) |
| Qatar | 38.6 | (0.8) | 39.4 | (0.7) | 42.3 | (0.7) | 42.5 | (0.6) | **-3.9** | (1.0) |
| Romania | 44.5 | (1.5) | 48.4 | (1.6) | 49.1 | (1.2) | 50.6 | (0.9) | **-6.1** | (1.7) |
| Russian Federation | 47.8 | (0.9) | 47.3 | (0.7) | 49.4 | (0.7) | 49.9 | (0.7) | -2.1 | (1.1) |
| Serbia | 56.3 | (0.8) | 55.2 | (1.0) | 57.9 | (0.9) | 58.0 | (0.8) | -2.0 | (1.1) |
| Slovenia | 52.3 | (0.9) | 53.9 | (0.8) | 56.3 | (0.9) | 60.4 | (0.8) | **-7.7** | (1.1) |
| Chinese Taipei | 67.6 | (0.8) | 64.6 | (0.7) | 62.8 | (0.7) | 59.8 | (0.6) | **7.6** | (1.0) |
| Thailand | 66.3 | (0.8) | 64.1 | (0.6) | 63.9 | (0.7) | 61.2 | (0.7) | **5.1** | (1.2) |
| Tunisia | 36.7 | (0.7) | 37.1 | (0.7) | 37.8 | (0.9) | 37.4 | (0.8) | -0.6 | (1.1) |
| Uruguay | 55.0 | (1.0) | 55.0 | (1.0) | 55.2 | (0.9) | 59.5 | (0.9) | **-4.2** | (1.4) |

*Note*: Values that are statistically significant at the 5% level (p < 0.05) are indicated in bold.

**Table 3.7a** Mean learning hours and allocation of total learning time in science,
[Part 6/7] by quarters of the PISA index of economic, social and cultural status (ESCS)

| | Allocation of total learning time in science for | | | | | | | | | |
|---|---|---|---|---|---|---|---|---|---|---|
| | Out-of-school-time lessons | | | | | | | | | |
| | Bottom quarter of ESCS | | Second quarter of ESCS | | Third quarter of ESCS | | Top quarter of ESCS | | Difference (bottom-top) | |
| | % | S.E. | % | S.E. | % | S.E. | % | S.E. | Dif. | S.E. |
| **OECD** Australia | 6.9 | (0.4) | 6.2 | (0.2) | 6.1 | (0.3) | 5.8 | (0.3) | 1.2 | (0.5) |
| Austria | 6.4 | (0.6) | 4.3 | (0.5) | 3.6 | (0.5) | 2.6 | (0.3) | 3.7 | (0.8) |
| Belgium | 8.3 | (0.5) | 7.2 | (0.5) | 5.8 | (0.4) | 4.9 | (0.3) | 3.4 | (0.6) |
| Canada | 9.3 | (0.4) | 8.4 | (0.4) | 8.4 | (0.4) | 7.8 | (0.3) | 1.6 | (0.5) |
| Czech Republic | 11.1 | (0.7) | 9.7 | (0.6) | 9.9 | (0.5) | 8.9 | (0.5) | 2.0 | (0.8) |
| Denmark | 13.6 | (0.5) | 12.4 | (0.5) | 12.7 | (0.5) | 13.5 | (0.4) | 0.1 | (0.7) |
| Finland | 6.7 | (0.4) | 6.1 | (0.4) | 6.0 | (0.3) | 4.9 | (0.4) | 1.7 | (0.5) |
| France | 12.0 | (0.7) | 11.8 | (0.6) | 10.4 | (0.5) | 8.6 | (0.6) | 3.5 | (0.9) |
| Germany | 10.5 | (0.6) | 8.0 | (0.5) | 8.2 | (0.6) | 7.2 | (0.4) | 3.5 | (0.6) |
| Greece | 24.0 | (0.6) | 26.9 | (0.7) | 27.7 | (0.7) | 26.2 | (0.9) | -2.4 | (1.1) |
| Hungary | 20.7 | (0.8) | 17.5 | (0.7) | 17.5 | (0.7) | 15.7 | (0.6) | 5.0 | (1.0) |
| Iceland | 4.9 | (0.4) | 4.2 | (0.4) | 5.9 | (0.5) | 5.3 | (0.4) | -0.4 | (0.6) |
| Ireland | 6.3 | (0.5) | 5.9 | (0.4) | 6.8 | (0.4) | 5.6 | (0.4) | 0.6 | (0.6) |
| Italy | 9.2 | (0.4) | 9.3 | (0.4) | 8.7 | (0.3) | 9.4 | (0.5) | -0.3 | (0.6) |
| Japan | 6.2 | (0.4) | 4.8 | (0.4) | 4.8 | (0.4) | 4.7 | (0.3) | 1.4 | (0.5) |
| Korea | 10.6 | (0.6) | 12.7 | (0.6) | 15.7 | (0.6) | 16.3 | (0.7) | -5.7 | (0.8) |
| Luxembourg | 12.2 | (0.7) | 11.3 | (0.6) | 8.6 | (0.6) | 7.7 | (0.5) | 4.7 | (0.9) |
| Mexico | 16.5 | (0.9) | 14.8 | (0.5) | 15.5 | (0.4) | 12.9 | (0.6) | 3.7 | (1.1) |
| Netherlands | 14.6 | (0.8) | 13.9 | (0.7) | 12.7 | (0.9) | 9.2 | (0.6) | 5.4 | (1.0) |
| New Zealand | 7.0 | (0.6) | 6.2 | (0.4) | 5.9 | (0.4) | 5.6 | (0.4) | 1.2 | (0.7) |
| Norway | 18.0 | (0.5) | 17.3 | (0.6) | 15.9 | (0.6) | 16.2 | (0.6) | 1.8 | (0.7) |
| Poland | 10.4 | (0.6) | 10.4 | (0.5) | 10.1 | (0.5) | 10.2 | (0.4) | 0.3 | (0.7) |
| Portugal | 10.4 | (0.7) | 9.5 | (0.6) | 8.8 | (0.4) | 8.5 | (0.4) | 2.1 | (0.8) |
| Slovak Republic | 12.3 | (0.6) | 10.5 | (0.7) | 11.6 | (0.7) | 12.4 | (0.5) | -0.1 | (0.8) |
| Spain | 11.3 | (0.5) | 11.4 | (0.5) | 10.5 | (0.5) | 9.6 | (0.6) | 1.8 | (0.9) |
| Sweden | 9.5 | (0.5) | 9.1 | (0.5) | 9.2 | (0.4) | 8.7 | (0.5) | 0.7 | (0.7) |
| Switzerland | 10.2 | (0.5) | 8.4 | (0.4) | 8.1 | (0.4) | 6.5 | (0.3) | 3.8 | (0.6) |
| Turkey | 20.7 | (0.8) | 18.4 | (0.8) | 20.9 | (0.8) | 23.9 | (0.7) | -2.9 | (1.1) |
| United Kingdom | 7.0 | (0.4) | 7.0 | (0.3) | 6.9 | (0.2) | 6.0 | (0.3) | 1.1 | (0.4) |
| United States | 15.0 | (1.1) | 13.1 | (0.6) | 12.4 | (0.5) | 9.6 | (0.5) | 5.3 | (1.3) |
| **OECD average** | 11.4 | (0.1) | 10.6 | (0.1) | 10.5 | (0.1) | 9.8 | (0.1) | 1.6 | (0.1) |
| **Partners** Argentina | 11.5 | (1.0) | 11.2 | (0.9) | 9.0 | (0.6) | 6.9 | (0.7) | 4.8 | (1.3) |
| Azerbaijan | 21.3 | (0.9) | 20.2 | (0.8) | 17.9 | (0.7) | 17.9 | (0.6) | 3.1 | (1.0) |
| Brazil | 13.8 | (0.8) | 13.9 | (0.7) | 14.6 | (0.6) | 14.3 | (0.6) | -0.3 | (1.0) |
| Bulgaria | 18.9 | (0.9) | 17.7 | (0.9) | 14.7 | (0.8) | 13.7 | (0.7) | 5.4 | (1.1) |
| Chile | 19.3 | (0.8) | 17.4 | (0.7) | 15.2 | (0.5) | 13.4 | (0.6) | 5.8 | (0.9) |
| Colombia | 13.6 | (0.7) | 13.5 | (0.7) | 12.8 | (0.6) | 12.4 | (0.7) | 1.2 | (1.0) |
| Croatia | 11.0 | (0.7) | 9.8 | (0.6) | 9.3 | (0.6) | 9.4 | (0.7) | 2.1 | (1.0) |
| Estonia | 13.5 | (0.6) | 13.6 | (0.6) | 12.3 | (0.6) | 11.0 | (0.7) | 2.5 | (0.9) |
| Hong Kong-China | 11.5 | (0.6) | 13.6 | (0.6) | 14.7 | (0.6) | 15.6 | (0.6) | -4.0 | (0.8) |
| Indonesia | 13.8 | (0.7) | 15.2 | (0.6) | 16.0 | (0.9) | 17.3 | (1.2) | -3.6 | (0.9) |
| Israel | 21.7 | (1.0) | 18.9 | (0.7) | 16.9 | (0.7) | 15.8 | (0.6) | 5.8 | (1.1) |
| Jordan | 20.8 | (0.7) | 20.3 | (0.6) | 20.5 | (0.7) | 19.4 | (0.8) | 1.4 | (1.1) |
| Kyrgyzstan | 27.1 | (1.0) | 27.7 | (0.9) | 26.6 | (1.1) | 22.0 | (0.7) | 5.1 | (1.2) |
| Latvia | 11.3 | (0.7) | 11.1 | (0.7) | 10.2 | (0.5) | 9.1 | (0.5) | 2.2 | (1.0) |
| Liechtenstein | 14.5 | (2.1) | 8.2 | (1.8) | 9.1 | (2.0) | 8.8 | (2.1) | 5.3 | (2.8) |
| Lithuania | 12.4 | (0.7) | 10.0 | (0.5) | 9.5 | (0.4) | 8.3 | (0.5) | 4.2 | (0.9) |
| Macao-China | 15.5 | (0.7) | 14.1 | (0.6) | 14.2 | (0.6) | 14.2 | (0.7) | 1.4 | (1.0) |
| Montenegro | 16.7 | (0.6) | 16.8 | (0.8) | 15.7 | (0.8) | 15.2 | (0.6) | 1.6 | (1.0) |
| Qatar | 26.5 | (0.6) | 25.2 | (0.6) | 24.0 | (0.8) | 23.5 | (0.6) | 3.1 | (0.9) |
| Romania | 22.2 | (1.5) | 19.7 | (1.5) | 18.0 | (0.8) | 18.0 | (0.8) | 4.0 | (1.8) |
| Russian Federation | 16.7 | (1.0) | 16.1 | (0.8) | 14.2 | (0.6) | 13.0 | (0.5) | 3.8 | (1.0) |
| Serbia | 14.2 | (0.7) | 14.3 | (0.6) | 13.4 | (0.7) | 11.4 | (0.5) | 3.0 | (1.0) |
| Slovenia | 15.0 | (0.6) | 13.6 | (0.5) | 13.2 | (0.6) | 10.8 | (0.5) | 4.2 | (0.8) |
| Chinese Taipei | 11.4 | (0.5) | 11.7 | (0.5) | 12.6 | (0.5) | 13.4 | (0.5) | -2.1 | (0.7) |
| Thailand | 6.9 | (0.5) | 9.0 | (0.6) | 9.6 | (0.5) | 14.3 | (0.7) | -7.4 | (0.9) |
| Tunisia | 25.9 | (0.8) | 26.1 | (0.7) | 25.3 | (0.8) | 26.1 | (0.5) | -0.2 | (1.0) |
| Uruguay | 12.8 | (0.7) | 12.5 | (0.7) | 13.0 | (0.6) | 9.8 | (0.5) | 3.0 | (1.0) |

*Note:* Values that are statistically significant at the 5% level (p < 0.05) are indicated in bold.

© OECD 2011 Quality Time for Students: Learning In and Out of School

**Table 3.7a** Mean learning hours and allocation of total learning time in science,
[Part 7/7] by quarters of the PISA index of economic, social and cultural status (ESCS)

| | | Allocation of total learning time in science for | | | | | | | | |
|---|---|---|---|---|---|---|---|---|---|---|
| | | | | | Individual study | | | | | |
| | | Bottom quarter of ESCS | | Second quarter of ESCS | | Third quarter of ESCS | | Top quarter of ESCS | | Difference (bottom-top) | |
| | | % | S.E. | % | S.E. | % | S.E. | % | S.E. | Dif. | S.E. |
| OECD | Australia | 21.0 | (0.4) | 21.9 | (0.5) | 23.3 | (0.4) | 25.0 | (0.4) | **-3.9** | (0.6) |
| | Austria | 35.3 | (0.9) | 33.0 | (0.9) | 30.9 | (1.0) | 27.4 | (0.8) | **7.7** | (1.2) |
| | Belgium | 29.5 | (0.7) | 29.4 | (0.6) | 30.5 | (0.5) | 30.2 | (0.5) | -0.3 | (0.9) |
| | Canada | 24.4 | (0.6) | 24.6 | (0.5) | 26.0 | (0.5) | 26.1 | (0.5) | **-1.6** | (0.7) |
| | Czech Republic | 22.6 | (0.9) | 23.0 | (1.1) | 20.4 | (0.8) | 19.6 | (0.7) | **2.7** | (1.1) |
| | Denmark | 20.0 | (0.6) | 20.1 | (0.6) | 20.8 | (0.5) | 20.2 | (0.5) | -0.4 | (0.8) |
| | Finland | 22.6 | (0.6) | 23.6 | (0.5) | 23.5 | (0.6) | 22.9 | (0.5) | -0.2 | (0.8) |
| | France | 26.1 | (0.7) | 26.1 | (0.7) | 26.6 | (0.6) | 26.4 | (0.5) | -0.1 | (0.8) |
| | Germany | 37.2 | (0.7) | 33.6 | (0.6) | 32.9 | (0.7) | 30.6 | (0.6) | **6.4** | (1.1) |
| | Greece | 27.4 | (0.6) | 25.0 | (0.7) | 25.2 | (0.6) | 24.2 | (0.5) | **3.3** | (0.7) |
| | Hungary | 30.9 | (0.6) | 31.4 | (0.7) | 30.5 | (0.7) | 29.7 | (0.5) | 1.3 | (0.8) |
| | Iceland | 24.8 | (0.6) | 24.9 | (0.6) | 24.1 | (0.6) | 25.4 | (0.6) | -0.6 | (0.8) |
| | Ireland | 25.7 | (0.7) | 27.3 | (0.8) | 28.3 | (0.6) | 29.1 | (0.7) | **-3.3** | (1.0) |
| | Italy | 36.0 | (0.6) | 36.4 | (0.3) | 37.4 | (0.5) | 37.7 | (0.4) | **-1.7** | (0.6) |
| | Japan | 14.1 | (0.5) | 16.0 | (0.6) | 17.4 | (0.7) | 18.3 | (0.5) | **-4.2** | (0.6) |
| | Korea | 17.0 | (0.6) | 16.9 | (0.5) | 19.1 | (0.5) | 21.9 | (0.7) | **-4.9** | (0.9) |
| | Luxembourg | 30.6 | (0.7) | 30.8 | (0.8) | 29.8 | (0.8) | 29.7 | (0.6) | 1.3 | (0.9) |
| | Mexico | 35.9 | (0.7) | 38.4 | (0.6) | 36.8 | (0.5) | 35.1 | (0.6) | 0.7 | (0.9) |
| | Netherlands | 32.1 | (0.9) | 30.5 | (0.7) | 31.3 | (0.8) | 30.1 | (0.7) | 2.0 | (1.1) |
| | New Zealand | 19.3 | (0.6) | 20.2 | (0.5) | 20.8 | (0.5) | 22.7 | (0.6) | **-3.4** | (0.8) |
| | Norway | 22.7 | (0.6) | 23.4 | (0.5) | 22.9 | (0.5) | 25.1 | (0.5) | **-2.2** | (0.8) |
| | Poland | 37.8 | (0.6) | 36.6 | (0.7) | 36.4 | (0.6) | 35.4 | (0.6) | **2.5** | (0.9) |
| | Portugal | 37.3 | (0.9) | 37.2 | (0.7) | 35.8 | (0.7) | 34.0 | (0.7) | **3.4** | (1.1) |
| | Slovak Republic | 31.5 | (0.9) | 29.9 | (0.9) | 29.1 | (0.8) | 27.7 | (0.7) | **3.9** | (1.3) |
| | Spain | 29.8 | (0.6) | 30.7 | (0.5) | 30.4 | (0.6) | 30.6 | (0.6) | -0.9 | (0.9) |
| | Sweden | 23.0 | (0.7) | 24.5 | (0.8) | 24.3 | (0.6) | 24.7 | (0.7) | **-1.8** | (0.8) |
| | Switzerland | 31.8 | (0.7) | 30.5 | (0.6) | 28.6 | (0.6) | 27.6 | (0.5) | **4.3** | (0.8) |
| | Turkey | 30.3 | (0.8) | 29.2 | (0.9) | 27.5 | (0.7) | 24.5 | (0.6) | **5.5** | (1.1) |
| | United Kingdom | 20.5 | (0.5) | 22.1 | (0.5) | 23.3 | (0.5) | 24.3 | (0.4) | **-3.8** | (0.6) |
| | United States | 28.9 | (0.6) | 28.4 | (0.7) | 28.6 | (0.7) | 29.6 | (0.5) | -0.9 | (0.8) |
| | **OECD average** | **27.5** | **(0.1)** | **27.5** | **(0.1)** | **27.4** | **(0.1)** | **27.2** | **(0.1)** | **0.4** | **(0.2)** |
| Partners | Argentina | 36.0 | (0.9) | 38.6 | (1.2) | 38.2 | (1.1) | 36.1 | (1.0) | 0.2 | (1.4) |
| | Azerbaijan | 36.9 | (0.8) | 37.9 | (0.9) | 38.3 | (0.7) | 37.1 | (0.6) | -0.1 | (1.0) |
| | Brazil | 37.9 | (0.9) | 35.3 | (0.8) | 36.4 | (0.8) | 32.7 | (0.6) | **5.1** | (1.2) |
| | Bulgaria | 34.7 | (1.1) | 34.5 | (0.8) | 35.7 | (0.8) | 34.8 | (0.6) | 0.1 | (1.2) |
| | Chile | 36.1 | (0.7) | 34.9 | (0.8) | 37.3 | (0.8) | 30.0 | (0.7) | **5.5** | (0.8) |
| | Colombia | 28.2 | (1.1) | 28.6 | (0.8) | 28.0 | (0.7) | 27.3 | (0.6) | 1.1 | (1.1) |
| | Croatia | 38.0 | (0.9) | 34.7 | (0.7) | 35.8 | (0.8) | 34.1 | (0.9) | **3.8** | (1.3) |
| | Estonia | 25.3 | (0.7) | 25.9 | (0.7) | 26.7 | (0.6) | 25.8 | (0.6) | -0.5 | (1.0) |
| | Hong Kong-China | 25.1 | (0.8) | 23.9 | (0.6) | 25.1 | (0.7) | 26.5 | (0.6) | -1.3 | (1.0) |
| | Indonesia | 31.9 | (0.7) | 30.6 | (0.6) | 30.4 | (0.7) | 26.4 | (0.7) | **5.4** | (0.9) |
| | Israel | 30.9 | (1.0) | 27.0 | (1.0) | 26.3 | (0.9) | 24.8 | (1.0) | **5.9** | (1.2) |
| | Jordan | 38.3 | (0.8) | 37.5 | (0.7) | 35.9 | (0.7) | 35.7 | (0.8) | **2.8** | (1.0) |
| | Kyrgyzstan | 40.1 | (0.8) | 39.3 | (0.9) | 38.4 | (0.9) | 37.1 | (0.7) | **2.8** | (1.0) |
| | Latvia | 33.9 | (0.7) | 33.7 | (0.9) | 33.3 | (0.6) | 32.9 | (0.6) | 0.7 | (0.9) |
| | Liechtenstein | 28.6 | (2.2) | 27.7 | (2.4) | 25.8 | (2.2) | 29.9 | (1.9) | -0.8 | (2.6) |
| | Lithuania | 32.6 | (0.6) | 31.6 | (0.7) | 32.6 | (0.6) | 34.6 | (0.6) | **-2.0** | (0.9) |
| | Macao-China | 19.8 | (0.7) | 19.6 | (0.6) | 21.1 | (0.6) | 22.4 | (0.6) | **-2.7** | (0.8) |
| | Montenegro | 39.0 | (0.8) | 36.8 | (1.0) | 37.3 | (0.9) | 35.3 | (0.8) | **3.5** | (1.1) |
| | Qatar | 34.9 | (0.7) | 35.5 | (0.6) | 33.5 | (0.6) | 34.0 | (0.6) | 0.8 | (0.9) |
| | Romania | 33.4 | (1.0) | 31.8 | (0.9) | 32.8 | (0.8) | 31.3 | (0.8) | 2.1 | (1.4) |
| | Russian Federation | 35.5 | (0.9) | 36.6 | (0.7) | 36.4 | (0.7) | 37.2 | (0.5) | -1.7 | (0.9) |
| | Serbia | 29.5 | (0.8) | 30.4 | (0.8) | 28.7 | (0.6) | 30.6 | (0.7) | -1.1 | (1.1) |
| | Slovenia | 32.6 | (0.8) | 32.7 | (0.8) | 30.5 | (0.7) | 28.7 | (0.6) | **3.6** | (1.0) |
| | Chinese Taipei | 21.1 | (0.6) | 23.7 | (0.5) | 24.6 | (0.6) | 26.8 | (0.5) | **-5.6** | (0.8) |
| | Thailand | 26.8 | (0.6) | 26.7 | (0.5) | 26.6 | (0.5) | 24.5 | (0.5) | **2.4** | (0.7) |
| | Tunisia | 37.4 | (0.9) | 36.7 | (0.8) | 36.8 | (0.8) | 36.5 | (0.6) | 0.9 | (1.1) |
| | Uruguay | 32.3 | (0.8) | 32.4 | (0.9) | 31.8 | (0.8) | 30.7 | (0.8) | 1.2 | (1.0) |

*Note:* Values that are statistically significant at the 5% level (p < 0.05) are indicated in bold.

119

Table 3.7b Mean learning hours and allocation of total learning time in mathematics,
[Part 1/7] by quarters of the PISA index of economic, social and cultural status (ESCS)

| | | Mean learning hours per week | | | | | | | | |
| | | Regular school lessons | | | | | | | | |
| | | Bottom quarter of ESCS | | Second quarter of ESCS | | Third quarter of ESCS | | Top quarter of ESCS | | Difference (bottom-top) | |
| | | Mean | S.E. | Mean | S.E. | Mean | S.E. | Mean | S.E. | Dif. | S.E. |
|---|---|---|---|---|---|---|---|---|---|---|---|
| OECD | Australia | 3.84 | (0.04) | 4.05 | (0.04) | 4.17 | (0.04) | 4.36 | (0.04) | **-0.53** | (0.05) |
| | Austria | 3.12 | (0.07) | 3.23 | (0.07) | 3.28 | (0.06) | 3.25 | (0.05) | -0.14 | (0.08) |
| | Belgium | 3.04 | (0.06) | 3.42 | (0.05) | 3.74 | (0.06) | 4.14 | (0.04) | **-1.07** | (0.07) |
| | Canada | 4.13 | (0.06) | 4.45 | (0.05) | 4.67 | (0.05) | 4.77 | (0.07) | **-0.64** | (0.07) |
| | Czech Republic | 3.90 | (0.07) | 3.97 | (0.07) | 4.01 | (0.07) | 4.10 | (0.05) | **-0.20** | (0.08) |
| | Denmark | 4.30 | (0.05) | 4.46 | (0.05) | 4.48 | (0.04) | 4.51 | (0.06) | **-0.22** | (0.07) |
| | Finland | 3.36 | (0.06) | 3.39 | (0.06) | 3.45 | (0.05) | 3.59 | (0.06) | **-0.23** | (0.07) |
| | France | 3.54 | (0.05) | 3.73 | (0.05) | 3.87 | (0.05) | 4.25 | (0.05) | **-0.71** | (0.07) |
| | Germany | 3.83 | (0.06) | 3.91 | (0.05) | 3.96 | (0.05) | 3.84 | (0.05) | -0.04 | (0.08) |
| | Greece | 3.11 | (0.08) | 3.34 | (0.06) | 3.46 | (0.06) | 3.90 | (0.07) | **-0.79** | (0.11) |
| | Hungary | 3.07 | (0.07) | 3.29 | (0.07) | 3.20 | (0.06) | 3.60 | (0.07) | **-0.53** | (0.09) |
| | Iceland | 4.71 | (0.05) | 4.77 | (0.05) | 4.67 | (0.05) | 4.83 | (0.05) | -0.12 | (0.06) |
| | Ireland | 3.62 | (0.07) | 3.54 | (0.05) | 3.71 | (0.05) | 3.76 | (0.05) | -0.14 | (0.08) |
| | Italy | 3.54 | (0.05) | 3.68 | (0.05) | 3.86 | (0.04) | 3.88 | (0.05) | **-0.34** | (0.06) |
| | Japan | 3.58 | (0.09) | 4.15 | (0.08) | 4.52 | (0.08) | 4.76 | (0.08) | **-1.18** | (0.10) |
| | Korea | 4.44 | (0.08) | 4.65 | (0.05) | 4.72 | (0.06) | 4.98 | (0.07) | **-0.54** | (0.11) |
| | Luxembourg | 3.60 | (0.05) | 3.79 | (0.05) | 3.95 | (0.05) | 4.09 | (0.05) | **-0.51** | (0.07) |
| | Mexico | 3.72 | (0.08) | 3.80 | (0.07) | 3.88 | (0.05) | 4.38 | (0.06) | **-0.65** | (0.10) |
| | Netherlands | 2.69 | (0.06) | 2.74 | (0.06) | 2.98 | (0.04) | 3.10 | (0.06) | **-0.40** | (0.09) |
| | New Zealand | 4.10 | (0.05) | 4.35 | (0.05) | 4.46 | (0.05) | 4.63 | (0.04) | **-0.53** | (0.07) |
| | Norway | 3.17 | (0.06) | 3.39 | (0.05) | 3.50 | (0.05) | 3.52 | (0.06) | **-0.35** | (0.08) |
| | Poland | 4.14 | (0.06) | 4.30 | (0.05) | 4.43 | (0.06) | 4.56 | (0.05) | **-0.42** | (0.06) |
| | Portugal | 3.20 | (0.07) | 3.53 | (0.07) | 3.65 | (0.07) | 4.05 | (0.07) | **-0.86** | (0.10) |
| | Slovak Republic | 3.14 | (0.07) | 3.19 | (0.06) | 3.33 | (0.09) | 3.48 | (0.07) | **-0.34** | (0.08) |
| | Spain | 3.16 | (0.05) | 3.39 | (0.04) | 3.45 | (0.04) | 3.69 | (0.05) | **-0.53** | (0.06) |
| | Sweden | 3.07 | (0.05) | 3.05 | (0.04) | 3.09 | (0.04) | 3.16 | (0.04) | -0.09 | (0.07) |
| | Switzerland | 3.80 | (0.06) | 3.87 | (0.05) | 3.93 | (0.06) | 3.84 | (0.05) | -0.04 | (0.07) |
| | Turkey | 3.50 | (0.09) | 3.59 | (0.08) | 3.80 | (0.08) | 4.39 | (0.09) | **-0.89** | (0.12) |
| | United Kingdom | 3.65 | (0.05) | 3.72 | (0.04) | 3.86 | (0.05) | 3.90 | (0.05) | **-0.25** | (0.06) |
| | United States | 3.21 | (0.08) | 3.61 | (0.06) | 3.95 | (0.06) | 4.33 | (0.07) | **-1.12** | (0.12) |
| | **OECD average** | 3.58 | (0.01) | 3.74 | (0.01) | 3.87 | (0.01) | 4.05 | (0.01) | **-0.48** | (0.02) |
| Partners | Argentina | 2.54 | (0.07) | 2.81 | (0.08) | 2.98 | (0.08) | 3.48 | (0.09) | **-0.97** | (0.11) |
| | Azerbaijan | 3.50 | (0.11) | 3.66 | (0.10) | 3.86 | (0.09) | 4.14 | (0.09) | **-0.65** | (0.14) |
| | Brazil | 2.91 | (0.07) | 2.95 | (0.06) | 3.21 | (0.05) | 3.52 | (0.06) | **-0.61** | (0.09) |
| | Bulgaria | 2.59 | (0.09) | 2.78 | (0.09) | 3.02 | (0.08) | 3.53 | (0.12) | **-0.93** | (0.15) |
| | Chile | 2.90 | (0.09) | 3.23 | (0.07) | 3.60 | (0.08) | 4.22 | (0.09) | **-1.31** | (0.13) |
| | Colombia | 4.00 | (0.10) | 4.06 | (0.09) | 4.17 | (0.08) | 4.63 | (0.10) | **-0.62** | (0.14) |
| | Croatia | 2.77 | (0.06) | 2.99 | (0.04) | 3.09 | (0.05) | 3.33 | (0.05) | **-0.55** | (0.07) |
| | Estonia | 4.01 | (0.08) | 4.17 | (0.05) | 4.19 | (0.06) | 4.40 | (0.06) | **-0.39** | (0.09) |
| | Hong Kong-China | 4.95 | (0.07) | 5.14 | (0.07) | 5.31 | (0.07) | 5.52 | (0.07) | **-0.58** | (0.10) |
| | Indonesia | 4.00 | (0.09) | 4.06 | (0.07) | 4.04 | (0.11) | 4.26 | (0.11) | **-0.26** | (0.12) |
| | Israel | 3.72 | (0.06) | 4.11 | (0.07) | 4.27 | (0.08) | 4.42 | (0.07) | **-0.69** | (0.09) |
| | Jordan | 3.01 | (0.08) | 3.35 | (0.08) | 3.56 | (0.07) | 4.00 | (0.07) | **-0.99** | (0.10) |
| | Kyrgyzstan | 2.59 | (0.09) | 2.62 | (0.10) | 2.92 | (0.08) | 3.40 | (0.08) | **-0.79** | (0.12) |
| | Latvia | 4.29 | (0.07) | 4.50 | (0.06) | 4.50 | (0.06) | 4.69 | (0.06) | **-0.40** | (0.08) |
| | Liechtenstein | 3.87 | (0.18) | 3.87 | (0.19) | 4.18 | (0.19) | 4.00 | (0.15) | -0.14 | (0.25) |
| | Lithuania | 3.10 | (0.08) | 3.45 | (0.06) | 3.62 | (0.06) | 3.84 | (0.06) | **-0.73** | (0.09) |
| | Macao-China | 5.23 | (0.06) | 5.55 | (0.05) | 5.29 | (0.06) | 5.57 | (0.06) | **-0.34** | (0.08) |
| | Montenegro | 2.88 | (0.07) | 3.00 | (0.07) | 3.06 | (0.08) | 3.40 | (0.07) | **-0.53** | (0.11) |
| | Qatar | 2.65 | (0.06) | 3.02 | (0.06) | 3.32 | (0.06) | 3.46 | (0.06) | **-0.81** | (0.09) |
| | Romania | 2.58 | (0.10) | 2.92 | (0.11) | 3.08 | (0.08) | 3.46 | (0.11) | **-0.89** | (0.11) |
| | Russian Federation | 3.35 | (0.07) | 3.44 | (0.08) | 3.69 | (0.07) | 4.06 | (0.06) | **-0.72** | (0.10) |
| | Serbia | 3.08 | (0.06) | 3.14 | (0.06) | 3.30 | (0.05) | 3.57 | (0.06) | **-0.49** | (0.08) |
| | Slovenia | 3.00 | (0.06) | 3.22 | (0.05) | 3.39 | (0.05) | 3.70 | (0.05) | **-0.69** | (0.08) |
| | Chinese Taipei | 3.57 | (0.08) | 4.01 | (0.07) | 4.54 | (0.07) | 4.92 | (0.06) | **-1.36** | (0.09) |
| | Thailand | 3.60 | (0.05) | 3.65 | (0.04) | 3.60 | (0.05) | 4.26 | (0.08) | **-0.65** | (0.09) |
| | Tunisia | 2.98 | (0.07) | 3.32 | (0.07) | 3.44 | (0.08) | 3.81 | (0.08) | **-0.82** | (0.11) |
| | Uruguay | 2.97 | (0.06) | 3.14 | (0.07) | 3.42 | (0.06) | 3.72 | (0.07) | **-0.76** | (0.08) |

*Note:* Values that are statistically significant at the 5% level (p < 0.05) are indicated in bold.

© OECD 2011 Quality Time for Students: Learning In and Out of School

**Table 3.7b** **Mean learning hours and allocation of total learning time in mathematics,**
[Part 2/7] **by quarters of the PISA index of economic, social and cultural status (ESCS)**

|  |  | Mean learning hours per week | | | | | | | | |
|  |  | Out-of-school-time lessons | | | | | | | | |
|  |  | Bottom quarter of ESCS | | Second quarter of ESCS | | Third quarter of ESCS | | Top quarter of ESCS | | Difference (bottom-top) | |
|  |  | Mean | S.E. | Mean | S.E. | Mean | S.E. | Mean | S.E. | Dif. | S.E. |
|---|---|---|---|---|---|---|---|---|---|---|---|
| OECD | Australia | 0.79 | (0.03) | 0.72 | (0.02) | 0.73 | (0.03) | 0.75 | (0.03) | 0.04 | (0.04) |
|  | Austria | 0.54 | (0.04) | 0.52 | (0.04) | 0.48 | (0.04) | 0.49 | (0.03) | 0.05 | (0.05) |
|  | Belgium | 0.57 | (0.03) | 0.54 | (0.03) | 0.54 | (0.03) | 0.53 | (0.03) | 0.04 | (0.04) |
|  | Canada | 0.91 | (0.03) | 0.88 | (0.03) | 0.99 | (0.04) | 0.96 | (0.04) | -0.05 | (0.05) |
|  | Czech Republic | 0.78 | (0.07) | 0.74 | (0.04) | 0.76 | (0.04) | 0.74 | (0.04) | 0.05 | (0.08) |
|  | Denmark | 1.39 | (0.05) | 1.31 | (0.05) | 1.44 | (0.05) | 1.31 | (0.05) | 0.09 | (0.07) |
|  | Finland | 0.38 | (0.03) | 0.38 | (0.03) | 0.38 | (0.03) | 0.34 | (0.03) | 0.04 | (0.04) |
|  | France | 0.97 | (0.03) | 0.94 | (0.04) | 0.94 | (0.03) | 0.85 | (0.04) | **0.12** | (0.05) |
|  | Germany | 0.92 | (0.05) | 0.83 | (0.04) | 0.84 | (0.05) | 0.67 | (0.04) | **0.25** | (0.07) |
|  | Greece | 1.69 | (0.08) | 2.19 | (0.07) | 2.42 | (0.07) | 2.63 | (0.09) | **-0.93** | (0.13) |
|  | Hungary | 1.29 | (0.05) | 1.25 | (0.05) | 1.30 | (0.05) | 1.30 | (0.05) | -0.01 | (0.08) |
|  | Iceland | 0.64 | (0.04) | 0.71 | (0.04) | 0.75 | (0.04) | 0.76 | (0.04) | **-0.12** | (0.06) |
|  | Ireland | 0.71 | (0.05) | 0.71 | (0.03) | 0.76 | (0.04) | 0.69 | (0.04) | 0.02 | (0.06) |
|  | Italy | 0.82 | (0.03) | 0.86 | (0.03) | 0.90 | (0.03) | 0.97 | (0.04) | **-0.16** | (0.05) |
|  | Japan | 0.54 | (0.03) | 0.61 | (0.04) | 0.77 | (0.05) | 0.93 | (0.05) | **-0.39** | (0.06) |
|  | Korea | 1.60 | (0.08) | 1.95 | (0.06) | 2.43 | (0.05) | 3.13 | (0.08) | **-1.52** | (0.12) |
|  | Luxembourg | 0.93 | (0.04) | 0.85 | (0.04) | 0.83 | (0.03) | 0.72 | (0.03) | **0.22** | (0.05) |
|  | Mexico | 1.38 | (0.07) | 1.09 | (0.04) | 1.19 | (0.04) | 1.06 | (0.05) | **0.33** | (0.10) |
|  | Netherlands | 0.73 | (0.05) | 0.72 | (0.04) | 0.68 | (0.04) | 0.61 | (0.03) | **0.12** | (0.05) |
|  | New Zealand | 0.77 | (0.04) | 0.65 | (0.04) | 0.65 | (0.04) | 0.66 | (0.04) | 0.11 | (0.06) |
|  | Norway | 1.05 | (0.04) | 1.02 | (0.04) | 1.02 | (0.04) | 1.10 | (0.04) | -0.04 | (0.06) |
|  | Poland | 0.78 | (0.04) | 0.75 | (0.04) | 0.76 | (0.04) | 0.82 | (0.04) | -0.04 | (0.06) |
|  | Portugal | 0.69 | (0.04) | 0.80 | (0.04) | 0.85 | (0.04) | 0.91 | (0.05) | **-0.23** | (0.07) |
|  | Slovak Republic | 0.81 | (0.04) | 0.82 | (0.04) | 0.88 | (0.04) | 1.02 | (0.05) | **-0.22** | (0.07) |
|  | Spain | 0.89 | (0.04) | 1.04 | (0.04) | 1.07 | (0.04) | 0.98 | (0.05) | -0.09 | (0.06) |
|  | Sweden | 0.62 | (0.04) | 0.60 | (0.03) | 0.61 | (0.03) | 0.59 | (0.03) | 0.04 | (0.04) |
|  | Switzerland | 0.86 | (0.04) | 0.68 | (0.03) | 0.68 | (0.03) | 0.59 | (0.03) | **0.27** | (0.05) |
|  | Turkey | 1.84 | (0.06) | 1.66 | (0.07) | 2.09 | (0.07) | 2.70 | (0.07) | **-0.84** | (0.10) |
|  | United Kingdom | 0.60 | (0.04) | 0.64 | (0.03) | 0.67 | (0.03) | 0.60 | (0.03) | 0.00 | (0.05) |
|  | United States | 1.21 | (0.04) | 1.18 | (0.05) | 1.17 | (0.05) | 1.02 | (0.05) | **0.20** | (0.06) |
|  | **OECD average** | 0.92 | (0.01) | 0.92 | (0.01) | 0.99 | (0.01) | 1.01 | (0.01) | **-0.09** | (0.01) |
| Partners | Argentina | 0.72 | (0.07) | 0.77 | (0.05) | 0.81 | (0.06) | 0.81 | (0.07) | -0.09 | (0.09) |
|  | Azerbaijan | 1.59 | (0.08) | 1.64 | (0.09) | 1.70 | (0.08) | 1.86 | (0.07) | **-0.27** | (0.10) |
|  | Brazil | 1.13 | (0.05) | 1.17 | (0.05) | 1.20 | (0.06) | 1.34 | (0.05) | **-0.20** | (0.07) |
|  | Bulgaria | 1.09 | (0.07) | 1.10 | (0.06) | 1.11 | (0.05) | 1.25 | (0.05) | -0.14 | (0.08) |
|  | Chile | 1.01 | (0.05) | 0.97 | (0.04) | 1.00 | (0.05) | 0.99 | (0.05) | 0.02 | (0.06) |
|  | Colombia | 1.24 | (0.06) | 1.27 | (0.06) | 1.16 | (0.06) | 1.24 | (0.04) | 0.01 | (0.07) |
|  | Croatia | 0.69 | (0.04) | 0.69 | (0.04) | 0.79 | (0.04) | 0.90 | (0.05) | **-0.20** | (0.06) |
|  | Estonia | 1.02 | (0.05) | 1.03 | (0.06) | 0.95 | (0.05) | 0.97 | (0.05) | 0.05 | (0.06) |
|  | Hong Kong-China | 1.07 | (0.05) | 1.29 | (0.06) | 1.43 | (0.05) | 1.75 | (0.06) | **-0.68** | (0.07) |
|  | Indonesia | 1.23 | (0.07) | 1.30 | (0.06) | 1.35 | (0.06) | 1.57 | (0.07) | **-0.33** | (0.09) |
|  | Israel | 2.10 | (0.06) | 2.15 | (0.07) | 2.17 | (0.08) | 2.23 | (0.08) | -0.12 | (0.10) |
|  | Jordan | 1.62 | (0.06) | 1.87 | (0.07) | 1.84 | (0.06) | 1.95 | (0.07) | **-0.33** | (0.10) |
|  | Kyrgyzstan | 1.64 | (0.08) | 1.55 | (0.06) | 1.54 | (0.05) | 1.49 | (0.06) | 0.14 | (0.09) |
|  | Latvia | 1.10 | (0.07) | 1.16 | (0.06) | 1.23 | (0.06) | 1.30 | (0.05) | **-0.21** | (0.08) |
|  | Liechtenstein | 0.73 | (0.11) | 0.36 | (0.07) | 0.61 | (0.12) | 0.53 | (0.10) | 0.20 | (0.16) |
|  | Lithuania | 0.69 | (0.04) | 0.75 | (0.04) | 0.73 | (0.04) | 0.79 | (0.04) | -0.10 | (0.05) |
|  | Macao-China | 1.10 | (0.06) | 1.14 | (0.04) | 1.16 | (0.06) | 1.41 | (0.07) | **-0.31** | (0.09) |
|  | Montenegro | 0.79 | (0.04) | 0.84 | (0.05) | 1.00 | (0.05) | 1.08 | (0.06) | **-0.29** | (0.08) |
|  | Qatar | 1.79 | (0.05) | 1.90 | (0.05) | 1.81 | (0.05) | 1.91 | (0.05) | -0.11 | (0.07) |
|  | Romania | 1.27 | (0.06) | 1.49 | (0.06) | 1.53 | (0.09) | 1.70 | (0.06) | **-0.44** | (0.08) |
|  | Russian Federation | 0.99 | (0.05) | 1.12 | (0.04) | 1.15 | (0.06) | 1.25 | (0.04) | **-0.26** | (0.06) |
|  | Serbia | 0.95 | (0.05) | 0.91 | (0.05) | 1.02 | (0.05) | 1.00 | (0.04) | -0.05 | (0.06) |
|  | Slovenia | 1.13 | (0.06) | 1.09 | (0.04) | 0.99 | (0.04) | 0.87 | (0.04) | **0.27** | (0.07) |
|  | Chinese Taipei | 1.00 | (0.04) | 1.36 | (0.05) | 1.69 | (0.04) | 2.07 | (0.05) | **-1.07** | (0.05) |
|  | Thailand | 0.63 | (0.04) | 0.78 | (0.05) | 0.89 | (0.05) | 1.39 | (0.06) | **-0.75** | (0.08) |
|  | Tunisia | 2.21 | (0.06) | 2.21 | (0.07) | 2.49 | (0.07) | 2.79 | (0.08) | **-0.57** | (0.10) |
|  | Uruguay | 0.71 | (0.04) | 0.80 | (0.04) | 0.94 | (0.05) | 0.90 | (0.05) | **-0.20** | (0.06) |

*Note*: Values that are statistically significant at the 5% level (p < 0.05) are indicated in bold.

121

**Table 3.7b** **Mean learning hours and allocation of total learning time in mathematics,**
[Part 3/7] **by quarters of the PISA index of economic, social and cultural status (ESCS)**

| | Mean learning hours per week | | | | | | | | | |
|---|---|---|---|---|---|---|---|---|---|---|
| | Individual study | | | | | | | | | |
| | Bottom quarter of ESCS | | Second quarter of ESCS | | Third quarter of ESCS | | Top quarter of ESCS | | Difference (bottom-top) | |
| | Mean | S.E. | Mean | S.E. | Mean | S.E. | Mean | S.E. | Dif. | S.E. |
| Australia | 1.55 | (0.04) | 1.69 | (0.03) | 1.83 | (0.04) | 2.11 | (0.04) | **-0.56** | (0.05) |
| Austria | 2.18 | (0.05) | 2.15 | (0.06) | 2.06 | (0.05) | 2.12 | (0.06) | 0.05 | (0.07) |
| Belgium | 1.43 | (0.04) | 1.66 | (0.04) | 1.91 | (0.05) | 2.16 | (0.05) | **-0.71** | (0.06) |
| Canada | 1.70 | (0.05) | 1.83 | (0.04) | 2.11 | (0.04) | 2.25 | (0.05) | **-0.55** | (0.06) |
| Czech Republic | 1.34 | (0.06) | 1.31 | (0.06) | 1.28 | (0.04) | 1.34 | (0.05) | -0.00 | (0.06) |
| Denmark | 1.65 | (0.05) | 1.71 | (0.04) | 1.81 | (0.04) | 1.79 | (0.04) | **-0.14** | (0.06) |
| Finland | 1.14 | (0.04) | 1.17 | (0.03) | 1.24 | (0.03) | 1.27 | (0.03) | **-0.14** | (0.04) |
| France | 1.49 | (0.04) | 1.62 | (0.05) | 1.82 | (0.05) | 2.03 | (0.06) | **-0.54** | (0.07) |
| Germany | 2.24 | (0.07) | 2.28 | (0.06) | 2.32 | (0.06) | 2.26 | (0.06) | -0.03 | (0.09) |
| Greece | 1.75 | (0.06) | 1.84 | (0.06) | 2.05 | (0.06) | 2.37 | (0.06) | **-0.62** | (0.08) |
| Hungary | 1.77 | (0.05) | 1.74 | (0.05) | 1.81 | (0.06) | 2.03 | (0.06) | **-0.26** | (0.08) |
| Iceland | 1.65 | (0.05) | 1.68 | (0.04) | 1.73 | (0.04) | 1.78 | (0.05) | -0.13 | (0.07) |
| Ireland | 1.57 | (0.06) | 1.65 | (0.05) | 1.89 | (0.05) | 1.94 | (0.05) | **-0.36** | (0.08) |
| Italy | 2.24 | (0.04) | 2.40 | (0.04) | 2.58 | (0.05) | 2.72 | (0.06) | **-0.48** | (0.06) |
| Japan | 1.01 | (0.05) | 1.42 | (0.07) | 1.61 | (0.07) | 1.91 | (0.09) | **-0.90** | (0.09) |
| Korea | 1.66 | (0.07) | 2.00 | (0.07) | 2.34 | (0.08) | 3.25 | (0.12) | **-1.58** | (0.14) |
| Luxembourg | 1.66 | (0.05) | 1.75 | (0.05) | 1.72 | (0.04) | 1.72 | (0.04) | -0.06 | (0.06) |
| Mexico | 2.32 | (0.06) | 2.25 | (0.05) | 2.28 | (0.04) | 2.19 | (0.04) | 0.14 | (0.06) |
| Netherlands | 1.31 | (0.05) | 1.34 | (0.05) | 1.56 | (0.05) | 1.68 | (0.04) | **-0.36** | (0.07) |
| New Zealand | 1.41 | (0.04) | 1.54 | (0.05) | 1.59 | (0.04) | 1.82 | (0.05) | **-0.41** | (0.06) |
| Norway | 1.26 | (0.05) | 1.36 | (0.04) | 1.43 | (0.05) | 1.55 | (0.05) | **-0.29** | (0.06) |
| Poland | 2.08 | (0.06) | 1.99 | (0.05) | 2.12 | (0.05) | 2.17 | (0.05) | -0.09 | (0.08) |
| Portugal | 1.70 | (0.06) | 1.92 | (0.06) | 2.04 | (0.05) | 2.19 | (0.06) | **-0.49** | (0.09) |
| Slovak Republic | 1.52 | (0.05) | 1.60 | (0.05) | 1.77 | (0.05) | 1.85 | (0.06) | **-0.32** | (0.08) |
| Spain | 1.72 | (0.05) | 1.94 | (0.05) | 2.04 | (0.05) | 2.15 | (0.04) | **-0.44** | (0.06) |
| Sweden | 1.09 | (0.04) | 1.13 | (0.04) | 1.26 | (0.04) | 1.24 | (0.04) | **-0.15** | (0.05) |
| Switzerland | 1.77 | (0.03) | 1.64 | (0.04) | 1.70 | (0.04) | 1.64 | (0.04) | 0.13 | (0.05) |
| Turkey | 2.13 | (0.06) | 2.14 | (0.07) | 2.30 | (0.07) | 2.65 | (0.08) | **-0.52** | (0.11) |
| United Kingdom | 1.30 | (0.03) | 1.40 | (0.03) | 1.57 | (0.04) | 1.69 | (0.04) | **-0.39** | (0.05) |
| United States | 1.77 | (0.05) | 1.82 | (0.05) | 2.20 | (0.06) | 2.38 | (0.06) | **-0.60** | (0.09) |
| **OECD average** | 1.65 | (0.01) | 1.73 | (0.01) | 1.87 | (0.01) | 2.01 | (0.01) | **-0.36** | (0.01) |
| Argentina | 1.73 | (0.07) | 1.81 | (0.08) | 1.87 | (0.07) | 1.88 | (0.05) | **-0.15** | (0.08) |
| Azerbaijan | 2.68 | (0.13) | 2.87 | (0.08) | 3.04 | (0.10) | 3.21 | (0.09) | **-0.52** | (0.14) |
| Brazil | 1.76 | (0.06) | 1.68 | (0.05) | 1.83 | (0.06) | 1.92 | (0.05) | **-0.16** | (0.08) |
| Bulgaria | 1.71 | (0.07) | 1.87 | (0.08) | 2.23 | (0.08) | 2.54 | (0.11) | **-0.83** | (0.12) |
| Chile | 1.50 | (0.05) | 1.51 | (0.04) | 1.69 | (0.07) | 1.70 | (0.05) | **-0.20** | (0.07) |
| Colombia | 1.84 | (0.06) | 2.04 | (0.06) | 1.81 | (0.06) | 2.03 | (0.05) | **-0.20** | (0.08) |
| Croatia | 1.65 | (0.05) | 1.82 | (0.05) | 1.83 | (0.05) | 1.92 | (0.05) | **-0.27** | (0.06) |
| Estonia | 1.78 | (0.05) | 1.98 | (0.05) | 1.94 | (0.05) | 2.13 | (0.06) | **-0.35** | (0.07) |
| Hong Kong-China | 1.94 | (0.07) | 2.16 | (0.07) | 2.24 | (0.06) | 2.61 | (0.08) | **-0.68** | (0.09) |
| Indonesia | 1.97 | (0.06) | 1.92 | (0.04) | 2.00 | (0.05) | 2.08 | (0.05) | -0.11 | (0.08) |
| Israel | 2.26 | (0.07) | 2.36 | (0.08) | 2.33 | (0.10) | 2.38 | (0.09) | -0.12 | (0.11) |
| Jordan | 2.42 | (0.07) | 2.68 | (0.07) | 2.74 | (0.06) | 2.93 | (0.08) | **-0.50** | (0.10) |
| Kyrgyzstan | 2.36 | (0.07) | 2.06 | (0.07) | 2.14 | (0.06) | 2.29 | (0.06) | 0.08 | (0.10) |
| Latvia | 2.23 | (0.07) | 2.50 | (0.07) | 2.48 | (0.07) | 2.56 | (0.07) | **-0.34** | (0.09) |
| Liechtenstein | 1.51 | (0.11) | 1.29 | (0.11) | 1.59 | (0.11) | 1.56 | (0.15) | -0.06 | (0.19) |
| Lithuania | 1.57 | (0.05) | 1.71 | (0.04) | 1.81 | (0.05) | 2.04 | (0.05) | **-0.47** | (0.08) |
| Macao-China | 1.81 | (0.06) | 1.97 | (0.06) | 2.09 | (0.05) | 2.39 | (0.07) | **-0.59** | (0.09) |
| Montenegro | 1.90 | (0.06) | 2.08 | (0.06) | 2.06 | (0.07) | 2.10 | (0.07) | **-0.21** | (0.09) |
| Qatar | 2.05 | (0.05) | 2.16 | (0.05) | 2.33 | (0.05) | 2.34 | (0.05) | **-0.30** | (0.07) |
| Romania | 1.89 | (0.08) | 2.19 | (0.09) | 2.19 | (0.07) | 2.37 | (0.08) | **-0.50** | (0.12) |
| Russian Federation | 1.98 | (0.08) | 2.19 | (0.06) | 2.29 | (0.06) | 2.46 | (0.05) | **-0.47** | (0.09) |
| Serbia | 1.63 | (0.05) | 1.66 | (0.05) | 1.87 | (0.06) | 2.11 | (0.06) | **-0.48** | (0.08) |
| Slovenia | 1.83 | (0.05) | 1.90 | (0.05) | 1.93 | (0.05) | 2.02 | (0.05) | **-0.20** | (0.07) |
| Chinese Taipei | 1.32 | (0.05) | 1.76 | (0.06) | 2.00 | (0.04) | 2.44 | (0.05) | **-1.11** | (0.07) |
| Thailand | 1.64 | (0.06) | 1.77 | (0.05) | 1.81 | (0.06) | 2.02 | (0.05) | **-0.37** | (0.09) |
| Tunisia | 2.47 | (0.08) | 2.56 | (0.07) | 2.45 | (0.07) | 2.78 | (0.06) | **-0.29** | (0.10) |
| Uruguay | 1.42 | (0.06) | 1.55 | (0.06) | 1.61 | (0.06) | 1.71 | (0.06) | **-0.29** | (0.07) |

*Note:* Values that are statistically significant at the 5% level (p < 0.05) are indicated in bold.

© OECD 2011 Quality Time for Students: Learning In and Out of School

**Table 3.7b** Mean learning hours and allocation of total learning time in mathematics,
[Part 4/7] by quarters of the PISA index of economic, social and cultural status (ESCS)

| | | Mean learning hours per week | | | | | | | | |
| | | Total learning hours | | | | | | | | |
| | | Bottom quarter of ESCS | | Second quarter of ESCS | | Third quarter of ESCS | | Top quarter of ESCS | | Difference (bottom-top) | |
| | | Mean | S.E. | Mean | S.E. | Mean | S.E. | Mean | S.E. | Dif. | S.E. |
|---|---|---|---|---|---|---|---|---|---|---|---|
| OECD | Australia | 6.20 | (0.09) | 6.48 | (0.07) | 6.73 | (0.07) | 7.20 | (0.07) | **-1.01** | (0.11) |
| | Austria | 5.88 | (0.12) | 5.92 | (0.12) | 5.83 | (0.10) | 5.87 | (0.12) | -0.02 | (0.14) |
| | Belgium | 5.07 | (0.10) | 5.62 | (0.09) | 6.21 | (0.10) | 6.83 | (0.09) | **-1.72** | (0.12) |
| | Canada | 6.78 | (0.10) | 7.21 | (0.09) | 7.78 | (0.09) | 8.01 | (0.13) | **-1.21** | (0.14) |
| | Czech Republic | 6.01 | (0.16) | 5.99 | (0.12) | 6.05 | (0.10) | 6.18 | (0.10) | -0.18 | (0.18) |
| | Denmark | 7.32 | (0.11) | 7.45 | (0.10) | 7.71 | (0.10) | 7.58 | (0.10) | -0.26 | (0.14) |
| | Finland | 4.88 | (0.10) | 4.94 | (0.09) | 5.08 | (0.08) | 5.20 | (0.08) | **-0.31** | (0.11) |
| | France | 6.03 | (0.09) | 6.29 | (0.08) | 6.63 | (0.09) | 7.12 | (0.10) | **-1.10** | (0.14) |
| | Germany | 7.03 | (0.14) | 7.04 | (0.10) | 7.15 | (0.10) | 6.76 | (0.11) | 0.22 | (0.18) |
| | Greece | 6.57 | (0.16) | 7.39 | (0.14) | 7.95 | (0.14) | 8.91 | (0.15) | **-2.34** | (0.23) |
| | Hungary | 6.16 | (0.13) | 6.27 | (0.14) | 6.34 | (0.13) | 6.91 | (0.15) | **-0.77** | (0.20) |
| | Iceland | 6.99 | (0.09) | 7.16 | (0.09) | 7.16 | (0.09) | 7.37 | (0.10) | **-0.40** | (0.13) |
| | Ireland | 5.89 | (0.14) | 5.91 | (0.10) | 6.37 | (0.10) | 6.38 | (0.10) | **-0.48** | (0.17) |
| | Italy | 6.63 | (0.08) | 6.96 | (0.09) | 7.34 | (0.09) | 7.55 | (0.12) | **-0.94** | (0.11) |
| | Japan | 5.13 | (0.14) | 6.17 | (0.15) | 6.90 | (0.15) | 7.60 | (0.17) | **-2.47** | (0.17) |
| | Korea | 7.78 | (0.19) | 8.62 | (0.14) | 9.54 | (0.14) | 11.34 | (0.23) | **-3.56** | (0.31) |
| | Luxembourg | 6.21 | (0.10) | 6.43 | (0.10) | 6.52 | (0.09) | 6.55 | (0.08) | **-0.33** | (0.11) |
| | Mexico | 7.36 | (0.13) | 7.13 | (0.11) | 7.34 | (0.09) | 7.59 | (0.10) | -0.19 | (0.16) |
| | Netherlands | 4.68 | (0.11) | 4.81 | (0.11) | 5.23 | (0.10) | 5.36 | (0.10) | **-0.67** | (0.14) |
| | New Zealand | 6.26 | (0.09) | 6.56 | (0.09) | 6.72 | (0.09) | 7.12 | (0.10) | **-0.83** | (0.12) |
| | Norway | 5.50 | (0.11) | 5.75 | (0.09) | 5.95 | (0.10) | 6.16 | (0.11) | **-0.65** | (0.15) |
| | Poland | 7.00 | (0.10) | 7.04 | (0.10) | 7.33 | (0.10) | 7.55 | (0.11) | **-0.54** | (0.14) |
| | Portugal | 5.60 | (0.12) | 6.24 | (0.13) | 6.55 | (0.12) | 7.13 | (0.14) | **-1.53** | (0.19) |
| | Slovak Republic | 5.49 | (0.14) | 5.62 | (0.13) | 6.00 | (0.14) | 6.37 | (0.14) | **-0.88** | (0.19) |
| | Spain | 5.85 | (0.09) | 6.41 | (0.10) | 6.56 | (0.09) | 6.84 | (0.07) | **-1.01** | (0.09) |
| | Sweden | 4.81 | (0.09) | 4.78 | (0.08) | 4.96 | (0.07) | 4.98 | (0.07) | -0.17 | (0.11) |
| | Switzerland | 6.44 | (0.08) | 6.20 | (0.08) | 6.32 | (0.09) | 6.10 | (0.09) | **0.34** | (0.12) |
| | Turkey | 7.42 | (0.17) | 7.38 | (0.19) | 8.14 | (0.20) | 9.72 | (0.21) | **-2.28** | (0.28) |
| | United Kingdom | 5.56 | (0.09) | 5.76 | (0.07) | 6.11 | (0.08) | 6.19 | (0.07) | **-0.63** | (0.11) |
| | United States | 6.26 | (0.13) | 6.67 | (0.12) | 7.37 | (0.12) | 7.73 | (0.13) | **-1.45** | (0.20) |
| | **OECD average** | 6.16 | (0.02) | 6.41 | (0.02) | 6.73 | (0.02) | 7.07 | (0.02) | **-0.91** | (0.03) |
| Partners | Argentina | 5.02 | (0.13) | 5.40 | (0.17) | 5.66 | (0.16) | 6.15 | (0.13) | **-1.17** | (0.18) |
| | Azerbaijan | 7.83 | (0.24) | 8.25 | (0.23) | 8.65 | (0.21) | 9.24 | (0.20) | **-1.41** | (0.31) |
| | Brazil | 5.81 | (0.12) | 5.78 | (0.13) | 6.23 | (0.12) | 6.75 | (0.11) | **-0.93** | (0.16) |
| | Bulgaria | 5.43 | (0.21) | 5.79 | (0.19) | 6.39 | (0.18) | 7.31 | (0.24) | **-1.84** | (0.29) |
| | Chile | 5.45 | (0.15) | 5.74 | (0.12) | 6.36 | (0.16) | 6.93 | (0.13) | **-1.48** | (0.19) |
| | Colombia | 7.04 | (0.13) | 7.37 | (0.12) | 7.14 | (0.14) | 7.95 | (0.14) | **-0.89** | (0.18) |
| | Croatia | 5.16 | (0.12) | 5.53 | (0.09) | 5.76 | (0.09) | 6.18 | (0.10) | **-1.03** | (0.13) |
| | Estonia | 6.83 | (0.11) | 7.16 | (0.11) | 7.08 | (0.12) | 7.51 | (0.11) | **-0.67** | (0.15) |
| | Hong Kong-China | 7.98 | (0.13) | 8.60 | (0.14) | 8.99 | (0.11) | 9.88 | (0.15) | **-1.90** | (0.18) |
| | Indonesia | 7.20 | (0.18) | 7.27 | (0.12) | 7.36 | (0.12) | 7.91 | (0.12) | **-0.72** | (0.17) |
| | Israel | 8.16 | (0.14) | 8.73 | (0.17) | 8.82 | (0.23) | 9.12 | (0.19) | **-0.94** | (0.23) |
| | Jordan | 7.07 | (0.15) | 7.90 | (0.17) | 8.04 | (0.13) | 8.86 | (0.12) | **-1.78** | (0.19) |
| | Kyrgyzstan | 6.78 | (0.18) | 6.24 | (0.18) | 6.60 | (0.15) | 7.21 | (0.13) | **-0.40** | (0.23) |
| | Latvia | 7.60 | (0.16) | 8.18 | (0.14) | 8.23 | (0.13) | 8.55 | (0.12) | **-0.95** | (0.18) |
| | Liechtenstein | 6.11 | (0.24) | 5.56 | (0.27) | 6.27 | (0.32) | 6.14 | (0.24) | -0.03 | (0.38) |
| | Lithuania | 5.34 | (0.13) | 5.93 | (0.10) | 6.16 | (0.11) | 6.65 | (0.10) | **-1.30** | (0.17) |
| | Macao-China | 8.14 | (0.12) | 8.65 | (0.11) | 8.54 | (0.11) | 9.37 | (0.14) | **-1.23** | (0.17) |
| | Montenegro | 5.54 | (0.12) | 5.93 | (0.12) | 6.13 | (0.17) | 6.52 | (0.14) | **-0.99** | (0.20) |
| | Qatar | 6.52 | (0.12) | 7.11 | (0.12) | 7.52 | (0.11) | 7.70 | (0.12) | **-1.17** | (0.17) |
| | Romania | 5.74 | (0.17) | 6.59 | (0.21) | 6.84 | (0.14) | 7.53 | (0.21) | **-1.82** | (0.24) |
| | Russian Federation | 6.32 | (0.13) | 6.76 | (0.14) | 7.13 | (0.14) | 7.77 | (0.11) | **-1.47** | (0.18) |
| | Serbia | 5.65 | (0.11) | 5.70 | (0.11) | 6.19 | (0.11) | 6.68 | (0.13) | **-1.04** | (0.16) |
| | Slovenia | 6.01 | (0.11) | 6.24 | (0.10) | 6.32 | (0.10) | 6.61 | (0.11) | **-0.60** | (0.15) |
| | Chinese Taipei | 5.98 | (0.16) | 7.20 | (0.15) | 8.29 | (0.12) | 9.45 | (0.12) | **-3.49** | (0.17) |
| | Thailand | 5.88 | (0.11) | 6.19 | (0.09) | 6.30 | (0.13) | 7.65 | (0.17) | **-1.76** | (0.22) |
| | Tunisia | 7.66 | (0.16) | 8.05 | (0.16) | 8.40 | (0.17) | 9.39 | (0.17) | **-1.68** | (0.24) |
| | Uruguay | 5.18 | (0.10) | 5.49 | (0.13) | 5.97 | (0.13) | 6.33 | (0.13) | **-1.18** | (0.15) |

*Note:* Values that are statistically significant at the 5% level (p < 0.05) are indicated in bold.

### Table 3.7b
**[Part 5/7]** **Mean learning hours and allocation of total learning time in mathematics, by quarters of the PISA index of economic, social and cultural status (ESCS)**

| | Allocation of total learning time in mathematics for | | | | | | | | | |
|---|---|---|---|---|---|---|---|---|---|---|
| | Regular school lessons | | | | | | | | | |
| | Bottom quarter of ESCS | | Second quarter of ESCS | | Third quarter of ESCS | | Top quarter of ESCS | | Difference (bottom-top) | |
| | % | S.E. | % | S.E. | % | S.E. | % | S.E. | Dif. | S.E. |
| **OECD** Australia | 66.5 | (0.6) | 66.7 | (0.4) | 65.7 | (0.4) | 64.2 | (0.4) | **2.3** | (0.7) |
| Austria | 57.0 | (0.9) | 58.0 | (0.8) | 60.0 | (0.7) | 59.0 | (0.7) | -1.9 | (1.1) |
| Belgium | 63.7 | (0.5) | 63.5 | (0.6) | 62.5 | (0.6) | 63.1 | (0.5) | 0.9 | (0.8) |
| Canada | 63.8 | (0.6) | 64.1 | (0.5) | 62.7 | (0.5) | 62.8 | (0.5) | 0.9 | (0.7) |
| Czech Republic | 69.4 | (0.9) | 70.2 | (0.7) | 70.8 | (0.7) | 70.9 | (0.7) | -1.6 | (1.2) |
| Denmark | 62.4 | (0.7) | 62.9 | (0.6) | 61.6 | (0.6) | 62.7 | (0.6) | -0.4 | (0.8) |
| Finland | 71.3 | (0.7) | 71.2 | (0.6) | 70.5 | (0.5) | 71.5 | (0.6) | -0.1 | (0.9) |
| France | 62.8 | (0.7) | 62.8 | (0.7) | 61.9 | (0.6) | 62.9 | (0.5) | 0.0 | (0.9) |
| Germany | 57.4 | (0.7) | 58.7 | (0.6) | 58.1 | (0.7) | 59.8 | (0.6) | **-2.3** | (0.8) |
| Greece | 53.0 | (0.8) | 49.6 | (0.8) | 47.8 | (0.8) | 47.0 | (0.9) | **6.0** | (1.1) |
| Hungary | 52.2 | (0.9) | 55.6 | (0.7) | 53.6 | (0.7) | 55.9 | (0.8) | **-3.6** | (1.3) |
| Iceland | 70.5 | (0.6) | 69.9 | (0.7) | 68.2 | (0.6) | 69.2 | (0.6) | 1.4 | (0.9) |
| Ireland | 65.6 | (0.8) | 63.6 | (0.7) | 62.6 | (0.6) | 62.7 | (0.6) | **3.0** | (1.0) |
| Italy | 56.0 | (0.5) | 55.3 | (0.4) | 54.9 | (0.4) | 53.9 | (0.5) | **2.1** | (0.7) |
| Japan | 74.8 | (0.6) | 72.8 | (0.7) | 70.6 | (0.9) | 68.5 | (0.9) | **6.3** | (1.0) |
| Korea | 63.9 | (0.9) | 61.2 | (0.7) | 54.8 | (0.7) | 47.8 | (0.7) | **16.2** | (1.2) |
| Luxembourg | 60.7 | (0.7) | 61.8 | (0.7) | 64.4 | (0.6) | 66.2 | (0.5) | **-5.8** | (1.0) |
| Mexico | 51.1 | (0.9) | 54.0 | (0.7) | 53.6 | (0.5) | 59.2 | (0.6) | **-8.1** | (1.1) |
| Netherlands | 60.3 | (1.1) | 59.6 | (0.8) | 59.3 | (0.8) | 61.0 | (0.7) | -0.7 | (1.5) |
| New Zealand | 69.2 | (0.8) | 69.9 | (0.7) | 70.0 | (0.7) | 68.9 | (0.6) | 0.4 | (1.0) |
| Norway | 62.4 | (0.8) | 63.3 | (0.7) | 62.1 | (0.7) | 61.0 | (0.7) | 1.4 | (1.0) |
| Poland | 60.9 | (0.6) | 62.9 | (0.6) | 62.8 | (0.6) | 63.3 | (0.5) | **-2.4** | (0.8) |
| Portugal | 59.1 | (1.0) | 58.7 | (0.8) | 58.6 | (0.7) | 59.1 | (0.7) | 0.0 | (1.2) |
| Slovak Republic | 61.6 | (0.9) | 61.5 | (0.8) | 59.7 | (0.8) | 59.6 | (0.9) | 2.1 | (1.2) |
| Spain | 58.6 | (0.7) | 57.6 | (0.6) | 56.8 | (0.5) | 57.8 | (0.6) | 0.9 | (0.9) |
| Sweden | 69.2 | (0.8) | 68.0 | (0.8) | 67.2 | (0.6) | 68.2 | (0.8) | 0.9 | (0.8) |
| Switzerland | 60.8 | (0.7) | 63.9 | (0.6) | 64.2 | (0.5) | 65.5 | (0.6) | **-4.7** | (0.9) |
| Turkey | 51.0 | (0.8) | 52.6 | (0.9) | 50.8 | (0.8) | 48.7 | (0.7) | 2.0 | (1.1) |
| United Kingdom | 69.0 | (0.6) | 67.7 | (0.5) | 66.1 | (0.5) | 65.8 | (0.5) | **3.3** | (0.8) |
| United States | 52.5 | (0.9) | 55.3 | (0.9) | 55.8 | (0.7) | 58.1 | (0.8) | **-5.7** | (1.3) |
| **OECD average** | 61.9 | (0.1) | 62.1 | (0.1) | 61.3 | (0.1) | 61.5 | (0.1) | **0.4** | (0.2) |
| **Partners** Argentina | 53.1 | (1.1) | 53.8 | (0.9) | 54.7 | (0.9) | 58.4 | (1.1) | **-5.8** | (1.5) |
| Azerbaijan | 47.3 | (1.0) | 46.2 | (1.0) | 46.9 | (0.8) | 47.9 | (0.7) | -0.8 | (1.1) |
| Brazil | 52.8 | (1.1) | 54.5 | (0.9) | 54.8 | (0.9) | 55.6 | (0.8) | **-2.8** | (1.4) |
| Bulgaria | 51.4 | (1.0) | 51.0 | (1.1) | 50.4 | (0.9) | 51.9 | (0.7) | -0.7 | (1.2) |
| Chile | 53.4 | (0.8) | 55.9 | (0.8) | 56.8 | (0.8) | 61.2 | (0.9) | **-7.8** | (1.2) |
| Colombia | 60.0 | (1.2) | 58.7 | (0.9) | 61.7 | (0.8) | 62.5 | (0.9) | -2.2 | (1.6) |
| Croatia | 57.8 | (0.7) | 58.7 | (0.8) | 58.1 | (0.8) | 58.8 | (0.7) | -0.9 | (0.8) |
| Estonia | 62.0 | (0.8) | 61.3 | (0.6) | 62.5 | (0.6) | 62.9 | (0.7) | -0.9 | (1.0) |
| Hong Kong-China | 65.5 | (0.8) | 63.4 | (0.8) | 62.4 | (0.6) | 59.2 | (0.5) | **6.4** | (0.8) |
| Indonesia | 57.7 | (0.8) | 57.5 | (0.7) | 56.9 | (1.2) | 56.6 | (1.0) | 1.1 | (1.4) |
| Israel | 48.9 | (0.9) | 51.0 | (1.0) | 52.7 | (1.0) | 52.7 | (1.0) | **-3.9** | (1.3) |
| Jordan | 41.1 | (1.0) | 42.8 | (0.9) | 43.6 | (0.8) | 45.3 | (0.9) | **-4.3** | (1.4) |
| Kyrgyzstan | 37.7 | (0.9) | 40.3 | (0.8) | 42.9 | (0.8) | 47.3 | (0.9) | **-9.6** | (1.3) |
| Latvia | 59.4 | (0.8) | 58.2 | (0.7) | 57.6 | (0.7) | 57.8 | (0.5) | 1.5 | (0.9) |
| Liechtenstein | 62.5 | (2.3) | 69.7 | (2.0) | 68.3 | (2.1) | 67.0 | (1.8) | -4.7 | (2.8) |
| Lithuania | 60.6 | (0.8) | 61.0 | (0.7) | 61.4 | (0.7) | 59.9 | (0.6) | 0.5 | (1.0) |
| Macao-China | 68.0 | (0.8) | 67.5 | (0.5) | 65.6 | (0.7) | 63.9 | (0.7) | **4.1** | (1.0) |
| Montenegro | 53.3 | (0.8) | 51.7 | (0.9) | 51.8 | (0.9) | 53.1 | (0.9) | -0.0 | (1.1) |
| Qatar | 40.8 | (0.7) | 42.2 | (0.6) | 44.7 | (0.6) | 45.3 | (0.6) | **-4.5** | (1.0) |
| Romania | 48.5 | (1.6) | 49.2 | (0.9) | 49.4 | (0.7) | 50.9 | (0.7) | -2.4 | (2.0) |
| Russian Federation | 54.6 | (0.9) | 52.6 | (0.8) | 53.8 | (0.8) | 54.8 | (0.6) | -0.1 | (1.1) |
| Serbia | 60.3 | (0.7) | 60.3 | (0.8) | 58.2 | (0.9) | 58.4 | (0.7) | 1.8 | (1.1) |
| Slovenia | 52.5 | (0.7) | 54.4 | (0.6) | 57.0 | (0.6) | 58.6 | (0.6) | **-6.0** | (1.0) |
| Chinese Taipei | 64.7 | (0.6) | 60.3 | (0.7) | 58.8 | (0.5) | 55.1 | (0.5) | **9.6** | (0.8) |
| Thailand | 66.0 | (0.9) | 63.4 | (0.7) | 63.1 | (0.6) | 61.1 | (0.6) | **4.8** | (1.2) |
| Tunisia | 40.5 | (0.8) | 42.1 | (0.9) | 42.3 | (0.7) | 41.9 | (0.7) | -1.4 | (1.2) |
| Uruguay | 59.8 | (0.9) | 60.2 | (0.9) | 61.1 | (0.8) | 62.1 | (0.6) | -2.2 | (1.2) |

*Note:* Values that are statistically significant at the 5% level (p < 0.05) are indicated in bold.

© OECD 2011 Quality Time for Students: Learning In and Out of School

## Table 3.7b Mean learning hours and allocation of total learning time in mathematics,
[Part 6/7] by quarters of the PISA index of economic, social and cultural status (ESCS)

| | Allocation of total learning time in mathematics for | | | | | | | | | |
|---|---|---|---|---|---|---|---|---|---|---|
| | Out-of-school-time lessons | | | | | | | | | |
| | Bottom quarter of ESCS | | Second quarter of ESCS | | Third quarter of ESCS | | Top quarter of ESCS | | Difference (bottom-top) | |
| | % | S.E. | % | S.E. | % | S.E. | % | S.E. | Dif. | S.E. |
| **OECD** | | | | | | | | | | |
| Australia | 10.4 | (0.4) | 9.1 | (0.3) | 9.0 | (0.3) | 8.5 | (0.3) | **1.9** | (0.4) |
| Austria | 6.7 | (0.4) | 6.9 | (0.5) | 6.5 | (0.4) | 6.5 | (0.4) | 0.1 | (0.6) |
| Belgium | 9.3 | (0.4) | 8.1 | (0.4) | 7.6 | (0.4) | 6.6 | (0.4) | **2.7** | (0.6) |
| Canada | 12.2 | (0.4) | 11.4 | (0.3) | 11.4 | (0.4) | 10.6 | (0.3) | **1.6** | (0.5) |
| Czech Republic | 10.2 | (0.5) | 9.7 | (0.4) | 10.1 | (0.4) | 9.3 | (0.4) | 1.0 | (0.8) |
| Denmark | 16.8 | (0.5) | 15.5 | (0.4) | 16.7 | (0.5) | 15.1 | (0.5) | **1.8** | (0.7) |
| Finland | 6.6 | (0.4) | 6.1 | (0.4) | 6.0 | (0.4) | 5.0 | (0.4) | **1.6** | (0.5) |
| France | 14.2 | (0.4) | 13.3 | (0.5) | 12.4 | (0.4) | 10.4 | (0.4) | **3.9** | (0.6) |
| Germany | 11.2 | (0.6) | 9.8 | (0.4) | 9.9 | (0.6) | 7.9 | (0.4) | **3.4** | (0.7) |
| Greece | 21.4 | (0.7) | 26.3 | (0.7) | 28.0 | (0.7) | 28.3 | (0.9) | **-6.9** | (1.1) |
| Hungary | 19.1 | (0.7) | 17.4 | (0.5) | 18.1 | (0.5) | 16.1 | (0.6) | **2.8** | (0.9) |
| Iceland | 8.0 | (0.5) | 8.2 | (0.5) | 9.0 | (0.4) | 8.7 | (0.4) | -0.7 | (0.6) |
| Ireland | 9.7 | (0.7) | 10.0 | (0.4) | 9.4 | (0.5) | 8.7 | (0.4) | 1.0 | (0.8) |
| Italy | 10.4 | (0.4) | 10.7 | (0.4) | 10.7 | (0.4) | 11.2 | (0.4) | -0.8 | (0.5) |
| Japan | 8.3 | (0.5) | 7.7 | (0.4) | 8.8 | (0.5) | 9.7 | (0.5) | **-1.5** | (0.6) |
| Korea | 16.9 | (0.6) | 18.8 | (0.5) | 22.5 | (0.4) | 25.5 | (0.5) | **-8.6** | (0.8) |
| Luxembourg | 13.1 | (0.5) | 11.9 | (0.5) | 10.4 | (0.4) | 8.9 | (0.4) | **4.3** | (0.7) |
| Mexico | 16.5 | (0.8) | 14.0 | (0.5) | 14.8 | (0.4) | 12.3 | (0.5) | **4.2** | (1.0) |
| Netherlands | 13.7 | (0.9) | 13.2 | (0.6) | 11.5 | (0.6) | 9.6 | (0.5) | **3.8** | (1.1) |
| New Zealand | 10.1 | (0.6) | 8.5 | (0.4) | 8.0 | (0.4) | 7.5 | (0.4) | **2.6** | (0.7) |
| Norway | 16.8 | (0.5) | 15.3 | (0.5) | 15.6 | (0.5) | 15.9 | (0.5) | 1.0 | (0.7) |
| Poland | 10.8 | (0.5) | 10.0 | (0.4) | 9.7 | (0.5) | 9.8 | (0.4) | 1.0 | (0.7) |
| Portugal | 11.8 | (0.6) | 11.8 | (0.6) | 11.3 | (0.5) | 11.3 | (0.5) | 0.6 | (0.8) |
| Slovak Republic | 12.1 | (0.5) | 12.3 | (0.5) | 12.4 | (0.5) | 13.5 | (0.5) | -1.4 | (0.8) |
| Spain | 13.0 | (0.4) | 13.3 | (0.5) | 13.8 | (0.4) | 12.1 | (0.5) | 1.1 | (0.7) |
| Sweden | 10.2 | (0.4) | 10.3 | (0.5) | 9.7 | (0.4) | 9.3 | (0.4) | 1.0 | (0.6) |
| Switzerland | 11.5 | (0.5) | 9.4 | (0.4) | 9.3 | (0.4) | 8.1 | (0.4) | **3.4** | (0.7) |
| Turkey | 22.1 | (0.7) | 20.2 | (0.6) | 22.9 | (0.6) | 25.6 | (0.6) | **-3.3** | (0.9) |
| United Kingdom | 8.8 | (0.5) | 9.1 | (0.3) | 9.2 | (0.3) | 8.3 | (0.4) | 0.6 | (0.6) |
| United States | 18.2 | (0.5) | 16.9 | (0.7) | 14.6 | (0.6) | 11.8 | (0.5) | **6.4** | (0.7) |
| **OECD average** | 12.7 | (0.1) | 12.2 | (0.1) | 12.3 | (0.1) | 11.7 | (0.1) | **1.0** | (0.1) |
| **Partners** | | | | | | | | | | |
| Argentina | 12.6 | (1.2) | 12.1 | (0.8) | 13.0 | (0.7) | 11.8 | (0.9) | 1.0 | (1.4) |
| Azerbaijan | 18.8 | (0.7) | 18.5 | (0.8) | 18.8 | (0.7) | 18.3 | (0.6) | 0.3 | (0.9) |
| Brazil | 17.0 | (0.9) | 18.0 | (0.7) | 17.0 | (0.7) | 17.4 | (0.6) | -0.5 | (1.1) |
| Bulgaria | 18.4 | (0.9) | 17.0 | (0.8) | 15.3 | (0.6) | 14.9 | (0.6) | **3.8** | (1.1) |
| Chile | 17.3 | (0.6) | 15.9 | (0.6) | 14.5 | (0.5) | 12.8 | (0.6) | **4.7** | (0.8) |
| Colombia | 15.0 | (0.7) | 14.2 | (0.8) | 13.9 | (0.5) | 13.8 | (0.5) | 1.2 | (0.8) |
| Croatia | 11.2 | (0.6) | 10.3 | (0.5) | 12.0 | (0.6) | 12.4 | (0.6) | -1.3 | (0.8) |
| Estonia | 13.4 | (0.5) | 13.2 | (0.6) | 11.9 | (0.5) | 10.9 | (0.4) | **2.4** | (0.7) |
| Hong Kong-China | 12.1 | (0.5) | 13.6 | (0.5) | 14.3 | (0.4) | 16.0 | (0.5) | **-3.7** | (0.7) |
| Indonesia | 15.3 | (0.7) | 16.0 | (0.6) | 16.4 | (0.7) | 17.7 | (0.8) | **-2.4** | (1.0) |
| Israel | 24.2 | (0.5) | 23.1 | (0.6) | 22.6 | (0.6) | 22.6 | (0.6) | **1.7** | (0.9) |
| Jordan | 23.4 | (0.7) | 22.4 | (0.7) | 22.2 | (0.7) | 21.3 | (1.0) | 2.2 | (1.1) |
| Kyrgyzstan | 25.5 | (0.9) | 25.7 | (0.8) | 25.0 | (0.9) | 20.0 | (0.7) | **5.3** | (1.2) |
| Latvia | 13.2 | (0.7) | 12.9 | (0.5) | 13.6 | (0.6) | 13.7 | (0.5) | -0.4 | (0.9) |
| Liechtenstein | 11.9 | (1.7) | 6.6 | (1.2) | 7.2 | (1.3) | 7.5 | (1.2) | **4.3** | (2.1) |
| Lithuania | 11.6 | (0.7) | 12.2 | (0.6) | 11.1 | (0.5) | 11.2 | (0.5) | 0.5 | (0.8) |
| Macao-China | 11.3 | (0.5) | 11.5 | (0.4) | 11.9 | (0.5) | 12.7 | (0.6) | -1.4 | (0.7) |
| Montenegro | 12.0 | (0.6) | 12.9 | (0.7) | 14.6 | (0.7) | 14.2 | (0.7) | **-2.2** | (1.0) |
| Qatar | 26.4 | (0.6) | 26.3 | (0.6) | 23.8 | (0.6) | 24.3 | (0.5) | **2.2** | (0.9) |
| Romania | 19.4 | (1.0) | 19.5 | (0.7) | 20.3 | (1.0) | 19.8 | (0.6) | -0.4 | (1.3) |
| Russian Federation | 15.9 | (1.1) | 16.3 | (0.7) | 15.4 | (0.8) | 15.1 | (0.5) | 0.8 | (1.1) |
| Serbia | 13.0 | (0.5) | 12.9 | (0.6) | 13.5 | (0.6) | 12.5 | (0.5) | 0.4 | (0.7) |
| Slovenia | 16.9 | (0.6) | 15.3 | (0.5) | 13.6 | (0.5) | 11.5 | (0.4) | **5.4** | (0.7) |
| Chinese Taipei | 13.7 | (0.5) | 15.9 | (0.4) | 18.2 | (0.4) | 19.9 | (0.4) | **-6.4** | (0.7) |
| Thailand | 8.2 | (0.5) | 9.6 | (0.5) | 10.6 | (0.5) | 14.2 | (0.5) | **-6.1** | (0.8) |
| Tunisia | 26.8 | (0.7) | 25.4 | (0.6) | 27.8 | (0.7) | 28.4 | (0.7) | -1.6 | (1.0) |
| Uruguay | 11.9 | (0.5) | 12.7 | (0.6) | 13.1 | (0.6) | 11.9 | (0.5) | -0.1 | (0.7) |

*Note:* Values that are statistically significant at the 5% level (p < 0.05) are indicated in bold.

### Table 3.7b Mean learning hours and allocation of total learning time in mathematics,
[Part 7/7] by quarters of the PISA index of economic, social and cultural status (ESCS)

| | | Allocation of total learning time in mathematics for | | | | | | | | |
|---|---|---|---|---|---|---|---|---|---|---|
| | | Individual study | | | | | | | | |
| | | Bottom quarter of ESCS | | Second quarter of ESCS | | Third quarter of ESCS | | Top quarter of ESCS | | Difference (bottom-top) | |
| | | % | S.E. | % | S.E. | % | S.E. | % | S.E. | Dif. | S.E. |
| OECD | Australia | 23.0 | (0.4) | 24.2 | (0.3) | 25.3 | (0.3) | 27.3 | (0.4) | **-4.3** | (0.5) |
| | Austria | 36.4 | (0.7) | 35.1 | (0.7) | 33.5 | (0.6) | 34.5 | (0.6) | **1.9** | (0.9) |
| | Belgium | 27.0 | (0.4) | 28.4 | (0.5) | 29.9 | (0.5) | 30.2 | (0.5) | **-3.7** | (0.6) |
| | Canada | 24.0 | (0.5) | 24.5 | (0.4) | 25.9 | (0.4) | 26.6 | (0.4) | **-2.5** | (0.5) |
| | Czech Republic | 20.5 | (0.7) | 20.0 | (0.5) | 19.1 | (0.6) | 19.9 | (0.6) | 0.5 | (0.9) |
| | Denmark | 20.8 | (0.4) | 21.5 | (0.4) | 21.9 | (0.4) | 22.3 | (0.5) | **-1.4** | (0.6) |
| | Finland | 22.1 | (0.5) | 22.6 | (0.4) | 23.5 | (0.4) | 23.5 | (0.4) | **-1.4** | (0.6) |
| | France | 22.9 | (0.5) | 23.9 | (0.5) | 25.8 | (0.5) | 26.7 | (0.5) | **-3.9** | (0.7) |
| | Germany | 31.3 | (0.5) | 31.5 | (0.5) | 32.0 | (0.6) | 32.3 | (0.6) | **-1.1** | (0.7) |
| | Greece | 25.6 | (0.7) | 24.1 | (0.6) | 24.1 | (0.6) | 24.8 | (0.5) | 0.8 | (0.9) |
| | Hungary | 28.7 | (0.6) | 27.0 | (0.6) | 28.3 | (0.6) | 27.9 | (0.6) | 0.9 | (0.8) |
| | Iceland | 21.5 | (0.5) | 22.0 | (0.4) | 22.7 | (0.4) | 22.2 | (0.5) | -0.7 | (0.7) |
| | Ireland | 24.7 | (0.6) | 26.4 | (0.5) | 27.9 | (0.5) | 28.6 | (0.6) | **-4.0** | (0.8) |
| | Italy | 33.6 | (0.4) | 34.0 | (0.4) | 34.4 | (0.4) | 34.9 | (0.4) | **-1.3** | (0.5) |
| | Japan | 16.9 | (0.5) | 19.5 | (0.6) | 20.5 | (0.7) | 21.8 | (0.7) | **-5.0** | (0.8) |
| | Korea | 19.1 | (0.5) | 20.1 | (0.6) | 22.6 | (0.6) | 26.7 | (0.6) | **-7.5** | (0.7) |
| | Luxembourg | 26.2 | (0.5) | 26.3 | (0.4) | 25.2 | (0.5) | 24.8 | (0.5) | 1.4 | (0.7) |
| | Mexico | 32.4 | (0.7) | 32.0 | (0.5) | 31.5 | (0.4) | 28.5 | (0.5) | **3.9** | (0.8) |
| | Netherlands | 26.0 | (0.7) | 27.3 | (0.6) | 29.2 | (0.5) | 29.3 | (0.6) | **-3.2** | (1.0) |
| | New Zealand | 20.6 | (0.4) | 21.6 | (0.5) | 21.9 | (0.4) | 23.7 | (0.5) | **-3.0** | (0.7) |
| | Norway | 20.7 | (0.5) | 21.5 | (0.5) | 22.2 | (0.5) | 23.2 | (0.5) | **-2.4** | (0.7) |
| | Poland | 28.2 | (0.6) | 27.1 | (0.5) | 27.6 | (0.5) | 26.9 | (0.4) | 1.4 | (0.7) |
| | Portugal | 29.1 | (0.7) | 29.4 | (0.6) | 30.0 | (0.5) | 29.7 | (0.6) | -0.5 | (0.8) |
| | Slovak Republic | 26.3 | (0.7) | 26.3 | (0.5) | 27.8 | (0.7) | 27.0 | (0.7) | -0.6 | (0.9) |
| | Spain | 28.5 | (0.6) | 29.1 | (0.5) | 29.4 | (0.5) | 30.2 | (0.5) | **-2.0** | (0.7) |
| | Sweden | 20.7 | (0.6) | 21.7 | (0.6) | 23.1 | (0.5) | 22.5 | (0.6) | **-1.7** | (0.6) |
| | Switzerland | 27.7 | (0.5) | 26.7 | (0.4) | 26.5 | (0.4) | 26.4 | (0.4) | **1.3** | (0.6) |
| | Turkey | 27.0 | (0.7) | 27.2 | (0.7) | 26.3 | (0.6) | 25.7 | (0.5) | 1.2 | (0.9) |
| | United Kingdom | 22.2 | (0.4) | 23.2 | (0.4) | 24.7 | (0.4) | 26.0 | (0.4) | **-3.8** | (0.5) |
| | United States | 29.3 | (0.7) | 27.8 | (0.5) | 29.6 | (0.6) | 30.2 | (0.5) | -0.8 | (0.9) |
| | **OECD average** | 25.4 | (0.1) | 25.7 | (0.1) | 26.4 | (0.1) | 26.8 | (0.1) | **-1.4** | (0.1) |
| Partners | Argentina | 34.2 | (0.8) | 34.3 | (1.1) | 32.2 | (0.8) | 29.9 | (0.7) | **4.8** | (1.1) |
| | Azerbaijan | 33.9 | (1.1) | 35.2 | (0.7) | 34.4 | (0.7) | 33.8 | (0.6) | 0.4 | (1.2) |
| | Brazil | 30.2 | (0.8) | 27.6 | (0.7) | 28.1 | (0.6) | 27.1 | (0.6) | **3.2** | (1.0) |
| | Bulgaria | 30.2 | (0.8) | 32.1 | (0.8) | 34.2 | (0.7) | 33.2 | (0.8) | **-3.1** | (1.1) |
| | Chile | 29.3 | (0.6) | 28.2 | (0.7) | 28.7 | (0.7) | 26.0 | (0.7) | **3.2** | (0.8) |
| | Colombia | 24.9 | (0.8) | 27.1 | (0.9) | 24.3 | (0.6) | 23.8 | (0.6) | 1.0 | (1.2) |
| | Croatia | 31.0 | (0.6) | 31.0 | (0.7) | 30.0 | (0.7) | 28.9 | (0.5) | **2.1** | (0.7) |
| | Estonia | 24.5 | (0.5) | 25.5 | (0.6) | 25.6 | (0.5) | 26.2 | (0.6) | **-1.6** | (0.7) |
| | Hong Kong-China | 22.4 | (0.6) | 22.9 | (0.6) | 23.2 | (0.5) | 24.9 | (0.5) | **-2.5** | (0.8) |
| | Indonesia | 27.0 | (0.5) | 26.5 | (0.5) | 26.7 | (0.6) | 25.7 | (0.5) | 1.3 | (0.8) |
| | Israel | 26.9 | (0.7) | 26.0 | (0.8) | 24.5 | (0.7) | 24.7 | (0.7) | **2.3** | (1.0) |
| | Jordan | 35.5 | (0.7) | 34.8 | (0.6) | 34.2 | (0.7) | 33.3 | (0.7) | **2.1** | (1.0) |
| | Kyrgyzstan | 36.9 | (0.7) | 34.0 | (0.8) | 32.3 | (0.8) | 32.6 | (0.7) | **4.4** | (1.0) |
| | Latvia | 27.4 | (0.8) | 29.0 | (0.7) | 28.7 | (0.5) | 28.5 | (0.5) | -1.1 | (0.9) |
| | Liechtenstein | 25.7 | (1.4) | 23.6 | (1.6) | 24.5 | (1.9) | 25.5 | (1.7) | 0.1 | (2.2) |
| | Lithuania | 27.9 | (0.6) | 26.9 | (0.6) | 27.5 | (0.5) | 28.9 | (0.5) | -1.0 | (0.8) |
| | Macao-China | 20.7 | (0.6) | 21.0 | (0.6) | 22.6 | (0.6) | 23.4 | (0.5) | **-2.7** | (0.8) |
| | Montenegro | 34.7 | (0.7) | 35.4 | (0.8) | 33.7 | (0.7) | 32.6 | (0.7) | **2.2** | (1.0) |
| | Qatar | 32.7 | (0.6) | 31.5 | (0.5) | 31.5 | (0.5) | 30.4 | (0.5) | **2.3** | (0.7) |
| | Romania | 32.1 | (1.6) | 31.3 | (0.7) | 30.3 | (0.8) | 29.3 | (0.6) | 2.8 | (1.8) |
| | Russian Federation | 29.4 | (0.8) | 31.2 | (0.6) | 30.7 | (0.4) | 30.2 | (0.5) | -0.7 | (0.8) |
| | Serbia | 26.8 | (0.6) | 26.9 | (0.6) | 28.3 | (0.7) | 29.0 | (0.7) | **-2.2** | (0.9) |
| | Slovenia | 30.7 | (0.7) | 30.2 | (0.6) | 29.4 | (0.6) | 29.9 | (0.5) | 0.7 | (1.0) |
| | Chinese Taipei | 21.6 | (0.4) | 23.8 | (0.5) | 23.2 | (0.4) | 24.9 | (0.4) | **-3.3** | (0.6) |
| | Thailand | 25.9 | (0.6) | 26.9 | (0.5) | 26.4 | (0.5) | 24.7 | (0.5) | 1.2 | (0.8) |
| | Tunisia | 32.6 | (0.8) | 32.5 | (0.8) | 29.9 | (0.7) | 29.8 | (0.6) | **3.0** | (0.9) |
| | Uruguay | 28.3 | (0.8) | 27.2 | (0.7) | 25.8 | (0.5) | 26.0 | (0.5) | **2.3** | (1.0) |

*Note:* Values that are statistically significant at the 5% level (p < 0.05) are indicated in bold.

© OECD 2011  Quality Time for Students: Learning In and Out of School

**Table 3.7c**
[Part 1/7]
**Mean learning hours and allocation of total learning time on the language of instruction, by quarters of the PISA index of economic, social and cultural status (ESCS)**

| | Mean learning hours per week | | | | | | | | | |
|---|---|---|---|---|---|---|---|---|---|---|
| | Regular school lessons | | | | | | | | | |
| | Bottom quarter of ESCS | | Second quarter of ESCS | | Third quarter of ESCS | | Top quarter of ESCS | | Difference (bottom-top) | |
| | Mean | S.E. | Mean | S.E. | Mean | S.E. | Mean | S.E. | Dif. | S.E. |
| **OECD** Australia | 3.83 | (0.04) | 4.02 | (0.03) | 4.13 | (0.04) | 4.28 | (0.04) | **-0.46** | (0.05) |
| Austria | 2.86 | (0.07) | 2.87 | (0.05) | 2.90 | (0.05) | 2.84 | (0.05) | 0.01 | (0.08) |
| Belgium | 3.22 | (0.06) | 3.39 | (0.05) | 3.62 | (0.04) | 3.72 | (0.05) | **-0.48** | (0.08) |
| Canada | 4.10 | (0.06) | 4.38 | (0.06) | 4.59 | (0.06) | 4.65 | (0.07) | **-0.56** | (0.08) |
| Czech Republic | 3.77 | (0.06) | 3.66 | (0.05) | 3.73 | (0.05) | 3.73 | (0.06) | 0.03 | (0.08) |
| Denmark | 5.39 | (0.07) | 5.51 | (0.05) | 5.57 | (0.05) | 5.55 | (0.05) | -0.16 | (0.08) |
| Finland | 3.05 | (0.06) | 3.11 | (0.06) | 3.13 | (0.06) | 3.24 | (0.06) | **-0.20** | (0.06) |
| France | 3.72 | (0.06) | 3.96 | (0.05) | 4.07 | (0.04) | 4.34 | (0.04) | **-0.61** | (0.07) |
| Germany | 3.65 | (0.07) | 3.70 | (0.06) | 3.74 | (0.05) | 3.55 | (0.05) | **0.07** | (0.09) |
| Greece | 2.88 | (0.07) | 3.12 | (0.07) | 3.31 | (0.07) | 3.39 | (0.06) | **-0.51** | (0.09) |
| Hungary | 2.79 | (0.06) | 3.19 | (0.07) | 3.26 | (0.07) | 3.50 | (0.07) | **-0.71** | (0.09) |
| Iceland | 4.51 | (0.05) | 4.55 | (0.05) | 4.43 | (0.06) | 4.59 | (0.05) | -0.09 | (0.07) |
| Ireland | 3.56 | (0.06) | 3.44 | (0.06) | 3.57 | (0.05) | 3.63 | (0.05) | -0.07 | (0.08) |
| Italy | 4.46 | (0.06) | 4.57 | (0.05) | 4.70 | (0.05) | 4.75 | (0.06) | **-0.30** | (0.08) |
| Japan | 3.41 | (0.07) | 3.74 | (0.05) | 4.04 | (0.05) | 4.11 | (0.05) | **-0.70** | (0.08) |
| Korea | 4.24 | (0.07) | 4.48 | (0.07) | 4.50 | (0.05) | 4.68 | (0.05) | **-0.44** | (0.08) |
| Luxembourg | 3.31 | (0.06) | 3.42 | (0.05) | 3.56 | (0.05) | 3.74 | (0.05) | **-0.43** | (0.07) |
| Mexico | 3.53 | (0.08) | 3.69 | (0.07) | 3.65 | (0.05) | 4.05 | (0.06) | **-0.51** | (0.09) |
| Netherlands | 2.92 | (0.05) | 2.94 | (0.04) | 2.95 | (0.05) | 2.87 | (0.04) | 0.05 | (0.07) |
| New Zealand | 4.11 | (0.06) | 4.38 | (0.05) | 4.49 | (0.05) | 4.63 | (0.04) | **-0.51** | (0.07) |
| Norway | 3.38 | (0.07) | 3.60 | (0.06) | 3.64 | (0.07) | 3.78 | (0.06) | **-0.40** | (0.09) |
| Poland | 4.38 | (0.05) | 4.62 | (0.05) | 4.72 | (0.06) | 4.84 | (0.04) | **-0.46** | (0.05) |
| Portugal | 3.04 | (0.05) | 3.23 | (0.05) | 3.32 | (0.05) | 3.48 | (0.05) | **-0.44** | (0.07) |
| Slovak Republic | 3.01 | (0.07) | 3.05 | (0.07) | 3.21 | (0.08) | 3.22 | (0.06) | **-0.21** | (0.07) |
| Spain | 3.46 | (0.05) | 3.56 | (0.05) | 3.62 | (0.04) | 3.79 | (0.05) | **-0.33** | (0.06) |
| Sweden | 3.06 | (0.04) | 3.09 | (0.05) | 3.11 | (0.04) | 3.21 | (0.06) | -0.15 | (0.08) |
| Switzerland | 3.57 | (0.05) | 3.60 | (0.06) | 3.68 | (0.05) | 3.75 | (0.05) | **-0.18** | (0.06) |
| Turkey | 3.71 | (0.09) | 3.89 | (0.07) | 4.06 | (0.08) | 4.31 | (0.06) | **-0.60** | (0.10) |
| United Kingdom | 3.75 | (0.05) | 3.84 | (0.04) | 3.97 | (0.05) | 4.03 | (0.05) | **-0.27** | (0.07) |
| United States | 3.04 | (0.09) | 3.45 | (0.07) | 3.80 | (0.05) | 4.29 | (0.06) | **-1.24** | (0.11) |
| **OECD average** | 3.59 | (0.01) | 3.73 | (0.01) | 3.84 | (0.01) | 3.95 | (0.01) | **-0.36** | (0.01) |
| **Partners** Argentina | 2.18 | (0.06) | 2.30 | (0.06) | 2.31 | (0.07) | 2.78 | (0.12) | **-0.58** | (0.14) |
| Azerbaijan | 3.34 | (0.07) | 3.59 | (0.09) | 3.87 | (0.08) | 3.95 | (0.08) | **-0.62** | (0.10) |
| Brazil | 2.90 | (0.09) | 2.96 | (0.07) | 3.16 | (0.05) | 3.38 | (0.05) | **-0.48** | (0.11) |
| Bulgaria | 2.59 | (0.10) | 2.77 | (0.07) | 3.02 | (0.07) | 3.27 | (0.06) | **-0.68** | (0.12) |
| Chile | 2.93 | (0.08) | 3.25 | (0.07) | 3.51 | (0.07) | 4.09 | (0.10) | **-1.15** | (0.13) |
| Colombia | 3.71 | (0.07) | 3.78 | (0.08) | 3.97 | (0.07) | 4.22 | (0.07) | **-0.51** | (0.10) |
| Croatia | 3.19 | (0.06) | 3.31 | (0.05) | 3.34 | (0.05) | 3.48 | (0.05) | **-0.29** | (0.07) |
| Estonia | 3.40 | (0.07) | 3.48 | (0.06) | 3.52 | (0.06) | 3.55 | (0.05) | **-0.14** | (0.07) |
| Hong Kong-China | 5.00 | (0.06) | 5.15 | (0.06) | 5.27 | (0.07) | 5.34 | (0.07) | **-0.35** | (0.09) |
| Indonesia | 3.61 | (0.10) | 3.64 | (0.08) | 3.56 | (0.06) | 3.75 | (0.05) | -0.14 | (0.10) |
| Israel | 2.78 | (0.07) | 2.91 | (0.08) | 3.06 | (0.08) | 3.38 | (0.07) | **-0.59** | (0.10) |
| Jordan | 3.33 | (0.09) | 3.44 | (0.09) | 3.60 | (0.07) | 3.89 | (0.08) | **-0.56** | (0.12) |
| Kyrgyzstan | 2.54 | (0.11) | 2.46 | (0.08) | 2.80 | (0.08) | 3.17 | (0.08) | **-0.61** | (0.12) |
| Latvia | 3.57 | (0.08) | 3.72 | (0.05) | 3.71 | (0.05) | 3.79 | (0.06) | **-0.21** | (0.11) |
| Liechtenstein | 3.54 | (0.17) | 3.72 | (0.19) | 3.78 | (0.18) | 3.62 | (0.14) | -0.07 | (0.24) |
| Lithuania | 3.39 | (0.07) | 3.62 | (0.06) | 3.71 | (0.07) | 3.92 | (0.08) | **-0.53** | (0.10) |
| Macao-China | 5.16 | (0.06) | 5.42 | (0.06) | 5.29 | (0.06) | 5.41 | (0.06) | **-0.24** | (0.08) |
| Montenegro | 2.55 | (0.08) | 2.80 | (0.07) | 2.96 | (0.07) | 3.42 | (0.08) | **-0.87** | (0.11) |
| Qatar | 2.58 | (0.06) | 2.82 | (0.07) | 3.05 | (0.07) | 3.12 | (0.06) | **-0.55** | (0.09) |
| Romania | 2.87 | (0.08) | 3.22 | (0.08) | 3.38 | (0.09) | 3.73 | (0.08) | **-0.87** | (0.11) |
| Russian Federation | 2.05 | (0.05) | 2.04 | (0.06) | 2.10 | (0.05) | 2.00 | (0.06) | 0.05 | (0.08) |
| Serbia | 3.05 | (0.05) | 2.97 | (0.05) | 3.24 | (0.05) | 3.45 | (0.05) | **-0.40** | (0.07) |
| Slovenia | 2.96 | (0.06) | 3.16 | (0.05) | 3.33 | (0.05) | 3.54 | (0.05) | **-0.58** | (0.08) |
| Chinese Taipei | 3.80 | (0.07) | 4.15 | (0.07) | 4.60 | (0.06) | 4.95 | (0.06) | **-1.16** | (0.08) |
| Thailand | 3.21 | (0.05) | 3.14 | (0.04) | 2.97 | (0.04) | 3.09 | (0.05) | 0.12 | (0.07) |
| Tunisia | 3.13 | (0.08) | 3.19 | (0.08) | 3.12 | (0.07) | 3.10 | (0.08) | 0.03 | (0.11) |
| Uruguay | 2.66 | (0.07) | 2.73 | (0.07) | 2.76 | (0.06) | 2.81 | (0.05) | -0.14 | (0.09) |

*Note*: Values that are statistically significant at the 5% level (p < 0.05) are indicated in bold.

**Table 3.7c** [Part 2/7] **Mean learning hours and allocation of total learning time on the language of instruction, by quarters of the PISA index of economic, social and cultural status (ESCS)**

| | | Mean learning hours per week | | | | | | | | |
| | | Out-of-school-time lessons | | | | | | | | |
| | | Bottom quarter of ESCS | | Second quarter of ESCS | | Third quarter of ESCS | | Top quarter of ESCS | | Difference (bottom-top) | |
| | | Mean | S.E. | Mean | S.E. | Mean | S.E. | Mean | S.E. | Dif. | S.E. |
|---|---|---|---|---|---|---|---|---|---|---|---|
| OECD | Australia | 0.71 | (0.03) | 0.66 | (0.03) | 0.65 | (0.02) | 0.62 | (0.03) | **0.10** | (0.04) |
| | Austria | 0.33 | (0.03) | 0.28 | (0.03) | 0.17 | (0.02) | 0.16 | (0.03) | **0.18** | (0.04) |
| | Belgium | 0.54 | (0.02) | 0.46 | (0.02) | 0.44 | (0.03) | 0.36 | (0.03) | **0.19** | (0.04) |
| | Canada | 0.85 | (0.03) | 0.83 | (0.04) | 0.92 | (0.04) | 0.86 | (0.04) | -0.02 | (0.04) |
| | Czech Republic | 0.67 | (0.03) | 0.59 | (0.04) | 0.58 | (0.04) | 0.60 | (0.03) | 0.08 | (0.05) |
| | Denmark | 1.75 | (0.06) | 1.60 | (0.05) | 1.69 | (0.06) | 1.69 | (0.06) | 0.06 | (0.09) |
| | Finland | 0.38 | (0.03) | 0.38 | (0.03) | 0.37 | (0.02) | 0.33 | (0.02) | 0.05 | (0.04) |
| | France | 0.95 | (0.04) | 0.77 | (0.03) | 0.74 | (0.03) | 0.60 | (0.04) | **0.36** | (0.06) |
| | Germany | 0.81 | (0.05) | 0.64 | (0.03) | 0.55 | (0.04) | 0.43 | (0.04) | **0.38** | (0.07) |
| | Greece | 1.46 | (0.07) | 1.61 | (0.04) | 1.77 | (0.07) | 1.67 | (0.06) | **-0.22** | (0.09) |
| | Hungary | 1.29 | (0.05) | 1.27 | (0.05) | 1.41 | (0.05) | 1.26 | (0.06) | 0.04 | (0.08) |
| | Iceland | 0.40 | (0.03) | 0.46 | (0.04) | 0.53 | (0.04) | 0.46 | (0.03) | -0.06 | (0.05) |
| | Ireland | 0.69 | (0.05) | 0.64 | (0.04) | 0.65 | (0.04) | 0.55 | (0.04) | **0.14** | (0.06) |
| | Italy | 0.85 | (0.03) | 0.82 | (0.04) | 0.76 | (0.03) | 0.75 | (0.04) | 0.10 | (0.05) |
| | Japan | 0.44 | (0.03) | 0.37 | (0.03) | 0.45 | (0.04) | 0.43 | (0.03) | -0.00 | (0.04) |
| | Korea | 1.05 | (0.06) | 1.28 | (0.06) | 1.55 | (0.06) | 1.90 | (0.08) | **-0.85** | (0.10) |
| | Luxembourg | 0.84 | (0.04) | 0.64 | (0.03) | 0.49 | (0.03) | 0.39 | (0.03) | **0.45** | (0.06) |
| | Mexico | 1.27 | (0.07) | 1.08 | (0.04) | 1.12 | (0.04) | 0.95 | (0.06) | **0.32** | (0.10) |
| | Netherlands | 0.77 | (0.04) | 0.74 | (0.03) | 0.60 | (0.04) | 0.47 | (0.03) | **0.31** | (0.06) |
| | New Zealand | 0.75 | (0.05) | 0.66 | (0.04) | 0.58 | (0.04) | 0.60 | (0.04) | **0.16** | (0.06) |
| | Norway | 1.17 | (0.04) | 1.14 | (0.04) | 1.11 | (0.05) | 1.19 | (0.05) | -0.02 | (0.06) |
| | Poland | 0.73 | (0.05) | 0.74 | (0.04) | 0.67 | (0.04) | 0.66 | (0.03) | 0.07 | (0.06) |
| | Portugal | 0.66 | (0.04) | 0.61 | (0.04) | 0.56 | (0.03) | 0.43 | (0.03) | **0.22** | (0.05) |
| | Slovak Republic | 0.89 | (0.05) | 0.83 | (0.04) | 0.88 | (0.04) | 0.95 | (0.04) | -0.06 | (0.07) |
| | Spain | 0.69 | (0.04) | 0.66 | (0.04) | 0.55 | (0.03) | 0.43 | (0.04) | **0.27** | (0.05) |
| | Sweden | 0.68 | (0.04) | 0.67 | (0.03) | 0.64 | (0.03) | 0.69 | (0.05) | -0.00 | (0.06) |
| | Switzerland | 0.63 | (0.03) | 0.50 | (0.03) | 0.44 | (0.03) | 0.38 | (0.03) | **0.25** | (0.04) |
| | Turkey | 1.81 | (0.07) | 1.83 | (0.07) | 1.87 | (0.07) | 1.75 | (0.09) | 0.05 | (0.11) |
| | United Kingdom | 0.62 | (0.04) | 0.60 | (0.03) | 0.64 | (0.03) | 0.51 | (0.03) | **0.11** | (0.04) |
| | United States | 1.17 | (0.08) | 1.12 | (0.04) | 1.14 | (0.06) | 1.03 | (0.05) | 0.14 | (0.09) |
| | **OECD average** | 0.86 | (0.01) | 0.82 | (0.01) | 0.82 | (0.01) | 0.77 | (0.01) | **0.09** | (0.01) |
| Partners | Argentina | 0.48 | (0.04) | 0.44 | (0.03) | 0.44 | (0.05) | 0.34 | (0.04) | **0.14** | (0.05) |
| | Azerbaijan | 1.69 | (0.08) | 1.70 | (0.07) | 1.79 | (0.07) | 2.01 | (0.07) | **-0.31** | (0.09) |
| | Brazil | 1.16 | (0.06) | 1.19 | (0.05) | 1.20 | (0.05) | 1.17 | (0.05) | 0.00 | (0.08) |
| | Bulgaria | 1.09 | (0.07) | 1.15 | (0.06) | 1.03 | (0.05) | 1.10 | (0.07) | -0.02 | (0.11) |
| | Chile | 1.10 | (0.05) | 1.03 | (0.05) | 1.03 | (0.05) | 0.83 | (0.05) | **0.27** | (0.06) |
| | Colombia | 1.20 | (0.06) | 1.22 | (0.08) | 1.06 | (0.04) | 1.12 | (0.06) | 0.08 | (0.07) |
| | Croatia | 0.44 | (0.04) | 0.40 | (0.03) | 0.34 | (0.03) | 0.37 | (0.02) | 0.07 | (0.04) |
| | Estonia | 0.95 | (0.05) | 0.94 | (0.05) | 0.87 | (0.05) | 0.78 | (0.05) | **0.17** | (0.05) |
| | Hong Kong-China | 0.82 | (0.05) | 0.85 | (0.06) | 0.75 | (0.04) | 0.81 | (0.06) | 0.01 | (0.07) |
| | Indonesia | 1.24 | (0.06) | 1.28 | (0.05) | 1.29 | (0.07) | 1.21 | (0.05) | 0.03 | (0.07) |
| | Israel | 1.51 | (0.06) | 1.36 | (0.06) | 1.24 | (0.06) | 1.25 | (0.05) | **0.27** | (0.08) |
| | Jordan | 1.81 | (0.06) | 1.81 | (0.06) | 1.85 | (0.06) | 1.63 | (0.07) | 0.18 | (0.09) |
| | Kyrgyzstan | 1.72 | (0.07) | 1.69 | (0.06) | 1.74 | (0.07) | 1.65 | (0.06) | 0.07 | (0.08) |
| | Latvia | 0.91 | (0.06) | 0.94 | (0.06) | 0.84 | (0.04) | 0.81 | (0.05) | 0.10 | (0.08) |
| | Liechtenstein | 0.45 | (0.09) | 0.30 | (0.08) | 0.28 | (0.08) | 0.22 | (0.06) | **0.22** | (0.11) |
| | Lithuania | 0.74 | (0.04) | 0.64 | (0.04) | 0.64 | (0.03) | 0.60 | (0.04) | **0.14** | (0.06) |
| | Macao-China | 1.01 | (0.05) | 1.02 | (0.04) | 1.01 | (0.05) | 1.19 | (0.07) | **-0.19** | (0.09) |
| | Montenegro | 0.69 | (0.04) | 0.75 | (0.05) | 0.80 | (0.05) | 0.75 | (0.05) | -0.06 | (0.06) |
| | Qatar | 1.57 | (0.05) | 1.64 | (0.05) | 1.61 | (0.06) | 1.52 | (0.05) | 0.06 | (0.06) |
| | Romania | 1.42 | (0.08) | 1.51 | (0.06) | 1.62 | (0.07) | 1.52 | (0.05) | -0.11 | (0.10) |
| | Russian Federation | 0.81 | (0.04) | 0.85 | (0.04) | 0.82 | (0.04) | 0.80 | (0.04) | 0.02 | (0.06) |
| | Serbia | 0.96 | (0.04) | 0.88 | (0.05) | 0.97 | (0.05) | 0.89 | (0.05) | 0.07 | (0.07) |
| | Slovenia | 0.85 | (0.03) | 0.77 | (0.04) | 0.73 | (0.04) | 0.58 | (0.03) | **0.27** | (0.05) |
| | Chinese Taipei | 0.64 | (0.03) | 0.71 | (0.04) | 0.70 | (0.04) | 0.72 | (0.04) | -0.09 | (0.05) |
| | Thailand | 0.61 | (0.05) | 0.66 | (0.04) | 0.56 | (0.03) | 0.42 | (0.04) | **0.20** | (0.06) |
| | Tunisia | 1.96 | (0.06) | 2.00 | (0.06) | 1.83 | (0.06) | 1.33 | (0.08) | **0.62** | (0.09) |
| | Uruguay | 0.64 | (0.04) | 0.73 | (0.05) | 0.68 | (0.04) | 0.52 | (0.04) | **0.12** | (0.06) |

*Note:* Values that are statistically significant at the 5% level (p < 0.05) are indicated in bold.

© OECD 2011  Quality Time for Students: Learning In and Out of School

**Table 3.7c** **Mean learning hours and allocation of total learning time on the language of**
[Part 3/7] **instruction, by quarters of the PISA index of economic, social and cultural status (ESCS)**

| | Mean learning hours per week | | | | | | | | | |
| | Individual study | | | | | | | | | |
| | Bottom quarter of ESCS | | Second quarter of ESCS | | Third quarter of ESCS | | Top quarter of ESCS | | Difference (bottom-top) | |
| | Mean | S.E. | Mean | S.E. | Mean | S.E. | Mean | S.E. | Dif. | S.E. |
|---|---|---|---|---|---|---|---|---|---|---|
| Australia | 1.52 | (0.03) | 1.64 | (0.03) | 1.76 | (0.04) | 1.94 | (0.04) | **-0.42** | (0.05) |
| Austria | 1.71 | (0.06) | 1.59 | (0.05) | 1.47 | (0.05) | 1.42 | (0.04) | **0.29** | (0.07) |
| Belgium | 1.24 | (0.04) | 1.30 | (0.03) | 1.42 | (0.03) | 1.43 | (0.03) | **-0.18** | (0.05) |
| Canada | 1.52 | (0.04) | 1.59 | (0.04) | 1.90 | (0.05) | 1.95 | (0.05) | **-0.43** | (0.06) |
| Czech Republic | 1.18 | (0.05) | 1.16 | (0.05) | 1.11 | (0.04) | 1.19 | (0.05) | -0.00 | (0.07) |
| Denmark | 2.08 | (0.06) | 2.09 | (0.05) | 2.24 | (0.05) | 2.25 | (0.05) | **-0.16** | (0.07) |
| Finland | 1.06 | (0.03) | 1.11 | (0.04) | 1.17 | (0.04) | 1.20 | (0.03) | **-0.13** | (0.04) |
| France | 1.36 | (0.05) | 1.44 | (0.04) | 1.55 | (0.04) | 1.72 | (0.05) | **-0.35** | (0.07) |
| Germany | 1.92 | (0.06) | 1.95 | (0.05) | 1.92 | (0.05) | 1.78 | (0.05) | 0.12 | (0.08) |
| Greece | 1.78 | (0.06) | 1.91 | (0.06) | 2.04 | (0.06) | 2.02 | (0.06) | **-0.23** | (0.07) |
| Hungary | 1.73 | (0.05) | 1.82 | (0.05) | 1.96 | (0.06) | 1.93 | (0.06) | **-0.19** | (0.07) |
| Iceland | 1.55 | (0.04) | 1.55 | (0.04) | 1.51 | (0.04) | 1.57 | (0.04) | -0.02 | (0.06) |
| Ireland | 1.59 | (0.06) | 1.66 | (0.05) | 1.83 | (0.05) | 1.92 | (0.06) | **-0.32** | (0.09) |
| Italy | 2.69 | (0.04) | 2.87 | (0.05) | 2.99 | (0.05) | 3.26 | (0.08) | **-0.57** | (0.08) |
| Japan | 0.74 | (0.03) | 0.91 | (0.04) | 1.05 | (0.05) | 1.08 | (0.05) | **-0.34** | (0.05) |
| Korea | 1.06 | (0.04) | 1.17 | (0.04) | 1.45 | (0.04) | 1.94 | (0.07) | **-0.88** | (0.08) |
| Luxembourg | 1.54 | (0.05) | 1.43 | (0.05) | 1.34 | (0.03) | 1.24 | (0.03) | **0.29** | (0.06) |
| Mexico | 2.07 | (0.06) | 2.09 | (0.04) | 2.07 | (0.05) | 2.00 | (0.05) | 0.07 | (0.07) |
| Netherlands | 1.37 | (0.05) | 1.29 | (0.04) | 1.31 | (0.04) | 1.35 | (0.04) | 0.02 | (0.06) |
| New Zealand | 1.42 | (0.05) | 1.58 | (0.04) | 1.54 | (0.04) | 1.78 | (0.05) | **-0.35** | (0.07) |
| Norway | 1.32 | (0.05) | 1.45 | (0.05) | 1.43 | (0.05) | 1.59 | (0.04) | **-0.27** | (0.06) |
| Poland | 2.19 | (0.05) | 2.19 | (0.05) | 2.23 | (0.05) | 2.29 | (0.05) | -0.12 | (0.07) |
| Portugal | 1.73 | (0.06) | 1.83 | (0.05) | 1.82 | (0.04) | 1.78 | (0.05) | -0.05 | (0.08) |
| Slovak Republic | 1.59 | (0.06) | 1.72 | (0.05) | 1.87 | (0.05) | 1.79 | (0.06) | **-0.20** | (0.07) |
| Spain | 1.76 | (0.05) | 1.85 | (0.05) | 1.95 | (0.05) | 1.99 | (0.04) | **-0.24** | (0.05) |
| Sweden | 1.13 | (0.04) | 1.22 | (0.04) | 1.29 | (0.03) | 1.39 | (0.05) | **-0.27** | (0.07) |
| Switzerland | 1.48 | (0.03) | 1.37 | (0.03) | 1.38 | (0.03) | 1.37 | (0.03) | 0.12 | (0.04) |
| Turkey | 2.17 | (0.06) | 2.32 | (0.06) | 2.26 | (0.06) | 1.96 | (0.09) | 0.20 | (0.10) |
| United Kingdom | 1.36 | (0.03) | 1.47 | (0.04) | 1.67 | (0.04) | 1.85 | (0.04) | **-0.49** | (0.05) |
| United States | 1.59 | (0.04) | 1.64 | (0.05) | 1.91 | (0.05) | 2.31 | (0.06) | **-0.71** | (0.07) |
| **OECD average** | 1.58 | (0.01) | 1.64 | (0.01) | 1.71 | (0.01) | 1.78 | (0.01) | **-0.19** | (0.01) |
| Argentina | 1.58 | (0.06) | 1.61 | (0.08) | 1.76 | (0.06) | 1.61 | (0.05) | -0.02 | (0.08) |
| Azerbaijan | 2.80 | (0.11) | 2.97 | (0.08) | 3.26 | (0.08) | 3.39 | (0.08) | **-0.58** | (0.14) |
| Brazil | 1.76 | (0.05) | 1.67 | (0.05) | 1.80 | (0.05) | 1.74 | (0.04) | 0.02 | (0.07) |
| Bulgaria | 1.69 | (0.08) | 2.00 | (0.08) | 2.18 | (0.08) | 2.35 | (0.08) | **-0.68** | (0.11) |
| Chile | 1.54 | (0.04) | 1.58 | (0.05) | 1.62 | (0.06) | 1.51 | (0.05) | 0.03 | (0.06) |
| Colombia | 1.78 | (0.07) | 1.87 | (0.08) | 1.78 | (0.06) | 1.92 | (0.07) | -0.14 | (0.11) |
| Croatia | 1.58 | (0.05) | 1.59 | (0.04) | 1.60 | (0.06) | 1.55 | (0.06) | 0.03 | (0.07) |
| Estonia | 1.60 | (0.05) | 1.62 | (0.04) | 1.64 | (0.05) | 1.62 | (0.05) | -0.02 | (0.07) |
| Hong Kong-China | 1.62 | (0.06) | 1.68 | (0.05) | 1.57 | (0.06) | 1.70 | (0.07) | -0.08 | (0.07) |
| Indonesia | 1.86 | (0.08) | 1.76 | (0.04) | 1.82 | (0.05) | 1.76 | (0.06) | 0.10 | (0.11) |
| Israel | 1.75 | (0.07) | 1.63 | (0.07) | 1.59 | (0.06) | 1.67 | (0.05) | 0.09 | (0.10) |
| Jordan | 2.66 | (0.07) | 2.55 | (0.06) | 2.59 | (0.06) | 2.56 | (0.08) | 0.11 | (0.11) |
| Kyrgyzstan | 2.38 | (0.08) | 2.26 | (0.06) | 2.37 | (0.06) | 2.35 | (0.06) | 0.03 | (0.09) |
| Latvia | 1.93 | (0.07) | 2.03 | (0.06) | 2.01 | (0.05) | 2.05 | (0.06) | -0.12 | (0.09) |
| Liechtenstein | 1.16 | (0.12) | 1.20 | (0.09) | 1.28 | (0.11) | 1.26 | (0.15) | -0.10 | (0.20) |
| Lithuania | 1.73 | (0.05) | 1.74 | (0.05) | 1.86 | (0.06) | 1.95 | (0.05) | **-0.21** | (0.07) |
| Macao-China | 1.36 | (0.05) | 1.45 | (0.05) | 1.48 | (0.05) | 1.67 | (0.06) | **-0.30** | (0.08) |
| Montenegro | 1.83 | (0.06) | 2.03 | (0.07) | 2.00 | (0.07) | 2.09 | (0.06) | **-0.26** | (0.10) |
| Qatar | 1.98 | (0.05) | 2.06 | (0.05) | 2.13 | (0.05) | 1.98 | (0.05) | 0.00 | (0.07) |
| Romania | 1.99 | (0.10) | 2.15 | (0.06) | 2.22 | (0.06) | 2.40 | (0.08) | **-0.42** | (0.09) |
| Russian Federation | 1.55 | (0.06) | 1.58 | (0.05) | 1.55 | (0.04) | 1.52 | (0.04) | 0.02 | (0.05) |
| Serbia | 1.64 | (0.05) | 1.61 | (0.05) | 1.74 | (0.05) | 1.81 | (0.06) | **-0.17** | (0.08) |
| Slovenia | 1.46 | (0.04) | 1.50 | (0.04) | 1.49 | (0.04) | 1.46 | (0.05) | -0.00 | (0.06) |
| Chinese Taipei | 1.43 | (0.04) | 1.68 | (0.05) | 1.90 | (0.05) | 2.07 | (0.04) | **-0.64** | (0.05) |
| Thailand | 1.78 | (0.06) | 1.81 | (0.05) | 1.67 | (0.05) | 1.56 | (0.04) | **0.22** | (0.07) |
| Tunisia | 2.31 | (0.07) | 2.25 | (0.06) | 2.07 | (0.06) | 1.84 | (0.07) | **0.46** | (0.09) |
| Uruguay | 1.30 | (0.05) | 1.32 | (0.06) | 1.34 | (0.05) | 1.44 | (0.04) | **-0.14** | (0.06) |

*Note*: Values that are statistically significant at the 5% level (p < 0.05) are indicated in bold.

129

**Table 3.7c** Mean learning hours and allocation of total learning time on the language of
[Part 4/7] instruction, by quarters of the PISA index of economic, social and cultural status (ESCS)

| | | Mean learning hours per week | | | | | | | | | |
| | | Total learning hours | | | | | | | | | |
| | | Bottom quarter of ESCS | | Second quarter of ESCS | | Third quarter of ESCS | | Top quarter of ESCS | | Difference (bottom-top) | |
| | | Mean | S.E. | Mean | S.E. | Mean | S.E. | Mean | S.E. | Dif. | S.E. |
|---|---|---|---|---|---|---|---|---|---|---|---|
| OECD | Australia | 6.09 | (0.07) | 6.33 | (0.06) | 6.52 | (0.07) | 6.81 | (0.07) | **-0.74** | (0.10) |
| | Austria | 4.89 | (0.13) | 4.77 | (0.11) | 4.53 | (0.09) | 4.43 | (0.08) | **0.46** | (0.14) |
| | Belgium | 5.04 | (0.10) | 5.16 | (0.06) | 5.48 | (0.06) | 5.51 | (0.06) | **-0.43** | (0.12) |
| | Canada | 6.50 | (0.10) | 6.84 | (0.09) | 7.42 | (0.11) | 7.48 | (0.12) | **-0.96** | (0.14) |
| | Czech Republic | 5.61 | (0.09) | 5.42 | (0.09) | 5.41 | (0.10) | 5.52 | (0.10) | 0.12 | (0.13) |
| | Denmark | 9.23 | (0.15) | 9.19 | (0.11) | 9.50 | (0.11) | 9.47 | (0.11) | -0.23 | (0.17) |
| | Finland | 4.49 | (0.10) | 4.60 | (0.09) | 4.67 | (0.09) | 4.76 | (0.08) | **-0.27** | (0.11) |
| | France | 6.06 | (0.10) | 6.18 | (0.08) | 6.37 | (0.07) | 6.65 | (0.09) | **-0.58** | (0.14) |
| | Germany | 6.42 | (0.13) | 6.28 | (0.10) | 6.23 | (0.08) | 5.75 | (0.11) | **0.60** | (0.18) |
| | Greece | 6.13 | (0.15) | 6.66 | (0.13) | 7.12 | (0.16) | 7.08 | (0.13) | **-0.96** | (0.18) |
| | Hungary | 5.85 | (0.13) | 6.29 | (0.13) | 6.65 | (0.14) | 6.67 | (0.15) | **-0.83** | (0.19) |
| | Iceland | 6.45 | (0.08) | 6.57 | (0.08) | 6.48 | (0.10) | 6.63 | (0.08) | -0.17 | (0.12) |
| | Ireland | 5.85 | (0.13) | 5.77 | (0.11) | 6.05 | (0.10) | 6.11 | (0.11) | -0.25 | (0.17) |
| | Italy | 8.03 | (0.09) | 8.26 | (0.10) | 8.45 | (0.10) | 8.74 | (0.13) | **-0.71** | (0.16) |
| | Japan | 4.59 | (0.09) | 5.02 | (0.09) | 5.55 | (0.10) | 5.63 | (0.11) | **-1.03** | (0.12) |
| | Korea | 6.38 | (0.14) | 6.95 | (0.11) | 7.54 | (0.11) | 8.50 | (0.17) | **-2.12** | (0.20) |
| | Luxembourg | 5.69 | (0.10) | 5.51 | (0.10) | 5.35 | (0.07) | 5.38 | (0.08) | **0.31** | (0.13) |
| | Mexico | 6.85 | (0.14) | 6.83 | (0.11) | 6.82 | (0.10) | 6.99 | (0.12) | -0.14 | (0.16) |
| | Netherlands | 5.05 | (0.08) | 4.99 | (0.08) | 4.85 | (0.09) | 4.67 | (0.07) | **0.40** | (0.10) |
| | New Zealand | 6.29 | (0.10) | 6.63 | (0.09) | 6.60 | (0.09) | 7.00 | (0.10) | **-0.70** | (0.13) |
| | Norway | 5.89 | (0.11) | 6.16 | (0.10) | 6.19 | (0.11) | 6.54 | (0.11) | **-0.66** | (0.15) |
| | Poland | 7.29 | (0.09) | 7.55 | (0.10) | 7.62 | (0.09) | 7.79 | (0.08) | **-0.50** | (0.12) |
| | Portugal | 5.46 | (0.10) | 5.68 | (0.10) | 5.70 | (0.10) | 5.65 | (0.10) | -0.21 | (0.14) |
| | Slovak Republic | 5.48 | (0.12) | 5.61 | (0.12) | 5.96 | (0.13) | 5.95 | (0.12) | **-0.50** | (0.15) |
| | Spain | 5.98 | (0.09) | 6.11 | (0.10) | 6.10 | (0.09) | 6.22 | (0.06) | **-0.25** | (0.11) |
| | Sweden | 4.89 | (0.09) | 4.98 | (0.09) | 5.03 | (0.07) | 5.30 | (0.14) | **-0.40** | (0.18) |
| | Switzerland | 5.69 | (0.07) | 5.47 | (0.08) | 5.51 | (0.07) | 5.49 | (0.08) | **0.20** | (0.10) |
| | Turkey | 7.62 | (0.17) | 8.04 | (0.16) | 8.20 | (0.17) | 7.97 | (0.18) | -0.39 | (0.22) |
| | United Kingdom | 5.75 | (0.10) | 5.91 | (0.08) | 6.28 | (0.09) | 6.39 | (0.09) | **-0.64** | (0.12) |
| | United States | 5.87 | (0.11) | 6.26 | (0.11) | 6.84 | (0.12) | 7.65 | (0.10) | **-1.76** | (0.15) |
| | **OECD average** | 6.05 | (0.02) | 6.20 | (0.02) | 6.37 | (0.02) | 6.49 | (0.02) | **-0.45** | (0.03) |
| Partners | Argentina | 4.27 | (0.12) | 4.33 | (0.12) | 4.50 | (0.12) | 4.70 | (0.14) | **-0.40** | (0.18) |
| | Azerbaijan | 7.93 | (0.20) | 8.32 | (0.20) | 9.01 | (0.20) | 9.36 | (0.18) | **-1.40** | (0.26) |
| | Brazil | 5.79 | (0.12) | 5.83 | (0.13) | 6.15 | (0.12) | 6.26 | (0.10) | **-0.43** | (0.17) |
| | Bulgaria | 5.42 | (0.19) | 5.95 | (0.16) | 6.24 | (0.16) | 6.70 | (0.16) | **-1.31** | (0.27) |
| | Chile | 5.60 | (0.12) | 5.87 | (0.11) | 6.20 | (0.14) | 6.45 | (0.13) | **-0.84** | (0.15) |
| | Colombia | 6.69 | (0.13) | 6.89 | (0.17) | 6.84 | (0.12) | 7.25 | (0.14) | **-0.57** | (0.18) |
| | Croatia | 5.25 | (0.11) | 5.32 | (0.09) | 5.29 | (0.09) | 5.42 | (0.09) | -0.17 | (0.13) |
| | Estonia | 5.97 | (0.09) | 6.03 | (0.10) | 6.03 | (0.11) | 5.94 | (0.10) | 0.03 | (0.12) |
| | Hong Kong-China | 7.44 | (0.12) | 7.69 | (0.12) | 7.58 | (0.11) | 7.86 | (0.16) | **-0.41** | (0.17) |
| | Indonesia | 6.72 | (0.19) | 6.67 | (0.13) | 6.64 | (0.14) | 6.71 | (0.12) | 0.00 | (0.22) |
| | Israel | 6.14 | (0.16) | 5.92 | (0.17) | 5.87 | (0.16) | 6.27 | (0.13) | -0.12 | (0.21) |
| | Jordan | 7.81 | (0.18) | 7.79 | (0.15) | 8.04 | (0.11) | 8.03 | (0.13) | -0.21 | (0.22) |
| | Kyrgyzstan | 6.77 | (0.18) | 6.46 | (0.15) | 6.96 | (0.16) | 7.21 | (0.13) | **-0.42** | (0.20) |
| | Latvia | 6.40 | (0.16) | 6.71 | (0.11) | 6.55 | (0.09) | 6.66 | (0.12) | -0.24 | (0.22) |
| | Liechtenstein | 5.18 | (0.23) | 5.16 | (0.24) | 5.29 | (0.24) | 5.15 | (0.23) | 0.05 | (0.37) |
| | Lithuania | 5.84 | (0.11) | 6.02 | (0.12) | 6.22 | (0.12) | 6.45 | (0.11) | **-0.62** | (0.15) |
| | Macao-China | 7.54 | (0.11) | 7.88 | (0.11) | 7.78 | (0.11) | 8.26 | (0.12) | **-0.73** | (0.16) |
| | Montenegro | 5.07 | (0.13) | 5.61 | (0.14) | 5.74 | (0.14) | 6.23 | (0.14) | **-1.16** | (0.20) |
| | Qatar | 6.16 | (0.11) | 6.52 | (0.12) | 6.77 | (0.13) | 6.58 | (0.12) | **-0.40** | (0.16) |
| | Romania | 6.29 | (0.17) | 6.89 | (0.16) | 7.25 | (0.17) | 7.64 | (0.14) | **-1.37** | (0.20) |
| | Russian Federation | 4.40 | (0.10) | 4.45 | (0.11) | 4.44 | (0.10) | 4.30 | (0.10) | 0.10 | (0.11) |
| | Serbia | 5.64 | (0.10) | 5.47 | (0.10) | 5.94 | (0.10) | 6.13 | (0.14) | **-0.51** | (0.17) |
| | Slovenia | 5.33 | (0.09) | 5.42 | (0.09) | 5.56 | (0.10) | 5.58 | (0.09) | **-0.28** | (0.13) |
| | Chinese Taipei | 5.95 | (0.10) | 6.56 | (0.11) | 7.23 | (0.10) | 7.75 | (0.10) | **-1.83** | (0.13) |
| | Thailand | 5.61 | (0.12) | 5.58 | (0.08) | 5.21 | (0.09) | 5.04 | (0.09) | **0.57** | (0.16) |
| | Tunisia | 7.39 | (0.14) | 7.46 | (0.15) | 7.09 | (0.12) | 6.25 | (0.18) | **1.12** | (0.21) |
| | Uruguay | 4.63 | (0.11) | 4.82 | (0.14) | 4.78 | (0.11) | 4.78 | (0.10) | -0.12 | (0.16) |

*Note:* Values that are statistically significant at the 5% level (p < 0.05) are indicated in bold.

130

**Table 3.7c** Mean learning hours and allocation of total learning time on the language of
[Part 5/7] instruction, by quarters of the PISA index of economic, social and cultural status (ESCS)

| | | Allocation of total learning time on the language of instruction for | | | | | | | | |
|---|---|---|---|---|---|---|---|---|---|---|
| | | Regular school lessons | | | | | | | | |
| | | Bottom quarter of ESCS | | Second quarter of ESCS | | Third quarter of ESCS | | Top quarter of ESCS | | Difference (bottom-top) | |
| | | % | S.E. | % | S.E. | % | S.E. | % | S.E. | Dif. | S.E. |
| OECD | Australia | 67.4 | (0.5) | 67.3 | (0.4) | 67.0 | (0.4) | 66.6 | (0.4) | 0.7 | (0.7) |
| | Austria | 62.9 | (0.8) | 64.7 | (0.7) | 67.1 | (0.7) | 67.4 | (0.7) | **-4.5** | (0.9) |
| | Belgium | 65.9 | (0.6) | 67.1 | (0.6) | 67.4 | (0.6) | 68.8 | (0.5) | **-2.8** | (0.7) |
| | Canada | 65.7 | (0.7) | 66.2 | (0.5) | 65.3 | (0.6) | 65.3 | (0.5) | 0.3 | (0.7) |
| | Czech Republic | 70.1 | (1.0) | 71.2 | (0.9) | 72.4 | (0.6) | 72.8 | (0.7) | **-2.7** | (1.2) |
| | Denmark | 61.6 | (0.7) | 62.9 | (0.5) | 62.1 | (0.6) | 62.1 | (0.6) | -0.6 | (0.8) |
| | Finland | 70.7 | (0.7) | 71.0 | (0.7) | 69.9 | (0.6) | 71.1 | (0.6) | -0.5 | (0.9) |
| | France | 65.2 | (0.8) | 66.9 | (0.8) | 67.2 | (0.6) | 68.7 | (0.7) | **-3.8** | (1.1) |
| | Germany | 59.4 | (0.7) | 61.9 | (0.6) | 63.0 | (0.7) | 65.0 | (0.7) | **-5.6** | (0.9) |
| | Greece | 51.8 | (1.0) | 49.7 | (0.8) | 49.9 | (0.9) | 52.5 | (0.9) | -0.6 | (1.3) |
| | Hungary | 49.8 | (0.9) | 54.2 | (0.7) | 52.6 | (0.7) | 56.4 | (0.7) | **-6.7** | (1.1) |
| | Iceland | 72.1 | (0.6) | 71.9 | (0.7) | 71.3 | (0.6) | 71.8 | (0.5) | 0.2 | (0.8) |
| | Ireland | 65.3 | (0.8) | 64.3 | (0.7) | 63.3 | (0.6) | 64.2 | (0.8) | 1.0 | (1.1) |
| | Italy | 57.2 | (0.5) | 57.4 | (0.5) | 57.8 | (0.4) | 56.4 | (0.5) | 0.9 | (0.7) |
| | Japan | 78.8 | (0.7) | 78.8 | (0.7) | 77.5 | (0.6) | 77.5 | (0.7) | 1.3 | (0.8) |
| | Korea | 71.9 | (0.7) | 69.3 | (0.8) | 64.5 | (0.7) | 59.7 | (0.9) | **12.1** | (1.2) |
| | Luxembourg | 62.2 | (0.9) | 65.5 | (0.7) | 69.7 | (0.6) | 71.9 | (0.6) | **-10.0** | (1.1) |
| | Mexico | 51.6 | (1.0) | 54.7 | (0.7) | 54.5 | (0.5) | 59.5 | (0.8) | **-7.7** | (1.3) |
| | Netherlands | 60.7 | (1.1) | 63.0 | (0.6) | 63.9 | (0.8) | 64.6 | (0.7) | **-3.8** | (1.4) |
| | New Zealand | 69.4 | (0.8) | 69.9 | (0.6) | 71.3 | (0.7) | 70.0 | (0.7) | -0.6 | (1.0) |
| | Norway | 62.1 | (0.8) | 62.6 | (0.8) | 62.1 | (0.9) | 62.1 | (0.8) | **0.2** | (1.1) |
| | Poland | 62.1 | (0.5) | 63.1 | (0.6) | 64.2 | (0.7) | 64.7 | (0.6) | **-2.7** | (0.7) |
| | Portugal | 58.5 | (1.0) | 59.6 | (0.8) | 61.8 | (0.6) | 64.3 | (0.7) | **-5.7** | (1.2) |
| | Slovak Republic | 60.2 | (0.9) | 58.6 | (0.7) | 58.0 | (0.9) | 59.0 | (0.8) | 1.3 | (1.1) |
| | Spain | 61.4 | (0.7) | 62.1 | (0.6) | 62.7 | (0.5) | 64.4 | (0.5) | **-3.1** | (0.9) |
| | Sweden | 67.7 | (0.9) | 66.3 | (0.8) | 66.9 | (0.6) | 66.3 | (0.8) | 1.4 | (1.0) |
| | Switzerland | 64.5 | (0.7) | 67.4 | (0.6) | 68.2 | (0.6) | 70.0 | (0.5) | **-5.4** | (0.8) |
| | Turkey | 52.3 | (1.0) | 52.7 | (0.7) | 55.1 | (0.8) | 58.7 | (1.3) | **-6.5** | (1.6) |
| | United Kingdom | 69.0 | (0.6) | 68.6 | (0.5) | 66.7 | (0.5) | 66.0 | (0.5) | **3.0** | (0.7) |
| | United States | 52.6 | (1.3) | 55.8 | (0.8) | 57.1 | (0.9) | 58.1 | (0.7) | **-5.5** | (1.5) |
| | **OECD average** | 63.0 | (0.1) | 63.8 | (0.1) | 64.0 | (0.1) | 64.9 | (0.1) | **-1.9** | (0.2) |
| Partners | Argentina | 53.6 | (0.9) | 53.8 | (1.0) | 52.9 | (1.1) | 60.7 | (1.2) | **-7.4** | (1.6) |
| | Azerbaijan | 44.6 | (1.1) | 44.6 | (1.0) | 45.3 | (0.7) | 44.9 | (0.8) | -0.7 | (1.3) |
| | Brazil | 53.0 | (1.1) | 53.9 | (1.0) | 53.9 | (0.9) | 56.9 | (0.8) | **-3.9** | (1.5) |
| | Bulgaria | 51.3 | (1.0) | 50.8 | (0.9) | 51.8 | (0.7) | 53.1 | (1.0) | -1.5 | (1.6) |
| | Chile | 51.9 | (0.8) | 55.9 | (0.9) | 57.7 | (0.8) | 64.0 | (1.0) | **-12.1** | (1.3) |
| | Colombia | 58.3 | (1.4) | 58.9 | (1.1) | 61.3 | (0.8) | 62.6 | (0.9) | **-4.0** | (1.7) |
| | Croatia | 65.3 | (0.8) | 66.1 | (0.7) | 66.9 | (0.7) | 68.9 | (0.8) | **-3.6** | (1.0) |
| | Estonia | 60.6 | (0.9) | 60.9 | (0.8) | 62.0 | (0.8) | 63.6 | (0.7) | **-3.0** | (0.9) |
| | Hong Kong-China | 70.1 | (0.8) | 69.9 | (0.7) | 72.2 | (0.8) | 71.5 | (0.7) | -1.5 | (1.0) |
| | Indonesia | 55.6 | (0.7) | 56.1 | (0.7) | 55.3 | (1.1) | 58.0 | (1.0) | -2.4 | (1.1) |
| | Israel | 48.6 | (1.1) | 52.2 | (0.9) | 56.3 | (1.1) | 58.8 | (0.9) | **-10.3** | (1.6) |
| | Jordan | 41.0 | (0.8) | 43.3 | (0.9) | 44.6 | (1.0) | 48.1 | (1.0) | **-7.2** | (1.3) |
| | Kyrgyzstan | 36.9 | (1.0) | 37.5 | (0.8) | 39.8 | (0.8) | 45.1 | (0.8) | **-8.1** | (1.3) |
| | Latvia | 58.6 | (0.9) | 58.4 | (0.7) | 59.6 | (0.7) | 60.4 | (0.6) | -1.8 | (1.1) |
| | Liechtenstein | 67.1 | (2.6) | 69.8 | (2.2) | 70.1 | (2.3) | 72.8 | (2.2) | -5.8 | (3.5) |
| | Lithuania | 60.8 | (0.9) | 63.2 | (0.7) | 62.6 | (0.7) | 62.8 | (0.7) | -2.1 | (1.1) |
| | Macao-China | 72.1 | (0.7) | 72.2 | (0.6) | 72.0 | (0.7) | 69.3 | (0.8) | **2.6** | (1.1) |
| | Montenegro | 50.9 | (0.9) | 51.9 | (0.8) | 53.2 | (0.8) | 56.1 | (0.8) | **-5.4** | (1.3) |
| | Qatar | 41.6 | (0.7) | 43.5 | (0.7) | 46.1 | (0.7) | 47.6 | (0.7) | **-5.9** | (1.0) |
| | Romania | 49.7 | (1.3) | 49.8 | (1.0) | 50.4 | (1.0) | 52.8 | (1.0) | **-3.0** | (1.4) |
| | Russian Federation | 48.6 | (1.0) | 47.1 | (0.8) | 48.5 | (0.9) | 48.8 | (0.8) | -0.3 | (1.2) |
| | Serbia | 59.5 | (0.7) | 59.6 | (0.8) | 59.6 | (0.8) | 62.0 | (0.8) | **-2.5** | (1.1) |
| | Slovenia | 57.2 | (0.8) | 59.2 | (0.7) | 62.4 | (0.7) | 64.7 | (0.9) | **-7.2** | (1.3) |
| | Chinese Taipei | 66.9 | (0.6) | 65.4 | (0.7) | 66.0 | (0.6) | 66.1 | (0.6) | 0.8 | (0.8) |
| | Thailand | 62.1 | (0.8) | 60.6 | (0.6) | 61.6 | (0.6) | 65.8 | (0.7) | **-3.8** | (1.1) |
| | Tunisia | 42.6 | (0.9) | 43.6 | (0.9) | 46.0 | (1.0) | 50.2 | (1.4) | **-7.6** | (1.6) |
| | Uruguay | 59.8 | (1.1) | 60.6 | (1.0) | 60.6 | (1.0) | 62.5 | (0.8) | **-2.9** | (1.3) |

*Note:* Values that are statistically significant at the 5% level (p < 0.05) are indicated in bold.

Table 3.7c Mean learning hours and allocation of total learning time on the language of
[Part 6/7] instruction, by quarters of the PISA index of economic, social and cultural status (ESCS)

| | Allocation of total learning time on the language of instruction for | | | | | | | | | |
| | Out-of-school-time lessons | | | | | | | | | |
| | Bottom quarter of ESCS | | Second quarter of ESCS | | Third quarter of ESCS | | Top quarter of ESCS | | Difference (bottom-top) | |
| | % | S.E. | % | S.E. | % | S.E. | % | S.E. | Dif. | S.E. |
|---|---|---|---|---|---|---|---|---|---|---|
| Australia | 9.6 | (0.3) | 8.5 | (0.3) | 7.9 | (0.3) | 7.1 | (0.3) | 2.6 | (0.4) |
| Austria | 4.7 | (0.4) | 4.0 | (0.4) | 2.5 | (0.3) | 2.3 | (0.3) | 2.5 | (0.5) |
| Belgium | 9.1 | (0.3) | 7.3 | (0.4) | 6.6 | (0.4) | 5.1 | (0.3) | 4.1 | (0.5) |
| Canada | 11.9 | (0.4) | 10.9 | (0.4) | 10.7 | (0.4) | 9.6 | (0.3) | 2.3 | (0.5) |
| Czech Republic | 10.2 | (0.4) | 8.8 | (0.5) | 8.8 | (0.4) | 8.1 | (0.4) | 2.3 | (0.6) |
| Denmark | 17.2 | (0.5) | 15.6 | (0.4) | 15.6 | (0.4) | 15.4 | (0.5) | 1.9 | (0.7) |
| Finland | 7.0 | (0.5) | 6.4 | (0.4) | 6.4 | (0.3) | 5.1 | (0.3) | 1.8 | (0.6) |
| France | 13.8 | (0.5) | 11.2 | (0.5) | 10.2 | (0.4) | 7.5 | (0.4) | 6.3 | (0.6) |
| Germany | 10.9 | (0.6) | 8.0 | (0.4) | 7.1 | (0.5) | 5.5 | (0.4) | 5.4 | (0.8) |
| Greece | 20.4 | (0.8) | 22.4 | (0.6) | 22.6 | (0.7) | 20.8 | (0.6) | -0.4 | (1.0) |
| Hungary | 20.8 | (0.7) | 17.9 | (0.6) | 18.3 | (0.5) | 16.0 | (0.6) | 4.9 | (0.9) |
| Iceland | 5.5 | (0.4) | 6.1 | (0.5) | 6.6 | (0.5) | 5.7 | (0.4) | -0.3 | (0.6) |
| Ireland | 9.3 | (0.6) | 8.8 | (0.4) | 7.9 | (0.4) | 6.5 | (0.4) | 2.9 | (0.6) |
| Italy | 9.6 | (0.4) | 8.4 | (0.3) | 7.7 | (0.3) | 7.5 | (0.3) | 2.1 | (0.5) |
| Japan | 7.3 | (0.4) | 5.7 | (0.4) | 6.1 | (0.4) | 6.0 | (0.3) | 1.3 | (0.5) |
| Korea | 13.1 | (0.6) | 15.2 | (0.6) | 17.9 | (0.6) | 19.7 | (0.7) | -6.5 | (0.9) |
| Luxembourg | 12.4 | (0.6) | 9.9 | (0.4) | 7.1 | (0.4) | 5.7 | (0.3) | 6.9 | (0.7) |
| Mexico | 17.2 | (0.9) | 14.2 | (0.5) | 15.1 | (0.4) | 11.9 | (0.6) | 5.3 | (1.1) |
| Netherlands | 13.1 | (0.7) | 12.3 | (0.4) | 10.2 | (0.5) | 7.8 | (0.4) | 5.2 | (0.8) |
| New Zealand | 9.8 | (0.6) | 8.2 | (0.4) | 7.2 | (0.4) | 6.6 | (0.4) | 3.2 | (0.7) |
| Norway | 17.7 | (0.5) | 16.3 | (0.5) | 16.1 | (0.6) | 15.5 | (0.5) | 2.2 | (0.7) |
| Poland | 9.5 | (0.6) | 8.9 | (0.4) | 8.1 | (0.5) | 7.4 | (0.4) | 2.1 | (0.7) |
| Portugal | 11.2 | (0.6) | 9.8 | (0.6) | 7.9 | (0.4) | 6.0 | (0.4) | 5.2 | (0.9) |
| Slovak Republic | 12.6 | (0.7) | 12.5 | (0.5) | 12.6 | (0.5) | 13.1 | (0.5) | -0.6 | (0.9) |
| Spain | 10.3 | (0.5) | 8.9 | (0.4) | 7.8 | (0.4) | 5.4 | (0.4) | 5.0 | (0.7) |
| Sweden | 11.2 | (0.5) | 10.6 | (0.5) | 9.9 | (0.4) | 9.3 | (0.4) | 1.9 | (0.6) |
| Switzerland | 9.2 | (0.5) | 7.3 | (0.4) | 6.4 | (0.4) | 5.3 | (0.3) | 4.0 | (0.6) |
| Turkey | 20.9 | (0.9) | 20.0 | (0.5) | 19.3 | (0.5) | 18.9 | (0.8) | 2.1 | (1.2) |
| United Kingdom | 8.7 | (0.4) | 8.0 | (0.3) | 8.0 | (0.3) | 6.5 | (0.4) | 2.2 | (0.5) |
| United States | 19.3 | (1.1) | 17.4 | (0.5) | 14.9 | (0.6) | 12.2 | (0.4) | 7.1 | (1.3) |
| **OECD average** | 12.1 | (0.1) | 11.0 | (0.1) | 10.4 | (0.1) | 9.3 | (0.1) | 2.8 | (0.1) |
| Argentina | 9.5 | (0.7) | 8.6 | (0.7) | 8.5 | (0.9) | 5.3 | (0.6) | 3.8 | (1.0) |
| Azerbaijan | 20.1 | (0.8) | 19.1 | (0.8) | 18.3 | (0.7) | 19.7 | (0.6) | 0.4 | (0.9) |
| Brazil | 17.7 | (0.9) | 18.8 | (0.7) | 18.1 | (0.6) | 16.4 | (0.7) | 1.3 | (1.2) |
| Bulgaria | 17.8 | (0.7) | 16.6 | (0.8) | 14.2 | (0.6) | 13.3 | (0.8) | 4.4 | (1.2) |
| Chile | 18.4 | (0.7) | 16.1 | (0.6) | 15.3 | (0.6) | 11.1 | (0.7) | 7.1 | (1.0) |
| Colombia | 16.6 | (0.7) | 14.9 | (0.8) | 13.8 | (0.5) | 12.5 | (0.6) | 4.0 | (0.8) |
| Croatia | 6.8 | (0.5) | 5.9 | (0.5) | 5.4 | (0.4) | 5.3 | (0.4) | 1.4 | (0.6) |
| Estonia | 14.4 | (0.8) | 13.9 | (0.7) | 12.7 | (0.6) | 11.3 | (0.6) | 3.1 | (0.7) |
| Hong Kong-China | 9.7 | (0.4) | 9.7 | (0.5) | 8.5 | (0.5) | 8.4 | (0.5) | 1.4 | (0.7) |
| Indonesia | 16.6 | (0.6) | 17.0 | (0.6) | 17.0 | (0.9) | 16.1 | (0.6) | 0.4 | (0.6) |
| Israel | 23.2 | (0.9) | 21.3 | (0.8) | 18.2 | (0.7) | 16.9 | (0.7) | 6.2 | (1.2) |
| Jordan | 23.5 | (0.7) | 22.7 | (0.7) | 22.7 | (0.7) | 19.6 | (0.7) | 4.0 | (1.0) |
| Kyrgyzstan | 27.2 | (1.0) | 28.2 | (0.8) | 26.6 | (0.9) | 22.3 | (0.8) | 4.8 | (1.3) |
| Latvia | 12.6 | (0.7) | 12.0 | (0.6) | 10.8 | (0.5) | 10.2 | (0.5) | 2.4 | (0.8) |
| Liechtenstein | 9.1 | (1.6) | 5.3 | (1.2) | 4.1 | (1.3) | 3.5 | (1.0) | 5.3 | (1.9) |
| Lithuania | 11.6 | (0.6) | 9.8 | (0.5) | 9.5 | (0.5) | 8.5 | (0.5) | 3.1 | (0.7) |
| Macao-China | 10.9 | (0.5) | 10.7 | (0.4) | 10.8 | (0.4) | 12.1 | (0.6) | -1.1 | (0.8) |
| Montenegro | 12.6 | (0.7) | 11.4 | (0.6) | 12.0 | (0.6) | 9.8 | (0.5) | 3.0 | (0.9) |
| Qatar | 25.4 | (0.6) | 24.5 | (0.6) | 22.4 | (0.6) | 22.1 | (0.6) | 3.4 | (0.8) |
| Romania | 20.3 | (0.9) | 20.2 | (0.8) | 20.4 | (0.8) | 18.0 | (0.7) | 2.1 | (1.3) |
| Russian Federation | 17.0 | (0.8) | 17.1 | (0.9) | 16.1 | (0.9) | 15.3 | (0.6) | 1.7 | (1.1) |
| Serbia | 13.9 | (0.6) | 13.2 | (0.7) | 13.1 | (0.6) | 11.2 | (0.5) | 2.7 | (0.8) |
| Slovenia | 14.5 | (0.5) | 12.9 | (0.5) | 11.4 | (0.5) | 9.4 | (0.5) | 4.9 | (0.7) |
| Chinese Taipei | 9.3 | (0.4) | 9.3 | (0.5) | 8.7 | (0.4) | 8.2 | (0.5) | 1.0 | (0.6) |
| Thailand | 7.8 | (0.5) | 8.3 | (0.5) | 7.6 | (0.4) | 5.7 | (0.4) | 2.2 | (0.7) |
| Tunisia | 25.6 | (0.7) | 25.8 | (0.8) | 24.0 | (0.7) | 19.1 | (0.8) | 6.4 | (1.1) |
| Uruguay | 11.8 | (0.6) | 12.3 | (0.7) | 12.8 | (0.7) | 8.2 | (0.5) | 3.4 | (0.8) |

*Note*: Values that are statistically significant at the 5% level (p < 0.05) are indicated in bold.

© OECD 2011 Quality Time for Students: Learning In and Out of School

**Table 3.7c** Mean learning hours and allocation of total learning time on the language of
[Part 7/7] instruction, by quarters of the PISA index of economic, social and cultural status (ESCS)

| | | Allocation of total learning time on the language of instruction for | | | | | | | | |
|---|---|---|---|---|---|---|---|---|---|---|
| | | Individual study | | | | | | | | |
| | | Bottom quarter of ESCS | | Second quarter of ESCS | | Third quarter of ESCS | | Top quarter of ESCS | | Difference (bottom-top) | |
| | | % | S.E. | % | S.E. | % | S.E. | % | S.E. | Dif. | S.E. |
| OECD | Australia | 23.0 | (0.3) | 24.2 | (0.3) | 25.2 | (0.3) | 26.3 | (0.3) | -3.3 | (0.5) |
| | Austria | 32.4 | (0.8) | 31.3 | (0.7) | 30.5 | (0.7) | 30.3 | (0.6) | 2.0 | (0.9) |
| | Belgium | 24.9 | (0.5) | 25.6 | (0.5) | 26.1 | (0.4) | 26.1 | (0.4) | -1.3 | (0.6) |
| | Canada | 22.5 | (0.4) | 22.7 | (0.4) | 24.1 | (0.4) | 25.1 | (0.4) | -2.5 | (0.5) |
| | Czech Republic | 19.7 | (0.7) | 20.0 | (0.6) | 18.8 | (0.4) | 19.2 | (0.6) | 0.5 | (0.9) |
| | Denmark | 21.3 | (0.4) | 21.4 | (0.3) | 22.4 | (0.4) | 22.5 | (0.4) | -1.3 | (0.6) |
| | Finland | 22.4 | (0.5) | 22.5 | (0.5) | 23.8 | (0.5) | 23.7 | (0.5) | -1.4 | (0.6) |
| | France | 21.2 | (0.6) | 21.8 | (0.5) | 22.6 | (0.4) | 23.8 | (0.4) | -2.6 | (0.8) |
| | Germany | 29.7 | (0.5) | 30.1 | (0.6) | 30.0 | (0.5) | 29.4 | (0.6) | 0.3 | (0.7) |
| | Greece | 27.7 | (0.7) | 27.9 | (0.6) | 27.5 | (0.5) | 26.7 | (0.6) | 1.1 | (0.8) |
| | Hungary | 29.3 | (0.6) | 27.9 | (0.4) | 29.1 | (0.6) | 27.7 | (0.4) | 1.8 | (0.7) |
| | Iceland | 22.4 | (0.5) | 21.9 | (0.5) | 22.1 | (0.4) | 22.4 | (0.4) | 0.1 | (0.6) |
| | Ireland | 25.3 | (0.7) | 27.0 | (0.6) | 28.7 | (0.5) | 29.2 | (0.7) | -3.9 | (1.0) |
| | Italy | 33.2 | (0.3) | 34.2 | (0.4) | 34.5 | (0.4) | 36.1 | (0.4) | -3.0 | (0.5) |
| | Japan | 14.0 | (0.5) | 15.5 | (0.6) | 16.4 | (0.5) | 16.5 | (0.6) | -2.6 | (0.6) |
| | Korea | 15.0 | (0.4) | 15.5 | (0.4) | 17.6 | (0.4) | 20.6 | (0.4) | -5.6 | (0.6) |
| | Luxembourg | 25.4 | (0.7) | 24.6 | (0.6) | 23.2 | (0.5) | 22.4 | (0.4) | 3.1 | (0.8) |
| | Mexico | 31.2 | (0.6) | 31.2 | (0.4) | 30.5 | (0.4) | 28.6 | (0.5) | 2.5 | (0.7) |
| | Netherlands | 26.3 | (0.6) | 24.7 | (0.5) | 25.9 | (0.6) | 27.7 | (0.6) | -1.4 | (0.9) |
| | New Zealand | 20.7 | (0.6) | 21.9 | (0.5) | 21.6 | (0.4) | 23.3 | (0.5) | -2.6 | (0.7) |
| | Norway | 20.2 | (0.5) | 21.1 | (0.5) | 21.8 | (0.5) | 22.4 | (0.5) | -2.3 | (0.7) |
| | Poland | 28.5 | (0.6) | 27.8 | (0.5) | 27.7 | (0.5) | 27.9 | (0.4) | 0.6 | (0.7) |
| | Portugal | 30.4 | (0.7) | 30.5 | (0.5) | 30.3 | (0.5) | 29.7 | (0.6) | 0.6 | (0.9) |
| | Slovak Republic | 27.2 | (1.2) | 29.0 | (0.5) | 29.4 | (0.7) | 27.8 | (0.7) | -0.6 | (1.3) |
| | Spain | 28.3 | (0.5) | 29.0 | (0.5) | 29.4 | (0.5) | 30.2 | (0.4) | -1.9 | (0.6) |
| | Sweden | 21.1 | (0.6) | 23.2 | (0.7) | 23.3 | (0.5) | 24.4 | (0.7) | -3.2 | (0.8) |
| | Switzerland | 26.2 | (0.5) | 25.3 | (0.4) | 25.3 | (0.5) | 24.7 | (0.4) | 1.5 | (0.6) |
| | Turkey | 26.8 | (0.4) | 27.2 | (0.5) | 25.5 | (0.5) | 22.4 | (0.7) | 4.4 | (0.8) |
| | United Kingdom | 22.3 | (0.4) | 23.4 | (0.4) | 25.2 | (0.4) | 27.5 | (0.4) | -5.1 | (0.5) |
| | United States | 28.1 | (0.5) | 26.9 | (0.5) | 28.0 | (0.5) | 29.7 | (0.6) | -1.5 | (0.8) |
| | **OECD average** | 24.9 | (0.1) | 25.2 | (0.1) | 25.6 | (0.1) | 25.8 | (0.1) | -0.9 | (0.1) |
| Partners | Argentina | 37.0 | (0.9) | 37.5 | (0.9) | 38.7 | (0.9) | 34.0 | (0.9) | 3.6 | (1.4) |
| | Azerbaijan | 35.3 | (1.1) | 36.3 | (0.7) | 36.3 | (0.6) | 35.5 | (0.6) | 0.3 | (1.2) |
| | Brazil | 29.2 | (0.7) | 27.5 | (0.6) | 28.0 | (0.6) | 26.8 | (0.5) | 2.5 | (0.8) |
| | Bulgaria | 30.9 | (0.8) | 32.6 | (0.8) | 34.1 | (0.6) | 33.6 | (0.7) | -2.8 | (1.0) |
| | Chile | 29.8 | (0.6) | 28.0 | (0.7) | 27.0 | (0.6) | 24.9 | (0.6) | 5.0 | (0.9) |
| | Colombia | 25.1 | (0.9) | 26.2 | (0.8) | 24.9 | (0.5) | 24.9 | (0.7) | 0.1 | (1.3) |
| | Croatia | 28.0 | (0.7) | 28.0 | (0.6) | 27.6 | (0.6) | 25.9 | (0.7) | 2.2 | (0.8) |
| | Estonia | 24.9 | (0.6) | 25.2 | (0.5) | 25.3 | (0.6) | 25.1 | (0.5) | -0.2 | (0.7) |
| | Hong Kong-China | 20.3 | (0.6) | 20.3 | (0.5) | 19.3 | (0.5) | 20.1 | (0.5) | 0.2 | (0.7) |
| | Indonesia | 27.9 | (0.6) | 26.9 | (0.6) | 27.7 | (0.5) | 25.8 | (0.7) | 2.0 | (1.0) |
| | Israel | 28.2 | (0.9) | 26.4 | (0.8) | 25.7 | (0.9) | 24.2 | (0.6) | 4.0 | (1.1) |
| | Jordan | 35.5 | (0.7) | 34.0 | (0.7) | 32.8 | (0.7) | 32.3 | (0.6) | 3.3 | (0.9) |
| | Kyrgyzstan | 35.8 | (0.8) | 34.4 | (0.7) | 33.5 | (0.7) | 32.6 | (0.7) | 3.4 | (1.0) |
| | Latvia | 28.8 | (0.8) | 29.6 | (0.7) | 29.6 | (0.5) | 29.3 | (0.5) | -0.6 | (1.0) |
| | Liechtenstein | 23.8 | (1.6) | 24.7 | (2.0) | 25.8 | (1.9) | 23.8 | (1.9) | 0.4 | (2.5) |
| | Lithuania | 27.6 | (0.7) | 26.9 | (0.6) | 28.0 | (0.6) | 28.7 | (0.5) | -1.0 | (0.8) |
| | Macao-China | 17.0 | (0.5) | 17.0 | (0.4) | 17.3 | (0.4) | 18.6 | (0.5) | -1.6 | (0.6) |
| | Montenegro | 36.7 | (0.9) | 36.5 | (0.7) | 34.8 | (0.7) | 34.2 | (0.7) | 2.3 | (1.1) |
| | Qatar | 33.0 | (0.6) | 32.0 | (0.6) | 31.4 | (0.5) | 30.4 | (0.6) | 2.5 | (0.9) |
| | Romania | 30.1 | (0.8) | 29.9 | (0.6) | 29.3 | (0.7) | 29.1 | (0.7) | 0.8 | (0.8) |
| | Russian Federation | 34.4 | (0.8) | 35.9 | (0.7) | 35.4 | (0.6) | 35.9 | (0.7) | -1.6 | (0.8) |
| | Serbia | 26.6 | (0.6) | 27.2 | (0.6) | 27.2 | (0.6) | 26.8 | (0.6) | -0.3 | (0.8) |
| | Slovenia | 28.3 | (0.7) | 27.8 | (0.6) | 26.4 | (0.6) | 25.9 | (0.6) | 2.3 | (1.0) |
| | Chinese Taipei | 23.8 | (0.4) | 25.2 | (0.5) | 25.3 | (0.5) | 25.6 | (0.4) | -1.9 | (0.6) |
| | Thailand | 30.1 | (0.6) | 31.1 | (0.5) | 30.7 | (0.5) | 28.5 | (0.5) | 1.7 | (0.8) |
| | Tunisia | 31.9 | (0.8) | 30.5 | (0.7) | 30.1 | (0.7) | 30.6 | (1.1) | 1.3 | (1.3) |
| | Uruguay | 28.5 | (0.8) | 27.1 | (0.8) | 26.7 | (0.9) | 29.3 | (0.6) | -0.6 | (1.0) |

*Note:* Values that are statistically significant at the 5% level (p < 0.05) are indicated in bold.

**Table 3.7d** **Mean learning hours and allocation of total learning time in science, in mathematics and on the**
[Part 1/7] **language of instruction, by quarters of the PISA index of economic, social and cultural status (ESCS)**

| | Mean learning hours per week | | | | | | | | | |
| | Regular school lessons | | | | | | | | | |
| | Bottom quarter of ESCS | | Second quarter of ESCS | | Third quarter of ESCS | | Top quarter of ESCS | | Difference (bottom-top) | |
| | Mean | S.E. | Mean | S.E. | Mean | S.E. | Mean | S.E. | Dif. | S.E. |
|---|---|---|---|---|---|---|---|---|---|---|
| Australia | 10.49 | (0.11) | 11.23 | (0.09) | 11.61 | (0.10) | 12.34 | (0.11) | **-1.86** | (0.14) |
| Austria | 7.98 | (0.12) | 8.34 | (0.13) | 8.80 | (0.13) | 9.11 | (0.13) | **-1.12** | (0.17) |
| Belgium | 8.25 | (0.17) | 9.27 | (0.13) | 10.22 | (0.15) | 11.15 | (0.11) | **-2.85** | (0.20) |
| Canada | 11.67 | (0.16) | 12.73 | (0.14) | 13.45 | (0.16) | 13.89 | (0.20) | **-2.23** | (0.20) |
| Czech Republic | 10.12 | (0.15) | 10.32 | (0.14) | 10.66 | (0.17) | 11.50 | (0.14) | **-1.36** | (0.17) |
| Denmark | 12.70 | (0.13) | 13.15 | (0.13) | 13.26 | (0.11) | 13.53 | (0.13) | **-0.83** | (0.18) |
| Finland | 9.27 | (0.16) | 9.52 | (0.14) | 9.74 | (0.13) | 10.30 | (0.15) | **-1.03** | (0.17) |
| France | 9.36 | (0.14) | 10.25 | (0.13) | 10.95 | (0.13) | 12.40 | (0.13) | **-3.05** | (0.18) |
| Germany | 9.88 | (0.18) | 10.61 | (0.15) | 10.99 | (0.14) | 11.00 | (0.12) | **-1.20** | (0.22) |
| Greece | 8.57 | (0.17) | 9.47 | (0.17) | 10.03 | (0.15) | 11.23 | (0.18) | **-2.68** | (0.24) |
| Hungary | 7.98 | (0.16) | 8.83 | (0.16) | 8.99 | (0.16) | 10.19 | (0.21) | **-2.21** | (0.25) |
| Iceland | 11.96 | (0.12) | 12.19 | (0.13) | 12.17 | (0.12) | 12.64 | (0.12) | **-0.69** | (0.15) |
| Ireland | 9.49 | (0.17) | 9.43 | (0.14) | 9.87 | (0.14) | 10.22 | (0.13) | **-0.74** | (0.21) |
| Italy | 10.71 | (0.14) | 11.17 | (0.10) | 11.67 | (0.11) | 11.53 | (0.14) | **-0.84** | (0.17) |
| Japan | 9.43 | (0.17) | 10.50 | (0.16) | 11.38 | (0.15) | 11.81 | (0.17) | **-2.39** | (0.21) |
| Korea | 11.94 | (0.18) | 12.67 | (0.14) | 12.87 | (0.14) | 13.54 | (0.19) | **-1.61** | (0.25) |
| Luxembourg | 8.94 | (0.12) | 9.48 | (0.11) | 9.98 | (0.12) | 10.50 | (0.12) | **-1.58** | (0.16) |
| Mexico | 10.43 | (0.24) | 10.51 | (0.18) | 10.62 | (0.15) | 11.80 | (0.16) | **-1.30** | (0.29) |
| Netherlands | 7.47 | (0.13) | 7.67 | (0.11) | 8.14 | (0.12) | 8.63 | (0.14) | **-1.14** | (0.20) |
| New Zealand | 11.80 | (0.17) | 12.71 | (0.16) | 13.19 | (0.14) | 13.72 | (0.12) | **-1.89** | (0.21) |
| Norway | 9.05 | (0.15) | 9.61 | (0.11) | 9.88 | (0.14) | 10.01 | (0.13) | **-0.98** | (0.20) |
| Poland | 11.05 | (0.13) | 11.47 | (0.13) | 11.91 | (0.14) | 12.44 | (0.12) | **-1.41** | (0.15) |
| Portugal | 8.81 | (0.18) | 9.79 | (0.17) | 10.31 | (0.16) | 11.42 | (0.19) | **-2.60** | (0.27) |
| Slovak Republic | 7.98 | (0.18) | 8.45 | (0.16) | 9.05 | (0.20) | 10.03 | (0.18) | **-2.07** | (0.22) |
| Spain | 9.26 | (0.11) | 9.84 | (0.12) | 10.26 | (0.12) | 11.23 | (0.16) | **-1.97** | (0.18) |
| Sweden | 8.82 | (0.11) | 8.88 | (0.12) | 9.08 | (0.09) | 9.28 | (0.12) | **-0.47** | (0.17) |
| Switzerland | 9.28 | (0.13) | 9.59 | (0.12) | 10.01 | (0.14) | 10.64 | (0.12) | **-1.36** | (0.15) |
| Turkey | 9.61 | (0.22) | 10.06 | (0.18) | 10.59 | (0.20) | 12.41 | (0.28) | **-2.81** | (0.34) |
| United Kingdom | 11.27 | (0.14) | 11.73 | (0.11) | 12.20 | (0.11) | 12.60 | (0.12) | **-1.32** | (0.16) |
| United States | 9.13 | (0.27) | 10.41 | (0.18) | 11.47 | (0.16) | 12.83 | (0.18) | **-3.68** | (0.35) |
| **OECD average** | 9.76 | (0.03) | 10.33 | (0.03) | 10.78 | (0.03) | 11.46 | (0.03) | **-1.71** | (0.04) |
| Argentina | 6.62 | (0.17) | 7.17 | (0.17) | 7.66 | (0.21) | 9.04 | (0.26) | **-2.45** | (0.32) |
| Azerbaijan | 9.51 | (0.18) | 10.10 | (0.21) | 10.71 | (0.19) | 11.18 | (0.20) | **-1.66** | (0.24) |
| Brazil | 7.73 | (0.19) | 7.84 | (0.16) | 8.51 | (0.12) | 9.76 | (0.14) | **-2.02** | (0.25) |
| Bulgaria | 7.28 | (0.26) | 7.90 | (0.20) | 8.86 | (0.19) | 10.17 | (0.23) | **-2.91** | (0.35) |
| Chile | 7.60 | (0.19) | 8.54 | (0.17) | 9.52 | (0.20) | 11.45 | (0.25) | **-3.82** | (0.30) |
| Colombia | 11.10 | (0.26) | 11.30 | (0.27) | 11.42 | (0.19) | 12.84 | (0.26) | **-1.68** | (0.31) |
| Croatia | 7.60 | (0.15) | 8.32 | (0.11) | 8.50 | (0.13) | 9.31 | (0.11) | **-1.70** | (0.17) |
| Estonia | 10.48 | (0.19) | 10.77 | (0.13) | 10.98 | (0.16) | 11.57 | (0.13) | **-1.07** | (0.20) |
| Hong Kong-China | 12.68 | (0.18) | 13.30 | (0.16) | 13.67 | (0.17) | 14.63 | (0.20) | **-1.96** | (0.28) |
| Indonesia | 10.47 | (0.24) | 10.71 | (0.21) | 10.76 | (0.23) | 11.96 | (0.19) | **-1.48** | (0.26) |
| Israel | 8.52 | (0.16) | 9.45 | (0.19) | 9.73 | (0.19) | 10.67 | (0.17) | **-2.10** | (0.25) |
| Jordan | 9.25 | (0.23) | 9.92 | (0.21) | 10.61 | (0.18) | 11.69 | (0.21) | **-2.48** | (0.31) |
| Kyrgyzstan | 7.13 | (0.31) | 7.07 | (0.21) | 7.88 | (0.21) | 9.11 | (0.22) | **-1.93** | (0.36) |
| Latvia | 10.47 | (0.19) | 11.01 | (0.17) | 11.13 | (0.14) | 11.64 | (0.14) | **-1.18** | (0.23) |
| Liechtenstein | 9.79 | (0.39) | 9.97 | (0.42) | 10.52 | (0.43) | 10.73 | (0.33) | -0.95 | (0.53) |
| Lithuania | 8.95 | (0.19) | 9.69 | (0.16) | 10.07 | (0.15) | 10.70 | (0.18) | **-1.77** | (0.23) |
| Macao-China | 13.87 | (0.16) | 14.96 | (0.16) | 14.26 | (0.16) | 14.78 | (0.16) | **-0.92** | (0.21) |
| Montenegro | 7.96 | (0.18) | 8.51 | (0.15) | 8.91 | (0.20) | 10.17 | (0.17) | **-2.25** | (0.28) |
| Qatar | 7.41 | (0.15) | 8.31 | (0.16) | 9.36 | (0.18) | 9.64 | (0.15) | **-2.24** | (0.23) |
| Romania | 7.32 | (0.19) | 8.18 | (0.23) | 8.71 | (0.20) | 10.10 | (0.24) | **-2.80** | (0.26) |
| Russian Federation | 8.83 | (0.21) | 9.06 | (0.18) | 9.62 | (0.16) | 10.16 | (0.12) | **-1.35** | (0.24) |
| Serbia | 8.55 | (0.15) | 8.77 | (0.14) | 9.47 | (0.16) | 10.49 | (0.14) | **-1.95** | (0.19) |
| Slovenia | 8.24 | (0.15) | 9.08 | (0.12) | 9.54 | (0.12) | 10.72 | (0.14) | **-2.44** | (0.22) |
| Chinese Taipei | 9.83 | (0.21) | 10.86 | (0.19) | 12.14 | (0.18) | 13.30 | (0.16) | **-3.49** | (0.24) |
| Thailand | 10.41 | (0.13) | 10.46 | (0.11) | 10.16 | (0.14) | 11.75 | (0.17) | **-1.34** | (0.22) |
| Tunisia | 8.49 | (0.17) | 8.96 | (0.16) | 9.18 | (0.17) | 10.04 | (0.23) | **-1.54** | (0.29) |
| Uruguay | 7.62 | (0.16) | 8.10 | (0.17) | 8.75 | (0.14) | 9.46 | (0.16) | **-1.81** | (0.20) |

*Note:* Values that are statistically significant at the 5% level (p < 0.05) are indicated in bold.

© OECD 2011 Quality Time for Students: Learning In and Out of School

**Table 3.7d** Mean learning hours and allocation of total learning time in science, in mathematics and on the
[Part 2/7] language of instruction, by quarters of the PISA index of economic, social and cultural status (ESCS)

| | Mean learning hours per week | | | | | | | | | |
|---|---|---|---|---|---|---|---|---|---|---|
| | Out-of-school-time lessons | | | | | | | | | |
| | Bottom quarter of ESCS | | Second quarter of ESCS | | Third quarter of ESCS | | Top quarter of ESCS | | Difference (bottom-top) | |
| | Mean | S.E. | Mean | S.E. | Mean | S.E. | Mean | S.E. | Dif. | S.E. |
| Australia | 1.85 | (0.07) | 1.72 | (0.06) | 1.72 | (0.06) | 1.75 | (0.06) | 0.10 | (0.10) |
| Austria | 1.14 | (0.08) | 0.99 | (0.07) | 0.83 | (0.06) | 0.82 | (0.06) | **0.31** | (0.09) |
| Belgium | 1.40 | (0.06) | 1.34 | (0.08) | 1.27 | (0.06) | 1.22 | (0.07) | **0.22** | (0.10) |
| Canada | 2.27 | (0.08) | 2.23 | (0.08) | 2.49 | (0.09) | 2.41 | (0.08) | -0.14 | (0.10) |
| Czech Republic | 1.97 | (0.09) | 1.80 | (0.10) | 1.89 | (0.08) | 1.90 | (0.09) | 0.07 | (0.14) |
| Denmark | 3.95 | (0.14) | 3.65 | (0.11) | 3.89 | (0.12) | 3.83 | (0.11) | 0.12 | (0.17) |
| Finland | 1.09 | (0.07) | 1.10 | (0.07) | 1.07 | (0.06) | 0.96 | (0.06) | 0.14 | (0.09) |
| France | 2.44 | (0.08) | 2.28 | (0.08) | 2.27 | (0.08) | 1.96 | (0.08) | **0.50** | (0.12) |
| Germany | 2.24 | (0.12) | 1.94 | (0.08) | 1.91 | (0.11) | 1.57 | (0.08) | **0.67** | (0.15) |
| Greece | 4.69 | (0.17) | 5.68 | (0.16) | 6.33 | (0.16) | 6.68 | (0.22) | **-2.00** | (0.28) |
| Hungary | 3.58 | (0.11) | 3.46 | (0.11) | 3.73 | (0.12) | 3.58 | (0.13) | -0.00 | (0.17) |
| Iceland | 1.28 | (0.08) | 1.38 | (0.09) | 1.65 | (0.10) | 1.52 | (0.07) | **-0.24** | (0.11) |
| Ireland | 1.66 | (0.09) | 1.64 | (0.07) | 1.75 | (0.09) | 1.55 | (0.09) | 0.10 | (0.12) |
| Italy | 2.19 | (0.07) | 2.23 | (0.08) | 2.25 | (0.07) | 2.33 | (0.08) | -0.14 | (0.11) |
| Japan | 1.25 | (0.08) | 1.21 | (0.08) | 1.46 | (0.09) | 1.62 | (0.08) | **-0.38** | (0.10) |
| Korea | 3.34 | (0.15) | 4.10 | (0.13) | 5.14 | (0.13) | 6.40 | (0.15) | **-3.05** | (0.22) |
| Luxembourg | 2.31 | (0.10) | 2.06 | (0.08) | 1.81 | (0.07) | 1.51 | (0.06) | **0.82** | (0.13) |
| Mexico | 3.80 | (0.19) | 3.10 | (0.09) | 3.31 | (0.10) | 2.88 | (0.16) | **0.93** | (0.26) |
| Netherlands | 2.12 | (0.11) | 2.03 | (0.08) | 1.83 | (0.09) | 1.54 | (0.08) | **0.58** | (0.14) |
| New Zealand | 1.94 | (0.11) | 1.71 | (0.09) | 1.64 | (0.10) | 1.69 | (0.10) | 0.26 | (0.15) |
| Norway | 3.16 | (0.09) | 3.14 | (0.10) | 3.00 | (0.09) | 3.23 | (0.11) | -0.06 | (0.14) |
| Poland | 2.12 | (0.11) | 2.09 | (0.09) | 2.04 | (0.09) | 2.16 | (0.08) | -0.04 | (0.14) |
| Portugal | 1.90 | (0.10) | 2.01 | (0.10) | 2.05 | (0.09) | 2.03 | (0.09) | -0.13 | (0.15) |
| Slovak Republic | 2.24 | (0.10) | 2.19 | (0.10) | 2.38 | (0.10) | 2.82 | (0.11) | **-0.60** | (0.16) |
| Spain | 2.19 | (0.09) | 2.36 | (0.10) | 2.30 | (0.09) | 2.10 | (0.12) | 0.10 | (0.16) |
| Sweden | 1.81 | (0.08) | 1.77 | (0.09) | 1.75 | (0.07) | 1.78 | (0.10) | 0.02 | (0.14) |
| Switzerland | 1.94 | (0.09) | 1.55 | (0.08) | 1.49 | (0.06) | 1.30 | (0.06) | **0.63** | (0.11) |
| Turkey | 4.76 | (0.15) | 4.54 | (0.14) | 5.24 | (0.15) | 6.36 | (0.13) | **-1.61** | (0.21) |
| United Kingdom | 1.65 | (0.09) | 1.71 | (0.07) | 1.81 | (0.06) | 1.61 | (0.07) | 0.05 | (0.11) |
| United States | 3.16 | (0.15) | 3.06 | (0.11) | 3.14 | (0.12) | 2.77 | (0.12) | **0.39** | (0.19) |
| **OECD average** | **2.38** | **(0.02)** | **2.34** | **(0.02)** | **2.45** | **(0.02)** | **2.46** | **(0.02)** | **-0.08** | **(0.03)** |
| Argentina | 1.68 | (0.12) | 1.71 | (0.10) | 1.69 | (0.12) | 1.56 | (0.12) | 0.13 | (0.17) |
| Azerbaijan | 4.63 | (0.19) | 4.67 | (0.16) | 4.78 | (0.16) | 5.36 | (0.16) | **-0.70** | (0.22) |
| Brazil | 2.98 | (0.12) | 3.01 | (0.12) | 3.18 | (0.14) | 3.43 | (0.14) | **-0.43** | (0.18) |
| Bulgaria | 3.12 | (0.16) | 3.26 | (0.15) | 3.07 | (0.12) | 3.35 | (0.11) | -0.22 | (0.20) |
| Chile | 2.91 | (0.10) | 2.78 | (0.09) | 2.83 | (0.10) | 2.70 | (0.10) | 0.21 | (0.12) |
| Colombia | 3.35 | (0.14) | 3.47 | (0.20) | 3.07 | (0.11) | 3.37 | (0.12) | 0.01 | (0.20) |
| Croatia | 1.53 | (0.08) | 1.48 | (0.08) | 1.54 | (0.07) | 1.76 | (0.09) | **-0.24** | (0.12) |
| Estonia | 2.76 | (0.11) | 2.71 | (0.11) | 2.55 | (0.12) | 2.50 | (0.11) | **0.26** | (0.13) |
| Hong Kong-China | 2.51 | (0.12) | 2.96 | (0.13) | 3.08 | (0.10) | 3.76 | (0.12) | **-1.25** | (0.16) |
| Indonesia | 3.31 | (0.15) | 3.53 | (0.12) | 3.68 | (0.17) | 4.14 | (0.18) | **-0.84** | (0.19) |
| Israel | 4.72 | (0.13) | 4.52 | (0.16) | 4.22 | (0.15) | 4.37 | (0.12) | 0.35 | (0.18) |
| Jordan | 4.83 | (0.16) | 5.13 | (0.14) | 5.22 | (0.14) | 5.19 | (0.18) | -0.36 | (0.24) |
| Kyrgyzstan | 4.73 | (0.15) | 4.66 | (0.14) | 4.64 | (0.14) | 4.36 | (0.13) | 0.36 | (0.19) |
| Latvia | 2.64 | (0.14) | 2.75 | (0.12) | 2.72 | (0.11) | 2.77 | (0.11) | -0.12 | (0.19) |
| Liechtenstein | 1.96 | (0.27) | 0.92 | (0.17) | 1.22 | (0.22) | 1.24 | (0.25) | 0.68 | (0.39) |
| Lithuania | 2.04 | (0.10) | 1.93 | (0.09) | 1.90 | (0.08) | 1.86 | (0.09) | 0.19 | (0.13) |
| Macao-China | 3.10 | (0.13) | 3.17 | (0.10) | 3.10 | (0.13) | 3.65 | (0.18) | **-0.54** | (0.22) |
| Montenegro | 2.42 | (0.11) | 2.63 | (0.11) | 2.81 | (0.12) | 2.86 | (0.13) | **-0.43** | (0.18) |
| Qatar | 4.81 | (0.11) | 4.92 | (0.11) | 4.92 | (0.13) | 4.96 | (0.12) | -0.14 | (0.16) |
| Romania | 3.71 | (0.20) | 3.94 | (0.13) | 4.16 | (0.15) | 4.35 | (0.10) | **-0.66** | (0.24) |
| Russian Federation | 2.94 | (0.11) | 3.10 | (0.09) | 3.07 | (0.13) | 3.16 | (0.10) | -0.22 | (0.15) |
| Serbia | 2.58 | (0.08) | 2.62 | (0.11) | 2.76 | (0.11) | 2.68 | (0.11) | -0.12 | (0.14) |
| Slovenia | 2.73 | (0.09) | 2.61 | (0.09) | 2.40 | (0.10) | 2.12 | (0.08) | **0.62** | (0.14) |
| Chinese Taipei | 2.19 | (0.07) | 2.76 | (0.09) | 3.21 | (0.10) | 3.85 | (0.11) | **-1.66** | (0.13) |
| Thailand | 1.82 | (0.13) | 2.17 | (0.12) | 2.27 | (0.11) | 3.33 | (0.13) | **-1.52** | (0.19) |
| Tunisia | 5.96 | (0.11) | 6.00 | (0.14) | 6.11 | (0.13) | 6.35 | (0.15) | **-0.39** | (0.20) |
| Uruguay | 1.90 | (0.10) | 2.08 | (0.10) | 2.31 | (0.10) | 2.03 | (0.09) | -0.13 | (0.14) |

*Note:* Values that are statistically significant at the 5% level (p < 0.05) are indicated in bold.

**Table 3.7d** **Mean learning hours and allocation of total learning time in science, in mathematics and on the**
[Part 3/7] **language of instruction, by quarters of the PISA index of economic, social and cultural status (ESCS)**

| | Mean learning hours per week | | | | | | | | | |
| | Individual study | | | | | | | | | |
| | Bottom quarter of ESCS | | Second quarter of ESCS | | Third quarter of ESCS | | Top quarter of ESCS | | Difference (bottom-top) | |
| | Mean | S.E. | Mean | S.E. | Mean | S.E. | Mean | S.E. | Dif. | S.E. |
|---|---|---|---|---|---|---|---|---|---|---|
| Australia | 3.97 | (0.08) | 4.43 | (0.08) | 4.78 | (0.10) | 5.54 | (0.09) | **-1.57** | (0.12) |
| Austria | 5.19 | (0.11) | 4.98 | (0.12) | 4.83 | (0.13) | 4.78 | (0.12) | 0.37 | (0.15) |
| Belgium | 3.64 | (0.10) | 4.10 | (0.09) | 4.67 | (0.10) | 5.15 | (0.09) | **-1.48** | (0.13) |
| Canada | 4.46 | (0.11) | 4.84 | (0.10) | 5.70 | (0.11) | 6.05 | (0.13) | **-1.60** | (0.15) |
| Czech Republic | 3.43 | (0.11) | 3.47 | (0.14) | 3.35 | (0.10) | 3.62 | (0.10) | -0.19 | (0.16) |
| Denmark | 4.75 | (0.12) | 4.82 | (0.10) | 5.17 | (0.09) | 5.23 | (0.10) | **-0.46** | (0.14) |
| Finland | 3.19 | (0.09) | 3.32 | (0.09) | 3.50 | (0.08) | 3.62 | (0.08) | **-0.43** | (0.11) |
| France | 3.89 | (0.11) | 4.23 | (0.11) | 4.72 | (0.11) | 5.45 | (0.13) | **-1.56** | (0.16) |
| Germany | 5.77 | (0.17) | 5.92 | (0.13) | 6.02 | (0.14) | 5.78 | (0.14) | -0.08 | (0.21) |
| Greece | 5.14 | (0.13) | 5.40 | (0.13) | 5.99 | (0.15) | 6.63 | (0.13) | **-1.50** | (0.17) |
| Hungary | 4.91 | (0.12) | 5.11 | (0.13) | 5.37 | (0.13) | 5.77 | (0.15) | **-0.85** | (0.19) |
| Iceland | 4.28 | (0.11) | 4.34 | (0.09) | 4.42 | (0.10) | 4.64 | (0.11) | **-0.37** | (0.15) |
| Ireland | 4.12 | (0.14) | 4.40 | (0.11) | 4.99 | (0.12) | 5.29 | (0.13) | **-1.15** | (0.19) |
| Italy | 6.81 | (0.08) | 7.32 | (0.11) | 7.83 | (0.12) | 8.17 | (0.12) | **-1.37** | (0.12) |
| Japan | 2.28 | (0.09) | 2.97 | (0.11) | 3.41 | (0.13) | 3.82 | (0.15) | **-1.53** | (0.15) |
| Korea | 3.62 | (0.12) | 4.20 | (0.12) | 5.05 | (0.13) | 6.86 | (0.24) | **-3.23** | (0.28) |
| Luxembourg | 4.35 | (0.11) | 4.49 | (0.11) | 4.29 | (0.08) | 4.22 | (0.09) | 0.12 | (0.14) |
| Mexico | 6.51 | (0.17) | 6.40 | (0.10) | 6.49 | (0.12) | 6.27 | (0.12) | 0.23 | (0.18) |
| Netherlands | 3.73 | (0.09) | 3.74 | (0.11) | 4.12 | (0.12) | 4.40 | (0.09) | **-0.64** | (0.12) |
| New Zealand | 3.84 | (0.10) | 4.31 | (0.12) | 4.47 | (0.10) | 5.13 | (0.13) | **-1.30** | (0.16) |
| Norway | 3.70 | (0.10) | 4.03 | (0.10) | 4.03 | (0.12) | 4.50 | (0.10) | **-0.79** | (0.13) |
| Poland | 6.30 | (0.14) | 6.08 | (0.12) | 6.38 | (0.12) | 6.60 | (0.11) | -0.31 | (0.19) |
| Portugal | 5.26 | (0.16) | 5.82 | (0.16) | 5.96 | (0.12) | 6.29 | (0.16) | **-1.04** | (0.24) |
| Slovak Republic | 4.29 | (0.13) | 4.58 | (0.11) | 5.06 | (0.14) | 5.31 | (0.16) | **-1.02** | (0.18) |
| Spain | 4.94 | (0.12) | 5.39 | (0.12) | 5.81 | (0.13) | 6.20 | (0.11) | **-1.30** | (0.15) |
| Sweden | 3.23 | (0.10) | 3.44 | (0.08) | 3.76 | (0.09) | 3.89 | (0.11) | **-0.67** | (0.17) |
| Switzerland | 4.31 | (0.07) | 4.07 | (0.08) | 4.18 | (0.09) | 4.23 | (0.07) | 0.07 | (0.10) |
| Turkey | 5.76 | (0.11) | 5.99 | (0.15) | 6.18 | (0.16) | 6.52 | (0.16) | **-0.76** | (0.21) |
| United Kingdom | 3.80 | (0.08) | 4.25 | (0.08) | 4.78 | (0.09) | 5.29 | (0.11) | **-1.51** | (0.13) |
| United States | 4.73 | (0.13) | 4.95 | (0.11) | 5.87 | (0.12) | 6.78 | (0.15) | **-2.04** | (0.21) |
| **OECD average** | 4.47 | (0.02) | 4.71 | (0.02) | 5.04 | (0.02) | 5.40 | (0.02) | **-0.93** | (0.03) |
| Argentina | 4.61 | (0.15) | 5.01 | (0.18) | 5.28 | (0.16) | 5.26 | (0.14) | **-0.64** | (0.19) |
| Azerbaijan | 7.98 | (0.29) | 8.42 | (0.17) | 9.04 | (0.21) | 9.40 | (0.20) | **-1.36** | (0.32) |
| Brazil | 5.18 | (0.13) | 4.85 | (0.12) | 5.36 | (0.15) | 5.44 | (0.12) | -0.23 | (0.18) |
| Bulgaria | 5.02 | (0.18) | 5.70 | (0.19) | 6.57 | (0.21) | 7.33 | (0.22) | **-2.31** | (0.28) |
| Chile | 4.43 | (0.10) | 4.50 | (0.10) | 4.97 | (0.16) | 4.84 | (0.11) | **-0.41** | (0.13) |
| Colombia | 5.39 | (0.18) | 5.73 | (0.16) | 5.28 | (0.15) | 5.91 | (0.17) | -0.52 | (0.29) |
| Croatia | 4.51 | (0.12) | 4.84 | (0.12) | 4.91 | (0.12) | 5.15 | (0.11) | **-0.65** | (0.15) |
| Estonia | 4.78 | (0.12) | 5.09 | (0.12) | 5.17 | (0.12) | 5.42 | (0.13) | **-0.63** | (0.17) |
| Hong Kong-China | 4.69 | (0.14) | 5.20 | (0.13) | 5.21 | (0.14) | 6.22 | (0.17) | **-1.53** | (0.18) |
| Indonesia | 5.55 | (0.16) | 5.38 | (0.11) | 5.63 | (0.14) | 5.75 | (0.16) | -0.20 | (0.24) |
| Israel | 5.49 | (0.16) | 5.43 | (0.19) | 5.09 | (0.18) | 5.39 | (0.18) | 0.12 | (0.25) |
| Jordan | 7.52 | (0.18) | 7.79 | (0.17) | 7.99 | (0.14) | 8.35 | (0.20) | **-0.83** | (0.26) |
| Kyrgyzstan | 6.89 | (0.20) | 6.47 | (0.16) | 6.66 | (0.15) | 6.78 | (0.15) | 0.09 | (0.25) |
| Latvia | 5.82 | (0.17) | 6.33 | (0.16) | 6.32 | (0.13) | 6.52 | (0.14) | **-0.71** | (0.21) |
| Liechtenstein | 3.79 | (0.26) | 3.46 | (0.25) | 4.00 | (0.25) | 4.37 | (0.38) | -0.60 | (0.49) |
| Lithuania | 4.90 | (0.13) | 4.99 | (0.12) | 5.36 | (0.13) | 5.86 | (0.13) | **-0.97** | (0.17) |
| Macao-China | 4.38 | (0.13) | 4.76 | (0.13) | 4.94 | (0.12) | 5.63 | (0.14) | **-1.25** | (0.18) |
| Montenegro | 5.77 | (0.15) | 6.21 | (0.15) | 6.35 | (0.18) | 6.48 | (0.16) | **-0.74** | (0.24) |
| Qatar | 5.82 | (0.10) | 6.18 | (0.12) | 6.59 | (0.12) | 6.50 | (0.11) | **-0.70** | (0.16) |
| Romania | 5.28 | (0.24) | 5.81 | (0.16) | 6.09 | (0.14) | 6.65 | (0.14) | **-1.41** | (0.29) |
| Russian Federation | 6.13 | (0.18) | 6.59 | (0.17) | 6.79 | (0.15) | 7.09 | (0.10) | **-0.96** | (0.18) |
| Serbia | 4.73 | (0.12) | 4.93 | (0.11) | 5.29 | (0.14) | 5.95 | (0.15) | **-1.23** | (0.18) |
| Slovenia | 4.70 | (0.10) | 4.98 | (0.12) | 4.93 | (0.13) | 5.12 | (0.12) | **-0.43** | (0.17) |
| Chinese Taipei | 3.59 | (0.11) | 4.54 | (0.13) | 5.21 | (0.11) | 6.20 | (0.12) | **-2.62** | (0.16) |
| Thailand | 5.13 | (0.18) | 5.29 | (0.12) | 5.23 | (0.15) | 5.61 | (0.12) | **-0.49** | (0.23) |
| Tunisia | 7.24 | (0.17) | 7.33 | (0.15) | 7.08 | (0.13) | 7.50 | (0.13) | -0.24 | (0.23) |
| Uruguay | 3.85 | (0.13) | 4.11 | (0.13) | 4.35 | (0.12) | 4.62 | (0.11) | **-0.79** | (0.16) |

*Note:* Values that are statistically significant at the 5% level (p < 0.05) are indicated in bold.

© OECD 2011 Quality Time for Students: Learning In and Out of School

**Table 3.7d** Mean learning hours and allocation of total learning time in science, in mathematics and on the
[Part 4/7] language of instruction, by quarters of the PISA index of economic, social and cultural status (ESCS)

| | | Mean learning hours per week | | | | | | | | |
|---|---|---|---|---|---|---|---|---|---|---|
| | | Total learning hours | | | | | | | | |
| | | Bottom quarter of ESCS | | Second quarter of ESCS | | Third quarter of ESCS | | Top quarter of ESCS | | Difference (bottom-top) | |
| | | Mean | S.E. | Mean | S.E. | Mean | S.E. | Mean | S.E. | Dif. | S.E. |
| **OECD** | Australia | 16.36 | (0.20) | 17.40 | (0.16) | 18.15 | (0.19) | 19.57 | (0.19) | **-3.22** | (0.26) |
| | Austria | 14.36 | (0.22) | 14.43 | (0.22) | 14.46 | (0.25) | 14.71 | (0.23) | -0.39 | (0.29) |
| | Belgium | 13.34 | (0.28) | 14.73 | (0.22) | 16.18 | (0.22) | 17.51 | (0.17) | **-4.05** | (0.32) |
| | Canada | 18.52 | (0.25) | 19.93 | (0.25) | 21.67 | (0.26) | 22.42 | (0.33) | **-3.89** | (0.35) |
| | Czech Republic | 15.42 | (0.25) | 15.55 | (0.25) | 15.95 | (0.28) | 17.02 | (0.23) | **-1.60** | (0.31) |
| | Denmark | 21.32 | (0.31) | 21.60 | (0.23) | 22.32 | (0.22) | 22.52 | (0.24) | **-1.20** | (0.34) |
| | Finland | 13.55 | (0.26) | 13.92 | (0.22) | 14.34 | (0.20) | 14.86 | (0.19) | **-1.32** | (0.28) |
| | France | 15.78 | (0.24) | 16.76 | (0.21) | 17.95 | (0.23) | 19.83 | (0.24) | **-4.05** | (0.34) |
| | Germany | 17.94 | (0.35) | 18.49 | (0.22) | 19.02 | (0.24) | 18.31 | (0.24) | -0.57 | (0.41) |
| | Greece | 18.36 | (0.37) | 20.68 | (0.35) | 22.28 | (0.35) | 24.61 | (0.34) | **-6.23** | (0.50) |
| | Hungary | 16.46 | (0.31) | 17.44 | (0.32) | 18.16 | (0.31) | 19.51 | (0.42) | **-3.05** | (0.51) |
| | Iceland | 17.44 | (0.20) | 17.99 | (0.19) | 18.26 | (0.22) | 18.81 | (0.20) | **-1.37** | (0.26) |
| | Ireland | 15.22 | (0.29) | 15.41 | (0.24) | 16.65 | (0.26) | 17.03 | (0.26) | **-1.81** | (0.39) |
| | Italy | 19.77 | (0.20) | 20.81 | (0.22) | 21.71 | (0.22) | 21.99 | (0.26) | **-2.22** | (0.25) |
| | Japan | 12.97 | (0.25) | 14.66 | (0.25) | 16.24 | (0.28) | 17.24 | (0.30) | **-4.32** | (0.33) |
| | Korea | 19.06 | (0.37) | 21.02 | (0.29) | 23.15 | (0.28) | 26.75 | (0.50) | **-7.70** | (0.65) |
| | Luxembourg | 15.60 | (0.21) | 16.10 | (0.22) | 16.01 | (0.18) | 16.24 | (0.18) | **-0.64** | (0.27) |
| | Mexico | 20.56 | (0.40) | 19.85 | (0.27) | 20.35 | (0.25) | 20.87 | (0.33) | -0.26 | (0.50) |
| | Netherlands | 13.24 | (0.23) | 13.53 | (0.23) | 14.04 | (0.24) | 14.48 | (0.21) | **-1.18** | (0.29) |
| | New Zealand | 17.58 | (0.24) | 18.77 | (0.25) | 19.31 | (0.22) | 20.56 | (0.25) | **-2.96** | (0.34) |
| | Norway | 15.93 | (0.25) | 16.71 | (0.21) | 16.90 | (0.24) | 17.68 | (0.26) | **-1.80** | (0.37) |
| | Poland | 19.49 | (0.25) | 19.68 | (0.23) | 20.36 | (0.22) | 21.23 | (0.22) | **-1.74** | (0.33) |
| | Portugal | 16.09 | (0.30) | 17.64 | (0.32) | 18.35 | (0.29) | 19.65 | (0.34) | **-3.63** | (0.48) |
| | Slovak Republic | 14.52 | (0.33) | 15.23 | (0.31) | 16.52 | (0.33) | 18.20 | (0.34) | **-3.72** | (0.42) |
| | Spain | 16.60 | (0.23) | 17.77 | (0.27) | 18.37 | (0.22) | 19.59 | (0.23) | **-3.02** | (0.27) |
| | Sweden | 13.89 | (0.22) | 14.09 | (0.19) | 14.55 | (0.18) | 14.92 | (0.25) | **-1.03** | (0.39) |
| | Switzerland | 15.52 | (0.16) | 15.26 | (0.19) | 15.68 | (0.19) | 16.17 | (0.18) | **-0.65** | (0.22) |
| | Turkey | 19.89 | (0.41) | 20.54 | (0.39) | 21.88 | (0.41) | 25.25 | (0.47) | **-5.39** | (0.65) |
| | United Kingdom | 16.79 | (0.25) | 17.72 | (0.19) | 18.77 | (0.21) | 19.50 | (0.22) | **-2.71** | (0.31) |
| | United States | 17.16 | (0.33) | 18.58 | (0.27) | 20.58 | (0.25) | 22.43 | (0.29) | **-5.24** | (0.48) |
| | **OECD average** | 16.63 | (0.05) | 17.41 | (0.05) | 18.27 | (0.05) | 19.32 | (0.05) | **-2.70** | (0.07) |
| **Partners** | Argentina | 12.89 | (0.28) | 14.01 | (0.32) | 14.59 | (0.33) | 15.80 | (0.32) | **-2.85** | (0.41) |
| | Azerbaijan | 22.29 | (0.50) | 23.39 | (0.45) | 24.80 | (0.45) | 25.92 | (0.42) | **-3.55** | (0.63) |
| | Brazil | 15.76 | (0.29) | 15.67 | (0.29) | 17.06 | (0.32) | 18.62 | (0.28) | **-2.72** | (0.40) |
| | Bulgaria | 15.58 | (0.50) | 16.93 | (0.42) | 18.65 | (0.42) | 20.76 | (0.41) | **-5.17** | (0.66) |
| | Chile | 15.05 | (0.29) | 15.86 | (0.25) | 17.47 | (0.38) | 19.07 | (0.31) | **-3.96** | (0.38) |
| | Colombia | 19.76 | (0.31) | 20.45 | (0.46) | 19.78 | (0.35) | 22.22 | (0.44) | **-2.43** | (0.57) |
| | Croatia | 13.74 | (0.26) | 14.70 | (0.22) | 15.00 | (0.23) | 16.33 | (0.21) | **-2.58** | (0.30) |
| | Estonia | 18.07 | (0.22) | 18.55 | (0.24) | 18.71 | (0.30) | 19.52 | (0.23) | **-1.43** | (0.32) |
| | Hong Kong-China | 19.95 | (0.32) | 21.46 | (0.30) | 21.89 | (0.28) | 24.60 | (0.40) | **-4.69** | (0.49) |
| | Indonesia | 19.30 | (0.43) | 19.55 | (0.32) | 19.98 | (0.32) | 21.85 | (0.33) | **-2.54** | (0.47) |
| | Israel | 18.94 | (0.35) | 19.46 | (0.40) | 19.05 | (0.44) | 20.47 | (0.37) | **-1.50** | (0.52) |
| | Jordan | 21.70 | (0.44) | 22.83 | (0.38) | 23.72 | (0.26) | 25.15 | (0.34) | **-3.49** | (0.56) |
| | Kyrgyzstan | 19.28 | (0.48) | 18.19 | (0.40) | 19.20 | (0.37) | 20.30 | (0.35) | -0.97 | (0.57) |
| | Latvia | 18.86 | (0.37) | 20.16 | (0.29) | 20.19 | (0.24) | 20.94 | (0.27) | **-2.06** | (0.49) |
| | Liechtenstein | 15.40 | (0.56) | 14.39 | (0.57) | 15.52 | (0.59) | 16.57 | (0.56) | -1.22 | (0.92) |
| | Lithuania | 15.79 | (0.30) | 16.70 | (0.29) | 17.30 | (0.25) | 18.40 | (0.28) | **-2.62** | (0.38) |
| | Macao-China | 21.38 | (0.26) | 22.83 | (0.29) | 22.36 | (0.27) | 23.98 | (0.31) | **-2.62** | (0.39) |
| | Montenegro | 16.18 | (0.34) | 17.38 | (0.28) | 18.02 | (0.40) | 19.36 | (0.32) | **-3.24** | (0.51) |
| | Qatar | 18.10 | (0.27) | 19.38 | (0.31) | 20.95 | (0.31) | 21.11 | (0.31) | **-3.02** | (0.42) |
| | Romania | 16.34 | (0.44) | 17.94 | (0.42) | 18.98 | (0.38) | 21.05 | (0.38) | **-4.80** | (0.58) |
| | Russian Federation | 17.87 | (0.34) | 18.81 | (0.34) | 19.43 | (0.33) | 20.43 | (0.21) | **-2.54** | (0.39) |
| | Serbia | 15.81 | (0.26) | 16.30 | (0.25) | 17.56 | (0.28) | 19.08 | (0.34) | **-3.33** | (0.41) |
| | Slovenia | 15.71 | (0.25) | 16.76 | (0.24) | 16.91 | (0.26) | 17.96 | (0.24) | **-2.22** | (0.36) |
| | Chinese Taipei | 15.81 | (0.35) | 18.30 | (0.34) | 20.72 | (0.31) | 23.42 | (0.30) | **-7.67** | (0.42) |
| | Thailand | 17.32 | (0.33) | 17.92 | (0.24) | 17.65 | (0.32) | 20.66 | (0.36) | **-3.38** | (0.54) |
| | Tunisia | 21.66 | (0.35) | 22.23 | (0.34) | 22.58 | (0.29) | 23.96 | (0.44) | **-2.26** | (0.56) |
| | Uruguay | 13.54 | (0.29) | 14.33 | (0.30) | 15.38 | (0.26) | 16.10 | (0.26) | **-2.52** | (0.36) |

*Note*: Values that are statistically significant at the 5% level (p < 0.05) are indicated in bold.

**Table 3.7d** Mean learning hours and allocation of total learning time in science, in mathematics and on the language of instruction, by quarters of the PISA index of economic, social and cultural status (ESCS)
[Part 5/7]

| | Allocation of total learning time in science, mathematics and the language of instruction for | | | | | | | | | |
|---|---|---|---|---|---|---|---|---|---|---|
| | Regular school lessons | | | | | | | | | |
| | Bottom quarter of ESCS | | Second quarter of ESCS | | Third quarter of ESCS | | Top quarter of ESCS | | Difference (bottom-top) | |
| | % | S.E. | % | S.E. | % | S.E. | % | S.E. | Dif. | S.E. |
| **Australia** | 67.2 | (0.5) | 67.2 | (0.4) | 66.4 | (0.4) | 65.5 | (0.4) | **1.7** | (0.6) |
| **Austria** | 59.2 | (0.7) | 61.0 | (0.6) | 63.4 | (0.6) | 63.9 | (0.6) | **-4.6** | (0.8) |
| **Belgium** | 63.7 | (0.5) | 64.7 | (0.6) | 64.1 | (0.5) | 65.0 | (0.4) | -1.1 | (0.7) |
| **Canada** | 64.3 | (0.6) | 64.7 | (0.5) | 63.5 | (0.5) | 63.5 | (0.4) | 0.7 | (0.7) |
| **Czech Republic** | 68.2 | (0.8) | 69.4 | (0.7) | 70.2 | (0.6) | 70.4 | (0.6) | **-2.2** | (1.0) |
| **Denmark** | 61.7 | (0.6) | 63.0 | (0.5) | 61.9 | (0.6) | 62.6 | (0.5) | -1.0 | (0.8) |
| **Finland** | 70.5 | (0.6) | 70.5 | (0.6) | 69.7 | (0.5) | 71.3 | (0.5) | -0.8 | (0.8) |
| **France** | 62.4 | (0.6) | 63.6 | (0.7) | 63.4 | (0.5) | 64.3 | (0.5) | **-2.0** | (0.8) |
| **Germany** | 56.9 | (0.6) | 59.4 | (0.6) | 59.9 | (0.7) | 61.8 | (0.5) | **-4.9** | (0.8) |
| **Greece** | 50.1 | (0.8) | 47.9 | (0.6) | 46.6 | (0.7) | 47.6 | (0.8) | **2.5** | (1.0) |
| **Hungary** | 50.0 | (0.7) | 53.0 | (0.6) | 52.0 | (0.7) | 54.4 | (0.6) | **-4.4** | (0.9) |
| **Iceland** | 70.4 | (0.5) | 70.2 | (0.6) | 68.9 | (0.6) | 69.4 | (0.5) | 1.0 | (0.7) |
| **Ireland** | 65.0 | (0.8) | 63.4 | (0.6) | 62.4 | (0.6) | 63.1 | (0.6) | 1.9 | (1.0) |
| **Italy** | 55.7 | (0.4) | 55.1 | (0.4) | 55.1 | (0.3) | 53.8 | (0.4) | **1.8** | (0.6) |
| **Japan** | 76.5 | (0.6) | 75.4 | (0.7) | 73.9 | (0.7) | 72.3 | (0.7) | **4.3** | (0.8) |
| **Korea** | 67.6 | (0.8) | 65.0 | (0.6) | 59.3 | (0.6) | 53.4 | (0.6) | **14.2** | (1.0) |
| **Luxembourg** | 60.0 | (0.7) | 61.5 | (0.6) | 64.6 | (0.5) | 66.7 | (0.5) | **-7.0** | (0.9) |
| **Mexico** | 51.0 | (0.9) | 53.2 | (0.6) | 53.0 | (0.5) | 57.7 | (0.6) | **-6.6** | (1.1) |
| **Netherlands** | 59.0 | (0.9) | 59.5 | (0.6) | 59.7 | (0.7) | 61.8 | (0.6) | **-2.9** | (1.2) |
| **New Zealand** | 69.2 | (0.8) | 69.8 | (0.6) | 70.5 | (0.6) | 69.1 | (0.6) | 0.1 | (0.9) |
| **Norway** | 60.5 | (0.7) | 60.8 | (0.7) | 61.0 | (0.7) | 59.5 | (0.7) | 0.9 | (1.0) |
| **Poland** | 58.6 | (0.5) | 59.9 | (0.5) | 60.4 | (0.6) | 60.6 | (0.4) | **-2.0** | (0.7) |
| **Portugal** | 57.3 | (0.9) | 57.4 | (0.7) | 58.5 | (0.5) | 59.9 | (0.6) | **-2.6** | (1.1) |
| **Slovak Republic** | 59.6 | (0.7) | 59.3 | (0.7) | 58.1 | (0.7) | 58.7 | (0.7) | 0.9 | (1.0) |
| **Spain** | 58.8 | (0.6) | 58.6 | (0.5) | 58.8 | (0.5) | 59.8 | (0.5) | -0.9 | (0.8) |
| **Sweden** | 67.0 | (0.7) | 66.0 | (0.7) | 65.8 | (0.5) | 66.0 | (0.6) | 1.0 | (0.8) |
| **Switzerland** | 61.4 | (0.7) | 64.2 | (0.5) | 65.0 | (0.5) | 66.6 | (0.4) | **-5.2** | (0.8) |
| **Turkey** | 51.0 | (0.6) | 51.7 | (0.6) | 51.6 | (0.6) | 51.5 | (0.6) | -0.6 | (0.9) |
| **United Kingdom** | 69.5 | (0.6) | 68.5 | (0.4) | 67.1 | (0.4) | 66.4 | (0.4) | **3.1** | (0.7) |
| **United States** | 52.7 | (1.1) | 55.5 | (0.7) | 56.2 | (0.6) | 58.1 | (0.6) | **-5.4** | (1.3) |
| **OECD average** | 61.5 | (0.1) | 62.0 | (0.1) | 61.7 | (0.1) | 62.2 | (0.1) | **-0.7** | (0.2) |
| **Argentina** | 53.8 | (0.9) | 52.5 | (0.9) | 53.4 | (0.8) | 58.3 | (0.9) | **-5.0** | (1.3) |
| **Azerbaijan** | 44.3 | (0.8) | 44.3 | (0.8) | 44.9 | (0.6) | 44.2 | (0.6) | -0.1 | (0.9) |
| **Brazil** | 51.8 | (0.9) | 52.7 | (0.8) | 52.5 | (0.8) | 54.9 | (0.7) | **-3.2** | (1.3) |
| **Bulgaria** | 50.0 | (1.0) | 49.3 | (0.9) | 49.8 | (0.6) | 50.9 | (0.6) | -1.1 | (1.2) |
| **Chile** | 50.3 | (0.7) | 53.4 | (0.7) | 54.8 | (0.6) | 59.8 | (0.8) | **-9.5** | (1.0) |
| **Colombia** | 58.7 | (1.3) | 58.5 | (1.0) | 59.9 | (0.7) | 61.0 | (0.7) | -1.9 | (1.5) |
| **Croatia** | 59.1 | (0.6) | 60.0 | (0.6) | 60.0 | (0.6) | 60.6 | (0.6) | **-1.5** | (0.7) |
| **Estonia** | 60.5 | (0.9) | 60.1 | (0.7) | 60.8 | (0.6) | 62.1 | (0.6) | -1.6 | (0.9) |
| **Hong Kong-China** | 66.0 | (0.7) | 64.4 | (0.7) | 64.3 | (0.6) | 61.8 | (0.5) | **4.3** | (0.7) |
| **Indonesia** | 55.8 | (0.7) | 56.0 | (0.7) | 55.4 | (1.2) | 56.7 | (1.0) | -0.9 | (1.1) |
| **Israel** | 48.5 | (0.9) | 51.3 | (0.8) | 53.9 | (0.9) | 55.1 | (0.7) | **-6.6** | (1.1) |
| **Jordan** | 41.3 | (0.8) | 43.0 | (0.7) | 44.3 | (0.7) | 46.0 | (0.8) | **-4.8** | (1.1) |
| **Kyrgyzstan** | 37.0 | (0.9) | 37.9 | (0.7) | 40.3 | (0.7) | 44.8 | (0.8) | **-7.8** | (1.1) |
| **Latvia** | 57.4 | (0.6) | 57.0 | (0.6) | 57.3 | (0.6) | 57.6 | (0.5) | -0.2 | (0.8) |
| **Liechtenstein** | 62.0 | (2.3) | 69.1 | (1.8) | 67.9 | (2.0) | 66.8 | (1.7) | -4.4 | (3.0) |
| **Lithuania** | 58.1 | (0.8) | 60.3 | (0.6) | 60.1 | (0.6) | 59.5 | (0.6) | -1.4 | (0.9) |
| **Macao-China** | 67.8 | (0.7) | 68.0 | (0.5) | 66.6 | (0.7) | 64.3 | (0.7) | **3.4** | (0.9) |
| **Montenegro** | 49.7 | (0.6) | 49.8 | (0.7) | 50.8 | (0.7) | 52.9 | (0.6) | **-3.2** | (1.0) |
| **Qatar** | 40.9 | (0.5) | 42.2 | (0.5) | 44.4 | (0.5) | 45.2 | (0.5) | **-4.4** | (0.8) |
| **Romania** | 47.8 | (1.3) | 48.4 | (0.8) | 48.5 | (0.7) | 50.1 | (0.6) | -2.2 | (1.4) |
| **Russian Federation** | 51.1 | (0.9) | 49.8 | (0.6) | 51.1 | (0.5) | 51.6 | (0.5) | -0.6 | (1.0) |
| **Serbia** | 57.9 | (0.6) | 57.8 | (0.7) | 57.3 | (0.7) | 57.9 | (0.6) | -0.0 | (0.9) |
| **Slovenia** | 53.8 | (0.6) | 55.3 | (0.5) | 58.1 | (0.6) | 60.6 | (0.6) | **-6.5** | (0.9) |
| **Chinese Taipei** | 64.9 | (0.5) | 61.4 | (0.7) | 60.8 | (0.5) | 58.6 | (0.5) | **6.4** | (0.7) |
| **Thailand** | 64.2 | (0.8) | 62.1 | (0.6) | 62.0 | (0.6) | 60.7 | (0.5) | **3.4** | (1.0) |
| **Tunisia** | 40.1 | (0.5) | 41.0 | (0.6) | 41.7 | (0.7) | 42.6 | (0.6) | **-2.3** | (0.9) |
| **Uruguay** | 58.6 | (0.9) | 58.5 | (0.7) | 59.0 | (0.6) | 60.7 | (0.6) | -2.1 | (1.1) |

*Note*: Values that are statistically significant at the 5% level (p < 0.05) are indicated in bold.

© OECD 2011 Quality Time for Students: Learning In and Out of School

**Table 3.7d** **Mean learning hours and allocation of total learning time in science, in mathematics and on the**
**[Part 6/7] language of instruction, by quarters of the PISA index of economic, social and cultural status (ESCS)**

| | | Allocation of total learning time in science, mathematics and the language of instruction for | | | | | | | | |
|---|---|---|---|---|---|---|---|---|---|---|
| | | Out-of-school-time lessons | | | | | | | | |
| | | Bottom quarter of ESCS | | Second quarter of ESCS | | Third quarter of ESCS | | Top quarter of ESCS | | Difference (bottom-top) | |
| | | % | S.E. | % | S.E. | % | S.E. | % | S.E. | Dif. | S.E. |
| OECD | Australia | 9.9 | (0.3) | 8.7 | (0.3) | 8.4 | (0.2) | 7.7 | (0.3) | **2.2** | (0.4) |
| | Austria | 6.3 | (0.4) | 5.8 | (0.4) | 4.7 | (0.3) | 4.7 | (0.3) | **1.6** | (0.5) |
| | Belgium | 9.6 | (0.3) | 8.0 | (0.4) | 7.3 | (0.3) | 6.0 | (0.3) | **3.5** | (0.5) |
| | Canada | 11.9 | (0.4) | 11.0 | (0.3) | 10.9 | (0.3) | 10.1 | (0.3) | **1.9** | (0.5) |
| | Czech Republic | 11.0 | (0.4) | 9.8 | (0.4) | 10.3 | (0.4) | 9.7 | (0.4) | **1.5** | (0.6) |
| | Denmark | 17.1 | (0.4) | 15.5 | (0.4) | 15.9 | (0.4) | 15.3 | (0.4) | **1.8** | (0.6) |
| | Finland | 7.2 | (0.4) | 6.7 | (0.4) | 6.5 | (0.3) | 5.4 | (0.3) | **1.8** | (0.5) |
| | France | 14.1 | (0.4) | 12.7 | (0.4) | 11.7 | (0.4) | 9.4 | (0.4) | **4.8** | (0.5) |
| | Germany | 11.4 | (0.5) | 9.2 | (0.4) | 9.0 | (0.5) | 7.6 | (0.3) | **3.9** | (0.6) |
| | Greece | 22.9 | (0.6) | 26.3 | (0.6) | 27.3 | (0.5) | 26.4 | (0.7) | **-3.5** | (1.0) |
| | Hungary | 20.6 | (0.5) | 18.5 | (0.5) | 18.8 | (0.4) | 17.0 | (0.5) | **3.6** | (0.7) |
| | Iceland | 6.7 | (0.4) | 6.9 | (0.4) | 7.9 | (0.4) | 7.2 | (0.3) | -0.6 | (0.5) |
| | Ireland | 9.2 | (0.5) | 9.2 | (0.3) | 8.8 | (0.4) | 7.6 | (0.3) | **1.7** | (0.6) |
| | Italy | 10.3 | (0.3) | 10.0 | (0.3) | 9.5 | (0.3) | 9.8 | (0.3) | 0.5 | (0.5) |
| | Japan | 7.8 | (0.4) | 6.7 | (0.4) | 7.3 | (0.4) | 7.9 | (0.4) | -0.1 | (0.5) |
| | Korea | 14.6 | (0.5) | 16.6 | (0.5) | 20.0 | (0.5) | 22.3 | (0.4) | **-7.7** | (0.7) |
| | Luxembourg | 13.3 | (0.5) | 11.6 | (0.4) | 9.6 | (0.4) | 8.1 | (0.3) | **5.4** | (0.6) |
| | Mexico | 16.7 | (0.8) | 14.3 | (0.4) | 15.2 | (0.4) | 12.6 | (0.5) | **4.1** | (1.0) |
| | Netherlands | 14.0 | (0.7) | 13.6 | (0.4) | 11.9 | (0.6) | 9.6 | (0.4) | **4.4** | (0.8) |
| | New Zealand | 9.9 | (0.6) | 8.3 | (0.4) | 7.6 | (0.4) | 7.1 | (0.4) | **2.9** | (0.6) |
| | Norway | 18.0 | (0.4) | 16.9 | (0.5) | 16.3 | (0.5) | 16.6 | (0.5) | **1.4** | (0.6) |
| | Poland | 10.6 | (0.5) | 10.2 | (0.4) | 9.7 | (0.4) | 9.7 | (0.3) | 0.9 | (0.6) |
| | Portugal | 11.2 | (0.6) | 10.8 | (0.5) | 9.8 | (0.4) | 9.2 | (0.3) | **2.1** | (0.7) |
| | Slovak Republic | 12.6 | (0.6) | 12.3 | (0.5) | 12.7 | (0.5) | 13.3 | (0.4) | -0.8 | (0.7) |
| | Spain | 12.0 | (0.4) | 11.7 | (0.4) | 11.4 | (0.4) | 9.8 | (0.5) | **2.3** | (0.7) |
| | Sweden | 11.0 | (0.4) | 10.3 | (0.5) | 10.1 | (0.4) | 9.5 | (0.4) | **1.5** | (0.5) |
| | Switzerland | 10.9 | (0.5) | 8.9 | (0.3) | 8.6 | (0.3) | 7.3 | (0.3) | **3.6** | (0.6) |
| | Turkey | 21.3 | (0.5) | 20.3 | (0.5) | 21.5 | (0.5) | 23.5 | (0.4) | **-2.1** | (0.6) |
| | United Kingdom | 8.6 | (0.4) | 8.4 | (0.3) | 8.3 | (0.2) | 7.3 | (0.3) | **1.3** | (0.4) |
| | United States | 18.2 | (0.8) | 16.5 | (0.5) | 14.6 | (0.5) | 11.8 | (0.5) | **6.4** | (0.9) |
| | **OECD average** | **12.6** | **(0.1)** | **11.9** | **(0.1)** | **11.7** | **(0.1)** | **11.0** | **(0.1)** | **1.7** | **(0.1)** |
| Partners | Argentina | 11.3 | (0.8) | 11.2 | (0.7) | 10.8 | (0.6) | 8.9 | (0.6) | **2.5** | (1.0) |
| | Azerbaijan | 20.4 | (0.7) | 19.6 | (0.7) | 18.9 | (0.5) | 20.0 | (0.5) | 0.2 | (0.8) |
| | Brazil | 16.8 | (0.7) | 17.8 | (0.6) | 17.2 | (0.6) | 16.8 | (0.5) | 0.1 | (0.9) |
| | Bulgaria | 18.8 | (0.6) | 17.8 | (0.7) | 15.5 | (0.6) | 15.2 | (0.6) | **3.8** | (0.9) |
| | Chile | 19.0 | (0.6) | 17.1 | (0.5) | 15.8 | (0.4) | 13.5 | (0.5) | **5.5** | (0.8) |
| | Colombia | 15.3 | (0.6) | 14.7 | (0.6) | 14.3 | (0.5) | 13.7 | (0.4) | **1.5** | (0.7) |
| | Croatia | 9.9 | (0.5) | 9.1 | (0.4) | 9.5 | (0.4) | 9.8 | (0.4) | 0.0 | (0.6) |
| | Estonia | 14.3 | (0.6) | 14.0 | (0.5) | 12.9 | (0.5) | 11.8 | (0.5) | **2.6** | (0.6) |
| | Hong Kong-China | 11.6 | (0.5) | 12.9 | (0.4) | 13.1 | (0.4) | 14.1 | (0.4) | **-2.4** | (0.6) |
| | Indonesia | 15.7 | (0.6) | 16.4 | (0.5) | 16.6 | (0.7) | 17.5 | (0.7) | **-1.7** | (0.6) |
| | Israel | 23.7 | (0.5) | 22.3 | (0.4) | 20.6 | (0.4) | 20.1 | (0.4) | **3.6** | (0.7) |
| | Jordan | 22.8 | (0.6) | 22.2 | (0.6) | 21.8 | (0.6) | 20.6 | (0.7) | **2.2** | (0.9) |
| | Kyrgyzstan | 25.8 | (0.8) | 26.9 | (0.6) | 26.0 | (0.7) | 22.0 | (0.6) | **3.7** | (1.0) |
| | Latvia | 13.2 | (0.6) | 12.9 | (0.6) | 12.4 | (0.5) | 12.4 | (0.5) | 0.8 | (0.8) |
| | Liechtenstein | 12.4 | (1.5) | 6.4 | (1.2) | 6.9 | (1.3) | 7.3 | (1.2) | **5.0** | (2.0) |
| | Lithuania | 12.6 | (0.6) | 11.3 | (0.5) | 10.5 | (0.4) | 10.0 | (0.5) | **2.6** | (0.7) |
| | Macao-China | 12.8 | (0.5) | 12.4 | (0.4) | 12.6 | (0.4) | 13.5 | (0.5) | -0.7 | (0.7) |
| | Montenegro | 14.5 | (0.5) | 14.9 | (0.6) | 14.9 | (0.6) | 13.8 | (0.6) | 0.8 | (0.8) |
| | Qatar | 26.1 | (0.5) | 25.4 | (0.4) | 23.5 | (0.5) | 23.6 | (0.4) | **2.6** | (0.6) |
| | Romania | 21.1 | (0.8) | 20.5 | (0.8) | 20.6 | (0.6) | 19.7 | (0.5) | 1.3 | (1.1) |
| | Russian Federation | 16.5 | (0.9) | 16.4 | (0.6) | 15.2 | (0.6) | 14.5 | (0.4) | **2.1** | (0.9) |
| | Serbia | 14.5 | (0.4) | 14.0 | (0.5) | 14.2 | (0.5) | 12.7 | (0.4) | **1.7** | (0.7) |
| | Slovenia | 16.3 | (0.5) | 14.7 | (0.5) | 13.4 | (0.4) | 11.2 | (0.4) | **5.0** | (0.6) |
| | Chinese Taipei | 12.4 | (0.4) | 13.7 | (0.4) | 14.4 | (0.4) | 15.4 | (0.3) | **-3.1** | (0.5) |
| | Thailand | 8.1 | (0.5) | 9.5 | (0.4) | 10.2 | (0.4) | 13.3 | (0.5) | **-5.2** | (0.7) |
| | Tunisia | 26.4 | (0.4) | 26.1 | (0.4) | 27.0 | (0.5) | 26.3 | (0.5) | -0.0 | (0.7) |
| | Uruguay | 12.6 | (0.5) | 13.1 | (0.5) | 13.6 | (0.5) | 11.1 | (0.4) | **1.4** | (0.7) |

*Note*: Values that are statistically significant at the 5% level (p < 0.05) are indicated in bold.

**Table 3.7d** Mean learning hours and allocation of total learning time in science, in mathematics and on the
[Part 7/7] language of instruction, by quarters of the PISA index of economic, social and cultural status (ESCS)

| | Allocation of total learning time in science, mathematics and the language of instruction for | | | | | | | | | |
|---|---|---|---|---|---|---|---|---|---|---|
| | Individual study | | | | | | | | | |
| | Bottom quarter of ESCS | | Second quarter of ESCS | | Third quarter of ESCS | | Top quarter of ESCS | | Difference (bottom-top) | |
| | % | S.E. | % | S.E. | % | S.E. | % | S.E. | Dif. | S.E. |
| **OECD** Australia | 23.0 | (0.3) | 24.2 | (0.3) | 25.2 | (0.3) | 26.9 | (0.3) | **-3.9** | (0.4) |
| Austria | 34.6 | (0.6) | 33.2 | (0.5) | 31.9 | (0.5) | 31.3 | (0.5) | **3.1** | (0.8) |
| Belgium | 26.7 | (0.4) | 27.3 | (0.4) | 28.6 | (0.4) | 29.0 | (0.4) | **-2.3** | (0.6) |
| Canada | 23.9 | (0.4) | 24.2 | (0.4) | 25.7 | (0.4) | 26.4 | (0.3) | **-2.5** | (0.4) |
| Czech Republic | 20.8 | (0.6) | 20.8 | (0.5) | 19.5 | (0.5) | 19.9 | (0.5) | 0.8 | (0.8) |
| Denmark | 21.2 | (0.4) | 21.6 | (0.3) | 22.2 | (0.3) | 22.0 | (0.3) | -0.9 | (0.5) |
| Finland | 22.4 | (0.4) | 22.8 | (0.4) | 23.8 | (0.4) | 23.3 | (0.4) | -1.0 | (0.5) |
| France | 23.4 | (0.5) | 23.7 | (0.5) | 24.9 | (0.4) | 26.2 | (0.4) | **-2.8** | (0.6) |
| Germany | 31.7 | (0.4) | 31.4 | (0.5) | 31.0 | (0.5) | 30.6 | (0.5) | 1.0 | (0.6) |
| Greece | 27.0 | (0.5) | 25.8 | (0.5) | 26.1 | (0.5) | 26.0 | (0.4) | 1.0 | (0.6) |
| Hungary | 29.3 | (0.5) | 28.5 | (0.4) | 29.2 | (0.5) | 28.6 | (0.4) | 0.8 | (0.6) |
| Iceland | 23.0 | (0.4) | 22.8 | (0.4) | 23.3 | (0.3) | 23.3 | (0.4) | -0.4 | (0.5) |
| Ireland | 25.8 | (0.6) | 27.4 | (0.5) | 28.8 | (0.4) | 29.4 | (0.6) | **-3.7** | (0.8) |
| Italy | 34.0 | (0.3) | 34.9 | (0.3) | 35.3 | (0.3) | 36.3 | (0.3) | **-2.4** | (0.4) |
| Japan | 15.7 | (0.4) | 17.8 | (0.5) | 18.8 | (0.5) | 19.9 | (0.5) | **-4.2** | (0.6) |
| Korea | 17.8 | (0.4) | 18.3 | (0.4) | 20.7 | (0.5) | 24.3 | (0.5) | **-6.6** | (0.6) |
| Luxembourg | 26.6 | (0.5) | 27.0 | (0.4) | 25.7 | (0.4) | 25.2 | (0.4) | **1.5** | (0.6) |
| Mexico | 32.2 | (0.5) | 32.5 | (0.4) | 31.8 | (0.4) | 29.7 | (0.4) | **2.4** | (0.7) |
| Netherlands | 27.0 | (0.5) | 27.0 | (0.5) | 28.4 | (0.4) | 28.7 | (0.5) | **-1.6** | (0.7) |
| New Zealand | 20.9 | (0.4) | 21.9 | (0.4) | 22.0 | (0.4) | 23.8 | (0.5) | **-3.0** | (0.6) |
| Norway | 21.5 | (0.4) | 22.4 | (0.5) | 22.6 | (0.4) | 23.9 | (0.4) | **-2.4** | (0.6) |
| Poland | 30.8 | (0.5) | 29.8 | (0.4) | 29.9 | (0.4) | 29.7 | (0.3) | 1.2 | (0.7) |
| Portugal | 31.5 | (0.6) | 31.8 | (0.5) | 31.7 | (0.4) | 31.0 | (0.5) | 0.5 | (0.8) |
| Slovak Republic | 27.7 | (0.7) | 28.5 | (0.4) | 29.1 | (0.6) | 28.0 | (0.6) | -0.2 | (0.9) |
| Spain | 29.2 | (0.5) | 29.6 | (0.4) | 29.8 | (0.4) | 30.4 | (0.4) | **-1.3** | (0.6) |
| Sweden | 22.0 | (0.5) | 23.6 | (0.6) | 24.2 | (0.4) | 24.5 | (0.5) | **-2.5** | (0.6) |
| Switzerland | 27.7 | (0.4) | 26.9 | (0.4) | 26.5 | (0.4) | 26.1 | (0.3) | **1.5** | (0.5) |
| Turkey | 27.7 | (0.4) | 28.1 | (0.5) | 26.9 | (0.4) | 25.0 | (0.4) | **2.7** | (0.6) |
| United Kingdom | 21.9 | (0.3) | 23.1 | (0.4) | 24.6 | (0.4) | 26.3 | (0.4) | **-4.4** | (0.4) |
| United States | 29.1 | (0.5) | 28.1 | (0.5) | 29.1 | (0.4) | 30.2 | (0.4) | -1.1 | (0.7) |
| **OECD average** | 25.9 | (0.1) | 26.2 | (0.1) | 26.6 | (0.1) | 26.9 | (0.1) | **-1.0** | (0.1) |
| **Partners** Argentina | 34.9 | (0.7) | 36.4 | (0.8) | 35.7 | (0.6) | 32.8 | (0.6) | **2.6** | (1.0) |
| Azerbaijan | 35.3 | (0.7) | 36.2 | (0.5) | 36.2 | (0.5) | 35.8 | (0.5) | -0.1 | (0.8) |
| Brazil | 31.5 | (0.7) | 29.4 | (0.5) | 30.3 | (0.5) | 28.3 | (0.5) | **3.1** | (0.8) |
| Bulgaria | 31.1 | (0.7) | 32.9 | (0.6) | 34.6 | (0.5) | 34.0 | (0.5) | **-2.8** | (0.9) |
| Chile | 30.7 | (0.5) | 29.5 | (0.5) | 29.5 | (0.5) | 26.7 | (0.5) | **4.0** | (0.6) |
| Colombia | 26.0 | (0.8) | 26.6 | (0.7) | 25.9 | (0.4) | 25.4 | (0.5) | 0.4 | (1.0) |
| Croatia | 31.0 | (0.5) | 30.8 | (0.5) | 30.5 | (0.6) | 29.6 | (0.5) | 1.4 | (0.7) |
| Estonia | 25.2 | (0.5) | 25.9 | (0.5) | 26.3 | (0.4) | 26.1 | (0.4) | -0.9 | (0.6) |
| Hong Kong-China | 22.3 | (0.6) | 22.7 | (0.5) | 22.6 | (0.5) | 24.2 | (0.4) | **-1.9** | (0.6) |
| Indonesia | 28.5 | (0.5) | 27.6 | (0.5) | 27.9 | (0.5) | 25.8 | (0.6) | **2.6** | (0.8) |
| Israel | 27.8 | (0.6) | 26.3 | (0.6) | 25.5 | (0.6) | 24.8 | (0.6) | **3.1** | (0.9) |
| Jordan | 36.0 | (0.5) | 34.8 | (0.5) | 33.9 | (0.5) | 33.4 | (0.5) | **2.6** | (0.7) |
| Kyrgyzstan | 37.2 | (0.5) | 35.2 | (0.6) | 33.8 | (0.6) | 33.2 | (0.5) | **4.1** | (0.7) |
| Latvia | 29.4 | (0.6) | 30.2 | (0.6) | 30.2 | (0.4) | 30.0 | (0.5) | -0.5 | (0.8) |
| Liechtenstein | 25.6 | (1.4) | 24.6 | (1.3) | 25.0 | (1.7) | 26.1 | (1.5) | -0.3 | (1.9) |
| Lithuania | 29.3 | (0.5) | 28.4 | (0.4) | 29.3 | (0.5) | 30.5 | (0.4) | **-1.3** | (0.6) |
| Macao-China | 19.4 | (0.5) | 19.6 | (0.4) | 20.7 | (0.5) | 22.1 | (0.4) | **-2.7** | (0.6) |
| Montenegro | 35.7 | (0.5) | 35.3 | (0.6) | 34.4 | (0.6) | 33.3 | (0.5) | **2.4** | (0.8) |
| Qatar | 33.1 | (0.4) | 32.5 | (0.3) | 32.1 | (0.3) | 31.2 | (0.4) | **1.9** | (0.6) |
| Romania | 31.2 | (0.7) | 31.1 | (0.5) | 31.0 | (0.6) | 30.2 | (0.4) | 0.9 | (0.7) |
| Russian Federation | 32.4 | (0.8) | 33.7 | (0.5) | 33.8 | (0.4) | 33.9 | (0.4) | **-1.5** | (0.6) |
| Serbia | 27.6 | (0.4) | 28.2 | (0.5) | 28.5 | (0.5) | 29.3 | (0.5) | **-1.7** | (0.6) |
| Slovenia | 29.9 | (0.5) | 29.9 | (0.5) | 28.4 | (0.5) | 28.3 | (0.5) | **1.6** | (0.8) |
| Chinese Taipei | 22.7 | (0.3) | 24.9 | (0.4) | 24.8 | (0.4) | 25.9 | (0.3) | **-3.3** | (0.5) |
| Thailand | 27.7 | (0.5) | 28.3 | (0.4) | 27.9 | (0.4) | 26.0 | (0.4) | **1.8** | (0.6) |
| Tunisia | 33.4 | (0.5) | 32.9 | (0.5) | 31.3 | (0.5) | 31.1 | (0.5) | **2.3** | (0.7) |
| Uruguay | 28.7 | (0.7) | 28.4 | (0.7) | 27.5 | (0.4) | 28.1 | (0.4) | 0.7 | (0.8) |

*Note*: Values that are statistically significant at the 5% level (p < 0.05) are indicated in bold.

© OECD 2011 Quality Time for Students: Learning In and Out of School

[Part 1/3]
## Table 3.8a Mean learning hours and allocation of total learning time in science, by immigrant status

| | | | | | | | | | | | | |
|---|---|---|---|---|---|---|---|---|---|---|---|---|
| | Mean learning hours per week | | | | | | | | | | | |
| | Regular school lessons | | | | | | Out-of-school-time lessons | | | | | |
| | Native students | | Students with an immigrant background | | Difference (native-immigrant) | | Native students | | Students with an immigrant background | | Difference (native-immigrant) | |
| | Mean | S.E. | Mean | S.E. | Dif. | S.E. | Mean | S.E. | Mean | S.E. | Dif. | S.E. |
| **OECD** | | | | | | | | | | | | |
| Australia | 3.18 | (0.04) | 3.51 | (0.06) | **-0.33** | (0.07) | 0.31 | (0.01) | 0.53 | (0.03) | **-0.22** | (0.03) |
| Austria | 2.51 | (0.07) | 2.15 | (0.10) | **0.36** | (0.11) | 0.19 | (0.01) | 0.35 | (0.05) | **-0.15** | (0.05) |
| Belgium | 2.66 | (0.04) | 2.38 | (0.10) | **0.29** | (0.09) | 0.29 | (0.01) | 0.51 | (0.05) | **-0.22** | (0.05) |
| Canada | 4.01 | (0.04) | 4.04 | (0.09) | -0.02 | (0.09) | 0.49 | (0.01) | 0.76 | (0.04) | **-0.26** | (0.04) |
| Czech Republic | 2.95 | (0.07) | 2.69 | (0.22) | 0.26 | (0.23) | 0.53 | (0.02) | 0.79 | (0.15) | -0.25 | (0.15) |
| Denmark | 3.23 | (0.04) | 2.96 | (0.13) | **0.27** | (0.12) | 0.75 | (0.02) | 1.05 | (0.07) | **-0.30** | (0.07) |
| Finland | 3.14 | (0.04) | 2.83 | (0.26) | 0.31 | (0.27) | 0.32 | (0.01) | 0.52 | (0.10) | **-0.20** | (0.10) |
| France | 2.91 | (0.05) | 2.55 | (0.12) | **0.36** | (0.13) | 0.53 | (0.02) | 0.74 | (0.06) | **-0.21** | (0.06) |
| Germany | 3.16 | (0.05) | 2.53 | (0.10) | **0.62** | (0.10) | 0.49 | (0.02) | 0.60 | (0.06) | **-0.11** | (0.06) |
| Greece | 3.24 | (0.05) | 2.61 | (0.14) | **0.63** | (0.14) | 2.04 | (0.04) | 1.40 | (0.12) | **0.63** | (0.12) |
| Hungary | 2.51 | (0.04) | 2.35 | (0.26) | 0.16 | (0.26) | 1.00 | (0.03) | 0.92 | (0.18) | 0.08 | (0.18) |
| Iceland | 2.97 | (0.02) | 2.86 | (0.20) | 0.11 | (0.20) | 0.28 | (0.01) | 0.57 | (0.14) | **-0.29** | (0.14) |
| Ireland | 2.53 | (0.04) | 2.65 | (0.14) | -0.12 | (0.14) | 0.31 | (0.01) | 0.47 | (0.07) | **-0.16** | (0.07) |
| Italy | 2.94 | (0.06) | 2.73 | (0.12) | 0.20 | (0.12) | 0.57 | (0.01) | 0.72 | (0.06) | **-0.15** | (0.07) |
| Japan | 2.70 | (0.05) | c | c | c | c | 0.26 | (0.01) | c | c | c | c |
| Korea | 3.60 | (0.06) | c | c | c | c | 1.03 | (0.04) | c | c | c | c |
| Luxembourg | 2.38 | (0.03) | 2.24 | (0.05) | 0.14 | (0.06) | 0.46 | (0.02) | 0.58 | (0.03) | **-0.12** | (0.03) |
| Mexico | 3.18 | (0.04) | 2.95 | (0.25) | **0.23** | (0.26) | 0.98 | (0.03) | 1.63 | (0.31) | **-0.65** | (0.31) |
| Netherlands | 2.22 | (0.04) | 1.83 | (0.12) | **0.39** | (0.12) | 0.51 | (0.02) | 0.76 | (0.05) | **-0.25** | (0.05) |
| New Zealand | 4.05 | (0.05) | 4.09 | (0.07) | -0.03 | (0.09) | 0.32 | (0.02) | 0.70 | (0.04) | **-0.38** | (0.04) |
| Norway | 2.64 | (0.03) | 2.70 | (0.10) | -0.06 | (0.10) | 0.91 | (0.02) | 1.30 | (0.09) | **-0.39** | (0.09) |
| Poland | 2.72 | (0.04) | c | c | c | c | 0.62 | (0.02) | c | c | c | c |
| Portugal | 3.25 | (0.05) | 2.71 | (0.19) | **0.54** | (0.19) | 0.63 | (0.02) | 0.67 | (0.09) | -0.04 | (0.10) |
| Slovak Republic | 2.46 | (0.07) | c | c | c | c | 0.65 | (0.03) | c | c | c | c |
| Spain | 3.14 | (0.04) | 2.89 | (0.14) | 0.26 | (0.14) | 0.68 | (0.03) | 0.64 | (0.05) | 0.03 | (0.06) |
| Sweden | 2.82 | (0.03) | 2.72 | (0.09) | 0.10 | (0.09) | 0.47 | (0.01) | 0.74 | (0.06) | **-0.27** | (0.06) |
| Switzerland | 2.46 | (0.05) | 2.08 | (0.05) | **0.38** | (0.06) | 0.36 | (0.01) | 0.50 | (0.03) | **-0.14** | (0.04) |
| Turkey | 2.88 | (0.09) | 3.13 | (0.33) | -0.25 | (0.31) | 1.36 | (0.05) | 1.11 | (0.34) | 0.24 | (0.33) |
| United Kingdom | 4.26 | (0.04) | 4.33 | (0.12) | -0.07 | (0.12) | 0.43 | (0.01) | 0.99 | (0.07) | **-0.56** | (0.07) |
| United States | 3.58 | (0.05) | 3.25 | (0.08) | **0.33** | (0.08) | 0.75 | (0.02) | 0.90 | (0.05) | **-0.15** | (0.05) |
| **OECD average** | 3.01 | (0.01) | 2.84 | (0.03) | **0.19** | (0.03) | 0.62 | (0.00) | 0.79 | (0.02) | **-0.17** | (0.02) |
| **Partners** | | | | | | | | | | | | |
| Argentina | 2.27 | (0.06) | 2.05 | (0.19) | 0.23 | (0.18) | 0.49 | (0.02) | 0.40 | (0.10) | 0.09 | (0.10) |
| Azerbaijan | 2.86 | (0.06) | 2.83 | (0.21) | 0.03 | (0.21) | 1.36 | (0.03) | 1.39 | (0.13) | -0.03 | (0.13) |
| Brazil | 2.23 | (0.03) | 1.61 | (0.12) | **0.62** | (0.12) | 0.78 | (0.02) | 0.81 | (0.12) | -0.03 | (0.11) |
| Bulgaria | 2.65 | (0.08) | c | c | c | c | 0.98 | (0.03) | c | c | c | c |
| Chile | 2.34 | (0.05) | c | c | c | c | 0.82 | (0.02) | c | c | c | c |
| Colombia | 3.53 | (0.11) | c | c | c | c | 0.95 | (0.04) | c | c | c | c |
| Croatia | 2.03 | (0.05) | 1.90 | (0.07) | 0.13 | (0.07) | 0.43 | (0.02) | 0.44 | (0.04) | -0.02 | (0.04) |
| Estonia | 3.29 | (0.04) | 3.24 | (0.11) | 0.06 | (0.11) | 0.73 | (0.02) | 0.94 | (0.07) | **-0.20** | (0.07) |
| Hong Kong-China | 3.14 | (0.08) | 3.16 | (0.08) | -0.02 | (0.11) | 0.99 | (0.04) | 0.74 | (0.04) | **0.24** | (0.05) |
| Indonesia | 3.24 | (0.07) | 1.85 | (0.39) | **1.39** | (0.40) | 1.04 | (0.04) | 1.06 | (0.16) | -0.02 | (0.16) |
| Israel | 2.41 | (0.06) | 2.57 | (0.10) | -0.17 | (0.10) | 0.94 | (0.03) | 1.00 | (0.05) | -0.06 | (0.05) |
| Jordan | 3.25 | (0.06) | 3.43 | (0.09) | -0.18 | (0.10) | 1.51 | (0.04) | 1.51 | (0.07) | 0.00 | (0.08) |
| Kyrgyzstan | 2.09 | (0.07) | 2.36 | (0.20) | -0.26 | (0.20) | 1.36 | (0.03) | 0.97 | (0.13) | **0.38** | (0.13) |
| Latvia | 2.86 | (0.06) | 3.02 | (0.14) | -0.16 | (0.13) | 0.63 | (0.02) | 0.90 | (0.07) | **-0.27** | (0.07) |
| Liechtenstein | 2.58 | (0.10) | 2.60 | (0.14) | -0.02 | (0.18) | 0.42 | (0.06) | 0.69 | (0.12) | **-0.27** | (0.13) |
| Lithuania | 2.70 | (0.04) | 2.75 | (0.22) | -0.05 | (0.21) | 0.56 | (0.02) | 0.50 | (0.08) | 0.06 | (0.08) |
| Macao-China | 3.47 | (0.07) | 3.86 | (0.04) | **-0.40** | (0.09) | 0.99 | (0.05) | 0.99 | (0.03) | -0.01 | (0.05) |
| Montenegro | 2.85 | (0.04) | 2.63 | (0.16) | 0.23 | (0.16) | 1.06 | (0.02) | 0.87 | (0.09) | 0.19 | (0.10) |
| Qatar | 2.33 | (0.04) | 3.20 | (0.05) | **-0.87** | (0.07) | 1.46 | (0.03) | 1.47 | (0.04) | -0.00 | (0.04) |
| Romania | 2.26 | (0.07) | c | c | c | c | 1.03 | (0.02) | c | c | c | c |
| Russian Federation | 3.75 | (0.09) | 3.56 | (0.16) | 0.19 | (0.16) | 1.12 | (0.03) | 1.14 | (0.08) | -0.02 | (0.08) |
| Serbia | 2.87 | (0.06) | 2.76 | (0.12) | 0.11 | (0.13) | 0.78 | (0.02) | 0.76 | (0.06) | 0.02 | (0.06) |
| Slovenia | 2.86 | (0.03) | 2.45 | (0.11) | **0.41** | (0.12) | 0.72 | (0.02) | 0.68 | (0.05) | 0.04 | (0.05) |
| Chinese Taipei | 2.91 | (0.05) | 2.15 | (0.32) | **0.76** | (0.31) | 0.78 | (0.02) | 0.80 | (0.23) | -0.02 | (0.23) |
| Thailand | 3.83 | (0.04) | c | c | c | c | 0.91 | (0.03) | c | c | c | c |
| Tunisia | 2.63 | (0.05) | 2.20 | (0.33) | 0.43 | (0.34) | 1.92 | (0.03) | 2.36 | (0.40) | -0.44 | (0.40) |
| Uruguay | 2.42 | (0.05) | c | c | c | c | 0.60 | (0.02) | c | c | c | c |

Note: Values that are statistically significant at the 5% level (p < 0.05) are indicated in bold.

[Part 2/3]
## Table 3.8a  Mean learning hours and allocation of total learning time in science, by immigrant status

| | Mean learning hours per week | | | | | | | | | | | |
| | Individual study | | | | | | Total learning hours | | | | | |
| | Native students | | Students with an immigrant background | | Difference (native-immigrant) | | Native students | | Students with an immigrant background | | Difference (native-immigrant) | |
| | Mean | S.E. | Mean | S.E. | Dif. | S.E. | Mean | S.E. | Mean | S.E. | Dif. | S.E. |
|---|---|---|---|---|---|---|---|---|---|---|---|---|
| Australia | 1.08 | (0.02) | 1.53 | (0.05) | **-0.45** | (0.04) | 4.56 | (0.05) | 5.56 | (0.11) | **-0.99** | (0.11) |
| Austria | 1.24 | (0.04) | 1.49 | (0.07) | -0.25 | (0.07) | 3.95 | (0.10) | 4.02 | (0.15) | -0.07 | (0.17) |
| Belgium | 1.25 | (0.02) | 1.26 | (0.06) | -0.00 | (0.06) | 4.22 | (0.06) | 4.10 | (0.16) | 0.12 | (0.15) |
| Canada | 1.42 | (0.02) | 2.05 | (0.06) | **-0.63** | (0.06) | 5.95 | (0.06) | 6.83 | (0.13) | **-0.88** | (0.14) |
| Czech Republic | 1.00 | (0.03) | 1.19 | (0.18) | -0.19 | (0.18) | 4.47 | (0.10) | 4.67 | (0.41) | -0.20 | (0.42) |
| Denmark | 1.06 | (0.02) | 1.46 | (0.08) | **-0.41** | (0.08) | 5.03 | (0.07) | 5.40 | (0.18) | **-0.37** | (0.17) |
| Finland | 1.07 | (0.02) | 1.12 | (0.11) | -0.05 | (0.11) | 4.53 | (0.06) | 4.49 | (0.34) | 0.04 | (0.34) |
| France | 1.30 | (0.03) | 1.38 | (0.08) | -0.08 | (0.08) | 4.75 | (0.09) | 4.69 | (0.19) | 0.06 | (0.21) |
| Germany | 1.70 | (0.03) | 1.70 | (0.07) | -0.00 | (0.07) | 5.36 | (0.07) | 4.77 | (0.15) | **0.59** | (0.16) |
| Greece | 1.87 | (0.04) | 1.54 | (0.11) | **0.33** | (0.11) | 7.15 | (0.10) | 5.53 | (0.29) | **1.61** | (0.27) |
| Hungary | 1.59 | (0.03) | 1.66 | (0.18) | -0.07 | (0.17) | 5.11 | (0.09) | 4.97 | (0.54) | 0.14 | (0.53) |
| Iceland | 1.16 | (0.02) | 1.37 | (0.18) | -0.21 | (0.18) | 4.42 | (0.04) | 4.84 | (0.37) | -0.42 | (0.36) |
| Ireland | 1.19 | (0.03) | 1.40 | (0.11) | -0.21 | (0.11) | 4.02 | (0.07) | 4.50 | (0.25) | -0.47 | (0.25) |
| Italy | 2.11 | (0.04) | 1.99 | (0.11) | 0.12 | (0.11) | 5.60 | (0.10) | 5.43 | (0.20) | 0.17 | (0.20) |
| Japan | 0.69 | (0.02) | c | c | c | c | 3.65 | (0.07) | c | c | c | c |
| Korea | 1.22 | (0.06) | c | c | c | c | 5.86 | (0.14) | c | c | c | c |
| Luxembourg | 1.25 | (0.02) | 1.24 | (0.04) | 0.01 | (0.04) | 4.10 | (0.06) | 4.05 | (0.08) | 0.05 | (0.10) |
| Mexico | 2.13 | (0.03) | 2.21 | (0.13) | -0.08 | (0.12) | 6.25 | (0.07) | 6.67 | (0.47) | -0.42 | (0.48) |
| Netherlands | 1.19 | (0.03) | 1.32 | (0.07) | -0.12 | (0.07) | 3.90 | (0.06) | 3.90 | (0.17) | 0.01 | (0.17) |
| New Zealand | 1.14 | (0.03) | 1.80 | (0.05) | **-0.66** | (0.06) | 5.52 | (0.07) | 6.58 | (0.10) | **-1.06** | (0.12) |
| Norway | 1.20 | (0.02) | 1.60 | (0.09) | **-0.40** | (0.09) | 4.75 | (0.05) | 5.63 | (0.20) | **-0.88** | (0.20) |
| Poland | 2.02 | (0.03) | c | c | c | c | 5.37 | (0.07) | c | c | c | c |
| Portugal | 2.08 | (0.04) | 2.15 | (0.15) | -0.07 | (0.15) | 5.97 | (0.08) | 5.43 | (0.36) | 0.53 | (0.37) |
| Slovak Republic | 1.39 | (0.04) | c | c | c | c | 4.52 | (0.12) | c | c | c | c |
| Spain | 1.73 | (0.03) | 1.76 | (0.09) | -0.03 | (0.09) | 5.58 | (0.08) | 5.29 | (0.17) | 0.29 | (0.19) |
| Sweden | 1.12 | (0.02) | 1.42 | (0.06) | **-0.30** | (0.06) | 4.41 | (0.04) | 4.89 | (0.13) | **-0.48** | (0.13) |
| Switzerland | 1.09 | (0.02) | 1.22 | (0.04) | **-0.13** | (0.04) | 3.90 | (0.06) | 3.80 | (0.10) | 0.10 | (0.11) |
| Turkey | 1.66 | (0.05) | 1.36 | (0.25) | 0.30 | (0.24) | 5.85 | (0.18) | 5.52 | (0.89) | 0.33 | (0.85) |
| United Kingdom | 1.40 | (0.02) | 1.95 | (0.07) | **-0.55** | (0.07) | 6.09 | (0.05) | 7.23 | (0.18) | **-1.13** | (0.18) |
| United States | 1.66 | (0.03) | 1.81 | (0.06) | **-0.15** | (0.06) | 6.02 | (0.07) | 5.98 | (0.14) | 0.04 | (0.15) |
| **OECD average** | 1.40 | (0.01) | 1.58 | (0.02) | **-0.16** | (0.02) | 5.03 | (0.02) | 5.18 | (0.06) | **-0.13** | (0.06) |
| Argentina | 1.59 | (0.04) | 1.54 | (0.14) | 0.05 | (0.13) | 4.33 | (0.09) | 4.02 | (0.25) | 0.31 | (0.26) |
| Azerbaijan | 2.65 | (0.05) | 2.63 | (0.27) | 0.03 | (0.28) | 6.87 | (0.11) | 6.76 | (0.41) | 0.11 | (0.41) |
| Brazil | 1.70 | (0.02) | 1.59 | (0.15) | 0.11 | (0.15) | 4.71 | (0.06) | 4.01 | (0.31) | **0.70** | (0.31) |
| Bulgaria | 2.01 | (0.06) | c | c | c | c | 5.65 | (0.13) | c | c | c | c |
| Chile | 1.52 | (0.03) | c | c | c | c | 4.70 | (0.07) | c | c | c | c |
| Colombia | 1.83 | (0.04) | c | c | c | c | 6.31 | (0.17) | c | c | c | c |
| Croatia | 1.47 | (0.04) | 1.43 | (0.07) | 0.04 | (0.07) | 3.94 | (0.09) | 3.81 | (0.14) | 0.14 | (0.13) |
| Estonia | 1.52 | (0.03) | 1.74 | (0.08) | -0.22 | (0.09) | 5.54 | (0.06) | 5.92 | (0.18) | **-0.38** | (0.18) |
| Hong Kong-China | 1.45 | (0.05) | 1.44 | (0.05) | 0.01 | (0.08) | 5.56 | (0.15) | 5.34 | (0.13) | 0.22 | (0.22) |
| Indonesia | 1.78 | (0.03) | 2.18 | (0.24) | -0.40 | (0.24) | 6.04 | (0.11) | 5.18 | (0.50) | 0.86 | (0.51) |
| Israel | 1.34 | (0.04) | 1.30 | (0.07) | 0.04 | (0.07) | 4.67 | (0.10) | 4.88 | (0.18) | -0.20 | (0.19) |
| Jordan | 2.62 | (0.05) | 2.82 | (0.10) | **-0.21** | (0.10) | 7.38 | (0.10) | 7.67 | (0.18) | -0.28 | (0.20) |
| Kyrgyzstan | 2.15 | (0.04) | 1.89 | (0.16) | 0.25 | (0.17) | 5.63 | (0.09) | 5.27 | (0.33) | 0.36 | (0.33) |
| Latvia | 1.79 | (0.03) | 2.01 | (0.10) | **-0.23** | (0.10) | 5.26 | (0.09) | 5.94 | (0.24) | **-0.68** | (0.24) |
| Liechtenstein | 1.23 | (0.08) | 1.14 | (0.11) | 0.09 | (0.15) | 4.26 | (0.14) | 4.38 | (0.22) | -0.12 | (0.30) |
| Lithuania | 1.69 | (0.03) | 1.58 | (0.15) | 0.11 | (0.14) | 4.94 | (0.06) | 4.85 | (0.32) | 0.09 | (0.32) |
| Macao-China | 1.38 | (0.05) | 1.37 | (0.03) | 0.01 | (0.06) | 5.84 | (0.13) | 6.22 | (0.07) | **-0.38** | (0.16) |
| Montenegro | 2.19 | (0.03) | 2.32 | (0.13) | -0.13 | (0.13) | 6.09 | (0.07) | 5.82 | (0.28) | 0.27 | (0.29) |
| Qatar | 1.86 | (0.03) | 2.28 | (0.04) | **-0.42** | (0.05) | 5.67 | (0.08) | 6.99 | (0.09) | **-1.32** | (0.11) |
| Romania | 1.61 | (0.05) | c | c | c | c | 4.87 | (0.11) | c | c | c | c |
| Russian Federation | 2.88 | (0.06) | 2.79 | (0.12) | 0.09 | (0.13) | 7.75 | (0.14) | 7.51 | (0.29) | 0.25 | (0.30) |
| Serbia | 1.71 | (0.04) | 1.66 | (0.10) | 0.06 | (0.10) | 5.37 | (0.10) | 5.17 | (0.22) | 0.21 | (0.22) |
| Slovenia | 1.56 | (0.02) | 1.32 | (0.06) | **0.24** | (0.07) | 5.15 | (0.05) | 4.47 | (0.17) | **0.68** | (0.18) |
| Chinese Taipei | 1.25 | (0.03) | 0.88 | (0.18) | **0.37** | (0.18) | 4.97 | (0.09) | 3.86 | (0.56) | **1.10** | (0.55) |
| Thailand | 1.82 | (0.03) | c | c | c | c | 6.55 | (0.07) | c | c | c | c |
| Tunisia | 2.61 | (0.04) | 3.13 | (0.44) | -0.53 | (0.45) | 7.14 | (0.10) | 7.73 | (0.80) | -0.59 | (0.80) |
| Uruguay | 1.33 | (0.03) | c | c | c | c | 4.37 | (0.08) | c | c | c | c |

*Note:* Values that are statistically significant at the 5% level (p < 0.05) are indicated in bold.

© OECD 2011  Quality Time for Students: Learning In and Out of School

[Part 3/3]
## Table 3.8a  Mean learning hours and allocation of total learning time in science, by immigrant status

| | | Allocation of total learning time in science for | | | | | | | | | | | | | | | | | |
| | | Regular school lessons | | | | | | Out-of-school-time lessons | | | | | | Individual study | | | | | |
| | | Native students | | Students with an immigrant background | | Difference (native-immigrant) | | Native students | | Students with an immigrant background | | Difference (native-immigrant) | | Native students | | Students with an immigrant background | | Difference (native-immigrant) | |
| | | % | S.E. | % | S.E. | Dif. | S.E. | % | S.E. | % | S.E. | Dif. | S.E. | % | S.E. | % | S.E. | Dif. | S.E. |
|---|---|---|---|---|---|---|---|---|---|---|---|---|---|---|---|---|---|---|---|
| OECD | Australia | 72.5 | (0.3) | 66.3 | (0.6) | **6.2** | (0.6) | 5.6 | (0.2) | 8.1 | (0.3) | **-2.5** | (0.3) | 21.9 | (0.2) | 25.6 | (0.5) | **-3.7** | (0.5) |
| | Austria | 65.2 | (0.6) | 57.1 | (1.3) | **8.1** | (1.3) | 3.8 | (0.2) | 7.0 | (0.9) | **-3.2** | (0.9) | 31.0 | (0.6) | 35.9 | (1.3) | **-4.9** | (1.3) |
| | Belgium | 64.2 | (0.4) | 59.2 | (1.2) | **4.9** | (1.2) | 6.0 | (0.2) | 10.5 | (0.8) | **-4.5** | (0.9) | 29.9 | (0.3) | 30.3 | (0.9) | -0.4 | (0.9) |
| | Canada | 68.3 | (0.3) | 59.8 | (0.8) | **8.5** | (0.8) | 7.9 | (0.2) | 10.2 | (0.5) | **-2.3** | (0.5) | 23.8 | (0.2) | 30.0 | (0.7) | **-6.2** | (0.7) |
| | Czech Republic | 68.9 | (0.6) | 63.2 | (3.4) | 5.7 | (3.5) | 9.8 | (0.3) | 13.2 | (2.2) | -3.4 | (2.2) | 21.3 | (0.4) | 23.6 | (3.4) | -2.3 | (3.5) |
| | Denmark | 67.4 | (0.5) | 56.9 | (1.8) | **10.5** | (1.8) | 12.7 | (0.3) | 17.1 | (1.0) | **-4.4** | (1.0) | 19.8 | (0.3) | 26.0 | (1.3) | **-6.2** | (1.3) |
| | Finland | 71.1 | (0.4) | 65.2 | (3.3) | 5.9 | (3.2) | 5.8 | (0.3) | 9.4 | (2.0) | -3.6 | (1.9) | 23.1 | (0.3) | 25.3 | (2.7) | -2.3 | (2.7) |
| | France | 63.6 | (0.5) | 58.7 | (1.1) | **4.9** | (1.1) | 10.4 | (0.3) | 13.5 | (0.9) | **-3.1** | (0.9) | 26.1 | (0.4) | 27.8 | (0.8) | -1.7 | (0.8) |
| | Germany | 58.9 | (0.5) | 53.3 | (1.2) | **5.6** | (1.2) | 8.0 | (0.3) | 11.4 | (1.0) | **-3.5** | (1.0) | 33.2 | (0.4) | 35.3 | (0.9) | -2.1 | (0.9) |
| | Greece | 48.4 | (0.6) | 50.3 | (2.1) | -1.9 | (2.1) | 26.3 | (0.5) | 23.6 | (1.8) | 2.7 | (1.9) | 25.3 | (0.4) | 26.1 | (1.7) | -0.8 | (1.7) |
| | Hungary | 51.6 | (0.5) | 50.6 | (2.8) | 1.1 | (2.7) | 17.9 | (0.5) | 13.9 | (2.1) | 3.9 | (2.1) | 30.5 | (0.5) | 35.5 | (2.7) | -5.0 | (2.7) |
| | Iceland | 70.3 | (0.3) | 60.2 | (3.2) | **10.1** | (3.1) | 4.9 | (0.2) | 12.2 | (2.6) | **-7.3** | (2.6) | 24.8 | (0.3) | 27.6 | (2.5) | -2.8 | (2.5) |
| | Ireland | 66.5 | (0.4) | 61.7 | (1.6) | **4.8** | (1.5) | 6.0 | (0.3) | 7.6 | (0.9) | -1.6 | (1.0) | 27.4 | (0.3) | 30.6 | (1.3) | **-3.2** | (1.3) |
| | Italy | 54.2 | (0.3) | 53.1 | (1.4) | 1.1 | (1.3) | 8.9 | (0.2) | 12.3 | (1.5) | **-3.4** | (1.5) | 36.9 | (0.2) | 34.6 | (1.2) | 2.3 | (1.2) |
| | Japan | 78.4 | (0.4) | c | c | c | c | 5.2 | (0.2) | c | c | c | c | 16.5 | (0.4) | c | c | c | c |
| | Korea | 67.5 | (0.6) | c | c | c | c | 13.8 | (0.4) | c | c | c | c | 18.7 | (0.4) | c | c | c | c |
| | Luxembourg | 61.5 | (0.5) | 57.1 | (0.8) | **4.4** | (1.1) | 8.6 | (0.3) | 12.4 | (0.6) | **-3.8** | (0.6) | 29.9 | (0.5) | 30.5 | (0.6) | -0.6 | (0.8) |
| | Mexico | 48.9 | (0.4) | 41.2 | (2.4) | **7.8** | (2.4) | 14.6 | (0.3) | 21.8 | (3.1) | **-7.3** | (3.0) | 36.5 | (0.4) | 37.0 | (2.4) | -0.5 | (2.4) |
| | Netherlands | 57.7 | (0.6) | 47.0 | (1.5) | **10.7** | (1.6) | 11.9 | (0.4) | 18.2 | (1.1) | **-6.3** | (1.3) | 30.4 | (0.4) | 34.8 | (1.5) | **-4.4** | (1.6) |
| | New Zealand | 75.4 | (0.4) | 64.9 | (0.8) | **10.5** | (0.9) | 5.1 | (0.2) | 9.7 | (0.6) | **-4.6** | (0.7) | 19.5 | (0.3) | 25.4 | (0.5) | **-5.9** | (0.6) |
| | Norway | 60.1 | (0.5) | 52.7 | (1.5) | **7.5** | (1.5) | 16.6 | (0.3) | 20.3 | (1.0) | **-3.8** | (1.0) | 23.3 | (0.3) | 27.0 | (1.0) | **-3.7** | (1.1) |
| | Poland | 53.2 | (0.4) | c | c | c | c | 10.2 | (0.3) | c | c | c | c | 36.5 | (0.4) | c | c | c | c |
| | Portugal | 54.9 | (0.5) | 50.5 | (2.2) | **4.4** | (2.3) | 9.3 | (0.3) | 9.5 | (1.0) | -0.3 | (1.0) | 35.8 | (0.4) | 40.0 | (2.0) | -4.2 | (2.1) |
| | Slovak Republic | 58.8 | (0.6) | c | c | c | c | 11.7 | (0.4) | c | c | c | c | 29.5 | (0.4) | c | c | c | c |
| | Spain | 59.3 | (0.4) | 56.5 | (1.6) | 2.8 | (1.6) | 10.6 | (0.3) | 10.7 | (0.8) | **-0.0** | (0.9) | 30.1 | (0.3) | 32.8 | (1.4) | -2.7 | (1.3) |
| | Sweden | 67.6 | (0.6) | 59.4 | (1.1) | **8.2** | (1.2) | 8.7 | (0.2) | 12.4 | (0.7) | **-3.7** | (0.8) | 23.6 | (0.5) | 28.1 | (0.8) | **-4.5** | (0.9) |
| | Switzerland | 63.5 | (0.4) | 57.4 | (0.8) | **6.1** | (0.8) | 7.6 | (0.2) | 10.6 | (0.5) | **-3.1** | (0.6) | 28.9 | (0.3) | 31.9 | (0.8) | **-3.0** | (0.8) |
| | Turkey | 51.1 | (0.6) | 56.9 | (4.6) | -5.7 | (4.5) | 21.0 | (0.4) | 16.7 | (3.6) | 4.3 | (3.6) | 27.9 | (0.5) | 26.4 | (2.9) | 1.5 | (3.0) |
| | United Kingdom | 71.8 | (0.3) | 61.4 | (1.0) | **10.4** | (1.0) | 6.1 | (0.2) | 12.5 | (0.9) | **-6.4** | (0.9) | 22.1 | (0.3) | 26.1 | (0.7) | **-4.0** | (0.7) |
| | United States | 59.4 | (0.5) | 54.9 | (0.9) | **4.5** | (1.0) | 12.0 | (0.4) | 14.4 | (0.7) | **-2.5** | (0.8) | 28.6 | (0.3) | 30.7 | (0.6) | **-2.1** | (0.6) |
| | **OECD average** | 62.7 | (0.1) | 56.8 | (0.4) | **5.6** | (0.4) | 10.2 | (0.1) | 13.1 | (0.3) | **-2.8** | (0.3) | 27.1 | (0.1) | 30.2 | (0.3) | **-2.8** | (0.3) |
| PARTNERS | Argentina | 53.2 | (0.8) | 51.8 | (3.3) | 1.4 | (3.3) | 9.6 | (0.4) | 11.0 | (3.2) | -1.4 | (3.1) | 37.3 | (0.7) | 37.2 | (2.3) | 0.0 | (2.4) |
| | Azerbaijan | 43.1 | (0.6) | 43.9 | (3.9) | -0.8 | (3.9) | 19.3 | (0.4) | 20.3 | (2.2) | -1.0 | (2.1) | 37.6 | (0.4) | 35.8 | (3.1) | 1.8 | (3.2) |
| | Brazil | 50.5 | (0.4) | 46.5 | (3.0) | 4.0 | (2.9) | 13.9 | (0.3) | 19.0 | (2.3) | -5.0 | (2.3) | 35.5 | (0.4) | 34.5 | (2.9) | 1.0 | (2.9) |
| | Bulgaria | 49.1 | (0.7) | c | c | c | c | 16.1 | (0.6) | c | c | c | c | 34.8 | (0.4) | c | c | c | c |
| | Chile | 49.2 | (0.6) | c | c | c | c | 16.2 | (0.4) | c | c | c | c | 34.6 | (0.4) | c | c | c | c |
| | Colombia | 59.1 | (0.6) | c | c | c | c | 13.0 | (0.3) | c | c | c | c | 28.0 | (0.4) | c | c | c | c |
| | Croatia | 54.8 | (0.5) | 52.6 | (1.4) | 2.3 | (1.4) | 9.6 | (0.4) | 11.1 | (0.9) | -1.5 | (0.9) | 35.6 | (0.5) | 36.3 | (1.2) | -0.8 | (1.2) |
| | Estonia | 62.2 | (0.5) | 57.3 | (1.2) | **5.0** | (1.2) | 12.1 | (0.3) | 15.1 | (1.1) | **-3.0** | (1.1) | 25.7 | (0.4) | 27.6 | (0.9) | **-2.0** | (1.0) |
| | Hong Kong-China | 59.5 | (0.6) | 62.8 | (0.9) | **-3.4** | (1.1) | 15.7 | (0.4) | 11.7 | (0.6) | **4.0** | (0.6) | 24.8 | (0.5) | 25.4 | (0.6) | -0.6 | (0.7) |
| | Indonesia | 54.8 | (0.9) | 38.5 | (7.8) | **16.3** | (7.8) | 15.4 | (0.6) | 18.8 | (2.5) | -3.4 | (2.6) | 29.8 | (0.4) | 42.7 | (6.4) | **-12.9** | (6.4) |
| | Israel | 54.9 | (0.8) | 55.6 | (1.2) | -0.7 | (1.4) | 17.9 | (0.5) | 18.0 | (0.7) | -0.1 | (0.9) | 27.2 | (0.6) | 26.4 | (1.0) | 0.8 | (1.0) |
| | Jordan | 43.4 | (0.6) | 42.5 | (1.0) | 0.8 | (1.2) | 20.1 | (0.4) | 19.7 | (0.9) | 0.4 | (1.0) | 36.5 | (0.4) | 37.8 | (0.8) | -1.2 | (0.9) |
| | Kyrgyzstan | 35.5 | (0.6) | 45.6 | (3.7) | **-10.1** | (3.7) | 25.7 | (0.6) | 19.2 | (2.6) | **6.5** | (2.6) | 38.8 | (0.4) | 35.2 | (2.9) | 3.6 | (3.0) |
| | Latvia | 56.3 | (0.5) | 53.1 | (1.2) | **3.2** | (1.2) | 10.2 | (0.3) | 13.3 | (0.9) | **-3.1** | (0.9) | 33.4 | (0.4) | 33.5 | (1.2) | -0.1 | (1.2) |
| | Liechtenstein | 62.5 | (1.6) | 60.9 | (2.8) | 1.6 | (3.2) | 8.7 | (1.0) | 12.6 | (2.0) | -3.9 | (2.2) | 28.8 | (1.5) | 26.5 | (2.0) | 2.3 | (2.3) |
| | Lithuania | 57.2 | (0.5) | 58.2 | (2.7) | -1.0 | (2.6) | 9.9 | (0.3) | 9.7 | (1.5) | 0.2 | (1.6) | 32.8 | (0.3) | 32.1 | (2.2) | 0.7 | (2.2) |
| | Macao-China | 63.3 | (0.8) | 65.4 | (0.5) | **-2.1** | (0.9) | 15.1 | (0.6) | 14.1 | (0.4) | 1.0 | (0.7) | 21.5 | (0.6) | 20.4 | (0.4) | 1.1 | (0.7) |
| | Montenegro | 47.1 | (0.4) | 45.4 | (2.0) | 1.7 | (2.0) | 16.1 | (0.3) | 13.2 | (1.4) | 2.9 | (1.4) | 36.8 | (0.5) | 41.4 | (1.7) | -4.6 | (1.7) |
| | Qatar | 38.7 | (0.5) | 44.6 | (0.5) | **-5.9** | (0.7) | 26.6 | (0.4) | 21.5 | (0.5) | **5.1** | (0.7) | 34.7 | (0.4) | 33.8 | (0.5) | 0.9 | (0.6) |
| | Romania | 48.1 | (0.6) | c | c | c | c | 19.5 | (0.5) | c | c | c | c | 32.4 | (0.5) | c | c | c | c |
| | Russian Federation | 48.6 | (0.5) | 48.9 | (1.1) | -0.3 | (1.2) | 14.9 | (0.5) | 14.9 | (1.0) | 0.1 | (1.0) | 36.4 | (0.5) | 36.2 | (1.0) | 0.2 | (1.0) |
| | Serbia | 56.9 | (0.6) | 57.2 | (1.3) | -0.3 | (1.5) | 13.3 | (0.4) | 13.4 | (1.0) | -0.1 | (1.0) | 29.8 | (0.5) | 29.4 | (1.2) | 0.4 | (1.3) |
| | Slovenia | 55.7 | (0.4) | 56.1 | (1.3) | -0.4 | (1.4) | 13.0 | (0.3) | 14.0 | (0.9) | -0.9 | (1.0) | 31.3 | (0.4) | 30.0 | (1.0) | 1.3 | (1.1) |
| | Chinese Taipei | 63.7 | (0.3) | 61.4 | (5.1) | 2.3 | (5.1) | 12.2 | (0.2) | 18.3 | (3.5) | -6.1 | (3.5) | 24.1 | (0.3) | 20.3 | (3.3) | 3.8 | (3.3) |
| | Thailand | 63.9 | (0.4) | c | c | c | c | 9.9 | (0.3) | c | c | c | c | 26.2 | (0.3) | c | c | c | c |
| | Tunisia | 37.5 | (0.4) | 28.9 | (4.3) | 8.6 | (4.2) | 25.8 | (0.4) | 27.6 | (3.4) | -1.8 | (3.4) | 36.8 | (0.4) | 43.5 | (4.1) | -6.8 | (4.1) |
| | Uruguay | 56.4 | (0.5) | c | c | c | c | 11.7 | (0.3) | c | c | c | c | 31.9 | (0.4) | c | c | c | c |

*Note:* Values that are statistically significant at the 5% level (p < 0.05) are indicated in bold.

[Part 1/3] **Table 3.8b  Mean learning hours and allocation of total learning time in mathematics, by immigrant status**

| | Mean learning hours per week | | | | | | | | | | | |
| | Regular school lessons | | | | | | Out-of-school-time lessons | | | | | |
| | Native students | | Students with an immigrant background | | Difference (native-immigrant) | | Native students | | Students with an immigrant background | | Difference (native-immigrant) | |
| | Mean | S.E. | Mean | S.E. | Dif. | S.E. | Mean | S.E. | Mean | S.E. | Dif. | S.E. |
|---|---|---|---|---|---|---|---|---|---|---|---|---|
| **OECD** Australia | 4.04 | (0.03) | 4.31 | (0.05) | **-0.27** | (0.05) | 0.63 | (0.01) | 1.13 | (0.05) | **-0.50** | (0.05) |
| Austria | 3.21 | (0.05) | 3.31 | (0.10) | -0.10 | (0.10) | 0.47 | (0.02) | 0.77 | (0.07) | **-0.30** | (0.08) |
| Belgium | 3.61 | (0.04) | 3.38 | (0.10) | **0.23** | (0.11) | 0.52 | (0.01) | 0.79 | (0.06) | **-0.27** | (0.06) |
| Canada | 4.52 | (0.04) | 4.50 | (0.07) | 0.02 | (0.07) | 0.83 | (0.02) | 1.30 | (0.05) | **-0.47** | (0.05) |
| Czech Republic | 4.00 | (0.05) | 3.98 | (0.19) | 0.02 | (0.20) | 0.75 | (0.02) | 0.82 | (0.17) | -0.06 | (0.18) |
| Denmark | 4.44 | (0.03) | 4.39 | (0.10) | 0.05 | (0.10) | 1.32 | (0.03) | 1.84 | (0.10) | **-0.52** | (0.10) |
| Finland | 3.46 | (0.04) | 3.11 | (0.17) | **0.35** | (0.17) | 0.36 | (0.02) | 0.76 | (0.17) | **-0.40** | (0.17) |
| France | 3.87 | (0.03) | 3.66 | (0.09) | **0.21** | (0.09) | 0.89 | (0.02) | 1.19 | (0.06) | **-0.30** | (0.07) |
| Germany | 3.86 | (0.04) | 4.02 | (0.08) | **-0.16** | (0.08) | 0.74 | (0.02) | 1.19 | (0.09) | **-0.45** | (0.09) |
| Greece | 3.48 | (0.05) | 3.20 | (0.14) | **0.28** | (0.14) | 2.31 | (0.06) | 1.31 | (0.10) | **1.00** | (0.12) |
| Hungary | 3.29 | (0.04) | 3.44 | (0.26) | -0.15 | (0.26) | 1.28 | (0.03) | 1.38 | (0.25) | -0.10 | (0.26) |
| Iceland | 4.74 | (0.02) | 4.66 | (0.25) | 0.08 | (0.25) | 0.71 | (0.02) | 1.09 | (0.17) | **-0.38** | (0.17) |
| Ireland | 3.64 | (0.03) | 3.80 | (0.11) | -0.15 | (0.11) | 0.70 | (0.02) | 0.93 | (0.12) | -0.23 | (0.12) |
| Italy | 3.76 | (0.03) | 3.63 | (0.11) | 0.13 | (0.11) | 0.88 | (0.02) | 1.02 | (0.07) | -0.14 | (0.07) |
| Japan | 4.24 | (0.07) | c | c | c | c | 0.71 | (0.03) | c | c | c | c |
| Korea | 4.71 | (0.04) | c | c | c | c | 2.28 | (0.04) | c | c | c | c |
| Luxembourg | 3.90 | (0.03) | 3.78 | (0.05) | **0.12** | (0.05) | 0.77 | (0.02) | 0.94 | (0.04) | **-0.18** | (0.04) |
| Mexico | 4.01 | (0.03) | 2.89 | (0.33) | **1.12** | (0.33) | 1.16 | (0.03) | 1.43 | (0.18) | -0.26 | (0.18) |
| Netherlands | 2.87 | (0.03) | 2.90 | (0.10) | -0.02 | (0.10) | 0.64 | (0.02) | 1.04 | (0.06) | **-0.40** | (0.06) |
| New Zealand | 4.40 | (0.03) | 4.34 | (0.07) | 0.06 | (0.07) | 0.55 | (0.02) | 1.15 | (0.05) | **-0.60** | (0.06) |
| Norway | 3.39 | (0.03) | 3.44 | (0.09) | -0.05 | (0.09) | 1.02 | (0.02) | 1.42 | (0.09) | **-0.40** | (0.09) |
| Poland | 4.36 | (0.04) | c | c | c | c | 0.77 | (0.02) | c | c | c | c |
| Portugal | 3.64 | (0.04) | 3.37 | (0.11) | **0.26** | (0.12) | 0.81 | (0.02) | 0.87 | (0.08) | -0.06 | (0.08) |
| Slovak Republic | 3.28 | (0.05) | c | c | c | c | 0.88 | (0.03) | c | c | c | c |
| Spain | 3.44 | (0.03) | 3.23 | (0.10) | **0.21** | (0.10) | 1.00 | (0.02) | 0.89 | (0.08) | 0.10 | (0.09) |
| Sweden | 3.09 | (0.02) | 3.16 | (0.08) | -0.08 | (0.07) | 0.56 | (0.01) | 1.00 | (0.07) | **-0.44** | (0.07) |
| Switzerland | 3.85 | (0.04) | 3.88 | (0.05) | -0.03 | (0.06) | 0.62 | (0.02) | 0.96 | (0.05) | **-0.34** | (0.05) |
| Turkey | 3.84 | (0.06) | 3.42 | (0.36) | 0.42 | (0.36) | 2.09 | (0.05) | 1.67 | (0.49) | 0.42 | (0.50) |
| United Kingdom | 3.77 | (0.03) | 3.88 | (0.10) | -0.10 | (0.10) | 0.57 | (0.01) | 1.24 | (0.07) | **-0.67** | (0.07) |
| United States | 3.84 | (0.05) | 3.49 | (0.07) | **0.35** | (0.08) | 1.10 | (0.03) | 1.35 | (0.06) | **-0.25** | (0.07) |
| **OECD average** | 3.82 | (0.01) | 3.66 | (0.03) | **0.11** | (0.03) | 0.93 | (0.00) | 1.13 | (0.03) | **-0.24** | (0.03) |
| **Partners** Argentina | 2.96 | (0.06) | 2.80 | (0.25) | 0.16 | (0.25) | 0.78 | (0.04) | 0.48 | (0.08) | **0.30** | (0.09) |
| Azerbaijan | 3.81 | (0.06) | 3.76 | (0.27) | 0.05 | (0.27) | 1.69 | (0.05) | 1.85 | (0.24) | -0.16 | (0.23) |
| Brazil | 3.18 | (0.04) | 2.50 | (0.20) | **0.67** | (0.20) | 1.20 | (0.03) | 1.20 | (0.16) | 0.01 | (0.16) |
| Bulgaria | 2.99 | (0.07) | c | c | c | c | 1.12 | (0.04) | c | c | c | c |
| Chile | 3.50 | (0.06) | c | c | c | c | 0.99 | (0.03) | c | c | c | c |
| Colombia | 4.24 | (0.06) | c | c | c | c | 1.22 | (0.03) | c | c | c | c |
| Croatia | 3.04 | (0.04) | 3.10 | (0.07) | -0.05 | (0.08) | 0.75 | (0.02) | 0.80 | (0.06) | -0.05 | (0.06) |
| Estonia | 4.21 | (0.04) | 4.21 | (0.10) | -0.01 | (0.10) | 0.98 | (0.03) | 1.08 | (0.05) | -0.10 | (0.06) |
| Hong Kong-China | 5.22 | (0.05) | 5.25 | (0.05) | -0.02 | (0.05) | 1.56 | (0.04) | 1.18 | (0.05) | **0.37** | (0.06) |
| Indonesia | 4.10 | (0.07) | 3.09 | (0.54) | 1.01 | (0.54) | 1.36 | (0.05) | 1.31 | (0.33) | 0.05 | (0.33) |
| Israel | 4.09 | (0.04) | 4.36 | (0.07) | **-0.27** | (0.08) | 2.11 | (0.05) | 2.29 | (0.07) | **-0.18** | (0.08) |
| Jordan | 3.48 | (0.05) | 3.62 | (0.09) | -0.14 | (0.11) | 1.81 | (0.04) | 1.84 | (0.07) | -0.03 | (0.08) |
| Kyrgyzstan | 2.88 | (0.05) | 3.42 | (0.20) | **-0.53** | (0.19) | 1.55 | (0.04) | 1.56 | (0.26) | -0.01 | (0.25) |
| Latvia | 4.51 | (0.04) | 4.39 | (0.10) | 0.12 | (0.10) | 1.19 | (0.04) | 1.30 | (0.07) | -0.10 | (0.08) |
| Liechtenstein | 4.05 | (0.10) | 3.81 | (0.14) | 0.25 | (0.16) | 0.51 | (0.06) | 0.70 | (0.10) | -0.19 | (0.13) |
| Lithuania | 3.51 | (0.04) | 3.72 | (0.18) | -0.21 | (0.18) | 0.74 | (0.02) | 0.71 | (0.12) | 0.03 | (0.13) |
| Macao-China | 5.39 | (0.06) | 5.44 | (0.03) | -0.05 | (0.07) | 1.27 | (0.05) | 1.18 | (0.03) | 0.09 | (0.06) |
| Montenegro | 3.10 | (0.04) | 2.99 | (0.14) | 0.11 | (0.15) | 0.92 | (0.02) | 0.86 | (0.12) | 0.06 | (0.12) |
| Qatar | 2.84 | (0.04) | 3.51 | (0.04) | **-0.66** | (0.06) | 1.90 | (0.04) | 1.73 | (0.04) | **0.17** | (0.06) |
| Romania | 3.01 | (0.07) | c | c | c | c | 1.50 | (0.03) | c | c | c | c |
| Russian Federation | 3.65 | (0.06) | 3.56 | (0.10) | 0.09 | (0.11) | 1.14 | (0.03) | 1.06 | (0.07) | 0.08 | (0.07) |
| Serbia | 3.27 | (0.04) | 3.35 | (0.09) | -0.08 | (0.09) | 0.97 | (0.03) | 1.02 | (0.08) | -0.06 | (0.09) |
| Slovenia | 3.34 | (0.03) | 3.18 | (0.08) | 0.17 | (0.09) | 1.01 | (0.02) | 1.11 | (0.07) | -0.10 | (0.08) |
| Chinese Taipei | 4.28 | (0.05) | 3.29 | (0.41) | **0.99** | (0.40) | 1.54 | (0.03) | 1.51 | (0.29) | 0.02 | (0.29) |
| Thailand | 3.79 | (0.03) | c | c | c | c | 0.92 | (0.03) | c | c | c | c |
| Tunisia | 3.41 | (0.04) | 3.18 | (0.31) | 0.22 | (0.32) | 2.42 | (0.04) | 2.44 | (0.22) | -0.02 | (0.23) |
| Uruguay | 3.33 | (0.03) | c | c | c | c | 0.83 | (0.03) | c | c | c | c |

*Note*: Values that are statistically significant at the 5% level (p < 0.05) are indicated in bold.

© OECD 2011  Quality Time for Students: Learning In and Out of School

[Part 2/3]
## Table 3.8b Mean learning hours and allocation of total learning time in mathematics, by immigrant status

| | Mean learning hours per week | | | | | | | | | | | |
| | Individual study | | | | | | Total learning hours | | | | | |
| | Native students | | Students with an immigrant background | | Difference (native-immigrant) | | Native students | | Students with an immigrant background | | Difference (native-immigrant) | |
| | Mean | S.E. | Mean | S.E. | Dif. | S.E. | Mean | S.E. | Mean | S.E. | Dif. | S.E. |
|---|---|---|---|---|---|---|---|---|---|---|---|---|
| **Australia** | 1.64 | (0.02) | 2.33 | (0.05) | **-0.69** | (0.05) | 6.32 | (0.04) | 7.79 | (0.12) | **-1.47** | (0.13) |
| Austria | 2.08 | (0.04) | 2.44 | (0.09) | **-0.36** | (0.10) | 5.77 | (0.09) | 6.57 | (0.20) | **-0.80** | (0.21) |
| Belgium | 1.81 | (0.03) | 1.71 | (0.07) | 0.09 | (0.07) | 5.96 | (0.06) | 5.86 | (0.18) | 0.10 | (0.18) |
| Canada | 1.84 | (0.02) | 2.47 | (0.08) | **-0.63** | (0.08) | 7.23 | (0.06) | 8.27 | (0.17) | **-1.03** | (0.17) |
| Czech Republic | 1.31 | (0.03) | 1.58 | (0.20) | -0.28 | (0.20) | 6.05 | (0.08) | 6.38 | (0.41) | -0.33 | (0.42) |
| Denmark | 1.72 | (0.03) | 2.05 | (0.09) | **-0.33** | (0.10) | 7.47 | (0.06) | 8.18 | (0.21) | **-0.71** | (0.21) |
| Finland | 1.20 | (0.02) | 1.40 | (0.13) | -0.21 | (0.12) | 5.02 | (0.06) | 5.27 | (0.26) | -0.26 | (0.26) |
| France | 1.73 | (0.03) | 1.85 | (0.09) | -0.12 | (0.10) | 6.49 | (0.06) | 6.68 | (0.18) | -0.19 | (0.18) |
| Germany | 2.23 | (0.04) | 2.52 | (0.08) | **-0.29** | (0.09) | 6.86 | (0.07) | 7.71 | (0.19) | **-0.86** | (0.19) |
| Greece | 2.02 | (0.04) | 1.75 | (0.10) | **0.27** | (0.11) | 7.83 | (0.10) | 6.25 | (0.27) | **1.58** | (0.29) |
| Hungary | 1.84 | (0.03) | 1.74 | (0.18) | 0.10 | (0.19) | 6.41 | (0.09) | 6.60 | (0.51) | -0.18 | (0.51) |
| Iceland | 1.71 | (0.02) | 1.85 | (0.23) | -0.14 | (0.23) | 7.16 | (0.05) | 7.63 | (0.41) | -0.47 | (0.41) |
| Ireland | 1.74 | (0.03) | 2.06 | (0.12) | **-0.31** | (0.12) | 6.09 | (0.07) | 6.78 | (0.26) | **-0.69** | (0.26) |
| Italy | 2.49 | (0.04) | 2.49 | (0.11) | 0.00 | (0.12) | 7.14 | (0.07) | 7.14 | (0.19) | 0.00 | (0.20) |
| Japan | 1.48 | (0.06) | c | c | c | c | 6.43 | (0.13) | c | c | c | c |
| Korea | 2.32 | (0.07) | c | c | c | c | 9.34 | (0.13) | c | c | c | c |
| Luxembourg | 1.72 | (0.03) | 1.68 | (0.04) | 0.04 | (0.05) | 6.41 | (0.06) | 6.44 | (0.08) | -0.03 | (0.10) |
| Mexico | 2.25 | (0.03) | 2.40 | (0.24) | -0.14 | (0.24) | 7.39 | (0.06) | 6.59 | (0.52) | 0.80 | (0.51) |
| Netherlands | 1.43 | (0.03) | 1.77 | (0.08) | **-0.33** | (0.08) | 4.94 | (0.07) | 5.64 | (0.20) | **-0.70** | (0.20) |
| New Zealand | 1.45 | (0.03) | 2.12 | (0.06) | **-0.68** | (0.07) | 6.41 | (0.05) | 7.61 | (0.12) | **-1.21** | (0.14) |
| Norway | 1.37 | (0.03) | 1.82 | (0.11) | **-0.44** | (0.11) | 5.78 | (0.06) | 6.70 | (0.21) | **-0.92** | (0.20) |
| Poland | 2.10 | (0.03) | c | c | c | c | 7.24 | (0.06) | c | c | c | c |
| Portugal | 1.95 | (0.03) | 2.11 | (0.12) | -0.16 | (0.12) | 6.39 | (0.07) | 6.32 | (0.24) | 0.07 | (0.24) |
| Slovak Republic | 1.69 | (0.03) | c | c | c | c | 5.87 | (0.10) | c | c | c | c |
| Spain | 1.96 | (0.03) | 2.00 | (0.12) | -0.04 | (0.12) | 6.44 | (0.06) | 6.12 | (0.18) | 0.31 | (0.18) |
| Sweden | 1.12 | (0.02) | 1.65 | (0.08) | **-0.53** | (0.09) | 4.77 | (0.04) | 5.86 | (0.15) | **-1.10** | (0.15) |
| Switzerland | 1.64 | (0.03) | 1.85 | (0.04) | **-0.22** | (0.05) | 6.13 | (0.07) | 6.71 | (0.09) | **-0.58** | (0.12) |
| Turkey | 2.32 | (0.05) | 1.85 | (0.37) | 0.47 | (0.38) | 8.21 | (0.14) | 6.88 | (1.23) | 1.33 | (1.25) |
| United Kingdom | 1.44 | (0.02) | 1.97 | (0.05) | **-0.52** | (0.06) | 5.79 | (0.05) | 7.07 | (0.12) | **-1.29** | (0.13) |
| United States | 2.04 | (0.03) | 2.09 | (0.07) | -0.05 | (0.09) | 7.03 | (0.07) | 6.95 | (0.16) | 0.08 | (0.18) |
| **OECD average** | 1.79 | (0.01) | 1.98 | (0.03) | **-0.21** | (0.03) | 6.55 | (0.01) | 6.77 | (0.07) | **-0.33** | (0.07) |
| Argentina | 1.83 | (0.04) | 1.55 | (0.13) | 0.28 | (0.14) | 5.58 | (0.11) | 4.89 | (0.38) | 0.69 | (0.40) |
| Azerbaijan | 2.96 | (0.07) | 3.08 | (0.19) | -0.12 | (0.19) | 8.51 | (0.14) | 8.75 | (0.52) | -0.23 | (0.50) |
| Brazil | 1.80 | (0.03) | 1.81 | (0.17) | -0.02 | (0.17) | 6.16 | (0.07) | 5.59 | (0.35) | 0.57 | (0.35) |
| Bulgaria | 2.08 | (0.07) | c | c | c | c | 6.23 | (0.15) | c | c | c | c |
| Chile | 1.60 | (0.03) | c | c | c | c | 6.13 | (0.10) | c | c | c | c |
| Colombia | 1.93 | (0.03) | c | c | c | c | 7.39 | (0.08) | c | c | c | c |
| Croatia | 1.79 | (0.03) | 1.88 | (0.08) | -0.09 | (0.09) | 5.62 | (0.06) | 5.82 | (0.16) | -0.20 | (0.17) |
| Estonia | 1.94 | (0.03) | 2.11 | (0.10) | -0.17 | (0.10) | 7.13 | (0.07) | 7.42 | (0.16) | -0.30 | (0.18) |
| Hong Kong-China | 2.28 | (0.05) | 2.19 | (0.05) | 0.09 | (0.06) | 9.06 | (0.09) | 8.63 | (0.11) | **0.43** | (0.11) |
| Indonesia | 1.99 | (0.03) | 1.81 | (0.23) | 0.19 | (0.23) | 7.45 | (0.10) | 6.30 | (0.55) | **1.15** | (0.56) |
| Israel | 2.32 | (0.06) | 2.36 | (0.08) | -0.05 | (0.09) | 8.60 | (0.13) | 9.10 | (0.18) | **-0.50** | (0.20) |
| Jordan | 2.68 | (0.04) | 2.79 | (0.10) | -0.11 | (0.11) | 7.96 | (0.09) | 8.17 | (0.18) | -0.21 | (0.21) |
| Kyrgyzstan | 2.22 | (0.03) | 2.35 | (0.21) | -0.13 | (0.21) | 6.71 | (0.09) | 7.32 | (0.59) | -0.61 | (0.57) |
| Latvia | 2.45 | (0.04) | 2.35 | (0.10) | 0.10 | (0.10) | 8.16 | (0.09) | 8.04 | (0.17) | 0.12 | (0.21) |
| Liechtenstein | 1.45 | (0.07) | 1.54 | (0.10) | -0.08 | (0.12) | 6.01 | (0.15) | 6.02 | (0.22) | -0.00 | (0.27) |
| Lithuania | 1.78 | (0.03) | 1.91 | (0.16) | -0.13 | (0.16) | 6.02 | (0.05) | 6.35 | (0.28) | -0.32 | (0.28) |
| Macao-China | 2.16 | (0.06) | 2.04 | (0.03) | 0.12 | (0.07) | 8.83 | (0.13) | 8.65 | (0.06) | 0.17 | (0.14) |
| Montenegro | 2.02 | (0.03) | 2.21 | (0.14) | -0.19 | (0.14) | 6.02 | (0.07) | 6.03 | (0.28) | -0.01 | (0.28) |
| Qatar | 2.05 | (0.03) | 2.46 | (0.04) | **-0.41** | (0.06) | 6.82 | (0.08) | 7.74 | (0.10) | **-0.92** | (0.14) |
| Romania | 2.16 | (0.04) | c | c | c | c | 6.67 | (0.11) | c | c | c | c |
| Russian Federation | 2.22 | (0.05) | 2.23 | (0.11) | -0.01 | (0.11) | 7.01 | (0.10) | 6.84 | (0.23) | 0.17 | (0.24) |
| Serbia | 1.81 | (0.03) | 1.85 | (0.10) | -0.04 | (0.11) | 6.05 | (0.08) | 6.24 | (0.18) | -0.20 | (0.20) |
| Slovenia | 1.93 | (0.02) | 1.87 | (0.09) | 0.06 | (0.10) | 6.30 | (0.05) | 6.18 | (0.19) | 0.12 | (0.20) |
| Chinese Taipei | 1.89 | (0.04) | 1.73 | (0.22) | 0.16 | (0.22) | 7.76 | (0.11) | 6.58 | (0.75) | 1.18 | (0.74) |
| Thailand | 1.82 | (0.03) | c | c | c | c | 6.52 | (0.07) | c | c | c | c |
| Tunisia | 2.56 | (0.04) | 2.13 | (0.42) | 0.43 | (0.43) | 8.39 | (0.10) | 7.73 | (0.63) | 0.66 | (0.64) |
| Uruguay | 1.57 | (0.03) | c | c | c | c | 5.75 | (0.07) | c | c | c | c |

*Note:* Values that are statistically significant at the 5% level (p < 0.05) are indicated in bold.

[Part 3/3]
## Table 3.8b Mean learning hours and allocation of total learning time in mathematics, by immigrant status

| | | Allocation of total learning time in mathematics for | | | | | | | | | | | | | | | | | | |
| | | Regular school lessons | | | | | | Out-of-school-time lessons | | | | | | Individual study | | | | | |
| | | Native students | | Students with an immigrant background | | Difference (native-immigrant) | | Native students | | Students with an immigrant background | | Difference (native-immigrant) | | Native students | | Students with an immigrant background | | Difference (native-immigrant) | |
| | | % | S.E. | % | S.E. | Dif. | S.E. | % | S.E. | % | S.E. | Dif. | S.E. | % | S.E. | % | S.E. | Dif. | S.E. |
|---|---|---|---|---|---|---|---|---|---|---|---|---|---|---|---|---|---|---|---|
| OECD | Australia | 67.6 | (0.3) | 59.7 | (0.5) | **7.9** | (0.5) | 8.4 | (0.2) | 12.2 | (0.4) | **-3.8** | (0.4) | 24.0 | (0.2) | 28.2 | (0.4) | **-4.1** | (0.4) |
| | Austria | 59.2 | (0.5) | 54.4 | (0.9) | **4.8** | (1.0) | 6.2 | (0.3) | 9.3 | (0.7) | **-3.1** | (0.8) | 34.6 | (0.4) | 36.3 | (0.9) | -1.6 | (0.9) |
| | Belgium | 63.5 | (0.3) | 60.3 | (0.8) | **3.2** | (0.9) | 7.4 | (0.2) | 11.7 | (0.9) | **-4.3** | (0.9) | 29.1 | (0.3) | 27.9 | (0.6) | 1.2 | (0.5) |
| | Canada | 65.2 | (0.3) | 57.2 | (0.7) | **8.0** | (0.7) | 10.5 | (0.2) | 14.3 | (0.4) | **-3.9** | (0.4) | 24.3 | (0.2) | 28.5 | (0.5) | **-4.2** | (0.6) |
| | Czech Republic | 70.5 | (0.4) | 67.1 | (2.6) | 3.4 | (2.6) | 9.8 | (0.2) | 9.8 | (1.6) | -0.0 | (1.7) | 19.8 | (0.3) | 23.1 | (2.4) | -3.4 | (2.3) |
| | Denmark | 62.8 | (0.3) | 56.7 | (1.2) | **6.1** | (1.2) | 15.7 | (0.3) | 20.0 | (0.8) | **-4.4** | (0.8) | 21.5 | (0.2) | 23.3 | (0.7) | -1.7 | (0.8) |
| | Finland | 71.4 | (0.3) | 61.8 | (2.5) | **9.6** | (2.4) | 5.8 | (0.2) | 11.6 | (2.4) | **-5.8** | (2.4) | 22.9 | (0.2) | 26.6 | (2.2) | -3.8 | (2.1) |
| | France | 63.2 | (0.4) | 58.2 | (0.9) | **5.0** | (1.0) | 12.1 | (0.3) | 16.3 | (0.8) | **-4.2** | (0.9) | 24.7 | (0.3) | 25.5 | (0.8) | -0.8 | (0.8) |
| | Germany | 59.1 | (0.3) | 55.0 | (1.0) | **4.1** | (1.1) | 9.0 | (0.3) | 13.4 | (0.9) | **-4.4** | (0.9) | 31.9 | (0.3) | 31.6 | (0.6) | 0.3 | (0.7) |
| | Greece | 49.0 | (0.5) | 55.0 | (1.5) | **-6.0** | (1.5) | 26.6 | (0.5) | 18.0 | (1.2) | **8.6** | (1.3) | 24.4 | (0.4) | 27.0 | (1.1) | -2.6 | (1.2) |
| | Hungary | 54.4 | (0.4) | 54.5 | (2.9) | -0.2 | (3.0) | 17.7 | (0.3) | 18.7 | (2.6) | -1.1 | (2.6) | 28.0 | (0.3) | 26.7 | (2.1) | 1.2 | (2.2) |
| | Iceland | 69.6 | (0.3) | 63.5 | (2.7) | **6.1** | (2.7) | 8.3 | (0.2) | 14.2 | (2.1) | **-5.9** | (2.1) | 22.1 | (0.2) | 22.3 | (2.0) | -0.2 | (2.0) |
| | Ireland | 63.8 | (0.4) | 60.5 | (1.6) | **3.3** | (1.6) | 9.4 | (0.3) | 10.5 | (1.3) | -1.2 | (1.4) | 26.8 | (0.3) | 28.9 | (1.2) | -2.1 | (1.2) |
| | Italy | 55.1 | (0.2) | 52.2 | (1.3) | **2.9** | (1.3) | 10.6 | (0.2) | 13.8 | (1.3) | **-3.2** | (1.3) | 34.3 | (0.2) | 34.0 | (1.1) | 0.3 | (1.2) |
| | Japan | 71.7 | (0.5) | c | c | c | c | 8.7 | (0.3) | c | c | c | c | 19.6 | (0.4) | c | c | c | c |
| | Korea | 56.9 | (0.5) | c | c | c | c | 20.9 | (0.3) | c | c | c | c | 22.2 | (0.4) | c | c | c | c |
| | Luxembourg | 64.4 | (0.4) | 61.5 | (0.6) | **2.9** | (0.7) | 10.0 | (0.3) | 12.9 | (0.4) | **-2.9** | (0.5) | 25.6 | (0.3) | 25.6 | (0.4) | -0.0 | (0.5) |
| | Mexico | 55.2 | (0.4) | 41.6 | (3.5) | **13.6** | (3.5) | 14.1 | (0.3) | 19.8 | (2.5) | **-5.7** | (2.4) | 30.7 | (0.3) | 38.7 | (2.9) | **-7.9** | (3.0) |
| | Netherlands | 60.9 | (0.4) | 53.4 | (1.1) | **7.5** | (1.2) | 11.5 | (0.3) | 16.3 | (1.0) | **-4.9** | (1.0) | 27.6 | (0.4) | 30.2 | (1.1) | -2.6 | (1.1) |
| | New Zealand | 72.0 | (0.4) | 60.9 | (0.8) | **11.0** | (0.9) | 7.2 | (0.2) | 13.1 | (0.6) | **-5.9** | (0.6) | 20.8 | (0.3) | 26.0 | (0.5) | **-5.1** | (0.6) |
| | Norway | 62.7 | (0.4) | 54.8 | (1.4) | **7.9** | (1.5) | 15.6 | (0.3) | 19.8 | (0.9) | **-4.1** | (1.0) | 21.7 | (0.3) | 25.4 | (1.0) | **-3.7** | (1.0) |
| | Poland | 62.5 | (0.3) | c | c | c | c | 10.0 | (0.3) | c | c | c | c | 27.5 | (0.3) | c | c | c | c |
| | Portugal | 59.1 | (0.4) | 57.5 | (1.6) | 1.6 | (1.7) | 11.5 | (0.3) | 12.3 | (1.1) | -0.9 | (1.1) | 29.5 | (0.4) | 30.2 | (1.3) | -0.7 | (1.4) |
| | Slovak Republic | 60.6 | (0.5) | c | c | c | c | 12.5 | (0.3) | c | c | c | c | 26.9 | (0.3) | c | c | c | c |
| | Spain | 57.9 | (0.3) | 56.1 | (1.1) | 1.7 | (1.1) | 13.0 | (0.3) | 12.6 | (0.9) | 0.4 | (1.0) | 29.1 | (0.3) | 31.3 | (1.0) | -2.2 | (1.1) |
| | Sweden | 69.3 | (0.5) | 58.9 | (1.1) | **10.4** | (1.2) | 9.2 | (0.2) | 14.8 | (0.9) | **-5.6** | (0.9) | 21.5 | (0.4) | 26.3 | (0.9) | **-4.8** | (1.0) |
| | Switzerland | 64.5 | (0.4) | 60.5 | (0.7) | **4.0** | (0.7) | 8.8 | (0.3) | 12.1 | (0.5) | **-3.3** | (0.5) | 26.6 | (0.2) | 27.4 | (0.5) | -0.7 | (0.5) |
| | Turkey | 50.6 | (0.4) | 53.8 | (4.0) | -3.2 | (4.0) | 22.7 | (0.4) | 19.5 | (3.9) | 3.2 | (3.9) | 26.6 | (0.3) | 26.7 | (1.5) | -0.1 | (1.6) |
| | United Kingdom | 68.1 | (0.3) | 58.0 | (1.0) | **10.1** | (1.1) | 8.2 | (0.2) | 15.0 | (1.0) | **-6.8** | (1.0) | 23.7 | (0.2) | 27.0 | (0.6) | **-3.3** | (0.7) |
| | United States | 56.2 | (0.5) | 52.0 | (1.0) | **4.2** | (1.1) | 14.7 | (0.4) | 18.1 | (0.7) | **-3.4** | (0.7) | 29.1 | (0.3) | 29.9 | (0.8) | -0.8 | (0.9) |
| | **OECD average** | 62.2 | (0.1) | 57.1 | (0.3) | **5.0** | (0.3) | 11.9 | (0.1) | 14.6 | (0.3) | **-2.9** | (0.3) | 25.9 | (0.1) | 28.2 | (0.3) | **-2.1** | (0.3) |
| Partners | Argentina | 55.0 | (0.6) | 56.6 | (2.3) | -1.7 | (2.4) | 12.4 | (0.5) | 9.3 | (1.4) | **3.2** | (1.4) | 32.6 | (0.4) | 34.1 | (2.3) | -1.5 | (2.3) |
| | Azerbaijan | 47.2 | (0.6) | 46.7 | (2.6) | 0.6 | (2.6) | 18.6 | (0.4) | 19.4 | (2.0) | -0.8 | (2.0) | 34.2 | (0.5) | 34.0 | (1.7) | 0.3 | (1.7) |
| | Brazil | 54.7 | (0.5) | 48.5 | (2.7) | **6.2** | (2.8) | 17.2 | (0.5) | 18.2 | (2.3) | -1.1 | (2.3) | 28.1 | (0.4) | 33.3 | (2.8) | **-5.2** | (2.8) |
| | Bulgaria | 51.4 | (0.5) | c | c | c | c | 16.2 | (0.5) | c | c | c | c | 32.3 | (0.5) | c | c | c | c |
| | Chile | 57.0 | (0.5) | c | c | c | c | 15.1 | (0.3) | c | c | c | c | 27.9 | (0.4) | c | c | c | c |
| | Colombia | 61.0 | (0.6) | c | c | c | c | 14.1 | (0.3) | c | c | c | c | 25.0 | (0.4) | c | c | c | c |
| | Croatia | 58.5 | (0.5) | 58.4 | (1.1) | 0.1 | (1.0) | 11.4 | (0.3) | 11.1 | (0.7) | **0.2** | (0.8) | 30.2 | (0.4) | 30.5 | (0.9) | -0.3 | (1.0) |
| | Estonia | 62.5 | (0.4) | 60.4 | (1.0) | **2.1** | (1.0) | 12.2 | (0.3) | 13.3 | (0.7) | -1.1 | (0.7) | 25.3 | (0.3) | 26.4 | (0.9) | -1.0 | (1.0) |
| | Hong Kong-China | 61.1 | (0.5) | 64.6 | (0.6) | **-3.5** | (0.8) | 15.5 | (0.4) | 12.2 | (0.5) | **3.3** | (0.6) | 23.4 | (0.3) | 23.3 | (0.4) | 0.2 | (0.5) |
| | Indonesia | 57.3 | (0.6) | 47.1 | (8.7) | 10.2 | (8.7) | 16.3 | (0.5) | 19.9 | (5.1) | -3.6 | (5.2) | 26.5 | (0.3) | 33.0 | (5.0) | -6.5 | (5.0) |
| | Israel | 51.8 | (0.7) | 51.7 | (0.9) | 0.1 | (1.0) | 22.8 | (0.4) | 23.5 | (0.5) | -0.8 | (0.6) | 25.5 | (0.5) | 24.7 | (0.6) | 0.7 | (0.6) |
| | Jordan | 43.4 | (0.6) | 43.3 | (1.2) | 0.2 | (1.3) | 22.0 | (0.5) | 22.4 | (0.9) | -0.3 | (1.0) | 34.5 | (0.4) | 34.4 | (0.7) | 0.1 | (0.8) |
| | Kyrgyzstan | 42.1 | (0.5) | 48.7 | (3.0) | **-6.6** | (3.0) | 24.1 | (0.5) | 19.6 | (2.2) | **4.5** | (2.1) | 33.9 | (0.4) | 31.7 | (1.7) | 2.2 | (1.8) |
| | Latvia | 58.4 | (0.4) | 56.9 | (1.0) | 1.5 | (1.1) | 13.2 | (0.4) | 15.6 | (0.8) | **-2.3** | (0.9) | 28.4 | (0.3) | 27.6 | (0.9) | 0.8 | (0.9) |
| | Liechtenstein | 67.9 | (1.3) | 64.7 | (2.0) | 3.3 | (2.3) | 7.3 | (0.7) | 10.5 | (1.3) | **-3.2** | (1.6) | 24.8 | (1.1) | 24.9 | (1.3) | -0.1 | (1.5) |
| | Lithuania | 60.8 | (0.4) | 61.4 | (2.1) | -0.6 | (2.1) | 11.4 | (0.3) | 10.3 | (1.6) | 1.2 | (1.7) | 27.8 | (0.3) | 28.3 | (1.9) | -0.5 | (1.9) |
| | Macao-China | 65.4 | (0.7) | 66.7 | (0.4) | -1.3 | (0.8) | 12.2 | (0.4) | 11.7 | (0.3) | 0.5 | (0.4) | 22.5 | (0.6) | 21.6 | (0.3) | 0.8 | (0.6) |
| | Montenegro | 52.8 | (0.4) | 49.7 | (1.9) | 3.1 | (2.0) | 13.3 | (0.3) | 13.4 | (1.5) | -0.0 | (1.5) | 33.9 | (0.4) | 36.9 | (1.7) | -3.0 | (1.7) |
| | Qatar | 41.5 | (0.4) | 46.1 | (0.5) | **-4.7** | (0.7) | 27.5 | (0.4) | 21.4 | (0.4) | **6.1** | (0.7) | 31.0 | (0.4) | 32.4 | (0.4) | **-1.4** | (0.5) |
| | Romania | 49.5 | (0.6) | c | c | c | c | 19.7 | (0.4) | c | c | c | c | 30.7 | (0.4) | c | c | c | c |
| | Russian Federation | 54.1 | (0.5) | 53.2 | (1.3) | 0.8 | (1.2) | 15.7 | (0.6) | 15.2 | (0.9) | 0.5 | (0.8) | 30.2 | (0.4) | 31.5 | (0.9) | -1.3 | (0.9) |
| | Serbia | 59.3 | (0.5) | 59.2 | (1.2) | 0.2 | (1.3) | 13.0 | (0.3) | 12.8 | (1.0) | 0.2 | (1.0) | 27.7 | (0.4) | 28.0 | (1.1) | -0.3 | (1.1) |
| | Slovenia | 55.9 | (0.3) | 53.0 | (0.8) | **2.9** | (0.9) | 14.0 | (0.2) | 16.7 | (0.7) | **-2.7** | (0.8) | 30.0 | (0.3) | 30.3 | (0.8) | -0.2 | (0.9) |
| | Chinese Taipei | 59.8 | (0.4) | 53.4 | (4.9) | 6.4 | (4.9) | 16.9 | (0.2) | 18.5 | (2.7) | -1.6 | (2.7) | 23.3 | (0.2) | 28.1 | (4.1) | -4.8 | (4.1) |
| | Thailand | 63.4 | (0.4) | c | c | c | c | 10.6 | (0.3) | c | c | c | c | 26.0 | (0.3) | c | c | c | c |
| | Tunisia | 41.8 | (0.4) | 39.0 | (4.2) | 2.8 | (4.3) | 27.0 | (0.3) | 33.1 | (2.4) | **-6.1** | (2.5) | 31.1 | (0.3) | 27.9 | (3.5) | 3.2 | (3.6) |
| | Uruguay | 61.0 | (0.4) | c | c | c | c | 12.3 | (0.3) | c | c | c | c | 26.7 | (0.3) | c | c | c | c |

*Note:* Values that are statistically significant at the 5% level (p < 0.05) are indicated in bold.

© OECD 2011 Quality Time for Students: Learning In and Out of School

### Table 3.8c [Part 1/3] Mean learning hours and allocation of total learning time on the language of instruction, by immigrant status

| | Mean learning hours per week | | | | | | | | | | | |
|---|---|---|---|---|---|---|---|---|---|---|---|---|
| | Regular school lessons | | | | | | Out-of-school-time lessons | | | | | |
| | Native students | | Students with an immigrant background | | Difference (native-immigrant) | | Native students | | Students with an immigrant background | | Difference (native-immigrant) | |
| | Mean | S.E. | Mean | S.E. | Dif. | S.E. | Mean | S.E. | Mean | S.E. | Dif. | S.E. |
| **OECD** | | | | | | | | | | | | |
| Australia | 4.02 | (0.03) | 4.22 | (0.05) | **-0.19** | (0.06) | 0.59 | (0.01) | 0.90 | (0.04) | **-0.31** | (0.04) |
| Austria | 2.81 | (0.03) | 3.25 | (0.12) | **-0.44** | (0.12) | 0.20 | (0.02) | 0.49 | (0.05) | **-0.30** | (0.04) |
| Belgium | 3.48 | (0.03) | 3.58 | (0.10) | -0.11 | (0.10) | 0.41 | (0.01) | 0.77 | (0.04) | **-0.37** | (0.05) |
| Canada | 4.47 | (0.04) | 4.34 | (0.08) | 0.13 | (0.08) | 0.79 | (0.02) | 1.12 | (0.05) | **-0.33** | (0.05) |
| Czech Republic | 3.72 | (0.03) | 3.72 | (0.17) | 0.01 | (0.16) | 0.60 | (0.01) | 0.88 | (0.18) | -0.28 | (0.18) |
| Denmark | 5.52 | (0.04) | 5.33 | (0.09) | **0.19** | (0.09) | 1.65 | (0.03) | 2.14 | (0.11) | **-0.50** | (0.11) |
| Finland | 3.14 | (0.05) | 2.90 | (0.26) | 0.24 | (0.26) | 0.36 | (0.01) | 0.75 | (0.12) | **-0.40** | (0.12) |
| France | 4.04 | (0.03) | 3.86 | (0.10) | 0.18 | (0.10) | 0.73 | (0.02) | 1.05 | (0.06) | **-0.33** | (0.06) |
| Germany | 3.63 | (0.03) | 3.83 | (0.08) | **-0.19** | (0.08) | 0.55 | (0.02) | 0.94 | (0.07) | **-0.39** | (0.08) |
| Greece | 3.23 | (0.04) | 2.69 | (0.14) | **0.54** | (0.13) | 1.66 | (0.04) | 1.23 | (0.11) | **0.43** | (0.11) |
| Hungary | 3.19 | (0.04) | 3.13 | (0.23) | 0.06 | (0.23) | 1.30 | (0.03) | 1.38 | (0.24) | -0.07 | (0.23) |
| Iceland | 4.52 | (0.02) | 4.29 | (0.23) | 0.23 | (0.23) | 0.45 | (0.02) | 0.85 | (0.18) | **-0.39** | (0.18) |
| Ireland | 3.54 | (0.03) | 3.74 | (0.11) | -0.20 | (0.11) | 0.61 | (0.02) | 0.98 | (0.13) | **-0.38** | (0.13) |
| Italy | 4.64 | (0.03) | 4.33 | (0.12) | **0.32** | (0.12) | 0.77 | (0.02) | 1.15 | (0.08) | **-0.38** | (0.09) |
| Japan | 3.82 | (0.04) | c | c | c | c | 0.43 | (0.02) | c | c | c | c |
| Korea | 4.49 | (0.04) | c | c | c | c | 1.45 | (0.04) | c | c | c | c |
| Luxembourg | 3.46 | (0.03) | 3.60 | (0.04) | **-0.14** | (0.05) | 0.48 | (0.02) | 0.80 | (0.03) | **-0.32** | (0.04) |
| Mexico | 3.80 | (0.04) | 2.78 | (0.28) | **1.02** | (0.29) | 1.09 | (0.03) | 1.36 | (0.21) | -0.27 | (0.22) |
| Netherlands | 2.91 | (0.03) | 2.97 | (0.09) | -0.05 | (0.09) | 0.58 | (0.02) | 1.12 | (0.06) | **-0.54** | (0.07) |
| New Zealand | 4.42 | (0.03) | 4.29 | (0.06) | 0.13 | (0.07) | 0.55 | (0.03) | 1.00 | (0.05) | **-0.45** | (0.06) |
| Norway | 3.60 | (0.04) | 3.60 | (0.13) | 0.01 | (0.14) | 1.12 | (0.02) | 1.59 | (0.12) | **-0.46** | (0.12) |
| Poland | 4.65 | (0.03) | c | c | c | c | 0.70 | (0.03) | c | c | c | c |
| Portugal | 3.29 | (0.03) | 3.10 | (0.13) | 0.20 | (0.13) | 0.55 | (0.02) | 0.79 | (0.10) | **-0.24** | (0.10) |
| Slovak Republic | 3.12 | (0.05) | c | c | c | c | 0.88 | (0.03) | c | c | c | c |
| Spain | 3.64 | (0.03) | 3.23 | (0.11) | **0.41** | (0.11) | 0.56 | (0.02) | 0.83 | (0.09) | **-0.27** | (0.09) |
| Sweden | 3.12 | (0.03) | 3.13 | (0.08) | -0.01 | (0.08) | 0.63 | (0.02) | 1.03 | (0.07) | **-0.40** | (0.07) |
| Switzerland | 3.64 | (0.04) | 3.70 | (0.05) | -0.06 | (0.05) | 0.39 | (0.02) | 0.79 | (0.05) | **-0.40** | (0.05) |
| Turkey | 3.99 | (0.05) | 4.29 | (0.24) | -0.30 | (0.23) | 1.82 | (0.05) | 1.62 | (0.24) | 0.20 | (0.25) |
| United Kingdom | 3.89 | (0.03) | 3.95 | (0.11) | -0.06 | (0.11) | 0.53 | (0.01) | 1.13 | (0.10) | **-0.59** | (0.10) |
| United States | 3.71 | (0.04) | 3.37 | (0.07) | **0.34** | (0.08) | 1.07 | (0.03) | 1.26 | (0.06) | **-0.19** | (0.07) |
| **OECD average** | 3.78 | (0.01) | 3.66 | (0.03) | **0.09** | (0.03) | 0.78 | (0.00) | 1.08 | (0.02) | **-0.31** | (0.02) |
| **Partners** | | | | | | | | | | | | |
| Argentina | 2.39 | (0.05) | 2.49 | (0.21) | -0.11 | (0.19) | 0.42 | (0.03) | 0.43 | (0.10) | -0.01 | (0.10) |
| Azerbaijan | 3.70 | (0.05) | 4.06 | (0.37) | -0.36 | (0.37) | 1.80 | (0.05) | 1.91 | (0.18) | -0.12 | (0.18) |
| Brazil | 3.13 | (0.04) | 2.64 | (0.23) | **0.49** | (0.24) | 1.18 | (0.03) | 1.15 | (0.13) | 0.02 | (0.13) |
| Bulgaria | 2.93 | (0.05) | c | c | c | c | 1.08 | (0.04) | c | c | c | c |
| Chile | 3.46 | (0.06) | c | c | c | c | 0.99 | (0.03) | c | c | c | c |
| Colombia | 3.95 | (0.05) | c | c | c | c | 1.15 | (0.03) | c | c | c | c |
| Croatia | 3.32 | (0.04) | 3.38 | (0.07) | -0.05 | (0.07) | 0.38 | (0.02) | 0.38 | (0.04) | -0.00 | (0.05) |
| Estonia | 3.48 | (0.04) | 3.61 | (0.09) | -0.13 | (0.10) | 0.86 | (0.03) | 0.99 | (0.06) | **-0.12** | (0.06) |
| Hong Kong-China | 5.15 | (0.05) | 5.25 | (0.05) | -0.10 | (0.06) | 0.82 | (0.04) | 0.79 | (0.04) | 0.03 | (0.05) |
| Indonesia | 3.65 | (0.05) | 2.27 | (0.32) | **1.37** | (0.31) | 1.25 | (0.04) | 1.11 | (0.25) | 0.14 | (0.24) |
| Israel | 3.07 | (0.05) | 2.91 | (0.09) | 0.16 | (0.09) | 1.32 | (0.03) | 1.27 | (0.07) | 0.05 | (0.08) |
| Jordan | 3.59 | (0.06) | 3.66 | (0.09) | -0.07 | (0.11) | 1.79 | (0.04) | 1.67 | (0.08) | 0.12 | (0.08) |
| Kyrgyzstan | 2.76 | (0.06) | 2.99 | (0.16) | -0.22 | (0.17) | 1.72 | (0.03) | 1.18 | (0.14) | **0.54** | (0.15) |
| Latvia | 3.73 | (0.04) | 3.29 | (0.10) | **0.45** | (0.11) | 0.87 | (0.04) | 0.90 | (0.06) | -0.02 | (0.07) |
| Liechtenstein | 3.76 | (0.10) | 3.51 | (0.16) | 0.25 | (0.19) | 0.25 | (0.04) | 0.44 | (0.07) | **-0.19** | (0.08) |
| Lithuania | 3.67 | (0.04) | 3.77 | (0.16) | -0.10 | (0.16) | 0.65 | (0.02) | 0.80 | (0.10) | -0.15 | (0.10) |
| Macao-China | 5.28 | (0.06) | 5.35 | (0.04) | -0.07 | (0.07) | 1.10 | (0.05) | 1.03 | (0.03) | 0.07 | (0.06) |
| Montenegro | 2.95 | (0.04) | 2.80 | (0.15) | 0.15 | (0.15) | 0.74 | (0.02) | 0.72 | (0.09) | 0.02 | (0.10) |
| Qatar | 2.68 | (0.04) | 3.22 | (0.04) | **-0.54** | (0.06) | 1.60 | (0.03) | 1.51 | (0.04) | 0.09 | (0.05) |
| Romania | 3.30 | (0.06) | c | c | c | c | 1.52 | (0.03) | c | c | c | c |
| Russian Federation | 2.02 | (0.03) | 2.26 | (0.09) | **-0.24** | (0.09) | 0.82 | (0.03) | 0.83 | (0.06) | -0.02 | (0.06) |
| Serbia | 3.18 | (0.04) | 3.13 | (0.10) | 0.06 | (0.10) | 0.93 | (0.03) | 0.82 | (0.08) | 0.11 | (0.08) |
| Slovenia | 3.26 | (0.03) | 3.12 | (0.09) | 0.14 | (0.10) | 0.73 | (0.02) | 0.74 | (0.05) | -0.01 | (0.05) |
| Chinese Taipei | 4.39 | (0.05) | 3.48 | (0.34) | **0.91** | (0.34) | 0.69 | (0.02) | 0.77 | (0.19) | -0.08 | (0.19) |
| Thailand | 3.11 | (0.02) | c | c | c | c | 0.55 | (0.02) | c | c | c | c |
| Tunisia | 3.15 | (0.05) | 2.91 | (0.37) | 0.24 | (0.37) | 1.78 | (0.04) | 1.98 | (0.35) | -0.20 | (0.36) |
| Uruguay | 2.76 | (0.04) | c | c | c | c | 0.64 | (0.03) | c | c | c | c |

*Note:* Values that are statistically significant at the 5% level (p < 0.05) are indicated in bold.

147

**Table 3.8c** [Part 2/3] **Mean learning hours and allocation of total learning time on the language of instruction, by immigrant status**

| | | Mean learning hours per week | | | | | | | | | | |
|---|---|---|---|---|---|---|---|---|---|---|---|---|
| | | Individual study | | | | | | Total learning hours | | | | |
| | | Native students | | Students with an immigrant background | | Difference (native-immigrant) | | Native students | | Students with an immigrant background | | Difference (native-immigrant) | |
| | | Mean | S.E. | Mean | S.E. | Dif. | S.E. | Mean | S.E. | Mean | S.E. | Dif. | S.E. |
| **OECD** | Australia | 1.63 | (0.02) | 1.99 | (0.05) | **-0.36** | (0.05) | 6.24 | (0.04) | 7.09 | (0.10) | **-0.85** | (0.11) |
| | Austria | 1.45 | (0.03) | 2.12 | (0.09) | **-0.67** | (0.09) | 4.47 | (0.06) | 5.83 | (0.21) | **-1.36** | (0.22) |
| | Belgium | 1.33 | (0.02) | 1.47 | (0.05) | **-0.14** | (0.05) | 5.23 | (0.04) | 5.84 | (0.14) | **-0.61** | (0.14) |
| | Canada | 1.63 | (0.02) | 2.14 | (0.07) | **-0.50** | (0.08) | 6.93 | (0.06) | 7.58 | (0.15) | **-0.65** | (0.15) |
| | Czech Republic | 1.16 | (0.02) | 1.27 | (0.16) | -0.11 | (0.15) | 5.48 | (0.05) | 5.87 | (0.37) | -0.39 | (0.37) |
| | Denmark | 2.14 | (0.03) | 2.45 | (0.09) | **-0.32** | (0.10) | 9.30 | (0.07) | 9.85 | (0.22) | **-0.55** | (0.21) |
| | Finland | 1.13 | (0.02) | 1.22 | (0.13) | -0.09 | (0.13) | 4.63 | (0.07) | 4.88 | (0.35) | -0.25 | (0.35) |
| | France | 1.50 | (0.02) | 1.66 | (0.07) | **-0.16** | (0.07) | 6.28 | (0.05) | 6.58 | (0.13) | **-0.30** | (0.13) |
| | Germany | 1.86 | (0.03) | 2.09 | (0.08) | **-0.23** | (0.08) | 6.06 | (0.05) | 6.80 | (0.17) | **-0.74** | (0.17) |
| | Greece | 1.95 | (0.03) | 1.65 | (0.10) | **0.31** | (0.10) | 6.85 | (0.08) | 5.55 | (0.28) | **1.30** | (0.29) |
| | Hungary | 1.86 | (0.03) | 1.76 | (0.18) | 0.11 | (0.18) | 6.37 | (0.08) | 6.31 | (0.52) | 0.06 | (0.51) |
| | Iceland | 1.54 | (0.02) | 1.63 | (0.20) | -0.08 | (0.20) | 6.52 | (0.04) | 6.81 | (0.35) | -0.30 | (0.35) |
| | Ireland | 1.73 | (0.03) | 2.11 | (0.12) | **-0.38** | (0.12) | 5.88 | (0.07) | 6.84 | (0.27) | **-0.96** | (0.29) |
| | Italy | 2.96 | (0.04) | 2.78 | (0.11) | 0.17 | (0.11) | 8.38 | (0.07) | 8.23 | (0.20) | 0.15 | (0.21) |
| | Japan | 0.94 | (0.03) | c | c | c | c | 5.19 | (0.07) | c | c | c | c |
| | Korea | 1.41 | (0.03) | c | c | c | c | 7.36 | (0.09) | c | c | c | c |
| | Luxembourg | 1.31 | (0.02) | 1.51 | (0.04) | **-0.21** | (0.05) | 5.24 | (0.05) | 5.90 | (0.07) | **-0.66** | (0.09) |
| | Mexico | 2.06 | (0.03) | 2.19 | (0.21) | -0.13 | (0.21) | 6.91 | (0.07) | 6.37 | (0.30) | 0.55 | (0.31) |
| | Netherlands | 1.29 | (0.02) | 1.63 | (0.07) | **-0.34** | (0.07) | 4.78 | (0.04) | 5.71 | (0.18) | **-0.93** | (0.18) |
| | New Zealand | 1.46 | (0.03) | 1.97 | (0.05) | **-0.51** | (0.06) | 6.44 | (0.07) | 7.25 | (0.10) | **-0.80** | (0.13) |
| | Norway | 1.42 | (0.03) | 1.90 | (0.10) | **-0.48** | (0.10) | 6.14 | (0.06) | 7.06 | (0.25) | **-0.92** | (0.24) |
| | Poland | 2.23 | (0.03) | c | c | c | c | 7.58 | (0.05) | c | c | c | c |
| | Portugal | 1.77 | (0.03) | 2.03 | (0.13) | -0.26 | (0.14) | 5.61 | (0.05) | 5.95 | (0.30) | -0.34 | (0.31) |
| | Slovak Republic | 1.74 | (0.03) | c | c | c | c | 5.75 | (0.08) | c | c | c | c |
| | Spain | 1.89 | (0.03) | 1.89 | (0.09) | -0.01 | (0.08) | 6.11 | (0.06) | 5.95 | (0.13) | 0.17 | (0.14) |
| | Sweden | 1.23 | (0.02) | 1.47 | (0.06) | **-0.23** | (0.06) | 4.99 | (0.05) | 5.65 | (0.15) | **-0.66** | (0.14) |
| | Switzerland | 1.35 | (0.02) | 1.57 | (0.04) | **-0.22** | (0.04) | 5.38 | (0.06) | 6.09 | (0.09) | **-0.71** | (0.10) |
| | Turkey | 2.18 | (0.05) | 2.19 | (0.25) | -0.01 | (0.26) | 7.97 | (0.12) | 8.16 | (0.51) | -0.19 | (0.54) |
| | United Kingdom | 1.55 | (0.02) | 1.95 | (0.09) | **-0.40** | (0.08) | 5.99 | (0.06) | 7.01 | (0.20) | **-1.03** | (0.19) |
| | United States | 1.87 | (0.04) | 1.90 | (0.08) | -0.04 | (0.09) | 6.69 | (0.07) | 6.54 | (0.16) | 0.15 | (0.18) |
| | **OECD average** | 1.65 | (0.01) | 1.87 | (0.02) | **-0.20** | (0.02) | 6.23 | (0.01) | 6.60 | (0.05) | **-0.42** | (0.05) |
| **Partners** | Argentina | 1.64 | (0.04) | 1.48 | (0.12) | 0.16 | (0.13) | 4.44 | (0.08) | 4.43 | (0.33) | 0.00 | (0.31) |
| | Azerbaijan | 3.11 | (0.05) | 3.28 | (0.25) | -0.17 | (0.26) | 8.65 | (0.11) | 9.35 | (0.69) | -0.70 | (0.71) |
| | Brazil | 1.75 | (0.03) | 1.49 | (0.16) | 0.26 | (0.16) | 6.04 | (0.06) | 5.34 | (0.34) | **0.69** | (0.33) |
| | Bulgaria | 2.05 | (0.05) | c | c | c | c | 6.09 | (0.11) | c | c | c | c |
| | Chile | 1.57 | (0.03) | c | c | c | c | 6.04 | (0.08) | c | c | c | c |
| | Colombia | 1.83 | (0.04) | c | c | c | c | 6.94 | (0.08) | c | c | c | c |
| | Croatia | 1.57 | (0.03) | 1.64 | (0.07) | -0.07 | (0.07) | 5.30 | (0.06) | 5.43 | (0.12) | -0.14 | (0.12) |
| | Estonia | 1.61 | (0.03) | 1.68 | (0.09) | -0.07 | (0.10) | 5.95 | (0.06) | 6.29 | (0.19) | -0.33 | (0.20) |
| | Hong Kong-China | 1.58 | (0.04) | 1.72 | (0.05) | **-0.14** | (0.05) | 7.55 | (0.09) | 7.77 | (0.10) | **-0.21** | (0.10) |
| | Indonesia | 1.80 | (0.03) | 1.88 | (0.39) | -0.08 | (0.39) | 6.68 | (0.10) | 5.24 | (0.76) | 1.44 | (0.74) |
| | Israel | 1.67 | (0.04) | 1.61 | (0.07) | 0.06 | (0.08) | 6.08 | (0.10) | 5.80 | (0.17) | 0.28 | (0.19) |
| | Jordan | 2.60 | (0.05) | 2.53 | (0.08) | 0.07 | (0.08) | 7.98 | (0.10) | 7.79 | (0.20) | 0.19 | (0.22) |
| | Kyrgyzstan | 2.35 | (0.04) | 2.35 | (0.18) | 0.00 | (0.18) | 6.89 | (0.10) | 6.62 | (0.30) | 0.27 | (0.31) |
| | Latvia | 2.02 | (0.03) | 1.96 | (0.08) | 0.06 | (0.09) | 6.63 | (0.08) | 6.17 | (0.18) | **0.45** | (0.21) |
| | Liechtenstein | 1.16 | (0.06) | 1.35 | (0.12) | -0.19 | (0.14) | 5.16 | (0.12) | 5.29 | (0.22) | -0.13 | (0.26) |
| | Lithuania | 1.82 | (0.03) | 1.79 | (0.17) | 0.04 | (0.16) | 6.14 | (0.06) | 6.37 | (0.31) | -0.24 | (0.31) |
| | Macao-China | 1.55 | (0.05) | 1.46 | (0.03) | 0.09 | (0.06) | 7.94 | (0.12) | 7.84 | (0.07) | 0.10 | (0.14) |
| | Montenegro | 1.98 | (0.03) | 2.03 | (0.14) | -0.05 | (0.15) | 5.66 | (0.07) | 5.56 | (0.29) | 0.11 | (0.30) |
| | Qatar | 1.92 | (0.04) | 2.18 | (0.04) | **-0.26** | (0.06) | 6.21 | (0.07) | 6.89 | (0.09) | **-0.68** | (0.11) |
| | Romania | 2.19 | (0.04) | c | c | c | c | 7.02 | (0.10) | c | c | c | c |
| | Russian Federation | 1.54 | (0.03) | 1.71 | (0.09) | **-0.17** | (0.08) | 4.35 | (0.07) | 4.76 | (0.18) | **-0.41** | (0.17) |
| | Serbia | 1.70 | (0.03) | 1.73 | (0.10) | -0.04 | (0.10) | 5.81 | (0.07) | 5.63 | (0.18) | 0.18 | (0.19) |
| | Slovenia | 1.48 | (0.02) | 1.45 | (0.05) | **0.04** | (0.06) | 5.49 | (0.04) | 5.34 | (0.14) | 0.16 | (0.14) |
| | Chinese Taipei | 1.78 | (0.03) | 1.38 | (0.22) | **0.40** | (0.21) | 6.89 | (0.08) | 5.64 | (0.59) | **1.25** | (0.58) |
| | Thailand | 1.71 | (0.03) | c | c | **c** | c | 5.37 | (0.05) | c | c | c | c |
| | Tunisia | 2.11 | (0.04) | 1.83 | (0.26) | **0.29** | (0.27) | 7.05 | (0.11) | 6.91 | (0.78) | 0.14 | (0.80) |
| | Uruguay | 1.36 | (0.02) | c | c | **c** | c | 4.77 | (0.06) | c | c | c | c |

*Note:* Values that are statistically significant at the 5% level (p < 0.05) are indicated in bold.

© OECD 2011 Quality Time for Students: Learning In and Out of School

## Table 3.8c [Part 3/3] Mean learning hours and allocation of total learning time on the language of instruction, by immigrant status

| | Allocation of total learning time on the language of instruction for | | | | | | | | | | | | | | | | | |
| | Regular school lessons | | | | | | Out-of-school-time lessons | | | | | | Individual study | | | | | |
| | Native students | | Students with an immigrant background | | Difference (native-immigrant) | | Native students | | Students with an immigrant background | | Difference (native-immigrant) | | Native students | | Students with an immigrant background | | Difference (native-immigrant) | |
| | % | S.E. | % | S.E. | Dif. | S.E. | % | S.E. | % | S.E. | Dif. | S.E. | % | S.E. | % | S.E. | Dif. | S.E. |
|---|---|---|---|---|---|---|---|---|---|---|---|---|---|---|---|---|---|---|
| **OECD** | | | | | | | | | | | | | | | | | | |
| Australia | 68.2 | (0.3) | 63.4 | (0.5) | **4.8** | (0.6) | 7.6 | (0.2) | 10.5 | (0.3) | **-2.9** | (0.4) | 24.2 | (0.2) | 26.1 | (0.4) | **-1.9** | (0.4) |
| Austria | 66.4 | (0.5) | 60.1 | (0.9) | **6.3** | (0.9) | 2.9 | (0.2) | 6.4 | (0.7) | **-3.6** | (0.6) | 30.7 | (0.4) | 33.5 | (0.7) | **-2.7** | (0.8) |
| Belgium | 67.8 | (0.3) | 64.0 | (1.0) | **3.8** | (1.1) | 6.4 | (0.2) | 11.8 | (0.7) | **-5.4** | (0.7) | 25.8 | (0.2) | 24.2 | (0.6) | **1.6** | (0.6) |
| Canada | 67.5 | (0.3) | 59.3 | (0.8) | **8.2** | (1.0) | 10.0 | (0.2) | 13.1 | (0.5) | **-3.1** | (0.5) | 22.5 | (0.2) | 27.6 | (0.6) | **-5.1** | (0.7) |
| Czech Republic | 71.7 | (0.4) | 68.3 | (2.8) | 3.4 | (2.8) | 8.9 | (0.2) | 11.6 | (1.8) | -2.7 | (1.9) | 19.4 | (0.4) | 20.0 | (1.9) | -0.7 | (1.8) |
| Denmark | 62.6 | (0.3) | 56.5 | (1.2) | **6.1** | (1.2) | 15.6 | (0.2) | 20.2 | (0.6) | **-4.6** | (0.8) | 21.8 | (0.2) | 23.3 | (0.7) | **-1.5** | (0.7) |
| Finland | 70.9 | (0.4) | 61.9 | (3.0) | **9.0** | (2.9) | 6.0 | (0.2) | 12.9 | (1.7) | **-6.9** | (1.7) | 23.0 | (0.3) | 25.2 | (2.6) | -2.1 | (2.6) |
| France | 67.7 | (0.4) | 61.7 | (1.1) | **6.0** | (1.2) | 10.1 | (0.3) | 14.8 | (0.8) | **-4.7** | (0.9) | 22.2 | (0.3) | 23.5 | (0.7) | -1.3 | (0.7) |
| Germany | 63.0 | (0.4) | 57.8 | (1.3) | **5.3** | (1.3) | 7.2 | (0.3) | 12.0 | (0.9) | **-4.9** | (1.0) | 29.8 | (0.3) | 30.2 | (0.7) | -0.4 | (0.7) |
| Greece | 51.1 | (0.6) | 52.3 | (1.4) | -1.2 | (1.5) | 21.8 | (0.4) | 18.8 | (1.4) | **3.0** | (1.4) | 27.2 | (0.4) | 28.9 | (1.1) | -1.7 | (1.1) |
| Hungary | 53.3 | (0.4) | 53.6 | (3.2) | -0.3 | (3.3) | 18.2 | (0.3) | 18.0 | (2.0) | 0.2 | (2.0) | 28.5 | (0.3) | 28.4 | (2.7) | 0.1 | (2.8) |
| Iceland | 71.9 | (0.3) | 63.7 | (3.2) | **8.3** | (3.2) | 5.8 | (0.2) | 13.3 | (2.4) | **-7.5** | (2.4) | 22.2 | (0.2) | 23.1 | (2.2) | -0.8 | (2.2) |
| Ireland | 64.6 | (0.5) | 61.0 | (1.5) | **3.6** | (1.5) | 8.0 | (0.3) | 9.7 | (1.1) | -1.7 | (1.1) | 27.5 | (0.4) | 29.3 | (1.1) | -1.8 | (1.1) |
| Italy | 57.5 | (0.3) | 53.6 | (1.1) | **3.9** | (1.1) | 8.0 | (0.2) | 13.2 | (0.8) | **-5.2** | (0.9) | 34.5 | (0.2) | 33.2 | (0.8) | 1.3 | (0.9) |
| Japan | 78.1 | (0.5) | c | c | c | c | 6.3 | (0.2) | c | c | c | c | 15.6 | (0.4) | c | c | c | c |
| Korea | 66.4 | (0.5) | c | c | c | c | 16.5 | (0.4) | c | c | c | c | 17.2 | (0.2) | c | c | c | c |
| Luxembourg | 69.2 | (0.4) | 64.4 | (0.7) | **4.7** | (0.8) | 7.2 | (0.3) | 11.4 | (0.4) | **-4.2** | (0.5) | 23.6 | (0.3) | 24.2 | (0.5) | -0.6 | (0.6) |
| Mexico | 55.8 | (0.4) | 43.2 | (3.3) | **12.5** | (3.3) | 14.2 | (0.3) | 21.5 | (2.8) | **-7.3** | (2.8) | 30.0 | (0.3) | 35.3 | (2.5) | **-5.2** | (2.6) |
| Netherlands | 64.0 | (0.4) | 55.0 | (1.1) | **9.0** | (1.1) | 10.1 | (0.3) | 17.0 | (0.6) | **-7.0** | (0.7) | 25.9 | (0.3) | 28.0 | (0.9) | **-2.1** | (0.9) |
| New Zealand | 72.1 | (0.5) | 63.1 | (0.9) | **9.0** | (1.0) | 6.9 | (0.3) | 11.8 | (0.6) | **-4.9** | (0.7) | 21.0 | (0.3) | 25.1 | (0.5) | **-4.1** | (0.6) |
| Norway | 62.8 | (0.4) | 54.0 | (1.7) | **8.8** | (1.7) | 16.1 | (0.3) | 21.1 | (1.2) | **-5.0** | (1.2) | 21.2 | (0.3) | 24.9 | (1.1) | **-3.8** | (1.1) |
| Poland | 63.6 | (0.3) | c | c | c | c | 8.4 | (0.3) | c | c | c | c | 27.9 | (0.3) | c | c | c | c |
| Portugal | 61.4 | (0.4) | 57.3 | (2.0) | 4.1 | (2.2) | 8.5 | (0.3) | 11.2 | (1.3) | **-2.7** | (1.3) | 30.1 | (0.3) | 31.5 | (1.4) | -1.4 | (1.5) |
| Slovak Republic | 58.9 | (0.5) | c | c | c | c | 12.7 | (0.3) | c | c | c | c | 28.4 | (0.5) | c | c | c | c |
| Spain | 63.2 | (0.3) | 56.8 | (1.6) | **6.4** | (1.5) | 7.7 | (0.2) | 13.3 | (1.5) | **-5.6** | (1.5) | 29.2 | (0.3) | 29.9 | (1.1) | -0.8 | (1.1) |
| Sweden | 67.6 | (0.6) | 60.3 | (1.2) | **7.3** | (1.4) | 9.7 | (0.2) | 14.8 | (0.9) | **-5.1** | (1.0) | 22.7 | (0.5) | 24.9 | (0.7) | **-2.1** | (0.9) |
| Switzerland | 68.7 | (0.4) | 63.8 | (0.7) | **4.9** | (0.7) | 5.9 | (0.3) | 10.8 | (0.5) | **-4.9** | (0.6) | 25.4 | (0.3) | 25.4 | (0.4) | -0.0 | (0.4) |
| Turkey | 54.7 | (0.7) | 56.2 | (3.5) | -1.5 | (3.5) | 19.9 | (0.4) | 18.1 | (1.9) | 1.7 | (1.9) | 25.5 | (0.3) | 25.7 | (2.2) | -0.2 | (2.2) |
| United Kingdom | 68.5 | (0.3) | 59.1 | (1.2) | **9.4** | (1.3) | 7.1 | (0.3) | 13.8 | (1.2) | **-6.7** | (1.2) | 24.3 | (0.3) | 27.1 | (0.8) | **-2.7** | (0.8) |
| United States | 56.8 | (0.6) | 52.3 | (0.9) | **4.5** | (1.0) | 15.3 | (0.4) | 18.3 | (0.7) | **-3.1** | (0.6) | 28.0 | (0.4) | 29.4 | (0.7) | -1.4 | (0.9) |
| **OECD average** | 64.5 | (0.1) | 58.6 | (0.4) | **5.6** | (0.4) | 10.3 | (0.1) | 14.2 | (0.3) | **-4.0** | (0.3) | 25.2 | (0.1) | 27.2 | (0.3) | **-1.6** | (0.3) |
| **Partners** | | | | | | | | | | | | | | | | | | |
| Argentina | 55.1 | (0.7) | 59.7 | (3.1) | -4.6 | (3.1) | 8.0 | (0.5) | 6.9 | (1.5) | 1.1 | (1.5) | 36.9 | (0.5) | 33.4 | (2.7) | 3.5 | (2.8) |
| Azerbaijan | 45.0 | (0.5) | 46.4 | (2.2) | -1.4 | (2.2) | 19.4 | (0.5) | 18.2 | (1.9) | 1.1 | (1.8) | 35.6 | (0.5) | 35.4 | (1.5) | 0.2 | (1.6) |
| Brazil | 54.7 | (0.5) | 53.5 | (2.8) | 1.2 | (2.9) | 17.5 | (0.3) | 19.6 | (2.1) | -2.1 | (2.0) | 27.8 | (0.3) | 27.0 | (2.5) | 0.9 | (2.6) |
| Bulgaria | 52.0 | (0.5) | c | c | c | c | 15.3 | (0.4) | c | c | c | c | 32.7 | (0.4) | c | c | c | c |
| Chile | 57.5 | (0.6) | c | c | c | c | 15.1 | (0.5) | c | c | c | c | 27.4 | (0.4) | c | c | c | c |
| Colombia | 60.5 | (0.6) | c | c | c | c | 14.3 | (0.4) | c | c | c | c | 25.2 | (0.4) | c | c | c | c |
| Croatia | 67.0 | (0.4) | 65.8 | (1.0) | 1.2 | (1.1) | 5.8 | (0.3) | 5.5 | (0.5) | 0.3 | (0.6) | 27.2 | (0.4) | 28.7 | (0.9) | -1.5 | (1.0) |
| Estonia | 62.0 | (0.5) | 61.5 | (1.0) | 0.5 | (1.1) | 12.8 | (0.4) | 14.1 | (0.8) | -1.3 | (0.8) | 25.2 | (0.3) | 24.4 | (0.7) | 0.8 | (0.8) |
| Hong Kong-China | 71.0 | (0.5) | 71.0 | (0.6) | 0.0 | (0.8) | 9.3 | (0.4) | 8.7 | (0.4) | 0.6 | (0.5) | 19.7 | (0.4) | 20.3 | (0.4) | -0.7 | (0.5) |
| Indonesia | 56.4 | (0.7) | 51.7 | (8.8) | 4.7 | (8.8) | 16.7 | (0.6) | 14.4 | (3.1) | 2.3 | (3.1) | 27.0 | (0.3) | 34.0 | (6.7) | -7.0 | (6.7) |
| Israel | 54.8 | (0.6) | 53.2 | (1.0) | 1.6 | (1.1) | 19.4 | (0.5) | 19.6 | (0.7) | -0.2 | (0.9) | 25.8 | (0.5) | 27.2 | (0.9) | -1.4 | (0.9) |
| Jordan | 44.4 | (0.7) | 45.1 | (0.9) | -0.6 | (0.9) | 22.2 | (0.5) | 21.1 | (0.8) | 1.1 | (0.9) | 33.4 | (0.4) | 33.9 | (0.7) | -0.5 | (0.8) |
| Kyrgyzstan | 39.9 | (0.5) | 47.4 | (2.0) | **-7.5** | (2.1) | 26.1 | (0.4) | 17.5 | (2.1) | **8.6** | (2.1) | 34.1 | (0.4) | 35.1 | (1.9) | -1.1 | (2.0) |
| Latvia | 59.5 | (0.4) | 56.4 | (1.0) | **3.0** | (1.0) | 11.3 | (0.4) | 12.7 | (0.8) | -1.4 | (0.8) | 29.3 | (0.4) | 30.9 | (0.8) | -1.6 | (0.8) |
| Liechtenstein | 71.8 | (1.3) | 66.6 | (2.3) | **5.1** | (2.6) | 4.4 | (0.7) | 7.6 | (1.1) | **-3.2** | (1.2) | 23.9 | (1.1) | 25.8 | (1.8) | -1.9 | (2.1) |
| Lithuania | 62.4 | (0.4) | 62.4 | (2.0) | -0.0 | (2.0) | 9.7 | (0.3) | 10.9 | (1.1) | -1.2 | (1.2) | 27.9 | (0.3) | 26.6 | (1.7) | 1.2 | (1.6) |
| Macao-China | 70.6 | (0.7) | 71.9 | (0.4) | -1.3 | (0.8) | 11.7 | (0.4) | 10.8 | (0.5) | **0.8** | (0.5) | 17.7 | (0.5) | 17.2 | (0.3) | 0.5 | (0.5) |
| Montenegro | 53.3 | (0.4) | 51.8 | (1.9) | 1.5 | (2.0) | 11.3 | (0.3) | 11.3 | (1.6) | 0.0 | (1.5) | 35.4 | (0.4) | 36.9 | (1.7) | -1.5 | (1.7) |
| Qatar | 43.5 | (0.5) | 47.0 | (0.5) | **-3.5** | (0.7) | 25.0 | (0.4) | 21.2 | (0.4) | **3.7** | (0.6) | 31.6 | (0.4) | 31.8 | (0.4) | -0.2 | (0.6) |
| Romania | 50.6 | (0.6) | c | c | c | c | 19.7 | (0.4) | c | c | c | c | 29.6 | (0.3) | c | c | c | c |
| Russian Federation | 48.2 | (0.6) | 49.0 | (1.1) | **-0.8** | (0.9) | 16.5 | (0.6) | 14.9 | (1.0) | 1.6 | (0.9) | 35.3 | (0.5) | 36.2 | (1.0) | -0.9 | (0.8) |
| Serbia | 60.3 | (0.5) | 60.1 | (1.6) | 0.2 | (1.7) | 12.9 | (0.4) | 11.4 | (1.0) | 1.5 | (1.0) | 26.8 | (0.3) | 28.5 | (1.3) | -1.7 | (1.3) |
| Slovenia | 61.0 | (0.4) | 59.4 | (1.0) | **1.7** | (1.1) | 11.9 | (0.3) | 12.7 | (0.8) | -0.7 | (0.9) | 27.0 | (0.3) | 28.0 | (0.9) | -0.9 | (1.0) |
| Chinese Taipei | 66.2 | (0.3) | 64.2 | (4.9) | 2.0 | (4.9) | 8.8 | (0.2) | 12.1 | (2.4) | -3.3 | (2.4) | 25.0 | (0.2) | 23.6 | (3.4) | 1.4 | (3.4) |
| Thailand | 62.6 | (0.4) | c | c | c | c | 7.2 | (0.3) | c | c | c | c | 30.2 | (0.3) | c | c | c | c |
| Tunisia | 45.8 | (0.7) | 38.7 | (3.8) | 7.1 | (3.8) | 23.6 | (0.5) | 31.4 | (3.9) | **-7.9** | (3.8) | 30.6 | (0.5) | 29.9 | (3.3) | 0.8 | (3.3) |
| Uruguay | 61.2 | (0.5) | c | c | c | c | 11.0 | (0.4) | c | c | c | c | 27.8 | (0.4) | c | c | c | c |

*Note:* Values that are statistically significant at the 5% level (p < 0.05) are indicated in bold.

### Table 3.8d  Mean learning hours and allocation of total learning time in science, in mathematics and on the language of instruction, by immigrant status
[Part 1/3]

| | Mean learning hours per week | | | | | | | | | | | | | | | |
| | Regular school lessons | | | | | | | | Out-of-school-time lessons | | | | | | | |
| | Native students | | Students with an immigrant background | | Difference (native-immigrant) | | Difference after accounting for ESCS and school average ESCS (native-immigrant) | | Native students | | Students with an immigrant background | | Difference (native-immigrant) | | Difference after accounting for ESCS and school average ESCS (native-immigrant) | |
| | Mean | S.E. | Mean | S.E. | Dif. | S.E. | Dif. | S.E. | Mean | S.E. | Mean | S.E. | Dif. | S.E. | Dif. | S.E. |
| **Australia** | 11.25 | (0.08) | 12.04 | (0.14) | **-0.79** | (0.16) | **-0.71** | (0.15) | 1.52 | (0.03) | 2.54 | (0.10) | **-1.01** | (0.10) | **-1.05** | (0.10) |
| **Austria** | 8.53 | (0.10) | 8.70 | (0.16) | -0.16 | (0.18) | **-0.65** | (0.22) | 0.85 | (0.04) | 1.58 | (0.13) | **-0.74** | (0.13) | **-0.65** | (0.14) |
| **Belgium** | 9.77 | (0.09) | 9.34 | (0.27) | 0.42 | (0.27) | **-1.00** | (0.29) | 1.21 | (0.03) | 2.04 | (0.12) | **-0.83** | (0.13) | **-0.71** | (0.13) |
| **Canada** | 13.00 | (0.11) | 12.87 | (0.22) | 0.13 | (0.22) | 0.17 | (0.21) | 2.11 | (0.04) | 3.17 | (0.11) | **-1.07** | (0.11) | **-1.11** | (0.11) |
| **Czech Republic** | 10.67 | (0.11) | 10.38 | (0.38) | 0.29 | (0.38) | 0.13 | (0.38) | 1.87 | (0.04) | 2.51 | (0.37) | **-0.64** | (0.39) | **-0.63** | (0.38) |
| **Denmark** | 13.20 | (0.08) | 12.69 | (0.25) | **0.51** | (0.25) | 0.15 | (0.25) | 3.74 | (0.06) | 5.01 | (0.23) | **-1.27** | (0.23) | **-1.28** | (0.23) |
| **Finland** | 9.74 | (0.11) | 8.84 | (0.62) | 0.90 | (0.62) | 0.73 | (0.62) | 1.03 | (0.04) | 2.03 | (0.35) | **-0.99** | (0.34) | **-1.01** | (0.35) |
| **France** | 10.83 | (0.10) | 10.09 | (0.27) | **0.74** | (0.26) | 0.10 | (0.22) | 2.13 | (0.04) | 2.99 | (0.15) | **-0.86** | (0.16) | **-0.83** | (0.16) |
| **Germany** | 10.66 | (0.09) | 10.40 | (0.20) | 0.26 | (0.21) | -0.17 | (0.21) | 1.77 | (0.05) | 2.72 | (0.19) | **-0.95** | (0.19) | **-0.70** | (0.19) |
| **Greece** | 9.96 | (0.12) | 8.55 | (0.34) | **1.40** | (0.32) | **0.66** | (0.33) | 6.00 | (0.11) | 3.95 | (0.27) | **2.04** | (0.28) | **1.62** | (0.29) |
| **Hungary** | 9.01 | (0.10) | 8.97 | (0.62) | 0.03 | (0.62) | 0.35 | (0.62) | 3.58 | (0.06) | 3.57 | (0.48) | 0.02 | (0.48) | -0.08 | (0.47) |
| **Iceland** | 12.24 | (0.06) | 11.83 | (0.58) | 0.41 | (0.57) | 0.25 | (0.56) | 1.43 | (0.04) | 2.51 | (0.42) | **-1.08** | (0.42) | **-1.12** | (0.42) |
| **Ireland** | 9.71 | (0.09) | 10.24 | (0.29) | -0.53 | (0.30) | -0.49 | (0.29) | 1.60 | (0.04) | 2.39 | (0.27) | **-0.78** | (0.28) | **-0.74** | (0.27) |
| **Italy** | 11.33 | (0.09) | 10.72 | (0.28) | **0.61** | (0.29) | 0.49 | (0.27) | 2.21 | (0.04) | 2.81 | (0.17) | **-0.60** | (0.18) | **-0.64** | (0.17) |
| **Japan** | 10.76 | (0.13) | c | c | c | c | c | c | 1.39 | (0.05) | c | c | c | c | c | c |
| **Korea** | 12.79 | (0.11) | c | c | c | c | c | c | 4.76 | (0.08) | c | c | c | c | c | c |
| **Luxembourg** | 9.77 | (0.07) | 9.64 | (0.10) | 0.13 | (0.12) | **-0.39** | (0.13) | 1.70 | (0.04) | 2.31 | (0.08) | **-0.61** | (0.09) | **-0.47** | (0.10) |
| **Mexico** | 10.99 | (0.10) | 8.61 | (0.82) | **2.38** | (0.82) | **1.81** | (0.84) | 3.23 | (0.08) | 4.35 | (0.61) | -1.13 | (0.61) | -0.70 | (0.62) |
| **Netherlands** | 8.01 | (0.07) | 7.74 | (0.24) | 0.26 | (0.26) | -0.38 | (0.22) | 1.74 | (0.05) | 2.95 | (0.14) | **-1.20** | (0.15) | **-1.01** | (0.18) |
| **New Zealand** | 12.88 | (0.10) | 12.73 | (0.18) | 0.16 | (0.21) | 0.24 | (0.17) | 1.43 | (0.06) | 2.84 | (0.13) | **-1.42** | (0.14) | **-1.43** | (0.14) |
| **Norway** | 9.63 | (0.08) | 9.75 | (0.28) | -0.12 | (0.28) | -0.25 | (0.30) | 3.05 | (0.05) | 4.30 | (0.25) | **-1.25** | (0.24) | **-1.35** | (0.24) |
| **Poland** | 11.74 | (0.09) | c | c | c | c | c | c | 2.10 | (0.06) | c | c | c | c | c | c |
| **Portugal** | 10.17 | (0.10) | 9.20 | (0.34) | **0.97** | (0.35) | **1.03** | (0.28) | 1.97 | (0.05) | 2.33 | (0.22) | -0.36 | (0.23) | -0.38 | (0.22) |
| **Slovak Republic** | 8.88 | (0.14) | c | c | c | c | c | c | 2.40 | (0.07) | c | c | c | c | c | c |
| **Spain** | 10.23 | (0.09) | 9.31 | (0.25) | **0.92** | (0.26) | **0.70** | (0.23) | 2.22 | (0.06) | 2.30 | (0.16) | -0.08 | (0.18) | -0.06 | (0.17) |
| **Sweden** | 9.03 | (0.07) | 9.03 | (0.20) | -0.00 | (0.19) | -0.05 | (0.19) | 1.66 | (0.03) | 2.77 | (0.18) | **-1.11** | (0.18) | **-1.03** | (0.16) |
| **Switzerland** | 9.96 | (0.10) | 9.65 | (0.11) | **0.30** | (0.12) | 0.05 | (0.13) | 1.37 | (0.05) | 2.23 | (0.11) | **-0.86** | (0.12) | **-0.81** | (0.12) |
| **Turkey** | 10.71 | (0.16) | 10.83 | (0.62) | -0.12 | (0.59) | 0.54 | (0.59) | 5.25 | (0.09) | 4.26 | (0.91) | 0.99 | (0.91) | 1.31 | (0.91) |
| **United Kingdom** | 11.93 | (0.10) | 12.17 | (0.29) | -0.24 | (0.29) | -0.49 | (0.29) | 1.53 | (0.03) | 3.36 | (0.22) | **-1.83** | (0.22) | **-1.85** | (0.20) |
| **United States** | 11.15 | (0.13) | 10.11 | (0.21) | **1.04** | (0.22) | -0.02 | (0.25) | 2.91 | (0.07) | 3.54 | (0.14) | **-0.63** | (0.15) | **-0.46** | (0.16) |
| **OECD average** | 10.62 | (0.02) | 10.17 | (0.07) | **0.38** | (0.07) | 0.11 | (0.07) | 2.33 | (0.01) | 2.98 | (0.06) | **-0.70** | (0.06) | **-0.66** | (0.06) |
| **Argentina** | 7.63 | (0.16) | 7.34 | (0.56) | 0.29 | (0.54) | -0.01 | (0.52) | 1.66 | (0.07) | 1.28 | (0.20) | 0.38 | (0.21) | 0.38 | (0.22) |
| **Azerbaijan** | 10.42 | (0.12) | 10.81 | (0.76) | -0.39 | (0.75) | -0.17 | (0.67) | 4.86 | (0.10) | 5.15 | (0.35) | -0.30 | (0.34) | -0.32 | (0.33) |
| **Brazil** | 8.54 | (0.08) | 6.83 | (0.45) | **1.71** | (0.46) | **1.44** | (0.44) | 3.14 | (0.07) | 2.88 | (0.29) | 0.26 | (0.28) | 0.21 | (0.28) |
| **Bulgaria** | 8.59 | (0.16) | c | c | c | c | c | c | 3.17 | (0.08) | c | c | c | c | c | c |
| **Chile** | 9.30 | (0.17) | c | c | c | c | c | c | 2.80 | (0.06) | c | c | c | c | c | c |
| **Colombia** | 11.74 | (0.20) | c | c | c | c | c | c | 3.32 | (0.07) | c | c | c | c | c | c |
| **Croatia** | 8.44 | (0.09) | 8.42 | (0.16) | 0.02 | (0.17) | -0.17 | (0.16) | 1.55 | (0.05) | 1.63 | (0.11) | -0.07 | (0.11) | -0.12 | (0.11) |
| **Estonia** | 10.97 | (0.10) | 11.05 | (0.22) | -0.08 | (0.23) | -0.13 | (0.24) | 2.56 | (0.07) | 3.01 | (0.13) | **-0.45** | (0.13) | **-0.42** | (0.13) |
| **Hong Kong-China** | 13.52 | (0.13) | 13.67 | (0.15) | -0.16 | (0.17) | **-0.73** | (0.16) | 3.36 | (0.10) | 2.72 | (0.11) | **0.65** | (0.13) | **0.40** | (0.15) |
| **Indonesia** | 11.00 | (0.17) | 7.14 | (0.83) | **3.86** | (0.84) | **3.26** | (0.79) | 3.65 | (0.11) | 3.48 | (0.68) | 0.17 | (0.69) | 0.10 | (0.68) |
| **Israel** | 9.56 | (0.11) | 9.84 | (0.21) | -0.28 | (0.21) | **-0.54** | (0.21) | 4.35 | (0.09) | 4.55 | (0.14) | -0.20 | (0.17) | -0.15 | (0.16) |
| **Jordan** | 10.39 | (0.15) | 10.75 | (0.24) | -0.36 | (0.28) | 0.04 | (0.30) | 5.09 | (0.11) | 5.01 | (0.19) | 0.08 | (0.20) | 0.04 | (0.20) |
| **Kyrgyzstan** | 7.81 | (0.15) | 8.77 | (0.49) | **-0.96** | (0.48) | -0.42 | (0.44) | 4.60 | (0.09) | 3.77 | (0.46) | 0.83 | (0.44) | 0.58 | (0.42) |
| **Latvia** | 11.11 | (0.11) | 10.72 | (0.26) | 0.40 | (0.26) | **0.50** | (0.25) | 2.70 | (0.08) | 3.09 | (0.15) | **-0.39** | (0.18) | **-0.43** | (0.17) |
| **Liechtenstein** | 10.43 | (0.24) | 9.91 | (0.35) | 0.52 | (0.43) | 0.21 | (0.42) | 1.13 | (0.12) | 1.77 | (0.19) | **-0.64** | (0.22) | -0.34 | (0.20) |
| **Lithuania** | 9.88 | (0.10) | 10.24 | (0.47) | -0.36 | (0.46) | -0.22 | (0.44) | 1.92 | (0.05) | 2.01 | (0.22) | -0.10 | (0.24) | -0.18 | (0.24) |
| **Macao-China** | 14.14 | (0.16) | 14.64 | (0.09) | **-0.50** | (0.19) | **-0.76** | (0.21) | 3.35 | (0.13) | 3.20 | (0.08) | 0.16 | (0.14) | 0.10 | (0.14) |
| **Montenegro** | 8.95 | (0.09) | 8.36 | (0.34) | 0.59 | (0.35) | **0.83** | (0.32) | 2.68 | (0.05) | 2.38 | (0.21) | 0.29 | (0.22) | 0.27 | (0.22) |
| **Qatar** | 7.85 | (0.10) | 9.95 | (0.11) | **-2.10** | (0.15) | **-1.98** | (0.15) | 4.94 | (0.08) | 4.71 | (0.10) | 0.24 | (0.13) | 0.16 | (0.13) |
| **Romania** | 8.57 | (0.15) | c | c | c | c | c | c | 4.04 | (0.07) | c | c | c | c | c | c |
| **Russian Federation** | 9.43 | (0.14) | 9.41 | (0.24) | 0.02 | (0.24) | 0.08 | (0.25) | 3.07 | (0.07) | 2.95 | (0.16) | 0.12 | (0.15) | 0.08 | (0.15) |
| **Serbia** | 9.34 | (0.11) | 9.21 | (0.24) | 0.13 | (0.25) | 0.40 | (0.23) | 2.65 | (0.06) | 2.61 | (0.18) | 0.04 | (0.18) | -0.01 | (0.18) |
| **Slovenia** | 9.47 | (0.07) | 8.77 | (0.25) | **0.70** | (0.26) | 0.27 | (0.26) | 2.45 | (0.05) | 2.51 | (0.12) | -0.06 | (0.13) | 0.10 | (0.14) |
| **Chinese Taipei** | 11.59 | (0.14) | 8.84 | (0.98) | **2.75** | (0.96) | **2.65** | (0.82) | 3.01 | (0.06) | 3.08 | (0.58) | -0.07 | (0.57) | -0.16 | (0.54) |
| **Thailand** | 10.73 | (0.08) | c | c | c | c | c | c | 2.39 | (0.07) | c | c | c | c | c | c |
| **Tunisia** | 9.21 | (0.12) | 8.33 | (0.81) | 0.88 | (0.83) | 0.58 | (0.87) | 6.09 | (0.06) | 6.69 | (0.76) | -0.60 | (0.77) | -0.49 | (0.76) |
| **Uruguay** | 8.53 | (0.09) | c | c | c | c | c | c | 2.06 | (0.06) | c | c | c | c | c | c |

*Note:* Values that are statistically significant at the 5% level (p < 0.05) are indicated in bold.

© OECD 2011  Quality Time for Students: Learning In and Out of School

**Table 3.8d** [Part 2/3] **Mean learning hours and allocation of total learning time in science, in mathematics and on the language of instruction, by immigrant status**

| | | Mean learning hours per week | | | | | | | | | | | | | |
|---|---|---|---|---|---|---|---|---|---|---|---|---|---|---|---|
| | | Individual study | | | | | | | | Total learning hours | | | | | |
| | | Native students | | Students with an immigrant background | | Difference (native-immigrant) | | Difference after accounting for ESCS and school average ESCS (native-immigrant) | | Native students | | Students with an immigrant background | | Difference (native-immigrant) | |
| | | Mean | S.E. | Mean | S.E. | Dif. | S.E. | Dif. | S.E. | Mean | S.E. | Mean | S.E. | Dif. | S.E. |
| **OECD** | Australia | 4.34 | (0.05) | 5.85 | (0.12) | **-1.51** | (0.12) | **-1.46** | (0.13) | 17.13 | (0.11) | 20.40 | (0.27) | **-3.27** | (0.29) |
| | Austria | 4.77 | (0.08) | 6.04 | (0.18) | **-1.27** | (0.20) | **-1.21** | (0.20) | 14.19 | (0.17) | 16.39 | (0.33) | **-2.20** | (0.37) |
| | Belgium | 4.39 | (0.05) | 4.44 | (0.16) | -0.05 | (0.15) | **-0.74** | (0.17) | 15.41 | (0.13) | 15.71 | (0.44) | -0.30 | (0.44) |
| | Canada | 4.90 | (0.06) | 6.64 | (0.20) | **-1.74** | (0.20) | **-1.69** | (0.20) | 20.12 | (0.16) | 22.60 | (0.41) | **-2.49** | (0.41) |
| | Czech Republic | 3.45 | (0.05) | 3.94 | (0.43) | -0.49 | (0.42) | -0.50 | (0.42) | 15.97 | (0.16) | 16.79 | (0.84) | -0.82 | (0.86) |
| | Denmark | 4.92 | (0.06) | 5.93 | (0.21) | **-1.01** | (0.21) | **-1.32** | (0.21) | 21.83 | (0.15) | 23.32 | (0.48) | **-1.49** | (0.47) |
| | Finland | 3.40 | (0.05) | 3.76 | (0.31) | -0.36 | (0.30) | -0.51 | (0.30) | 14.16 | (0.16) | 14.65 | (0.82) | -0.49 | (0.82) |
| | France | 4.53 | (0.08) | 4.91 | (0.20) | -0.39 | (0.20) | **-0.76** | (0.20) | 17.53 | (0.15) | 18.03 | (0.41) | -0.51 | (0.41) |
| | Germany | 5.79 | (0.08) | 6.32 | (0.19) | **-0.52** | (0.20) | **-0.53** | (0.20) | 18.28 | (0.16) | 19.26 | (0.37) | **-0.98** | (0.39) |
| | Greece | 5.84 | (0.09) | 4.93 | (0.25) | **0.91** | (0.25) | **0.56** | (0.26) | 21.82 | (0.24) | 17.43 | (0.74) | **4.39** | (0.73) |
| | Hungary | 5.29 | (0.08) | 5.16 | (0.38) | 0.13 | (0.38) | 0.20 | (0.39) | 17.89 | (0.20) | 17.83 | (1.20) | 0.06 | (1.19) |
| | Iceland | 4.42 | (0.05) | 4.92 | (0.51) | -0.50 | (0.51) | -0.60 | (0.52) | 18.10 | (0.09) | 19.35 | (0.85) | -1.25 | (0.84) |
| | Ireland | 4.65 | (0.08) | 5.50 | (0.27) | **-0.85** | (0.27) | **-0.74** | (0.27) | 15.95 | (0.16) | 18.01 | (0.58) | **-2.06** | (0.61) |
| | Italy | 7.56 | (0.08) | 7.31 | (0.26) | 0.25 | (0.27) | 0.04 | (0.25) | 21.11 | (0.17) | 20.88 | (0.48) | 0.23 | (0.49) |
| | Japan | 3.11 | (0.09) | c | c | c | c | c | c | 15.26 | (0.22) | c | c | c | c |
| | Korea | 4.95 | (0.12) | c | c | c | c | c | c | 22.55 | (0.25) | c | c | c | c |
| | Luxembourg | 4.26 | (0.06) | 4.42 | (0.09) | -0.16 | (0.11) | -0.12 | (0.12) | 15.74 | (0.12) | 16.35 | (0.18) | **-0.62** | (0.22) |
| | Mexico | 6.41 | (0.08) | 6.71 | (0.56) | -0.30 | (0.55) | -0.23 | (0.54) | 20.50 | (0.19) | 19.53 | (1.21) | 0.97 | (1.21) |
| | Netherlands | 3.91 | (0.06) | 4.62 | (0.15) | **-0.72** | (0.15) | **-1.09** | (0.17) | 13.63 | (0.13) | 15.24 | (0.44) | **-1.61** | (0.46) |
| | New Zealand | 4.04 | (0.08) | 5.87 | (0.13) | **-1.84** | (0.16) | **-1.76** | (0.16) | 18.37 | (0.16) | 21.43 | (0.27) | **-3.06** | (0.33) |
| | Norway | 3.99 | (0.06) | 5.27 | (0.25) | **-1.28** | (0.25) | **-1.56** | (0.24) | 16.65 | (0.12) | 19.32 | (0.50) | **-2.67** | (0.50) |
| | Poland | 6.36 | (0.07) | c | c | c | c | c | c | 20.23 | (0.14) | c | c | c | c |
| | Portugal | 5.80 | (0.08) | 6.22 | (0.37) | -0.42 | (0.38) | -0.39 | (0.37) | 17.97 | (0.17) | 17.81 | (0.76) | 0.16 | (0.78) |
| | Slovak Republic | 4.81 | (0.09) | c | c | c | c | c | c | 16.13 | (0.25) | c | c | c | c |
| | Spain | 5.58 | (0.08) | 5.59 | (0.23) | -0.01 | (0.23) | -0.15 | (0.24) | 18.15 | (0.17) | 17.21 | (0.33) | **0.94** | (0.37) |
| | Sweden | 3.47 | (0.05) | 4.55 | (0.16) | **-1.08** | (0.17) | **-1.22** | (0.19) | 14.14 | (0.10) | 16.42 | (0.36) | **-2.28** | (0.33) |
| | Switzerland | 4.08 | (0.05) | 4.61 | (0.10) | **-0.53** | (0.11) | **-0.55** | (0.12) | 15.40 | (0.15) | 16.53 | (0.21) | **-1.13** | (0.26) |
| | Turkey | 6.14 | (0.09) | 5.37 | (0.72) | 0.77 | (0.73) | 0.94 | (0.72) | 21.99 | (0.29) | 20.38 | (2.16) | 1.60 | (2.17) |
| | United Kingdom | 4.39 | (0.06) | 5.89 | (0.16) | **-1.50** | (0.16) | **-1.81** | (0.16) | 17.87 | (0.13) | 21.43 | (0.39) | **-3.56** | (0.38) |
| | United States | 5.56 | (0.08) | 5.79 | (0.18) | -0.23 | (0.21) | **-0.90** | (0.21) | 19.76 | (0.16) | 19.43 | (0.40) | 0.33 | (0.43) |
| | **OECD average** | 4.84 | (0.01) | 5.41 | (0.06) | **-0.56** | (0.06) | **-0.70** | (0.06) | 17.79 | (0.03) | 18.53 | (0.14) | **-0.85** | (0.14) |
| **Partners** | Argentina | 5.04 | (0.10) | 4.52 | (0.32) | 0.52 | (0.33) | 0.42 | (0.34) | 14.34 | (0.24) | 13.30 | (0.81) | 1.04 | (0.81) |
| | Azerbaijan | 8.74 | (0.14) | 9.10 | (0.39) | -0.36 | (0.40) | -0.35 | (0.42) | 24.16 | (0.27) | 25.09 | (1.11) | -0.93 | (1.11) |
| | Brazil | 5.21 | (0.07) | 4.93 | (0.42) | 0.27 | (0.42) | 0.23 | (0.42) | 16.84 | (0.17) | 14.68 | (0.95) | **2.16** | (0.94) |
| | Bulgaria | 6.15 | (0.16) | c | c | c | c | c | c | 17.99 | (0.33) | c | c | c | c |
| | Chile | 4.68 | (0.08) | c | c | c | c | c | c | 16.88 | (0.23) | c | c | c | c |
| | Colombia | 5.57 | (0.10) | c | c | c | c | c | c | 20.62 | (0.27) | c | c | c | c |
| | Croatia | 4.83 | (0.07) | 4.96 | (0.19) | -0.13 | (0.20) | -0.19 | (0.20) | 14.91 | (0.15) | 15.09 | (0.34) | -0.18 | (0.34) |
| | Estonia | 5.07 | (0.07) | 5.51 | (0.22) | -0.43 | (0.24) | -0.46 | (0.24) | 18.62 | (0.16) | 19.66 | (0.40) | **-1.05** | (0.45) |
| | Hong Kong-China | 5.33 | (0.10) | 5.35 | (0.13) | -0.02 | (0.15) | **-0.46** | (0.16) | 22.19 | (0.24) | 21.75 | (0.29) | 0.44 | (0.33) |
| | Indonesia | 5.56 | (0.08) | 5.94 | (0.66) | -0.38 | (0.66) | -0.39 | (0.66) | 20.17 | (0.25) | 16.42 | (1.23) | **3.74** | (1.23) |
| | Israel | 5.34 | (0.12) | 5.24 | (0.17) | 0.10 | (0.18) | 0.16 | (0.18) | 19.32 | (0.27) | 19.71 | (0.42) | -0.39 | (0.43) |
| | Jordan | 7.89 | (0.12) | 8.11 | (0.23) | -0.21 | (0.24) | -0.23 | (0.23) | 23.39 | (0.24) | 23.65 | (0.51) | -0.26 | (0.56) |
| | Kyrgyzstan | 6.73 | (0.09) | 6.56 | (0.42) | 0.17 | (0.42) | 0.08 | (0.43) | 19.26 | (0.25) | 19.16 | (0.98) | 0.10 | (0.94) |
| | Latvia | 6.25 | (0.09) | 6.32 | (0.21) | -0.07 | (0.23) | -0.07 | (0.22) | 20.06 | (0.20) | 20.16 | (0.46) | -0.11 | (0.53) |
| | Liechtenstein | 3.87 | (0.18) | 4.00 | (0.30) | -0.14 | (0.36) | -0.11 | (0.37) | 15.50 | (0.33) | 15.48 | (0.45) | 0.02 | (0.62) |
| | Lithuania | 5.28 | (0.07) | 5.27 | (0.42) | 0.01 | (0.41) | 0.06 | (0.40) | 17.06 | (0.14) | 17.55 | (0.74) | -0.49 | (0.72) |
| | Macao-China | 5.09 | (0.14) | 4.87 | (0.08) | 0.22 | (0.16) | -0.30 | (0.16) | 22.60 | (0.31) | 22.69 | (0.17) | -0.10 | (0.34) |
| | Montenegro | 6.17 | (0.08) | 6.50 | (0.32) | -0.33 | (0.32) | -0.25 | (0.32) | 17.75 | (0.17) | 17.15 | (0.68) | 0.61 | (0.70) |
| | Qatar | 5.80 | (0.08) | 6.92 | (0.10) | **-1.12** | (0.14) | **-1.15** | (0.14) | 18.60 | (0.20) | 21.65 | (0.24) | **-3.05** | (0.31) |
| | Romania | 5.96 | (0.10) | c | c | c | c | c | c | 18.57 | (0.26) | c | c | c | c |
| | Russian Federation | 6.65 | (0.12) | 6.71 | (0.26) | -0.06 | (0.23) | -0.03 | (0.24) | 19.15 | (0.24) | 18.99 | (0.53) | 0.16 | (0.53) |
| | Serbia | 5.23 | (0.08) | 5.20 | (0.20) | 0.03 | (0.21) | 0.13 | (0.21) | 17.22 | (0.20) | 16.94 | (0.40) | 0.28 | (0.44) |
| | Slovenia | 4.98 | (0.06) | 4.62 | (0.18) | 0.36 | (0.19) | 0.30 | (0.18) | 16.94 | (0.12) | 15.96 | (0.41) | **0.98** | (0.42) |
| | Chinese Taipei | 4.91 | (0.09) | 3.91 | (0.48) | **1.00** | (0.48) | 0.83 | (0.44) | 19.63 | (0.26) | 15.76 | (1.69) | **3.87** | (1.66) |
| | Thailand | 5.34 | (0.08) | c | c | c | c | c | c | 18.44 | (0.16) | c | c | c | c |
| | Tunisia | 7.28 | (0.08) | 7.08 | (0.70) | 0.20 | (0.70) | 0.31 | (0.71) | 22.61 | (0.21) | 22.57 | (1.76) | 0.05 | (1.77) |
| | Uruguay | 4.25 | (0.06) | c | c | c | c | c | c | 14.87 | (0.15) | c | c | c | c |

*Note:* Values that are statistically significant at the 5% level (p < 0.05) are indicated in bold.

### Table 3.8d
[Part 3/3]

## Mean learning hours and allocation of total learning time in science, in mathematics and on the language of instruction, by immigrant status

| | Allocation of total learning time in science, mathematics and the language of instruction for | | | | | | | | | | | | | | | | | |
| | Regular school lessons | | | | | | Out-of-school-time lessons | | | | | | Individual study | | | | | |
| | Native students | | Students with an immigrant background | | Difference (native-immigrant) | | Native students | | Students with an immigrant background | | Difference (native-immigrant) | | Native students | | Students with an immigrant background | | Difference (native-immigrant) | |
| | % | S.E. | % | S.E. | Dif. | S.E. | % | S.E. | % | S.E. | Dif. | S.E. | % | S.E. | % | S.E. | Dif. | S.E. |
|---|---|---|---|---|---|---|---|---|---|---|---|---|---|---|---|---|---|---|
| **OECD** | | | | | | | | | | | | | | | | | | |
| Australia | 68.1 | (0.2) | 61.7 | (0.4) | **6.4** | (0.5) | 7.9 | (0.2) | 11.0 | (0.3) | **-3.1** | (0.3) | 24.0 | (0.2) | 27.3 | (0.3) | **-3.3** | (0.3) |
| Austria | 62.7 | (0.4) | 56.7 | (0.8) | **6.0** | (0.9) | 4.9 | (0.2) | 8.3 | (0.6) | **-3.4** | (0.6) | 32.4 | (0.3) | 35.0 | (0.8) | **-2.6** | (0.8) |
| Belgium | 64.8 | (0.2) | 61.2 | (0.8) | **3.5** | (0.8) | 7.2 | (0.2) | 11.9 | (0.7) | **-4.8** | (0.7) | 28.1 | (0.2) | 26.8 | (0.5) | **1.2** | (0.5) |
| Canada | 65.8 | (0.3) | 57.8 | (0.7) | **8.0** | (0.7) | 10.2 | (0.2) | 13.3 | (0.4) | **-3.1** | (0.4) | 24.0 | (0.2) | 28.9 | (0.6) | **-4.9** | (0.6) |
| Czech Republic | 69.7 | (0.4) | 66.1 | (2.5) | 3.6 | (2.5) | 10.1 | (0.2) | 12.5 | (1.5) | -2.4 | (1.5) | 20.2 | (0.3) | 21.4 | (1.8) | -1.2 | (1.8) |
| Denmark | 62.8 | (0.3) | 55.5 | (1.2) | **7.3** | (1.2) | 15.6 | (0.3) | 20.2 | (0.9) | **-4.6** | (0.9) | 21.6 | (0.2) | 24.3 | (0.6) | **-2.7** | (0.7) |
| Finland | 70.7 | (0.3) | 62.5 | (2.6) | **8.2** | (2.5) | 6.3 | (0.2) | 12.0 | (1.8) | **-5.8** | (1.8) | 23.0 | (0.2) | 25.5 | (2.2) | -2.5 | (2.1) |
| France | 64.1 | (0.3) | 58.4 | (0.8) | **5.7** | (0.9) | 11.5 | (0.2) | 15.9 | (0.7) | **-4.4** | (0.8) | 24.4 | (0.3) | 25.7 | (0.5) | **-1.3** | (0.6) |
| Germany | 60.2 | (0.3) | 55.3 | (1.0) | **4.9** | (1.1) | 8.6 | (0.3) | 13.0 | (0.9) | **-4.4** | (0.9) | 31.2 | (0.3) | 31.7 | (0.5) | -0.5 | (0.5) |
| Greece | 48.0 | (0.5) | 51.4 | (1.3) | **-3.5** | (1.2) | 26.0 | (0.3) | 20.9 | (1.2) | **5.2** | (1.2) | 26.0 | (0.3) | 27.7 | (1.0) | -1.7 | (1.0) |
| Hungary | 52.5 | (0.4) | 52.0 | (2.1) | 0.4 | (2.1) | 18.7 | (0.3) | 18.5 | (1.8) | 0.2 | (1.9) | 28.8 | (0.3) | 29.5 | (1.5) | -0.7 | (1.6) |
| Iceland | 69.9 | (0.3) | 62.2 | (2.7) | **7.6** | (2.6) | 7.0 | (0.2) | 13.2 | (2.0) | **-6.1** | (2.0) | 23.1 | (0.2) | 24.6 | (1.9) | -1.5 | (1.9) |
| Ireland | 63.7 | (0.4) | 60.2 | (1.2) | **3.5** | (1.2) | 8.6 | (0.2) | 10.1 | (1.0) | -1.5 | (1.1) | 27.7 | (0.3) | 29.7 | (0.9) | **-1.9** | (0.9) |
| Italy | 55.1 | (0.2) | 52.2 | (1.0) | **2.9** | (1.0) | 9.7 | (0.2) | 13.6 | (1.0) | **-3.9** | (1.0) | 35.2 | (0.2) | 34.2 | (0.7) | 1.0 | (0.7) |
| Japan | 74.5 | (0.5) | c | c | c | c | 7.5 | (0.3) | c | c | c | c | 18.0 | (0.4) | c | c | c | c |
| Korea | 61.3 | (0.4) | c | c | c | c | 18.4 | (0.2) | c | c | c | c | 20.3 | (0.3) | c | c | c | c |
| Luxembourg | 64.6 | (0.3) | 61.1 | (0.6) | **3.5** | (0.7) | 9.4 | (0.2) | 12.9 | (0.4) | **-3.5** | (0.4) | 26.0 | (0.2) | 26.0 | (0.4) | -0.1 | (0.5) |
| Mexico | 54.3 | (0.3) | 43.5 | (2.7) | **10.8** | (2.7) | 14.4 | (0.3) | 19.6 | (2.4) | **-5.2** | (2.3) | 31.3 | (0.3) | 36.9 | (2.4) | **-5.6** | (2.4) |
| Netherlands | 60.9 | (0.4) | 53.2 | (1.0) | **7.7** | (1.0) | 11.6 | (0.3) | 17.3 | (0.6) | **-5.7** | (0.6) | 27.5 | (0.3) | 29.5 | (0.7) | **-2.0** | (0.8) |
| New Zealand | 71.9 | (0.4) | 61.6 | (0.7) | **10.4** | (0.9) | 7.0 | (0.2) | 12.3 | (0.6) | **-5.2** | (0.6) | 21.0 | (0.3) | 26.2 | (0.4) | **-5.1** | (0.5) |
| Norway | 60.9 | (0.4) | 52.9 | (1.3) | **8.0** | (1.3) | 16.7 | (0.3) | 20.9 | (0.9) | **-4.2** | (0.9) | 22.4 | (0.3) | 26.2 | (0.8) | **-3.8** | (0.9) |
| Poland | 59.9 | (0.3) | c | c | c | c | 10.0 | (0.3) | c | c | c | c | 30.0 | (0.3) | c | c | c | c |
| Portugal | 58.5 | (0.4) | 55.6 | (1.6) | 3.0 | (1.7) | 10.1 | (0.2) | 11.7 | (0.8) | -1.6 | (0.9) | 31.4 | (0.3) | 32.8 | (1.3) | -1.4 | (1.4) |
| Slovak Republic | 58.9 | (0.5) | c | c | c | c | 12.7 | (0.3) | c | c | c | c | 28.4 | (0.3) | c | c | c | c |
| Spain | 59.3 | (0.3) | 56.1 | (1.1) | **3.3** | (1.1) | 11.1 | (0.2) | 12.5 | (0.9) | -1.4 | (0.9) | 29.6 | (0.3) | 31.5 | (1.1) | -1.9 | (1.1) |
| Sweden | 67.2 | (0.5) | 58.4 | (1.0) | **8.8** | (1.1) | 9.7 | (0.2) | 14.7 | (0.8) | **-5.0** | (0.8) | 23.2 | (0.4) | 26.9 | (0.6) | **-3.8** | (0.7) |
| Switzerland | 65.3 | (0.3) | 60.8 | (0.6) | **4.6** | (0.6) | 8.0 | (0.2) | 11.9 | (0.5) | **-3.9** | (0.5) | 26.6 | (0.2) | 27.4 | (0.4) | -0.7 | (0.4) |
| Turkey | 51.3 | (0.3) | 55.8 | (3.9) | -4.5 | (3.9) | 21.7 | (0.3) | 18.7 | (3.0) | 3.0 | (3.0) | 27.0 | (0.3) | 25.5 | (1.3) | 1.4 | (1.3) |
| United Kingdom | 68.8 | (0.3) | 58.8 | (0.9) | **10.0** | (1.0) | 7.5 | (0.1) | 14.2 | (0.9) | **-6.7** | (0.9) | 23.6 | (0.2) | 27.0 | (0.5) | **-3.4** | (0.5) |
| United States | 56.5 | (0.5) | 51.8 | (0.8) | **4.7** | (0.9) | 14.6 | (0.4) | 17.9 | (0.6) | **-3.3** | (0.6) | 28.9 | (0.3) | 30.3 | (0.6) | -1.4 | (0.7) |
| **OECD average** | 62.4 | (0.1) | 57.0 | (0.3) | **5.2** | (0.3) | 11.4 | (0.0) | 14.6 | (0.2) | **-3.3** | (0.2) | 26.2 | (0.0) | 28.4 | (0.2) | **-1.9** | (0.2) |
| **Partners** | | | | | | | | | | | | | | | | | | |
| Argentina | 54.5 | (0.6) | 55.9 | (1.8) | -1.5 | (1.8) | 10.5 | (0.4) | 9.1 | (1.3) | 1.5 | (1.3) | 35.0 | (0.4) | 35.0 | (1.5) | 0.0 | (1.5) |
| Azerbaijan | 44.5 | (0.5) | 44.1 | (2.3) | 0.4 | (2.3) | 19.7 | (0.4) | 20.4 | (1.5) | -0.7 | (1.4) | 35.8 | (0.3) | 35.5 | (1.3) | 0.3 | (1.5) |
| Brazil | 53.2 | (0.4) | 51.6 | (2.3) | 1.6 | (2.3) | 17.0 | (0.3) | 17.7 | (1.8) | -0.7 | (1.7) | 29.8 | (0.3) | 30.7 | (1.9) | -0.9 | (2.0) |
| Bulgaria | 50.3 | (0.5) | c | c | c | c | 16.7 | (0.4) | c | c | c | c | 33.1 | (0.4) | c | c | c | c |
| Chile | 54.7 | (0.5) | c | c | c | c | 16.3 | (0.3) | c | c | c | c | 29.1 | (0.3) | c | c | c | c |
| Colombia | 59.7 | (0.6) | c | c | c | c | 14.4 | (0.3) | c | c | c | c | 25.9 | (0.4) | c | c | c | c |
| Croatia | 60.1 | (0.4) | 59.2 | (0.9) | 0.9 | (0.9) | 9.5 | (0.3) | 9.5 | (0.5) | 0.1 | (0.6) | 30.4 | (0.3) | 31.3 | (0.8) | -1.0 | (0.8) |
| Estonia | 61.3 | (0.4) | 58.5 | (0.9) | **2.8** | (0.8) | 12.9 | (0.3) | 14.7 | (0.7) | **-1.8** | (0.7) | 25.8 | (0.2) | 26.8 | (0.7) | -1.0 | (0.8) |
| Hong Kong-China | 63.1 | (0.5) | 65.5 | (0.6) | **-2.4** | (0.8) | 14.1 | (0.3) | 11.4 | (0.4) | **2.7** | (0.5) | 22.8 | (0.3) | 23.1 | (0.4) | -0.3 | (0.5) |
| Indonesia | 56.1 | (0.7) | 45.0 | (5.0) | **11.1** | (5.1) | 16.5 | (0.5) | 17.8 | (3.2) | -1.3 | (3.2) | 27.4 | (0.3) | 37.2 | (3.6) | **-9.8** | (3.6) |
| Israel | 52.8 | (0.5) | 52.2 | (0.8) | 0.5 | (0.8) | 21.2 | (0.3) | 22.0 | (0.4) | -0.7 | (0.6) | 26.0 | (0.4) | 25.8 | (0.6) | 0.2 | (0.6) |
| Jordan | 43.9 | (0.5) | 43.5 | (0.9) | 0.4 | (1.0) | 21.7 | (0.4) | 21.5 | (0.7) | 0.3 | (0.8) | 34.3 | (0.4) | 35.0 | (0.6) | -0.7 | (0.6) |
| Kyrgyzstan | 40.1 | (0.5) | 46.1 | (2.5) | **-6.0** | (2.5) | 25.2 | (0.4) | 19.4 | (2.2) | **5.8** | (2.1) | 34.7 | (0.3) | 34.6 | (1.7) | 0.2 | (1.7) |
| Latvia | 57.5 | (0.3) | 55.6 | (0.8) | **2.0** | (0.8) | 12.6 | (0.3) | 14.4 | (0.5) | **-1.8** | (0.6) | 29.9 | (0.3) | 30.0 | (0.6) | -0.2 | (0.7) |
| Liechtenstein | 67.5 | (1.2) | 64.4 | (2.0) | 3.1 | (2.3) | 7.0 | (0.6) | 10.6 | (1.1) | **-3.7** | (1.2) | 25.6 | (1.0) | 25.0 | (1.3) | 0.6 | (1.5) |
| Lithuania | 59.6 | (0.3) | 60.2 | (1.8) | -0.6 | (1.8) | 11.0 | (0.3) | 10.8 | (1.2) | 0.2 | (1.2) | 29.4 | (0.2) | 29.0 | (1.5) | 0.3 | (1.5) |
| Macao-China | 65.6 | (0.6) | 67.2 | (0.4) | **-1.7** | (0.7) | 13.4 | (0.4) | 12.5 | (0.2) | **0.9** | (0.4) | 21.0 | (0.4) | 20.2 | (0.3) | 0.8 | (0.5) |
| Montenegro | 51.1 | (0.3) | 49.3 | (1.5) | 1.8 | (1.5) | 14.5 | (0.3) | 12.8 | (1.0) | 1.8 | (1.0) | 34.4 | (0.3) | 37.9 | (1.3) | **-3.6** | (1.3) |
| Qatar | 41.7 | (0.4) | 45.9 | (0.4) | **-4.2** | (0.6) | 26.4 | (0.3) | 21.6 | (0.4) | **4.8** | (0.5) | 32.0 | (0.3) | 32.5 | (0.3) | -0.5 | (0.5) |
| Romania | 48.7 | (0.4) | c | c | c | c | 20.5 | (0.3) | c | c | c | c | 30.9 | (0.2) | c | c | c | c |
| Russian Federation | 50.9 | (0.5) | 51.1 | (0.7) | -0.2 | (0.6) | 15.7 | (0.5) | 15.2 | (0.7) | 0.5 | (0.6) | 33.4 | (0.4) | 33.7 | (0.6) | -0.2 | (0.5) |
| Serbia | 57.8 | (0.4) | 57.3 | (1.1) | 0.5 | (1.2) | 13.8 | (0.3) | 13.7 | (0.9) | 0.1 | (0.9) | 28.4 | (0.3) | 29.0 | (0.9) | -0.6 | (1.0) |
| Slovenia | 57.2 | (0.3) | 55.3 | (0.8) | **1.9** | (0.8) | 13.7 | (0.2) | 15.4 | (0.6) | **-1.8** | (0.6) | 29.1 | (0.3) | 29.3 | (0.7) | -0.1 | (0.7) |
| Chinese Taipei | 61.5 | (0.3) | 57.5 | (4.3) | 4.0 | (4.3) | 13.9 | (0.2) | 16.2 | (2.4) | -2.3 | (2.4) | 24.6 | (0.2) | 26.3 | (3.3) | -1.8 | (3.2) |
| Thailand | 62.3 | (0.4) | c | c | c | c | 10.2 | (0.3) | c | c | c | c | 27.5 | (0.3) | c | c | c | c |
| Tunisia | 41.5 | (0.3) | 36.1 | (2.4) | **5.4** | (2.4) | 26.4 | (0.2) | 30.6 | (2.0) | **-4.2** | (1.9) | 32.1 | (0.3) | 33.3 | (2.4) | -1.2 | (2.5) |
| Uruguay | 59.4 | (0.4) | c | c | c | c | 12.4 | (0.3) | c | c | c | c | 28.2 | (0.3) | c | c | c | c |

*Note:* Values that are statistically significant at the 5% level (p < 0.05) are indicated in bold.

© OECD 2011  Quality Time for Students: Learning In and Out of School

[Part 1/2]
## Table 3.9a Within- and between-school variance in learning time in science

| | | Regular school lessons | | | | | | Out-of-school-time lessons | | | | | | |
|---|---|---|---|---|---|---|---|---|---|---|---|---|---|---|
| | | Between-school variance | Within-school variance | Proportion of between school variance | Mean hours per week | | Standard deviation | | Between-school variance | Within-school variance | Proportion of between school variance | Mean hours per week | | Standard deviation | |
| | | | | | Mean | S.E. | S.D. | S.E. | | | | Mean | S.E. | S.D. | S.E. |
| OECD | Australia | 0.56 | 3.33 | 0.14 | 3.24 | (0.02) | 1.97 | (0.02) | 0.01 | 0.72 | 0.02 | 0.36 | (0.01) | 0.86 | (0.02) |
| | Austria | 1.08 | 2.87 | 0.27 | 2.47 | (0.04) | 1.98 | (0.04) | 0.04 | 0.53 | 0.08 | 0.21 | (0.01) | 0.76 | (0.04) |
| | Belgium | 0.89 | 3.20 | 0.22 | 2.63 | (0.02) | 2.03 | (0.02) | 0.03 | 0.71 | 0.04 | 0.32 | (0.01) | 0.86 | (0.03) |
| | Canada | 0.55 | 4.58 | 0.11 | 4.00 | (0.02) | 2.29 | (0.02) | 0.04 | 1.04 | 0.03 | 0.55 | (0.01) | 1.05 | (0.02) |
| | Czech Republic | 1.81 | 3.42 | 0.35 | 2.93 | (0.03) | 2.25 | (0.03) | 0.04 | 1.08 | 0.04 | 0.54 | (0.02) | 1.07 | (0.03) |
| | Denmark | 0.26 | 1.96 | 0.12 | 3.21 | (0.03) | 1.49 | (0.03) | 0.03 | 1.06 | 0.03 | 0.77 | (0.02) | 1.05 | (0.02) |
| | Finland | 0.18 | 2.45 | 0.07 | 3.13 | (0.02) | 1.62 | (0.02) | 0.01 | 0.54 | 0.01 | 0.32 | (0.01) | 0.74 | (0.03) |
| | France | 1.29 | 2.60 | 0.33 | 2.85 | (0.02) | 1.98 | (0.02) | 0.02 | 0.88 | 0.02 | 0.55 | (0.02) | 0.95 | (0.03) |
| | Germany | 0.99 | 3.39 | 0.23 | 3.06 | (0.02) | 2.08 | (0.02) | 0.03 | 1.07 | 0.03 | 0.51 | (0.02) | 1.05 | (0.03) |
| | Greece | 0.69 | 3.17 | 0.18 | 3.18 | (0.02) | 1.95 | (0.02) | 0.30 | 3.34 | 0.08 | 1.99 | (0.04) | 1.90 | (0.02) |
| | Hungary | 0.50 | 2.69 | 0.16 | 2.51 | (0.03) | 1.79 | (0.03) | 0.07 | 1.67 | 0.04 | 1.00 | (0.03) | 1.32 | (0.03) |
| | Iceland | 0.23 | 2.03 | 0.10 | 2.97 | (0.02) | 1.50 | (0.02) | 0.02 | 0.59 | 0.03 | 0.29 | (0.01) | 0.78 | (0.03) |
| | Ireland | 0.20 | 2.54 | 0.07 | 2.54 | (0.02) | 1.65 | (0.02) | 0.01 | 0.62 | 0.01 | 0.32 | (0.01) | 0.80 | (0.03) |
| | Italy | 0.92 | 3.24 | 0.22 | 2.91 | (0.03) | 2.05 | (0.03) | 0.06 | 1.33 | 0.05 | 0.58 | (0.01) | 1.19 | (0.02) |
| | Japan | 0.72 | 1.11 | 0.39 | 2.70 | (0.04) | 1.34 | (0.04) | 0.01 | 0.48 | 0.02 | 0.26 | (0.01) | 0.70 | (0.03) |
| | Korea | 0.67 | 1.47 | 0.31 | 3.58 | (0.06) | 1.47 | (0.06) | 0.35 | 1.57 | 0.18 | 1.02 | (0.04) | 1.39 | (0.05) |
| | Luxembourg | 0.31 | 3.20 | 0.09 | 2.33 | (0.02) | 1.85 | (0.02) | 0.02 | 1.06 | 0.02 | 0.50 | (0.02) | 1.04 | (0.03) |
| | Mexico | 0.32 | 5.64 | 0.05 | 3.15 | (0.01) | 2.47 | (0.01) | 0.12 | 1.98 | 0.06 | 1.01 | (0.03) | 1.48 | (0.03) |
| | Netherlands | 0.60 | 3.24 | 0.16 | 2.17 | (0.02) | 1.96 | (0.02) | 0.02 | 0.97 | 0.02 | 0.54 | (0.02) | 1.00 | (0.03) |
| | New Zealand | 0.30 | 3.37 | 0.08 | 4.06 | (0.03) | 1.91 | (0.03) | 0.02 | 0.83 | 0.03 | 0.41 | (0.02) | 0.92 | (0.03) |
| | Norway | 0.09 | 1.32 | 0.06 | 2.64 | (0.02) | 1.19 | (0.02) | 0.02 | 1.27 | 0.02 | 0.93 | (0.02) | 1.14 | (0.02) |
| | Poland | 0.16 | 2.59 | 0.06 | 2.72 | (0.02) | 1.66 | (0.02) | 0.04 | 1.05 | 0.03 | 0.62 | (0.02) | 1.04 | (0.03) |
| | Portugal | 0.35 | 5.46 | 0.06 | 3.21 | (0.02) | 2.41 | (0.02) | 0.01 | 1.44 | 0.01 | 0.63 | (0.02) | 1.21 | (0.03) |
| | Slovak Republic | 1.65 | 2.88 | 0.36 | 2.46 | (0.04) | 2.15 | (0.04) | 0.11 | 1.21 | 0.08 | 0.65 | (0.03) | 1.16 | (0.03) |
| | Spain | 0.31 | 3.64 | 0.08 | 3.12 | (0.02) | 2.01 | (0.02) | 0.09 | 1.73 | 0.05 | 0.68 | (0.02) | 1.35 | (0.03) |
| | Sweden | 0.19 | 1.31 | 0.13 | 2.81 | (0.02) | 1.21 | (0.02) | 0.01 | 0.77 | 0.02 | 0.50 | (0.01) | 0.89 | (0.02) |
| | Switzerland | 0.87 | 2.49 | 0.26 | 2.36 | (0.03) | 1.90 | (0.03) | 0.05 | 0.75 | 0.06 | 0.39 | (0.01) | 0.89 | (0.02) |
| | Turkey | 1.46 | 5.02 | 0.22 | 2.86 | (0.03) | 2.55 | (0.03) | 0.35 | 3.18 | 0.10 | 1.35 | (0.05) | 1.88 | (0.04) |
| | United Kingdom | 0.35 | 2.56 | 0.12 | 4.25 | (0.03) | 1.71 | (0.03) | 0.04 | 0.79 | 0.05 | 0.48 | (0.02) | 0.92 | (0.02) |
| | United States | 0.23 | 4.76 | 0.05 | 3.51 | (0.03) | 2.24 | (0.03) | 0.03 | 1.56 | 0.02 | 0.78 | (0.02) | 1.26 | (0.03) |
| | **OECD average** | 0.62 | 3.05 | 0.17 | 0.55 | (0.03) | 0.35 | (0.03) | 0.07 | 1.19 | 0.04 | 0.13 | (0.02) | 0.21 | (0.03) |
| Partners | Argentina | 0.35 | 3.10 | 0.10 | 2.26 | (0.03) | 1.87 | (0.03) | 0.04 | 1.04 | 0.04 | 0.49 | (0.02) | 1.05 | (0.03) |
| | Azerbaijan | 0.45 | 3.83 | 0.10 | 2.84 | (0.04) | 2.06 | (0.04) | 0.10 | 2.77 | 0.04 | 1.36 | (0.03) | 1.70 | (0.03) |
| | Brazil | 0.39 | 2.22 | 0.15 | 2.21 | (0.03) | 1.62 | (0.03) | 0.09 | 1.42 | 0.06 | 0.79 | (0.02) | 1.23 | (0.04) |
| | Bulgaria | 0.85 | 3.86 | 0.18 | 2.63 | (0.03) | 2.16 | (0.03) | 0.06 | 1.98 | 0.03 | 0.98 | (0.03) | 1.43 | (0.03) |
| | Chile | 0.63 | 3.49 | 0.15 | 2.33 | (0.03) | 2.02 | (0.03) | 0.02 | 1.45 | 0.01 | 0.83 | (0.02) | 1.22 | (0.02) |
| | Colombia | 0.46 | 3.21 | 0.12 | 3.50 | (0.05) | 1.95 | (0.05) | 0.04 | 1.82 | 0.02 | 0.95 | (0.03) | 1.37 | (0.04) |
| | Croatia | 0.51 | 2.46 | 0.17 | 2.02 | (0.02) | 1.72 | (0.02) | 0.02 | 0.93 | 0.02 | 0.43 | (0.02) | 0.98 | (0.03) |
| | Estonia | 0.18 | 3.68 | 0.05 | 3.27 | (0.02) | 1.97 | (0.02) | 0.04 | 1.36 | 0.03 | 0.76 | (0.02) | 1.18 | (0.03) |
| | Hong Kong-China | 0.42 | 7.66 | 0.05 | 3.14 | (0.02) | 2.84 | (0.02) | 0.06 | 2.17 | 0.03 | 0.88 | (0.03) | 1.49 | (0.03) |
| | Indonesia | 1.00 | 2.78 | 0.26 | 3.23 | (0.03) | 1.99 | (0.03) | 0.15 | 1.66 | 0.09 | 1.04 | (0.04) | 1.36 | (0.03) |
| | Israel | 0.34 | 4.46 | 0.07 | 2.43 | (0.03) | 2.19 | (0.03) | 0.17 | 1.86 | 0.08 | 0.98 | (0.03) | 1.42 | (0.03) |
| | Jordan | 0.43 | 4.80 | 0.08 | 3.25 | (0.02) | 2.30 | (0.02) | 0.09 | 2.82 | 0.03 | 1.52 | (0.02) | 1.71 | (0.02) |
| | Kyrgyzstan | 0.44 | 4.07 | 0.10 | 2.09 | (0.05) | 2.15 | (0.05) | 0.12 | 2.44 | 0.05 | 1.36 | (0.03) | 1.61 | (0.03) |
| | Latvia | 0.34 | 3.32 | 0.09 | 2.86 | (0.03) | 1.91 | (0.03) | 0.03 | 1.23 | 0.03 | 0.65 | (0.02) | 1.12 | (0.03) |
| | Liechtenstein | 0.35 | 2.38 | 0.13 | 2.57 | (0.06) | 1.69 | (0.06) | 0.05 | 0.94 | 0.05 | 0.52 | (0.06) | 1.00 | (0.08) |
| | Lithuania | 0.15 | 3.05 | 0.05 | 2.69 | (0.02) | 1.79 | (0.02) | 0.02 | 1.06 | 0.02 | 0.57 | (0.02) | 1.04 | (0.03) |
| | Macao-China | 0.31 | 5.35 | 0.05 | 3.74 | (0.02) | 2.38 | (0.02) | 0.03 | 2.47 | 0.01 | 1.00 | (0.03) | 1.58 | (0.04) |
| | Montenegro | 0.41 | 4.37 | 0.09 | 2.83 | (0.02) | 2.20 | (0.02) | 0.02 | 2.29 | 0.01 | 1.05 | (0.02) | 1.52 | (0.03) |
| | Qatar | 0.82 | 4.39 | 0.16 | 2.66 | (0.02) | 2.25 | (0.02) | 0.05 | 2.56 | 0.02 | 1.48 | (0.02) | 1.61 | (0.02) |
| | Romania | 0.56 | 3.69 | 0.13 | 2.26 | (0.04) | 2.06 | (0.04) | 0.03 | 1.91 | 0.01 | 1.03 | (0.02) | 1.39 | (0.03) |
| | Russian Federation | 0.91 | 4.77 | 0.16 | 3.73 | (0.02) | 2.38 | (0.02) | 0.11 | 2.06 | 0.05 | 1.12 | (0.03) | 1.48 | (0.03) |
| | Serbia | 0.71 | 3.82 | 0.16 | 2.86 | (0.02) | 2.13 | (0.02) | 0.02 | 1.64 | 0.01 | 0.78 | (0.02) | 1.29 | (0.03) |
| | Slovenia | 1.09 | 3.39 | 0.24 | 2.82 | (0.02) | 2.14 | (0.02) | 0.05 | 1.22 | 0.04 | 0.72 | (0.02) | 1.11 | (0.03) |
| | Chinese Taipei | 1.15 | 2.90 | 0.28 | 2.89 | (0.02) | 2.01 | (0.02) | 0.25 | 1.55 | 0.14 | 0.78 | (0.02) | 1.36 | (0.03) |
| | Thailand | 0.63 | 2.01 | 0.24 | 3.81 | (0.02) | 1.65 | (0.02) | 0.35 | 1.88 | 0.16 | 0.91 | (0.03) | 1.50 | (0.03) |
| | Tunisia | 0.42 | 3.84 | 0.10 | 2.62 | (0.03) | 2.07 | (0.03) | 0.09 | 3.11 | 0.03 | 1.93 | (0.03) | 1.79 | (0.02) |
| | Uruguay | 0.66 | 3.53 | 0.16 | 2.40 | (0.02) | 2.05 | (0.02) | 0.03 | 1.30 | 0.03 | 0.61 | (0.02) | 1.16 | (0.03) |

153

[Part 2/2]
## Table 3.9a Within- and between-school variance in learning time in science

| | Individual study | | | | | | | Total learning hours | | | | | | |
|---|---|---|---|---|---|---|---|---|---|---|---|---|---|---|
| | Between-school variance | Within-school variance | Proportion of between school variance | Mean hours per week | | Standard deviation | | Between-school variance | Within-school variance | Proportion of between school variance | Mean hours per week | | Standard deviation | |
| | | | | Mean | S.E. | S.D. | S.E. | | | | Mean | S.E. | S.D. | S.E. |
| **OECD** | | | | | | | | | | | | | | |
| Australia | 0.15 | 1.55 | 0.09 | 1.17 | (0.02) | 1.30 | (0.02) | 1.25 | 8.55 | 0.13 | 4.77 | (0.05) | 3.12 | (0.03) |
| Austria | 0.17 | 2.09 | 0.08 | 1.28 | (0.03) | 1.50 | (0.03) | 1.74 | 7.53 | 0.19 | 3.96 | (0.09) | 3.02 | (0.06) |
| Belgium | 0.15 | 1.46 | 0.09 | 1.25 | (0.02) | 1.27 | (0.02) | 1.68 | 7.84 | 0.18 | 4.20 | (0.07) | 3.10 | (0.04) |
| Canada | 0.21 | 2.06 | 0.09 | 1.55 | (0.02) | 1.53 | (0.02) | 1.33 | 10.89 | 0.11 | 6.13 | (0.06) | 3.55 | (0.04) |
| Czech Republic | 0.13 | 1.43 | 0.08 | 1.00 | (0.03) | 1.26 | (0.03) | 3.10 | 8.02 | 0.28 | 4.47 | (0.10) | 3.32 | (0.06) |
| Denmark | 0.06 | 1.04 | 0.06 | 1.09 | (0.02) | 1.05 | (0.02) | 0.69 | 5.90 | 0.11 | 5.06 | (0.07) | 2.56 | (0.05) |
| Finland | 0.02 | 0.93 | 0.02 | 1.07 | (0.02) | 0.97 | (0.02) | 0.27 | 5.17 | 0.05 | 4.52 | (0.06) | 2.33 | (0.05) |
| France | 0.21 | 1.53 | 0.12 | 1.31 | (0.03) | 1.32 | (0.03) | 2.60 | 7.24 | 0.26 | 4.72 | (0.08) | 3.14 | (0.05) |
| Germany | 0.06 | 2.31 | 0.02 | 1.71 | (0.03) | 1.54 | (0.03) | 1.17 | 9.37 | 0.11 | 5.28 | (0.07) | 3.24 | (0.05) |
| Greece | 0.14 | 2.96 | 0.05 | 1.85 | (0.04) | 1.76 | (0.03) | 2.32 | 16.02 | 0.13 | 7.02 | (0.10) | 4.26 | (0.06) |
| Hungary | 0.13 | 2.14 | 0.06 | 1.60 | (0.03) | 1.51 | (0.03) | 1.21 | 10.61 | 0.10 | 5.10 | (0.08) | 3.45 | (0.06) |
| Iceland | 0.06 | 1.21 | 0.04 | 1.16 | (0.02) | 1.13 | (0.03) | 0.47 | 5.09 | 0.08 | 4.42 | (0.04) | 2.35 | (0.05) |
| Ireland | 0.06 | 1.69 | 0.04 | 1.20 | (0.03) | 1.32 | (0.02) | 0.50 | 7.38 | 0.06 | 4.05 | (0.07) | 2.81 | (0.05) |
| Italy | 0.45 | 2.76 | 0.14 | 2.10 | (0.04) | 1.81 | (0.02) | 2.57 | 11.12 | 0.19 | 5.58 | (0.10) | 3.74 | (0.06) |
| Japan | 0.07 | 0.69 | 0.09 | 0.69 | (0.02) | 0.87 | (0.02) | 1.11 | 2.88 | 0.28 | 3.65 | (0.07) | 1.99 | (0.05) |
| Korea | 0.28 | 1.52 | 0.16 | 1.22 | (0.06) | 1.35 | (0.09) | 3.12 | 6.22 | 0.33 | 5.84 | (0.14) | 3.09 | (0.23) |
| Luxembourg | 0.04 | 1.83 | 0.02 | 1.25 | (0.02) | 1.36 | (0.03) | 0.63 | 8.73 | 0.07 | 4.09 | (0.05) | 3.03 | (0.05) |
| Mexico | 0.16 | 3.15 | 0.05 | 2.12 | (0.03) | 1.84 | (0.02) | 0.94 | 15.68 | 0.06 | 6.24 | (0.07) | 4.14 | (0.04) |
| Netherlands | 0.09 | 1.62 | 0.05 | 1.21 | (0.03) | 1.31 | (0.03) | 1.01 | 9.58 | 0.10 | 3.90 | (0.06) | 3.25 | (0.05) |
| New Zealand | 0.11 | 1.63 | 0.07 | 1.28 | (0.02) | 1.32 | (0.02) | 0.73 | 8.25 | 0.08 | 5.74 | (0.06) | 3.00 | (0.05) |
| Norway | 0.04 | 1.27 | 0.03 | 1.23 | (0.02) | 1.15 | (0.02) | 0.22 | 6.01 | 0.04 | 4.80 | (0.05) | 2.50 | (0.05) |
| Poland | 0.06 | 2.65 | 0.02 | 2.02 | (0.03) | 1.65 | (0.02) | 0.39 | 9.59 | 0.04 | 5.36 | (0.07) | 3.16 | (0.05) |
| Portugal | 0.08 | 3.26 | 0.02 | 2.09 | (0.04) | 1.83 | (0.02) | 0.58 | 16.63 | 0.03 | 5.93 | (0.08) | 4.16 | (0.04) |
| Slovak Republic | 0.34 | 1.98 | 0.15 | 1.39 | (0.04) | 1.53 | (0.03) | 4.35 | 8.98 | 0.33 | 4.51 | (0.12) | 3.69 | (0.07) |
| Spain | 0.11 | 2.54 | 0.04 | 1.74 | (0.03) | 1.64 | (0.02) | 0.88 | 11.28 | 0.07 | 5.56 | (0.07) | 3.53 | (0.04) |
| Sweden | 0.03 | 1.12 | 0.03 | 1.15 | (0.02) | 1.08 | (0.03) | 0.36 | 4.45 | 0.08 | 4.45 | (0.04) | 2.18 | (0.05) |
| Switzerland | 0.11 | 1.22 | 0.08 | 1.12 | (0.02) | 1.16 | (0.02) | 1.61 | 6.34 | 0.20 | 3.87 | (0.06) | 2.86 | (0.04) |
| Turkey | 0.31 | 3.11 | 0.09 | 1.64 | (0.05) | 1.85 | (0.03) | 5.29 | 21.49 | 0.20 | 5.81 | (0.18) | 5.18 | (0.09) |
| United Kingdom | 0.10 | 1.40 | 0.07 | 1.45 | (0.02) | 1.23 | (0.02) | 0.66 | 6.32 | 0.09 | 6.18 | (0.05) | 2.66 | (0.04) |
| United States | 0.08 | 2.39 | 0.03 | 1.68 | (0.03) | 1.57 | (0.02) | 0.31 | 12.80 | 0.02 | 6.01 | (0.06) | 3.62 | (0.04) |
| **OECD average** | 0.13 | 1.89 | 0.07 | 0.27 | (0.03) | 0.26 | (0.03) | 1.44 | 9.20 | 0.13 | 0.93 | (0.08) | 0.60 | (0.06) |
| **Partners** | | | | | | | | | | | | | | |
| Argentina | 0.13 | 2.32 | 0.05 | 1.59 | (0.04) | 1.58 | (0.03) | 0.72 | 9.02 | 0.07 | 4.32 | (0.09) | 3.14 | (0.05) |
| Azerbaijan | 0.27 | 4.46 | 0.06 | 2.64 | (0.05) | 2.17 | (0.03) | 1.58 | 16.91 | 0.09 | 6.83 | (0.10) | 4.29 | (0.08) |
| Brazil | 0.14 | 2.41 | 0.05 | 1.70 | (0.02) | 1.59 | (0.02) | 0.99 | 8.57 | 0.10 | 4.70 | (0.06) | 3.09 | (0.06) |
| Bulgaria | 0.36 | 3.38 | 0.10 | 2.00 | (0.06) | 1.93 | (0.03) | 2.20 | 15.23 | 0.13 | 5.65 | (0.13) | 4.17 | (0.06) |
| Chile | 0.06 | 2.15 | 0.03 | 1.52 | (0.03) | 1.49 | (0.02) | 1.15 | 11.33 | 0.09 | 4.70 | (0.07) | 3.53 | (0.05) |
| Colombia | 0.08 | 2.77 | 0.03 | 1.83 | (0.04) | 1.69 | (0.02) | 0.77 | 11.33 | 0.06 | 6.28 | (0.17) | 3.53 | (0.12) |
| Croatia | 0.34 | 2.32 | 0.13 | 1.46 | (0.04) | 1.63 | (0.03) | 1.86 | 8.64 | 0.18 | 3.93 | (0.09) | 3.24 | (0.05) |
| Estonia | 0.08 | 2.13 | 0.04 | 1.54 | (0.03) | 1.49 | (0.03) | 0.45 | 9.80 | 0.04 | 5.57 | (0.06) | 3.20 | (0.06) |
| Hong Kong-China | 0.17 | 3.22 | 0.05 | 1.44 | (0.03) | 1.84 | (0.03) | 1.33 | 25.73 | 0.05 | 5.45 | (0.10) | 5.20 | (0.05) |
| Indonesia | 0.15 | 2.10 | 0.07 | 1.78 | (0.03) | 1.51 | (0.02) | 2.38 | 9.19 | 0.21 | 6.04 | (0.11) | 3.47 | (0.08) |
| Israel | 0.34 | 2.32 | 0.13 | 1.35 | (0.04) | 1.63 | (0.03) | 1.71 | 14.44 | 0.11 | 4.75 | (0.10) | 4.02 | (0.06) |
| Jordan | 0.18 | 3.92 | 0.04 | 2.65 | (0.04) | 2.03 | (0.02) | 0.74 | 16.23 | 0.04 | 7.40 | (0.09) | 4.15 | (0.05) |
| Kyrgyzstan | 0.15 | 4.31 | 0.03 | 2.14 | (0.03) | 2.12 | (0.02) | 0.90 | 15.75 | 0.05 | 5.63 | (0.09) | 4.11 | (0.06) |
| Latvia | 0.09 | 2.38 | 0.04 | 1.80 | (0.03) | 1.57 | (0.03) | 0.82 | 10.07 | 0.08 | 5.30 | (0.09) | 3.30 | (0.05) |
| Liechtenstein | 0.01 | 1.44 | 0.01 | 1.20 | (0.06) | 1.20 | (0.09) | 0.46 | 5.82 | 0.07 | 4.29 | (0.10) | 2.52 | (0.11) |
| Lithuania | 0.04 | 2.29 | 0.02 | 1.69 | (0.03) | 1.53 | (0.02) | 0.27 | 9.31 | 0.03 | 4.94 | (0.06) | 3.09 | (0.04) |
| Macao-China | 0.10 | 2.39 | 0.04 | 1.37 | (0.03) | 1.57 | (0.03) | 0.73 | 16.25 | 0.04 | 6.11 | (0.06) | 4.12 | (0.06) |
| Montenegro | 0.14 | 3.64 | 0.04 | 2.20 | (0.03) | 1.95 | (0.02) | 1.06 | 16.31 | 0.06 | 6.08 | (0.07) | 4.18 | (0.05) |
| Qatar | 0.10 | 2.99 | 0.03 | 2.04 | (0.02) | 1.75 | (0.02) | 1.41 | 15.27 | 0.08 | 6.21 | (0.06) | 4.07 | (0.05) |
| Romania | 0.15 | 2.86 | 0.05 | 1.61 | (0.05) | 1.74 | (0.03) | 1.27 | 14.47 | 0.08 | 4.88 | (0.11) | 3.96 | (0.07) |
| Russian Federation | 0.51 | 4.08 | 0.11 | 2.87 | (0.06) | 2.14 | (0.02) | 2.74 | 15.88 | 0.15 | 7.72 | (0.13) | 4.31 | (0.06) |
| Serbia | 0.28 | 2.96 | 0.09 | 1.71 | (0.04) | 1.80 | (0.03) | 1.96 | 13.11 | 0.13 | 5.35 | (0.10) | 3.89 | (0.06) |
| Slovenia | 0.11 | 1.99 | 0.05 | 1.53 | (0.02) | 1.44 | (0.02) | 1.80 | 9.43 | 0.16 | 5.08 | (0.05) | 3.35 | (0.04) |
| Chinese Taipei | 0.26 | 1.71 | 0.13 | 1.24 | (0.03) | 1.41 | (0.02) | 3.83 | 9.30 | 0.29 | 4.94 | (0.10) | 3.65 | (0.05) |
| Thailand | 0.20 | 2.12 | 0.09 | 1.80 | (0.03) | 1.53 | (0.03) | 2.66 | 8.95 | 0.23 | 6.52 | (0.07) | 3.46 | (0.05) |
| Tunisia | 0.09 | 4.00 | 0.02 | 2.61 | (0.04) | 2.02 | (0.02) | 1.47 | 17.39 | 0.08 | 7.14 | (0.10) | 4.35 | (0.07) |
| Uruguay | 0.13 | 1.80 | 0.07 | 1.32 | (0.03) | 1.40 | (0.03) | 1.31 | 10.37 | 0.11 | 4.35 | (0.07) | 3.43 | (0.06) |

154

[Part 1/2]
## Table 3.9b Within- and between-school variance in learning time in mathematics

| | | Regular school lessons | | | | | | | Out-of-school-time lessons | | | | | | |
|---|---|---|---|---|---|---|---|---|---|---|---|---|---|---|---|
| | | Between-school variance | Within-school variance | Proportion of between school variance | Mean hours per week | | Standard deviation | | Between-school variance | Within-school variance | Proportion of between school variance | Mean hours per week | | Standard deviation | |
| | | | | | Mean | S.E. | S.D. | S.E. | | | | Mean | S.E. | S.D. | S.E. |
| OECD | Australia | 0.24 | 2.42 | 0.09 | 4.10 | (0.03) | 1.63 | (0.01) | 0.05 | 1.57 | 0.03 | 0.75 | (0.02) | 1.28 | (0.02) |
| | Austria | 0.42 | 1.97 | 0.17 | 3.22 | (0.05) | 1.55 | (0.03) | 0.07 | 1.20 | 0.06 | 0.51 | (0.02) | 1.13 | (0.03) |
| | Belgium | 0.74 | 2.44 | 0.23 | 3.58 | (0.04) | 1.79 | (0.02) | 0.07 | 1.17 | 0.05 | 0.55 | (0.01) | 1.12 | (0.02) |
| | Canada | 0.28 | 3.88 | 0.07 | 4.50 | (0.04) | 2.06 | (0.02) | 0.07 | 1.92 | 0.04 | 0.94 | (0.02) | 1.43 | (0.02) |
| | Czech Republic | 0.31 | 2.02 | 0.13 | 4.00 | (0.05) | 1.55 | (0.02) | 0.04 | 1.49 | 0.03 | 0.76 | (0.02) | 1.25 | (0.03) |
| | Denmark | 0.17 | 1.80 | 0.09 | 4.44 | (0.03) | 1.40 | (0.02) | 0.08 | 1.94 | 0.04 | 1.36 | (0.03) | 1.42 | (0.02) |
| | Finland | 0.20 | 1.64 | 0.11 | 3.45 | (0.04) | 1.35 | (0.02) | 0.01 | 0.69 | 0.01 | 0.37 | (0.02) | 0.84 | (0.03) |
| | France | 0.24 | 1.90 | 0.11 | 3.84 | (0.03) | 1.46 | (0.02) | 0.03 | 1.49 | 0.02 | 0.93 | (0.02) | 1.23 | (0.02) |
| | Germany | 0.20 | 2.35 | 0.08 | 3.88 | (0.04) | 1.60 | (0.03) | 0.12 | 1.73 | 0.07 | 0.82 | (0.03) | 1.36 | (0.03) |
| | Greece | 0.33 | 2.70 | 0.11 | 3.45 | (0.04) | 1.73 | (0.02) | 0.55 | 3.59 | 0.13 | 2.23 | (0.05) | 2.02 | (0.02) |
| | Hungary | 0.30 | 2.53 | 0.10 | 3.29 | (0.04) | 1.68 | (0.02) | 0.06 | 2.16 | 0.02 | 1.29 | (0.03) | 1.49 | (0.02) |
| | Iceland | 0.11 | 2.27 | 0.05 | 4.74 | (0.02) | 1.54 | (0.02) | 0.09 | 1.42 | 0.06 | 0.72 | (0.02) | 1.23 | (0.03) |
| | Ireland | 0.05 | 2.61 | 0.02 | 3.66 | (0.03) | 1.63 | (0.02) | 0.01 | 1.53 | 0.01 | 0.72 | (0.02) | 1.24 | (0.03) |
| | Italy | 0.44 | 2.61 | 0.14 | 3.74 | (0.03) | 1.75 | (0.01) | 0.09 | 1.96 | 0.04 | 0.89 | (0.02) | 1.43 | (0.02) |
| | Japan | 1.34 | 1.40 | 0.49 | 4.24 | (0.07) | 1.65 | (0.04) | 0.13 | 1.45 | 0.08 | 0.71 | (0.02) | 1.26 | (0.04) |
| | Korea | 0.50 | 1.75 | 0.22 | 4.70 | (0.04) | 1.50 | (0.03) | 0.93 | 3.41 | 0.21 | 2.28 | (0.04) | 2.08 | (0.03) |
| | Luxembourg | 0.10 | 2.59 | 0.04 | 3.86 | (0.03) | 1.63 | (0.02) | 0.03 | 1.73 | 0.02 | 0.83 | (0.02) | 1.33 | (0.02) |
| | Mexico | 0.40 | 4.34 | 0.08 | 3.94 | (0.03) | 2.21 | (0.02) | 0.13 | 2.34 | 0.05 | 1.18 | (0.03) | 1.61 | (0.03) |
| | Netherlands | 0.16 | 2.09 | 0.07 | 2.87 | (0.03) | 1.51 | (0.03) | 0.04 | 1.14 | 0.03 | 0.69 | (0.02) | 1.09 | (0.02) |
| | New Zealand | 0.09 | 2.12 | 0.04 | 4.38 | (0.03) | 1.49 | (0.02) | 0.07 | 1.44 | 0.05 | 0.68 | (0.02) | 1.23 | (0.03) |
| | Norway | 0.10 | 1.92 | 0.05 | 3.39 | (0.03) | 1.43 | (0.02) | 0.03 | 1.52 | 0.02 | 1.05 | (0.02) | 1.25 | (0.03) |
| | Poland | 0.14 | 2.93 | 0.05 | 4.36 | (0.04) | 1.75 | (0.02) | 0.05 | 1.25 | 0.04 | 0.78 | (0.02) | 1.14 | (0.03) |
| | Portugal | 0.30 | 3.40 | 0.08 | 3.61 | (0.04) | 1.92 | (0.02) | 0.04 | 1.45 | 0.03 | 0.81 | (0.02) | 1.22 | (0.03) |
| | Slovak Republic | 0.92 | 1.58 | 0.37 | 3.29 | (0.05) | 1.56 | (0.02) | 0.09 | 1.33 | 0.06 | 0.88 | (0.03) | 1.19 | (0.03) |
| | Spain | 0.17 | 1.98 | 0.08 | 3.42 | (0.03) | 1.48 | (0.02) | 0.12 | 2.30 | 0.05 | 0.99 | (0.02) | 1.56 | (0.02) |
| | Sweden | 0.07 | 1.22 | 0.06 | 3.09 | (0.03) | 1.13 | (0.02) | 0.02 | 1.02 | 0.02 | 0.61 | (0.02) | 1.02 | (0.02) |
| | Switzerland | 0.37 | 2.30 | 0.14 | 3.86 | (0.04) | 1.67 | (0.02) | 0.10 | 1.28 | 0.07 | 0.70 | (0.02) | 1.18 | (0.03) |
| | Turkey | 0.66 | 3.36 | 0.16 | 3.82 | (0.06) | 2.01 | (0.04) | 0.29 | 4.01 | 0.07 | 2.08 | (0.05) | 2.08 | (0.03) |
| | United Kingdom | 0.15 | 1.84 | 0.08 | 3.78 | (0.03) | 1.42 | (0.02) | 0.05 | 1.06 | 0.05 | 0.63 | (0.02) | 1.06 | (0.02) |
| | United States | 0.16 | 4.53 | 0.03 | 3.77 | (0.05) | 2.17 | (0.03) | 0.07 | 2.33 | 0.03 | 1.15 | (0.03) | 1.55 | (0.03) |
| | **OECD average** | 0.32 | 0.46 | 0.12 | 0.70 | (0.04) | 0.30 | (0.02) | 0.12 | 1.76 | 0.05 | 0.20 | (0.02) | 0.25 | (0.03) |
| Partners | Argentina | 0.36 | 3.21 | 0.10 | 2.95 | (0.06) | 1.90 | (0.03) | 0.08 | 1.78 | 0.04 | 0.78 | (0.04) | 1.37 | (0.04) |
| | Azerbaijan | 0.50 | 4.95 | 0.09 | 3.79 | (0.06) | 2.33 | (0.02) | 0.21 | 3.86 | 0.05 | 1.70 | (0.05) | 2.02 | (0.03) |
| | Brazil | 0.31 | 3.17 | 0.09 | 3.15 | (0.04) | 1.87 | (0.02) | 0.12 | 2.29 | 0.05 | 1.21 | (0.03) | 1.55 | (0.03) |
| | Bulgaria | 0.55 | 3.40 | 0.14 | 2.98 | (0.07) | 1.99 | (0.04) | 0.05 | 2.42 | 0.02 | 1.14 | (0.04) | 1.58 | (0.04) |
| | Chile | 0.74 | 4.41 | 0.14 | 3.49 | (0.06) | 2.26 | (0.02) | 0.05 | 1.77 | 0.03 | 0.99 | (0.03) | 1.35 | (0.02) |
| | Colombia | 0.44 | 3.02 | 0.13 | 4.21 | (0.06) | 1.86 | (0.03) | 0.07 | 2.37 | 0.03 | 1.23 | (0.03) | 1.56 | (0.03) |
| | Croatia | 0.30 | 1.91 | 0.14 | 3.05 | (0.04) | 1.48 | (0.02) | 0.07 | 1.60 | 0.04 | 0.77 | (0.02) | 1.29 | (0.03) |
| | Estonia | 0.14 | 2.82 | 0.05 | 4.19 | (0.04) | 1.72 | (0.03) | 0.06 | 1.83 | 0.03 | 0.99 | (0.03) | 1.37 | (0.03) |
| | Hong Kong-China | 0.28 | 3.25 | 0.08 | 5.23 | (0.04) | 1.88 | (0.03) | 0.09 | 2.76 | 0.03 | 1.39 | (0.04) | 1.69 | (0.03) |
| | Indonesia | 0.56 | 3.04 | 0.16 | 4.09 | (0.07) | 1.91 | (0.03) | 0.22 | 2.05 | 0.10 | 1.36 | (0.05) | 1.52 | (0.03) |
| | Israel | 0.39 | 3.67 | 0.10 | 4.12 | (0.04) | 2.01 | (0.03) | 0.22 | 3.88 | 0.05 | 2.15 | (0.04) | 2.03 | (0.02) |
| | Jordan | 0.32 | 5.07 | 0.06 | 3.48 | (0.05) | 2.33 | (0.02) | 0.13 | 3.51 | 0.04 | 1.82 | (0.04) | 1.92 | (0.03) |
| | Kyrgyzstan | 0.49 | 4.81 | 0.09 | 2.88 | (0.05) | 2.32 | (0.02) | 0.13 | 3.06 | 0.04 | 1.55 | (0.04) | 1.79 | (0.03) |
| | Latvia | 0.16 | 2.66 | 0.06 | 4.49 | (0.04) | 1.68 | (0.02) | 0.09 | 1.95 | 0.04 | 1.20 | (0.04) | 1.43 | (0.03) |
| | Liechtenstein | 0.19 | 2.74 | 0.07 | 3.98 | (0.08) | 1.69 | (0.05) | 0.08 | 0.91 | 0.08 | 0.58 | (0.05) | 1.00 | (0.07) |
| | Lithuania | 0.26 | 3.12 | 0.08 | 3.50 | (0.04) | 1.84 | (0.02) | 0.03 | 1.23 | 0.03 | 0.74 | (0.02) | 1.12 | (0.02) |
| | Macao-China | 0.22 | 3.11 | 0.07 | 5.41 | (0.03) | 1.81 | (0.02) | 0.06 | 3.05 | 0.02 | 1.20 | (0.03) | 1.76 | (0.03) |
| | Montenegro | 0.22 | 4.24 | 0.05 | 3.09 | (0.04) | 2.10 | (0.02) | 0.03 | 2.41 | 0.01 | 0.93 | (0.02) | 1.56 | (0.03) |
| | Qatar | 0.58 | 4.39 | 0.12 | 3.11 | (0.03) | 2.20 | (0.01) | 0.10 | 3.63 | 0.03 | 1.85 | (0.03) | 1.93 | (0.02) |
| | Romania | 0.57 | 2.89 | 0.16 | 3.01 | (0.07) | 1.86 | (0.05) | 0.11 | 2.82 | 0.04 | 1.50 | (0.03) | 1.71 | (0.03) |
| | Russian Federation | 0.59 | 2.73 | 0.18 | 3.63 | (0.06) | 1.82 | (0.03) | 0.10 | 1.66 | 0.06 | 1.13 | (0.03) | 1.33 | (0.03) |
| | Serbia | 0.27 | 2.45 | 0.10 | 3.27 | (0.04) | 1.65 | (0.02) | 0.03 | 2.15 | 0.01 | 0.97 | (0.02) | 1.48 | (0.03) |
| | Slovenia | 0.49 | 2.45 | 0.17 | 3.33 | (0.03) | 1.70 | (0.01) | 0.09 | 1.92 | 0.04 | 1.02 | (0.02) | 1.40 | (0.03) |
| | Chinese Taipei | 1.28 | 3.02 | 0.30 | 4.26 | (0.05) | 2.08 | (0.02) | 0.48 | 2.61 | 0.16 | 1.53 | (0.04) | 1.77 | (0.02) |
| | Thailand | 0.52 | 1.45 | 0.26 | 3.77 | (0.03) | 1.43 | (0.02) | 0.23 | 1.79 | 0.11 | 0.92 | (0.03) | 1.42 | (0.03) |
| | Tunisia | 0.25 | 4.09 | 0.06 | 3.39 | (0.04) | 2.08 | (0.02) | 0.05 | 4.50 | 0.01 | 2.42 | (0.03) | 2.13 | (0.02) |
| | Uruguay | 0.33 | 2.89 | 0.10 | 3.31 | (0.03) | 1.80 | (0.02) | 0.04 | 1.82 | 0.02 | 0.84 | (0.03) | 1.37 | (0.03) |

[Part 2/2]
## Table 3.9b Within- and between-school variance in learning time in mathematics

| | | Individual study | | | | | | | Total learning hours | | | | | | |
|---|---|---|---|---|---|---|---|---|---|---|---|---|---|---|---|
| | | Between-school variance | Within-school variance | Proportion of between school variance | Mean hours per week | | Standard deviation | | Between-school variance | Within-school variance | Proportion of between school variance | Mean hours per week | | Standard deviation | |
| | | | | | Mean | S.E. | S.D. | S.E. | | | | Mean | S.E. | S.D. | S.E. |
| **OECD** | Australia | 0.22 | 2.19 | 0.09 | 1.79 | (0.02) | 1.55 | (0.02) | 0.94 | 9.26 | 0.09 | 6.65 | (0.05) | 3.19 | (0.04) |
| | Austria | 0.15 | 2.84 | 0.05 | 2.13 | (0.04) | 1.73 | (0.02) | 1.15 | 8.61 | 0.12 | 5.88 | (0.08) | 3.13 | (0.05) |
| | Belgium | 0.26 | 2.02 | 0.11 | 1.79 | (0.03) | 1.52 | (0.02) | 1.81 | 8.13 | 0.18 | 5.93 | (0.06) | 3.17 | (0.04) |
| | Canada | 0.23 | 2.78 | 0.08 | 1.97 | (0.03) | 1.76 | (0.02) | 0.92 | 12.60 | 0.07 | 7.45 | (0.07) | 3.72 | (0.04) |
| | Czech Republic | 0.07 | 1.82 | 0.04 | 1.32 | (0.03) | 1.39 | (0.04) | 0.65 | 7.84 | 0.08 | 6.06 | (0.08) | 2.95 | (0.07) |
| | Denmark | 0.07 | 1.82 | 0.04 | 1.74 | (0.02) | 1.38 | (0.02) | 0.62 | 8.32 | 0.07 | 7.52 | (0.06) | 2.99 | (0.05) |
| | Finland | 0.03 | 0.98 | 0.03 | 1.20 | (0.02) | 1.00 | (0.02) | 0.29 | 4.50 | 0.06 | 5.02 | (0.06) | 2.19 | (0.05) |
| | France | 0.16 | 1.98 | 0.08 | 1.74 | (0.03) | 1.46 | (0.02) | 0.66 | 7.41 | 0.08 | 6.50 | (0.06) | 2.84 | (0.04) |
| | Germany | 0.14 | 2.70 | 0.05 | 2.27 | (0.03) | 1.69 | (0.02) | 0.86 | 9.92 | 0.08 | 6.99 | (0.07) | 3.29 | (0.06) |
| | Greece | 0.10 | 3.29 | 0.03 | 2.01 | (0.03) | 1.84 | (0.02) | 1.95 | 15.29 | 0.11 | 7.71 | (0.10) | 4.13 | (0.05) |
| | Hungary | 0.12 | 2.30 | 0.05 | 1.84 | (0.03) | 1.56 | (0.03) | 0.81 | 11.67 | 0.06 | 6.42 | (0.09) | 3.53 | (0.06) |
| | Iceland | 0.08 | 2.11 | 0.04 | 1.71 | (0.02) | 1.48 | (0.02) | 0.42 | 7.54 | 0.05 | 7.18 | (0.05) | 2.81 | (0.05) |
| | Ireland | 0.07 | 2.31 | 0.03 | 1.76 | (0.03) | 1.54 | (0.03) | 0.14 | 9.89 | 0.01 | 6.14 | (0.06) | 3.17 | (0.06) |
| | Italy | 0.40 | 2.90 | 0.12 | 2.48 | (0.03) | 1.83 | (0.02) | 1.72 | 10.96 | 0.14 | 7.12 | (0.07) | 3.58 | (0.03) |
| | Japan | 0.74 | 1.79 | 0.29 | 1.48 | (0.06) | 1.59 | (0.05) | 4.60 | 5.99 | 0.43 | 6.43 | (0.13) | 3.26 | (0.08) |
| | Korea | 0.93 | 3.38 | 0.22 | 2.31 | (0.06) | 2.08 | (0.05) | 5.81 | 12.37 | 0.32 | 9.32 | (0.13) | 4.25 | (0.09) |
| | Luxembourg | 0.02 | 2.22 | 0.01 | 1.71 | (0.02) | 1.50 | (0.02) | 0.19 | 8.89 | 0.02 | 6.42 | (0.05) | 3.01 | (0.04) |
| | Mexico | 0.15 | 3.10 | 0.04 | 2.26 | (0.03) | 1.83 | (0.02) | 0.82 | 13.76 | 0.06 | 7.35 | (0.07) | 3.88 | (0.05) |
| | Netherlands | 0.10 | 1.61 | 0.06 | 1.47 | (0.03) | 1.31 | (0.03) | 0.41 | 7.30 | 0.05 | 5.02 | (0.07) | 2.79 | (0.06) |
| | New Zealand | 0.11 | 2.01 | 0.05 | 1.59 | (0.03) | 1.46 | (0.03) | 0.38 | 7.95 | 0.05 | 6.66 | (0.05) | 2.89 | (0.06) |
| | Norway | 0.07 | 1.71 | 0.04 | 1.40 | (0.03) | 1.33 | (0.03) | 0.23 | 7.63 | 0.03 | 5.84 | (0.06) | 2.81 | (0.05) |
| | Poland | 0.06 | 2.80 | 0.02 | 2.09 | (0.03) | 1.69 | (0.02) | 0.37 | 9.80 | 0.04 | 7.23 | (0.06) | 3.19 | (0.04) |
| | Portugal | 0.05 | 2.77 | 0.02 | 1.96 | (0.03) | 1.68 | (0.02) | 0.61 | 11.74 | 0.05 | 6.38 | (0.07) | 3.52 | (0.05) |
| | Slovak Republic | 0.20 | 2.12 | 0.09 | 1.69 | (0.03) | 1.52 | (0.03) | 2.50 | 7.43 | 0.25 | 5.87 | (0.10) | 3.12 | (0.05) |
| | Spain | 0.13 | 2.53 | 0.05 | 1.96 | (0.03) | 1.64 | (0.02) | 0.63 | 9.28 | 0.06 | 6.41 | (0.06) | 3.17 | (0.04) |
| | Sweden | 0.05 | 1.26 | 0.04 | 1.18 | (0.02) | 1.14 | (0.03) | 0.19 | 5.34 | 0.03 | 4.88 | (0.04) | 2.35 | (0.06) |
| | Switzerland | 0.11 | 1.70 | 0.06 | 1.69 | (0.02) | 1.35 | (0.02) | 0.86 | 7.00 | 0.11 | 6.26 | (0.06) | 2.85 | (0.05) |
| | Turkey | 0.26 | 3.61 | 0.07 | 2.31 | (0.05) | 1.97 | (0.02) | 3.24 | 20.08 | 0.14 | 8.17 | (0.14) | 4.83 | (0.08) |
| | United Kingdom | 0.08 | 1.39 | 0.06 | 1.49 | (0.02) | 1.22 | (0.02) | 0.41 | 6.10 | 0.06 | 5.90 | (0.05) | 2.56 | (0.04) |
| | United States | 0.06 | 3.08 | 0.02 | 2.05 | (0.03) | 1.77 | (0.02) | 0.19 | 15.98 | 0.01 | 7.01 | (0.07) | 4.02 | (0.06) |
| | **OECD average** | 0.17 | 2.30 | 0.07 | 0.34 | (0.03) | 0.29 | (0.03) | 1.15 | 9.62 | 0.10 | 1.22 | (0.07) | 0.60 | (0.05) |
| **Partners** | Argentina | 0.09 | 2.81 | 0.03 | 1.82 | (0.04) | 1.71 | (0.03) | 0.90 | 10.73 | 0.08 | 5.56 | (0.10) | 3.42 | (0.07) |
| | Azerbaijan | 0.29 | 5.23 | 0.05 | 2.95 | (0.06) | 2.36 | (0.02) | 1.82 | 23.41 | 0.07 | 8.49 | (0.13) | 5.04 | (0.07) |
| | Brazil | 0.13 | 2.63 | 0.05 | 1.80 | (0.03) | 1.66 | (0.03) | 0.83 | 11.93 | 0.06 | 6.14 | (0.07) | 3.56 | (0.05) |
| | Bulgaria | 0.39 | 3.36 | 0.10 | 2.08 | (0.06) | 1.94 | (0.04) | 2.06 | 16.16 | 0.11 | 6.23 | (0.15) | 4.27 | (0.09) |
| | Chile | 0.06 | 2.25 | 0.03 | 1.60 | (0.03) | 1.52 | (0.02) | 1.27 | 12.61 | 0.09 | 6.12 | (0.10) | 3.73 | (0.04) |
| | Colombia | 0.04 | 2.91 | 0.01 | 1.93 | (0.03) | 1.72 | (0.03) | 0.69 | 12.38 | 0.05 | 7.37 | (0.08) | 3.62 | (0.08) |
| | Croatia | 0.15 | 2.53 | 0.06 | 1.80 | (0.03) | 1.64 | (0.02) | 0.84 | 8.44 | 0.09 | 5.66 | (0.06) | 3.05 | (0.05) |
| | Estonia | 0.06 | 2.88 | 0.02 | 1.96 | (0.03) | 1.71 | (0.02) | 0.40 | 10.75 | 0.04 | 7.15 | (0.07) | 3.34 | (0.06) |
| | Hong Kong-China | 0.24 | 3.29 | 0.07 | 2.24 | (0.04) | 1.88 | (0.03) | 1.01 | 13.91 | 0.07 | 8.87 | (0.08) | 3.86 | (0.05) |
| | Indonesia | 0.12 | 2.35 | 0.05 | 1.99 | (0.03) | 1.57 | (0.02) | 1.47 | 10.31 | 0.12 | 7.44 | (0.10) | 3.44 | (0.06) |
| | Israel | 0.22 | 3.91 | 0.05 | 2.33 | (0.05) | 2.04 | (0.03) | 1.45 | 20.12 | 0.07 | 8.69 | (0.11) | 4.64 | (0.07) |
| | Jordan | 0.17 | 4.16 | 0.04 | 2.69 | (0.04) | 2.09 | (0.02) | 0.77 | 19.61 | 0.04 | 7.96 | (0.08) | 4.55 | (0.06) |
| | Kyrgyzstan | 0.10 | 4.44 | 0.02 | 2.22 | (0.03) | 2.14 | (0.02) | 0.85 | 20.15 | 0.04 | 6.71 | (0.09) | 4.62 | (0.06) |
| | Latvia | 0.09 | 3.07 | 0.03 | 2.44 | (0.04) | 1.78 | (0.02) | 0.52 | 10.89 | 0.05 | 8.14 | (0.09) | 3.38 | (0.05) |
| | Liechtenstein | 0.05 | 1.31 | 0.03 | 1.49 | (0.06) | 1.16 | (0.06) | 0.50 | 5.97 | 0.08 | 6.04 | (0.12) | 2.52 | (0.11) |
| | Lithuania | 0.08 | 2.48 | 0.03 | 1.78 | (0.03) | 1.60 | (0.02) | 0.58 | 9.55 | 0.06 | 6.02 | (0.06) | 3.18 | (0.05) |
| | Macao-China | 0.58 | 3.03 | 0.16 | 2.07 | (0.03) | 1.86 | (0.02) | 1.50 | 12.75 | 0.11 | 8.68 | (0.06) | 3.72 | (0.04) |
| | Montenegro | 0.04 | 3.57 | 0.01 | 2.03 | (0.03) | 1.90 | (0.02) | 0.42 | 15.35 | 0.03 | 6.03 | (0.07) | 3.97 | (0.04) |
| | Qatar | 0.08 | 3.47 | 0.02 | 2.22 | (0.02) | 1.88 | (0.01) | 0.86 | 18.97 | 0.04 | 7.21 | (0.06) | 4.44 | (0.04) |
| | Romania | 0.22 | 3.51 | 0.06 | 2.16 | (0.04) | 1.93 | (0.03) | 1.95 | 16.66 | 0.10 | 6.67 | (0.11) | 4.30 | (0.08) |
| | Russian Federation | 0.36 | 2.83 | 0.11 | 2.23 | (0.05) | 1.78 | (0.03) | 1.97 | 10.77 | 0.15 | 6.99 | (0.10) | 3.55 | (0.06) |
| | Serbia | 0.10 | 2.86 | 0.03 | 1.82 | (0.03) | 1.72 | (0.02) | 0.77 | 11.71 | 0.06 | 6.06 | (0.07) | 3.53 | (0.05) |
| | Slovenia | 0.18 | 2.49 | 0.07 | 1.92 | (0.02) | 1.62 | (0.02) | 1.16 | 11.00 | 0.10 | 6.30 | (0.05) | 3.44 | (0.04) |
| | Chinese Taipei | 0.52 | 2.44 | 0.18 | 1.88 | (0.04) | 1.72 | (0.02) | 5.51 | 11.74 | 0.32 | 7.72 | (0.12) | 4.17 | (0.04) |
| | Thailand | 0.22 | 2.09 | 0.09 | 1.81 | (0.03) | 1.52 | (0.02) | 2.23 | 7.73 | 0.22 | 6.50 | (0.07) | 3.22 | (0.05) |
| | Tunisia | 0.08 | 4.47 | 0.02 | 2.57 | (0.04) | 2.13 | (0.02) | 0.91 | 21.24 | 0.04 | 8.38 | (0.10) | 4.70 | (0.06) |
| | Uruguay | 0.08 | 2.22 | 0.03 | 1.57 | (0.03) | 1.52 | (0.03) | 0.60 | 10.60 | 0.05 | 5.74 | (0.07) | 3.36 | (0.07) |

© OECD 2011 Quality Time for Students: Learning In and Out of School

[Part 1/2]

## Table 3.9c  Within- and between-school variance in learning time on the language of instruction

| | | Regular school lessons | | | | | | Out-of-school-time lessons | | | | | | |
|---|---|---|---|---|---|---|---|---|---|---|---|---|---|---|
| | | Between-school variance | Within-school variance | Proportion of between school variance | Mean hours per week | | Standard deviation | | Between-school variance | Within-school variance | Proportion of between school variance | Mean hours per week | | Standard deviation | |
| | | | | | Mean | S.E. | S.D. | S.E. | | | | Mean | S.E. | S.D. | S.E. |
| OECD | Australia | 0.25 | 2.26 | 0.10 | 4.06 | (0.03) | 1.58 | (0.01) | 0.04 | 1.49 | 0.02 | 0.66 | (0.02) | 1.24 | (0.02) |
| | Austria | 0.34 | 1.62 | 0.17 | 2.87 | (0.03) | 1.39 | (0.03) | 0.06 | 0.59 | 0.09 | 0.24 | (0.02) | 0.80 | (0.04) |
| | Belgium | 0.47 | 2.43 | 0.16 | 3.49 | (0.03) | 1.71 | (0.02) | 0.06 | 1.03 | 0.05 | 0.46 | (0.01) | 1.05 | (0.03) |
| | Canada | 0.27 | 4.13 | 0.06 | 4.43 | (0.04) | 2.12 | (0.02) | 0.08 | 2.03 | 0.04 | 0.86 | (0.02) | 1.47 | (0.02) |
| | Czech Republic | 0.19 | 1.83 | 0.10 | 3.72 | (0.03) | 1.44 | (0.02) | 0.02 | 1.13 | 0.02 | 0.61 | (0.01) | 1.08 | (0.02) |
| | Denmark | 0.24 | 2.16 | 0.10 | 5.50 | (0.03) | 1.55 | (0.02) | 0.08 | 2.78 | 0.03 | 1.68 | (0.03) | 1.69 | (0.02) |
| | Finland | 0.23 | 1.43 | 0.14 | 3.13 | (0.05) | 1.29 | (0.04) | 0.01 | 0.71 | 0.01 | 0.36 | (0.01) | 0.85 | (0.03) |
| | France | 0.24 | 1.94 | 0.11 | 4.01 | (0.03) | 1.47 | (0.02) | 0.06 | 1.30 | 0.05 | 0.77 | (0.02) | 1.17 | (0.02) |
| | Germany | 0.18 | 2.36 | 0.07 | 3.66 | (0.03) | 1.60 | (0.03) | 0.14 | 1.38 | 0.09 | 0.61 | (0.02) | 1.23 | (0.03) |
| | Greece | 0.39 | 3.31 | 0.11 | 3.18 | (0.04) | 1.91 | (0.02) | 0.14 | 3.01 | 0.04 | 1.63 | (0.03) | 1.77 | (0.03) |
| | Hungary | 0.36 | 2.44 | 0.13 | 3.18 | (0.04) | 1.66 | (0.02) | 0.08 | 2.31 | 0.03 | 1.31 | (0.03) | 1.54 | (0.03) |
| | Iceland | 0.14 | 2.30 | 0.06 | 4.52 | (0.02) | 1.56 | (0.02) | 0.06 | 0.98 | 0.06 | 0.46 | (0.02) | 1.02 | (0.04) |
| | Ireland | 0.07 | 2.64 | 0.03 | 3.55 | (0.03) | 1.65 | (0.02) | 0.03 | 1.68 | 0.02 | 0.63 | (0.02) | 1.31 | (0.03) |
| | Italy | 0.40 | 3.51 | 0.10 | 4.62 | (0.03) | 1.99 | (0.01) | 0.15 | 2.18 | 0.06 | 0.79 | (0.02) | 1.53 | (0.02) |
| | Japan | 0.63 | 1.41 | 0.31 | 3.82 | (0.04) | 1.42 | (0.03) | 0.06 | 0.82 | 0.06 | 0.43 | (0.02) | 0.93 | (0.03) |
| | Korea | 0.39 | 1.73 | 0.18 | 4.48 | (0.04) | 1.45 | (0.03) | 0.40 | 2.21 | 0.15 | 1.45 | (0.04) | 1.61 | (0.02) |
| | Luxembourg | 0.26 | 2.55 | 0.09 | 3.50 | (0.03) | 1.65 | (0.01) | 0.05 | 1.44 | 0.03 | 0.60 | (0.02) | 1.22 | (0.02) |
| | Mexico | 0.31 | 4.41 | 0.07 | 3.73 | (0.04) | 2.20 | (0.01) | 0.13 | 2.13 | 0.06 | 1.10 | (0.03) | 1.53 | (0.03) |
| | Netherlands | 0.07 | 1.59 | 0.04 | 2.92 | (0.03) | 1.29 | (0.02) | 0.09 | 1.07 | 0.08 | 0.64 | (0.02) | 1.08 | (0.02) |
| | New Zealand | 0.09 | 2.09 | 0.04 | 4.39 | (0.03) | 1.48 | (0.03) | 0.08 | 1.50 | 0.05 | 0.65 | (0.03) | 1.26 | (0.04) |
| | Norway | 0.23 | 2.19 | 0.09 | 3.60 | (0.04) | 1.56 | (0.02) | 0.04 | 1.89 | 0.02 | 1.16 | (0.02) | 1.39 | (0.03) |
| | Poland | 0.09 | 2.94 | 0.03 | 4.64 | (0.03) | 1.74 | (0.02) | 0.06 | 1.25 | 0.05 | 0.70 | (0.03) | 1.15 | (0.03) |
| | Portugal | 0.10 | 2.21 | 0.04 | 3.27 | (0.03) | 1.52 | (0.02) | 0.06 | 1.03 | 0.06 | 0.57 | (0.02) | 1.05 | (0.02) |
| | Slovak Republic | 0.76 | 1.47 | 0.34 | 3.12 | (0.05) | 1.48 | (0.02) | 0.07 | 1.34 | 0.05 | 0.89 | (0.03) | 1.19 | (0.02) |
| | Spain | 0.25 | 2.03 | 0.11 | 3.60 | (0.03) | 1.53 | (0.02) | 0.07 | 1.53 | 0.04 | 0.58 | (0.02) | 1.27 | (0.03) |
| | Sweden | 0.09 | 1.35 | 0.07 | 3.12 | (0.03) | 1.20 | (0.03) | 0.02 | 1.40 | 0.01 | 0.68 | (0.02) | 1.19 | (0.04) |
| | Switzerland | 0.43 | 2.28 | 0.16 | 3.65 | (0.04) | 1.66 | (0.02) | 0.09 | 1.03 | 0.08 | 0.49 | (0.02) | 1.06 | (0.03) |
| | Turkey | 0.49 | 2.60 | 0.16 | 3.99 | (0.05) | 1.77 | (0.02) | 0.22 | 3.25 | 0.06 | 1.81 | (0.05) | 1.87 | (0.03) |
| | United Kingdom | 0.16 | 1.88 | 0.08 | 3.89 | (0.04) | 1.44 | (0.02) | 0.06 | 1.13 | 0.05 | 0.59 | (0.02) | 1.10 | (0.02) |
| | United States | 0.20 | 4.63 | 0.04 | 3.64 | (0.04) | 2.20 | (0.03) | 0.06 | 2.32 | 0.03 | 1.11 | (0.03) | 1.54 | (0.03) |
| | **OECD average** | 0.28 | 0.46 | 0.11 | 0.70 | (0.04) | 0.30 | (0.02) | 0.08 | 1.60 | 0.05 | 0.17 | (0.02) | 0.24 | (0.03) |
| Partners | Argentina | 0.25 | 2.47 | 0.09 | 2.39 | (0.05) | 1.66 | (0.05) | 0.07 | 0.88 | 0.07 | 0.43 | (0.03) | 0.98 | (0.04) |
| | Azerbaijan | 0.28 | 4.32 | 0.06 | 3.69 | (0.05) | 2.14 | (0.02) | 0.17 | 4.01 | 0.04 | 1.80 | (0.05) | 2.05 | (0.03) |
| | Brazil | 0.28 | 3.32 | 0.08 | 3.10 | (0.04) | 1.90 | (0.02) | 0.10 | 2.15 | 0.05 | 1.18 | (0.03) | 1.50 | (0.03) |
| | Bulgaria | 0.26 | 3.16 | 0.08 | 2.91 | (0.05) | 1.85 | (0.02) | 0.10 | 2.32 | 0.04 | 1.09 | (0.04) | 1.56 | (0.03) |
| | Chile | 0.60 | 4.25 | 0.12 | 3.45 | (0.06) | 2.20 | (0.02) | 0.06 | 1.86 | 0.03 | 1.00 | (0.03) | 1.39 | (0.03) |
| | Colombia | 0.27 | 2.65 | 0.09 | 3.92 | (0.05) | 1.71 | (0.03) | 0.06 | 2.11 | 0.03 | 1.15 | (0.03) | 1.48 | (0.03) |
| | Croatia | 0.17 | 1.95 | 0.08 | 3.33 | (0.03) | 1.46 | (0.02) | 0.05 | 0.92 | 0.05 | 0.39 | (0.02) | 0.98 | (0.03) |
| | Estonia | 0.12 | 2.43 | 0.05 | 3.48 | (0.04) | 1.60 | (0.02) | 0.06 | 1.53 | 0.04 | 0.88 | (0.03) | 1.26 | (0.03) |
| | Hong Kong-China | 0.20 | 3.32 | 0.06 | 5.19 | (0.04) | 1.88 | (0.03) | 0.13 | 1.68 | 0.07 | 0.81 | (0.03) | 1.34 | (0.03) |
| | Indonesia | 0.63 | 2.66 | 0.19 | 3.64 | (0.05) | 1.83 | (0.04) | 0.16 | 1.84 | 0.08 | 1.25 | (0.04) | 1.42 | (0.02) |
| | Israel | 0.19 | 4.10 | 0.04 | 3.03 | (0.04) | 2.08 | (0.02) | 0.17 | 2.75 | 0.06 | 1.33 | (0.03) | 1.71 | (0.03) |
| | Jordan | 0.39 | 5.24 | 0.07 | 3.56 | (0.05) | 2.38 | (0.02) | 0.14 | 3.25 | 0.04 | 1.77 | (0.04) | 1.85 | (0.02) |
| | Kyrgyzstan | 0.37 | 4.32 | 0.08 | 2.74 | (0.06) | 2.18 | (0.02) | 0.14 | 3.30 | 0.04 | 1.70 | (0.03) | 1.86 | (0.03) |
| | Latvia | 0.17 | 2.21 | 0.07 | 3.69 | (0.04) | 1.54 | (0.02) | 0.07 | 1.51 | 0.05 | 0.88 | (0.03) | 1.26 | (0.03) |
| | Liechtenstein | 0.00 | 2.76 | 0.00 | 3.66 | (0.08) | 1.66 | (0.05) | 0.04 | 0.52 | 0.07 | 0.32 | (0.04) | 0.75 | (0.08) |
| | Lithuania | 0.21 | 3.30 | 0.06 | 3.66 | (0.04) | 1.87 | (0.02) | 0.04 | 1.32 | 0.03 | 0.66 | (0.02) | 1.17 | (0.03) |
| | Macao-China | 0.23 | 3.19 | 0.07 | 5.32 | (0.03) | 1.83 | (0.02) | 0.06 | 2.67 | 0.02 | 1.06 | (0.03) | 1.65 | (0.03) |
| | Montenegro | 0.22 | 4.41 | 0.05 | 2.93 | (0.04) | 2.15 | (0.02) | 0.03 | 2.05 | 0.02 | 0.75 | (0.02) | 1.44 | (0.03) |
| | Qatar | 0.52 | 4.21 | 0.11 | 2.90 | (0.03) | 2.13 | (0.02) | 0.12 | 2.97 | 0.04 | 1.59 | (0.03) | 1.76 | (0.02) |
| | Romania | 0.63 | 2.55 | 0.20 | 3.30 | (0.06) | 1.77 | (0.04) | 0.12 | 2.64 | 0.04 | 1.52 | (0.03) | 1.66 | (0.03) |
| | Russian Federation | 0.16 | 1.97 | 0.07 | 2.04 | (0.04) | 1.46 | (0.02) | 0.08 | 1.21 | 0.06 | 0.82 | (0.03) | 1.14 | (0.03) |
| | Serbia | 0.23 | 2.35 | 0.09 | 3.17 | (0.04) | 1.61 | (0.02) | 0.05 | 2.10 | 0.02 | 0.93 | (0.03) | 1.47 | (0.03) |
| | Slovenia | 0.34 | 2.72 | 0.11 | 3.25 | (0.03) | 1.73 | (0.01) | 0.08 | 1.23 | 0.06 | 0.73 | (0.02) | 1.13 | (0.02) |
| | Chinese Taipei | 0.79 | 2.97 | 0.21 | 4.37 | (0.05) | 1.94 | (0.02) | 0.09 | 1.57 | 0.06 | 0.69 | (0.02) | 1.29 | (0.02) |
| | Thailand | 0.50 | 0.78 | 0.39 | 3.10 | (0.02) | 1.18 | (0.02) | 0.15 | 1.12 | 0.12 | 0.56 | (0.02) | 1.12 | (0.03) |
| | Tunisia | 0.34 | 4.02 | 0.08 | 3.14 | (0.05) | 2.09 | (0.02) | 0.17 | 3.14 | 0.05 | 1.78 | (0.04) | 1.82 | (0.03) |
| | Uruguay | 0.20 | 2.68 | 0.07 | 2.74 | (0.04) | 1.70 | (0.02) | 0.06 | 1.41 | 0.04 | 0.65 | (0.02) | 1.22 | (0.04) |

[Part 2/2]

## Table 3.9c  Within- and between-school variance in learning time on the language of instruction

| | | Individual study | | | | | | Total learning hours | | | | | |
|---|---|---|---|---|---|---|---|---|---|---|---|---|---|
| | | Between-school variance | Within-school variance | Proportion of between school variance | Mean hours per week | | Standard deviation | | Between-school variance | Within-school variance | Proportion of between school variance | Mean hours per week | | Standard deviation | |
| | | | | | Mean | S.E. | S.D. | S.E. | | | | Mean | S.E. | S.D. | S.E. |
| OECD | Australia | 0.13 | 2.12 | 0.06 | 1.71 | (0.02) | 1.50 | (0.02) | 0.64 | 8.66 | 0.07 | 6.43 | (0.04) | 3.05 | (0.04) |
| | Austria | 0.21 | 2.03 | 0.09 | 1.55 | (0.04) | 1.50 | (0.03) | 1.11 | 5.95 | 0.16 | 4.66 | (0.07) | 2.64 | (0.06) |
| | Belgium | 0.06 | 1.37 | 0.04 | 1.35 | (0.02) | 1.20 | (0.02) | 0.80 | 6.21 | 0.11 | 5.30 | (0.04) | 2.67 | (0.04) |
| | Canada | 0.24 | 2.53 | 0.09 | 1.74 | (0.03) | 1.70 | (0.02) | 0.97 | 13.03 | 0.07 | 7.06 | (0.06) | 3.80 | (0.04) |
| | Czech Republic | 0.07 | 1.35 | 0.05 | 1.16 | (0.02) | 1.20 | (0.03) | 0.35 | 6.00 | 0.06 | 5.49 | (0.05) | 2.54 | (0.05) |
| | Denmark | 0.06 | 2.36 | 0.02 | 2.16 | (0.03) | 1.56 | (0.03) | 0.69 | 10.91 | 0.06 | 9.34 | (0.07) | 3.40 | (0.05) |
| | Finland | 0.03 | 1.05 | 0.02 | 1.13 | (0.02) | 1.04 | (0.03) | 0.38 | 4.37 | 0.08 | 4.63 | (0.07) | 2.18 | (0.06) |
| | France | 0.08 | 1.70 | 0.05 | 1.51 | (0.02) | 1.34 | (0.02) | 0.42 | 6.84 | 0.06 | 6.30 | (0.04) | 2.69 | (0.04) |
| | Germany | 0.13 | 2.32 | 0.05 | 1.89 | (0.03) | 1.57 | (0.02) | 0.91 | 8.59 | 0.10 | 6.17 | (0.05) | 3.08 | (0.07) |
| | Greece | 0.07 | 3.04 | 0.02 | 1.94 | (0.03) | 1.76 | (0.02) | 1.12 | 16.61 | 0.06 | 6.75 | (0.08) | 4.20 | (0.06) |
| | Hungary | 0.13 | 2.31 | 0.05 | 1.86 | (0.03) | 1.56 | (0.02) | 0.91 | 12.18 | 0.07 | 6.36 | (0.08) | 3.61 | (0.05) |
| | Iceland | 0.08 | 1.67 | 0.05 | 1.54 | (0.02) | 1.32 | (0.02) | 0.39 | 6.27 | 0.06 | 6.54 | (0.04) | 2.57 | (0.05) |
| | Ireland | 0.06 | 2.52 | 0.02 | 1.75 | (0.03) | 1.61 | (0.03) | 0.24 | 10.59 | 0.02 | 5.94 | (0.07) | 3.29 | (0.06) |
| | Italy | 0.59 | 3.23 | 0.15 | 2.95 | (0.04) | 1.97 | (0.02) | 1.76 | 12.35 | 0.12 | 8.37 | (0.07) | 3.78 | (0.04) |
| | Japan | 0.19 | 1.05 | 0.16 | 0.94 | (0.03) | 1.12 | (0.04) | 1.47 | 4.18 | 0.26 | 5.19 | (0.07) | 2.38 | (0.07) |
| | Korea | 0.20 | 1.90 | 0.09 | 1.40 | (0.03) | 1.45 | (0.03) | 2.28 | 7.94 | 0.22 | 7.34 | (0.09) | 3.19 | (0.05) |
| | Luxembourg | 0.03 | 1.89 | 0.01 | 1.38 | (0.02) | 1.39 | (0.02) | 0.30 | 8.19 | 0.04 | 5.48 | (0.04) | 2.90 | (0.04) |
| | Mexico | 0.13 | 2.73 | 0.04 | 2.06 | (0.03) | 1.71 | (0.02) | 0.70 | 12.75 | 0.05 | 6.87 | (0.07) | 3.73 | (0.04) |
| | Netherlands | 0.04 | 1.31 | 0.03 | 1.33 | (0.02) | 1.16 | (0.03) | 0.33 | 5.25 | 0.06 | 4.89 | (0.05) | 2.37 | (0.05) |
| | New Zealand | 0.10 | 2.06 | 0.05 | 1.57 | (0.03) | 1.47 | (0.03) | 0.44 | 8.06 | 0.05 | 6.62 | (0.06) | 2.92 | (0.07) |
| | Norway | 0.07 | 1.81 | 0.04 | 1.44 | (0.03) | 1.37 | (0.03) | 0.48 | 8.80 | 0.05 | 6.19 | (0.06) | 3.05 | (0.06) |
| | Poland | 0.05 | 2.87 | 0.02 | 2.22 | (0.03) | 1.71 | (0.02) | 0.22 | 9.72 | 0.02 | 7.56 | (0.05) | 3.15 | (0.04) |
| | Portugal | 0.06 | 2.14 | 0.03 | 1.79 | (0.03) | 1.48 | (0.02) | 0.22 | 7.54 | 0.03 | 5.63 | (0.05) | 2.79 | (0.05) |
| | Slovak Republic | 0.16 | 2.15 | 0.07 | 1.74 | (0.03) | 1.52 | (0.02) | 1.64 | 7.20 | 0.19 | 5.75 | (0.08) | 2.96 | (0.05) |
| | Spain | 0.13 | 2.37 | 0.05 | 1.89 | (0.03) | 1.59 | (0.02) | 0.65 | 7.72 | 0.08 | 6.10 | (0.05) | 2.93 | (0.04) |
| | Sweden | 0.04 | 1.44 | 0.03 | 1.26 | (0.02) | 1.22 | (0.04) | 0.26 | 6.42 | 0.04 | 5.06 | (0.06) | 2.58 | (0.10) |
| | Switzerland | 0.08 | 1.30 | 0.06 | 1.40 | (0.02) | 1.17 | (0.02) | 0.83 | 6.16 | 0.12 | 5.54 | (0.05) | 2.66 | (0.04) |
| | Turkey | 0.22 | 3.10 | 0.07 | 2.18 | (0.05) | 1.83 | (0.03) | 1.92 | 15.45 | 0.11 | 7.96 | (0.12) | 4.18 | (0.07) |
| | United Kingdom | 0.09 | 1.65 | 0.05 | 1.59 | (0.02) | 1.33 | (0.02) | 0.45 | 6.64 | 0.06 | 6.08 | (0.06) | 2.68 | (0.04) |
| | United States | 0.10 | 2.78 | 0.04 | 1.87 | (0.03) | 1.70 | (0.02) | 0.30 | 15.34 | 0.02 | 6.65 | (0.06) | 3.95 | (0.05) |
| | **OECD average** | 0.12 | 2.07 | 0.05 | 0.31 | (0.03) | 0.27 | (0.02) | 0.77 | 8.86 | 0.08 | 1.16 | (0.06) | 0.57 | (0.05) |
| Partners | Argentina | 0.12 | 2.17 | 0.05 | 1.64 | (0.04) | 1.52 | (0.04) | 0.56 | 7.29 | 0.07 | 4.45 | (0.08) | 2.82 | (0.07) |
| | Azerbaijan | 0.21 | 5.07 | 0.04 | 3.10 | (0.05) | 2.30 | (0.02) | 0.89 | 22.54 | 0.04 | 8.66 | (0.11) | 4.85 | (0.07) |
| | Brazil | 0.12 | 2.57 | 0.04 | 1.74 | (0.03) | 1.64 | (0.02) | 0.60 | 11.86 | 0.05 | 6.01 | (0.06) | 3.52 | (0.05) |
| | Bulgaria | 0.32 | 3.12 | 0.09 | 2.05 | (0.05) | 1.85 | (0.03) | 1.22 | 15.11 | 0.07 | 6.08 | (0.11) | 4.04 | (0.07) |
| | Chile | 0.06 | 2.19 | 0.02 | 1.56 | (0.03) | 1.50 | (0.03) | 0.81 | 12.30 | 0.06 | 6.03 | (0.08) | 3.63 | (0.06) |
| | Colombia | 0.07 | 2.61 | 0.03 | 1.84 | (0.04) | 1.64 | (0.03) | 0.50 | 10.32 | 0.05 | 6.92 | (0.08) | 3.29 | (0.07) |
| | Croatia | 0.09 | 2.12 | 0.04 | 1.58 | (0.03) | 1.49 | (0.02) | 0.38 | 6.89 | 0.05 | 5.32 | (0.06) | 2.70 | (0.05) |
| | Estonia | 0.05 | 2.09 | 0.03 | 1.62 | (0.03) | 1.46 | (0.02) | 0.31 | 8.40 | 0.04 | 5.99 | (0.06) | 2.95 | (0.05) |
| | Hong Kong-China | 0.05 | 2.40 | 0.02 | 1.64 | (0.03) | 1.56 | (0.03) | 0.41 | 10.62 | 0.04 | 7.64 | (0.08) | 3.32 | (0.06) |
| | Indonesia | 0.18 | 1.89 | 0.09 | 1.80 | (0.03) | 1.44 | (0.04) | 1.67 | 8.66 | 0.16 | 6.68 | (0.10) | 3.24 | (0.07) |
| | Israel | 0.17 | 3.05 | 0.05 | 1.66 | (0.04) | 1.80 | (0.03) | 0.83 | 17.00 | 0.05 | 6.04 | (0.09) | 4.24 | (0.07) |
| | Jordan | 0.14 | 3.81 | 0.04 | 2.59 | (0.04) | 2.00 | (0.02) | 0.64 | 18.61 | 0.03 | 7.92 | (0.09) | 4.41 | (0.06) |
| | Kyrgyzstan | 0.08 | 4.51 | 0.02 | 2.34 | (0.04) | 2.15 | (0.02) | 0.79 | 20.54 | 0.04 | 6.85 | (0.09) | 4.64 | (0.06) |
| | Latvia | 0.07 | 2.19 | 0.03 | 2.01 | (0.03) | 1.51 | (0.02) | 0.58 | 8.25 | 0.07 | 6.58 | (0.07) | 2.98 | (0.05) |
| | Liechtenstein | 0.00 | 1.18 | 0.00 | 1.24 | (0.06) | 1.09 | (0.10) | 0.02 | 4.73 | 0.00 | 5.21 | (0.10) | 2.18 | (0.10) |
| | Lithuania | 0.06 | 2.51 | 0.02 | 1.82 | (0.03) | 1.60 | (0.02) | 0.30 | 9.86 | 0.03 | 6.13 | (0.06) | 3.19 | (0.05) |
| | Macao-China | 0.16 | 2.17 | 0.07 | 1.49 | (0.03) | 1.51 | (0.03) | 0.78 | 11.09 | 0.07 | 7.86 | (0.06) | 3.41 | (0.05) |
| | Montenegro | 0.05 | 3.51 | 0.01 | 1.99 | (0.03) | 1.88 | (0.02) | 0.43 | 16.35 | 0.03 | 5.66 | (0.07) | 4.08 | (0.06) |
| | Qatar | 0.06 | 3.35 | 0.02 | 2.04 | (0.02) | 1.85 | (0.02) | 0.68 | 16.70 | 0.04 | 6.51 | (0.06) | 4.16 | (0.04) |
| | Romania | 0.21 | 3.17 | 0.06 | 2.19 | (0.04) | 1.84 | (0.02) | 1.96 | 13.87 | 0.12 | 7.02 | (0.10) | 3.96 | (0.09) |
| | Russian Federation | 0.11 | 1.70 | 0.06 | 1.55 | (0.04) | 1.35 | (0.03) | 0.58 | 7.31 | 0.07 | 4.40 | (0.07) | 2.81 | (0.06) |
| | Serbia | 0.07 | 2.69 | 0.03 | 1.70 | (0.03) | 1.66 | (0.03) | 0.53 | 11.56 | 0.04 | 5.80 | (0.07) | 3.48 | (0.06) |
| | Slovenia | 0.08 | 1.67 | 0.04 | 1.48 | (0.02) | 1.31 | (0.02) | 0.42 | 8.18 | 0.05 | 5.47 | (0.04) | 2.89 | (0.04) |
| | Chinese Taipei | 0.17 | 2.18 | 0.07 | 1.77 | (0.03) | 1.54 | (0.02) | 1.55 | 9.21 | 0.14 | 6.87 | (0.08) | 3.29 | (0.04) |
| | Thailand | 0.20 | 1.86 | 0.10 | 1.71 | (0.03) | 1.44 | (0.03) | 1.82 | 5.11 | 0.26 | 5.36 | (0.05) | 2.66 | (0.05) |
| | Tunisia | 0.12 | 3.35 | 0.03 | 2.12 | (0.04) | 1.86 | (0.03) | 0.75 | 17.24 | 0.04 | 7.05 | (0.10) | 4.24 | (0.06) |
| | Uruguay | 0.07 | 1.78 | 0.04 | 1.35 | (0.02) | 1.37 | (0.02) | 0.42 | 9.23 | 0.04 | 4.76 | (0.06) | 3.12 | (0.07) |

© OECD 2011  Quality Time for Students: Learning In and Out of School

**Table 3.9d** **Within- and between-school variance in learning time in science, in mathematics and on**
[Part 1/2] **the language of instruction**

| | | Regular school lessons | | | | | | | Out-of-school-time lessons | | | | | | |
|---|---|---|---|---|---|---|---|---|---|---|---|---|---|---|---|
| | | Between-school variance | Within-school variance | Proportion of between school variance | Mean hours per week | | Standard deviation | | Between-school variance | Within-school variance | Proportion of between school variance | Mean hours per week | | Standard deviation | |
| | | | | | Mean | S.E. | S.D. | S.E. | | | | Mean | S.E. | S.D. | S.E. |
| OECD | Australia | 2.43 | 17.00 | 0.12 | 11.40 | (0.07) | 4.41 | (0.03) | 0.24 | 7.77 | 0.03 | 1.76 | (0.04) | 2.83 | (0.04) |
| | Austria | 2.42 | 9.56 | 0.20 | 8.56 | (0.09) | 3.44 | (0.06) | 0.33 | 3.69 | 0.08 | 0.94 | (0.04) | 2.00 | (0.07) |
| | Belgium | 5.34 | 15.70 | 0.25 | 9.70 | (0.10) | 4.61 | (0.04) | 0.40 | 5.63 | 0.07 | 1.32 | (0.03) | 2.47 | (0.05) |
| | Canada | 2.66 | 29.59 | 0.08 | 12.93 | (0.11) | 5.75 | (0.05) | 0.40 | 9.87 | 0.04 | 2.35 | (0.04) | 3.24 | (0.04) |
| | Czech Republic | 2.54 | 11.73 | 0.18 | 10.65 | (0.11) | 3.80 | (0.04) | 0.15 | 6.51 | 0.02 | 1.89 | (0.04) | 2.60 | (0.05) |
| | Denmark | 1.02 | 10.54 | 0.09 | 13.16 | (0.07) | 3.40 | (0.05) | 0.43 | 10.92 | 0.04 | 3.83 | (0.07) | 3.37 | (0.04) |
| | Finland | 1.24 | 10.03 | 0.11 | 9.71 | (0.11) | 3.36 | (0.06) | 0.07 | 4.01 | 0.02 | 1.06 | (0.04) | 2.02 | (0.06) |
| | France | 3.84 | 10.82 | 0.26 | 10.71 | (0.10) | 3.83 | (0.05) | 0.26 | 7.03 | 0.04 | 2.24 | (0.04) | 2.70 | (0.04) |
| | Germany | 1.34 | 14.74 | 0.08 | 10.61 | (0.08) | 4.01 | (0.05) | 0.70 | 7.75 | 0.08 | 1.92 | (0.06) | 2.91 | (0.07) |
| | Greece | 3.62 | 14.84 | 0.20 | 9.82 | (0.12) | 4.25 | (0.05) | 2.39 | 15.85 | 0.13 | 5.84 | (0.11) | 4.25 | (0.04) |
| | Hungary | 2.79 | 13.41 | 0.17 | 8.99 | (0.10) | 4.00 | (0.05) | 0.40 | 10.53 | 0.04 | 3.59 | (0.06) | 3.30 | (0.05) |
| | Iceland | 0.75 | 12.87 | 0.06 | 12.24 | (0.06) | 3.68 | (0.04) | 0.38 | 5.49 | 0.06 | 1.46 | (0.04) | 2.42 | (0.07) |
| | Ireland | 0.53 | 15.98 | 0.03 | 9.75 | (0.08) | 4.07 | (0.06) | 0.13 | 7.14 | 0.02 | 1.65 | (0.05) | 2.70 | (0.06) |
| | Italy | 3.34 | 17.21 | 0.16 | 11.27 | (0.09) | 4.55 | (0.05) | 0.62 | 9.94 | 0.06 | 2.25 | (0.04) | 3.26 | (0.05) |
| | Japan | 5.84 | 7.32 | 0.44 | 10.75 | (0.13) | 3.60 | (0.07) | 0.32 | 5.71 | 0.05 | 1.40 | (0.05) | 2.46 | (0.06) |
| | Korea | 3.56 | 10.37 | 0.26 | 12.76 | (0.11) | 3.73 | (0.09) | 4.17 | 13.94 | 0.23 | 4.74 | (0.08) | 4.25 | (0.06) |
| | Luxembourg | 1.44 | 13.29 | 0.10 | 9.71 | (0.06) | 3.78 | (0.04) | 0.28 | 7.68 | 0.03 | 1.93 | (0.04) | 2.82 | (0.06) |
| | Mexico | 2.25 | 29.51 | 0.07 | 10.84 | (0.09) | 5.73 | (0.04) | 0.93 | 12.99 | 0.07 | 3.28 | (0.08) | 3.82 | (0.07) |
| | Netherlands | 1.23 | 10.64 | 0.10 | 7.97 | (0.07) | 3.45 | (0.04) | 0.39 | 5.93 | 0.06 | 1.88 | (0.05) | 2.52 | (0.05) |
| | New Zealand | 1.06 | 17.33 | 0.06 | 12.84 | (0.09) | 4.29 | (0.06) | 0.42 | 7.90 | 0.05 | 1.74 | (0.06) | 2.89 | (0.07) |
| | Norway | 0.96 | 10.32 | 0.09 | 9.63 | (0.08) | 3.37 | (0.05) | 0.19 | 9.40 | 0.02 | 3.13 | (0.05) | 3.10 | (0.04) |
| | Poland | 0.72 | 16.25 | 0.04 | 11.71 | (0.09) | 4.12 | (0.05) | 0.29 | 6.13 | 0.04 | 2.11 | (0.05) | 2.53 | (0.06) |
| | Portugal | 1.86 | 20.68 | 0.08 | 10.08 | (0.10) | 4.75 | (0.05) | 0.22 | 7.77 | 0.03 | 1.99 | (0.05) | 2.83 | (0.06) |
| | Slovak Republic | 6.12 | 8.92 | 0.41 | 8.88 | (0.14) | 3.86 | (0.06) | 0.62 | 7.90 | 0.07 | 2.40 | (0.07) | 2.93 | (0.06) |
| | Spain | 1.50 | 13.95 | 0.10 | 10.15 | (0.09) | 3.98 | (0.05) | 0.58 | 11.34 | 0.05 | 2.24 | (0.05) | 3.47 | (0.06) |
| | Sweden | 0.60 | 7.15 | 0.08 | 9.01 | (0.07) | 2.78 | (0.05) | 0.13 | 6.69 | 0.02 | 1.79 | (0.05) | 2.61 | (0.06) |
| | Switzerland | 2.36 | 12.24 | 0.16 | 9.88 | (0.09) | 3.93 | (0.05) | 0.47 | 5.52 | 0.08 | 1.57 | (0.04) | 2.46 | (0.06) |
| | Turkey | 5.79 | 16.63 | 0.26 | 10.67 | (0.16) | 4.75 | (0.06) | 1.24 | 17.04 | 0.07 | 5.22 | (0.09) | 4.28 | (0.05) |
| | United Kingdom | 1.15 | 13.48 | 0.08 | 11.92 | (0.09) | 3.86 | (0.05) | 0.38 | 6.07 | 0.06 | 1.70 | (0.05) | 2.56 | (0.05) |
| | United States | 1.57 | 33.39 | 0.04 | 10.95 | (0.13) | 5.92 | (0.07) | 0.42 | 11.88 | 0.03 | 3.04 | (0.07) | 3.51 | (0.04) |
| | **OECD average** | 2.40 | 2.94 | 0.15 | 1.95 | (0.10) | 0.76 | (0.05) | 0.60 | 8.53 | 0.06 | 0.49 | (0.05) | 0.55 | (0.06) |
| Partners | Argentina | 2.20 | 17.13 | 0.11 | 7.62 | (0.16) | 4.44 | (0.10) | 0.43 | 6.68 | 0.06 | 1.66 | (0.07) | 2.68 | (0.08) |
| | Azerbaijan | 2.74 | 21.27 | 0.11 | 10.37 | (0.12) | 4.87 | (0.07) | 0.86 | 17.94 | 0.05 | 4.86 | (0.10) | 4.35 | (0.06) |
| | Brazil | 2.36 | 17.92 | 0.12 | 8.46 | (0.09) | 4.51 | (0.05) | 0.64 | 11.15 | 0.05 | 3.15 | (0.07) | 3.42 | (0.07) |
| | Bulgaria | 4.21 | 19.11 | 0.18 | 8.55 | (0.17) | 4.81 | (0.07) | 0.47 | 11.91 | 0.04 | 3.20 | (0.08) | 3.53 | (0.07) |
| | Chile | 5.43 | 25.50 | 0.18 | 9.28 | (0.17) | 5.54 | (0.06) | 0.25 | 8.89 | 0.03 | 2.81 | (0.06) | 3.03 | (0.05) |
| | Colombia | 2.70 | 17.17 | 0.14 | 11.66 | (0.20) | 4.48 | (0.09) | 0.37 | 12.00 | 0.03 | 3.31 | (0.07) | 3.52 | (0.07) |
| | Croatia | 2.03 | 10.68 | 0.16 | 8.43 | (0.09) | 3.56 | (0.04) | 0.23 | 5.83 | 0.04 | 1.58 | (0.05) | 2.46 | (0.06) |
| | Estonia | 0.81 | 17.30 | 0.04 | 10.95 | (0.09) | 4.25 | (0.07) | 0.39 | 8.95 | 0.04 | 2.63 | (0.07) | 3.06 | (0.07) |
| | Hong Kong-China | 2.06 | 24.07 | 0.08 | 13.57 | (0.11) | 5.11 | (0.06) | 0.47 | 11.28 | 0.04 | 3.08 | (0.08) | 3.43 | (0.06) |
| | Indonesia | 4.67 | 17.58 | 0.21 | 10.98 | (0.17) | 4.74 | (0.08) | 1.07 | 11.07 | 0.09 | 3.66 | (0.11) | 3.51 | (0.05) |
| | Israel | 1.66 | 20.90 | 0.07 | 9.58 | (0.11) | 4.74 | (0.07) | 1.26 | 13.79 | 0.08 | 4.44 | (0.08) | 3.87 | (0.06) |
| | Jordan | 2.89 | 31.85 | 0.08 | 10.36 | (0.14) | 5.94 | (0.05) | 0.86 | 17.56 | 0.05 | 5.10 | (0.10) | 4.32 | (0.05) |
| | Kyrgyzstan | 3.18 | 23.19 | 0.12 | 7.80 | (0.16) | 5.19 | (0.08) | 0.97 | 13.90 | 0.07 | 4.60 | (0.09) | 3.88 | (0.05) |
| | Latvia | 1.04 | 14.20 | 0.07 | 11.06 | (0.11) | 3.91 | (0.05) | 0.35 | 7.82 | 0.04 | 2.72 | (0.08) | 2.87 | (0.05) |
| | Liechtenstein | 0.53 | 14.85 | 0.03 | 10.23 | (0.19) | 3.91 | (0.12) | 0.42 | 3.53 | 0.11 | 1.37 | (0.10) | 2.00 | (0.13) |
| | Lithuania | 1.61 | 19.07 | 0.08 | 9.85 | (0.10) | 4.54 | (0.05) | 0.22 | 6.70 | 0.03 | 1.93 | (0.05) | 2.63 | (0.05) |
| | Macao-China | 1.45 | 21.99 | 0.06 | 14.46 | (0.07) | 4.80 | (0.05) | 0.30 | 16.73 | 0.02 | 3.25 | (0.07) | 4.12 | (0.08) |
| | Montenegro | 2.10 | 22.64 | 0.08 | 8.89 | (0.09) | 4.98 | (0.05) | 0.17 | 10.91 | 0.01 | 2.68 | (0.05) | 3.32 | (0.06) |
| | Qatar | 5.55 | 26.71 | 0.17 | 8.68 | (0.08) | 5.52 | (0.05) | 0.56 | 16.92 | 0.03 | 4.90 | (0.07) | 4.18 | (0.04) |
| | Romania | 4.02 | 14.30 | 0.22 | 8.58 | (0.15) | 4.27 | (0.12) | 0.53 | 11.88 | 0.04 | 4.04 | (0.07) | 3.52 | (0.05) |
| | Russian Federation | 3.01 | 12.82 | 0.19 | 9.41 | (0.13) | 3.96 | (0.05) | 0.59 | 7.95 | 0.07 | 3.07 | (0.07) | 2.93 | (0.06) |
| | Serbia | 2.77 | 15.02 | 0.16 | 9.32 | (0.11) | 4.22 | (0.05) | 0.22 | 10.15 | 0.02 | 2.66 | (0.06) | 3.22 | (0.05) |
| | Slovenia | 4.83 | 16.77 | 0.22 | 9.39 | (0.07) | 4.66 | (0.04) | 0.49 | 8.15 | 0.06 | 2.47 | (0.04) | 2.90 | (0.05) |
| | Chinese Taipei | 8.33 | 19.95 | 0.29 | 11.52 | (0.15) | 5.32 | (0.05) | 1.37 | 10.10 | 0.12 | 3.00 | (0.06) | 3.41 | (0.05) |
| | Thailand | 4.11 | 6.78 | 0.38 | 10.69 | (0.08) | 3.42 | (0.05) | 1.44 | 9.07 | 0.14 | 2.40 | (0.07) | 3.24 | (0.06) |
| | Tunisia | 2.60 | 18.36 | 0.12 | 9.17 | (0.12) | 4.58 | (0.05) | 0.14 | 15.18 | 0.01 | 6.10 | (0.06) | 3.91 | (0.04) |
| | Uruguay | 2.36 | 16.43 | 0.13 | 8.49 | (0.09) | 4.34 | (0.06) | 0.23 | 8.14 | 0.03 | 2.08 | (0.06) | 2.91 | (0.07) |

**Table 3.9d** **Within- and between-school variance in learning time in science, in mathematics and on**
[Part 2/2] **the language of instruction**

| | | Individual study | | | | | | Total learning hours | | | | | | |
|---|---|---|---|---|---|---|---|---|---|---|---|---|---|---|
| | Between-school variance | Within-school variance | Proportion of between school variance | Mean hours per week | | Standard deviation | | Between-school variance | Within-school variance | Proportion of between school variance | Mean hours per week | | Standard deviation | |
| | | | | Mean | S.E. | S.D. | S.E. | | | | Mean | S.E. | S.D. | S.E. |
| Australia | 1.30 | 11.53 | 0.10 | 4.67 | (0.06) | 3.58 | (0.05) | 6.48 | 52.43 | 0.11 | 17.85 | (0.12) | 7.67 | (0.09) |
| Austria | 0.80 | 12.86 | 0.06 | 4.95 | (0.08) | 3.69 | (0.06) | 5.17 | 36.59 | 0.12 | 14.49 | (0.16) | 6.44 | (0.11) |
| Belgium | 1.06 | 9.20 | 0.10 | 4.39 | (0.06) | 3.22 | (0.04) | 10.41 | 41.41 | 0.20 | 15.43 | (0.14) | 7.25 | (0.08) |
| Canada | 1.54 | 15.00 | 0.09 | 5.26 | (0.07) | 4.15 | (0.06) | 7.34 | 75.91 | 0.09 | 20.63 | (0.17) | 9.26 | (0.09) |
| Czech Republic | 0.41 | 8.16 | 0.05 | 3.47 | (0.05) | 2.95 | (0.06) | 4.31 | 35.77 | 0.11 | 15.98 | (0.15) | 6.37 | (0.10) |
| Denmark | 0.37 | 9.48 | 0.04 | 5.00 | (0.06) | 3.13 | (0.04) | 3.26 | 45.50 | 0.07 | 21.94 | (0.15) | 6.98 | (0.10) |
| Finland | 0.16 | 5.79 | 0.03 | 3.41 | (0.05) | 2.44 | (0.06) | 1.84 | 26.76 | 0.06 | 14.16 | (0.16) | 5.35 | (0.11) |
| France | 1.21 | 9.43 | 0.11 | 4.56 | (0.07) | 3.27 | (0.06) | 7.96 | 36.03 | 0.18 | 17.55 | (0.15) | 6.63 | (0.09) |
| Germany | 0.58 | 14.33 | 0.04 | 5.87 | (0.08) | 3.87 | (0.06) | 2.71 | 50.95 | 0.05 | 18.44 | (0.15) | 7.33 | (0.13) |
| Greece | 0.82 | 15.72 | 0.05 | 5.79 | (0.08) | 4.06 | (0.04) | 14.71 | 75.01 | 0.16 | 21.48 | (0.24) | 9.40 | (0.12) |
| Hungary | 0.85 | 11.99 | 0.07 | 5.29 | (0.08) | 3.58 | (0.05) | 6.31 | 59.91 | 0.10 | 17.89 | (0.19) | 8.13 | (0.11) |
| Iceland | 0.29 | 10.07 | 0.03 | 4.42 | (0.05) | 3.22 | (0.05) | 2.20 | 36.31 | 0.06 | 18.14 | (0.09) | 6.19 | (0.11) |
| Ireland | 0.36 | 12.71 | 0.03 | 4.70 | (0.08) | 3.62 | (0.06) | 1.33 | 53.45 | 0.02 | 16.08 | (0.15) | 7.41 | (0.11) |
| Italy | 3.05 | 16.63 | 0.16 | 7.53 | (0.07) | 4.46 | (0.05) | 10.94 | 60.88 | 0.15 | 21.07 | (0.17) | 8.52 | (0.09) |
| Japan | 2.06 | 6.74 | 0.23 | 3.11 | (0.10) | 2.97 | (0.09) | 14.61 | 25.41 | 0.37 | 15.26 | (0.22) | 6.31 | (0.13) |
| Korea | 3.21 | 12.63 | 0.20 | 4.93 | (0.12) | 3.98 | (0.10) | 27.01 | 51.88 | 0.34 | 22.49 | (0.25) | 8.87 | (0.21) |
| Luxembourg | 0.15 | 10.57 | 0.01 | 4.33 | (0.05) | 3.27 | (0.05) | 2.22 | 41.68 | 0.05 | 15.98 | (0.10) | 6.57 | (0.09) |
| Mexico | 1.03 | 18.64 | 0.05 | 6.42 | (0.08) | 4.51 | (0.06) | 5.46 | 85.23 | 0.06 | 20.41 | (0.19) | 9.71 | (0.11) |
| Netherlands | 0.43 | 8.03 | 0.05 | 3.99 | (0.06) | 2.92 | (0.06) | 2.28 | 35.55 | 0.06 | 13.82 | (0.12) | 6.16 | (0.10) |
| New Zealand | 0.81 | 11.53 | 0.07 | 4.42 | (0.07) | 3.52 | (0.06) | 3.30 | 48.76 | 0.06 | 19.02 | (0.14) | 7.23 | (0.11) |
| Norway | 0.34 | 9.42 | 0.03 | 4.06 | (0.06) | 3.13 | (0.05) | 1.54 | 42.87 | 0.03 | 16.79 | (0.12) | 6.68 | (0.11) |
| Poland | 0.31 | 17.36 | 0.02 | 6.34 | (0.07) | 4.20 | (0.04) | 1.38 | 58.44 | 0.02 | 20.19 | (0.14) | 7.74 | (0.09) |
| Portugal | 0.46 | 17.24 | 0.03 | 5.83 | (0.08) | 4.21 | (0.06) | 3.06 | 67.92 | 0.04 | 17.94 | (0.18) | 8.44 | (0.10) |
| Slovak Republic | 1.43 | 12.23 | 0.10 | 4.81 | (0.09) | 3.69 | (0.06) | 16.43 | 43.01 | 0.28 | 16.11 | (0.25) | 7.70 | (0.11) |
| Spain | 0.88 | 15.60 | 0.05 | 5.58 | (0.08) | 4.09 | (0.06) | 4.70 | 53.56 | 0.08 | 18.08 | (0.16) | 7.72 | (0.11) |
| Sweden | 0.28 | 7.04 | 0.04 | 3.58 | (0.05) | 2.71 | (0.08) | 1.34 | 30.36 | 0.04 | 14.37 | (0.12) | 5.63 | (0.16) |
| Switzerland | 0.46 | 7.56 | 0.06 | 4.20 | (0.04) | 2.84 | (0.04) | 3.95 | 33.70 | 0.10 | 15.66 | (0.13) | 6.24 | (0.10) |
| Turkey | 1.08 | 15.91 | 0.06 | 6.11 | (0.09) | 4.12 | (0.05) | 19.65 | 84.77 | 0.19 | 21.88 | (0.29) | 10.21 | (0.14) |
| United Kingdom | 0.66 | 8.72 | 0.07 | 4.52 | (0.06) | 3.09 | (0.04) | 2.88 | 38.38 | 0.07 | 18.16 | (0.14) | 6.48 | (0.10) |
| United States | 0.58 | 16.07 | 0.03 | 5.59 | (0.07) | 4.08 | (0.05) | 1.63 | 89.82 | 0.02 | 19.69 | (0.15) | 9.56 | (0.10) |
| **OECD average** | 0.90 | 11.94 | 0.07 | 0.91 | (0.07) | 0.66 | (0.06) | 6.55 | 50.61 | 0.11 | 3.30 | (0.16) | 1.38 | (0.11) |
| Argentina | 0.68 | 14.24 | 0.05 | 5.04 | (0.10) | 3.89 | (0.09) | 4.67 | 50.41 | 0.08 | 14.32 | (0.23) | 7.47 | (0.15) |
| Azerbaijan | 1.68 | 25.47 | 0.06 | 8.71 | (0.13) | 5.21 | (0.07) | 7.27 | 104.17 | 0.07 | 24.10 | (0.27) | 10.56 | (0.14) |
| Brazil | 0.96 | 15.80 | 0.06 | 5.21 | (0.07) | 4.09 | (0.06) | 5.71 | 66.13 | 0.08 | 16.78 | (0.17) | 8.44 | (0.11) |
| Bulgaria | 3.00 | 18.61 | 0.14 | 6.15 | (0.16) | 4.62 | (0.06) | 14.12 | 85.61 | 0.14 | 17.98 | (0.33) | 9.95 | (0.13) |
| Chile | 0.41 | 11.91 | 0.03 | 4.69 | (0.08) | 3.52 | (0.05) | 8.15 | 68.56 | 0.11 | 16.86 | (0.23) | 8.76 | (0.09) |
| Colombia | 0.46 | 16.78 | 0.03 | 5.58 | (0.09) | 4.16 | (0.06) | 3.98 | 66.42 | 0.06 | 20.55 | (0.27) | 8.44 | (0.18) |
| Croatia | 1.08 | 13.55 | 0.07 | 4.85 | (0.07) | 3.82 | (0.05) | 5.54 | 43.01 | 0.11 | 14.94 | (0.15) | 6.97 | (0.09) |
| Estonia | 0.37 | 13.64 | 0.03 | 5.11 | (0.06) | 3.74 | (0.06) | 1.79 | 55.60 | 0.03 | 18.71 | (0.14) | 7.56 | (0.14) |
| Hong Kong-China | 0.94 | 15.47 | 0.06 | 5.33 | (0.08) | 4.05 | (0.06) | 5.26 | 80.77 | 0.06 | 21.98 | (0.21) | 9.28 | (0.11) |
| Indonesia | 1.00 | 13.36 | 0.07 | 5.58 | (0.08) | 3.80 | (0.06) | 11.12 | 59.77 | 0.16 | 20.17 | (0.25) | 8.46 | (0.15) |
| Israel | 1.71 | 15.78 | 0.10 | 5.34 | (0.11) | 4.19 | (0.06) | 7.24 | 86.04 | 0.08 | 19.44 | (0.24) | 9.66 | (0.16) |
| Jordan | 1.16 | 22.46 | 0.05 | 7.90 | (0.11) | 4.89 | (0.06) | 4.55 | 106.16 | 0.04 | 23.35 | (0.22) | 10.61 | (0.13) |
| Kyrgyzstan | 0.93 | 24.77 | 0.04 | 6.70 | (0.09) | 5.09 | (0.06) | 6.16 | 103.23 | 0.06 | 19.24 | (0.25) | 10.54 | (0.14) |
| Latvia | 0.43 | 14.69 | 0.03 | 6.25 | (0.08) | 3.89 | (0.06) | 2.64 | 50.96 | 0.05 | 20.03 | (0.19) | 7.33 | (0.10) |
| Liechtenstein | 0.00 | 8.09 | 0.00 | 3.93 | (0.15) | 2.84 | (0.21) | 0.00 | 29.66 | 0.00 | 15.51 | (0.23) | 5.45 | (0.21) |
| Lithuania | 0.38 | 15.10 | 0.02 | 5.27 | (0.07) | 3.93 | (0.06) | 2.40 | 56.72 | 0.04 | 17.04 | (0.14) | 7.69 | (0.10) |
| Macao-China | 1.72 | 14.07 | 0.11 | 4.93 | (0.07) | 3.91 | (0.06) | 5.10 | 73.71 | 0.06 | 22.63 | (0.15) | 8.79 | (0.12) |
| Montenegro | 0.59 | 19.56 | 0.03 | 6.20 | (0.08) | 4.49 | (0.05) | 4.74 | 83.31 | 0.05 | 17.73 | (0.16) | 9.39 | (0.11) |
| Qatar | 0.53 | 18.55 | 0.03 | 6.27 | (0.06) | 4.36 | (0.04) | 6.98 | 103.04 | 0.06 | 19.89 | (0.16) | 10.42 | (0.11) |
| Romania | 1.31 | 15.93 | 0.08 | 5.96 | (0.10) | 4.15 | (0.06) | 11.28 | 74.37 | 0.13 | 18.57 | (0.26) | 9.22 | (0.15) |
| Russian Federation | 2.27 | 14.28 | 0.14 | 6.65 | (0.12) | 4.06 | (0.07) | 10.14 | 52.84 | 0.16 | 19.13 | (0.24) | 7.90 | (0.14) |
| Serbia | 0.94 | 15.60 | 0.06 | 5.22 | (0.08) | 4.07 | (0.06) | 6.94 | 64.44 | 0.10 | 17.19 | (0.18) | 8.45 | (0.13) |
| Slovenia | 0.74 | 12.02 | 0.06 | 4.93 | (0.05) | 3.53 | (0.05) | 7.80 | 55.81 | 0.12 | 16.84 | (0.12) | 7.89 | (0.09) |
| Chinese Taipei | 2.43 | 12.26 | 0.17 | 4.88 | (0.09) | 3.83 | (0.05) | 26.30 | 61.64 | 0.30 | 19.53 | (0.27) | 9.43 | (0.11) |
| Thailand | 1.57 | 12.91 | 0.11 | 5.31 | (0.08) | 3.82 | (0.06) | 15.96 | 42.34 | 0.27 | 18.37 | (0.16) | 7.81 | (0.09) |
| Tunisia | 0.39 | 17.88 | 0.02 | 7.29 | (0.08) | 4.27 | (0.05) | 5.30 | 84.90 | 0.06 | 22.60 | (0.21) | 9.49 | (0.12) |
| Uruguay | 0.44 | 10.39 | 0.04 | 4.23 | (0.06) | 3.31 | (0.05) | 3.64 | 51.68 | 0.07 | 14.84 | (0.15) | 7.47 | (0.12) |

© OECD 2011 Quality Time for Students: Learning In and Out of School

### Table 3.10a
[Part 1/3]
**Mean learning hours and allocation of total learning time in science, by lower and upper secondary schools**

| | Mean learning hours per week | | | | | | | | | | | |
|---|---|---|---|---|---|---|---|---|---|---|---|---|
| | Regular school lessons | | | | | | Out-of-school-time lessons | | | | | |
| | Lower secondary school | | Upper secondary school | | Difference (lower-upper) | | Lower secondary school | | Upper secondary school | | Difference (lower-upper) | |
| | Mean | S.E. | Mean | S.E. | Dif. | S.E. | Mean | S.E. | Mean | S.E. | Dif. | S.E. |
| **OECD** Australia | 3.39 | (0.03) | 2.66 | (0.08) | **0.73** | (0.08) | 0.35 | (0.01) | 0.38 | (0.02) | -0.03 | (0.02) |
| Austria | 2.08 | (0.13) | 2.49 | (0.07) | -0.41 | (0.16) | 0.60 | (0.14) | 0.19 | (0.01) | **0.41** | (0.14) |
| Belgium | 2.29 | (0.17) | 2.64 | (0.04) | -0.35 | (0.17) | 0.66 | (0.09) | 0.31 | (0.01) | **0.36** | (0.09) |
| Canada | 2.72 | (0.08) | 4.22 | (0.05) | -1.51 | (0.09) | 0.52 | (0.02) | 0.56 | (0.01) | -0.04 | (0.03) |
| Czech Republic | 2.94 | (0.06) | 2.93 | (0.12) | 0.01 | (0.13) | 0.60 | (0.02) | 0.48 | (0.03) | **0.12** | (0.04) |
| Denmark | 3.20 | (0.04) | 4.35 | (0.45) | -1.16 | (0.46) | 0.77 | (0.02) | 1.15 | (0.25) | -0.38 | (0.25) |
| Finland | 3.13 | (0.04) | c | c | c | c | 0.32 | (0.01) | c | c | c | c |
| France | 1.75 | (0.04) | 3.55 | (0.08) | -1.80 | (0.09) | 0.56 | (0.02) | 0.55 | (0.02) | 0.01 | (0.03) |
| Germany | 3.11 | (0.05) | 1.51 | (0.37) | **1.60** | (0.38) | 0.51 | (0.02) | 0.39 | (0.08) | 0.12 | (0.08) |
| Greece | 2.25 | (0.15) | 3.26 | (0.15) | -1.01 | (0.15) | 1.41 | (0.13) | 2.04 | (0.05) | **-0.63** | (0.14) |
| Hungary | 1.93 | (0.10) | 2.55 | (0.05) | -0.63 | (0.11) | 1.28 | (0.11) | 0.98 | (0.03) | **0.30** | (0.12) |
| Iceland | 2.96 | (0.02) | c | c | c | c | 0.29 | (0.01) | c | c | c | c |
| Ireland | 2.69 | (0.05) | 2.30 | (0.06) | **0.39** | (0.07) | 0.38 | (0.02) | 0.22 | (0.02) | **0.16** | (0.02) |
| Italy | 1.81 | (0.22) | 2.93 | (0.05) | -1.12 | (0.23) | 0.79 | (0.15) | 0.58 | (0.01) | 0.21 | (0.15) |
| Japan | a | a | 2.70 | (0.05) | a | a | a | a | 0.26 | (0.01) | a | a |
| Korea | 3.50 | (0.13) | 3.59 | (0.06) | -0.08 | (0.14) | 1.21 | (0.18) | 1.02 | (0.04) | 0.19 | (0.18) |
| Luxembourg | 1.92 | (0.03) | 3.06 | (0.05) | -1.14 | (0.05) | 0.57 | (0.02) | 0.38 | (0.02) | **0.19** | (0.03) |
| Mexico | 3.16 | (0.07) | 3.15 | (0.04) | 0.02 | (0.08) | 1.18 | (0.06) | 0.88 | (0.02) | **0.30** | (0.06) |
| Netherlands | 1.93 | (0.04) | 2.81 | (0.07) | **-0.88** | (0.09) | 0.59 | (0.02) | 0.38 | (0.02) | 0.21 | (0.04) |
| New Zealand | 3.36 | (0.12) | 4.10 | (0.04) | -0.74 | (0.13) | 0.52 | (0.06) | 0.40 | (0.02) | 0.12 | (0.06) |
| Norway | 2.63 | (0.03) | c | c | c | c | 0.94 | (0.02) | c | c | c | c |
| Poland | 2.71 | (0.04) | 4.32 | (0.18) | -1.61 | (0.18) | 0.62 | (0.02) | 0.49 | (0.10) | 0.13 | (0.10) |
| Portugal | 2.45 | (0.04) | 3.97 | (0.07) | -1.52 | (0.08) | 0.69 | (0.03) | 0.58 | (0.02) | **0.11** | (0.03) |
| Slovak Republic | 2.38 | (0.10) | 2.50 | (0.10) | -0.12 | (0.14) | 0.61 | (0.03) | 0.67 | (0.04) | -0.06 | (0.04) |
| Spain | 3.12 | (0.04) | c | c | c | c | 0.68 | (0.02) | c | c | c | c |
| Sweden | 2.82 | (0.03) | 2.39 | (0.43) | 0.43 | (0.43) | 0.50 | (0.01) | 0.50 | (0.09) | 0.00 | (0.09) |
| Switzerland | 2.17 | (0.04) | 3.30 | (0.17) | -1.13 | (0.16) | 0.42 | (0.01) | 0.27 | (0.03) | **0.14** | (0.03) |
| Turkey | 2.83 | (0.32) | 2.87 | (0.09) | -0.04 | (0.34) | 1.72 | (0.23) | 1.33 | (0.05) | 0.39 | (0.24) |
| United Kingdom | 2.88 | (0.32) | 4.25 | (0.04) | -1.37 | (0.32) | 0.40 | (0.12) | 0.48 | (0.02) | -0.08 | (0.12) |
| United States | 2.51 | (0.16) | 3.64 | (0.04) | -1.14 | (0.16) | 1.10 | (0.08) | 0.74 | (0.02) | **0.36** | (0.08) |
| **OECD average** | 2.64 | (0.02) | 3.16 | (0.03) | -0.58 | (0.04) | 0.72 | (0.02) | 0.62 | (0.01) | **0.10** | (0.02) |
| **Partners** Argentina | 1.77 | (0.07) | 2.46 | (0.08) | -0.69 | (0.10) | 0.64 | (0.05) | 0.42 | (0.02) | **0.21** | (0.05) |
| Azerbaijan | 2.98 | (0.06) | 2.63 | (0.07) | **0.35** | (0.08) | 1.32 | (0.04) | 1.42 | (0.05) | -0.10 | (0.07) |
| Brazil | 2.04 | (0.05) | 2.29 | (0.04) | -0.25 | (0.07) | 0.80 | (0.04) | 0.78 | (0.03) | 0.02 | (0.05) |
| Bulgaria | 2.10 | (0.27) | 2.67 | (0.08) | -0.57 | (0.27) | 1.02 | (0.10) | 0.98 | (0.03) | 0.03 | (0.10) |
| Chile | 1.15 | (0.13) | 2.38 | (0.05) | -1.23 | (0.14) | 0.79 | (0.14) | 0.83 | (0.02) | -0.04 | (0.14) |
| Colombia | 3.38 | (0.08) | 3.58 | (0.15) | -0.21 | (0.12) | 0.99 | (0.04) | 0.93 | (0.05) | 0.06 | (0.07) |
| Croatia | c | c | 2.02 | (0.04) | -1.02 | (0.36) | c | c | 0.43 | (0.02) | 0.05 | (0.36) |
| Estonia | 3.26 | (0.04) | 3.94 | (0.19) | -0.68 | (0.19) | 0.76 | (0.02) | 0.72 | (0.12) | 0.04 | (0.12) |
| Hong Kong-China | 3.02 | (0.08) | 3.22 | (0.08) | -0.19 | (0.12) | 0.65 | (0.05) | 1.01 | (0.04) | **-0.36** | (0.07) |
| Indonesia | 2.89 | (0.05) | 3.61 | (0.12) | -0.72 | (0.14) | 1.05 | (0.03) | 1.04 | (0.09) | 0.01 | (0.09) |
| Israel | 2.53 | (0.09) | 2.42 | (0.06) | 0.11 | (0.11) | 1.06 | (0.07) | 0.97 | (0.03) | 0.09 | (0.07) |
| Jordan | 3.25 | (0.06) | a | a | a | a | 1.52 | (0.03) | a | a | a | a |
| Kyrgyzstan | 2.04 | (0.06) | 2.26 | (0.12) | -0.22 | (0.10) | 1.34 | (0.03) | 1.42 | (0.06) | -0.08 | (0.06) |
| Latvia | 2.83 | (0.06) | 3.74 | (0.19) | -0.91 | (0.19) | 0.65 | (0.02) | 0.58 | (0.09) | 0.07 | (0.09) |
| Liechtenstein | 2.42 | (0.08) | 3.69 | (0.30) | -1.26 | (0.30) | 0.55 | (0.06) | 0.24 | (0.12) | **0.31** | (0.11) |
| Lithuania | 2.69 | (0.04) | c | c | -2.31 | (0.04) | 0.57 | (0.02) | c | c | **0.57** | (0.02) |
| Macao-China | 3.56 | (0.04) | 4.05 | (0.05) | -0.48 | (0.06) | 1.05 | (0.03) | 0.90 | (0.04) | **0.16** | (0.05) |
| Montenegro | c | c | 2.83 | (0.04) | -1.71 | (0.40) | c | c | 1.05 | (0.02) | -0.28 | (0.20) |
| Qatar | 2.09 | (0.05) | 2.82 | (0.04) | -0.73 | (0.06) | 1.52 | (0.05) | 1.47 | (0.03) | 0.04 | (0.06) |
| Romania | 2.26 | (0.07) | a | a | a | a | 1.03 | (0.02) | a | a | a | a |
| Russian Federation | 3.35 | (0.14) | 3.95 | (0.08) | -0.60 | (0.13) | 1.16 | (0.05) | 1.10 | (0.04) | 0.06 | (0.07) |
| Serbia | 2.66 | (0.35) | 2.86 | (0.06) | -0.20 | (0.35) | 0.72 | (0.22) | 0.78 | (0.02) | -0.06 | (0.22) |
| Slovenia | 1.52 | (0.24) | 2.87 | (0.03) | -1.34 | (0.24) | 0.91 | (0.20) | 0.71 | (0.02) | 0.21 | (0.20) |
| Chinese Taipei | 3.80 | (0.07) | 2.44 | (0.07) | **1.36** | (0.10) | 1.37 | (0.05) | 0.49 | (0.02) | **0.88** | (0.06) |
| Thailand | 3.47 | (0.05) | 3.97 | (0.05) | -0.50 | (0.06) | 0.83 | (0.05) | 0.95 | (0.04) | -0.11 | (0.07) |
| Tunisia | 2.02 | (0.05) | 3.17 | (0.07) | -1.15 | (0.08) | 1.73 | (0.04) | 2.11 | (0.04) | **-0.38** | (0.06) |
| Uruguay | 2.04 | (0.06) | 2.58 | (0.06) | -0.53 | (0.08) | 0.70 | (0.04) | 0.56 | (0.02) | **0.14** | (0.05) |

*Note:* Values that are statistically significant at the 5% level (p < 0.05) are indicated in bold.

**Table 3.10a** **Mean learning hours and allocation of total learning time in science,**
[Part 2/3] **by lower and upper secondary schools**

| | | Mean learning hours per week | | | | | | | | | | |
|---|---|---|---|---|---|---|---|---|---|---|---|---|
| | | Individual study | | | | | | Total learning hours | | | | |
| | | Lower secondary school | | Upper secondary school | | Difference (lower-upper) | | Lower secondary school | | Upper secondary school | | Difference (lower-upper) |
| | | Mean | S.E. | Mean | S.E. | Dif. | S.E. | Mean | S.E. | Mean | S.E. | Dif. | S.E. |
| **OECD** | Australia | 1.15 | (0.02) | 1.28 | (0.04) | **-0.14** | (0.05) | 4.89 | (0.05) | 4.31 | (0.13) | **0.58** | (0.14) |
| | Austria | 1.65 | (0.15) | 1.25 | (0.03) | **0.40** | (0.15) | 4.37 | (0.28) | 3.94 | (0.10) | 0.43 | (0.29) |
| | Belgium | 1.21 | (0.09) | 1.25 | (0.02) | -0.04 | (0.09) | 4.20 | (0.23) | 4.20 | (0.07) | -0.00 | (0.23) |
| | Canada | 1.10 | (0.05) | 1.63 | (0.03) | **-0.54** | (0.09) | 4.37 | (0.14) | 6.43 | (0.06) | **-2.07** | (0.15) |
| | Czech Republic | 1.06 | (0.03) | 0.95 | (0.05) | **0.11** | (0.05) | 4.59 | (0.08) | 4.36 | (0.17) | 0.23 | (0.18) |
| | Denmark | 1.08 | (0.02) | 1.84 | (0.32) | **-0.76** | (0.32) | 5.03 | (0.07) | 7.35 | (0.95) | **-2.31** | (0.96) |
| | Finland | 1.07 | (0.02) | c | c | c | c | 4.52 | (0.06) | c | c | c | c |
| | France | 0.96 | (0.03) | 1.54 | (0.04) | **-0.57** | (0.05) | 3.27 | (0.07) | 5.65 | (0.12) | **-2.38** | (0.13) |
| | Germany | 1.72 | (0.03) | 1.23 | (0.19) | **0.49** | (0.19) | 5.35 | (0.07) | 3.12 | (0.54) | **2.23** | (0.55) |
| | Greece | 1.56 | (0.15) | 1.87 | (0.04) | **-0.31** | (0.15) | 5.20 | (0.30) | 7.17 | (0.11) | **-1.97** | (0.31) |
| | Hungary | 1.56 | (0.12) | 1.60 | (0.04) | -0.04 | (0.13) | 4.75 | (0.23) | 5.13 | (0.09) | -0.38 | (0.26) |
| | Iceland | 1.16 | (0.02) | c | c | c | c | 4.41 | (0.04) | c | c | c | c |
| | Ireland | 1.35 | (0.03) | 0.97 | (0.04) | **0.38** | (0.05) | 4.40 | (0.08) | 3.50 | (0.10) | **0.91** | (0.12) |
| | Italy | 1.65 | (0.25) | 2.10 | (0.04) | -0.45 | (0.26) | 4.38 | (0.58) | 5.60 | (0.10) | **-1.23** | (0.59) |
| | Japan | a | a | 0.69 | (0.02) | a | a | a | a | 3.65 | (0.07) | a | a |
| | Korea | 1.35 | (0.08) | 1.22 | (0.06) | 0.13 | (0.10) | 6.00 | (0.19) | 5.83 | (0.14) | 0.17 | (0.24) |
| | Luxembourg | 1.21 | (0.02) | 1.31 | (0.04) | **-0.09** | (0.04) | 3.71 | (0.05) | 4.74 | (0.07) | **-1.03** | (0.08) |
| | Mexico | 2.18 | (0.06) | 2.08 | (0.02) | 0.11 | (0.06) | 6.46 | (0.13) | 6.08 | (0.07) | **0.39** | (0.15) |
| | Netherlands | 1.14 | (0.03) | 1.40 | (0.05) | **-0.27** | (0.05) | 3.64 | (0.07) | 4.59 | (0.13) | **-0.95** | (0.15) |
| | New Zealand | 1.25 | (0.07) | 1.28 | (0.03) | -0.03 | (0.07) | 5.09 | (0.17) | 5.78 | (0.07) | **-0.69** | (0.18) |
| | Norway | 1.23 | (0.02) | c | c | c | c | 4.79 | (0.05) | c | c | c | c |
| | Poland | 2.02 | (0.03) | 2.63 | (0.23) | **-0.61** | (0.23) | 5.35 | (0.07) | 7.44 | (0.39) | **-2.09** | (0.39) |
| | Portugal | 1.93 | (0.05) | 2.24 | (0.05) | **-0.31** | (0.07) | 5.08 | (0.08) | 6.76 | (0.12) | **-1.69** | (0.14) |
| | Slovak Republic | 1.36 | (0.05) | 1.41 | (0.06) | -0.05 | (0.08) | 4.37 | (0.13) | 4.59 | (0.18) | -0.22 | (0.22) |
| | Spain | 1.74 | (0.03) | c | c | c | c | 5.55 | (0.07) | c | c | c | c |
| | Sweden | 1.15 | (0.02) | 1.05 | (0.20) | 0.10 | (0.21) | 4.46 | (0.04) | 3.95 | (0.69) | 0.51 | (0.69) |
| | Switzerland | 1.08 | (0.02) | 1.29 | (0.05) | **-0.21** | (0.05) | 3.66 | (0.05) | 4.84 | (0.21) | **-1.18** | (0.20) |
| | Turkey | 2.11 | (0.19) | 1.62 | (0.05) | **0.50** | (0.20) | 6.60 | (0.43) | 5.77 | (0.19) | 0.83 | (0.48) |
| | United Kingdom | 0.58 | (0.11) | 1.45 | (0.02) | **-0.87** | (0.11) | 3.91 | (0.31) | 6.19 | (0.05) | **-2.28** | (0.31) |
| | United States | 1.49 | (0.07) | 1.71 | (0.03) | **-0.22** | (0.07) | 5.20 | (0.16) | 6.12 | (0.06) | **-0.91** | (0.16) |
| | **OECD average** | 1.38 | (0.02) | 1.50 | (0.02) | **-0.13** | (0.03) | 4.75 | (0.04) | 5.27 | (0.06) | **-0.60** | (0.07) |
| **Partners** | Argentina | 1.39 | (0.05) | 1.67 | (0.05) | **-0.28** | (0.07) | 3.77 | (0.11) | 4.54 | (0.11) | **-0.76** | (0.15) |
| | Azerbaijan | 2.72 | (0.06) | 2.52 | (0.06) | **0.20** | (0.08) | 7.01 | (0.12) | 6.57 | (0.15) | **0.44** | (0.17) |
| | Brazil | 1.70 | (0.05) | 1.70 | (0.03) | 0.01 | (0.06) | 4.55 | (0.11) | 4.77 | (0.07) | -0.22 | (0.13) |
| | Bulgaria | 1.69 | (0.16) | 2.03 | (0.06) | **-0.34** | (0.16) | 4.81 | (0.37) | 5.71 | (0.13) | **-0.90** | (0.36) |
| | Chile | 1.07 | (0.13) | 1.54 | (0.03) | **-0.47** | (0.14) | 3.04 | (0.34) | 4.77 | (0.07) | **-1.72** | (0.35) |
| | Colombia | 1.80 | (0.04) | 1.85 | (0.05) | -0.05 | (0.06) | 6.17 | (0.11) | 6.35 | (0.23) | -0.18 | (0.20) |
| | Croatia | c | c | 1.46 | (0.04) | c | c | c | c | 3.93 | (0.09) | c | c |
| | Estonia | 1.53 | (0.03) | 1.81 | (0.17) | -0.28 | (0.17) | 5.56 | (0.06) | 6.48 | (0.33) | **-0.92** | (0.33) |
| | Hong Kong-China | 1.32 | (0.05) | 1.51 | (0.04) | **-0.19** | (0.06) | 4.98 | (0.14) | 5.73 | (0.13) | **-0.74** | (0.21) |
| | Indonesia | 1.84 | (0.04) | 1.72 | (0.07) | 0.11 | (0.09) | 5.75 | (0.08) | 6.36 | (0.23) | **-0.61** | (0.26) |
| | Israel | 1.42 | (0.08) | 1.34 | (0.04) | 0.07 | (0.09) | 5.02 | (0.19) | 4.71 | (0.11) | 0.30 | (0.21) |
| | Jordan | 2.65 | (0.04) | a | a | a | a | 7.40 | (0.09) | a | a | a | a |
| | Kyrgyzstan | 2.07 | (0.04) | 2.33 | (0.08) | **-0.26** | (0.09) | 5.52 | (0.08) | 5.96 | (0.18) | **-0.44** | (0.17) |
| | Latvia | 1.80 | (0.03) | 1.84 | (0.13) | -0.05 | (0.14) | 5.27 | (0.09) | 6.15 | (0.33) | **-0.88** | (0.34) |
| | Liechtenstein | 1.16 | (0.07) | 1.44 | (0.22) | -0.28 | (0.24) | 4.14 | (0.10) | 5.37 | (0.46) | **-1.23** | (0.48) |
| | Lithuania | 1.69 | (0.03) | c | c | c | c | 4.94 | (0.06) | c | c | c | c |
| | Macao-China | 1.26 | (0.03) | 1.56 | (0.04) | **-0.30** | (0.05) | 5.87 | (0.07) | 6.50 | (0.10) | **-0.62** | (0.13) |
| | Montenegro | c | c | 2.20 | (0.03) | c | c | c | c | 6.09 | (0.07) | **-2.46** | (0.80) |
| | Qatar | 1.92 | (0.05) | 2.07 | (0.03) | **-0.15** | (0.05) | 5.53 | (0.10) | 6.40 | (0.07) | **-0.87** | (0.12) |
| | Romania | 1.61 | (0.05) | a | a | a | a | 4.88 | (0.11) | a | a | a | a |
| | Russian Federation | 2.75 | (0.09) | 2.94 | (0.06) | **-0.19** | (0.10) | 7.25 | (0.23) | 8.00 | (0.14) | **-0.75** | (0.25) |
| | Serbia | 1.34 | (0.22) | 1.72 | (0.04) | -0.37 | (0.22) | 4.75 | (0.67) | 5.36 | (0.10) | -0.62 | (0.67) |
| | Slovenia | 1.37 | (0.15) | 1.54 | (0.02) | -0.17 | (0.16) | 3.71 | (0.47) | 5.13 | (0.04) | **-1.42** | (0.47) |
| | Chinese Taipei | 1.55 | (0.05) | 1.08 | (0.03) | **0.47** | (0.06) | 6.79 | (0.14) | 4.03 | (0.11) | **2.76** | (0.18) |
| | Thailand | 1.84 | (0.07) | 1.79 | (0.03) | 0.05 | (0.08) | 6.13 | (0.11) | 6.70 | (0.09) | **-0.57** | (0.14) |
| | Tunisia | 2.39 | (0.05) | 2.81 | (0.06) | **-0.43** | (0.08) | 6.11 | (0.10) | 8.08 | (0.15) | **-1.97** | (0.18) |
| | Uruguay | 1.16 | (0.05) | 1.39 | (0.03) | **-0.23** | (0.06) | 3.97 | (0.12) | 4.53 | (0.09) | **-0.57** | (0.13) |

*Note:* Values that are statistically significant at the 5% level (p < 0.05) are indicated in bold.

© OECD 2011 Quality Time for Students: Learning In and Out of School

## Table 3.10a [Part 3/3] Mean learning hours and allocation of total learning time in science, by lower and upper secondary schools

| | | Allocation of total learning time in science for | | | | | | | | | | | | | | | | |
|---|---|---|---|---|---|---|---|---|---|---|---|---|---|---|---|---|---|---|
| | | Regular school lessons | | | | | | Out-of-school-time lessons | | | | | | Individual study | | | | | |
| | | Lower secondary school | | Upper secondary school | | Difference (lower-upper) | | Lower secondary school | | Upper secondary school | | Difference (lower-upper) | | Lower secondary school | | Upper secondary school | | Difference (lower-upper) | |
| | | % | S.E | % | S.E | Dif. | S.E. | % | S.E | % | S.E | Dif. | S.E. | % | S.E | % | S.E | Dif. | S.E. |
| OECD | Australia | 72.1 | (0.3) | 64.1 | (0.6) | **8.0** | (0.7) | 5.9 | (0.2) | 8.2 | (0.4) | **-2.3** | (0.4) | 22.0 | (0.3) | 27.7 | (0.4) | **-5.7** | (0.5) |
| | Austria | 52.6 | (2.6) | 64.9 | (0.6) | **-12.3** | (2.7) | 9.9 | (1.6) | 3.8 | (0.2) | **6.0** | (1.7) | 37.5 | (2.4) | 31.3 | (0.6) | **6.3** | (2.4) |
| | Belgium | 58.2 | (3.1) | 63.7 | (0.3) | -5.6 | (3.1) | 13.0 | (1.7) | 6.3 | (0.2) | **6.6** | (1.7) | 28.9 | (1.9) | 30.0 | (0.3) | -1.1 | (1.9) |
| | Canada | 63.3 | (0.7) | 66.7 | (0.4) | **-3.4** | (0.7) | 10.9 | (0.4) | 8.1 | (0.2) | **2.8** | (0.4) | 25.8 | (0.6) | 25.2 | (0.3) | 0.6 | (0.7) |
| | Czech Republic | 67.2 | (0.6) | 70.3 | (1.1) | -3.2 | (1.3) | 10.3 | (0.4) | 9.4 | (0.5) | 0.9 | (0.6) | 22.5 | (0.4) | 20.2 | (0.8) | **2.3** | (0.9) |
| | Denmark | 66.7 | (0.5) | 61.8 | (2.6) | 5.0 | (2.6) | 13.0 | (0.3) | 15.0 | (1.8) | -2.0 | (1.8) | 20.3 | (0.3) | 23.2 | (1.3) | -3.0 | (1.4) |
| | Finland | 70.9 | (0.4) | c | c | c | c | 5.9 | (0.2) | c | c | c | c | 23.1 | (0.3) | c | c | c | c |
| | France | 59.5 | (0.9) | 65.0 | (0.6) | **-5.5** | (1.1) | 13.7 | (0.5) | 9.0 | (0.4) | **4.7** | (0.7) | 26.8 | (0.7) | 26.0 | (0.4) | 0.8 | (0.8) |
| | Germany | 58.2 | (0.5) | 47.8 | (5.4) | 10.4 | (5.5) | 8.4 | (0.3) | 11.7 | (3.6) | -3.3 | (3.6) | 33.4 | (0.3) | 40.4 | (5.4) | -7.1 | (5.4) |
| | Greece | 46.2 | (2.6) | 48.5 | (0.6) | -2.3 | (2.7) | 25.0 | (1.9) | 26.3 | (0.5) | -1.3 | (2.0) | 28.8 | (2.3) | 25.2 | (0.4) | 3.6 | (2.3) |
| | Hungary | 42.1 | (2.5) | 52.3 | (0.6) | **-10.2** | (2.6) | 25.7 | (2.1) | 17.2 | (0.4) | **8.5** | (2.2) | 32.2 | (1.5) | 30.5 | (0.4) | 1.7 | (1.6) |
| | Iceland | 70.2 | (0.4) | c | c | c | c | 5.1 | (0.2) | c | c | c | c | 24.7 | (0.3) | c | c | c | c |
| | Ireland | 64.0 | (0.5) | 70.1 | (0.7) | **-6.1** | (0.9) | 6.9 | (0.3) | 4.8 | (0.3) | **2.2** | (0.4) | 29.1 | (0.4) | 25.1 | (0.6) | **4.0** | (0.7) |
| | Italy | 48.6 | (2.7) | 54.1 | (0.3) | **-5.5** | (2.7) | 15.2 | (2.1) | 9.1 | (0.2) | **6.1** | (2.1) | 36.3 | (2.3) | 36.9 | (0.2) | -0.6 | (2.3) |
| | Japan | a | a | 78.4 | (0.4) | a | a | a | a | 5.2 | (0.2) | a | a | a | a | 16.4 | (0.4) | a | a |
| | Korea | 61.9 | (1.9) | 67.6 | (0.6) | -5.7 | (2.0) | 17.3 | (1.7) | 13.7 | (0.4) | 3.6 | (1.8) | 20.8 | (1.0) | 18.7 | (0.4) | 2.1 | (1.1) |
| | Luxembourg | 56.2 | (0.5) | 66.3 | (0.5) | **-10.1** | (0.8) | 11.8 | (0.4) | 6.8 | (0.3) | **5.0** | (0.5) | 32.0 | (0.5) | 26.9 | (0.5) | **5.0** | (0.7) |
| | Mexico | 47.5 | (0.8) | 49.4 | (0.4) | **-1.9** | (0.9) | 16.6 | (0.7) | 13.6 | (0.2) | **3.0** | (0.7) | 36.0 | (0.7) | 37.0 | (0.3) | -1.0 | (0.8) |
| | Netherlands | 54.0 | (0.7) | 62.5 | (0.7) | **-8.5** | (0.9) | 14.5 | (0.4) | 7.8 | (0.4) | **6.6** | (0.6) | 31.5 | (0.5) | 29.7 | (0.6) | **1.9** | (0.7) |
| | New Zealand | 67.1 | (1.5) | 73.5 | (0.4) | **-6.4** | (1.5) | 8.8 | (0.9) | 6.0 | (0.2) | **2.8** | (1.0) | 24.1 | (1.1) | 20.5 | (0.3) | **3.6** | (1.1) |
| | Norway | 59.6 | (0.5) | c | c | c | c | 16.9 | (0.3) | c | c | c | c | 23.5 | (0.3) | c | c | c | c |
| | Poland | 53.1 | (0.4) | 62.0 | (2.6) | **-8.9** | (2.5) | 10.3 | (0.3) | 4.4 | (0.9) | **5.9** | (0.9) | 36.6 | (0.4) | 33.6 | (2.2) | 3.0 | (2.1) |
| | Portugal | 50.3 | (0.6) | 59.8 | (0.4) | **-9.4** | (0.7) | 11.2 | (0.4) | 7.0 | (0.3) | **4.2** | (0.5) | 38.4 | (0.6) | 33.2 | (0.4) | **5.2** | (0.7) |
| | Slovak Republic | 58.9 | (0.8) | 58.6 | (0.8) | 0.2 | (1.1) | 11.7 | (0.5) | 11.7 | (0.6) | -0.1 | (0.7) | 29.5 | (0.7) | 29.6 | (0.5) | -0.2 | (0.9) |
| | Spain | 58.9 | (0.3) | c | c | c | c | 10.7 | (0.3) | c | c | c | c | 30.4 | (0.3) | c | c | c | c |
| | Sweden | 66.7 | (0.6) | 63.4 | (2.9) | 3.3 | (3.0) | 9.1 | (0.2) | 11.2 | (1.2) | -2.0 | (1.2) | 24.1 | (0.5) | 25.4 | (2.6) | -1.3 | (2.6) |
| | Switzerland | 61.0 | (0.4) | 67.3 | (1.1) | **-6.3** | (1.1) | 9.0 | (0.2) | 4.8 | (0.5) | **4.2** | (0.6) | 30.0 | (0.3) | 27.8 | (0.9) | **2.2** | (1.0) |
| | Turkey | 46.5 | (2.9) | 51.5 | (0.6) | -5.0 | (3.0) | 21.5 | (1.9) | 20.9 | (0.5) | 0.6 | (2.0) | 32.0 | (2.7) | 27.6 | (0.4) | 4.4 | (2.7) |
| | United Kingdom | 76.4 | (5.3) | 70.7 | (0.3) | 5.7 | (5.4) | 8.8 | (2.9) | 6.7 | (0.2) | 2.0 | (2.9) | 14.8 | (3.1) | 22.6 | (0.3) | **-7.8** | (3.1) |
| | United States | 48.9 | (2.4) | 59.8 | (0.4) | **-10.9** | (2.5) | 21.1 | (2.0) | 11.4 | (0.3) | **9.6** | (2.1) | 30.0 | (0.9) | 28.8 | (0.3) | 1.2 | (1.0) |
| | **OECD average** | 58.9 | (0.3) | 62.3 | (0.3) | **-3.8** | (0.5) | 12.7 | (0.2) | 10.0 | (0.2) | **3.0** | (0.3) | 28.4 | (0.2) | 27.7 | (0.3) | 0.8 | (0.4) |
| Partners | Argentina | 48.3 | (1.3) | 55.0 | (0.9) | **-6.7** | (1.6) | 14.4 | (1.0) | 7.8 | (0.3) | **6.6** | (1.0) | 37.3 | (1.2) | 37.2 | (0.7) | 0.1 | (1.4) |
| | Azerbaijan | 43.7 | (0.8) | 42.2 | (0.8) | 1.5 | (1.1) | 18.8 | (0.6) | 20.1 | (0.6) | -1.3 | (0.8) | 37.5 | (0.5) | 37.7 | (0.7) | -0.2 | (0.8) |
| | Brazil | 48.6 | (0.7) | 51.1 | (0.6) | **-2.4** | (1.0) | 15.1 | (0.7) | 13.6 | (0.4) | **1.5** | (0.7) | 36.2 | (0.7) | 35.3 | (0.4) | 0.9 | (0.9) |
| | Bulgaria | 44.9 | (3.6) | 49.1 | (0.7) | -4.1 | (3.7) | 18.8 | (2.1) | 16.1 | (0.6) | 2.7 | (2.2) | 36.2 | (3.2) | 34.8 | (0.4) | 1.4 | (3.2) |
| | Chile | 33.9 | (3.0) | 49.4 | (0.6) | **-15.6** | (3.0) | 31.1 | (4.3) | 16.0 | (0.4) | **15.1** | (4.4) | 35.0 | (3.3) | 34.6 | (0.4) | 0.4 | (3.4) |
| | Colombia | 58.3 | (0.8) | 59.3 | (0.8) | -1.0 | (0.9) | 13.8 | (0.6) | 12.6 | (0.5) | 1.2 | (0.8) | 27.9 | (0.6) | 28.1 | (0.5) | -0.2 | (0.7) |
| | Croatia | c | c | 54.7 | (0.5) | c | c | c | c | 9.8 | (0.4) | c | c | 59.4 | (11.9) | 35.5 | (0.5) | **23.8** | (11.8) |
| | Estonia | 61.4 | (0.5) | 64.3 | (2.4) | -2.8 | (2.4) | 12.7 | (0.4) | 9.4 | (1.3) | **3.3** | (1.4) | 25.9 | (0.3) | 26.3 | (2.1) | -0.4 | (2.1) |
| | Hong Kong-China | 63.7 | (0.9) | 58.7 | (0.5) | **5.0** | (1.0) | 11.3 | (0.6) | 16.1 | (0.5) | **-4.8** | (0.6) | 25.0 | (0.6) | 25.3 | (0.4) | -0.2 | (0.7) |
| | Indonesia | 51.9 | (0.7) | 57.7 | (1.5) | **-5.8** | (1.6) | 16.4 | (0.5) | 14.7 | (1.0) | 1.7 | (1.0) | 31.8 | (0.6) | 27.6 | (0.7) | **4.2** | (1.1) |
| | Israel | 52.8 | (1.4) | 54.7 | (0.8) | -1.8 | (1.6) | 19.6 | (1.1) | 18.1 | (0.4) | 1.5 | (1.1) | 27.6 | (1.1) | 27.3 | (0.6) | 0.3 | (1.3) |
| | Jordan | 42.9 | (0.6) | a | a | a | a | 20.3 | (0.4) | a | a | a | a | 36.8 | (0.4) | a | a | a | a |
| | Kyrgyzstan | 35.3 | (0.7) | 35.7 | (1.2) | -0.4 | (1.2) | 26.1 | (0.6) | 25.0 | (1.1) | 1.2 | (1.2) | 38.5 | (0.6) | 39.3 | (1.0) | -0.8 | (1.3) |
| | Latvia | 55.9 | (0.5) | 62.7 | (1.7) | **-6.8** | (1.8) | 10.5 | (0.3) | 7.4 | (1.0) | **3.2** | (1.1) | 33.6 | (0.4) | 30.0 | (1.8) | 3.6 | (1.9) |
| | Liechtenstein | 61.0 | (1.5) | 67.7 | (3.7) | -6.7 | (3.9) | 11.0 | (1.1) | 3.5 | (2.1) | **7.5** | (2.1) | 28.0 | (1.3) | 28.8 | (3.0) | -0.8 | (3.0) |
| | Lithuania | 57.1 | (0.5) | c | c | c | c | 10.1 | (0.3) | c | c | **10.1** | (0.3) | 32.8 | (0.3) | 37.5 | (0.0) | **-4.7** | (0.3) |
| | Macao-China | 64.7 | (0.5) | 64.9 | (0.6) | -0.2 | (0.7) | 15.4 | (0.4) | 12.8 | (0.5) | **2.6** | (0.6) | 19.9 | (0.4) | 22.4 | (0.5) | **-2.4** | (0.6) |
| | Montenegro | c | c | 46.8 | (0.4) | c | c | c | c | 16.1 | (0.3) | c | c | 37.3 | (17.0) | 37.1 | (0.5) | 0.2 | (17.1) |
| | Qatar | 36.6 | (0.7) | 41.9 | (0.4) | **-5.2** | (0.8) | 27.8 | (0.6) | 23.9 | (0.4) | **3.9** | (0.8) | 35.5 | (0.7) | 34.2 | (0.3) | 1.3 | (0.8) |
| | Romania | 48.1 | (0.6) | a | a | a | a | 19.5 | (0.5) | a | a | a | a | 32.4 | (0.5) | a | a | a | a |
| | Russian Federation | 45.7 | (0.9) | 50.3 | (0.5) | **-4.6** | (1.0) | 17.1 | (0.9) | 13.8 | (0.5) | **3.3** | (0.9) | 37.2 | (0.9) | 36.0 | (0.5) | 1.3 | (0.9) |
| | Serbia | 57.4 | (4.3) | 56.8 | (0.5) | 0.6 | (4.4) | 13.8 | (3.8) | 13.4 | (0.4) | 0.4 | (3.8) | 28.8 | (4.5) | 29.8 | (0.4) | -1.0 | (4.5) |
| | Slovenia | 43.3 | (3.8) | 56.2 | (0.4) | **-12.9** | (3.8) | 20.0 | (3.3) | 12.9 | (0.3) | **7.1** | (3.3) | 36.7 | (3.7) | 30.9 | (0.3) | 5.8 | (3.7) |
| | Chinese Taipei | 60.1 | (0.7) | 65.6 | (0.4) | **-5.5** | (0.9) | 17.6 | (0.5) | 9.4 | (0.3) | **8.2** | (0.7) | 22.3 | (0.5) | 25.0 | (0.4) | **-2.7** | (0.6) |
| | Thailand | 62.2 | (0.7) | 64.7 | (0.4) | **-2.5** | (0.8) | 10.7 | (0.6) | 9.6 | (0.4) | 1.0 | (0.7) | 27.1 | (0.7) | 25.7 | (0.3) | **1.4** | (0.7) |
| | Tunisia | 34.2 | (0.6) | 40.1 | (0.4) | **-5.9** | (0.8) | 27.3 | (0.7) | 24.6 | (0.4) | **2.7** | (0.8) | 38.5 | (0.7) | 35.4 | (0.4) | **3.2** | (0.8) |
| | Uruguay | 51.6 | (1.0) | 58.3 | (0.6) | **-6.6** | (1.2) | 16.3 | (0.8) | 10.0 | (0.3) | **6.3** | (0.9) | 32.0 | (0.6) | 31.7 | (0.6) | 0.4 | (0.8) |

*Note:* Values that are statistically significant at the 5% level (p < 0.05) are indicated in bold.

### Table 3.10b [Part 1/3]  Mean learning hours and allocation of total learning time in mathematics, by lower and upper secondary schools

| | Mean learning hours per week | | | | | | | | | | | |
| | Regular school lessons | | | | | | Out-of-school-time lessons | | | | | |
| | Lower secondary school | | Upper secondary school | | Difference (lower-upper) | | Lower secondary school | | Upper secondary school | | Difference (lower-upper) | |
| | Mean | S.E. | Mean | S.E. | Dif. | S.E. | Mean | S.E. | Mean | S.E. | Dif. | S.E. |
|---|---|---|---|---|---|---|---|---|---|---|---|---|
| **OECD** | | | | | | | | | | | | |
| Australia | 4.13 | (0.03) | 3.98 | (0.05) | **0.15** | (0.05) | 0.74 | (0.02) | 0.79 | (0.03) | -0.05 | (0.03) |
| Austria | 3.45 | (0.11) | 3.21 | (0.05) | 0.24 | (0.12) | 0.93 | (0.15) | 0.48 | (0.02) | **0.45** | (0.15) |
| Belgium | 3.39 | (0.17) | 3.59 | (0.04) | -0.20 | (0.18) | 0.95 | (0.08) | 0.53 | (0.01) | **0.42** | (0.08) |
| Canada | 4.06 | (0.05) | 4.58 | (0.04) | **-0.52** | (0.07) | 1.13 | (0.04) | 0.90 | (0.02) | **0.22** | (0.04) |
| Czech Republic | 4.28 | (0.04) | 3.73 | (0.08) | **0.54** | (0.09) | 0.78 | (0.02) | 0.74 | (0.03) | 0.04 | (0.04) |
| Denmark | 4.43 | (0.03) | 4.51 | (0.32) | -0.07 | (0.33) | 1.36 | (0.03) | 1.40 | (0.29) | -0.04 | (0.29) |
| Finland | 3.45 | (0.04) | c | c | c | c | 0.37 | (0.02) | c | c | c | c |
| France | 3.66 | (0.04) | 3.96 | (0.04) | **-0.30** | (0.06) | 1.11 | (0.03) | 0.81 | (0.02) | **0.30** | (0.04) |
| Germany | 3.91 | (0.04) | 2.86 | (0.24) | **1.05** | (0.25) | 0.82 | (0.03) | 0.75 | (0.26) | 0.07 | (0.26) |
| Greece | 3.16 | (0.19) | 3.48 | (0.05) | -0.32 | (0.20) | 1.14 | (0.10) | 2.32 | (0.05) | **-1.19** | (0.12) |
| Hungary | 2.76 | (0.16) | 3.33 | (0.04) | **-0.57** | (0.17) | 1.59 | (0.14) | 1.26 | (0.03) | **0.33** | (0.14) |
| Iceland | 4.74 | (0.02) | c | c | c | c | 0.72 | (0.02) | c | c | c | c |
| Ireland | 3.75 | (0.04) | 3.51 | (0.05) | **0.25** | (0.06) | 0.87 | (0.03) | 0.47 | (0.03) | **0.40** | (0.04) |
| Italy | 3.03 | (0.23) | 3.75 | (0.03) | **-0.72** | (0.23) | 1.00 | (0.25) | 0.88 | (0.02) | 0.11 | (0.25) |
| Japan | a | a | 4.24 | (0.07) | a | a | a | a | 0.71 | (0.03) | a | a |
| Korea | 3.84 | (0.10) | 4.72 | (0.05) | **-0.88** | (0.11) | 1.87 | (0.24) | 2.28 | (0.04) | -0.41 | (0.24) |
| Luxembourg | 3.87 | (0.03) | 3.82 | (0.04) | 0.05 | (0.05) | 0.97 | (0.03) | 0.58 | (0.03) | **0.39** | (0.04) |
| Mexico | 3.63 | (0.07) | 4.19 | (0.04) | **-0.56** | (0.08) | 1.33 | (0.06) | 1.07 | (0.02) | **0.26** | (0.07) |
| Netherlands | 2.79 | (0.04) | 3.10 | (0.05) | **-0.31** | (0.07) | 0.74 | (0.03) | 0.54 | (0.03) | **0.21** | (0.04) |
| New Zealand | 3.89 | (0.10) | 4.41 | (0.03) | **-0.53** | (0.11) | 0.93 | (0.10) | 0.67 | (0.02) | **0.26** | (0.10) |
| Norway | 3.39 | (0.03) | c | c | c | c | 1.05 | (0.02) | c | c | c | c |
| Poland | 4.36 | (0.04) | 4.13 | (0.21) | 0.23 | (0.21) | 0.78 | (0.02) | 0.50 | (0.09) | **0.28** | (0.09) |
| Portugal | 3.07 | (0.05) | 4.14 | (0.05) | **-1.08** | (0.06) | 0.84 | (0.03) | 0.79 | (0.04) | 0.05 | (0.04) |
| Slovak Republic | 4.20 | (0.07) | 2.74 | (0.06) | **1.46** | (0.09) | 1.06 | (0.04) | 0.78 | (0.03) | **0.28** | (0.05) |
| Spain | 3.42 | (0.03) | c | c | c | c | 0.99 | (0.02) | c | c | c | c |
| Sweden | 3.09 | (0.03) | 3.28 | (0.20) | -0.19 | (0.20) | 0.61 | (0.02) | 0.54 | (0.06) | 0.07 | (0.06) |
| Switzerland | 4.01 | (0.04) | 3.13 | (0.11) | **0.88** | (0.12) | 0.76 | (0.03) | 0.42 | (0.03) | **0.35** | (0.04) |
| Turkey | 3.47 | (0.22) | 3.84 | (0.06) | -0.36 | (0.23) | 1.83 | (0.20) | 2.09 | (0.05) | -0.26 | (0.20) |
| United Kingdom | 3.61 | (0.29) | 3.78 | (0.03) | -0.16 | (0.29) | 0.73 | (0.17) | 0.63 | (0.02) | 0.10 | (0.17) |
| United States | 3.02 | (0.12) | 3.87 | (0.04) | **-0.86** | (0.12) | 1.42 | (0.07) | 1.11 | (0.03) | **0.32** | (0.07) |
| **OECD average** | 3.65 | (0.02) | 3.76 | (0.02) | **-0.11** | (0.03) | 1.01 | (0.02) | 0.92 | (0.02) | **0.12** | (0.03) |
| **Partners** | | | | | | | | | | | | |
| Argentina | 2.41 | (0.06) | 3.17 | (0.08) | **-0.77** | (0.10) | 0.87 | (0.05) | 0.74 | (0.04) | **0.14** | (0.06) |
| Azerbaijan | 3.96 | (0.07) | 3.54 | (0.09) | **0.43** | (0.11) | 1.62 | (0.06) | 1.81 | (0.06) | **-0.19** | (0.08) |
| Brazil | 2.75 | (0.06) | 3.34 | (0.04) | **-0.59** | (0.08) | 1.22 | (0.04) | 1.21 | (0.04) | 0.01 | (0.06) |
| Bulgaria | 2.58 | (0.19) | 3.01 | (0.07) | **-0.43** | (0.20) | 1.02 | (0.11) | 1.14 | (0.04) | -0.12 | (0.12) |
| Chile | 2.31 | (0.20) | 3.54 | (0.06) | **-1.22** | (0.21) | 1.37 | (0.14) | 0.98 | (0.03) | **0.40** | (0.14) |
| Colombia | 3.86 | (0.08) | 4.45 | (0.07) | **-0.59** | (0.09) | 1.21 | (0.05) | 1.24 | (0.04) | -0.03 | (0.07) |
| Croatia | c | c | 3.05 | (0.04) | c | c | c | c | 0.76 | (0.02) | c | c |
| Estonia | 4.19 | (0.04) | 4.45 | (0.17) | -0.26 | (0.18) | 1.00 | (0.03) | 0.73 | (0.12) | **0.26** | (0.13) |
| Hong Kong-China | 4.89 | (0.06) | 5.43 | (0.05) | **-0.54** | (0.07) | 1.20 | (0.06) | 1.51 | (0.04) | **-0.31** | (0.07) |
| Indonesia | 4.04 | (0.08) | 4.13 | (0.10) | -0.09 | (0.12) | 1.56 | (0.06) | 1.15 | (0.07) | **0.41** | (0.10) |
| Israel | 4.08 | (0.11) | 4.13 | (0.04) | -0.05 | (0.11) | 2.08 | (0.10) | 2.16 | (0.05) | -0.09 | (0.10) |
| Jordan | 3.48 | (0.05) | a | a | a | a | 1.82 | (0.04) | a | a | a | a |
| Kyrgyzstan | 2.88 | (0.05) | 2.89 | (0.09) | -0.01 | (0.09) | 1.57 | (0.04) | 1.49 | (0.06) | 0.08 | (0.06) |
| Latvia | 4.49 | (0.04) | 4.39 | (0.15) | 0.11 | (0.15) | 1.21 | (0.04) | 0.86 | (0.08) | **0.35** | (0.09) |
| Liechtenstein | 4.05 | (0.09) | 3.42 | (0.20) | **0.63** | (0.21) | 0.63 | (0.05) | 0.24 | (0.08) | **0.39** | (0.10) |
| Lithuania | 3.50 | (0.04) | c | c | c | c | 0.74 | (0.02) | c | c | c | c |
| Macao-China | 5.18 | (0.04) | 5.80 | (0.04) | **-0.62** | (0.05) | 1.26 | (0.03) | 1.10 | (0.05) | **0.16** | (0.06) |
| Montenegro | c | c | 3.09 | (0.04) | c | c | c | c | 0.93 | (0.02) | c | c |
| Qatar | 2.70 | (0.06) | 3.23 | (0.03) | **-0.52** | (0.07) | 1.95 | (0.06) | 1.82 | (0.03) | **0.13** | (0.06) |
| Romania | 3.01 | (0.07) | a | a | a | a | 1.50 | (0.03) | a | a | a | a |
| Russian Federation | 3.41 | (0.07) | 3.76 | (0.07) | **-0.35** | (0.07) | 1.20 | (0.05) | 1.09 | (0.04) | 0.11 | (0.06) |
| Serbia | 3.50 | (0.36) | 3.27 | (0.04) | 0.23 | (0.35) | 1.28 | (0.25) | 0.96 | (0.02) | 0.32 | (0.25) |
| Slovenia | 2.97 | (0.32) | 3.34 | (0.03) | -0.37 | (0.32) | 1.35 | (0.30) | 1.01 | (0.02) | 0.34 | (0.30) |
| Chinese Taipei | 4.21 | (0.06) | 4.28 | (0.08) | -0.06 | (0.10) | 1.76 | (0.06) | 1.41 | (0.05) | **0.35** | (0.08) |
| Thailand | 3.68 | (0.04) | 3.82 | (0.04) | **-0.14** | (0.05) | 0.99 | (0.05) | 0.89 | (0.04) | 0.10 | (0.07) |
| Tunisia | 2.92 | (0.05) | 3.82 | (0.05) | **-0.91** | (0.07) | 2.24 | (0.04) | 2.59 | (0.05) | **-0.35** | (0.07) |
| Uruguay | 2.82 | (0.07) | 3.56 | (0.04) | **-0.74** | (0.08) | 0.89 | (0.05) | 0.81 | (0.03) | 0.08 | (0.05) |

*Note*: Values that are statistically significant at the 5% level (p < 0.05) are indicated in bold.

© OECD 2011  Quality Time for Students: Learning In and Out of School

**Table 3.10b** Mean learning hours and allocation of total learning time in mathematics,
[Part 2/3] by lower and upper secondary schools

| | | Mean learning hours per week | | | | | | | | | | |
| | | Individual study | | | | | | Total learning hours | | | | |
| | | Lower secondary school | | Upper secondary school | | Difference (lower-upper) | | Lower secondary school | | Upper secondary school | | Difference (lower-upper) |
| | | Mean | S.E. | Mean | S.E. | Dif. | S.E. | Mean | S.E. | Mean | S.E. | Dif. | S.E. |
|---|---|---|---|---|---|---|---|---|---|---|---|---|---|
| OECD | Australia | 1.74 | (0.03) | 1.99 | (0.04) | **-0.25** | (0.04) | 6.62 | (0.05) | 6.76 | (0.08) | -0.15 | (0.08) |
| | Austria | 2.67 | (0.13) | 2.09 | (0.04) | **0.57** | (0.13) | 7.12 | (0.24) | 5.80 | (0.08) | **1.33** | (0.24) |
| | Belgium | 1.65 | (0.10) | 1.79 | (0.03) | -0.14 | (0.10) | 6.02 | (0.26) | 5.93 | (0.06) | 0.08 | (0.25) |
| | Canada | 1.72 | (0.05) | 2.01 | (0.03) | **-0.30** | (0.05) | 6.98 | (0.11) | 7.53 | (0.07) | **-0.55** | (0.12) |
| | Czech Republic | 1.35 | (0.03) | 1.29 | (0.05) | 0.06 | (0.06) | 6.39 | (0.06) | 5.75 | (0.13) | **0.65** | (0.14) |
| | Denmark | 1.74 | (0.02) | 2.36 | (0.43) | -0.63 | (0.44) | 7.51 | (0.06) | 8.27 | (0.92) | -0.76 | (0.94) |
| | Finland | 1.20 | (0.02) | c | c | c | c | 5.02 | (0.06) | 9.00 | (0.00) | **-3.98** | (0.06) |
| | France | 1.52 | (0.04) | 1.88 | (0.05) | **-0.36** | (0.06) | 6.29 | (0.08) | 6.64 | (0.08) | **-0.35** | (0.11) |
| | Germany | 2.28 | (0.03) | 1.98 | (0.20) | 0.30 | (0.20) | 7.03 | (0.07) | 5.65 | (0.59) | **1.38** | (0.59) |
| | Greece | 1.68 | (0.11) | 2.03 | (0.04) | **-0.35** | (0.12) | 6.00 | (0.28) | 7.85 | (0.10) | **-1.85** | (0.30) |
| | Hungary | 1.88 | (0.14) | 1.84 | (0.04) | 0.05 | (0.14) | 6.20 | (0.32) | 6.44 | (0.09) | -0.24 | (0.33) |
| | Iceland | 1.71 | (0.02) | c | c | c | c | 7.17 | (0.05) | 7.48 | (0.48) | -0.31 | (0.48) |
| | Ireland | 1.93 | (0.04) | 1.50 | (0.05) | **0.43** | (0.05) | 6.55 | (0.08) | 5.48 | (0.10) | **1.07** | (0.12) |
| | Italy | 1.92 | (0.32) | 2.49 | (0.03) | -0.58 | (0.33) | 6.22 | (0.72) | 7.13 | (0.07) | -0.91 | (0.73) |
| | Japan | a | a | 1.48 | (0.06) | a | a | a | a | 6.43 | (0.13) | a | a |
| | Korea | 1.77 | (0.25) | 2.32 | (0.07) | **-0.55** | (0.25) | 7.46 | (0.28) | 9.36 | (0.13) | **-1.89** | (0.30) |
| | Luxembourg | 1.76 | (0.03) | 1.62 | (0.03) | **0.14** | (0.04) | 6.64 | (0.06) | 6.04 | (0.07) | **0.60** | (0.09) |
| | Mexico | 2.26 | (0.06) | 2.26 | (0.02) | -0.01 | (0.07) | 7.15 | (0.14) | 7.50 | (0.06) | **-0.35** | (0.15) |
| | Netherlands | 1.37 | (0.04) | 1.74 | (0.04) | **-0.37** | (0.06) | 4.89 | (0.08) | 5.37 | (0.08) | **-0.49** | (0.11) |
| | New Zealand | 1.49 | (0.09) | 1.59 | (0.03) | -0.10 | (0.09) | 6.28 | (0.20) | 6.68 | (0.05) | **-0.41** | (0.20) |
| | Norway | 1.40 | (0.03) | c | c | c | c | 5.83 | (0.06) | 6.55 | (0.84) | -0.72 | (0.84) |
| | Poland | 2.09 | (0.03) | 2.31 | (0.18) | -0.22 | (0.19) | 7.23 | (0.06) | 6.92 | (0.38) | 0.31 | (0.39) |
| | Portugal | 1.77 | (0.04) | 2.16 | (0.04) | **-0.39** | (0.06) | 5.67 | (0.09) | 7.08 | (0.08) | **-1.40** | (0.11) |
| | Slovak Republic | 1.89 | (0.05) | 1.56 | (0.04) | **0.32** | (0.07) | 7.18 | (0.13) | 5.09 | (0.11) | **2.09** | (0.17) |
| | Spain | 1.96 | (0.03) | c | c | c | c | 6.41 | (0.06) | 6.48 | (0.56) | -0.07 | (0.56) |
| | Sweden | 1.18 | (0.02) | 1.39 | (0.24) | -0.22 | (0.24) | 4.87 | (0.04) | 5.23 | (0.44) | -0.36 | (0.44) |
| | Switzerland | 1.74 | (0.02) | 1.44 | (0.05) | **0.30** | (0.05) | 6.53 | (0.06) | 4.99 | (0.15) | **1.54** | (0.16) |
| | Turkey | 1.92 | (0.12) | 2.32 | (0.05) | **-0.41** | (0.13) | 7.16 | (0.36) | 8.22 | (0.14) | **-1.06** | (0.39) |
| | United Kingdom | 1.20 | (0.31) | 1.49 | (0.02) | -0.29 | (0.31) | 5.64 | (0.49) | 5.90 | (0.05) | -0.26 | (0.50) |
| | United States | 1.82 | (0.09) | 2.08 | (0.03) | **-0.25** | (0.09) | 6.39 | (0.19) | 7.09 | (0.07) | **-0.70** | (0.19) |
| | **OECD average** | 1.75 | (0.02) | 1.89 | (0.02) | **-0.13** | (0.03) | 6.43 | (0.04) | 6.69 | (0.06) | **-0.27** | (0.07) |
| Partners | Argentina | 1.72 | (0.08) | 1.86 | (0.05) | -0.14 | (0.10) | 5.04 | (0.14) | 5.76 | (0.13) | **-0.72** | (0.19) |
| | Azerbaijan | 2.96 | (0.08) | 2.92 | (0.08) | 0.04 | (0.10) | 8.61 | (0.17) | 8.32 | (0.18) | 0.30 | (0.23) |
| | Brazil | 1.71 | (0.05) | 1.84 | (0.04) | -0.12 | (0.06) | 5.64 | (0.12) | 6.38 | (0.08) | **-0.74** | (0.15) |
| | Bulgaria | 1.81 | (0.18) | 2.10 | (0.06) | -0.29 | (0.18) | 5.32 | (0.37) | 6.29 | (0.15) | **-0.98** | (0.39) |
| | Chile | 1.69 | (0.22) | 1.60 | (0.03) | 0.09 | (0.21) | 5.48 | (0.53) | 6.15 | (0.09) | -0.67 | (0.52) |
| | Colombia | 1.82 | (0.05) | 2.00 | (0.04) | **-0.18** | (0.06) | 6.91 | (0.12) | 7.67 | (0.11) | **-0.75** | (0.16) |
| | Croatia | c | c | 1.80 | (0.03) | c | c | 6.38 | (0.87) | 5.66 | (0.06) | 0.73 | (0.87) |
| | Estonia | 1.95 | (0.03) | 2.23 | (0.20) | -0.27 | (0.20) | 7.14 | (0.07) | 7.44 | (0.36) | -0.29 | (0.36) |
| | Hong Kong-China | 1.99 | (0.07) | 2.38 | (0.05) | **-0.39** | (0.09) | 8.08 | (0.14) | 9.32 | (0.09) | **-1.24** | (0.16) |
| | Indonesia | 2.07 | (0.04) | 1.91 | (0.05) | **0.16** | (0.06) | 7.66 | (0.15) | 7.20 | (0.13) | **0.46** | (0.18) |
| | Israel | 2.24 | (0.10) | 2.34 | (0.06) | -0.10 | (0.11) | 8.47 | (0.24) | 8.73 | (0.11) | -0.26 | (0.24) |
| | Jordan | 2.69 | (0.04) | a | a | a | a | 7.96 | (0.08) | a | a | a | a |
| | Kyrgyzstan | 2.19 | (0.04) | 2.28 | (0.07) | -0.09 | (0.08) | 6.73 | (0.10) | 6.65 | (0.17) | 0.08 | (0.18) |
| | Latvia | 2.46 | (0.04) | 2.01 | (0.14) | **0.45** | (0.14) | 8.17 | (0.09) | 7.26 | (0.30) | **0.91** | (0.30) |
| | Liechtenstein | 1.50 | (0.07) | 1.44 | (0.15) | 0.05 | (0.16) | 6.17 | (0.13) | 5.10 | (0.28) | **1.07** | (0.32) |
| | Lithuania | 1.78 | (0.03) | c | c | c | c | 6.02 | (0.06) | 6.00 | (0.00) | 0.02 | (0.06) |
| | Macao-China | 1.80 | (0.03) | 2.51 | (0.05) | **-0.71** | (0.05) | 8.24 | (0.07) | 9.41 | (0.09) | **-1.17** | (0.12) |
| | Montenegro | c | c | 2.03 | (0.03) | c | c | 4.14 | (0.84) | 6.03 | (0.07) | **-1.89** | (0.85) |
| | Qatar | 2.17 | (0.05) | 2.24 | (0.03) | -0.07 | (0.05) | 6.81 | (0.12) | 7.32 | (0.07) | **-0.51** | (0.13) |
| | Romania | 2.16 | (0.04) | a | a | a | a | 6.67 | (0.11) | a | a | a | a |
| | Russian Federation | 2.16 | (0.07) | 2.26 | (0.05) | -0.10 | (0.08) | 6.77 | (0.13) | 7.12 | (0.12) | **-0.35** | (0.15) |
| | Serbia | 1.75 | (0.26) | 1.82 | (0.03) | -0.07 | (0.26) | 6.63 | (0.64) | 6.04 | (0.07) | 0.59 | (0.63) |
| | Slovenia | 1.67 | (0.21) | 1.93 | (0.02) | -0.26 | (0.21) | 5.99 | (0.59) | 6.31 | (0.05) | -0.31 | (0.60) |
| | Chinese Taipei | 1.78 | (0.05) | 1.93 | (0.05) | -0.15 | (0.07) | 7.82 | (0.14) | 7.67 | (0.16) | 0.15 | (0.21) |
| | Thailand | 1.83 | (0.05) | 1.80 | (0.03) | 0.03 | (0.06) | 6.48 | (0.09) | 6.51 | (0.09) | -0.02 | (0.12) |
| | Tunisia | 2.39 | (0.05) | 2.73 | (0.06) | **-0.34** | (0.08) | 7.54 | (0.10) | 9.13 | (0.14) | **-1.59** | (0.17) |
| | Uruguay | 1.45 | (0.05) | 1.64 | (0.03) | **-0.19** | (0.06) | 5.21 | (0.12) | 6.00 | (0.08) | **-0.79** | (0.14) |

*Note:* Values that are statistically significant at the 5% level (p < 0.05) are indicated in bold.

### Table 3.10b Mean learning hours and allocation of total learning time in mathematics, [Part 3/3] by lower and upper secondary schools

| | Allocation of total learning time in mathematics for | | | | | | | | | | | | | | | | | |
| | Regular school lessons | | | | | | Out-of-school-time lessons | | | | | | Individual study | | | | | |
| | Lower secondary school | | Upper secondary school | | Difference (lower-upper) | | Lower secondary school | | Upper secondary school | | Difference (lower-upper) | | Lower secondary school | | Upper secondary school | | Difference (lower-upper) | |
| | % | S.E | % | S.E | Dif. | S.E. | % | S.E | % | S.E | Dif. | S.E. | % | S.E | % | S.E | Dif. | S.E. |
|---|---|---|---|---|---|---|---|---|---|---|---|---|---|---|---|---|---|---|
| Australia | 66.5 | (0.3) | 63.0 | (0.6) | **3.5** | (0.6) | 9.1 | (0.2) | 9.9 | (0.4) | **-0.9** | (0.4) | 24.4 | (0.3) | 27.1 | (0.4) | **-2.7** | (0.4) |
| Austria | 51.0 | (2.1) | 59.0 | (0.5) | **-8.0** | (2.2) | 12.1 | (1.6) | 6.3 | (0.2) | **5.8** | (1.6) | 36.9 | (1.7) | 34.7 | (0.4) | 2.2 | (1.7) |
| Belgium | 57.7 | (1.9) | 63.3 | (0.3) | **-5.7** | (1.9) | 15.8 | (1.5) | 7.7 | (0.2) | **8.1** | (1.5) | 26.6 | (1.1) | 29.0 | (0.3) | **-2.4** | (1.2) |
| Canada | 61.2 | (0.6) | 63.7 | (0.3) | **-2.5** | (0.6) | 14.5 | (0.4) | 10.9 | (0.2) | **3.6** | (0.4) | 24.3 | (0.4) | 25.4 | (0.2) | -1.1 | (0.5) |
| Czech Republic | 70.5 | (0.6) | 70.2 | (0.7) | 0.3 | (0.9) | 9.9 | (0.3) | 9.7 | (0.3) | 0.2 | (0.4) | 19.6 | (0.4) | 20.1 | (0.5) | -0.6 | (0.7) |
| Denmark | 62.4 | (0.3) | 56.8 | (2.5) | **5.6** | (2.5) | 16.0 | (0.3) | 16.2 | (2.5) | -0.2 | (2.5) | 21.6 | (0.2) | 26.9 | (2.2) | **-5.3** | (2.2) |
| Finland | 71.1 | (0.3) | c | c | c | c | 6.0 | (0.2) | c | c | c | c | 22.9 | (0.2) | c | c | c | c |
| France | 61.7 | (0.6) | 63.1 | (0.4) | **-1.4** | (0.7) | 15.9 | (0.4) | 10.6 | (0.3) | **5.3** | (0.5) | 22.5 | (0.4) | 26.3 | (0.4) | **-3.8** | (0.5) |
| Germany | 58.5 | (0.3) | 53.5 | (1.9) | **5.1** | (1.9) | 9.8 | (0.3) | 11.2 | (2.7) | -1.4 | (2.8) | 31.7 | (0.3) | 35.3 | (1.4) | **-3.6** | (1.4) |
| Greece | 56.1 | (2.2) | 48.8 | (0.5) | **7.3** | (2.3) | 16.3 | (1.3) | 26.8 | (0.5) | **-10.4** | (1.4) | 27.6 | (1.8) | 24.4 | (0.4) | 3.2 | (1.9) |
| Hungary | 45.2 | (2.3) | 55.0 | (0.4) | **-9.8** | (2.3) | 23.8 | (1.6) | 17.3 | (0.3) | **6.5** | (1.7) | 31.0 | (1.2) | 27.8 | (0.3) | **3.3** | (1.2) |
| Iceland | 69.4 | (0.3) | c | c | c | c | 8.5 | (0.2) | c | c | c | c | 22.1 | (0.2) | c | c | c | c |
| Ireland | 60.6 | (0.4) | 68.4 | (0.6) | **-7.8** | (0.7) | 11.2 | (0.3) | 6.7 | (0.3) | **4.5** | (0.4) | 28.2 | (0.4) | 24.9 | (0.5) | **3.3** | (0.6) |
| Italy | 54.2 | (3.5) | 55.0 | (0.2) | -0.8 | (3.5) | 15.0 | (3.1) | 10.7 | (0.2) | 4.3 | (3.2) | 30.7 | (2.7) | 34.3 | (0.2) | -3.5 | (2.7) |
| Japan | a | a | 71.7 | (0.5) | a | a | a | a | 8.7 | (0.3) | a | a | a | a | 19.6 | (0.4) | a | a |
| Korea | 58.9 | (2.8) | 56.9 | (0.5) | 1.9 | (2.8) | 21.2 | (2.3) | 20.9 | (0.3) | 0.3 | (2.3) | 20.0 | (2.6) | 22.2 | (0.4) | -2.2 | (2.7) |
| Luxembourg | 61.5 | (0.4) | 66.4 | (0.5) | **-4.9** | (0.7) | 12.9 | (0.3) | 8.0 | (0.3) | **4.9** | (0.5) | 25.6 | (0.3) | 25.6 | (0.4) | -0.1 | (0.5) |
| Mexico | 50.5 | (0.7) | 57.5 | (0.4) | **-7.0** | (0.8) | 16.7 | (0.6) | 12.7 | (0.3) | **4.0** | (0.7) | 32.9 | (0.5) | 29.8 | (0.3) | **3.1** | (0.6) |
| Netherlands | 59.6 | (0.6) | 61.0 | (0.7) | -1.3 | (1.0) | 13.6 | (0.5) | 8.4 | (0.4) | **5.1** | (0.6) | 26.8 | (0.4) | 30.6 | (0.5) | **-3.8** | (0.7) |
| New Zealand | 64.7 | (1.4) | 69.9 | (0.4) | **-5.1** | (1.4) | 12.1 | (1.0) | 8.3 | (0.3) | **3.9** | (1.0) | 23.1 | (0.9) | 21.8 | (0.3) | 1.3 | (1.0) |
| Norway | 62.2 | (0.4) | c | c | c | c | 16.0 | (0.3) | c | c | c | c | 21.9 | (0.3) | c | c | c | c |
| Poland | 62.5 | (0.3) | 63.4 | (1.8) | -0.9 | (1.7) | 10.1 | (0.3) | 5.6 | (0.8) | **4.5** | (0.8) | 27.4 | (0.3) | 31.0 | (1.6) | **-3.6** | (1.6) |
| Portugal | 56.9 | (0.6) | 60.9 | (0.4) | **-4.0** | (0.6) | 13.6 | (0.4) | 9.5 | (0.4) | **4.0** | (0.6) | 29.5 | (0.5) | 29.6 | (0.4) | -0.1 | (0.6) |
| Slovak Republic | 62.4 | (0.7) | 59.6 | (0.7) | **2.8** | (1.0) | 13.0 | (0.4) | 12.3 | (0.4) | 0.7 | (0.5) | 24.6 | (0.5) | 28.2 | (0.5) | **-3.6** | (0.7) |
| Spain | 57.7 | (0.3) | c | c | **c** | c | 13.1 | (0.2) | c | c | c | c | 29.3 | (0.3) | c | c | c | c |
| Sweden | 68.1 | (0.5) | 66.6 | (2.3) | 1.5 | (2.3) | 9.9 | (0.2) | 10.4 | (1.8) | -0.5 | (1.8) | 22.0 | (0.4) | 23.0 | (2.1) | -1.0 | (2.1) |
| Switzerland | 63.4 | (0.4) | 64.2 | (0.9) | -0.7 | (1.0) | 10.2 | (0.3) | 6.9 | (0.5) | **3.3** | (0.6) | 26.4 | (0.2) | 28.9 | (0.7) | **-2.6** | (0.8) |
| Turkey | 49.8 | (3.5) | 50.8 | (0.4) | -1.0 | (3.5) | 23.9 | (2.9) | 22.6 | (0.4) | 1.2 | (2.9) | 26.3 | (2.7) | 26.6 | (0.3) | -0.2 | (2.7) |
| United Kingdom | 68.9 | (4.2) | 67.1 | (0.3) | 1.8 | (4.2) | 10.8 | (2.3) | 8.9 | (0.2) | 2.0 | (2.4) | 20.3 | (3.6) | 24.0 | (0.2) | **-3.7** | (3.6) |
| United States | 47.3 | (1.8) | 56.5 | (0.4) | **-9.1** | (1.9) | 22.3 | (1.0) | 14.4 | (0.4) | **7.9** | (1.0) | 30.3 | (1.1) | 29.1 | (0.3) | 1.2 | (1.2) |
| **OECD average** | 60.0 | (0.3) | 61.2 | (0.2) | **-1.6** | (0.4) | 13.4 | (0.2) | 11.6 | (0.2) | **2.6** | (0.3) | 26.1 | (0.2) | 27.2 | (0.2) | **-1.1** | (0.3) |
| Argentina | 50.3 | (1.1) | 56.7 | (0.7) | **-6.5** | (1.3) | 15.1 | (1.0) | 11.4 | (0.5) | **3.7** | (1.1) | 34.7 | (0.8) | 31.9 | (0.5) | **2.7** | (1.0) |
| Azerbaijan | 48.4 | (0.7) | 45.4 | (0.6) | **3.0** | (0.8) | 17.6 | (0.5) | 20.0 | (0.6) | **-2.4** | (0.8) | 34.1 | (0.6) | 34.6 | (0.6) | -0.5 | (0.8) |
| Brazil | 51.7 | (0.8) | 55.6 | (0.6) | **-3.9** | (0.9) | 19.3 | (0.8) | 16.4 | (0.8) | **2.8** | (0.9) | 29.0 | (0.6) | 27.9 | (0.5) | 1.1 | (0.7) |
| Bulgaria | 50.2 | (3.0) | 51.3 | (0.5) | -1.1 | (3.0) | 18.6 | (1.5) | 16.3 | (0.5) | 2.4 | (1.5) | 31.2 | (2.5) | 32.5 | (0.4) | -1.3 | (2.5) |
| Chile | 43.8 | (1.5) | 57.4 | (0.5) | **-13.6** | (1.7) | 26.4 | (2.4) | 14.7 | (0.3) | **11.7** | (2.5) | 29.9 | (2.2) | 28.0 | (0.4) | 1.9 | (2.3) |
| Colombia | 58.5 | (0.9) | 62.1 | (0.5) | **-3.6** | (0.9) | 15.4 | (0.7) | 13.5 | (0.4) | **2.0** | (0.8) | 26.0 | (0.6) | 24.4 | (0.4) | **1.6** | (0.6) |
| Croatia | c | c | 58.4 | (0.5) | c | c | c | c | c | c | 16.5 | (17.7) | c | c | 30.2 | (0.4) | c | c |
| Estonia | 62.2 | (0.4) | 63.6 | (2.0) | -1.4 | (2.0) | 12.4 | (0.3) | 8.5 | (1.4) | **3.9** | (1.5) | 25.4 | (0.3) | 27.9 | (1.7) | -2.4 | (1.7) |
| Hong Kong-China | 63.9 | (0.9) | 61.9 | (0.5) | 2.0 | (1.0) | 13.3 | (0.5) | 14.5 | (0.3) | **-1.2** | (0.5) | 22.8 | (0.6) | 23.7 | (0.3) | -0.8 | (0.7) |
| Indonesia | 54.0 | (0.6) | 60.5 | (1.0) | **-6.5** | (1.3) | 18.9 | (0.5) | 13.6 | (0.2) | **5.3** | (0.9) | 27.1 | (0.4) | 25.9 | (0.5) | 1.2 | (0.7) |
| Israel | 52.0 | (1.1) | 51.3 | (0.7) | 0.7 | (1.2) | 23.0 | (0.8) | 23.1 | (0.3) | -0.2 | (0.9) | 25.0 | (0.8) | 25.6 | (0.5) | -0.5 | (0.9) |
| Jordan | 43.2 | (0.5) | c | c | c | c | 22.3 | (0.5) | c | c | c | c | 34.5 | (0.4) | c | c | c | c |
| Kyrgyzstan | 41.8 | (0.6) | 42.7 | (0.8) | -0.9 | (0.9) | 24.8 | (0.6) | 22.0 | (0.7) | **2.7** | (0.8) | 33.5 | (0.5) | 35.3 | (0.8) | -1.8 | (1.0) |
| Latvia | 58.0 | (0.4) | 64.1 | (1.8) | **-6.1** | (1.9) | 13.4 | (0.4) | 11.2 | (1.4) | 2.2 | (1.5) | 28.6 | (0.3) | 24.7 | (1.5) | **3.9** | (1.5) |
| Liechtenstein | 66.3 | (1.2) | 69.7 | (2.8) | -3.4 | (2.9) | 9.1 | (0.7) | 3.7 | (1.2) | **5.4** | (1.5) | 24.5 | (1.0) | 26.6 | (2.4) | -2.0 | (2.3) |
| Lithuania | 60.7 | (0.4) | a | a | a | a | 11.5 | (0.3) | a | a | a | a | 27.8 | (0.3) | a | a | a | a |
| Macao-China | 66.7 | (0.5) | 65.4 | (0.4) | **1.3** | (0.6) | 12.9 | (0.3) | 10.0 | (0.4) | **2.9** | (0.5) | 20.3 | (0.4) | 24.6 | (0.4) | **-4.2** | (0.5) |
| Montenegro | c | c | 52.4 | (0.4) | c | c | c | c | 13.5 | (0.3) | c | c | c | c | 34.1 | (0.4) | c | c |
| Qatar | 39.2 | (0.7) | 44.4 | (0.3) | **-5.2** | (0.8) | 28.1 | (0.7) | 24.3 | (0.3) | **3.8** | (0.8) | 32.6 | (0.6) | 31.3 | (0.3) | **1.4** | (0.6) |
| Romania | 49.5 | (0.6) | a | a | a | a | 19.7 | (0.4) | a | a | a | a | 30.7 | (0.4) | a | a | a | a |
| Russian Federation | 51.5 | (0.9) | 55.3 | (0.5) | **-3.8** | (0.9) | 17.8 | (1.0) | 14.4 | (0.5) | **3.4** | (0.9) | 30.7 | (0.6) | 30.2 | (0.4) | 0.4 | (0.7) |
| Serbia | 59.6 | (4.6) | 59.3 | (0.5) | 0.4 | (4.6) | 16.6 | (2.6) | 12.9 | (0.3) | 3.7 | (2.5) | 23.8 | (3.0) | 27.8 | (0.4) | -4.0 | (3.1) |
| Slovenia | 48.8 | (3.2) | 55.9 | (0.3) | **-7.0** | (3.2) | 20.6 | (2.3) | 14.1 | (0.2) | **6.5** | (2.3) | 30.6 | (4.5) | 30.0 | (0.3) | 0.5 | (4.5) |
| Chinese Taipei | 57.7 | (0.6) | 60.7 | (0.5) | **-3.0** | (0.8) | 19.9 | (0.5) | 15.4 | (0.3) | **4.5** | (0.7) | 22.4 | (0.3) | 23.9 | (0.3) | **-1.5** | (0.4) |
| Thailand | 62.4 | (0.9) | 63.9 | (0.4) | -1.5 | (0.9) | 12.2 | (0.9) | 9.9 | (0.3) | **2.3** | (0.7) | 25.4 | (0.6) | 26.2 | (0.3) | -0.8 | (0.7) |
| Tunisia | 39.3 | (0.6) | 43.8 | (0.4) | **-4.5** | (0.8) | 28.1 | (0.5) | 26.2 | (0.3) | **1.8** | (0.6) | 32.6 | (0.5) | 30.0 | (0.4) | **2.6** | (0.7) |
| Uruguay | 56.0 | (0.9) | 62.9 | (0.5) | **-6.9** | (1.0) | 15.5 | (0.7) | 11.0 | (0.3) | **4.4** | (0.8) | 28.5 | (0.7) | 26.0 | (0.3) | **2.5** | (0.7) |

*Note:* Values that are statistically significant at the 5% level (p < 0.05) are indicated in bold.

© OECD 2011 Quality Time for Students: Learning In and Out of School

**Table 3.10c** [Part 1/3] **Mean learning hours and allocation of total learning time on the language of instruction, by lower and upper secondary schools**

| | Mean learning hours per week | | | | | | | | | | | |
|---|---|---|---|---|---|---|---|---|---|---|---|---|
| | Regular school lessons | | | | | | Out-of-school-time lessons | | | | | |
| | Lower secondary school | | Upper secondary school | | Difference (lower-upper) | | Lower secondary school | | Upper secondary school | | Difference (lower-upper) | |
| | Mean | S.E. | Mean | S.E. | Dif. | S.E. | Mean | S.E. | Mean | S.E. | Dif. | S.E. |
| Australia | 4.07 | (0.03) | 4.02 | (0.05) | 0.05 | (0.05) | 0.65 | (0.02) | 0.71 | (0.03) | -0.07 | (0.04) |
| Austria | 3.56 | (0.13) | 2.82 | (0.04) | **0.74** | (0.14) | 0.54 | (0.12) | 0.22 | (0.02) | **0.32** | (0.12) |
| Belgium | 3.52 | (0.19) | 3.48 | (0.03) | 0.04 | (0.19) | 0.96 | (0.10) | 0.44 | (0.01) | **0.52** | (0.10) |
| Canada | 4.14 | (0.06) | 4.48 | (0.04) | **-0.34** | (0.07) | 0.98 | (0.04) | 0.84 | (0.02) | **0.14** | (0.04) |
| Czech Republic | 4.03 | (0.04) | 3.43 | (0.05) | **0.60** | (0.06) | 0.62 | (0.02) | 0.61 | (0.02) | 0.01 | (0.03) |
| Denmark | 5.52 | (0.04) | 3.96 | (0.16) | **1.56** | (0.17) | 1.69 | (0.03) | 1.17 | (0.19) | **0.52** | (0.20) |
| Finland | 3.13 | (0.05) | c | c | c | c | 0.36 | (0.01) | c | c | c | c |
| France | 3.81 | (0.05) | 4.14 | (0.03) | **-0.33** | (0.06) | 1.00 | (0.03) | 0.62 | (0.03) | **0.38** | (0.04) |
| Germany | 3.68 | (0.03) | 2.99 | (0.21) | **0.69** | (0.21) | 0.61 | (0.02) | 0.52 | (0.22) | 0.09 | (0.22) |
| Greece | 2.68 | (0.21) | 3.22 | (0.04) | **-0.53** | (0.21) | 1.42 | (0.16) | 1.65 | (0.03) | -0.23 | (0.16) |
| Hungary | 2.46 | (0.13) | 3.24 | (0.04) | **-0.78** | (0.14) | 1.52 | (0.13) | 1.29 | (0.03) | 0.23 | (0.13) |
| Iceland | 4.53 | (0.02) | c | c | c | c | 0.46 | (0.02) | c | c | c | c |
| Ireland | 3.61 | (0.04) | 3.45 | (0.05) | **0.16** | (0.06) | 0.72 | (0.03) | 0.49 | (0.03) | **0.23** | (0.03) |
| Italy | 3.92 | (0.20) | 4.63 | (0.03) | **-0.71** | (0.21) | 1.55 | (0.26) | 0.78 | (0.02) | **0.77** | (0.27) |
| Japan | a | a | 3.82 | (0.04) | a | a | a | a | 0.43 | (0.02) | a | a |
| Korea | 3.86 | (0.19) | 4.49 | (0.04) | **-0.63** | (0.20) | 1.29 | (0.26) | 1.45 | (0.04) | -0.16 | (0.26) |
| Luxembourg | 3.53 | (0.03) | 3.46 | (0.04) | 0.08 | (0.05) | 0.77 | (0.02) | 0.28 | (0.02) | **0.49** | (0.03) |
| Mexico | 3.64 | (0.07) | 3.80 | (0.04) | -0.16 | (0.09) | 1.29 | (0.06) | 0.96 | (0.02) | **0.33** | (0.06) |
| Netherlands | 2.97 | (0.03) | 2.79 | (0.04) | **0.18** | (0.05) | 0.76 | (0.02) | 0.31 | (0.02) | **0.45** | (0.03) |
| New Zealand | 3.81 | (0.10) | 4.43 | (0.03) | **-0.62** | (0.10) | 0.87 | (0.09) | 0.64 | (0.03) | **0.23** | (0.10) |
| Norway | 3.60 | (0.04) | c | c | c | c | 1.16 | (0.02) | c | c | c | c |
| Poland | 4.64 | (0.03) | 4.97 | (0.19) | -0.33 | (0.19) | 0.71 | (0.03) | 0.32 | (0.08) | **0.39** | (0.08) |
| Portugal | 3.01 | (0.04) | 3.52 | (0.03) | **-0.52** | (0.05) | 0.78 | (0.03) | 0.35 | (0.02) | **0.44** | (0.03) |
| Slovak Republic | 4.07 | (0.07) | 2.56 | (0.05) | **1.51** | (0.09) | 1.03 | (0.03) | 0.80 | (0.03) | **0.23** | (0.05) |
| Spain | 3.60 | (0.03) | c | c | c | c | 0.58 | (0.02) | c | c | c | c |
| Sweden | 3.12 | (0.03) | 3.07 | (0.15) | 0.05 | (0.15) | 0.68 | (0.02) | 0.73 | (0.11) | -0.05 | (0.11) |
| Switzerland | 3.75 | (0.03) | 3.20 | (0.12) | **0.55** | (0.13) | 0.54 | (0.02) | 0.26 | (0.04) | **0.28** | (0.04) |
| Turkey | 4.20 | (0.23) | 3.98 | (0.05) | 0.22 | (0.23) | 1.90 | (0.21) | 1.81 | (0.05) | 0.09 | (0.22) |
| United Kingdom | 3.68 | (0.25) | 3.89 | (0.04) | -0.21 | (0.26) | 0.93 | (0.19) | 0.59 | (0.02) | 0.34 | (0.19) |
| United States | 2.77 | (0.11) | 3.76 | (0.04) | **-0.98** | (0.11) | 1.38 | (0.13) | 1.08 | (0.03) | **0.30** | (0.14) |
| **OECD average** | 3.69 | (0.02) | 3.68 | (0.02) | 0.01 | (0.03) | 0.96 | (0.02) | 0.74 | (0.01) | **0.25** | (0.03) |
| Argentina | 2.19 | (0.06) | 2.47 | (0.07) | **-0.29** | (0.09) | 0.67 | (0.04) | 0.33 | (0.03) | **0.34** | (0.05) |
| Azerbaijan | 3.64 | (0.05) | 3.75 | (0.07) | -0.11 | (0.08) | 1.65 | (0.06) | 2.02 | (0.07) | **-0.36** | (0.08) |
| Brazil | 2.77 | (0.07) | 3.26 | (0.05) | **-0.49** | (0.09) | 1.20 | (0.04) | 1.17 | (0.03) | 0.03 | (0.05) |
| Bulgaria | 2.64 | (0.21) | 2.93 | (0.05) | -0.30 | (0.22) | 1.09 | (0.14) | 1.09 | (0.04) | -0.00 | (0.15) |
| Chile | 2.41 | (0.19) | 3.49 | (0.06) | **-1.08** | (0.20) | 1.43 | (0.17) | 0.98 | (0.03) | **0.45** | (0.17) |
| Colombia | 3.58 | (0.07) | 4.14 | (0.07) | **-0.55** | (0.10) | 1.19 | (0.04) | 1.12 | (0.04) | 0.06 | (0.05) |
| Croatia | c | c | 3.33 | (0.03) | c | c | c | c | 0.39 | (0.02) | c | c |
| Estonia | 3.47 | (0.04) | 4.14 | (0.16) | **-0.67** | (0.16) | 0.89 | (0.03) | 0.87 | (0.15) | 0.02 | (0.15) |
| Hong Kong-China | 5.00 | (0.07) | 5.30 | (0.05) | **-0.30** | (0.07) | 0.83 | (0.04) | 0.79 | (0.03) | 0.03 | (0.05) |
| Indonesia | 3.87 | (0.09) | 3.40 | (0.06) | **0.47** | (0.10) | 1.52 | (0.04) | 0.97 | (0.04) | **0.56** | (0.06) |
| Israel | 2.80 | (0.11) | 3.06 | (0.05) | **-0.26** | (0.12) | 1.26 | (0.08) | 1.35 | (0.04) | -0.08 | (0.09) |
| Jordan | 3.56 | (0.05) | a | a | a | a | 1.77 | (0.04) | a | a | a | a |
| Kyrgyzstan | 2.69 | (0.05) | 2.89 | (0.11) | -0.20 | (0.10) | 1.68 | (0.03) | 1.78 | (0.06) | -0.10 | (0.07) |
| Latvia | 3.71 | (0.04) | 3.16 | (0.15) | **0.55** | (0.15) | 0.89 | (0.03) | 0.60 | (0.08) | **0.29** | (0.08) |
| Liechtenstein | 3.70 | (0.08) | 3.39 | (0.31) | 0.30 | (0.31) | 0.35 | (0.05) | 0.11 | (0.05) | **0.24** | (0.07) |
| Lithuania | 3.66 | (0.04) | c | c | c | c | 0.66 | (0.02) | c | c | c | c |
| Macao-China | 5.13 | (0.03) | 5.63 | (0.05) | **-0.49** | (0.06) | 1.17 | (0.04) | 0.86 | (0.05) | **0.32** | (0.06) |
| Montenegro | c | c | 2.94 | (0.04) | c | c | c | c | 0.75 | (0.02) | c | c |
| Qatar | 2.60 | (0.06) | 2.98 | (0.03) | **-0.38** | (0.07) | 1.83 | (0.05) | 1.52 | (0.03) | **0.31** | (0.05) |
| Romania | 3.30 | (0.06) | a | a | a | a | 1.52 | (0.03) | a | a | a | a |
| Russian Federation | 2.47 | (0.05) | 1.79 | (0.05) | **0.68** | (0.06) | 0.96 | (0.04) | 0.74 | (0.03) | **0.23** | (0.04) |
| Serbia | 3.36 | (0.41) | 3.17 | (0.04) | 0.19 | (0.41) | 1.09 | (0.20) | 0.92 | (0.03) | 0.16 | (0.21) |
| Slovenia | 2.80 | (0.24) | 3.26 | (0.03) | -0.46 | (0.24) | 1.13 | (0.13) | 0.72 | (0.02) | **0.41** | (0.13) |
| Chinese Taipei | 4.51 | (0.06) | 4.30 | (0.07) | 0.21 | (0.09) | 0.95 | (0.04) | 0.57 | (0.02) | **0.39** | (0.05) |
| Thailand | 3.58 | (0.05) | 2.88 | (0.02) | **0.70** | (0.05) | 0.86 | (0.05) | 0.42 | (0.02) | **0.43** | (0.06) |
| Tunisia | 2.74 | (0.08) | 3.50 | (0.06) | **-0.76** | (0.10) | 2.05 | (0.05) | 1.53 | (0.07) | **0.52** | (0.08) |
| Uruguay | 2.60 | (0.07) | 2.81 | (0.04) | **-0.20** | (0.08) | 0.81 | (0.05) | 0.56 | (0.02) | **0.25** | (0.05) |

*Note*: Values that are statistically significant at the 5% level (p < 0.05) are indicated in bold.

### Table 3.10c Mean learning hours and allocation of total learning time on the language of instruction, by lower and upper secondary schools
[Part 2/3]

| | Mean learning hours per week | | | | | | | | | | | |
|---|---|---|---|---|---|---|---|---|---|---|---|---|
| | Individual study | | | | | | Total learning hours | | | | | |
| | Lower secondary school | | Upper secondary school | | Difference (lower-upper) | | Lower secondary school | | Upper secondary school | | Difference (lower-upper) | |
| | Mean | S.E. | Mean | S.E. | Dif. | S.E. | Mean | S.E. | Mean | S.E. | Dif. | S.E. |
| Australia | 1.66 | (0.02) | 1.92 | (0.04) | **-0.27** | (0.04) | 6.38 | (0.05) | 6.65 | (0.08) | -0.27 | (0.09) |
| Austria | 2.41 | (0.17) | 1.49 | (0.04) | **0.92** | (0.17) | 6.54 | (0.24) | 4.54 | (0.07) | 2.00 | (0.25) |
| Belgium | 1.52 | (0.10) | 1.34 | (0.02) | 0.18 | (0.10) | 6.10 | (0.27) | 5.27 | (0.04) | 0.83 | (0.27) |
| Canada | 1.45 | (0.04) | 1.79 | (0.03) | **-0.34** | (0.05) | 6.63 | (0.11) | 7.14 | (0.07) | -0.50 | (0.13) |
| Czech Republic | 1.16 | (0.03) | 1.16 | (0.03) | 0.01 | (0.05) | 5.81 | (0.07) | 5.19 | (0.07) | 0.61 | (0.09) |
| Denmark | 2.16 | (0.03) | 2.21 | (0.26) | -0.05 | (0.25) | 9.37 | (0.07) | 7.35 | (0.27) | 2.02 | (0.27) |
| Finland | 1.13 | (0.02) | c | c | c | c | 4.63 | (0.07) | c | c | c | c |
| France | 1.36 | (0.03) | 1.62 | (0.03) | **-0.26** | (0.04) | 6.19 | (0.08) | 6.38 | (0.05) | -0.19 | (0.09) |
| Germany | 1.90 | (0.03) | 1.63 | (0.19) | 0.27 | (0.20) | 6.20 | (0.05) | 5.16 | (0.52) | 1.04 | (0.53) |
| Greece | 1.77 | (0.14) | 1.95 | (0.03) | -0.18 | (0.14) | 5.91 | (0.46) | 6.82 | (0.07) | -0.91 | (0.45) |
| Hungary | 1.84 | (0.14) | 1.86 | (0.04) | -0.02 | (0.14) | 5.79 | (0.30) | 6.41 | (0.09) | -0.62 | (0.32) |
| Iceland | 1.54 | (0.02) | c | c | c | c | 6.54 | (0.04) | c | c | c | c |
| Ireland | 1.87 | (0.04) | 1.57 | (0.05) | **0.30** | (0.06) | 6.20 | (0.08) | 5.53 | (0.10) | 0.67 | (0.12) |
| Italy | 2.28 | (0.21) | 2.96 | (0.04) | **-0.68** | (0.22) | 7.80 | (0.44) | 8.38 | (0.07) | -0.58 | (0.45) |
| Japan | a | a | 0.94 | (0.03) | a | a | a | a | 5.19 | (0.07) | a | a |
| Korea | 1.27 | (0.08) | 1.41 | (0.04) | -0.13 | (0.09) | 6.41 | (0.34) | 7.36 | (0.09) | -0.95 | (0.35) |
| Luxembourg | 1.51 | (0.03) | 1.15 | (0.03) | **0.36** | (0.05) | 5.82 | (0.06) | 4.89 | (0.06) | 0.94 | (0.09) |
| Mexico | 2.13 | (0.05) | 2.00 | (0.02) | **0.13** | (0.06) | 7.05 | (0.15) | 6.73 | (0.06) | 0.32 | (0.16) |
| Netherlands | 1.34 | (0.03) | 1.29 | (0.04) | 0.06 | (0.05) | 5.08 | (0.06) | 4.38 | (0.07) | 0.70 | (0.09) |
| New Zealand | 1.55 | (0.10) | 1.57 | (0.03) | -0.02 | (0.10) | 6.15 | (0.20) | 6.65 | (0.06) | -0.51 | (0.20) |
| Norway | 1.45 | (0.03) | c | c | c | c | 6.20 | (0.06) | c | c | c | c |
| Poland | 2.22 | (0.03) | 2.36 | (0.20) | -0.14 | (0.20) | 7.56 | (0.05) | 7.65 | (0.38) | -0.09 | (0.38) |
| Portugal | 1.78 | (0.04) | 1.80 | (0.03) | -0.02 | (0.06) | 5.59 | (0.08) | 5.67 | (0.06) | -0.08 | (0.10) |
| Slovak Republic | 1.78 | (0.05) | 1.71 | (0.05) | 0.07 | (0.07) | 6.88 | (0.11) | 5.07 | (0.09) | 1.81 | (0.15) |
| Spain | 1.89 | (0.03) | c | c | c | c | 6.10 | (0.05) | c | c | c | c |
| Sweden | 1.26 | (0.02) | 1.29 | (0.15) | -0.03 | (0.15) | 5.05 | (0.06) | 5.10 | (0.35) | -0.05 | (0.36) |
| Switzerland | 1.44 | (0.02) | 1.20 | (0.04) | **0.24** | (0.04) | 5.73 | (0.04) | 4.65 | (0.17) | 1.08 | (0.17) |
| Turkey | 2.30 | (0.12) | 2.17 | (0.05) | 0.13 | (0.13) | 8.29 | (0.35) | 7.94 | (0.13) | 0.35 | (0.38) |
| United Kingdom | 1.39 | (0.33) | 1.59 | (0.02) | -0.20 | (0.33) | 6.11 | (0.48) | 6.08 | (0.06) | 0.03 | (0.48) |
| United States | 1.60 | (0.08) | 1.90 | (0.04) | **-0.30** | (0.09) | 5.82 | (0.21) | 6.77 | (0.07) | -0.95 | (0.23) |
| **OECD average** | **1.69** | **(0.02)** | **1.69** | **(0.02)** | **0.00** | **(0.03)** | **6.34** | **(0.04)** | **6.11** | **(0.03)** | **0.27** | **(0.06)** |
| Argentina | 1.69 | (0.10) | 1.61 | (0.04) | 0.07 | (0.10) | 4.59 | (0.15) | 4.39 | (0.09) | 0.20 | (0.17) |
| Azerbaijan | 2.99 | (0.06) | 3.27 | (0.08) | -0.28 | (0.09) | 8.35 | (0.14) | 9.12 | (0.16) | -0.77 | (0.21) |
| Brazil | 1.80 | (0.04) | 1.72 | (0.03) | 0.09 | (0.06) | 5.76 | (0.11) | 6.13 | (0.08) | -0.37 | (0.13) |
| Bulgaria | 1.65 | (0.18) | 2.08 | (0.05) | -0.43 | (0.18) | 5.34 | (0.43) | 6.13 | (0.11) | -0.79 | (0.43) |
| Chile | 1.63 | (0.16) | 1.56 | (0.03) | 0.06 | (0.17) | 5.50 | (0.47) | 6.05 | (0.08) | -0.55 | (0.46) |
| Colombia | 1.78 | (0.05) | 1.88 | (0.05) | -0.10 | (0.07) | 6.59 | (0.11) | 7.13 | (0.11) | -0.54 | (0.14) |
| Croatia | c | c | 1.58 | (0.03) | c | c | c | c | 5.32 | (0.06) | c | c |
| Estonia | 1.61 | (0.02) | 1.77 | (0.15) | -0.15 | (0.15) | 5.98 | (0.06) | 6.77 | (0.34) | -0.79 | (0.34) |
| Hong Kong-China | 1.71 | (0.06) | 1.60 | (0.03) | 0.11 | (0.06) | 7.54 | (0.13) | 7.70 | (0.08) | -0.16 | (0.12) |
| Indonesia | 1.91 | (0.05) | 1.69 | (0.06) | 0.22 | (0.09) | 7.28 | (0.14) | 6.04 | (0.12) | 1.24 | (0.20) |
| Israel | 1.53 | (0.08) | 1.68 | (0.04) | -0.15 | (0.08) | 5.56 | (0.19) | 6.11 | (0.10) | -0.54 | (0.22) |
| Jordan | 2.59 | (0.04) | a | a | a | a | 7.92 | (0.09) | a | a | a | a |
| Kyrgyzstan | 2.27 | (0.04) | 2.54 | (0.07) | -0.28 | (0.07) | 6.72 | (0.09) | 7.22 | (0.18) | -0.50 | (0.18) |
| Latvia | 2.02 | (0.03) | 1.55 | (0.12) | 0.48 | (0.13) | 6.63 | (0.07) | 5.30 | (0.27) | 1.32 | (0.28) |
| Liechtenstein | 1.25 | (0.06) | 1.10 | (0.22) | 0.16 | (0.24) | 5.29 | (0.11) | 4.60 | (0.41) | 0.69 | (0.44) |
| Lithuania | 1.82 | (0.03) | c | c | c | c | 6.13 | (0.06) | c | c | c | c |
| Macao-China | 1.43 | (0.03) | 1.59 | (0.04) | -0.15 | (0.05) | 7.75 | (0.07) | 8.06 | (0.10) | -0.31 | (0.12) |
| Montenegro | c | c | 1.99 | (0.03) | c | c | c | c | 5.67 | (0.07) | c | c |
| Qatar | 2.21 | (0.05) | 1.99 | (0.03) | 0.23 | (0.06) | 6.60 | (0.12) | 6.49 | (0.07) | 0.12 | (0.13) |
| Romania | 2.19 | (0.04) | a | a | a | a | 7.02 | (0.10) | a | a | a | a |
| Russian Federation | 1.76 | (0.05) | 1.43 | (0.04) | 0.33 | (0.06) | 5.18 | (0.08) | 3.94 | (0.09) | 1.24 | (0.12) |
| Serbia | 1.59 | (0.27) | 1.70 | (0.03) | -0.11 | (0.27) | 6.02 | (0.53) | 5.79 | (0.07) | 0.22 | (0.54) |
| Slovenia | 1.55 | (0.17) | 1.47 | (0.02) | 0.07 | (0.18) | 5.53 | (0.35) | 5.47 | (0.05) | 0.06 | (0.35) |
| Chinese Taipei | 1.85 | (0.04) | 1.73 | (0.04) | 0.12 | (0.06) | 7.36 | (0.11) | 6.62 | (0.10) | 0.74 | (0.14) |
| Thailand | 1.92 | (0.06) | 1.61 | (0.03) | 0.31 | (0.06) | 6.35 | (0.10) | 4.90 | (0.06) | 1.45 | (0.11) |
| Tunisia | 2.28 | (0.06) | 1.97 | (0.05) | 0.31 | (0.08) | 7.12 | (0.14) | 6.99 | (0.15) | 0.13 | (0.20) |
| Uruguay | 1.30 | (0.04) | 1.38 | (0.03) | -0.08 | (0.04) | 4.77 | (0.09) | 4.75 | (0.07) | 0.02 | (0.11) |

*Note*: Values that are statistically significant at the 5% level (p < 0.05) are indicated in bold.

168

## Table 3.10c [Part 3/3] Mean learning hours and allocation of total learning time on the language of instruction, by lower and upper secondary schools

| | Allocation of total learning time on the language of instruction for | | | | | | | | | | | | | | | | | |
| | Regular school lessons | | | | | | Out-of-school-time lessons | | | | | | Individual study | | | | | |
| | Lower secondary school | | Upper secondary school | | Difference (lower-upper) | | Lower secondary school | | Upper secondary school | | Difference (lower-upper) | | Lower secondary school | | Upper secondary school | | Difference (lower-upper) | |
| | % | S.E | % | S.E | Dif. | S.E. | % | S.E | % | S.E | Dif. | S.E. | % | S.E | % | S.E | Dif. | S.E. |
|---|---|---|---|---|---|---|---|---|---|---|---|---|---|---|---|---|---|---|
| **OECD** | | | | | | | | | | | | | | | | | | |
| Australia | 67.7 | (0.3) | 64.5 | (0.5) | **3.2** | (0.6) | 8.2 | (0.2) | 8.8 | (0.4) | -0.7 | (0.4) | 24.1 | (0.2) | 26.7 | (0.4) | **-2.5** | (0.4) |
| Austria | 58.0 | (2.2) | 66.0 | (0.4) | **-8.0** | (2.2) | 6.8 | (1.2) | 3.1 | (0.3) | **3.7** | (1.3) | 35.2 | (1.8) | 30.9 | (0.4) | **4.3** | (1.8) |
| Belgium | 58.5 | (1.9) | 67.6 | (0.3) | **-9.1** | (1.9) | 15.4 | (1.6) | 6.8 | (0.2) | **8.6** | (1.7) | 26.2 | (1.3) | 25.6 | (0.2) | 0.5 | (1.3) |
| Canada | 65.0 | (0.7) | 65.7 | (0.3) | -0.8 | (0.7) | 12.9 | (0.4) | 10.4 | (0.2) | **2.5** | (0.4) | 22.1 | (0.5) | 23.8 | (0.3) | -1.7 | (0.6) |
| Czech Republic | 72.4 | (0.6) | 70.8 | (0.7) | 1.6 | (0.9) | 8.8 | (0.2) | 9.1 | (0.3) | -0.3 | (0.4) | 18.7 | (0.4) | 20.0 | (0.6) | -1.3 | (0.7) |
| Denmark | 62.2 | (0.3) | 56.1 | (2.4) | **6.1** | (2.4) | 16.0 | (0.2) | 14.6 | (2.8) | 1.4 | (2.8) | 21.8 | (0.2) | 29.3 | (2.7) | **-7.5** | (2.6) |
| Finland | 70.7 | (0.4) | c | c | c | c | 6.2 | (0.2) | c | c | c | c | 23.1 | (0.3) | c | c | c | c |
| France | 64.7 | (0.6) | 68.4 | (0.5) | **-3.7** | (0.8) | 14.6 | (0.4) | 8.2 | (0.4) | **6.4** | (0.5) | 20.7 | (0.4) | 23.4 | (0.3) | **-2.7** | (0.5) |
| Germany | 62.3 | (0.4) | 60.9 | (1.7) | 1.4 | (1.8) | 7.9 | (0.3) | 8.5 | (1.9) | -0.6 | (2.0) | 29.8 | (0.3) | 30.6 | (1.9) | -0.8 | (1.9) |
| Greece | 50.6 | (2.2) | 51.0 | (0.6) | -0.4 | (2.3) | 21.0 | (2.0) | 21.6 | (0.3) | -0.6 | (2.0) | 28.4 | (1.4) | 27.4 | (0.3) | 1.0 | (1.4) |
| Hungary | 43.0 | (2.4) | 54.0 | (0.4) | **-11.0** | (2.5) | 26.0 | (1.7) | 17.7 | (0.3) | **8.3** | (1.8) | 31.0 | (1.5) | 28.3 | (0.3) | **2.7** | (1.5) |
| Iceland | 71.8 | (0.3) | c | c | c | c | 6.0 | (0.2) | c | c | c | c | 22.2 | (0.2) | c | c | c | c |
| Ireland | 62.2 | (0.5) | 67.5 | (0.7) | **-5.3** | (0.7) | 9.1 | (0.3) | 6.6 | (0.3) | **2.5** | (0.4) | 28.6 | (0.4) | 25.9 | (0.5) | 2.7 | (0.6) |
| Italy | 51.0 | (3.9) | 57.3 | (0.2) | -6.3 | (3.9) | 19.3 | (3.0) | 8.1 | (0.2) | **11.2** | (3.0) | 29.7 | (1.6) | 34.6 | (0.2) | **-4.9** | (1.7) |
| Japan | a | a | 78.1 | (0.5) | a | a | a | a | 6.3 | (0.3) | a | a | a | a | 15.5 | (0.4) | a | a |
| Korea | 65.6 | (2.8) | 66.4 | (0.5) | -0.8 | (2.8) | 16.0 | (3.4) | 16.5 | (0.4) | -0.4 | (3.4) | 18.4 | (1.5) | 17.2 | (0.2) | 1.2 | (1.5) |
| Luxembourg | 64.5 | (0.4) | 72.3 | (0.6) | **-7.8** | (0.7) | 11.1 | (0.3) | 4.8 | (0.3) | **6.3** | (0.4) | 24.4 | (0.4) | 22.9 | (0.5) | **1.5** | (0.6) |
| Mexico | 51.6 | (0.8) | 57.7 | (0.4) | **-6.0** | (0.9) | 17.0 | (0.7) | 12.7 | (0.3) | **4.3** | (0.8) | 31.3 | (0.6) | 29.6 | (0.3) | **1.7** | (0.7) |
| Netherlands | 61.7 | (0.5) | 66.6 | (0.7) | **-5.0** | (0.9) | 12.8 | (0.4) | 5.6 | (0.3) | **7.2** | (0.5) | 25.6 | (0.3) | 27.7 | (0.7) | **-2.2** | (0.8) |
| New Zealand | 65.6 | (1.5) | 70.5 | (0.4) | **-4.9** | (1.5) | 11.5 | (1.0) | 7.7 | (0.3) | **3.8** | (1.0) | 22.9 | (1.2) | 21.8 | (0.3) | 1.1 | (1.2) |
| Norway | 62.1 | (0.5) | c | c | c | c | 16.5 | (0.3) | c | c | c | c | 21.4 | (0.3) | c | c | c | c |
| Poland | 63.5 | (0.3) | 68.4 | (1.9) | -4.9 | (1.9) | 8.5 | (0.3) | 3.0 | (0.7) | **5.5** | (0.8) | 27.9 | (0.3) | 28.6 | (1.8) | -0.6 | (1.9) |
| Portugal | 56.4 | (0.6) | 65.5 | (0.4) | **-9.1** | (0.7) | 13.1 | (0.5) | 4.5 | (0.2) | **8.6** | (0.5) | 30.5 | (0.6) | 30.0 | (0.3) | 0.5 | (0.6) |
| Slovak Republic | 63.4 | (0.7) | 56.3 | (0.7) | **7.1** | (1.0) | 12.9 | (0.5) | 12.6 | (0.4) | 0.4 | (0.6) | 23.7 | (0.5) | 31.1 | (0.6) | **-7.5** | (0.8) |
| Spain | 62.6 | (0.3) | c | c | c | c | 8.1 | (0.3) | c | c | c | c | 29.2 | (0.3) | c | c | c | c |
| Sweden | 66.8 | (0.5) | 63.9 | (2.2) | 2.9 | (2.2) | 10.2 | (0.2) | 11.9 | (1.5) | -1.7 | (1.5) | 23.0 | (0.4) | 24.3 | (1.5) | -1.3 | (1.6) |
| Switzerland | 67.1 | (0.4) | 69.7 | (0.8) | **-2.6** | (0.8) | 7.7 | (0.3) | 4.2 | (0.6) | **3.4** | (0.6) | 25.3 | (0.3) | 26.1 | (0.6) | -0.8 | (0.7) |
| Turkey | 51.3 | (2.3) | 54.9 | (0.6) | -3.7 | (2.3) | 21.2 | (2.1) | 19.7 | (0.4) | 1.5 | (2.1) | 27.6 | (2.2) | 25.4 | (0.3) | 2.2 | (2.3) |
| United Kingdom | 66.3 | (5.1) | 67.6 | (0.3) | -1.2 | (5.1) | 13.6 | (2.8) | 7.8 | (0.2) | **5.8** | (2.9) | 20.1 | (3.4) | 24.6 | (0.3) | **-4.6** | (3.4) |
| United States | 48.1 | (1.8) | 56.9 | (0.6) | **-8.8** | (1.8) | 24.0 | (1.7) | 14.9 | (0.3) | **9.0** | (1.8) | 28.0 | (0.8) | 28.2 | (0.4) | -0.2 | (0.8) |
| **OECD average** | 61.3 | (0.3) | 64.0 | (0.2) | **-3.1** | (0.4) | 13.2 | (0.2) | 9.8 | (0.2) | **3.8** | (0.3) | 25.5 | (0.2) | 26.1 | (0.2) | **-0.8** | (0.3) |
| **Partners** | | | | | | | | | | | | | | | | | | |
| Argentina | 49.0 | (1.0) | 57.6 | (0.7) | **-8.7** | (1.3) | 13.2 | (0.8) | 6.0 | (0.5) | **7.2** | (0.9) | 37.8 | (1.1) | 36.4 | (0.6) | 1.5 | (1.3) |
| Azerbaijan | 45.6 | (0.7) | 43.8 | (0.8) | 1.8 | (1.0) | 18.5 | (0.6) | 20.4 | (0.6) | **-1.8** | (0.7) | 35.8 | (0.6) | 35.9 | (0.7) | -0.0 | (0.8) |
| Brazil | 50.8 | (0.7) | 56.1 | (0.6) | **-5.3** | (1.0) | 19.6 | (0.6) | 16.9 | (0.4) | **2.7** | (0.7) | 29.7 | (0.6) | 27.0 | (0.4) | **2.6** | (0.8) |
| Bulgaria | 53.1 | (3.1) | 51.7 | (0.5) | 1.3 | (3.2) | 17.6 | (1.7) | 15.3 | (0.5) | 2.3 | (1.9) | 29.3 | (2.4) | 33.0 | (0.4) | -3.7 | (2.4) |
| Chile | 45.1 | (2.6) | 57.8 | (0.7) | **-12.7** | (2.8) | 22.9 | (2.5) | 14.9 | (0.5) | **8.0** | (2.6) | 31.9 | (2.2) | 27.2 | (0.4) | **4.7** | (2.3) |
| Colombia | 57.0 | (0.9) | 62.3 | (0.7) | **-5.4** | (1.1) | 16.6 | (0.6) | 13.1 | (0.4) | **3.6** | (0.6) | 26.4 | (0.5) | 24.6 | (0.5) | **1.8** | (0.6) |
| Croatia | c | c | 66.8 | (0.4) | c | c | c | c | 5.8 | (0.2) | c | c | c | c | 27.4 | (0.4) | c | c |
| Estonia | 61.7 | (0.5) | 65.1 | (1.9) | -3.4 | (2.1) | 13.1 | (0.4) | 10.5 | (1.7) | **2.6** | (1.8) | 25.2 | (0.3) | 24.4 | (1.5) | 0.8 | (1.5) |
| Hong Kong-China | 69.1 | (0.7) | 72.0 | (0.4) | **-2.9** | (0.7) | 9.6 | (0.4) | 8.8 | (0.3) | **0.8** | (0.5) | 21.3 | (0.5) | 19.2 | (0.3) | **2.1** | (0.5) |
| Indonesia | 53.9 | (0.6) | 58.7 | (1.0) | **-4.8** | (1.1) | 19.7 | (0.6) | 13.4 | (0.5) | **6.3** | (0.5) | 26.3 | (0.5) | 27.9 | (0.7) | -1.5 | (0.9) |
| Israel | 53.2 | (1.7) | 54.2 | (0.6) | -0.9 | (1.8) | 20.0 | (1.0) | 19.8 | (0.4) | 0.2 | (1.1) | 26.8 | (1.2) | 26.0 | (0.5) | 0.8 | (1.2) |
| Jordan | 44.2 | (0.6) | a | a | a | a | 22.2 | (0.5) | a | a | a | a | 33.6 | (0.4) | a | a | a | a |
| Kyrgyzstan | 39.7 | (0.6) | 40.4 | (0.9) | -0.8 | (1.1) | 26.5 | (0.5) | 24.9 | (0.9) | 1.7 | (0.9) | 33.8 | (0.5) | 34.7 | (0.6) | -0.9 | (0.8) |
| Latvia | 59.2 | (0.4) | 61.5 | (1.7) | -2.4 | (1.9) | 11.5 | (0.4) | 9.8 | (1.5) | 1.6 | (1.5) | 29.4 | (0.4) | 28.6 | (1.8) | 0.7 | (1.9) |
| Liechtenstein | 69.3 | (1.2) | 73.6 | (4.1) | -4.3 | (4.1) | 6.0 | (0.7) | 2.3 | (1.2) | **3.7** | (1.4) | 24.7 | (0.9) | 24.1 | (3.3) | 0.6 | (3.3) |
| Lithuania | 62.3 | (0.4) | c | c | c | c | 9.9 | (0.3) | c | c | c | c | 27.8 | (0.3) | c | c | c | c |
| Macao-China | 70.0 | (0.5) | 73.7 | (0.5) | **-3.7** | (0.7) | 12.8 | (0.3) | 8.4 | (0.3) | **4.4** | (0.5) | 17.2 | (0.3) | 17.9 | (0.4) | -0.8 | (0.5) |
| Montenegro | c | c | 53.0 | (0.4) | c | c | c | c | 11.4 | (0.3) | c | c | c | c | 35.6 | (0.4) | c | c |
| Qatar | 39.2 | (0.7) | 46.2 | (0.4) | **-7.0** | (0.8) | 27.3 | (0.6) | 22.6 | (0.3) | **4.7** | (0.6) | 33.5 | (0.6) | 31.2 | (0.3) | **2.3** | (0.7) |
| Romania | 50.6 | (0.6) | a | a | a | a | 19.7 | (0.4) | a | a | a | a | 29.6 | (0.3) | a | a | a | a |
| Russian Federation | 48.6 | (0.9) | 48.0 | (0.7) | 0.6 | (1.0) | 17.9 | (1.0) | 15.5 | (0.5) | **2.5** | (1.0) | 33.5 | (0.6) | 36.5 | (0.6) | **-3.0** | (0.7) |
| Serbia | 58.0 | (3.6) | 60.2 | (0.5) | -2.2 | (3.6) | 18.7 | (2.4) | 12.8 | (0.4) | **5.9** | (2.4) | 23.2 | (2.8) | 27.0 | (0.3) | -3.8 | (2.9) |
| Slovenia | 51.6 | (3.3) | 61.2 | (0.4) | **-9.6** | (3.4) | 19.3 | (2.5) | 11.8 | (0.2) | **7.5** | (2.5) | 29.1 | (3.2) | 27.0 | (0.3) | 2.1 | (3.3) |
| Chinese Taipei | 63.2 | (0.5) | 67.5 | (0.4) | **-4.4** | (0.7) | 11.6 | (0.5) | 7.6 | (0.3) | **4.1** | (0.5) | 25.2 | (0.3) | 24.9 | (0.3) | 0.3 | (0.4) |
| Thailand | 62.2 | (0.7) | 62.7 | (0.4) | -0.5 | (0.7) | 10.3 | (0.6) | 6.0 | (0.2) | **4.3** | (0.6) | 27.5 | (0.5) | 31.3 | (0.3) | **-3.8** | (0.6) |
| Tunisia | 38.6 | (0.9) | 52.1 | (0.8) | **-13.5** | (1.2) | 28.5 | (0.6) | 19.1 | (0.6) | **9.5** | (0.8) | 32.9 | (0.6) | 28.8 | (0.7) | **4.0** | (0.9) |
| Uruguay | 55.6 | (1.0) | 63.3 | (0.4) | **-7.8** | (1.1) | 15.8 | (0.9) | 9.2 | (0.3) | **6.6** | (0.9) | 28.7 | (0.6) | 27.5 | (0.4) | 1.1 | (0.7) |

*Note*: Values that are statistically significant at the 5% level (p < 0.05) are indicated in bold.

**Table 3.10d** Mean learning hours and allocation of total learning time in science, in mathematics and on language of instruction, by lower and upper secondary schools
[Part 1/3]

| | | Mean learning hours per week | | | | | | | | | | |
|---|---|---|---|---|---|---|---|---|---|---|---|---|
| | | Regular school lessons | | | | | | Out-of-school-time lessons | | | | | |
| | | Lower secondary school | | Upper secondary school | | Difference (lower-upper) | | Lower secondary school | | Upper secondary school | | Difference (lower-upper) | |
| | | Mean | S.E. | Mean | S.E. | Dif. | S.E. | Mean | S.E. | Mean | S.E. | Dif. | S.E. |
| OECD | Australia | 11.59 | (0.08) | 10.66 | (0.13) | **0.93** | (0.15) | 1.73 | (0.04) | 1.87 | (0.07) | -0.14 | (0.07) |
| | Austria | 9.08 | (0.30) | 8.53 | (0.10) | 0.56 | (0.31) | 1.97 | (0.29) | 0.88 | (0.04) | **1.09** | (0.29) |
| | Belgium | 9.26 | (0.46) | 9.72 | (0.10) | -0.46 | (0.48) | 2.53 | (0.21) | 1.27 | (0.03) | **1.26** | (0.21) |
| | Canada | 10.93 | (0.17) | 13.28 | (0.13) | **-2.35** | (0.22) | 2.63 | (0.08) | 2.30 | (0.05) | **0.33** | (0.09) |
| | Czech Republic | 11.24 | (0.10) | 10.09 | (0.17) | **1.15** | (0.20) | 1.98 | (0.05) | 1.80 | (0.07) | **0.18** | (0.08) |
| | Denmark | 13.16 | (0.08) | 12.82 | (0.71) | 0.34 | (0.73) | 3.83 | (0.07) | 3.72 | (0.60) | 0.11 | (0.61) |
| | Finland | 9.71 | (0.11) | c | c | c | c | 1.06 | (0.04) | c | c | c | c |
| | France | 9.24 | (0.11) | 11.66 | (0.14) | **-2.41** | (0.18) | 2.67 | (0.07) | 1.97 | (0.06) | **0.70** | (0.09) |
| | Germany | 10.70 | (0.08) | 7.45 | (0.66) | **3.25** | (0.68) | 1.93 | (0.06) | 1.62 | (0.54) | 0.31 | (0.55) |
| | Greece | 8.17 | (0.45) | 9.96 | (0.12) | **-1.78** | (0.46) | 3.93 | (0.30) | 6.00 | (0.11) | **-2.08** | (0.31) |
| | Hungary | 7.16 | (0.32) | 9.14 | (0.11) | **-1.98** | (0.34) | 4.30 | (0.30) | 3.54 | (0.07) | **0.77** | (0.31) |
| | Iceland | 12.24 | (0.06) | c | c | c | c | 1.47 | (0.04) | c | c | c | c |
| | Ireland | 10.06 | (0.10) | 9.26 | (0.14) | **0.80** | (0.16) | 1.95 | (0.06) | 1.18 | (0.06) | **0.77** | (0.07) |
| | Italy | 8.77 | (0.49) | 11.31 | (0.09) | **-2.55** | (0.49) | 3.14 | (0.48) | 2.23 | (0.04) | 0.91 | (0.49) |
| | Japan | c | c | 10.75 | (0.13) | c | c | c | c | 1.40 | (0.05) | c | c |
| | Korea | 11.20 | (0.22) | 12.79 | (0.12) | **-1.59** | (0.25) | 4.38 | (0.56) | 4.75 | (0.08) | -0.37 | (0.56) |
| | Luxembourg | 9.33 | (0.08) | 10.38 | (0.10) | **-1.04** | (0.12) | 2.31 | (0.06) | 1.25 | (0.05) | **1.07** | (0.08) |
| | Mexico | 10.45 | (0.19) | 11.13 | (0.10) | **-0.68** | (0.22) | 3.76 | (0.17) | 2.91 | (0.06) | **0.85** | (0.18) |
| | Netherlands | 7.69 | (0.09) | 8.70 | (0.11) | **-1.01** | (0.14) | 2.12 | (0.06) | 1.25 | (0.06) | **0.87** | (0.09) |
| | New Zealand | 11.09 | (0.28) | 12.95 | (0.09) | **-1.86** | (0.29) | 2.30 | (0.21) | 1.71 | (0.06) | **0.59** | (0.22) |
| | Norway | 9.62 | (0.08) | c | c | c | c | 3.14 | (0.05) | c | c | c | c |
| | Poland | 11.71 | (0.09) | 13.42 | (0.39) | **-1.71** | (0.39) | 2.11 | (0.05) | 1.32 | (0.19) | **0.79** | (0.19) |
| | Portugal | 8.52 | (0.10) | 11.64 | (0.12) | **-3.12** | (0.14) | 2.28 | (0.07) | 1.71 | (0.06) | **0.56** | (0.08) |
| | Slovak Republic | 10.67 | (0.21) | 7.80 | (0.14) | **2.87** | (0.26) | 2.69 | (0.08) | 2.23 | (0.09) | **0.46** | (0.11) |
| | Spain | 10.15 | (0.09) | 11.45 | (2.07) | -1.31 | (2.07) | 2.24 | (0.05) | c | c | c | c |
| | Sweden | 9.02 | (0.07) | 8.68 | (0.59) | 0.34 | (0.58) | 1.79 | (0.04) | 1.81 | (0.17) | -0.02 | (0.18) |
| | Switzerland | 9.93 | (0.07) | 9.63 | (0.36) | 0.30 | (0.36) | 1.70 | (0.05) | 0.95 | (0.09) | **0.75** | (0.10) |
| | Turkey | 10.68 | (0.54) | 10.67 | (0.17) | 0.02 | (0.56) | 5.43 | (0.60) | 5.21 | (0.09) | 0.22 | (0.61) |
| | United Kingdom | 10.19 | (0.66) | 11.93 | (0.09) | -1.75 | (0.67) | 2.06 | (0.35) | 1.70 | (0.05) | 0.36 | (0.36) |
| | United States | 8.41 | (0.33) | 11.28 | (0.11) | **-2.88** | (0.33) | 3.86 | (0.23) | 2.93 | (0.07) | **0.93** | (0.25) |
| | **OECD average** | 10.00 | (0.05) | 10.63 | (0.09) | **-0.69** | (0.11) | 2.66 | (0.04) | 2.29 | (0.03) | **0.45** | (0.06) |
| Partners | Argentina | 6.37 | (0.14) | 8.12 | (0.20) | **-1.75** | (0.23) | 2.14 | (0.11) | 1.47 | (0.08) | **0.66** | (0.13) |
| | Azerbaijan | 10.67 | (0.13) | 9.95 | (0.17) | **0.72** | (0.19) | 4.60 | (0.13) | 5.25 | (0.13) | **-0.65** | (0.18) |
| | Brazil | 7.55 | (0.17) | 8.89 | (0.10) | **-1.34** | (0.21) | 3.15 | (0.09) | 3.15 | (0.09) | 0.00 | (0.12) |
| | Bulgaria | 7.34 | (0.61) | 8.64 | (0.17) | **-1.30** | (0.62) | 3.13 | (0.27) | 3.21 | (0.09) | -0.08 | (0.29) |
| | Chile | 5.78 | (0.44) | 9.41 | (0.17) | **-3.64** | (0.46) | 3.45 | (0.41) | 2.78 | (0.05) | 0.67 | (0.40) |
| | Colombia | 10.87 | (0.19) | 12.17 | (0.25) | **-1.30** | (0.28) | 3.34 | (0.10) | 3.29 | (0.10) | 0.05 | (0.14) |
| | Croatia | c | c | 8.44 | (0.08) | c | c | c | c | 1.57 | (0.05) | c | c |
| | Estonia | 10.92 | (0.10) | 12.48 | (0.36) | **-1.56** | (0.38) | 2.63 | (0.07) | 2.33 | (0.32) | 0.31 | (0.33) |
| | Hong Kong-China | 12.92 | (0.20) | 13.94 | (0.12) | **-1.03** | (0.22) | 2.68 | (0.13) | 3.32 | (0.09) | **-0.64** | (0.15) |
| | Indonesia | 10.82 | (0.21) | 11.15 | (0.24) | -0.33 | (0.30) | 4.12 | (0.11) | 3.17 | (0.18) | **0.95** | (0.23) |
| | Israel | 9.41 | (0.25) | 9.60 | (0.11) | -0.19 | (0.26) | 4.40 | (0.19) | 4.45 | (0.09) | -0.04 | (0.20) |
| | Jordan | 10.36 | (0.14) | a | a | a | a | 5.10 | (0.10) | a | a | a | a |
| | Kyrgyzstan | 7.69 | (0.14) | 8.11 | (0.31) | -0.42 | (0.27) | 4.57 | (0.09) | 4.68 | (0.13) | -0.11 | (0.14) |
| | Latvia | 11.05 | (0.11) | 11.27 | (0.36) | -0.22 | (0.36) | 2.74 | (0.08) | 2.04 | (0.16) | **0.70** | (0.18) |
| | Liechtenstein | 10.20 | (0.20) | 10.50 | (0.49) | -0.30 | (0.51) | 1.47 | (0.11) | 0.59 | (0.17) | **0.88** | (0.19) |
| | Lithuania | 9.85 | (0.10) | c | c | c | c | 1.93 | (0.05) | c | c | c | c |
| | Macao-China | 13.86 | (0.09) | 15.47 | (0.12) | **-1.61** | (0.15) | 3.49 | (0.09) | 2.85 | (0.12) | **0.64** | (0.16) |
| | Montenegro | c | c | 8.90 | (0.09) | c | c | c | c | 2.69 | (0.05) | c | c |
| | Qatar | 7.39 | (0.15) | 9.05 | (0.09) | **-1.66** | (0.17) | 5.28 | (0.13) | 4.80 | (0.07) | **0.49** | (0.14) |
| | Romania | 8.58 | (0.15) | a | a | a | a | 4.04 | (0.07) | a | a | a | a |
| | Russian Federation | 9.25 | (0.22) | 9.51 | (0.13) | -0.26 | (0.22) | 3.31 | (0.11) | 2.93 | (0.09) | **0.38** | (0.14) |
| | Serbia | 9.69 | (0.93) | 9.32 | (0.11) | 0.37 | (0.92) | 2.88 | (0.35) | 2.66 | (0.06) | 0.22 | (0.35) |
| | Slovenia | 7.13 | (0.59) | 9.48 | (0.07) | **-2.35** | (0.60) | 3.46 | (0.53) | 2.43 | (0.04) | 1.03 | (0.53) |
| | Chinese Taipei | 12.53 | (0.19) | 11.02 | (0.19) | **1.51** | (0.26) | 4.08 | (0.12) | 2.47 | (0.07) | **1.61** | (0.15) |
| | Thailand | 10.73 | (0.13) | 10.66 | (0.09) | 0.07 | (0.14) | 2.68 | (0.14) | 2.27 | (0.08) | **0.41** | (0.16) |
| | Tunisia | 7.68 | (0.14) | 10.53 | (0.15) | **-2.84** | (0.20) | 5.96 | (0.08) | 6.23 | (0.10) | -0.26 | (0.14) |
| | Uruguay | 7.51 | (0.18) | 8.94 | (0.10) | **-1.43** | (0.21) | 2.37 | (0.11) | 1.94 | (0.05) | **0.44** | (0.11) |

*Note*: Values that are statistically significant at the 5% level (p < 0.05) are indicated in bold.

© OECD 2011 Quality Time for Students: Learning In and Out of School

**Table 3.10d** Mean learning hours and allocation of total learning time in science, in mathematics
[Part 2/3] and on language of instruction, by lower and upper secondary schools

| | | Mean learning hours per week | | | | | | | | | | |
|---|---|---|---|---|---|---|---|---|---|---|---|---|
| | | Individual study | | | | | | Total learning hours | | | | |
| | | Lower secondary school | | Upper secondary school | | Difference (lower-upper) | | Lower secondary school | | Upper secondary school | | Difference (lower-upper) |
| | | Mean | S.E. | Mean | S.E. | Dif. | S.E. | Mean | S.E. | Mean | S.E. | Dif. | S.E. |
| **OECD** | Australia | 4.54 | (0.06) | 5.19 | (0.09) | **-0.65** | (0.11) | 17.88 | (0.13) | 17.72 | (0.22) | 0.16 | (0.24) |
| | Austria | 6.74 | (0.39) | 4.83 | (0.07) | **1.90** | (0.39) | 17.95 | (0.57) | 14.27 | (0.16) | **3.68** | (0.58) |
| | Belgium | 4.39 | (0.23) | 4.39 | (0.05) | 0.01 | (0.22) | 16.41 | (0.62) | 15.39 | (0.14) | 1.02 | (0.60) |
| | Canada | 4.26 | (0.12) | 5.44 | (0.08) | **-1.18** | (0.13) | 17.99 | (0.31) | 21.08 | (0.19) | **-3.09** | (0.36) |
| | Czech Republic | 3.56 | (0.08) | 3.38 | (0.07) | 0.18 | (0.10) | 16.77 | (0.15) | 15.25 | (0.24) | **1.52** | (0.27) |
| | Denmark | 4.98 | (0.06) | 6.41 | (0.86) | -1.44 | (0.86) | 21.93 | (0.15) | 22.96 | (1.92) | -1.03 | (1.94) |
| | Finland | 3.40 | (0.05) | c | c | c | c | 14.16 | (0.16) | c | c | c | c |
| | France | 3.82 | (0.07) | 5.04 | (0.10) | **-1.22** | (0.12) | 15.74 | (0.20) | 18.69 | (0.21) | **-2.94** | (0.29) |
| | Germany | 5.90 | (0.08) | 4.88 | (0.52) | 1.02 | (0.53) | 18.57 | (0.14) | 14.06 | (1.34) | **4.51** | (1.36) |
| | Greece | 5.04 | (0.29) | 5.85 | (0.09) | **-0.81** | (0.30) | 17.13 | (0.83) | 21.84 | (0.24) | **-4.70** | (0.85) |
| | Hungary | 5.19 | (0.33) | 5.30 | (0.08) | -0.11 | (0.35) | 16.48 | (0.74) | 18.00 | (0.20) | -1.52 | (0.77) |
| | Iceland | 4.42 | (0.05) | c | c | c | c | 18.14 | (0.09) | c | c | c | c |
| | Ireland | 5.13 | (0.09) | 4.03 | (0.11) | **1.11** | (0.13) | 17.08 | (0.19) | 14.47 | (0.24) | **2.61** | (0.28) |
| | Italy | 5.83 | (0.67) | 7.56 | (0.08) | **-1.73** | (0.69) | 18.31 | (1.39) | 21.11 | (0.17) | -2.80 | (1.42) |
| | Japan | c | c | 3.11 | (0.10) | c | c | c | c | 15.26 | (0.22) | c | c |
| | Korea | 4.40 | (0.32) | 4.94 | (0.12) | -0.55 | (0.34) | 19.87 | (0.57) | 22.54 | (0.25) | -2.67 | (0.62) |
| | Luxembourg | 4.46 | (0.06) | 4.08 | (0.07) | **0.39** | (0.10) | 16.14 | (0.12) | 15.69 | (0.14) | **0.45** | (0.19) |
| | Mexico | 6.52 | (0.16) | 6.34 | (0.07) | 0.18 | (0.16) | 20.54 | (0.39) | 20.31 | (0.16) | 0.24 | (0.42) |
| | Netherlands | 3.83 | (0.07) | 4.43 | (0.09) | **-0.60** | (0.11) | 13.59 | (0.15) | 14.40 | (0.18) | **-0.81** | (0.23) |
| | New Zealand | 4.22 | (0.21) | 4.44 | (0.07) | -0.21 | (0.22) | 17.49 | (0.46) | 19.12 | (0.14) | -1.64 | (0.47) |
| | Norway | 4.06 | (0.06) | c | c | c | c | 16.79 | (0.12) | c | c | c | c |
| | Poland | 6.33 | (0.07) | 7.30 | (0.50) | -0.97 | (0.50) | 20.18 | (0.14) | 22.06 | (0.92) | -1.88 | (0.92) |
| | Portugal | 5.47 | (0.12) | 6.20 | (0.10) | **-0.73** | (0.15) | 16.33 | (0.20) | 19.51 | (0.21) | **-3.18** | (0.27) |
| | Slovak Republic | 5.02 | (0.12) | 4.68 | (0.12) | 0.33 | (0.17) | 18.43 | (0.31) | 14.74 | (0.28) | **3.69** | (0.43) |
| | Spain | 5.58 | (0.08) | c | c | c | c | 18.08 | (0.16) | c | c | c | c |
| | Sweden | 3.58 | (0.05) | 3.78 | (0.45) | -0.20 | (0.45) | 14.37 | (0.12) | 14.38 | (1.04) | -0.01 | (1.03) |
| | Switzerland | 4.26 | (0.04) | 3.93 | (0.11) | **0.32** | (0.11) | 15.92 | (0.11) | 14.46 | (0.45) | **1.45** | (0.47) |
| | Turkey | 6.35 | (0.40) | 6.10 | (0.09) | 0.25 | (0.42) | 22.06 | (1.15) | 21.88 | (0.30) | 0.19 | (1.21) |
| | United Kingdom | 3.16 | (0.67) | 4.53 | (0.06) | **-1.37** | (0.67) | 15.62 | (0.80) | 18.17 | (0.14) | **-2.56** | (0.81) |
| | United States | 4.92 | (0.22) | 5.68 | (0.07) | **-0.76** | (0.23) | 17.50 | (0.46) | 19.97 | (0.15) | **-2.47** | (0.46) |
| | **OECD average** | 4.81 | (0.05) | 5.07 | (0.05) | **-0.27** | (0.07) | 17.50 | (0.09) | 17.97 | (0.11) | **-0.47** | (0.16) |
| **Partners** | Argentina | 4.75 | (0.19) | 5.15 | (0.12) | -0.41 | (0.22) | 13.30 | (0.34) | 14.71 | (0.27) | **-1.41** | (0.41) |
| | Azerbaijan | 8.68 | (0.17) | 8.75 | (0.19) | -0.07 | (0.23) | 24.13 | (0.35) | 24.06 | (0.37) | 0.07 | (0.48) |
| | Brazil | 5.15 | (0.12) | 5.23 | (0.09) | -0.08 | (0.16) | 15.74 | (0.29) | 17.24 | (0.20) | **-1.49** | (0.37) |
| | Bulgaria | 5.10 | (0.46) | 6.22 | (0.16) | **-1.12** | (0.46) | 15.17 | (1.01) | 18.16 | (0.34) | **-2.99** | (1.03) |
| | Chile | 4.31 | (0.45) | 4.70 | (0.08) | -0.39 | (0.45) | 13.68 | (1.36) | 16.98 | (0.22) | **-3.30** | (1.33) |
| | Colombia | 5.38 | (0.11) | 5.71 | (0.12) | **-0.32** | (0.15) | 19.61 | (0.23) | 21.13 | (0.36) | **-1.52** | (0.38) |
| | Croatia | c | c | 4.85 | (0.07) | c | c | c | c | 14.93 | (0.15) | c | c |
| | Estonia | 5.10 | (0.06) | 5.82 | (0.41) | -0.72 | (0.40) | 18.67 | (0.14) | 20.69 | (0.75) | **-2.01** | (0.75) |
| | Hong Kong-China | 5.02 | (0.16) | 5.51 | (0.09) | **-0.49** | (0.18) | 20.61 | (0.38) | 22.76 | (0.21) | **-2.15** | (0.42) |
| | Indonesia | 5.81 | (0.12) | 5.33 | (0.15) | 0.48 | (0.22) | 20.69 | (0.34) | 19.60 | (0.41) | 1.09 | (0.55) |
| | Israel | 5.19 | (0.20) | 5.36 | (0.12) | -0.16 | (0.23) | 19.08 | (0.52) | 19.49 | (0.26) | -0.41 | (0.55) |
| | Jordan | 7.90 | (0.11) | a | a | a | a | 23.35 | (0.22) | a | a | a | a |
| | Kyrgyzstan | 6.53 | (0.10) | 7.20 | (0.19) | **-0.67** | (0.20) | 19.01 | (0.24) | 19.93 | (0.48) | **-0.93** | (0.46) |
| | Latvia | 6.28 | (0.08) | 5.40 | (0.33) | **0.87** | (0.34) | 20.08 | (0.19) | 18.60 | (0.65) | **1.48** | (0.67) |
| | Liechtenstein | 3.92 | (0.16) | 3.98 | (0.50) | -0.06 | (0.55) | 15.57 | (0.28) | 15.07 | (0.71) | 0.50 | (0.84) |
| | Lithuania | 5.27 | (0.07) | c | c | c | c | 17.04 | (0.14) | c | c | c | c |
| | Macao-China | 4.49 | (0.08) | 5.67 | (0.11) | **-1.18** | (0.13) | 21.84 | (0.18) | 23.98 | (0.26) | **-2.14** | (0.32) |
| | Montenegro | c | c | 6.21 | (0.08) | c | c | c | c | 17.75 | (0.16) | c | c |
| | Qatar | 6.26 | (0.12) | 6.28 | (0.06) | -0.02 | (0.14) | 18.92 | (0.30) | 20.16 | (0.17) | **-1.24** | (0.32) |
| | Romania | 5.96 | (0.10) | a | a | a | a | 18.57 | (0.26) | a | a | a | a |
| | Russian Federation | 6.67 | (0.20) | 6.64 | (0.12) | 0.04 | (0.20) | 19.23 | (0.40) | 19.08 | (0.26) | 0.15 | (0.45) |
| | Serbia | 4.71 | (0.60) | 5.23 | (0.08) | -0.52 | (0.61) | 17.53 | (1.66) | 17.18 | (0.18) | 0.35 | (1.65) |
| | Slovenia | 4.59 | (0.27) | 4.95 | (0.05) | -0.36 | (0.28) | 15.03 | (1.17) | 16.91 | (0.12) | -1.87 | (1.18) |
| | Chinese Taipei | 5.18 | (0.13) | 4.73 | (0.11) | **0.45** | (0.17) | 21.99 | (0.37) | 18.33 | (0.34) | **3.65** | (0.49) |
| | Thailand | 5.58 | (0.17) | 5.19 | (0.08) | **0.39** | (0.19) | 18.93 | (0.29) | 18.11 | (0.19) | **0.82** | (0.34) |
| | Tunisia | 7.02 | (0.12) | 7.53 | (0.12) | **-0.51** | (0.17) | 20.69 | (0.25) | 24.29 | (0.31) | **-3.61** | (0.40) |
| | Uruguay | 3.85 | (0.10) | 4.42 | (0.07) | **-0.57** | (0.12) | 13.86 | (0.24) | 15.28 | (0.18) | **-1.42** | (0.28) |

*Note:* Values that are statistically significant at the 5% level (p < 0.05) are indicated in bold.

### Table 3.10d [Part 3/3] Mean learning hours and allocation of total learning time in science, in mathematics and on language of instruction, by lower and upper secondary schools

| | Allocation of total learning time in science, in mathematics and on the language of instruction for | | | | | | | | | | | | | | | | | |
|---|---|---|---|---|---|---|---|---|---|---|---|---|---|---|---|---|---|---|
| | Regular school lessons | | | | | | Out-of-school-time lessons | | | | | | Individual study | | | | | |
| | Lower secondary school | | Upper secondary school | | Difference (lower-upper) | | Lower secondary school | | Upper secondary school | | Difference (lower-upper) | | Lower secondary school | | Upper secondary school | | Difference (lower-upper) | |
| | % | S.E | % | S.E | Dif. | S.E. | % | S.E | % | S.E | Dif. | S.E. | % | S.E | % | S.E | Dif. | S.E. |
| **OECD** Australia | 67.4 | (0.3) | 63.3 | (0.4) | **4.1** | (0.5) | 8.4 | (0.2) | 9.6 | (0.3) | **-1.1** | (0.4) | 24.2 | (0.2) | 27.1 | (0.3) | **-3.0** | (0.4) |
| Austria | 53.6 | (2.1) | 62.4 | (0.4) | **-8.9** | (2.2) | 10.1 | (1.3) | 5.1 | (0.2) | **5.1** | (1.3) | 36.3 | (1.6) | 32.5 | (0.3) | **3.8** | (1.6) |
| Belgium | 59.0 | (1.8) | 64.5 | (0.3) | **-5.5** | (1.8) | 14.6 | (1.3) | 7.5 | (0.2) | **7.1** | (1.4) | 26.4 | (0.8) | 28.0 | (0.2) | -1.6 | (0.8) |
| Canada | 62.3 | (0.6) | 64.3 | (0.3) | **-2.0** | (0.6) | 13.7 | (0.4) | 10.5 | (0.2) | **3.2** | (0.4) | 24.0 | (0.4) | 25.2 | (0.2) | **-1.2** | (0.4) |
| Czech Republic | 69.5 | (0.5) | 69.6 | (0.6) | -0.1 | (0.8) | 10.4 | (0.3) | 10.0 | (0.3) | 0.4 | (0.4) | 20.1 | (0.4) | 20.4 | (0.5) | -0.3 | (0.5) |
| Denmark | 62.3 | (0.3) | 57.7 | (2.4) | 4.7 | (2.4) | 15.9 | (0.2) | 15.5 | (2.0) | 0.5 | (2.0) | 21.7 | (0.2) | 26.8 | (2.0) | **-5.1** | (2.0) |
| Finland | 70.5 | (0.3) | c | c | c | c | 6.4 | (0.2) | c | c | c | c | 23.1 | (0.2) | c | c | c | c |
| France | 61.5 | (0.5) | 64.6 | (0.4) | **-3.1** | (0.6) | 15.6 | (0.3) | 9.8 | (0.3) | **5.8** | (0.5) | 22.9 | (0.3) | 25.6 | (0.3) | **-2.6** | (0.4) |
| Germany | 59.6 | (0.3) | 56.2 | (1.9) | 3.4 | (2.0) | 9.3 | (0.3) | 10.5 | (2.5) | -1.2 | (2.5) | 31.1 | (0.2) | 33.4 | (1.2) | -2.2 | (1.3) |
| Greece | 51.1 | (1.9) | 47.8 | (0.5) | 3.3 | (2.0) | 20.7 | (1.3) | 26.1 | (0.3) | **-5.4** | (1.3) | 28.2 | (1.1) | 26.1 | (0.3) | 2.1 | (1.2) |
| Hungary | 44.3 | (2.2) | 53.0 | (0.4) | **-8.7** | (2.3) | 25.1 | (1.5) | 18.3 | (0.5) | **6.8** | (1.5) | 30.6 | (1.1) | 28.8 | (0.2) | 1.9 | (1.1) |
| Iceland | 69.7 | (0.3) | c | c | c | c | 7.2 | (0.2) | c | c | c | c | 23.0 | (0.2) | c | c | c | c |
| Ireland | 61.0 | (0.4) | 67.4 | (0.6) | **-6.4** | (0.6) | 9.9 | (0.3) | 6.7 | (0.3) | **3.2** | (0.3) | 29.1 | (0.3) | 25.9 | (0.5) | **3.2** | (0.5) |
| Italy | 51.9 | (2.3) | 55.0 | (0.2) | -3.1 | (2.3) | 17.2 | (1.6) | 9.8 | (0.2) | **7.4** | (1.6) | 30.9 | (2.0) | 35.2 | (0.2) | **-4.3** | (2.0) |
| Japan | c | c | 74.5 | (0.5) | c | c | c | c | 7.5 | (0.3) | c | c | c | c | 18.0 | (0.4) | c | c |
| Korea | 61.0 | (2.4) | 61.4 | (0.4) | -0.4 | (2.5) | 18.5 | (2.3) | 18.4 | (0.3) | 0.1 | (2.4) | 20.5 | (0.8) | 20.3 | (0.3) | 0.3 | (0.9) |
| Luxembourg | 60.8 | (0.4) | 67.5 | (0.4) | **-6.8** | (0.6) | 12.7 | (0.3) | 7.3 | (0.3) | **5.4** | (0.4) | 26.6 | (0.3) | 25.2 | (0.3) | **1.4** | (0.5) |
| Mexico | 50.5 | (0.6) | 56.1 | (0.4) | **-5.6** | (0.7) | 16.9 | (0.6) | 13.1 | (0.2) | **3.9** | (0.6) | 32.5 | (0.5) | 30.8 | (0.2) | **1.7** | (0.4) |
| Netherlands | 58.9 | (0.5) | 62.8 | (0.5) | **-3.9** | (0.8) | 14.0 | (0.4) | 7.8 | (0.3) | **6.1** | (0.5) | 27.2 | (0.3) | 29.4 | (0.5) | **-2.2** | (0.6) |
| New Zealand | 65.0 | (1.3) | 70.0 | (0.4) | **-5.0** | (1.3) | 11.6 | (0.8) | 8.0 | (0.3) | **3.6** | (0.9) | 23.4 | (0.9) | 22.0 | (0.2) | 1.4 | (0.9) |
| Norway | 60.4 | (0.4) | c | c | c | c | 17.0 | (0.3) | c | c | c | c | 22.6 | (0.3) | c | c | c | c |
| Poland | 59.9 | (0.3) | 63.2 | (1.8) | -3.3 | (1.8) | 10.1 | (0.3) | 5.1 | (0.7) | **5.0** | (0.7) | 30.0 | (0.3) | 31.8 | (1.5) | -1.7 | (1.5) |
| Portugal | 54.7 | (0.5) | 61.7 | (0.3) | **-7.0** | (0.6) | 13.1 | (0.4) | 7.4 | (0.3) | **5.7** | (0.5) | 32.2 | (0.5) | 30.8 | (0.3) | **1.3** | (0.5) |
| Slovak Republic | 61.6 | (0.6) | 57.4 | (0.5) | **4.2** | (0.8) | 13.1 | (0.3) | 12.5 | (0.4) | 0.6 | (0.5) | 25.3 | (0.4) | 30.1 | (0.4) | **-4.8** | (0.6) |
| Spain | 59.0 | (0.3) | c | c | c | c | 11.2 | (0.2) | c | c | c | c | 29.7 | (0.3) | c | c | c | c |
| Sweden | 66.2 | (0.5) | 63.0 | (1.6) | 3.2 | (1.6) | 10.3 | (0.2) | 11.7 | (1.3) | -1.4 | (1.3) | 23.5 | (0.4) | 25.3 | (1.2) | -1.8 | (1.3) |
| Switzerland | 63.8 | (0.3) | 66.3 | (0.8) | **-2.5** | (0.9) | 9.6 | (0.2) | 5.9 | (0.6) | **3.7** | (0.6) | 26.6 | (0.2) | 27.8 | (0.6) | **-1.2** | (0.6) |
| Turkey | 50.3 | (1.9) | 51.5 | (0.4) | 1.2 | (1.9) | 22.1 | (1.6) | 21.6 | (0.3) | 0.5 | (1.6) | 27.6 | (2.5) | 26.9 | (0.2) | 0.7 | (2.5) |
| United Kingdom | 68.3 | (4.5) | 67.8 | (0.3) | 0.5 | (4.5) | 12.1 | (2.3) | 8.2 | (0.2) | 3.9 | (2.4) | 19.6 | (3.2) | 24.0 | (0.2) | **-4.4** | (3.2) |
| United States | 48.0 | (1.8) | 56.6 | (0.4) | **-8.6** | (1.9) | 22.3 | (1.1) | 14.4 | (0.3) | **7.9** | (1.1) | 29.7 | (0.9) | 29.1 | (0.2) | 0.7 | (0.9) |
| **OECD average** | 59.7 | (0.3) | 61.7 | (0.2) | **-2.3** | (0.4) | 13.8 | (0.2) | 11.1 | (0.1) | **3.1** | (0.3) | 26.5 | (0.2) | 27.2 | (0.1) | **-0.7** | (0.3) |
| **Partners** Argentina | 49.7 | (0.9) | 56.3 | (0.7) | **-6.5** | (1.1) | 14.2 | (0.7) | 9.2 | (0.4) | **5.0** | (0.8) | 36.1 | (0.8) | 34.6 | (0.4) | 1.5 | (0.9) |
| Azerbaijan | 45.6 | (0.6) | 42.8 | (0.6) | **2.8** | (0.7) | 18.6 | (0.5) | 21.3 | (0.5) | **-2.7** | (0.6) | 35.8 | (0.4) | 35.9 | (0.5) | -0.1 | (0.6) |
| Brazil | 50.6 | (0.7) | 54.0 | (0.5) | **-3.4** | (0.9) | 18.5 | (0.4) | 16.5 | (0.4) | **2.0** | (0.6) | 30.9 | (0.5) | 29.4 | (0.4) | **1.4** | (0.7) |
| Bulgaria | 50.1 | (2.9) | 50.0 | (0.5) | 0.0 | (2.9) | 18.9 | (1.3) | 16.7 | (0.4) | 2.2 | (1.4) | 31.1 | (2.3) | 33.3 | (0.3) | -2.2 | (2.3) |
| Chile | 43.6 | (1.3) | 55.0 | (0.5) | **-11.4** | (1.5) | 24.4 | (1.5) | 16.0 | (0.3) | **8.4** | (1.6) | 32.0 | (1.7) | 29.0 | (0.3) | 3.0 | (1.7) |
| Colombia | 57.4 | (0.7) | 60.8 | (0.6) | **-3.4** | (0.8) | 15.9 | (0.5) | 13.6 | (0.3) | **2.3** | (0.6) | 26.6 | (0.5) | 25.6 | (0.4) | **1.0** | (0.5) |
| Croatia | c | c | 60.0 | (0.4) | c | c | c | c | 9.5 | (0.2) | c | c | c | c | 30.5 | (0.3) | c | c |
| Estonia | 60.8 | (0.4) | 63.3 | (1.7) | -2.5 | (1.8) | 13.3 | (0.3) | 10.1 | (1.2) | **3.2** | (1.3) | 25.9 | (0.2) | 26.6 | (1.4) | -0.7 | (1.4) |
| Hong Kong-China | 65.0 | (0.8) | 63.7 | (0.4) | 1.3 | (0.9) | 11.9 | (0.4) | 13.5 | (0.3) | **-1.6** | (0.4) | 23.1 | (0.5) | 22.8 | (0.3) | 0.3 | (0.6) |
| Indonesia | 53.1 | (0.6) | 59.1 | (1.0) | **-5.9** | (1.2) | 18.9 | (0.4) | 14.1 | (0.6) | **4.8** | (0.7) | 28.0 | (0.5) | 26.9 | (0.6) | 1.2 | (0.8) |
| Israel | 51.6 | (1.1) | 52.4 | (0.5) | -0.8 | (1.2) | 22.2 | (0.7) | 21.6 | (0.5) | 0.7 | (0.7) | 26.2 | (0.7) | 26.1 | (0.4) | 0.1 | (0.8) |
| Jordan | 43.6 | (0.5) | a | a | a | a | 21.9 | (0.4) | a | a | a | a | 34.5 | (0.3) | a | a | a | a |
| Kyrgyzstan | 39.9 | (0.5) | 40.4 | (0.8) | -0.5 | (0.9) | 25.7 | (0.5) | 23.8 | (0.7) | **1.9** | (0.8) | 34.4 | (0.4) | 35.9 | (0.5) | **-1.5** | (0.7) |
| Latvia | 57.2 | (0.3) | 62.6 | (1.1) | **-5.4** | (1.3) | 12.8 | (0.3) | 10.5 | (0.9) | **2.3** | (0.9) | 30.1 | (0.3) | 26.9 | (1.3) | **3.1** | (1.4) |
| Liechtenstein | 65.5 | (1.1) | 71.7 | (2.8) | -6.2 | (2.7) | 9.0 | (0.7) | 3.4 | (1.2) | **5.6** | (1.2) | 25.4 | (0.9) | 24.9 | (2.2) | 0.5 | (2.2) |
| Lithuania | 59.5 | (0.3) | 75.0 | (0.0) | **-15.5** | (0.3) | 11.1 | (0.3) | c | c | c | c | 29.4 | (0.2) | c | c | c | c |
| Macao-China | 66.3 | (0.4) | 67.2 | (0.4) | -0.9 | (0.6) | 14.3 | (0.3) | 10.5 | (0.3) | **3.8** | (0.4) | 19.4 | (0.3) | 22.3 | (0.3) | **-2.9** | (0.4) |
| Montenegro | c | c | 50.8 | (0.4) | c | c | c | c | 14.5 | (0.3) | c | c | c | c | 34.7 | (0.3) | c | c |
| Qatar | 38.9 | (0.2) | 44.4 | (0.3) | **-5.5** | (0.6) | 27.6 | (0.5) | 23.8 | (0.2) | **3.8** | (0.5) | 33.5 | (0.4) | 31.8 | (0.2) | **1.7** | (0.5) |
| Romania | 48.7 | (0.4) | a | a | a | a | 20.5 | (0.3) | a | a | a | a | 30.9 | (0.2) | a | a | a | a |
| Russian Federation | 48.9 | (0.8) | 52.0 | (0.4) | **-3.1** | (0.7) | 17.6 | (0.8) | 14.6 | (0.4) | **3.0** | (0.8) | 33.5 | (0.6) | 33.5 | (0.4) | 0.0 | (0.5) |
| Serbia | 60.1 | (3.4) | 57.7 | (0.4) | 2.5 | (3.5) | 16.9 | (1.5) | 13.8 | (0.3) | 3.1 | (1.6) | 22.9 | (2.4) | 28.5 | (0.3) | **-5.6** | (2.4) |
| Slovenia | 49.9 | (2.3) | 57.2 | (0.3) | **-7.3** | (2.3) | 21.0 | (1.9) | 13.6 | (0.2) | **7.3** | (1.9) | 29.1 | (2.7) | 29.1 | (0.2) | -0.0 | (2.7) |
| Chinese Taipei | 58.5 | (0.5) | 62.8 | (0.3) | **-4.3** | (0.7) | 17.6 | (0.4) | 12.2 | (0.3) | **5.3** | (0.5) | 23.9 | (0.3) | 24.9 | (0.3) | **-1.0** | (0.4) |
| Thailand | 61.1 | (0.7) | 62.8 | (0.3) | **-1.7** | (0.8) | 11.7 | (0.6) | 9.6 | (0.3) | **2.0** | (0.6) | 27.3 | (0.6) | 27.6 | (0.3) | -0.3 | (0.6) |
| Tunisia | 38.1 | (0.5) | 44.3 | (0.3) | **-6.2** | (0.6) | 28.1 | (0.4) | 25.0 | (0.3) | **3.1** | (0.4) | 33.9 | (0.4) | 30.7 | (0.3) | **3.2** | (0.5) |
| Uruguay | 54.9 | (0.8) | 61.2 | (0.4) | **-6.3** | (0.9) | 16.1 | (0.6) | 11.0 | (0.3) | **5.1** | (0.7) | 29.0 | (0.5) | 27.8 | (0.3) | **1.2** | (0.5) |

*Note*: Values that are statistically significant at the 5% level (p < 0.05) are indicated in bold.

© OECD 2011 Quality Time for Students: Learning In and Out of School

## Table 3.11a [Part 1/3] Mean learning hours and allocation of total learning time in science, by public and private schools

| | Mean learning hours per week | | | | | | | | | | | |
| | Regular school lessons | | | | | | Out-of-school-time lessons | | | | | |
| | Public schools | | Private schools | | Difference (public-private) | | Public schools | | Private schools | | Difference (public-private) | |
| | Mean | S.E. | Mean | S.E. | Dif. | S.E. | Mean | S.E. | Mean | S.E. | Dif. | S.E. |
|---|---|---|---|---|---|---|---|---|---|---|---|---|
| **OECD** | | | | | | | | | | | | |
| Australia | w | w | w | w | w | w | w | w | w | w | w | w |
| Austria | 2.45 | (0.07) | 2.67 | (0.21) | -0.22 | (0.22) | 0.21 | (0.02) | 0.21 | (0.05) | 0.00 | (0.05) |
| Belgium | w | w | w | w | w | w | w | w | w | w | w | w |
| Canada | 4.03 | (0.04) | 3.97 | (0.12) | 0.05 | (0.13) | 0.56 | (0.01) | 0.54 | (0.04) | 0.02 | (0.04) |
| Czech Republic | 3.00 | (0.07) | 2.06 | (0.34) | **0.94** | (0.36) | 0.54 | (0.02) | 0.46 | (0.12) | 0.08 | (0.12) |
| Denmark | 3.20 | (0.05) | 3.26 | (0.12) | -0.06 | (0.13) | 0.79 | (0.02) | 0.71 | (0.05) | 0.08 | (0.06) |
| Finland | 3.11 | (0.04) | 3.53 | (0.21) | -0.42 | (0.22) | 0.32 | (0.01) | 0.50 | (0.12) | -0.18 | (0.12) |
| France | w | w | w | w | w | w | w | w | w | w | w | w |
| Germany | 3.05 | (0.05) | 3.36 | (0.33) | -0.31 | (0.34) | 0.51 | (0.02) | 0.48 | (0.07) | 0.03 | (0.07) |
| Greece | 3.10 | (0.05) | 4.55 | (0.23) | **-1.45** | (0.24) | 2.01 | (0.05) | 1.66 | (0.08) | **0.35** | (0.09) |
| Hungary | 2.44 | (0.06) | 2.81 | (0.20) | -0.37 | (0.22) | 1.00 | (0.03) | 1.00 | (0.10) | -0.00 | (0.10) |
| Iceland | 2.97 | (0.02) | 3.20 | (0.25) | -0.23 | (0.25) | 0.29 | (0.01) | 0.28 | (0.13) | 0.01 | (0.13) |
| Ireland | 2.52 | (0.07) | 2.57 | (0.05) | -0.04 | (0.09) | 0.35 | (0.02) | 0.30 | (0.02) | **0.05** | (0.03) |
| Italy | 2.94 | (0.06) | 2.45 | (0.18) | **0.49** | (0.20) | 0.58 | (0.01) | 0.58 | (0.06) | 0.00 | (0.07) |
| Japan | 2.59 | (0.05) | 2.93 | (0.12) | **-0.34** | (0.13) | 0.26 | (0.01) | 0.26 | (0.02) | -0.00 | (0.02) |
| Korea | 3.72 | (0.10) | 3.42 | (0.09) | 0.30 | (0.15) | 1.13 | (0.08) | 0.90 | (0.06) | **0.23** | (0.11) |
| Luxembourg | 2.31 | (0.03) | 2.45 | (0.07) | **-0.14** | (0.07) | 0.50 | (0.02) | 0.53 | (0.04) | -0.03 | (0.04) |
| Mexico | 3.08 | (0.04) | 3.57 | (0.12) | **-0.50** | (0.13) | 1.05 | (0.03) | 0.76 | (0.06) | **0.30** | (0.06) |
| Netherlands | 2.17 | (0.11) | 2.17 | (0.06) | -0.00 | (0.14) | 0.54 | (0.03) | 0.53 | (0.02) | 0.01 | (0.04) |
| New Zealand | 4.02 | (0.04) | 4.55 | (0.20) | **-0.53** | (0.20) | 0.40 | (0.02) | 0.49 | (0.08) | -0.09 | (0.08) |
| Norway | 2.62 | (0.03) | 3.00 | (0.10) | **-0.38** | (0.11) | 0.94 | (0.02) | 0.71 | (0.10) | **0.23** | (0.10) |
| Poland | 2.70 | (0.04) | 3.44 | (0.13) | **-0.73** | (0.14) | 0.62 | (0.02) | 0.64 | (0.08) | -0.01 | (0.09) |
| Portugal | 3.19 | (0.05) | 3.37 | (0.13) | -0.18 | (0.13) | 0.63 | (0.02) | 0.67 | (0.08) | -0.04 | (0.08) |
| Slovak Republic | 2.43 | (0.08) | 2.77 | (0.24) | -0.34 | (0.27) | 0.66 | (0.03) | 0.55 | (0.08) | 0.10 | (0.09) |
| Spain | 2.84 | (0.05) | 3.62 | (0.07) | **-0.78** | (0.08) | 0.66 | (0.03) | 0.72 | (0.05) | -0.06 | (0.06) |
| Sweden | 2.83 | (0.03) | 2.57 | (0.16) | 0.26 | (0.15) | 0.51 | (0.01) | 0.45 | (0.05) | 0.06 | (0.05) |
| Switzerland | 2.38 | (0.05) | 2.42 | (0.19) | -0.04 | (0.21) | 0.39 | (0.01) | 0.45 | (0.06) | -0.06 | (0.06) |
| Turkey | 2.87 | (0.09) | 2.67 | (0.44) | 0.20 | (0.45) | 1.35 | (0.05) | 1.28 | (0.22) | 0.08 | (0.23) |
| United Kingdom | 4.23 | (0.04) | 4.81 | (0.26) | **-0.58** | (0.26) | 0.50 | (0.02) | 0.26 | (0.04) | **0.23** | (0.05) |
| United States | 3.46 | (0.05) | 4.13 | (0.12) | **-0.67** | (0.13) | 0.79 | (0.02) | 0.66 | (0.06) | **0.14** | (0.06) |
| **OECD average** | 2.95 | (0.01) | 3.18 | (0.04) | **-0.23** | (0.04) | 0.66 | (0.01) | 0.60 | (0.02) | **0.06** | (0.02) |
| **Partners** | | | | | | | | | | | | |
| Argentina | 2.04 | (0.06) | 2.65 | (0.08) | **-0.61** | (0.10) | 0.52 | (0.03) | 0.42 | (0.03) | **0.10** | (0.04) |
| Azerbaijan | 2.83 | (0.06) | 3.47 | (0.05) | **-0.64** | (0.08) | 1.36 | (0.03) | 1.63 | (0.02) | **-0.27** | (0.04) |
| Brazil | 2.03 | (0.03) | 3.31 | (0.12) | **-1.28** | (0.13) | 0.76 | (0.03) | 0.95 | (0.08) | **-0.19** | (0.08) |
| Bulgaria | m | m | m | m | m | m | m | m | m | m | m | m |
| Chile | 2.02 | (0.08) | 2.57 | (0.06) | **-0.55** | (0.10) | 0.86 | (0.03) | 0.80 | (0.02) | 0.05 | (0.04) |
| Colombia | 3.44 | (0.14) | 3.80 | (0.15) | -0.36 | (0.21) | 0.99 | (0.04) | 0.80 | (0.05) | **0.19** | (0.06) |
| Croatia | 2.01 | (0.04) | 2.61 | (0.00) | **-0.60** | (0.04) | 0.43 | (0.02) | 0.56 | (0.00) | **-0.13** | (0.02) |
| Estonia | 3.27 | (0.04) | 3.41 | (0.28) | -0.14 | (0.28) | 0.77 | (0.02) | 0.37 | (0.11) | **0.40** | (0.11) |
| Hong Kong-China | 3.10 | (0.20) | 3.15 | (0.06) | -0.05 | (0.21) | 0.89 | (0.10) | 0.88 | (0.03) | 0.02 | (0.10) |
| Indonesia | 3.54 | (0.09) | 2.77 | (0.10) | **0.77** | (0.14) | 1.11 | (0.06) | 0.95 | (0.05) | **0.16** | (0.07) |
| Israel | 2.50 | (0.05) | 2.32 | (0.14) | 0.18 | (0.15) | 1.07 | (0.03) | 0.78 | (0.06) | **0.29** | (0.08) |
| Jordan | 3.15 | (0.06) | 3.55 | (0.11) | **-0.40** | (0.12) | 1.52 | (0.04) | 1.56 | (0.08) | -0.04 | (0.09) |
| Kyrgyzstan | 2.06 | (0.06) | 2.83 | (0.36) | **-0.77** | (0.37) | 1.36 | (0.03) | 1.07 | (0.35) | 0.29 | (0.36) |
| Latvia | 2.86 | (0.06) | a | a | a | a | 0.65 | (0.02) | a | a | a | a |
| Liechtenstein | 2.65 | (0.09) | c | c | c | c | 0.54 | (0.06) | c | c | c | c |
| Lithuania | 2.68 | (0.04) | c | c | c | c | 0.57 | (0.02) | c | c | c | c |
| Macao-China | 2.85 | (0.11) | 3.78 | (0.03) | **-0.93** | (0.11) | 0.79 | (0.08) | 1.00 | (0.03) | **-0.21** | (0.09) |
| Montenegro | 2.85 | (0.04) | a | a | a | a | 1.05 | (0.02) | a | a | a | a |
| Qatar | 2.53 | (0.04) | 3.44 | (0.08) | **-0.91** | (0.09) | 1.48 | (0.03) | 1.46 | (0.06) | 0.02 | (0.06) |
| Romania | 2.26 | (0.07) | a | a | a | a | 1.03 | (0.02) | a | a | a | a |
| Russian Federation | 3.73 | (0.08) | a | a | a | a | 1.12 | (0.03) | a | a | a | a |
| Serbia | 2.86 | (0.06) | c | c | c | c | 0.79 | (0.02) | c | c | c | c |
| Slovenia | 2.79 | (0.03) | 4.31 | (0.19) | **-1.53** | (0.19) | 0.72 | (0.02) | 0.59 | (0.10) | 0.12 | (0.10) |
| Chinese Taipei | 3.13 | (0.07) | 2.46 | (0.14) | **0.67** | (0.17) | 0.92 | (0.03) | 0.52 | (0.04) | **0.39** | (0.06) |
| Thailand | 3.94 | (0.04) | 3.18 | (0.10) | **0.76** | (0.11) | 0.94 | (0.03) | 0.74 | (0.11) | 0.20 | (0.12) |
| Tunisia | 2.64 | (0.05) | 1.82 | (0.29) | **0.82** | (0.30) | 1.94 | (0.03) | 1.62 | (0.27) | 0.32 | (0.27) |
| Uruguay | 2.22 | (0.05) | 3.36 | (0.11) | **-1.14** | (0.12) | 0.61 | (0.02) | 0.61 | (0.04) | -0.00 | (0.05) |

*Note*: Values that are statistically significant at the 5% level (p < 0.05) are indicated in bold.

**Table 3.11a** [Part 2/3] **Mean learning hours and allocation of total learning time in science, by public and private schools**

| | Mean learning hours per week | | | | | | | | | | | |
|---|---|---|---|---|---|---|---|---|---|---|---|---|
| | Individual study | | | | | | Total learning hours | | | | | |
| | Public schools | | Private schools | | Difference (public-private) | | Public schools | | Private schools | | Difference (public-private) | |
| | Mean | S.E. | Mean | S.E. | Dif. | S.E. | Mean | S.E. | Mean | S.E. | Dif. | S.E. |
| Australia | w | w | w | w | w | w | w | w | w | w | w | w |
| Austria | 1.26 | (0.04) | 1.46 | (0.11) | -0.21 | (0.11) | 3.92 | (0.10) | 4.36 | (0.27) | -0.44 | (0.29) |
| Belgium | w | w | w | w | w | w | w | w | w | w | w | w |
| Canada | 1.56 | (0.03) | 1.67 | (0.08) | -0.11 | (0.08) | 6.17 | (0.06) | 6.16 | (0.19) | 0.01 | (0.20) |
| Czech Republic | 1.03 | (0.03) | 0.66 | (0.17) | **0.37** | (0.18) | 4.56 | (0.11) | 3.18 | (0.59) | **1.39** | (0.64) |
| Denmark | 1.07 | (0.03) | 1.10 | (0.06) | -0.03 | (0.07) | 5.04 | (0.08) | 5.05 | (0.20) | -0.01 | (0.22) |
| Finland | 1.07 | (0.02) | 1.29 | (0.17) | -0.22 | (0.16) | 4.49 | (0.06) | 5.38 | (0.22) | **-0.88** | (0.22) |
| France | w | w | w | w | w | w | w | w | w | w | w | w |
| Germany | 1.70 | (0.03) | 1.71 | (0.12) | -0.01 | (0.12) | 5.27 | (0.07) | 5.55 | (0.43) | -0.29 | (0.44) |
| Greece | 1.83 | (0.04) | 2.11 | (0.11) | **-0.28** | (0.12) | 6.94 | (0.11) | 8.35 | (0.27) | **-1.41** | (0.30) |
| Hungary | 1.57 | (0.04) | 1.71 | (0.11) | -0.15 | (0.12) | 5.01 | (0.10) | 5.51 | (0.35) | -0.50 | (0.38) |
| Iceland | 1.17 | (0.02) | 1.36 | (0.21) | -0.19 | (0.21) | 4.43 | (0.04) | 4.84 | (0.35) | -0.41 | (0.35) |
| Ireland | 1.16 | (0.04) | 1.24 | (0.03) | -0.07 | (0.05) | 4.03 | (0.12) | 4.09 | (0.08) | -0.07 | (0.14) |
| Italy | 2.12 | (0.04) | 1.65 | (0.12) | **0.47** | (0.14) | 5.63 | (0.11) | 4.71 | (0.30) | **0.92** | (0.34) |
| Japan | 0.68 | (0.02) | 0.72 | (0.04) | -0.04 | (0.04) | 3.53 | (0.07) | 3.92 | (0.15) | **-0.39** | (0.16) |
| Korea | 1.27 | (0.10) | 1.16 | (0.04) | 0.12 | (0.12) | 6.14 | (0.26) | 5.49 | (0.16) | 0.65 | (0.35) |
| Luxembourg | 1.23 | (0.02) | 1.35 | (0.06) | **-0.12** | (0.06) | 4.05 | (0.05) | 4.30 | (0.11) | **-0.25** | (0.13) |
| Mexico | 2.15 | (0.03) | 2.00 | (0.07) | 0.15 | (0.07) | 6.23 | (0.08) | 6.31 | (0.14) | -0.08 | (0.16) |
| Netherlands | 1.25 | (0.05) | 1.20 | (0.03) | 0.05 | (0.06) | 77.43 | (0.13) | 3.88 | (0.09) | 0.06 | (0.18) |
| New Zealand | 1.24 | (0.03) | 1.86 | (0.09) | **-0.62** | (0.09) | 5.67 | (0.07) | 6.90 | (0.23) | **-1.23** | (0.24) |
| Norway | 1.23 | (0.02) | 1.22 | (0.25) | 0.00 | (0.25) | 4.79 | (0.05) | 4.94 | (0.39) | -0.15 | (0.40) |
| Poland | 2.01 | (0.03) | 2.38 | (0.12) | **-0.36** | (0.13) | 5.34 | (0.07) | 6.44 | (0.27) | **-1.10** | (0.28) |
| Portugal | 2.09 | (0.04) | 2.09 | (0.15) | -0.00 | (0.15) | 5.91 | (0.08) | 6.12 | (0.27) | -0.22 | (0.28) |
| Slovak Republic | 1.39 | (0.04) | 1.41 | (0.13) | -0.02 | (0.13) | 4.49 | (0.14) | 4.76 | (0.42) | -0.28 | (0.45) |
| Spain | 1.64 | (0.03) | 1.90 | (0.05) | **-0.26** | (0.06) | 5.16 | (0.08) | 6.27 | (0.13) | **-1.12** | (0.15) |
| Sweden | 1.14 | (0.02) | 1.26 | (0.10) | -0.12 | (0.10) | 4.47 | (0.04) | 4.27 | (0.23) | 0.20 | (0.23) |
| Switzerland | 1.12 | (0.02) | 1.20 | (0.11) | -0.08 | (0.12) | 3.89 | (0.06) | 4.05 | (0.32) | -0.16 | (0.34) |
| Turkey | 1.64 | (0.05) | 1.62 | (0.17) | 0.02 | (0.18) | 5.82 | (0.19) | 5.43 | (0.66) | 0.38 | (0.69) |
| United Kingdom | 1.41 | (0.03) | 1.95 | (0.09) | **-0.54** | (0.10) | 6.14 | (0.05) | 7.01 | (0.36) | **-0.87** | (0.36) |
| United States | 1.65 | (0.03) | 2.10 | (0.15) | **-0.46** | (0.16) | 5.94 | (0.07) | 6.88 | (0.22) | **-0.94** | (0.24) |
| **OECD average** | 1.42 | (0.01) | 1.52 | (0.02) | **-0.10** | (0.02) | 7.66 | (0.02) | 5.30 | (0.06) | **-0.27** | (0.06) |
| Argentina | 1.52 | (0.05) | 1.71 | (0.07) | **-0.19** | (0.08) | 4.07 | (0.11) | 4.76 | (0.12) | **-0.69** | (0.16) |
| Azerbaijan | 2.64 | (0.05) | 2.60 | (0.10) | 0.04 | (0.10) | 6.82 | (0.11) | 7.68 | (0.14) | **-0.86** | (0.16) |
| Brazil | 1.66 | (0.03) | 1.91 | (0.05) | **-0.25** | (0.06) | 4.45 | (0.06) | 6.16 | (0.20) | **-1.71** | (0.20) |
| Bulgaria | m | m | m | m | m | m | m | m | m | m | m | m |
| Chile | 1.48 | (0.04) | 1.55 | (0.04) | -0.07 | (0.06) | 4.38 | (0.11) | 4.94 | (0.10) | **-0.56** | (0.15) |
| Colombia | 1.85 | (0.04) | 1.75 | (0.07) | 0.10 | (0.08) | 6.27 | (0.21) | 6.35 | (0.21) | -0.08 | (0.30) |
| Croatia | 1.46 | (0.04) | 1.54 | (0.00) | -0.08 | (0.04) | 3.92 | (0.09) | 4.70 | (0.01) | **-0.79** | (0.09) |
| Estonia | 1.55 | (0.03) | 1.22 | (0.08) | **0.33** | (0.08) | 5.58 | (0.06) | 4.97 | (0.36) | 0.62 | (0.36) |
| Hong Kong-China | 1.42 | (0.14) | 1.44 | (0.03) | -0.03 | (0.14) | 5.41 | (0.39) | 5.46 | (0.10) | -0.05 | (0.41) |
| Indonesia | 1.88 | (0.06) | 1.63 | (0.05) | **0.25** | (0.08) | 6.52 | (0.15) | 5.33 | (0.16) | **1.19** | (0.23) |
| Israel | 1.46 | (0.05) | 1.14 | (0.10) | **0.33** | (0.12) | 5.02 | (0.10) | 4.24 | (0.25) | **0.78** | (0.28) |
| Jordan | 2.62 | (0.05) | 2.72 | (0.10) | -0.10 | (0.11) | 7.31 | (0.10) | 7.73 | (0.18) | **-0.42** | (0.21) |
| Kyrgyzstan | 2.13 | (0.04) | 2.18 | (0.35) | -0.05 | (0.35) | 5.59 | (0.09) | 6.12 | (0.89) | -0.53 | (0.90) |
| Latvia | 1.80 | (0.03) | a | a | a | a | 5.30 | (0.09) | a | a | a | a |
| Liechtenstein | 1.18 | (0.06) | c | c | c | c | 4.37 | (0.11) | c | c | c | c |
| Lithuania | 1.68 | (0.03) | c | c | c | c | 4.93 | (0.06) | c | c | c | c |
| Macao-China | 0.86 | (0.08) | 1.39 | (0.03) | **-0.54** | (0.09) | 4.51 | (0.19) | 6.17 | (0.06) | **-1.66** | (0.20) |
| Montenegro | 2.21 | (0.03) | a | a | a | a | 6.11 | (0.07) | a | a | a | a |
| Qatar | 2.00 | (0.03) | 2.32 | (0.07) | **-0.32** | (0.08) | 6.02 | (0.07) | 7.28 | (0.15) | **-1.26** | (0.16) |
| Romania | 1.61 | (0.05) | a | a | a | a | 4.88 | (0.11) | a | a | a | a |
| Russian Federation | 2.87 | (0.06) | a | a | a | a | 7.72 | (0.13) | a | a | a | a |
| Serbia | 1.71 | (0.04) | c | c | c | c | 5.36 | (0.10) | c | c | c | c |
| Slovenia | 1.53 | (0.02) | 1.76 | (0.12) | -0.23 | (0.12) | 5.04 | (0.05) | 6.69 | (0.27) | **-1.65** | (0.28) |
| Chinese Taipei | 1.36 | (0.04) | 1.02 | (0.06) | **0.33** | (0.08) | 5.43 | (0.12) | 4.02 | (0.23) | **1.41** | (0.29) |
| Thailand | 1.89 | (0.04) | 1.36 | (0.07) | **0.53** | (0.08) | 6.77 | (0.07) | 5.27 | (0.22) | **1.49** | (0.23) |
| Tunisia | 2.62 | (0.04) | 2.12 | (0.13) | **0.50** | (0.14) | 7.19 | (0.10) | 5.36 | (0.47) | **1.83** | (0.48) |
| Uruguay | 1.27 | (0.03) | 1.59 | (0.07) | **-0.32** | (0.08) | 4.12 | (0.08) | 5.58 | (0.17) | **-1.46** | (0.19) |

*Note*: Values that are statistically significant at the 5% level (p < 0.05) are indicated in bold.

© OECD 2011 Quality Time for Students: Learning In and Out of School

## Table 3.11a [Part 3/3] Mean learning hours and allocation of total learning time in science, by public and private schools

| | Allocation of total learning time in science for | | | | | | | | | | | | | | | | | |
| | Regular school lessons | | | | | | Out-of-school-time lessons | | | | | | Individual study | | | | | |
| | Public schools | | Private schools | | Difference (public-private) | | Public schools | | Private schools | | Difference (public-private) | | Public schools | | Private schools | | Difference (public-private) | |
| | % | S.E | % | S.E | Dif. | S.E. | % | S.E | % | S.E | Dif. | S.E. | % | S.E | % | S.E | Dif. | S.E. |
|---|---|---|---|---|---|---|---|---|---|---|---|---|---|---|---|---|---|---|
| **OECD** | | | | | | | | | | | | | | | | | | |
| Australia | w | w | w | w | w | w | w | w | w | w | w | w | w | w | w | w | w | w |
| Austria | 64.1 | (0.6) | 63.8 | (2.1) | 0.3 | (2.1) | 4.3 | (0.3) | 3.2 | (0.7) | 1.1 | (0.8) | 31.5 | (0.6) | 33.0 | (1.8) | -1.5 | (1.8) |
| Belgium | w | w | w | w | w | w | w | w | w | w | w | w | w | w | w | w | w | w |
| Canada | 66.1 | (0.4) | 66.7 | (0.8) | -0.6 | (0.9) | 8.6 | (0.2) | 7.1 | (0.5) | **1.5** | (0.5) | 25.3 | (0.3) | 26.2 | (0.6) | -0.9 | (0.7) |
| Czech Republic | 68.7 | (0.7) | 69.2 | (3.5) | -0.5 | (3.7) | 9.7 | (0.3) | 12.2 | (1.8) | -2.5 | (1.7) | 21.6 | (0.5) | 18.6 | (2.4) | 3.0 | (2.7) |
| Denmark | 66.8 | (0.6) | 67.5 | (1.2) | -0.7 | (1.3) | 13.3 | (0.3) | 12.1 | (0.6) | 1.1 | (0.7) | 19.9 | (0.4) | 20.3 | (0.8) | -0.4 | (0.9) |
| Finland | 71.0 | (0.4) | 69.2 | (3.9) | 1.8 | (3.8) | 5.9 | (0.2) | 6.9 | (1.3) | -1.0 | (1.3) | 23.1 | (0.3) | 23.9 | (3.0) | -0.8 | (3.0) |
| France | w | w | w | w | w | w | w | w | w | w | w | w | w | w | w | w | w | w |
| Germany | 58.0 | (0.6) | 60.8 | (2.3) | -2.8 | (2.4) | 8.5 | (0.4) | 7.6 | (1.2) | 1.0 | (1.3) | 33.5 | (0.3) | 31.6 | (1.5) | 1.8 | (1.5) |
| Greece | 47.8 | (0.6) | 58.4 | (1.2) | **-10.6** | (1.3) | 26.7 | (0.4) | 18.2 | (1.3) | **8.5** | (1.4) | 25.6 | (0.4) | 23.4 | (1.0) | **2.2** | (1.0) |
| Hungary | 51.1 | (0.6) | 54.0 | (1.2) | **-2.8** | (1.3) | 18.1 | (0.5) | 16.1 | (1.1) | 2.0 | (1.3) | 30.8 | (0.4) | 30.0 | (0.7) | 0.8 | (0.7) |
| Iceland | 70.1 | (0.4) | 70.2 | (3.4) | -0.1 | (3.4) | 5.1 | (0.2) | 4.9 | (2.1) | 0.2 | (2.1) | 24.8 | (0.3) | 24.9 | (3.1) | -0.1 | (3.1) |
| Ireland | 66.0 | (0.7) | 66.4 | (0.6) | -0.4 | (0.9) | 6.9 | (0.4) | 5.7 | (0.3) | 1.1 | (0.5) | 27.2 | (0.6) | 27.9 | (0.4) | -0.7 | (0.7) |
| Italy | 54.0 | (0.3) | 53.9 | (1.6) | 0.0 | (1.6) | 9.1 | (0.2) | 11.3 | (1.5) | -2.2 | (1.5) | 36.9 | (0.2) | 34.8 | (1.1) | 2.2 | (1.1) |
| Japan | 78.3 | (0.5) | 78.5 | (0.7) | -0.2 | (0.7) | 5.2 | (0.3) | 5.2 | (0.3) | -0.1 | (0.4) | 16.5 | (0.5) | 16.2 | (0.7) | 0.3 | (0.8) |
| Korea | 67.0 | (1.0) | 68.0 | (1.0) | -1.0 | (1.6) | 14.7 | (0.6) | 12.8 | (0.7) | 1.8 | (1.2) | 18.4 | (0.6) | 19.2 | (0.5) | -0.8 | (0.8) |
| Luxembourg | 60.2 | (0.4) | 57.5 | (1.1) | **2.7** | (1.2) | 9.9 | (0.3) | 10.8 | (0.7) | -1.0 | (0.7) | 29.9 | (0.4) | 31.7 | (0.9) | -1.8 | (1.0) |
| Mexico | 47.3 | (0.4) | 55.0 | (1.4) | **-7.7** | (1.5) | 15.7 | (0.3) | 10.9 | (0.7) | **4.8** | (0.8) | 37.0 | (0.4) | 34.1 | (1.2) | **2.9** | (1.2) |
| Netherlands | 56.4 | (1.1) | 56.4 | (0.7) | 0.1 | (1.3) | 12.3 | (0.9) | 12.7 | (0.5) | -0.4 | (1.1) | 31.2 | (0.6) | 30.9 | (0.5) | 0.3 | (0.7) |
| New Zealand | 73.4 | (0.4) | 68.9 | (1.2) | **4.5** | (1.2) | 6.2 | (0.2) | 5.9 | (1.1) | 0.3 | (1.1) | 20.4 | (0.3) | 25.2 | (0.5) | **-4.8** | (0.6) |
| Norway | 59.4 | (0.5) | 64.6 | (3.6) | -5.2 | (3.7) | 17.0 | (0.3) | 10.9 | (1.8) | **6.1** | (1.9) | 23.5 | (0.3) | 24.4 | (2.4) | -0.9 | (2.4) |
| Poland | 53.2 | (0.4) | 55.1 | (1.5) | -2.0 | (1.6) | 10.3 | (0.3) | 8.9 | (0.8) | 1.4 | (0.9) | 36.5 | (0.4) | 36.0 | (1.1) | 0.6 | (1.2) |
| Portugal | 54.5 | (0.5) | 56.4 | (2.1) | -1.9 | (2.1) | 9.3 | (0.3) | 9.6 | (0.7) | -0.4 | (0.8) | 36.3 | (0.4) | 34.0 | (1.5) | 2.3 | (1.5) |
| Slovak Republic | 58.4 | (0.6) | 63.0 | (1.9) | **-4.6** | (2.0) | 11.9 | (0.4) | 9.8 | (0.9) | **2.1** | (1.0) | 29.7 | (0.4) | 27.2 | (1.2) | **2.5** | (1.3) |
| Spain | 58.2 | (0.5) | 60.2 | (0.5) | **-2.0** | (0.7) | 11.0 | (0.4) | 10.1 | (0.5) | 1.0 | (0.7) | 30.7 | (0.4) | 29.7 | (0.4) | 1.0 | (0.6) |
| Sweden | 67.0 | (0.6) | 63.9 | (2.3) | 3.1 | (2.3) | 9.2 | (0.2) | 8.6 | (0.8) | 0.6 | (0.9) | 23.8 | (0.5) | 27.5 | (1.6) | **-3.7** | (1.6) |
| Switzerland | 62.2 | (0.4) | 60.6 | (2.0) | 1.5 | (2.1) | 8.2 | (0.2) | 9.2 | (1.0) | -1.1 | (1.1) | 29.7 | (0.3) | 30.1 | (1.2) | -0.5 | (1.3) |
| Turkey | 51.2 | (0.5) | 53.3 | (3.3) | -2.1 | (3.3) | 21.0 | (0.4) | 19.5 | (1.9) | 1.5 | (2.0) | 27.9 | (0.4) | 27.3 | (2.6) | 0.6 | (2.6) |
| United Kingdom | 70.9 | (0.4) | 69.3 | (0.5) | **1.6** | (0.6) | 7.0 | (0.2) | 3.1 | (0.5) | **3.9** | (0.5) | 22.1 | (0.3) | 27.6 | (0.4) | **-5.5** | (0.5) |
| United States | 58.2 | (0.6) | 62.7 | (0.7) | **-4.5** | (0.9) | 12.9 | (0.4) | 8.1 | (0.8) | **4.8** | (0.9) | 28.9 | (0.3) | 29.2 | (1.3) | -0.3 | (1.3) |
| **OECD average** | 61.5 | (0.1) | 62.8 | (0.4) | **-1.3** | (0.4) | 10.9 | (0.1) | 9.5 | (0.2) | **1.4** | (0.2) | 27.6 | (0.1) | 27.7 | (0.3) | -0.1 | (0.3) |
| **Partners** | | | | | | | | | | | | | | | | | | |
| Argentina | 0.0 | (0.8) | 56.6 | (1.3) | **-5.5** | (1.4) | 10.8 | (0.5) | 7.7 | (0.6) | **3.1** | (0.8) | 38.1 | (0.6) | 35.7 | (1.1) | 2.4 | (1.3) |
| Azerbaijan | 100.0 | (0.6) | 49.9 | (1.3) | **-6.8** | (1.4) | 19.4 | (0.5) | 18.2 | (0.3) | **1.2** | (0.0) | 37.6 | (0.4) | 32.0 | (1.3) | **5.7** | (1.4) |
| Brazil | 100.0 | (0.5) | 56.1 | (1.0) | **-6.8** | (1.2) | 14.3 | (0.4) | 13.2 | (0.7) | 1.1 | (0.8) | 36.4 | (0.4) | 30.7 | (0.7) | **5.7** | (0.0) |
| Bulgaria | m | m | m | m | m | m | m | m | m | m | m | m | m | m | m | m | m | m |
| Chile | 45.3 | (0.9) | 51.8 | (0.6) | **-6.5** | (1.1) | 18.4 | (0.7) | 14.8 | (0.5) | **3.6** | (0.9) | 36.3 | (0.6) | 33.4 | (0.5) | **2.9** | (0.8) |
| Colombia | 58.1 | (0.8) | 62.7 | (1.3) | **-4.6** | (1.5) | 13.5 | (0.4) | 11.0 | (0.8) | **2.5** | (0.9) | 28.4 | (0.5) | 26.4 | (0.7) | **2.1** | (0.9) |
| Croatia | 54.4 | (0.5) | 59.1 | (0.1) | **-4.6** | (0.5) | 9.8 | (0.4) | 12.0 | (0.0) | **-2.2** | (0.4) | 35.8 | (0.5) | 28.9 | (0.1) | **6.8** | (0.5) |
| Estonia | 61.3 | (0.5) | 68.8 | (2.3) | **-7.4** | (2.4) | 12.7 | (0.4) | 7.2 | (1.8) | **5.6** | (1.8) | 26.0 | (0.3) | 24.1 | (1.3) | 1.9 | (1.5) |
| Hong Kong-China | 61.1 | (1.8) | 61.0 | (0.6) | 0.1 | (1.9) | 14.1 | (1.2) | 13.9 | (0.4) | 0.2 | (1.3) | 24.9 | (0.7) | 25.2 | (0.4) | -0.3 | (0.8) |
| Indonesia | 56.0 | (1.1) | 52.4 | (0.9) | **3.6** | (1.4) | 15.1 | (0.7) | 16.3 | (0.8) | -1.1 | (1.0) | 28.9 | (0.6) | 31.3 | (0.7) | **-2.4** | (0.7) |
| Israel | 52.0 | (1.0) | 60.1 | (2.0) | **-8.2** | (2.5) | 19.4 | (0.5) | 15.7 | (0.8) | **3.7** | (1.1) | 28.6 | (0.7) | 24.1 | (1.4) | **4.5** | (1.7) |
| Jordan | 42.4 | (0.6) | 44.1 | (1.4) | -1.7 | (1.5) | 20.6 | (0.4) | 19.7 | (1.1) | 0.9 | (1.1) | 37.0 | (0.4) | 36.2 | (0.9) | 0.8 | (1.0) |
| Kyrgyzstan | 35.0 | (0.7) | 48.1 | (1.2) | **-13.1** | (1.4) | 26.1 | (0.6) | 15.4 | (4.5) | **10.7** | (4.7) | 38.8 | (0.4) | 36.5 | (4.1) | 2.3 | (4.1) |
| Latvia | 56.1 | (0.5) | a | a | a | a | 10.4 | (0.3) | a | a | a | a | 33.5 | (0.4) | a | a | a | a |
| Liechtenstein | 62.0 | (1.5) | c | c | c | c | 10.3 | (1.1) | c | c | c | c | 27.7 | (1.3) | c | c | c | c |
| Lithuania | 57.1 | (0.5) | c | c | c | c | 10.1 | (0.3) | c | c | c | c | 32.8 | (0.3) | c | c | c | c |
| Macao-China | 67.7 | (2.0) | 64.6 | (0.4) | 3.1 | (2.0) | 15.1 | (1.4) | 14.5 | (0.3) | 0.6 | (1.4) | 17.2 | (1.3) | 20.9 | (0.3) | **-3.7** | (1.3) |
| Montenegro | 46.9 | (0.4) | a | a | a | a | 16.0 | (0.3) | a | a | a | a | 37.1 | (0.5) | a | a | a | a |
| Qatar | 39.6 | (0.4) | 46.8 | (0.9) | **-7.1** | (1.0) | 25.5 | (0.3) | 20.7 | (0.8) | **4.8** | (0.8) | 34.9 | (0.4) | 32.5 | (0.7) | **2.4** | (0.9) |
| Romania | 48.1 | (0.6) | a | a | a | a | 19.5 | (0.5) | a | a | a | a | 32.4 | (0.5) | a | a | a | a |
| Russian Federation | 48.6 | (0.5) | a | a | a | a | 15.0 | (0.5) | a | a | a | a | 36.4 | (0.5) | a | a | a | a |
| Serbia | 56.8 | (0.5) | c | c | c | c | 13.4 | (0.4) | c | c | c | c | 29.8 | (0.4) | c | c | c | c |
| Slovenia | m | m | 66.4 | (1.9) | m | m | 13.3 | (0.3) | 7.7 | (1.2) | **5.5** | (1.2) | 31.3 | (0.4) | 25.8 | (1.6) | **5.4** | (1.7) |
| Chinese Taipei | 62.4 | (0.5) | 66.3 | (0.8) | **-3.9** | (1.0) | 13.1 | (0.3) | 10.4 | (0.5) | **2.7** | (0.7) | 24.5 | (0.4) | 23.3 | (0.5) | 1.2 | (0.6) |
| Thailand | 63.5 | (0.4) | 65.7 | (1.1) | -2.2 | (1.1) | 10.2 | (0.4) | 8.4 | (1.0) | 1.9 | (1.1) | 26.2 | (0.3) | 25.9 | (0.7) | 0.3 | (0.8) |
| Tunisia | 37.4 | (0.4) | 33.8 | (5.6) | 3.6 | (5.6) | 25.8 | (0.4) | 29.4 | (4.5) | -3.6 | (4.5) | 36.8 | (0.4) | 36.8 | (3.0) | 0.0 | (3.0) |
| Uruguay | 55.1 | (0.6) | 61.2 | (1.1) | **-6.1** | (1.2) | 12.5 | (0.4) | 9.8 | (0.6) | **2.7** | (0.7) | 32.4 | (0.5) | 29.0 | (0.9) | **3.4** | (1.0) |

*Note:* Values that are statistically significant at the 5% level (p < 0.05) are indicated in bold.

## Table 3.11b Mean learning hours and allocation of total learning time in mathematics by public and private schools
[Part 1/3]

| | Mean learning hours per week | | | | | | | | | | | |
| | Regular school lessons | | | | | | Out-of-school-time lessons | | | | | |
| | Public schools | | Private schools | | Difference (public-private) | | Public schools | | Private schools | | Difference (public-private) | |
| | Mean | S.E. | Mean | S.E. | Dif. | S.E. | Mean | S.E. | Mean | S.E. | Dif. | S.E. |
|---|---|---|---|---|---|---|---|---|---|---|---|---|
| Australia | w | w | w | w | w | w | w | w | w | w | w | w |
| Austria | 3.24 | (0.05) | 3.08 | (0.11) | 0.16 | (0.12) | 0.51 | (0.02) | 0.47 | (0.07) | 0.04 | (0.07) |
| Belgium | w | w | w | w | w | w | w | w | w | w | w | w |
| Canada | 4.51 | (0.04) | 4.50 | (0.08) | 0.01 | (0.09) | 0.93 | (0.02) | 1.02 | (0.06) | -0.08 | (0.07) |
| Czech Republic | 4.01 | (0.05) | 3.90 | (0.35) | 0.11 | (0.36) | 0.75 | (0.03) | 0.83 | (0.19) | -0.08 | (0.20) |
| Denmark | 4.45 | (0.04) | 4.45 | (0.10) | 0.00 | (0.11) | 1.44 | (0.03) | 1.16 | (0.07) | **0.29** | (0.08) |
| Finland | 3.45 | (0.04) | 3.32 | (0.25) | 0.14 | (0.25) | 0.36 | (0.02) | 0.58 | (0.10) | **-0.22** | (0.10) |
| France | w | w | w | w | w | w | w | w | w | w | w | w |
| Germany | 3.90 | (0.04) | 3.62 | (0.21) | 0.28 | (0.21) | 0.81 | (0.03) | 0.81 | (0.14) | -0.00 | (0.14) |
| Greece | 3.41 | (0.04) | 4.22 | (0.18) | **-0.81** | (0.19) | 2.25 | (0.06) | 1.83 | (0.11) | **0.42** | (0.12) |
| Hungary | 3.28 | (0.05) | 3.36 | (0.12) | -0.08 | (0.14) | 1.31 | (0.03) | 1.21 | (0.08) | 0.10 | (0.08) |
| Iceland | 4.75 | (0.02) | 5.47 | (0.27) | **-0.73** | (0.27) | 0.73 | (0.02) | 0.80 | (0.18) | -0.07 | (0.19) |
| Ireland | 3.60 | (0.06) | 3.70 | (0.03) | -0.09 | (0.07) | 0.78 | (0.04) | 0.68 | (0.03) | **0.10** | (0.04) |
| Italy | 3.76 | (0.04) | 3.22 | (0.17) | **0.54** | (0.18) | 0.90 | (0.02) | 0.68 | (0.06) | **0.22** | (0.06) |
| Japan | 4.19 | (0.07) | 4.34 | (0.15) | -0.15 | (0.16) | 0.68 | (0.04) | 0.79 | (0.05) | **-0.12** | (0.06) |
| Korea | 4.58 | (0.08) | 4.84 | (0.07) | -0.26 | (0.12) | 2.18 | (0.09) | 2.39 | (0.10) | -0.22 | (0.16) |
| Luxembourg | 3.85 | (0.03) | 3.86 | (0.06) | -0.01 | (0.06) | 0.82 | (0.02) | 0.94 | (0.06) | -0.12 | (0.07) |
| Mexico | 3.87 | (0.04) | 4.33 | (0.13) | -0.45 | (0.13) | 1.23 | (0.03) | 0.90 | (0.06) | **0.33** | (0.06) |
| Netherlands | 2.88 | (0.07) | 2.87 | (0.05) | 0.01 | (0.09) | 0.74 | (0.03) | 0.66 | (0.03) | 0.08 | (0.05) |
| New Zealand | 4.36 | (0.03) | 4.70 | (0.14) | -0.33 | (0.15) | 0.68 | (0.02) | 0.73 | (0.08) | -0.05 | (0.08) |
| Norway | 3.37 | (0.03) | 3.74 | (0.15) | -0.36 | (0.15) | 1.05 | (0.02) | 0.78 | (0.15) | 0.28 | (0.15) |
| Poland | 4.35 | (0.04) | 4.54 | (0.09) | -0.19 | (0.10) | 0.78 | (0.02) | 0.70 | (0.13) | 0.07 | (0.13) |
| Portugal | 3.57 | (0.04) | 3.93 | (0.16) | -0.36 | (0.17) | 0.81 | (0.02) | 0.82 | (0.11) | -0.00 | (0.12) |
| Slovak Republic | 3.31 | (0.06) | 3.14 | (0.34) | 0.17 | (0.35) | 0.89 | (0.03) | 0.78 | (0.11) | 0.11 | (0.12) |
| Spain | 3.29 | (0.03) | 3.66 | (0.05) | **-0.37** | (0.06) | 0.99 | (0.03) | 1.00 | (0.04) | -0.00 | (0.05) |
| Sweden | 3.11 | (0.02) | 2.85 | (0.13) | **0.26** | (0.13) | 0.61 | (0.02) | 0.61 | (0.05) | 0.00 | (0.05) |
| Switzerland | 3.90 | (0.04) | 3.64 | (0.20) | 0.27 | (0.22) | 0.70 | (0.02) | 0.77 | (0.07) | -0.07 | (0.07) |
| Turkey | 3.79 | (0.06) | 5.16 | (0.28) | **-1.38** | (0.29) | 2.06 | (0.05) | 2.50 | (0.08) | **-0.44** | (0.10) |
| United Kingdom | 3.74 | (0.03) | 4.09 | (0.12) | **-0.34** | (0.12) | 0.64 | (0.02) | 0.35 | (0.06) | **0.29** | (0.07) |
| United States | 3.75 | (0.05) | 4.10 | (0.11) | **-0.36** | (0.12) | 1.17 | (0.03) | 0.85 | (0.09) | **0.32** | (0.09) |
| **OECD average** | **3.77** | **(0.01)** | **3.94** | **(0.03)** | **-0.17** | **(0.03)** | **0.98** | **(0.01)** | **0.93** | **(0.02)** | **0.05** | **(0.02)** |
| Argentina | 2.70 | (0.06) | 3.40 | (0.09) | **-0.70** | (0.10) | 0.79 | (0.05) | 0.76 | (0.05) | 0.03 | (0.07) |
| Azerbaijan | 3.78 | (0.06) | 4.66 | (0.24) | **-0.88** | (0.25) | 1.69 | (0.05) | 2.28 | (0.24) | **-0.59** | (0.25) |
| Brazil | 3.02 | (0.04) | 3.90 | (0.07) | **-0.87** | (0.09) | 1.19 | (0.03) | 1.32 | (0.06) | -0.13 | (0.07) |
| Bulgaria | m | m | m | m | m | m | m | m | m | m | m | m |
| Chile | 3.08 | (0.10) | 3.81 | (0.08) | **-0.73** | (0.13) | 1.01 | (0.05) | 0.98 | (0.03) | 0.03 | (0.06) |
| Colombia | 4.10 | (0.07) | 4.77 | (0.21) | **-0.67** | (0.22) | 1.26 | (0.04) | 1.07 | (0.05) | **0.19** | (0.07) |
| Croatia | 3.04 | (0.04) | 3.40 | (0.00) | **-0.36** | (0.04) | 0.76 | (0.03) | 1.17 | (0.00) | **-0.41** | (0.03) |
| Estonia | 4.20 | (0.04) | 3.79 | (0.21) | **0.41** | (0.20) | 1.00 | (0.03) | 0.45 | (0.13) | **0.55** | (0.13) |
| Hong Kong-China | 5.39 | (0.18) | 5.22 | (0.04) | 0.17 | (0.19) | 1.38 | (0.09) | 1.39 | (0.04) | -0.01 | (0.10) |
| Indonesia | 4.29 | (0.09) | 3.78 | (0.08) | **0.51** | (0.12) | 1.46 | (0.06) | 1.22 | (0.06) | **0.24** | (0.09) |
| Israel | 4.10 | (0.05) | 4.16 | (0.11) | -0.06 | (0.13) | 2.28 | (0.05) | 1.84 | (0.10) | **0.44** | (0.11) |
| Jordan | 3.38 | (0.05) | 3.86 | (0.11) | **-0.47** | (0.12) | 1.82 | (0.04) | 1.89 | (0.09) | -0.07 | (0.10) |
| Kyrgyzstan | 2.87 | (0.06) | 3.40 | (0.22) | **-0.54** | (0.23) | 1.55 | (0.04) | 1.24 | (0.18) | 0.31 | (0.20) |
| Latvia | 4.49 | (0.04) | a | a | a | a | 1.20 | (0.04) | a | a | a | a |
| Liechtenstein | 3.92 | (0.09) | c | c | c | c | 0.59 | (0.05) | c | c | c | c |
| Lithuania | 3.49 | (0.04) | c | c | c | c | 0.74 | (0.02) | c | c | c | c |
| Macao-China | 5.00 | (0.12) | 5.42 | (0.03) | **-0.42** | (0.12) | 1.08 | (0.12) | 1.21 | (0.03) | -0.13 | (0.13) |
| Montenegro | 3.09 | (0.04) | c | c | c | c | 0.93 | (0.03) | c | c | c | c |
| Qatar | 2.98 | (0.04) | 3.82 | (0.06) | **-0.84** | (0.08) | 1.84 | (0.03) | 1.87 | (0.06) | -0.03 | (0.07) |
| Romania | 3.01 | (0.07) | a | a | a | a | 1.50 | (0.03) | a | a | a | a |
| Russian Federation | 3.63 | (0.06) | a | a | a | a | 1.13 | (0.03) | a | a | a | a |
| Serbia | 3.28 | (0.04) | c | c | c | c | 0.97 | (0.03) | c | c | c | c |
| Slovenia | 3.31 | (0.03) | 4.23 | (0.12) | **-0.92** | (0.12) | 1.03 | (0.02) | 0.80 | (0.09) | **0.23** | (0.10) |
| Chinese Taipei | 4.35 | (0.07) | 4.08 | (0.17) | 0.27 | (0.22) | 1.72 | (0.05) | 1.17 | (0.08) | **0.55** | (0.10) |
| Thailand | 3.90 | (0.04) | 3.14 | (0.07) | **0.76** | (0.08) | 0.97 | (0.03) | 0.67 | (0.06) | **0.30** | (0.07) |
| Tunisia | 3.42 | (0.04) | 2.78 | (0.28) | **0.63** | (0.29) | 2.43 | (0.04) | 2.35 | (0.06) | 0.08 | (0.07) |
| Uruguay | 3.18 | (0.04) | 4.04 | (0.13) | **-0.86** | (0.14) | 0.83 | (0.03) | 0.89 | (0.04) | -0.06 | (0.05) |

*Note:* Values that are statistically significant at the 5% level (p < 0.05) are indicated in bold.

© OECD 2011 Quality Time for Students: Learning In and Out of School

**Table 3.11b** **Mean learning hours and allocation of total learning time in mathematics**
[Part 2/3] **by public and private schools**

| | | Mean learning hours per week | | | | | | | | | | |
|---|---|---|---|---|---|---|---|---|---|---|---|---|
| | | Individual study | | | | | | Total learning hours | | | | |
| | | Public schools | | Private schools | | Difference (public-private) | | Public schools | | Private schools | | Difference (public-private) |
| | | Mean | S.E. | Mean | S.E. | Dif. | S.E. | Mean | S.E. | Mean | S.E. | Dif. | S.E. |
| OECD | Australia | w | w | w | w | w | w | w | w | w | w | w | w |
| | Austria | 2.11 | (0.04) | 2.34 | (0.09) | **-0.24** | (0.11) | 5.87 | (0.09) | 5.90 | (0.16) | -0.03 | (0.19) |
| | Belgium | w | w | w | w | w | w | w | w | w | w | w | w |
| | Canada | 1.95 | (0.03) | 2.35 | (0.07) | **-0.40** | (0.08) | 7.43 | (0.08) | 7.87 | (0.14) | **-0.45** | (0.17) |
| | Czech Republic | 1.32 | (0.03) | 1.24 | (0.17) | 0.08 | (0.17) | 6.07 | (0.09) | 5.97 | (0.65) | 0.10 | (0.68) |
| | Denmark | 1.74 | (0.03) | 1.75 | (0.06) | -0.01 | (0.08) | 7.62 | (0.07) | 7.31 | (0.17) | 0.31 | (0.21) |
| | Finland | 1.19 | (0.02) | 1.58 | (0.15) | **-0.38** | (0.15) | 5.01 | (0.06) | 5.51 | (0.28) | -0.50 | (0.29) |
| | France | w | w | w | w | w | w | w | w | w | w | w | w |
| | Germany | 2.26 | (0.04) | 2.29 | (0.18) | -0.03 | (0.19) | 6.99 | (0.08) | 6.72 | (0.43) | 0.27 | (0.44) |
| | Greece | 2.00 | (0.04) | 2.12 | (0.11) | -0.12 | (0.11) | 7.68 | (0.11) | 8.23 | (0.27) | -0.55 | (0.29) |
| | Hungary | 1.84 | (0.04) | 1.88 | (0.10) | -0.04 | (0.10) | 6.43 | (0.09) | 6.47 | (0.23) | -0.03 | (0.25) |
| | Iceland | 1.71 | (0.02) | 1.90 | (0.33) | -0.19 | (0.33) | 7.19 | (0.05) | 8.17 | (0.48) | **-0.98** | (0.47) |
| | Ireland | 1.71 | (0.05) | 1.81 | (0.04) | -0.09 | (0.06) | 6.09 | (0.11) | 6.18 | (0.08) | -0.10 | (0.13) |
| | Italy | 2.51 | (0.03) | 1.97 | (0.14) | **0.54** | (0.14) | 7.18 | (0.07) | 5.91 | (0.30) | **1.27** | (0.32) |
| | Japan | 1.50 | (0.07) | 1.43 | (0.09) | 0.07 | (0.11) | 6.37 | (0.13) | 6.57 | (0.25) | -0.20 | (0.26) |
| | Korea | 2.23 | (0.12) | 2.41 | (0.09) | -0.18 | (0.17) | 9.02 | (0.25) | 9.67 | (0.22) | -0.65 | (0.41) |
| | Luxembourg | 1.68 | (0.02) | 1.88 | (0.06) | **-0.19** | (0.07) | 6.38 | (0.05) | 6.69 | (0.13) | **-0.31** | (0.14) |
| | Mexico | 2.29 | (0.03) | 2.09 | (0.06) | **0.20** | (0.07) | 7.36 | (0.07) | 7.33 | (0.13) | 0.03 | (0.13) |
| | Netherlands | 1.51 | (0.06) | 1.45 | (0.04) | 0.06 | (0.06) | 5.11 | (0.10) | 4.97 | (0.09) | 0.14 | (0.14) |
| | New Zealand | 1.56 | (0.03) | 2.00 | (0.08) | **-0.44** | (0.08) | 6.61 | (0.05) | 7.41 | (0.17) | **-0.79** | (0.18) |
| | Norway | 1.39 | (0.03) | 1.31 | (0.17) | 0.08 | (0.17) | 5.82 | (0.06) | 5.81 | (0.26) | 0.00 | (0.26) |
| | Poland | 2.09 | (0.03) | 2.27 | (0.09) | **-0.19** | (0.09) | 7.22 | (0.06) | 7.51 | (0.14) | **-0.29** | (0.15) |
| | Portugal | 1.95 | (0.03) | 2.05 | (0.14) | -0.10 | (0.15) | 6.34 | (0.07) | 6.77 | (0.33) | -0.43 | (0.34) |
| | Slovak Republic | 1.70 | (0.04) | 1.55 | (0.14) | 0.15 | (0.15) | 5.91 | (0.10) | 5.51 | (0.55) | 0.40 | (0.57) |
| | Spain | 1.91 | (0.04) | 2.06 | (0.05) | **-0.15** | (0.06) | 6.23 | (0.07) | 6.74 | (0.10) | **-0.50** | (0.12) |
| | Sweden | 1.16 | (0.02) | 1.35 | (0.08) | **-0.18** | (0.08) | 4.89 | (0.05) | 4.81 | (0.19) | 0.08 | (0.19) |
| | Switzerland | 1.70 | (0.02) | 1.81 | (0.06) | -0.12 | (0.07) | 6.32 | (0.06) | 6.25 | (0.28) | 0.07 | (0.30) |
| | Turkey | 2.30 | (0.05) | 2.47 | (0.14) | -0.17 | (0.14) | 8.12 | (0.15) | 10.03 | (0.24) | **-1.92** | (0.30) |
| | United Kingdom | 1.46 | (0.02) | 1.87 | (0.07) | **-0.40** | (0.07) | 5.85 | (0.05) | 6.31 | (0.19) | **-0.46** | (0.19) |
| | United States | 2.01 | (0.03) | 2.48 | (0.10) | **-0.47** | (0.10) | 6.98 | (0.07) | 7.43 | (0.15) | **-0.45** | (0.16) |
| | **OECD average** | 1.80 | (0.01) | 1.91 | (0.02) | **-0.11** | (0.02) | 6.56 | (0.02) | 6.79 | (0.05) | **-0.23** | (0.06) |
| Partners | Argentina | 1.82 | (0.05) | 1.83 | (0.05) | -0.01 | (0.06) | 5.31 | (0.13) | 5.98 | (0.13) | **-0.67** | (0.17) |
| | Azerbaijan | 2.94 | (0.06) | 3.33 | (0.13) | **-0.38** | (0.14) | 8.47 | (0.14) | 10.30 | (0.07) | **-1.83** | (0.15) |
| | Brazil | 1.76 | (0.03) | 2.06 | (0.06) | **-0.30** | (0.07) | 5.96 | (0.08) | 7.25 | (0.13) | **-1.29** | (0.15) |
| | Bulgaria | m | m | m | m | m | m | m | m | m | m | m | m |
| | Chile | 1.58 | (0.06) | 1.61 | (0.04) | -0.03 | (0.07) | 5.72 | (0.17) | 6.43 | (0.12) | **-0.72** | (0.22) |
| | Colombia | 1.94 | (0.04) | 1.91 | (0.06) | 0.03 | (0.08) | 7.30 | (0.08) | 7.77 | (0.27) | -0.48 | (0.29) |
| | Croatia | 1.80 | (0.03) | 1.90 | (0.00) | **-0.10** | (0.03) | 5.65 | (0.06) | 6.48 | (0.01) | **-0.84** | (0.06) |
| | Estonia | 1.97 | (0.03) | 1.38 | (0.13) | **0.59** | (0.14) | 7.18 | (0.06) | 5.60 | (0.32) | **1.58** | (0.31) |
| | Hong Kong-China | 2.23 | (0.12) | 2.24 | (0.04) | -0.01 | (0.12) | 9.02 | (0.34) | 8.85 | (0.09) | 0.17 | (0.35) |
| | Indonesia | 2.09 | (0.04) | 1.85 | (0.04) | **0.24** | (0.07) | 7.84 | (0.13) | 6.83 | (0.14) | **1.01** | (0.19) |
| | Israel | 2.47 | (0.06) | 2.00 | (0.11) | **0.46** | (0.13) | 8.93 | (0.13) | 8.09 | (0.25) | **0.84** | (0.30) |
| | Jordan | 2.65 | (0.04) | 2.82 | (0.10) | -0.17 | (0.11) | 7.84 | (0.09) | 8.49 | (0.17) | **-0.64** | (0.20) |
| | Kyrgyzstan | 2.21 | (0.04) | 2.07 | (0.24) | 0.14 | (0.25) | 6.69 | (0.09) | 6.82 | (0.54) | -0.13 | (0.55) |
| | Latvia | 2.44 | (0.04) | a | a | a | a | 8.14 | (0.09) | a | a | a | a |
| | Liechtenstein | 1.46 | (0.06) | c | c | c | c | 5.97 | (0.13) | c | c | c | c |
| | Lithuania | 1.77 | (0.03) | c | c | c | c | 6.00 | (0.06) | c | c | c | c |
| | Macao-China | 1.32 | (0.10) | 2.10 | (0.03) | **-0.77** | (0.11) | 7.42 | (0.25) | 8.73 | (0.06) | **-1.31** | (0.26) |
| | Montenegro | 2.04 | (0.03) | c | c | c | c | 6.05 | (0.07) | c | c | c | c |
| | Qatar | 2.17 | (0.03) | 2.56 | (0.07) | **-0.39** | (0.07) | 7.01 | (0.08) | 8.26 | (0.15) | **-1.25** | (0.17) |
| | Romania | 2.16 | (0.04) | a | a | a | a | 6.67 | (0.11) | a | a | a | a |
| | Russian Federation | 2.23 | (0.05) | a | a | a | a | 6.99 | (0.10) | a | a | a | a |
| | Serbia | 1.82 | (0.03) | c | c | c | c | 6.07 | (0.07) | c | c | c | c |
| | Slovenia | 1.92 | (0.02) | 2.35 | (0.14) | **-0.43** | (0.14) | 6.28 | (0.05) | 7.38 | (0.26) | **-1.11** | (0.27) |
| | Chinese Taipei | 1.99 | (0.04) | 1.67 | (0.08) | **0.31** | (0.10) | 8.11 | (0.13) | 6.98 | (0.32) | **1.13** | (0.40) |
| | Thailand | 1.90 | (0.03) | 1.35 | (0.06) | **0.55** | (0.07) | 6.77 | (0.08) | 5.16 | (0.15) | **1.61** | (0.16) |
| | Tunisia | 2.58 | (0.04) | 2.12 | (0.41) | 0.45 | (0.41) | 8.41 | (0.10) | 7.52 | (0.67) | 0.89 | (0.68) |
| | Uruguay | 1.54 | (0.03) | 1.72 | (0.07) | **-0.18** | (0.08) | 5.57 | (0.07) | 6.64 | (0.20) | **-1.08** | (0.21) |

*Note:* Values that are statistically significant at the 5% level (p < 0.05) are indicated in bold.

## Table 3.11b Mean learning hours and allocation of total learning time in mathematics by public and private schools
[Part 3/3]

| | Allocation of total learning time in mathematics for | | | | | | | | | | | | | | | | | |
| | Regular school lessons | | | | | | Out-of-school-time lessons | | | | | | Individual study | | | | | |
| | Public schools | | Private schools | | Difference (public-private) | | Public schools | | Private schools | | Difference (public-private) | | Public schools | | Private schools | | Difference (public-private) | |
| | % | S.E | % | S.E | Dif. | S.E. | % | S.E | % | S.E | Dif. | S.E. | % | S.E | % | S.E | Dif. | S.E. |
|---|---|---|---|---|---|---|---|---|---|---|---|---|---|---|---|---|---|---|
| **OECD** | | | | | | | | | | | | | | | | | | |
| Australia | w | w | w | w | w | w | w | w | w | w | w | w | w | w | w | w | w | w |
| Austria | 58.8 | (0.5) | 55.4 | (1.1) | 3.4 | (1.3) | 6.7 | (0.3) | 6.3 | (0.7) | 0.3 | (0.7) | 34.5 | (0.4) | 38.3 | (1.3) | -3.7 | (1.4) |
| Belgium | w | w | w | w | w | w | w | w | w | w | w | w | w | w | w | w | w | w |
| Canada | 63.5 | (0.3) | 61.0 | (0.7) | 2.4 | (0.8) | 11.5 | (0.2) | 10.9 | (0.6) | 0.6 | (0.6) | 25.1 | (0.2) | 28.1 | (0.6) | -3.0 | (0.7) |
| Czech Republic | 70.4 | (0.5) | 70.0 | (2.7) | 0.4 | (2.8) | 9.7 | (0.2) | 10.7 | (1.7) | -1.0 | (1.7) | 19.9 | (0.4) | 19.3 | (1.5) | 0.6 | (1.6) |
| Denmark | 61.9 | (0.4) | 64.3 | (0.9) | -2.3 | (1.0) | 16.7 | (0.3) | 13.7 | (0.6) | 3.0 | (0.6) | 21.3 | (0.2) | 22.0 | (0.6) | -0.7 | (0.6) |
| Finland | 71.3 | (0.3) | 65.6 | (2.6) | 5.7 | (2.6) | 5.9 | (0.2) | 7.8 | (1.2) | -1.9 | (1.2) | 22.8 | (0.2) | 26.6 | (1.5) | -3.7 | (1.5) |
| France | w | w | w | w | w | w | w | w | w | w | w | w | w | w | w | w | w | w |
| Germany | 58.7 | (0.4) | 56.4 | (1.6) | 2.3 | (1.7) | 9.7 | (0.3) | 9.5 | (1.5) | 0.2 | (1.5) | 31.5 | (0.3) | 34.1 | (0.8) | -2.6 | (0.8) |
| Greece | 49.0 | (0.5) | 55.5 | (1.3) | -6.5 | (1.3) | 26.3 | (0.5) | 20.8 | (1.7) | 5.4 | (1.8) | 24.7 | (0.4) | 23.7 | (1.1) | 1.0 | (1.2) |
| Hungary | 54.1 | (0.5) | 55.6 | (0.9) | -1.5 | (1.1) | 18.0 | (0.3) | 16.3 | (1.0) | 1.7 | (1.1) | 27.9 | (0.3) | 28.1 | (0.8) | -0.2 | (0.8) |
| Iceland | 69.4 | (0.3) | 70.7 | (3.6) | -1.3 | (3.6) | 8.6 | (0.2) | 8.5 | (2.0) | 0.1 | (2.0) | 22.0 | (0.2) | 20.8 | (2.7) | 1.2 | (2.7) |
| Ireland | 63.2 | (0.6) | 63.8 | (0.5) | -0.6 | (0.8) | 10.5 | (0.5) | 8.8 | (0.3) | 1.7 | (0.5) | 26.3 | (0.4) | 27.4 | (0.4) | -1.2 | (0.6) |
| Italy | 54.9 | (0.2) | 57.3 | (1.0) | -2.4 | (1.0) | 10.8 | (0.2) | 9.8 | (0.8) | 1.0 | (0.8) | 34.3 | (0.2) | 32.9 | (1.3) | 1.4 | (1.3) |
| Japan | 71.9 | (0.6) | 71.2 | (0.9) | 0.7 | (1.1) | 8.3 | (0.4) | 9.5 | (0.4) | -1.2 | (0.5) | 19.8 | (0.5) | 19.2 | (0.8) | 0.6 | (0.8) |
| Korea | 57.5 | (1.0) | 56.4 | (0.9) | 1.1 | (1.7) | 20.5 | (0.6) | 21.4 | (0.6) | -0.9 | (1.1) | 22.0 | (0.6) | 22.2 | (0.5) | -0.2 | (0.9) |
| Luxembourg | 63.6 | (0.3) | 61.3 | (0.9) | 2.3 | (1.0) | 10.9 | (0.3) | 12.3 | (0.6) | -1.4 | (0.7) | 25.5 | (0.3) | 26.4 | (0.7) | -0.9 | (0.7) |
| Mexico | 53.4 | (0.4) | 60.4 | (1.3) | -7.1 | (1.4) | 15.1 | (0.3) | 10.8 | (0.7) | 4.3 | (0.7) | 31.5 | (0.3) | 28.8 | (1.0) | 2.7 | (1.1) |
| Netherlands | 59.4 | (0.9) | 60.3 | (0.6) | -0.9 | (1.1) | 12.7 | (0.7) | 11.7 | (0.4) | 0.9 | (0.9) | 27.9 | (0.6) | 28.0 | (0.5) | -0.0 | (0.9) |
| New Zealand | 69.8 | (0.4) | 66.5 | (1.0) | 3.3 | (1.1) | 8.6 | (0.3) | 8.0 | (0.8) | 0.5 | (0.8) | 21.7 | (0.3) | 25.5 | (0.7) | -3.8 | (0.7) |
| Norway | 62.1 | (0.4) | 67.4 | (3.2) | -5.3 | (3.3) | 16.0 | (0.4) | 12.1 | (1.7) | 4.0 | (1.7) | 21.9 | (0.3) | 20.5 | (1.7) | 1.3 | (1.7) |
| Poland | 62.4 | (0.3) | 64.3 | (1.3) | -1.9 | (1.3) | 10.1 | (0.3) | 7.9 | (1.3) | 2.2 | (1.4) | 27.4 | (0.3) | 27.7 | (0.7) | -0.3 | (0.8) |
| Portugal | 58.7 | (0.4) | 60.5 | (2.3) | -1.8 | (2.3) | 11.7 | (0.3) | 11.0 | (1.3) | 0.7 | (1.3) | 29.7 | (0.4) | 28.5 | (1.3) | 1.1 | (1.4) |
| Slovak Republic | 60.4 | (0.5) | 63.8 | (2.0) | -3.4 | (2.0) | 12.7 | (0.3) | 10.7 | (1.2) | 2.1 | (1.3) | 26.9 | (0.4) | 25.6 | (1.5) | 1.3 | (1.6) |
| Spain | 57.4 | (0.4) | 58.1 | (0.4) | -0.6 | (0.6) | 13.4 | (0.3) | 12.5 | (0.4) | 0.9 | (0.5) | 29.2 | (0.3) | 29.5 | (0.4) | -0.3 | (0.6) |
| Sweden | 68.5 | (0.5) | 63.5 | (1.7) | 5.0 | (1.7) | 9.9 | (0.2) | 10.5 | (0.6) | -0.6 | (0.6) | 21.6 | (0.4) | 26.0 | (1.4) | -4.4 | (1.4) |
| Switzerland | 63.8 | (0.4) | 60.4 | (1.4) | 3.4 | (1.5) | 9.6 | (0.3) | 10.3 | (0.8) | -0.8 | (0.8) | 26.6 | (0.3) | 29.2 | (1.4) | -2.6 | (1.4) |
| Turkey | 50.7 | (0.4) | 53.8 | (1.6) | -3.1 | (1.6) | 22.7 | (0.4) | 22.8 | (0.6) | -0.1 | (0.6) | 26.6 | (0.3) | 23.4 | (2.1) | 3.2 | (2.2) |
| United Kingdom | 67.1 | (0.4) | 67.2 | (0.9) | -0.1 | (1.0) | 9.1 | (0.3) | 4.2 | (0.6) | 4.9 | (0.8) | 23.8 | (0.3) | 28.6 | (0.5) | -4.8 | (0.5) |
| United States | 55.3 | (0.5) | 57.4 | (0.7) | -2.1 | (0.8) | 15.8 | (0.4) | 10.0 | (1.0) | 5.8 | (1.0) | 28.9 | (0.3) | 32.6 | (0.9) | -3.7 | (1.0) |
| **OECD average** | 61.4 | (0.1) | 61.8 | (0.3) | -0.4 | (0.3) | 12.5 | (0.1) | 11.3 | (0.2) | 1.2 | (0.2) | 26.0 | (0.1) | 26.9 | (0.2) | -0.8 | (0.2) |
| **Partners** | | | | | | | | | | | | | | | | | | |
| Argentina | 53.0 | (0.7) | 58.3 | (0.8) | -5.4 | (1.0) | 12.9 | (0.6) | 11.5 | (0.6) | 1.3 | (0.9) | 34.2 | (0.5) | 30.1 | (0.6) | 4.0 | (0.8) |
| Azerbaijan | 47.1 | (0.5) | 48.6 | (2.8) | -1.5 | (2.9) | 18.6 | (0.4) | 21.1 | (1.8) | -2.5 | (1.9) | 34.3 | (0.5) | 30.3 | (1.3) | 4.0 | (1.4) |
| Brazil | 53.9 | (0.5) | 57.6 | (1.0) | -3.7 | (1.1) | 17.6 | (0.5) | 15.7 | (0.6) | 1.9 | (0.8) | 28.5 | (0.4) | 26.7 | (0.6) | 1.8 | (0.7) |
| Bulgaria | c | c | c | c | c | c | c | c | c | c | c | c | c | c | c | c | c | c |
| Chile | 53.8 | (0.8) | 59.3 | (0.5) | -5.5 | (0.9) | 16.9 | (0.5) | 13.8 | (0.4) | 3.2 | (0.6) | 29.3 | (0.6) | 26.9 | (0.4) | 2.3 | (0.7) |
| Colombia | 60.1 | (0.7) | 63.8 | (1.2) | -3.7 | (1.4) | 14.6 | (0.4) | 12.5 | (0.6) | 2.1 | (0.8) | 25.3 | (0.4) | 23.7 | (0.8) | 1.6 | (0.9) |
| Croatia | 58.3 | (0.5) | 60.6 | (0.1) | -2.3 | (0.5) | 11.4 | (0.3) | 14.7 | (0.0) | -3.3 | (0.3) | 30.3 | (0.3) | 24.7 | (0.0) | 5.6 | (0.4) |
| Estonia | 62.0 | (0.4) | 69.5 | (1.3) | -7.4 | (1.4) | 12.5 | (0.3) | 6.5 | (2.1) | 5.9 | (2.1) | 25.5 | (0.3) | 24.0 | (1.7) | 1.5 | (1.7) |
| Hong Kong-China | 63.3 | (0.5) | 62.5 | (0.5) | 0.8 | (0.7) | 13.6 | (0.4) | 14.1 | (0.3) | -0.5 | (0.6) | 23.1 | (0.9) | 23.4 | (0.3) | -0.3 | (0.9) |
| Indonesia | 57.1 | (0.9) | 57.2 | (0.9) | -0.1 | (1.4) | 16.6 | (0.4) | 16.0 | (0.7) | 0.6 | (0.8) | 26.3 | (0.4) | 26.8 | (0.5) | -0.6 | (0.7) |
| Israel | 49.2 | (0.7) | 56.8 | (1.3) | -7.6 | (1.6) | 24.2 | (0.4) | 20.4 | (0.7) | 3.8 | (0.8) | 26.7 | (0.5) | 22.9 | (0.9) | 3.8 | (1.0) |
| Jordan | 42.7 | (0.5) | 44.8 | (1.6) | -2.1 | (1.7) | 22.6 | (0.5) | 22.0 | (1.2) | 0.6 | (1.3) | 34.7 | (0.5) | 33.3 | (0.7) | 1.5 | (0.8) |
| Kyrgyzstan | 41.8 | (0.6) | 55.6 | (1.7) | -13.9 | (1.7) | 24.1 | (0.5) | 16.6 | (2.4) | 7.6 | (2.5) | 34.1 | (0.4) | 27.8 | (2.5) | 6.3 | (2.5) |
| Latvia | 58.2 | (0.3) | a | a | a | a | 13.3 | (0.4) | a | a | a | a | 28.4 | (0.3) | a | a | a | a |
| Liechtenstein | 66.5 | (1.2) | c | c | c | c | 8.6 | (0.6) | c | c | c | c | 24.9 | (1.0) | c | c | c | c |
| Lithuania | 60.7 | (0.4) | c | c | c | c | 11.5 | (0.3) | c | c | c | c | 27.7 | (0.3) | c | c | c | c |
| Macao-China | 71.9 | (1.5) | 66.0 | (0.4) | 5.9 | (1.5) | 11.7 | (1.1) | 11.9 | (0.2) | -0.2 | (1.1) | 16.4 | (0.9) | 22.1 | (0.3) | -5.7 | (0.9) |
| Montenegro | 52.4 | (0.4) | c | c | c | c | 13.5 | (0.3) | c | c | c | c | 34.1 | (0.4) | c | c | c | c |
| Qatar | 42.5 | (0.3) | 47.6 | (0.8) | -5.1 | (0.9) | 25.6 | (0.3) | 21.9 | (0.8) | 3.7 | (0.9) | 31.9 | (0.3) | 30.6 | (0.6) | 1.3 | (0.6) |
| Romania | 49.5 | (0.6) | a | a | a | a | 19.7 | (0.4) | a | a | a | a | 30.7 | (0.4) | a | a | a | a |
| Russian Federation | 53.9 | (0.5) | a | a | a | a | 15.7 | (0.6) | a | a | a | a | 30.4 | (0.4) | a | a | a | a |
| Serbia | 59.2 | (0.5) | c | c | c | c | 13.0 | (0.3) | c | c | c | c | 27.8 | (0.4) | c | c | c | c |
| Slovenia | 55.4 | (0.3) | 62.5 | (1.3) | -7.0 | (1.3) | 14.5 | (0.2) | 9.3 | (1.0) | 5.1 | (1.0) | 30.1 | (0.3) | 28.2 | (1.1) | 1.9 | (1.1) |
| Chinese Taipei | 57.9 | (0.4) | 63.3 | (0.9) | -5.4 | (1.0) | 18.3 | (0.3) | 14.1 | (0.6) | 4.2 | (0.8) | 23.8 | (0.3) | 22.6 | (0.5) | 1.2 | (0.6) |
| Thailand | 63.0 | (0.5) | 65.4 | (0.6) | -2.3 | (0.7) | 11.1 | (0.3) | 8.3 | (0.7) | 2.8 | (0.8) | 25.9 | (0.4) | 26.4 | (0.4) | -0.5 | (0.9) |
| Tunisia | 41.7 | (0.4) | 43.9 | (1.3) | -2.2 | (1.4) | 27.1 | (0.3) | 28.2 | (5.4) | -1.1 | (5.4) | 31.2 | (0.3) | 27.9 | (5.0) | 3.3 | (5.0) |
| Uruguay | 60.2 | (0.5) | 63.6 | (0.7) | -3.3 | (0.8) | 12.6 | (0.4) | 11.5 | (0.6) | 1.1 | (0.6) | 27.2 | (0.3) | 25.0 | (0.7) | 2.2 | (0.8) |

*Note:* Values that are statistically significant at the 5% level (p < 0.05) are indicated in bold.

© OECD 2011 Quality Time for Students: Learning In and Out of School

## Table 3.11c [Part 1/3] Mean learning hours and allocation of total learning time on the language of instruction, by public and private schools

| | | Mean learning hours per week | | | | | | | | | | |
|---|---|---|---|---|---|---|---|---|---|---|---|---|
| | | Regular school lessons | | | | | | Out-of-school-time lessons | | | | |
| | | Public schools | | Private schools | | Difference (public-private) | | Public schools | | Private schools | | Difference (public-private) |
| | | Mean | S.E. | Mean | S.E. | Dif. | S.E. | Mean | S.E. | Mean | S.E. | Dif. | S.E. |

| | | Mean | S.E. | Mean | S.E. | Dif. | S.E. | Mean | S.E. | Mean | S.E. | Dif. | S.E. |
|---|---|---|---|---|---|---|---|---|---|---|---|---|---|
| OECD | Australia | w | w | w | w | w | w | w | w | w | w | w | w |
| | Austria | 2.84 | (0.03) | 3.18 | (0.18) | -0.34 | (0.18) | 0.24 | (0.02) | 0.22 | (0.07) | 0.01 | (0.07) |
| | Belgium | w | w | w | w | w | w | w | w | w | w | w | w |
| | Canada | 4.44 | (0.04) | 4.30 | (0.09) | 0.14 | (0.10) | 0.89 | (0.02) | 0.65 | (0.03) | **0.25** | (0.03) |
| | Czech Republic | 3.73 | (0.04) | 3.64 | (0.14) | 0.10 | (0.16) | 0.61 | (0.02) | 0.65 | (0.07) | -0.04 | (0.07) |
| | Denmark | 5.62 | (0.03) | 5.20 | (0.14) | **0.42** | (0.14) | 1.78 | (0.04) | 1.43 | (0.08) | **0.35** | (0.08) |
| | Finland | 3.14 | (0.05) | 2.85 | (0.26) | 0.29 | (0.26) | 0.36 | (0.01) | 0.57 | (0.15) | -0.21 | (0.15) |
| | France | w | w | w | w | w | w | w | w | w | w | w | w |
| | Germany | 3.68 | (0.03) | 3.49 | (0.11) | 0.19 | (0.11) | 0.61 | (0.02) | 0.46 | (0.10) | 0.15 | (0.10) |
| | Greece | 3.15 | (0.04) | 3.57 | (0.09) | **-0.42** | (0.10) | 1.65 | (0.04) | 1.17 | (0.04) | **0.48** | (0.05) |
| | Hungary | 3.17 | (0.05) | 3.32 | (0.14) | -0.15 | (0.16) | 1.33 | (0.03) | 1.24 | (0.08) | 0.09 | (0.08) |
| | Iceland | 4.52 | (0.03) | 5.16 | (0.29) | **-0.64** | (0.29) | 0.47 | (0.02) | 0.61 | (0.18) | -0.15 | (0.18) |
| | Ireland | 3.50 | (0.05) | 3.58 | (0.04) | -0.08 | (0.06) | 0.76 | (0.04) | 0.56 | (0.03) | **0.20** | (0.05) |
| | Italy | 4.64 | (0.03) | 4.27 | (0.17) | **0.37** | (0.18) | 0.79 | (0.02) | 0.78 | (0.10) | 0.01 | (0.09) |
| | Japan | 3.72 | (0.05) | 4.04 | (0.07) | **-0.32** | (0.09) | 0.42 | (0.03) | 0.45 | (0.03) | -0.03 | (0.04) |
| | Korea | 4.37 | (0.07) | 4.59 | (0.07) | **-0.22** | (0.11) | 1.39 | (0.07) | 1.51 | (0.06) | -0.11 | (0.10) |
| | Luxembourg | 3.51 | (0.03) | 3.49 | (0.06) | 0.02 | (0.06) | 0.58 | (0.02) | 0.67 | (0.05) | -0.09 | (0.06) |
| | Mexico | 3.67 | (0.04) | 4.04 | (0.13) | **-0.37** | (0.14) | 1.17 | (0.03) | 0.77 | (0.05) | **0.40** | (0.06) |
| | Netherlands | 2.93 | (0.04) | 2.91 | (0.04) | 0.02 | (0.06) | 0.68 | (0.05) | 0.62 | (0.03) | 0.05 | (0.06) |
| | New Zealand | 4.38 | (0.03) | 4.66 | (0.13) | **-0.28** | (0.14) | 0.65 | (0.03) | 0.66 | (0.06) | -0.01 | (0.07) |
| | Norway | 3.58 | (0.04) | 3.98 | (0.10) | **-0.39** | (0.12) | 1.16 | (0.02) | 1.03 | (0.10) | 0.14 | (0.10) |
| | Poland | 4.63 | (0.03) | 4.86 | (0.12) | -0.23 | (0.13) | 0.71 | (0.03) | 0.57 | (0.08) | 0.14 | (0.08) |
| | Portugal | 3.25 | (0.03) | 3.41 | (0.08) | -0.16 | (0.08) | 0.57 | (0.02) | 0.55 | (0.08) | 0.01 | (0.08) |
| | Slovak Republic | 3.13 | (0.06) | 3.01 | (0.29) | 0.13 | (0.30) | 0.90 | (0.03) | 0.69 | (0.07) | **0.21** | (0.08) |
| | Spain | 3.54 | (0.03) | 3.72 | (0.05) | **-0.17** | (0.05) | 0.64 | (0.03) | 0.48 | (0.03) | **0.16** | (0.04) |
| | Sweden | 3.14 | (0.03) | 2.90 | (0.17) | 0.24 | (0.17) | 0.68 | (0.02) | 0.68 | (0.10) | 0.00 | (0.11) |
| | Switzerland | 3.67 | (0.04) | 3.54 | (0.16) | 0.14 | (0.17) | 0.49 | (0.02) | 0.50 | (0.06) | -0.01 | (0.07) |
| | Turkey | 3.96 | (0.06) | 4.97 | (0.17) | **-1.01** | (0.18) | 1.81 | (0.05) | 2.04 | (0.19) | -0.23 | (0.20) |
| | United Kingdom | 3.86 | (0.04) | 4.01 | (0.20) | -0.15 | (0.20) | 0.60 | (0.02) | 0.30 | (0.04) | **0.30** | (0.05) |
| | United States | 3.60 | (0.04) | 4.09 | (0.15) | **-0.48** | (0.16) | 1.13 | (0.03) | 0.89 | (0.09) | **0.24** | (0.09) |
| | **OECD average** | 3.74 | (0.01) | 3.87 | (0.03) | **-0.12** | (0.03) | 0.84 | (0.01) | 0.76 | (0.02) | **0.09** | (0.02) |
| Partners | Argentina | 2.25 | (0.05) | 2.65 | (0.09) | **-0.40** | (0.11) | 0.50 | (0.03) | 0.30 | (0.04) | **0.19** | (0.04) |
| | Azerbaijan | 3.69 | (0.05) | 3.47 | (0.24) | 0.22 | (0.25) | 1.79 | (0.05) | 2.27 | (0.23) | **-0.47** | (0.23) |
| | Brazil | 3.03 | (0.05) | 3.56 | (0.07) | **-0.53** | (0.09) | 1.21 | (0.03) | 1.02 | (0.07) | **0.18** | (0.07) |
| | Bulgaria | m | m | m | m | m | m | m | m | m | m | m | m |
| | Chile | 3.09 | (0.08) | 3.71 | (0.08) | **-0.62** | (0.12) | 1.06 | (0.04) | 0.94 | (0.05) | 0.12 | (0.07) |
| | Colombia | 3.90 | (0.06) | 4.09 | (0.14) | -0.19 | (0.16) | 1.21 | (0.03) | 0.89 | (0.07) | **0.32** | (0.08) |
| | Croatia | 3.33 | (0.03) | 3.53 | (0.00) | **-0.21** | (0.03) | 0.39 | (0.02) | 0.57 | (0.00) | **-0.19** | (0.02) |
| | Estonia | 3.49 | (0.04) | 3.28 | (0.19) | 0.21 | (0.19) | 0.89 | (0.03) | 0.65 | (0.13) | 0.24 | (0.14) |
| | Hong Kong-China | 5.39 | (0.15) | 5.17 | (0.05) | 0.21 | (0.16) | 0.57 | (0.07) | 0.83 | (0.03) | **-0.26** | (0.08) |
| | Indonesia | 3.90 | (0.07) | 3.25 | (0.08) | **0.65** | (0.11) | 1.32 | (0.05) | 1.16 | (0.06) | **0.16** | (0.06) |
| | Israel | 3.07 | (0.06) | 2.94 | (0.09) | 0.13 | (0.12) | 1.45 | (0.04) | 1.04 | (0.05) | **0.41** | (0.07) |
| | Jordan | 3.52 | (0.05) | 3.70 | (0.13) | -0.18 | (0.14) | 1.80 | (0.04) | 1.69 | (0.10) | 0.11 | (0.11) |
| | Kyrgyzstan | 2.74 | (0.06) | 2.89 | (0.13) | -0.14 | (0.15) | 1.71 | (0.03) | 1.37 | (0.26) | 0.33 | (0.27) |
| | Latvia | 3.69 | (0.04) | a | a | a | a | 0.88 | (0.03) | a | a | a | a |
| | Liechtenstein | 3.65 | (0.09) | c | c | c | c | 0.33 | (0.04) | c | c | c | c |
| | Lithuania | 3.65 | (0.04) | c | c | c | c | 0.66 | (0.02) | c | c | c | c |
| | Macao-China | 4.93 | (0.12) | 5.33 | (0.03) | **-0.40** | (0.12) | 0.98 | (0.11) | 1.06 | (0.03) | -0.08 | (0.12) |
| | Montenegro | 2.97 | (0.04) | c | c | c | c | 0.75 | (0.02) | c | c | c | c |
| | Qatar | 2.75 | (0.03) | 3.72 | (0.07) | **-0.96** | (0.08) | 1.60 | (0.03) | 1.54 | (0.06) | 0.06 | (0.07) |
| | Romania | 3.30 | (0.06) | a | a | a | a | 1.52 | (0.03) | a | a | a | a |
| | Russian Federation | 2.04 | (0.04) | a | a | a | a | 0.82 | (0.03) | a | a | a | a |
| | Serbia | 3.18 | (0.04) | c | c | c | c | 0.93 | (0.03) | c | c | c | c |
| | Slovenia | 3.24 | (0.03) | 4.03 | (0.11) | **-0.79** | (0.11) | 0.74 | (0.02) | 0.46 | (0.07) | **0.27** | (0.07) |
| | Chinese Taipei | 4.44 | (0.06) | 4.23 | (0.15) | 0.21 | (0.18) | 0.69 | (0.02) | 0.70 | (0.03) | -0.01 | (0.04) |
| | Thailand | 3.24 | (0.03) | 2.39 | (0.06) | **0.85** | (0.06) | 0.59 | (0.03) | 0.43 | (0.02) | **0.16** | (0.04) |
| | Tunisia | 3.18 | (0.05) | 1.81 | (0.56) | **1.37** | (0.56) | 1.78 | (0.04) | 1.73 | (0.27) | 0.05 | (0.27) |
| | Uruguay | 2.72 | (0.04) | 2.83 | (0.06) | -0.11 | (0.07) | 0.69 | (0.03) | 0.43 | (0.04) | **0.26** | (0.05) |

*Note*: Values that are statistically significant at the 5% level (p < 0.05) are indicated in bold.

## Table 3.11c Mean learning hours and allocation of total learning time on the language of instruction, by public and private schools
[Part 2/3]

| | Mean learning hours per week | | | | | | | | | | | |
| | Individual study | | | | | | Total learning hours | | | | | |
| | Public schools | | Private schools | | Difference (public-private) | | Public schools | | Private schools | | Difference (public-private) | |
| | Mean | S.E. | Mean | S.E. | Dif. | S.E. | Mean | S.E. | Mean | S.E. | Dif. | S.E. |
|---|---|---|---|---|---|---|---|---|---|---|---|---|
| Australia | w | w | w | w | w | w | w | w | w | w | w | w |
| Austria | 1.51 | (0.04) | 1.90 | (0.09) | **-0.39** | (0.10) | 4.59 | (0.07) | 5.34 | (0.28) | **-0.75** | (0.29) |
| Belgium | w | w | w | w | w | w | w | w | w | w | w | w |
| Canada | 1.77 | (0.03) | 1.61 | (0.05) | **0.15** | (0.06) | 7.13 | (0.07) | 6.55 | (0.11) | **0.57** | (0.13) |
| Czech Republic | 1.16 | (0.02) | 1.17 | (0.14) | -0.01 | (0.14) | 5.50 | (0.05) | 5.47 | (0.31) | 0.03 | (0.33) |
| Denmark | 2.18 | (0.03) | 2.13 | (0.08) | 0.05 | (0.09) | 9.57 | (0.07) | 8.75 | (0.25) | **0.82** | (0.27) |
| Finland | 1.13 | (0.02) | 1.25 | (0.16) | -0.12 | (0.16) | 4.63 | (0.07) | 4.70 | (0.36) | -0.07 | (0.36) |
| France | w | w | w | w | w | w | w | w | w | w | w | w |
| Germany | 1.88 | (0.03) | 1.91 | (0.12) | -0.03 | (0.13) | 6.18 | (0.06) | 5.86 | (0.18) | 0.32 | (0.20) |
| Greece | 1.95 | (0.03) | 1.68 | (0.09) | **0.28** | (0.10) | 6.76 | (0.08) | 6.46 | (0.13) | 0.30 | (0.16) |
| Hungary | 1.86 | (0.03) | 1.88 | (0.12) | -0.01 | (0.12) | 6.38 | (0.09) | 6.43 | (0.27) | -0.06 | (0.29) |
| Iceland | 1.55 | (0.02) | 1.28 | (0.18) | 0.27 | (0.18) | 6.55 | (0.04) | 7.05 | (0.38) | -0.51 | (0.38) |
| Ireland | 1.70 | (0.06) | 1.79 | (0.04) | -0.09 | (0.07) | 5.96 | (0.11) | 5.94 | (0.08) | 0.02 | (0.14) |
| Italy | 2.97 | (0.04) | 2.53 | (0.16) | **0.45** | (0.17) | 8.41 | (0.07) | 7.62 | (0.27) | **0.79** | (0.28) |
| Japan | 0.97 | (0.04) | 0.88 | (0.05) | 0.09 | (0.06) | 5.11 | (0.09) | 5.37 | (0.12) | -0.27 | (0.14) |
| Korea | 1.37 | (0.05) | 1.44 | (0.05) | -0.07 | (0.08) | 7.15 | (0.16) | 7.55 | (0.14) | -0.40 | (0.25) |
| Luxembourg | 1.36 | (0.02) | 1.51 | (0.05) | **-0.15** | (0.06) | 5.46 | (0.05) | 5.62 | (0.11) | -0.16 | (0.12) |
| Mexico | 2.09 | (0.03) | 1.86 | (0.07) | **0.23** | (0.07) | 6.91 | (0.08) | 6.67 | (0.14) | 0.24 | (0.15) |
| Netherlands | 1.34 | (0.04) | 1.32 | (0.03) | 0.01 | (0.05) | 4.94 | (0.09) | 4.86 | (0.06) | 0.08 | (0.13) |
| New Zealand | 1.55 | (0.03) | 1.99 | (0.09) | **-0.45** | (0.09) | 6.58 | (0.06) | 7.31 | (0.24) | **-0.73** | (0.24) |
| Norway | 1.44 | (0.03) | 1.46 | (0.12) | -0.02 | (0.13) | 6.18 | (0.06) | 6.41 | (0.16) | -0.22 | (0.17) |
| Poland | 2.22 | (0.03) | 2.28 | (0.08) | -0.06 | (0.09) | 7.56 | (0.05) | 7.70 | (0.15) | -0.15 | (0.16) |
| Portugal | 1.80 | (0.03) | 1.68 | (0.08) | 0.12 | (0.09) | 5.63 | (0.05) | 5.64 | (0.17) | -0.01 | (0.18) |
| Slovak Republic | 1.77 | (0.03) | 1.42 | (0.07) | **0.34** | (0.08) | 5.80 | (0.09) | 5.15 | (0.37) | 0.65 | (0.38) |
| Spain | 1.84 | (0.04) | 1.97 | (0.05) | **-0.13** | (0.05) | 6.06 | (0.06) | 6.18 | (0.08) | -0.12 | (0.09) |
| Sweden | 1.24 | (0.02) | 1.45 | (0.14) | -0.20 | (0.15) | 5.06 | (0.05) | 5.02 | (0.32) | 0.03 | (0.33) |
| Switzerland | 1.40 | (0.02) | 1.45 | (0.08) | -0.05 | (0.09) | 5.57 | (0.06) | 5.49 | (0.15) | 0.08 | (0.17) |
| Turkey | 2.17 | (0.05) | 2.29 | (0.40) | -0.12 | (0.40) | 7.93 | (0.12) | 9.25 | (0.57) | **-1.32** | (0.57) |
| United Kingdom | 1.55 | (0.03) | 2.05 | (0.15) | **-0.50** | (0.16) | 6.02 | (0.06) | 6.37 | (0.35) | -0.36 | (0.35) |
| United States | 1.82 | (0.03) | 2.34 | (0.17) | **-0.52** | (0.17) | 6.59 | (0.07) | 7.29 | (0.27) | **-0.70** | (0.29) |
| **OECD average** | 1.68 | (0.01) | 1.71 | (0.02) | **-0.03** | (0.02) | 6.27 | (0.01) | 6.33 | (0.05) | -0.07 | (0.05) |
| Argentina | 1.63 | (0.05) | 1.64 | (0.05) | -0.00 | (0.06) | 4.39 | (0.09) | 4.55 | (0.13) | -0.15 | (0.15) |
| Azerbaijan | 3.10 | (0.05) | 3.09 | (0.16) | 0.01 | (0.17) | 8.65 | (0.11) | 8.85 | (0.38) | -0.19 | (0.40) |
| Brazil | 1.75 | (0.03) | 1.73 | (0.05) | 0.02 | (0.06) | 5.96 | (0.07) | 6.29 | (0.13) | **-0.33** | (0.15) |
| Bulgaria | m | m | m | m | m | m | m | m | m | m | m | m |
| Chile | 1.58 | (0.04) | 1.55 | (0.05) | 0.03 | (0.06) | 5.75 | (0.12) | 6.23 | (0.13) | **-0.48** | (0.20) |
| Colombia | 1.87 | (0.04) | 1.71 | (0.10) | 0.16 | (0.10) | 6.99 | (0.09) | 6.67 | (0.26) | 0.32 | (0.28) |
| Croatia | 1.58 | (0.03) | 1.82 | (0.01) | **-0.25** | (0.03) | 5.31 | (0.06) | 5.92 | (0.02) | **-0.60** | (0.06) |
| Estonia | 1.62 | (0.03) | 1.52 | (0.06) | 0.10 | (0.06) | 6.00 | (0.06) | 5.42 | (0.35) | 0.59 | (0.36) |
| Hong Kong-China | 1.61 | (0.12) | 1.64 | (0.04) | -0.04 | (0.13) | 7.56 | (0.24) | 7.65 | (0.09) | -0.08 | (0.25) |
| Indonesia | 1.88 | (0.06) | 1.68 | (0.04) | **0.21** | (0.07) | 7.09 | (0.09) | 6.06 | (0.14) | **1.03** | (0.20) |
| Israel | 1.77 | (0.05) | 1.37 | (0.06) | **0.40** | (0.08) | 6.31 | (0.11) | 5.37 | (0.15) | **0.94** | (0.19) |
| Jordan | 2.62 | (0.05) | 2.49 | (0.10) | 0.12 | (0.11) | 7.95 | (0.10) | 7.82 | (0.19) | 0.12 | (0.21) |
| Kyrgyzstan | 2.34 | (0.04) | 2.18 | (0.09) | 0.16 | (0.09) | 6.86 | (0.10) | 6.50 | (0.46) | 0.36 | (0.48) |
| Latvia | 2.01 | (0.03) | a | a | a | a | 6.58 | (0.07) | a | a | a | a |
| Liechtenstein | 1.22 | (0.06) | c | c | c | c | 5.18 | (0.11) | c | c | c | c |
| Lithuania | 1.82 | (0.03) | c | c | c | c | 6.12 | (0.06) | c | c | c | c |
| Macao-China | 1.17 | (0.09) | 1.50 | (0.03) | **-0.34** | (0.09) | 7.09 | (0.23) | 7.89 | (0.06) | **-0.81** | (0.23) |
| Montenegro | 2.01 | (0.03) | c | c | c | c | 5.73 | (0.07) | c | c | c | c |
| Qatar | 2.03 | (0.03) | 2.15 | (0.07) | -0.12 | (0.08) | 6.38 | (0.07) | 7.37 | (0.13) | **-0.99** | (0.15) |
| Romania | 2.19 | (0.04) | a | a | a | a | 7.02 | (0.10) | a | a | a | a |
| Russian Federation | 1.55 | (0.04) | a | a | a | a | 4.40 | (0.07) | a | a | a | a |
| Serbia | 1.70 | (0.03) | c | c | c | c | 5.80 | (0.07) | c | c | c | c |
| Slovenia | 1.47 | (0.02) | 1.61 | (0.10) | -0.14 | (0.10) | 5.46 | (0.05) | 6.11 | (0.19) | **-0.64** | (0.19) |
| Chinese Taipei | 1.84 | (0.03) | 1.62 | (0.06) | **0.22** | (0.07) | 7.01 | (0.09) | 6.60 | (0.21) | 0.42 | (0.24) |
| Thailand | 1.79 | (0.04) | 1.26 | (0.04) | **0.53** | (0.05) | 5.62 | (0.06) | 4.08 | (0.09) | **1.54** | (0.12) |
| Tunisia | 2.12 | (0.04) | 1.95 | (0.32) | 0.16 | (0.33) | 7.09 | (0.10) | 5.66 | (1.13) | 1.42 | (1.13) |
| Uruguay | 1.35 | (0.03) | 1.36 | (0.05) | -0.00 | (0.06) | 4.78 | (0.07) | 4.61 | (0.12) | 0.17 | (0.14) |

*Note:* Values that are statistically significant at the 5% level (p < 0.05) are indicated in bold.

© OECD 2011 Quality Time for Students: Learning In and Out of School

## Table 3.11c [Part 3/3] Mean learning hours and allocation of total learning time on the language of instruction, by public and private schools

| | Allocation of total learning time on the language of instruction for | | | | | | | | | | | | | | | | |
| --- | --- | --- | --- | --- | --- | --- | --- | --- | --- | --- | --- | --- | --- | --- | --- | --- | --- |
| | Regular school lessons | | | | | | Out-of-school-time lessons | | | | | | Individual study | | | | | |
| | Public schools | | Private schools | | Difference (public-private) | | Public schools | | Private schools | | Difference (public-private) | | Public schools | | Private schools | | Difference (public-private) | |
| | % | S.E | % | S.E | Dif. | S.E. | % | S.E | % | S.E | Dif. | S.E. | % | S.E | % | S.E | Dif. | S.E. |
| **OECD** Australia | w | w | w | w | w | w | w | w | w | w | w | w | w | w | w | w | w | w |
| Austria | 65.8 | (0.5) | 62.7 | (1.2) | **3.1** | (1.4) | 3.4 | (0.3) | 3.0 | (0.8) | 0.4 | (0.9) | 30.8 | (0.4) | 34.3 | (1.3) | **-3.5** | (1.4) |
| Belgium | w | w | w | w | w | w | w | w | w | w | w | w | w | w | w | w | w | w |
| Canada | 65.1 | (0.3) | 68.8 | (0.8) | **-3.6** | (0.9) | 11.1 | (0.2) | 7.9 | (0.3) | **3.2** | (0.4) | 23.8 | (0.3) | 23.3 | (0.8) | 0.5 | (0.8) |
| Czech Republic | 71.7 | (0.5) | 70.4 | (2.4) | 1.3 | (2.5) | 9.0 | (0.2) | 9.4 | (0.8) | -0.5 | (0.9) | 19.3 | (0.4) | 20.1 | (1.9) | -0.8 | (2.0) |
| Denmark | 62.0 | (0.4) | 63.2 | (0.8) | -1.2 | (0.9) | 16.6 | (0.3) | 14.1 | (0.6) | 2.4 | (0.6) | 21.4 | (0.2) | 22.7 | (0.4) | **-1.3** | (0.5) |
| Finland | 70.8 | (0.4) | 65.9 | (2.9) | 4.9 | (2.9) | 6.1 | (0.2) | 9.7 | (1.6) | -3.6 | (1.6) | 23.1 | (0.3) | 24.5 | (1.8) | -1.4 | (1.8) |
| France | w | w | w | w | w | w | w | w | w | w | w | w | w | w | w | w | w | w |
| Germany | 62.4 | (0.4) | 63.3 | (2.3) | -0.9 | (2.3) | 7.9 | (0.3) | 6.1 | (1.2) | 1.8 | (1.3) | 29.7 | (0.3) | 30.6 | (1.5) | -0.9 | (1.6) |
| Greece | 50.4 | (0.5) | 60.8 | (1.6) | **-10.4** | (1.6) | 21.9 | (0.4) | 15.4 | (0.8) | **6.5** | (0.9) | 27.7 | (0.3) | 23.8 | (1.5) | **3.9** | (1.5) |
| Hungary | 53.0 | (0.5) | 54.2 | (1.2) | -1.2 | (1.4) | 18.4 | (0.4) | 17.3 | (1.1) | 1.2 | (1.2) | 28.5 | (0.3) | 28.5 | (0.8) | 0.0 | (0.8) |
| Iceland | 71.8 | (0.3) | 75.5 | (3.1) | -3.8 | (3.1) | 6.0 | (0.2) | 8.1 | (2.3) | -2.0 | (2.3) | 22.2 | (0.2) | 16.4 | (1.8) | **5.8** | (1.8) |
| Ireland | 63.5 | (0.8) | 64.7 | (0.5) | -1.2 | (1.0) | 9.6 | (0.4) | 7.2 | (0.3) | **2.4** | (0.5) | 26.8 | (0.6) | 28.1 | (0.4) | -1.3 | (0.7) |
| Italy | 57.1 | (0.3) | 57.7 | (1.0) | -0.5 | (1.1) | 8.3 | (0.2) | 8.9 | (1.1) | -0.7 | (1.1) | 34.6 | (0.2) | 33.4 | (1.1) | 1.2 | (1.1) |
| Japan | 77.7 | (0.6) | 79.1 | (0.7) | -1.4 | (0.8) | 6.3 | (0.3) | 6.4 | (0.3) | -0.1 | (0.5) | 16.0 | (0.5) | 14.5 | (0.6) | **1.5** | (0.7) |
| Korea | 66.7 | (0.9) | 66.0 | (0.7) | 0.6 | (1.3) | 16.1 | (0.7) | 16.9 | (0.6) | -0.8 | (1.0) | 17.3 | (0.4) | 17.1 | (0.3) | 0.2 | (0.6) |
| Luxembourg | 67.7 | (0.4) | 64.8 | (0.8) | **2.9** | (0.9) | 8.6 | (0.3) | 10.0 | (0.7) | **-1.4** | (0.7) | 23.7 | (0.3) | 25.2 | (0.6) | **-1.5** | (0.6) |
| Mexico | 53.9 | (0.4) | 61.6 | (1.4) | **-7.7** | (1.4) | 15.4 | (0.3) | 10.1 | (0.8) | **5.4** | (0.9) | 30.7 | (0.3) | 28.4 | (1.0) | **2.4** | (1.0) |
| Netherlands | 62.7 | (0.9) | 63.2 | (0.5) | -0.5 | (1.1) | 11.3 | (0.7) | 10.6 | (0.4) | 0.7 | (0.9) | 26.1 | (0.5) | 26.2 | (0.4) | -0.1 | (0.7) |
| New Zealand | 70.3 | (0.4) | 67.4 | (0.9) | **3.0** | (1.0) | 8.0 | (0.3) | 6.9 | (0.4) | **1.2** | (0.5) | 21.6 | (0.3) | 25.7 | (0.7) | **-4.1** | (0.7) |
| Norway | 62.0 | (0.5) | 65.3 | (1.4) | **-3.3** | (1.5) | 16.6 | (0.3) | 12.6 | (0.9) | **4.0** | (0.9) | 21.4 | (0.3) | 22.0 | (1.1) | -0.6 | (1.1) |
| Poland | 63.5 | (0.3) | 65.2 | (1.5) | -1.7 | (1.5) | 8.5 | (0.3) | 6.3 | (1.2) | 2.2 | (1.2) | 27.9 | (0.3) | 28.5 | (0.9) | -0.6 | (0.9) |
| Portugal | 60.7 | (0.4) | 64.0 | (1.8) | -3.3 | (1.9) | 8.7 | (0.3) | 8.4 | (1.0) | 0.3 | (1.1) | 30.6 | (0.4) | 27.6 | (0.9) | **3.0** | (1.0) |
| Slovak Republic | 58.7 | (0.5) | 62.3 | (1.9) | -3.6 | (1.9) | 12.9 | (0.4) | 10.9 | (0.8) | **2.0** | (0.9) | 28.4 | (0.5) | 26.8 | (1.9) | 1.7 | (2.0) |
| Spain | 62.2 | (0.2) | 63.4 | (0.4) | -1.2 | (0.6) | 9.0 | (0.4) | 6.6 | (0.4) | **2.4** | (0.5) | 28.8 | (0.4) | 30.0 | (0.4) | **-1.2** | (0.5) |
| Sweden | 67.3 | (0.5) | 61.4 | (2.5) | **5.9** | (2.6) | 10.3 | (0.3) | 10.3 | (0.9) | -0.0 | (1.0) | 22.5 | (0.4) | 28.3 | (2.1) | **-5.9** | (2.1) |
| Switzerland | 67.7 | (0.4) | 66.0 | (2.0) | 1.7 | (2.1) | 7.0 | (0.3) | 7.6 | (0.9) | -0.6 | (1.0) | 25.3 | (0.2) | 26.4 | (1.7) | -1.1 | (1.8) |
| Turkey | 54.6 | (0.6) | 57.4 | (2.4) | -2.8 | (2.6) | 19.8 | (0.4) | 20.0 | (0.4) | -0.2 | (0.6) | 25.6 | (0.3) | 22.5 | (2.8) | 3.1 | (2.9) |
| United Kingdom | 67.8 | (0.4) | 65.7 | (1.2) | 2.1 | (1.3) | 8.0 | (0.2) | 3.7 | (0.5) | **4.2** | (0.6) | 24.2 | (0.3) | 30.6 | (1.0) | **-6.4** | (1.1) |
| United States | 55.6 | (0.6) | 59.1 | (1.9) | -3.5 | (2.0) | 16.4 | (0.5) | 10.5 | (1.2) | **5.9** | (1.3) | 28.0 | (0.3) | 30.4 | (1.6) | -2.4 | (1.6) |
| **OECD average** | **63.5** | **(0.1)** | **64.5** | **(0.3)** | **-1.0** | **(0.3)** | **11.1** | **(0.1)** | **9.7** | **(0.2)** | **1.4** | **(0.2)** | **25.4** | **(0.1)** | **25.8** | **(0.2)** | **-0.4** | **(0.3)** |
| **Partners** Argentina | 52.7 | (0.7) | 59.6 | (0.9) | **-6.9** | (1.1) | 9.6 | (0.5) | 5.3 | (0.7) | **4.2** | (0.7) | 37.8 | (0.6) | 35.1 | (0.7) | **2.7** | (0.9) |
| Azerbaijan | 44.9 | (0.6) | 44.7 | (1.9) | 0.2 | (2.0) | 19.3 | (0.5) | 22.2 | (2.1) | -2.9 | (2.1) | 35.9 | (0.5) | 33.2 | (1.2) | 2.7 | (1.3) |
| Brazil | 53.5 | (0.5) | 60.1 | (1.0) | **-6.7** | (1.1) | 18.4 | (0.4) | 13.9 | (0.8) | **4.4** | (0.8) | 28.2 | (0.4) | 25.9 | (0.6) | **2.2** | (0.7) |
| Bulgaria | c | c | c | c | c | c | c | c | c | c | c | c | c | c | c | c | c | c |
| Chile | 53.6 | (0.8) | 60.3 | (0.8) | **-6.7** | (1.1) | 16.9 | (0.6) | 13.8 | (0.6) | **3.1** | (0.9) | 29.5 | (0.6) | 25.9 | (0.4) | **3.6** | (0.7) |
| Colombia | 59.5 | (0.7) | 64.2 | (1.5) | **-4.7** | (1.6) | 15.2 | (0.4) | 11.2 | (0.8) | **3.9** | (1.0) | 25.3 | (0.5) | 24.5 | (0.9) | 0.8 | (1.0) |
| Croatia | 66.8 | (0.4) | 64.9 | (0.1) | **1.9** | (0.5) | 5.8 | (0.2) | 9.1 | (0.0) | **-3.3** | (0.2) | 27.4 | (0.4) | 26.0 | (0.1) | **1.4** | (0.4) |
| Estonia | 61.7 | (0.5) | 63.7 | (1.9) | -2.0 | (1.9) | 13.1 | (0.4) | 9.5 | (1.7) | **3.6** | (1.7) | 25.1 | (0.3) | 26.7 | (0.7) | **-1.6** | (0.7) |
| Hong Kong-China | 74.7 | (0.6) | 70.6 | (0.5) | **4.0** | (0.7) | 6.0 | (0.8) | 9.3 | (0.3) | **-3.3** | (0.8) | 19.3 | (1.2) | 20.0 | (0.3) | -0.7 | (1.3) |
| Indonesia | 57.0 | (0.8) | 55.1 | (0.7) | **2.0** | (0.8) | 16.7 | (0.5) | 16.6 | (0.9) | 0.1 | (0.8) | 26.2 | (0.5) | 28.3 | (0.6) | **-2.1** | (0.8) |
| Israel | 51.7 | (0.8) | 59.9 | (1.2) | **-8.2** | (1.7) | 21.1 | (0.6) | 16.5 | (0.7) | **4.6** | (1.0) | 27.1 | (0.5) | 23.6 | (1.0) | **3.5** | (1.2) |
| Jordan | 43.5 | (0.6) | 46.5 | (1.6) | -3.0 | (1.7) | 22.5 | (0.5) | 21.2 | (1.1) | 1.3 | (1.2) | 34.0 | (0.4) | 32.3 | (1.0) | 1.7 | (1.1) |
| Kyrgyzstan | 39.7 | (0.5) | 47.6 | (1.7) | **-7.9** | (1.7) | 26.3 | (0.5) | 17.3 | (3.4) | **9.0** | (3.5) | 34.0 | (0.4) | 35.1 | (3.1) | -1.1 | (3.1) |
| Latvia | 59.2 | (0.4) | a | a | a | a | 11.4 | (0.4) | a | a | a | a | 29.3 | (0.3) | a | a | a | a |
| Liechtenstein | 69.7 | (1.3) | c | c | c | c | 5.8 | (0.7) | c | c | c | c | 24.5 | (1.0) | c | c | c | c |
| Lithuania | 62.2 | (0.4) | c | c | c | c | 9.9 | (0.3) | c | c | c | c | 27.8 | (0.3) | c | c | c | c |
| Macao-China | 72.9 | (1.5) | 71.3 | (0.3) | 1.6 | (1.5) | 11.7 | (1.1) | 11.1 | (0.8) | 0.6 | (1.1) | 15.4 | (0.9) | 17.5 | (0.3) | **-2.2** | (0.9) |
| Montenegro | 53.0 | (0.4) | c | c | c | c | 11.5 | (0.3) | c | c | c | c | 35.6 | (0.4) | c | c | c | c |
| Qatar | 43.5 | (0.4) | 51.7 | (0.8) | **-8.1** | (1.0) | 24.1 | (0.3) | 20.1 | (0.8) | **4.1** | (0.9) | 32.3 | (0.4) | 28.3 | (0.7) | **4.1** | (0.9) |
| Romania | 50.6 | (0.6) | a | a | a | a | 19.7 | (0.4) | a | a | a | a | 29.6 | (0.3) | a | a | a | a |
| Russian Federation | 48.2 | (0.6) | a | a | a | a | 16.4 | (0.6) | a | a | a | a | 35.4 | (0.5) | a | a | a | a |
| Serbia | 60.1 | (0.5) | c | c | c | c | 12.9 | (0.4) | c | c | c | c | 27.0 | (0.3) | c | c | c | c |
| Slovenia | 60.7 | (0.4) | 68.6 | (1.3) | **-7.9** | (1.4) | 12.2 | (0.3) | 6.6 | (1.0) | **5.6** | (1.0) | 27.1 | (0.3) | 24.8 | (1.1) | **2.3** | (1.1) |
| Chinese Taipei | 65.7 | (0.4) | 66.8 | (0.8) | -1.1 | (0.9) | 8.6 | (0.3) | 9.4 | (0.5) | -0.8 | (0.6) | 25.6 | (0.3) | 23.8 | (0.4) | **1.9** | (0.5) |
| Thailand | 63.0 | (0.4) | 60.3 | (0.7) | **2.7** | (0.8) | 7.5 | (0.3) | 6.6 | (0.4) | 0.9 | (0.5) | 29.5 | (0.3) | 33.1 | (0.7) | **-3.6** | (0.8) |
| Tunisia | 46.0 | (0.7) | 33.0 | (5.6) | 12.9 | (5.6) | 23.5 | (0.5) | 27.7 | (3.2) | -4.2 | (3.2) | 30.5 | (0.4) | 39.2 | (4.0) | -8.7 | (4.0) |
| Uruguay | 60.0 | (0.5) | 64.7 | (0.8) | **-4.7** | (0.9) | 12.2 | (0.4) | 7.0 | (0.5) | **5.1** | (0.7) | 27.8 | (0.4) | 28.3 | (0.6) | -0.5 | (0.7) |

*Note*: Values that are statistically significant at the 5% level (p < 0.05) are indicated in bold.

### Table 3.11d  Mean learning hours and allocation of total learning time in science, in mathematics and on the language of instruction, by public and private schools
[Part 1/3]

| | | Mean learning hours per week | | | | | | | | | | | | | | |
|---|---|---|---|---|---|---|---|---|---|---|---|---|---|---|---|---|
| | | Regular school lessons | | | | | | | | Out-of-school-time lessons | | | | | | |
| | | Public schools | | Private schools | | Difference (public-private) | | Difference after accounting for ESCS and school average ESCS (public-private) | | Public schools | | Private schools | | Difference (public-private) | | Difference after accounting for ESCS and school average ESCS (public-private) | |
| | | Mean | S.E. | Mean | S.E. | Dif. | S.E. | Dif. | S.E. | Mean | S.E. | Mean | S.E. | Dif. | S.E. | Dif. | S.E. |
| OECD | Australia | w | w | w | w | w | w | w | w | w | w | w | w | w | w | w | w |
| | Austria | 8.52 | (0.10) | 8.92 | (0.27) | -0.40 | (0.30) | -0.23 | (0.41) | 0.95 | (0.04) | 0.88 | (0.11) | 0.07 | (0.12) | 0.01 | (0.13) |
| | Belgium | w | w | w | w | w | w | w | w | w | w | w | w | w | w | w | w |
| | Canada | 12.97 | (0.12) | 12.77 | (0.26) | 0.20 | (0.30) | **1.37** | (0.38) | 2.38 | (0.05) | 2.20 | (0.11) | 0.18 | (0.12) | 0.13 | (0.13) |
| | Czech Republic | 10.74 | (0.11) | 9.59 | (0.42) | **1.15** | (0.44) | **1.42** | (0.29) | 1.89 | (0.04) | 1.93 | (0.29) | -0.04 | (0.30) | -0.07 | (0.31) |
| | Denmark | 13.28 | (0.09) | 12.93 | (0.26) | 0.35 | (0.29) | 0.51 | (0.31) | 4.04 | (0.08) | 3.28 | (0.18) | **0.76** | (0.20) | **0.72** | (0.20) |
| | Finland | 9.71 | (0.11) | 9.67 | (0.57) | 0.04 | (0.59) | 0.25 | (0.63) | 1.04 | (0.04) | 1.67 | (0.33) | -0.63 | (0.33) | **-0.73** | (0.33) |
| | France | w | w | w | w | w | w | w | w | w | w | w | w | w | w | w | w |
| | Germany | 10.64 | (0.09) | 10.47 | (0.62) | 0.17 | (0.63) | 0.61 | (0.60) | 1.91 | (0.06) | 1.75 | (0.27) | 0.16 | (0.28) | -0.33 | (0.27) |
| | Greece | 9.68 | (0.11) | 12.36 | (0.44) | **-2.68** | (0.46) | 0.21 | (0.38) | 5.91 | (0.11) | 4.66 | (0.20) | **1.24** | (0.23) | **3.80** | (0.41) |
| | Hungary | 8.91 | (0.13) | 9.50 | (0.42) | -0.59 | (0.47) | 0.34 | (0.38) | 3.62 | (0.07) | 3.46 | (0.21) | 0.16 | (0.23) | -0.06 | (0.20) |
| | Iceland | 12.25 | (0.06) | 13.84 | (0.70) | -1.59 | (0.69) | **-1.56** | (0.69) | 1.49 | (0.04) | 1.69 | (0.38) | -0.21 | (0.38) | -0.09 | (0.38) |
| | Ireland | 9.64 | (0.16) | 9.84 | (0.09) | -0.20 | (0.18) | -0.02 | (0.20) | 1.85 | (0.08) | 1.53 | (0.06) | **0.32** | (0.10) | 0.14 | (0.10) |
| | Italy | 11.34 | (0.10) | 9.96 | (0.39) | **1.38** | (0.43) | **1.72** | (0.36) | 2.26 | (0.04) | 2.05 | (0.18) | 0.21 | (0.18) | 0.07 | (0.18) |
| | Japan | 10.50 | (0.13) | 11.32 | (0.29) | **-0.82** | (0.31) | 0.43 | (0.28) | 1.35 | (0.07) | 1.51 | (0.07) | -0.16 | (0.09) | -0.07 | (0.09) |
| | Korea | 12.68 | (0.19) | 12.85 | (0.20) | -0.17 | (0.32) | -0.30 | (0.28) | 4.70 | (0.19) | 4.80 | (0.19) | -0.10 | (0.34) | -0.30 | (0.22) |
| | Luxembourg | 9.69 | (0.07) | 9.84 | (0.13) | -0.15 | (0.15) | **-0.34** | (0.15) | 1.89 | (0.04) | 2.15 | (0.11) | **-0.26** | (0.12) | -0.15 | (0.13) |
| | Mexico | 10.63 | (0.10) | 11.94 | (0.35) | **-1.31** | (0.37) | -0.11 | (0.38) | 3.45 | (0.08) | 2.40 | (0.16) | **1.05** | (0.16) | 0.27 | (0.21) |
| | Netherlands | 8.01 | (0.17) | 7.95 | (0.11) | 0.05 | (0.24) | -0.00 | (0.19) | 1.98 | (0.10) | 1.83 | (0.07) | 0.14 | (0.13) | 0.18 | (0.11) |
| | New Zealand | 12.77 | (0.09) | 13.92 | (0.40) | -1.15 | (0.41) | -0.07 | (0.32) | 1.74 | (0.06) | 1.89 | (0.17) | -0.15 | (0.18) | -0.37 | (0.19) |
| | Norway | 9.58 | (0.08) | 10.72 | (0.23) | **-1.14** | (0.26) | **-0.90** | (0.32) | 3.15 | (0.06) | 2.56 | (0.26) | **0.59** | (0.27) | **0.64** | (0.27) |
| | Poland | 11.70 | (0.09) | 12.85 | (0.24) | **-1.16** | (0.25) | -0.37 | (0.23) | 2.11 | (0.05) | 1.91 | (0.24) | 0.20 | (0.24) | -0.07 | (0.24) |
| | Portugal | 10.01 | (0.11) | 10.69 | (0.32) | **-0.68** | (0.34) | -0.18 | (0.31) | 1.99 | (0.05) | 2.03 | (0.25) | -0.04 | (0.25) | -0.12 | (0.27) |
| | Slovak Republic | 8.88 | (0.15) | 8.95 | (0.69) | -0.07 | (0.73) | 0.61 | (0.76) | 2.44 | (0.07) | 2.03 | (0.22) | 0.41 | (0.24) | **0.65** | (0.23) |
| | Spain | 9.67 | (0.09) | 11.00 | (0.16) | **-1.33** | (0.17) | **-0.70** | (0.17) | 2.27 | (0.07) | 2.18 | (0.10) | 0.09 | (0.13) | -0.10 | (0.13) |
| | Sweden | 9.08 | (0.07) | 8.28 | (0.38) | **0.80** | (0.37) | **0.93** | (0.35) | 1.79 | (0.04) | 1.74 | (0.17) | 0.06 | (0.18) | -0.02 | (0.18) |
| | Switzerland | 9.97 | (0.10) | 9.63 | (0.46) | 0.34 | (0.51) | **1.33** | (0.52) | 1.57 | (0.05) | 1.72 | (0.14) | -0.15 | (0.15) | **-0.68** | (0.20) |
| | Turkey | 10.62 | (0.17) | 12.79 | (0.31) | **-2.17** | (0.36) | -0.46 | (0.31) | 5.21 | (0.09) | 5.76 | (0.09) | **-0.55** | (0.12) | 0.12 | (0.28) |
| | United Kingdom | 11.85 | (0.09) | 12.91 | (0.49) | **-1.07** | (0.49) | -0.16 | (0.49) | 1.73 | (0.05) | 0.91 | (0.14) | **0.82** | (0.15) | 0.35 | (0.22) |
| | United States | 10.84 | (0.13) | 12.32 | (0.39) | **-1.48** | (0.40) | -0.02 | (0.38) | 3.08 | (0.07) | 2.38 | (0.22) | **0.70** | (0.22) | 0.08 | (0.21) |
| | **OECD average** | 10.48 | (0.02) | 10.99 | (0.07) | **-0.52** | (0.08) | **0.17** | (0.08) | 2.48 | (0.01) | 2.29 | (0.04) | **0.19** | (0.04) | **0.15** | (0.04) |
| Partners | Argentina | 7.00 | (0.16) | 8.71 | (0.21) | **-1.71** | (0.25) | -0.48 | (0.32) | 1.78 | (0.08) | 1.45 | (0.10) | **0.33** | (0.13) | 0.20 | (0.18) |
| | Azerbaijan | 10.36 | (0.12) | 11.67 | (0.31) | **-1.31** | (0.34) | 0.35 | (0.59) | 4.85 | (0.10) | 6.16 | (0.51) | **-1.32** | (0.53) | **-1.24** | (0.60) |
| | Brazil | 8.07 | (0.11) | 10.77 | (0.21) | **-2.69** | (0.24) | **-0.88** | (0.33) | 3.12 | (0.08) | 3.32 | (0.18) | -0.20 | (0.20) | -0.11 | (0.25) |
| | Bulgaria | m | m | m | m | m | m | m | m | m | m | m | m | m | m | m | m |
| | Chile | 8.20 | (0.24) | 10.10 | (0.20) | **-1.89** | (0.31) | -0.31 | (0.34) | 2.91 | (0.10) | 2.72 | (0.08) | 0.19 | (0.13) | 0.00 | (0.15) |
| | Colombia | 11.46 | (0.24) | 12.66 | (0.45) | **-1.20** | (0.51) | 0.30 | (0.74) | 3.44 | (0.08) | 2.77 | (0.15) | **0.66** | (0.17) | **0.43** | (0.22) |
| | Croatia | 8.42 | (0.09) | 9.55 | (0.01) | **-1.14** | (0.09) | **0.41** | (0.16) | 1.57 | (0.05) | 2.34 | (0.01) | **-0.77** | (0.05) | **-0.87** | (0.08) |
| | Estonia | 10.96 | (0.09) | 10.48 | (0.52) | 0.48 | (0.51) | **1.00** | (0.45) | 2.65 | (0.07) | 1.47 | (0.28) | **1.18** | (0.28) | **0.93** | (0.26) |
| | Hong Kong-China | 13.87 | (0.44) | 13.54 | (0.12) | 0.32 | (0.45) | -0.10 | (0.35) | 2.85 | (0.19) | 3.10 | (0.08) | -0.25 | (0.21) | -0.24 | (0.21) |
| | Indonesia | 11.74 | (0.18) | 9.81 | (0.21) | **1.92** | (0.27) | **1.67** | (0.26) | 3.87 | (0.16) | 3.34 | (0.14) | **0.53** | (0.19) | **0.50** | (0.18) |
| | Israel | 9.66 | (0.12) | 9.42 | (0.26) | 0.24 | (0.31) | 0.32 | (0.28) | 4.77 | (0.10) | 3.64 | (0.17) | **1.13** | (0.21) | **1.03** | (0.21) |
| | Jordan | 10.14 | (0.14) | 11.17 | (0.31) | **-1.04** | (0.34) | -0.18 | (0.33) | 5.12 | (0.10) | 5.14 | (0.25) | -0.02 | (0.26) | -0.12 | (0.27) |
| | Kyrgyzstan | 7.75 | (0.16) | 9.15 | (0.72) | -1.40 | (0.75) | 0.83 | (1.07) | 4.61 | (0.09) | 3.75 | (0.78) | 0.85 | (0.81) | -0.08 | (0.87) |
| | Latvia | 11.06 | (0.11) | a | a | a | a | a | a | 2.72 | (0.08) | a | a | a | a | a | a |
| | Liechtenstein | 10.24 | (0.21) | c | c | c | c | c | c | 1.40 | (0.11) | c | c | c | c | c | c |
| | Lithuania | 9.82 | (0.10) | c | c | c | c | c | c | 1.94 | (0.05) | c | c | c | c | c | c |
| | Macao-China | 12.78 | (0.27) | 14.53 | (0.07) | **-1.75** | (0.28) | **-1.48** | (0.29) | 2.82 | (0.28) | 3.27 | (0.07) | -0.46 | (0.29) | -0.42 | (0.31) |
| | Montenegro | 8.94 | (0.09) | c | c | c | c | c | c | 2.70 | (0.05) | c | c | c | c | c | c |
| | Qatar | 8.27 | (0.10) | 11.01 | (0.17) | **-2.75** | (0.21) | **-1.60** | (0.22) | 4.90 | (0.07) | 4.91 | (0.14) | -0.01 | (0.15) | **-0.37** | (0.18) |
| | Romania | 8.58 | (0.15) | a | a | a | a | a | a | 4.04 | (0.07) | a | a | a | a | a | a |
| | Russian Federation | 9.41 | (0.13) | a | a | a | a | a | a | 3.07 | (0.07) | a | a | a | a | a | a |
| | Serbia | 9.33 | (0.11) | c | c | c | c | c | c | 2.67 | (0.06) | c | c | c | c | c | c |
| | Slovenia | 9.33 | (0.07) | 12.57 | (0.32) | **-3.23** | (0.31) | **-1.11** | (0.33) | 2.48 | (0.04) | 1.82 | (0.21) | **0.66** | (0.22) | 0.21 | (0.24) |
| | Chinese Taipei | 11.92 | (0.17) | 10.77 | (0.44) | **1.15** | (0.54) | **1.11** | (0.31) | 3.32 | (0.08) | 2.40 | (0.13) | **0.93** | (0.17) | **0.90** | (0.11) |
| | Thailand | 11.08 | (0.09) | 8.70 | (0.18) | **2.38** | (0.20) | **2.74** | (0.23) | 2.50 | (0.08) | 1.85 | (0.16) | **0.66** | (0.18) | **0.91** | (0.12) |
| | Tunisia | 9.27 | (0.11) | 6.23 | (0.82) | **3.04** | (0.83) | **3.32** | (0.78) | 6.12 | (0.06) | 5.50 | (0.35) | 0.62 | (0.35) | 0.60 | (0.35) |
| | Uruguay | 8.15 | (0.09) | 10.24 | (0.25) | **-2.09** | (0.27) | **-0.89** | (0.34) | 2.11 | (0.06) | 1.93 | (0.07) | **0.18** | (0.09) | **-0.29** | (0.14) |

*Note:* Values that are statistically significant at the 5% level (p < 0.05) are indicated in bold.

© OECD 2011  Quality Time for Students: Learning In and Out of School

**Table 3.11d** [Part 2/3] **Mean learning hours and allocation of total learning time in science, in mathematics and on the language of instruction, by public and private schools**

| | Mean learning hours per week | | | | | | | | | | | |
| | Individual study | | | | | | | | Total learning hours | | | |
| | Public schools | | Private schools | | Difference (public-private) | | Difference after accounting for ESCS and school average ESCS (public-private) | | Public schools | | Private schools | | Difference (public-private) | |
| | Mean | S.E. | Mean | S.E. | Dif. | S.E. | Dif. | S.E. | Mean | S.E. | Mean | S.E. | Dif. | S.E. |
|---|---|---|---|---|---|---|---|---|---|---|---|---|---|---|
| Australia | w | w | w | w | w | w | w | w | w | w | w | w | w | w |
| Austria | 4.87 | (0.08) | 5.71 | (0.18) | **-0.83** | (0.20) | **-0.88** | (0.22) | 14.38 | (0.17) | 15.57 | (0.31) | **-1.19** | (0.37) |
| Belgium | w | w | w | w | **w** | w | w | w | w | w | w | w | **w** | w |
| Canada | 5.27 | (0.08) | 5.64 | (0.15) | -0.37 | (0.18) | **0.62** | (0.24) | 20.72 | (0.19) | 20.58 | (0.39) | 0.14 | (0.44) |
| Czech Republic | 3.50 | (0.05) | 3.08 | (0.40) | 0.42 | (0.40) | 0.44 | (0.39) | 16.09 | (0.15) | 14.67 | (1.03) | 1.42 | (1.05) |
| Denmark | 4.99 | (0.07) | 4.99 | (0.17) | -0.00 | (0.20) | 0.14 | (0.20) | 22.26 | (0.16) | 21.08 | (0.51) | **1.18** | (0.57) |
| Finland | 3.39 | (0.05) | 4.13 | (0.39) | -0.74 | (0.39) | -0.73 | (0.39) | 14.12 | (0.16) | 15.59 | (0.36) | **-1.47** | (0.37) |
| France | w | w | w | w | w | w | w | w | w | w | w | w | w | w |
| Germany | 5.84 | (0.09) | 5.91 | (0.35) | -0.07 | (0.37) | -0.12 | (0.41) | 18.44 | (0.16) | 18.13 | (0.90) | 0.31 | (0.92) |
| Greece | 5.78 | (0.09) | 5.92 | (0.19) | -0.14 | (0.22) | **1.38** | (0.32) | 21.38 | (0.25) | 23.08 | (0.49) | **-1.70** | (0.58) |
| Hungary | 5.26 | (0.09) | 5.48 | (0.26) | -0.23 | (0.28) | 0.01 | (0.26) | 17.81 | (0.22) | 18.46 | (0.73) | -0.65 | (0.80) |
| Iceland | 4.43 | (0.05) | 4.53 | (0.57) | -0.10 | (0.57) | -0.12 | (0.56) | 18.18 | (0.09) | 20.06 | (0.93) | **-1.89** | (0.92) |
| Ireland | 4.55 | (0.12) | 4.82 | (0.10) | -0.26 | (0.15) | -0.19 | (0.18) | 15.96 | (0.26) | 16.19 | (0.19) | -0.24 | (0.32) |
| Italy | 7.60 | (0.08) | 6.08 | (0.34) | **1.52** | (0.36) | **1.97** | (0.35) | 21.21 | (0.18) | 18.26 | (0.63) | **2.95** | (0.70) |
| Japan | 3.15 | (0.11) | 3.03 | (0.15) | 0.12 | (0.18) | **0.84** | (0.20) | 14.99 | (0.23) | 15.85 | (0.44) | -0.86 | (0.46) |
| Korea | 4.88 | (0.23) | 5.00 | (0.16) | -0.12 | (0.32) | -0.32 | (0.20) | 22.30 | (0.53) | 22.70 | (0.46) | -0.40 | (0.87) |
| Luxembourg | 4.26 | (0.05) | 4.73 | (0.13) | **-0.47** | (0.14) | **-0.42** | (0.14) | 15.86 | (0.11) | 16.67 | (0.25) | **-0.81** | (0.28) |
| Mexico | 6.50 | (0.09) | 5.95 | (0.18) | 0.56 | (0.19) | **0.60** | (0.23) | 20.44 | (0.21) | 20.22 | (0.36) | 0.22 | (0.39) |
| Netherlands | 4.08 | (0.10) | 3.96 | (0.08) | 0.12 | (0.13) | 0.09 | (0.13) | 14.04 | (0.24) | 13.71 | (0.19) | 0.33 | (0.35) |
| New Zealand | 4.34 | (0.07) | 5.83 | (0.17) | **-1.50** | (0.18) | **-0.66** | (0.18) | 18.86 | (0.14) | 21.61 | (0.45) | **-2.75** | (0.47) |
| Norway | 4.05 | (0.06) | 4.04 | (0.47) | 0.01 | (0.47) | 0.29 | (0.46) | 16.75 | (0.13) | 17.30 | (0.42) | -0.55 | (0.43) |
| Poland | 6.33 | (0.07) | 6.94 | (0.17) | **-0.61** | (0.30) | **-0.64** | (0.30) | 20.16 | (0.14) | 21.71 | (0.28) | **-1.55** | (0.31) |
| Portugal | 5.84 | (0.08) | 5.82 | (0.34) | 0.01 | (0.35) | 0.09 | (0.38) | 17.86 | (0.17) | 18.58 | (0.68) | -0.72 | (0.70) |
| Slovak Republic | 4.85 | (0.09) | 4.37 | (0.30) | 0.48 | (0.31) | **0.86** | (0.33) | 16.19 | (0.26) | 15.46 | (1.10) | 0.72 | (1.16) |
| Spain | 5.39 | (0.09) | 5.93 | (0.13) | **-0.54** | (0.15) | -0.36 | (0.18) | 17.46 | (0.18) | 19.19 | (0.28) | **-1.73** | (0.31) |
| Sweden | 3.53 | (0.05) | 4.04 | (0.25) | **-0.51** | (0.25) | -0.41 | (0.25) | 14.40 | (0.11) | 14.03 | (0.61) | 0.37 | (0.61) |
| Switzerland | 4.21 | (0.04) | 4.45 | (0.20) | -0.24 | (0.20) | -0.32 | (0.22) | 15.76 | (0.14) | 15.81 | (0.60) | -0.05 | (0.66) |
| Turkey | 6.10 | (0.09) | 6.35 | (0.46) | -0.24 | (0.46) | 0.21 | (0.55) | 21.82 | (0.30) | 24.49 | (0.26) | **-2.67** | (0.38) |
| United Kingdom | 4.42 | (0.06) | 5.87 | (0.27) | **-1.45** | (0.28) | **-0.69** | (0.30) | 18.02 | (0.14) | 19.78 | (0.75) | **-1.76** | (0.75) |
| United States | 5.47 | (0.06) | 6.92 | (0.39) | **-1.44** | (0.40) | **-0.82** | (0.35) | 19.52 | (0.16) | 21.59 | (0.61) | **-2.07** | (0.64) |
| **OECD average** | 4.89 | (0.02) | 5.14 | (0.05) | -0.25 | (0.06) | 0.03 | (0.06) | 17.85 | (0.04) | 18.43 | (0.11) | **-0.58** | (0.12) |
| Argentina | 4.96 | (0.12) | 5.17 | (0.13) | -0.21 | (0.16) | -0.00 | (0.24) | 13.77 | (0.29) | 15.25 | (0.28) | **-1.48** | (0.37) |
| Azerbaijan | 8.70 | (0.13) | 9.01 | (0.34) | -0.31 | (0.35) | 0.19 | (0.61) | 24.07 | (0.27) | 26.85 | (0.46) | **-2.78** | (0.52) |
| Brazil | 5.12 | (0.08) | 5.69 | (0.15) | **-0.57** | (0.16) | **-0.62** | (0.26) | 16.26 | (0.20) | 19.77 | (0.39) | **-3.51** | (0.44) |
| Bulgaria | m | m | m | m | m | m | m | m | m | m | m | m | m | m |
| Chile | 4.64 | (0.12) | 4.72 | (0.11) | -0.08 | (0.17) | 0.03 | (0.20) | 15.86 | (0.37) | 17.60 | (0.30) | **-1.74** | (0.49) |
| Colombia | 5.64 | (0.11) | 5.35 | (0.18) | 0.30 | (0.21) | **0.61** | (0.24) | 20.52 | (0.32) | 20.81 | (0.65) | -0.28 | (0.73) |
| Croatia | 4.85 | (0.07) | 5.25 | (0.02) | **-0.40** | (0.08) | **0.48** | (0.15) | 14.91 | (0.14) | 17.13 | (0.04) | **-2.22** | (0.15) |
| Estonia | 5.13 | (0.06) | 4.12 | (0.15) | **1.01** | (0.17) | **1.21** | (0.16) | 18.77 | (0.14) | 15.98 | (0.62) | **2.79** | (0.61) |
| Hong Kong-China | 5.26 | (0.27) | 5.34 | (0.09) | -0.08 | (0.29) | **-0.40** | (0.18) | 22.01 | (0.76) | 21.97 | (0.21) | 0.04 | (0.79) |
| Indonesia | 5.85 | (0.14) | 5.16 | (0.12) | **0.70** | (0.21) | **0.72** | (0.20) | 21.43 | (0.34) | 18.24 | (0.37) | **3.19** | (0.51) |
| Israel | 5.69 | (0.12) | 4.53 | (0.24) | **1.16** | (0.28) | **1.06** | (0.30) | 20.23 | (0.26) | 17.64 | (0.54) | **2.59** | (0.61) |
| Jordan | 7.88 | (0.12) | 7.97 | (0.27) | -0.09 | (0.29) | -0.14 | (0.30) | 23.18 | (0.24) | 24.05 | (0.49) | -0.87 | (0.55) |
| Kyrgyzstan | 6.70 | (0.09) | 6.51 | (0.73) | 0.19 | (0.73) | -0.18 | (0.74) | 19.20 | (0.24) | 19.79 | (1.91) | -0.59 | (1.93) |
| Latvia | 6.25 | (0.08) | a | a | a | a | a | a | 20.03 | (0.19) | a | a | a | a |
| Liechtenstein | 3.86 | (0.14) | c | c | c | c | c | c | 15.48 | (0.24) | c | c | c | c |
| Lithuania | 5.26 | (0.07) | c | c | c | c | c | c | 17.01 | (0.14) | c | c | c | c |
| Macao-China | 3.34 | (0.21) | 4.99 | (0.07) | **-1.65** | (0.22) | **-0.66** | (0.25) | 18.99 | (0.57) | 22.78 | (0.15) | **-3.79** | (0.58) |
| Montenegro | 6.25 | (0.08) | c | c | c | c | c | c | 17.86 | (0.16) | c | c | c | c |
| Qatar | 6.16 | (0.06) | 7.03 | (0.15) | **-0.87** | (0.17) | **-0.82** | (0.20) | 19.34 | (0.19) | 23.05 | (0.32) | **-3.71** | (0.37) |
| Romania | 5.96 | (0.10) | a | a | a | a | a | a | 18.57 | (0.26) | a | a | a | a |
| Russian Federation | 6.65 | (0.12) | a | a | a | a | a | a | 19.13 | (0.24) | a | a | a | a |
| Serbia | 5.23 | (0.08) | c | c | c | c | c | c | 17.22 | (0.19) | c | c | c | c |
| Slovenia | 4.92 | (0.06) | 5.72 | (0.29) | **-0.80** | (0.30) | -0.34 | (0.32) | 16.78 | (0.12) | 20.15 | (0.61) | **-3.38** | (0.61) |
| Chinese Taipei | 5.18 | (0.10) | 4.32 | (0.20) | **0.86** | (0.24) | **0.83** | (0.15) | 20.56 | (0.30) | 17.61 | (0.74) | **2.95** | (0.90) |
| Thailand | 5.58 | (0.09) | 3.96 | (0.16) | **1.62** | (0.18) | **1.72** | (0.18) | 19.14 | (0.18) | 14.52 | (0.37) | **4.63** | (0.42) |
| Tunisia | 7.31 | (0.08) | 5.98 | (0.70) | 1.34 | (0.71) | 1.32 | (0.71) | 22.74 | (0.21) | 17.97 | (0.70) | **4.77** | (0.72) |
| Uruguay | 4.15 | (0.07) | 4.66 | (0.15) | **-0.51** | (0.16) | -0.04 | (0.26) | 14.45 | (0.16) | 16.83 | (0.39) | **-2.38** | (0.42) |

*Note:* Values that are statistically significant at the 5% level (p < 0.05) are indicated in bold.

183

### Table 3.11d [Part 3/3] Mean learning hours and allocation of total learning time in science, in mathematics and on the language of instruction, by public and private schools

| | Allocation of total learning time in science, in mathematics and on the language of instruction for | | | | | | | | | | | | | | | | | |
| | Regular school lessons | | | | | | Out-of-school-time lessons | | | | | | Individual study | | | | | |
| | Public schools | | Private schools | | Difference (public-private) | | Public schools | | Private schools | | Difference (public-private) | | Public schools | | Private schools | | Difference (public-private) | |
| | % | S.E | % | S.E | Dif. | S.E. | % | S.E | % | S.E | Dif. | S.E. | % | S.E | % | S.E | Dif. | S.E. |
|---|---|---|---|---|---|---|---|---|---|---|---|---|---|---|---|---|---|---|
| **OECD** | | | | | | | | | | | | | | | | | | |
| Australia | w | w | w | w | w | w | w | w | w | w | w | w | w | w | w | w | w | w |
| Austria | 62.1 | (0.4) | 59.9 | (1.1) | 2.1 | (1.2) | 5.4 | (0.2) | 5.1 | (0.6) | 0.3 | (0.6) | 32.5 | (0.4) | 34.9 | (1.1) | -2.4 | (1.2) |
| Belgium | w | w | w | w | w | w | w | w | w | w | w | w | w | w | w | w | w | w |
| Canada | 63.8 | (0.3) | 63.9 | (0.7) | -0.1 | (0.8) | 11.1 | (0.2) | 9.3 | (0.5) | **1.8** | (0.5) | 25.0 | (0.2) | 26.8 | (0.6) | **-1.7** | (0.6) |
| Czech Republic | 69.6 | (0.4) | 69.1 | (2.5) | 0.5 | (2.6) | 10.1 | (0.2) | 11.1 | (1.3) | -1.0 | (1.3) | 20.3 | (0.3) | 19.8 | (1.6) | 0.4 | (1.7) |
| Denmark | 62.0 | (0.3) | 63.8 | (0.8) | -1.7 | (0.9) | 16.5 | (0.3) | 14.0 | (0.6) | **2.5** | (0.6) | 21.4 | (0.2) | 22.2 | (0.4) | -0.8 | (0.5) |
| Finland | 70.6 | (0.3) | 66.0 | (2.9) | 4.6 | (2.9) | 6.4 | (0.2) | 9.0 | (1.6) | -2.7 | (1.6) | 23.0 | (0.2) | 25.0 | (1.7) | -2.0 | (1.7) |
| France | w | w | w | w | w | w | w | w | w | w | w | w | w | w | w | w | w | w |
| Germany | 59.6 | (0.4) | 59.8 | (1.8) | -0.1 | (1.9) | 9.3 | (0.3) | 8.5 | (1.4) | 0.8 | (1.4) | 31.1 | (0.3) | 31.8 | (0.8) | -0.7 | (0.9) |
| Greece | 47.6 | (0.4) | 56.1 | (1.2) | **-8.5** | (1.3) | 26.1 | (0.3) | 19.4 | (1.1) | **6.7** | (1.1) | 26.3 | (0.3) | 24.5 | (0.6) | **1.8** | (0.7) |
| Hungary | 52.2 | (0.5) | 53.5 | (0.9) | -1.3 | (1.1) | 18.9 | (0.3) | 17.5 | (0.9) | 1.5 | (1.0) | 28.9 | (0.3) | 29.0 | (0.6) | -0.1 | (0.6) |
| Iceland | 69.7 | (0.3) | 71.3 | (3.0) | -1.7 | (3.0) | 7.3 | (0.2) | 7.8 | (1.6) | -0.6 | (1.6) | 23.1 | (0.2) | 20.9 | (2.1) | 2.2 | (2.1) |
| Ireland | 63.0 | (0.6) | 63.7 | (0.5) | -0.7 | (0.8) | 9.9 | (0.4) | 8.0 | (0.3) | **1.9** | (0.5) | 27.1 | (0.5) | 28.4 | (0.4) | **-1.3** | (0.6) |
| Italy | 54.9 | (0.2) | 56.2 | (0.8) | -1.4 | (0.9) | 9.9 | (0.2) | 10.2 | (0.9) | -0.2 | (0.9) | 35.2 | (0.2) | 33.6 | (0.9) | 1.6 | (0.9) |
| Japan | 74.4 | (0.5) | 74.9 | (0.7) | -0.5 | (0.8) | 7.3 | (0.3) | 7.8 | (0.4) | -0.5 | (0.4) | 18.3 | (0.4) | 17.3 | (0.6) | 1.0 | (0.7) |
| Korea | 61.6 | (0.9) | 61.0 | (0.8) | 0.6 | (1.5) | 18.2 | (0.6) | 18.6 | (0.5) | -0.3 | (1.0) | 20.1 | (0.5) | 20.4 | (0.4) | -0.3 | (0.7) |
| Luxembourg | 63.5 | (0.3) | 61.3 | (0.7) | **2.3** | (0.8) | 10.5 | (0.2) | 12.0 | (0.6) | **-1.5** | (0.6) | 26.0 | (0.2) | 26.7 | (0.5) | -0.7 | (0.6) |
| Mexico | 52.5 | (0.3) | 59.9 | (1.2) | **-7.3** | (1.3) | 15.4 | (0.3) | 10.9 | (0.7) | **4.6** | (0.7) | 32.0 | (0.3) | 29.2 | (0.9) | **2.8** | (0.9) |
| Netherlands | 59.5 | (0.8) | 60.2 | (0.5) | -0.6 | (1.0) | 12.6 | (0.6) | 12.1 | (0.4) | 0.5 | (0.8) | 27.9 | (0.5) | 27.7 | (0.4) | 0.2 | (0.7) |
| New Zealand | 69.9 | (0.4) | 66.5 | (0.7) | **3.4** | (0.8) | 8.3 | (0.3) | 7.3 | (0.7) | 0.9 | (0.8) | 21.9 | (0.2) | 26.2 | (0.5) | **-4.3** | (0.5) |
| Norway | 60.3 | (0.4) | 64.8 | (2.1) | **-4.5** | (2.2) | 17.1 | (0.3) | 12.4 | (0.8) | **4.7** | (0.9) | 22.6 | (0.3) | 22.8 | (1.9) | -0.2 | (1.9) |
| Poland | 59.9 | (0.3) | 61.4 | (1.5) | -1.5 | (1.4) | 10.1 | (0.3) | 8.1 | (1.2) | 2.0 | (1.2) | 30.0 | (0.3) | 30.5 | (0.6) | -0.5 | (0.7) |
| Portugal | 58.0 | (0.3) | 60.4 | (1.9) | -2.4 | (1.9) | 10.3 | (0.2) | 10.0 | (0.9) | 0.3 | (0.9) | 31.7 | (0.3) | 29.6 | (1.1) | 2.1 | (1.1) |
| Slovak Republic | 58.7 | (0.5) | 62.0 | (1.4) | **-3.3** | (1.5) | 12.9 | (0.3) | 10.8 | (0.9) | **2.1** | (1.0) | 28.4 | (0.3) | 27.2 | (1.4) | 1.2 | (1.4) |
| Spain | 58.6 | (0.4) | 59.8 | (0.4) | **-1.2** | (0.6) | 11.7 | (0.3) | 10.4 | (0.4) | **1.3** | (0.5) | 29.7 | (0.3) | 29.8 | (0.3) | -0.1 | (0.5) |
| Sweden | 66.6 | (0.5) | 61.5 | (1.6) | **5.1** | (1.7) | 10.3 | (0.2) | 10.7 | (0.7) | -0.4 | (0.7) | 23.1 | (0.4) | 27.9 | (1.2) | **-4.8** | (1.2) |
| Switzerland | 64.4 | (0.3) | 62.0 | (1.6) | 2.5 | (1.7) | 8.8 | (0.2) | 9.7 | (0.7) | -0.8 | (0.8) | 26.7 | (0.2) | 28.3 | (1.3) | -1.6 | (1.4) |
| Turkey | 51.4 | (0.4) | 53.8 | (1.2) | -2.4 | (1.3) | 21.6 | (0.3) | 22.1 | (0.6) | -0.4 | (0.7) | 27.0 | (0.2) | 24.2 | (1.8) | 2.8 | (1.8) |
| United Kingdom | 67.9 | (0.4) | 67.2 | (0.7) | 0.7 | (0.8) | 8.4 | (0.2) | 3.8 | (0.5) | **4.6** | (0.6) | 23.7 | (0.2) | 29.0 | (0.5) | **-5.3** | (0.5) |
| United States | 55.4 | (0.5) | 58.7 | (1.0) | **-3.3** | (1.0) | 15.7 | (0.4) | 9.9 | (1.0) | **5.8** | (1.0) | 28.9 | (0.2) | 31.4 | (1.2) | **-2.5** | (1.2) |
| **OECD average** | **61.5** | **(0.1)** | **62.3** | **(0.3)** | **-0.8** | **(0.3)** | **12.1** | **(0.1)** | **10.8** | **(0.2)** | **1.3** | **(0.2)** | **26.4** | **(0.1)** | **26.9** | **(0.2)** | **-0.5** | **(0.2)** |
| **Partners** | | | | | | | | | | | | | | | | | | |
| Argentina | 52.5 | (0.5) | 57.8 | (0.8) | **-5.3** | (0.9) | 11.5 | (0.4) | 9.0 | (0.5) | **2.4** | (0.7) | 36.0 | (0.4) | 33.2 | (0.5) | **2.9** | (0.6) |
| Azerbaijan | 44.4 | (0.5) | 46.6 | (1.4) | -2.2 | (1.5) | 19.7 | (0.4) | 21.4 | (1.5) | -1.7 | (1.6) | 35.9 | (0.3) | 31.9 | (0.8) | **4.0** | (0.9) |
| Brazil | 52.2 | (0.4) | 57.3 | (0.9) | **-5.1** | (1.0) | 17.5 | (0.3) | 15.2 | (0.6) | **2.2** | (0.7) | 30.3 | (0.3) | 27.4 | (0.5) | **2.9** | (0.6) |
| Bulgaria | c | c | c | c | c | c | c | c | c | c | c | c | c | c | c | c | c | c |
| Chile | 51.4 | (0.8) | 57.1 | (0.5) | **-5.7** | (0.9) | 18.2 | (0.5) | 14.9 | (0.4) | **3.2** | (0.6) | 30.5 | (0.4) | 28.0 | (0.3) | **2.4** | (0.5) |
| Colombia | 58.8 | (0.7) | 62.9 | (1.2) | **-4.2** | (1.4) | 15.0 | (0.3) | 12.2 | (0.7) | **2.8** | (0.8) | 26.2 | (0.5) | 24.9 | (0.7) | 1.3 | (0.8) |
| Croatia | 59.9 | (0.4) | 60.7 | (0.1) | -0.8 | (0.4) | 9.6 | (0.3) | 12.7 | (0.0) | **-3.1** | (0.3) | 30.5 | (0.3) | 26.7 | (0.1) | **3.9** | (0.4) |
| Estonia | 60.8 | (0.4) | 66.1 | (1.8) | **-5.3** | (1.8) | 13.3 | (0.3) | 8.8 | (1.7) | **4.5** | (1.7) | 25.9 | (0.2) | 25.1 | (1.0) | 0.8 | (1.0) |
| Hong Kong-China | 65.5 | (0.6) | 64.0 | (0.4) | **1.5** | (0.7) | 11.7 | (0.5) | 13.0 | (0.3) | **-1.3** | (0.6) | 22.7 | (0.7) | 23.0 | (0.3) | -0.2 | (0.8) |
| Indonesia | 56.5 | (0.9) | 55.2 | (0.8) | 1.3 | (1.0) | 16.6 | (0.6) | 16.5 | (0.7) | 0.1 | (0.8) | 26.9 | (0.5) | 28.3 | (0.5) | -1.4 | (0.7) |
| Israel | 50.2 | (0.6) | 57.2 | (1.2) | **-7.0** | (1.6) | 22.7 | (0.3) | 19.0 | (0.6) | **3.7** | (0.8) | 27.1 | (0.4) | 23.8 | (0.9) | **3.3** | (1.1) |
| Jordan | 43.1 | (0.5) | 45.1 | (1.4) | -2.1 | (1.4) | 22.2 | (0.4) | 21.4 | (1.0) | 0.8 | (1.0) | 34.8 | (0.4) | 33.5 | (0.6) | 1.3 | (0.7) |
| Kyrgyzstan | 39.7 | (0.5) | 50.3 | (1.4) | **-10.6** | (1.5) | 25.3 | (0.5) | 17.6 | (3.3) | **7.8** | (3.5) | 34.9 | (0.3) | 32.1 | (2.3) | 2.8 | (2.3) |
| Latvia | 57.4 | (0.3) | a | a | a | a | 12.7 | (0.3) | a | a | a | a | 30.0 | (0.3) | a | a | a | a |
| Liechtenstein | 66.1 | (1.1) | c | c | c | c | 8.6 | (0.7) | c | c | c | c | 25.3 | (0.9) | c | c | c | c |
| Lithuania | 59.5 | (0.3) | c | c | c | c | 11.2 | (0.3) | c | c | c | c | 29.3 | (0.2) | c | c | c | c |
| Macao-China | 70.3 | (1.4) | 66.5 | (0.3) | 3.8 | (1.4) | 13.0 | (0.9) | 12.8 | (0.2) | 0.1 | (1.0) | 16.7 | (0.8) | 20.6 | (0.2) | **-3.9** | (0.8) |
| Montenegro | 50.8 | (0.3) | c | c | c | c | 14.6 | (0.3) | c | c | c | c | 34.6 | (0.3) | c | c | c | c |
| Qatar | 42.3 | (0.3) | 48.1 | (0.7) | **-5.8** | (0.8) | 25.1 | (0.2) | 21.3 | (0.6) | **3.8** | (0.6) | 32.6 | (0.2) | 30.6 | (0.5) | **2.0** | (0.6) |
| Romania | 48.7 | (0.4) | a | a | a | a | 20.5 | (0.3) | a | a | a | a | 30.9 | (0.2) | a | a | a | a |
| Russian Federation | 50.9 | (0.5) | a | a | a | a | 15.7 | (0.5) | a | a | a | a | 33.5 | (0.4) | a | a | a | a |
| Serbia | 57.7 | (0.4) | c | c | c | c | 13.9 | (0.3) | c | c | c | c | 28.5 | (0.3) | c | c | c | c |
| Slovenia | 56.8 | (0.3) | 65.1 | (1.2) | **-8.3** | (1.3) | 14.0 | (0.2) | 8.3 | (0.9) | **5.7** | (0.9) | 29.2 | (0.2) | 26.6 | (1.1) | **2.6** | (1.1) |
| Chinese Taipei | 60.2 | (0.3) | 63.8 | (0.8) | **-3.6** | (0.9) | 14.8 | (0.2) | 12.4 | (0.5) | **2.4** | (0.6) | 25.0 | (0.2) | 23.8 | (0.4) | **1.2** | (0.5) |
| Thailand | 62.0 | (0.4) | 63.4 | (0.6) | -1.4 | (0.8) | 10.6 | (0.3) | 8.7 | (0.8) | **1.9** | (0.8) | 27.4 | (0.3) | 27.8 | (0.6) | -0.4 | (0.7) |
| Tunisia | 41.6 | (0.3) | 37.8 | (3.1) | 3.8 | (3.1) | 26.4 | (0.2) | 30.0 | (2.9) | -3.6 | (2.9) | 32.1 | (0.2) | 32.3 | (1.8) | -0.2 | (1.8) |
| Uruguay | 58.5 | (0.4) | 62.9 | (0.6) | **-4.4** | (0.7) | 13.1 | (0.3) | 10.2 | (0.4) | **2.8** | (0.5) | 28.4 | (0.3) | 26.9 | (0.5) | **1.6** | (0.6) |

*Note*: Values that are statistically significant at the 5% level (p < 0.05) are indicated in bold.

© OECD 2011  Quality Time for Students: Learning In and Out of School

## Table 3.12a [Part 1/3] Mean learning hours and allocation of total learning time in science, by academic and vocational orientation of schools

| | Mean learning hours per week | | | | | | | | | | | |
|---|---|---|---|---|---|---|---|---|---|---|---|---|
| | Regular school lessons | | | | | | Out-of-school-time lessons | | | | | |
| | Academic schools | | Vocational schools | | Difference (academic-vocational) | | Academic schools | | Vocational schools | | Difference (academic-vocational) | |
| | Mean | S.E. | Mean | S.E. | Dif. | S.E. | Mean | S.E. | Mean | S.E. | Dif. | S.E. |
| **OECD** | | | | | | | | | | | | |
| Australia | 3.40 | (0.03) | 1.91 | (0.10) | **1.49** | (0.10) | 0.37 | (0.01) | 0.28 | (0.02) | **0.09** | (0.03) |
| Austria | 3.10 | (0.09) | 2.20 | (0.08) | **0.90** | (0.12) | 0.21 | (0.03) | 0.21 | (0.02) | -0.00 | (0.04) |
| Belgium | 3.47 | (0.04) | 1.58 | (0.06) | **1.90** | (0.07) | 0.33 | (0.02) | 0.32 | (0.02) | 0.01 | (0.03) |
| Canada | 4.00 | (0.04) | a | a | a | a | 0.55 | (0.01) | a | a | a | a |
| Czech Republic | 3.39 | (0.07) | 2.28 | (0.11) | **1.11** | (0.12) | 0.62 | (0.02) | 0.43 | (0.03) | **0.19** | (0.04) |
| Denmark | 3.21 | (0.04) | a | a | a | a | 0.77 | (0.02) | a | a | a | a |
| Finland | 3.13 | (0.04) | a | a | a | a | 0.32 | (0.01) | a | a | a | a |
| France | 2.99 | (0.05) | 1.46 | (0.14) | **1.53** | (0.16) | 0.57 | (0.02) | 0.37 | (0.04) | **0.20** | (0.05) |
| Germany | 3.11 | (0.05) | 1.27 | (0.37) | **1.84** | (0.38) | 0.51 | (0.02) | 0.43 | (0.08) | 0.08 | (0.08) |
| Greece | 3.40 | (0.05) | 1.74 | (0.08) | **1.66** | (0.10) | 2.12 | (0.05) | 1.17 | (0.09) | **0.95** | (0.11) |
| Hungary | 2.91 | (0.08) | 2.20 | (0.05) | **0.72** | (0.09) | 1.08 | (0.05) | 0.94 | (0.03) | **0.14** | (0.06) |
| Iceland | 2.97 | (0.02) | c | c | c | c | 0.29 | (0.01) | c | c | c | c |
| Ireland | 2.55 | (0.04) | 1.40 | (0.30) | **1.16** | (0.30) | 0.32 | (0.01) | 0.35 | (0.13) | -0.03 | (0.13) |
| Italy | 2.79 | (0.11) | 3.01 | (0.04) | -0.21 | (0.11) | 0.49 | (0.02) | 0.65 | (0.02) | **-0.16** | (0.03) |
| Japan | 2.92 | (0.06) | 2.02 | (0.11) | **0.90** | (0.13) | 0.25 | (0.01) | 0.28 | (0.03) | -0.03 | (0.03) |
| Korea | 3.85 | (0.07) | 2.69 | (0.16) | **1.16** | (0.17) | 1.26 | (0.05) | 0.25 | (0.03) | **1.00** | (0.06) |
| Luxembourg | 2.28 | (0.02) | 2.71 | (0.09) | **-0.43** | (0.09) | 0.50 | (0.02) | 0.51 | (0.04) | -0.00 | (0.04) |
| Mexico | 3.26 | (0.05) | 2.93 | (0.05) | **0.34** | (0.06) | 1.06 | (0.04) | 0.90 | (0.02) | **0.16** | (0.04) |
| Netherlands | 2.55 | (0.04) | 1.24 | (0.07) | **1.30** | (0.08) | 0.52 | (0.02) | 0.57 | (0.04) | -0.05 | (0.05) |
| New Zealand | 4.06 | (0.04) | a | a | a | a | 0.41 | (0.02) | a | a | a | a |
| Norway | 2.64 | (0.03) | a | a | a | a | 0.93 | (0.02) | a | a | a | a |
| Poland | 2.72 | (0.04) | a | a | a | a | 0.62 | (0.02) | a | a | a | a |
| Portugal | 3.23 | (0.05) | 3.06 | (0.14) | 0.17 | (0.14) | 0.65 | (0.02) | 0.52 | (0.04) | **0.14** | (0.05) |
| Slovak Republic | 3.07 | (0.09) | 1.67 | (0.10) | **1.39** | (0.14) | 0.81 | (0.03) | 0.44 | (0.04) | **0.37** | (0.05) |
| Spain | 3.12 | (0.04) | a | a | a | a | 0.68 | (0.02) | a | a | a | a |
| Sweden | 2.81 | (0.03) | c | c | c | c | 0.50 | (0.01) | c | c | c | c |
| Switzerland | 2.42 | (0.04) | 1.55 | (0.13) | **0.88** | (0.13) | 0.40 | (0.01) | 0.26 | (0.05) | **0.14** | (0.06) |
| Turkey | 3.42 | (0.14) | 2.06 | (0.10) | **1.35** | (0.17) | 1.65 | (0.08) | 0.92 | (0.05) | **0.72** | (0.10) |
| United Kingdom | 4.25 | (0.04) | a | a | a | a | 0.48 | (0.02) | a | a | a | a |
| United States | 3.51 | (0.05) | a | a | a | a | 0.78 | (0.02) | a | a | a | a |
| **OECD average** | **3.15** | **(0.01)** | **2.05** | **(0.03)** | **1.01** | **(0.04)** | **0.67** | **(0.01)** | **0.52** | **(0.01)** | **0.21** | **(0.01)** |
| **Partners** | | | | | | | | | | | | |
| Argentina | 2.26 | (0.06) | 2.13 | (0.35) | 0.13 | (0.36) | 0.49 | (0.02) | 0.50 | (0.18) | -0.02 | (0.18) |
| Azerbaijan | 2.85 | (0.06) | 1.71 | (0.37) | **1.13** | (0.38) | 1.36 | (0.03) | 1.41 | (0.38) | -0.04 | (0.38) |
| Brazil | 2.21 | (0.03) | a | a | a | a | 0.79 | (0.02) | a | a | a | a |
| Bulgaria | 2.94 | (0.11) | 2.28 | (0.09) | **0.66** | (0.14) | 0.96 | (0.04) | 1.01 | (0.04) | -0.06 | (0.06) |
| Chile | 2.38 | (0.05) | 0.71 | (0.11) | **1.66** | (0.12) | 0.84 | (0.02) | 0.33 | (0.06) | **0.52** | (0.07) |
| Colombia | 3.53 | (0.08) | 3.35 | (0.39) | 0.19 | (0.35) | 0.95 | (0.03) | 0.98 | (0.10) | -0.03 | (0.10) |
| Croatia | 2.85 | (0.07) | 1.68 | (0.05) | **1.17** | (0.09) | 0.48 | (0.03) | 0.41 | (0.02) | 0.06 | (0.04) |
| Estonia | 3.27 | (0.04) | a | a | a | a | 0.76 | (0.02) | a | a | a | a |
| Hong Kong-China | 3.23 | (0.06) | 2.03 | (0.17) | **1.20** | (0.17) | 0.90 | (0.03) | 0.65 | (0.07) | **0.25** | (0.08) |
| Indonesia | 3.41 | (0.07) | 2.38 | (0.39) | **1.03** | (0.39) | 1.14 | (0.04) | 0.59 | (0.06) | **0.55** | (0.07) |
| Israel | 2.47 | (0.06) | 2.23 | (0.10) | **0.24** | (0.12) | 0.96 | (0.03) | 1.08 | (0.07) | -0.12 | (0.08) |
| Jordan | 3.25 | (0.06) | a | a | a | a | 1.52 | (0.03) | a | a | a | a |
| Kyrgyzstan | 2.09 | (0.07) | 2.28 | (0.26) | -0.19 | (0.27) | 1.36 | (0.03) | 1.18 | (0.18) | 0.19 | (0.18) |
| Latvia | 2.83 | (0.06) | 3.74 | (0.19) | **-0.91** | (0.19) | 0.65 | (0.02) | 0.58 | (0.09) | 0.07 | (0.09) |
| Liechtenstein | 2.57 | (0.08) | a | a | a | a | 0.52 | (0.06) | a | a | a | a |
| Lithuania | 2.69 | (0.04) | c | c | c | c | 0.56 | (0.02) | c | c | c | c |
| Macao-China | 3.75 | (0.03) | 3.39 | (0.26) | 0.36 | (0.26) | 1.00 | (0.03) | 0.77 | (0.17) | 0.23 | (0.17) |
| Montenegro | 3.62 | (0.06) | 2.45 | (0.05) | **1.17** | (0.07) | 0.98 | (0.04) | 1.09 | (0.03) | **-0.11** | (0.05) |
| Qatar | 2.66 | (0.03) | a | a | a | a | 1.48 | (0.02) | a | a | a | a |
| Romania | 2.47 | (0.07) | 1.57 | (0.07) | **0.91** | (0.09) | 1.00 | (0.02) | 1.11 | (0.05) | -0.11 | (0.05) |
| Russian Federation | 3.78 | (0.10) | 3.41 | (0.23) | 0.37 | (0.27) | 1.13 | (0.03) | 1.10 | (0.11) | 0.03 | (0.11) |
| Serbia | 3.97 | (0.06) | 2.46 | (0.06) | **1.50** | (0.09) | 0.85 | (0.04) | 0.76 | (0.03) | 0.09 | (0.05) |
| Slovenia | 3.66 | (0.05) | 2.00 | (0.03) | **1.67** | (0.06) | 0.69 | (0.03) | 0.74 | (0.02) | -0.05 | (0.03) |
| Chinese Taipei | 3.54 | (0.05) | 1.70 | (0.08) | **1.84** | (0.09) | 1.02 | (0.03) | 0.35 | (0.03) | **0.67** | (0.04) |
| Thailand | 4.08 | (0.04) | 2.28 | (0.10) | **1.80** | (0.11) | 1.04 | (0.04) | 0.17 | (0.04) | **0.87** | (0.06) |
| Tunisia | 2.62 | (0.05) | a | a | a | a | 1.93 | (0.03) | a | a | a | a |
| Uruguay | 2.52 | (0.04) | 1.49 | (0.25) | **1.03** | (0.25) | 0.63 | (0.02) | 0.47 | (0.05) | **0.16** | (0.05) |

*Note:* Values that are statistically significant at the 5% level ($p < 0.05$) are indicated in bold.

### Table 3.12a [Part 2/3] Mean learning hours and allocation of total learning time in science, by academic and vocational orientation of schools

| | Mean learning hours per week | | | | | | | | | | | |
| | Individual study | | | | | | Total learning hours | | | | | |
| | Academic schools | | Vocational schools | | Difference (academic-vocational) | | Academic schools | | Vocational schools | | Difference (academic-vocational) | |
| | Mean | S.E. | Mean | S.E. | Dif. | S.E. | Mean | S.E. | Mean | S.E. | Dif. | S.E. |
|---|---|---|---|---|---|---|---|---|---|---|---|---|
| **OECD** | | | | | | | | | | | | |
| Australia | 1.23 | (0.02) | 0.71 | (0.04) | **0.52** | (0.05) | 4.99 | (0.05) | 2.88 | (0.14) | **2.12** | (0.14) |
| Austria | 1.36 | (0.06) | 1.24 | (0.04) | 0.12 | (0.07) | 4.68 | (0.12) | 3.67 | (0.11) | **1.01** | (0.17) |
| Belgium | 1.57 | (0.03) | 0.87 | (0.03) | **0.71** | (0.04) | 5.35 | (0.05) | 2.77 | (0.10) | **2.58** | (0.11) |
| Canada | 1.55 | (0.02) | a | a | a | a | 6.13 | (0.06) | a | a | a | a |
| Czech Republic | 1.14 | (0.03) | 0.80 | (0.04) | **0.34** | (0.05) | 5.14 | (0.10) | 3.50 | (0.15) | **1.64** | (0.17) |
| Denmark | 1.09 | (0.02) | a | a | a | a | 5.06 | (0.07) | a | a | a | a |
| Finland | 1.07 | (0.02) | a | a | a | a | 4.52 | (0.06) | a | a | a | a |
| France | 1.38 | (0.03) | 0.67 | (0.08) | **0.71** | (0.08) | 4.95 | (0.08) | 2.50 | (0.23) | **2.45** | (0.25) |
| Germany | 1.72 | (0.03) | 1.15 | (0.19) | **0.57** | (0.19) | 5.35 | (0.07) | 2.85 | (0.55) | **2.50** | (0.56) |
| Greece | 1.92 | (0.04) | 1.40 | (0.12) | **0.52** | (0.12) | 7.43 | (0.10) | 4.35 | (0.22) | **3.08** | (0.25) |
| Hungary | 1.79 | (0.05) | 1.45 | (0.05) | **0.35** | (0.07) | 5.79 | (0.14) | 4.58 | (0.11) | **1.20** | (0.18) |
| Iceland | 1.16 | (0.02) | c | c | c | c | 4.43 | (0.04) | c | c | c | c |
| Ireland | 1.21 | (0.03) | 0.86 | (0.19) | 0.35 | (0.20) | 4.07 | (0.07) | 2.71 | (0.54) | **1.36** | (0.55) |
| Italy | 2.31 | (0.08) | 1.93 | (0.03) | **0.38** | (0.09) | 5.57 | (0.20) | 5.59 | (0.07) | -0.03 | (0.21) |
| Japan | 0.76 | (0.03) | 0.48 | (0.03) | **0.28** | (0.04) | 3.93 | (0.08) | 2.78 | (0.15) | **1.15** | (0.17) |
| Korea | 1.40 | (0.07) | 0.62 | (0.04) | **0.79** | (0.08) | 6.51 | (0.17) | 3.57 | (0.20) | **2.94** | (0.26) |
| Luxembourg | 1.23 | (0.02) | 1.39 | (0.07) | **-0.16** | (0.07) | 4.01 | (0.04) | 4.57 | (0.15) | **-0.56** | (0.15) |
| Mexico | 2.16 | (0.04) | 2.05 | (0.03) | **0.11** | (0.05) | 6.44 | (0.10) | 5.84 | (0.07) | **0.60** | (0.13) |
| Netherlands | 1.32 | (0.03) | 0.93 | (0.05) | **0.40** | (0.06) | 4.37 | (0.07) | 2.74 | (0.13) | **1.63** | (0.16) |
| New Zealand | 1.28 | (0.02) | a | a | a | a | 5.74 | (0.06) | a | a | a | a |
| Norway | 1.23 | (0.02) | a | a | a | a | 4.80 | (0.05) | a | a | a | a |
| Poland | 2.02 | (0.03) | a | a | a | a | 5.36 | (0.07) | a | a | a | a |
| Portugal | 2.13 | (0.04) | 1.82 | (0.12) | **0.31** | (0.12) | 6.02 | (0.08) | 5.38 | (0.27) | **0.64** | (0.28) |
| Slovak Republic | 1.65 | (0.05) | 1.06 | (0.06) | **0.59** | (0.07) | 5.54 | (0.13) | 3.18 | (0.18) | **2.36** | (0.23) |
| Spain | 1.74 | (0.03) | a | a | a | a | 5.56 | (0.07) | a | a | a | a |
| Sweden | 1.16 | (0.02) | 0.56 | (0.15) | **0.60** | (0.15) | 4.47 | (0.05) | c | c | c | c |
| Switzerland | 1.13 | (0.02) | 0.88 | (0.09) | **0.25** | (0.09) | 3.95 | (0.06) | 2.69 | (0.22) | **1.26** | (0.23) |
| Turkey | 1.91 | (0.07) | 1.26 | (0.06) | **0.64** | (0.09) | 6.93 | (0.28) | 4.20 | (0.20) | **2.73** | (0.34) |
| United Kingdom | 1.45 | (0.02) | a | a | a | a | 6.18 | (0.05) | a | a | a | a |
| United States | 1.68 | (0.03) | a | a | a | a | 6.01 | (0.06) | a | a | a | a |
| **OECD average** | **1.49** | **(0.01)** | **1.11** | **(0.02)** | **0.42** | **(0.02)** | **5.31** | **(0.02)** | **3.70** | **(0.05)** | **1.61** | **(0.06)** |
| **Partners** | | | | | | | | | | | | |
| Argentina | 1.60 | (0.04) | 1.45 | (0.25) | 0.15 | (0.26) | 4.33 | (0.09) | 4.10 | (0.66) | 0.23 | (0.67) |
| Azerbaijan | 2.65 | (0.05) | 1.85 | (0.46) | 0.80 | (0.47) | 6.85 | (0.10) | 4.71 | (0.82) | **2.14** | (0.83) |
| Brazil | 1.70 | (0.02) | a | a | a | a | 4.70 | (0.06) | a | a | a | a |
| Bulgaria | 2.20 | (0.09) | 1.78 | (0.06) | **0.42** | (0.10) | 6.13 | (0.20) | 5.11 | (0.14) | **1.02** | (0.23) |
| Chile | 1.55 | (0.03) | 0.53 | (0.09) | **1.02** | (0.10) | 4.79 | (0.07) | 1.57 | (0.22) | **3.23** | (0.24) |
| Colombia | 1.79 | (0.03) | 2.01 | (0.18) | -0.22 | (0.19) | 6.27 | (0.11) | 6.33 | (0.66) | -0.06 | (0.62) |
| Croatia | 2.15 | (0.05) | 1.19 | (0.05) | **0.96** | (0.07) | 5.49 | (0.11) | 3.29 | (0.11) | **2.20** | (0.15) |
| Estonia | 1.54 | (0.03) | a | a | a | a | 5.57 | (0.06) | a | a | a | a |
| Hong Kong-China | 1.49 | (0.04) | 0.75 | (0.06) | **0.75** | (0.07) | 5.61 | (0.10) | 3.45 | (0.28) | **2.16** | (0.29) |
| Indonesia | 1.91 | (0.03) | 1.15 | (0.05) | **0.76** | (0.06) | 6.44 | (0.12) | 4.13 | (0.39) | **2.31** | (0.38) |
| Israel | 1.35 | (0.04) | 1.36 | (0.07) | -0.01 | (0.10) | 4.76 | (0.11) | 4.71 | (0.19) | 0.05 | (0.23) |
| Jordan | 2.65 | (0.04) | a | a | a | a | 7.40 | (0.09) | a | a | a | a |
| Kyrgyzstan | 2.15 | (0.04) | 1.68 | (0.13) | **0.46** | (0.13) | 5.64 | (0.09) | 5.20 | (0.30) | 0.44 | (0.32) |
| Latvia | 1.80 | (0.03) | 1.84 | (0.13) | -0.05 | (0.14) | 5.27 | (0.09) | 6.15 | (0.33) | **-0.88** | (0.34) |
| Liechtenstein | 1.20 | (0.06) | a | a | a | a | 4.29 | (0.10) | a | a | a | a |
| Lithuania | 1.69 | (0.03) | c | c | c | c | 4.94 | (0.06) | c | c | c | c |
| Macao-China | 1.37 | (0.03) | 1.35 | (0.21) | 0.02 | (0.21) | 6.12 | (0.06) | 5.46 | (0.46) | 0.65 | (0.46) |
| Montenegro | 2.66 | (0.06) | 1.98 | (0.04) | **0.68** | (0.07) | 7.25 | (0.12) | 5.50 | (0.08) | **1.74** | (0.14) |
| Qatar | 2.04 | (0.02) | a | a | a | a | 6.21 | (0.06) | a | a | a | a |
| Romania | 1.68 | (0.06) | 1.41 | (0.06) | **0.27** | (0.08) | 5.12 | (0.13) | 4.05 | (0.14) | **1.07** | (0.18) |
| Russian Federation | 2.99 | (0.06) | 2.13 | (0.17) | **0.85** | (0.18) | 7.89 | (0.15) | 6.68 | (0.40) | **1.21** | (0.45) |
| Serbia | 2.36 | (0.07) | 1.48 | (0.04) | **0.88** | (0.08) | 7.19 | (0.14) | 4.70 | (0.10) | **2.50** | (0.17) |
| Slovenia | 1.76 | (0.03) | 1.32 | (0.03) | **0.44** | (0.04) | 6.11 | (0.08) | 4.08 | (0.05) | **2.03** | (0.10) |
| Chinese Taipei | 1.53 | (0.03) | 0.71 | (0.04) | **0.82** | (0.05) | 6.12 | (0.09) | 2.76 | (0.13) | **3.35** | (0.16) |
| Thailand | 1.96 | (0.04) | 0.93 | (0.03) | **1.02** | (0.05) | 7.07 | (0.08) | 3.38 | (0.13) | **3.69** | (0.16) |
| Tunisia | 2.61 | (0.04) | a | a | a | a | 7.14 | (0.10) | a | a | a | a |
| Uruguay | 1.39 | (0.03) | 0.77 | (0.06) | **0.62** | (0.07) | 4.56 | (0.07) | 2.73 | (0.31) | **1.83** | (0.33) |

*Note:* Values that are statistically significant at the 5% level ($p < 0.05$) are indicated in bold.

© OECD 2011  Quality Time for Students: Learning In and Out of School

## Table 3.12a Mean learning hours and allocation of total learning time in science, by academic and vocational orientation of schools
[Part 3/3]

| | Allocation of total learning time in science for | | | | | | | | | | | | | | | | | |
| | Regular school lessons | | | | | | Out-of-school-time lessons | | | | | | Individual study | | | | | |
| | Academic schools | | Vocational schools | | Difference (academic-vocational) | | Academic schools | | Vocational schools | | Difference (academic-vocational) | | Academic schools | | Vocational schools | | Difference (academic-vocational) | |
| | % | S.E | % | S.E | Dif. | S.E. | % | S.E | % | S.E | Dif. | S.E. | % | S.E | % | S.E | Dif. | S.E. |
|---|---|---|---|---|---|---|---|---|---|---|---|---|---|---|---|---|---|---|
| Australia | 71.2 | (0.3) | 68.2 | (1.2) | **3.0** | (1.2) | 6.1 | (0.2) | 8.7 | (0.7) | **-2.6** | (0.7) | 22.8 | (0.2) | 23.2 | (0.8) | -0.4 | (0.9) |
| Austria | 67.9 | (1.1) | 62.3 | (0.7) | **5.6** | (1.3) | 3.4 | (0.5) | 4.6 | (0.3) | **-1.2** | (0.6) | 28.7 | (0.9) | 33.1 | (0.7) | **-4.3** | (1.1) |
| Belgium | 66.0 | (0.4) | 59.3 | (0.7) | **6.8** | (0.7) | 4.9 | (0.2) | 9.4 | (0.4) | **-4.5** | (0.5) | 29.1 | (0.3) | 31.3 | (0.5) | **-2.2** | (0.6) |
| Canada | 66.3 | (0.4) | a | a | a | a | 8.5 | (0.2) | a | a | a | a | 25.2 | (0.3) | a | a | a | a |
| Czech Republic | 68.3 | (0.5) | 69.5 | (1.4) | -1.2 | (1.5) | 9.9 | (0.4) | 9.8 | (0.6) | 0.1 | (0.7) | 21.8 | (0.4) | 20.7 | (1.0) | 1.1 | (1.0) |
| Denmark | 66.7 | (0.5) | a | a | a | a | 13.0 | (0.3) | a | a | a | a | 20.3 | (0.3) | a | a | a | a |
| Finland | 70.9 | (0.4) | a | a | a | a | 5.9 | (0.2) | a | a | a | a | 23.1 | (0.3) | a | a | a | a |
| France | 62.9 | (0.5) | 63.1 | (2.2) | -0.2 | (2.3) | 10.7 | (0.3) | 11.5 | (2.1) | -0.7 | (2.1) | 26.4 | (0.4) | 25.4 | (1.4) | 1.0 | (1.3) |
| Germany | 58.2 | (0.5) | 44.8 | (6.0) | **13.4** | (6.1) | 8.4 | (0.3) | 13.5 | (3.9) | -5.2 | (3.9) | 33.4 | (0.3) | 41.6 | (6.3) | -8.2 | (6.3) |
| Greece | 48.9 | (0.5) | 44.7 | (2.5) | 4.1 | (2.5) | 26.4 | (0.4) | 24.8 | (1.7) | 1.6 | (1.8) | 24.7 | (0.4) | 30.5 | (1.2) | **-5.7** | (1.2) |
| Hungary | 52.1 | (0.8) | 51.1 | (0.8) | 1.0 | (1.1) | 17.6 | (0.8) | 18.1 | (0.5) | -0.5 | (0.9) | 30.3 | (0.5) | 30.9 | (0.5) | -0.5 | (0.7) |
| Iceland | 70.1 | (0.4) | c | c | c | c | 5.1 | (0.2) | c | c | c | c | 24.8 | (0.3) | c | c | c | c |
| Ireland | 66.3 | (0.4) | 59.1 | (6.7) | 7.2 | (6.7) | 6.1 | (0.3) | 8.5 | (2.5) | -2.4 | (2.6) | 27.6 | (0.4) | 32.4 | (6.1) | -4.8 | (6.1) |
| Italy | 52.4 | (0.3) | 55.1 | (0.4) | **-2.7** | (0.5) | 7.3 | (0.3) | 10.5 | (0.3) | **-3.2** | (0.4) | 40.3 | (0.2) | 34.4 | (0.4) | **5.9** | (0.4) |
| Japan | 78.2 | (0.5) | 79.1 | (0.8) | -0.9 | (0.9) | 4.9 | (0.2) | 6.3 | (0.4) | **-1.5** | (0.5) | 17.0 | (0.5) | 14.6 | (0.9) | **2.4** | (1.0) |
| Korea | 64.2 | (0.7) | 79.4 | (1.1) | **-15.2** | (1.3) | 16.2 | (0.4) | 5.2 | (0.5) | **10.9** | (0.7) | 19.6 | (0.5) | 15.4 | (0.8) | **4.3** | (0.9) |
| Luxembourg | 59.9 | (0.5) | 59.2 | (1.2) | 0.7 | (1.4) | 9.9 | (0.3) | 10.7 | (0.8) | -0.8 | (0.9) | 30.2 | (0.4) | 30.1 | (0.9) | 0.1 | (1.1) |
| Mexico | 49.3 | (0.5) | 46.9 | (0.5) | **2.4** | (0.7) | 15.1 | (0.4) | 14.5 | (0.3) | 0.6 | (0.5) | 35.6 | (0.5) | 38.6 | (0.4) | **-3.0** | (0.6) |
| Netherlands | 59.0 | (0.6) | 48.5 | (1.4) | **10.4** | (1.5) | 10.9 | (0.4) | 17.8 | (0.7) | **-6.9** | (0.8) | 30.1 | (0.4) | 33.7 | (0.9) | **-3.5** | (1.0) |
| New Zealand | 73.1 | (0.4) | a | a | a | a | 6.2 | (0.2) | a | a | a | a | 20.7 | (0.3) | a | a | a | a |
| Norway | 59.6 | (0.5) | a | a | a | a | 16.9 | (0.3) | a | a | a | a | 23.5 | (0.3) | a | a | a | a |
| Poland | 53.2 | (0.4) | a | a | a | a | 10.3 | (0.3) | a | a | a | a | 36.5 | (0.4) | a | a | a | a |
| Portugal | 54.2 | (0.5) | 57.8 | (1.1) | **-3.6** | (1.2) | 9.5 | (0.3) | 7.8 | (0.7) | 1.8 | (0.7) | 36.3 | (0.4) | 34.4 | (1.0) | 1.9 | (1.1) |
| Slovak Republic | 58.6 | (0.7) | 58.9 | (1.1) | -0.3 | (1.3) | 12.4 | (0.4) | 10.7 | (0.8) | 1.7 | (0.8) | 29.0 | (0.6) | 30.4 | (0.6) | -1.4 | (0.8) |
| Spain | 58.9 | (0.3) | a | a | a | a | 10.7 | (0.3) | a | a | a | a | 30.4 | (0.3) | a | a | a | a |
| Sweden | 66.7 | (0.6) | c | c | c | c | 9.2 | (0.2) | c | c | c | c | 24.1 | (0.5) | c | c | c | c |
| Switzerland | 62.3 | (0.4) | 57.9 | (1.4) | **4.4** | (1.5) | 8.3 | (0.2) | 7.3 | (1.2) | 1.0 | (1.2) | 29.4 | (0.3) | 34.8 | (1.2) | **-5.4** | (1.3) |
| Turkey | 51.5 | (0.8) | 50.9 | (0.7) | 0.6 | (1.0) | 21.6 | (0.5) | 19.9 | (0.7) | 1.7 | (0.8) | 26.9 | (0.5) | 29.2 | (0.8) | **-2.3** | (0.9) |
| United Kingdom | 70.7 | (0.3) | a | a | a | a | 6.8 | (0.2) | a | a | a | a | 22.5 | (0.3) | a | a | a | a |
| United States | 58.5 | (0.5) | a | a | a | a | 12.5 | (0.4) | a | a | a | a | 28.9 | (0.3) | a | a | a | a |
| **OECD average** | **62.2** | **(0.1)** | **58.7** | **(0.5)** | **1.9** | **(0.6)** | **10.5** | **(0.1)** | **11.6** | **(0.3)** | **-0.5** | **(0.3)** | **27.3** | **(0.1)** | **29.7** | **(0.5)** | **-1.3** | **(0.5)** |
| Argentina | 53.2 | (0.8) | 52.1 | (3.9) | 1.1 | (3.9) | 9.6 | (0.4) | 9.1 | (2.3) | 0.5 | (2.3) | 37.2 | (0.6) | 38.8 | (3.7) | -1.6 | (3.7) |
| Azerbaijan | 43.2 | (0.6) | 32.4 | (4.2) | **10.8** | (4.3) | 19.2 | (0.5) | 30.6 | (7.3) | -11.4 | (7.3) | 37.6 | (0.4) | 37.0 | (8.2) | 0.6 | (8.2) |
| Brazil | 50.3 | (0.4) | a | a | a | a | 14.1 | (0.3) | a | a | a | a | 35.6 | (0.3) | a | a | a | a |
| Bulgaria | 49.9 | (0.8) | 47.6 | (1.2) | 2.3 | (1.4) | 14.6 | (0.6) | 18.2 | (1.0) | **-3.5** | (1.2) | 35.5 | (0.6) | 34.3 | (0.6) | 1.2 | (0.8) |
| Chile | 49.0 | (0.6) | 48.2 | (4.4) | 0.8 | (4.4) | 16.4 | (0.4) | 18.3 | (4.8) | -2.0 | (4.6) | 34.6 | (0.4) | 33.5 | (3.9) | 1.2 | (3.8) |
| Colombia | 59.6 | (0.6) | 55.3 | (1.5) | **4.4** | (1.5) | 13.0 | (0.4) | 13.5 | (0.9) | -0.6 | (1.0) | 27.4 | (0.5) | 31.2 | (1.2) | **-3.8** | (1.4) |
| Croatia | 55.1 | (0.8) | 54.2 | (0.7) | 0.9 | (1.1) | 7.4 | (0.5) | 11.2 | (0.5) | **-3.8** | (0.7) | 37.5 | (0.8) | 34.6 | (0.6) | **2.9** | (1.0) |
| Estonia | 61.5 | (0.5) | a | a | a | a | 12.6 | (0.4) | a | a | a | a | 25.9 | (0.3) | a | a | a | a |
| Hong Kong-China | 60.9 | (0.6) | 61.9 | (2.2) | -1.0 | (2.2) | 13.7 | (0.4) | 15.8 | (0.9) | **-2.0** | (1.0) | 25.4 | (0.4) | 22.3 | (1.9) | 3.0 | (2.0) |
| Indonesia | 54.3 | (0.5) | 56.2 | (5.0) | -1.9 | (4.9) | 15.7 | (0.4) | 15.1 | (3.0) | 0.6 | (2.8) | 30.0 | (0.4) | 28.7 | (2.1) | 1.3 | (2.2) |
| Israel | 55.7 | (0.8) | 47.3 | (2.5) | **8.4** | (2.8) | 17.4 | (0.4) | 23.0 | (1.5) | **-5.5** | (1.6) | 26.9 | (0.6) | 29.7 | (1.5) | -2.8 | (1.7) |
| Jordan | 42.9 | (0.6) | a | a | a | a | 20.3 | (0.4) | a | a | a | a | 36.8 | (0.4) | a | a | a | a |
| Kyrgyzstan | 35.2 | (0.6) | 45.8 | (3.1) | **-10.5** | (3.1) | 25.9 | (0.6) | 24.4 | (4.2) | 1.4 | (4.2) | 38.9 | (0.4) | 29.8 | (1.7) | **9.1** | (1.7) |
| Latvia | 55.9 | (0.5) | 62.7 | (1.7) | **-6.8** | (1.8) | 10.5 | (0.3) | 7.4 | (1.0) | **3.2** | (1.1) | 33.6 | (0.4) | 30.0 | (1.8) | 3.6 | (1.9) |
| Liechtenstein | 61.8 | (1.4) | a | a | a | a | 10.2 | (1.0) | a | a | a | a | 28.1 | (1.3) | a | a | a | a |
| Lithuania | 57.1 | (0.5) | c | c | c | c | 10.0 | (0.3) | c | c | c | c | 32.9 | (0.3) | c | c | c | c |
| Macao-China | 64.7 | (0.4) | 68.0 | (3.2) | -3.3 | (3.2) | 14.6 | (0.3) | 11.1 | (2.0) | 3.4 | (2.0) | 20.7 | (0.3) | 20.9 | (2.1) | -0.2 | (2.1) |
| Montenegro | 51.3 | (0.6) | 44.5 | (0.5) | **6.8** | (0.7) | 12.3 | (0.5) | 18.1 | (0.4) | **-5.8** | (0.7) | 36.4 | (0.6) | 37.4 | (0.6) | -1.0 | (0.8) |
| Qatar | 40.7 | (0.3) | a | a | a | a | 24.8 | (0.3) | a | a | a | a | 34.5 | (0.3) | a | a | a | a |
| Romania | 51.0 | (0.6) | 37.5 | (1.1) | **13.4** | (1.3) | 17.6 | (0.5) | 26.8 | (1.3) | **-9.2** | (1.4) | 31.5 | (0.6) | 35.7 | (1.1) | **-4.3** | (1.3) |
| Russian Federation | 48.0 | (0.6) | 52.3 | (1.9) | **-4.2** | (2.0) | 14.8 | (0.6) | 16.6 | (1.4) | -1.9 | (1.5) | 37.2 | (0.5) | 31.1 | (1.3) | **6.1** | (1.3) |
| Serbia | 58.2 | (0.8) | 56.3 | (0.7) | 2.0 | (1.2) | 10.8 | (0.5) | 14.4 | (0.5) | **-3.6** | (0.7) | 31.0 | (0.6) | 29.3 | (0.5) | 1.7 | (0.9) |
| Slovenia | 60.2 | (0.6) | 51.2 | (0.6) | **9.0** | (0.9) | 10.6 | (0.4) | 15.9 | (0.4) | **-5.3** | (0.5) | 29.3 | (0.5) | 33.0 | (0.4) | **-3.7** | (0.7) |
| Chinese Taipei | 62.5 | (0.4) | 66.4 | (1.0) | **-3.9** | (1.1) | 13.3 | (0.3) | 9.8 | (0.5) | **3.5** | (0.6) | 24.2 | (0.4) | 23.8 | (0.7) | 0.4 | (0.8) |
| Thailand | 62.9 | (0.4) | 69.5 | (1.0) | **-6.5** | (1.1) | 11.2 | (0.4) | 2.9 | (0.6) | **8.3** | (0.7) | 25.9 | (0.3) | 27.7 | (0.9) | -1.8 | (1.0) |
| Tunisia | 37.3 | (0.4) | a | a | a | a | 25.9 | (0.4) | a | a | a | a | 36.9 | (0.4) | a | a | a | a |
| Uruguay | 56.3 | (0.5) | 54.3 | (3.6) | 2.0 | (3.7) | 11.8 | (0.3) | 14.8 | (2.1) | -3.0 | (2.1) | 31.9 | (0.4) | 30.9 | (2.6) | 0.9 | (2.7) |

*Note:* Values that are statistically significant at the 5% level (p < 0.05) are indicated in bold.

### Table 3.12b [Part 1/3] Mean learning hours and allocation of total learning time in mathematics, by academic and vocational orientation of schools

| | Mean learning hours per week | | | | | | | | | | | |
| | Regular school lessons | | | | | | Out-of-school-time lessons | | | | | |
| | Academic schools | | Vocational schools | | Difference (academic-vocational) | | Academic schools | | Vocational schools | | Difference (academic-vocational) | |
| | Mean | S.E. | Mean | S.E. | Dif. | S.E. | Mean | S.E. | Mean | S.E. | Dif. | S.E. |
|---|---|---|---|---|---|---|---|---|---|---|---|---|
| Australia | 4.15 | (0.03) | 3.69 | (0.07) | **0.46** | (0.08) | 0.74 | (0.02) | 0.81 | (0.05) | -0.07 | (0.05) |
| Austria | 3.48 | (0.04) | 3.11 | (0.06) | 0.37 | (0.07) | 0.61 | (0.04) | 0.46 | (0.02) | **0.15** | (0.05) |
| Belgium | 4.34 | (0.04) | 2.64 | (0.04) | **1.69** | (0.06) | 0.55 | (0.02) | 0.55 | (0.02) | 0.01 | (0.03) |
| Canada | 4.50 | (0.04) | a | a | a | a | 0.94 | (0.02) | a | a | a | a |
| Czech Republic | 4.19 | (0.04) | 3.72 | (0.09) | **0.48** | (0.10) | 0.73 | (0.02) | 0.79 | (0.04) | -0.06 | (0.05) |
| Denmark | 4.44 | (0.03) | a | a | a | a | 1.36 | (0.03) | a | a | a | a |
| Finland | 3.45 | (0.04) | a | a | a | a | 0.37 | (0.02) | a | a | a | a |
| France | 3.96 | (0.03) | 2.70 | (0.08) | **1.25** | (0.09) | 0.94 | (0.02) | 0.76 | (0.06) | **0.18** | (0.07) |
| Germany | 3.91 | (0.04) | 2.86 | (0.27) | **1.05** | (0.28) | 0.82 | (0.03) | 0.83 | (0.28) | -0.01 | (0.29) |
| Greece | 3.58 | (0.04) | 2.59 | (0.07) | **0.99** | (0.08) | 2.40 | (0.06) | 1.19 | (0.11) | **1.21** | (0.13) |
| Hungary | 3.36 | (0.06) | 3.23 | (0.05) | 0.12 | (0.08) | 1.26 | (0.05) | 1.31 | (0.04) | -0.04 | (0.06) |
| Iceland | 4.74 | (0.02) | c | c | c | c | 0.72 | (0.02) | c | c | c | c |
| Ireland | 3.66 | (0.03) | 3.08 | (0.21) | **0.59** | (0.21) | 0.72 | (0.02) | 0.62 | (0.14) | 0.10 | (0.14) |
| Italy | 3.94 | (0.06) | 3.57 | (0.04) | **0.37** | (0.07) | 0.86 | (0.03) | 0.91 | (0.03) | -0.05 | (0.04) |
| Japan | 4.69 | (0.07) | 2.85 | (0.11) | **1.84** | (0.14) | 0.79 | (0.04) | 0.46 | (0.03) | **0.33** | (0.05) |
| Korea | 4.96 | (0.05) | 3.82 | (0.10) | **1.14** | (0.11) | 2.72 | (0.05) | 0.81 | (0.07) | **1.91** | (0.09) |
| Luxembourg | 3.98 | (0.03) | 3.02 | (0.06) | **0.96** | (0.07) | 0.86 | (0.02) | 0.64 | (0.05) | **0.22** | (0.06) |
| Mexico | 3.96 | (0.04) | 3.91 | (0.05) | 0.05 | (0.06) | 1.24 | (0.04) | 1.05 | (0.02) | **0.19** | (0.05) |
| Netherlands | 3.04 | (0.04) | 2.45 | (0.07) | **0.60** | (0.07) | 0.65 | (0.02) | 0.78 | (0.04) | **-0.13** | (0.05) |
| New Zealand | 4.38 | (0.03) | a | a | a | a | 0.68 | (0.02) | a | a | a | a |
| Norway | 3.39 | (0.03) | a | a | a | a | 1.05 | (0.02) | a | a | a | a |
| Poland | 4.36 | (0.04) | a | a | a | a | 0.78 | (0.02) | a | a | a | a |
| Portugal | 3.63 | (0.04) | 3.45 | (0.12) | 0.18 | (0.12) | 0.83 | (0.02) | 0.72 | (0.06) | **0.12** | (0.06) |
| Slovak Republic | 3.88 | (0.06) | 2.52 | (0.07) | **1.36** | (0.09) | 1.08 | (0.03) | 0.64 | (0.04) | **0.44** | (0.05) |
| Spain | 3.42 | (0.03) | a | a | a | a | 0.99 | (0.02) | a | a | a | a |
| Sweden | 3.09 | (0.03) | c | c | c | c | 0.61 | (0.02) | c | c | c | c |
| Switzerland | 3.98 | (0.03) | 2.15 | (0.15) | **1.83** | (0.15) | 0.72 | (0.02) | 0.50 | (0.08) | **0.22** | (0.08) |
| Turkey | 4.25 | (0.07) | 3.20 | (0.11) | **1.05** | (0.12) | 2.41 | (0.06) | 1.59 | (0.06) | **0.82** | (0.08) |
| United Kingdom | 3.78 | (0.03) | a | a | a | a | 0.63 | (0.02) | a | a | a | a |
| United States | 3.77 | (0.05) | a | a | a | a | 1.15 | (0.03) | a | a | a | a |
| **OECD average** | **3.94** | **(0.01)** | **3.08** | **(0.03)** | **0.86** | **(0.03)** | **1.01** | **(0.01)** | **0.81** | **(0.02)** | **0.29** | **(0.02)** |
| Argentina | 2.95 | (0.06) | 2.79 | (0.43) | 0.16 | (0.43) | 0.77 | (0.03) | 0.96 | (0.21) | -0.19 | (0.21) |
| Azerbaijan | 3.80 | (0.06) | 2.54 | (0.54) | **1.26** | (0.54) | 1.70 | (0.05) | 1.39 | (0.42) | 0.31 | (0.42) |
| Brazil | 3.15 | (0.04) | a | a | a | a | 1.21 | (0.03) | a | a | a | a |
| Bulgaria | 3.22 | (0.10) | 2.71 | (0.07) | **0.51** | (0.12) | 1.17 | (0.05) | 1.10 | (0.05) | 0.08 | (0.06) |
| Chile | 3.52 | (0.07) | 2.58 | (0.12) | **0.93** | (0.13) | 1.00 | (0.03) | 0.79 | (0.18) | 0.21 | (0.19) |
| Colombia | 4.20 | (0.07) | 4.26 | (0.11) | -0.06 | (0.13) | 1.23 | (0.04) | 1.23 | (0.08) | 0.00 | (0.10) |
| Croatia | 3.66 | (0.05) | 2.80 | (0.05) | **0.86** | (0.07) | 0.81 | (0.04) | 0.75 | (0.03) | 0.06 | (0.05) |
| Estonia | 4.19 | (0.04) | a | a | a | a | 0.99 | (0.03) | a | a | a | a |
| Hong Kong-China | 5.31 | (0.04) | 4.23 | (0.13) | **1.07** | (0.14) | 1.41 | (0.04) | 1.12 | (0.10) | **0.29** | (0.11) |
| Indonesia | 4.05 | (0.06) | 4.29 | (0.23) | -0.24 | (0.23) | 1.46 | (0.05) | 0.91 | (0.07) | **0.55** | (0.08) |
| Israel | 4.18 | (0.04) | 3.83 | (0.15) | **0.35** | (0.17) | 2.13 | (0.05) | 2.28 | (0.13) | -0.15 | (0.14) |
| Jordan | 3.48 | (0.05) | a | a | a | a | 1.82 | (0.04) | a | a | a | a |
| Kyrgyzstan | 2.88 | (0.05) | 2.86 | (0.36) | 0.02 | (0.36) | 1.55 | (0.04) | 1.52 | (0.09) | 0.04 | (0.10) |
| Latvia | 4.49 | (0.04) | 4.39 | (0.15) | 0.11 | (0.15) | 1.21 | (0.04) | 0.86 | (0.08) | **0.35** | (0.09) |
| Liechtenstein | 3.98 | (0.08) | a | a | a | a | 0.58 | (0.05) | a | a | a | a |
| Lithuania | 3.50 | (0.04) | c | c | c | c | 0.74 | (0.02) | c | c | c | c |
| Macao-China | 5.41 | (0.03) | 4.95 | (0.15) | **0.46** | (0.15) | 1.21 | (0.03) | 0.78 | (0.10) | **0.43** | (0.10) |
| Montenegro | 3.69 | (0.06) | 2.80 | (0.04) | **0.89** | (0.07) | 0.88 | (0.04) | 0.95 | (0.03) | -0.07 | (0.06) |
| Qatar | 3.11 | (0.03) | a | a | a | a | 1.85 | (0.03) | a | a | a | a |
| Romania | 3.23 | (0.09) | 2.25 | (0.06) | **0.99** | (0.11) | 1.51 | (0.04) | 1.46 | (0.07) | 0.05 | (0.08) |
| Russian Federation | 3.74 | (0.06) | 2.91 | (0.14) | **0.83** | (0.16) | 1.15 | (0.03) | 0.99 | (0.10) | 0.16 | (0.11) |
| Serbia | 3.87 | (0.07) | 3.06 | (0.04) | **0.81** | (0.08) | 1.04 | (0.04) | 0.95 | (0.03) | 0.09 | (0.05) |
| Slovenia | 3.89 | (0.04) | 2.78 | (0.03) | **1.11** | (0.05) | 0.96 | (0.04) | 1.09 | (0.03) | **-0.13** | (0.05) |
| Chinese Taipei | 4.77 | (0.05) | 3.30 | (0.09) | **1.48** | (0.10) | 1.91 | (0.04) | 0.83 | (0.04) | **1.08** | (0.05) |
| Thailand | 4.04 | (0.04) | 2.27 | (0.04) | **1.77** | (0.06) | 1.05 | (0.03) | 0.19 | (0.03) | **0.86** | (0.04) |
| Tunisia | 3.39 | (0.04) | a | a | a | a | 2.42 | (0.03) | a | a | a | a |
| Uruguay | 3.32 | (0.04) | 3.28 | (0.10) | 0.04 | (0.11) | 0.85 | (0.03) | 0.76 | (0.10) | 0.09 | (0.11) |

*Note*: Values that are statistically significant at the 5% level (p < 0.05) are indicated in bold.

© OECD 2011 Quality Time for Students: Learning In and Out of School

## Table 3.12b [Part 2/3] Mean learning hours and allocation of total learning time in mathematics, by academic and vocational orientation of schools

| | Mean learning hours per week | | | | | | | | | | | |
| | Individual study | | | | | | Total learning hours | | | | | |
| | Academic schools | | Vocational schools | | Difference (academic-vocational) | | Academic schools | | Vocational schools | | Difference (academic-vocational) | |
| | Mean | S.E. | Mean | S.E. | Dif. | S.E. | Mean | S.E. | Mean | S.E. | Dif. | S.E. |
|---|---|---|---|---|---|---|---|---|---|---|---|---|
| **OECD** | | | | | | | | | | | | |
| Australia | 1.82 | (0.03) | 1.52 | (0.05) | **0.30** | (0.06) | 6.72 | (0.05) | 6.03 | (0.12) | **0.69** | (0.13) |
| Austria | 2.42 | (0.05) | 2.01 | (0.05) | **0.42** | (0.07) | 6.54 | (0.09) | 5.60 | (0.10) | **0.94** | (0.13) |
| Belgium | 2.17 | (0.04) | 1.33 | (0.03) | **0.84** | (0.05) | 7.05 | (0.08) | 4.55 | (0.07) | **2.50** | (0.10) |
| Canada | 1.97 | (0.03) | a | a | a | a | 7.45 | (0.07) | a | a | a | a |
| Czech Republic | 1.34 | (0.03) | 1.28 | (0.06) | 0.06 | (0.07) | 6.26 | (0.06) | 5.77 | (0.16) | **0.48** | (0.17) |
| Denmark | 1.74 | (0.02) | a | a | a | a | 7.52 | (0.06) | a | a | a | a |
| Finland | 1.20 | (0.02) | a | a | a | a | 5.02 | (0.06) | a | a | a | a |
| France | 1.80 | (0.03) | 1.06 | (0.06) | **0.74** | (0.06) | 6.71 | (0.06) | 4.51 | (0.15) | **2.20** | (0.16) |
| Germany | 2.28 | (0.03) | 1.96 | (0.22) | 0.32 | (0.22) | 7.03 | (0.07) | 5.72 | (0.66) | **1.31** | (0.66) |
| Greece | 2.05 | (0.03) | 1.70 | (0.13) | 0.35 | (0.14) | 8.05 | (0.10) | 5.51 | (0.26) | **2.54** | (0.29) |
| Hungary | 1.94 | (0.05) | 1.76 | (0.04) | **0.18** | (0.07) | 6.55 | (0.12) | 6.32 | (0.12) | 0.23 | (0.17) |
| Iceland | 1.71 | (0.02) | c | c | c | c | 7.18 | (0.05) | c | c | c | c |
| Ireland | 1.77 | (0.03) | 1.27 | (0.22) | **0.50** | (0.22) | 6.15 | (0.06) | 5.12 | (0.36) | **1.03** | (0.35) |
| Italy | 2.88 | (0.06) | 2.17 | (0.03) | **0.71** | (0.07) | 7.68 | (0.13) | 6.66 | (0.08) | **1.02** | (0.14) |
| Japan | 1.70 | (0.07) | 0.81 | (0.04) | **0.89** | (0.08) | 7.18 | (0.16) | 4.12 | (0.15) | **3.06** | (0.22) |
| Korea | 2.70 | (0.08) | 1.03 | (0.07) | **1.68** | (0.11) | 10.39 | (0.15) | 5.69 | (0.21) | **4.70** | (0.25) |
| Luxembourg | 1.74 | (0.02) | 1.53 | (0.06) | **0.21** | (0.06) | 6.61 | (0.05) | 5.19 | (0.13) | **1.42** | (0.13) |
| Mexico | 2.29 | (0.04) | 2.20 | (0.03) | 0.09 | (0.05) | 7.45 | (0.09) | 7.14 | (0.06) | **0.32** | (0.11) |
| Netherlands | 1.58 | (0.03) | 1.21 | (0.06) | **0.37** | (0.06) | 5.26 | (0.07) | 4.41 | (0.14) | **0.85** | (0.15) |
| New Zealand | 1.59 | (0.03) | a | a | a | a | 6.66 | (0.05) | a | a | a | a |
| Norway | 1.40 | (0.03) | a | a | a | a | 5.84 | (0.06) | a | a | a | a |
| Poland | 2.09 | (0.03) | a | a | a | a | 7.23 | (0.06) | a | a | a | a |
| Portugal | 1.98 | (0.03) | 1.85 | (0.09) | 0.13 | (0.10) | 6.44 | (0.07) | 6.03 | (0.22) | 0.41 | (0.23) |
| Slovak Republic | 1.88 | (0.04) | 1.43 | (0.05) | **0.45** | (0.07) | 6.86 | (0.11) | 4.60 | (0.14) | **2.26** | (0.17) |
| Spain | 1.96 | (0.03) | a | a | a | a | 6.41 | (0.06) | a | a | a | a |
| Sweden | 1.18 | (0.02) | 0.77 | (0.07) | **0.41** | (0.07) | 4.89 | (0.04) | c | c | c | c |
| Switzerland | 1.72 | (0.02) | 1.31 | (0.08) | **0.40** | (0.08) | 6.43 | (0.05) | 3.97 | (0.27) | **2.46** | (0.27) |
| Turkey | 2.56 | (0.06) | 1.94 | (0.08) | **0.62** | (0.10) | 9.19 | (0.16) | 6.70 | (0.21) | **2.49** | (0.27) |
| United Kingdom | 1.49 | (0.02) | a | a | a | a | 5.90 | (0.05) | a | a | a | a |
| United States | 2.05 | (0.03) | a | a | a | a | 7.01 | (0.07) | a | a | a | a |
| **OECD average** | **1.90** | **(0.01)** | **1.51** | **(0.02)** | **0.48** | **(0.02)** | **6.86** | **(0.02)** | **5.45** | **(0.05)** | **1.63** | **(0.06)** |
| **Partners** | | | | | | | | | | | | |
| Argentina | 1.81 | (0.04) | 2.26 | (0.28) | -0.44 | (0.28) | 5.54 | (0.10) | 6.16 | (0.64) | -0.62 | (0.63) |
| Azerbaijan | 2.96 | (0.06) | 1.54 | (0.26) | **1.42** | (0.27) | 8.52 | (0.13) | 5.36 | (0.93) | **3.16** | (0.93) |
| Brazil | 1.80 | (0.03) | a | a | a | a | 6.14 | (0.07) | a | a | a | a |
| Bulgaria | 2.28 | (0.09) | 1.87 | (0.07) | **0.41** | (0.10) | 6.69 | (0.21) | 5.71 | (0.14) | **0.98** | (0.22) |
| Chile | 1.61 | (0.03) | 1.30 | (0.09) | **0.31** | (0.10) | 6.16 | (0.10) | 4.68 | (0.31) | **1.48** | (0.32) |
| Colombia | 1.90 | (0.04) | 2.07 | (0.09) | -0.17 | (0.09) | 7.33 | (0.11) | 7.56 | (0.21) | -0.23 | (0.25) |
| Croatia | 2.22 | (0.06) | 1.64 | (0.03) | **0.58** | (0.06) | 6.70 | (0.08) | 5.24 | (0.07) | **1.46** | (0.11) |
| Estonia | 1.96 | (0.03) | a | a | a | a | 7.15 | (0.07) | a | a | a | a |
| Hong Kong-China | 2.31 | (0.04) | 1.37 | (0.15) | **0.94** | (0.16) | 9.03 | (0.08) | 6.76 | (0.34) | **2.27** | (0.36) |
| Indonesia | 2.05 | (0.03) | 1.74 | (0.07) | **0.30** | (0.08) | 7.54 | (0.11) | 6.95 | (0.24) | **0.59** | (0.24) |
| Israel | 2.31 | (0.06) | 2.41 | (0.11) | -0.10 | (0.12) | 8.67 | (0.12) | 8.81 | (0.33) | -0.14 | (0.36) |
| Jordan | 2.69 | (0.04) | a | a | a | a | 7.96 | (0.08) | a | a | a | a |
| Kyrgyzstan | 2.23 | (0.03) | 1.71 | (0.13) | **0.51** | (0.13) | 6.72 | (0.09) | 6.04 | (0.43) | 0.68 | (0.43) |
| Latvia | 2.46 | (0.04) | 2.01 | (0.14) | **0.45** | (0.14) | 8.17 | (0.09) | 7.26 | (0.30) | **0.91** | (0.30) |
| Liechtenstein | 1.49 | (0.06) | a | a | a | a | 6.04 | (0.12) | a | a | a | a |
| Lithuania | 1.78 | (0.03) | c | c | c | c | 6.02 | (0.05) | c | c | c | c |
| Macao-China | 2.07 | (0.03) | 1.77 | (0.17) | 0.30 | (0.17) | 8.69 | (0.06) | 7.47 | (0.29) | **1.22** | (0.30) |
| Montenegro | 2.27 | (0.06) | 1.92 | (0.04) | **0.34** | (0.07) | 6.80 | (0.11) | 5.64 | (0.09) | **1.16** | (0.15) |
| Qatar | 2.22 | (0.02) | a | a | a | a | 7.21 | (0.06) | a | a | a | a |
| Romania | 2.24 | (0.05) | 1.91 | (0.05) | **0.33** | (0.08) | 6.99 | (0.15) | 5.61 | (0.13) | **1.37** | (0.20) |
| Russian Federation | 2.33 | (0.05) | 1.56 | (0.11) | **0.77** | (0.11) | 7.23 | (0.10) | 5.50 | (0.29) | **1.73** | (0.31) |
| Serbia | 2.16 | (0.07) | 1.69 | (0.03) | **0.47** | (0.08) | 7.07 | (0.13) | 5.69 | (0.08) | **1.38** | (0.16) |
| Slovenia | 2.21 | (0.04) | 1.65 | (0.03) | **0.57** | (0.05) | 7.06 | (0.09) | 5.55 | (0.06) | **1.52** | (0.11) |
| Chinese Taipei | 2.17 | (0.04) | 1.34 | (0.06) | **0.83** | (0.08) | 8.91 | (0.10) | 5.52 | (0.17) | **3.39** | (0.20) |
| Thailand | 1.97 | (0.03) | 0.90 | (0.02) | **1.07** | (0.04) | 7.05 | (0.07) | 3.36 | (0.06) | **3.69** | (0.10) |
| Tunisia | 2.57 | (0.04) | a | a | a | a | 8.38 | (0.10) | a | a | a | a |
| Uruguay | 1.59 | (0.03) | 1.47 | (0.12) | 0.12 | (0.12) | 5.76 | (0.07) | 5.57 | (0.24) | 0.20 | (0.24) |

*Note*: Values that are statistically significant at the 5% level (p < 0.05) are indicated in bold.

### Table 3.12b [Part 3/3] Mean learning hours and allocation of total learning time in mathematics, by academic and vocational orientation of schools

| | Allocation of total learning time in mathematics for | | | | | | | | | | | | | | | | | |
| | Regular school lessons | | | | | | Out-of-school-time lessons | | | | | | Individual study | | | | | |
| | Academic schools | | Vocational schools | | Difference (academic-vocational) | | Academic schools | | Vocational schools | | Difference (academic-vocational) | | Academic schools | | Vocational schools | | Difference (academic-vocational) | |
| | % | S.E | % | S.E | Dif. | S.E. | % | S.E | % | S.E | Dif. | S.E. | % | S.E | % | S.E | Dif. | S.E. |
|---|---|---|---|---|---|---|---|---|---|---|---|---|---|---|---|---|---|---|
| Australia | 65.8 | (0.3) | 65.4 | (0.9) | 0.4 | (0.9) | 16.0 | (0.5) | 24.6 | (2.1) | **-8.6** | (2.1) | 25.2 | (0.2) | 23.2 | (0.6) | **1.9** | (0.6) |
| Austria | 57.3 | (0.7) | 59.0 | (0.6) | -1.7 | (0.9) | 18.0 | (1.7) | 15.6 | (0.9) | 2.4 | (2.0) | 35.0 | (0.6) | 34.8 | (0.5) | 0.2 | (0.8) |
| Belgium | 63.9 | (0.4) | 62.1 | (0.5) | **1.8** | (0.6) | 11.6 | (0.5) | 20.5 | (1.1) | **-8.9** | (1.3) | 29.4 | (0.4) | 28.3 | (0.4) | **1.1** | (0.5) |
| Canada | 63.3 | (0.3) | a | a | a | a | 18.6 | (0.5) | a | a | a | a | 25.2 | (0.2) | a | a | a | a |
| Czech Republic | 70.6 | (0.5) | 69.9 | (0.8) | 0.7 | (1.0) | 21.1 | (1.0) | 29.6 | (3.1) | **-8.5** | (3.3) | 19.9 | (0.4) | 19.8 | (0.7) | 0.1 | (0.8) |
| Denmark | 62.3 | (0.3) | a | a | a | a | 31.1 | (0.9) | a | a | a | a | 21.6 | (0.2) | a | a | a | a |
| Finland | 71.1 | (0.3) | a | a | a | a | 9.0 | (0.4) | a | a | a | a | 22.9 | (0.2) | a | a | a | a |
| France | 62.3 | (0.3) | 65.4 | (1.2) | **-3.1** | (1.2) | 26.1 | (0.7) | 34.0 | (4.5) | -7.9 | (4.7) | 25.2 | (0.3) | 21.2 | (1.0) | **4.0** | (0.9) |
| Germany | 58.6 | (0.3) | 52.8 | (1.9) | **5.8** | (2.0) | 20.1 | (1.0) | 34.2 | (8.1) | -14.1 | (8.2) | 31.7 | (0.3) | 35.0 | (1.5) | **-3.3** | (1.5) |
| Greece | 48.4 | (0.5) | 55.5 | (1.9) | **-7.0** | (2.0) | 38.7 | (1.1) | 34.5 | (4.0) | 4.2 | (4.2) | 24.3 | (0.3) | 27.2 | (1.2) | **-2.9** | (1.2) |
| Hungary | 54.5 | (0.7) | 54.1 | (0.5) | 0.5 | (0.9) | 27.0 | (1.2) | 35.5 | (1.6) | **-8.5** | (2.0) | 28.5 | (0.5) | 27.6 | (0.3) | 1.0 | (0.6) |
| Iceland | 69.4 | (0.3) | c | c | c | c | 19.1 | (0.9) | c | c | c | c | 22.1 | (0.2) | c | c | c | c |
| Ireland | 63.6 | (0.4) | 67.1 | (4.0) | -3.5 | (4.0) | 18.5 | (0.9) | 16.8 | (5.9) | 1.6 | (5.9) | 27.0 | (0.3) | 22.8 | (2.9) | 4.1 | (2.9) |
| Italy | 54.1 | (0.3) | 55.7 | (0.3) | **-1.6** | (0.5) | 17.9 | (0.8) | 21.1 | (0.8) | **-3.2** | (1.2) | 36.3 | (0.3) | 32.5 | (0.3) | **3.8** | (0.4) |
| Japan | 70.7 | (0.7) | 74.9 | (0.8) | **-4.2** | (1.0) | 21.9 | (1.4) | 13.0 | (1.2) | **9.0** | (1.9) | 20.5 | (0.5) | 17.1 | (0.8) | **3.4** | (0.8) |
| Korea | 52.1 | (0.5) | 73.6 | (1.1) | **-21.5** | (1.2) | 46.9 | (1.6) | 23.5 | (2.5) | **23.4** | (3.0) | 23.9 | (0.4) | 16.0 | (0.8) | **7.9** | (0.9) |
| Luxembourg | 63.4 | (0.3) | 62.7 | (0.9) | 0.7 | (1.0) | 27.0 | (0.9) | 18.3 | (2.1) | **8.7** | (2.3) | 25.3 | (0.3) | 27.8 | (0.8) | **-2.5** | (0.8) |
| Mexico | 53.9 | (0.5) | 55.9 | (0.5) | **-2.0** | (0.7) | 22.7 | (0.9) | 22.1 | (0.7) | 0.6 | (1.1) | 31.3 | (0.3) | 30.6 | (0.3) | 0.7 | (0.4) |
| Netherlands | 60.8 | (0.5) | 57.7 | (1.0) | **3.1** | (1.2) | 16.6 | (0.7) | 25.9 | (1.6) | **-9.3** | (1.8) | 28.6 | (0.4) | 26.1 | (0.7) | **2.5** | (0.8) |
| New Zealand | 69.6 | (0.4) | a | a | a | a | 12.2 | (0.5) | a | a | a | a | 21.9 | (0.3) | a | a | a | a |
| Norway | 62.2 | (0.4) | a | a | a | a | 23.0 | (0.6) | a | a | a | a | 21.9 | (0.3) | a | a | a | a |
| Poland | 62.5 | (0.3) | a | a | a | a | 18.0 | (0.7) | a | a | a | a | 27.4 | (0.3) | a | a | a | a |
| Portugal | 58.7 | (0.4) | 60.0 | (0.9) | -1.3 | (1.0) | 15.6 | (0.5) | 12.6 | (1.0) | **3.0** | (1.1) | 29.5 | (0.4) | 30.2 | (0.8) | -0.7 | (0.9) |
| Slovak Republic | 60.5 | (0.6) | 60.7 | (0.9) | -0.2 | (1.1) | 28.1 | (1.1) | 24.9 | (2.2) | 3.2 | (2.3) | 25.8 | (0.5) | 28.2 | (0.6) | **-2.4** | (0.8) |
| Spain | 57.7 | (0.3) | a | a | a | a | 19.4 | (0.5) | a | a | a | a | 29.3 | (0.3) | a | a | a | a |
| Sweden | 68.1 | (0.5) | c | c | c | c | 13.5 | (0.4) | c | c | c | c | 22.0 | (0.4) | c | c | c | c |
| Switzerland | 64.1 | (0.4) | 56.2 | (0.9) | **7.9** | (1.0) | 23.9 | (0.9) | 22.1 | (6.5) | 1.8 | (6.6) | 26.3 | (0.2) | 33.9 | (1.0) | **-7.6** | (1.0) |
| Turkey | 49.7 | (0.5) | 52.3 | (0.7) | **-2.6** | (0.9) | 41.9 | (2.4) | 46.7 | (2.8) | -4.8 | (3.7) | 26.4 | (0.4) | 26.8 | (0.5) | -0.4 | (0.7) |
| United Kingdom | 67.1 | (0.3) | a | a | a | a | 11.0 | (0.5) | a | a | a | a | 24.0 | (0.2) | a | a | a | a |
| United States | 55.4 | (0.5) | a | a | a | a | 23.9 | (0.9) | a | a | a | a | 29.2 | (0.3) | a | a | a | a |
| **OECD average** | **61.4** | **(0.1)** | **61.1** | **(0.3)** | **-1.5** | **(0.3)** | **21.9** | **(0.2)** | **25.0** | **(0.8)** | **-0.8** | **(0.8)** | **26.3** | **(0.1)** | **26.8** | **(0.2)** | **0.6** | **(0.2)** |
| Argentina | 55.1 | (0.6) | 49.6 | (3.5) | 5.5 | (3.6) | 22.2 | (1.1) | 33.9 | (5.2) | **-11.7** | (5.3) | 32.6 | (0.4) | 35.9 | (2.2) | -3.3 | (2.2) |
| Azerbaijan | 47.1 | (0.5) | 50.5 | (9.2) | -3.4 | (9.2) | 34.0 | (1.3) | 28.4 | (7.5) | 5.7 | (7.8) | 34.3 | (0.5) | 28.2 | (3.9) | 6.2 | (3.9) |
| Brazil | 54.4 | (0.5) | a | a | a | a | 30.3 | (0.9) | a | a | a | a | 28.3 | (0.4) | a | a | a | a |
| Bulgaria | 51.7 | (0.7) | 50.7 | (0.9) | 1.0 | (1.1) | 24.0 | (1.0) | 28.6 | (1.6) | **-4.6** | (1.8) | 32.8 | (0.6) | 32.0 | (0.6) | 0.8 | (0.8) |
| Chile | 56.8 | (0.5) | 59.0 | (2.4) | -2.2 | (2.5) | 26.2 | (0.9) | 34.8 | (12.7) | -8.6 | (12.9) | 28.0 | (0.4) | 28.3 | (1.9) | -0.3 | (1.9) |
| Colombia | 60.5 | (0.6) | 62.1 | (1.0) | -1.6 | (1.0) | 23.8 | (0.9) | 23.9 | (3.1) | -0.1 | (3.2) | 25.1 | (0.4) | 24.9 | (0.7) | 0.2 | (0.7) |
| Croatia | 59.1 | (0.7) | 58.0 | (0.6) | 1.0 | (0.9) | 17.4 | (1.3) | 23.4 | (1.2) | **-6.0** | (1.7) | 30.8 | (0.3) | 30.0 | (0.5) | 0.8 | (0.8) |
| Estonia | 62.2 | (0.4) | a | a | a | a | 22.4 | (0.7) | a | a | a | a | 25.5 | (0.3) | a | a | a | a |
| Hong Kong-China | 62.2 | (0.4) | 68.0 | (2.3) | **-5.8** | (2.3) | 24.0 | (1.1) | 32.7 | (4.0) | **-8.7** | (4.3) | 23.8 | (0.3) | 17.6 | (1.6) | **6.2** | (1.6) |
| Indonesia | 55.7 | (0.5) | 64.1 | (1.5) | **-8.5** | (1.6) | 24.6 | (0.8) | 27.1 | (4.5) | -2.5 | (4.6) | 26.9 | (0.4) | 24.7 | (0.9) | **2.2** | (0.9) |
| Israel | 52.2 | (0.7) | 47.2 | (1.6) | **5.0** | (1.7) | 56.7 | (2.0) | 63.4 | (3.9) | -6.7 | (4.7) | 25.0 | (0.5) | 27.9 | (1.1) | **-2.9** | (1.2) |
| Jordan | 43.2 | (0.5) | a | a | a | a | 30.2 | (0.9) | a | a | a | a | 34.5 | (0.4) | a | a | a | a |
| Kyrgyzstan | 41.8 | (0.5) | 52.3 | (2.1) | **-10.5** | (2.1) | 40.1 | (1.4) | 34.2 | (4.7) | 5.9 | (4.8) | 34.1 | (0.4) | 25.8 | (1.7) | **8.3** | (1.7) |
| Latvia | 58.0 | (0.4) | 64.1 | (1.8) | **-6.1** | (1.9) | 30.4 | (1.3) | 17.7 | (2.0) | **12.6** | (2.4) | 28.6 | (0.3) | 24.7 | (1.5) | **3.9** | (1.5) |
| Liechtenstein | 66.7 | (1.2) | a | a | a | a | 14.4 | (1.4) | a | a | a | a | 24.8 | (1.0) | a | a | a | a |
| Lithuania | 60.7 | (0.4) | c | c | c | c | 19.1 | (0.6) | c | c | c | c | 27.8 | (0.3) | c | c | c | c |
| Macao-China | 66.2 | (0.4) | 69.7 | (1.6) | **-3.5** | (1.6) | 23.9 | (0.8) | 16.6 | (3.0) | **7.2** | (3.0) | 21.9 | (0.3) | 22.5 | (1.5) | -0.6 | (1.5) |
| Montenegro | 55.9 | (0.6) | 50.7 | (0.5) | **5.3** | (0.8) | 16.2 | (1.2) | 23.1 | (1.2) | **-7.0** | (1.8) | 32.9 | (0.6) | 34.7 | (0.5) | **-1.8** | (0.8) |
| Qatar | 43.3 | (0.3) | a | a | a | a | 38.5 | (0.8) | a | a | a | a | 31.6 | (0.3) | c | c | c | c |
| Romania | 50.8 | (0.7) | 45.1 | (1.0) | **5.8** | (1.3) | 42.1 | (2.3) | 51.2 | (4.8) | -9.1 | (5.4) | 30.4 | (0.5) | a | a | a | a |
| Russian Federation | 53.3 | (0.6) | 57.8 | (1.9) | **-4.5** | (2.0) | 19.7 | (0.9) | 20.3 | (2.0) | -0.6 | (2.2) | 31.0 | (0.4) | 26.3 | (1.3) | **4.7** | (1.3) |
| Serbia | 59.0 | (0.8) | 59.4 | (0.6) | -0.3 | (1.0) | 18.1 | (1.2) | 25.1 | (1.2) | **-7.0** | (1.6) | 28.6 | (0.7) | 27.4 | (0.4) | 1.2 | (0.9) |
| Slovenia | 57.8 | (0.5) | 53.4 | (0.5) | **4.4** | (0.7) | 20.5 | (1.1) | 32.8 | (1.1) | **-12.3** | (1.6) | 30.5 | (0.5) | 29.6 | (0.4) | 0.9 | (0.6) |
| Chinese Taipei | 57.1 | (0.4) | 64.7 | (0.8) | **-7.6** | (0.9) | 38.4 | (0.9) | 32.3 | (1.7) | **6.1** | (1.8) | 23.5 | (0.2) | 23.1 | (0.5) | 0.4 | (0.6) |
| Thailand | 62.5 | (0.4) | 68.5 | (1.0) | **-6.0** | (1.1) | 13.8 | (0.5) | 5.2 | (0.6) | **8.6** | (0.8) | 25.7 | (0.3) | 27.7 | (0.9) | **-2.1** | (0.9) |
| Tunisia | 41.7 | (0.4) | a | a | a | a | 44.7 | (1.1) | a | a | a | a | 31.2 | (0.3) | a | a | a | a |
| Uruguay | 60.5 | (0.4) | 63.1 | (1.8) | -2.6 | (1.9) | 23.0 | (1.1) | 26.5 | (5.5) | -3.5 | (5.7) | 27.0 | (0.3) | 25.6 | (1.3) | 1.4 | (1.3) |

*Note:* Values that are statistically significant at the 5% level (p < 0.05) are indicated in bold.

© OECD 2011 Quality Time for Students: Learning In and Out of School

## Table 3.12c [Part 1/3] Mean learning hours and allocation of total learning time on the language of instruction, by academic and vocational orientation of schools

| | Mean learning hours per week | | | | | | | | | | | |
|---|---|---|---|---|---|---|---|---|---|---|---|---|
| | Regular school lessons | | | | | | Out-of-school-time lessons | | | | | |
| | Academic schools | | Vocational schools | | Difference (academic-vocational) | | Academic schools | | Vocational schools | | Difference (academic-vocational) | |
| | Mean | S.E. | Mean | S.E. | Dif. | S.E. | Mean | S.E. | Mean | S.E. | Dif. | S.E. |
| **OECD** | | | | | | | | | | | | |
| Australia | 4.09 | (0.03) | 3.83 | (0.07) | **0.26** | (0.08) | 0.64 | (0.02) | 0.81 | (0.05) | **-0.17** | (0.05) |
| Austria | 3.21 | (0.04) | 2.73 | (0.05) | **0.49** | (0.06) | 0.18 | (0.03) | 0.26 | (0.02) | **-0.08** | (0.04) |
| Belgium | 3.92 | (0.03) | 2.95 | (0.04) | **0.97** | (0.05) | 0.38 | (0.02) | 0.55 | (0.02) | **-0.17** | (0.03) |
| Canada | 4.43 | (0.04) | a | a | a | a | 0.86 | (0.02) | a | a | a | a |
| Czech Republic | 3.94 | (0.04) | 3.41 | (0.05) | **0.53** | (0.06) | 0.61 | (0.02) | 0.62 | (0.03) | -0.01 | (0.03) |
| Denmark | 5.50 | (0.03) | a | a | a | a | 1.68 | (0.03) | a | a | a | a |
| Finland | 3.13 | (0.05) | a | a | a | a | 0.36 | (0.01) | a | a | a | a |
| France | 4.10 | (0.03) | 3.15 | (0.09) | **0.95** | (0.10) | 0.77 | (0.02) | 0.77 | (0.07) | -0.01 | (0.08) |
| Germany | 3.67 | (0.03) | 3.02 | (0.23) | **0.65** | (0.23) | 0.61 | (0.02) | 0.57 | (0.23) | 0.04 | (0.24) |
| Greece | 3.36 | (0.04) | 1.94 | (0.07) | **1.42** | (0.08) | 1.69 | (0.04) | 1.22 | (0.08) | **0.48** | (0.09) |
| Hungary | 3.36 | (0.07) | 3.05 | (0.05) | **0.31** | (0.09) | 1.32 | (0.05) | 1.30 | (0.03) | 0.02 | (0.06) |
| Iceland | 4.52 | (0.02) | c | c | c | c | 0.46 | (0.02) | c | c | c | c |
| Ireland | 3.56 | (0.03) | 2.94 | (0.24) | **0.61** | (0.23) | 0.63 | (0.02) | 0.73 | (0.20) | -0.10 | (0.20) |
| Italy | 4.94 | (0.05) | 4.36 | (0.04) | **0.58** | (0.07) | 0.66 | (0.03) | 0.89 | (0.03) | **-0.23** | (0.04) |
| Japan | 4.08 | (0.05) | 3.01 | (0.08) | **1.07** | (0.09) | 0.44 | (0.02) | 0.41 | (0.03) | 0.03 | (0.04) |
| Korea | 4.70 | (0.04) | 3.70 | (0.12) | **1.00** | (0.13) | 1.72 | (0.05) | 0.55 | (0.06) | **1.17** | (0.08) |
| Luxembourg | 3.65 | (0.03) | 2.51 | (0.05) | **1.15** | (0.06) | 0.63 | (0.02) | 0.35 | (0.04) | **0.28** | (0.04) |
| Mexico | 3.74 | (0.05) | 3.72 | (0.05) | 0.01 | (0.07) | 1.15 | (0.04) | 1.00 | (0.02) | **0.15** | (0.05) |
| Netherlands | 2.95 | (0.03) | 2.84 | (0.05) | 0.11 | (0.06) | 0.54 | (0.02) | 0.90 | (0.04) | **-0.36** | (0.05) |
| New Zealand | 4.39 | (0.03) | a | a | a | a | 0.65 | (0.03) | a | a | a | a |
| Norway | 3.60 | (0.04) | a | a | a | a | 1.16 | (0.02) | a | a | a | a |
| Poland | 4.64 | (0.03) | a | a | a | a | 0.70 | (0.03) | a | a | a | a |
| Portugal | 3.27 | (0.03) | 3.23 | (0.06) | 0.04 | (0.07) | 0.58 | (0.02) | 0.49 | (0.05) | 0.08 | (0.05) |
| Slovak Republic | 3.66 | (0.06) | 2.44 | (0.06) | **1.22** | (0.08) | 1.03 | (0.03) | 0.70 | (0.04) | **0.33** | (0.05) |
| Spain | 3.60 | (0.03) | a | a | a | a | 0.58 | (0.02) | a | a | a | a |
| Sweden | 3.12 | (0.03) | c | c | c | c | 0.68 | (0.02) | c | c | c | c |
| Switzerland | 3.76 | (0.03) | 2.12 | (0.17) | **1.64** | (0.17) | 0.50 | (0.02) | 0.34 | (0.07) | **0.16** | (0.07) |
| Turkey | 4.46 | (0.05) | 3.30 | (0.08) | **1.17** | (0.09) | 1.96 | (0.07) | 1.60 | (0.06) | **0.36** | (0.09) |
| United Kingdom | 3.89 | (0.04) | a | a | a | a | 0.59 | (0.02) | a | a | a | a |
| United States | 3.64 | (0.04) | a | a | a | a | 1.11 | (0.03) | a | a | a | a |
| **OECD average** | **3.90** | **(0.01)** | **3.07** | **(0.02)** | **0.75** | **(0.03)** | **0.83** | **(0.01)** | **0.74** | **(0.02)** | **0.10** | **(0.02)** |
| **Partners** | | | | | | | | | | | | |
| Argentina | 2.40 | (0.05) | 1.90 | (0.32) | 0.51 | (0.32) | 0.42 | (0.03) | 0.63 | (0.19) | -0.21 | (0.19) |
| Azerbaijan | 3.70 | (0.05) | 2.71 | (0.43) | **0.98** | (0.43) | 1.80 | (0.05) | 1.71 | (0.44) | 0.09 | (0.44) |
| Brazil | 3.10 | (0.04) | a | a | a | a | 1.18 | (0.03) | a | a | a | a |
| Bulgaria | 3.10 | (0.06) | 2.71 | (0.07) | **0.39** | (0.08) | 1.06 | (0.05) | 1.12 | (0.04) | -0.05 | (0.07) |
| Chile | 3.47 | (0.06) | 2.58 | (0.13) | **0.89** | (0.15) | 1.01 | (0.03) | 0.52 | (0.09) | **0.49** | (0.10) |
| Colombia | 3.89 | (0.05) | 4.05 | (0.19) | -0.16 | (0.20) | 1.15 | (0.03) | 1.13 | (0.07) | 0.02 | (0.07) |
| Croatia | 3.81 | (0.05) | 3.14 | (0.04) | **0.67** | (0.07) | 0.26 | (0.02) | 0.44 | (0.02) | **-0.17** | (0.03) |
| Estonia | 3.48 | (0.04) | a | a | a | a | 0.88 | (0.03) | a | a | a | a |
| Hong Kong-China | 5.25 | (0.05) | 4.45 | (0.14) | **0.80** | (0.15) | 0.80 | (0.03) | 0.96 | (0.11) | -0.16 | (0.12) |
| Indonesia | 3.83 | (0.05) | 2.72 | (0.19) | **1.11** | (0.18) | 1.35 | (0.03) | 0.81 | (0.06) | **0.54** | (0.07) |
| Israel | 3.10 | (0.05) | 2.64 | (0.10) | **0.47** | (0.12) | 1.32 | (0.04) | 1.40 | (0.07) | -0.08 | (0.08) |
| Jordan | 3.56 | (0.05) | a | a | a | a | 1.77 | (0.04) | a | a | a | a |
| Kyrgyzstan | 2.75 | (0.06) | 2.61 | (0.17) | 0.13 | (0.18) | 1.71 | (0.03) | 1.38 | (0.20) | 0.33 | (0.20) |
| Latvia | 3.71 | (0.04) | 3.16 | (0.15) | **0.55** | (0.15) | 0.89 | (0.03) | 0.60 | (0.08) | **0.29** | (0.08) |
| Liechtenstein | 3.66 | (0.08) | a | a | a | a | 0.32 | (0.04) | a | a | a | a |
| Lithuania | 3.66 | (0.04) | c | c | c | c | 0.65 | (0.02) | c | c | c | c |
| Macao-China | 5.32 | (0.03) | 5.31 | (0.15) | 0.01 | (0.15) | 1.06 | (0.03) | 0.82 | (0.14) | 0.24 | (0.14) |
| Montenegro | 3.53 | (0.06) | 2.64 | (0.04) | **0.89** | (0.07) | 0.61 | (0.04) | 0.81 | (0.03) | **-0.20** | (0.05) |
| Qatar | 2.90 | (0.03) | a | a | a | a | 1.59 | (0.03) | a | a | a | a |
| Romania | 3.64 | (0.06) | 2.17 | (0.07) | **1.47** | (0.09) | 1.52 | (0.03) | 1.50 | (0.08) | 0.02 | (0.08) |
| Russian Federation | 2.06 | (0.04) | 1.91 | (0.09) | 0.15 | (0.09) | 0.84 | (0.03) | 0.68 | (0.06) | **0.17** | (0.07) |
| Serbia | 3.86 | (0.06) | 2.93 | (0.03) | **0.93** | (0.07) | 0.91 | (0.05) | 0.93 | (0.03) | -0.02 | (0.06) |
| Slovenia | 3.68 | (0.04) | 2.83 | (0.03) | **0.85** | (0.05) | 0.60 | (0.02) | 0.86 | (0.02) | **-0.27** | (0.03) |
| Chinese Taipei | 4.81 | (0.04) | 3.55 | (0.08) | **1.26** | (0.09) | 0.72 | (0.03) | 0.64 | (0.04) | 0.08 | (0.04) |
| Thailand | 3.41 | (0.02) | 1.35 | (0.06) | **2.06** | (0.06) | 0.63 | (0.03) | 0.18 | (0.02) | **0.45** | (0.03) |
| Tunisia | 3.14 | (0.05) | a | a | a | a | 1.78 | (0.04) | a | a | a | a |
| Uruguay | 2.84 | (0.03) | 1.99 | (0.11) | **0.84** | (0.11) | 0.66 | (0.02) | 0.57 | (0.08) | 0.09 | (0.08) |

*Note:* Values that are statistically significant at the 5% level (p < 0.05) are indicated in bold.

### Table 3.12c [Part 2/3] Mean learning hours and allocation of total learning time on the language of instruction, by academic and vocational orientation of schools

| | | Mean learning hours per week | | | | | | | | | | |
|---|---|---|---|---|---|---|---|---|---|---|---|---|
| | | Individual study | | | | | | Total learning hours | | | | |
| | | Academic schools | | Vocational schools | | Difference (academic-vocational) | | Academic schools | | Vocational schools | | Difference (academic-vocational) |
| | | Mean | S.E. | Mean | S.E. | Dif. | S.E. | Mean | S.E. | Mean | S.E. | Dif. | S.E. |
| OECD | Australia | 1.72 | (0.02) | 1.64 | (0.05) | 0.08 | (0.05) | 6.45 | (0.05) | 6.27 | (0.13) | 0.18 | (0.14) |
| | Austria | 1.69 | (0.07) | 1.49 | (0.04) | **0.21** | (0.08) | 5.09 | (0.10) | 4.48 | (0.09) | **0.61** | (0.13) |
| | Belgium | 1.46 | (0.02) | 1.22 | (0.03) | **0.24** | (0.03) | 5.76 | (0.05) | 4.74 | (0.06) | **1.01** | (0.07) |
| | Canada | 1.74 | (0.03) | a | a | a | a | 7.06 | (0.06) | a | a | a | a |
| | Czech Republic | 1.19 | (0.03) | 1.12 | (0.04) | 0.07 | (0.05) | 5.73 | (0.06) | 5.14 | (0.08) | **0.59** | (0.10) |
| | Denmark | 2.16 | (0.03) | a | a | a | a | 9.34 | (0.07) | a | a | a | a |
| | Finland | 1.13 | (0.02) | a | a | a | a | 4.63 | (0.07) | a | a | a | a |
| | France | 1.56 | (0.02) | 1.07 | (0.07) | **0.49** | (0.07) | 6.44 | (0.05) | 5.01 | (0.14) | **1.43** | (0.14) |
| | Germany | 1.90 | (0.03) | 1.60 | (0.20) | 0.30 | (0.21) | 6.20 | (0.05) | 5.21 | (0.58) | 0.98 | (0.59) |
| | Greece | 2.01 | (0.03) | 1.47 | (0.08) | **0.54** | (0.09) | 7.07 | (0.08) | 4.65 | (0.17) | **2.43** | (0.19) |
| | Hungary | 1.99 | (0.06) | 1.77 | (0.04) | **0.22** | (0.08) | 6.66 | (0.14) | 6.14 | (0.11) | **0.53** | (0.19) |
| | Iceland | 1.54 | (0.02) | c | c | c | c | 6.54 | (0.04) | c | c | c | c |
| | Ireland | 1.76 | (0.03) | 1.44 | (0.25) | 0.31 | (0.24) | 5.95 | (0.06) | 5.27 | (0.46) | 0.69 | (0.45) |
| | Italy | 3.51 | (0.07) | 2.51 | (0.04) | **1.00** | (0.08) | 9.10 | (0.13) | 7.79 | (0.08) | **1.30** | (0.15) |
| | Japan | 1.03 | (0.04) | 0.69 | (0.04) | **0.33** | (0.06) | 5.54 | (0.09) | 4.12 | (0.10) | **1.42** | (0.13) |
| | Korea | 1.60 | (0.03) | 0.77 | (0.04) | **0.82** | (0.05) | 8.01 | (0.10) | 5.05 | (0.18) | **2.96** | (0.21) |
| | Luxembourg | 1.43 | (0.02) | 1.08 | (0.05) | **0.35** | (0.06) | 5.72 | (0.04) | 3.91 | (0.11) | **1.80** | (0.12) |
| | Mexico | 2.07 | (0.04) | 2.03 | (0.03) | 0.03 | (0.05) | 6.93 | (0.10) | 6.74 | (0.06) | 0.20 | (0.12) |
| | Netherlands | 1.33 | (0.03) | 1.33 | (0.05) | -0.01 | (0.06) | 4.80 | (0.06) | 5.10 | (0.11) | **-0.30** | (0.14) |
| | New Zealand | 1.57 | (0.03) | a | a | a | a | 6.62 | (0.06) | a | a | a | a |
| | Norway | 1.44 | (0.03) | a | a | a | a | 6.19 | (0.06) | a | a | a | a |
| | Poland | 2.22 | (0.03) | a | a | a | a | 7.56 | (0.05) | a | a | a | a |
| | Portugal | 1.81 | (0.03) | 1.68 | (0.07) | 0.13 | (0.08) | 5.66 | (0.06) | 5.42 | (0.12) | 0.24 | (0.14) |
| | Slovak Republic | 1.82 | (0.04) | 1.64 | (0.05) | **0.19** | (0.07) | 6.51 | (0.09) | 4.78 | (0.11) | **1.73** | (0.14) |
| | Spain | 1.89 | (0.03) | m | m | m | m | 6.10 | (0.05) | m | m | m | m |
| | Sweden | 1.26 | (0.02) | c | c | c | c | 5.06 | (0.06) | c | c | c | c |
| | Switzerland | 1.43 | (0.01) | 1.01 | (0.07) | **0.42** | (0.07) | 5.70 | (0.04) | 3.46 | (0.30) | **2.24** | (0.30) |
| | Turkey | 2.32 | (0.07) | 1.97 | (0.05) | **0.34** | (0.09) | 8.72 | (0.14) | 6.86 | (0.17) | **1.86** | (0.23) |
| | United Kingdom | 1.59 | (0.02) | a | a | a | a | 6.08 | (0.06) | a | a | a | a |
| | United States | 1.87 | (0.03) | a | a | a | a | 6.65 | (0.06) | a | a | a | a |
| | **OECD average** | **1.73** | **(0.01)** | **1.45** | **(0.02)** | **0.32** | **(0.02)** | **6.46** | **(0.01)** | **5.27** | **(0.05)** | **1.15** | **(0.05)** |
| Partners | Argentina | 1.64 | (0.04) | 1.49 | (0.17) | 0.15 | (0.16) | 4.46 | (0.08) | 4.00 | (0.61) | 0.46 | (0.60) |
| | Azerbaijan | 3.12 | (0.05) | 1.80 | (0.27) | **1.32** | (0.27) | 8.68 | (0.11) | 6.22 | (0.56) | **2.46** | (0.57) |
| | Brazil | 1.74 | (0.03) | a | a | a | a | 6.01 | (0.06) | a | a | a | a |
| | Bulgaria | 2.17 | (0.08) | 1.92 | (0.06) | **0.26** | (0.10) | 6.35 | (0.15) | 5.77 | (0.12) | **0.58** | (0.18) |
| | Chile | 1.57 | (0.03) | 1.22 | (0.10) | **0.35** | (0.10) | 6.08 | (0.09) | 4.33 | (0.26) | **1.75** | (0.28) |
| | Colombia | 1.80 | (0.04) | 2.02 | (0.08) | **-0.21** | (0.09) | 6.87 | (0.08) | 7.18 | (0.26) | -0.31 | (0.27) |
| | Croatia | 1.83 | (0.06) | 1.48 | (0.04) | **0.35** | (0.07) | 5.90 | (0.11) | 5.09 | (0.07) | **0.82** | (0.13) |
| | Estonia | 1.62 | (0.03) | a | a | a | a | 5.99 | (0.06) | a | a | a | a |
| | Hong Kong-China | 1.67 | (0.04) | 1.34 | (0.10) | **0.32** | (0.11) | 7.71 | (0.08) | 6.76 | (0.31) | **0.94** | (0.33) |
| | Indonesia | 1.87 | (0.04) | 1.49 | (0.08) | **0.37** | (0.10) | 7.04 | (0.09) | 5.01 | (0.09) | **2.03** | (0.12) |
| | Israel | 1.63 | (0.05) | 1.77 | (0.09) | -0.14 | (0.10) | 6.05 | (0.11) | 5.96 | (0.22) | 0.10 | (0.25) |
| | Jordan | 2.59 | (0.04) | a | a | a | a | 7.92 | (0.09) | a | a | a | a |
| | Kyrgyzstan | 2.34 | (0.04) | 2.04 | (0.08) | **0.30** | (0.09) | 6.87 | (0.09) | 6.05 | (0.39) | **0.82** | (0.39) |
| | Latvia | 2.02 | (0.03) | 1.55 | (0.12) | **0.48** | (0.13) | 6.63 | (0.07) | 5.30 | (0.27) | **1.32** | (0.28) |
| | Liechtenstein | 1.24 | (0.06) | a | a | a | a | 5.21 | (0.10) | a | a | a | a |
| | Lithuania | 1.82 | (0.03) | c | c | c | c | 6.13 | (0.06) | c | c | c | c |
| | Macao-China | 1.49 | (0.03) | 1.57 | (0.17) | -0.09 | (0.17) | 7.87 | (0.06) | 7.69 | (0.36) | 0.18 | (0.36) |
| | Montenegro | 2.15 | (0.05) | 1.91 | (0.04) | **0.25** | (0.07) | 6.27 | (0.11) | 5.37 | (0.08) | **0.90** | (0.14) |
| | Qatar | 2.04 | (0.02) | a | a | a | a | 6.51 | (0.06) | a | a | a | a |
| | Romania | 2.33 | (0.04) | 1.74 | (0.05) | **0.59** | (0.07) | 7.50 | (0.10) | 5.40 | (0.17) | **2.09** | (0.20) |
| | Russian Federation | 1.62 | (0.04) | 1.14 | (0.06) | **0.47** | (0.05) | 4.50 | (0.07) | 3.73 | (0.17) | **0.77** | (0.17) |
| | Serbia | 1.97 | (0.06) | 1.60 | (0.03) | **0.37** | (0.07) | 6.74 | (0.12) | 5.46 | (0.06) | **1.28** | (0.14) |
| | Slovenia | 1.55 | (0.03) | 1.40 | (0.02) | **0.15** | (0.04) | 5.83 | (0.07) | 5.13 | (0.05) | **0.71** | (0.08) |
| | Chinese Taipei | 1.95 | (0.03) | 1.44 | (0.06) | **0.51** | (0.06) | 7.51 | (0.07) | 5.67 | (0.13) | **1.84** | (0.14) |
| | Thailand | 1.84 | (0.03) | 0.91 | (0.02) | **0.93** | (0.04) | 5.87 | (0.05) | 2.44 | (0.08) | **3.43** | (0.10) |
| | Tunisia | 2.12 | (0.04) | a | a | a | a | 7.05 | (0.10) | a | a | a | a |
| | Uruguay | 1.40 | (0.02) | 0.98 | (0.07) | **0.42** | (0.07) | 4.90 | (0.06) | 3.61 | (0.21) | **1.29** | (0.22) |

*Note:* Values that are statistically significant at the 5% level (p < 0.05) are indicated in bold.

© OECD 2011 Quality Time for Students: Learning In and Out of School

## Table 3.12c [Part 3/3] Mean learning hours and allocation of total learning time on the language of instruction, by academic and vocational orientation of schools

| | Allocation of total learning time on the language of instruction for | | | | | | | | | | | | | | | | | |
| | Regular school lessons | | | | | | Out-of-school-time lessons | | | | | | Individual study | | | | | |
| | Academic schools | | Vocational schools | | Difference (academic-vocational) | | Academic schools | | Vocational schools | | Difference (academic-vocational) | | Academic schools | | Vocational schools | | Difference (academic-vocational) | |
| | % | S.E | % | S.E | Dif. | S.E. | % | S.E | % | S.E | Dif. | S.E. | % | S.E | % | S.E | Dif. | S.E. |
|---|---|---|---|---|---|---|---|---|---|---|---|---|---|---|---|---|---|---|
| **OECD** | | | | | | | | | | | | | | | | | | |
| Australia | 65.8 | (0.3) | 65.4 | (0.9) | 0.4 | (0.9) | 9.0 | (0.2) | 11.4 | (0.7) | **-2.4** | (0.7) | 25.2 | (0.2) | 23.2 | (0.6) | **1.9** | (0.6) |
| Austria | 57.3 | (0.7) | 59.0 | (0.6) | -1.7 | (0.9) | 7.7 | (0.5) | 6.2 | (0.3) | **1.5** | (0.5) | 35.0 | (0.6) | 34.8 | (0.5) | 0.2 | (0.8) |
| Belgium | 63.9 | (0.4) | 62.1 | (0.5) | **1.8** | (0.6) | 6.7 | (0.3) | 9.6 | (0.4) | **-2.9** | (0.5) | 29.4 | (0.4) | 28.3 | (0.4) | **1.1** | (0.5) |
| Canada | 63.3 | (0.3) | a | a | a | a | 11.4 | (0.2) | a | a | a | a | 25.2 | (0.2) | a | a | a | a |
| Czech Republic | 70.6 | (0.5) | 69.9 | (0.8) | 0.7 | (1.0) | 9.5 | (0.3) | 10.3 | (0.3) | -0.8 | (0.5) | 19.9 | (0.4) | 19.8 | (0.7) | 0.1 | (0.8) |
| Denmark | 62.3 | (0.3) | a | a | a | a | 16.0 | (0.3) | a | a | a | a | 21.6 | (0.2) | a | a | a | a |
| Finland | 71.1 | (0.3) | a | a | a | a | 6.0 | (0.2) | a | a | a | a | 22.9 | (0.2) | a | a | a | a |
| France | 62.3 | (0.3) | 65.4 | (1.2) | **-3.1** | (1.2) | 12.6 | (0.2) | 13.5 | (0.8) | -0.9 | (0.8) | 25.2 | (0.3) | 21.2 | (1.0) | **4.0** | (0.9) |
| Germany | 58.6 | (0.3) | 52.8 | (1.9) | **5.8** | (2.0) | 9.7 | (0.3) | 12.2 | (2.9) | -2.5 | (3.0) | 31.7 | (0.3) | 35.0 | (1.5) | **-3.3** | (1.5) |
| Greece | 48.4 | (0.5) | 55.5 | (1.9) | **-7.0** | (2.0) | 27.3 | (0.5) | 17.4 | (1.0) | **9.9** | (1.2) | 24.3 | (0.3) | 27.2 | (1.2) | **-2.9** | (1.2) |
| Hungary | 54.5 | (0.7) | 54.1 | (0.5) | 0.5 | (0.9) | 16.9 | (0.5) | 18.3 | (0.4) | **-1.4** | (0.7) | 28.5 | (0.5) | 27.6 | (0.3) | 1.0 | (0.6) |
| Iceland | 69.4 | (0.3) | c | c | c | c | 8.5 | (0.2) | c | c | c | c | 22.1 | (0.2) | c | c | c | c |
| Ireland | 63.6 | (0.4) | 67.1 | (4.0) | -3.5 | (4.0) | 9.5 | (0.3) | 10.1 | (2.0) | -0.7 | (2.0) | 27.0 | (0.3) | 22.8 | (2.9) | 4.1 | (2.9) |
| Italy | 54.1 | (0.3) | 55.7 | (0.3) | **-1.6** | (0.5) | 9.5 | (0.3) | 11.8 | (0.3) | **-2.2** | (0.4) | 36.3 | (0.3) | 32.5 | (0.3) | **3.8** | (0.4) |
| Japan | 70.7 | (0.7) | 74.9 | (0.8) | **-4.2** | (1.0) | 8.9 | (0.4) | 8.1 | (0.5) | 0.8 | (0.6) | 20.5 | (0.5) | 17.1 | (0.8) | **3.4** | (0.9) |
| Korea | 52.1 | (0.5) | 73.6 | (1.1) | **-21.5** | (1.2) | 24.0 | (0.3) | 10.3 | (0.6) | **13.7** | (0.7) | 23.9 | (0.4) | 16.0 | (0.8) | **7.9** | (0.9) |
| Luxembourg | 63.4 | (0.3) | 62.7 | (0.9) | 0.7 | (1.0) | 11.4 | (0.3) | 9.5 | (0.6) | **1.8** | (0.7) | 25.3 | (0.3) | 27.8 | (0.8) | **-2.5** | (0.8) |
| Mexico | 53.9 | (0.5) | 55.9 | (0.5) | **-2.0** | (0.7) | 14.8 | (0.4) | 13.5 | (0.3) | **1.3** | (0.5) | 31.3 | (0.3) | 30.6 | (0.3) | 0.7 | (0.4) |
| Netherlands | 60.8 | (0.5) | 57.7 | (1.0) | **3.1** | (1.2) | 10.6 | (0.3) | 16.2 | (0.7) | **-5.6** | (0.8) | 28.6 | (0.4) | 26.1 | (0.7) | **2.5** | (0.8) |
| New Zealand | 69.6 | (0.4) | a | a | a | a | 8.5 | (0.3) | a | a | a | a | 21.9 | (0.3) | a | a | a | a |
| Norway | 62.2 | (0.4) | a | a | a | a | 15.9 | (0.3) | a | a | a | a | 21.9 | (0.3) | a | a | a | a |
| Poland | 62.5 | (0.3) | a | a | a | a | 10.1 | (0.3) | a | a | a | a | 27.4 | (0.3) | a | a | a | a |
| Portugal | 58.7 | (0.4) | 60.0 | (0.9) | -1.3 | (1.0) | 11.9 | (0.3) | 9.9 | (0.8) | **2.0** | (0.8) | 29.5 | (0.4) | 30.2 | (0.8) | -0.7 | (0.9) |
| Slovak Republic | 60.5 | (0.6) | 60.7 | (0.9) | -0.2 | (1.1) | 13.7 | (0.3) | 11.1 | (0.5) | **2.6** | (0.6) | 25.8 | (0.5) | 28.2 | (0.6) | **-2.4** | (0.8) |
| Spain | 57.7 | (0.3) | m | m | m | m | 13.1 | (0.2) | m | m | m | m | 29.3 | (0.3) | m | m | m | m |
| Sweden | 68.1 | (0.5) | c | c | c | c | 9.9 | (0.2) | c | c | c | c | 22.0 | (0.4) | c | c | c | c |
| Switzerland | 64.1 | (0.4) | 56.2 | (0.9) | **7.9** | (1.0) | 9.6 | (0.3) | 9.9 | (1.0) | -0.3 | (1.0) | 26.3 | (0.2) | 33.9 | (1.0) | **-7.6** | (1.0) |
| Turkey | 49.7 | (0.5) | 52.3 | (0.7) | **-2.6** | (0.9) | 23.9 | (0.5) | 20.9 | (0.7) | **3.0** | (0.8) | 26.4 | (0.4) | 26.8 | (0.5) | -0.4 | (0.7) |
| United Kingdom | 67.1 | (0.3) | a | a | a | a | 8.9 | (0.2) | a | a | a | a | 24.0 | (0.2) | a | a | a | a |
| United States | 55.4 | (0.5) | a | a | a | a | 15.4 | (0.4) | a | a | a | a | 29.2 | (0.3) | a | a | a | a |
| **OECD average** | **61.4** | **(0.1)** | **61.1** | **(0.3)** | **-1.5** | **(0.3)** | **12.4** | **(0.1)** | **12.1** | **(0.2)** | **0.9** | **(0.2)** | **26.3** | **(0.1)** | **26.8** | **(0.2)** | **0.6** | **(0.2)** |
| **Partners** | | | | | | | | | | | | | | | | | | |
| Argentina | 55.1 | (0.6) | 49.6 | (3.5) | 5.5 | (3.6) | 12.3 | (0.5) | 14.5 | (2.0) | -2.2 | (2.1) | 32.6 | (0.4) | 35.9 | (2.2) | -3.3 | (2.2) |
| Azerbaijan | 47.1 | (0.5) | 50.5 | (9.2) | -3.4 | (9.2) | 18.6 | (0.4) | 21.3 | (5.4) | -2.8 | (5.5) | 34.3 | (0.5) | 28.2 | (3.9) | 6.2 | (3.9) |
| Brazil | 54.4 | (0.5) | a | a | a | a | 17.3 | (0.4) | a | a | a | a | 28.3 | (0.4) | a | a | a | a |
| Bulgaria | 51.7 | (0.7) | 50.7 | (0.9) | 1.0 | (1.1) | 15.5 | (0.6) | 17.4 | (0.8) | -1.8 | (1.0) | 32.8 | (0.6) | 32.0 | (0.6) | 0.8 | (0.8) |
| Chile | 56.8 | (0.5) | 59.0 | (2.4) | -2.2 | (2.5) | 15.2 | (0.3) | 12.7 | (2.4) | 2.5 | (2.4) | 28.0 | (0.4) | 28.3 | (1.9) | -0.3 | (1.9) |
| Colombia | 60.5 | (0.6) | 62.1 | (1.0) | -1.6 | (1.0) | 14.5 | (0.4) | 13.0 | (0.7) | 1.5 | (0.8) | 25.1 | (0.4) | 24.9 | (0.7) | 0.2 | (0.7) |
| Croatia | 59.1 | (0.7) | 58.0 | (0.6) | 1.0 | (0.9) | 10.1 | (0.5) | 12.0 | (0.4) | **-1.9** | (0.7) | 30.8 | (0.7) | 30.0 | (0.5) | 0.8 | (0.8) |
| Estonia | 62.2 | (0.4) | a | a | a | a | 12.3 | (0.3) | a | a | a | a | 25.5 | (0.3) | a | a | a | a |
| Hong Kong-China | 62.2 | (0.4) | 68.0 | (2.3) | -5.8 | (2.3) | 14.0 | (0.3) | 14.4 | (0.9) | -0.4 | (1.0) | 23.8 | (0.3) | 17.6 | (1.6) | **6.2** | (1.6) |
| Indonesia | 55.7 | (0.5) | 64.1 | (1.5) | **-8.5** | (1.6) | 17.4 | (0.4) | 11.2 | (0.8) | **6.2** | (0.9) | 26.9 | (0.3) | 24.7 | (0.9) | **2.2** | (1.0) |
| Israel | 52.2 | (0.7) | 47.2 | (1.6) | **5.0** | (1.7) | 22.8 | (0.3) | 24.9 | (0.8) | **-2.1** | (0.9) | 25.0 | (0.5) | 27.9 | (1.1) | **-2.9** | (1.2) |
| Jordan | 43.2 | (0.5) | a | a | a | a | 22.3 | (0.5) | a | a | a | a | 34.5 | (0.4) | a | a | a | a |
| Kyrgyzstan | 41.8 | (0.5) | 52.3 | (2.1) | **-10.5** | (2.1) | 24.1 | (0.5) | 21.8 | (2.5) | 2.3 | (2.5) | 34.1 | (0.4) | 25.8 | (1.7) | **8.3** | (1.7) |
| Latvia | 58.0 | (0.4) | 64.1 | (1.8) | **-6.1** | (1.9) | 13.4 | (0.4) | 11.2 | (1.4) | 2.2 | (1.5) | 28.6 | (0.3) | 24.7 | (1.5) | **3.9** | (1.5) |
| Liechtenstein | 66.7 | (1.2) | a | a | a | a | 8.5 | (0.6) | a | a | a | a | 24.8 | (1.0) | a | a | a | a |
| Lithuania | 60.7 | (0.4) | c | c | c | c | 11.5 | (0.3) | c | c | c | c | 27.8 | (0.3) | c | c | c | c |
| Macao-China | 66.2 | (0.4) | 69.7 | (1.6) | -3.5 | (1.6) | 11.9 | (0.2) | 7.8 | (1.1) | **4.1** | (1.1) | 21.9 | (0.3) | 22.5 | (1.5) | -0.6 | (1.5) |
| Montenegro | 55.9 | (0.6) | 50.7 | (0.5) | **5.3** | (0.8) | 11.2 | (0.5) | 14.6 | (0.4) | **-3.4** | (0.7) | 32.9 | (0.6) | 34.7 | (0.5) | **-1.8** | (0.8) |
| Qatar | 43.3 | (0.3) | a | a | a | a | 25.2 | (0.3) | a | a | a | a | 31.6 | (0.3) | a | a | a | a |
| Romania | 50.8 | (0.7) | 45.1 | (1.0) | **5.8** | (1.3) | 18.7 | (0.4) | 23.1 | (0.8) | **-4.4** | (0.9) | 30.4 | (0.5) | 31.8 | (0.5) | **-1.4** | (0.7) |
| Russian Federation | 53.3 | (0.6) | 57.8 | (1.9) | **-4.5** | (2.0) | 15.7 | (0.7) | 15.8 | (1.2) | -0.2 | (1.4) | 31.0 | (0.4) | 26.3 | (1.3) | **4.7** | (1.3) |
| Serbia | 59.0 | (0.8) | 59.4 | (0.6) | -0.3 | (0.9) | 12.3 | (0.4) | 13.2 | (0.3) | -0.9 | (0.5) | 28.6 | (0.7) | 27.4 | (0.4) | 1.2 | (0.9) |
| Slovenia | 57.8 | (0.5) | 53.4 | (0.5) | **4.4** | (0.7) | 11.7 | (0.3) | 17.0 | (0.3) | **-5.3** | (0.5) | 30.5 | (0.3) | 29.6 | (0.4) | 0.9 | (0.6) |
| Chinese Taipei | 57.1 | (0.4) | 64.7 | (0.8) | **-7.6** | (0.9) | 19.4 | (0.3) | 12.2 | (0.5) | **7.2** | (0.5) | 23.5 | (0.2) | 23.1 | (0.5) | 0.4 | (0.6) |
| Thailand | 62.5 | (0.4) | 68.5 | (1.0) | **-6.0** | (1.1) | 11.8 | (0.3) | 3.8 | (0.4) | **8.1** | (0.5) | 25.7 | (0.3) | 27.7 | (0.9) | **-2.1** | (0.9) |
| Tunisia | 41.7 | (0.4) | a | a | a | a | 27.1 | (0.3) | a | a | a | a | 31.2 | (0.3) | a | a | a | a |
| Uruguay | 60.5 | (0.4) | 63.1 | (1.8) | -2.6 | (1.9) | 12.5 | (0.4) | 11.4 | (1.1) | 1.2 | (1.2) | 27.0 | (0.3) | 25.6 | (1.3) | 1.4 | (1.3) |

*Note:* Values that are statistically significant at the 5% level (p < 0.05) are indicated in bold.

Table 3.12d [Part 1/3] **Mean learning hours and allocation of total learning time in science, in mathematics and on the language of instruction, by academic and vocational orientation of schools**

| | Mean learning hours per week | | | | | | | | | | | | | | | |
|---|---|---|---|---|---|---|---|---|---|---|---|---|---|---|---|---|
| | Regular school lessons | | | | | | | | Out-of-school-time lessons | | | | | | | |
| | Academic schools | | Vocational schools | | Difference (academic-vocational) | | Difference after accounting for ESCS and school average ESCS (academic-vocational) | | Academic schools | | Vocational schools | | Difference (academic-vocational) | | Difference after accounting for ESCS and school average ESCS (academic-vocational) | |
| | Mean | S.E. | Mean | S.E. | Dif. | S.E. | Dif. | S.E. | Mean | S.E. | Mean | S.E. | Dif. | S.E. | Dif. | S.E. |
| **OECD** | | | | | | | | | | | | | | | | |
| Australia | 11.63 | (0.07) | 9.43 | (0.20) | **2.20** | (0.21) | **1.80** | (0.22) | 1.75 | (0.04) | 1.90 | (0.11) | -0.16 | (0.11) | -0.10 | (0.12) |
| Austria | 9.80 | (0.12) | 8.04 | (0.11) | **1.76** | (0.16) | **1.19** | (0.22) | 0.98 | (0.08) | 0.93 | (0.04) | 0.05 | (0.09) | **0.45** | (0.13) |
| Belgium | 11.73 | (0.09) | 7.17 | (0.10) | **4.55** | (0.14) | **4.09** | (0.15) | 1.25 | (0.05) | 1.39 | (0.06) | -0.14 | (0.08) | **0.19** | (0.09) |
| Canada | 12.93 | (0.11) | a | a | a | a | a | a | 2.35 | (0.05) | a | a | a | a | a | a |
| Czech Republic | 11.52 | (0.10) | 9.40 | (0.17) | **2.13** | (0.20) | **1.85** | (0.20) | 1.95 | (0.05) | 1.80 | (0.08) | 0.15 | (0.09) | **0.20** | (0.09) |
| Denmark | 13.16 | (0.07) | a | a | a | a | a | a | 3.83 | (0.07) | a | a | a | a | a | a |
| Finland | 9.71 | (0.11) | a | a | a | a | a | a | 1.06 | (0.04) | a | a | a | a | a | a |
| France | 11.06 | (0.10) | 7.32 | (0.22) | **3.74** | (0.25) | **2.69** | (0.24) | 2.28 | (0.05) | 1.92 | (0.14) | **0.36** | (0.15) | **0.57** | (0.16) |
| Germany | 10.70 | (0.08) | 7.25 | (0.70) | **3.45** | (0.72) | **3.13** | (0.66) | 1.92 | (0.06) | 1.79 | (0.59) | 0.13 | (0.60) | 0.59 | (0.70) |
| Greece | 10.37 | (0.10) | 6.27 | (0.16) | **4.09** | (0.19) | **3.20** | (0.25) | 6.21 | (0.11) | 3.52 | (0.27) | **2.69** | (0.30) | **2.34** | (0.35) |
| Hungary | 9.65 | (0.18) | 8.49 | (0.12) | **1.16** | (0.21) | 0.23 | (0.23) | 3.65 | (0.12) | 3.55 | (0.08) | 0.10 | (0.15) | **0.41** | (0.16) |
| Iceland | 12.25 | (0.06) | c | c | c | c | c | c | 1.46 | (0.04) | c | c | c | c | c | c |
| Ireland | 9.78 | (0.08) | 7.46 | (0.64) | **2.32** | (0.64) | **2.12** | (0.64) | 1.65 | (0.05) | 1.68 | (0.43) | -0.03 | (0.43) | 0.07 | (0.43) |
| Italy | 11.69 | (0.16) | 10.94 | (0.09) | **0.75** | (0.19) | -0.09 | (0.30) | 2.00 | (0.05) | 2.45 | (0.06) | **-0.45** | (0.08) | -0.19 | (0.12) |
| Japan | 11.69 | (0.15) | 7.88 | (0.20) | **3.81** | (0.25) | **2.55** | (0.30) | 1.48 | (0.07) | 1.15 | (0.08) | **0.33** | (0.10) | **0.27** | (0.11) |
| Korea | 13.51 | (0.12) | 10.20 | (0.28) | **3.31** | (0.30) | **3.05** | (0.39) | 5.69 | (0.10) | 1.62 | (0.14) | **4.07** | (0.17) | **2.86** | (0.25) |
| Luxembourg | 9.92 | (0.06) | 8.28 | (0.15) | **1.64** | (0.16) | **1.38** | (0.17) | 1.99 | (0.04) | 1.50 | (0.10) | **0.49** | (0.11) | **0.76** | (0.12) |
| Mexico | 10.97 | (0.12) | 10.55 | (0.12) | **0.42** | (0.17) | **0.41** | (0.17) | 3.43 | (0.11) | 2.95 | (0.05) | **0.48** | (0.12) | **0.49** | (0.11) |
| Netherlands | 8.54 | (0.08) | 6.55 | (0.12) | **1.99** | (0.15) | **1.61** | (0.18) | 1.72 | (0.06) | 2.28 | (0.10) | **-0.56** | (0.13) | -0.01 | (0.15) |
| New Zealand | 12.84 | (0.09) | a | a | a | a | a | a | 1.74 | (0.06) | a | a | a | a | a | a |
| Norway | 9.63 | (0.08) | a | a | a | a | a | a | 3.13 | (0.05) | a | a | a | a | a | a |
| Poland | 11.71 | (0.09) | a | a | a | a | a | a | 2.11 | (0.05) | a | a | a | a | a | a |
| Portugal | 10.14 | (0.10) | 9.75 | (0.27) | 0.39 | (0.27) | 0.40 | (0.26) | 2.04 | (0.05) | 1.69 | (0.13) | **0.35** | (0.13) | **0.29** | (0.13) |
| Slovak Republic | 10.63 | (0.16) | 6.63 | (0.14) | **4.00** | (0.22) | **3.74** | (0.23) | 2.90 | (0.07) | 1.76 | (0.10) | **1.14** | (0.12) | **1.03** | (0.12) |
| Spain | 10.15 | (0.09) | a | a | a | a | a | a | 2.24 | (0.05) | a | a | a | a | a | a |
| Sweden | 9.02 | (0.07) | c | c | c | c | c | c | 1.79 | (0.04) | c | c | c | c | c | c |
| Switzerland | 10.17 | (0.07) | 5.82 | (0.33) | **4.35** | (0.34) | **4.26** | (0.33) | 1.61 | (0.05) | 1.10 | (0.18) | **0.51** | (0.19) | **0.55** | (0.18) |
| Turkey | 12.14 | (0.19) | 8.54 | (0.23) | **3.60** | (0.30) | **2.87** | (0.31) | 6.01 | (0.10) | 4.10 | (0.11) | **1.91** | (0.15) | **1.71** | (0.18) |
| United Kingdom | 11.92 | (0.09) | a | a | a | a | a | a | 1.70 | (0.05) | a | a | a | a | a | a |
| United States | 10.94 | (0.13) | a | a | a | a | a | a | 3.04 | (0.07) | a | a | a | a | a | a |
| **OECD average** | **11.00** | **(0.02)** | **8.21** | **(0.06)** | **2.61** | **(0.07)** | **1.57** | **(0.07)** | **2.50** | **(0.01)** | **2.06** | **(0.05)** | **0.60** | **(0.05)** | **0.46** | **(0.04)** |
| **Partners** | | | | | | | | | | | | | | | | |
| Argentina | 7.63 | (0.16) | 6.85 | (0.93) | 0.78 | (0.94) | 0.38 | (0.84) | 1.65 | (0.07) | 2.07 | (0.47) | -0.42 | (0.47) | -0.35 | (0.48) |
| Azerbaijan | 10.41 | (0.12) | 6.84 | (1.06) | **3.57** | (1.08) | **3.21** | (1.14) | 4.87 | (0.10) | 4.41 | (1.15) | 0.46 | (1.16) | 0.42 | (1.15) |
| Brazil | 8.46 | (0.09) | a | a | a | a | a | a | 3.15 | (0.07) | a | a | a | a | a | a |
| Bulgaria | 9.28 | (0.24) | 7.73 | (0.19) | **1.55** | (0.30) | **1.03** | (0.26) | 3.19 | (0.11) | 3.21 | (0.12) | -0.02 | (0.16) | 0.01 | (0.16) |
| Chile | 9.38 | (0.17) | 5.84 | (0.30) | **3.54** | (0.33) | **2.69** | (0.34) | 2.84 | (0.06) | 1.67 | (0.20) | **1.17** | (0.21) | **1.30** | (0.21) |
| Colombia | 11.66 | (0.16) | 11.67 | (0.65) | -0.01 | (0.63) | 0.09 | (0.61) | 3.31 | (0.08) | 3.34 | (0.18) | -0.03 | (0.20) | -0.03 | (0.19) |
| Croatia | 10.35 | (0.13) | 7.66 | (0.10) | **2.69** | (0.16) | **2.38** | (0.21) | 1.54 | (0.08) | 1.59 | (0.06) | -0.05 | (0.10) | -0.02 | (0.14) |
| Estonia | 10.95 | (0.09) | a | a | a | a | a | a | 2.63 | (0.07) | a | a | a | a | a | a |
| Hong Kong-China | 13.79 | (0.11) | 10.72 | (0.36) | **3.07** | (0.38) | **2.35** | (0.36) | 3.11 | (0.08) | 2.73 | (0.23) | 0.38 | (0.25) | 0.40 | (0.26) |
| Indonesia | 11.30 | (0.15) | 9.41 | (0.81) | **1.88** | (0.78) | **1.93** | (0.62) | 3.94 | (0.10) | 2.32 | (0.16) | **1.62** | (0.19) | **1.64** | (0.20) |
| Israel | 9.77 | (0.12) | 8.61 | (0.28) | **1.16** | (0.32) | **0.92** | (0.32) | 4.39 | (0.09) | 4.67 | (0.21) | -0.28 | (0.23) | -0.13 | (0.23) |
| Jordan | 10.36 | (0.14) | a | a | a | a | a | a | 5.10 | (0.10) | a | a | a | a | a | a |
| Kyrgyzstan | 7.80 | (0.16) | 7.76 | (0.70) | 0.04 | (0.72) | 1.59 | (1.05) | 4.61 | (0.09) | 3.93 | (0.30) | **0.68** | (0.30) | 0.11 | (0.37) |
| Latvia | 11.05 | (0.11) | 11.27 | (0.36) | -0.22 | (0.36) | -0.04 | (0.37) | 2.74 | (0.08) | 2.04 | (0.16) | **0.70** | (0.18) | **0.72** | (0.17) |
| Liechtenstein | 10.23 | (0.19) | a | a | a | a | a | a | 1.37 | (0.10) | a | a | a | a | a | a |
| Lithuania | 9.86 | (0.10) | c | c | c | c | c | c | 1.93 | (0.05) | c | c | c | c | c | c |
| Macao-China | 14.47 | (0.07) | 13.65 | (0.40) | **0.82** | (0.40) | 0.53 | (0.41) | 3.27 | (0.07) | 2.40 | (0.34) | **0.87** | (0.34) | **0.83** | (0.35) |
| Montenegro | 10.84 | (0.14) | 7.92 | (0.11) | **2.91** | (0.16) | **2.58** | (0.23) | 2.41 | (0.10) | 2.81 | (0.06) | **-0.40** | (0.12) | **-0.31** | (0.13) |
| Qatar | 8.68 | (0.08) | a | a | a | a | a | a | 4.90 | (0.07) | a | a | a | a | a | a |
| Romania | 9.35 | (0.17) | 5.98 | (0.17) | **3.37** | (0.23) | **2.55** | (0.30) | 4.03 | (0.08) | 4.05 | (0.15) | -0.02 | (0.17) | -0.01 | (0.21) |
| Russian Federation | 9.59 | (0.15) | 8.26 | (0.36) | **1.34** | (0.41) | **1.22** | (0.39) | 3.12 | (0.08) | 2.76 | (0.21) | 0.36 | (0.23) | 0.39 | (0.23) |
| Serbia | 11.71 | (0.15) | 8.46 | (0.11) | **3.25** | (0.18) | **2.50** | (0.29) | 2.78 | (0.11) | 2.62 | (0.07) | 0.16 | (0.13) | **0.45** | (0.17) |
| Slovenia | 11.23 | (0.12) | 7.61 | (0.07) | **3.62** | (0.14) | **2.35** | (0.20) | 2.25 | (0.07) | 2.69 | (0.05) | **-0.44** | (0.09) | 0.08 | (0.20) |
| Chinese Taipei | 13.12 | (0.12) | 8.54 | (0.20) | **4.58** | (0.23) | **3.41** | (0.24) | 3.65 | (0.07) | 1.82 | (0.09) | **1.83** | (0.11) | **1.57** | (0.13) |
| Thailand | 11.52 | (0.07) | 5.90 | (0.13) | **5.63** | (0.15) | **5.58** | (0.17) | 2.72 | (0.08) | 0.54 | (0.08) | **2.18** | (0.11) | **2.14** | (0.11) |
| Tunisia | 9.17 | (0.12) | a | a | a | a | a | a | 6.10 | (0.06) | a | a | a | a | a | a |
| Uruguay | 8.70 | (0.09) | 6.83 | (0.29) | **1.87** | (0.30) | **1.56** | (0.27) | 2.12 | (0.06) | 1.79 | (0.17) | 0.33 | (0.17) | **0.42** | (0.17) |

*Note*: Values that are statistically significant at the 5% level (p < 0.05) are indicated in bold.

© OECD 2011 Quality Time for Students: Learning In and Out of School

**Table 3.12d** [Part 2/3] **Mean learning hours and allocation of total learning time in science, in mathematics and on the language of instruction, by academic and vocational orientation of schools**

| | Mean learning hours per week | | | | | | | | | | | | | |
|---|---|---|---|---|---|---|---|---|---|---|---|---|---|---|
| | Individual study | | | | | | | | Total learning hours | | | | | |
| | Academic schools | | Vocational schools | | Difference (academic-vocational) | | Difference after accounting for ESCS and school average ESCS (academic-vocational) | | Academic schools | | Vocational schools | | Difference (academic-vocational) | |
| | Mean | S.E. | Mean | S.E. | Dif. | S.E. | Dif. | S.E. | Mean | S.E. | Mean | S.E. | Dif. | S.E. |
| **OECD** | | | | | | | | | | | | | | |
| Australia | 4.77 | (0.06) | 3.86 | (0.11) | 0.91 | (0.13) | 0.56 | (0.12) | 18.16 | (0.13) | 15.16 | (0.32) | 3.01 | (0.35) |
| Austria | 5.48 | (0.14) | 4.73 | (0.09) | 0.75 | (0.16) | 1.31 | (0.19) | 16.30 | (0.20) | 13.74 | (0.20) | 2.56 | (0.28) |
| Belgium | 5.19 | (0.08) | 3.41 | (0.07) | 1.79 | (0.10) | 1.48 | (0.12) | 18.13 | (0.14) | 12.04 | (0.18) | 6.10 | (0.22) |
| Canada | 5.26 | (0.07) | a | a | a | a | a | a | 20.63 | (0.17) | a | a | a | a |
| Czech Republic | 3.67 | (0.07) | 3.18 | (0.08) | 0.48 | (0.11) | 0.47 | (0.11) | 17.12 | (0.16) | 14.35 | (0.23) | 2.77 | (0.28) |
| Denmark | 5.00 | (0.06) | a | a | a | a | a | a | 21.94 | (0.15) | a | a | a | a |
| Finland | 3.41 | (0.05) | a | a | a | a | a | a | 14.16 | (0.16) | a | a | a | a |
| France | 4.74 | (0.07) | 2.78 | (0.18) | 1.96 | (0.18) | 1.41 | (0.21) | 18.11 | (0.15) | 12.02 | (0.39) | 6.09 | (0.41) |
| Germany | 5.90 | (0.08) | 4.76 | (0.54) | 1.15 | (0.55) | 1.21 | (0.57) | 18.56 | (0.14) | 13.92 | (1.48) | 4.65 | (1.49) |
| Greece | 5.99 | (0.09) | 4.50 | (0.31) | 1.49 | (0.32) | 1.12 | (0.34) | 22.56 | (0.22) | 14.39 | (0.57) | 8.17 | (0.64) |
| Hungary | 5.72 | (0.13) | 4.97 | (0.11) | 0.75 | (0.18) | 0.58 | (0.21) | 19.00 | (0.33) | 17.05 | (0.26) | 1.95 | (0.43) |
| Iceland | 4.42 | (0.05) | c | c | c | c | c | c | 18.14 | (0.09) | c | c | c | c |
| Ireland | 4.72 | (0.08) | 3.64 | (0.59) | 1.08 | (0.59) | 0.83 | (0.58) | 16.11 | (0.15) | 13.13 | (1.13) | 2.99 | (1.13) |
| Italy | 8.69 | (0.14) | 6.61 | (0.08) | 2.08 | (0.16) | 1.59 | (0.21) | 22.38 | (0.31) | 20.02 | (0.18) | 2.35 | (0.36) |
| Japan | 3.48 | (0.12) | 1.98 | (0.08) | 1.50 | (0.15) | 0.71 | (0.15) | 16.64 | (0.27) | 11.02 | (0.27) | 5.62 | (0.39) |
| Korea | 5.70 | (0.15) | 2.41 | (0.12) | 3.28 | (0.19) | 1.95 | (0.24) | 24.91 | (0.29) | 14.32 | (0.43) | 10.59 | (0.52) |
| Luxembourg | 4.37 | (0.05) | 3.99 | (0.13) | 0.38 | (0.14) | 0.53 | (0.15) | 16.31 | (0.10) | 13.72 | (0.27) | 2.59 | (0.28) |
| Mexico | 6.48 | (0.11) | 6.28 | (0.07) | 0.20 | (0.13) | 0.21 | (0.13) | 20.74 | (0.27) | 19.72 | (0.15) | 1.02 | (0.32) |
| Netherlands | 4.21 | (0.07) | 3.44 | (0.13) | 0.77 | (0.15) | 0.66 | (0.18) | 14.44 | (0.15) | 12.27 | (0.30) | 2.17 | (0.36) |
| New Zealand | 4.42 | (0.07) | a | a | a | a | a | a | 19.02 | (0.14) | a | a | a | a |
| Norway | 4.06 | (0.06) | a | a | a | a | a | a | 16.79 | (0.12) | a | a | a | a |
| Poland | 6.34 | (0.07) | a | a | a | a | a | a | 20.19 | (0.14) | a | a | a | a |
| Portugal | 5.92 | (0.09) | 5.34 | (0.24) | 0.58 | (0.27) | 0.52 | (0.26) | 18.12 | (0.17) | 16.80 | (0.52) | 1.32 | (0.56) |
| Slovak Republic | 5.34 | (0.11) | 4.12 | (0.12) | 1.22 | (0.17) | 1.00 | (0.16) | 18.92 | (0.25) | 12.52 | (0.28) | 6.40 | (0.38) |
| Spain | 5.58 | (0.08) | a | a | a | a | a | a | 18.08 | (0.16) | a | a | a | a |
| Sweden | 3.59 | (0.05) | c | c | c | c | c | c | 14.39 | (0.12) | c | c | c | c |
| Switzerland | 4.27 | (0.04) | 3.20 | (0.19) | 1.07 | (0.19) | 1.07 | (0.19) | 16.07 | (0.11) | 10.14 | (0.64) | 5.93 | (0.64) |
| Turkey | 6.78 | (0.12) | 5.14 | (0.12) | 1.64 | (0.17) | 1.55 | (0.18) | 24.86 | (0.34) | 17.65 | (0.41) | 7.20 | (0.54) |
| United Kingdom | 4.52 | (0.06) | a | a | a | a | a | a | 18.16 | (0.14) | a | a | a | a |
| United States | 5.59 | (0.07) | a | a | a | a | a | a | 19.69 | (0.15) | a | a | a | a |
| **OECD average** | 5.12 | (0.02) | 4.12 | (0.05) | 1.21 | (0.06) | 0.68 | (0.05) | 18.62 | (0.04) | 14.42 | (0.12) | 4.39 | (0.13) |
| **Partners** | | | | | | | | | | | | | | |
| Argentina | 5.03 | (0.10) | 5.20 | (0.62) | -0.16 | (0.61) | -0.21 | (0.61) | 14.32 | (0.23) | 14.18 | (1.76) | 0.14 | (1.73) |
| Azerbaijan | 8.74 | (0.13) | 5.02 | (1.07) | 3.72 | (1.08) | 3.64 | (1.10) | 24.18 | (0.27) | 15.91 | (2.50) | 8.27 | (2.51) |
| Brazil | 5.21 | 0.03 | a | a | a | a | a | a | 16.78 | (0.17) | a | a | a | a |
| Bulgaria | 6.67 | (0.22) | 5.57 | (0.17) | 1.10 | (0.26) | 0.69 | (0.23) | 19.18 | (0.47) | 16.63 | (0.34) | 2.54 | (0.52) |
| Chile | 4.74 | (0.08) | 3.04 | (0.20) | 1.69 | (0.22) | 1.67 | (0.22) | 17.05 | (0.23) | 10.59 | (0.53) | 6.46 | (0.60) |
| Colombia | 5.47 | (0.10) | 6.10 | (0.30) | -0.63 | (0.33) | -0.62 | (0.32) | 20.43 | (0.22) | 21.12 | (1.01) | -0.69 | (1.01) |
| Croatia | 6.21 | (0.11) | 4.31 | (0.08) | 1.90 | (0.13) | 2.05 | (0.18) | 18.14 | (0.20) | 13.65 | (0.18) | 4.49 | (0.27) |
| Estonia | 5.11 | (0.06) | a | a | a | a | a | a | 18.71 | (0.14) | a | a | a | a |
| Hong Kong-China | 5.48 | (0.09) | 3.46 | (0.24) | 2.01 | (0.26) | 1.39 | (0.26) | 22.36 | (0.20) | 17.01 | (0.74) | 5.35 | (0.77) |
| Indonesia | 5.83 | (0.09) | 4.40 | (0.11) | 1.43 | (0.16) | 1.43 | (0.16) | 21.01 | (0.27) | 16.12 | (0.66) | 4.89 | (0.62) |
| Israel | 5.31 | (0.13) | 5.48 | (0.23) | -0.18 | (0.28) | 0.03 | (0.27) | 19.49 | (0.27) | 19.17 | (0.61) | 0.32 | (0.68) |
| Jordan | 7.90 | (0.11) | a | a | a | a | a | a | 23.35 | (0.22) | a | a | a | a |
| Kyrgyzstan | 6.73 | (0.09) | 5.41 | (0.26) | 1.31 | (0.26) | 1.20 | (0.25) | 19.29 | (0.25) | 17.26 | (0.94) | 2.03 | (0.96) |
| Latvia | 6.28 | (0.08) | 5.40 | (0.33) | 0.87 | (0.34) | 0.96 | (0.34) | 20.08 | (0.19) | 18.60 | (0.65) | 1.48 | (0.67) |
| Liechtenstein | 3.93 | (0.15) | a | a | a | a | a | a | 15.51 | (0.23) | a | a | a | a |
| Lithuania | 5.28 | (0.07) | c | c | c | c | c | c | 17.05 | (0.14) | c | c | c | c |
| Macao-China | 4.93 | (0.07) | 4.70 | (0.42) | 0.23 | (0.42) | -0.77 | (0.43) | 22.66 | (0.15) | 20.63 | (0.79) | 2.03 | (0.79) |
| Montenegro | 7.06 | (0.13) | 5.79 | (0.10) | 1.27 | (0.17) | 1.27 | (0.22) | 20.23 | (0.26) | 16.48 | (0.21) | 3.75 | (0.34) |
| Qatar | 6.27 | (0.06) | a | a | a | a | a | a | 19.89 | (0.16) | a | a | a | a |
| Romania | 6.24 | (0.11) | 5.03 | (0.16) | 1.22 | (0.20) | 0.74 | (0.21) | 19.63 | (0.27) | 15.01 | (0.41) | 4.62 | (0.50) |
| Russian Federation | 6.93 | (0.13) | 4.85 | (0.30) | 2.09 | (0.31) | 2.02 | (0.29) | 19.63 | (0.25) | 15.91 | (0.68) | 3.72 | (0.72) |
| Serbia | 6.50 | (0.16) | 4.76 | (0.07) | 1.74 | (0.18) | 1.35 | (0.25) | 21.01 | (0.31) | 15.81 | (0.17) | 5.20 | (0.36) |
| Slovenia | 5.53 | (0.08) | 4.37 | (0.06) | 1.16 | (0.10) | 1.15 | (0.14) | 19.00 | (0.20) | 14.74 | (0.13) | 4.26 | (0.23) |
| Chinese Taipei | 5.65 | (0.09) | 3.48 | (0.14) | 2.17 | (0.17) | 1.38 | (0.17) | 22.55 | (0.22) | 13.94 | (0.37) | 8.60 | (0.43) |
| Thailand | 5.76 | (0.09) | 2.75 | (0.05) | 3.02 | (0.10) | 3.00 | (0.11) | 19.99 | (0.16) | 9.19 | (0.20) | 10.79 | (0.26) |
| Tunisia | 7.29 | (0.08) | a | a | a | a | a | a | 22.60 | (0.21) | a | a | a | a |
| Uruguay | 4.36 | (0.06) | 3.23 | (0.19) | 1.13 | (0.20) | 1.04 | (0.20) | 15.20 | (0.14) | 11.94 | (0.40) | 3.26 | (0.41) |

*Note:* Values that are statistically significant at the 5% level (p < 0.05) are indicated in bold.

### Table 3.12d [Part 3/3] Mean learning hours and allocation of total learning time in science, in mathematics and on the language of instruction, by academic and vocational orientation of schools

| | Allocation of total learning time in science, in mathematics and on the language of instruction for | | | | | | | | |
| | Regular school lessons | | | Out-of-school-time lessons | | | Individual study | | |
| | Academic schools | Vocational schools | Difference (academic-vocational) | Academic schools | Vocational schools | Difference (academic-vocational) | Academic schools | Vocational schools | Difference (academic-vocational) |
| | % S.E | % S.E | Dif. S.E. | % S.E | % S.E | Dif. S.E. | % S.E | % S.E | Dif. S.E. |
|---|---|---|---|---|---|---|---|---|---|
| **OECD** | | | | | | | | | |
| Australia | 67.2 (0.3) | 65.6 (0.8) | 1.6 (0.8) | 8.0 (0.2) | 10.6 (0.6) | **-2.5** (0.6) | 24.8 (0.2) | 23.8 (0.5) | 0.9 (0.5) |
| Austria | 66.8 (0.8) | 65.0 (0.5) | 1.8 (1.0) | 2.2 (0.3) | 3.8 (0.3) | **-1.6** (0.4) | 31.0 (0.8) | 31.2 (0.5) | -0.2 (0.9) |
| Belgium | 69.4 (0.3) | 64.5 (0.5) | **5.0** (0.6) | 5.2 (0.3) | 9.4 (0.2) | **-4.2** (0.5) | 25.3 (0.3) | 26.1 (0.4) | -0.8 (0.5) |
| Canada | 65.6 (0.3) | a a | a a | 10.8 (0.2) | a a | a a | 23.6 (0.2) | a a | a a |
| Czech Republic | 72.0 (0.5) | 71.0 (0.8) | 1.1 (1.0) | 8.7 (0.2) | 9.4 (0.3) | -0.6 (0.4) | 19.2 (0.4) | 19.6 (0.7) | -0.4 (0.8) |
| Denmark | 62.2 (0.3) | a a | a a | 16.0 (0.2) | a a | a a | 21.9 (0.2) | a a | a a |
| Finland | 70.7 (0.4) | a a | a a | 6.2 (0.2) | a a | a a | 23.1 (0.3) | a a | a a |
| France | 66.8 (0.4) | 68.4 (1.6) | -1.6 (1.7) | 10.5 (0.3) | 12.3 (1.0) | -1.8 (1.1) | 22.7 (0.3) | 19.3 (1.0) | **3.3** (1.0) |
| Germany | 62.3 (0.4) | 60.9 (1.7) | 1.5 (1.8) | 7.9 (0.3) | 9.2 (2.0) | -1.3 (2.1) | 29.8 (0.3) | 29.9 (1.8) | -0.1 (1.8) |
| Greece | 51.5 (0.5) | 47.5 (2.2) | 4.0 (2.3) | 21.4 (0.4) | 22.8 (1.1) | -1.4 (1.2) | 27.1 (0.3) | 29.7 (1.3) | **-2.6** (1.3) |
| Hungary | 53.6 (0.7) | 52.9 (0.5) | 0.7 (0.9) | 17.6 (0.6) | 18.8 (0.4) | -1.3 (0.8) | 28.8 (0.4) | 28.3 (0.4) | 0.6 (0.6) |
| Iceland | 71.8 (0.3) | c c | c c | 6.0 (0.2) | c c | c c | 22.2 (0.2) | c c | c c |
| Ireland | 64.3 (0.4) | 64.8 (4.3) | -0.6 (4.3) | 8.1 (0.3) | 10.9 (2.3) | -2.8 (2.3) | 27.6 (0.3) | 24.3 (3.0) | 3.3 (3.0) |
| Italy | 56.7 (0.4) | 57.6 (0.4) | -0.8 (0.6) | 5.9 (0.2) | 10.2 (0.3) | **-4.3** (0.4) | 37.4 (0.3) | 32.2 (0.2) | **5.2** (0.4) |
| Japan | 78.0 (0.5) | 78.6 (1.0) | -0.6 (1.1) | 6.0 (0.3) | 7.1 (0.5) | -1.1 (0.6) | 16.0 (0.4) | 14.3 (0.8) | 1.7 (0.9) |
| Korea | 63.0 (0.5) | 78.1 (1.0) | **-15.1** (1.1) | 18.8 (0.5) | 8.3 (0.7) | **10.6** (0.9) | 18.2 (0.3) | 13.7 (0.5) | **4.5** (0.6) |
| Luxembourg | 67.3 (0.3) | 67.3 (1.0) | -0.0 (1.1) | 9.1 (0.2) | 6.8 (0.7) | **2.3** (0.6) | 23.6 (0.3) | 25.9 (0.8) | **-2.3** (0.9) |
| Mexico | 54.6 (0.5) | 56.1 (0.4) | **-1.6** (0.6) | 15.1 (0.5) | 13.6 (0.3) | **1.5** (0.6) | 30.4 (0.4) | 30.3 (0.3) | 0.1 (0.5) |
| Netherlands | 64.4 (0.5) | 59.5 (1.0) | **4.9** (1.2) | 9.0 (0.3) | 15.5 (0.6) | **-6.5** (0.7) | 26.6 (0.4) | 25.0 (0.6) | **1.6** (0.7) |
| New Zealand | 70.2 (0.4) | a a | a a | 8.0 (0.3) | a a | a a | 21.9 (0.3) | a a | a a |
| Norway | 62.2 (0.5) | a a | a a | 16.4 (0.3) | a a | a a | 21.4 (0.3) | a a | a a |
| Poland | 63.5 (0.3) | a a | a a | 8.5 (0.3) | a a | a a | 27.9 (0.3) | a a | a a |
| Portugal | 60.6 (0.5) | 63.5 (0.9) | **-3.0** (1.0) | 9.0 (0.3) | 7.1 (0.8) | **1.9** (0.8) | 30.4 (0.4) | 29.4 (0.8) | 1.0 (0.9) |
| Slovak Republic | 60.5 (0.6) | 57.0 (0.7) | **3.4** (1.1) | 13.6 (0.3) | 11.5 (0.5) | **2.1** (0.6) | 25.9 (0.5) | 31.4 (0.7) | **-5.5** (0.9) |
| Spain | 62.7 (0.3) | a a | a a | 8.1 (0.3) | a a | a a | 29.2 (0.3) | a a | a a |
| Sweden | 66.7 (0.5) | c c | c c | 10.3 (0.2) | c c | c c | 23.0 (0.4) | c c | c c |
| Switzerland | 67.8 (0.4) | 62.7 (0.7) | **5.1** (0.8) | 7.1 (0.3) | 6.8 (1.0) | 0.3 (1.0) | 25.1 (0.2) | 30.4 (1.2) | **-5.3** (1.2) |
| Turkey | 56.0 (0.9) | 52.9 (0.7) | **3.1** (1.1) | 19.6 (0.5) | 20.1 (0.7) | -0.5 (0.8) | 24.4 (0.5) | 27.0 (0.4) | **-2.6** (0.6) |
| United Kingdom | 67.6 (0.3) | a a | a a | 7.8 (0.2) | a a | a a | 24.6 (0.3) | a a | a a |
| United States | 55.8 (0.6) | a a | a a | 16.0 (0.4) | a a | a a | 28.2 (0.3) | a a | a a |
| **OECD average** | 64.1 (0.1) | 62.8 (0.3) | 0.5 (0.3) | 10.6 (0.1) | 11.3 (0.2) | **-0.6** (0.2) | 25.4 (0.1) | 25.9 (0.2) | 0.1 (0.3) |
| **Partners** | | | | | | | | | |
| Argentina | 55.4 (0.6) | 48.5 (3.1) | **6.8** (3.2) | 7.9 (0.5) | 12.8 (3.6) | -4.9 (3.7) | 36.7 (0.5) | 38.7 (2.3) | -1.9 (2.3) |
| Azerbaijan | 44.9 (0.6) | 46.1 (8.4) | -1.3 (8.3) | 19.2 (0.5) | 26.9 (6.0) | -7.6 (6.0) | 35.9 (0.5) | 27.0 (2.6) | **8.9** (2.5) |
| Brazil | 54.4 (0.4) | a a | a a | 17.7 (0.4) | a a | a a | 27.8 (0.3) | a a | a a |
| Bulgaria | 52.8 (0.8) | 50.7 (0.8) | 2.1 (1.1) | 14.2 (0.5) | 16.8 (0.7) | **-2.6** (0.9) | 33.0 (0.6) | 32.5 (0.6) | 0.5 (0.9) |
| Chile | 57.2 (0.7) | 62.4 (2.0) | **-5.2** (2.1) | 15.4 (0.5) | 8.8 (1.5) | **6.7** (1.6) | 27.4 (0.4) | 28.8 (1.6) | -1.4 (1.7) |
| Colombia | 60.1 (0.6) | 61.2 (1.3) | -1.1 (1.2) | 14.8 (0.4) | 13.0 (0.7) | **1.8** (0.7) | 25.2 (0.5) | 25.8 (0.7) | -0.7 (0.8) |
| Croatia | 68.4 (0.7) | 66.1 (0.5) | **2.2** (0.9) | 3.5 (0.3) | 6.8 (0.3) | **-3.4** (0.4) | 28.2 (0.7) | 27.0 (0.4) | 1.1 (0.8) |
| Estonia | 61.8 (0.5) | a a | a a | 13.1 (0.4) | a a | a a | 25.2 (0.3) | a a | a a |
| Hong Kong-China | 71.1 (0.5) | 68.7 (1.3) | 2.5 (1.4) | 8.8 (0.3) | 12.3 (1.0) | **-3.5** (1.1) | 20.1 (0.5) | 19.1 (0.8) | 1.0 (0.9) |
| Indonesia | 56.1 (0.4) | 56.8 (2.9) | -0.7 (2.9) | 17.4 (0.4) | 13.1 (1.1) | **4.3** (1.0) | 26.4 (0.3) | 30.1 (2.0) | -3.6 (2.1) |
| Israel | 55.2 (0.7) | 47.5 (1.5) | **7.8** (1.8) | 19.4 (0.4) | 22.4 (1.2) | **-3.0** (1.3) | 25.4 (0.5) | 30.1 (1.1) | **-4.7** (1.2) |
| Jordan | 44.2 (0.6) | a a | a a | 22.2 (0.5) | a a | a a | 33.6 (0.4) | a a | a a |
| Kyrgyzstan | 39.7 (0.5) | 47.3 (1.3) | **-7.7** (1.4) | 26.3 (0.4) | 19.1 (1.7) | **7.1** (1.7) | 34.0 (0.4) | 33.5 (1.9) | 0.5 (1.9) |
| Latvia | 59.2 (0.4) | 61.5 (1.7) | -2.4 (1.9) | 11.5 (0.4) | 9.8 (1.5) | 1.6 (1.5) | 29.4 (0.4) | 28.6 (1.8) | 0.7 (1.9) |
| Liechtenstein | 69.8 (1.2) | a a | a a | 5.6 (0.7) | a a | a a | 24.6 (0.9) | a a | a a |
| Lithuania | 62.3 (0.4) | c c | c c | 9.8 (0.3) | c c | c c | 27.9 (0.3) | c c | c c |
| Macao-China | 71.4 (0.3) | 73.0 (2.0) | -1.6 (2.0) | 11.2 (0.2) | 8.2 (1.2) | **2.9** (1.2) | 17.4 (0.3) | 18.8 (1.2) | -1.3 (1.2) |
| Montenegro | 57.9 (0.7) | 50.6 (0.5) | **7.4** (0.9) | 8.0 (0.5) | 13.2 (0.3) | **-5.1** (0.6) | 34.1 (0.6) | 36.3 (0.5) | **-2.2** (0.8) |
| Qatar | 44.7 (0.3) | a a | a a | 23.6 (0.3) | a a | a a | 31.7 (0.3) | a a | a a |
| Romania | 52.8 (0.7) | 43.1 (1.1) | **9.7** (1.3) | 18.0 (0.5) | 25.8 (0.8) | **-7.8** (0.9) | 29.2 (0.4) | 31.1 (0.6) | **-1.9** (0.7) |
| Russian Federation | 46.9 (0.5) | 57.2 (1.6) | **-10.2** (1.5) | 16.8 (0.7) | 13.6 (1.2) | **3.1** (1.5) | 36.3 (0.5) | 29.2 (1.7) | **7.1** (1.7) |
| Serbia | 62.1 (0.8) | 59.4 (0.6) | **2.7** (1.0) | 11.0 (0.6) | 13.6 (0.4) | **-2.6** (0.7) | 26.8 (0.6) | 27.0 (0.4) | -0.1 (0.7) |
| Slovenia | 64.7 (0.5) | 57.1 (0.6) | **7.6** (0.8) | 9.0 (0.3) | 15.0 (0.3) | **-6.0** (0.4) | 26.2 (0.4) | 27.9 (0.4) | **-1.7** (0.6) |
| Chinese Taipei | 66.1 (0.4) | 66.2 (0.8) | -0.1 (0.9) | 8.6 (0.3) | 9.6 (0.5) | -1.0 (0.6) | 25.4 (0.2) | 24.3 (0.5) | **1.1** (0.5) |
| Thailand | 63.6 (0.4) | 56.0 (0.8) | **7.7** (1.0) | 7.8 (0.3) | 4.7 (0.4) | **3.1** (0.5) | 28.5 (0.3) | 39.3 (0.9) | **-10.8** (1.0) |
| Tunisia | 45.6 (0.7) | a a | a a | 23.6 (0.5) | a a | a a | 30.8 (0.5) | a a | a a |
| Uruguay | 60.7 (0.5) | 62.0 (1.4) | -1.3 (1.5) | 11.2 (0.4) | 12.1 (1.4) | -0.9 (1.4) | 28.1 (0.3) | 25.9 (1.5) | 2.2 (1.5) |

*Note*: Values that are statistically significant at the 5% level (p < 0.05) are indicated in bold.

© OECD 2011 Quality Time for Students: Learning In and Out of School

[Part 1/3]
## Table 3.13a  Mean learning hours and allocation of total learning time in science, by school location

| | Regular school lessons | | | | | | Out-of-school-time lessons | | | | | |
| | Rural (fewer than 100 000 people) | | City (over 100 000 people) | | Difference (rural-city) | | Rural (fewer than 100 000 people) | | City (over 100 000 people) | | Difference (rural-city) | |
| | Mean | S.E. | Mean | S.E. | Dif. | S.E. | Mean | S.E. | Mean | S.E. | Dif. | S.E. |
|---|---|---|---|---|---|---|---|---|---|---|---|---|
| Australia | 3.04 | (0.06) | 3.37 | (0.04) | **-0.33** | (0.08) | 0.33 | (0.01) | 0.38 | (0.01) | **-0.04** | (0.02) |
| Austria | 2.37 | (0.09) | 2.67 | (0.13) | -0.30 | (0.17) | 0.23 | (0.02) | 0.19 | (0.02) | 0.04 | (0.03) |
| Belgium | 2.56 | (0.05) | 2.85 | (0.15) | -0.29 | (0.17) | 0.30 | (0.01) | 0.41 | (0.04) | **-0.11** | (0.04) |
| Canada | 3.97 | (0.05) | 4.12 | (0.08) | -0.15 | (0.09) | 0.52 | (0.02) | 0.60 | (0.02) | **-0.08** | (0.03) |
| Czech Republic | 2.82 | (0.09) | 3.35 | (0.22) | **-0.53** | (0.26) | 0.55 | (0.02) | 0.48 | (0.04) | 0.06 | (0.05) |
| Denmark | 3.20 | (0.05) | 3.32 | (0.14) | -0.12 | (0.15) | 0.76 | (0.02) | 0.90 | (0.05) | **-0.15** | (0.06) |
| Finland | 3.10 | (0.05) | 3.24 | (0.11) | -0.14 | (0.11) | 0.33 | (0.01) | 0.31 | (0.03) | 0.02 | (0.03) |
| France | a | a | 2.85 | (0.05) | a | a | a | a | 0.55 | (0.02) | a | a |
| Germany | 2.96 | (0.06) | 3.44 | (0.15) | **-0.48** | (0.18) | 0.49 | (0.02) | 0.56 | (0.05) | -0.07 | (0.05) |
| Greece | 3.09 | (0.08) | 3.38 | (0.12) | -0.29 | (0.16) | 2.02 | (0.06) | 1.95 | (0.07) | 0.07 | (0.10) |
| Hungary | 2.46 | (0.07) | 2.56 | (0.10) | -0.09 | (0.13) | 1.05 | (0.03) | 0.94 | (0.05) | **0.11** | (0.06) |
| Iceland | 3.04 | (0.03) | 2.84 | (0.05) | **0.20** | (0.05) | 0.30 | (0.02) | 0.27 | (0.02) | 0.03 | (0.03) |
| Ireland | 2.57 | (0.05) | 2.49 | (0.09) | 0.08 | (0.10) | 0.34 | (0.02) | 0.27 | (0.02) | **0.06** | (0.03) |
| Italy | 2.92 | (0.06) | 2.93 | (0.11) | -0.01 | (0.12) | 0.58 | (0.02) | 0.56 | (0.03) | 0.02 | (0.04) |
| Japan | 2.46 | (0.09) | 2.82 | (0.07) | **-0.36** | (0.12) | 0.27 | (0.02) | 0.26 | (0.02) | 0.01 | (0.03) |
| Korea | 3.25 | (0.18) | 3.64 | (0.07) | -0.39 | (0.20) | 0.66 | (0.08) | 1.09 | (0.05) | **-0.43** | (0.10) |
| Luxembourg | 2.35 | (0.03) | 2.17 | (0.07) | **0.18** | (0.07) | 0.51 | (0.02) | 0.43 | (0.04) | 0.08 | (0.04) |
| Mexico | 3.11 | (0.06) | 3.20 | (0.06) | -0.09 | (0.09) | 1.14 | (0.04) | 0.88 | (0.03) | **0.26** | (0.05) |
| Netherlands | 2.12 | (0.05) | 2.32 | (0.12) | -0.20 | (0.15) | 0.53 | (0.02) | 0.54 | (0.03) | -0.01 | (0.04) |
| New Zealand | 3.91 | (0.07) | 4.18 | (0.05) | **-0.27** | (0.09) | 0.35 | (0.02) | 0.46 | (0.02) | **-0.11** | (0.03) |
| Norway | 2.61 | (0.03) | 2.80 | (0.07) | **-0.19** | (0.08) | 0.94 | (0.02) | 0.94 | (0.06) | -0.01 | (0.06) |
| Poland | 2.66 | (0.04) | 2.90 | (0.07) | -0.24 | (0.08) | 0.62 | (0.02) | 0.63 | (0.04) | -0.01 | (0.05) |
| Portugal | 3.19 | (0.06) | 3.27 | (0.12) | -0.08 | (0.14) | 0.63 | (0.02) | 0.66 | (0.04) | -0.03 | (0.05) |
| Slovak Republic | 2.40 | (0.08) | 2.81 | (0.34) | -0.41 | (0.37) | 0.64 | (0.03) | 0.72 | (0.12) | -0.09 | (0.13) |
| Spain | 2.97 | (0.06) | 3.34 | (0.08) | **-0.37** | (0.10) | 0.71 | (0.03) | 0.63 | (0.03) | 0.08 | (0.05) |
| Sweden | 2.79 | (0.03) | 2.85 | (0.07) | -0.06 | (0.08) | 0.49 | (0.01) | 0.53 | (0.04) | -0.03 | (0.04) |
| Switzerland | 2.34 | (0.05) | 2.59 | (0.21) | -0.25 | (0.22) | 0.40 | (0.01) | 0.31 | (0.04) | **0.09** | (0.04) |
| Turkey | 2.72 | (0.13) | 3.01 | (0.15) | -0.30 | (0.23) | 1.26 | (0.07) | 1.44 | (0.09) | -0.17 | (0.12) |
| United Kingdom | 4.32 | (0.04) | 4.17 | (0.09) | 0.15 | (0.10) | 0.45 | (0.02) | 0.54 | (0.04) | -0.09 | (0.05) |
| United States | 3.62 | (0.05) | 3.33 | (0.11) | **0.28** | (0.13) | 0.73 | (0.02) | 0.88 | (0.04) | **-0.16** | (0.05) |
| **OECD average** | 2.93 | (0.01) | 3.09 | (0.02) | **-0.17** | (0.03) | 0.62 | (0.01) | 0.64 | (0.01) | **-0.02** | (0.01) |
| Argentina | 2.16 | (0.08) | 2.41 | (0.10) | -0.25 | (0.14) | 0.51 | (0.03) | 0.46 | (0.03) | 0.05 | (0.05) |
| Azerbaijan | 2.80 | (0.07) | 2.95 | (0.08) | -0.15 | (0.10) | 1.40 | (0.04) | 1.25 | (0.06) | **0.15** | (0.07) |
| Brazil | 2.14 | (0.05) | 2.32 | (0.06) | **-0.18** | (0.09) | 0.78 | (0.03) | 0.80 | (0.04) | -0.02 | (0.05) |
| Bulgaria | 2.48 | (0.09) | 2.89 | (0.15) | **-0.41** | (0.17) | 1.00 | (0.04) | 0.97 | (0.03) | 0.02 | (0.05) |
| Chile | 2.20 | (0.10) | 2.40 | (0.07) | -0.20 | (0.13) | 0.91 | (0.03) | 0.77 | (0.02) | **0.13** | (0.04) |
| Colombia | 3.60 | (0.19) | 3.41 | (0.08) | 0.19 | (0.21) | 1.00 | (0.06) | 0.88 | (0.03) | 0.12 | (0.07) |
| Croatia | 1.92 | (0.05) | 2.18 | (0.08) | **-0.26** | (0.10) | 0.41 | (0.02) | 0.47 | (0.03) | -0.06 | (0.04) |
| Estonia | 3.20 | (0.05) | 3.45 | (0.09) | **-0.25** | (0.10) | 0.75 | (0.03) | 0.80 | (0.04) | -0.05 | (0.05) |
| Hong Kong-China | a | a | 3.14 | (0.05) | a | a | a | a | 0.88 | (0.03) | a | a |
| Indonesia | 3.16 | (0.08) | 3.57 | (0.20) | -0.42 | (0.23) | 1.06 | (0.04) | 1.00 | (0.17) | 0.06 | (0.18) |
| Israel | 2.42 | (0.07) | 2.48 | (0.10) | -0.05 | (0.13) | 1.04 | (0.05) | 0.91 | (0.04) | 0.14 | (0.07) |
| Jordan | 3.09 | (0.08) | 3.47 | (0.09) | **-0.39** | (0.13) | 1.53 | (0.04) | 1.51 | (0.06) | 0.02 | (0.08) |
| Kyrgyzstan | 2.00 | (0.07) | 2.59 | (0.14) | **-0.59** | (0.16) | 1.43 | (0.03) | 1.01 | (0.09) | **0.42** | (0.09) |
| Latvia | 2.76 | (0.06) | 3.08 | (0.12) | **-0.32** | (0.13) | 0.64 | (0.02) | 0.67 | (0.04) | -0.03 | (0.05) |
| Liechtenstein | 2.61 | (0.08) | a | a | a | a | 0.49 | (0.06) | a | a | a | a |
| Lithuania | 2.63 | (0.04) | 2.79 | (0.06) | **-0.16** | (0.07) | 0.61 | (0.02) | 0.50 | (0.02) | **0.10** | (0.03) |
| Macao-China | 3.42 | (0.07) | 3.81 | (0.04) | **-0.39** | (0.08) | 1.07 | (0.05) | 0.98 | (0.03) | 0.08 | (0.06) |
| Montenegro | 2.79 | (0.05) | 2.90 | (0.07) | -0.11 | (0.08) | 1.08 | (0.03) | 1.00 | (0.05) | 0.08 | (0.05) |
| Qatar | 2.58 | (0.04) | 2.96 | (0.06) | **-0.37** | (0.07) | 1.50 | (0.03) | 1.43 | (0.04) | 0.07 | (0.05) |
| Romania | 2.15 | (0.08) | 2.37 | (0.12) | -0.22 | (0.17) | 1.07 | (0.04) | 0.98 | (0.03) | **0.09** | (0.05) |
| Russian Federation | 3.69 | (0.11) | 3.78 | (0.09) | -0.09 | (0.12) | 1.17 | (0.04) | 1.06 | (0.05) | 0.11 | (0.07) |
| Serbia | 2.72 | (0.08) | 3.07 | (0.11) | **-0.35** | (0.15) | 0.80 | (0.03) | 0.76 | (0.03) | 0.04 | (0.04) |
| Slovenia | 2.77 | (0.03) | 2.91 | (0.05) | **-0.14** | (0.06) | 0.77 | (0.03) | 0.62 | (0.03) | **0.16** | (0.04) |
| Chinese Taipei | 2.83 | (0.12) | 2.93 | (0.09) | -0.09 | (0.18) | 0.62 | (0.04) | 0.86 | (0.04) | **-0.24** | (0.07) |
| Thailand | 3.71 | (0.06) | 4.10 | (0.15) | **-0.39** | (0.19) | 0.82 | (0.04) | 1.18 | (0.13) | **-0.36** | (0.16) |
| Tunisia | 2.58 | (0.05) | 2.89 | (0.22) | -0.31 | (0.24) | 1.92 | (0.03) | 2.00 | (0.11) | -0.08 | (0.12) |
| Uruguay | 2.33 | (0.06) | 2.51 | (0.07) | -0.18 | (0.10) | 0.63 | (0.03) | 0.59 | (0.03) | 0.03 | (0.04) |

*Note:* Values that are statistically significant at the 5% level (p < 0.05) are indicated in bold.

197

[Part 2/3]
## Table 3.13a Mean learning hours and allocation of total learning time in science, by school location

| | | Mean learning hours per week | | | | | | | | | | |
|---|---|---|---|---|---|---|---|---|---|---|---|---|
| | | Individual study | | | | | | Total learning hours | | | | |
| | | Rural (fewer than 100 000 people) | | City (over 100 000 people) | | Difference (rural-city) | | Rural (fewer than 100 000 people) | | City (over 100 000 people) | | Difference (rural-city) |
| | | Mean | S.E. | Mean | S.E. | Dif. | S.E. | Mean | S.E. | Mean | S.E. | Dif. | S.E. |
| **OECD** | Australia | 0.99 | (0.02) | 1.30 | (0.03) | **-0.31** | (0.04) | 4.36 | (0.08) | 5.04 | (0.07) | **-0.67** | (0.12) |
| | Austria | 1.27 | (0.04) | 1.29 | (0.05) | -0.02 | (0.06) | 3.87 | (0.12) | 4.15 | (0.16) | -0.28 | (0.21) |
| | Belgium | 1.23 | (0.03) | 1.35 | (0.06) | -0.12 | (0.07) | 4.09 | (0.08) | 4.61 | (0.20) | **-0.52** | (0.23) |
| | Canada | 1.40 | (0.03) | 1.80 | (0.05) | **-0.40** | (0.06) | 5.91 | (0.08) | 6.52 | (0.11) | **-0.61** | (0.15) |
| | Czech Republic | 1.01 | (0.03) | 0.94 | (0.07) | 0.06 | (0.08) | 4.36 | (0.13) | 4.77 | (0.32) | -0.40 | (0.37) |
| | Denmark | 1.06 | (0.03) | 1.18 | (0.06) | **-0.12** | (0.06) | 5.00 | (0.08) | 5.37 | (0.18) | -0.37 | (0.20) |
| | Finland | 1.06 | (0.02) | 1.11 | (0.05) | -0.05 | (0.05) | 4.48 | (0.06) | 4.67 | (0.13) | -0.19 | (0.14) |
| | France | a | a | 1.31 | (0.03) | a | a | a | a | 4.72 | (0.08) | a | a |
| | Germany | 1.68 | (0.03) | 1.76 | (0.05) | -0.08 | (0.07) | 5.14 | (0.09) | 5.77 | (0.16) | **-0.63** | (0.20) |
| | Greece | 1.84 | (0.05) | 1.86 | (0.07) | -0.02 | (0.08) | 6.95 | (0.16) | 7.20 | (0.21) | -0.26 | (0.28) |
| | Hungary | 1.59 | (0.04) | 1.59 | (0.06) | -0.01 | (0.08) | 5.10 | (0.11) | 5.07 | (0.18) | 0.03 | (0.23) |
| | Iceland | 1.21 | (0.02) | 1.08 | (0.03) | **0.13** | (0.04) | 4.56 | (0.04) | 4.19 | (0.07) | **0.37** | (0.08) |
| | Ireland | 1.22 | (0.03) | 1.19 | (0.05) | 0.03 | (0.06) | 4.11 | (0.08) | 3.94 | (0.14) | 0.17 | (0.16) |
| | Italy | 2.09 | (0.04) | 2.10 | (0.08) | -0.01 | (0.09) | 5.58 | (0.11) | 5.60 | (0.20) | -0.02 | (0.22) |
| | Japan | 0.61 | (0.03) | 0.74 | (0.03) | **-0.13** | (0.04) | 3.34 | (0.11) | 3.82 | (0.09) | **-0.48** | (0.15) |
| | Korea | 0.97 | (0.06) | 1.26 | (0.07) | **-0.29** | (0.09) | 4.91 | (0.28) | 6.00 | (0.16) | **-1.08** | (0.34) |
| | Luxembourg | 1.26 | (0.02) | 1.12 | (0.07) | 0.14 | (0.07) | 4.13 | (0.05) | 3.71 | (0.13) | **0.42** | (0.14) |
| | Mexico | 2.14 | (0.05) | 2.11 | (0.03) | 0.03 | (0.06) | 6.34 | (0.11) | 6.16 | (0.09) | 0.18 | (0.15) |
| | Netherlands | 1.17 | (0.03) | 1.32 | (0.06) | **-0.15** | (0.06) | 3.81 | (0.08) | 4.15 | (0.16) | -0.34 | (0.20) |
| | New Zealand | 1.12 | (0.04) | 1.41 | (0.04) | **-0.30** | (0.05) | 5.38 | (0.11) | 6.06 | (0.08) | **-0.68** | (0.14) |
| | Norway | 1.21 | (0.02) | 1.30 | (0.05) | -0.09 | (0.05) | 4.76 | (0.06) | 5.03 | (0.12) | **-0.27** | (0.13) |
| | Poland | 2.03 | (0.03) | 1.99 | (0.06) | 0.04 | (0.07) | 5.32 | (0.08) | 5.50 | (0.12) | -0.19 | (0.14) |
| | Portugal | 2.08 | (0.04) | 2.12 | (0.07) | -0.04 | (0.09) | 5.90 | (0.09) | 6.03 | (0.20) | -0.13 | (0.24) |
| | Slovak Republic | 1.39 | (0.04) | 1.42 | (0.19) | -0.04 | (0.19) | 4.44 | (0.13) | 4.98 | (0.63) | -0.54 | (0.67) |
| | Spain | 1.67 | (0.03) | 1.85 | (0.04) | **-0.18** | (0.05) | 5.38 | (0.10) | 5.83 | (0.11) | **-0.46** | (0.15) |
| | Sweden | 1.11 | (0.02) | 1.27 | (0.05) | **-0.16** | (0.05) | 4.38 | (0.05) | 4.65 | (0.12) | **-0.27** | (0.13) |
| | Switzerland | 1.11 | (0.02) | 1.17 | (0.06) | -0.05 | (0.07) | 3.86 | (0.06) | 4.05 | (0.25) | -0.19 | (0.26) |
| | Turkey | 1.60 | (0.07) | 1.68 | (0.08) | -0.08 | (0.11) | 5.53 | (0.25) | 6.09 | (0.31) | -0.55 | (0.43) |
| | United Kingdom | 1.44 | (0.03) | 1.49 | (0.06) | -0.05 | (0.08) | 6.21 | (0.06) | 6.19 | (0.14) | 0.02 | (0.17) |
| | United States | 1.62 | (0.03) | 1.80 | (0.05) | **-0.18** | (0.06) | 6.01 | (0.07) | 6.02 | (0.12) | -0.01 | (0.15) |
| | **OECD average** | **1.38** | **(0.01)** | **1.46** | **(0.01)** | **-0.08** | **(0.01)** | **4.94** | **(0.02)** | **5.17** | **(0.04)** | **-0.25** | **(0.04)** |
| **Partners** | Argentina | 1.58 | (0.05) | 1.61 | (0.07) | -0.02 | (0.09) | 4.22 | (0.13) | 4.49 | (0.14) | -0.27 | (0.21) |
| | Azerbaijan | 2.67 | (0.06) | 2.55 | (0.06) | 0.11 | (0.08) | 6.86 | (0.13) | 6.72 | (0.15) | 0.14 | (0.20) |
| | Brazil | 1.71 | (0.04) | 1.68 | (0.04) | 0.03 | (0.06) | 4.64 | (0.08) | 4.79 | (0.11) | -0.15 | (0.16) |
| | Bulgaria | 1.92 | (0.06) | 2.16 | (0.12) | -0.24 | (0.14) | 5.42 | (0.14) | 6.06 | (0.27) | **-0.64** | (0.31) |
| | Chile | 1.59 | (0.05) | 1.47 | (0.03) | **0.13** | (0.06) | 4.72 | (0.14) | 4.67 | (0.10) | 0.06 | (0.18) |
| | Colombia | 1.88 | (0.07) | 1.76 | (0.04) | 0.12 | (0.08) | 6.50 | (0.32) | 6.05 | (0.11) | 0.45 | (0.34) |
| | Croatia | 1.41 | (0.04) | 1.56 | (0.07) | -0.15 | (0.09) | 3.75 | (0.10) | 4.23 | (0.17) | **-0.48** | (0.20) |
| | Estonia | 1.46 | (0.03) | 1.76 | (0.05) | **-0.30** | (0.06) | 5.41 | (0.07) | 6.00 | (0.12) | **-0.59** | (0.14) |
| | Hong Kong-China | a | a | 1.44 | (0.03) | a | a | a | a | 5.45 | (0.10) | a | a |
| | Indonesia | 1.82 | (0.04) | 1.63 | (0.15) | 0.19 | (0.17) | 6.01 | (0.13) | 6.21 | (0.42) | -0.20 | (0.48) |
| | Israel | 1.45 | (0.07) | 1.25 | (0.05) | **0.20** | (0.09) | 4.89 | (0.16) | 4.64 | (0.15) | 0.25 | (0.23) |
| | Jordan | 2.64 | (0.06) | 2.65 | (0.07) | -0.01 | (0.09) | 7.25 | (0.12) | 7.62 | (0.13) | **-0.37** | (0.19) |
| | Kyrgyzstan | 2.16 | (0.04) | 2.03 | (0.10) | 0.12 | (0.10) | 5.64 | (0.10) | 5.61 | (0.23) | 0.02 | (0.25) |
| | Latvia | 1.76 | (0.04) | 1.87 | (0.07) | -0.11 | (0.08) | 5.15 | (0.09) | 5.61 | (0.19) | **-0.47** | (0.21) |
| | Liechtenstein | 1.20 | (0.06) | a | a | a | a | 4.31 | (0.10) | a | a | a | a |
| | Lithuania | 1.69 | (0.03) | 1.68 | (0.05) | 0.01 | (0.05) | 4.91 | (0.07) | 4.97 | (0.10) | -0.06 | (0.11) |
| | Macao-China | 1.35 | (0.05) | 1.38 | (0.03) | -0.03 | (0.06) | 5.83 | (0.13) | 6.16 | (0.07) | **-0.34** | (0.16) |
| | Montenegro | 2.23 | (0.04) | 2.14 | (0.06) | 0.09 | (0.07) | 6.10 | (0.09) | 6.03 | (0.11) | 0.07 | (0.15) |
| | Qatar | 2.03 | (0.03) | 2.12 | (0.05) | -0.09 | (0.06) | 6.14 | (0.07) | 6.52 | (0.12) | **-0.38** | (0.13) |
| | Romania | 1.59 | (0.05) | 1.64 | (0.09) | -0.05 | (0.11) | 4.79 | (0.14) | 4.96 | (0.20) | -0.17 | (0.27) |
| | Russian Federation | 2.97 | (0.08) | 2.72 | (0.07) | **0.25** | (0.09) | 7.82 | (0.19) | 7.58 | (0.15) | 0.25 | (0.22) |
| | Serbia | 1.65 | (0.06) | 1.79 | (0.07) | -0.14 | (0.10) | 5.18 | (0.14) | 5.61 | (0.18) | 0.43 | (0.25) |
| | Slovenia | 1.58 | (0.02) | 1.46 | (0.04) | 0.13 | (0.04) | 5.14 | (0.06) | 4.98 | (0.09) | 0.16 | (0.11) |
| | Chinese Taipei | 1.12 | (0.06) | 1.30 | (0.04) | **-0.18** | (0.08) | 4.60 | (0.20) | 5.12 | (0.16) | -0.52 | (0.31) |
| | Thailand | 1.81 | (0.04) | 1.79 | (0.08) | 0.03 | (0.11) | 6.34 | (0.12) | 7.06 | (0.33) | -0.72 | (0.42) |
| | Tunisia | 2.61 | (0.04) | 2.62 | (0.12) | -0.01 | (0.12) | 7.09 | (0.11) | 7.50 | (0.42) | -0.41 | (0.45) |
| | Uruguay | 1.35 | (0.04) | 1.28 | (0.05) | 0.07 | (0.06) | 4.33 | (0.10) | 4.40 | (0.11) | -0.07 | (0.15) |

*Note:* Values that are statistically significant at the 5% level (p < 0.05) are indicated in bold.

© OECD 2011 Quality Time for Students: Learning In and Out of School

## Table 3.13a  Mean learning hours and allocation of total learning time in science, by school location

| | Allocation of total learning time in science for | | | | | | | | | | | | | | | | | |
| | Regular school lessons | | | | | | Out-of-school-time lessons | | | | | | Individual study | | | | | |
| | Rural (fewer than 100 000 people) | | City (over 100 000 people) | | Difference (rural-city) | | Rural (fewer than 100 000 people) | | City (over 100 000 people) | | Difference (rural-city) | | Rural (fewer than 100 000 people) | | City (over 100 000 people) | | Difference (rural-city) | |
| | % | S.E | % | S.E | Dif. | S.E. | % | S.E | % | S.E | Dif. | S.E. | % | S.E | % | S.E | Dif. | S.E. |
|---|---|---|---|---|---|---|---|---|---|---|---|---|---|---|---|---|---|---|
| **OECD** | | | | | | | | | | | | | | | | | | |
| Australia | 72.4 | (0.6) | 70.1 | (0.4) | **2.3** | (0.7) | 6.4 | (0.3) | 6.2 | (0.2) | 0.2 | (0.3) | 21.2 | (0.4) | 23.8 | (0.3) | **-2.5** | (0.6) |
| Austria | 63.4 | (0.9) | 65.5 | (1.1) | -2.0 | (1.5) | 4.7 | (0.4) | 3.2 | (0.4) | **1.5** | (0.6) | 31.9 | (0.7) | 31.3 | (1.0) | 0.6 | (1.3) |
| Belgium | 63.6 | (0.4) | 63.2 | (1.0) | 0.4 | (1.1) | 6.3 | (0.2) | 7.4 | (0.4) | -1.1 | (0.7) | 30.1 | (0.3) | 29.4 | (0.7) | 0.7 | (0.7) |
| Canada | 67.9 | (0.4) | 64.2 | (0.5) | **3.7** | (0.6) | 8.4 | (0.2) | 8.6 | (0.3) | -0.2 | (0.4) | 23.8 | (0.3) | 27.2 | (0.5) | **-3.4** | (0.6) |
| Czech Republic | 67.9 | (0.8) | 72.4 | (0.9) | **-4.5** | (1.2) | 10.4 | (0.4) | 7.8 | (0.5) | **2.6** | (0.6) | 21.7 | (0.5) | 19.8 | (0.9) | 1.9 | (1.0) |
| Denmark | 67.2 | (0.5) | 65.4 | (1.4) | 1.9 | (1.5) | 12.9 | (0.3) | 14.1 | (0.8) | -1.2 | (0.9) | 19.9 | (0.4) | 20.6 | (0.8) | -0.6 | (0.9) |
| Finland | 70.9 | (0.4) | 70.9 | (0.9) | 0.0 | (1.0) | 6.1 | (0.2) | 5.3 | (0.4) | 0.7 | (0.5) | 23.0 | (0.3) | 23.7 | (0.8) | -0.7 | (0.8) |
| France | a | a | 62.9 | (0.5) | a | a | a | a | 10.8 | (0.3) | a | a | a | a | 26.3 | (0.4) | a | a |
| Germany | 57.7 | (0.7) | 59.7 | (1.4) | -1.9 | (1.7) | 8.4 | (0.4) | 8.8 | (0.8) | -0.4 | (0.9) | 33.9 | (0.4) | 31.6 | (0.9) | **2.3** | (1.0) |
| Greece | 47.5 | (0.7) | 49.9 | (0.9) | **-2.4** | (1.2) | 26.6 | (0.5) | 25.8 | (0.8) | 0.8 | (1.0) | 25.9 | (0.6) | 24.3 | (0.6) | 1.6 | (0.9) |
| Hungary | 50.5 | (0.7) | 53.0 | (1.0) | **-2.5** | (1.2) | 19.0 | (0.6) | 16.2 | (0.6) | **2.9** | (0.9) | 30.4 | (0.4) | 30.8 | (0.6) | -0.4 | (0.8) |
| Iceland | 69.9 | (0.4) | 70.4 | (0.7) | -0.5 | (0.7) | 5.1 | (0.3) | 5.1 | (0.4) | -0.0 | (0.5) | 25.0 | (0.3) | 24.5 | (0.6) | 0.5 | (0.6) |
| Ireland | 66.0 | (0.6) | 67.0 | (0.9) | -1.0 | (1.1) | 6.4 | (0.3) | 5.4 | (0.4) | 1.0 | (0.5) | 27.6 | (0.5) | 27.6 | (0.7) | 0.0 | (0.9) |
| Italy | 53.9 | (0.3) | 54.6 | (0.6) | -0.7 | (0.8) | 9.3 | (0.3) | 8.7 | (0.5) | 0.6 | (0.6) | 36.8 | (0.3) | 36.7 | (0.5) | 0.0 | (0.6) |
| Japan | 78.5 | (0.7) | 78.3 | (0.5) | 0.3 | (0.9) | 5.5 | (0.4) | 5.0 | (0.3) | 0.4 | (0.5) | 16.0 | (0.7) | 16.7 | (0.5) | -0.7 | (0.8) |
| Korea | 71.8 | (1.2) | 66.7 | (0.7) | **5.1** | (1.4) | 10.1 | (1.1) | 14.5 | (0.4) | **-4.4** | (1.3) | 18.1 | (0.9) | 18.8 | (0.4) | -0.7 | (1.0) |
| Luxembourg | 59.6 | (0.4) | 62.5 | (1.3) | **-3.0** | (1.4) | 10.2 | (0.3) | 8.4 | (0.7) | **1.7** | (0.7) | 30.3 | (0.4) | 29.0 | (1.2) | 1.2 | (1.3) |
| Mexico | 47.1 | (0.6) | 49.9 | (0.6) | **-2.8** | (0.9) | 16.6 | (0.5) | 13.3 | (0.6) | **3.2** | (0.6) | 36.4 | (0.6) | 36.8 | (0.5) | -0.4 | (0.8) |
| Netherlands | 56.1 | (0.8) | 57.3 | (1.1) | -1.2 | (1.4) | 12.8 | (0.5) | 12.1 | (0.8) | 0.7 | (1.0) | 31.2 | (0.5) | 30.6 | (0.7) | 0.5 | (0.9) |
| New Zealand | 75.2 | (0.6) | 71.4 | (0.5) | **3.7** | (0.8) | 5.5 | (0.3) | 6.8 | (0.4) | **-1.3** | (0.5) | 19.4 | (0.4) | 21.8 | (0.4) | -2.5 | (0.5) |
| Norway | 59.6 | (0.5) | 59.2 | (1.4) | 0.4 | (1.4) | 16.9 | (0.3) | 16.8 | (1.0) | 0.1 | (1.0) | 23.5 | (0.3) | 24.0 | (0.8) | -0.5 | (0.8) |
| Poland | 52.6 | (0.4) | 55.0 | (0.7) | **-2.3** | (0.8) | 10.4 | (0.4) | 9.8 | (0.6) | 0.6 | (0.7) | 36.9 | (0.4) | 35.2 | (0.7) | **1.7** | (0.8) |
| Portugal | 54.3 | (0.6) | 55.7 | (0.9) | -1.3 | (1.1) | 9.4 | (0.3) | 9.3 | (0.5) | 0.1 | (0.7) | 36.3 | (0.5) | 35.0 | (0.7) | 1.3 | (0.9) |
| Slovak Republic | 58.3 | (0.6) | 61.7 | (1.9) | -3.4 | (2.0) | 11.8 | (0.4) | 11.3 | (1.2) | 0.5 | (1.3) | 30.0 | (0.4) | 27.0 | (1.1) | **2.9** | (1.2) |
| Spain | 58.6 | (0.5) | 59.4 | (0.6) | -0.7 | (0.8) | 11.3 | (0.4) | 9.8 | (0.5) | **1.5** | (0.6) | 30.1 | (0.3) | 30.8 | (0.5) | -0.8 | (0.6) |
| Sweden | 67.4 | (0.7) | 64.7 | (0.9) | **2.6** | (1.1) | 9.1 | (0.3) | 9.4 | (0.5) | -0.3 | (0.6) | 23.5 | (0.6) | 25.9 | (0.7) | **-2.3** | (0.9) |
| Switzerland | 61.8 | (0.4) | 63.7 | (1.4) | -1.9 | (1.5) | 8.5 | (0.2) | 6.7 | (0.8) | **1.8** | (0.9) | 29.7 | (0.3) | 29.6 | (1.3) | 0.1 | (1.3) |
| Turkey | 50.9 | (0.7) | 51.6 | (0.9) | -0.7 | (1.1) | 20.7 | (0.6) | 21.2 | (0.6) | -0.5 | (0.9) | 28.4 | (0.5) | 27.2 | (0.7) | 1.2 | (0.9) |
| United Kingdom | 71.5 | (0.4) | 69.4 | (0.8) | **2.1** | (1.0) | 6.3 | (0.2) | 7.5 | (0.6) | -1.3 | (0.7) | 22.2 | (0.3) | 23.1 | (0.6) | -0.8 | (0.8) |
| United States | 60.5 | (0.5) | 55.1 | (1.2) | **5.4** | (1.4) | 11.5 | (0.3) | 14.4 | (1.1) | **-2.9** | (1.2) | 28.0 | (0.4) | 30.5 | (0.5) | **-2.5** | (0.6) |
| OECD average | 62.2 | (0.1) | 62.4 | (0.2) | -0.2 | (0.2) | 10.6 | (0.1) | 10.3 | (0.1) | 0.3 | (0.1) | 27.3 | (0.1) | 27.3 | (0.1) | -0.1 | (0.2) |
| **Partners** | | | | | | | | | | | | | | | | | | |
| Argentina | 51.9 | (1.0) | 54.9 | (1.2) | **-3.0** | (1.6) | 10.2 | (0.6) | 8.7 | (0.5) | 1.5 | (0.9) | 37.9 | (0.8) | 36.4 | (1.1) | 1.5 | (1.3) |
| Azerbaijan | 42.1 | (0.7) | 46.5 | (1.1) | **-4.4** | (1.3) | 19.9 | (0.5) | 17.6 | (0.9) | **2.3** | (1.1) | 38.0 | (0.5) | 36.0 | (0.7) | **2.1** | (0.8) |
| Brazil | 49.4 | (0.6) | 51.6 | (0.7) | **-2.2** | (1.0) | 14.2 | (0.5) | 13.9 | (0.4) | 0.3 | (0.6) | 36.4 | (0.5) | 34.5 | (0.5) | **1.9** | (0.8) |
| Bulgaria | 48.2 | (1.0) | 49.7 | (0.8) | -1.5 | (1.2) | 17.2 | (0.7) | 14.8 | (0.8) | **2.4** | (1.1) | 34.6 | (0.6) | 35.5 | (0.5) | -0.9 | (0.9) |
| Chile | 46.8 | (1.0) | 50.4 | (0.6) | **-3.6** | (1.0) | 18.6 | (0.9) | 14.9 | (0.5) | **3.7** | (1.0) | 34.6 | (0.5) | 34.7 | (0.5) | -0.1 | (0.8) |
| Colombia | 58.9 | (0.8) | 59.3 | (1.0) | -0.4 | (1.2) | 13.4 | (0.5) | 12.5 | (0.5) | 0.9 | (0.6) | 27.8 | (0.6) | 28.2 | (0.6) | -0.5 | (0.9) |
| Croatia | 54.1 | (0.6) | 55.1 | (1.0) | -1.0 | (1.2) | 9.8 | (0.5) | 9.8 | (0.5) | -0.0 | (0.7) | 36.0 | (0.5) | 35.0 | (0.9) | 1.0 | (1.0) |
| Estonia | 62.2 | (0.6) | 59.7 | (0.9) | **2.5** | (1.2) | 12.7 | (0.4) | 12.4 | (0.6) | 0.3 | (0.7) | 25.1 | (0.4) | 27.9 | (0.6) | **-2.8** | (0.8) |
| Hong Kong-China | a | a | 61.0 | (0.5) | a | a | a | a | 13.9 | (0.4) | a | a | a | a | 25.2 | (0.4) | a | a |
| Indonesia | 53.7 | (0.7) | 58.7 | (2.9) | -5.0 | (2.9) | 15.8 | (0.6) | 14.6 | (1.9) | 1.2 | (1.8) | 30.5 | (0.4) | 26.7 | (1.3) | **3.8** | (1.4) |
| Israel | 52.7 | (1.2) | 56.5 | (1.4) | -3.8 | (2.1) | 19.1 | (0.7) | 17.4 | (0.7) | 1.6 | (1.1) | 28.2 | (0.8) | 26.1 | (1.0) | 2.1 | (1.4) |
| Jordan | 41.7 | (0.8) | 44.7 | (1.0) | **-3.0** | (1.3) | 21.0 | (0.5) | 19.2 | (0.8) | 1.8 | (1.1) | 37.4 | (0.5) | 36.1 | (0.6) | 1.3 | (0.7) |
| Kyrgyzstan | 33.1 | (0.7) | 47.5 | (1.8) | **-14.4** | (1.9) | 27.5 | (0.6) | 18.0 | (1.4) | **9.4** | (1.6) | 39.4 | (0.4) | 34.4 | (1.0) | **5.0** | (1.0) |
| Latvia | 55.9 | (0.6) | 56.6 | (0.9) | -0.7 | (1.1) | 10.6 | (0.4) | 10.0 | (0.5) | 0.6 | (0.7) | 33.5 | (0.4) | 33.4 | (0.6) | 0.0 | (0.7) |
| Liechtenstein | 62.2 | (1.4) | a | a | a | a | 9.7 | (1.0) | a | a | a | a | 28.1 | (1.3) | a | a | a | a |
| Lithuania | 56.6 | (0.5) | 57.9 | (0.8) | -1.4 | (0.9) | 10.8 | (0.4) | 9.0 | (0.4) | **1.8** | (0.5) | 32.7 | (0.4) | 33.1 | (0.6) | -0.4 | (0.8) |
| Macao-China | 62.2 | (0.9) | 65.2 | (0.4) | **-3.0** | (0.9) | 16.2 | (0.7) | 14.2 | (0.3) | **2.0** | (0.7) | 21.6 | (0.7) | 20.6 | (0.3) | 1.0 | (0.7) |
| Montenegro | 45.9 | (0.5) | 48.5 | (0.9) | **-2.7** | (1.0) | 16.6 | (0.4) | 15.2 | (0.6) | 1.3 | (0.7) | 37.5 | (0.5) | 36.2 | (0.9) | 1.3 | (1.0) |
| Qatar | 40.2 | (0.4) | 42.7 | (0.7) | **-2.5** | (0.8) | 25.1 | (0.4) | 23.7 | (0.6) | 1.4 | (0.6) | 34.7 | (0.3) | 33.6 | (0.6) | 1.1 | (0.7) |
| Romania | 46.2 | (0.8) | 50.1 | (1.1) | **-3.9** | (1.4) | 20.6 | (0.7) | 18.4 | (0.9) | 2.2 | (1.2) | 33.2 | (0.6) | 31.5 | (0.8) | 1.6 | (0.9) |
| Russian Federation | 47.2 | (0.7) | 50.6 | (0.8) | **-3.4** | (1.1) | 15.6 | (0.6) | 14.2 | (0.7) | 1.4 | (0.9) | 37.3 | (0.7) | 35.2 | (0.6) | **2.1** | (0.9) |
| Serbia | 56.1 | (0.6) | 57.9 | (0.9) | -1.8 | (1.1) | 14.3 | (0.5) | 12.0 | (0.6) | **2.2** | (0.7) | 29.6 | (0.5) | 30.1 | (0.7) | -0.5 | (0.9) |
| Slovenia | 54.2 | (0.5) | 58.3 | (0.6) | **-4.1** | (0.7) | 14.2 | (0.4) | 11.4 | (0.4) | **2.8** | (0.6) | 31.6 | (0.4) | 30.3 | (0.5) | **1.2** | (0.6) |
| Chinese Taipei | 65.8 | (0.9) | 62.6 | (0.4) | **3.2** | (1.0) | 10.9 | (0.5) | 13.0 | (0.4) | **-2.1** | (0.7) | 23.3 | (0.6) | 24.5 | (0.3) | -1.2 | (0.7) |
| Thailand | 63.8 | (0.5) | 64.2 | (0.9) | -0.4 | (1.0) | 9.5 | (0.4) | 11.2 | (1.0) | -1.7 | (1.2) | 26.7 | (0.4) | 24.6 | (0.7) | **2.1** | (0.8) |
| Tunisia | 37.2 | (0.4) | 38.0 | (1.2) | -0.8 | (1.4) | 26.0 | (0.4) | 25.7 | (0.8) | 0.2 | (0.9) | 36.8 | (0.4) | 36.2 | (0.9) | 0.6 | (1.1) |
| Uruguay | 55.3 | (0.7) | 57.3 | (0.8) | -1.9 | (1.2) | 12.2 | (0.5) | 11.8 | (0.6) | 0.3 | (0.5) | 32.5 | (0.6) | 30.9 | (0.6) | **1.6** | (0.8) |

Note: Values that are statistically significant at the 5% level (p < 0.05) are indicated in bold.

### Table 3.13b Mean learning hours and allocation of total learning time in mathematics, by school location
[Part 1/3]

| | Mean learning hours per week | | | | | | | | | | | |
| | Regular school lessons | | | | | | Out-of-school-time lessons | | | | | |
| | Rural (fewer than 100 000 people) | | City (over 100 000 people) | | Difference (rural-city) | | Rural (fewer than 100 000 people) | | City (over 100 000 people) | | Difference (rural-city) | |
| | Mean | S.E. | Mean | S.E. | Dif. | S.E. | Mean | S.E. | Mean | S.E. | Dif. | S.E. |
|---|---|---|---|---|---|---|---|---|---|---|---|---|
| **OECD** | | | | | | | | | | | | |
| Australia | 3.99 | (0.05) | 4.17 | (0.04) | **-0.18** | (0.06) | 0.68 | (0.02) | 0.79 | (0.02) | **-0.11** | (0.03) |
| Austria | 3.16 | (0.06) | 3.35 | (0.09) | -0.19 | (0.11) | 0.50 | (0.03) | 0.52 | (0.03) | -0.02 | (0.04) |
| Belgium | 3.52 | (0.05) | 3.79 | (0.14) | -0.27 | (0.17) | 0.52 | (0.01) | 0.67 | (0.04) | **-0.15** | (0.04) |
| Canada | 4.51 | (0.04) | 4.53 | (0.07) | -0.02 | (0.08) | 0.88 | (0.02) | 1.02 | (0.04) | **-0.14** | (0.04) |
| Czech Republic | 3.98 | (0.05) | 4.12 | (0.11) | -0.14 | (0.13) | 0.77 | (0.02) | 0.68 | (0.04) | 0.09 | (0.05) |
| Denmark | 4.43 | (0.04) | 4.59 | (0.08) | -0.15 | (0.08) | 1.36 | (0.03) | 1.46 | (0.09) | -0.10 | (0.11) |
| Finland | 3.46 | (0.04) | 3.42 | (0.09) | 0.04 | (0.10) | 0.37 | (0.02) | 0.37 | (0.03) | -0.00 | (0.04) |
| France | a | a | 3.84 | (0.03) | a | a | a | a | 0.93 | (0.02) | a | a |
| Germany | 3.94 | (0.04) | 3.70 | (0.06) | **0.25** | (0.07) | 0.80 | (0.03) | 0.85 | (0.07) | -0.05 | (0.09) |
| Greece | 3.40 | (0.06) | 3.54 | (0.08) | -0.14 | (0.11) | 2.27 | (0.08) | 2.16 | (0.08) | 0.12 | (0.13) |
| Hungary | 3.26 | (0.06) | 3.32 | (0.07) | -0.06 | (0.08) | 1.31 | (0.03) | 1.26 | (0.05) | 0.05 | (0.06) |
| Iceland | 4.74 | (0.03) | 4.80 | (0.04) | -0.06 | (0.05) | 0.69 | (0.03) | 0.82 | (0.04) | **-0.14** | (0.05) |
| Ireland | 3.64 | (0.04) | 3.72 | (0.05) | -0.09 | (0.06) | 0.72 | (0.03) | 0.70 | (0.04) | 0.03 | (0.05) |
| Italy | 3.74 | (0.04) | 3.73 | (0.06) | 0.01 | (0.08) | 0.89 | (0.02) | 0.86 | (0.03) | 0.03 | (0.04) |
| Japan | 4.05 | (0.14) | 4.34 | (0.09) | -0.29 | (0.19) | 0.67 | (0.06) | 0.74 | (0.04) | -0.07 | (0.07) |
| Korea | 4.44 | (0.13) | 4.74 | (0.05) | **-0.30** | (0.14) | 1.69 | (0.14) | 2.38 | (0.05) | **-0.69** | (0.15) |
| Luxembourg | 3.85 | (0.03) | 3.86 | (0.07) | -0.01 | (0.08) | 0.84 | (0.02) | 0.78 | (0.06) | 0.06 | (0.06) |
| Mexico | 3.73 | (0.06) | 4.15 | (0.05) | **-0.42** | (0.08) | 1.31 | (0.05) | 1.06 | (0.04) | **0.25** | (0.06) |
| Netherlands | 2.87 | (0.04) | 2.89 | (0.08) | -0.02 | (0.09) | 0.67 | (0.02) | 0.73 | (0.05) | -0.06 | (0.06) |
| New Zealand | 4.38 | (0.04) | 4.38 | (0.04) | -0.00 | (0.06) | 0.61 | (0.04) | 0.75 | (0.03) | **-0.14** | (0.06) |
| Norway | 3.37 | (0.03) | 3.45 | (0.08) | -0.07 | (0.08) | 1.03 | (0.02) | 1.13 | (0.06) | -0.09 | (0.06) |
| Poland | 4.31 | (0.04) | 4.51 | (0.08) | **-0.20** | (0.09) | 0.77 | (0.03) | 0.81 | (0.04) | -0.05 | (0.05) |
| Portugal | 3.56 | (0.05) | 3.78 | (0.10) | -0.23 | (0.13) | 0.79 | (0.03) | 0.91 | (0.05) | **-0.12** | (0.06) |
| Slovak Republic | 3.31 | (0.06) | 3.15 | (0.15) | **1.78** | (0.17) | 0.87 | (0.03) | 1.00 | (0.11) | -0.14 | (0.11) |
| Spain | 3.38 | (0.04) | 3.48 | (0.05) | -0.10 | (0.06) | 1.06 | (0.03) | 0.90 | (0.04) | **0.16** | (0.05) |
| Sweden | 3.08 | (0.03) | 3.09 | (0.06) | -0.01 | (0.07) | 0.60 | (0.02) | 0.65 | (0.03) | -0.05 | (0.04) |
| Switzerland | 3.90 | (0.04) | 3.73 | (0.12) | 0.17 | (0.14) | 0.72 | (0.02) | 0.62 | (0.06) | 0.10 | (0.06) |
| Turkey | 3.76 | (0.09) | 3.88 | (0.11) | -0.11 | (0.16) | 1.99 | (0.06) | 2.16 | (0.08) | -0.17 | (0.11) |
| United Kingdom | 3.78 | (0.03) | 3.74 | (0.07) | 0.05 | (0.08) | 0.56 | (0.02) | 0.74 | (0.05) | **-0.18** | (0.05) |
| United States | 3.85 | (0.05) | 3.64 | (0.08) | **0.20** | (0.10) | 1.06 | (0.03) | 1.30 | (0.06) | **-0.23** | (0.06) |
| **OECD average** | 3.77 | (0.01) | 3.85 | (0.02) | -0.02 | (0.02) | 0.93 | (0.01) | 0.99 | (0.01) | **-0.06** | (0.01) |
| **Partners** | | | | | | | | | | | | |
| Argentina | 2.87 | (0.09) | 3.07 | (0.08) | -0.20 | (0.13) | 0.80 | (0.04) | 0.75 | (0.05) | 0.05 | (0.07) |
| Azerbaijan | 3.65 | (0.06) | 4.26 | (0.13) | **-0.61** | (0.14) | 1.66 | (0.05) | 1.83 | (0.09) | -0.17 | (0.10) |
| Brazil | 3.03 | (0.05) | 3.33 | (0.05) | **-0.30** | (0.08) | 1.18 | (0.03) | 1.26 | (0.05) | -0.09 | (0.06) |
| Bulgaria | 2.91 | (0.08) | 3.11 | (0.12) | -0.20 | (0.14) | 1.16 | (0.05) | 1.10 | (0.04) | 0.06 | (0.07) |
| Chile | 3.25 | (0.13) | 3.65 | (0.08) | **-0.40** | (0.17) | 1.08 | (0.05) | 0.94 | (0.03) | **0.14** | (0.06) |
| Colombia | 4.15 | (0.07) | 4.31 | (0.11) | -0.16 | (0.13) | 1.25 | (0.05) | 1.20 | (0.04) | 0.04 | (0.07) |
| Croatia | 3.01 | (0.04) | 3.11 | (0.07) | -0.10 | (0.08) | 0.73 | (0.03) | 0.83 | (0.04) | -0.09 | (0.05) |
| Estonia | 4.20 | (0.05) | 4.18 | (0.07) | 0.03 | (0.08) | 1.00 | (0.03) | 0.97 | (0.05) | 0.02 | (0.06) |
| Hong Kong-China | a | a | 5.23 | (0.04) | a | a | a | a | 1.39 | (0.04) | a | a |
| Indonesia | 4.04 | (0.07) | 4.30 | (0.18) | -0.25 | (0.18) | 1.37 | (0.05) | 1.28 | (0.12) | 0.09 | (0.14) |
| Israel | 4.03 | (0.06) | 4.24 | (0.07) | **-0.21** | (0.10) | 2.16 | (0.06) | 2.13 | (0.07) | 0.03 | (0.09) |
| Jordan | 3.38 | (0.07) | 3.63 | (0.09) | **-0.25** | (0.12) | 1.84 | (0.05) | 1.79 | (0.07) | 0.05 | (0.09) |
| Kyrgyzstan | 2.76 | (0.06) | 3.50 | (0.14) | **-0.74** | (0.15) | 1.59 | (0.04) | 1.42 | (0.10) | 0.16 | (0.11) |
| Latvia | 4.48 | (0.05) | 4.51 | (0.08) | -0.02 | (0.10) | 1.19 | (0.05) | 1.21 | (0.06) | -0.02 | (0.08) |
| Liechtenstein | 3.98 | (0.09) | a | a | a | a | 0.54 | (0.05) | a | a | a | a |
| Lithuania | 3.40 | (0.05) | 3.65 | (0.06) | **-0.25** | (0.08) | 0.76 | (0.02) | 0.71 | (0.03) | 0.05 | (0.03) |
| Macao-China | 5.38 | (0.06) | 5.41 | (0.03) | -0.03 | (0.07) | 1.35 | (0.06) | 1.17 | (0.03) | **0.18** | (0.07) |
| Montenegro | 3.14 | (0.04) | 2.98 | (0.06) | **0.16** | (0.08) | 0.91 | (0.02) | 0.96 | (0.05) | -0.04 | (0.06) |
| Qatar | 3.01 | (0.04) | 3.43 | (0.05) | **-0.42** | (0.06) | 1.87 | (0.03) | 1.80 | (0.05) | 0.07 | (0.06) |
| Romania | 2.99 | (0.08) | 3.02 | (0.12) | -0.03 | (0.15) | 1.51 | (0.05) | 1.49 | (0.06) | 0.02 | (0.08) |
| Russian Federation | 3.63 | (0.07) | 3.64 | (0.09) | -0.01 | (0.11) | 1.16 | (0.05) | 1.08 | (0.04) | 0.08 | (0.07) |
| Serbia | 3.21 | (0.06) | 3.37 | (0.07) | -0.16 | (0.09) | 0.96 | (0.03) | 0.98 | (0.04) | -0.02 | (0.05) |
| Slovenia | 3.28 | (0.03) | 3.42 | (0.04) | **-0.14** | (0.05) | 1.05 | (0.03) | 0.98 | (0.04) | 0.07 | (0.05) |
| Chinese Taipei | 4.06 | (0.14) | 4.36 | (0.10) | -0.29 | (0.21) | 1.21 | (0.07) | 1.69 | (0.06) | **-0.49** | (0.11) |
| Thailand | 3.71 | (0.06) | 3.97 | (0.15) | -0.26 | (0.20) | 0.87 | (0.04) | 1.06 | (0.10) | -0.19 | (0.12) |
| Tunisia | 3.34 | (0.05) | 3.66 | (0.13) | **-0.32** | (0.14) | 2.38 | (0.04) | 2.63 | (0.09) | **-0.24** | (0.10) |
| Uruguay | 3.26 | (0.05) | 3.39 | (0.05) | -0.13 | (0.08) | 0.83 | (0.04) | 0.85 | (0.04) | -0.01 | (0.05) |

*Note:* Values that are statistically significant at the 5% level (p < 0.05) are indicated in bold.

© OECD 2011 Quality Time for Students: Learning In and Out of School

## Table 3.13b Mean learning hours and allocation of total learning time in mathematics, by school location
[Part 2/3]

| | | Mean learning hours per week | | | | | | | | | | |
| | | Individual study | | | | | | Total learning hours | | | | |
| | | Rural (fewer than 100 000 people) | | City (over 100 000 people) | | Difference (rural-city) | | Rural (fewer than 100 000 people) | | City (over 100 000 people) | | Difference (rural-city) | |
| | | Mean | S.E. | Mean | S.E. | Dif. | S.E. | Mean | S.E. | Mean | S.E. | Dif. | S.E. |
|---|---|---|---|---|---|---|---|---|---|---|---|---|---|
| OECD | Australia | 1.50 | (0.03) | 1.98 | (0.04) | **-0.48** | (0.05) | 6.19 | (0.07) | 6.94 | (0.07) | **-0.75** | (0.11) |
| | Austria | 2.08 | (0.05) | 2.22 | (0.05) | **-0.13** | (0.07) | 5.77 | (0.10) | 6.10 | (0.13) | -0.33 | (0.17) |
| | Belgium | 1.78 | (0.03) | 1.82 | (0.09) | -0.05 | (0.10) | 5.83 | (0.07) | 6.28 | (0.23) | -0.45 | (0.27) |
| | Canada | 1.78 | (0.03) | 2.23 | (0.06) | **-0.45** | (0.07) | 7.21 | (0.07) | 7.81 | (0.13) | **-0.60** | (0.14) |
| | Czech Republic | 1.32 | (0.04) | 1.28 | (0.06) | 0.04 | (0.08) | 6.06 | (0.09) | 6.07 | (0.18) | -0.00 | (0.20) |
| | Denmark | 1.73 | (0.03) | 1.84 | (0.10) | -0.11 | (0.11) | 7.50 | (0.07) | 7.85 | (0.21) | -0.35 | (0.24) |
| | Finland | 1.20 | (0.02) | 1.21 | (0.04) | -0.00 | (0.04) | 5.03 | (0.06) | 5.00 | (0.11) | 0.04 | (0.12) |
| | France | a | a | 1.74 | (0.03) | a | a | a | a | 6.50 | (0.06) | a | a |
| | Germany | 2.30 | (0.04) | 2.14 | (0.06) | **0.16** | (0.07) | 7.06 | (0.09) | 6.69 | (0.15) | **0.37** | (0.17) |
| | Greece | 2.03 | (0.04) | 1.97 | (0.06) | 0.05 | (0.08) | 7.71 | (0.15) | 7.71 | (0.15) | 0.00 | (0.24) |
| | Hungary | 1.86 | (0.04) | 1.81 | (0.06) | 0.05 | (0.07) | 6.44 | (0.10) | 6.40 | (0.14) | 0.04 | (0.17) |
| | Iceland | 1.69 | (0.03) | 1.76 | (0.05) | -0.06 | (0.06) | 7.12 | (0.05) | 7.37 | (0.09) | **-0.25** | (0.11) |
| | Ireland | 1.76 | (0.04) | 1.80 | (0.06) | -0.04 | (0.07) | 6.12 | (0.08) | 6.22 | (0.11) | -0.11 | (0.14) |
| | Italy | 2.50 | (0.04) | 2.46 | (0.06) | 0.03 | (0.07) | 7.14 | (0.09) | 7.07 | (0.12) | 0.07 | (0.14) |
| | Japan | 1.39 | (0.10) | 1.53 | (0.07) | -0.14 | (0.13) | 6.11 | (0.25) | 6.60 | (0.18) | -0.49 | (0.33) |
| | Korea | 1.83 | (0.10) | 2.40 | (0.08) | **-0.57** | (0.13) | 8.05 | (0.29) | 9.54 | (0.14) | **-1.50** | (0.34) |
| | Luxembourg | 1.72 | (0.02) | 1.57 | (0.06) | **0.16** | (0.06) | 6.44 | (0.05) | 6.21 | (0.13) | 0.23 | (0.14) |
| | Mexico | 2.28 | (0.05) | 2.24 | (0.03) | 0.04 | (0.06) | 7.27 | (0.10) | 7.44 | (0.08) | -0.16 | (0.13) |
| | Netherlands | 1.42 | (0.04) | 1.61 | (0.06) | **-0.19** | (0.07) | 4.95 | (0.08) | 5.21 | (0.15) | -0.26 | (0.17) |
| | New Zealand | 1.45 | (0.05) | 1.71 | (0.04) | **-0.26** | (0.06) | 6.45 | (0.09) | 6.84 | (0.07) | **-0.40** | (0.13) |
| | Norway | 1.36 | (0.03) | 1.61 | (0.09) | **-0.25** | (0.09) | 5.77 | (0.06) | 6.15 | (0.17) | **-0.37** | (0.18) |
| | Poland | 2.09 | (0.03) | 2.10 | (0.04) | -0.01 | (0.05) | 7.16 | (0.08) | 7.43 | (0.10) | **-0.27** | (0.12) |
| | Portugal | 1.94 | (0.04) | 2.04 | (0.07) | -0.10 | (0.08) | 6.29 | (0.09) | 6.72 | (0.17) | **-0.44** | (0.21) |
| | Slovak Republic | 1.68 | (0.04) | 1.73 | (0.12) | -0.05 | (0.12) | 5.87 | (0.11) | 5.89 | (0.33) | -0.02 | (0.36) |
| | Spain | 1.93 | (0.04) | 2.01 | (0.05) | -0.07 | (0.06) | 6.41 | (0.08) | 6.41 | (0.09) | 0.00 | (0.12) |
| | Sweden | 1.13 | (0.03) | 1.35 | (0.04) | **-0.21** | (0.05) | 4.82 | (0.05) | 5.09 | (0.11) | **-0.28** | (0.12) |
| | Switzerland | 1.70 | (0.02) | 1.67 | (0.05) | 0.03 | (0.06) | 6.34 | (0.06) | 6.03 | (0.17) | 0.31 | (0.19) |
| | Turkey | 2.28 | (0.05) | 2.33 | (0.08) | -0.05 | (0.09) | 8.00 | (0.19) | 8.34 | (0.25) | -0.34 | (0.34) |
| | United Kingdom | 1.47 | (0.02) | 1.54 | (0.05) | -0.07 | (0.06) | 5.82 | (0.05) | 6.02 | (0.12) | -0.20 | (0.12) |
| | United States | 1.99 | (0.03) | 2.17 | (0.04) | **-0.19** | (0.06) | 6.96 | (0.08) | 7.12 | (0.11) | -0.16 | (0.14) |
| | **OECD average** | 1.77 | (0.01) | 1.86 | (0.01) | **-0.10** | (0.01) | 6.48 | (0.02) | 6.70 | (0.03) | **-0.23** | (0.04) |
| Partners | Argentina | 1.83 | (0.05) | 1.82 | (0.06) | 0.02 | (0.07) | 5.51 | (0.14) | 5.64 | (0.14) | -0.13 | (0.20) |
| | Azerbaijan | 2.88 | (0.07) | 3.17 | (0.13) | -0.29 | (0.15) | 8.24 | (0.15) | 9.33 | (0.29) | **-1.09** | (0.32) |
| | Brazil | 1.78 | (0.04) | 1.84 | (0.05) | -0.06 | (0.07) | 5.95 | (0.10) | 6.43 | (0.13) | **-0.48** | (0.17) |
| | Bulgaria | 2.01 | (0.07) | 2.22 | (0.14) | -0.21 | (0.15) | 6.10 | (0.18) | 6.47 | (0.27) | -0.37 | (0.32) |
| | Chile | 1.63 | (0.06) | 1.58 | (0.04) | 0.05 | (0.07) | 5.99 | (0.20) | 6.21 | (0.11) | -0.21 | (0.24) |
| | Colombia | 1.93 | (0.05) | 1.94 | (0.05) | -0.00 | (0.06) | 7.31 | (0.11) | 7.46 | (0.14) | -0.15 | (0.18) |
| | Croatia | 1.82 | (0.04) | 1.77 | (0.05) | 0.05 | (0.06) | 5.60 | (0.07) | 5.76 | (0.09) | -0.16 | (0.12) |
| | Estonia | 1.92 | (0.04) | 2.04 | (0.05) | **-0.12** | (0.06) | 7.13 | (0.08) | 7.19 | (0.12) | -0.06 | (0.14) |
| | Hong Kong-China | a | a | 2.24 | (0.04) | a | a | a | a | 8.87 | (0.08) | a | a |
| | Indonesia | 2.01 | (0.03) | 1.90 | (0.07) | 0.11 | (0.08) | 7.42 | (0.11) | 7.49 | (0.17) | -0.08 | (0.19) |
| | Israel | 2.32 | (0.07) | 2.33 | (0.08) | -0.01 | (0.10) | 8.56 | (0.15) | 8.82 | (0.17) | -0.26 | (0.23) |
| | Jordan | 2.68 | (0.05) | 2.71 | (0.07) | -0.03 | (0.09) | 7.88 | (0.12) | 8.09 | (0.13) | -0.22 | (0.19) |
| | Kyrgyzstan | 2.22 | (0.04) | 2.16 | (0.07) | 0.06 | (0.08) | 6.63 | (0.11) | 7.12 | (0.18) | **-0.48** | (0.21) |
| | Latvia | 2.48 | (0.05) | 2.36 | (0.06) | 0.12 | (0.08) | 8.17 | (0.10) | 8.08 | (0.16) | 0.09 | (0.20) |
| | Liechtenstein | 1.49 | (0.07) | a | a | a | a | 6.00 | (0.13) | a | a | a | a |
| | Lithuania | 1.74 | (0.04) | 1.84 | (0.04) | -0.10 | (0.06) | 5.89 | (0.08) | 6.21 | (0.10) | **-0.31** | (0.14) |
| | Macao-China | 1.90 | (0.06) | 2.10 | (0.03) | **-0.20** | (0.06) | 8.63 | (0.11) | 8.69 | (0.06) | -0.06 | (0.13) |
| | Montenegro | 2.07 | (0.04) | 1.97 | (0.06) | 0.10 | (0.07) | 6.10 | (0.08) | 5.88 | (0.12) | 0.22 | (0.14) |
| | Qatar | 2.21 | (0.03) | 2.31 | (0.04) | **-0.10** | (0.05) | 7.12 | (0.08) | 7.56 | (0.12) | **-0.44** | (0.14) |
| | Romania | 2.12 | (0.06) | 2.20 | (0.07) | -0.07 | (0.11) | 6.63 | (0.17) | 6.71 | (0.19) | -0.08 | (0.29) |
| | Russian Federation | 2.30 | (0.06) | 2.13 | (0.06) | **0.17** | (0.08) | 7.08 | (0.12) | 6.86 | (0.15) | 0.22 | (0.19) |
| | Serbia | 1.77 | (0.04) | 1.88 | (0.05) | -0.11 | (0.07) | 5.94 | (0.10) | 6.24 | (0.13) | -0.30 | (0.18) |
| | Slovenia | 1.94 | (0.03) | 1.91 | (0.04) | 0.03 | (0.05) | 6.30 | (0.06) | 6.32 | (0.09) | -0.02 | (0.11) |
| | Chinese Taipei | 1.69 | (0.07) | 1.97 | (0.06) | **-0.28** | (0.11) | 7.01 | (0.27) | 8.09 | (0.20) | **-1.08** | (0.41) |
| | Thailand | 1.80 | (0.04) | 1.82 | (0.08) | -0.02 | (0.11) | 6.37 | (0.12) | 6.86 | (0.31) | -0.48 | (0.40) |
| | Tunisia | 2.57 | (0.05) | 2.57 | (0.09) | -0.00 | (0.10) | 8.28 | (0.11) | 8.88 | (0.26) | **-0.60** | (0.29) |
| | Uruguay | 1.56 | (0.04) | 1.59 | (0.04) | -0.04 | (0.06) | 5.67 | (0.10) | 5.85 | (0.10) | -0.18 | (0.14) |

*Note:* Values that are statistically significant at the 5% level (p < 0.05) are indicated in bold.

### Table 3.13b [Part 3/3] Mean learning hours and allocation of total learning time in mathematics, by school location

| | Allocation of total learning time in mathematics for | | | | | | | | | | | | | | | | | |
| | Regular school lessons | | | | | | Out-of-school-time lessons | | | | | | Individual study | | | | | |
| | Rural (fewer than 100 000 people) | | City (over 100 000 people) | | Difference (rural-city) | | Rural (fewer than 100 000 people) | | City (over 100 000 people) | | Difference (rural-city) | | Rural (fewer than 100 000 people) | | City (over 100 000 people) | | Difference (rural-city) | |
| | % | S.E | % | S.E | Dif. | S.E. | % | S.E | % | S.E | Dif. | S.E. | % | S.E | % | S.E | Dif. | S.E. |
|---|---|---|---|---|---|---|---|---|---|---|---|---|---|---|---|---|---|---|
| **OECD** | | | | | | | | | | | | | | | | | | |
| Australia | 68.1 | (0.5) | 64.3 | (0.4) | **3.8** | (0.7) | 9.2 | (0.3) | 9.3 | (0.2) | -0.1 | (0.4) | 22.7 | (0.4) | 26.4 | (0.3) | **-3.7** | (0.5) |
| Austria | 58.3 | (0.6) | 58.9 | (0.7) | -0.5 | (0.9) | 6.8 | (0.4) | 6.3 | (0.3) | 0.5 | (0.5) | 34.9 | (0.5) | 34.8 | (0.6) | 0.1 | (0.8) |
| Belgium | 63.3 | (0.3) | 62.4 | (0.7) | 0.9 | (0.7) | 7.6 | (0.2) | 9.4 | (0.7) | **-1.8** | (0.7) | 29.2 | (0.3) | 28.2 | (0.6) | 0.9 | (0.6) |
| Canada | 65.2 | (0.3) | 60.9 | (0.5) | **4.3** | (0.6) | 11.0 | (0.2) | 11.8 | (0.3) | -0.8 | (0.4) | 23.7 | (0.3) | 27.3 | (0.4) | **-3.6** | (0.5) |
| Czech Republic | 70.1 | (0.5) | 71.9 | (0.8) | -1.8 | (1.0) | 10.0 | (0.2) | 8.8 | (0.5) | 1.2 | (0.5) | 19.9 | (0.4) | 19.3 | (0.6) | 0.6 | (0.8) |
| Denmark | 62.5 | (0.4) | 62.5 | (1.0) | 0.0 | (1.1) | 16.0 | (0.3) | 16.1 | (0.8) | -0.1 | (0.9) | 21.5 | (0.2) | 21.4 | (0.7) | 0.1 | (0.8) |
| Finland | 71.1 | (0.4) | 71.1 | (0.9) | 0.0 | (0.9) | 6.0 | (0.2) | 5.7 | (0.5) | 0.3 | (0.5) | 22.9 | (0.3) | 23.2 | (0.6) | -0.4 | (0.6) |
| France | a | a | 62.6 | (0.3) | a | a | a | a | 12.6 | (0.2) | a | a | a | a | 24.8 | (0.3) | a | a |
| Germany | 58.7 | (0.4) | 58.4 | (0.8) | 0.3 | (1.0) | 9.4 | (0.4) | 10.7 | (0.7) | -1.2 | (0.9) | 31.9 | (0.3) | 30.9 | (0.5) | 1.0 | (0.6) |
| Greece | 48.8 | (0.6) | 50.1 | (1.0) | -1.4 | (1.1) | 26.3 | (0.7) | 25.5 | (0.9) | 0.8 | (1.2) | 24.9 | (0.5) | 24.3 | (0.6) | 0.6 | (0.7) |
| Hungary | 53.5 | (0.6) | 55.3 | (0.9) | **-1.8** | (0.9) | 18.2 | (0.4) | 17.2 | (0.5) | 1.0 | (0.7) | 28.3 | (0.4) | 27.5 | (0.5) | 0.8 | (0.7) |
| Iceland | 69.7 | (0.4) | 68.7 | (0.6) | 1.0 | (0.7) | 8.2 | (0.3) | 9.3 | (0.4) | **-1.1** | (0.5) | 22.0 | (0.3) | 22.0 | (0.4) | 0.1 | (0.5) |
| Ireland | 63.4 | (0.5) | 63.9 | (0.7) | -0.4 | (0.9) | 9.7 | (0.4) | 8.9 | (0.3) | 0.8 | (0.5) | 26.9 | (0.4) | 27.3 | (0.7) | -0.4 | (0.7) |
| Italy | 54.8 | (0.3) | 55.5 | (0.5) | -0.7 | (0.6) | 10.8 | (0.2) | 10.5 | (0.4) | 0.3 | (0.5) | 34.4 | (0.2) | 34.0 | (0.4) | 0.4 | (0.5) |
| Japan | 72.2 | (1.0) | 71.5 | (0.6) | 0.7 | (1.1) | 8.4 | (0.5) | 8.8 | (0.4) | -0.3 | (0.6) | 19.4 | (0.8) | 19.8 | (0.5) | -0.4 | (0.9) |
| Korea | 62.4 | (1.4) | 56.0 | (0.5) | **6.4** | (1.6) | 17.5 | (1.2) | 21.5 | (0.3) | **-4.0** | (1.3) | 20.1 | (0.6) | 22.5 | (0.4) | **-2.4** | (0.8) |
| Luxembourg | 63.1 | (0.3) | 64.7 | (1.1) | -1.5 | (1.1) | 11.1 | (0.2) | 10.8 | (0.7) | 0.3 | (0.7) | 25.7 | (0.3) | 24.5 | (0.7) | 1.2 | (0.7) |
| Mexico | 51.9 | (0.7) | 56.9 | (0.5) | **-5.0** | (0.9) | 16.1 | (0.5) | 12.8 | (0.4) | 3.3 | (0.7) | 32.0 | (0.4) | 30.3 | (0.4) | 1.7 | (0.6) |
| Netherlands | 60.7 | (0.5) | 58.3 | (0.8) | 2.4 | (1.0) | 11.9 | (0.4) | 12.3 | (0.9) | -0.3 | (1.0) | 27.4 | (0.5) | 29.4 | (0.8) | **-2.0** | (1.0) |
| New Zealand | 71.7 | (0.7) | 67.7 | (0.5) | **4.0** | (0.9) | 7.7 | (0.4) | 9.2 | (0.4) | **-1.5** | (0.6) | 20.5 | (0.4) | 23.1 | (0.4) | **-2.6** | (0.6) |
| Norway | 62.5 | (0.5) | 60.0 | (0.8) | 2.4 | (1.0) | 15.9 | (0.3) | 16.3 | (0.7) | -0.4 | (0.8) | 21.6 | (0.3) | 23.7 | (0.8) | **-2.1** | (0.8) |
| Poland | 62.2 | (0.4) | 63.3 | (0.5) | -1.1 | (0.6) | 10.0 | (0.3) | 10.3 | (0.5) | -0.3 | (0.6) | 27.8 | (0.3) | 26.4 | (0.5) | 1.3 | (0.6) |
| Portugal | 58.8 | (0.5) | 59.1 | (0.6) | -0.3 | (0.8) | 11.5 | (0.4) | 11.9 | (0.5) | -0.3 | (0.6) | 29.7 | (0.4) | 29.0 | (0.8) | 0.6 | (0.9) |
| Slovak Republic | 60.8 | (0.6) | 59.1 | (1.4) | 1.7 | (1.5) | 12.3 | (0.4) | 13.9 | (0.9) | -1.6 | (0.9) | 26.9 | (0.4) | 27.0 | (0.9) | -0.1 | (1.0) |
| Spain | 57.3 | (0.4) | 58.2 | (0.6) | -0.9 | (0.8) | 13.9 | (0.3) | 11.8 | (0.5) | 2.2 | (0.6) | 28.8 | (0.3) | 30.0 | (0.5) | **-1.2** | (0.6) |
| Sweden | 68.9 | (0.6) | 65.5 | (0.8) | **3.4** | (1.0) | 9.8 | (0.3) | 10.0 | (0.4) | -0.2 | (0.5) | 21.3 | (0.4) | 24.5 | (0.4) | **-3.2** | (0.8) |
| Switzerland | 63.5 | (0.4) | 64.0 | (1.1) | -0.5 | (1.2) | 9.8 | (0.3) | 8.5 | (0.7) | 1.3 | (0.7) | 26.7 | (0.2) | 27.5 | (0.9) | -0.8 | (1.0) |
| Turkey | 51.1 | (0.6) | 50.4 | (0.6) | 0.7 | (0.8) | 22.3 | (0.6) | 23.0 | (0.5) | -0.7 | (0.8) | 26.6 | (0.5) | 26.6 | (0.4) | 0.0 | (0.6) |
| United Kingdom | 67.8 | (0.4) | 65.5 | (0.7) | **2.3** | (0.8) | 8.1 | (0.2) | 10.1 | (0.6) | **-2.0** | (0.7) | 24.1 | (0.3) | 24.4 | (0.5) | -0.3 | (0.5) |
| United States | 57.1 | (0.4) | 52.3 | (1.0) | **4.8** | (1.2) | 14.2 | (0.4) | 17.3 | (0.8) | **-3.1** | (0.9) | 28.7 | (0.3) | 30.3 | (0.5) | **-1.7** | (0.6) |
| **OECD average** | 62.1 | (0.1) | 61.3 | (0.1) | **0.8** | (0.2) | 12.1 | (0.1) | 12.4 | (0.1) | -0.3 | (0.1) | 25.9 | (0.1) | 26.3 | (0.1) | **-0.5** | (0.1) |
| **Partners** | | | | | | | | | | | | | | | | | | |
| Argentina | 54.2 | (0.8) | 56.2 | (1.0) | -2.0 | (1.3) | 12.9 | (0.7) | 11.6 | (0.6) | 1.3 | (0.9) | 32.9 | (0.5) | 32.3 | (0.8) | **0.7** | (1.0) |
| Azerbaijan | 46.4 | (0.6) | 49.5 | (1.0) | -3.1 | (1.2) | 18.8 | (0.5) | 17.9 | (0.7) | 0.9 | (0.8) | 34.8 | (0.5) | 32.6 | (0.9) | **2.2** | (1.0) |
| Brazil | 53.9 | (0.6) | 55.1 | (0.7) | -1.1 | (0.9) | 17.3 | (0.5) | 17.3 | (0.6) | 0.0 | (0.8) | 28.7 | (0.4) | 27.7 | (0.5) | 1.1 | (0.6) |
| Bulgaria | 51.0 | (0.7) | 51.5 | (0.7) | -0.5 | (1.0) | 17.3 | (0.7) | 15.0 | (0.5) | 2.3 | (0.9) | 31.7 | (0.6) | 33.5 | (0.7) | -1.8 | (0.9) |
| Chile | 54.4 | (1.0) | 58.7 | (0.6) | **-4.3** | (1.2) | 16.7 | (0.5) | 14.1 | (0.4) | 2.6 | (0.7) | 28.9 | (0.7) | 27.2 | (0.5) | 1.7 | (0.9) |
| Colombia | 60.5 | (0.7) | 61.1 | (0.9) | -0.6 | (1.1) | 14.2 | (0.5) | 14.1 | (0.5) | 0.1 | (0.7) | 25.3 | (0.5) | 24.8 | (0.5) | 0.5 | (0.7) |
| Croatia | 58.1 | (0.6) | 58.8 | (0.9) | -0.7 | (1.0) | 11.1 | (0.4) | 12.2 | (0.5) | -1.1 | (0.7) | 30.9 | (0.5) | 29.1 | (0.7) | 1.8 | (0.8) |
| Estonia | 62.7 | (0.5) | 60.9 | (0.7) | 1.8 | (0.8) | 12.3 | (0.3) | 12.4 | (0.7) | -0.1 | (0.8) | 25.0 | (0.3) | 26.7 | (0.6) | **-1.7** | (0.6) |
| Hong Kong-China | a | a | 62.6 | (0.4) | a | a | a | a | 14.0 | (0.3) | a | a | a | a | 23.4 | (0.3) | a | a |
| Indonesia | 56.7 | (0.6) | 59.4 | (2.2) | -2.7 | (2.3) | 16.5 | (0.5) | 15.5 | (1.4) | 1.0 | (1.5) | 26.8 | (0.4) | 25.1 | (0.8) | 1.7 | (0.9) |
| Israel | 50.7 | (0.9) | 52.3 | (1.0) | -1.6 | (1.4) | 23.5 | (0.5) | 22.5 | (0.4) | 1.0 | (0.7) | 25.8 | (0.6) | 25.2 | (0.7) | 0.6 | (0.9) |
| Jordan | 42.3 | (0.6) | 44.5 | (1.0) | -2.3 | (1.3) | 22.9 | (0.6) | 21.5 | (0.8) | 1.4 | (1.1) | 34.8 | (0.5) | 34.0 | (0.7) | 0.8 | (0.9) |
| Kyrgyzstan | 40.0 | (0.5) | 51.7 | (1.8) | **-11.7** | (1.9) | 25.3 | (0.6) | 18.4 | (1.3) | **6.8** | (1.4) | 34.7 | (0.5) | 29.8 | (1.1) | **4.9** | (1.1) |
| Latvia | 58.0 | (0.5) | 58.8 | (0.6) | -0.9 | (0.8) | 13.2 | (0.5) | 13.5 | (0.5) | -0.3 | (0.7) | 28.8 | (0.4) | 27.7 | (0.4) | 1.1 | (0.6) |
| Liechtenstein | 67.1 | (1.2) | a | a | a | a | 7.9 | (0.6) | a | a | a | a | 24.9 | (1.0) | a | a | a | a |
| Lithuania | 60.3 | (0.5) | 61.4 | (0.5) | -1.1 | (0.7) | 12.1 | (0.4) | 10.6 | (0.4) | 1.5 | (0.6) | 27.6 | (0.4) | 28.1 | (0.6) | -0.4 | (0.7) |
| Macao-China | 66.6 | (0.8) | 66.2 | (0.4) | 0.4 | (0.9) | 13.2 | (0.5) | 11.6 | (0.3) | 1.6 | (0.6) | 20.3 | (0.6) | 22.2 | (0.3) | **-2.0** | (0.6) |
| Montenegro | 52.3 | (0.4) | 52.8 | (0.9) | -0.5 | (0.9) | 13.2 | (0.3) | 13.8 | (0.7) | -0.6 | (0.8) | 34.5 | (0.4) | 33.4 | (0.7) | 1.1 | (0.7) |
| Qatar | 42.7 | (0.4) | 45.3 | (0.5) | **-2.6** | (0.7) | 25.5 | (0.4) | 23.6 | (0.5) | 1.8 | (0.7) | 31.8 | (0.3) | 31.0 | (0.4) | 0.8 | (0.6) |
| Romania | 49.1 | (0.7) | 50.0 | (0.9) | -0.9 | (1.2) | 20.3 | (0.5) | 19.2 | (0.6) | 1.2 | (0.8) | 30.6 | (0.4) | 30.9 | (0.6) | -0.3 | (0.8) |
| Russian Federation | 52.7 | (0.7) | 55.6 | (0.6) | **-2.9** | (0.8) | 16.4 | (0.8) | 14.8 | (0.6) | 1.6 | (0.8) | 30.9 | (0.6) | 29.6 | (0.6) | 1.3 | (0.8) |
| Serbia | 59.2 | (0.6) | 59.3 | (0.7) | -0.1 | (0.9) | 12.9 | (0.3) | 13.1 | (0.5) | -0.2 | (0.6) | 27.9 | (0.5) | 27.6 | (0.5) | 0.3 | (0.7) |
| Slovenia | 54.7 | (0.4) | 57.0 | (0.5) | **-2.2** | (0.7) | 14.9 | (0.3) | 13.6 | (0.4) | 1.3 | (0.5) | 30.4 | (0.4) | 29.4 | (0.4) | 1.0 | (0.6) |
| Chinese Taipei | 62.3 | (0.9) | 58.4 | (0.5) | **4.0** | (1.2) | 14.4 | (0.7) | 18.2 | (0.4) | **-3.7** | (1.0) | 23.2 | (0.5) | 23.5 | (0.3) | -0.2 | (0.6) |
| Thailand | 63.3 | (0.5) | 63.6 | (0.7) | -0.2 | (1.0) | 10.5 | (0.4) | 11.1 | (0.8) | -0.6 | (1.1) | 26.2 | (0.3) | 25.3 | (0.6) | 0.9 | (0.7) |
| Tunisia | 41.6 | (0.4) | 42.4 | (1.2) | -0.8 | (1.3) | 26.9 | (0.3) | 27.9 | (0.8) | -1.0 | (0.9) | 31.5 | (0.4) | 29.7 | (0.8) | 1.8 | (1.0) |
| Uruguay | 60.6 | (0.6) | 61.1 | (0.5) | -0.5 | (0.8) | 12.4 | (0.5) | 12.5 | (0.4) | -0.1 | (0.6) | 27.0 | (0.4) | 26.5 | (0.4) | 0.6 | (0.6) |

*Note:* Values that are statistically significant at the 5% level (p < 0.05) are indicated in bold.

© OECD 2011 Quality Time for Students: Learning In and Out of School

**Table 3.13c** Mean learning hours and allocation of total learning time on the language of
[Part 1/3] instruction, by school location

| | | Mean learning hours per week | | | | | | | | | | |
|---|---|---|---|---|---|---|---|---|---|---|---|---|
| | | Regular school lessons | | | | | | Out-of-school-time lessons | | | | | |
| | | Rural (fewer than 100 000 people) | | City (over 100 000 people) | | Difference (rural-city) | | Rural (fewer than 100 000 people) | | City (over 100 000 people) | | Difference (rural-city) | |
| | | Mean | S.E. | Mean | S.E. | Dif. | S.E. | Mean | S.E. | Mean | S.E. | Dif. | S.E. |
| **OECD** | Australia | 3.97 | (0.05) | 4.12 | (0.04) | **-0.15** | (0.07) | 0.64 | (0.02) | 0.67 | (0.02) | -0.04 | (0.03) |
| | Austria | 2.84 | (0.04) | 2.94 | (0.09) | -0.10 | (0.10) | 0.24 | (0.02) | 0.22 | (0.03) | 0.02 | (0.04) |
| | Belgium | 3.39 | (0.04) | 3.82 | (0.10) | **-0.43** | (0.13) | 0.44 | (0.02) | 0.51 | (0.04) | -0.07 | (0.05) |
| | Canada | 4.44 | (0.04) | 4.44 | (0.07) | 0.00 | (0.08) | 0.84 | (0.02) | 0.91 | (0.04) | -0.07 | (0.04) |
| | Czech Republic | 3.73 | (0.04) | 3.69 | (0.10) | 0.04 | (0.11) | 0.63 | (0.02) | 0.52 | (0.04) | **0.11** | (0.04) |
| | Denmark | 5.51 | (0.05) | 5.56 | (0.10) | -0.05 | (0.11) | 1.70 | (0.04) | 1.69 | (0.10) | 0.01 | (0.10) |
| | Finland | 3.13 | (0.05) | 3.14 | (0.10) | -0.01 | (0.11) | 0.37 | (0.02) | 0.35 | (0.02) | 0.01 | (0.03) |
| | France | a | a | 4.01 | (0.03) | a | a | a | a | 0.77 | (0.02) | a | a |
| | Germany | 3.69 | (0.04) | 3.58 | (0.06) | 0.12 | (0.08) | 0.59 | (0.03) | 0.62 | (0.07) | -0.03 | (0.08) |
| | Greece | 3.13 | (0.06) | 3.26 | (0.08) | -0.13 | (0.11) | 1.63 | (0.05) | 1.62 | (0.07) | 0.01 | (0.09) |
| | Hungary | 3.12 | (0.06) | 3.27 | (0.08) | -0.15 | (0.10) | 1.31 | (0.04) | 1.31 | (0.04) | 0.01 | (0.06) |
| | Iceland | 4.51 | (0.03) | 4.58 | (0.04) | -0.07 | (0.05) | 0.46 | (0.02) | 0.50 | (0.03) | -0.04 | (0.04) |
| | Ireland | 3.54 | (0.04) | 3.58 | (0.06) | -0.05 | (0.07) | 0.67 | (0.03) | 0.54 | (0.05) | **0.13** | (0.06) |
| | Italy | 4.61 | (0.04) | 4.62 | (0.08) | -0.01 | (0.09) | 0.82 | (0.03) | 0.71 | (0.04) | **0.11** | (0.05) |
| | Japan | 3.67 | (0.07) | 3.90 | (0.07) | **-0.22** | (0.11) | 0.45 | (0.04) | 0.42 | (0.03) | 0.03 | (0.05) |
| | Korea | 4.37 | (0.13) | 4.49 | (0.05) | -0.12 | (0.13) | 1.16 | (0.11) | 1.50 | (0.04) | **-0.34** | (0.12) |
| | Luxembourg | 3.49 | (0.03) | 3.69 | (0.09) | **-0.20** | (0.09) | 0.60 | (0.02) | 0.53 | (0.06) | 0.07 | (0.06) |
| | Mexico | 3.54 | (0.05) | 3.92 | (0.05) | **-0.38** | (0.08) | 1.23 | (0.04) | 0.98 | (0.04) | **0.25** | (0.06) |
| | Netherlands | 2.94 | (0.03) | 2.85 | (0.06) | 0.09 | (0.08) | 0.64 | (0.03) | 0.63 | (0.06) | 0.01 | (0.07) |
| | New Zealand | 4.38 | (0.04) | 4.40 | (0.04) | -0.02 | (0.06) | 0.62 | (0.05) | 0.68 | (0.02) | -0.05 | (0.05) |
| | Norway | 3.57 | (0.04) | 3.74 | (0.09) | -0.17 | (0.10) | 1.15 | (0.03) | 1.27 | (0.08) | **-0.12** | (0.08) |
| | Poland | 4.58 | (0.04) | 4.83 | (0.06) | **-0.25** | (0.07) | 0.72 | (0.03) | 0.65 | (0.04) | 0.07 | (0.05) |
| | Portugal | 3.24 | (0.03) | 3.38 | (0.07) | -0.15 | (0.08) | 0.59 | (0.02) | 0.47 | (0.04) | 0.12 | (0.05) |
| | Slovak Republic | 3.15 | (0.06) | 2.94 | (0.14) | 0.20 | (0.16) | 0.89 | (0.03) | 0.87 | (0.09) | 0.02 | (0.10) |
| | Spain | 3.59 | (0.04) | 3.63 | (0.06) | -0.05 | (0.08) | 0.61 | (0.03) | 0.54 | (0.04) | 0.07 | (0.05) |
| | Sweden | 3.10 | (0.04) | 3.13 | (0.07) | -0.03 | (0.07) | 0.66 | (0.02) | 0.73 | (0.04) | -0.07 | (0.05) |
| | Switzerland | 3.66 | (0.04) | 3.66 | (0.16) | 0.01 | (0.16) | 0.49 | (0.02) | 0.46 | (0.07) | 0.03 | (0.08) |
| | Turkey | 3.97 | (0.09) | 4.01 | (0.08) | -0.04 | (0.13) | 1.85 | (0.07) | 1.78 | (0.07) | 0.07 | (0.10) |
| | United Kingdom | 3.90 | (0.04) | 3.83 | (0.08) | 0.07 | (0.09) | 0.52 | (0.02) | 0.70 | (0.05) | **-0.18** | (0.05) |
| | United States | 3.72 | (0.05) | 3.49 | (0.08) | **0.23** | (0.10) | 1.04 | (0.03) | 1.25 | (0.06) | **-0.21** | (0.07) |
| | **OECD average** | 3.74 | (0.01) | 3.82 | (0.01) | **-0.07** | (0.02) | 0.81 | (0.01) | 0.81 | (0.01) | -0.00 | (0.01) |
| **Partners** | Argentina | 2.30 | (0.06) | 2.53 | (0.10) | **-0.23** | (0.12) | 0.46 | (0.04) | 0.38 | (0.04) | 0.08 | (0.06) |
| | Azerbaijan | 3.60 | (0.05) | 4.00 | (0.08) | **-0.40** | (0.10) | 1.79 | (0.05) | 1.84 | (0.10) | -0.05 | (0.11) |
| | Brazil | 3.00 | (0.06) | 3.24 | (0.05) | **-0.24** | (0.07) | 1.17 | (0.03) | 1.21 | (0.05) | -0.03 | (0.06) |
| | Bulgaria | 2.84 | (0.06) | 3.03 | (0.06) | **-0.19** | (0.09) | 1.10 | (0.05) | 1.08 | (0.05) | 0.02 | (0.07) |
| | Chile | 3.29 | (0.12) | 3.54 | (0.08) | -0.25 | (0.16) | 1.15 | (0.06) | 0.89 | (0.03) | **0.26** | (0.06) |
| | Colombia | 3.94 | (0.08) | 3.92 | (0.07) | 0.02 | (0.11) | 1.18 | (0.04) | 1.11 | (0.04) | 0.06 | (0.06) |
| | Croatia | 3.31 | (0.05) | 3.37 | (0.06) | -0.06 | (0.08) | 0.42 | (0.02) | 0.34 | (0.03) | **0.08** | (0.03) |
| | Estonia | 3.50 | (0.04) | 3.43 | (0.06) | 0.07 | (0.07) | 0.90 | (0.03) | 0.84 | (0.05) | 0.06 | (0.06) |
| | Hong Kong-China | a | a | 5.19 | (0.04) | a | a | a | a | 0.81 | (0.03) | a | a |
| | Indonesia | 3.67 | (0.07) | 3.49 | (0.09) | 0.19 | (0.12) | 1.31 | (0.04) | 0.98 | (0.08) | **0.33** | (0.08) |
| | Israel | 3.03 | (0.06) | 3.03 | (0.07) | -0.00 | (0.09) | 1.41 | (0.05) | 1.22 | (0.06) | **0.19** | (0.09) |
| | Jordan | 3.47 | (0.08) | 3.71 | (0.09) | -0.24 | (0.13) | 1.85 | (0.05) | 1.66 | (0.07) | **0.19** | (0.09) |
| | Kyrgyzstan | 2.66 | (0.06) | 3.22 | (0.13) | **-0.57** | (0.14) | 1.77 | (0.04) | 1.38 | (0.09) | **0.39** | (0.10) |
| | Latvia | 3.77 | (0.05) | 3.55 | (0.06) | **0.22** | (0.09) | 0.93 | (0.05) | 0.77 | (0.03) | **0.16** | (0.06) |
| | Liechtenstein | 3.68 | (0.09) | a | a | a | a | 0.30 | (0.04) | a | a | a | a |
| | Lithuania | 3.62 | (0.04) | 3.72 | (0.06) | -0.11 | (0.07) | 0.72 | (0.03) | 0.56 | (0.02) | **0.16** | (0.04) |
| | Macao-China | 5.24 | (0.07) | 5.33 | (0.03) | -0.10 | (0.08) | 1.14 | 0.05 | 1.04 | (0.03) | 0.10 | (0.07) |
| | Montenegro | 2.91 | (0.04) | 2.97 | (0.07) | -0.05 | (0.08) | 0.74 | (0.02) | 0.75 | (0.04) | -0.01 | (0.05) |
| | Qatar | 2.79 | (0.04) | 3.26 | (0.06) | **-0.47** | (0.07) | 1.60 | (0.03) | 1.57 | (0.05) | 0.03 | (0.05) |
| | Romania | 3.23 | (0.07) | 3.36 | (0.10) | -0.13 | (0.13) | 1.57 | (0.05) | 1.46 | (0.05) | 0.11 | (0.08) |
| | Russian Federation | 2.06 | (0.04) | 2.01 | (0.06) | 0.06 | (0.06) | 0.89 | (0.03) | 0.72 | (0.03) | **0.17** | (0.04) |
| | Serbia | 3.14 | (0.05) | 3.23 | (0.06) | -0.09 | (0.09) | 0.98 | (0.03) | 0.85 | (0.04) | **0.13** | (0.05) |
| | Slovenia | 3.18 | (0.03) | 3.37 | (0.04) | **-0.20** | (0.05) | 0.79 | (0.02) | 0.64 | (0.03) | **0.16** | (0.03) |
| | Chinese Taipei | 4.19 | (0.11) | 4.46 | (0.09) | -0.27 | (0.17) | 0.68 | (0.04) | 0.70 | (0.03) | -0.02 | (0.05) |
| | Thailand | 3.16 | (0.05) | 2.94 | (0.13) | 0.22 | (0.18) | 0.63 | (0.03) | 0.36 | (0.04) | **0.27** | (0.05) |
| | Tunisia | 3.16 | (0.06) | 3.07 | (0.15) | 0.09 | (0.16) | 1.88 | (0.04) | 1.32 | (0.12) | **0.56** | (0.12) |
| | Uruguay | 2.73 | (0.06) | 2.75 | (0.04) | -0.02 | (0.07) | 0.67 | (0.03) | 0.62 | (0.03) | 0.05 | (0.05) |

*Note:* Values that are statistically significant at the 5% level (p < 0.05) are indicated in bold.

**Table 3.13c** **Mean learning hours and allocation of total learning time on the language of instruction, by school location**
[Part 2/3]

| | | Mean learning hours per week | | | | | | | | | | |
| | | Individual study | | | | | | Total learning hours | | | | | |
| | | Rural (fewer than 100 000 people) | | City (over 100 000 people) | | Difference (rural-city) | | Rural (fewer than 100 000 people) | | City (over 100 000 people) | | Difference (rural-city) | |
| | | Mean | S.E. | Mean | S.E. | Dif. | S.E. | Mean | S.E. | Mean | S.E. | Dif. | S.E. |
|---|---|---|---|---|---|---|---|---|---|---|---|---|---|
| **OECD** | Australia | 1.53 | (0.03) | 1.83 | (0.03) | **-0.29** | (0.05) | 6.15 | (0.07) | 6.61 | (0.06) | **-0.47** | (0.11) |
| | Austria | 1.54 | (0.04) | 1.55 | (0.07) | -0.01 | (0.08) | 4.63 | (0.07) | 4.73 | (0.16) | -0.10 | (0.18) |
| | Belgium | 1.32 | (0.02) | 1.46 | (0.04) | **-0.14** | (0.05) | 5.16 | (0.06) | 5.80 | (0.13) | **-0.64** | (0.16) |
| | Canada | 1.58 | (0.03) | 1.98 | (0.05) | **-0.40** | (0.07) | 6.90 | (0.07) | 7.34 | (0.11) | **-0.45** | (0.14) |
| | Czech Republic | 1.17 | (0.03) | 1.08 | (0.04) | 0.10 | (0.05) | 5.53 | (0.06) | 5.28 | (0.14) | 0.25 | (0.15) |
| | Denmark | 2.16 | (0.03) | 2.20 | (0.09) | -0.03 | (0.10) | 9.37 | (0.09) | 9.44 | (0.19) | -0.07 | (0.21) |
| | Finland | 1.13 | (0.02) | 1.15 | (0.05) | -0.01 | (0.05) | 4.63 | (0.07) | 4.64 | (0.13) | -0.01 | (0.14) |
| | France | a | a | 1.51 | (0.02) | a | a | a | a | 6.30 | (0.04) | a | a |
| | Germany | 1.88 | (0.03) | 1.88 | (0.06) | -0.00 | (0.08) | 6.18 | (0.07) | 6.11 | (0.15) | 0.06 | (0.18) |
| | Greece | 1.97 | (0.04) | 1.88 | (0.05) | 0.08 | (0.07) | 6.74 | (0.12) | 6.77 | (0.15) | -0.03 | (0.22) |
| | Hungary | 1.87 | (0.04) | 1.84 | (0.06) | 0.04 | (0.07) | 6.33 | (0.12) | 6.42 | (0.14) | -0.09 | (0.20) |
| | Iceland | 1.55 | (0.03) | 1.54 | (0.04) | 0.01 | (0.05) | 6.52 | (0.05) | 6.61 | (0.08) | -0.09 | (0.10) |
| | Ireland | 1.74 | (0.04) | 1.78 | (0.06) | -0.03 | (0.07) | 5.96 | (0.08) | 5.90 | (0.13) | 0.06 | (0.15) |
| | Italy | 2.98 | (0.04) | 2.90 | (0.09) | 0.08 | (0.10) | 8.42 | (0.08) | 8.23 | (0.16) | 0.19 | (0.19) |
| | Japan | 0.89 | (0.05) | 0.97 | (0.04) | -0.09 | (0.07) | 5.02 | (0.12) | 5.28 | (0.11) | -0.26 | (0.18) |
| | Korea | 1.20 | (0.07) | 1.44 | (0.03) | **-0.25** | (0.08) | 6.77 | (0.24) | 7.44 | (0.10) | **-0.67** | (0.26) |
| | Luxembourg | 1.39 | (0.02) | 1.36 | (0.07) | 0.03 | (0.07) | 5.47 | (0.04) | 5.57 | (0.16) | -0.10 | (0.17) |
| | Mexico | 2.09 | (0.04) | 2.02 | (0.04) | 0.07 | (0.06) | 6.84 | (0.10) | 6.90 | (0.11) | -0.07 | (0.15) |
| | Netherlands | 1.30 | (0.03) | 1.42 | (0.04) | **-0.12** | (0.05) | 4.89 | (0.06) | 4.88 | (0.13) | 0.01 | (0.16) |
| | New Zealand | 1.49 | (0.05) | 1.65 | (0.03) | **-0.16** | (0.07) | 6.51 | (0.11) | 6.72 | (0.07) | -0.21 | (0.14) |
| | Norway | 1.42 | (0.03) | 1.63 | (0.09) | **-0.22** | (0.10) | 6.13 | (0.07) | 6.61 | (0.19) | **-0.48** | (0.21) |
| | Poland | 2.23 | (0.03) | 2.20 | (0.06) | 0.03 | (0.07) | 7.52 | (0.06) | 7.67 | (0.10) | -0.15 | (0.12) |
| | Portugal | 1.81 | (0.03) | 1.72 | (0.07) | 0.08 | (0.08) | 5.65 | (0.06) | 5.57 | (0.11) | 0.08 | (0.12) |
| | Slovak Republic | 1.77 | (0.04) | 1.57 | (0.11) | 0.20 | (0.12) | 5.81 | (0.09) | 5.36 | (0.30) | 0.46 | (0.32) |
| | Spain | 1.87 | (0.04) | 1.91 | (0.05) | -0.04 | (0.06) | 6.10 | (0.08) | 6.11 | (0.08) | -0.01 | (0.12) |
| | Sweden | 1.22 | (0.02) | 1.39 | (0.06) | **-0.16** | (0.07) | 4.98 | (0.06) | 5.27 | (0.14) | -0.29 | (0.16) |
| | Switzerland | 1.40 | (0.02) | 1.39 | (0.06) | 0.01 | (0.06) | 5.56 | (0.05) | 5.51 | (0.25) | 0.05 | (0.26) |
| | Turkey | 2.24 | (0.06) | 2.11 | (0.07) | 0.13 | (0.09) | 8.04 | (0.18) | 7.88 | (0.17) | 0.16 | (0.26) |
| | United Kingdom | 1.55 | (0.03) | 1.67 | (0.07) | -0.12 | (0.07) | 5.97 | (0.06) | 6.20 | (0.14) | -0.22 | (0.15) |
| | United States | 1.79 | (0.04) | 2.00 | (0.05) | **-0.21** | (0.07) | 6.62 | (0.07) | 6.73 | (0.12) | -0.11 | (0.15) |
| | **OECD average** | 1.66 | (0.01) | 1.70 | (0.01) | **-0.05** | (0.01) | 6.22 | (0.02) | 6.33 | (0.03) | **-0.11** | (0.03) |
| **Partners** | Argentina | 1.61 | (0.05) | 1.66 | (0.06) | -0.05 | (0.07) | 4.36 | (0.09) | 4.57 | (0.14) | -0.22 | (0.17) |
| | Azerbaijan | 3.10 | (0.05) | 3.11 | (0.11) | -0.01 | (0.12) | 8.55 | (0.12) | 9.01 | (0.25) | -0.45 | (0.27) |
| | Brazil | 1.77 | (0.04) | 1.72 | (0.04) | 0.04 | (0.06) | 5.93 | (0.08) | 6.16 | (0.12) | -0.23 | (0.14) |
| | Bulgaria | 1.96 | (0.07) | 2.22 | (0.09) | **-0.26** | (0.11) | 5.92 | (0.15) | 6.37 | (0.15) | **-0.46** | (0.21) |
| | Chile | 1.65 | (0.05) | 1.49 | (0.04) | **0.16** | (0.06) | 6.10 | (0.18) | 5.95 | (0.10) | 0.15 | (0.22) |
| | Colombia | 1.82 | (0.06) | 1.85 | (0.05) | -0.03 | (0.08) | 6.95 | (0.11) | 6.88 | (0.12) | 0.07 | (0.16) |
| | Croatia | 1.60 | (0.03) | 1.54 | (0.06) | 0.06 | (0.07) | 5.35 | (0.07) | 5.27 | (0.12) | 0.08 | (0.14) |
| | Estonia | 1.59 | (0.03) | 1.69 | (0.04) | **-0.10** | (0.05) | 6.00 | (0.07) | 5.97 | (0.11) | 0.03 | (0.12) |
| | Hong Kong-China | a | a | 1.64 | (0.03) | a | a | a | a | 7.64 | (0.08) | a | a |
| | Indonesia | 1.84 | (0.04) | 1.59 | (0.09) | **0.25** | (0.10) | 6.82 | (0.11) | 6.03 | (0.19) | **0.79** | (0.24) |
| | Israel | 1.68 | (0.05) | 1.62 | (0.07) | 0.06 | (0.10) | 6.12 | (0.13) | 5.91 | (0.17) | 0.21 | (0.22) |
| | Jordan | 2.69 | (0.06) | 2.44 | (0.06) | **0.25** | (0.09) | 8.01 | (0.13) | 7.79 | (0.13) | 0.22 | (0.19) |
| | Kyrgyzstan | 2.35 | (0.04) | 2.28 | (0.07) | 0.07 | (0.08) | 6.86 | (0.11) | 6.92 | (0.22) | -0.06 | (0.25) |
| | Latvia | 2.07 | (0.03) | 1.87 | (0.07) | **0.20** | (0.08) | 6.77 | (0.10) | 6.20 | (0.12) | **0.56** | (0.17) |
| | Liechtenstein | 1.22 | (0.06) | a | a | a | a | 5.20 | (0.10) | a | a | a | a |
| | Lithuania | 1.81 | (0.04) | 1.83 | (0.06) | -0.02 | (0.07) | 6.13 | (0.07) | 6.12 | (0.10) | 0.01 | (0.12) |
| | Macao-China | 1.44 | (0.05) | 1.50 | (0.03) | -0.06 | (0.06) | 7.82 | (0.12) | 7.87 | (0.06) | -0.06 | (0.13) |
| | Montenegro | 1.98 | (0.03) | 2.01 | (0.06) | -0.03 | (0.07) | 5.62 | (0.08) | 5.73 | (0.13) | -0.10 | (0.15) |
| | Qatar | 2.04 | (0.03) | 2.06 | (0.06) | -0.02 | (0.06) | 6.43 | (0.07) | 6.89 | (0.12) | **-0.45** | (0.14) |
| | Romania | 2.17 | (0.05) | 2.21 | (0.07) | -0.05 | (0.09) | 6.99 | (0.13) | 7.04 | (0.17) | -0.05 | (0.24) |
| | Russian Federation | 1.64 | (0.05) | 1.42 | (0.04) | **0.23** | (0.06) | 4.57 | (0.09) | 4.13 | (0.09) | **0.45** | (0.13) |
| | Serbia | 1.73 | (0.04) | 1.66 | (0.04) | 0.07 | (0.06) | 5.84 | (0.09) | 5.73 | (0.10) | 0.11 | (0.15) |
| | Slovenia | 1.52 | (0.02) | 1.41 | (0.03) | **0.11** | (0.03) | 5.51 | (0.05) | 5.43 | (0.07) | 0.08 | (0.08) |
| | Chinese Taipei | 1.64 | (0.05) | 1.83 | (0.04) | **-0.19** | (0.07) | 6.54 | (0.15) | 7.03 | (0.12) | **-0.49** | (0.23) |
| | Thailand | 1.79 | (0.04) | 1.47 | (0.06) | **0.32** | (0.09) | 5.57 | (0.10) | 4.76 | (0.19) | **0.81** | (0.27) |
| | Tunisia | 2.20 | (0.04) | 1.74 | (0.10) | **0.46** | (0.11) | 7.25 | (0.10) | 6.13 | (0.24) | **1.13** | (0.26) |
| | Uruguay | 1.40 | (0.03) | 1.29 | (0.03) | **0.11** | (0.05) | 4.82 | (0.09) | 4.68 | (0.08) | 0.14 | (0.12) |

*Note:* Values that are statistically significant at the 5% level (p < 0.05) are indicated in bold.

© OECD 2011  Quality Time for Students: Learning In and Out of School

## Table 3.13c [Part 3/3] Mean learning hours and allocation of total learning time on the language of instruction, by school location

| | Regular school lessons | | | | | | Out-of-school-time lessons | | | | | | Individual study | | | | | |
| | Rural (fewer than 100 000 people) | | City (over 100 000 people) | | Difference (rural-city) | | Rural (fewer than 100 000 people) | | City (over 100 000 people) | | Difference (rural-city) | | Rural (fewer than 100 000 people) | | City (over 100 000 people) | | Difference (rural-city) | |
| | % | S.E | % | S.E | Dif. | S.E. | % | S.E | % | S.E | Dif. | S.E. | % | S.E | % | S.E | Dif. | S.E. |
|---|---|---|---|---|---|---|---|---|---|---|---|---|---|---|---|---|---|---|
| **OECD** | | | | | | | | | | | | | | | | | | |
| Australia | 68.3 | (0.5) | 66.3 | (0.4) | **2.0** | (0.6) | 8.5 | (0.3) | 8.1 | (0.2) | 0.4 | (0.4) | 23.2 | (0.3) | 25.6 | (0.3) | **-2.4** | (0.5) |
| Austria | 65.3 | (0.6) | 65.9 | (0.7) | -0.6 | (1.0) | 3.5 | (0.4) | 2.9 | (0.3) | 0.6 | (0.5) | 31.1 | (0.6) | 31.2 | (0.6) | -0.0 | (0.9) |
| Belgium | 67.3 | (0.4) | 67.1 | (0.8) | 0.1 | (0.9) | 6.9 | (0.2) | 7.6 | (0.6) | -0.7 | (0.7) | 25.8 | (0.3) | 25.3 | (0.6) | 0.6 | (0.7) |
| Canada | 67.3 | (0.4) | 63.1 | (0.5) | **4.1** | (0.6) | 10.9 | (0.2) | 10.8 | (0.4) | 0.1 | (0.5) | 21.9 | (0.3) | 26.1 | (0.4) | **-4.3** | (0.5) |
| Czech Republic | 71.2 | (0.5) | 74.0 | (0.8) | **-2.9** | (1.0) | 9.3 | (0.2) | 7.6 | (0.4) | **1.7** | (0.5) | 19.5 | (0.4) | 18.4 | (0.8) | 1.1 | (0.9) |
| Denmark | 62.3 | (0.4) | 62.1 | (1.1) | 0.2 | (1.1) | 16.0 | (0.3) | 15.9 | (0.8) | 0.1 | (0.8) | 21.7 | (0.2) | 22.0 | (0.7) | -0.3 | (0.7) |
| Finland | 70.8 | (0.4) | 70.2 | (1.0) | 0.6 | (1.1) | 6.2 | (0.2) | 6.1 | (0.5) | 0.1 | (0.5) | 23.0 | (0.3) | 23.7 | (0.7) | -0.7 | (0.8) |
| France | a | a | 67.0 | (0.4) | a | a | a | a | 10.7 | (0.3) | a | a | a | a | 22.3 | (0.3) | a | a |
| Germany | 62.6 | (0.5) | 61.8 | (0.9) | 0.9 | (1.2) | 7.8 | (0.4) | 8.1 | (0.8) | -0.3 | (1.0) | 29.6 | (0.3) | 30.2 | (0.6) | -0.5 | (0.7) |
| Greece | 50.2 | (0.7) | 52.6 | (1.0) | **-2.4** | (1.2) | 21.8 | (0.4) | 21.1 | (0.7) | 0.7 | (0.9) | 28.0 | (0.4) | 26.3 | (0.7) | **1.7** | (0.8) |
| Hungary | 52.1 | (0.7) | 54.6 | (0.6) | **-2.4** | (1.0) | 18.8 | (0.5) | 17.6 | (0.5) | 1.3 | (0.7) | 29.0 | (0.4) | 27.8 | (0.4) | **1.2** | (0.6) |
| Iceland | 71.8 | (0.4) | 71.7 | (0.5) | 0.2 | (0.7) | 5.9 | (0.3) | 6.4 | (0.4) | -0.5 | (0.4) | 22.2 | (0.3) | 21.9 | (0.4) | 0.3 | (0.5) |
| Ireland | 63.8 | (0.5) | 65.4 | (0.9) | -1.6 | (1.0) | 8.7 | (0.3) | 6.7 | (0.5) | **2.0** | (0.6) | 27.5 | (0.4) | 27.9 | (0.6) | -0.4 | (0.7) |
| Italy | 56.8 | (0.3) | 58.3 | (0.4) | **-1.5** | (0.6) | 8.5 | (0.3) | 7.6 | (0.4) | 1.0 | (0.5) | 34.7 | (0.2) | 34.2 | (0.4) | 0.5 | (0.5) |
| Japan | 77.8 | (0.8) | 78.3 | (0.6) | -0.5 | (1.0) | 6.8 | (0.5) | 6.1 | (0.4) | 0.7 | (0.6) | 15.4 | (0.6) | 15.6 | (0.5) | -0.3 | (0.8) |
| Korea | 70.2 | (1.4) | 65.7 | (0.5) | **4.6** | (1.5) | 13.9 | (1.1) | 16.9 | (0.4) | **-3.0** | (1.2) | 15.9 | (0.6) | 17.4 | (0.3) | **-1.6** | (0.6) |
| Luxembourg | 67.2 | (0.3) | 68.2 | (1.2) | -1.0 | (1.2) | 8.9 | (0.2) | 8.0 | (0.8) | 1.0 | (0.8) | 23.9 | (0.3) | 23.9 | (0.9) | 0.0 | (0.9) |
| Mexico | 52.1 | (0.6) | 57.8 | (0.6) | **-5.7** | (0.8) | 16.5 | (0.5) | 12.7 | (0.4) | **3.8** | (0.7) | 31.3 | (0.4) | 29.5 | (0.4) | **1.9** | (0.5) |
| Netherlands | 63.6 | (0.5) | 61.5 | (0.9) | **2.1** | (1.0) | 10.9 | (0.4) | 10.5 | (0.4) | 0.5 | (1.0) | 25.5 | (0.3) | 28.1 | (0.4) | **-2.6** | (0.8) |
| New Zealand | 71.4 | (0.7) | 69.1 | (0.5) | **2.3** | (0.8) | 7.7 | (0.4) | 8.2 | (0.3) | -0.5 | (0.5) | 20.9 | (0.4) | 22.7 | (0.4) | **-1.8** | (0.6) |
| Norway | 62.4 | (0.5) | 60.1 | (1.2) | 2.3 | (1.3) | 16.4 | (0.3) | 17.2 | (0.9) | -0.8 | (0.9) | 21.2 | (0.4) | 22.7 | (0.9) | -1.5 | (1.0) |
| Poland | 63.1 | (0.4) | 65.0 | (0.7) | **-1.9** | (0.8) | 8.7 | (0.4) | 8.0 | (0.5) | 0.7 | (0.6) | 28.2 | (0.3) | 27.0 | (0.6) | 1.2 | (0.7) |
| Portugal | 60.2 | (0.5) | 63.7 | (1.1) | **-3.5** | (1.2) | 9.2 | (0.4) | 7.1 | (0.6) | **2.0** | (0.8) | 30.6 | (0.3) | 29.2 | (1.0) | 1.4 | (1.1) |
| Slovak Republic | 58.7 | (0.6) | 60.3 | (1.4) | -1.6 | (1.6) | 12.6 | (0.4) | 13.3 | (0.8) | -0.7 | (0.9) | 28.7 | (0.6) | 26.4 | (1.0) | 2.3 | (1.2) |
| Spain | 62.5 | (0.4) | 62.8 | (0.7) | -0.3 | (0.8) | 8.5 | (0.3) | 7.5 | (0.5) | 1.0 | (0.7) | 28.9 | (0.3) | 29.6 | (0.5) | -0.7 | (0.6) |
| Sweden | 67.3 | (0.6) | 64.6 | (1.0) | **2.6** | (1.2) | 10.2 | (0.3) | 10.4 | (0.4) | -0.1 | (0.5) | 22.5 | (0.5) | 25.0 | (0.9) | **-2.5** | (1.0) |
| Switzerland | 67.4 | (0.4) | 68.2 | (1.2) | -0.8 | (1.3) | 7.1 | (0.3) | 6.6 | (0.9) | 0.5 | (1.0) | 25.4 | (0.3) | 25.2 | (0.7) | 0.3 | (0.8) |
| Turkey | 53.6 | (0.9) | 55.9 | (0.9) | -2.3 | (1.4) | 20.3 | (0.7) | 19.3 | (0.5) | 1.0 | (0.9) | 26.1 | (0.5) | 24.8 | (0.5) | 1.3 | (0.7) |
| United Kingdom | 68.6 | (0.4) | 65.5 | (0.8) | **3.1** | (0.9) | 7.0 | (0.2) | 9.0 | (0.6) | **-2.0** | (0.7) | 24.4 | (0.3) | 25.5 | (0.6) | -1.1 | (0.7) |
| United States | 57.6 | (0.7) | 52.8 | (1.1) | **4.8** | (1.3) | 14.8 | (0.4) | 17.9 | (1.0) | **-3.1** | (1.1) | 27.6 | (0.4) | 29.3 | (0.5) | **-1.7** | (0.7) |
| **OECD average** | **63.9** | **(0.1)** | **64.0** | **(0.2)** | **0.0** | **(0.2)** | **10.8** | **(0.1)** | **10.5** | **(0.1)** | **0.3** | **(0.1)** | **25.3** | **(0.1)** | **25.5** | **(0.1)** | **-0.3** | **(0.1)** |
| **Partners** | | | | | | | | | | | | | | | | | | |
| Argentina | 54.8 | (0.8) | 55.8 | (1.1) | -1.0 | (1.4) | 8.7 | (0.6) | 7.0 | (0.7) | 1.7 | (0.9) | 36.4 | (0.6) | 37.2 | (0.8) | -0.7 | (1.1) |
| Azerbaijan | 44.2 | (0.7) | 47.3 | (1.0) | **-3.1** | (1.2) | 19.4 | (0.5) | 19.0 | (0.8) | 0.3 | (0.9) | 36.5 | (0.6) | 33.7 | (0.7) | **2.8** | (0.9) |
| Brazil | 53.6 | (0.6) | 55.4 | (0.7) | **-1.8** | (1.0) | 17.7 | (0.4) | 17.8 | (0.6) | -0.0 | (0.7) | 28.7 | (0.5) | 26.9 | (0.4) | **1.8** | (0.7) |
| Bulgaria | 51.6 | (0.7) | 52.0 | (0.7) | -0.4 | (1.0) | 16.3 | (0.5) | 14.0 | (0.8) | **2.3** | (1.0) | 32.1 | (0.6) | 34.0 | (0.7) | **-1.9** | (0.9) |
| Chile | 54.1 | (1.0) | 59.6 | (0.6) | **-5.5** | (1.3) | 17.0 | (0.7) | 13.9 | (0.5) | **3.1** | (0.8) | 28.8 | (0.7) | 26.5 | (0.4) | **2.4** | (0.9) |
| Colombia | 60.1 | (0.8) | 60.8 | (0.9) | -0.7 | (1.2) | 15.1 | (0.6) | 13.6 | (0.5) | 1.5 | (0.8) | 24.7 | (0.6) | 25.6 | (0.5) | -0.9 | (0.9) |
| Croatia | 66.0 | (0.5) | 68.1 | (0.8) | **-2.1** | (0.9) | 6.4 | (0.3) | 4.9 | (0.3) | **1.4** | (0.4) | 27.6 | (0.4) | 26.9 | (0.6) | 0.7 | (0.7) |
| Estonia | 62.1 | (0.6) | 61.0 | (0.7) | 1.1 | (0.9) | 13.2 | (0.5) | 12.7 | (0.8) | 0.5 | (0.9) | 24.7 | (0.4) | 26.3 | (0.4) | **-1.5** | (0.6) |
| Hong Kong-China | a | a | 70.9 | (0.4) | a | a | a | a | 9.1 | (0.3) | a | a | a | a | 20.0 | (0.3) | a | a |
| Indonesia | 55.6 | (0.5) | 59.6 | (1.9) | **-4.0** | (1.9) | 17.2 | (0.5) | 14.0 | (1.0) | **3.2** | (0.9) | 27.2 | (0.4) | 26.4 | (1.2) | 0.8 | (1.3) |
| Israel | 52.9 | (0.9) | 55.9 | (1.1) | **-3.0** | (1.7) | 20.8 | (0.6) | 18.4 | (0.6) | **2.5** | (1.0) | 26.3 | (0.6) | 25.8 | (0.8) | 0.5 | (1.1) |
| Jordan | 42.3 | (0.8) | 47.0 | (1.2) | **-4.7** | (1.5) | 23.2 | (0.6) | 20.6 | (0.8) | **2.6** | (1.0) | 34.5 | (0.5) | 32.3 | (0.7) | **2.1** | (0.9) |
| Kyrgyzstan | 37.9 | (0.5) | 49.8 | (1.4) | **-11.9** | (1.3) | 27.7 | (0.5) | 18.3 | (1.2) | **9.4** | (1.3) | 34.5 | (0.4) | 31.9 | (1.0) | **2.5** | (1.1) |
| Latvia | 58.6 | (0.5) | 60.5 | (0.7) | **-1.9** | (0.9) | 12.0 | (0.5) | 10.3 | (0.4) | **1.6** | (0.7) | 29.4 | (0.4) | 29.2 | (0.7) | 0.2 | (0.8) |
| Liechtenstein | 70.4 | (1.3) | a | a | a | a | 5.3 | (0.6) | a | a | a | a | 24.3 | (1.0) | a | a | a | a |
| Lithuania | 61.7 | (0.5) | 63.3 | (0.7) | -1.5 | (0.9) | 10.7 | (0.4) | 8.6 | (0.5) | **2.1** | (0.6) | 27.6 | (0.4) | 28.1 | (0.6) | -0.5 | (0.8) |
| Macao-China | 70.9 | (0.7) | 71.5 | (0.4) | -0.7 | (0.9) | 12.2 | (0.5) | 10.9 | (0.3) | **1.3** | (0.7) | 16.9 | (0.5) | 17.6 | (0.3) | -0.7 | (0.6) |
| Montenegro | 52.4 | (0.4) | 54.1 | (0.8) | -1.8 | (1.0) | 11.7 | (0.4) | 10.9 | (0.5) | 0.8 | (0.6) | 35.9 | (0.4) | 34.9 | (0.7) | 1.0 | (0.7) |
| Qatar | 43.9 | (0.4) | 47.6 | (0.6) | **-3.7** | (0.8) | 24.0 | (0.4) | 22.0 | (0.5) | **2.0** | (0.7) | 32.1 | (0.4) | 30.3 | (0.5) | **1.7** | (0.6) |
| Romania | 49.8 | (0.7) | 51.5 | (1.1) | -1.7 | (1.3) | 20.4 | (0.7) | 19.1 | (0.7) | 1.4 | (1.0) | 29.8 | (0.4) | 29.4 | (0.6) | 0.4 | (0.7) |
| Russian Federation | 46.3 | (0.6) | 51.0 | (1.0) | **-4.7** | (1.1) | 17.6 | (0.7) | 14.6 | (0.7) | **3.0** | (0.9) | 36.1 | (0.6) | 34.4 | (0.9) | 1.7 | (0.9) |
| Serbia | 59.2 | (0.5) | 61.6 | (0.7) | **-2.3** | (0.9) | 13.5 | (0.5) | 12.0 | (0.5) | **1.5** | (0.7) | 27.3 | (0.3) | 26.5 | (0.5) | 0.8 | (0.6) |
| Slovenia | 59.2 | (0.5) | 63.6 | (0.6) | **-4.4** | (0.7) | 13.0 | (0.3) | 10.5 | (0.4) | **2.6** | (0.5) | 27.7 | (0.3) | 25.9 | (0.4) | **1.8** | (0.5) |
| Chinese Taipei | 66.3 | (0.7) | 66.0 | (0.4) | 0.3 | (0.8) | 9.1 | (0.5) | 8.8 | (0.4) | 0.3 | (0.7) | 24.6 | (0.4) | 25.2 | (0.3) | -0.7 | (0.5) |
| Thailand | 61.6 | (0.5) | 65.1 | (1.1) | **-3.5** | (1.3) | 8.1 | (0.3) | 5.2 | (0.4) | **3.0** | (0.5) | 30.3 | (0.4) | 29.7 | (1.0) | 0.5 | (1.2) |
| Tunisia | 44.6 | (0.7) | 50.8 | (2.2) | **-6.2** | (2.4) | 24.4 | (0.5) | 19.5 | (1.4) | **4.9** | (1.5) | 31.0 | (0.5) | 29.7 | (1.5) | 1.3 | (1.6) |
| Uruguay | 60.1 | (0.6) | 61.8 | (0.8) | -1.7 | (1.1) | 11.3 | (0.5) | 11.2 | (0.5) | 0.1 | (0.8) | 28.5 | (0.4) | 27.0 | (0.5) | **1.6** | (0.7) |

*Note:* Values that are statistically significant at the 5% level (p < 0.05) are indicated in bold.

### Table 3.13d Mean learning hours and allocation of total learning time in science, in mathematics
[Part 1/3] and on the language of instruction, by school location

| | Mean learning hours per week | | | | | | | | | | | | | | | |
| | Regular school lessons | | | | | | | | Out-of-school-time lessons | | | | | | | |
| | Rural (fewer than 100 000 people) | | City (over 100 000 people) | | Difference (rural-city) | | Difference after accounting for ESCS and school average ESCS (rural-city) | | Rural (fewer than 100 000 people) | | City (over 100 000 people) | | Difference (rural-city) | | Difference after accounting for ESCS and school average ESCS (rural-city) | |
| | Mean | S.E. | Mean | S.E. | Dif. | S.E. | Dif. | S.E. | Mean | S.E. | Mean | S.E. | Dif. | S.E. | Dif. | S.E. |
|---|---|---|---|---|---|---|---|---|---|---|---|---|---|---|---|---|
| **OECD** | | | | | | | | | | | | | | | | |
| Australia | 11.00 | (0.14) | 11.66 | (0.10) | **-0.66** | (0.19) | -0.01 | (0.21) | 1.65 | (0.05) | 1.83 | (0.05) | **-0.18** | (0.07) | **-0.35** | (0.09) |
| Austria | 8.36 | (0.13) | 8.97 | (0.18) | **-0.61** | (0.25) | -0.31 | (0.24) | 0.95 | (0.06) | 0.94 | (0.06) | 0.01 | (0.09) | -0.08 | (0.09) |
| Belgium | 9.48 | (0.12) | 10.49 | (0.36) | **-1.01** | (0.43) | **-1.05** | (0.35) | 1.24 | (0.04) | 1.57 | (0.10) | **-0.33** | (0.11) | **-0.33** | (0.10) |
| Canada | 12.91 | (0.13) | 13.08 | (0.20) | -0.17 | (0.23) | 0.18 | (0.20) | 2.24 | (0.04) | 2.52 | (0.09) | **-0.28** | (0.09) | **-0.32** | (0.10) |
| Czech Republic | 10.53 | (0.13) | 11.14 | (0.27) | -0.62 | (0.32) | 0.14 | (0.35) | 1.93 | (0.05) | 1.69 | (0.10) | **0.24** | (0.11) | 0.18 | (0.12) |
| Denmark | 13.15 | (0.09) | 13.49 | (0.24) | -0.34 | (0.27) | -0.25 | (0.27) | 3.83 | (0.08) | 4.05 | (0.21) | -0.22 | (0.23) | -0.32 | (0.21) |
| Finland | 9.68 | (0.11) | 9.79 | (0.27) | -0.11 | (0.28) | 0.11 | (0.28) | 1.06 | (0.04) | 1.04 | (0.07) | 0.02 | (0.09) | -0.06 | (0.10) |
| France | a | a | 10.71 | (0.10) | a | a | a | a | a | a | 2.24 | (0.04) | a | a | a | a |
| Germany | 10.60 | (0.11) | 10.74 | (0.17) | -0.13 | (0.23) | -0.10 | (0.20) | 1.87 | (0.07) | 2.00 | (0.16) | -0.13 | (0.19) | -0.18 | (0.14) |
| Greece | 9.64 | (0.18) | 10.19 | (0.23) | -0.55 | (0.33) | 0.23 | (0.24) | 5.92 | (0.16) | 5.72 | (0.20) | 0.20 | (0.28) | **0.65** | (0.27) |
| Hungary | 8.86 | (0.15) | 9.16 | (0.20) | -0.30 | (0.27) | **0.46** | (0.23) | 3.67 | (0.09) | 3.49 | (0.10) | 0.18 | (0.13) | 0.02 | (0.13) |
| Iceland | 12.29 | (0.07) | 12.22 | (0.09) | 0.07 | (0.12) | 0.12 | (0.12) | 1.44 | (0.05) | 1.58 | (0.08) | -0.14 | (0.09) | -0.05 | (0.10) |
| Ireland | 9.75 | (0.10) | 9.78 | (0.16) | -0.03 | (0.18) | 0.12 | (0.20) | 1.71 | (0.06) | 1.51 | (0.09) | 0.20 | (0.11) | 0.08 | (0.10) |
| Italy | 11.26 | (0.12) | 11.30 | (0.15) | -0.03 | (0.20) | **0.44** | (0.21) | 2.28 | (0.06) | 2.12 | (0.08) | 0.16 | (0.11) | -0.02 | (0.11) |
| Japan | 10.18 | (0.23) | 11.06 | (0.20) | **-0.88** | (0.34) | 0.18 | (0.29) | 1.37 | (0.10) | 1.41 | (0.07) | -0.03 | (0.12) | 0.04 | (0.13) |
| Korea | 12.08 | (0.36) | 12.87 | (0.12) | **-0.80** | (0.40) | 0.42 | (0.45) | 3.51 | (0.26) | 4.96 | (0.09) | **-1.45** | (0.30) | 0.54 | (0.36) |
| Luxembourg | 9.71 | (0.06) | 9.73 | (0.18) | -0.02 | (0.18) | 0.18 | (0.19) | 1.95 | (0.04) | 1.73 | (0.13) | 0.22 | (0.13) | 0.09 | (0.14) |
| Mexico | 10.39 | (0.15) | 11.26 | (0.15) | **-0.87** | (0.23) | 0.21 | (0.20) | 3.67 | (0.12) | 2.92 | (0.11) | **0.75** | (0.16) | 0.10 | (0.13) |
| Netherlands | 7.93 | (0.08) | 8.07 | (0.21) | -0.14 | (0.24) | 0.10 | (0.22) | 1.87 | (0.06) | 1.92 | (0.13) | -0.06 | (0.15) | **-0.22** | (0.11) |
| New Zealand | 12.69 | (0.13) | 12.96 | (0.12) | -0.27 | (0.19) | 0.20 | (0.16) | 1.58 | (0.10) | 1.88 | (0.07) | **-0.30** | (0.13) | **-0.42** | (0.16) |
| Norway | 9.55 | (0.09) | 9.99 | (0.22) | -0.43 | (0.23) | -0.19 | (0.23) | 3.11 | (0.06) | 3.35 | (0.17) | -0.23 | (0.17) | -0.19 | (0.19) |
| Poland | 11.55 | (0.10) | 12.24 | (0.18) | **-0.70** | (0.20) | -0.37 | (0.24) | 2.11 | (0.06) | 2.10 | (0.09) | 0.01 | (0.11) | -0.15 | (0.12) |
| Portugal | 9.98 | (0.13) | 10.43 | (0.26) | -0.45 | (0.31) | **0.60** | (0.30) | 1.99 | (0.06) | 2.01 | (0.10) | -0.02 | (0.12) | -0.22 | (0.14) |
| Slovak Republic | 8.87 | (0.16) | 8.92 | (0.54) | -0.06 | (0.59) | **0.91** | (0.45) | 2.38 | (0.08) | 2.57 | (0.29) | -0.19 | (0.31) | 0.11 | (0.29) |
| Spain | 9.94 | (0.11) | 10.46 | (0.16) | **-0.51** | (0.19) | -0.06 | (0.16) | 2.37 | (0.07) | 2.05 | (0.10) | **0.32** | (0.13) | **0.27** | (0.13) |
| Sweden | 8.97 | (0.08) | 9.09 | (0.17) | -0.11 | (0.19) | -0.07 | (0.19) | 1.75 | (0.04) | 1.90 | (0.11) | -0.15 | (0.12) | -0.13 | (0.11) |
| Switzerland | 9.91 | (0.09) | 9.98 | (0.40) | -0.06 | (0.42) | 0.50 | (0.44) | 1.61 | (0.05) | 1.39 | (0.16) | 0.21 | (0.17) | -0.06 | (0.15) |
| Turkey | 10.46 | (0.25) | 10.87 | (0.30) | -0.41 | (0.45) | **0.78** | (0.33) | 5.08 | (0.13) | 5.36 | (0.14) | -0.28 | (0.21) | 0.16 | (0.17) |
| United Kingdom | 12.01 | (0.09) | 11.76 | (0.22) | 0.24 | (0.24) | -0.00 | (0.22) | 1.53 | (0.05) | 1.97 | (0.13) | **-0.44** | (0.14) | **-0.32** | (0.12) |
| United States | 11.21 | (0.14) | 10.50 | (0.24) | **0.70** | (0.29) | **0.62** | (0.24) | 2.82 | (0.07) | 3.41 | (0.14) | **-0.59** | (0.16) | **-0.57** | (0.14) |
| **OECD average** | 10.45 | (0.03) | 10.76 | (0.04) | **-0.32** | (0.05) | **0.14** | (0.05) | 2.36 | (0.02) | 2.44 | (0.02) | **-0.09** | (0.03) | **-0.06** | (0.03) |
| **Partners** | | | | | | | | | | | | | | | | |
| Argentina | 7.34 | (0.21) | 8.04 | (0.25) | **-0.70** | (0.34) | -0.06 | (0.23) | 1.73 | (0.09) | 1.56 | (0.11) | 0.17 | (0.15) | 0.10 | (0.16) |
| Azerbaijan | 10.12 | (0.14) | 11.23 | (0.24) | **-1.12** | (0.26) | -0.46 | (0.31) | 4.84 | (0.11) | 4.93 | (0.20) | -0.09 | (0.23) | 0.02 | (0.25) |
| Brazil | 8.15 | (0.14) | 8.90 | (0.14) | **-0.75** | (0.22) | 0.03 | (0.17) | 3.08 | (0.07) | 3.25 | (0.13) | -0.17 | (0.15) | -0.15 | (0.17) |
| Bulgaria | 8.24 | (0.20) | 9.12 | (0.27) | **-0.88** | (0.34) | **0.72** | (0.29) | 3.24 | (0.12) | 3.16 | (0.10) | 0.08 | (0.16) | -0.00 | (0.16) |
| Chile | 8.76 | (0.34) | 9.60 | (0.20) | **-0.83** | (0.42) | **0.78** | (0.35) | 3.11 | (0.10) | 2.60 | (0.06) | **0.51** | (0.11) | **0.41** | (0.13) |
| Colombia | 11.71 | (0.31) | 11.66 | (0.23) | 0.05 | (0.39) | **1.46** | (0.41) | 3.42 | (0.10) | 3.20 | (0.10) | 0.22 | (0.14) | -0.06 | (0.19) |
| Croatia | 8.28 | (0.11) | 8.70 | (0.16) | **-0.42** | (0.20) | 0.45 | (0.24) | 1.55 | (0.06) | 1.62 | (0.08) | -0.07 | (0.10) | -0.12 | (0.12) |
| Estonia | 10.90 | (0.11) | 11.06 | (0.18) | -0.16 | (0.21) | 0.30 | (0.22) | 2.64 | (0.08) | 2.60 | (0.13) | 0.03 | (0.15) | -0.24 | (0.17) |
| Hong Kong-China | a | a | 13.57 | (0.11) | a | a | a | a | a | a | 3.08 | (0.08) | a | a | a | a |
| Indonesia | 10.89 | (0.18) | 11.38 | (0.36) | -0.49 | (0.40) | 0.55 | (0.37) | 3.74 | (0.11) | 3.27 | (0.35) | 0.47 | (0.38) | **0.78** | (0.38) |
| Israel | 9.46 | (0.14) | 9.75 | (0.18) | -0.29 | (0.24) | -0.26 | (0.24) | 4.59 | (0.14) | 4.23 | (0.13) | 0.36 | (0.21) | 0.30 | (0.19) |
| Jordan | 10.03 | (0.19) | 10.86 | (0.24) | **-0.83** | (0.34) | -0.21 | (0.36) | 5.19 | (0.12) | 4.96 | (0.18) | 0.23 | (0.22) | 0.20 | (0.23) |
| Kyrgyzstan | 7.50 | (0.17) | 9.33 | (0.38) | **-1.83** | (0.41) | -0.75 | (0.47) | 4.77 | (0.09) | 3.79 | (0.24) | **0.99** | (0.26) | **0.71** | (0.29) |
| Latvia | 11.03 | (0.13) | 11.12 | (0.21) | -0.09 | (0.26) | 0.29 | (0.28) | 2.75 | (0.11) | 2.65 | (0.08) | 0.10 | (0.13) | -0.05 | (0.12) |
| Liechtenstein | 10.29 | (0.20) | a | a | a | a | a | a | 1.27 | (0.10) | a | a | a | a | a | a |
| Lithuania | 9.64 | (0.12) | 10.17 | (0.16) | **-0.53** | (0.19) | 0.40 | (0.22) | 2.05 | (0.06) | 1.75 | (0.06) | **0.30** | (0.08) | -0.07 | (0.10) |
| Macao-China | 14.04 | (0.17) | 14.55 | (0.08) | **-0.51** | (0.19) | **-0.42** | (0.19) | 3.55 | (0.14) | 3.19 | (0.08) | **0.35** | (0.17) | **0.38** | (0.17) |
| Montenegro | 8.88 | (0.10) | 8.91 | (0.14) | -0.03 | (0.19) | 0.28 | (0.18) | 2.71 | (0.05) | 2.64 | (0.10) | 0.07 | (0.11) | 0.00 | (0.11) |
| Qatar | 8.40 | (0.09) | 9.65 | (0.14) | **-1.25** | (0.16) | **-0.51** | (0.17) | 4.95 | (0.08) | 4.79 | (0.11) | 0.16 | (0.13) | -0.01 | (0.13) |
| Romania | 8.37 | (0.19) | 8.78 | (0.26) | -0.41 | (0.34) | **0.90** | (0.34) | 4.14 | (0.12) | 3.93 | (0.11) | 0.21 | (0.18) | 0.25 | (0.20) |
| Russian Federation | 9.39 | (0.15) | 9.44 | (0.19) | -0.05 | (0.21) | **0.53** | (0.25) | 3.20 | (0.10) | 2.87 | (0.09) | **0.34** | (0.13) | **0.33** | (0.14) |
| Serbia | 9.08 | (0.16) | 9.69 | (0.21) | **-0.61** | (0.30) | 0.37 | (0.23) | 2.71 | (0.07) | 2.58 | (0.09) | 0.13 | (0.11) | 0.09 | (0.12) |
| Slovenia | 9.22 | (0.07) | 9.70 | (0.11) | **-0.48** | (0.12) | 0.22 | (0.13) | 2.62 | (0.06) | 2.23 | (0.07) | **0.39** | (0.10) | **0.25** | (0.10) |
| Chinese Taipei | 11.09 | (0.34) | 11.75 | (0.26) | -0.65 | (0.52) | **1.07** | (0.41) | 2.50 | (0.13) | 3.26 | (0.10) | **-0.75** | (0.20) | -0.31 | (0.17) |
| Thailand | 10.57 | (0.16) | 11.01 | (0.54) | -0.44 | (0.54) | 0.41 | (0.60) | 2.32 | (0.10) | 2.61 | (0.22) | -0.28 | (0.28) | 0.39 | (0.25) |
| Tunisia | 9.11 | (0.13) | 9.61 | (0.45) | -0.51 | (0.50) | 0.66 | (0.41) | 6.16 | (0.07) | 5.89 | (0.17) | 0.27 | (0.19) | **0.35** | (0.13) |
| Uruguay | 8.36 | (0.13) | 8.68 | (0.13) | -0.32 | (0.19) | 0.28 | (0.19) | 2.11 | (0.09) | 2.05 | (0.07) | 0.06 | (0.12) | -0.06 | (0.11) |

*Note:* Values that are statistically significant at the 5% level (p < 0.05) are indicated in bold.

© OECD 2011  Quality Time for Students: Learning In and Out of School

**Table 3.13d** [Part 2/3] **Mean learning hours and allocation of total learning time in science, in mathematics and on the language of instruction, by school location**

| | Individual study | | | | | | | | Total learning hours | | | | | |
| | Rural (fewer than 100 000 people) | | City (over 100 000 people) | | Difference (rural-city) | | Difference after accounting for ESCS and school average ESCS (rural-city) | | Rural (fewer than 100 000 people) | | City (over 100 000 people) | | Difference (rural-city) | |
| | Mean | S.E. | Mean | S.E. | Dif. | S.E. | Dif. | S.E. | Mean | S.E. | Mean | S.E. | Dif. | S.E. |
|---|---|---|---|---|---|---|---|---|---|---|---|---|---|---|
| **OECD** | | | | | | | | | | | | | | |
| Australia | 4.02 | (0.07) | 5.10 | (0.09) | **-1.09** | (0.13) | **-0.67** | (0.13) | 16.70 | (0.18) | 18.59 | (0.18) | **-1.89** | (0.29) |
| Austria | 4.90 | (0.09) | 5.06 | (0.12) | -0.16 | (0.15) | -0.23 | (0.15) | 14.25 | (0.20) | 15.01 | (0.28) | **-0.77** | (0.35) |
| Belgium | 4.32 | (0.07) | 4.63 | (0.18) | -0.31 | (0.20) | **-0.33** | (0.16) | 15.08 | (0.18) | 16.67 | (0.50) | **-1.60** | (0.60) |
| Canada | 4.76 | (0.07) | 6.01 | (0.15) | **-1.25** | (0.18) | **-0.99** | (0.16) | 20.03 | (0.19) | 21.65 | (0.33) | **-1.61** | (0.40) |
| Czech Republic | 3.49 | (0.07) | 3.30 | (0.13) | 0.19 | (0.16) | 0.28 | (0.16) | 15.91 | (0.19) | 16.13 | (0.44) | -0.22 | (0.50) |
| Denmark | 4.95 | (0.07) | 5.22 | (0.18) | -0.26 | (0.20) | -0.18 | (0.21) | 21.88 | (0.19) | 22.70 | (0.41) | -0.82 | (0.50) |
| Finland | 3.39 | (0.06) | 3.46 | (0.11) | -0.07 | (0.12) | -0.04 | (0.13) | 14.13 | (0.16) | 14.28 | (0.34) | -0.15 | (0.35) |
| France | a | a | 4.56 | (0.07) | a | a | a | a | a | a | 17.55 | (0.15) | a | a |
| Germany | 5.86 | (0.10) | 5.78 | (0.13) | 0.08 | (0.16) | 0.09 | (0.16) | 18.39 | (0.19) | 18.52 | (0.26) | -0.14 | (0.32) |
| Greece | 5.83 | (0.11) | 5.73 | (0.15) | 0.10 | (0.19) | **0.44** | (0.17) | 21.41 | (0.38) | 21.68 | (0.44) | -0.28 | (0.66) |
| Hungary | 5.31 | (0.10) | 5.24 | (0.15) | 0.07 | (0.18) | 0.30 | (0.17) | 17.89 | (0.27) | 17.88 | (0.36) | 0.01 | (0.49) |
| Iceland | 4.45 | (0.06) | 4.38 | (0.10) | 0.07 | (0.13) | 0.07 | (0.14) | 18.21 | (0.11) | 18.17 | (0.19) | 0.04 | (0.23) |
| Ireland | 4.70 | (0.09) | 4.74 | (0.13) | -0.03 | (0.17) | 0.05 | (0.18) | 16.14 | (0.18) | 15.99 | (0.29) | 0.15 | (0.34) |
| Italy | 7.57 | (0.10) | 7.44 | (0.14) | 0.13 | (0.17) | **0.82** | (0.18) | 21.13 | (0.22) | 20.90 | (0.26) | 0.22 | (0.34) |
| Japan | 2.88 | (0.16) | 3.23 | (0.13) | -0.35 | (0.21) | 0.21 | (0.19) | 14.45 | (0.32) | 15.69 | (0.32) | **-1.25** | (0.54) |
| Korea | 4.01 | (0.19) | 5.10 | (0.14) | **-1.09** | (0.25) | **0.78** | (0.28) | 19.77 | (0.67) | 22.97 | (0.28) | **-3.20** | (0.77) |
| Luxembourg | 4.36 | (0.05) | 4.02 | (0.15) | **0.34** | (0.16) | **0.33** | (0.16) | 16.03 | (0.10) | 15.46 | (0.32) | 0.57 | (0.35) |
| Mexico | 6.47 | (0.13) | 6.37 | (0.10) | 0.10 | (0.15) | 0.01 | (0.15) | 20.35 | (0.28) | 20.48 | (0.27) | -0.13 | (0.39) |
| Netherlands | 3.87 | (0.06) | 4.34 | (0.13) | **-0.47** | (0.14) | **-0.41** | (0.14) | 13.66 | (0.14) | 14.24 | (0.36) | -0.58 | (0.39) |
| New Zealand | 4.03 | (0.11) | 4.76 | (0.09) | **-0.73** | (0.16) | **-0.39** | (0.15) | 18.33 | (0.24) | 19.62 | (0.19) | **-1.30** | (0.33) |
| Norway | 3.99 | (0.06) | 4.55 | (0.17) | **-0.57** | (0.19) | -0.30 | (0.18) | 16.62 | (0.14) | 17.79 | (0.38) | **-1.16** | (0.42) |
| Poland | 6.36 | (0.08) | 6.27 | (0.13) | 0.08 | (0.15) | 0.14 | (0.17) | 20.04 | (0.16) | 20.64 | (0.25) | **-0.60** | (0.30) |
| Portugal | 5.82 | (0.10) | 5.87 | (0.17) | -0.05 | (0.20) | 0.16 | (0.22) | 17.84 | (0.21) | 18.27 | (0.39) | -0.43 | (0.48) |
| Slovak Republic | 4.83 | (0.09) | 4.71 | (0.36) | 0.12 | (0.38) | 0.64 | (0.36) | 16.12 | (0.26) | 16.20 | (1.12) | -0.09 | (1.20) |
| Spain | 5.47 | (0.10) | 5.76 | (0.13) | -0.29 | (0.15) | -0.14 | (0.16) | 17.91 | (0.22) | 18.34 | (0.23) | -0.42 | (0.30) |
| Sweden | 3.46 | (0.05) | 3.98 | (0.13) | **-0.52** | (0.14) | **-0.45** | (0.14) | 14.17 | (0.12) | 14.97 | (0.32) | **-0.80** | (0.34) |
| Switzerland | 4.21 | (0.04) | 4.22 | (0.12) | -0.00 | (0.13) | -0.03 | (0.13) | 15.75 | (0.12) | 15.57 | (0.51) | 0.18 | (0.52) |
| Turkey | 6.10 | (0.11) | 6.12 | (0.14) | -0.02 | (0.18) | 0.30 | (0.18) | 21.50 | (0.42) | 22.27 | (0.53) | -0.77 | (0.77) |
| United Kingdom | 4.46 | (0.07) | 4.71 | (0.16) | -0.25 | (0.19) | **-0.48** | (0.16) | 18.02 | (0.14) | 18.47 | (0.37) | -0.45 | (0.40) |
| United States | 5.39 | (0.08) | 5.98 | (0.13) | **-0.58** | (0.16) | **-0.62** | (0.14) | 19.61 | (0.18) | 19.88 | (0.30) | -0.27 | (0.35) |
| **OECD average** | 4.80 | (0.02) | 5.02 | (0.03) | **-0.23** | (0.03) | -0.02 | (0.03) | 17.63 | (0.05) | 18.22 | (0.07) | **-0.61** | (0.09) |
| **Partners** | | | | | | | | | | | | | | |
| Argentina | 5.01 | (0.13) | 5.08 | (0.15) | -0.06 | (0.19) | 0.04 | (0.19) | 14.06 | (0.30) | 14.70 | (0.36) | -0.64 | (0.48) |
| Azerbaijan | 8.66 | (0.15) | 8.86 | (0.26) | -0.20 | (0.30) | 0.06 | (0.40) | 23.78 | (0.30) | 25.14 | (0.57) | **-1.36** | (0.63) |
| Brazil | 5.21 | (0.10) | 5.23 | (0.11) | -0.02 | (0.16) | 0.06 | (0.16) | 16.40 | (0.24) | 17.35 | (0.31) | **-0.95** | (0.42) |
| Bulgaria | 5.88 | (0.17) | 6.63 | (0.31) | **-0.75** | (0.35) | 0.53 | (0.28) | 17.40 | (0.41) | 19.04 | (0.56) | **-1.64** | (0.70) |
| Chile | 4.87 | (0.13) | 4.55 | (0.09) | **0.33** | (0.16) | **0.51** | (0.19) | 16.80 | (0.49) | 16.85 | (0.27) | -0.05 | (0.58) |
| Colombia | 5.62 | (0.15) | 5.52 | (0.12) | 0.10 | (0.19) | 0.25 | (0.25) | 20.75 | (0.45) | 20.37 | (0.30) | 0.39 | (0.54) |
| Croatia | 4.85 | (0.08) | 4.87 | (0.14) | -0.02 | (0.16) | **0.51** | (0.19) | 14.74 | (0.18) | 15.29 | (0.28) | -0.55 | (0.35) |
| Estonia | 4.97 | (0.08) | 5.50 | (0.11) | **-0.53** | (0.13) | **-0.50** | (0.15) | 18.54 | (0.16) | 19.15 | (0.27) | -0.61 | (0.31) |
| Hong Kong-China | a | a | 5.33 | (0.08) | a | a | a | a | a | a | 21.98 | (0.21) | a | a |
| Indonesia | 5.67 | (0.10) | 5.12 | (0.30) | 0.55 | (0.34) | **0.71** | (0.34) | 20.24 | (0.31) | 19.74 | (0.67) | 0.51 | (0.79) |
| Israel | 5.45 | (0.16) | 5.19 | (0.17) | 0.26 | (0.25) | 0.20 | (0.24) | 19.50 | (0.35) | 19.37 | (0.38) | 0.13 | (0.53) |
| Jordan | 7.98 | (0.15) | 7.80 | (0.17) | 0.18 | (0.23) | 0.21 | (0.25) | 23.20 | (0.32) | 23.55 | (0.32) | -0.35 | (0.48) |
| Kyrgyzstan | 6.74 | (0.10) | 6.49 | (0.22) | 0.25 | (0.24) | 0.11 | (0.27) | 19.16 | (0.27) | 19.77 | (0.58) | -0.60 | (0.64) |
| Latvia | 6.32 | (0.10) | 6.10 | (0.16) | 0.21 | (0.20) | 0.32 | (0.24) | 20.10 | (0.24) | 19.87 | (0.37) | 0.23 | (0.47) |
| Liechtenstein | 3.93 | (0.15) | a | a | a | a | a | a | 15.50 | (0.24) | a | a | a | a |
| Lithuania | 5.22 | (0.08) | 5.35 | (0.13) | -0.13 | (0.16) | 0.23 | (0.20) | 16.86 | (0.18) | 17.31 | (0.24) | -0.45 | (0.30) |
| Macao-China | 4.68 | (0.12) | 4.98 | (0.08) | **-0.30** | (0.14) | -0.02 | (0.14) | 22.27 | (0.27) | 22.71 | (0.17) | -0.44 | (0.32) |
| Montenegro | 6.24 | (0.09) | 6.12 | (0.14) | 0.13 | (0.16) | 0.24 | (0.16) | 17.81 | (0.18) | 17.59 | (0.28) | 0.22 | (0.32) |
| Qatar | 6.26 | (0.07) | 6.47 | (0.12) | -0.22 | (0.14) | -0.12 | (0.15) | 19.65 | (0.19) | 20.92 | (0.29) | **-1.27** | (0.33) |
| Romania | 5.86 | (0.14) | 6.06 | (0.18) | -0.20 | (0.25) | 0.41 | (0.29) | 18.40 | (0.37) | 18.74 | (0.44) | -0.33 | (0.64) |
| Russian Federation | 6.91 | (0.16) | 6.27 | (0.14) | **0.64** | (0.19) | **1.15** | (0.20) | 19.47 | (0.31) | 18.62 | (0.30) | **0.85** | (0.40) |
| Serbia | 5.15 | (0.11) | 5.34 | (0.13) | -0.20 | (0.18) | **0.34** | (0.16) | 16.93 | (0.28) | 17.57 | (0.34) | -0.64 | (0.50) |
| Slovenia | 5.04 | (0.06) | 4.77 | (0.09) | **0.27** | (0.10) | **0.45** | (0.11) | 16.95 | (0.14) | 16.71 | (0.20) | 0.24 | (0.23) |
| Chinese Taipei | 4.44 | (0.16) | 5.11 | (0.13) | **-0.67** | (0.24) | 0.26 | (0.22) | 18.15 | (0.58) | 20.25 | (0.45) | **-2.10** | (0.89) |
| Thailand | 5.40 | (0.12) | 5.08 | (0.21) | 0.32 | (0.29) | 0.59 | (0.34) | 18.26 | (0.31) | 18.69 | (0.77) | -0.43 | (1.03) |
| Tunisia | 7.37 | (0.10) | 6.96 | (0.19) | 0.40 | (0.22) | **0.44** | (0.22) | 22.69 | (0.24) | 22.52 | (0.73) | 0.17 | (0.82) |
| Uruguay | 4.29 | (0.09) | 4.16 | (0.08) | 0.14 | (0.13) | **0.33** | (0.13) | 14.78 | (0.22) | 14.95 | (0.19) | -0.16 | (0.30) |

*Note*: Values that are statistically significant at the 5% level (p < 0.05) are indicated in bold.

### Table 3.13d Mean learning hours and allocation of total learning time in science, in mathematics
[Part 3/3] and on the language of instruction, by school location

| | Allocation of total learning time in science, in mathematics and on the language of instruction for | | | | | | | | | | | | | | | | | |
| | Regular school lessons | | | | | | Out-of-school-time lessons | | | | | | Individual study | | | | | |
| | Rural (fewer than 100 000 people) | | City (over 100 000 people) | | Difference (rural-city) | | Rural (fewer than 100 000 people) | | City (over 100 000 people) | | Difference (rural-city) | | Rural (fewer than 100 000 people) | | City (over 100 000 people) | | Difference (rural-city) | |
| | % | S.E | % | S.E | Dif. | S.E. | % | S.E | % | S.E | Dif. | S.E. | % | S.E | % | S.E | Dif. | S.E. |
|---|---|---|---|---|---|---|---|---|---|---|---|---|---|---|---|---|---|---|
| Australia | 68.3 | (0.5) | 65.4 | (0.3) | **2.8** | (0.6) | 8.8 | (0.3) | 8.6 | (0.2) | 0.2 | (0.4) | 23.0 | (0.3) | 26.0 | (0.3) | **-3.0** | (0.5) |
| Austria | 61.6 | (0.5) | 62.4 | (0.6) | -0.7 | (0.9) | 5.5 | (0.3) | 5.1 | (0.3) | 0.4 | (0.4) | 32.9 | (0.4) | 32.5 | (0.5) | 0.3 | (0.7) |
| Belgium | 64.4 | (0.3) | 63.9 | (0.6) | 0.5 | (0.7) | 7.5 | (0.2) | 8.7 | (0.6) | -1.2 | (0.7) | 28.1 | (0.2) | 27.4 | (0.5) | 0.7 | (0.5) |
| Canada | 65.7 | (0.3) | 61.6 | (0.5) | **4.1** | (0.5) | 10.8 | (0.2) | 11.2 | (0.4) | -0.4 | (0.4) | 23.5 | (0.2) | 27.2 | (0.4) | **-3.7** | (0.5) |
| Czech Republic | 69.1 | (0.5) | 71.9 | (0.6) | **-2.8** | (0.8) | 10.5 | (0.2) | 9.0 | (0.4) | **1.5** | (0.5) | 20.5 | (0.4) | 19.1 | (0.5) | **1.3** | (0.7) |
| Denmark | 62.5 | (0.3) | 61.7 | (1.0) | 0.8 | (1.0) | 15.9 | (0.3) | 16.2 | (0.7) | -0.2 | (0.8) | 21.5 | (0.2) | 22.1 | (0.6) | -0.6 | (0.6) |
| Finland | 70.5 | (0.3) | 70.4 | (0.8) | 0.1 | (0.9) | 6.5 | (0.2) | 6.1 | (0.4) | 0.4 | (0.5) | 23.0 | (0.2) | 23.5 | (0.5) | -0.5 | (0.6) |
| France | a | a | 63.4 | (0.3) | a | a | a | a | 12.1 | (0.2) | a | a | a | a | 24.5 | (0.3) | a | a |
| Germany | 59.5 | (0.4) | 60.0 | (1.0) | -0.5 | (1.1) | 9.1 | (0.4) | 9.7 | (0.7) | -0.6 | (0.9) | 31.4 | (0.3) | 30.3 | (0.5) | 1.1 | (0.6) |
| Greece | 47.2 | (0.5) | 49.5 | (0.9) | **-2.3** | (1.0) | 26.1 | (0.4) | 25.1 | (0.7) | 1.0 | (0.9) | 26.7 | (0.4) | 25.4 | (0.5) | **1.3** | (0.5) |
| Hungary | 51.5 | (0.5) | 53.6 | (0.6) | **-2.1** | (0.8) | 19.4 | (0.4) | 17.9 | (0.4) | **1.5** | (0.6) | 29.1 | (0.3) | 28.5 | (0.4) | 0.6 | (0.5) |
| Iceland | 69.9 | (0.4) | 69.3 | (0.5) | 0.6 | (0.6) | 7.0 | (0.2) | 7.8 | (0.3) | **-0.9** | (0.4) | 23.1 | (0.2) | 22.9 | (0.4) | 0.3 | (0.4) |
| Ireland | 63.2 | (0.5) | 64.1 | (0.7) | -0.9 | (0.8) | 9.1 | (0.3) | 7.6 | (0.3) | **1.5** | (0.5) | 27.7 | (0.4) | 28.3 | (0.6) | -0.6 | (0.7) |
| Italy | 54.6 | (0.3) | 55.7 | (0.4) | **-1.1** | (0.5) | 10.1 | (0.2) | 9.4 | (0.3) | 0.7 | (0.5) | 35.3 | (0.2) | 34.9 | (0.4) | 0.4 | (0.4) |
| Japan | 74.8 | (0.8) | 74.4 | (0.5) | 0.4 | (0.9) | 7.5 | (0.4) | 7.4 | (0.3) | 0.1 | (0.6) | 17.7 | (0.6) | 18.2 | (0.5) | -0.5 | (0.7) |
| Korea | 66.2 | (1.2) | 60.5 | (0.5) | **5.7** | (1.4) | 15.1 | (1.0) | 19.0 | (0.3) | **-3.8** | (1.1) | 18.7 | (0.6) | 20.5 | (0.4) | **-1.9** | (0.7) |
| Luxembourg | 63.1 | (0.3) | 64.5 | (0.9) | -1.4 | (0.9) | 10.8 | (0.2) | 10.0 | (0.6) | 0.8 | (0.6) | 26.1 | (0.2) | 25.5 | (0.6) | 0.6 | (0.6) |
| Mexico | 51.3 | (0.6) | 55.9 | (0.5) | **-4.6** | (0.8) | 16.4 | (0.4) | 13.2 | (0.4) | **3.3** | (0.6) | 32.3 | (0.4) | 30.9 | (0.4) | **1.4** | (0.5) |
| Netherlands | 60.4 | (0.5) | 58.9 | (0.8) | 1.5 | (0.9) | 12.5 | (0.4) | 11.7 | (0.7) | 0.8 | (0.9) | 27.2 | (0.3) | 29.4 | (0.6) | **-2.2** | (0.7) |
| New Zealand | 71.5 | (0.6) | 68.2 | (0.5) | **3.3** | (0.8) | 7.7 | (0.4) | 8.7 | (0.3) | -1.0 | (0.5) | 20.8 | (0.3) | 23.2 | (0.3) | **-2.3** | (0.5) |
| Norway | 60.6 | (0.4) | 58.5 | (1.0) | 2.1 | (1.0) | 17.0 | (0.3) | 17.4 | (0.9) | -0.4 | (0.9) | 22.4 | (0.3) | 24.1 | (0.6) | **-1.6** | (0.7) |
| Poland | 59.5 | (0.3) | 61.0 | (0.5) | **-1.5** | (0.6) | 10.1 | (0.4) | 9.9 | (0.5) | 0.3 | (0.5) | 30.3 | (0.3) | 29.1 | (0.5) | 1.2 | (0.6) |
| Portugal | 58.0 | (0.5) | 59.3 | (0.7) | -1.3 | (0.9) | 10.3 | (0.3) | 10.0 | (0.4) | 0.4 | (0.6) | 31.7 | (0.4) | 30.8 | (0.7) | 0.9 | (0.7) |
| Slovak Republic | 58.8 | (0.5) | 59.2 | (1.2) | -0.4 | (1.3) | 12.7 | (0.4) | 13.4 | (0.8) | -0.7 | (0.8) | 28.5 | (0.3) | 27.4 | (0.8) | 1.1 | (0.9) |
| Spain | 58.7 | (0.4) | 59.6 | (0.6) | -0.9 | (0.8) | 11.9 | (0.3) | 10.2 | (0.5) | **1.6** | (0.6) | 29.5 | (0.3) | 30.2 | (0.4) | -0.7 | (0.5) |
| Sweden | 66.8 | (0.5) | 64.0 | (0.8) | **2.8** | (0.9) | 10.2 | (0.2) | 10.4 | (0.4) | -0.2 | (0.5) | 23.0 | (0.4) | 25.6 | (0.6) | **-2.6** | (0.7) |
| Switzerland | 64.2 | (0.4) | 65.0 | (1.0) | -0.9 | (1.1) | 9.1 | (0.2) | 7.7 | (0.7) | 1.3 | (0.8) | 26.8 | (0.2) | 27.3 | (0.8) | -0.5 | (0.9) |
| Turkey | 51.3 | (0.5) | 51.6 | (0.5) | 0.3 | (0.7) | 21.5 | (0.4) | 21.8 | (0.3) | -0.3 | (0.6) | 27.2 | (0.4) | 26.6 | (0.4) | 0.7 | (0.5) |
| United Kingdom | 68.7 | (0.3) | 66.1 | (0.7) | **2.6** | (0.8) | 7.5 | (0.2) | 9.2 | (0.6) | **-1.7** | (0.7) | 23.8 | (0.3) | 24.7 | (0.5) | -0.9 | (0.6) |
| United States | 57.4 | (0.4) | 52.2 | (1.0) | **5.2** | (1.1) | 14.2 | (0.3) | 17.2 | (0.8) | **-3.0** | (0.9) | 28.4 | (0.4) | 30.6 | (0.4) | **-2.2** | (0.5) |
| **OECD average** | **62.0** | **(0.1)** | **61.7** | **(0.1)** | **0.4** | **(0.2)** | **11.7** | **(0.1)** | **11.7** | **(0.1)** | **0.0** | **(0.1)** | **26.2** | **(0.1)** | **26.6** | **(0.1)** | **-0.4** | **(0.1)** |
| Argentina | 53.7 | (0.7) | 55.6 | (0.9) | -1.9 | (1.1) | 11.1 | (0.5) | 9.7 | (0.5) | **1.4** | (0.7) | 35.2 | (0.4) | 34.7 | (0.6) | 0.4 | (0.8) |
| Azerbaijan | 43.9 | (0.6) | 46.2 | (0.9) | **-2.4** | (1.0) | 19.8 | (0.4) | 19.3 | (0.6) | 0.6 | (0.7) | 36.3 | (0.4) | 34.5 | (0.5) | **1.8** | (0.7) |
| Brazil | 52.4 | (0.5) | 53.8 | (0.6) | -1.4 | (0.8) | 17.1 | (0.3) | 17.1 | (0.5) | 0.0 | (0.6) | 30.5 | (0.4) | 29.1 | (0.3) | **1.4** | (0.5) |
| Bulgaria | 49.7 | (0.7) | 50.5 | (0.6) | -0.7 | (0.9) | 17.7 | (0.5) | 15.4 | (0.7) | **2.2** | (0.9) | 32.6 | (0.5) | 34.1 | (0.6) | **-1.5** | (0.7) |
| Chile | 51.8 | (0.9) | 56.4 | (0.5) | **-4.6** | (1.1) | 18.1 | (0.5) | 15.2 | (0.4) | **2.9** | (0.7) | 30.1 | (0.5) | 28.4 | (0.4) | **1.7** | (0.7) |
| Colombia | 59.3 | (0.7) | 59.9 | (0.8) | -0.7 | (1.1) | 15.0 | (0.4) | 13.9 | (0.4) | 1.1 | (0.6) | 25.8 | (0.4) | 26.2 | (0.5) | -0.4 | (0.8) |
| Croatia | 59.6 | (0.4) | 60.4 | (0.7) | -0.8 | (0.9) | 9.6 | (0.4) | 9.7 | (0.4) | -0.1 | (0.5) | 30.8 | (0.3) | 29.9 | (0.6) | 0.9 | (0.7) |
| Estonia | 61.4 | (0.5) | 59.5 | (0.7) | 1.8 | (0.8) | 13.3 | (0.4) | 13.0 | (0.6) | 0.3 | (0.7) | 25.3 | (0.3) | 27.4 | (0.4) | **-2.2** | (0.5) |
| Hong Kong-China | a | a | 64.1 | (0.4) | a | a | a | a | 12.9 | (0.3) | a | a | a | a | 22.9 | (0.2) | a | a |
| Indonesia | 55.3 | (0.5) | 59.2 | (2.1) | -3.9 | (2.2) | 16.9 | (0.4) | 15.0 | (1.3) | 1.9 | (1.3) | 27.8 | (0.4) | 25.8 | (1.0) | 2.0 | (1.1) |
| Israel | 51.3 | (0.8) | 53.5 | (0.9) | -2.1 | (1.4) | 22.1 | (0.4) | 21.0 | (0.4) | 1.2 | (0.7) | 26.5 | (0.6) | 25.5 | (0.6) | 1.0 | (0.9) |
| Jordan | 42.4 | (0.7) | 45.3 | (0.9) | **-2.9** | (1.2) | 22.6 | (0.5) | 20.9 | (0.7) | 1.7 | (1.0) | 35.0 | (0.4) | 33.8 | (0.6) | 1.2 | (0.7) |
| Kyrgyzstan | 38.1 | (0.5) | 49.1 | (1.4) | **-10.9** | (1.5) | 26.5 | (0.5) | 18.7 | (1.0) | **7.8** | (1.2) | 35.3 | (0.3) | 32.2 | (0.9) | **3.1** | (0.9) |
| Latvia | 57.0 | (0.4) | 58.1 | (0.6) | -1.1 | (0.7) | 12.8 | (0.4) | 12.5 | (0.3) | 0.3 | (0.6) | 30.2 | (0.3) | 29.4 | (0.4) | 0.9 | (0.5) |
| Liechtenstein | 66.7 | (1.1) | a | a | a | a | 7.9 | (0.6) | a | a | a | a | 25.4 | (0.9) | a | a | a | a |
| Lithuania | 58.9 | (0.4) | 60.4 | (0.5) | **-1.5** | (0.7) | 11.8 | (0.3) | 10.0 | (0.4) | **1.8** | (0.5) | 29.2 | (0.3) | 29.5 | (0.5) | -0.3 | (0.6) |
| Macao-China | 66.0 | (0.7) | 66.8 | (0.3) | -0.9 | (0.8) | 14.2 | (0.5) | 12.6 | (0.3) | **1.7** | (0.6) | 19.8 | (0.5) | 20.6 | (0.3) | -0.8 | (0.5) |
| Montenegro | 50.3 | (0.3) | 51.7 | (0.6) | **-1.4** | (0.7) | 14.6 | (0.3) | 14.4 | (0.3) | 0.2 | (0.6) | 35.1 | (0.3) | 33.8 | (0.5) | **1.2** | (0.6) |
| Qatar | 42.6 | (0.3) | 45.4 | (0.5) | **-2.8** | (0.6) | 25.0 | (0.3) | 23.1 | (0.4) | **1.8** | (0.5) | 32.5 | (0.2) | 31.5 | (0.4) | **1.0** | (0.5) |
| Romania | 47.8 | (0.5) | 49.5 | (0.8) | -1.7 | (1.0) | 21.2 | (0.5) | 19.8 | (0.6) | 1.4 | (0.8) | 31.0 | (0.3) | 30.7 | (0.4) | 0.3 | (0.6) |
| Russian Federation | 49.4 | (0.5) | 53.0 | (0.7) | **-3.6** | (0.8) | 16.4 | (0.6) | 14.7 | (0.6) | **1.7** | (0.7) | 34.2 | (0.5) | 32.4 | (0.6) | **1.8** | (0.7) |
| Serbia | 57.3 | (0.4) | 58.4 | (0.6) | -1.1 | (0.7) | 14.2 | (0.4) | 13.2 | (0.5) | 1.0 | (0.6) | 28.5 | (0.3) | 28.4 | (0.4) | 0.1 | (0.5) |
| Slovenia | 55.8 | (0.3) | 58.8 | (0.5) | **-3.0** | (0.6) | 14.6 | (0.2) | 12.7 | (0.3) | **1.9** | (0.4) | 29.6 | (0.3) | 28.4 | (0.3) | **1.1** | (0.4) |
| Chinese Taipei | 63.3 | (0.7) | 60.5 | (0.4) | **2.8** | (0.9) | 12.5 | (0.5) | 14.7 | (0.3) | **-2.2** | (0.7) | 24.2 | (0.4) | 24.8 | (0.3) | -0.5 | (0.5) |
| Thailand | 62.0 | (0.4) | 63.0 | (0.6) | -1.0 | (0.7) | 10.1 | (0.4) | 10.7 | (0.7) | -0.6 | (0.9) | 27.9 | (0.3) | 26.3 | (0.6) | **1.5** | (0.7) |
| Tunisia | 41.0 | (0.3) | 43.2 | (1.1) | -2.2 | (1.2) | 26.6 | (0.2) | 25.6 | (0.5) | 1.1 | (0.6) | 32.4 | (0.3) | 31.2 | (0.8) | 1.1 | (0.9) |
| Uruguay | 58.9 | (0.5) | 59.7 | (0.5) | -0.8 | (0.8) | 12.6 | (0.4) | 12.6 | (0.3) | -0.0 | (0.6) | 28.6 | (0.4) | 27.7 | (0.4) | 0.9 | (0.5) |

*Note:* Values that are statistically significant at the 5% level (p < 0.05) are indicated in bold.

208

[Part 1/3]
## Table 3.14 Percentage of students by different types of out-of-school-time lessons, by gender

| | Proportion of students participating in out-of-school-time lessons | | | | | | Proportion of students participating in out-of-school lessons with non-school teachers | | | | | | | | | | | |
| | | | | | | | One-to-one lessons | | | | | | Small group lessons | | | | | |
| | Male students | | Female students | | Difference (male-female) | | Male students | | Female students | | Difference (male-female) | | Male students | | Female students | | Difference (male-female) | |
| | % | S.E. | % | S.E. | Dif. | S.E. | % | S.E. | % | S.E. | Dif. | S.E. | % | S.E. | % | S.E. | Dif. | S.E. |
|---|---|---|---|---|---|---|---|---|---|---|---|---|---|---|---|---|---|---|
| Australia | 32.0 | (0.8) | 30.4 | (0.8) | 1.6 | (1.0) | 16.0 | (0.6) | 17.2 | (0.6) | -1.2 | (0.9) | 8.6 | (0.5) | 7.6 | (0.4) | 1.0 | 0.6 |
| Austria | 36.1 | (1.4) | 36.4 | (1.4) | -0.3 | (1.6) | 16.1 | (0.9) | 17.4 | (1.1) | -1.3 | (1.3) | 9.2 | (0.7) | 6.2 | (0.7) | **2.9** | 0.8 |
| Belgium | 29.9 | (0.8) | 30.9 | (0.9) | -1.0 | (1.2) | 16.1 | (0.7) | 19.6 | (0.9) | **-3.5** | (1.1) | 7.9 | (0.5) | 6.8 | (0.5) | 1.1 | 0.7 |
| Canada | 34.0 | (1.0) | 37.7 | (0.8) | **-3.7** | (1.1) | 15.3 | (0.6) | 17.6 | (0.6) | **-2.3** | (0.8) | 8.8 | (0.5) | 8.1 | (0.4) | 0.7 | 0.6 |
| Czech Republic | 36.0 | (1.3) | 39.0 | (1.2) | -3.1 | (1.6) | 14.4 | (0.8) | 17.8 | (1.0) | **-3.3** | (1.1) | 8.0 | (0.6) | 7.8 | (0.9) | 0.2 | 1.0 |
| Denmark | 21.5 | (0.9) | 19.7 | (1.1) | 1.8 | (1.2) | 5.2 | (0.5) | 5.5 | (0.5) | -0.2 | (0.6) | 4.8 | (0.6) | 4.4 | (0.4) | 0.4 | 0.7 |
| Finland | 23.5 | (1.0) | 23.5 | (0.9) | 0.0 | (1.3) | 5.9 | (0.6) | 4.8 | (0.5) | 1.1 | (0.8) | 3.2 | (0.3) | 1.7 | (0.3) | **1.5** | 0.4 |
| France | 40.6 | (1.3) | 42.6 | (1.1) | -1.9 | (1.6) | 20.8 | (1.2) | 23.8 | (1.0) | **-3.0** | (1.2) | 9.4 | (0.7) | 8.9 | (0.7) | 0.6 | 0.8 |
| Germany | 37.4 | (1.1) | 36.7 | (1.0) | 0.7 | (1.6) | 20.7 | (1.0) | 22.3 | (0.8) | -1.5 | (1.3) | 8.3 | (0.6) | 6.3 | (0.5) | **2.0** | 0.8 |
| Greece | 73.3 | (1.3) | 79.5 | (1.1) | **-6.3** | (1.6) | 42.1 | (1.3) | 47.5 | (1.5) | **-5.5** | (1.7) | 41.8 | (1.4) | 50.1 | (1.7) | **-8.3** | 1.5 |
| Hungary | 50.3 | (1.4) | 58.4 | (1.3) | **-8.1** | (1.7) | 27.6 | (1.2) | 37.8 | (1.3) | **-10.2** | (1.6) | 10.5 | (0.8) | 11.2 | (0.8) | -0.7 | 1.1 |
| Iceland | 37.3 | (1.2) | 43.4 | (1.0) | **-6.2** | (1.5) | 13.4 | (0.8) | 16.0 | (0.9) | **-2.6** | (1.2) | 7.2 | (0.6) | 6.2 | (0.5) | 1.0 | 0.7 |
| Ireland | 38.1 | (1.2) | 38.2 | (1.1) | -0.1 | (1.4) | 19.8 | (1.0) | 23.0 | (1.0) | **-3.3** | (1.4) | 9.1 | (0.8) | 10.4 | (0.7) | -1.3 | 1.1 |
| Italy | 67.1 | (0.8) | 65.8 | (1.0) | 1.2 | (1.4) | 37.7 | (0.9) | 36.8 | (0.8) | 0.9 | (1.2) | 15.7 | (0.7) | 12.6 | (0.5) | **3.1** | 0.7 |
| Japan | 47.0 | (1.6) | 44.3 | (1.7) | 2.7 | (1.8) | 9.0 | (0.6) | 9.8 | (0.9) | -0.8 | (0.9) | 9.1 | (0.6) | 7.8 | (0.8) | 1.4 | 0.8 |
| Korea | 77.2 | (1.4) | 81.2 | (1.2) | **-4.0** | (1.8) | 29.0 | (1.2) | 33.7 | (1.1) | **-4.7** | (1.7) | 29.5 | (1.4) | 33.1 | (1.1) | **-3.6** | 1.8 |
| Luxembourg | 43.0 | (0.9) | 44.7 | (1.0) | -1.7 | (1.4) | 22.0 | (0.9) | 24.2 | (0.8) | -2.2 | (1.2) | 8.5 | (0.7) | 5.6 | (0.5) | **2.9** | 0.8 |
| Mexico | 50.2 | (1.2) | 45.3 | (1.1) | **4.9** | (1.5) | 18.9 | (0.8) | 17.0 | (0.8) | 1.9 | (1.0) | 18.2 | (0.8) | 14.4 | (0.7) | **3.8** | 0.9 |
| Netherlands | 21.5 | (1.1) | 22.7 | (1.0) | -1.3 | (1.3) | 7.2 | (0.6) | 7.6 | (0.6) | -0.5 | (0.8) | 4.5 | (0.6) | 2.6 | (0.3) | **1.9** | 0.6 |
| New Zealand | 33.6 | (1.2) | 33.9 | (1.3) | -0.3 | (1.8) | 17.0 | (0.9) | 17.3 | (0.8) | -0.3 | (1.1) | 10.8 | (0.7) | 9.0 | (0.7) | 1.8 | 1.0 |
| Norway | 31.1 | (1.2) | 23.4 | (1.0) | **7.7** | (1.3) | 7.2 | (0.7) | 3.4 | (0.4) | **3.8** | (0.7) | 7.0 | (0.6) | 2.7 | (0.4) | **4.4** | 0.7 |
| Poland | 54.8 | (1.2) | 57.5 | (1.3) | -2.7 | (1.4) | 19.6 | (0.9) | 19.1 | (0.9) | 0.5 | (0.9) | 11.4 | (0.7) | 9.9 | (0.7) | 1.5 | 0.8 |
| Portugal | 67.8 | (1.3) | 69.7 | (1.3) | -1.9 | (1.8) | 26.1 | (1.2) | 27.1 | (1.1) | -1.0 | (1.5) | 14.6 | (0.9) | 14.7 | (1.0) | -0.1 | 1.2 |
| Slovak Republic | 52.2 | (1.3) | 59.4 | (1.8) | **-7.2** | (1.8) | 22.9 | (1.2) | 28.3 | (1.3) | **-5.4** | (1.5) | 11.5 | (0.7) | 10.9 | (0.6) | 0.6 | 0.9 |
| Spain | 52.6 | (0.9) | 55.2 | (0.9) | **-2.6** | (1.0) | 26.6 | (0.9) | 30.7 | (1.0) | **-4.1** | (1.1) | 24.0 | (0.8) | 28.3 | (0.9) | **-4.3** | 1.1 |
| Sweden | 35.4 | (1.3) | 28.3 | (1.0) | **7.1** | (1.7) | 7.9 | (0.5) | 7.0 | (0.6) | 0.9 | (0.7) | 7.0 | (0.6) | 4.5 | (0.4) | **2.6** | 0.7 |
| Switzerland | 39.0 | (1.0) | 41.1 | (0.7) | -2.2 | (1.2) | 18.1 | (0.7) | 21.7 | (0.8) | **-3.6** | (1.0) | 6.8 | (0.6) | 5.8 | (0.4) | 1.1 | 0.6 |
| Turkey | 37.4 | (1.4) | 36.3 | (1.5) | 1.1 | (1.8) | 13.5 | (0.8) | 13.4 | (0.9) | 0.1 | (1.1) | 11.8 | (0.7) | 9.9 | (0.8) | 1.9 | 1.0 |
| United Kingdom | 43.3 | (1.2) | 47.8 | (1.0) | **-4.5** | (1.4) | 16.2 | (0.7) | 18.5 | (0.8) | **-2.3** | (1.0) | 8.0 | (0.7) | 6.9 | (0.6) | 1.1 | 0.8 |
| United States | 42.4 | (1.5) | 42.2 | (1.3) | 0.1 | (1.6) | 17.0 | (1.0) | 17.7 | (0.9) | -0.7 | (1.1) | 13.3 | (0.9) | 11.8 | (1.0) | 1.5 | 1.0 |
| **OECD average** | 42.8 | (0.2) | 43.8 | (0.2) | **-1.0** | (0.3) | 18.3 | (0.2) | 20.1 | (0.2) | **-1.8** | (0.2) | 11.6 | (0.1) | 10.9 | (0.1) | **0.8** | 0.2 |
| Argentina | 47.8 | (1.5) | 49.1 | (1.5) | -1.3 | (1.7) | 28.3 | (1.5) | 33.6 | (1.5) | **-5.3** | (1.7) | 18.9 | (1.2) | 19.4 | (1.2) | -0.5 | 1.5 |
| Azerbaijan | 78.9 | (1.5) | 80.2 | (1.2) | -1.4 | (1.4) | 32.8 | (1.7) | 28.3 | (1.1) | **4.5** | (1.9) | 42.4 | (1.5) | 39.0 | (1.5) | 3.4 | 2.0 |
| Brazil | 49.5 | (1.2) | 47.5 | (1.2) | 2.0 | (1.6) | 19.6 | (0.9) | 19.8 | (0.8) | -0.2 | (1.2) | 18.2 | (0.8) | 17.5 | (0.7) | 0.7 | 1.0 |
| Bulgaria | 55.2 | (1.6) | 53.2 | (1.7) | 2.0 | (1.7) | 26.4 | (1.2) | 27.4 | (1.2) | -1.0 | (1.6) | 20.9 | (1.3) | 14.0 | (1.0) | **6.8** | 1.4 |
| Chile | 38.3 | (1.5) | 38.2 | (1.5) | 0.1 | (1.7) | 12.4 | (0.8) | 14.4 | (1.2) | -2.0 | (1.3) | 9.8 | (0.8) | 8.9 | (0.7) | 0.9 | 1.2 |
| Colombia | 51.1 | (1.4) | 50.8 | (1.4) | 0.3 | (1.7) | 23.2 | (1.2) | 27.3 | (1.1) | **-4.1** | (1.9) | 16.6 | (1.1) | 18.8 | (1.1) | -2.1 | 1.5 |
| Croatia | 44.6 | (1.2) | 46.2 | (1.3) | -1.6 | (1.7) | 24.6 | (0.9) | 31.1 | (1.1) | **-6.5** | (1.3) | 10.3 | (0.8) | 9.2 | (0.6) | 1.1 | 1.0 |
| Estonia | 43.9 | (1.5) | 48.3 | (1.3) | **-4.4** | (2.1) | 15.4 | (0.8) | 19.2 | (1.0) | **-3.8** | (1.2) | 8.0 | (0.7) | 8.3 | (0.7) | -0.3 | 1.0 |
| Hong Kong-China | 74.6 | (1.1) | 76.1 | (1.3) | -1.5 | (1.5) | 23.2 | (1.3) | 25.0 | (1.8) | -1.8 | (1.9) | 19.4 | (1.2) | 16.3 | (0.8) | **3.1** | 1.4 |
| Indonesia | 64.1 | (3.5) | 67.6 | (2.1) | -3.5 | (3.5) | 17.4 | (1.2) | 17.5 | (0.8) | -0.2 | (1.4) | 20.2 | (1.1) | 18.6 | (0.9) | 1.6 | 1.3 |
| Israel | 65.7 | (1.5) | 63.2 | (1.5) | 2.5 | (2.0) | 41.3 | (1.4) | 43.1 | (1.5) | -1.7 | (1.9) | 22.6 | (1.2) | 18.0 | (0.9) | **4.5** | 1.4 |
| Jordan | 73.2 | (1.3) | 72.0 | (1.2) | 1.3 | (1.9) | 36.0 | (1.0) | 32.8 | (1.2) | **3.2** | (1.6) | 30.5 | (1.3) | 20.1 | (1.0) | **10.4** | 1.6 |
| Kyrgyzstan | 84.6 | (1.1) | 85.7 | (1.1) | -1.1 | (1.1) | 28.4 | (1.1) | 24.8 | (1.1) | **3.6** | (1.5) | 30.9 | (1.2) | 23.8 | (1.1) | **7.1** | 1.4 |
| Latvia | 67.6 | (1.4) | 75.2 | (1.2) | **-7.5** | (1.5) | 29.2 | (1.2) | 35.2 | (1.6) | **-6.0** | (1.6) | 14.7 | (0.9) | 13.5 | (0.7) | 1.2 | 1.3 |
| Liechtenstein | 28.1 | (3.6) | 27.5 | (3.1) | 0.6 | (4.8) | 11.7 | (2.3) | 16.1 | (2.6) | -4.4 | (3.4) | 5.3 | (1.8) | 0.6 | (0.6) | **4.7** | 1.7 |
| Lithuania | 45.4 | (1.4) | 52.4 | (1.4) | **-7.0** | (1.8) | 15.7 | (0.9) | 19.9 | (1.1) | **-4.2** | (1.2) | 7.3 | (0.6) | 6.7 | (0.6) | 0.6 | 0.7 |
| Macao-China | 66.7 | (1.1) | 57.8 | (1.0) | **8.8** | (1.5) | 21.7 | (1.1) | 22.0 | (1.0) | -0.3 | (1.6) | 22.5 | (1.1) | 18.7 | (0.9) | **3.8** | 1.4 |
| Montenegro | 63.2 | (1.1) | 60.9 | (1.0) | 2.2 | (1.6) | 36.1 | (1.1) | 38.9 | (1.2) | -2.9 | (1.7) | 22.1 | (0.8) | 19.3 | (0.9) | **2.8** | 1.2 |
| Qatar | 69.1 | (0.9) | 58.3 | (0.8) | **10.7** | (1.2) | 35.3 | (1.0) | 37.1 | (1.0) | -1.8 | (1.4) | 30.2 | (0.9) | 20.8 | (0.7) | **9.4** | 1.2 |
| Romania | 60.7 | (1.4) | 53.0 | (2.2) | **7.7** | (2.3) | 27.3 | (1.5) | 28.5 | (1.8) | -1.2 | (1.4) | 21.4 | (1.4) | 18.2 | (1.5) | 3.2 | 1.8 |
| Russian Federation | 67.6 | (1.7) | 71.0 | (1.7) | -3.4 | (1.8) | 21.3 | (1.1) | 22.0 | (1.0) | -0.7 | (1.4) | 13.3 | (1.1) | 11.7 | (0.9) | 1.6 | 1.3 |
| Serbia | 53.5 | (1.1) | 54.2 | (1.5) | -0.7 | (1.6) | 35.5 | (1.3) | 41.6 | (1.5) | **-6.1** | (1.7) | 12.8 | (0.8) | 13.0 | (0.7) | -0.3 | 1.0 |
| Slovenia | 40.5 | (0.9) | 42.7 | (1.1) | -2.2 | (1.6) | 24.4 | (0.8) | 29.0 | (1.0) | **-4.6** | (1.3) | 7.6 | (0.6) | 5.5 | (0.5) | **2.2** | 0.8 |
| Chinese Taipei | 76.4 | (0.8) | 73.5 | (0.8) | **2.9** | (1.3) | 24.6 | (0.7) | 22.7 | (0.7) | 1.8 | (1.0) | 25.9 | (0.7) | 21.1 | (0.6) | **4.8** | 1.0 |
| Thailand | 64.4 | (1.5) | 62.9 | (1.5) | 1.5 | (1.8) | 23.0 | (1.1) | 18.6 | (0.9) | **4.4** | (1.3) | 27.6 | (1.2) | 21.4 | (1.0) | **6.1** | 1.3 |
| Tunisia | 72.3 | (1.1) | 68.7 | (1.5) | 3.7 | (1.6) | 31.4 | (1.5) | 30.2 | (1.7) | 1.1 | (1.8) | 30.6 | (1.3) | 26.1 | (1.5) | **4.5** | 1.7 |
| Uruguay | 43.4 | (1.5) | 45.9 | (1.2) | -2.5 | (1.9) | 25.8 | (1.1) | 32.3 | (1.1) | **-6.6** | (1.3) | 19.6 | (1.1) | 22.5 | (0.9) | **-2.9** | 1.3 |

*Note:* Values that are statistically significant at the 5% level (p < 0.05) are indicated in bold.

[Part 2/3]
## Table 3.14 Percentage of students by different types of out-of-school-time lessons, by gender

| | Proportion of students participating in out-of-school lessons with non-school teachers | | | | | | | | | | | | Proportion of students participating in out-of-school lessons with school teachers | | | | | |
| | Large group lessons | | | | | | At least one of these types of out-of-school lessons | | | | | | One-to-one lessons | | | | | |
| | Male students | | Female students | | Difference (male-female) | | Male students | | Female students | | Difference (male-female) | | Male students | | Female students | | Difference (male-female) | |
| | % | S.E. | % | S.E. | Dif. | S.E. | % | S.E. | % | S.E. | Dif. | S.E. | % | S.E. | % | S.E. | Dif. | S.E. |
|---|---|---|---|---|---|---|---|---|---|---|---|---|---|---|---|---|---|---|
| **OECD** | | | | | | | | | | | | | | | | | | |
| Australia | 8.1 | (0.6) | 6.3 | (0.4) | **1.8** | (0.6) | 22.6 | (0.8) | 23.7 | (0.8) | -1.1 | (1.1) | 8.4 | (0.5) | 5.0 | (0.4) | **3.4** | (0.5) |
| Austria | 8.0 | (0.8) | 4.3 | (0.6) | **3.7** | (0.8) | 25.1 | (1.0) | 23.2 | (1.3) | 1.8 | (1.4) | 6.7 | (0.6) | 4.1 | (0.6) | **2.7** | (0.6) |
| Belgium | 5.0 | (0.7) | 3.6 | (0.4) | **1.4** | (0.6) | 21.7 | (0.8) | 23.4 | (0.9) | -1.7 | (1.2) | 8.2 | (0.5) | 6.3 | (0.5) | **1.9** | (0.6) |
| Canada | 7.9 | (0.6) | 6.3 | (0.5) | **1.6** | (0.6) | 22.1 | (0.8) | 23.6 | (0.7) | -1.5 | (1.0) | 12.2 | (0.6) | 12.4 | (0.6) | -0.2 | (0.8) |
| Czech Republic | 6.4 | (1.0) | 4.7 | (0.7) | **1.6** | (0.8) | 20.2 | (1.0) | 23.8 | (1.2) | **-3.6** | (1.4) | 15.5 | (0.9) | 12.7 | (1.0) | **2.8** | (1.3) |
| Denmark | 5.3 | (0.7) | 2.6 | (0.4) | **2.7** | (0.6) | 10.9 | (0.8) | 9.9 | (0.7) | 1.0 | (0.9) | 7.1 | (0.6) | 3.5 | (0.4) | **3.7** | (0.7) |
| Finland | 3.9 | (0.4) | 3.6 | (0.4) | 0.3 | (0.6) | 9.0 | (0.6) | 8.1 | (0.6) | 0.9 | (0.8) | 7.6 | (0.6) | 8.7 | (0.7) | -1.1 | (0.7) |
| France | 6.0 | (0.8) | 3.9 | (0.5) | **2.1** | (0.8) | 26.3 | (1.3) | 26.4 | (1.1) | -0.1 | (1.1) | 7.3 | (0.7) | 6.8 | (0.7) | 0.5 | (0.9) |
| Germany | 4.9 | (0.8) | 2.7 | (0.4) | **2.2** | (0.7) | 27.4 | (1.1) | 27.3 | (0.8) | 0.1 | (1.4) | 6.9 | (0.6) | 4.6 | (0.6) | **2.3** | (0.8) |
| Greece | 20.3 | (1.5) | 16.7 | (1.2) | **3.6** | (1.3) | 66.2 | (1.4) | 75.1 | (1.2) | **-8.9** | (1.6) | 16.7 | (1.3) | 7.3 | (0.7) | **9.3** | (1.3) |
| Hungary | 9.6 | (1.1) | 7.9 | (0.6) | 1.6 | (1.1) | 34.4 | (1.3) | 42.5 | (1.4) | **-8.1** | (1.7) | 14.9 | (0.9) | 14.4 | (0.9) | 0.5 | (1.0) |
| Iceland | 5.4 | (0.7) | 4.8 | (0.5) | 0.7 | (0.7) | 18.4 | (0.9) | 21.2 | (1.0) | **-2.8** | (1.3) | 12.0 | (0.7) | 8.8 | (0.7) | **3.1** | (1.0) |
| Ireland | 7.3 | (1.1) | 6.1 | (0.7) | 1.2 | (0.9) | 27.4 | (1.2) | 30.4 | (1.0) | **-3.0** | (1.5) | 7.7 | (0.7) | 6.3 | (0.7) | 1.4 | (0.8) |
| Italy | 10.9 | (0.7) | 7.1 | (0.4) | **3.8** | (0.6) | 47.3 | (0.9) | 44.5 | (0.8) | **2.8** | (1.2) | a | a | a | a | a | a |
| Japan | 9.9 | (0.8) | 6.6 | (0.7) | **3.3** | (0.8) | 20.9 | (1.1) | 19.6 | (1.4) | 1.3 | (1.4) | 4.5 | (0.4) | 2.9 | (0.4) | **1.6** | (0.5) |
| Korea | 27.6 | (1.8) | 26.2 | (1.2) | 1.4 | (1.7) | 55.7 | (1.7) | 60.0 | (1.5) | -4.3 | (2.5) | 9.4 | (0.6) | 9.7 | (0.7) | -0.3 | (0.9) |
| Luxembourg | 7.4 | (0.8) | 3.6 | (0.4) | **3.9** | (0.7) | 28.2 | (0.9) | 27.7 | (0.9) | 0.5 | (1.3) | 15.4 | (0.6) | 12.1 | (0.6) | **3.3** | (0.9) |
| Mexico | 18.6 | (0.9) | 13.9 | (0.7) | **4.7** | (1.2) | 33.0 | (1.1) | 28.1 | (1.0) | **4.8** | (1.3) | 20.2 | (1.0) | 14.8 | (0.8) | **5.4** | (1.0) |
| Netherlands | 4.8 | (0.6) | 2.5 | (0.4) | **2.2** | (0.5) | 12.2 | (0.8) | 10.0 | (0.7) | **2.1** | (0.9) | 7.6 | (0.6) | 7.4 | (0.6) | 0.2 | (0.8) |
| New Zealand | 8.4 | (1.0) | 5.5 | (0.5) | **2.9** | (0.8) | 24.4 | (1.0) | 23.4 | (0.9) | 0.9 | (1.3) | 8.6 | (0.9) | 9.6 | (1.2) | -1.0 | (1.5) |
| Norway | 7.6 | (0.7) | 2.4 | (0.4) | **5.2** | (0.7) | 13.0 | (0.9) | 6.6 | (0.5) | **6.4** | (1.0) | 11.6 | (0.7) | 5.2 | (0.6) | **6.4** | (0.8) |
| Poland | 11.9 | (0.8) | 8.1 | (0.6) | **3.8** | (0.9) | 29.8 | (1.0) | 28.1 | (1.2) | 1.6 | (1.2) | 17.5 | (0.8) | 11.8 | (0.8) | **5.7** | (1.0) |
| Portugal | 8.8 | (1.2) | 7.7 | (0.7) | 1.1 | (0.9) | 34.8 | (1.3) | 35.8 | (1.2) | -1.0 | (1.5) | 23.9 | (1.3) | 20.2 | (1.0) | **3.7** | (1.4) |
| Slovak Republic | 7.4 | (0.9) | 7.3 | (0.7) | 0.1 | (0.7) | 27.6 | (1.2) | 31.9 | (1.4) | **-4.2** | (1.6) | 29.0 | (1.4) | 31.8 | (1.7) | -2.8 | (1.6) |
| Spain | 11.3 | (1.1) | 9.7 | (0.6) | 1.5 | (0.9) | 40.5 | (1.0) | 46.4 | (0.9) | **-5.9** | (1.0) | 10.9 | (0.7) | 6.2 | (0.6) | **4.7** | (0.9) |
| Sweden | 8.9 | (0.7) | 5.0 | (0.6) | **3.9** | (0.8) | 15.3 | (0.8) | 10.9 | (0.7) | **4.3** | (1.0) | 10.8 | (0.7) | 6.7 | (0.7) | **4.1** | (0.8) |
| Switzerland | 5.8 | (0.6) | 3.7 | (0.3) | **2.1** | (0.5) | 23.5 | (0.9) | 25.8 | (0.8) | **-2.3** | (1.2) | 7.8 | (0.5) | 5.7 | (0.4) | **2.1** | (0.6) |
| Turkey | 15.7 | (1.0) | 14.2 | (1.2) | 1.4 | (1.3) | 26.9 | (1.4) | 26.0 | (1.4) | 0.8 | (1.5) | 9.5 | (0.9) | 5.4 | (0.6) | **4.1** | (1.0) |
| United Kingdom | 8.4 | (0.8) | 6.3 | (0.5) | **2.1** | (0.8) | 23.0 | (0.9) | 25.2 | (1.0) | -2.2 | (1.3) | 11.8 | (0.6) | 10.8 | (0.6) | 1.0 | (0.9) |
| United States | 12.9 | (1.0) | 10.4 | (0.9) | **2.5** | (0.9) | 25.6 | (1.4) | 24.9 | (1.2) | 0.7 | (1.6) | 23.7 | (1.3) | 21.0 | (1.1) | 2.7 | (1.2) |
| **OECD average** | 9.5 | (0.2) | 7.1 | (0.1) | **2.3** | (0.2) | 27.1 | (0.2) | 27.8 | (0.2) | **-0.7** | (0.2) | 12.2 | (0.2) | 9.7 | (0.1) | **2.5** | (0.2) |
| **Partners** | | | | | | | | | | | | | | | | | | |
| Argentina | 14.6 | (1.5) | 11.8 | (1.1) | 2.8 | (1.5) | 38.2 | (1.4) | 41.5 | (1.5) | -3.3 | (1.8) | 13.7 | (1.0) | 8.1 | (1.2) | **5.6** | (1.2) |
| Azerbaijan | 40.5 | (2.0) | 37.3 | (1.2) | **3.2** | (1.4) | 63.5 | (1.4) | 61.8 | (1.2) | 1.8 | (1.6) | 40.8 | (1.5) | 36.9 | (1.5) | **3.9** | (1.6) |
| Brazil | 17.7 | (1.0) | 13.5 | (0.7) | **4.2** | (1.1) | 33.9 | (1.1) | 32.3 | (0.9) | 1.6 | (1.4) | 15.2 | (0.7) | 12.2 | (0.7) | **2.9** | (0.9) |
| Bulgaria | 21.4 | (1.4) | 12.1 | (0.9) | **9.3** | (1.3) | 39.9 | (1.4) | 36.1 | (1.2) | **3.8** | (1.6) | 26.2 | (1.6) | 17.6 | (1.7) | **8.7** | (1.9) |
| Chile | 9.8 | (1.2) | 6.5 | (0.5) | **3.3** | (0.9) | 21.5 | (1.0) | 21.3 | (1.0) | 0.1 | (1.6) | 8.8 | (0.7) | 7.5 | (0.6) | 1.3 | (1.0) |
| Colombia | 17.4 | (1.5) | 15.6 | (0.8) | 1.8 | (1.3) | 35.7 | (1.4) | 37.6 | (1.2) | -1.8 | (2.1) | 17.3 | (1.2) | 13.1 | (1.4) | **4.2** | (1.4) |
| Croatia | 9.9 | (1.0) | 5.8 | (0.5) | **4.1** | (0.9) | 32.0 | (1.0) | 36.0 | (1.2) | **-3.9** | (1.4) | 16.4 | (0.9) | 9.9 | (0.8) | **6.5** | (1.2) |
| Estonia | 7.9 | (1.0) | 6.7 | (0.6) | 1.2 | (0.8) | 21.8 | (1.0) | 25.2 | (1.1) | **-3.3** | (1.5) | 19.0 | (1.2) | 17.8 | (1.0) | 1.3 | (1.4) |
| Hong Kong-China | 30.9 | (1.4) | 29.2 | (1.5) | 1.7 | (1.6) | 52.2 | (1.5) | 51.9 | (1.7) | 0.3 | (2.1) | 6.7 | (0.7) | 5.1 | (0.6) | 1.6 | (0.9) |
| Indonesia | 18.2 | (1.3) | 16.8 | (0.9) | 1.4 | (1.4) | 34.6 | (1.5) | 33.5 | (1.2) | 1.1 | (1.9) | 32.4 | (3.1) | 30.7 | (2.0) | 1.7 | (2.4) |
| Israel | 19.0 | (1.4) | 11.9 | (0.8) | **7.1** | (1.4) | 54.2 | (1.7) | 51.3 | (1.5) | 2.9 | (2.1) | 25.2 | (1.0) | 16.5 | (1.1) | **8.7** | (1.7) |
| Jordan | 27.1 | (1.6) | 17.0 | (0.9) | **10.0** | (1.6) | 52.7 | (1.2) | 43.5 | (1.2) | **9.2** | (1.7) | 35.4 | (1.7) | 19.5 | (1.0) | **15.9** | (1.9) |
| Kyrgyzstan | 37.4 | (1.4) | 27.1 | (1.1) | **10.3** | (1.7) | 53.0 | (1.5) | 44.9 | (1.2) | **8.1** | (1.9) | 63.3 | (1.2) | 64.2 | (1.3) | -0.9 | (1.3) |
| Latvia | 19.1 | (1.3) | 15.2 | (1.0) | **3.9** | (1.5) | 41.1 | (1.2) | 43.4 | (1.6) | -2.4 | (1.9) | 34.2 | (1.4) | 35.2 | (1.6) | -1.0 | (1.8) |
| Liechtenstein | 4.0 | (1.7) | 1.1 | (0.8) | 2.8 | (1.7) | 14.3 | (2.6) | 17.7 | (2.9) | -3.5 | (3.6) | 7.3 | (2.1) | 4.5 | (1.6) | 2.8 | (2.7) |
| Lithuania | 7.5 | (0.7) | 5.7 | (0.5) | **1.8** | (0.8) | 22.4 | (0.9) | 24.5 | (1.1) | -2.2 | (1.3) | 12.3 | (0.9) | 11.6 | (0.8) | 0.8 | (1.1) |
| Macao-China | 22.5 | (1.4) | 16.3 | (1.0) | **6.2** | (1.4) | 41.6 | (1.3) | 36.6 | (1.0) | **5.0** | (1.6) | 17.5 | (0.9) | 10.9 | (0.8) | **6.5** | (1.2) |
| Montenegro | 20.1 | (1.2) | 14.6 | (0.8) | **5.5** | (1.1) | 47.4 | (1.1) | 47.5 | (1.2) | -0.1 | (1.7) | 30.1 | (0.9) | 19.9 | (0.9) | **10.2** | (1.5) |
| Qatar | 28.6 | (1.2) | 17.3 | (0.7) | **11.3** | (1.1) | 51.3 | (1.0) | 45.9 | (0.9) | **5.4** | (1.4) | 45.8 | (0.9) | 22.6 | (0.7) | **23.1** | (1.2) |
| Romania | 19.0 | (1.8) | 12.0 | (1.4) | **7.0** | (1.3) | 39.3 | (1.5) | 37.7 | (1.8) | 1.6 | (2.1) | 32.1 | (1.4) | 21.8 | (1.7) | **10.3** | (1.7) |
| Russian Federation | 14.5 | (1.3) | 11.1 | (1.0) | **3.5** | (1.3) | 32.2 | (1.3) | 30.3 | (1.5) | 1.9 | (1.8) | 31.2 | (1.2) | 30.3 | (1.2) | 0.9 | (1.6) |
| Serbia | 10.2 | (1.0) | 7.3 | (0.7) | **2.9** | (0.9) | 41.2 | (1.3) | 45.4 | (1.5) | **-4.2** | (1.7) | 12.9 | (0.8) | 7.7 | (0.8) | **5.2** | (1.0) |
| Slovenia | 6.1 | (0.8) | 4.0 | (0.6) | **2.1** | (0.9) | 29.2 | (0.9) | 33.1 | (1.1) | **-3.9** | (1.6) | 10.8 | (0.6) | 7.0 | (0.7) | **3.8** | (1.0) |
| Chinese Taipei | 41.7 | (1.0) | 38.8 | (1.2) | 2.9 | (1.6) | 58.1 | (1.0) | 55.6 | (1.2) | 2.5 | (1.6) | 16.1 | (0.8) | 12.5 | (0.7) | **3.6** | (1.0) |
| Thailand | 34.3 | (1.3) | 29.0 | (1.2) | **5.4** | (1.9) | 47.3 | (1.7) | 42.0 | (1.4) | **5.3** | (1.8) | 25.4 | (1.2) | 17.7 | (0.8) | **7.7** | (1.3) |
| Tunisia | 23.6 | (1.7) | 15.4 | (0.9) | **8.3** | (1.3) | 48.1 | (1.6) | 41.9 | (1.7) | **6.2** | (1.9) | 44.7 | (1.5) | 40.7 | (1.7) | 4.1 | (1.8) |
| Uruguay | 13.1 | (1.3) | 11.0 | (0.8) | 2.1 | (1.2) | 35.3 | (1.2) | 39.7 | (1.2) | **-4.4** | (1.4) | 11.5 | (1.4) | 7.6 | (0.7) | **3.9** | (1.6) |

*Note:* Values that are statistically significant at the 5% level (p < 0.05) are indicated in bold.

© OECD 2011 Quality Time for Students: Learning In and Out of School

[Part 3/3]
## Table 3.14 Percentage of students by different types of out-of-school-time lessons, by gender

| | Proportion of students participating in out-of-school lessons with school teachers | | | | | | | | | | | | At least one of these types of out-of-school lessons | | | | | |
|---|---|---|---|---|---|---|---|---|---|---|---|---|---|---|---|---|---|---|
| | Small group lessons | | | | | | Large group lessons | | | | | | | | | | | |
| | Male students | | Female students | | Difference (male-female) | | Male students | | Female students | | Difference (male-female) | | Male students | | Female students | | Difference (male-female) | |
| | % | S.E. | % | S.E. | Dif. | S.E. | % | S.E. | % | S.E. | Dif. | S.E. | % | S.E. | % | S.E. | Dif. | S.E. |
| Australia | 8.5 | (0.5) | 5.9 | (0.4) | **2.6** | (0.5) | 10.4 | (0.5) | 5.9 | (0.4) | **4.5** | (0.6) | 16.6 | (0.7) | 11.4 | (0.6) | **5.2** | (0.7) |
| Austria | 14.1 | (1.0) | 12.0 | (1.0) | 2.2 | (1.1) | 15.3 | (1.0) | 16.0 | (1.1) | -0.6 | (1.2) | 24.1 | (1.4) | 22.6 | (1.4) | 1.4 | (1.6) |
| Belgium | 8.8 | (0.6) | 6.8 | (0.5) | **2.0** | (0.7) | 7.4 | (0.4) | 4.5 | (0.4) | **3.0** | (0.5) | 15.9 | (0.7) | 12.4 | (0.7) | **3.5** | (0.9) |
| Canada | 10.9 | (0.5) | 10.0 | (0.5) | 0.9 | (0.6) | 12.3 | (0.6) | 10.2 | (0.5) | **2.1** | (0.7) | 21.5 | (0.7) | 21.2 | (0.7) | 0.3 | (0.9) |
| Czech Republic | 11.9 | (0.8) | 9.7 | (0.9) | **2.3** | (1.1) | 14.9 | (1.0) | 11.5 | (0.9) | **3.4** | (1.3) | 25.1 | (1.3) | 20.9 | (1.4) | **4.2** | (1.8) |
| Denmark | 8.8 | (0.7) | 7.1 | (0.7) | 1.7 | (0.9) | 9.9 | (0.7) | 6.2 | (0.6) | **3.8** | (0.8) | 16.2 | (0.9) | 12.0 | (0.9) | **4.2** | (1.1) |
| Finland | 9.6 | (0.7) | 9.3 | (0.7) | 0.3 | (0.9) | 14.2 | (0.8) | 10.1 | (0.7) | **4.0** | (0.9) | 18.8 | (0.9) | 17.6 | (0.8) | 1.2 | (1.1) |
| France | 17.8 | (1.0) | 18.0 | (1.0) | -0.2 | (1.3) | 10.9 | (0.8) | 9.8 | (0.7) | 1.1 | (0.9) | 24.0 | (1.1) | 23.8 | (1.0) | 0.2 | (1.4) |
| Germany | 7.7 | (0.6) | 7.8 | (0.8) | -0.1 | (0.9) | 11.1 | (0.8) | 9.6 | (0.8) | 1.6 | (1.0) | 18.8 | (0.9) | 16.4 | (1.0) | **2.5** | (1.2) |
| Greece | 17.9 | (1.1) | 11.6 | (1.0) | **6.2** | (1.3) | 13.1 | (1.1) | 6.2 | (0.7) | **7.0** | (1.2) | 27.4 | (1.5) | 16.6 | (1.1) | **10.8** | (1.6) |
| Hungary | 12.4 | (1.0) | 13.1 | (0.9) | -0.7 | (1.2) | 16.3 | (1.0) | 15.4 | (0.9) | 1.0 | (1.2) | 29.4 | (1.3) | 29.3 | (1.3) | 0.1 | (1.5) |
| Iceland | 15.3 | (0.9) | 13.7 | (0.7) | 1.6 | (1.1) | 11.9 | (0.8) | 16.2 | (0.9) | **-4.3** | (1.1) | 25.8 | (1.1) | 28.2 | (1.0) | -2.4 | (1.5) |
| Ireland | 9.9 | (0.8) | 8.1 | (0.7) | **1.8** | (0.9) | 11.4 | (0.8) | 8.3 | (0.6) | **3.0** | (1.0) | 18.9 | (1.0) | 15.0 | (1.0) | **3.9** | (1.2) |
| Italy | 36.1 | (1.0) | 36.6 | (1.0) | -0.5 | (1.2) | 27.0 | (0.8) | 24.7 | (0.8) | **2.4** | (1.0) | 46.2 | (1.1) | 45.3 | (1.0) | 1.0 | (1.2) |
| Japan | 8.1 | (0.6) | 5.1 | (0.5) | **3.1** | (0.8) | 32.3 | (1.4) | 28.6 | (1.5) | **3.6** | (1.5) | 37.0 | (1.5) | 32.8 | (1.5) | **4.2** | (1.6) |
| Korea | 17.1 | (0.8) | 16.3 | (0.8) | 0.8 | (1.1) | 34.9 | (1.4) | 37.6 | (1.9) | -2.6 | (2.1) | 49.5 | (1.3) | 51.3 | (1.7) | -1.8 | (2.0) |
| Luxembourg | 14.5 | (0.8) | 14.7 | (0.8) | -0.2 | (1.1) | 10.8 | (0.7) | 8.9 | (0.6) | **1.9** | (0.9) | 25.9 | (0.8) | 24.8 | (0.9) | 1.1 | (1.1) |
| Mexico | 20.3 | (1.0) | 15.1 | (0.8) | **5.2** | (1.1) | 27.2 | (1.0) | 20.7 | (0.9) | **6.5** | (1.1) | 37.9 | (1.1) | 29.1 | (1.0) | **8.7** | (1.3) |
| Netherlands | 8.7 | (0.7) | 8.7 | (0.7) | 0.0 | (0.9) | 7.4 | (0.8) | 7.0 | (0.6) | 0.4 | (0.9) | 15.4 | (1.1) | 15.6 | (0.9) | -0.2 | (1.1) |
| New Zealand | 9.5 | (0.6) | 9.9 | (1.0) | -0.5 | (1.2) | 10.7 | (0.8) | 7.6 | (0.7) | **3.1** | (1.0) | 18.2 | (1.1) | 17.3 | (1.3) | 0.8 | (1.7) |
| Norway | 14.2 | (0.9) | 9.5 | (0.7) | **4.8** | (1.1) | 20.4 | (1.0) | 14.0 | (0.9) | **6.5** | (1.2) | 27.4 | (1.1) | 20.1 | (0.9) | **7.3** | (1.3) |
| Poland | 22.8 | (1.1) | 23.4 | (1.0) | -0.6 | (1.4) | 27.2 | (1.0) | 26.2 | (1.1) | 1.0 | (1.0) | 41.5 | (1.2) | 41.0 | (1.2) | 0.6 | (1.4) |
| Portugal | 31.7 | (1.4) | 32.0 | (1.3) | -0.3 | (1.4) | 25.7 | (1.2) | 22.0 | (1.3) | **3.7** | (1.2) | 48.5 | (1.5) | 47.2 | (1.6) | 1.2 | (1.7) |
| Slovak Republic | 17.4 | (1.0) | 18.8 | (1.3) | -1.4 | (1.3) | 22.9 | (1.3) | 25.0 | (1.5) | -2.2 | (1.5) | 37.5 | (1.5) | 39.7 | (1.9) | -2.2 | (1.9) |
| Spain | 13.2 | (0.6) | 8.3 | (0.5) | **4.9** | (0.8) | 11.6 | (0.6) | 7.9 | (0.6) | **3.7** | (0.8) | 22.5 | (0.8) | 14.6 | (0.8) | **7.9** | (1.0) |
| Sweden | 15.9 | (0.8) | 12.5 | (0.7) | **3.4** | (1.1) | 24.3 | (0.9) | 17.2 | (1.0) | **7.1** | (1.4) | 30.2 | (1.2) | 22.5 | (1.0) | **7.7** | (1.4) |
| Switzerland | 10.7 | (0.5) | 9.4 | (0.6) | 1.3 | (0.8) | 14.9 | (0.8) | 13.2 | (0.7) | **1.8** | (0.9) | 23.8 | (0.8) | 21.1 | (0.8) | **2.7** | (0.9) |
| Turkey | 10.9 | (0.8) | 7.4 | (0.6) | 3.6 | (1.0) | 13.8 | (1.0) | 11.6 | (0.9) | 2.2 | (1.3) | 21.9 | (1.2) | 17.1 | (1.1) | **4.8** | (1.5) |
| United Kingdom | 17.3 | (0.8) | 18.1 | (0.8) | **-0.9** | (1.0) | 19.8 | (0.9) | 19.2 | (0.9) | 0.6 | (1.0) | 31.6 | (1.1) | 31.9 | (1.1) | -0.2 | (1.4) |
| United States | 20.9 | (1.2) | 17.2 | (0.9) | **3.7** | (1.3) | 21.1 | (1.4) | 15.1 | (0.9) | **6.0** | (1.3) | 34.5 | (1.6) | 30.2 | (1.2) | **4.3** | (1.5) |
| **OECD average** | 14.8 | (0.2) | 13.2 | (0.2) | **1.6** | (0.2) | 17.0 | (0.2) | 14.5 | (0.2) | **2.5** | (0.2) | 27.7 | (0.2) | 25.0 | (0.2) | **2.8** | (0.3) |
| Argentina | 15.9 | (1.4) | 9.6 | (0.9) | **6.3** | (1.4) | 14.4 | (1.3) | 8.6 | (1.0) | **5.8** | (1.2) | 25.3 | (1.6) | 15.6 | (1.3) | **9.7** | (1.3) |
| Azerbaijan | 39.0 | (1.7) | 35.3 | (1.6) | 3.7 | (2.1) | 49.6 | (1.8) | 47.0 | (1.5) | 2.6 | (1.8) | 68.5 | (1.7) | 66.7 | (1.6) | 1.8 | (1.5) |
| Brazil | 25.5 | (1.1) | 21.8 | (1.0) | **3.7** | (1.4) | 23.7 | (1.0) | 17.6 | (0.9) | **6.1** | (1.2) | 37.8 | (1.2) | 31.4 | (1.2) | **6.4** | (1.6) |
| Bulgaria | 22.3 | (1.6) | 15.9 | (1.2) | **6.4** | (1.8) | 26.6 | (1.4) | 18.8 | (1.4) | **7.9** | (1.4) | 39.2 | (1.8) | 30.4 | (1.9) | **8.8** | (2.0) |
| Chile | 16.7 | (1.0) | 15.6 | (1.0) | 1.0 | (1.2) | 19.2 | (1.0) | 15.9 | (1.0) | **3.3** | (1.2) | 28.0 | (1.4) | 26.2 | (1.4) | 1.8 | (1.8) |
| Colombia | 22.8 | (1.7) | 17.8 | (1.4) | **5.1** | (2.0) | 22.3 | (1.3) | 17.0 | (1.2) | **5.3** | (1.4) | 33.1 | (1.4) | 26.2 | (1.5) | **6.9** | (1.4) |
| Croatia | 13.3 | (0.8) | 9.0 | (0.7) | **4.4** | (1.0) | 15.4 | (1.0) | 8.6 | (0.8) | **6.8** | (1.2) | 25.6 | (1.2) | 18.1 | (1.2) | **7.5** | (1.6) |
| Estonia | 13.9 | (0.9) | 13.5 | (1.0) | 0.3 | (1.3) | 20.2 | (1.0) | 17.1 | (1.1) | **3.1** | (1.5) | 33.3 | (1.5) | 30.8 | (1.3) | 2.5 | (1.9) |
| Hong Kong-China | 18.6 | (1.0) | 15.3 | (1.2) | **3.4** | (1.5) | 42.2 | (1.6) | 41.8 | (1.6) | 0.4 | (1.9) | 49.3 | (1.6) | 47.9 | (1.6) | 1.4 | (2.0) |
| Indonesia | 26.3 | (2.6) | 26.6 | (1.7) | -0.3 | (2.2) | 34.6 | (2.8) | 35.1 | (2.3) | -0.5 | (2.3) | 51.3 | (4.0) | 52.3 | (2.7) | -1.0 | (3.3) |
| Israel | 23.7 | (1.2) | 18.1 | (1.1) | **5.6** | (1.3) | 22.5 | (1.3) | 17.9 | (0.8) | **4.5** | (1.4) | 39.2 | (1.4) | 31.4 | (1.3) | **7.7** | (1.7) |
| Jordan | 36.3 | (1.3) | 27.2 | (1.2) | **9.2** | (1.9) | 41.9 | (1.3) | 39.9 | (1.4) | 2.0 | (1.9) | 60.0 | (1.7) | 53.2 | (1.5) | **6.8** | (2.2) |
| Kyrgyzstan | 45.0 | (1.4) | 43.3 | (1.4) | 1.8 | (1.6) | 52.9 | (1.4) | 52.9 | (1.4) | -0.0 | (1.4) | 78.8 | (1.3) | 78.2 | (1.3) | 0.6 | (1.2) |
| Latvia | 25.3 | (1.2) | 25.8 | (1.3) | -0.6 | (1.4) | 28.0 | (1.7) | 30.0 | (1.6) | -2.0 | (2.3) | 48.8 | (1.8) | 52.2 | (1.5) | -3.4 | (2.1) |
| Liechtenstein | 11.2 | (2.4) | 16.1 | (3.1) | **6.3** | (3.1) | 15.8 | (3.0) | 6.1 | (1.8) | **9.7** | (3.7) | 21.7 | (3.3) | 12.3 | (2.3) | **9.3** | (4.1) |
| Lithuania | 16.8 | (1.0) | 18.5 | (1.0) | -1.6 | (1.2) | 19.5 | (1.0) | 19.2 | (1.1) | 0.3 | (1.3) | 33.1 | (1.2) | 35.8 | (1.3) | -2.6 | (1.6) |
| Macao-China | 27.7 | (1.0) | 17.6 | (0.8) | **10.1** | (1.3) | 39.7 | (1.2) | 30.0 | (1.1) | **9.7** | (1.7) | 53.8 | (1.1) | 39.4 | (1.1) | **14.4** | (1.6) |
| Montenegro | 21.4 | (0.8) | 13.9 | (0.9) | **7.5** | (1.2) | 26.1 | (1.0) | 17.0 | (0.8) | **9.1** | (1.3) | 40.0 | (1.1) | 29.1 | (1.1) | **10.8** | (1.5) |
| Qatar | 39.5 | (0.8) | 19.3 | (0.6) | **20.2** | (1.0) | 38.0 | (1.0) | 21.4 | (0.7) | **16.6** | (1.3) | 58.1 | (0.8) | 33.2 | (0.8) | **24.9** | (1.1) |
| Romania | 27.5 | (1.4) | 21.4 | (1.4) | **6.1** | (1.9) | 27.2 | (1.4) | 16.6 | (2.1) | **10.5** | (2.0) | 46.2 | (1.5) | 34.1 | (2.2) | **12.1** | (2.2) |
| Russian Federation | 30.6 | (1.4) | 32.4 | (1.4) | -1.8 | (1.6) | 36.7 | (1.6) | 36.7 | (1.5) | 0.0 | (1.7) | 56.2 | (1.6) | 58.9 | (1.6) | -2.7 | (1.9) |
| Serbia | 15.2 | (0.9) | 9.2 | (0.7) | **5.9** | (1.0) | 17.8 | (1.1) | 11.4 | (0.8) | **6.4** | (1.2) | 27.3 | (1.1) | 19.9 | (1.1) | **7.5** | (1.4) |
| Slovenia | 9.8 | (0.7) | 8.0 | (0.8) | 1.7 | (1.1) | 14.2 | (0.8) | 9.2 | (0.6) | **5.0** | (1.0) | 23.1 | (0.9) | 17.3 | (0.9) | **5.8** | (1.2) |
| Chinese Taipei | 25.4 | (0.9) | 20.0 | (1.1) | **5.3** | (1.3) | 38.4 | (1.0) | 31.5 | (1.1) | **6.8** | (1.4) | 48.5 | (1.1) | 41.3 | (1.4) | **7.2** | (1.7) |
| Thailand | 31.7 | (1.5) | 23.2 | (0.9) | **8.5** | (1.5) | 41.6 | (1.4) | 37.1 | (1.4) | **4.6** | (1.4) | 50.6 | (1.6) | 44.9 | (1.2) | **5.7** | (1.6) |
| Tunisia | 35.9 | (1.4) | 29.9 | (1.4) | **6.0** | (1.7) | 33.4 | (1.3) | 27.9 | (1.1) | **5.5** | (1.6) | 56.8 | (1.4) | 51.4 | (1.6) | **5.3** | (1.9) |
| Uruguay | 10.9 | (0.9) | 7.1 | (0.7) | **3.8** | (1.1) | 11.5 | (0.9) | 6.0 | (0.6) | **5.5** | (1.1) | 20.8 | (1.6) | 13.6 | (0.9) | **7.1** | (1.8) |

Note: Values that are statistically significant at the 5% level (p < 0.05) are indicated in bold.

211

**Table 3.15** **Percentage of students by different types of out-of-school-time lessons, by quarters**
[Part 1/5] **of the PISA index of economic, social and cultural status (ESCS)**

| | | Proportion of students participating in out-of-school-time lessons | | | | | | | | |
|---|---|---|---|---|---|---|---|---|---|---|
| | | Bottom quarter of ESCS | | Second quarter of ESCS | | Third quarter of ESCS | | Top quarter of ESCS | | Difference (bottom-top) | |
| | | % | S.E. | % | S.E. | % | S.E. | % | S.E. | Dif. | S.E. |
| OECD | Australia | 26.8 | (1.1) | 28.1 | (0.9) | 31.8 | (1.1) | 37.9 | (1.0) | **-11.0** | (1.4) |
| | Austria | 34.9 | (2.1) | 33.4 | (1.5) | 37.5 | (1.4) | 39.3 | (1.8) | -4.5 | (2.6) |
| | Belgium | 25.5 | (1.2) | 28.4 | (1.3) | 32.2 | (1.1) | 35.4 | (1.4) | **-9.8** | (2.0) |
| | Canada | 31.5 | (1.2) | 33.5 | (1.1) | 37.5 | (1.3) | 40.8 | (1.3) | **-9.4** | (1.8) |
| | Czech Republic | 36.5 | (1.8) | 33.5 | (1.8) | 37.3 | (1.6) | 41.7 | (1.6) | **-5.6** | (2.4) |
| | Denmark | 24.8 | (1.5) | 19.8 | (1.5) | 18.6 | (1.4) | 18.7 | (1.2) | **6.0** | (1.9) |
| | Finland | 22.6 | (1.1) | 25.8 | (1.4) | 22.9 | (1.3) | 22.4 | (1.4) | 0.1 | (1.6) |
| | France | 36.9 | (1.6) | 39.6 | (1.5) | 42.4 | (1.6) | 47.6 | (1.9) | **-11.0** | (2.5) |
| | Germany | 31.8 | (1.6) | 36.9 | (1.6) | 41.2 | (1.6) | 38.0 | (1.6) | **-6.2** | (2.3) |
| | Greece | 64.6 | (2.0) | 74.1 | (1.4) | 80.2 | (1.3) | 86.6 | (1.1) | **-22.0** | (2.4) |
| | Hungary | 46.6 | (1.9) | 48.5 | (1.8) | 56.9 | (1.8) | 64.9 | (1.8) | **-18.6** | (2.6) |
| | Iceland | 37.9 | (1.8) | 39.2 | (1.4) | 43.5 | (1.6) | 40.8 | (1.5) | -2.7 | (2.6) |
| | Ireland | 30.8 | (1.9) | 35.8 | (1.8) | 43.0 | (1.7) | 42.9 | (1.5) | **-12.3** | (2.4) |
| | Italy | 57.6 | (1.2) | 64.0 | (1.0) | 70.0 | (1.1) | 74.2 | (0.8) | **-16.7** | (1.3) |
| | Japan | 41.6 | (2.0) | 42.7 | (1.8) | 45.8 | (1.9) | 52.0 | (2.2) | **-10.5** | (2.8) |
| | Korea | 68.8 | (1.9) | 74.7 | (1.4) | 82.0 | (1.3) | 91.2 | (1.0) | **-22.4** | (2.4) |
| | Luxembourg | 41.5 | (1.6) | 48.1 | (1.6) | 44.9 | (1.4) | 40.5 | (1.4) | 1.1 | (2.1) |
| | Mexico | 51.1 | (2.0) | 44.2 | (1.3) | 47.9 | (1.2) | 47.5 | (1.2) | 3.6 | (2.5) |
| | Netherlands | 21.6 | (1.7) | 21.5 | (1.4) | 23.0 | (1.3) | 22.1 | (1.6) | -0.8 | (2.3) |
| | New Zealand | 29.3 | (1.6) | 29.6 | (1.4) | 35.7 | (1.6) | 39.9 | (1.6) | **-10.6** | (2.3) |
| | Norway | 32.1 | (1.6) | 27.4 | (1.6) | 25.5 | (1.3) | 23.5 | (1.3) | **8.5** | (1.8) |
| | Poland | 49.9 | (1.9) | 51.1 | (1.8) | 56.9 | (1.4) | 66.6 | (1.5) | **-16.8** | (2.4) |
| | Portugal | 63.4 | (2.0) | 68.2 | (1.7) | 68.7 | (1.6) | 74.7 | (1.6) | **-11.3** | (2.6) |
| | Slovak Republic | 49.3 | (1.7) | 53.3 | (2.1) | 60.2 | (1.8) | 60.3 | (2.1) | **-11.3** | (2.5) |
| | Spain | 49.5 | (1.6) | 50.3 | (1.3) | 56.5 | (1.4) | 59.1 | (1.6) | **-9.5** | (2.3) |
| | Sweden | 38.5 | (1.5) | 33.8 | (1.5) | 28.8 | (1.4) | 26.3 | (1.5) | **12.3** | (2.1) |
| | Switzerland | 39.2 | (1.3) | 37.7 | (1.2) | 40.9 | (1.3) | 41.9 | (1.6) | -2.7 | (2.1) |
| | Turkey | 28.1 | (1.6) | 30.1 | (1.7) | 37.2 | (1.3) | 52.5 | (1.9) | **-24.1** | (2.4) |
| | United Kingdom | 42.3 | (1.5) | 44.5 | (1.4) | 45.9 | (1.6) | 49.5 | (1.6) | **-7.1** | (2.1) |
| | United States | 44.9 | (2.3) | 43.5 | (2.0) | 42.2 | (1.6) | 39.0 | (1.4) | **6.2** | (2.6) |
| | **OECD average** | **40.0** | **(0.3)** | **41.4** | **(0.3)** | **44.6** | **(0.3)** | **47.3** | **(0.3)** | **-7.3** | **(0.4)** |
| Partners | Argentina | 42.1 | (2.0) | 45.7 | (2.4) | 50.9 | (2.0) | 55.5 | (2.2) | **-13.0** | (3.0) |
| | Azerbaijan | 72.8 | (2.1) | 78.6 | (1.8) | 81.4 | (1.7) | 85.1 | (1.2) | **-12.3** | (2.3) |
| | Brazil | 44.4 | (1.7) | 44.2 | (1.7) | 47.2 | (1.6) | 58.1 | (1.9) | **-13.9** | (2.7) |
| | Bulgaria | 52.5 | (3.0) | 51.0 | (2.3) | 55.5 | (1.5) | 57.9 | (1.6) | -5.0 | (3.5) |
| | Chile | 37.4 | (1.9) | 35.8 | (1.5) | 37.3 | (1.8) | 42.3 | (2.3) | -5.0 | (2.9) |
| | Colombia | 50.6 | (1.9) | 46.9 | (2.0) | 51.4 | (1.6) | 54.8 | (1.9) | -4.1 | (2.8) |
| | Croatia | 38.7 | (1.5) | 44.4 | (1.5) | 47.3 | (1.5) | 51.4 | (1.6) | **-12.6** | (2.0) |
| | Estonia | 46.4 | (1.6) | 48.0 | (1.9) | 44.6 | (1.7) | 45.1 | (1.9) | 1.4 | (2.4) |
| | Hong Kong-China | 63.6 | (1.6) | 73.1 | (1.5) | 80.4 | (1.4) | 84.3 | (1.0) | **-20.8** | (1.9) |
| | Indonesia | 64.9 | (3.0) | 66.0 | (1.9) | 61.9 | (4.0) | 70.3 | (2.6) | -5.3 | (3.1) |
| | Israel | 62.0 | (2.0) | 61.0 | (1.9) | 65.0 | (1.6) | 69.9 | (1.6) | **-7.9** | (2.4) |
| | Jordan | 70.1 | (1.4) | 72.8 | (1.5) | 75.3 | (1.4) | 72.0 | (1.8) | -1.7 | (2.2) |
| | Kyrgyzstan | 84.9 | (2.0) | 86.9 | (1.3) | 85.7 | (1.5) | 83.5 | (1.4) | 1.5 | (2.5) |
| | Latvia | 70.0 | (1.8) | 69.5 | (1.7) | 72.4 | (1.4) | 74.1 | (1.4) | -4.3 | (2.0) |
| | Liechtenstein | 35.4 | (4.6) | 17.6 | (4.0) | 29.0 | (5.7) | 27.4 | (5.5) | **7.3** | (7.2) |
| | Lithuania | 42.3 | (1.5) | 44.1 | (1.9) | 51.8 | (1.9) | 57.1 | (1.7) | **-15.0** | (2.4) |
| | Macao-China | 60.4 | (1.7) | 61.6 | (1.8) | 60.5 | (1.7) | 66.5 | (1.6) | **-6.0** | (2.1) |
| | Montenegro | 55.8 | (1.6) | 58.5 | (1.6) | 65.9 | (1.6) | 68.0 | (1.6) | **-12.4** | (2.3) |
| | Qatar | 62.8 | (1.4) | 64.5 | (1.2) | 60.8 | (1.2) | 66.2 | (1.2) | -3.3 | (1.8) |
| | Romania | 58.0 | (1.8) | 53.2 | (2.8) | 56.6 | (2.1) | 59.6 | (2.0) | -1.3 | (2.4) |
| | Russian Federation | 68.4 | (2.1) | 67.4 | (1.9) | 69.5 | (1.9) | 72.4 | (1.7) | -4.0 | (2.4) |
| | Serbia | 45.7 | (1.5) | 51.2 | (1.6) | 56.8 | (1.8) | 61.6 | (1.9) | **-15.9** | (2.2) |
| | Slovenia | 40.4 | (1.5) | 42.0 | (1.5) | 42.2 | (1.4) | 41.9 | (1.4) | -1.4 | (2.1) |
| | Chinese Taipei | 70.3 | (1.1) | 73.3 | (1.0) | 76.2 | (1.0) | 80.6 | (0.9) | **-10.3** | (1.4) |
| | Thailand | 51.9 | (1.8) | 60.9 | (1.9) | 64.2 | (1.9) | 77.1 | (1.7) | **-25.4** | (2.5) |
| | Tunisia | 59.3 | (1.8) | 68.7 | (1.6) | 74.4 | (1.4) | 79.3 | (1.5) | **-20.0** | (2.1) |
| | Uruguay | 31.9 | (1.7) | 41.1 | (2.0) | 47.8 | (2.2) | 57.9 | (1.6) | **-26.0** | (2.3) |

*Note:* Values that are statistically significant at the 5% level (p < 0.05) are indicated in bold.

© OECD 2011  Quality Time for Students: Learning In and Out of School

**Table 3.15** Percentage of students by different types of out-of-school-time lessons,
[Part 2/5] by quarters of the PISA index of economic, social and cultural status (ESCS)

| | | Proportion of students participating in out-of-school lessons with non-school teachers | | | | | | | | | | | | | | | | | |
| | | One-to-one lessons | | | | | | | | | | Small group lessons | | | | | | | | |
| | | Bottom quarter of ESCS | | Second quarter of ESCS | | Third quarter of ESCS | | Top quarter of ESCS | | Difference (bottom-top) | | Bottom quarter of ESCS | | Second quarter of ESCS | | Third quarter of ESCS | | Top quarter of ESCS | | Difference (bottom-top) | |
| | | % | S.E. | % | S.E. | % | S.E. | % | S.E. | Dif. | S.E. | % | S.E. | % | S.E. | % | S.E. | % | S.E. | Dif. | S.E. |
|---|---|---|---|---|---|---|---|---|---|---|---|---|---|---|---|---|---|---|---|---|---|
| OECD | Australia | 11.5 | (0.7) | 14.0 | (0.7) | 17.2 | (0.8) | 23.6 | (0.9) | **-12.1** | (1.1) | 8.9 | (0.8) | 7.3 | (0.6) | 7.6 | (0.6) | 8.5 | (0.6) | 0.4 | (1.0) |
| | Austria | 12.1 | (1.1) | 13.4 | (1.1) | 18.4 | (1.1) | 23.0 | (1.4) | **-10.8** | (1.7) | 9.3 | (1.0) | 7.6 | (0.7) | 6.7 | (0.8) | 7.4 | (1.2) | 2.0 | (1.5) |
| | Belgium | 10.3 | (0.9) | 16.0 | (1.1) | 19.9 | (0.9) | 25.0 | (1.3) | **-14.6** | (1.5) | 7.6 | (0.7) | 6.4 | (0.8) | 7.2 | (0.6) | 8.4 | (0.7) | -0.8 | (1.1) |
| | Canada | 12.2 | (0.7) | 13.6 | (0.7) | 17.4 | (1.0) | 22.7 | (0.9) | **-10.6** | (1.3) | 7.2 | (0.6) | 8.5 | (0.7) | 9.0 | (0.7) | 9.0 | (0.7) | **-1.9** | (0.9) |
| | Czech Republic | 9.9 | (1.1) | 13.4 | (1.3) | 16.1 | (1.1) | 24.3 | (1.4) | **-14.1** | (1.7) | 6.9 | (1.0) | 7.0 | (0.9) | 8.3 | (0.9) | 9.4 | (0.8) | **-2.8** | (1.2) |
| | Denmark | 6.4 | (0.7) | 4.7 | (0.7) | 4.6 | (0.7) | 5.7 | (0.8) | 0.7 | (1.2) | 6.6 | (0.9) | 3.7 | (0.6) | 3.5 | (0.6) | 4.5 | (0.7) | 2.2 | (1.0) |
| | Finland | 3.2 | (0.5) | 5.4 | (0.7) | 5.3 | (0.7) | 7.5 | (1.0) | **-4.2** | (1.0) | 2.3 | (0.4) | 3.1 | (0.6) | 2.4 | (0.4) | 1.9 | (0.4) | 0.4 | (0.6) |
| | France | 14.2 | (1.3) | 19.7 | (1.2) | 23.8 | (1.6) | 32.4 | (1.8) | **-18.1** | (2.3) | 10.0 | (0.9) | 9.9 | (1.0) | 7.7 | (1.0) | 8.6 | (0.9) | 1.4 | (1.3) |
| | Germany | 15.3 | (1.2) | 21.8 | (1.3) | 25.4 | (1.4) | 23.7 | (1.4) | **-8.8** | (2.0) | 6.4 | (0.8) | 5.7 | (0.7) | 8.4 | (0.9) | 8.6 | (0.9) | **-2.1** | (1.2) |
| | Greece | 30.4 | (1.8) | 41.3 | (1.9) | 48.4 | (1.8) | 58.9 | (1.5) | **-28.6** | (2.5) | 39.1 | (1.8) | 47.0 | (1.8) | 48.8 | (1.9) | 48.8 | (2.5) | **-9.9** | (2.9) |
| | Hungary | 17.7 | (1.2) | 27.7 | (1.6) | 37.1 | (1.8) | 47.5 | (1.8) | **-29.7** | (2.2) | 9.3 | (1.1) | 10.2 | (1.1) | 11.5 | (1.1) | 12.2 | (0.9) | **-2.7** | (1.5) |
| | Iceland | 9.9 | (1.0) | 13.5 | (1.1) | 17.2 | (1.3) | 18.0 | (1.2) | **-8.1** | (1.7) | 5.2 | (0.8) | 5.7 | (0.8) | 7.6 | (0.8) | 8.2 | (0.8) | **-3.1** | (1.1) |
| | Ireland | 12.3 | (1.0) | 18.7 | (1.1) | 25.6 | (1.4) | 28.9 | (1.3) | **-16.5** | (1.7) | 7.2 | (1.0) | 9.0 | (0.9) | 9.8 | (1.0) | 12.8 | (1.1) | **-5.6** | (1.5) |
| | Italy | 22.5 | (1.0) | 33.5 | (1.0) | 42.5 | (1.1) | 50.4 | (1.0) | **-27.8** | (1.3) | 14.3 | (0.8) | 14.4 | (0.9) | 13.0 | (0.8) | 14.7 | (0.7) | -0.4 | (1.0) |
| | Japan | 5.8 | (0.7) | 7.7 | (0.8) | 9.9 | (1.1) | 14.1 | (1.3) | **-8.2** | (1.5) | 5.5 | (0.7) | 7.6 | (0.8) | 8.3 | (0.9) | 12.3 | (1.1) | **-6.8** | (1.2) |
| | Korea | 20.3 | (1.4) | 27.4 | (1.4) | 33.8 | (1.5) | 43.7 | (1.6) | **-23.4** | (2.1) | 19.7 | (1.4) | 28.8 | (1.1) | 31.0 | (1.6) | 45.6 | (1.9) | **-25.9** | (2.6) |
| | Luxembourg | 17.1 | (1.2) | 25.0 | (1.3) | 27.0 | (1.4) | 23.3 | (1.3) | **-6.4** | (1.7) | 9.0 | (0.9) | 7.4 | (0.9) | 5.5 | (0.7) | 6.0 | (0.7) | 2.9 | (1.1) |
| | Mexico | 13.3 | (1.3) | 14.9 | (0.9) | 19.6 | (0.9) | 23.9 | (0.9) | **-10.7** | (1.5) | 14.5 | (1.4) | 13.8 | (0.9) | 17.8 | (0.9) | 18.5 | (0.9) | **-4.3** | (1.6) |
| | Netherlands | 4.2 | (0.7) | 6.3 | (0.8) | 8.6 | (0.9) | 10.7 | (1.0) | **-6.4** | (1.2) | 3.8 | (0.6) | 4.2 | (0.8) | 3.4 | (0.6) | 2.8 | (0.6) | 0.8 | (0.8) |
| | New Zealand | 11.1 | (1.1) | 13.6 | (1.0) | 20.3 | (1.2) | 24.1 | (1.4) | **-13.2** | (1.8) | 10.8 | (1.1) | 7.3 | (0.8) | 11.1 | (1.1) | 9.8 | (0.8) | 1.0 | (1.3) |
| | Norway | 4.2 | (0.7) | 4.2 | (0.7) | 6.4 | (0.8) | 6.1 | (0.7) | **-1.9** | (0.9) | 5.1 | (0.9) | 3.7 | (0.7) | 5.1 | (0.7) | 5.0 | (0.7) | 0.1 | (1.1) |
| | Poland | 9.0 | (0.9) | 11.8 | (1.1) | 21.2 | (1.3) | 35.0 | (1.5) | **-26.0** | (1.7) | 7.9 | (0.9) | 7.5 | (0.7) | 10.6 | (0.9) | 16.5 | (1.4) | **-8.6** | (1.6) |
| | Portugal | 14.3 | (1.3) | 23.2 | (1.3) | 28.2 | (1.7) | 40.9 | (2.2) | **-26.9** | (2.8) | 10.6 | (1.2) | 12.3 | (1.2) | 15.3 | (1.2) | 20.2 | (1.6) | **-9.6** | (2.0) |
| | Slovak Republic | 13.7 | (1.1) | 20.3 | (1.3) | 32.3 | (2.0) | 35.9 | (1.7) | **-22.6** | (2.1) | 8.2 | (0.8) | 10.0 | (0.9) | 13.0 | (1.1) | 13.6 | (1.2) | **-5.4** | (1.3) |
| | Spain | 20.9 | (1.2) | 26.2 | (1.2) | 31.7 | (1.3) | 35.8 | (1.3) | **-14.9** | (1.7) | 20.8 | (1.1) | 25.7 | (1.0) | 28.8 | (1.2) | 29.3 | (1.6) | **-8.5** | (2.1) |
| | Sweden | 6.8 | (0.8) | 6.1 | (0.7) | 7.7 | (0.8) | 8.7 | (1.1) | -1.9 | (1.4) | 5.9 | (0.9) | 5.4 | (0.7) | 5.5 | (0.6) | 5.8 | (0.7) | 0.1 | (1.1) |
| | Switzerland | 16.0 | (1.0) | 16.8 | (1.0) | 20.5 | (1.0) | 26.1 | (1.3) | **-10.0** | (1.7) | 6.6 | (0.7) | 4.7 | (0.5) | 7.1 | (0.7) | 6.6 | (0.7) | 0.1 | (0.9) |
| | Turkey | 8.1 | (1.2) | 9.5 | (1.0) | 13.7 | (1.1) | 22.7 | (1.6) | **-14.5** | (2.0) | 7.8 | (1.0) | 8.9 | (1.0) | 11.1 | (0.8) | 16.0 | (1.4) | **-8.0** | (1.7) |
| | United Kingdom | 12.1 | (1.0) | 15.4 | (0.8) | 18.3 | (1.0) | 23.9 | (1.2) | **-11.8** | (1.7) | 7.8 | (0.9) | 7.4 | (0.8) | 7.1 | (0.8) | 7.3 | (0.7) | 0.4 | (1.1) |
| | United States | 17.3 | (1.6) | 16.7 | (1.2) | 18.0 | (1.3) | 17.5 | (1.4) | -0.4 | (2.2) | 15.9 | (1.6) | 13.8 | (1.4) | 11.5 | (0.9) | 8.9 | (1.0) | **7.1** | (1.9) |
| | **OECD average** | 12.7 | (0.2) | 16.7 | (0.2) | 21.2 | (0.2) | 26.1 | (0.2) | **-13.4** | (0.3) | 10.0 | (0.2) | 10.5 | (0.2) | 11.5 | (0.2) | 12.9 | (0.2) | **-2.9** | (0.3) |
| Partners | Argentina | 20.3 | (1.4) | 27.2 | (1.9) | 36.4 | (1.9) | 40.9 | (1.9) | **-20.7** | (2.3) | 15.3 | (1.3) | 16.9 | (1.3) | 22.2 | (1.9) | 22.4 | (1.6) | **-6.5** | (1.9) |
| | Azerbaijan | 22.1 | (1.9) | 29.0 | (2.4) | 30.4 | (1.3) | 41.1 | (1.6) | **-19.0** | (2.4) | 37.2 | (2.2) | 42.7 | (1.7) | 41.3 | (1.6) | 42.0 | (1.6) | -4.9 | (2.7) |
| | Brazil | 11.7 | (1.0) | 15.8 | (1.0) | 20.9 | (1.3) | 30.4 | (1.4) | **-18.3** | (1.8) | 14.0 | (1.3) | 17.3 | (1.0) | 19.0 | (1.2) | 21.2 | (1.3) | **-7.2** | (1.9) |
| | Bulgaria | 19.1 | (1.5) | 25.1 | (1.4) | 30.9 | (1.6) | 32.3 | (1.5) | **-13.0** | (2.1) | 20.3 | (1.7) | 15.8 | (1.3) | 17.5 | (1.6) | 16.4 | (1.1) | 4.0 | (1.8) |
| | Chile | 7.6 | (1.1) | 9.8 | (1.2) | 11.5 | (1.1) | 24.2 | (1.6) | **-16.5** | (1.9) | 10.0 | (1.0) | 8.3 | (1.1) | 7.9 | (0.7) | 11.2 | (1.0) | -0.9 | (1.4) |
| | Colombia | 21.1 | (1.7) | 19.5 | (1.5) | 28.8 | (2.0) | 32.1 | (1.7) | **-11.3** | (2.3) | 16.1 | (1.2) | 17.1 | (1.4) | 18.9 | (1.5) | 19.0 | (1.3) | -2.8 | (1.8) |
| | Croatia | 19.0 | (1.2) | 26.8 | (1.5) | 29.7 | (1.4) | 36.1 | (1.4) | **-17.2** | (1.9) | 9.9 | (1.0) | 10.5 | (0.8) | 8.5 | (0.9) | 10.2 | (0.8) | -0.2 | (1.1) |
| | Estonia | 11.4 | (1.3) | 18.0 | (1.4) | 19.3 | (1.3) | 20.2 | (1.2) | **-8.6** | (1.9) | 6.1 | (1.0) | 7.8 | (0.8) | 9.2 | (0.8) | 9.3 | (0.9) | **-3.3** | (1.3) |
| | Hong Kong-China | 12.4 | (1.0) | 18.3 | (1.4) | 28.3 | (2.1) | 37.6 | (2.1) | **-25.2** | (2.4) | 12.8 | (1.3) | 14.0 | (1.3) | 21.1 | (1.5) | 23.4 | (1.5) | **-10.7** | (1.9) |
| | Indonesia | 10.9 | (1.2) | 14.3 | (0.9) | 16.0 | (1.1) | 28.5 | (2.1) | **-17.5** | (2.3) | 13.8 | (1.1) | 18.4 | (1.1) | 20.5 | (1.6) | 25.1 | (1.6) | **-11.4** | (1.9) |
| | Israel | 32.2 | (1.8) | 38.4 | (2.0) | 46.8 | (1.9) | 52.2 | (1.7) | **-19.8** | (2.4) | 24.4 | (1.7) | 18.7 | (1.5) | 17.9 | (1.5) | 19.6 | (1.2) | **4.9** | (1.9) |
| | Jordan | 27.8 | (1.3) | 32.8 | (1.5) | 39.6 | (1.5) | 37.3 | (1.5) | **-9.6** | (1.8) | 25.5 | (1.5) | 25.1 | (1.3) | 27.2 | (1.4) | 23.0 | (1.2) | 2.3 | (2.0) |
| | Kyrgyzstan | 23.9 | (1.5) | 27.2 | (1.5) | 24.7 | (1.3) | 29.9 | (1.6) | **-5.9** | (2.2) | 25.7 | (1.7) | 28.9 | (1.7) | 26.4 | (1.5) | 26.9 | (1.4) | -1.2 | (2.2) |
| | Latvia | 20.9 | (1.7) | 27.5 | (1.7) | 35.2 | (1.7) | 45.3 | (1.9) | **-24.4** | (2.4) | 9.3 | (0.9) | 13.7 | (1.2) | 15.8 | (1.1) | 17.5 | (1.2) | **-8.1** | (1.5) |
| | Liechtenstein | 15.4 | (3.3) | 10.4 | (3.6) | 11.4 | (3.8) | 18.1 | (4.7) | -2.6 | (5.2) | 3.7 | (2.1) | 1.2 | (1.2) | 2.5 | (1.7) | 2.5 | (1.7) | 1.3 | (2.7) |
| | Lithuania | 7.7 | (0.8) | 12.0 | (1.0) | 20.6 | (1.6) | 31.0 | (1.6) | **-23.4** | (1.8) | 4.9 | (0.6) | 6.6 | (0.8) | 7.4 | (0.8) | 9.0 | (1.1) | **-4.0** | (1.3) |
| | Macao-China | 19.6 | (1.4) | 18.1 | (1.1) | 22.2 | (1.4) | 27.7 | (1.5) | **-8.1** | (1.8) | 20.2 | (1.3) | 17.4 | (1.2) | 20.6 | (1.3) | 24.2 | (1.5) | **-4.1** | (2.0) |
| | Montenegro | 25.2 | (1.4) | 33.1 | (1.7) | 41.6 | (1.7) | 50.0 | (1.8) | **-25.3** | (2.1) | 19.8 | (1.3) | 19.0 | (1.4) | 22.3 | (1.3) | 21.7 | (1.3) | -1.9 | (2.1) |
| | Qatar | 30.9 | (1.2) | 34.6 | (1.4) | 37.0 | (1.4) | 42.2 | (1.3) | **-11.1** | (1.7) | 26.0 | (1.2) | 26.3 | (1.2) | 24.6 | (1.2) | 24.7 | (1.1) | 1.4 | (1.5) |
| | Romania | 22.9 | (1.8) | 26.2 | (2.0) | 27.8 | (1.7) | 34.7 | (2.4) | **-12.0** | (2.9) | 18.7 | (1.6) | 20.1 | (2.3) | 18.4 | (1.3) | 21.9 | (2.0) | -3.6 | (2.8) |
| | Russian Federation | 13.9 | (1.1) | 18.2 | (1.2) | 23.6 | (1.3) | 30.9 | (1.4) | **-17.0** | (1.7) | 11.6 | (1.2) | 11.6 | (1.0) | 12.5 | (1.1) | 14.3 | (1.2) | **-2.7** | (1.3) |
| | Serbia | 27.0 | (1.6) | 35.7 | (1.5) | 42.2 | (2.0) | 49.1 | (1.7) | **-22.2** | (2.2) | 11.4 | (0.9) | 12.0 | (0.9) | 13.2 | (1.1) | 15.0 | (1.2) | **-3.6** | (1.5) |
| | Slovenia | 22.0 | (1.2) | 27.9 | (1.4) | 29.4 | (1.5) | 27.5 | (1.4) | **-5.5** | (1.9) | 5.8 | (0.7) | 6.7 | (0.8) | 6.4 | (0.8) | 7.1 | (0.8) | -1.5 | (0.9) |
| | Chinese Taipei | 20.4 | (1.0) | 21.8 | (0.9) | 24.3 | (0.9) | 28.5 | (1.2) | **-8.2** | (1.5) | 22.6 | (0.9) | 22.8 | (0.9) | 25.0 | (1.1) | 24.2 | (0.9) | -1.5 | (1.3) |
| | Thailand | 13.4 | (1.2) | 19.1 | (1.4) | 21.9 | (1.3) | 27.6 | (1.3) | **-14.3** | (1.6) | 18.3 | (1.2) | 24.3 | (1.5) | 25.4 | (1.5) | 28.1 | (1.6) | **-9.9** | (1.9) |
| | Tunisia | 21.1 | (1.4) | 25.8 | (1.6) | 31.9 | (1.5) | 44.3 | (2.7) | **-23.0** | (3.0) | 22.7 | (1.4) | 25.3 | (1.6) | 27.7 | (1.4) | 37.5 | (1.8) | **-14.8** | (2.2) |
| | Uruguay | 17.2 | (1.4) | 25.6 | (1.6) | 32.2 | (1.6) | 41.7 | (1.5) | **-24.7** | (2.3) | 12.9 | (1.3) | 17.6 | (1.6) | 23.8 | (1.5) | 30.0 | (1.5) | **-16.9** | (2.0) |

*Note:* Values that are statistically significant at the 5% level (p < 0.05) are indicated in bold.

### Table 3.15 Percentage of students by different types of out-of-school-time lessons,
[Part 3/5] by quarters of the PISA index of economic, social and cultural status (ESCS)

| | | Proportion of students participating in out-of-school lessons with non-school teachers | | | | | | | | | | | | | | | | | | |
| | | Large group lessons | | | | | | | | | | At least one of these types of out-of-school lessons | | | | | | | | | |
| | | Bottom quarter of ESCS | | Second quarter of ESCS | | Third quarter of ESCS | | Top quarter of ESCS | | Difference (bottom-top) | | Bottom quarter of ESCS | | Second quarter of ESCS | | Third quarter of ESCS | | Top quarter of ESCS | | Difference (bottom-top) | |
| | | % | S.E. | % | S.E. | % | S.E. | % | S.E. | Dif. | S.E. | % | S.E. | % | S.E. | % | S.E. | % | S.E. | Dif. | S.E. |
| OECD | Australia | 7.9 | (0.7) | 6.6 | (0.6) | 7.1 | (0.5) | 7.1 | (0.4) | 0.8 | (0.7) | 18.5 | (1.0) | 20.3 | (0.9) | 23.7 | (1.0) | 29.9 | (0.9) | **-11.3** | (1.4) |
| | Austria | 9.1 | (1.4) | 7.3 | (0.8) | 5.7 | (0.7) | 2.6 | (0.5) | **6.6** | (1.5) | 21.9 | (1.9) | 21.9 | (1.2) | 25.4 | (1.3) | 27.6 | (1.6) | **-5.7** | (2.3) |
| | Belgium | 4.9 | (0.6) | 4.5 | (0.6) | 4.0 | (0.6) | 3.9 | (0.6) | 0.9 | (0.8) | 16.4 | (0.9) | 20.0 | (1.3) | 24.6 | (1.0) | 29.2 | (1.4) | **-12.6** | (1.7) |
| | Canada | 7.4 | (0.6) | 7.0 | (0.6) | 7.3 | (0.6) | 6.5 | (0.6) | 0.9 | (0.8) | 18.4 | (1.0) | 20.1 | (0.9) | 24.2 | (1.1) | 28.5 | (1.1) | **-10.1** | (1.5) |
| | Czech Republic | 5.7 | (1.0) | 5.4 | (0.8) | 5.9 | (0.8) | 5.5 | (0.8) | -0.2 | (1.3) | 15.7 | (1.5) | 18.0 | (1.5) | 22.9 | (1.3) | 30.5 | (1.4) | **-15.1** | (2.1) |
| | Denmark | 5.1 | (0.8) | 3.7 | (0.8) | 3.0 | (0.6) | 3.6 | (0.5) | 1.4 | (0.9) | 12.2 | (1.2) | 9.4 | (1.1) | 8.9 | (0.9) | 10.9 | (1.2) | 1.4 | (1.7) |
| | Finland | 2.8 | (0.4) | 4.0 | (0.5) | 4.1 | (0.6) | 3.9 | (0.5) | -1.0 | (0.7) | 6.2 | (0.7) | 8.8 | (1.0) | 8.6 | (0.8) | 10.3 | (1.0) | **-4.1** | (1.1) |
| | France | 7.5 | (1.1) | 5.6 | (0.8) | 3.9 | (0.6) | 2.3 | (0.6) | **5.2** | (1.3) | 20.0 | (1.5) | 23.1 | (1.4) | 27.1 | (1.6) | 35.4 | (1.9) | **-15.6** | (2.4) |
| | Germany | 4.9 | (0.7) | 3.7 | (0.7) | 2.7 | (0.6) | 3.5 | (0.7) | 1.4 | (0.9) | 21.2 | (1.2) | 26.8 | (1.4) | 30.6 | (1.5) | 30.4 | (1.5) | **-9.4** | (2.1) |
| | Greece | 18.7 | (1.8) | 18.1 | (1.3) | 21.1 | (1.4) | 16.1 | (1.7) | 2.6 | (2.2) | 56.5 | (1.9) | 68.0 | (1.7) | 75.0 | (1.4) | 83.0 | (1.3) | **-26.4** | (2.4) |
| | Hungary | 11.6 | (1.4) | 7.3 | (0.8) | 7.3 | (0.8) | 8.7 | (1.0) | 3.0 | (1.8) | 26.6 | (1.7) | 32.6 | (1.7) | 42.5 | (1.9) | 51.6 | (1.7) | **-25.1** | (2.3) |
| | Iceland | 4.1 | (0.6) | 4.2 | (0.7) | 6.3 | (0.8) | 5.9 | (0.7) | -1.7 | (0.9) | 14.2 | (1.2) | 18.1 | (1.2) | 23.2 | (1.4) | 23.5 | (1.3) | **-9.3** | (1.7) |
| | Ireland | 5.6 | (0.9) | 6.0 | (0.7) | 7.0 | (1.0) | 8.2 | (1.0) | -2.6 | (1.4) | 18.9 | (1.6) | 25.7 | (1.3) | 33.6 | (1.7) | 37.4 | (1.3) | **-18.6** | (2.1) |
| | Italy | 9.6 | (0.7) | 8.8 | (0.7) | 9.2 | (0.7) | 8.3 | (0.6) | 1.2 | (0.9) | 34.2 | (1.2) | 42.3 | (1.0) | 50.1 | (1.2) | 57.1 | (1.0) | **-23.0** | (1.5) |
| | Japan | 7.5 | (0.8) | 6.4 | (0.9) | 8.5 | (1.0) | 10.2 | (1.0) | **-2.6** | (1.1) | 14.8 | (1.1) | 15.9 | (1.3) | 21.4 | (1.6) | 28.7 | (1.8) | **-14.0** | (1.9) |
| | Korea | 18.5 | (1.4) | 25.8 | (1.3) | 28.1 | (1.3) | 35.4 | (1.5) | **-16.9** | (2.0) | 39.0 | (1.7) | 54.6 | (1.5) | 61.1 | (1.6) | 76.7 | (1.6) | **-37.4** | (2.5) |
| | Luxembourg | 9.5 | (0.9) | 6.0 | (0.8) | 3.6 | (0.5) | 2.8 | (0.5) | **6.7** | (1.1) | 24.1 | (1.3) | 30.6 | (1.5) | 30.3 | (1.4) | 27.0 | (1.3) | -3.0 | (1.8) |
| | Mexico | 17.7 | (1.6) | 15.5 | (1.1) | 16.6 | (0.9) | 14.9 | (0.7) | 2.8 | (1.8) | 26.4 | (1.8) | 26.9 | (1.2) | 32.0 | (1.1) | 36.5 | (1.2) | **-10.2** | (2.0) |
| | Netherlands | 4.9 | (0.8) | 4.3 | (0.7) | 3.0 | (0.6) | 2.5 | (0.5) | 2.5 | (0.9) | 9.9 | (1.1) | 10.2 | (1.1) | 11.4 | (1.0) | 13.0 | (1.1) | **-3.0** | (1.5) |
| | New Zealand | 8.6 | (0.9) | 6.5 | (0.8) | 5.5 | (0.7) | 6.7 | (0.7) | 1.8 | (1.2) | 19.2 | (1.4) | 19.7 | (1.3) | 26.2 | (1.4) | 30.4 | (1.4) | **-11.1** | (2.0) |
| | Norway | 4.8 | (0.6) | 4.7 | (0.7) | 5.4 | (0.8) | 4.8 | (0.6) | 0.1 | (0.8) | 9.9 | (1.0) | 8.2 | (1.0) | 10.5 | (1.0) | 10.2 | (0.8) | -0.2 | (1.3) |
| | Poland | 8.7 | (0.8) | 8.9 | (0.8) | 10.3 | (1.0) | 12.1 | (1.0) | **-3.4** | (1.3) | 16.8 | (1.3) | 20.5 | (1.2) | 30.3 | (1.5) | 47.9 | (1.8) | **-31.1** | (2.2) |
| | Portugal | 9.6 | (1.2) | 6.5 | (1.0) | 9.4 | (1.1) | 7.0 | (0.9) | 2.1 | (1.5) | 22.2 | (1.5) | 29.5 | (1.3) | 37.1 | (1.7) | 52.1 | (2.6) | **-30.7** | (3.2) |
| | Slovak Republic | 6.4 | (0.8) | 5.7 | (0.7) | 8.2 | (1.1) | 9.2 | (1.1) | **-2.7** | (1.3) | 18.6 | (1.2) | 24.1 | (1.4) | 35.4 | (1.9) | 40.7 | (1.8) | **-22.4** | (2.0) |
| | Spain | 9.9 | (0.7) | 9.7 | (0.8) | 11.8 | (0.7) | 10.5 | (0.9) | -0.6 | (1.2) | 33.4 | (1.3) | 40.0 | (1.2) | 47.3 | (1.4) | 53.2 | (1.5) | **-19.7** | (2.1) |
| | Sweden | 7.1 | (0.8) | 6.7 | (0.9) | 6.8 | (0.8) | 6.9 | (0.7) | 0.2 | (1.2) | 13.1 | (1.2) | 12.0 | (1.1) | 13.1 | (1.0) | 13.8 | (1.0) | -0.8 | (1.6) |
| | Switzerland | 6.6 | (0.7) | 4.8 | (0.6) | 3.4 | (0.5) | 4.0 | (0.5) | **2.5** | (0.8) | 21.8 | (1.1) | 21.5 | (1.1) | 25.3 | (1.0) | 29.8 | (1.3) | **-7.8** | (1.6) |
| | Turkey | 10.0 | (1.2) | 11.2 | (1.2) | 14.3 | (1.2) | 24.6 | (1.9) | **-14.5** | (2.1) | 17.8 | (1.7) | 19.4 | (1.5) | 25.6 | (1.3) | 43.5 | (2.2) | **-25.6** | (2.8) |
| | United Kingdom | 8.7 | (0.9) | 7.4 | (0.7) | 6.4 | (0.7) | 6.5 | (0.7) | 2.2 | (1.2) | 20.5 | (1.4) | 21.6 | (1.0) | 24.2 | (1.2) | 30.1 | (1.4) | **-9.6** | (1.9) |
| | United States | 15.2 | (1.5) | 13.7 | (1.4) | 10.4 | (1.0) | 7.3 | (0.8) | **7.8** | (1.6) | 26.8 | (?.?) | 25.8 | (1.6) | 25.6 | (1.5) | 22.9 | (1.6) | 3.7 | (2.7) |
| | **OECD average** | 8.6 | (0.2) | 7.9 | (0.2) | 8.2 | (0.2) | 8.4 | (0.2) | 0.2 | (0.2) | 21.2 | (0.3) | 24.5 | (0.2) | 29.2 | (0.2) | 34.7 | (0.3) | **-13.6** | (0.4) |
| Partners | Argentina | 13.9 | (1.5) | 13.2 | (1.4) | 14.4 | (1.8) | 10.8 | (1.1) | **3.6** | (1.8) | 30.4 | (1.8) | 36.6 | (1.9) | 43.5 | (1.9) | 49.3 | (2.1) | **-18.8** | (2.8) |
| | Azerbaijan | 39.1 | (2.9) | 39.6 | (1.6) | 39.7 | (2.0) | 37.5 | (1.5) | 0.9 | (3.4) | 57.4 | (2.3) | 62.4 | (1.7) | 62.9 | (1.7) | 67.8 | (1.5) | **-10.7** | (2.8) |
| | Brazil | 13.9 | (1.0) | 16.6 | (1.1) | 14.6 | (0.9) | 16.8 | (1.3) | **-3.1** | (1.6) | 24.8 | (1.4) | 30.4 | (1.3) | 33.2 | (1.2) | 44.0 | (1.6) | **-19.3** | (2.2) |
| | Bulgaria | 21.2 | (1.6) | 17.2 | (1.4) | 15.4 | (1.6) | 13.7 | (1.3) | **8.0** | (2.1) | 31.8 | (1.9) | 33.9 | (1.6) | 42.3 | (1.8) | 44.1 | (1.6) | **-12.2** | (2.5) |
| | Chile | 10.3 | (1.1) | 9.1 | (1.0) | 7.2 | (0.6) | 6.5 | (0.8) | **4.0** | (1.4) | 17.7 | (1.4) | 18.0 | (1.3) | 18.8 | (1.1) | 31.1 | (1.6) | **-13.3** | (2.1) |
| | Colombia | 15.8 | (1.4) | 14.2 | (1.4) | 15.7 | (1.7) | 19.7 | (2.2) | -4.0 | (3.0) | 31.3 | (1.9) | 32.2 | (1.6) | 38.2 | (1.8) | 45.1 | (1.5) | **-13.9** | (2.8) |
| | Croatia | 8.9 | (1.0) | 7.8 | (0.8) | 8.2 | (0.8) | 6.4 | (0.8) | 2.4 | (1.3) | 26.2 | (1.6) | 32.6 | (1.4) | 36.1 | (1.6) | 41.2 | (1.5) | **-15.1** | (2.2) |
| | Estonia | 5.8 | (0.9) | 6.7 | (0.7) | 8.4 | (0.8) | 8.4 | (0.9) | **-2.5** | (1.2) | 16.6 | (1.5) | 23.5 | (1.5) | 25.8 | (1.3) | 27.9 | (1.4) | **-11.3** | (2.1) |
| | Hong Kong-China | 20.7 | (1.4) | 26.3 | (1.5) | 32.7 | (2.0) | 40.6 | (2.1) | **-19.8** | (2.3) | 33.8 | (1.6) | 44.5 | (1.8) | 59.7 | (1.9) | 70.4 | (1.8) | **-36.4** | (2.3) |
| | Indonesia | 12.3 | (1.2) | 16.6 | (1.1) | 18.3 | (1.9) | 22.9 | (1.5) | **-10.6** | (1.7) | 23.9 | (1.5) | 31.3 | (1.3) | 32.9 | (2.3) | 48.1 | (2.1) | **-24.3** | (2.8) |
| | Israel | 18.3 | (1.7) | 15.7 | (1.3) | 12.4 | (1.1) | 14.7 | (1.1) | 3.7 | (2.1) | 46.7 | (2.0) | 48.5 | (2.1) | 54.4 | (2.0) | 61.3 | (1.6) | **-14.8** | (2.3) |
| | Jordan | 22.3 | (1.4) | 22.3 | (1.4) | 22.4 | (1.4) | 20.6 | (1.4) | 1.7 | (2.0) | 43.2 | (1.6) | 48.0 | (1.4) | 52.3 | (1.6) | 48.6 | (1.5) | **-5.6** | (2.1) |
| | Kyrgyzstan | 33.7 | (1.8) | 33.7 | (1.6) | 32.1 | (1.6) | 27.6 | (1.8) | **6.3** | (2.4) | 48.4 | (1.9) | 50.2 | (1.5) | 47.3 | (1.5) | 48.5 | (1.8) | -0.1 | (2.7) |
| | Latvia | 14.2 | (1.4) | 18.0 | (1.4) | 18.4 | (1.3) | 17.9 | (1.3) | -3.6 | (2.1) | 28.4 | (1.7) | 39.2 | (1.7) | 47.1 | (1.7) | 54.4 | (1.5) | **-25.9** | (2.0) |
| | Liechtenstein | 4.9 | (2.4) | 0.0 | (0.0) | 0.2 | (0.8) | 3.4 | (2.1) | 1.2 | (3.1) | 20.1 | (4.3) | 10.4 | (3.6) | 14.5 | (4.1) | 18.8 | (4.8) | 0.5 | (5.7) |
| | Lithuania | 6.6 | (0.6) | 7.0 | (0.8) | 6.8 | (0.9) | 5.9 | (0.7) | 0.7 | (0.9) | 13.9 | (0.9) | 18.6 | (1.4) | 25.6 | (1.7) | 35.5 | (1.7) | **-21.6** | (2.1) |
| | Macao-China | 18.7 | (1.3) | 18.8 | (1.4) | 19.3 | (1.4) | 20.6 | (1.7) | -1.8 | (2.3) | 36.2 | (1.6) | 34.9 | (1.6) | 38.6 | (1.7) | 46.5 | (1.8) | **-10.1** | (2.4) |
| | Montenegro | 18.8 | (1.3) | 14.8 | (1.2) | 17.4 | (1.2) | 18.6 | (1.3) | 0.3 | (1.8) | 36.8 | (1.7) | 43.2 | (1.7) | 52.4 | (1.7) | 57.4 | (1.7) | **-20.8** | (2.4) |
| | Qatar | 24.4 | (1.2) | 24.9 | (1.1) | 20.6 | (1.1) | 21.3 | (0.9) | **3.3** | (1.5) | 45.1 | (1.3) | 48.9 | (1.4) | 47.9 | (1.4) | 52.1 | (1.2) | **-7.1** | (1.7) |
| | Romania | 20.6 | (1.4) | 16.2 | (2.0) | 13.8 | (2.0) | 11.1 | (1.5) | **9.5** | (2.1) | 36.1 | (1.8) | 35.7 | (2.0) | 38.4 | (1.8) | 43.9 | (2.1) | **-8.0** | (2.5) |
| | Russian Federation | 12.1 | (0.9) | 13.0 | (1.1) | 11.6 | (1.1) | 14.2 | (1.2) | -2.1 | (1.5) | 24.3 | (1.6) | 27.7 | (1.6) | 32.3 | (1.6) | 40.7 | (1.4) | **-16.1** | (1.9) |
| | Serbia | 9.5 | (0.9) | 10.4 | (1.0) | 8.4 | (1.0) | 6.4 | (0.8) | **3.2** | (1.2) | 32.4 | (1.6) | 40.4 | (1.5) | 46.7 | (1.9) | 53.4 | (1.9) | **-21.2** | (2.4) |
| | Slovenia | 6.8 | (0.6) | 4.7 | (0.6) | 4.8 | (0.7) | 3.7 | (0.6) | **3.1** | (0.9) | 27.1 | (1.2) | 32.3 | (1.4) | 33.5 | (1.5) | 32.0 | (1.5) | **-5.1** | (2.0) |
| | Chinese Taipei | 31.9 | (1.2) | 37.8 | (1.3) | 43.3 | (1.1) | 48.4 | (1.4) | **-16.5** | (1.7) | 45.6 | (1.1) | 52.7 | (1.4) | 60.9 | (1.0) | 68.7 | (1.0) | **-23.0** | (1.4) |
| | Thailand | 24.4 | (1.3) | 28.6 | (1.7) | 30.5 | (1.5) | 41.6 | (2.8) | **-17.1** | (3.0) | 33.7 | (1.6) | 40.2 | (1.8) | 44.7 | (1.8) | 58.3 | (2.6) | **-24.7** | (2.8) |
| | Tunisia | 21.6 | (1.4) | 20.5 | (1.5) | 18.1 | (1.4) | 17.0 | (1.8) | **4.4** | (2.2) | 38.3 | (1.6) | 40.8 | (1.7) | 45.3 | (1.6) | 55.2 | (2.7) | **-17.0** | (3.0) |
| | Uruguay | 9.3 | (0.8) | 12.0 | (1.1) | 12.7 | (1.3) | 14.0 | (1.1) | **-4.8** | (1.4) | 23.7 | (1.6) | 34.1 | (1.7) | 41.4 | (2.0) | 51.2 | (1.6) | **-27.7** | (2.3) |

Note: Values that are statistically significant at the 5% level (p < 0.05) are indicated in bold.

© OECD 2011 Quality Time for Students: Learning In and Out of School

### Table 3.15 Percentage of students by different types of out-of-school-time lessons, by quarters of the PISA index of economic, social and cultural status (ESCS)
[Part 4/5]

**Proportion of students participating in out-of-school lessons with school teachers**

| | One-to-one lessons | | | | | | | | | | Small group lessons | | | | | | | | | |
| | Bottom quarter of ESCS | | Second quarter of ESCS | | Third quarter of ESCS | | Top quarter of ESCS | | Difference (bottom-top) | | Bottom quarter of ESCS | | Second quarter of ESCS | | Third quarter of ESCS | | Top quarter of ESCS | | Difference (bottom-top) | |
| | % | S.E. | % | S.E. | % | S.E. | % | S.E. | % | S.E. | % | S.E. | % | S.E. | % | S.E. | % | S.E. | % | S.E. |
|---|---|---|---|---|---|---|---|---|---|---|---|---|---|---|---|---|---|---|---|---|
| Australia | 7.1 | (0.6) | 6.3 | (0.5) | 6.5 | (0.5) | 6.9 | (0.6) | 0.2 | (0.8) | 7.5 | (0.6) | 7.0 | (0.5) | 7.5 | (0.6) | 6.7 | (0.6) | 0.8 | (0.8) |
| Austria | 6.4 | (1.0) | 6.6 | (0.9) | 5.1 | (0.7) | 3.6 | (0.6) | **2.9** | (1.1) | 16.3 | (1.5) | 13.0 | (1.2) | 12.3 | (1.1) | 10.7 | (1.2) | **5.9** | (1.7) |
| Belgium | 7.3 | (0.9) | 7.6 | (0.8) | 7.2 | (0.8) | 6.9 | (0.6) | 0.6 | (1.1) | 8.9 | (1.0) | 8.0 | (0.8) | 8.1 | (0.8) | 6.3 | (0.7) | **2.6** | (1.1) |
| Canada | 12.6 | (0.8) | 12.4 | (0.8) | 11.7 | (0.7) | 12.6 | (0.8) | -0.0 | (1.2) | 11.3 | (0.8) | 10.5 | (0.7) | 10.9 | (0.7) | 9.2 | (0.8) | 2.1 | (1.2) |
| Czech Republic | 17.2 | (1.7) | 14.4 | (1.2) | 13.6 | (1.1) | 11.5 | (1.3) | **5.2** | (2.4) | 12.5 | (1.1) | 11.0 | (1.0) | 10.1 | (0.9) | 10.0 | (1.0) | 2.0 | (1.4) |
| Denmark | 8.9 | (1.0) | 4.3 | (0.8) | 4.6 | (0.7) | 3.1 | (0.5) | **5.7** | (1.0) | 10.3 | (1.0) | 8.0 | (0.9) | 6.9 | (0.9) | 6.4 | (0.8) | **3.8** | (1.1) |
| Finland | 8.5 | (0.9) | 9.5 | (0.9) | 7.1 | (0.8) | 7.3 | (0.8) | 1.2 | (1.0) | 11.2 | (1.0) | 11.0 | (1.0) | 8.6 | (0.8) | 6.6 | (0.7) | **4.7** | (1.2) |
| France | 9.8 | (0.9) | 7.2 | (1.0) | 5.1 | (0.8) | 5.7 | (0.9) | **4.2** | (1.1) | 19.1 | (1.3) | 19.7 | (1.2) | 18.8 | (1.3) | 14.2 | (1.3) | **5.0** | (1.7) |
| Germany | 5.5 | (0.9) | 6.0 | (0.8) | 5.7 | (0.8) | 5.7 | (0.8) | -0.0 | (1.2) | 7.8 | (1.0) | 7.4 | (1.0) | 8.0 | (0.8) | 7.2 | (1.1) | 0.5 | (1.4) |
| Greece | 13.3 | (1.4) | 12.1 | (1.2) | 12.9 | (1.2) | 9.8 | (1.0) | **3.4** | (1.7) | 16.4 | (1.3) | 15.9 | (1.5) | 15.5 | (1.3) | 11.3 | (1.1) | **5.0** | (1.6) |
| Hungary | 14.9 | (1.3) | 13.4 | (1.2) | 15.2 | (1.3) | 15.4 | (1.3) | -0.6 | (1.9) | 15.2 | (1.2) | 9.8 | (1.0) | 12.7 | (1.1) | 13.3 | (1.4) | 1.9 | (1.9) |
| Iceland | 14.2 | (0.9) | 9.0 | (0.9) | 10.1 | (1.0) | 8.3 | (0.8) | **5.9** | (1.3) | 17.3 | (1.1) | 16.2 | (1.2) | 13.1 | (1.1) | 11.3 | (1.0) | **6.0** | (1.5) |
| Ireland | 8.0 | (1.4) | 6.1 | (1.0) | 7.1 | (0.9) | 6.7 | (0.8) | 1.1 | (1.6) | 11.0 | (1.3) | 9.2 | (1.1) | 9.8 | (1.0) | 6.0 | (0.8) | **4.9** | (1.6) |
| Italy | a | a | a | a | a | a | a | a | a | a | 33.3 | (1.0) | 37.6 | (1.1) | 38.0 | (1.5) | 36.5 | (1.4) | -3.2 | (1.6) |
| Japan | 4.4 | (0.7) | 4.2 | (0.6) | 2.8 | (0.5) | 3.2 | (0.6) | 1.2 | (0.8) | 8.2 | (0.9) | 7.3 | (0.8) | 4.8 | (0.6) | 5.7 | (0.7) | **2.5** | (1.3) |
| Korea | 10.3 | (1.0) | 9.7 | (0.8) | 10.3 | (0.9) | 7.9 | (0.9) | 2.3 | (1.4) | 17.3 | (1.1) | 16.2 | (1.0) | 16.1 | (1.3) | 17.3 | (1.1) | 0.1 | (1.5) |
| Luxembourg | 15.8 | (1.0) | 14.7 | (1.1) | 11.5 | (1.0) | 12.8 | (1.0) | **3.0** | (1.5) | 18.7 | (1.1) | 15.6 | (1.3) | 12.5 | (1.0) | 11.4 | (1.0) | **7.4** | (1.5) |
| Mexico | 24.8 | (1.8) | 16.7 | (1.4) | 16.9 | (0.9) | 11.1 | (0.8) | **13.9** | (2.0) | 24.0 | (1.4) | 19.0 | (1.1) | 16.8 | (1.1) | 10.6 | (0.7) | **13.4** | (1.7) |
| Netherlands | 8.4 | (0.9) | 7.6 | (0.9) | 7.3 | (0.8) | 6.8 | (0.9) | 1.3 | (1.1) | 10.5 | (1.0) | 8.0 | (0.9) | 8.7 | (0.8) | 7.4 | (0.9) | **2.9** | (1.3) |
| New Zealand | 10.4 | (1.2) | 8.1 | (1.0) | 9.4 | (1.2) | 8.0 | (1.3) | 2.4 | (1.6) | 13.0 | (1.2) | 6.8 | (0.8) | 9.1 | (1.1) | 9.8 | (1.1) | 3.2 | (1.6) |
| Norway | 10.7 | (1.2) | 8.0 | (1.1) | 8.5 | (0.9) | 6.5 | (0.9) | **4.1** | (1.4) | 17.1 | (1.3) | 12.6 | (1.2) | 10.3 | (1.0) | 7.3 | (0.8) | **9.9** | (1.7) |
| Poland | 17.0 | (1.3) | 15.2 | (1.1) | 13.6 | (0.9) | 12.6 | (0.9) | **4.4** | (1.6) | 24.5 | (1.4) | 24.0 | (1.3) | 23.0 | (1.1) | 20.8 | (1.3) | **3.9** | (1.8) |
| Portugal | 25.4 | (2.1) | 24.0 | (1.5) | 20.4 | (1.4) | 17.8 | (1.3) | **7.2** | (2.5) | 36.8 | (1.9) | 32.3 | (2.1) | 32.5 | (1.8) | 25.6 | (1.6) | **11.5** | (2.5) |
| Slovak Republic | 32.1 | (2.0) | 31.3 | (2.0) | 31.8 | (2.0) | 26.3 | (1.6) | **5.9** | (2.3) | 19.3 | (1.3) | 19.7 | (1.6) | 17.9 | (1.5) | 15.3 | (1.6) | **3.7** | (1.8) |
| Spain | 10.1 | (1.1) | 8.7 | (0.7) | 9.0 | (0.7) | 6.3 | (0.5) | **3.8** | (1.1) | 14.0 | (0.9) | 9.9 | (0.8) | 11.3 | (0.6) | 7.9 | (0.7) | **6.2** | (1.1) |
| Sweden | 10.3 | (1.1) | 10.1 | (1.0) | 8.0 | (0.8) | 5.8 | (0.8) | **4.5** | (1.3) | 21.1 | (1.3) | 17.0 | (1.2) | 11.3 | (0.9) | 7.2 | (0.9) | **14.0** | (1.6) |
| Switzerland | 9.1 | (0.7) | 6.6 | (0.6) | 5.4 | (0.5) | 6.0 | (0.7) | **3.1** | (1.0) | 13.1 | (0.9) | 9.8 | (0.8) | 9.3 | (0.8) | 7.8 | (0.7) | **5.3** | (1.1) |
| Turkey | 7.4 | (1.1) | 8.2 | (1.2) | 7.8 | (0.8) | 7.0 | (0.9) | 0.1 | (1.3) | 8.9 | (0.9) | 9.2 | (1.0) | 10.3 | (1.0) | 9.0 | (0.9) | -0.0 | (1.2) |
| United Kingdom | 13.1 | (1.0) | 11.1 | (0.8) | 10.6 | (0.8) | 10.2 | (1.0) | 2.8 | (1.4) | 17.4 | (1.1) | 18.7 | (1.1) | 18.0 | (1.2) | 16.1 | (1.1) | 1.2 | (1.5) |
| United States | 26.7 | (2.0) | 23.9 | (1.7) | 21.2 | (1.4) | 18.0 | (1.2) | **8.8** | (2.3) | 25.5 | (1.7) | 19.5 | (1.6) | 17.0 | (1.2) | 14.5 | (1.2) | **11.0** | (2.0) |
| **OECD average** | 12.8 | (0.2) | 11.1 | (0.2) | 10.6 | (0.2) | 9.3 | (0.2) | **3.4** | (0.3) | 16.2 | (0.2) | 14.3 | (0.2) | 13.6 | (0.2) | 11.7 | (0.2) | **4.6** | (0.3) |
| Argentina | 8.1 | (1.1) | 11.3 | (1.6) | 12.7 | (1.7) | 10.3 | (1.7) | -1.9 | (2.1) | 17.9 | (1.8) | 11.8 | (1.3) | 12.4 | (1.7) | 8.1 | (1.6) | **9.7** | (2.5) |
| Azerbaijan | 31.9 | (2.3) | 38.4 | (2.3) | 41.4 | (1.7) | 44.1 | (1.7) | **-12.1** | (3.0) | 33.6 | (1.8) | 37.3 | (2.3) | 37.5 | (1.9) | 40.4 | (1.6) | **-6.8** | (2.2) |
| Brazil | 12.7 | (1.1) | 12.5 | (1.0) | 13.4 | (1.0) | 15.7 | (1.3) | -3.3 | (1.5) | 25.1 | (1.2) | 23.3 | (1.4) | 21.6 | (1.3) | 24.2 | (1.6) | 1.2 | (2.0) |
| Bulgaria | 31.8 | (2.6) | 23.3 | (2.1) | 19.7 | (1.7) | 13.3 | (1.3) | **18.9** | (2.9) | 25.7 | (1.9) | 20.4 | (1.8) | 16.4 | (1.4) | 14.4 | (1.3) | **11.5** | (2.3) |
| Chile | 8.4 | (1.1) | 9.1 | (0.9) | 8.0 | (0.8) | 7.4 | (1.0) | 1.0 | (1.6) | 20.0 | (1.3) | 16.9 | (1.3) | 16.2 | (1.4) | 11.6 | (1.4) | **8.2** | (2.0) |
| Colombia | 20.4 | (1.5) | 14.0 | (1.4) | 13.6 | (1.4) | 12.1 | (2.0) | **8.3** | (2.3) | 27.3 | (1.9) | 20.3 | (1.9) | 19.4 | (1.9) | 13.4 | (1.3) | **13.7** | (2.0) |
| Croatia | 15.0 | (1.1) | 13.2 | (1.0) | 13.0 | (0.9) | 11.5 | (1.1) | **3.5** | (1.5) | 13.3 | (1.2) | 11.4 | (1.0) | 9.7 | (0.9) | 10.3 | (1.0) | **3.0** | (1.4) |
| Estonia | 21.0 | (1.6) | 17.7 | (1.5) | 17.5 | (1.3) | 14.1 | (1.2) | **7.1** | (1.9) | 16.4 | (1.1) | 14.7 | (1.4) | 12.0 | (1.1) | 11.9 | (1.3) | **4.6** | (1.5) |
| Hong Kong-China | 6.5 | (0.7) | 4.9 | (0.8) | 7.6 | (0.9) | 4.6 | (0.7) | 1.8 | (0.9) | 18.3 | (1.3) | 16.9 | (1.4) | 18.7 | (1.6) | 13.7 | (1.4) | **4.6** | (2.0) |
| Indonesia | 38.1 | (2.6) | 33.4 | (2.2) | 31.1 | (3.1) | 23.6 | (2.7) | **14.5** | (2.7) | 29.5 | (2.3) | 27.4 | (1.8) | 27.6 | (2.9) | 21.5 | (2.7) | **8.0** | (2.5) |
| Israel | 25.8 | (1.7) | 20.4 | (1.6) | 19.2 | (1.5) | 17.5 | (1.3) | **8.5** | (2.0) | 26.5 | (1.8) | 24.0 | (1.7) | 18.5 | (1.4) | 14.0 | (1.1) | **12.1** | (2.0) |
| Jordan | 27.9 | (1.6) | 26.1 | (1.5) | 28.5 | (1.5) | 26.8 | (1.9) | 1.2 | (2.4) | 31.5 | (1.5) | 32.3 | (1.5) | 32.6 | (1.5) | 30.2 | (1.8) | 1.1 | (2.3) |
| Kyrgyzstan | 64.9 | (1.7) | 66.4 | (1.6) | 67.4 | (1.8) | 56.6 | (1.9) | **8.0** | (2.5) | 45.0 | (2.0) | 45.0 | (1.7) | 46.5 | (1.8) | 39.9 | (1.7) | 4.9 | (2.6) |
| Latvia | 41.3 | (2.2) | 36.9 | (2.0) | 31.8 | (1.8) | 28.6 | (1.8) | **12.6** | (2.7) | 33.0 | (2.2) | 26.0 | (1.9) | 23.3 | (1.3) | 19.8 | (1.4) | **12.8** | (2.2) |
| Liechtenstein | 9.7 | (3.4) | 2.5 | (1.8) | 4.9 | (2.5) | 6.2 | (2.8) | 3.6 | (4.4) | 12.9 | (3.8) | 3.9 | (2.2) | 6.3 | (2.7) | 7.3 | (2.5) | 5.6 | (5.0) |
| Lithuania | 9.7 | (1.0) | 11.7 | (1.2) | 12.8 | (1.2) | 13.7 | (1.0) | **-4.0** | (1.3) | 19.3 | (1.3) | 18.4 | (1.4) | 17.1 | (1.2) | 15.7 | (1.3) | 3.5 | (1.8) |
| Macao-China | 17.1 | (1.3) | 12.6 | (1.0) | 13.2 | (1.1) | 14.0 | (1.1) | **3.0** | (1.6) | 24.9 | (1.3) | 22.4 | (1.5) | 22.3 | (1.5) | 21.3 | (1.4) | 3.4 | (1.9) |
| Montenegro | 28.1 | (1.3) | 24.6 | (1.3) | 25.7 | (1.4) | 21.9 | (1.5) | **6.2** | (2.0) | 18.7 | (1.1) | 19.7 | (1.4) | 17.8 | (1.1) | 14.8 | (1.2) | **4.1** | (1.5) |
| Qatar | 35.3 | (1.3) | 36.6 | (1.3) | 31.1 | (1.3) | 32.7 | (0.9) | 2.4 | (1.5) | 30.2 | (1.2) | 32.0 | (1.3) | 26.2 | (1.0) | 28.0 | (1.2) | 2.3 | (1.6) |
| Romania | 27.9 | (2.3) | 26.5 | (2.7) | 27.2 | (1.9) | 26.0 | (1.7) | 1.9 | (3.0) | 32.9 | (2.1) | 20.9 | (2.5) | 22.3 | (1.6) | 21.5 | (1.5) | **11.3** | (2.3) |
| Russian Federation | 33.4 | (1.7) | 28.6 | (1.6) | 29.9 | (1.9) | 31.1 | (1.2) | 2.5 | (1.8) | 34.7 | (1.8) | 33.1 | (1.8) | 30.9 | (1.9) | 27.5 | (1.6) | **7.2** | (2.3) |
| Serbia | 10.5 | (1.0) | 10.2 | (1.1) | 11.4 | (1.2) | 9.1 | (0.8) | 1.5 | (1.2) | 14.1 | (1.1) | 13.8 | (1.2) | 12.2 | (1.1) | 9.0 | (1.0) | **4.9** | (1.4) |
| Slovenia | 11.8 | (1.0) | 9.6 | (0.9) | 6.7 | (0.7) | 7.3 | (0.9) | **4.3** | (1.2) | 10.5 | (1.3) | 8.3 | (0.8) | 8.2 | (1.0) | 8.4 | (0.8) | 2.1 | (1.5) |
| Chinese Taipei | 18.3 | (1.4) | 15.8 | (1.0) | 12.1 | (0.9) | 11.4 | (0.8) | **7.0** | (1.6) | 28.7 | (1.6) | 24.2 | (1.1) | 20.4 | (1.1) | 17.8 | (1.0) | **11.0** | (2.0) |
| Thailand | 18.8 | (1.3) | 22.5 | (1.4) | 23.6 | (1.3) | 19.2 | (1.2) | -0.2 | (1.7) | 22.3 | (1.4) | 29.7 | (2.0) | 31.0 | (1.4) | 24.3 | (1.3) | -1.9 | (1.8) |
| Tunisia | 34.8 | (1.8) | 42.5 | (1.8) | 47.3 | (1.6) | 45.7 | (3.0) | **-10.9** | (3.0) | 30.2 | (1.5) | 34.8 | (1.7) | 34.7 | (1.7) | 31.4 | (2.3) | -1.3 | (2.6) |
| Uruguay | 7.2 | (0.9) | 10.6 | (1.6) | 10.2 | (1.3) | 10.2 | (1.0) | **-3.0** | (1.1) | 7.7 | (1.0) | 9.7 | (1.0) | 8.9 | (1.3) | 9.5 | (1.0) | -1.7 | (1.4) |

*Note:* Values that are statistically significant at the 5% level (p < 0.05) are indicated in bold.

**Table 3.15** Percentage of students by different types of out-of-school-time lessons,
[Part 5/5] by quarters of the PISA index of economic, social and cultural status (ESCS)

| | Proportion of students participating in out-of-school lessons with school teachers | | | | | | | | | | | | | | | | | | | |
| --- | --- | --- | --- | --- | --- | --- | --- | --- | --- | --- | --- | --- | --- | --- | --- | --- | --- | --- | --- | --- |
| | Large group lessons | | | | | | | | | | At least one of these types of out-of-school lessons | | | | | | | | | |
| | Bottom quarter of ESCS | | Second quarter of ESCS | | Third quarter of ESCS | | Top quarter of ESCS | | Difference (bottom-top) | | Bottom quarter of ESCS | | Second quarter of ESCS | | Third quarter of ESCS | | Top quarter of ESCS | | Difference (bottom-top) | |
| | % | S.E. | % | S.E. | % | S.E. | % | S.E. | % | S.E. | % | S.E. | % | S.E. | % | S.E. | % | S.E. | % | S.E. |
| Australia | 9.7 | (0.6) | 7.2 | (0.5) | 7.7 | (0.6) | 7.9 | (0.6) | **1.8** | (0.8) | 14.5 | (0.8) | 13.2 | (0.7) | 13.9 | (0.8) | 14.4 | (0.9) | **0.1** | (1.1) |
| Austria | 17.7 | (1.6) | 15.0 | (1.3) | 15.2 | (1.1) | 14.7 | (1.6) | 3.0 | (2.1) | 26.7 | (1.9) | 22.6 | (1.5) | 22.8 | (1.4) | 21.4 | (1.8) | **5.5** | (2.3) |
| Belgium | 7.9 | (0.9) | 6.1 | (0.7) | 5.8 | (0.7) | 4.3 | (0.5) | **3.6** | (1.1) | 15.7 | (1.4) | 14.4 | (1.1) | 14.3 | (1.0) | 12.7 | (0.8) | 3.0 | (1.6) |
| Canada | 12.5 | (0.8) | 11.3 | (0.6) | 11.6 | (0.7) | 9.7 | (0.7) | **2.7** | (1.0) | 21.5 | (1.0) | 21.4 | (0.9) | 21.9 | (0.9) | 20.7 | (1.1) | 0.7 | (1.5) |
| Czech Republic | 18.1 | (1.4) | 14.1 | (1.4) | 12.5 | (1.2) | 8.7 | (1.1) | **9.0** | (1.7) | 29.1 | (1.7) | 23.6 | (1.6) | 21.2 | (1.5) | 18.8 | (1.4) | **10.1** | (2.0) |
| Denmark | 9.2 | (0.9) | 7.6 | (1.0) | 8.6 | (1.0) | 6.6 | (0.7) | **2.5** | (1.2) | 17.7 | (1.4) | 14.1 | (1.3) | 13.0 | (1.1) | 11.1 | (0.9) | **6.7** | (1.5) |
| Finland | 12.9 | (1.1) | 14.2 | (1.1) | 11.8 | (1.1) | 9.6 | (0.9) | **3.4** | (1.3) | 19.5 | (1.1) | 21.5 | (1.4) | 16.9 | (1.2) | 14.7 | (1.1) | **4.7** | (1.3) |
| France | 12.7 | (1.2) | 11.0 | (1.1) | 8.9 | (0.9) | 8.6 | (1.0) | **4.1** | (1.5) | 25.8 | (1.5) | 24.6 | (1.5) | 23.9 | (1.4) | 20.9 | (1.5) | **4.9** | (2.0) |
| Germany | 12.6 | (1.3) | 10.1 | (1.0) | 10.1 | (0.9) | 8.2 | (0.9) | **4.5** | (1.7) | 18.9 | (1.5) | 18.5 | (1.4) | 16.7 | (1.2) | 15.9 | (1.3) | 3.0 | (2.1) |
| Greece | 12.6 | (1.2) | 10.3 | (1.0) | 9.2 | (1.0) | 6.3 | (0.8) | **6.2** | (1.2) | 25.8 | (1.8) | 23.1 | (1.7) | 21.7 | (1.5) | 17.5 | (1.4) | **8.3** | (2.3) |
| Hungary | 21.4 | (1.6) | 13.4 | (1.1) | 15.1 | (1.3) | 13.4 | (1.2) | **7.9** | (1.9) | 33.5 | (1.7) | 25.6 | (1.5) | 28.7 | (1.7) | 29.5 | (2.0) | 3.8 | (2.3) |
| Iceland | 12.1 | (1.1) | 14.5 | (1.1) | 15.0 | (1.1) | 14.7 | (1.2) | -2.6 | (1.6) | 29.3 | (1.4) | 27.6 | (1.5) | 27.8 | (1.4) | 23.5 | (1.2) | **5.8** | (1.9) |
| Ireland | 11.5 | (1.1) | 10.4 | (1.1) | 10.2 | (1.2) | 7.3 | (0.9) | **4.1** | (1.4) | 18.9 | (1.7) | 16.9 | (1.3) | 17.9 | (1.4) | 13.9 | (1.3) | **4.9** | (2.0) |
| Italy | 22.9 | (1.0) | 25.7 | (1.1) | 27.4 | (1.0) | 27.3 | (1.0) | **-4.4** | (1.5) | 42.1 | (1.1) | 46.0 | (1.1) | 48.0 | (1.5) | 47.0 | (1.4) | **-4.9** | (1.6) |
| Japan | 31.2 | (2.0) | 30.1 | (1.7) | 29.4 | (1.7) | 30.6 | (1.8) | 0.7 | (2.3) | 36.6 | (1.9) | 34.9 | (1.8) | 33.0 | (1.7) | 34.7 | (1.9) | 2.0 | (2.5) |
| Korea | 36.0 | (1.7) | 36.4 | (1.7) | 35.9 | (1.9) | 36.5 | (2.4) | -0.5 | (2.8) | 50.5 | (1.6) | 48.6 | (1.7) | 50.3 | (1.9) | 51.9 | (2.0) | -1.4 | (2.5) |
| Luxembourg | 14.3 | (1.2) | 11.7 | (1.0) | 7.6 | (0.9) | 5.6 | (0.7) | **8.8** | (1.4) | 29.2 | (1.3) | 27.8 | (1.4) | 22.8 | (1.4) | 21.2 | (1.3) | **8.1** | (1.9) |
| Mexico | 34.2 | (1.9) | 25.1 | (1.1) | 21.6 | (1.2) | 14.4 | (0.9) | **19.9** | (2.2) | 45.1 | (2.1) | 33.9 | (1.3) | 31.8 | (1.1) | 22.5 | (1.2) | **22.8** | (2.6) |
| Netherlands | 8.5 | (1.0) | 7.7 | (0.9) | 7.8 | (0.8) | 4.4 | (0.7) | **4.1** | (1.3) | 17.5 | (1.6) | 15.9 | (1.2) | 15.6 | (1.2) | 13.0 | (1.4) | 4.0 | (2.1) |
| New Zealand | 11.1 | (1.2) | 8.8 | (1.0) | 8.4 | (1.0) | 7.4 | (0.8) | **3.7** | (1.3) | 20.2 | (1.6) | 16.3 | (1.3) | 17.1 | (1.6) | 16.6 | (1.5) | 3.8 | (2.0) |
| Norway | 20.0 | (1.4) | 18.2 | (1.4) | 15.7 | (1.2) | 14.7 | (1.0) | **5.5** | (1.6) | 29.4 | (1.5) | 25.0 | (1.5) | 21.5 | (1.4) | 18.9 | (1.2) | **10.7** | (1.9) |
| Poland | 30.6 | (1.6) | 28.7 | (1.6) | 27.2 | (1.5) | 20.3 | (1.2) | **10.3** | (1.9) | 45.8 | (1.8) | 42.8 | (1.8) | 40.4 | (1.5) | 35.9 | (1.4) | **10.0** | (2.3) |
| Portugal | 30.1 | (1.9) | 26.8 | (1.6) | 23.2 | (1.7) | 15.3 | (1.5) | **15.3** | (2.5) | 54.8 | (2.2) | 53.1 | (2.2) | 45.7 | (1.9) | 37.7 | (1.9) | **17.9** | (2.9) |
| Slovak Republic | 27.1 | (1.9) | 24.1 | (1.8) | 23.4 | (1.7) | 21.2 | (1.7) | **5.7** | (2.1) | 39.8 | (2.1) | 39.5 | (2.2) | 39.4 | (2.0) | 35.7 | (2.1) | 4.1 | (2.7) |
| Spain | 14.6 | (1.0) | 9.3 | (0.8) | 8.9 | (0.7) | 6.1 | (0.6) | **8.6** | (1.0) | 24.3 | (1.3) | 17.8 | (0.8) | 18.2 | (0.8) | 13.8 | (0.8) | **10.4** | (1.3) |
| Sweden | 27.8 | (1.4) | 23.6 | (1.3) | 17.4 | (1.2) | 13.9 | (1.1) | **14.1** | (1.7) | 35.1 | (1.4) | 30.1 | (1.5) | 22.5 | (1.3) | 17.7 | (1.3) | **17.4** | (2.1) |
| Switzerland | 16.2 | (1.0) | 15.9 | (1.0) | 14.5 | (1.3) | 9.4 | (0.8) | **6.7** | (1.2) | 26.0 | (1.2) | 23.7 | (1.1) | 22.2 | (1.3) | 18.0 | (1.3) | **8.1** | (1.8) |
| Turkey | 14.0 | (1.4) | 12.2 | (1.2) | 12.8 | (1.2) | 12.2 | (1.2) | 2.0 | (1.8) | 19.9 | (1.6) | 19.6 | (1.6) | 20.3 | (1.3) | 19.2 | (1.6) | 0.9 | (2.3) |
| United Kingdom | 20.8 | (1.2) | 20.0 | (1.1) | 18.7 | (1.4) | 18.3 | (1.2) | 2.5 | (1.7) | 32.6 | (1.5) | 32.0 | (1.3) | 31.1 | (1.5) | 30.6 | (1.5) | 2.0 | (2.2) |
| United States | 24.6 | (2.4) | 20.4 | (1.4) | 15.7 | (1.2) | 12.1 | (0.9) | **12.6** | (2.5) | 38.6 | (2.2) | 34.7 | (2.0) | 30.9 | (1.7) | 25.6 | (1.2) | **13.0** | (2.5) |
| **OECD average** | 18.5 | (0.3) | 16.3 | (0.2) | 15.2 | (0.2) | 13.0 | (0.2) | **5.5** | (0.3) | 29.5 | (0.3) | 27.0 | (0.3) | 25.7 | (0.3) | 23.2 | (0.3) | **6.3** | (0.4) |
| Argentina | 15.7 | (1.9) | 10.9 | (1.4) | 12.2 | (1.7) | 6.2 | (1.2) | **9.8** | (2.2) | 24.4 | (1.9) | 19.7 | (2.0) | 21.4 | (2.3) | 15.0 | (2.1) | **9.6** | (2.8) |
| Azerbaijan | 45.1 | (2.4) | 52.6 | (2.0) | 51.4 | (1.6) | 44.3 | (2.1) | 0.2 | (2.8) | 60.8 | (2.8) | 68.1 | (2.2) | 70.1 | (1.8) | 71.4 | (2.0) | **-10.6** | (3.1) |
| Brazil | 22.9 | (1.2) | 20.8 | (1.1) | 18.9 | (1.3) | 19.2 | (1.3) | 3.6 | (1.9) | 35.7 | (1.5) | 33.2 | (1.6) | 32.7 | (1.5) | 35.7 | (1.7) | -0.2 | (2.3) |
| Bulgaria | 29.0 | (2.0) | 24.8 | (2.4) | 19.9 | (1.8) | 17.7 | (1.4) | **11.7** | (2.4) | 44.7 | (3.0) | 35.8 | (2.6) | 31.0 | (2.0) | 28.4 | (1.7) | **16.7** | (3.5) |
| Chile | 21.7 | (1.5) | 19.4 | (1.1) | 17.3 | (1.5) | 12.4 | (1.3) | **8.7** | (2.1) | 31.8 | (1.8) | 28.9 | (1.5) | 26.8 | (1.8) | 21.2 | (1.9) | **10.3** | (2.7) |
| Colombia | 26.3 | (1.8) | 18.9 | (1.7) | 19.1 | (1.7) | 13.2 | (1.6) | **13.1** | (2.1) | 37.9 | (1.8) | 29.3 | (2.1) | 29.2 | (2.0) | 20.9 | (1.9) | **17.2** | (2.5) |
| Croatia | 15.2 | (1.1) | 12.2 | (1.0) | 12.1 | (1.1) | 8.6 | (1.0) | **6.5** | (1.3) | 24.7 | (1.3) | 22.4 | (1.3) | 21.5 | (1.2) | 18.7 | (1.6) | **6.1** | (1.9) |
| Estonia | 25.4 | (1.8) | 19.2 | (1.1) | 16.5 | (1.3) | 13.5 | (1.3) | **11.9** | (2.4) | 39.6 | (1.6) | 33.8 | (1.8) | 28.7 | (1.7) | 26.2 | (1.8) | **13.7** | (2.2) |
| Hong Kong-China | 42.0 | (1.7) | 43.4 | (1.6) | 44.5 | (1.9) | 37.7 | (2.1) | 4.1 | (2.5) | 48.9 | (1.8) | 50.1 | (1.6) | 51.2 | (1.8) | 43.9 | (2.4) | 5.0 | (2.9) |
| Indonesia | 40.6 | (2.9) | 37.2 | (2.1) | 34.0 | (3.1) | 27.7 | (3.1) | **12.7** | (3.8) | 59.5 | (3.0) | 55.8 | (2.3) | 49.3 | (4.2) | 42.6 | (4.4) | **16.7** | (4.5) |
| Israel | 25.9 | (1.6) | 20.9 | (1.5) | 18.7 | (1.3) | 15.0 | (1.2) | **10.6** | (2.0) | 43.4 | (2.0) | 37.6 | (1.8) | 31.5 | (1.7) | 28.1 | (1.4) | **15.0** | (2.3) |
| Jordan | 41.8 | (1.8) | 44.0 | (1.6) | 39.4 | (1.5) | 38.1 | (1.6) | 3.8 | (2.5) | 57.3 | (1.8) | 58.8 | (1.9) | 56.7 | (1.7) | 53.3 | (2.1) | 3.9 | (2.8) |
| Kyrgyzstan | 54.7 | (2.0) | 53.1 | (1.8) | 54.6 | (1.8) | 49.4 | (1.7) | **5.3** | (2.3) | 81.4 | (2.0) | 81.0 | (1.5) | 79.7 | (1.7) | 72.0 | (1.9) | **9.2** | (2.7) |
| Latvia | 37.3 | (1.6) | 30.8 | (1.6) | 26.1 | (1.9) | 21.7 | (1.6) | **15.6** | (2.1) | 59.2 | (2.0) | 51.1 | (2.1) | 46.6 | (1.7) | 44.6 | (1.8) | **14.5** | (2.5) |
| Liechtenstein | 16.5 | (4.1) | 8.9 | (3.3) | 11.2 | (3.5) | 6.1 | (2.6) | 10.2 | (5.3) | 23.8 | (4.5) | 10.1 | (3.5) | 17.2 | (4.3) | 14.7 | (4.3) | 9.6 | (6.4) |
| Lithuania | 23.2 | (1.6) | 17.8 | (1.3) | 20.9 | (1.5) | 15.6 | (1.1) | **7.5** | (2.0) | 35.9 | (1.6) | 33.8 | (1.7) | 35.0 | (1.7) | 32.9 | (1.5) | 2.9 | (2.1) |
| Macao-China | 37.9 | (1.5) | 39.2 | (1.7) | 32.6 | (1.4) | 29.8 | (1.5) | **8.0** | (2.1) | 50.4 | (1.6) | 49.7 | (1.8) | 44.6 | (1.6) | 41.9 | (1.5) | **8.7** | (1.8) |
| Montenegro | 25.9 | (1.4) | 21.8 | (1.4) | 21.0 | (1.3) | 18.0 | (1.3) | **7.9** | (2.0) | 40.0 | (1.4) | 34.8 | (1.6) | 35.0 | (1.6) | 28.7 | (1.6) | **11.5** | (2.1) |
| Qatar | 31.7 | (1.3) | 32.0 | (1.3) | 25.3 | (0.9) | 28.8 | (1.0) | 2.9 | (1.6) | 48.2 | (1.3) | 48.7 | (1.3) | 40.7 | (1.1) | 43.6 | (1.3) | 4.6 | (1.6) |
| Romania | 31.6 | (2.4) | 22.8 | (2.7) | 18.8 | (2.3) | 14.4 | (1.4) | **16.9** | (3.0) | 47.9 | (2.0) | 38.0 | (3.3) | 39.3 | (2.3) | 35.2 | (2.2) | **12.9** | (3.0) |
| Russian Federation | 41.5 | (2.1) | 38.1 | (2.0) | 35.1 | (1.6) | 32.0 | (1.5) | **9.6** | (2.4) | 60.7 | (2.0) | 58.0 | (1.8) | 56.4 | (1.9) | 55.5 | (1.6) | **5.0** | (2.2) |
| Serbia | 18.8 | (1.4) | 14.9 | (1.2) | 14.1 | (1.1) | 10.5 | (1.0) | **8.4** | (1.6) | 26.8 | (1.5) | 24.4 | (1.4) | 23.6 | (1.6) | 19.7 | (1.2) | **7.0** | (1.7) |
| Slovenia | 14.2 | (1.1) | 12.6 | (1.0) | 10.2 | (0.8) | 9.6 | (0.9) | **4.6** | (1.4) | 23.6 | (1.5) | 20.9 | (1.1) | 17.7 | (1.2) | 18.2 | (1.2) | **5.4** | (1.7) |
| Chinese Taipei | 39.7 | (1.6) | 38.2 | (1.5) | 33.4 | (1.1) | 29.1 | (1.3) | **10.6** | (2.0) | 51.4 | (1.7) | 48.3 | (1.6) | 42.9 | (1.2) | 37.6 | (1.5) | **13.7** | (2.1) |
| Thailand | 33.0 | (1.9) | 41.4 | (1.9) | 40.9 | (1.9) | 41.0 | (2.0) | **-8.3** | (2.8) | 39.6 | (1.8) | 48.8 | (2.0) | 49.7 | (1.8) | 51.4 | (1.9) | **-11.9** | (2.7) |
| Tunisia | 32.2 | (1.9) | 32.7 | (1.8) | 30.2 | (1.5) | 26.9 | (1.7) | 5.5 | (2.5) | 48.8 | (1.8) | 55.7 | (1.7) | 57.1 | (1.6) | 54.3 | (2.4) | **-5.5** | (2.7) |
| Uruguay | 9.9 | (1.1) | 10.1 | (1.0) | 7.6 | (1.1) | 7.1 | (0.8) | **2.9** | (1.4) | 16.1 | (1.5) | 18.7 | (1.8) | 16.9 | (1.7) | 16.7 | (1.5) | -0.7 | (1.9) |

*Note:* Values that are statistically significant at the 5% level (p < 0.05) are indicated in bold.

© OECD 2011 Quality Time for Students: Learning In and Out of School

## Table 3.16 Percentage of students by different types of out-of-school-time lessons, by immigrant status
[Part 1/5]

| | Proportion of students participating in out-of-school-time lessons | | | | | | Proportion of students participating in out-of-school lessons with non-school teachers — One-to-one lessons | | | | | | If students' ESCS was equal to the national average ESCS, and schools' average ESCS was equal to the national average of schools' average ESCS | | |
| | Native students | | Students with an immigrant background | | Difference (native-immigrant) | | Native students | | Students with an immigrant background | | Difference (native-immigrant) | | Difference (native-immigrant) | Increase in the logit of participating in out-of-school-time lessons by being a native student | |
| | % | S.E. | % | S.E. | Dif. | S.E. | % | S.E. | % | S.E. | Dif. | S.E. | Dif. | Logistic regression coefficient | S.E. |
|---|---|---|---|---|---|---|---|---|---|---|---|---|---|---|---|
| **OECD** | | | | | | | | | | | | | | | |
| Australia | 27.5 | (0.6) | 43.8 | (1.3) | **-16.3** | (1.4) | 14.3 | (0.4) | 24.7 | (1.2) | **-10.4** | (1.2) | **-10.1** | **-0.67** | (0.07) |
| Austria | 35.1 | (1.1) | 43.3 | (2.5) | **-8.2** | (2.4) | 16.8 | (0.8) | 16.0 | (1.8) | 0.8 | (1.9) | -2.7 | -0.19 | (0.17) |
| Belgium | 29.0 | (0.6) | 37.3 | (1.8) | **-8.3** | (1.9) | 17.8 | (0.6) | 17.3 | (1.1) | 0.5 | (1.2) | **-3.8** | **-0.26** | (0.09) |
| Canada | 32.6 | (0.8) | 46.5 | (1.4) | **-14.0** | (1.5) | 14.6 | (0.5) | 22.7 | (1.3) | **-8.1** | (1.4) | **-8.0** | **-0.55** | (0.09) |
| Czech Republic | 36.9 | (0.9) | 46.4 | (6.9) | -9.5 | (6.9) | 15.8 | (0.7) | 18.7 | (4.2) | -2.8 | (4.2) | -3.8 | -0.27 | (0.27) |
| Denmark | 19.0 | (0.8) | 39.8 | (2.9) | **-20.9** | (3.1) | 4.8 | (0.4) | 11.5 | (1.9) | **-6.8** | (2.1) | **-6.9** | **-0.97** | (0.24) |
| Finland | 23.2 | (0.7) | 39.4 | (6.0) | **-16.2** | (6.1) | 5.3 | (0.3) | 9.9 | (4.2) | -4.6 | (4.2) | -6.4 | -0.89 | (0.46) |
| France | 40.5 | (0.9) | 49.6 | (2.8) | **-9.1** | (2.8) | 22.1 | (1.0) | 24.4 | (2.4) | -2.4 | (2.4) | **-7.1** | **-0.39** | (0.13) |
| Germany | 36.1 | (0.9) | 41.0 | (2.4) | -4.9 | (2.7) | 21.2 | (0.8) | 21.1 | (2.0) | 0.0 | (2.3) | -3.2 | -0.19 | (0.15) |
| Greece | 78.3 | (0.9) | 51.1 | (4.2) | **27.2** | (4.3) | 46.3 | (1.2) | 23.4 | (2.5) | **22.9** | (2.8) | **18.1** | **0.79** | (0.15) |
| Hungary | 54.1 | (1.1) | 59.5 | (6.8) | -5.4 | (7.0) | 32.4 | (1.0) | 38.4 | (5.5) | -6.0 | (5.4) | -4.5 | -0.20 | (0.25) |
| Iceland | 40.1 | (0.8) | 50.1 | (6.9) | -10.0 | (7.0) | 14.6 | (0.6) | 15.4 | (5.4) | -0.8 | (5.6) | -2.1 | -0.17 | (0.43) |
| Ireland | 37.9 | (1.0) | 41.1 | (3.6) | -3.3 | (3.7) | 21.5 | (0.7) | 18.6 | (2.8) | 2.9 | (3.1) | 3.9 | 0.26 | (0.21) |
| Italy | 66.1 | (0.6) | 68.9 | (2.9) | -2.8 | (2.9) | 37.2 | (0.6) | 34.1 | (2.4) | 3.1 | (2.3) | -2.1 | -0.09 | (0.11) |
| Japan | 45.6 | (1.4) | c | c | c | c | 9.4 | (0.6) | c | c | c | c | c | c | c |
| Korea | 79.3 | (0.9) | c | c | c | c | 31.4 | (0.8) | c | c | c | c | c | c | c |
| Luxembourg | 43.7 | (0.8) | 43.4 | (1.4) | 0.4 | (1.6) | 25.5 | (0.8) | 18.8 | (1.1) | **6.7** | (1.2) | **5.4** | **0.31** | (0.08) |
| Mexico | 46.1 | (0.8) | 76.8 | (3.9) | **-30.7** | (3.9) | 17.4 | (0.6) | 19.1 | (4.1) | -1.7 | (4.2) | -4.5 | -0.29 | (0.27) |
| Netherlands | 21.2 | (0.9) | 28.7 | (2.6) | **-7.5** | (2.8) | 7.4 | (0.5) | 7.9 | (1.2) | -0.4 | (1.3) | **-3.4** | **-0.45** | (0.19) |
| New Zealand | 30.5 | (1.1) | 44.7 | (1.8) | **-14.2** | (2.2) | 14.7 | (0.7) | 25.4 | (1.5) | **-10.7** | (1.6) | **-9.4** | **-0.62** | (0.09) |
| Norway | 26.1 | (0.8) | 41.1 | (3.6) | **-14.9** | (3.7) | 4.9 | (0.4) | 9.6 | (2.1) | **-4.7** | (2.0) | **-6.2** | **-0.90** | (0.25) |
| Poland | 56.0 | (1.0) | c | c | c | c | 19.3 | (0.8) | c | c | c | c | c | c | c |
| Portugal | 68.7 | (1.0) | 66.7 | (3.3) | 2.1 | (3.5) | 27.1 | (0.9) | 18.7 | (3.7) | **8.4** | (3.8) | 8.8 | 0.52 | (0.29) |
| Slovak Republic | 55.6 | (1.3) | c | c | c | c | 25.4 | (1.0) | c | c | c | c | c | c | c |
| Spain | 53.7 | (0.8) | 53.0 | (3.4) | 0.7 | (3.5) | 28.7 | (0.8) | 27.4 | (2.5) | 1.4 | (2.6) | -0.3 | -0.01 | (0.14) |
| Sweden | 29.4 | (0.9) | 50.8 | (2.7) | **-21.4** | (2.9) | 6.5 | (0.5) | 15.5 | (1.8) | **-9.1** | (1.9) | **-9.2** | **-1.00** | (0.18) |
| Switzerland | 38.6 | (0.7) | 43.9 | (1.4) | **-5.3** | (1.6) | 19.4 | (0.6) | 21.0 | (1.0) | -1.6 | (1.1) | **-3.5** | **-0.22** | (0.06) |
| Turkey | 37.0 | (1.2) | 35.5 | (8.1) | 1.5 | (8.2) | 13.5 | (0.7) | 9.4 | (4.2) | 4.0 | (4.5) | 5.2 | 0.60 | (0.54) |
| United Kingdom | 44.0 | (0.9) | 59.2 | (2.6) | **-15.2** | (2.6) | 16.2 | (0.6) | 27.9 | (1.6) | **-11.6** | (1.8) | **-13.7** | **-0.81** | (0.10) |
| United States | 39.8 | (1.3) | 53.1 | (2.2) | **-13.3** | (2.4) | 16.5 | (0.8) | 21.6 | (2.0) | -5.1 | (2.2) | -4.8 | -0.32 | (0.14) |
| **OECD average** | **42.4** | **(0.2)** | **48.3** | **(0.8)** | **-8.4** | **(0.8)** | **18.9** | **(0.1)** | **19.9** | **(0.6)** | **-1.4** | **(0.6)** | **-3.9** | **-0.27** | **(0.05)** |
| **Partners** | | | | | | | | | | | | | | | |
| Argentina | 48.3 | (1.2) | 54.2 | (5.7) | -5.9 | (5.7) | 31.4 | (1.3) | 26.2 | (4.3) | 5.2 | (4.7) | 2.3 | 0.11 | (0.22) |
| Azerbaijan | 79.6 | (1.1) | 74.9 | (3.6) | 4.7 | (3.7) | 30.3 | (1.1) | 27.8 | (5.1) | 2.5 | (5.1) | 5.0 | 0.25 | (0.24) |
| Brazil | 47.9 | (0.9) | 60.1 | (4.8) | **-12.3** | (4.8) | 19.7 | (0.6) | 16.5 | (3.9) | 3.2 | (3.8) | 0.9 | 0.06 | (0.29) |
| Bulgaria | 54.0 | (1.4) | c | c | c | c | 26.8 | (0.9) | c | c | c | c | c | c | c |
| Chile | 38.0 | (1.2) | c | c | c | c | 13.2 | (0.8) | c | c | c | c | c | c | c |
| Colombia | 50.5 | (1.1) | c | c | c | c | 25.3 | (0.7) | c | c | c | c | c | c | c |
| Croatia | 45.4 | (0.9) | 43.7 | (2.3) | 1.7 | (2.3) | 28.0 | (0.9) | 26.1 | (2.0) | 2.0 | (2.1) | -0.3 | -0.02 | (0.11) |
| Estonia | 43.6 | (0.9) | 60.7 | (2.5) | **-17.1** | (2.5) | 15.4 | (0.6) | 30.1 | (2.3) | **-14.6** | (2.3) | **-15.5** | **-0.91** | (0.10) |
| Hong Kong-China | 80.4 | (0.9) | 68.9 | (1.3) | **11.5** | (1.3) | 29.7 | (1.4) | 17.1 | (1.4) | **12.5** | (1.4) | **6.5** | **0.38** | (0.09) |
| Indonesia | 65.6 | (2.3) | 83.6 | (5.8) | **-18.0** | (6.2) | 17.2 | (0.8) | 22.7 | (5.3) | -5.5 | (5.4) | -9.2 | -0.57 | (0.35) |
| Israel | 63.4 | (1.1) | 66.4 | (1.9) | -3.0 | (2.0) | 42.3 | (1.2) | 42.2 | (2.3) | 0.2 | (2.6) | -2.3 | -0.10 | (0.12) |
| Jordan | 72.4 | (0.9) | 71.1 | (2.3) | 1.2 | (2.3) | 34.4 | (0.9) | 33.8 | (1.9) | 0.6 | (2.1) | 1.8 | 0.08 | (0.10) |
| Kyrgyzstan | 85.4 | (1.0) | 75.8 | (5.0) | 9.6 | (5.0) | 26.0 | (0.9) | 26.7 | (4.6) | -0.7 | (4.8) | 0.8 | 0.04 | (0.24) |
| Latvia | 71.7 | (1.1) | 73.1 | (2.0) | -1.4 | (2.2) | 32.0 | (1.3) | 37.3 | (3.0) | -5.3 | (3.1) | -3.1 | -0.14 | (0.13) |
| Liechtenstein | 21.8 | (2.7) | 37.4 | (4.4) | **-15.6** | (5.3) | 14.3 | (2.2) | 13.2 | (2.7) | 1.2 | (3.2) | 1.4 | 0.12 | (0.29) |
| Lithuania | 48.4 | (1.0) | 53.4 | (5.0) | -5.0 | (4.9) | 17.5 | (0.8) | 22.0 | (4.0) | -4.5 | (4.1) | -3.4 | -0.24 | (0.24) |
| Macao-China | 65.6 | (1.4) | 60.9 | (0.9) | **4.7** | (1.7) | 24.7 | (1.2) | 20.4 | (0.8) | 4.2 | (1.4) | 2.5 | 0.15 | (0.08) |
| Montenegro | 62.3 | (0.7) | 55.7 | (3.3) | 6.6 | (3.4) | 37.3 | (0.8) | 35.7 | (3.2) | 1.6 | (3.2) | 3.9 | 0.17 | (0.14) |
| Qatar | 72.4 | (0.7) | 48.6 | (1.0) | **23.8** | (1.4) | 43.8 | (0.9) | 24.2 | (0.9) | **19.5** | (1.1) | **19.2** | **0.88** | (0.05) |
| Romania | 56.8 | (1.5) | c | c | c | c | 27.9 | (1.4) | c | c | c | c | c | c | c |
| Russian Federation | 69.3 | (1.4) | 70.3 | (2.7) | -1.0 | (2.4) | 21.5 | (0.9) | 24.1 | (2.0) | -2.6 | (2.1) | -2.6 | -0.15 | (0.12) |
| Serbia | 53.8 | (1.1) | 52.8 | (2.1) | 1.0 | (2.1) | 38.7 | (1.1) | 37.3 | (2.1) | 1.4 | (2.0) | 2.2 | 0.09 | (0.08) |
| Slovenia | 41.2 | (0.7) | 44.7 | (2.6) | -3.4 | (2.8) | 26.6 | (0.7) | 27.3 | (2.3) | -0.7 | (2.6) | -2.3 | -0.12 | (0.13) |
| Chinese Taipei | 75.1 | (0.5) | 65.6 | (7.8) | 9.5 | (7.9) | 23.7 | (0.5) | 20.2 | (5.6) | 3.5 | (5.7) | 2.9 | 0.17 | (0.37) |
| Thailand | 63.4 | (1.2) | c | c | c | c | 20.2 | (0.8) | c | c | c | c | -12.7 | -0.67 | (0.56) |
| Tunisia | 70.1 | (1.0) | 93.6 | (4.4) | **-23.4** | (4.6) | 30.6 | (1.4) | 39.3 | (7.6) | -8.6 | (7.7) | -11.0 | -0.49 | (0.33) |
| Uruguay | 44.4 | (1.0) | c | c | c | c | 29.0 | (0.9) | c | c | c | c | -6.9 | -0.32 | (0.41) |

*Note:* Values that are statistically significant at the 5% level (p < 0.05) are indicated in bold.

217

### Table 3.16 Percentage of students by different types of out-of-school-time lessons, by immigrant status
[Part 2/5]

| | | Proportion of students participating in out-of-school lessons with non-school teachers | | | | | | | | | | |
| | | Small group lessons | | | | | | Large group lessons | | | | |
| | | Native students | | Students with an immigrant background | | Difference (native-immigrant) | | Native students | | Students with an immigrant background | | Difference (native-immigrant) | |
| | | % | S.E. | % | S.E. | Dif. | S.E. | % | S.E. | % | S.E. | Dif. | S.E. |
|---|---|---|---|---|---|---|---|---|---|---|---|---|---|
| OECD | Australia | 6.3 | (0.3) | 14.4 | (1.0) | **-8.0** | (1.0) | 5.7 | (0.3) | 12.5 | (0.9) | **-6.8** | (0.9) |
| | Austria | 6.9 | (0.5) | 12.4 | (1.5) | **-5.5** | (1.5) | 5.4 | (0.4) | 10.7 | (2.1) | **-5.3** | (2.1) |
| | Belgium | 6.6 | (0.4) | 11.9 | (1.2) | **-5.2** | (1.2) | 3.6 | (0.3) | 9.3 | (1.4) | **-5.8** | (1.3) |
| | Canada | 6.6 | (0.3) | 14.6 | (0.9) | **-8.1** | (0.9) | 5.6 | (0.3) | 11.8 | (0.8) | **-6.1** | (0.7) |
| | Czech Republic | 7.7 | (0.6) | 11.3 | (3.3) | -3.6 | (3.2) | 5.5 | (0.5) | 6.5 | (2.7) | -1.0 | (2.6) |
| | Denmark | 3.9 | (0.4) | 13.4 | (1.8) | **-9.5** | (1.8) | 3.3 | (0.4) | 11.2 | (2.2) | **-8.0** | (2.2) |
| | Finland | 2.2 | (0.2) | 14.8 | (3.9) | **-12.6** | (3.9) | 3.5 | (0.3) | 14.7 | (4.5) | **-11.2** | (4.5) |
| | France | 8.2 | (0.5) | 15.4 | (1.9) | **-7.2** | (1.9) | 3.9 | (0.4) | 11.1 | (2.1) | **-7.1** | (2.1) |
| | Germany | 6.9 | (0.4) | 9.6 | (1.6) | -2.7 | (1.7) | 3.0 | (0.3) | 8.0 | (1.6) | **-5.0** | (1.5) |
| | Greece | 47.4 | (1.4) | 26.5 | (3.1) | **20.9** | (3.2) | 18.7 | (1.0) | 14.8 | (1.7) | **3.9** | (1.8) |
| | Hungary | 10.7 | (0.6) | 13.8 | (5.1) | -3.0 | (5.1) | 8.6 | (0.6) | 16.1 | (4.9) | -7.5 | (5.0) |
| | Iceland | 6.4 | (0.4) | 13.8 | (4.5) | -7.4 | (4.5) | 5.0 | (0.4) | 7.2 | (3.3) | -2.2 | (3.4) |
| | Ireland | 9.3 | (0.5) | 16.3 | (2.8) | **-7.1** | (2.8) | 6.4 | (0.5) | 9.2 | (1.9) | -2.8 | (1.9) |
| | Italy | 13.6 | (0.5) | 19.5 | (2.2) | **-5.9** | (2.3) | 8.6 | (0.4) | 14.5 | (2.1) | **-6.0** | (2.1) |
| | Japan | 8.4 | (0.6) | c | c | c | c | 8.2 | (0.6) | c | c | c | c |
| | Korea | 31.4 | (0.9) | c | c | c | c | 27.0 | (0.8) | c | c | c | c |
| | Luxembourg | 5.3 | (0.5) | 9.6 | (0.9) | **-4.4** | (0.9) | 3.4 | (0.3) | 8.7 | (0.8) | **-5.3** | (0.9) |
| | Mexico | 15.5 | (0.6) | 29.1 | (5.5) | **-13.6** | (5.5) | 15.1 | (0.5) | 32.9 | (5.0) | **-17.8** | (5.1) |
| | Netherlands | 3.0 | (0.4) | 8.1 | (1.5) | **-5.0** | (1.6) | 3.1 | (0.3) | 8.6 | (1.4) | **-5.6** | (1.5) |
| | New Zealand | 8.0 | (0.5) | 16.5 | (1.1) | **-8.5** | (1.2) | 6.0 | (0.5) | 9.7 | (1.0) | **-3.7** | (1.2) |
| | Norway | 4.2 | (0.4) | 12.2 | (2.1) | **-7.9** | (2.1) | 4.6 | (0.4) | 8.7 | (1.7) | **-4.1** | (1.8) |
| | Poland | 10.6 | (0.6) | c | c | c | c | 9.7 | (0.5) | c | c | c | c |
| | Portugal | 14.5 | (0.8) | 14.7 | (3.4) | -0.2 | (3.6) | 7.6 | (0.5) | 13.3 | (4.2) | -5.7 | (4.2) |
| | Slovak Republic | 11.0 | (0.5) | c | c | c | c | 7.4 | (0.6) | c | c | c | c |
| | Spain | 26.6 | (0.7) | 19.1 | (2.0) | **7.5** | (2.2) | 10.3 | (0.5) | 13.3 | (1.5) | **-3.0** | (1.5) |
| | Sweden | 4.5 | (0.4) | 14.4 | (1.5) | **-9.8** | (1.5) | 6.1 | (0.4) | 13.0 | (1.9) | **-6.9** | (2.1) |
| | Switzerland | 5.4 | (0.4) | 9.2 | (0.8) | **-3.8** | (0.8) | 3.8 | (0.3) | 7.8 | (0.9) | **-4.0** | (1.0) |
| | Turkey | 11.0 | (0.6) | 7.5 | (3.8) | 3.6 | (3.9) | 15.0 | (1.0) | 15.5 | (3.5) | -0.5 | (3.4) |
| | United Kingdom | 6.7 | (0.4) | 13.6 | (1.8) | **-6.9** | (1.8) | 6.6 | (0.4) | 14.1 | (2.5) | **-7.5** | (2.6) |
| | United States | 11.2 | (0.8) | 17.5 | (1.9) | **-6.3** | (1.9) | 10.4 | (0.8) | 16.1 | (2.0) | **-5.6** | (2.0) |
| | **OECD average** | 10.7 | (0.1) | 14.6 | (0.5) | **-4.6** | (0.5) | 7.7 | (0.1) | 12.3 | (0.5) | **-5.4** | (0.5) |
| Partners | Argentina | 19.3 | (0.9) | 15.4 | (3.8) | 3.9 | (3.8) | 12.9 | (0.8) | 11.4 | (2.5) | 1.5 | (2.6) |
| | Azerbaijan | 40.7 | (1.1) | 37.0 | (4.5) | 3.6 | (4.5) | 39.1 | (1.1) | 38.5 | (5.2) | 0.7 | (5.3) |
| | Brazil | 17.6 | (0.5) | 22.8 | (3.7) | -5.3 | (3.8) | 15.1 | (0.5) | 24.4 | (4.0) | **-9.3** | (4.0) |
| | Bulgaria | 17.1 | (1.0) | c | c | c | c | 16.5 | (1.0) | c | c | c | c |
| | Chile | 9.2 | (0.5) | c | c | c | c | 8.1 | (0.5) | c | c | c | c |
| | Colombia | 17.6 | (0.8) | c | c | c | c | 16.3 | (0.7) | c | c | c | c |
| | Croatia | 9.4 | (0.6) | 10.8 | (1.2) | -1.4 | (1.3) | 7.8 | (0.5) | 7.1 | (1.1) | 0.7 | (1.1) |
| | Estonia | 6.8 | (0.4) | 16.0 | (1.5) | **-9.2** | (1.5) | 6.2 | (0.4) | 12.5 | (1.8) | **-6.2** | (1.8) |
| | Hong Kong-China | 20.5 | (0.9) | 14.3 | (0.9) | **6.2** | (1.1) | 33.1 | (1.4) | 26.3 | (1.3) | **6.7** | (1.5) |
| | Indonesia | 19.3 | (0.8) | 26.4 | (8.1) | -7.1 | (8.2) | 17.3 | (0.9) | 37.1 | (9.6) | **-19.8** | (9.5) |
| | Israel | 19.7 | (0.9) | 20.2 | (1.5) | -0.5 | (1.6) | 15.2 | (0.9) | 13.1 | (1.3) | 2.2 | (1.3) |
| | Jordan | 25.0 | (1.0) | 23.7 | (1.8) | 1.3 | (2.1) | 21.5 | (0.9) | 19.8 | (1.6) | 1.7 | (1.7) |
| | Kyrgyzstan | 26.4 | (0.9) | 26.4 | (3.7) | 0.1 | (3.9) | 31.3 | (1.0) | 22.4 | (4.4) | **8.9** | (4.4) |
| | Latvia | 13.8 | (0.6) | 15.9 | (1.8) | -2.1 | (2.0) | 17.1 | (0.7) | 16.3 | (2.2) | 0.8 | (2.2) |
| | Liechtenstein | 1.5 | (0.8) | 5.2 | (2.0) | -3.7 | (2.0) | 0.5 | (0.5) | 5.8 | (2.2) | **-5.4** | (2.2) |
| | Lithuania | 6.7 | (0.4) | 11.6 | (3.5) | -4.9 | (3.5) | 6.4 | (0.5) | 8.4 | (2.7) | -2.0 | (2.8) |
| | Macao-China | 26.5 | (1.4) | 18.0 | (0.7) | **8.5** | (1.4) | 19.6 | (1.5) | 19.1 | (0.8) | 0.5 | (1.6) |
| | Montenegro | 20.5 | (0.5) | 21.3 | (2.5) | -0.7 | (2.7) | 17.2 | (0.7) | 16.7 | (2.6) | 0.5 | (2.6) |
| | Qatar | 29.4 | (0.8) | 17.9 | (0.9) | **11.5** | (1.2) | 26.5 | (0.8) | 15.3 | (0.8) | **11.1** | (1.3) |
| | Romania | 19.8 | (1.2) | c | c | c | c | 15.5 | (1.2) | c | c | c | c |
| | Russian Federation | 12.4 | (0.9) | 13.0 | (1.6) | -0.6 | (1.7) | 12.6 | (0.6) | 13.2 | (1.6) | -0.5 | (1.6) |
| | Serbia | 12.9 | (0.6) | 10.3 | (1.5) | 2.5 | (1.6) | 8.6 | (0.6) | 8.2 | (1.3) | 0.3 | (1.4) |
| | Slovenia | 6.5 | (0.4) | 6.1 | (1.1) | 0.4 | (1.2) | 5.0 | (0.3) | 5.0 | (0.9) | 0.1 | (1.1) |
| | Chinese Taipei | 23.6 | (0.5) | 25.3 | (5.5) | -1.7 | (5.5) | 40.4 | (0.9) | 37.0 | (6.2) | 3.4 | (6.5) |
| | Thailand | 23.9 | (0.9) | c | c | c | c | 31.1 | (1.2) | c | c | c | c |
| | Tunisia | 28.2 | (1.1) | 31.3 | (7.4) | -3.1 | (7.5) | 19.1 | (0.9) | 29.5 | (9.8) | -10.5 | (9.8) |
| | Uruguay | 20.9 | (0.7) | c | c | c | c | 11.7 | (0.6) | c | c | c | c |

*Note*: Values that are statistically significant at the 5% level (p < 0.05) are indicated in bold.

© OECD 2011 Quality Time for Students: Learning In and Out of School

**Table 3.16** Percentage of students by different types of out-of-school-time lessons,
[Part 3/5] by immigrant status

| | | | | | | | | | |
|---|---|---|---|---|---|---|---|---|---|
| | Proportion of students participating in out-of-school lessons with non-school teachers | | | | | | | | |
| | At least one of these types of out-of-school lessons | | | | | | | | |
| | Native students | | Students with an immigrant background | | Difference (native-immigrant) | | If students' ESCS was equal to the national average ESCS, and schools' average ESCS was equal to the national average of schools' average ESCS | | |
| | | | | | | | Difference (native-immigrant) | Increase in the logit of participating in out-of-school-time lessons by being a native student | |
| | % | S.E. | % | S.E. | Dif. | S.E. | Dif. in % | Logistic regression coefficient | S.E. |
| **OECD** Australia | 19.4 | (0.5) | 36.5 | (1.5) | **-17.1** | (1.5) | **-16.9** | **-0.87** | (0.07) |
| Austria | 23.4 | (0.8) | 29.1 | (2.5) | **-5.7** | (2.4) | **-8.3** | **-0.42** | (0.13) |
| Belgium | 21.7 | (0.7) | 27.2 | (1.6) | **-5.5** | (1.7) | **-10.0** | **-0.53** | (0.09) |
| Canada | 19.6 | (0.5) | 33.9 | (1.6) | **-14.3** | (1.7) | **-14.3** | **-0.75** | (0.08) |
| Czech Republic | 21.6 | (0.9) | 24.8 | (4.5) | -3.1 | (4.4) | -4.3 | -0.24 | (0.23) |
| Denmark | 9.2 | (0.7) | 23.5 | (2.3) | **-14.2** | (2.5) | **-14.4** | **-1.11** | (0.16) |
| Finland | 8.2 | (0.4) | 25.0 | (6.6) | **-16.7** | (6.6) | **-19.2** | **-1.45** | (0.37) |
| France | 25.4 | (1.0) | 32.7 | (2.7) | **-7.2** | (2.8) | **-11.5** | **-0.55** | (0.13) |
| Germany | 26.8 | (0.8) | 28.3 | (2.4) | -1.5 | (2.7) | -4.7 | -0.23 | (0.15) |
| Greece | 72.8 | (1.0) | 43.3 | (3.7) | **29.4** | (3.7) | **22.1** | **0.97** | (0.17) |
| Hungary | 38.2 | (1.0) | 44.8 | (5.7) | -6.6 | (5.6) | -5.6 | -0.23 | (0.25) |
| Iceland | 19.7 | (0.7) | 21.2 | (5.9) | -1.5 | (6.0) | -3.5 | -0.21 | (0.36) |
| Ireland | 28.9 | (0.8) | 28.6 | (3.2) | 0.3 | (3.3) | 1.6 | 0.08 | (0.18) |
| Italy | 45.5 | (0.6) | 48.1 | (2.6) | -2.6 | (2.6) | **-7.0** | **-0.28** | (0.11) |
| Japan | 20.1 | (1.0) | c | c | c | c | c | c | c |
| Korea | 58.0 | (1.0) | c | c | c | c | c | c | c |
| Luxembourg | 29.0 | (0.8) | 25.8 | (1.3) | **3.2** | (1.5) | 2.5 | 0.13 | (0.08) |
| Mexico | 29.4 | (0.8) | 42.3 | (5.3) | **-12.8** | (5.2) | **-15.1** | **-0.66** | (0.22) |
| Netherlands | 10.4 | (0.6) | 16.8 | (1.8) | **-6.3** | (1.8) | **-8.2** | **-0.69** | (0.15) |
| New Zealand | 20.4 | (0.7) | 35.6 | (1.6) | **-15.2** | (1.8) | **-14.4** | **-0.74** | (0.09) |
| Norway | 9.0 | (0.6) | 19.3 | (2.7) | **-10.3** | (2.8) | **-11.5** | **-0.97** | (0.20) |
| Poland | 28.7 | (0.9) | c | c | c | c | c | c | c |
| Portugal | 35.4 | (1.0) | 28.8 | (4.6) | 6.7 | (4.7) | 7.3 | 0.34 | (0.26) |
| Slovak Republic | 29.5 | (1.0) | c | c | c | c | c | c | c |
| Spain | 43.9 | (0.9) | 35.4 | (2.3) | **8.5** | (2.5) | **6.6** | **0.28** | (0.11) |
| Sweden | 11.3 | (0.6) | 27.3 | (2.1) | **-16.0** | (2.2) | **-16.2** | **-1.10** | (0.13) |
| Switzerland | 23.5 | (0.7) | 27.9 | (1.1) | **-4.4** | (1.1) | **-6.3** | **-0.33** | (0.05) |
| Turkey | 26.6 | (1.2) | 23.6 | (5.0) | 3.0 | (5.0) | 7.0 | 0.42 | (0.31) |
| United Kingdom | 22.5 | (0.7) | 38.2 | (1.7) | **-15.7** | (1.8) | **-17.2** | **-0.82** | (0.09) |
| United States | 23.5 | (1.0) | 31.9 | (2.5) | **-8.3** | (2.5) | **-6.7** | **-0.34** | (0.14) |
| **OECD average** | 26.7 | (0.2) | 30.8 | (0.7) | **-5.2** | (0.7) | **-7.8** | **-0.40** | (0.04) |
| **Partners** Argentina | 40.1 | (1.2) | 33.2 | (4.3) | 6.9 | (4.6) | 4.5 | 0.19 | (0.20) |
| Azerbaijan | 62.7 | (1.0) | 58.9 | (3.6) | 3.8 | (3.7) | 4.9 | 0.21 | (0.16) |
| Brazil | 32.6 | (0.7) | 40.4 | (4.8) | -7.8 | (4.8) | **-10.7** | **-0.46** | (0.20) |
| Bulgaria | 37.7 | (1.1) | c | c | c | c | c | c | c |
| Chile | 21.1 | (0.9) | c | c | c | c | c | c | c |
| Colombia | 36.6 | (0.8) | c | c | c | c | c | c | c |
| Croatia | 34.0 | (0.9) | 33.0 | (2.1) | 1.0 | (2.3) | -1.3 | -0.06 | (0.10) |
| Estonia | 21.1 | (0.6) | 38.4 | (2.6) | **-17.3** | (2.6) | **-18.3** | **-0.90** | (0.11) |
| Hong Kong-China | 59.5 | (1.3) | 42.7 | (1.5) | **16.8** | (1.6) | **8.4** | **0.34** | (0.07) |
| Indonesia | 33.7 | (0.9) | 52.8 | (8.0) | -19.0 | (7.8) | -23.5 | **-0.97** | (0.30) |
| Israel | 52.1 | (1.3) | 53.3 | (2.2) | -1.2 | (2.3) | -2.8 | -0.11 | (0.09) |
| Jordan | 47.8 | (1.0) | 46.6 | (2.0) | 1.1 | (2.3) | 1.0 | 0.04 | (0.10) |
| Kyrgyzstan | 48.0 | (1.1) | 48.3 | (4.7) | -0.3 | (5.0) | -0.7 | -0.03 | (0.21) |
| Latvia | 42.0 | (1.1) | 46.4 | (2.4) | -4.4 | (2.6) | -1.9 | -0.08 | (0.10) |
| Liechtenstein | 15.3 | (2.3) | 17.3 | (3.6) | -2.0 | (4.0) | -2.1 | -0.16 | (0.32) |
| Lithuania | 22.9 | (0.8) | 29.9 | (4.8) | -7.0 | (4.8) | -5.7 | -0.31 | (0.23) |
| Macao-China | 45.4 | (1.8) | 36.4 | (0.9) | **9.0** | (1.9) | **7.7** | **0.32** | (0.08) |
| Montenegro | 47.2 | (0.8) | 46.8 | (3.2) | 0.4 | (3.3) | 2.2 | 0.09 | (0.14) |
| Qatar | 57.0 | (0.9) | 33.7 | (1.1) | **23.3** | (1.4) | **22.6** | **0.93** | (0.06) |
| Romania | 38.5 | (1.3) | c | c | c | c | c | c | c |
| Russian Federation | 31.0 | (1.2) | 32.9 | (1.9) | -1.9 | (1.9) | -2.0 | -0.09 | (0.08) |
| Serbia | 43.4 | (1.1) | 41.7 | (2.3) | 1.7 | (2.2) | 2.2 | 0.09 | (0.09) |
| Slovenia | 31.2 | (0.8) | 30.6 | (2.4) | 0.7 | (2.7) | -0.8 | -0.04 | (0.13) |
| Chinese Taipei | 57.1 | (0.8) | 47.7 | (6.6) | 9.4 | (6.7) | 8.6 | 0.35 | (0.27) |
| Thailand | 44.0 | (1.3) | c | c | c | c | **-32.0** | **-1.39** | (0.51) |
| Tunisia | 44.7 | (1.4) | 57.5 | (9.1) | -12.7 | (9.4) | -12.8 | -0.52 | (0.39) |
| Uruguay | 37.3 | (1.0) | c | c | c | c | -1.9 | -0.08 | (0.41) |

*Note:* Values that are statistically significant at the 5% level (p < 0.05) are indicated in bold.

**Table 3.16** [Part 4/5] **Percentage of students by different types of out-of-school-time lessons, by immigrant status**

| | | | | | | | \multicolumn{9}{Proportion of students participating in out-of-school lessons with school teachers} | | | | | | | |
|---|---|---|---|---|---|---|---|---|---|---|---|---|---|---|---|
| | \multicolumn{8}{One-to-one lessons} | | | | | | | | \multicolumn{6}{Small group lessons} | | | | | |
| | | | | | | | \multicolumn{3}{If students' ESCS was equal to the national average ESCS, and schools' average ESCS was equal to the national average of schools' average ESCS} | | | | | | | |
| | Native students | | Students with an immigrant background | | Difference (native-immigrant) | | Difference (native-immigrant) | Increase in the logit of participating in out-of-school-time lessons by being a native student | | Native students | | Students with an immigrant background | | Difference (native-immigrant) | |
| | | | | | | | | Logistic regression coefficient | | | | | | | |
| | % | S.E. | % | S.E. | Dif. | S.E. | Dif. in % | | S.E. | % | S.E. | % | S.E. | Dif. | S.E. |
| Australia | 6.6 | (0.4) | 6.8 | (0.6) | -0.2 | (0.7) | -0.4 | -0.06 | (0.11) | 6.6 | (0.4) | 8.9 | (0.6) | **-2.2** | (0.7) |
| Austria | 5.1 | (0.5) | 6.8 | (1.0) | -1.7 | (1.1) | 0.4 | 0.09 | (0.24) | 12.0 | (0.9) | 19.6 | (1.8) | **-7.6** | (2.0) |
| Belgium | 6.5 | (0.3) | 11.6 | (1.5) | **-5.1** | (1.5) | **-4.7** | **-0.59** | (0.14) | 6.9 | (0.4) | 13.1 | (1.7) | **-6.2** | (1.8) |
| Canada | 11.3 | (0.4) | 14.8 | (1.3) | **-3.4** | (1.4) | **-3.8** | **-0.33** | (0.11) | 9.7 | (0.4) | 12.5 | (0.9) | **-2.8** | (1.0) |
| Czech Republic | 13.9 | (0.7) | 24.6 | (4.5) | **-10.7** | (4.4) | **-9.4** | **-0.65** | (0.23) | 10.6 | (0.6) | 19.0 | (4.4) | **-8.4** | (4.3) |
| Denmark | 4.3 | (0.4) | 17.4 | (2.6) | **-13.0** | (2.6) | **-8.2** | **-1.18** | (0.20) | 7.2 | (0.5) | 17.3 | (2.4) | **-10.2** | (2.4) |
| Finland | 8.0 | (0.5) | 10.2 | (3.3) | -2.2 | (3.3) | -2.1 | -0.26 | (0.38) | 9.3 | (0.5) | 12.8 | (4.4) | -3.5 | (4.3) |
| France | 5.9 | (0.5) | 14.3 | (1.9) | **-8.4** | (1.9) | **-6.8** | **-0.86** | (0.18) | 17.4 | (0.8) | 21.9 | (1.9) | **-4.5** | (1.8) |
| Germany | 4.9 | (0.4) | 10.5 | (1.9) | **-5.6** | (1.9) | **-5.6** | **-0.84** | (0.21) | 6.9 | (0.6) | 12.1 | (1.4) | **-5.2** | (1.5) |
| Greece | 11.9 | (0.8) | 10.8 | (2.0) | 1.1 | (2.0) | 2.8 | 0.31 | (0.23) | 14.5 | (0.8) | 16.6 | (3.0) | -2.0 | (3.0) |
| Hungary | 14.5 | (0.7) | 21.5 | (5.0) | -7.0 | (5.2) | -7.5 | -0.51 | (0.31) | 12.7 | (0.7) | 18.7 | (4.5) | -6.1 | (4.4) |
| Iceland | 9.9 | (0.5) | 29.7 | (5.3) | **-19.8** | (5.3) | **-17.6** | **-1.25** | (0.27) | 14.2 | (0.6) | 24.7 | (5.7) | -10.5 | (5.7) |
| Ireland | 6.5 | (0.5) | 14.4 | (3.6) | -7.9 | (3.5) | -7.0 | **-0.84** | (0.24) | 8.6 | (0.6) | 12.9 | (3.4) | -4.2 | (3.5) |
| Italy | a | a | a | a | a | a | a | a | a | 35.9 | (0.8) | 45.2 | (3.6) | **-9.3** | (3.5) |
| Japan | 3.7 | (0.3) | c | c | c | c | c | c | c | 6.6 | (0.3) | c | c | c | c |
| Korea | 9.6 | (0.5) | c | c | c | c | c | c | c | 16.7 | (0.6) | c | c | c | c |
| Luxembourg | 12.2 | (0.6) | 16.0 | (1.0) | -3.8 | (1.3) | -3.4 | -0.29 | (0.11) | 11.7 | (0.6) | 19.1 | (1.1) | **-7.4** | (1.2) |
| Mexico | 15.8 | (0.7) | 42.4 | (5.9) | **-26.6** | (5.9) | **-18.4** | **-1.04** | (0.26) | 16.4 | (0.6) | 38.3 | (5.8) | **-21.9** | (5.9) |
| Netherlands | 6.9 | (0.5) | 11.7 | (1.7) | **-4.7** | (1.7) | **-3.3** | **-0.43** | (0.18) | 8.1 | (0.6) | 13.3 | (2.1) | **-5.2** | (2.2) |
| New Zealand | 8.5 | (0.9) | 10.9 | (1.3) | -2.4 | (1.5) | -2.5 | -0.29 | (0.18) | 8.9 | (0.7) | 11.9 | (1.2) | **-2.9** | (1.3) |
| Norway | 7.6 | (0.5) | 19.0 | (2.4) | **-11.5** | (2.5) | **-10.6** | **-1.00** | (0.18) | 11.3 | (0.5) | 18.8 | (2.7) | **-7.6** | (2.8) |
| Poland | 14.4 | (0.6) | c | c | c | c | c | c | c | 23.1 | (0.8) | c | c | c | c |
| Portugal | 21.1 | (0.9) | 32.1 | (4.1) | **-11.0** | (4.2) | **-11.6** | **-0.61** | (0.19) | 30.7 | (1.2) | 43.7 | (2.8) | **-13.0** | (3.1) |
| Slovak Republic | 30.2 | (1.3) | c | c | c | c | c | c | c | 17.9 | (1.0) | c | c | c | c |
| Spain | 7.8 | (0.5) | 15.4 | (2.6) | **-7.6** | (2.6) | **-7.1** | **-0.73** | (0.20) | 10.0 | (0.4) | 20.1 | (2.4) | **-10.1** | (2.3) |
| Sweden | 7.2 | (0.5) | 19.1 | (1.7) | **-11.9** | (1.7) | **-9.5** | **-0.95** | (0.14) | 12.8 | (0.6) | 24.1 | (2.0) | **-11.2** | (2.0) |
| Switzerland | 5.0 | (0.3) | 12.1 | (1.0) | **-7.1** | (1.1) | **-6.5** | **-0.90** | (0.11) | 8.4 | (0.4) | 15.2 | (1.0) | **-6.7** | (1.1) |
| Turkey | 7.6 | (0.6) | 11.5 | (3.5) | -3.9 | (3.6) | -4.5 | -0.53 | (0.41) | 9.3 | (0.6) | 7.6 | (3.7) | 1.6 | (3.7) |
| United Kingdom | 10.4 | (0.4) | 19.6 | (1.8) | **-9.2** | (1.7) | **-8.5** | **-0.70** | (0.11) | 17.1 | (0.7) | 23.1 | (1.8) | **-6.0** | (1.9) |
| United States | 20.7 | (1.1) | 28.2 | (1.9) | **-7.4** | (2.1) | **-4.3** | -0.24 | (0.12) | 17.5 | (1.0) | 26.0 | (1.8) | **-8.5** | (1.7) |
| **OECD average** | 10.3 | (0.1) | 17.2 | (0.6) | **-7.6** | (0.6) | **-5.9** | **-0.59** | (0.04) | 13.3 | (0.1) | 19.9 | (0.6) | **-7.0** | (0.6) |
| Argentina | 10.1 | (1.0) | 19.7 | (4.7) | -9.6 | (4.6) | **-10.3** | **-0.85** | (0.30) | 12.2 | (1.0) | 22.4 | (5.5) | -10.2 | (5.3) |
| Azerbaijan | 38.5 | (1.3) | 40.3 | (4.7) | -1.8 | (4.7) | -1.3 | -0.05 | (0.21) | 37.4 | (1.3) | 32.5 | (5.5) | 4.9 | (5.8) |
| Brazil | 13.0 | (0.6) | 26.0 | (4.7) | **-13.0** | (4.7) | **-13.5** | **-0.89** | (0.24) | 23.1 | (0.8) | 34.1 | (4.4) | **-10.9** | (4.6) |
| Bulgaria | 21.7 | (1.4) | c | c | c | c | c | c | c | 19.1 | (1.1) | c | c | c | c |
| Chile | 8.0 | (0.5) | c | c | c | c | c | c | c | 16.1 | (0.8) | c | c | c | c |
| Colombia | 14.4 | (1.1) | c | c | c | c | c | c | c | 19.5 | (1.2) | c | c | c | c |
| Croatia | 12.8 | (0.5) | 14.1 | (1.5) | -1.4 | (1.5) | -1.0 | -0.09 | (0.13) | 10.6 | (0.6) | 13.2 | (1.5) | -2.6 | (1.7) |
| Estonia | 17.6 | (0.9) | 22.7 | (2.1) | **-5.1** | (2.1) | -4.5 | -0.29 | (0.13) | 12.7 | (0.6) | 19.6 | (1.8) | **-6.9** | (1.8) |
| Hong Kong-China | 5.7 | (0.6) | 5.8 | (0.5) | -0.1 | (0.8) | 0.2 | 0.03 | (0.15) | 16.4 | (1.0) | 17.4 | (1.0) | -1.0 | (1.2) |
| Indonesia | 31.3 | (2.3) | 59.7 | (7.5) | **-28.4** | (7.7) | **-17.7** | **-0.75** | (0.37) | 26.5 | (2.0) | 36.6 | (8.7) | -10.2 | (8.9) |
| Israel | 19.9 | (1.0) | 19.1 | (1.6) | 0.9 | (1.6) | 1.5 | 0.10 | (0.10) | 19.7 | (0.9) | 22.2 | (2.2) | -2.6 | (2.2) |
| Jordan | 27.0 | (1.0) | 23.9 | (2.1) | 3.1 | (1.9) | 1.5 | 0.08 | (0.09) | 31.4 | (1.0) | 30.8 | (2.0) | 0.6 | (2.2) |
| Kyrgyzstan | 64.2 | (1.0) | 46.0 | (6.1) | **18.2** | (5.9) | **11.7** | **0.48** | (0.22) | 44.2 | (1.1) | 32.3 | (6.1) | **11.9** | (6.0) |
| Latvia | 34.9 | (1.2) | 31.7 | (2.2) | 3.2 | (2.3) | -0.5 | -0.02 | (0.11) | 25.6 | (1.1) | 25.5 | (2.2) | 0.1 | (2.3) |
| Liechtenstein | 2.5 | (1.1) | 11.7 | (3.0) | **-9.2** | (3.3) | **-9.2** | **-1.64** | (0.60) | 4.9 | (1.3) | 11.5 | (2.7) | **-6.6** | (3.1) |
| Lithuania | 11.5 | (0.6) | 14.6 | (3.6) | -3.0 | (3.7) | -3.4 | -0.30 | (0.30) | 17.3 | (0.8) | 17.8 | (3.4) | -0.4 | (3.6) |
| Macao-China | 13.8 | (1.1) | 14.1 | (0.7) | -0.3 | (1.3) | 0.7 | 0.06 | (0.11) | 23.0 | (1.2) | 22.6 | (0.8) | 0.4 | (1.4) |
| Montenegro | 25.0 | (0.6) | 24.9 | (2.8) | 0.1 | (2.7) | -1.5 | -0.08 | (0.14) | 17.9 | (0.6) | 17.4 | (2.2) | 0.5 | (2.2) |
| Qatar | 38.8 | (0.8) | 23.8 | (0.8) | **15.0** | (1.1) | **13.9** | **0.66** | (0.05) | 32.4 | (0.7) | 22.2 | (0.8) | **10.2** | (1.1) |
| Romania | 26.9 | (1.3) | c | c | c | c | c | c | c | 24.4 | (1.1) | c | c | c | c |
| Russian Federation | 30.3 | (0.9) | 33.4 | (2.3) | -3.1 | (2.3) | -3.9 | -0.18 | (0.11) | 31.5 | (1.2) | 30.9 | (2.4) | 0.6 | (2.2) |
| Serbia | 10.2 | (0.7) | 9.6 | (1.5) | 0.6 | (1.6) | -0.4 | -0.04 | (0.17) | 12.0 | (0.6) | 10.9 | (1.3) | 1.1 | (1.4) |
| Slovenia | 8.4 | (0.4) | 12.0 | (1.5) | **-3.6** | (1.7) | -2.6 | -0.32 | (0.18) | 8.5 | (0.5) | 11.7 | (1.8) | -3.2 | (1.8) |
| Chinese Taipei | 14.0 | (0.6) | 16.1 | (4.8) | -2.1 | (4.8) | -2.1 | -0.17 | (0.35) | 22.5 | (0.7) | 19.9 | (6.8) | 2.6 | (6.8) |
| Thailand | 20.7 | (0.7) | c | c | c | c | c | c | c | 26.7 | (0.9) | c | c | c | c |
| Tunisia | 42.4 | (1.4) | 56.1 | (8.2) | -13.7 | (8.2) | -9.6 | -0.38 | (0.34) | 32.6 | (1.1) | 58.9 | (10.3) | **-26.3** | (10.2) |
| Uruguay | 9.3 | (0.8) | c | c | c | c | c | c | c | 8.9 | (0.6) | c | c | c | c |

*Note*: Values that are statistically significant at the 5% level (p < 0.05) are indicated in bold.

© OECD 2011 Quality Time for Students: Learning In and Out of School

## Table 3.16 Percentage of students by different types of out-of-school-time lessons, by immigrant status
[Part 5/5]

Proportion of students participating in out-of-school lessons with school teachers

| | Large group lessons | | | | | | At least one of these types of out-of-school lessons | | | | | | If students' ESCS was equal to the national average ESCS, and schools' average ESCS was equal to the national average of schools' average ESCS | | |
| | Native students | | Students with an immigrant background | | Difference (native-immigrant) | | Native students | | Students with an immigrant background | | Difference (native-immigrant) | | Difference (native-immigrant) | Increase in the logit of participating in out-of-school-time lessons by being a native student | |
| | % | S.E. | % | S.E. | Dif. | S.E. | % | S.E. | % | S.E. | Dif. | S.E. | Dif. in % | Logistic regression coefficient | S.E. |
|---|---|---|---|---|---|---|---|---|---|---|---|---|---|---|---|
| **OECD** | | | | | | | | | | | | | | | |
| Australia | 7.8 | (0.4) | 9.3 | (0.7) | -1.5 | (0.8) | 13.5 | (0.6) | 15.3 | (1.0) | -1.9 | (1.0) | **-2.1** | **-0.17** | (0.08) |
| Austria | 14.9 | (0.9) | 20.0 | (2.0) | **-5.1** | (1.9) | 22.1 | (1.1) | 30.7 | (2.1) | **-8.6** | (1.9) | **-6.8** | **-0.36** | (0.10) |
| Belgium | 5.1 | (0.2) | 11.0 | (1.2) | **-5.8** | (1.2) | 12.8 | (0.4) | 22.4 | (2.0) | **-9.6** | (2.0) | **-7.9** | **-0.58** | (0.12) |
| Canada | 10.7 | (0.4) | 12.8 | (0.8) | -2.1 | (0.9) | 20.3 | (0.6) | 23.8 | (1.1) | -3.5 | (1.3) | -4.2 | -0.25 | (0.07) |
| Czech Republic | 13.1 | (0.7) | 26.1 | (5.6) | **-13.0** | (5.5) | 22.8 | (1.0) | 35.7 | (6.1) | -12.9 | (6.1) | **-11.7** | **-0.58** | (0.27) |
| Denmark | 7.5 | (0.5) | 13.7 | (2.3) | **-6.1** | (2.3) | 12.9 | (0.7) | 28.4 | (3.2) | **-15.5** | (3.1) | **-12.2** | **-0.81** | (0.16) |
| Finland | 12.0 | (0.6) | 19.3 | (4.9) | -7.3 | (5.0) | 18.0 | (0.7) | 26.2 | (5.2) | -8.1 | (5.2) | -7.2 | -0.43 | (0.28) |
| France | 9.5 | (0.5) | 15.4 | (1.9) | **-5.9** | (1.9) | 22.8 | (0.9) | 31.1 | (2.3) | **-8.3** | (2.4) | **-6.9** | **-0.36** | (0.12) |
| Germany | 9.3 | (0.6) | 15.8 | (2.1) | **-6.5** | (2.1) | 16.3 | (0.8) | 25.5 | (2.4) | **-9.2** | (2.6) | **-7.9** | **-0.50** | (0.15) |
| Greece | 9.3 | (0.7) | 11.3 | (2.1) | -2.0 | (2.2) | 21.7 | (1.0) | 23.5 | (3.5) | -1.8 | (3.4) | 1.3 | 0.08 | (0.21) |
| Hungary | 15.6 | (0.8) | 28.3 | (6.0) | -12.7 | (6.4) | 29.2 | (1.1) | 39.8 | (5.1) | -10.6 | (5.4) | **-11.1** | **-0.49** | (0.23) |
| Iceland | 14.0 | (0.6) | 16.2 | (5.2) | -2.2 | (5.3) | 26.6 | (0.7) | 44.3 | (5.9) | -17.7 | (6.0) | -16.0 | -0.72 | (0.25) |
| Ireland | 9.4 | (0.6) | 15.5 | (3.2) | -6.1 | (3.2) | 16.3 | (0.8) | 25.2 | (3.9) | -8.9 | (3.8) | -8.0 | -0.51 | (0.17) |
| Italy | 25.7 | (0.6) | 28.4 | (2.4) | -2.7 | (2.4) | 45.4 | (0.8) | 51.2 | (3.8) | -5.8 | (3.7) | -6.8 | -0.27 | (0.15) |
| Japan | 30.4 | (1.2) | c | c | c | c | 34.8 | (1.2) | c | c | c | c | c | c | c |
| Korea | 36.2 | (1.3) | c | c | c | c | 50.4 | (1.2) | c | c | c | c | c | c | c |
| Luxembourg | 7.7 | (0.5) | 13.2 | (0.9) | **-5.4** | (1.1) | 22.7 | (0.7) | 29.3 | (1.3) | **-6.6** | (1.6) | **-4.8** | **-0.25** | (0.09) |
| Mexico | 22.3 | (0.5) | 51.0 | (5.3) | **-28.6** | (5.4) | 31.3 | (0.7) | 71.2 | (3.9) | **-39.8** | (3.8) | **-32.6** | **-1.36** | (0.18) |
| Netherlands | 6.5 | (0.6) | 11.9 | (1.8) | **-5.3** | (1.9) | 14.6 | (0.9) | 22.8 | (2.5) | **-8.2** | (2.6) | **-5.1** | **-0.36** | (0.18) |
| New Zealand | 8.1 | (0.5) | 12.3 | (1.5) | -4.2 | (1.6) | 16.8 | (1.1) | 20.5 | (1.8) | -3.7 | (2.0) | -4.0 | -0.26 | (0.13) |
| Norway | 16.6 | (0.7) | 23.8 | (2.7) | -7.2 | (2.7) | 22.9 | (0.7) | 34.1 | (3.3) | **-11.2** | (3.3) | **-8.4** | **-0.43** | (0.16) |
| Poland | 26.5 | (0.9) | c | c | c | c | 41.0 | (1.0) | c | c | c | c | c | c | c |
| Portugal | 23.5 | (1.1) | 26.2 | (4.1) | -2.7 | (4.1) | 46.9 | (1.4) | 58.0 | (3.0) | **-11.0** | (3.3) | **-12.3** | **-0.50** | (0.14) |
| Slovak Republic | 24.0 | (1.2) | c | c | c | c | 38.4 | (1.4) | c | c | c | c | c | c | c |
| Spain | 9.1 | (0.5) | 16.9 | (2.1) | **-7.8** | (2.1) | 17.4 | (0.6) | 29.9 | (2.6) | **-12.4** | (2.7) | **-11.3** | **-0.65** | (0.12) |
| Sweden | 19.3 | (0.6) | 31.5 | (2.9) | **-12.3** | (3.1) | 24.5 | (0.8) | 39.9 | (2.4) | **-15.4** | (2.6) | **-11.3** | **-0.54** | (0.11) |
| Switzerland | 13.3 | (0.6) | 16.8 | (1.3) | **-3.5** | (1.4) | 20.8 | (0.7) | 27.9 | (1.5) | **-7.1** | (1.6) | **-6.0** | **-0.34** | (0.08) |
| Turkey | 12.7 | (0.7) | 13.0 | (5.5) | -0.3 | (5.5) | 19.6 | (1.0) | 23.8 | (5.6) | -4.2 | (5.6) | -5.5 | -0.32 | (0.31) |
| United Kingdom | 18.8 | (0.7) | 26.5 | (2.6) | **-7.7** | (2.6) | 30.8 | (0.9) | 39.7 | (2.5) | **-8.9** | (2.4) | -7.3 | -0.32 | (0.10) |
| United States | 16.5 | (1.0) | 24.7 | (2.0) | **-8.2** | (1.9) | 30.1 | (1.2) | 40.9 | (2.0) | **-10.8** | (2.1) | **-6.4** | **-0.29** | (0.10) |
| **OECD average** | 15.2 | (0.1) | 19.6 | (0.6) | **-6.6** | (0.6) | 25.5 | (0.2) | 33.1 | (0.7) | **-10.1** | (0.7) | **-8.6** | **-0.44** | (0.03) |
| **Partners** | | | | | | | | | | | | | | | |
| Argentina | 11.0 | (1.0) | 21.4 | (5.3) | **-10.4** | (5.3) | 19.6 | (1.4) | 32.0 | (5.8) | **-12.4** | (5.5) | **-11.6** | **-0.63** | (0.25) |
| Azerbaijan | 48.2 | (1.4) | 42.3 | (5.3) | 6.0 | (5.1) | 67.6 | (1.5) | 61.0 | (4.3) | 6.7 | (4.4) | 6.8 | 0.30 | (0.19) |
| Brazil | 19.9 | (0.8) | 30.1 | (4.8) | **-10.3** | (5.1) | 33.6 | (0.9) | 51.2 | (5.1) | **-17.6** | (5.1) | **-18.1** | **-0.75** | (0.20) |
| Bulgaria | 22.6 | (1.2) | c | c | c | c | 34.6 | (1.6) | c | c | c | c | c | c | c |
| Chile | 17.5 | (0.8) | c | c | c | c | 27.0 | (1.1) | c | c | c | c | c | c | c |
| Colombia | 18.9 | (1.0) | c | c | c | c | 28.6 | (1.3) | c | c | c | c | c | c | c |
| Croatia | 11.6 | (0.7) | 13.3 | (1.5) | -1.7 | (1.6) | 21.4 | (0.9) | 23.2 | (2.0) | -1.8 | (2.0) | -1.2 | -0.07 | (0.12) |
| Estonia | 18.1 | (0.7) | 20.4 | (1.8) | -2.3 | (1.8) | 31.0 | (1.0) | 36.8 | (2.5) | -5.8 | (2.4) | -4.8 | -0.22 | (0.12) |
| Hong Kong-China | 41.8 | (1.4) | 42.1 | (1.6) | -0.3 | (1.5) | 48.7 | (1.5) | 48.3 | (1.5) | 0.3 | (1.6) | 2.6 | 0.10 | (0.07) |
| Indonesia | 34.7 | (2.3) | 57.9 | (9.4) | **-23.2** | (9.7) | 51.5 | (3.0) | 75.1 | (7.3) | **-23.5** | (7.9) | -15.1 | -0.63 | (0.48) |
| Israel | 18.9 | (0.9) | 21.1 | (1.3) | -2.1 | (1.5) | 33.5 | (1.1) | 36.8 | (2.1) | -3.3 | (2.3) | -1.7 | -0.07 | (0.10) |
| Jordan | 40.7 | (1.0) | 39.9 | (2.1) | 0.8 | (2.4) | 56.3 | (1.2) | 54.8 | (2.2) | 1.5 | (2.1) | -0.7 | -0.03 | (0.08) |
| Kyrgyzstan | 53.3 | (1.2) | 36.6 | (5.4) | **16.7** | (5.3) | 78.8 | (1.1) | 61.7 | (6.6) | **17.1** | (6.5) | 9.4 | 0.51 | (0.30) |
| Latvia | 29.5 | (1.3) | 24.6 | (2.3) | **4.8** | (2.4) | 50.8 | (1.3) | 47.2 | (2.8) | 3.6 | (3.0) | -0.4 | -0.01 | (0.12) |
| Liechtenstein | 7.3 | (1.8) | 15.9 | (3.5) | **-8.6** | (4.3) | 10.2 | (2.0) | 26.7 | (4.0) | **-16.1** | (4.7) | **-14.8** | **-1.08** | (0.34) |
| Lithuania | 19.1 | (0.9) | 17.7 | (5.4) | 1.4 | (5.4) | 33.9 | (1.0) | 38.1 | (5.0) | -4.2 | (5.1) | -5.6 | -0.24 | (0.23) |
| Macao-China | 31.9 | (1.5) | 35.7 | (0.9) | **-3.7** | (1.8) | 44.3 | (1.5) | 47.4 | (1.0) | -3.1 | (1.8) | -0.1 | -0.00 | (0.08) |
| Montenegro | 21.7 | (0.7) | 19.9 | (2.8) | 1.8 | (2.9) | 34.7 | (0.8) | 34.1 | (3.5) | 0.6 | (3.5) | -1.5 | -0.07 | (0.15) |
| Qatar | 33.3 | (0.8) | 22.0 | (0.8) | **11.3** | (1.1) | 50.9 | (0.8) | 34.6 | (1.0) | **16.3** | (1.3) | **15.4** | **0.63** | (0.06) |
| Romania | 21.9 | (1.5) | c | c | c | c | 40.1 | (1.6) | c | c | c | c | c | c | c |
| Russian Federation | 36.5 | (1.3) | 38.7 | (2.4) | -2.2 | (2.0) | 57.4 | (1.3) | 59.4 | (2.5) | -2.0 | (2.1) | -2.8 | -0.11 | (0.09) |
| Serbia | 14.5 | (0.8) | 14.4 | (1.9) | 0.0 | (1.8) | 23.4 | (0.9) | 22.1 | (2.0) | 1.4 | (2.0) | -0.0 | -0.00 | (0.11) |
| Slovenia | 11.3 | (0.5) | 15.0 | (1.8) | -3.6 | (1.9) | 19.7 | (0.6) | 23.9 | (2.4) | -4.2 | (2.5) | -3.4 | -0.20 | (0.14) |
| Chinese Taipei | 34.9 | (0.7) | 39.3 | (9.0) | -4.5 | (8.9) | 44.7 | (0.9) | 46.0 | (8.7) | -1.2 | (8.5) | -1.1 | -0.05 | (0.33) |
| Thailand | 39.2 | (1.2) | c | c | c | c | 47.4 | (1.2) | c | c | c | c | c | c | c |
| Tunisia | 30.2 | (0.9) | 61.7 | (9.8) | **-31.5** | (9.8) | 53.7 | (1.2) | 82.3 | (7.8) | **-28.6** | (7.6) | **-25.6** | **-1.20** | (0.53) |
| Uruguay | 8.5 | (0.6) | c | c | c | c | 16.9 | (1.2) | c | c | c | c | c | c | c |

Note: Values that are statistically significant at the 5% level (p < 0.05) are indicated in bold.

### Table 3.17 Percentage of students by different types of out-of-school-time lessons, by lower and upper secondary schools
[Part 1/3]

| | Proportion of students participating in out-of-school-time lessons | | | | | | Proportion of students participating in out-of-school lessons with non-school teachers | | | | | | | | | | | |
| | | | | | | | One-to-one lessons | | | | | | Small group lessons | | | | | |
| | Lower secondary school | | Upper secondary school | | Difference (lower-upper) | | Lower secondary school | | Upper secondary school | | Difference (lower-upper) | | Lower secondary school | | Upper secondary school | | Difference (lower-upper) | |
| | % | S.E. | % | S.E. | Dif. | S.E. | % | S.E. | % | S.E. | Dif. | S.E. | % | S.E. | % | S.E. | Dif. | S.E. |
|---|---|---|---|---|---|---|---|---|---|---|---|---|---|---|---|---|---|---|
| **OECD** | | | | | | | | | | | | | | | | | | |
| Australia | 30.3 | (0.7) | 34.9 | (1.3) | **-4.6** | (1.4) | 16.5 | (0.5) | 16.8 | (0.9) | -0.3 | (1.0) | 8.0 | (0.4) | 8.6 | (0.7) | -0.6 | (0.7) |
| Austria | 51.3 | (5.8) | 35.3 | (1.1) | **16.0** | (5.8) | 22.3 | (3.5) | 16.3 | (0.8) | 6.0 | (3.6) | 19.0 | (3.6) | 7.0 | (0.5) | **12.0** | (3.6) |
| Belgium | 45.3 | (3.4) | 29.7 | (0.7) | **15.7** | (3.5) | 16.5 | (2.5) | 17.8 | (0.6) | -1.3 | (2.6) | 14.0 | (2.2) | 7.1 | (0.4) | **6.9** | (2.3) |
| Canada | 38.7 | (1.6) | 35.3 | (0.8) | **3.3** | (1.7) | 16.5 | (1.0) | 16.5 | (0.5) | 0.0 | (1.0) | 9.3 | (0.8) | 8.3 | (0.4) | 1.0 | (0.8) |
| Czech Republic | 42.6 | (1.3) | 32.4 | (1.4) | **10.2** | (2.0) | 17.5 | (1.1) | 14.3 | (1.0) | **3.2** | (1.5) | 8.7 | (0.8) | 7.1 | (0.7) | 1.6 | (1.0) |
| Denmark | 20.8 | (0.8) | 5.8 | (3.0) | **15.0** | (3.1) | 5.4 | (0.4) | 3.8 | (3.1) | 1.5 | (3.2) | 4.6 | (0.4) | 2.0 | (1.8) | 2.7 | (1.9) |
| Finland | 23.4 | (0.7) | c | c | c | c | 5.3 | (0.3) | c | c | c | c | 2.4 | (0.2) | c | c | c | c |
| France | 38.5 | (1.3) | 43.8 | (1.2) | **-5.3** | (1.7) | 20.0 | (1.4) | 24.0 | (1.1) | **-4.0** | (1.7) | 10.7 | (0.9) | 8.1 | (0.6) | **2.6** | (1.1) |
| Germany | 37.4 | (0.8) | 23.1 | (7.4) | 14.3 | (7.6) | 21.8 | (0.6) | 11.7 | (4.6) | **10.1** | (4.7) | 7.5 | (0.4) | 1.4 | (1.2) | **6.1** | (1.3) |
| Greece | 46.9 | (3.5) | 78.9 | (0.9) | **-32.0** | (3.7) | 20.4 | (2.4) | 46.9 | (1.1) | **-26.4** | (2.7) | 22.5 | (2.2) | 47.9 | (1.4) | **-25.5** | (2.6) |
| Hungary | 67.5 | (2.9) | 53.1 | (1.2) | **14.4** | (3.2) | 18.9 | (2.6) | 33.6 | (1.1) | **-14.7** | (2.9) | 14.2 | (2.6) | 10.5 | (0.6) | 3.7 | (2.7) |
| Iceland | 40.6 | (0.8) | a | a | a | a | 14.7 | (0.6) | a | a | a | a | 6.7 | (0.5) | a | a | a | a |
| Ireland | 44.8 | (1.3) | 27.8 | (1.2) | **17.0** | (1.7) | 24.0 | (0.8) | 17.2 | (1.0) | **6.8** | (1.3) | 11.1 | (0.7) | 7.5 | (0.7) | **3.6** | (1.0) |
| Italy | 70.2 | (9.3) | 66.4 | (0.6) | 3.9 | (9.4) | 29.9 | (4.4) | 37.3 | (0.6) | -7.5 | (4.4) | 23.4 | (7.9) | 14.0 | (0.5) | 9.4 | (8.0) |
| Japan | a | a | 45.6 | (1.4) | a | a | a | a | 9.4 | (0.6) | a | a | a | a | 8.4 | (0.6) | a | a |
| Korea | 74.3 | (9.5) | 79.3 | (0.9) | -5.0 | (9.5) | 27.3 | (7.7) | 31.4 | (0.8) | -4.1 | (7.8) | 34.4 | (3.9) | 31.2 | (0.9) | 3.2 | (4.0) |
| Luxembourg | 47.4 | (0.9) | 37.5 | (1.0) | **9.8** | (1.3) | 23.5 | (0.7) | 22.5 | (1.2) | 1.0 | (1.2) | 8.8 | (0.6) | 4.0 | (0.6) | **4.8** | (0.8) |
| Mexico | 56.2 | (1.5) | 40.9 | (0.9) | **15.3** | (1.8) | 20.4 | (1.2) | 15.9 | (0.6) | **4.5** | (1.3) | 19.3 | (1.2) | 13.7 | (0.4) | **5.6** | (1.2) |
| Netherlands | 23.0 | (1.0) | 19.6 | (1.5) | 3.4 | (1.8) | 7.3 | (0.5) | 7.8 | (0.7) | -0.5 | (0.8) | 4.4 | (0.5) | 1.4 | (0.3) | **3.0** | (0.6) |
| New Zealand | 36.2 | (2.8) | 33.6 | (0.9) | 2.6 | (2.9) | 17.9 | (2.2) | 17.1 | (0.7) | 0.7 | (2.3) | 13.0 | (2.3) | 9.6 | (0.5) | 3.4 | (2.3) |
| Norway | 27.4 | (0.8) | c | c | c | c | 5.4 | (0.4) | c | c | c | c | 4.9 | (0.4) | c | c | c | c |
| Poland | 56.1 | (1.0) | 59.5 | (6.6) | -3.3 | (6.7) | 19.2 | (0.8) | 33.7 | (5.1) | **-14.5** | (5.1) | 10.6 | (0.6) | 17.9 | (4.8) | -7.3 | (4.8) |
| Portugal | 69.4 | (1.3) | 68.0 | (1.4) | 1.5 | (1.9) | 19.7 | (1.0) | 34.6 | (1.6) | **-14.9** | (2.0) | 13.6 | (0.8) | 15.9 | (1.2) | -2.4 | (1.4) |
| Slovak Republic | 77.1 | (1.7) | 42.8 | (1.5) | **34.3** | (2.4) | 28.4 | (2.0) | 23.8 | (1.1) | 4.6 | (2.3) | 12.9 | (1.0) | 10.2 | (0.6) | **2.8** | (1.2) |
| Spain | 53.9 | (0.7) | c | c | c | c | 28.7 | (0.8) | c | c | c | c | 26.2 | (0.7) | c | c | c | c |
| Sweden | 32.4 | (0.8) | 13.3 | (3.4) | **19.1** | (3.6) | 7.5 | (0.5) | 3.4 | (1.9) | **4.1** | (2.0) | 5.8 | (0.4) | 2.7 | (1.8) | 3.1 | (1.9) |
| Switzerland | 40.4 | (0.7) | 38.2 | (1.9) | 2.1 | (2.1) | 18.6 | (0.5) | 26.2 | (1.7) | **-7.6** | (1.7) | 6.0 | (0.4) | 7.9 | (1.2) | -1.9 | (1.2) |
| Turkey | 35.9 | (6.8) | 37.0 | (1.1) | -1.1 | (6.9) | 9.0 | (5.1) | 13.7 | (0.6) | -4.7 | (5.1) | 11.6 | (2.9) | 10.9 | (0.6) | 0.7 | (3.0) |
| United Kingdom | 63.4 | (5.6) | 45.5 | (0.9) | **17.9** | (5.6) | 25.9 | (7.5) | 17.4 | (0.5) | 8.5 | (7.6) | 31.5 | (5.7) | 7.4 | (0.5) | **24.1** | (5.7) |
| United States | 57.7 | (3.9) | 40.2 | (1.1) | **17.5** | (4.0) | 23.9 | (2.9) | 16.4 | (0.8) | **7.4** | (3.0) | 25.0 | (3.2) | 10.8 | (0.6) | **14.2** | (3.2) |
| **OECD average** | **46.5** | **(0.7)** | **41.0** | **(0.5)** | **7.3** | **(0.9)** | **18.4** | **(0.5)** | **20.4** | **(0.3)** | **-1.7** | **(0.7)** | **13.5** | **(0.5)** | **10.8** | **(0.3)** | **3.1** | **(0.6)** |
| **Partners** | | | | | | | | | | | | | | | | | | |
| Argentina | 54.5 | (2.4) | 46.1 | (1.4) | **8.5** | (2.8) | 26.8 | (1.9) | 33.0 | (1.6) | **-6.1** | (2.5) | 22.8 | (2.3) | 17.7 | (0.8) | **5.1** | (2.4) |
| Azerbaijan | 78.4 | (1.3) | 81.1 | (1.4) | -2.7 | (1.4) | 26.9 | (1.3) | 36.2 | (1.8) | **-9.3** | (2.0) | 39.6 | (1.2) | 42.5 | (1.5) | -2.8 | (1.8) |
| Brazil | 56.9 | (1.2) | 44.4 | (1.1) | **12.5** | (1.6) | 19.9 | (1.0) | 19.6 | (0.8) | 0.3 | (1.3) | 21.6 | (0.9) | 16.0 | (0.7) | **5.6** | (1.2) |
| Bulgaria | 55.2 | (5.3) | 54.1 | (1.4) | 1.1 | (5.5) | 17.9 | (2.9) | 27.5 | (1.0) | **-9.6** | (3.1) | 26.2 | (4.0) | 16.9 | (1.1) | **9.4** | (4.3) |
| Chile | 53.5 | (5.4) | 37.6 | (1.2) | **15.9** | (5.5) | 15.6 | (4.1) | 13.2 | (0.8) | 2.5 | (4.1) | 18.5 | (3.9) | 9.0 | (0.5) | **9.5** | (3.9) |
| Colombia | 57.0 | (1.8) | 47.0 | (1.5) | **10.0** | (2.3) | 26.5 | (1.2) | 24.7 | (1.2) | 1.8 | (1.9) | 19.5 | (1.1) | 16.7 | (0.9) | **2.8** | (1.3) |
| Croatia | c | c | 45.4 | (0.9) | c | c | c | c | 28.0 | (0.8) | c | c | c | c | 9.8 | (0.5) | c | c |
| Estonia | 46.0 | (0.9) | 48.1 | (4.9) | -2.1 | (5.1) | 17.1 | (0.7) | 23.8 | (4.3) | -6.6 | (4.3) | 8.1 | (0.5) | 9.6 | (3.7) | -1.5 | (3.8) |
| Hong Kong-China | 66.3 | (1.5) | 80.6 | (0.8) | **-14.3** | (1.5) | 22.3 | (1.5) | 25.2 | (1.3) | **-2.9** | (1.4) | 18.5 | (1.0) | 17.4 | (0.9) | 1.0 | (1.2) |
| Indonesia | 81.0 | (1.3) | 49.1 | (2.4) | **31.9** | (2.5) | 18.0 | (1.0) | 16.8 | (1.4) | 1.2 | (1.8) | 20.4 | (1.0) | 18.4 | (1.1) | 2.1 | (1.4) |
| Israel | 65.2 | (2.3) | 64.3 | (1.1) | 0.9 | (2.5) | 42.4 | (2.6) | 42.2 | (1.1) | 0.3 | (2.8) | 21.9 | (2.8) | 20.0 | (0.8) | 1.9 | (2.8) |
| Jordan | 72.6 | (0.9) | a | a | a | a | 34.4 | (0.8) | a | a | a | a | 25.2 | (0.8) | a | a | a | a |
| Kyrgyzstan | 85.5 | (1.1) | 84.3 | (1.5) | 1.2 | (1.5) | 26.9 | (0.8) | 25.0 | (1.6) | 1.9 | (1.7) | 27.6 | (1.0) | 25.1 | (1.4) | 2.5 | (1.6) |
| Latvia | 71.5 | (1.1) | 70.4 | (3.7) | 1.2 | (3.6) | 32.2 | (1.2) | 34.0 | (4.4) | -1.8 | (4.4) | 14.0 | (0.5) | 16.0 | (3.9) | -2.0 | (4.0) |
| Liechtenstein | 27.2 | (2.4) | 32.7 | (8.8) | -5.5 | (9.1) | 13.8 | (1.8) | 15.7 | (6.5) | -1.9 | (6.6) | 2.8 | (1.0) | 2.7 | (2.6) | 0.1 | (2.4) |
| Lithuania | 48.8 | (1.1) | c | c | c | c | 17.8 | (0.8) | c | c | c | c | 7.0 | (0.4) | c | c | c | c |
| Macao-China | 66.8 | (0.9) | 54.7 | (1.3) | **12.0** | (1.5) | 25.4 | (0.9) | 15.7 | (0.9) | **9.7** | (1.2) | 22.8 | (0.9) | 17.0 | (1.0) | **5.8** | (1.2) |
| Montenegro | c | c | 62.0 | (0.7) | c | c | c | c | 37.5 | (0.8) | c | c | c | c | 20.7 | (0.6) | c | c |
| Qatar | 69.8 | (1.1) | 61.8 | (0.6) | **8.0** | (1.4) | 33.9 | (1.5) | 36.9 | (0.8) | -3.0 | (1.6) | 31.0 | (1.3) | 23.8 | (0.7) | **7.2** | (1.6) |
| Romania | 56.8 | (1.5) | a | a | a | a | 27.9 | (1.4) | a | a | a | a | 19.8 | (1.2) | a | a | a | a |
| Russian Federation | 74.0 | (1.6) | 66.6 | (1.7) | **7.4** | (2.0) | 20.8 | (1.2) | 22.1 | (1.0) | -1.3 | (1.4) | 14.3 | (1.2) | 11.4 | (0.7) | **2.9** | (1.1) |
| Serbia | 44.4 | (5.9) | 54.0 | (1.1) | -9.6 | (6.0) | 22.9 | (9.7) | 38.8 | (1.1) | -15.9 | (9.8) | 4.5 | (2.6) | 13.0 | (0.6) | **-8.5** | (2.6) |
| Slovenia | 67.5 | (6.4) | 40.6 | (0.6) | **26.9** | (6.4) | 14.0 | (4.5) | 27.2 | (0.7) | **-13.3** | (4.6) | 9.6 | (4.6) | 6.4 | (0.3) | 3.2 | (4.6) |
| Chinese Taipei | 79.5 | (0.9) | 72.8 | (0.7) | **6.8** | (1.2) | 25.2 | (1.0) | 22.9 | (0.6) | 2.3 | (1.3) | 27.0 | (1.0) | 22.0 | (0.5) | **5.0** | (1.1) |
| Thailand | 63.8 | (1.6) | 63.4 | (1.6) | 0.4 | (2.2) | 21.9 | (1.4) | 19.8 | (0.9) | 2.1 | (1.7) | 25.4 | (1.2) | 23.4 | (1.1) | 2.0 | (1.6) |
| Tunisia | 74.8 | (1.3) | 66.4 | (1.6) | **8.4** | (2.0) | 29.3 | (1.3) | 32.1 | (2.3) | -2.8 | (2.6) | 29.0 | (1.2) | 27.6 | (1.8) | 1.4 | (2.1) |
| Uruguay | 39.3 | (1.6) | 47.4 | (1.2) | **-8.0** | (1.9) | 21.3 | (1.2) | 33.2 | (1.1) | **-11.9** | (1.6) | 14.8 | (1.1) | 24.2 | (0.9) | **-9.4** | (1.2) |

Note: Values that are statistically significant at the 5% level (p < 0.05) are indicated in bold.

© OECD 2011 Quality Time for Students: Learning In and Out of School

## Table 3.17 Percentage of students by different types of out-of-school-time lessons, by lower and upper secondary schools
[Part 2/3]

| | Proportion of students participating in out-of-school lessons with non-school teachers | | | | | | | | | | | | Proportion of students participating in out-of-school lessons with school teachers | | | | | |
|---|---|---|---|---|---|---|---|---|---|---|---|---|---|---|---|---|---|---|
| | Large group lessons | | | | | | At least one of these types of out-of-school lessons | | | | | | One-to-one lessons | | | | | |
| | Lower secondary school | | Upper secondary school | | Difference (lower-upper) | | Lower secondary school | | Upper secondary school | | Difference (lower-upper) | | Lower secondary school | | Upper secondary school | | Difference (lower-upper) | |
| | % | S.E. | % | S.E. | Dif. | S.E. | % | S.E. | % | S.E. | Dif. | S.E. | % | S.E. | % | S.E. | Dif. | S.E. |
| **OECD** | | | | | | | | | | | | | | | | | | |
| Australia | 7.3 | (0.4) | 7.0 | (0.6) | 0.4 | (0.7) | 22.9 | (0.6) | 24.0 | (1.1) | -1.1 | (1.2) | 6.4 | (0.4) | 7.9 | (0.8) | -1.5 | (0.8) |
| Austria | 13.7 | (3.3) | 5.7 | (0.4) | **8.0** | (3.3) | 38.3 | (5.6) | 23.3 | (0.9) | **15.0** | (5.7) | 15.4 | (3.6) | 4.8 | (0.4) | **10.6** | (3.6) |
| Belgium | 10.2 | (1.9) | 4.1 | (0.4) | **6.2** | (1.9) | 28.1 | (3.4) | 22.2 | (0.6) | 5.9 | (3.4) | 19.9 | (2.9) | 6.7 | (0.4) | **13.2** | (2.9) |
| Canada | 8.0 | (0.7) | 6.9 | (0.4) | 1.1 | (0.8) | 23.0 | (1.1) | 22.8 | (0.6) | 0.2 | (1.2) | 15.9 | (1.1) | 11.7 | (0.4) | **4.3** | (1.1) |
| Czech Republic | 6.8 | (0.7) | 4.6 | (0.7) | 2.1 | (1.0) | 23.5 | (1.2) | 20.2 | (1.2) | 3.3 | (1.7) | 17.2 | (1.1) | 11.6 | (1.0) | **5.6** | (1.5) |
| Denmark | 3.9 | (0.4) | a | a | a | a | 10.4 | (0.6) | 5.8 | (3.0) | 4.7 | (3.1) | 5.4 | (0.4) | a | a | a | a |
| Finland | 3.7 | (0.3) | c | c | c | c | 8.5 | (0.4) | c | c | c | c | 8.1 | (0.5) | c | c | c | c |
| France | 8.4 | (1.0) | 2.5 | (0.4) | 5.9 | (1.0) | 25.9 | (1.5) | 26.7 | (1.2) | -0.7 | (1.9) | 9.8 | (0.9) | 5.2 | (0.9) | **4.6** | (1.1) |
| Germany | 3.9 | (0.4) | 0.9 | (1.0) | 2.9 | (1.1) | 27.7 | (0.6) | 14.0 | (4.1) | **13.7** | (4.1) | 5.9 | (0.5) | 1.3 | (1.0) | **4.6** | (1.1) |
| Greece | 18.6 | (3.2) | 18.5 | (1.0) | 0.0 | (3.3) | 39.2 | (2.6) | 73.3 | (1.0) | **-34.1** | (2.8) | 16.1 | (4.1) | 11.7 | (0.8) | 4.4 | (4.2) |
| Hungary | 22.2 | (3.5) | 7.7 | (0.5) | **14.5** | (3.6) | 33.6 | (3.6) | 38.7 | (1.1) | -5.0 | (3.9) | 30.2 | (3.0) | 13.4 | (0.8) | **16.8** | (3.0) |
| Iceland | 5.1 | (0.4) | a | a | a | a | 19.9 | (0.7) | a | a | a | a | 10.5 | (0.5) | a | a | a | a |
| Ireland | 7.5 | (0.7) | 5.4 | (0.6) | 2.2 | (0.9) | 32.7 | (1.1) | 22.9 | (1.1) | **9.9** | (1.5) | 9.1 | (0.8) | 3.8 | (0.5) | **5.3** | (0.9) |
| Italy | 22.8 | (4.3) | 8.8 | (1.0) | 14.0 | (4.4) | 48.6 | (7.9) | 45.9 | (0.7) | 2.8 | (8.0) | a | a | a | a | a | a |
| Japan | a | a | 8.2 | (0.6) | a | a | a | a | 20.2 | (1.0) | a | a | a | a | 7.5 | (0.6) | a | a |
| Korea | 28.3 | (12.6) | 26.9 | (0.8) | 1.5 | (12.6) | 54.4 | (11.2) | 57.9 | (1.0) | -3.5 | (11.2) | 8.7 | (2.6) | 9.6 | (0.5) | -0.9 | (2.6) |
| Luxembourg | 7.3 | (0.5) | 2.3 | (0.4) | 5.0 | (0.6) | 29.6 | (0.7) | 25.0 | (1.3) | **4.6** | (1.4) | 16.3 | (0.7) | 9.3 | (0.7) | **7.0** | (1.1) |
| Mexico | 21.7 | (1.2) | 11.8 | (0.5) | 9.8 | (1.3) | 35.5 | (1.5) | 26.4 | (0.8) | **9.1** | (1.6) | 25.6 | (1.6) | 10.8 | (0.4) | **14.8** | (1.7) |
| Netherlands | 4.5 | (0.4) | 1.5 | (0.3) | 3.0 | (0.5) | 11.8 | (0.7) | 9.3 | (0.8) | **2.5** | (1.0) | 8.7 | (0.6) | 4.3 | (0.9) | **4.4** | (1.0) |
| New Zealand | 12.3 | (2.0) | 6.6 | (0.4) | 5.7 | (2.0) | 26.0 | (2.6) | 23.8 | (0.7) | 2.3 | (2.6) | 11.4 | (1.7) | 9.0 | (0.8) | 2.4 | (1.7) |
| Norway | 5.0 | (0.4) | c | c | c | c | 9.9 | (0.6) | c | c | c | c | 8.5 | (0.5) | c | c | c | c |
| Poland | 10.0 | (0.4) | 11.8 | (3.5) | -1.8 | (3.4) | 28.8 | (0.9) | 49.7 | (6.8) | **-20.8** | (6.8) | 14.7 | (0.6) | 6.4 | (2.5) | **8.3** | (2.5) |
| Portugal | 10.8 | (1.0) | 5.1 | (0.5) | 5.7 | (1.1) | 28.2 | (1.1) | 43.5 | (1.7) | **-15.3** | (2.1) | 28.6 | (1.5) | 14.2 | (0.9) | **14.4** | (1.8) |
| Slovak Republic | 10.3 | (1.2) | 5.6 | (0.6) | 4.7 | (1.3) | 33.9 | (2.0) | 27.1 | (1.1) | **6.8** | (2.3) | 53.3 | (2.4) | 16.5 | (1.1) | **36.9** | (2.6) |
| Spain | 10.5 | (0.5) | c | c | c | c | 43.5 | (0.8) | c | c | c | c | 8.5 | (0.5) | c | c | c | c |
| Sweden | 7.1 | (0.4) | 1.5 | (1.0) | 5.6 | (1.1) | 13.3 | (0.6) | 5.8 | (1.9) | **7.5** | (2.0) | 8.9 | (0.6) | 0.8 | (0.6) | **8.1** | (0.8) |
| Switzerland | 5.3 | (0.4) | 2.5 | (0.7) | 2.8 | (0.8) | 23.6 | (0.6) | 29.8 | (1.9) | **-6.2** | (1.9) | 7.3 | (0.3) | 4.0 | (0.8) | **3.3** | (0.8) |
| Turkey | 13.4 | (2.2) | 15.1 | (1.0) | -1.7 | (2.5) | 21.4 | (3.8) | 26.8 | (1.2) | -5.3 | (4.1) | 12.6 | (8.0) | 7.4 | (0.5) | 5.2 | (8.1) |
| United Kingdom | 31.1 | (8.6) | 7.3 | (0.4) | **23.8** | (8.6) | 51.8 | (4.9) | 24.0 | (0.7) | **27.9** | (5.0) | 20.6 | (6.7) | 11.3 | (0.4) | 9.3 | (6.7) |
| United States | 23.2 | (3.4) | 10.0 | (0.6) | **13.2** | (3.5) | 39.8 | (3.8) | 23.2 | (0.9) | **16.6** | (3.9) | 36.9 | (4.2) | 20.4 | (0.8) | **16.5** | (4.3) |
| **OECD average** | 11.8 | (0.6) | 7.5 | (0.2) | **5.6** | (0.8) | 28.8 | (0.6) | 28.1 | (0.4) | **1.6** | (0.8) | 15.7 | (0.5) | 8.7 | (0.2) | **8.6** | (0.6) |
| **Partners** | | | | | | | | | | | | | | | | | | |
| Argentina | 22.2 | (1.4) | 9.3 | (0.8) | 12.9 | (1.5) | 40.2 | (2.2) | 39.8 | (1.4) | 0.4 | (2.6) | 18.2 | (2.0) | 7.6 | (0.8) | **10.6** | (2.1) |
| Azerbaijan | 38.2 | (1.5) | 40.0 | (1.4) | -1.8 | (2.0) | 60.6 | (1.2) | 65.7 | (1.6) | **-5.1** | (1.8) | 35.8 | (1.3) | 43.6 | (1.6) | **-7.8** | (1.5) |
| Brazil | 20.4 | (1.0) | 13.1 | (0.6) | 7.3 | (1.2) | 37.0 | (1.2) | 31.1 | (0.8) | **5.9** | (1.6) | 19.5 | (1.3) | 10.7 | (0.6) | **8.7** | (1.5) |
| Bulgaria | 26.9 | (3.5) | 16.1 | (1.1) | 10.8 | (3.6) | 35.9 | (4.8) | 38.2 | (1.1) | -2.3 | (4.9) | 38.0 | (4.5) | 20.8 | (1.5) | **17.2** | (4.8) |
| Chile | 19.8 | (5.3) | 7.8 | (0.4) | 11.9 | (5.3) | 33.2 | (5.4) | 20.9 | (0.8) | **12.3** | (5.4) | 22.3 | (4.5) | 7.7 | (0.5) | **14.7** | (4.5) |
| Colombia | 18.7 | (1.5) | 14.9 | (0.9) | 3.8 | (2.0) | 39.0 | (1.6) | 35.2 | (1.3) | 3.8 | (2.3) | 23.2 | (1.6) | 9.6 | (1.4) | **13.7** | (2.0) |
| Croatia | c | c | 7.8 | (0.5) | c | c | c | c | 34.1 | (0.9) | c | c | c | c | 13.0 | (0.5) | c | c |
| Estonia | 7.3 | (0.5) | 7.7 | (3.4) | -0.3 | (3.5) | 23.3 | (0.7) | 31.5 | (5.5) | -8.2 | (5.6) | 18.5 | (0.9) | 13.8 | (3.8) | 4.7 | (4.0) |
| Hong Kong-China | 21.0 | (1.3) | 35.3 | (1.5) | -14.3 | (1.6) | 43.5 | (1.7) | 57.0 | (1.3) | **-13.5** | (1.7) | 9.0 | (0.8) | 4.1 | (0.4) | **4.8** | (0.9) |
| Indonesia | 20.0 | (1.1) | 14.8 | (1.0) | 5.3 | (1.4) | 35.8 | (1.2) | 32.1 | (1.6) | 3.7 | (2.2) | 48.4 | (1.9) | 13.2 | (1.4) | **35.1** | (2.0) |
| Israel | 14.8 | (1.9) | 15.5 | (0.8) | -0.6 | (1.9) | 54.4 | (2.7) | 52.5 | (1.3) | 1.9 | (2.7) | 17.5 | (2.0) | 21.3 | (1.1) | -3.8 | (2.1) |
| Jordan | 21.9 | (0.8) | a | a | a | a | 48.0 | (0.9) | a | a | a | a | 27.4 | (1.0) | a | a | a | a |
| Kyrgyzstan | 33.2 | (1.1) | 27.6 | (1.3) | 5.6 | (1.5) | 49.9 | (1.1) | 44.5 | (1.6) | **5.4** | (1.8) | 63.7 | (1.2) | 63.9 | (1.7) | -0.2 | (2.0) |
| Latvia | 17.3 | (0.7) | 10.9 | (2.8) | 6.4 | (3.1) | 42.3 | (1.1) | 42.7 | (5.1) | -0.5 | (5.1) | 35.0 | (1.2) | 25.3 | (4.0) | **9.7** | (4.4) |
| Liechtenstein | 2.7 | (1.0) | 0.0 | (0.0) | 2.7 | (1.0) | 15.9 | (2.1) | 18.3 | (6.8) | -2.4 | (7.0) | 5.9 | (1.4) | 5.3 | (3.7) | 0.6 | (4.2) |
| Lithuania | 6.6 | (0.5) | c | c | c | c | 23.4 | (0.8) | c | c | c | c | 12.0 | (0.6) | c | c | c | c |
| Macao-China | 21.7 | (0.9) | 15.5 | (1.0) | 6.2 | (1.3) | 43.5 | (1.0) | 31.6 | (1.3) | **11.9** | (1.5) | 17.8 | (0.8) | 8.2 | (0.7) | **9.7** | (1.0) |
| Montenegro | c | c | 17.4 | (0.6) | c | c | c | c | 47.5 | (0.8) | c | c | c | c | 25.1 | (0.6) | c | c |
| Qatar | 29.7 | (1.2) | 20.9 | (0.6) | 8.9 | (1.4) | 52.1 | (1.3) | 47.5 | (0.8) | **4.7** | (1.5) | 45.2 | (1.5) | 30.7 | (0.5) | **14.6** | (1.7) |
| Romania | 15.5 | (1.2) | a | a | a | a | 38.5 | (1.3) | a | a | a | a | 26.9 | (1.3) | a | a | a | a |
| Russian Federation | 14.5 | (1.0) | 11.7 | (0.7) | 2.9 | (1.2) | 31.2 | (1.8) | 31.3 | (1.2) | -0.0 | (1.9) | 35.3 | (1.2) | 28.0 | (1.2) | **7.3** | (1.5) |
| Serbia | 9.3 | (4.0) | 8.7 | (0.5) | 0.6 | (4.0) | 27.2 | (8.5) | 43.6 | (1.1) | -16.4 | (8.5) | 6.7 | (3.4) | 10.4 | (0.7) | -3.7 | (3.4) |
| Slovenia | 12.8 | (2.5) | 4.8 | (0.3) | 8.1 | (2.5) | 29.3 | (4.8) | 31.3 | (0.6) | -1.9 | (4.9) | 29.2 | (5.8) | 8.1 | (0.3) | **21.1** | (5.8) |
| Chinese Taipei | 43.2 | (1.9) | 39.0 | (1.0) | 4.2 | (2.1) | 62.0 | (1.4) | 54.4 | (0.9) | **7.6** | (1.6) | 13.3 | (1.0) | 14.9 | (0.8) | -1.6 | (1.4) |
| Thailand | 31.8 | (1.3) | 31.1 | (1.5) | 0.8 | (1.8) | 44.2 | (1.3) | 44.3 | (1.7) | -0.1 | (2.0) | 26.5 | (1.4) | 18.5 | (0.7) | **8.1** | (1.6) |
| Tunisia | 27.1 | (1.4) | 12.1 | (0.8) | 15.0 | (1.6) | 48.7 | (1.3) | 41.3 | (2.4) | **7.4** | (2.7) | 49.7 | (1.6) | 36.0 | (2.2) | **13.7** | (2.6) |
| Uruguay | 13.7 | (1.2) | 11.1 | (0.7) | 2.6 | (1.5) | 30.0 | (1.4) | 41.4 | (1.1) | **-11.4** | (1.9) | 12.7 | (1.2) | 7.9 | (1.0) | **4.8** | (1.5) |

Note: Values that are statistically significant at the 5% level (p < 0.05) are indicated in bold.

### Table 3.17 Percentage of students by different types of out-of-school-time lessons, by lower and upper secondary schools
[Part 3/3]

| | Proportion of students participating in out-of-school lessons with school teachers | | | | | | | | | | | | | | | | | |
| | Small group lessons | | | | | | Large group lessons | | | | | | At least one of these types of out-of-school lessons | | | | | |
| | Lower secondary school | | Upper secondary school | | Difference (lower-upper) | | Lower secondary school | | Upper secondary school | | Difference (lower-upper) | | Lower secondary school | | Upper secondary school | | Difference (lower-upper) | |
| | % | S.E. | % | S.E. | Dif. | S.E. | % | S.E. | % | S.E. | Dif. | S.E. | % | S.E. | % | S.E. | Dif. | S.E. |
|---|---|---|---|---|---|---|---|---|---|---|---|---|---|---|---|---|---|---|
| **OECD** | | | | | | | | | | | | | | | | | | |
| Australia | 6.6 | (0.4) | 10.1 | (1.0) | -3.5 | (1.0) | 7.9 | (0.4) | 9.4 | (0.7) | -1.5 | (0.7) | 13.2 | (0.6) | 17.4 | (1.2) | -4.2 | (1.3) |
| Austria | 29.8 | (4.2) | 12.0 | (0.8) | 17.8 | (4.2) | 25.4 | (3.8) | 15.0 | (0.9) | 10.3 | (4.0) | 43.2 | (5.2) | 22.1 | (1.1) | 21.2 | (5.2) |
| Belgium | 22.8 | (2.5) | 7.2 | (0.4) | 15.6 | (2.6) | 19.5 | (3.1) | 5.4 | (0.3) | 14.1 | (3.1) | 35.9 | (2.9) | 13.3 | (0.5) | 22.6 | (3.0) |
| Canada | 14.6 | (1.0) | 9.8 | (0.4) | 4.9 | (1.1) | 15.5 | (0.9) | 10.6 | (0.4) | 4.9 | (1.0) | 26.7 | (1.3) | 20.4 | (0.6) | 6.3 | (1.5) |
| Czech Republic | 13.6 | (1.0) | 8.5 | (0.9) | 5.1 | (1.3) | 16.5 | (0.9) | 10.5 | (1.2) | 6.0 | (1.5) | 28.1 | (1.3) | 18.7 | (1.6) | 9.4 | (2.1) |
| Denmark | 8.1 | (0.5) | a | a | a | a | 8.1 | (0.5) | a | a | a | a | 14.2 | (0.7) | a | a | a | a |
| Finland | 9.4 | (0.5) | c | c | c | c | 12.1 | (0.6) | c | c | c | c | 18.2 | (0.7) | c | c | c | c |
| France | 16.1 | (0.9) | 19.2 | (1.1) | -3.2 | (1.5) | 10.7 | (0.8) | 10.2 | (0.7) | 0.5 | (1.1) | 23.0 | (1.2) | 24.5 | (1.2) | -1.5 | (1.7) |
| Germany | 7.8 | (0.6) | 5.6 | (1.5) | 2.2 | (1.6) | 10.5 | (0.6) | 6.3 | (4.4) | 4.2 | (4.5) | 17.8 | (0.7) | 11.3 | (6.0) | 6.5 | (6.1) |
| Greece | 17.2 | (3.5) | 14.6 | (0.9) | 2.6 | (3.6) | 17.8 | (2.8) | 9.0 | (0.7) | 8.8 | (2.9) | 27.0 | (4.1) | 21.6 | (1.1) | 5.4 | (4.3) |
| Hungary | 22.6 | (2.9) | 11.9 | (0.7) | 10.7 | (3.0) | 38.2 | (4.5) | 14.0 | (0.7) | 24.2 | (4.6) | 54.8 | (3.7) | 27.3 | (1.1) | 27.5 | (3.9) |
| Iceland | 14.6 | (0.6) | a | a | a | a | 14.2 | (0.6) | c | c | c | c | 27.2 | (0.7) | c | c | c | c |
| Ireland | 11.5 | (0.8) | 5.1 | (0.6) | 6.4 | (0.9) | 13.0 | (0.9) | 4.9 | (0.5) | 8.0 | (1.1) | 21.9 | (1.2) | 9.2 | (0.7) | 12.6 | (1.4) |
| Italy | 39.2 | (6.5) | 36.3 | (0.8) | 2.9 | (6.7) | 36.9 | (7.7) | 25.6 | (0.6) | 11.3 | (7.7) | 49.8 | (7.7) | 45.7 | (0.9) | 4.1 | (7.7) |
| Japan | a | a | 6.6 | (0.3) | a | a | a | a | 30.5 | (1.2) | a | a | a | a | 34.9 | (1.2) | a | a |
| Korea | 12.6 | (8.0) | 16.8 | (0.6) | -4.2 | (8.0) | 21.4 | (9.0) | 36.5 | (1.3) | -15.1 | (9.1) | 34.0 | (11.8) | 50.7 | (1.2) | -16.7 | (11.9) |
| Luxembourg | 17.2 | (0.7) | 9.9 | (0.7) | 7.4 | (1.0) | 13.1 | (0.7) | 4.1 | (0.5) | 8.9 | (0.9) | 29.5 | (0.8) | 17.8 | (0.9) | 11.7 | (1.3) |
| Mexico | 24.6 | (1.5) | 12.0 | (0.5) | 12.6 | (1.7) | 32.6 | (1.8) | 16.8 | (0.6) | 15.7 | (2.0) | 44.7 | (1.9) | 24.3 | (0.7) | 20.4 | (2.1) |
| Netherlands | 9.9 | (0.6) | 5.5 | (1.1) | 4.3 | (1.1) | 7.5 | (0.6) | 6.4 | (1.1) | 1.1 | (1.3) | 16.6 | (0.9) | 12.5 | (1.6) | 4.2 | (1.7) |
| New Zealand | 14.9 | (2.2) | 9.4 | (0.6) | 5.5 | (2.2) | 12.7 | (2.0) | 8.8 | (0.6) | 3.9 | (2.2) | 21.0 | (2.4) | 17.5 | (1.0) | 3.5 | (2.5) |
| Norway | 12.0 | (0.5) | c | c | c | c | 17.3 | (0.7) | c | c | c | c | 23.9 | (0.8) | m | m | m | m |
| Poland | 23.2 | (0.8) | 11.2 | (3.5) | 11.9 | (3.7) | 26.8 | (0.9) | 12.7 | (3.6) | 14.1 | (3.6) | 41.3 | (1.0) | 20.9 | (4.6) | 20.4 | (4.6) |
| Portugal | 38.3 | (1.5) | 24.3 | (1.4) | 14.1 | (1.8) | 32.7 | (1.7) | 13.4 | (1.2) | 19.4 | (2.1) | 58.3 | (1.8) | 35.5 | (1.5) | 22.8 | (2.2) |
| Slovak Republic | 28.6 | (1.7) | 11.6 | (1.1) | 17.0 | (1.9) | 45.9 | (2.1) | 10.6 | (1.0) | 35.3 | (2.3) | 64.9 | (2.3) | 22.7 | (1.4) | 42.2 | (2.7) |
| Spain | 10.8 | (0.4) | m | m | m | m | 9.8 | (0.5) | c | c | c | c | 18.6 | (0.6) | c | c | c | c |
| Sweden | 14.4 | (0.6) | 7.4 | (3.7) | 7.0 | (3.8) | 21.1 | (0.7) | 6.3 | (2.6) | 14.8 | (2.7) | 26.8 | (0.8) | 9.7 | (3.4) | 17.1 | (3.5) |
| Switzerland | 11.1 | (0.4) | 5.1 | (0.6) | 6.0 | (0.8) | 15.7 | (0.7) | 6.1 | (0.7) | 9.6 | (1.1) | 24.6 | (0.8) | 12.5 | (1.1) | 12.1 | (1.5) |
| Turkey | 20.6 | (6.3) | 8.8 | (0.10) | 11.9 | (6.3) | 22.1 | (4.8) | 12.3 | (0.8) | 9.8 | (4.9) | 32.1 | (6.5) | 19.1 | (1.0) | 13.0 | (6.6) |
| United Kingdom | 32.5 | (6.6) | 17.6 | (0.6) | 14.9 | (6.6) | 29.2 | (8.4) | 19.5 | (0.7) | 9.7 | (8.4) | 54.7 | (5.1) | 31.7 | (0.9) | 23.0 | (5.1) |
| United States | 31.6 | (2.9) | 17.4 | (0.8) | 14.2 | (3.0) | 32.7 | (4.2) | 16.1 | (0.7) | 16.6 | (4.2) | 50.4 | (4.4) | 29.9 | (1.0) | 20.6 | (4.4) |
| **OECD average** | 18.5 | (0.6) | 12.1 | (0.3) | 7.7 | (0.7) | 20.2 | (0.6) | 12.8 | (0.3) | 9.8 | (0.8) | 32.5 | (0.7) | 22.9 | (0.4) | 12.7 | (0.9) |
| **Partners** | | | | | | | | | | | | | | | | | | |
| Argentina | 23.0 | (1.7) | 8.3 | (0.9) | 14.8 | (1.9) | 22.4 | (1.9) | 6.7 | (0.9) | 15.7 | (1.8) | 35.1 | (2.5) | 14.0 | (1.2) | 21.0 | (2.7) |
| Azerbaijan | 34.9 | (1.3) | 40.7 | (1.7) | -5.8 | (1.6) | 48.9 | (1.4) | 47.7 | (1.8) | 1.1 | (1.7) | 66.6 | (1.6) | 69.1 | (1.7) | -2.5 | (1.5) |
| Brazil | 30.1 | (1.2) | 20.4 | (0.9) | 9.8 | (1.5) | 28.7 | (1.2) | 16.4 | (0.9) | 12.3 | (1.5) | 44.6 | (1.4) | 29.3 | (1.1) | 15.3 | (1.8) |
| Bulgaria | 29.5 | (4.4) | 18.5 | (1.1) | 11.0 | (4.5) | 36.6 | (4.2) | 21.8 | (1.3) | 14.8 | (4.5) | 48.1 | (5.1) | 33.9 | (1.7) | 14.1 | (5.3) |
| Chile | 31.5 | (4.6) | 15.6 | (0.8) | 15.9 | (4.6) | 32.8 | (4.0) | 17.1 | (0.8) | 15.7 | (4.1) | 47.2 | (5.4) | 26.4 | (1.1) | 20.9 | (5.6) |
| Colombia | 30.4 | (1.7) | 13.3 | (1.3) | 17.1 | (2.2) | 28.1 | (1.8) | 13.6 | (1.2) | 14.5 | (2.0) | 40.8 | (2.0) | 21.8 | (1.4) | 19.0 | (2.1) |
| Croatia | c | c | 11.1 | (0.6) | c | c | c | c | 12.0 | (0.7) | c | c | c | c | 21.7 | (0.8) | c | c |
| Estonia | 13.9 | (0.7) | 6.6 | (2.6) | 7.2 | (2.6) | 18.7 | (0.7) | 13.4 | (3.3) | 5.4 | (3.4) | 32.2 | (1.1) | 25.1 | (4.7) | 7.1 | (4.8) |
| Hong Kong-China | 18.4 | (1.1) | 16.0 | (0.9) | 2.4 | (1.1) | 36.6 | (1.6) | 45.1 | (1.6) | -8.5 | (1.8) | 44.2 | (1.7) | 51.1 | (1.5) | -6.9 | (1.8) |
| Indonesia | 36.0 | (1.8) | 16.1 | (1.9) | 19.8 | (2.3) | 50.7 | (1.8) | 17.6 | (1.8) | 33.1 | (2.3) | 72.7 | (1.6) | 28.8 | (2.8) | 43.8 | (2.8) |
| Israel | 17.4 | (1.6) | 21.4 | (1.0) | -4.0 | (1.8) | 19.8 | (2.0) | 20.2 | (0.9) | -0.4 | (2.2) | 32.9 | (1.7) | 35.6 | (1.2) | -2.6 | (2.0) |
| Jordan | 31.7 | (0.9) | a | a | a | a | 40.9 | (0.9) | a | a | a | a | 56.6 | (1.1) | a | a | a | a |
| Kyrgyzstan | 43.6 | (1.3) | 45.4 | (1.8) | -1.8 | (2.0) | 53.5 | (1.3) | 51.2 | (2.1) | 2.3 | (2.2) | 79.0 | (1.3) | 77.1 | (1.6) | 1.8 | (1.8) |
| Latvia | 25.8 | (1.1) | 19.7 | (3.1) | 6.1 | (3.3) | 29.2 | (1.2) | 22.9 | (3.9) | 6.3 | (4.0) | 50.8 | (1.3) | 42.8 | (5.3) | 8.0 | (5.5) |
| Liechtenstein | 7.5 | (1.4) | 11.0 | (5.3) | -3.6 | (5.7) | 10.9 | (1.6) | 8.6 | (4.6) | 2.3 | (4.6) | 16.0 | (1.9) | 22.0 | (6.3) | -6.0 | (6.4) |
| Lithuania | 17.6 | (0.8) | c | c | c | c | 19.4 | (0.8) | c | c | c | c | 34.4 | (1.0) | c | c | c | c |
| Macao-China | 25.7 | (0.8) | 17.5 | (1.1) | 8.2 | (1.5) | 38.0 | (0.9) | 29.7 | (1.4) | 8.3 | (1.8) | 51.5 | (0.9) | 38.7 | (1.4) | 12.8 | (1.7) |
| Montenegro | c | c | 17.8 | (0.6) | c | c | c | c | 21.6 | (0.6) | c | c | c | c | 34.6 | (0.8) | c | c |
| Qatar | 35.7 | (1.1) | 27.3 | (0.6) | 8.5 | (1.4) | 37.2 | (1.1) | 27.3 | (0.6) | 9.8 | (1.2) | 57.3 | (1.2) | 41.9 | (0.7) | 15.4 | (1.4) |
| Romania | 24.4 | (1.1) | a | a | a | a | 21.9 | (1.5) | a | a | a | a | 40.1 | (1.6) | a | a | a | a |
| Russian Federation | 37.8 | (1.5) | 27.9 | (1.3) | 9.9 | (1.7) | 39.4 | (1.8) | 35.0 | (1.6) | 4.3 | (2.3) | 63.5 | (1.4) | 54.1 | (1.7) | 9.4 | (2.0) |
| Serbia | 15.3 | (5.8) | 12.2 | (0.6) | 3.1 | (5.9) | 17.5 | (5.4) | 14.6 | (0.8) | 2.9 | (2.9) | 28.5 | (7.5) | 23.6 | (0.9) | 5.0 | (7.6) |
| Slovenia | 30.1 | (8.0) | 8.1 | (0.4) | 22.0 | (8.1) | 28.9 | (4.9) | 11.0 | (0.4) | 17.9 | (4.9) | 60.0 | (5.9) | 18.6 | (0.5) | 41.3 | (6.0) |
| Chinese Taipei | 20.6 | (1.2) | 23.9 | (0.9) | -3.4 | (1.6) | 36.1 | (1.2) | 34.6 | (0.9) | 1.5 | (1.4) | 45.7 | (1.5) | 44.7 | (1.2) | 1.0 | (1.9) |
| Thailand | 30.5 | (1.7) | 25.1 | (1.0) | 5.4 | (1.9) | 41.7 | (2.2) | 37.8 | (1.3) | 3.9 | (2.5) | 51.1 | (2.1) | 45.6 | (1.4) | 5.4 | (2.4) |
| Tunisia | 39.4 | (1.7) | 26.7 | (1.5) | 12.7 | (2.3) | 39.9 | (1.4) | 21.8 | (0.9) | 18.0 | (1.6) | 63.3 | (1.7) | 45.3 | (1.7) | 17.9 | (2.4) |
| Uruguay | 12.0 | (1.1) | 7.4 | (0.6) | 4.5 | (1.2) | 14.2 | (1.1) | 5.9 | (0.4) | 8.3 | (1.2) | 23.0 | (1.4) | 14.1 | (1.1) | 8.8 | (1.8) |

*Note:* Values that are statistically significant at the 5% level (p < 0.05) are indicated in bold.

© OECD 2011 Quality Time for Students: Learning In and Out of School

**Table 3.18** **Percentage of students by different types of out-of-school-time lessons, by public and private schools**
[Part 1/6]

| | Proportion of students participating in out-of-school-time lessons | | | | | |
| | Public schools | | Private schools | | Difference (public-private) | |
| | % | S.E. | % | S.E. | Dif. | S.E. |
|---|---|---|---|---|---|---|
| **OECD** | | | | | | |
| Australia | w | w | w | w | w | w |
| Austria | 36.0 | (1.1) | 39.0 | (4.5) | -3.0 | (4.5) |
| Belgium | w | w | w | w | w | w |
| Canada | 35.1 | (0.8) | 46.1 | (2.7) | **-11.0** | (2.9) |
| Czech Republic | 37.2 | (0.9) | 37.2 | (4.4) | -0.0 | (4.4) |
| Denmark | 19.1 | (1.0) | 23.5 | (1.4) | **-4.4** | (1.9) |
| Finland | 23.3 | (0.7) | 27.6 | (2.6) | -4.3 | (2.7) |
| France | w | w | w | w | w | w |
| Germany | 36.6 | (0.9) | 41.4 | (5.1) | -4.8 | (5.4) |
| Greece | 76.3 | (1.0) | 78.7 | (2.5) | -2.4 | (2.7) |
| Hungary | 53.3 | (1.3) | 59.3 | (3.5) | -6.0 | (3.9) |
| Iceland | 40.7 | (0.9) | 43.7 | (7.8) | -3.0 | (8.1) |
| Ireland | 41.2 | (1.8) | 36.3 | (0.9) | **4.8** | (2.0) |
| Italy | 66.6 | (0.6) | 65.0 | (3.2) | 1.5 | (3.3) |
| Japan | 42.9 | (1.5) | 51.7 | (2.5) | **-8.8** | (2.8) |
| Korea | 77.5 | (1.5) | 81.1 | (1.3) | -3.6 | (2.3) |
| Luxembourg | 42.3 | (0.8) | 52.5 | (2.1) | **-10.2** | (2.3) |
| Mexico | 48.2 | (0.8) | 45.2 | (3.1) | 3.0 | (3.1) |
| Netherlands | 21.9 | (1.6) | 22.2 | (1.1) | -0.3 | (2.1) |
| New Zealand | 32.9 | (0.9) | 47.8 | (2.7) | **-15.0** | (2.8) |
| Norway | 27.6 | (0.9) | 17.6 | (6.4) | 10.0 | (6.6) |
| Poland | 56.0 | (1.0) | 67.7 | (6.1) | -11.7 | (6.1) |
| Portugal | 69.1 | (0.9) | 65.5 | (5.2) | 3.7 | (5.3) |
| Slovak Republic | 55.8 | (1.4) | 54.1 | (6.2) | 1.7 | (6.7) |
| Spain | 52.8 | (0.9) | 55.7 | (1.3) | -2.8 | (1.6) |
| Sweden | 31.8 | (0.8) | 32.3 | (3.3) | -0.5 | (3.3) |
| Switzerland | 39.7 | (0.7) | 43.0 | (3.2) | -3.2 | (3.3) |
| Turkey | 36.3 | (1.1) | 58.9 | (3.2) | **-22.6** | (3.5) |
| United Kingdom | 45.7 | (0.9) | 42.0 | (3.4) | 3.7 | (3.4) |
| United States | 42.8 | (1.2) | 36.1 | (2.8) | **6.8** | (3.0) |
| **OECD average** | 43.6 | (0.2) | 46.5 | (0.7) | **-2.9** | (0.8) |
| **Partners** | | | | | | |
| Argentina | 46.5 | (1.6) | 52.2 | (1.7) | **-5.8** | (2.2) |
| Azerbaijan | 79.4 | (1.2) | 89.9 | (3.3) | **-10.5** | (3.6) |
| Brazil | 47.1 | (0.9) | 56.7 | (2.6) | **-9.7** | (2.7) |
| Bulgaria | m | m | m | m | m | m |
| Chile | 37.5 | (1.6) | 39.1 | (1.6) | -1.6 | (2.4) |
| Colombia | 51.1 | (1.2) | 49.1 | (3.0) | 2.1 | (3.3) |
| Croatia | 45.1 | (0.9) | 67.6 | (0.1) | **-22.5** | (0.9) |
| Estonia | 46.4 | (0.9) | 29.1 | (2.9) | **17.3** | (3.0) |
| Hong Kong-China | 77.4 | (3.6) | 75.2 | (0.9) | 2.2 | (3.8) |
| Indonesia | 67.6 | (3.0) | 63.1 | (2.9) | 4.5 | (3.4) |
| Israel | 67.9 | (1.2) | 55.8 | (2.5) | **12.1** | (2.8) |
| Jordan | 72.7 | (0.9) | 72.5 | (2.7) | 0.2 | (2.9) |
| Kyrgyzstan | 85.3 | (1.0) | 78.9 | (5.0) | 6.3 | (5.2) |
| Latvia | 71.5 | (1.1) | a | a | a | a |
| Liechtenstein | 28.3 | (2.5) | 21.0 | (9.1) | 7.3 | (9.4) |
| Lithuania | 48.8 | (1.1) | 46.4 | (0.0) | **2.4** | (1.1) |
| Macao-China | 69.3 | (3.0) | 62.0 | (0.8) | **7.2** | (3.0) |
| Montenegro | 62.3 | (0.7) | 90.7 | (9.1) | **-28.4** | (9.1) |
| Qatar | 63.5 | (0.6) | 62.2 | (1.7) | 1.3 | (1.9) |
| Romania | 56.8 | (1.5) | a | a | a | a |
| Russian Federation | 69.4 | (1.4) | a | a | a | a |
| Serbia | 53.7 | (1.0) | c | c | c | c |
| Slovenia | 41.8 | (0.6) | 38.1 | (4.8) | 3.7 | (4.8) |
| Chinese Taipei | 76.5 | (0.8) | 72.2 | (1.0) | **4.3** | (1.4) |
| Thailand | 64.0 | (1.3) | 61.3 | (2.7) | 2.7 | (2.9) |
| Tunisia | 70.4 | (1.0) | 74.3 | (11.7) | -3.9 | (11.8) |
| Uruguay | 42.5 | (1.2) | 56.1 | (1.8) | **-13.5** | (2.2) |

*Note*: Values that are statistically significant at the 5% level (p < 0.05) are indicated in bold.

**Table 3.18** [Part 2/6] **Percentage of students by different types of out-of-school-time lessons, by public and private schools**

| | Proportion of students participating in out-of-school lessons with non-school teachers | | | | | | | | | | | | | |
|---|---|---|---|---|---|---|---|---|---|---|---|---|---|---|
| | One-to-one lessons | | | | | | | | | | Small group lessons | | | |
| | | | | | | | If students' ESCS was equal to the national average ESCS, and schools' average ESCS was equal to the national average of schools' average ESCS | | | | | | | |
| | Public schools | | Private schools | | Difference (public-private) | | Difference (public-private) | Increase in the logit of participating in out-of-school-time lessons by being in a public school | | Public schools | | Private schools | | Difference (public-private) |
| | % | S.E. | % | S.E. | Dif. | S.E. | Dif. in % | Logistic regression coefficient | S.E. | % | S.E. | % | S.E. | Dif. | S.E. |
| **OECD** | | | | | | | | | | | | | | | |
| Australia | w | w | w | w | w | w | w | w | w | w | w | w | w | w | w |
| Austria | 16.0 | (0.7) | 23.3 | (3.4) | **-7.3** | (3.5) | -5.1 | -0.34 | (0.26) | 7.4 | (0.5) | 10.7 | (2.3) | -3.3 | (2.3) |
| Belgium | w | w | w | w | w | w | w | w | w | w | w | w | w | w | w |
| Canada | 16.0 | (0.5) | 23.9 | (1.4) | **-7.9** | (1.5) | **-2.9** | **-0.20** | (0.10) | 8.5 | (0.4) | 8.1 | (1.0) | 0.4 | (1.0) |
| Czech Republic | 15.4 | (0.7) | 21.0 | (2.8) | **-5.6** | (2.7) | **-4.2** | **-0.31** | (0.13) | 8.0 | (0.6) | 6.6 | (1.0) | 1.4 | (1.0) |
| Denmark | 5.3 | (0.6) | 5.5 | (0.9) | -0.2 | (1.2) | 0.3 | 0.07 | (0.24) | 4.9 | (0.5) | 4.2 | (0.7) | 0.7 | (0.9) |
| Finland | 5.3 | (0.3) | 8.5 | (1.4) | **-3.3** | (1.5) | **-2.7** | **-0.46** | (0.22) | 2.4 | (0.3) | 3.7 | (1.1) | -1.3 | (1.2) |
| France | w | w | w | w | w | w | w | w | w | w | w | w | w | w | w |
| Germany | 21.5 | (0.7) | 23.8 | (5.9) | -2.4 | (6.0) | -0.5 | -0.03 | (0.33) | 7.4 | (0.4) | 6.2 | (1.4) | 1.2 | (1.5) |
| Greece | 43.8 | (1.2) | 63.1 | (3.7) | **-19.2** | (4.0) | 7.2 | 0.30 | (0.16) | 47.3 | (1.3) | 21.4 | (4.3) | **25.9** | (4.5) |
| Hungary | 31.6 | (1.2) | 38.3 | (2.9) | **-6.6** | (3.3) | 3.5 | 0.16 | (0.11) | 10.7 | (0.7) | 11.8 | (1.6) | -1.1 | (1.7) |
| Iceland | 14.9 | (0.6) | 14.9 | (6.9) | 0.1 | (7.0) | 4.1 | 0.39 | (0.61) | 6.9 | (0.5) | 5.5 | (3.9) | 1.4 | (4.0) |
| Ireland | 20.6 | (1.0) | 22.0 | (0.9) | -1.4 | (1.4) | 2.0 | 0.12 | (0.09) | 10.2 | (0.7) | 9.5 | (0.7) | 0.8 | (1.0) |
| Italy | 37.3 | (0.6) | 37.2 | (2.9) | 0.1 | (3.1) | 5.4 | 0.24 | (0.14) | 14.0 | (0.5) | 16.7 | (1.9) | -2.7 | (2.1) |
| Japan | 7.6 | (0.5) | 13.4 | (1.7) | **-5.8** | (1.8) | **-2.8** | **-0.35** | (0.14) | 8.1 | (0.5) | 9.2 | (1.3) | -1.1 | (1.4) |
| Korea | 30.7 | (1.3) | 32.0 | (1.3) | -1.4 | (2.0) | -2.4 | -0.11 | (0.08) | 32.3 | (1.6) | 30.1 | (1.3) | 2.1 | (2.4) |
| Luxembourg | 23.0 | (0.7) | 23.9 | (1.8) | -0.9 | (2.0) | -1.1 | -0.06 | (0.11) | 7.1 | (0.5) | 6.9 | (1.8) | 0.2 | (1.2) |
| Mexico | 17.0 | (0.6) | 23.2 | (2.5) | **-6.3** | (2.5) | -2.4 | -0.16 | (0.16) | 16.1 | (0.5) | 16.4 | (1.9) | -0.3 | (1.8) |
| Netherlands | 7.7 | (0.9) | 7.3 | (0.6) | 0.5 | (1.1) | 0.3 | 0.04 | (0.14) | 4.3 | (0.8) | 3.2 | (0.5) | 1.0 | (1.1) |
| New Zealand | 16.7 | (0.7) | 25.3 | (2.4) | **-8.7** | (2.4) | 0.8 | 0.06 | (0.14) | 9.8 | (0.5) | 10.5 | (2.2) | -0.7 | (2.2) |
| Norway | 5.3 | (0.4) | 8.1 | (2.5) | -2.8 | (2.6) | -2.3 | -0.39 | (0.38) | 5.0 | (0.4) | 1.2 | (1.1) | **3.8** | (1.2) |
| Poland | 19.0 | (0.8) | 41.3 | (5.0) | **-22.4** | (5.0) | 1.0 | 0.07 | (0.20) | 10.6 | (0.6) | 15.0 | (1.8) | **-4.5** | (1.8) |
| Portugal | 25.9 | (1.0) | 33.0 | (2.5) | **-7.1** | (2.7) | -1.1 | -0.06 | (0.12) | 15.0 | (0.8) | 11.7 | (2.7) | 3.3 | (2.8) |
| Slovak Republic | 25.5 | (1.0) | 25.7 | (4.0) | -0.3 | (4.0) | 4.1 | 0.24 | (0.21) | 11.4 | (0.5) | 8.4 | (2.0) | 2.9 | (2.1) |
| Spain | 27.5 | (1.0) | 30.8 | (1.2) | **-3.3** | (1.5) | 2.0 | 0.10 | (0.08) | 27.2 | (0.8) | 24.3 | (1.3) | 2.9 | (1.5) |
| Sweden | 7.2 | (0.5) | 10.0 | (1.3) | **-2.9** | (1.4) | **-3.4** | **-0.43** | (0.19) | 5.7 | (0.4) | 5.8 | (1.0) | -0.1 | (1.2) |
| Switzerland | 19.6 | (0.6) | 23.9 | (3.1) | -4.3 | (3.2) | 1.6 | 0.10 | (0.17) | 6.2 | (0.4) | 6.7 | (1.8) | -0.5 | (1.9) |
| Turkey | 13.2 | (0.7) | 22.0 | (2.3) | **-8.8** | (2.4) | -3.4 | -0.28 | (0.23) | 10.9 | (0.6) | 12.1 | (4.2) | -1.3 | (4.2) |
| United Kingdom | 17.1 | (0.6) | 21.0 | (2.6) | -3.9 | (2.7) | 0.6 | 0.04 | (0.19) | 7.5 | (0.5) | 6.1 | (1.4) | 1.4 | (1.4) |
| United States | 17.6 | (0.8) | 13.7 | (2.4) | 3.9 | (2.5) | -0.1 | -0.01 | (0.23) | 12.9 | (0.9) | 6.9 | (1.4) | **6.0** | (1.7) |
| **OECD average** | **18.8** | **(0.2)** | **23.4** | **(0.6)** | **-4.6** | **(0.6)** | **-0.6** | **-0.04** | **(0.04)** | **11.6** | **(0.1)** | **10.2** | **(0.4)** | **1.4** | **(0.4)** |
| **Partners** | | | | | | | | | | | | | | | |
| Argentina | 26.1 | (1.3) | 40.2 | (2.0) | **-14.1** | (2.3) | **-5.4** | **0.25** | (0.13) | 18.0 | (1.1) | 21.3 | (1.4) | -3.3 | (1.8) |
| Azerbaijan | 30.5 | (1.1) | 47.3 | (5.6) | **-16.8** | (5.8) | 2.3 | 0.11 | (0.26) | 40.9 | (1.1) | 35.8 | (6.7) | 5.0 | (7.0) |
| Brazil | 18.0 | (0.6) | 30.0 | (2.1) | **-11.9** | (2.2) | 1.6 | 0.11 | (0.16) | 17.5 | (0.6) | 20.1 | (1.7) | -2.6 | (1.9) |
| Bulgaria | m | m | m | m | m | m | m | m | m | m | m | m | m | m | m |
| Chile | 10.0 | (1.0) | 16.0 | (1.2) | **-6.0** | (1.6) | -0.7 | -0.06 | (0.13) | 10.0 | (0.7) | 9.0 | (0.7) | 0.9 | (1.0) |
| Colombia | 24.8 | (0.7) | 28.6 | (2.6) | -3.8 | (2.7) | 2.9 | 0.16 | (0.13) | 18.2 | (0.9) | 16.2 | (1.9) | 2.0 | (2.1) |
| Croatia | 27.9 | (0.9) | 27.6 | (0.0) | 0.3 | (0.9) | **8.8** | **0.50** | (0.07) | 9.6 | (0.6) | 20.1 | (0.0) | **-10.5** | (0.5) |
| Estonia | 17.3 | (0.7) | 17.1 | (2.2) | 0.2 | (2.3) | 3.9 | 0.30 | (0.19) | 8.1 | (0.4) | 8.0 | (3.2) | 0.1 | (3.1) |
| Hong Kong-China | 24.9 | (3.0) | 24.1 | (1.4) | 0.8 | (3.3) | -2.7 | -0.16 | (0.23) | 20.0 | (2.1) | 17.6 | (0.8) | 2.3 | (2.2) |
| Indonesia | 18.1 | (1.2) | 16.5 | (1.0) | 1.6 | (1.6) | -0.1 | -0.01 | (0.12) | 19.6 | (1.1) | 19.2 | (1.1) | 0.4 | (1.4) |
| Israel | 45.1 | (1.3) | 34.1 | (2.7) | **11.1** | (3.2) | **12.8** | **0.54** | (0.14) | 21.8 | (1.1) | 15.9 | (1.5) | **6.0** | (1.8) |
| Jordan | 34.9 | (0.8) | 32.6 | (2.3) | 2.3 | (2.4) | 5.4 | 0.24 | (0.13) | 26.5 | (0.9) | 20.8 | (1.9) | **5.6** | (2.1) |
| Kyrgyzstan | 26.2 | (0.8) | 35.0 | (11.2) | -8.8 | (11.1) | -3.9 | -0.19 | (0.46) | 26.9 | (0.9) | 27.9 | (11.3) | -1.0 | (11.4) |
| Latvia | 32.3 | (1.2) | a | a | a | a | a | a | a | 14.1 | (0.5) | a | a | a | a |
| Liechtenstein | 14.5 | (2.0) | c | c | c | c | c | c | c | 3.0 | (1.1) | m | m | m | m |
| Lithuania | 17.7 | (0.8) | c | c | c | c | c | c | c | 7.0 | (0.4) | m | m | m | m |
| Macao-China | 21.7 | (2.6) | 21.8 | (0.7) | -0.2 | (2.6) | 2.8 | 0.16 | (0.17) | 26.9 | (3.2) | 20.4 | (0.8) | 6.6 | (3.5) |
| Montenegro | 38.0 | (0.8) | c | c | c | c | 21.3 | 1.15 | (0.81) | 21.0 | (0.6) | c | c | c | c |
| Qatar | 36.2 | (0.8) | 36.8 | (1.6) | -0.6 | (1.8) | 0.4 | 0.02 | (0.09) | 26.0 | (0.7) | 21.9 | (1.4) | **4.1** | (1.6) |
| Romania | 27.9 | (1.4) | a | a | a | a | a | a | a | 19.8 | (1.2) | a | a | a | a |
| Russian Federation | 21.7 | (0.8) | a | a | a | a | a | a | a | 12.5 | (0.8) | a | a | a | a |
| Serbia | 38.3 | (1.1) | c | c | c | c | c | c | c | 12.9 | (0.6) | c | c | c | c |
| Slovenia | 26.9 | (0.7) | 23.2 | (4.1) | 3.8 | (4.2) | 6.9 | 0.39 | (0.24) | 6.6 | (0.4) | 5.2 | (2.3) | 1.4 | (2.2) |
| Chinese Taipei | 21.2 | (0.6) | 28.4 | (1.2) | **-7.3** | (1.5) | **-7.3** | **-0.40** | (0.08) | 23.7 | (0.7) | 23.4 | (1.0) | 0.3 | (1.3) |
| Thailand | 20.3 | (0.9) | 21.4 | (1.8) | -1.1 | (2.0) | -0.1 | -0.01 | (0.12) | 23.9 | (1.0) | 24.9 | (1.8) | -1.0 | (2.0) |
| Tunisia | 30.6 | (1.4) | 40.9 | (10.1) | -10.3 | (10.2) | -7.4 | -0.34 | (0.48) | 28.1 | (1.1) | 39.7 | (10.0) | -11.6 | (10.0) |
| Uruguay | 27.0 | (1.0) | 40.3 | (1.8) | **-13.3** | (2.1) | 3.1 | 0.16 | (0.15) | 19.8 | (0.8) | 28.2 | (2.0) | **-8.3** | (2.2) |

*Note:* Values that are statistically significant at the 5% level (p < 0.05) are indicated in bold.

© OECD 2011 Quality Time for Students: Learning In and Out of School

## Table 3.18 Percentage of students by different types of out-of-school-time lessons, by public and private schools
[Part 3/6]

| | Proportion of students participating in out-of-school lessons with non-school teachers | | | | | | | | | | | | | | |
| | Large group lessons | | | | | | At least one of these types of out-of-school lessons | | | | | | | If students' ESCS was equal to the national average ESCS, and schools' average ESCS was equal to the national average of schools' average ESCS | |
| | | | | | | | | | | | | | | Difference (public-private) | Increase in the logit of participating in out-of-school-time lessons by being in a public school | |
| | Public schools | | Private schools | | Difference (public-private) | | Public schools | | Private schools | | Difference (public-private) | | | | | |
| | % | S.E. | % | S.E. | Dif. | S.E. | % | S.E. | % | S.E. | Dif. | S.E. | Dif. in % | Logistic regression coefficient | S.E. |
|---|---|---|---|---|---|---|---|---|---|---|---|---|---|---|---|
| Australia | w | w | w | w | w | w | w | w | w | w | w | w | w | w | w |
| Austria | 6.1 | (0.4) | 6.8 | (2.8) | -0.7 | (2.8) | 23.5 | (0.8) | 31.1 | (4.5) | -7.7 | (4.6) | -6.8 | -0.35 | (0.26) |
| Belgium | w | w | w | w | w | w | w | w | w | w | w | w | w | w | w |
| Canada | 7.4 | (0.4) | 4.4 | (0.8) | 2.9 | (0.9) | 22.5 | (0.6) | 29.2 | (1.8) | -6.7 | (2.0) | -1.3 | -0.08 | (0.10) |
| Czech Republic | 5.7 | (0.5) | 3.7 | (0.9) | 2.0 | (1.1) | 21.3 | (0.8) | 25.5 | (2.5) | -4.2 | (2.5) | -3.1 | -0.18 | (0.12) |
| Denmark | 3.6 | (0.5) | 3.9 | (0.7) | -0.3 | (0.8) | 10.1 | (0.8) | 10.9 | (1.1) | -0.8 | (1.4) | -0.7 | -0.07 | (0.17) |
| Finland | 3.7 | (0.3) | 4.3 | (1.7) | -0.6 | (1.7) | 8.4 | (0.5) | 12.5 | (2.3) | -4.1 | (2.4) | -3.3 | -0.38 | (0.22) |
| France | w | w | w | w | w | w | w | w | w | w | w | w | w | w | w |
| Germany | 4.0 | (0.4) | 2.0 | (1.0) | 1.9 | (1.1) | 27.3 | (0.7) | 28.4 | (5.1) | -1.0 | (5.3) | 0.1 | 0.00 | (0.26) |
| Greece | 19.1 | (1.0) | 8.1 | (2.5) | 11.0 | (2.7) | 70.4 | (1.1) | 75.4 | (2.7) | -5.0 | (3.0) | 37.3 | 1.59 | (0.23) |
| Hungary | 8.7 | (0.6) | 8.4 | (1.5) | 0.3 | (1.6) | 37.7 | (1.3) | 42.8 | (2.9) | -5.2 | (3.3) | 2.2 | 0.09 | (0.12) |
| Iceland | 5.3 | (0.4) | 0.0 | (0.0) | 5.3 | (0.4) | 20.2 | (0.7) | 14.9 | (6.9) | 5.3 | (7.0) | 8.3 | 0.65 | (0.61) |
| Ireland | 7.5 | (0.7) | 6.3 | (0.6) | 1.2 | (0.9) | 28.3 | (1.2) | 29.5 | (1.0) | -1.3 | (1.5) | 2.5 | 0.12 | (0.08) |
| Italy | 8.9 | (0.4) | 10.0 | (2.1) | -1.0 | (2.1) | 45.9 | (0.7) | 47.9 | (2.5) | -2.1 | (2.7) | 1.2 | 0.05 | (0.11) |
| Japan | 8.3 | (0.7) | 8.1 | (1.1) | 0.1 | (1.2) | 18.6 | (1.0) | 23.9 | (2.4) | -5.3 | (2.5) | 0.6 | 0.04 | (0.13) |
| Korea | 27.2 | (1.3) | 26.5 | (1.5) | 0.7 | (2.4) | 58.4 | (2.1) | 57.1 | (1.9) | 1.4 | (3.5) | -1.4 | -0.06 | (0.09) |
| Luxembourg | 5.7 | (0.4) | 4.5 | (0.8) | 1.2 | (0.9) | 28.0 | (0.8) | 28.0 | (1.9) | -0.1 | (2.1) | 0.0 | 0.00 | (0.11) |
| Mexico | 17.0 | (0.6) | 11.2 | (1.4) | 5.8 | (1.6) | 29.9 | (0.8) | 33.4 | (3.4) | -3.4 | (3.4) | -1.7 | -0.08 | (0.19) |
| Netherlands | 3.6 | (0.8) | 3.7 | (0.4) | -0.0 | (1.0) | 11.9 | (1.2) | 10.8 | (0.7) | 1.1 | (1.4) | 1.0 | 0.10 | (0.14) |
| New Zealand | 6.9 | (0.4) | 7.0 | (1.5) | -0.0 | (1.6) | 23.4 | (0.7) | 31.1 | (2.9) | -7.6 | (3.0) | -1.0 | -0.06 | (0.15) |
| Norway | 5.1 | (0.4) | 2.4 | (1.1) | 2.7 | (1.2) | 9.9 | (0.6) | 10.4 | (2.3) | -0.5 | (2.4) | -0.2 | -0.02 | (0.26) |
| Poland | 10.0 | (0.4) | 10.7 | (2.2) | -0.7 | (2.2) | 28.6 | (0.9) | 52.1 | (4.6) | -23.5 | (4.7) | 3.4 | 0.18 | (0.16) |
| Portugal | 8.5 | (0.6) | 5.7 | (1.8) | 2.8 | (1.9) | 34.9 | (1.1) | 39.0 | (3.5) | -4.1 | (3.6) | 2.1 | 0.09 | (0.15) |
| Slovak Republic | 7.6 | (0.6) | 5.0 | (1.8) | 2.6 | (1.9) | 29.8 | (1.0) | 28.5 | (4.0) | 1.3 | (4.2) | 5.5 | 0.28 | (0.21) |
| Spain | 10.9 | (0.5) | 9.8 | (0.9) | 1.0 | (1.0) | 42.1 | (1.0) | 45.8 | (1.4) | -3.7 | (1.6) | 3.3 | 0.13 | (0.08) |
| Sweden | 6.9 | (0.4) | 6.6 | (1.6) | 0.3 | (1.6) | 13.0 | (0.6) | 14.0 | (1.8) | -1.0 | (1.8) | -2.0 | -0.17 | (0.18) |
| Switzerland | 4.8 | (0.3) | 4.0 | (1.3) | 0.8 | (1.3) | 24.4 | (0.6) | 28.0 | (3.3) | -3.6 | (3.4) | 1.2 | 0.07 | (0.17) |
| Turkey | 14.7 | (1.0) | 26.4 | (4.0) | -11.7 | (4.1) | 26.0 | (1.2) | 41.8 | (3.5) | -15.8 | (3.8) | -4.0 | -0.20 | (0.14) |
| United Kingdom | 7.5 | (0.5) | 3.6 | (0.7) | 3.9 | (0.9) | 23.9 | (0.8) | 26.3 | (2.9) | -2.4 | (3.0) | -0.8 | -0.05 | (0.18) |
| United States | 11.8 | (0.8) | 8.1 | (2.6) | 3.7 | (2.6) | 25.5 | (1.1) | 20.4 | (2.8) | 5.2 | (2.9) | -3.1 | -0.16 | (0.19) |
| **OECD average** | 8.6 | (0.1) | 7.3 | (0.3) | 1.3 | (0.3) | 27.3 | (0.2) | 30.8 | (0.6) | -3.4 | (0.6) | 1.1 | 0.06 | (0.04) |
| Argentina | 14.2 | (0.8) | 11.0 | (1.4) | 3.2 | (1.6) | 35.3 | (1.5) | 48.1 | (1.7) | -12.8 | (2.2) | -8.2 | 0.34 | (0.12) |
| Azerbaijan | 39.0 | (1.1) | 33.5 | (8.3) | 5.5 | (8.4) | 62.6 | (1.1) | 72.0 | (6.9) | -9.4 | (7.2) | -2.9 | -0.12 | (0.38) |
| Brazil | 16.3 | (0.6) | 10.5 | (1.1) | 5.8 | (1.3) | 32.0 | (0.7) | 39.7 | (2.3) | -7.8 | (2.5) | 1.1 | 0.05 | (0.16) |
| Bulgaria | m | m | m | m | m | m | c | c | c | c | c | c | c | c | c |
| Chile | 10.3 | (0.9) | 6.8 | (0.5) | 3.5 | (1.0) | 19.9 | (1.2) | 22.8 | (1.3) | -2.8 | (1.9) | 0.9 | 0.05 | (0.11) |
| Colombia | 16.4 | (0.7) | 15.8 | (1.8) | 0.5 | (1.9) | 36.3 | (0.8) | 38.9 | (2.9) | -2.6 | (3.0) | 3.1 | 0.14 | (0.16) |
| Croatia | 7.7 | (0.5) | 15.1 | (0.1) | -7.3 | (0.5) | 33.8 | (0.9) | 45.2 | (0.0) | -11.3 | (0.9) | -3.0 | -0.13 | (0.07) |
| Estonia | 7.3 | (0.5) | 11.0 | (3.8) | -3.7 | (3.8) | 23.5 | (0.7) | 21.9 | (3.6) | 1.6 | (3.6) | 5.6 | 0.35 | (0.17) |
| Hong Kong-China | 38.0 | (6.7) | 29.4 | (1.1) | 8.6 | (6.8) | 58.4 | (5.4) | 51.6 | (1.3) | 6.8 | (5.5) | 1.6 | 0.07 | (0.11) |
| Indonesia | 18.1 | (1.2) | 16.7 | (1.1) | 1.4 | (1.5) | 35.4 | (1.4) | 32.0 | (1.4) | 3.4 | (2.1) | 1.6 | 0.07 | (0.10) |
| Israel | 16.9 | (0.9) | 12.2 | (1.7) | 4.7 | (1.9) | 56.5 | (1.3) | 43.2 | (3.2) | 13.2 | (3.4) | 14.9 | 0.60 | (0.13) |
| Jordan | 23.1 | (0.9) | 17.9 | (1.9) | 5.2 | (2.1) | 48.8 | (0.9) | 45.6 | (2.0) | 3.2 | (2.2) | 2.2 | 0.09 | (0.10) |
| Kyrgyzstan | 32.0 | (0.9) | 22.9 | (9.7) | 9.1 | (9.7) | 48.5 | (1.0) | 49.9 | (11.1) | -1.4 | (11.0) | -4.0 | -0.16 | (0.45) |
| Latvia | 17.1 | (0.7) | a | a | a | a | 42.3 | (1.1) | a | a | a | a | a | a | a |
| Liechtenstein | 2.6 | (0.9) | c | c | c | c | 16.8 | (2.2) | c | c | c | c | c | c | c |
| Lithuania | 6.6 | (0.5) | c | c | c | c | 23.4 | (0.8) | c | c | c | c | c | c | c |
| Macao-China | 23.0 | (2.5) | 19.3 | (0.7) | 3.7 | (2.6) | 40.8 | (3.3) | 39.0 | (0.8) | 1.7 | (3.4) | 4.4 | 0.18 | (0.15) |
| Montenegro | 17.6 | (0.6) | c | c | c | c | 48.0 | (0.8) | c | c | c | c | 25.6 | 1.17 | (0.81) |
| Qatar | 23.6 | (0.6) | 17.0 | (1.3) | 6.7 | (1.4) | 48.7 | (0.8) | 47.2 | (1.7) | 1.5 | (1.8) | -2.4 | -0.10 | (0.08) |
| Romania | 15.5 | (1.2) | a | a | a | a | 38.5 | (1.3) | a | a | a | a | a | a | a |
| Russian Federation | 12.7 | (0.6) | a | a | a | a | 31.2 | (1.1) | a | a | a | a | a | a | a |
| Serbia | 8.7 | (0.6) | c | c | c | c | 43.1 | (1.1) | c | c | c | c | c | c | c |
| Slovenia | 5.1 | (0.3) | 3.0 | (1.7) | 2.1 | (1.7) | 31.4 | (0.6) | 27.6 | (4.4) | 3.8 | (4.5) | 5.7 | 0.28 | (0.24) |
| Chinese Taipei | 45.2 | (1.2) | 31.5 | (1.2) | 13.7 | (1.8) | 60.4 | (1.0) | 50.5 | (1.6) | 10.0 | (2.1) | 10.0 | 0.41 | (0.06) |
| Thailand | 31.3 | (1.2) | 31.1 | (3.2) | 0.2 | (3.4) | 44.6 | (1.4) | 42.6 | (3.2) | 2.0 | (3.4) | 6.2 | 0.26 | (0.11) |
| Tunisia | 18.8 | (0.8) | 37.5 | (12.7) | -18.7 | (12.7) | 44.5 | (1.4) | 60.1 | (11.1) | -15.6 | (11.2) | -14.0 | -0.57 | (0.49) |
| Uruguay | 12.1 | (0.7) | 10.6 | (1.2) | 1.5 | (1.5) | 35.4 | (1.1) | 49.3 | (2.0) | -14.0 | (2.4) | 1.4 | 0.06 | (0.15) |

*Note:* Values that are statistically significant at the 5% level (p < 0.05) are indicated in bold.

227

**Table 3.18** **Percentage of students by different types of out-of-school-time lessons,**
[Part 4/6] **by public and private schools**

| | | Proportion of students participating in out-of-school lessons with school teachers | | | | | | | |
|---|---|---|---|---|---|---|---|---|---|
| | | One-to-one lessons | | | | | | | |
| | | | | | | | | If students' ESCS was equal to the national average ESCS, and schools' average ESCS was equal to the national average of schools' average ESCS | | |
| | | Public schools | | Private schools | | Difference (public-private) | | Difference (public-private) | Increase in the logit of participating in out-of-school-time lessons by being in a public school | |
| | | % | S.E. | % | S.E. | Dif. | S.E. | Dif. in % | Logistic regression coefficient | S.E. |
| OECD | Australia | w | w | w | w | w | w | w | w | w |
| | Austria | 5.2 | (0.4) | 7.3 | (2.3) | -2.0 | (2.3) | -1.3 | -0.27 | (0.32) |
| | Belgium | w | w | w | w | w | w | w | w | w |
| | Canada | 12.1 | (0.4) | 15.9 | (1.9) | -3.9 | (2.0) | **-6.5** | **-0.51** | (0.16) |
| | Czech Republic | 14.4 | (0.7) | 11.2 | (2.8) | 3.2 | (2.8) | 1.0 | 0.09 | (0.29) |
| | Denmark | 5.0 | (0.5) | 5.5 | (0.9) | -0.5 | (1.0) | -1.4 | -0.30 | (0.22) |
| | Finland | 8.2 | (0.6) | 5.2 | (3.2) | 3.1 | (3.3) | 2.4 | 0.38 | (0.68) |
| | France | w | w | w | w | w | w | w | w | w |
| | Germany | 5.4 | (0.4) | 8.1 | (2.8) | -2.7 | (2.9) | -4.4 | -0.67 | (0.43) |
| | Greece | 12.3 | (0.8) | 6.4 | (1.5) | **5.9** | (1.7) | -1.7 | -0.16 | (0.38) |
| | Hungary | 14.6 | (0.8) | 14.8 | (2.4) | -0.2 | (2.5) | -0.9 | -0.07 | (0.20) |
| | Iceland | 10.5 | (0.5) | 26.1 | (6.3) | **-15.7** | (6.4) | **-17.1** | **-1.19** | (0.34) |
| | Ireland | 9.5 | (1.1) | 5.4 | (0.5) | **4.1** | (1.2) | **2.3** | **0.37** | (0.16) |
| | Italy | a | a | a | a | a | a | a | a | a |
| | Japan | 3.4 | (0.3) | 4.4 | (0.7) | -1.0 | (0.9) | **-1.9** | **-0.51** | (0.24) |
| | Korea | 9.6 | (0.6) | 9.5 | (0.7) | 0.0 | (0.9) | 0.0 | 0.01 | (0.10) |
| | Luxembourg | 13.7 | (0.5) | 14.5 | (1.3) | -0.9 | (1.4) | -0.6 | -0.05 | (0.11) |
| | Mexico | 18.6 | (0.9) | 10.6 | (1.2) | **8.0** | (1.6) | -2.7 | -0.19 | (0.15) |
| | Netherlands | 7.6 | (1.0) | 7.4 | (0.5) | 0.1 | (1.2) | 0.2 | 0.03 | (0.17) |
| | New Zealand | 8.8 | (0.8) | 14.1 | (3.8) | -5.3 | (3.9) | **-11.2** | **-0.99** | (0.44) |
| | Norway | 8.6 | (0.5) | 2.3 | (1.1) | **6.3** | (1.2) | **5.9** | **1.27** | (0.57) |
| | Poland | 14.7 | (0.6) | 11.5 | (3.7) | 3.2 | (3.8) | -0.5 | -0.04 | (0.38) |
| | Portugal | 22.6 | (1.0) | 15.8 | (0.8) | **6.9** | (1.3) | **4.8** | **0.31** | (0.09) |
| | Slovak Republic | 30.4 | (1.3) | 30.4 | (8.4) | 0.1 | (8.6) | -3.7 | -0.17 | (0.41) |
| | Spain | 8.9 | (0.6) | 7.9 | (0.7) | 1.0 | (0.9) | -0.6 | -0.08 | (0.14) |
| | Sweden | 8.3 | (0.5) | 13.4 | (3.0) | -5.1 | (3.1) | **-7.8** | **-0.79** | (0.29) |
| | Switzerland | 6.4 | (0.3) | 11.8 | (2.1) | **-5.4** | (2.1) | **-8.8** | **-0.99** | (0.20) |
| | Turkey | 7.5 | (0.6) | 10.9 | (3.5) | -3.4 | (3.5) | **-7.2** | **-0.78** | (0.31) |
| | United Kingdom | 11.2 | (0.4) | 8.8 | (1.6) | 2.4 | (1.6) | -3.0 | -0.28 | (0.26) |
| | United States | 22.7 | (1.1) | 18.0 | (3.1) | 4.7 | (3.2) | -3.7 | -0.20 | (0.24) |
| | **OECD average** | 11.4 | (0.1) | 11.3 | (0.6) | 0.1 | (0.6) | -2.1 | **-0.22** | (0.06) |
| Partners | Argentina | 12.3 | (1.2) | 7.7 | (1.3) | **4.7** | (1.7) | 2.0 | -0.23 | (0.26) |
| | Azerbaijan | 39.0 | (1.3) | 38.1 | (5.4) | 0.9 | (5.7) | 5.9 | 0.26 | (0.29) |
| | Brazil | 13.7 | (0.6) | 12.8 | (1.5) | 1.0 | (1.6) | -2.5 | -0.20 | (0.19) |
| | Bulgaria | c | c | c | c | c | c | c | c | c |
| | Chile | 9.4 | (0.8) | 7.5 | (0.6) | 1.9 | (1.1) | 0.4 | 0.06 | (0.13) |
| | Colombia | 16.0 | (1.3) | 9.7 | (1.8) | **6.3** | (2.2) | 0.1 | 0.01 | (0.34) |
| | Croatia | 12.9 | (0.5) | 29.7 | (0.0) | **-16.7** | (0.5) | **-36.3** | **-1.93** | (0.11) |
| | Estonia | 18.6 | (0.9) | 8.8 | (4.0) | **9.8** | (4.2) | 6.3 | 0.50 | (0.43) |
| | Hong Kong-China | 3.7 | (0.9) | 6.1 | (0.5) | **-2.4** | (1.0) | -1.7 | -0.36 | (0.22) |
| | Indonesia | 31.6 | (2.6) | 31.5 | (3.1) | 0.2 | (3.2) | 5.2 | 0.25 | (0.15) |
| | Israel | 21.6 | (1.3) | 18.7 | (1.9) | 2.8 | (2.3) | 1.5 | 0.10 | (0.14) |
| | Jordan | 28.3 | (1.1) | 24.1 | (2.8) | 4.2 | (3.0) | -1.2 | -0.06 | (0.14) |
| | Kyrgyzstan | 64.2 | (1.1) | 40.5 | (13.2) | 23.7 | (13.3) | -3.1 | -0.14 | (0.53) |
| | Latvia | 34.7 | (1.2) | a | a | a | a | a | a | a |
| | Liechtenstein | 5.6 | (1.3) | c | c | c | c | c | c | c |
| | Lithuania | 12.1 | (0.6) | c | c | c | c | c | c | c |
| | Macao-China | 27.0 | (2.8) | 13.7 | (0.6) | **13.3** | (2.9) | **11.9** | **0.77** | (0.17) |
| | Montenegro | 24.9 | (0.6) | c | c | c | c | **-58.0** | **-2.67** | (0.81) |
| | Qatar | 34.7 | (0.7) | 27.7 | (1.5) | **7.1** | (1.7) | -2.1 | -0.09 | (0.09) |
| | Romania | 26.9 | (1.3) | a | a | a | a | a | a | a |
| | Russian Federation | 30.7 | (0.9) | a | a | a | a | a | a | a |
| | Serbia | 10.4 | (0.7) | c | c | c | c | c | c | c |
| | Slovenia | 8.8 | (0.4) | 9.7 | (3.3) | -0.9 | (3.3) | -7.5 | -0.74 | (0.44) |
| | Chinese Taipei | 12.3 | (0.7) | 18.3 | (1.3) | **-6.1** | (1.6) | **-5.4** | **-0.44** | (0.09) |
| | Thailand | 21.1 | (0.8) | 20.8 | (1.1) | 0.3 | (1.3) | -1.3 | -0.08 | (0.08) |
| | Tunisia | 42.7 | (1.3) | 41.5 | (11.8) | 1.2 | (11.9) | 0.7 | 0.03 | (0.50) |
| | Uruguay | 9.8 | (0.9) | 8.5 | (0.9) | 1.3 | (1.3) | 1.0 | 0.12 | (0.29) |

*Note:* Values that are statistically significant at the 5% level (p < 0.05) are indicated in bold.

© OECD 2011 Quality Time for Students: Learning In and Out of School

## Table 3.18 Percentage of students by different types of out-of-school-time lessons, by public and private schools
[Part 5/6]

| | | Proportion of students participating in out-of-school lessons with school teachers | | | | | | | | | |
| | | Small group lessons | | | | | | Large group lessons | | | |
| | | Public schools | | Private schools | | Difference (public-private) | | Public schools | | Private schools | | Difference (public-private) |
| | | % | S.E. | % | S.E. | Dif. | S.E. | % | S.E. | % | S.E. | Dif. | S.E. |
|---|---|---|---|---|---|---|---|---|---|---|---|---|---|
| OECD | Australia | w | w | w | w | w | w | w | w | w | w | w | w |
| | Austria | 13.2 | (0.8) | 12.0 | (2.9) | 1.2 | (2.9) | 15.9 | (0.9) | 13.0 | (2.8) | 2.9 | (2.9) |
| | Belgium | w | w | w | w | w | w | w | w | w | w | w | w |
| | Canada | 10.2 | (0.4) | 11.9 | (1.8) | -1.7 | (1.9) | 11.1 | (0.4) | 12.0 | (1.6) | -0.9 | (1.7) |
| | Czech Republic | 11.1 | (0.7) | 8.3 | (1.7) | 2.8 | (1.8) | 13.4 | (0.7) | 12.2 | (3.7) | 1.2 | (3.7) |
| | Denmark | 7.4 | (0.5) | 8.9 | (1.0) | -1.5 | (1.2) | 6.8 | (0.6) | 11.1 | (1.0) | **-4.3** | (1.2) |
| | Finland | 9.5 | (0.5) | 7.4 | (2.1) | 2.1 | (2.1) | 12.2 | (0.6) | 11.4 | (2.0) | 0.8 | (2.1) |
| | France | w | w | w | w | w | w | w | w | w | w | w | w |
| | Germany | 7.4 | (0.5) | 12.2 | (4.3) | -4.9 | (4.4) | 10.4 | (0.7) | 8.1 | (3.3) | 2.3 | (3.5) |
| | Greece | 15.2 | (0.9) | 6.9 | (2.4) | **8.4** | (2.6) | 10.1 | (0.7) | 2.5 | (0.6) | 7.5 | (1.0) |
| | Hungary | 12.2 | (0.8) | 15.1 | (2.1) | -2.9 | (2.3) | 15.3 | (0.8) | 17.2 | (1.5) | -1.9 | (1.6) |
| | Iceland | 14.3 | (0.6) | 28.9 | (7.0) | **-14.5** | (7.1) | 14.3 | (0.6) | 0.0 | (0.0) | **14.3** | (0.6) |
| | Ireland | 12.4 | (1.1) | 6.8 | (0.7) | **5.6** | (1.3) | 13.3 | (1.2) | 7.7 | (0.6) | **5.6** | (1.3) |
| | Italy | 36.4 | (0.8) | 34.3 | (3.1) | 2.1 | (3.3) | 26.0 | (0.6) | 23.2 | (2.7) | 2.8 | (2.8) |
| | Japan | 6.1 | (0.5) | 7.7 | (0.7) | -1.6 | (0.9) | 28.9 | (1.3) | 33.9 | (2.6) | -4.9 | (2.9) |
| | Korea | 17.3 | (0.9) | 16.0 | (0.9) | 1.4 | (1.3) | 33.7 | (1.8) | 39.1 | (1.8) | **-5.4** | (2.5) |
| | Luxembourg | 13.7 | (0.6) | 20.1 | (1.7) | **-6.4** | (1.9) | 9.0 | (0.5) | 14.9 | (1.4) | **-5.9** | (1.5) |
| | Mexico | 18.8 | (0.8) | 11.5 | (1.5) | 7.3 | (1.9) | 25.9 | (0.9) | 12.6 | (1.3) | **13.3** | (1.7) |
| | Netherlands | 8.9 | (1.2) | 8.6 | (0.6) | 0.4 | (1.4) | 6.4 | (1.0) | 7.6 | (0.7) | -1.2 | (1.4) |
| | New Zealand | 9.4 | (0.7) | 14.7 | (1.6) | **-5.4** | (1.7) | 9.1 | (0.6) | 8.6 | (2.4) | 0.5 | (2.4) |
| | Norway | 12.1 | (0.6) | 4.6 | (2.1) | **7.6** | (2.2) | 17.6 | (0.7) | 7.1 | (3.8) | **10.5** | (3.9) |
| | Poland | 23.2 | (0.8) | 19.1 | (5.8) | 4.0 | (5.6) | 26.9 | (0.9) | 14.8 | (3.5) | **12.1** | (3.5) |
| | Portugal | 33.4 | (1.1) | 17.4 | (4.9) | **16.0** | (5.0) | 23.9 | (1.2) | 23.0 | (2.7) | 1.0 | (2.9) |
| | Slovak Republic | 18.2 | (1.1) | 15.9 | (4.2) | 2.3 | (4.5) | 24.4 | (1.2) | 20.2 | (7.1) | 4.2 | (7.3) |
| | Spain | 11.0 | (0.6) | 10.4 | (0.6) | 0.6 | (0.9) | 10.9 | (0.6) | 7.8 | (0.6) | **3.1** | (0.8) |
| | Sweden | 14.0 | (0.6) | 15.6 | (2.1) | -1.7 | (2.2) | 21.1 | (0.7) | 16.4 | (1.7) | **4.7** | (1.6) |
| | Switzerland | 10.0 | (0.4) | 12.7 | (2.0) | -2.7 | (2.0) | 14.3 | (0.6) | 10.4 | (1.9) | **3.9** | (2.0) |
| | Turkey | 9.0 | (0.6) | 21.6 | (1.4) | **-12.5** | (1.5) | 12.6 | (0.7) | 23.1 | (2.8) | **-10.5** | (2.9) |
| | United Kingdom | 17.9 | (0.6) | 12.9 | (2.0) | **5.0** | (2.0) | 20.0 | (0.8) | 10.6 | (2.2) | **9.4** | (2.4) |
| | United States | 19.5 | (0.9) | 13.7 | (2.8) | **5.8** | (2.9) | 18.8 | (1.1) | 9.1 | (1.7) | **9.7** | (1.9) |
| | **OECD average** | 14.3 | (0.1) | 13.7 | (0.5) | 0.7 | (0.6) | 16.4 | (0.2) | 13.7 | (0.5) | 2.7 | (0.5) |
| Partners | Argentina | 15.8 | (1.1) | 6.8 | (1.2) | **9.1** | (1.5) | 14.4 | (1.2) | 5.7 | (1.2) | **8.7** | (1.5) |
| | Azerbaijan | 37.2 | (1.3) | 39.3 | (7.5) | -2.0 | (7.5) | 48.5 | (1.3) | 38.7 | (9.1) | 9.8 | (8.9) |
| | Brazil | 23.7 | (0.8) | 22.8 | (2.8) | 0.8 | (2.9) | 20.5 | (0.7) | 20.2 | (2.0) | 0.2 | (2.1) |
| | Bulgaria | c | c | c | c | c | c | c | c | c | c | c | c |
| | Chile | 18.2 | (1.1) | 14.8 | (1.2) | **3.4** | (1.6) | 19.9 | (0.9) | 16.1 | (1.1) | **3.7** | (1.5) |
| | Colombia | 21.5 | (1.4) | 12.7 | (2.3) | **8.7** | (2.7) | 20.5 | (1.2) | 12.5 | (1.9) | **8.0** | (2.3) |
| | Croatia | 11.0 | (0.6) | 24.8 | (0.1) | **-13.9** | (0.6) | 11.8 | (0.6) | 29.9 | (0.0) | **-18.1** | (0.6) |
| | Estonia | 13.9 | (0.7) | 7.0 | (3.4) | **6.9** | (3.5) | 18.8 | (0.7) | 9.9 | (4.8) | 8.9 | (4.9) |
| | Hong Kong-China | 13.0 | (3.0) | 17.2 | (0.8) | -4.2 | (3.1) | 40.4 | (5.1) | 42.1 | (1.4) | -1.7 | (5.3) |
| | Indonesia | 26.2 | (2.1) | 27.0 | (2.4) | -0.8 | (2.1) | 34.4 | (2.5) | 35.6 | (3.2) | -1.2 | (3.2) |
| | Israel | 21.8 | (1.3) | 19.0 | (1.7) | 2.8 | (2.4) | 21.8 | (1.1) | 17.1 | (1.8) | **4.7** | (2.3) |
| | Jordan | 31.6 | (0.9) | 32.8 | (2.6) | -1.3 | (2.7) | 40.6 | (1.0) | 42.1 | (2.3) | -1.5 | (2.5) |
| | Kyrgyzstan | 44.4 | (1.2) | 29.9 | (2.5) | **14.5** | (2.7) | 53.1 | (1.3) | 34.7 | (11.2) | 18.4 | (11.3) |
| | Latvia | 25.6 | (1.1) | a | a | a | a | 29.0 | (1.2) | a | a | a | a |
| | Liechtenstein | 8.5 | (1.4) | c | c | c | c | 11.1 | (1.7) | c | c | c | c |
| | Lithuania | 17.8 | (0.8) | c | c | c | c | 19.4 | (0.8) | c | c | c | c |
| | Macao-China | 39.8 | (3.3) | 22.0 | (0.7) | **17.8** | (3.4) | 42.2 | (3.3) | 34.7 | (0.7) | **7.5** | (3.2) |
| | Montenegro | 17.5 | (0.6) | c | c | c | c | 21.3 | (0.6) | c | c | c | c |
| | Qatar | 29.6 | (0.6) | 25.2 | (1.3) | **4.3** | (1.5) | 30.5 | (0.7) | 22.2 | (1.4) | **8.3** | (1.6) |
| | Romania | 24.4 | (1.1) | a | a | a | a | 21.9 | (1.5) | a | a | a | a |
| | Russian Federation | 31.6 | (1.2) | a | a | a | a | 36.7 | (1.3) | a | a | a | a |
| | Serbia | 12.3 | (0.6) | c | c | c | c | 14.7 | (0.8) | c | c | c | c |
| | Slovenia | 8.9 | (0.5) | 7.1 | (2.1) | 1.7 | (2.1) | 11.7 | (0.5) | 8.8 | (2.5) | 2.9 | (2.5) |
| | Chinese Taipei | 19.7 | (0.8) | 28.6 | (1.4) | **-8.8** | (1.8) | 32.9 | (0.8) | 39.2 | (1.5) | **-6.3** | (1.8) |
| | Thailand | 26.5 | (1.0) | 28.4 | (1.5) | -1.9 | (1.8) | 39.4 | (1.4) | 37.2 | (1.9) | 2.2 | (2.3) |
| | Tunisia | 32.7 | (1.1) | 43.2 | (14.6) | -10.5 | (14.7) | 30.3 | (0.9) | 34.7 | (10.1) | -4.3 | (10.1) |
| | Uruguay | 9.1 | (0.6) | 8.6 | (1.2) | 0.5 | (1.3) | 8.7 | (0.6) | 8.6 | (1.0) | 0.2 | (1.2) |

*Note:* Values that are statistically significant at the 5% level (p < 0.05) are indicated in bold.

### Table 3.18 Percentage of students by different types of out-of-school-time lessons, by public and private schools
[Part 6/6]

| | | Proportion of students participating in out-of-school lessons with school teachers | | | | | | | |
|---|---|---|---|---|---|---|---|---|---|
| | | At least one of these types of out-of-school lessons | | | | | | | |
| | | | | | | | If students' ESCS was equal to the national average ESCS, and schools' average ESCS was equal to the national average of schools' average ESCS | | |
| | | Public schools | | Private schools | | Difference (public-private) | | Difference (public-private) | Increase in the logit of participating in out-of-school-time lessons by being in a public school | |
| | | % | S.E. | % | S.E. | Dif. | S.E. | Dif. in % | Logistic regression coefficient | S.E. |
| OECD | Australia | w | w | w | w | w | w | w | w | w |
| | Austria | 23.6 | (1.1) | 20.9 | (3.7) | 2.7 | (3.8) | 2.2 | 0.12 | (0.21) |
| | Belgium | w | w | w | w | w | w | w | w | w |
| | Canada | 20.8 | (0.6) | 26.2 | (2.4) | -5.4 | (2.5) | -10.0 | -0.53 | (0.14) |
| | Czech Republic | 23.2 | (1.0) | 22.2 | (4.8) | 1.0 | (4.7) | -2.1 | -0.12 | (0.27) |
| | Denmark | 12.6 | (0.8) | 16.9 | (1.3) | -4.3 | (1.5) | -5.9 | -0.47 | (0.12) |
| | Finland | 18.2 | (0.7) | 17.7 | (3.4) | 0.5 | (3.5) | -1.1 | -0.07 | (0.21) |
| | France | w | w | w | w | w | w | w | w | w |
| | Germany | 17.1 | (0.7) | 20.7 | (4.3) | -3.7 | (4.6) | -8.0 | -0.50 | (0.32) |
| | Greece | 22.6 | (1.1) | 13.3 | (2.8) | 9.3 | (3.0) | -2.5 | -0.15 | (0.30) |
| | Hungary | 28.4 | (1.1) | 32.6 | (3.6) | -4.2 | (3.7) | -5.7 | -0.27 | (0.18) |
| | Iceland | 27.1 | (0.8) | 31.7 | (6.4) | -4.6 | (6.7) | -3.4 | -0.17 | (0.30) |
| | Ireland | 22.7 | (1.6) | 13.2 | (0.8) | 9.4 | (1.7) | 5.5 | 0.40 | (0.11) |
| | Italy | 46.0 | (0.9) | 41.1 | (2.9) | 4.9 | (3.2) | 5.5 | 0.22 | (0.13) |
| | Japan | 33.1 | (1.4) | 39.1 | (2.3) | -6.0 | (2.7) | -10.2 | -0.44 | (0.12) |
| | Korea | 48.2 | (1.6) | 52.9 | (1.8) | -4.7 | (2.3) | -4.8 | -0.19 | (0.09) |
| | Luxembourg | 23.8 | (0.7) | 34.4 | (2.0) | -10.6 | (2.2) | -10.0 | -0.50 | (0.10) |
| | Mexico | 35.5 | (1.0) | 21.8 | (2.1) | 13.7 | (2.5) | -4.9 | -0.22 | (0.17) |
| | Netherlands | 14.8 | (1.6) | 15.9 | (1.1) | -1.1 | (2.0) | -1.0 | -0.08 | (0.16) |
| | New Zealand | 17.3 | (1.0) | 24.2 | (3.8) | -6.9 | (3.9) | -14.1 | -0.79 | (0.28) |
| | Norway | 24.3 | (0.8) | 8.3 | (4.7) | 15.9 | (4.8) | 14.9 | 1.15 | (0.71) |
| | Poland | 41.4 | (1.0) | 31.3 | (4.5) | 10.1 | (4.4) | -2.4 | -0.10 | (0.21) |
| | Portugal | 48.9 | (1.3) | 37.7 | (5.2) | 11.2 | (5.4) | 6.5 | 0.26 | (0.25) |
| | Slovak Republic | 38.9 | (1.5) | 36.1 | (8.8) | 2.7 | (9.1) | -0.8 | -0.03 | (0.40) |
| | Spain | 19.2 | (0.8) | 17.5 | (0.8) | 1.7 | (1.1) | -2.1 | -0.14 | (0.08) |
| | Sweden | 26.6 | (0.8) | 24.1 | (2.9) | 2.5 | (2.8) | -3.1 | -0.16 | (0.19) |
| | Switzerland | 22.6 | (0.7) | 22.8 | (2.0) | -0.2 | (2.2) | -6.6 | -0.36 | (0.15) |
| | Turkey | 19.6 | (1.0) | 29.1 | (1.1) | -9.6 | (1.4) | -17.0 | -0.87 | (0.12) |
| | United Kingdom | 32.0 | (0.9) | 24.2 | (2.9) | 7.8 | (2.9) | -3.0 | -0.14 | (0.21) |
| | United States | 32.9 | (1.3) | 25.7 | (3.5) | 7.2 | (3.6) | -4.7 | -0.21 | (0.21) |
| | **OECD average** | 27.0 | (0.2) | 25.5 | (0.7) | 1.5 | (0.7) | -3.1 | -0.16 | (0.05) |
| Partners | Argentina | 24.7 | (1.5) | 12.1 | (1.9) | 12.6 | (2.3) | 6.1 | -0.41 | (0.23) |
| | Azerbaijan | 67.7 | (1.4) | 62.8 | (7.4) | 4.9 | (7.3) | 7.8 | 0.34 | (0.40) |
| | Brazil | 34.3 | (1.0) | 34.7 | (2.3) | -0.4 | (2.4) | -14.9 | -0.63 | (0.17) |
| | Bulgaria | c | c | c | c | c | c | c | c | c |
| | Chile | 29.5 | (1.4) | 25.6 | (1.5) | 3.9 | (2.1) | -0.3 | -0.02 | (0.11) |
| | Colombia | 31.0 | (1.5) | 20.1 | (2.6) | 10.9 | (3.0) | -1.8 | -0.09 | (0.27) |
| | Croatia | 21.4 | (0.8) | 48.7 | (0.1) | -27.2 | (0.8) | -45.0 | -2.00 | (0.13) |
| | Estonia | 32.4 | (1.1) | 15.9 | (6.1) | 16.6 | (6.3) | 10.2 | 0.53 | (0.35) |
| | Hong Kong-China | 47.9 | (5.6) | 48.7 | (1.3) | -0.8 | (5.8) | 4.2 | 0.17 | (0.20) |
| | Indonesia | 52.5 | (3.6) | 50.7 | (3.8) | 1.7 | (4.0) | 7.5 | 0.30 | (0.17) |
| | Israel | 36.5 | (1.4) | 32.5 | (2.3) | 4.0 | (3.0) | 2.4 | 0.10 | (0.12) |
| | Jordan | 56.5 | (1.2) | 57.4 | (3.2) | -0.9 | (3.4) | -8.7 | -0.36 | (0.12) |
| | Kyrgyzstan | 78.8 | (1.2) | 58.0 | (11.1) | 20.8 | (11.2) | -5.2 | -0.36 | (0.46) |
| | Latvia | 50.5 | (1.3) | a | a | a | a | a | a | a |
| | Liechtenstein | 17.0 | (1.9) | c | c | c | c | c | c | c |
| | Lithuania | 34.6 | (1.0) | c | c | c | c | c | c | c |
| | Macao-China | 57.6 | (3.4) | 46.3 | (0.8) | 11.3 | (3.3) | 5.5 | 0.22 | (0.15) |
| | Montenegro | 34.3 | (0.8) | c | c | c | c | c | c | c |
| | Qatar | 46.1 | (0.6) | 38.9 | (1.6) | 7.2 | (1.8) | -1.8 | -0.07 | (0.08) |
| | Romania | 40.1 | (1.6) | a | a | a | a | a | a | a |
| | Russian Federation | 57.6 | (1.3) | a | a | a | a | a | a | a |
| | Serbia | 23.6 | (0.9) | c | c | c | c | c | c | c |
| | Slovenia | 20.2 | (0.5) | 17.4 | (3.9) | 2.8 | (3.8) | -3.8 | -0.23 | (0.29) |
| | Chinese Taipei | 41.7 | (1.1) | 51.3 | (1.7) | -9.7 | (2.1) | -9.5 | -0.39 | (0.07) |
| | Thailand | 47.9 | (1.3) | 44.8 | (1.9) | 3.1 | (2.3) | 4.2 | 0.17 | (0.09) |
| | Tunisia | 54.0 | (1.2) | 58.8 | (13.8) | -4.8 | (13.9) | -6.3 | -0.26 | (0.56) |
| | Uruguay | 17.4 | (1.0) | 16.0 | (1.6) | 1.5 | (1.8) | -8.1 | -0.51 | (0.24) |

*Note:* Values that are statistically significant at the 5% level (p < 0.05) are indicated in bold.

230

Table 3.19 **Percentage of students by different types of out-of-school-time lessons,**
[Part 1/5] **by academic and vocational orientation of schools**

| | | Proportion of students participating in out-of-school-time lessons | | | | | |
|---|---|---|---|---|---|---|---|
| | | Academic schools | | Vocational schools | | Difference (academic-vocational) | |
| | | % | S.E. | % | S.E. | Dif. | S.E. |
| OECD | Australia | 31.4 | (0.6) | 30.0 | (1.7) | **1.3** | (1.7) |
| | Austria | 44.2 | (2.3) | 33.0 | (1.3) | **11.3** | (2.6) |
| | Belgium | 33.5 | (1.0) | 26.9 | (0.9) | **6.5** | (1.5) |
| | Canada | 35.8 | (0.7) | a | a | a | a |
| | Czech Republic | 40.7 | (1.1) | 32.4 | (1.7) | **8.3** | (2.0) |
| | Denmark | 20.6 | (0.8) | a | a | a | a |
| | Finland | 23.5 | (0.7) | a | a | a | a |
| | France | 43.2 | (0.9) | 27.0 | (1.6) | **16.3** | (1.8) |
| | Germany | 37.3 | (0.8) | 24.8 | (8.1) | 12.5 | (8.3) |
| | Greece | 80.1 | (1.0) | 52.4 | (2.8) | **27.7** | (3.2) |
| | Hungary | 64.5 | (1.5) | 46.5 | (1.6) | **18.0** | (2.2) |
| | Iceland | 40.4 | (0.8) | c | c | c | c |
| | Ireland | 38.1 | (0.9) | 38.3 | (6.4) | -0.2 | (6.3) |
| | Italy | 70.0 | (1.0) | 63.6 | (0.8) | **6.4** | (1.3) |
| | Japan | 46.5 | (1.6) | 43.0 | (2.3) | 3.5 | (2.8) |
| | Korea | 85.2 | (0.8) | 58.8 | (2.8) | **26.4** | (2.9) |
| | Luxembourg | 44.8 | (0.7) | 37.4 | (1.8) | **7.4** | (2.0) |
| | Mexico | 50.7 | (1.2) | 41.3 | (0.9) | **9.4** | (1.6) |
| | Netherlands | 21.7 | (0.9) | 23.1 | (1.4) | -1.4 | (1.6) |
| | New Zealand | 33.7 | (0.9) | a | a | a | a |
| | Norway | 27.3 | (0.8) | a | a | a | a |
| | Poland | 56.2 | (1.0) | a | a | a | a |
| | Portugal | 70.0 | (1.1) | 60.9 | (2.8) | **9.1** | (3.0) |
| | Slovak Republic | 68.7 | (1.5) | 39.1 | (1.5) | **29.6** | (2.2) |
| | Spain | 53.8 | (0.7) | a | a | a | a |
| | Sweden | 32.1 | (0.8) | c | c | c | c |
| | Switzerland | 40.6 | (0.7) | 31.8 | (3.9) | **8.8** | (4.0) |
| | Turkey | 42.5 | (1.7) | 28.8 | (1.4) | **13.7** | (2.2) |
| | United Kingdom | 45.5 | (0.9) | a | a | a | a |
| | United States | 42.3 | (1.2) | a | a | a | a |
| | **OECD average** | 45.5 | (0.2) | 38.9 | (0.7) | **11.3** | (0.8) |
| Partners | Argentina | 48.3 | (1.2) | 59.2 | (5.5) | -10.9 | (5.6) |
| | Azerbaijan | 79.4 | (1.2) | 84.8 | (5.3) | -5.4 | (5.4) |
| | Brazil | 48.4 | (0.9) | a | a | a | a |
| | Bulgaria | 56.1 | (1.7) | 52.2 | (1.8) | 3.9 | (2.2) |
| | Chile | 38.6 | (1.2) | 26.0 | (4.2) | **12.6** | (4.3) |
| | Colombia | 51.5 | (1.2) | 48.1 | (2.9) | 3.4 | (2.9) |
| | Croatia | 49.2 | (1.8) | 44.0 | (1.0) | **5.2** | (2.0) |
| | Estonia | 46.0 | (0.9) | a | a | a | a |
| | Hong Kong-China | 76.0 | (0.9) | 67.1 | (4.4) | **8.9** | (4.5) |
| | Indonesia | 72.3 | (1.4) | 34.2 | (2.3) | **38.1** | (2.6) |
| | Israel | 64.5 | (1.1) | 64.3 | (2.6) | 0.2 | (2.7) |
| | Jordan | 72.6 | (0.9) | a | a | a | a |
| | Kyrgyzstan | 85.3 | (1.0) | 80.4 | (5.9) | 4.9 | (5.8) |
| | Latvia | 71.5 | (1.1) | 70.4 | (3.7) | 1.2 | (3.6) |
| | Liechtenstein | 27.8 | (2.4) | a | a | a | a |
| | Lithuania | 48.8 | (1.1) | c | c | c | c |
| | Macao-China | 62.4 | (0.8) | 54.4 | (5.7) | 8.0 | (5.7) |
| | Montenegro | 61.6 | (1.3) | 62.3 | (0.9) | -0.7 | (1.7) |
| | Qatar | 63.6 | (0.5) | a | a | a | a |
| | Romania | 52.9 | (1.5) | 69.5 | (1.7) | **-16.6** | (2.3) |
| | Russian Federation | 71.8 | (1.5) | 54.2 | (2.8) | **17.6** | (3.0) |
| | Serbia | 58.6 | (2.2) | 52.2 | (1.1) | **6.4** | (2.4) |
| | Slovenia | 44.1 | (1.1) | 39.2 | (0.9) | **4.9** | (1.6) |
| | Chinese Taipei | 79.1 | (0.5) | 67.5 | (1.0) | **11.6** | (1.1) |
| | Thailand | 65.8 | (1.2) | 50.3 | (3.6) | **15.5** | (3.7) |
| | Tunisia | 70.4 | (1.0) | a | a | a | a |
| | Uruguay | 45.5 | (1.1) | 37.7 | (4.2) | 7.9 | (4.3) |

*Note:* Values that are statistically significant at the 5% level (p < 0.05) are indicated in bold.

231

### Table 3.19 Percentage of students by different types of out-of-school-time lessons, by academic and vocational orientation of schools
[Part 2/5]

Proportion of students participating in out-of-school lessons with non-school teachers

| | One-to-one lessons | | | | | | If students' ESCS was equal to the national average ESCS, and schools' average ESCS was equal to the national average of schools' average ESCS | | | Small group lessons | | | | | |
| | Academic schools | | Vocational schools | | Difference (academic-vocational) | | Difference (academic-vocational) | Increase in the logit of participating in out-of-school-time lessons by being in an academic school | | Academic schools | | Vocational schools | | Difference (academic-vocational) | |
| | % | S.E. | % | S.E. | Dif. | S.E. | Dif. in % | Logistic regression coefficient | S.E. | % | S.E. | % | S.E. | Dif. | S.E. |
|---|---|---|---|---|---|---|---|---|---|---|---|---|---|---|---|
| Australia | 17.1 | (0.4) | 12.4 | (0.9) | **4.7** | (1.0) | **3.1** | **0.25** | (0.09) | 7.9 | (0.4) | 10.1 | (0.9) | **-2.2** | (1.0) |
| Austria | 23.9 | (1.4) | 13.7 | (0.8) | **10.2** | (1.5) | **6.1** | **0.43** | (0.14) | 9.8 | (1.2) | 6.9 | (0.5) | **2.9** | (1.3) |
| Belgium | 22.5 | (0.9) | 12.6 | (0.7) | **9.9** | (1.1) | **7.5** | **0.54** | (0.09) | 7.4 | (0.5) | 7.4 | (0.6) | 0.1 | (0.7) |
| Canada | 16.5 | (0.5) | a | a | a | a | a | a | a | 8.5 | (0.4) | a | a | a | a |
| Czech Republic | 17.5 | (0.9) | 13.5 | (1.1) | **4.0** | (1.5) | 2.2 | 0.18 | (0.12) | 8.6 | (0.7) | 6.9 | (0.8) | 1.7 | (1.1) |
| Denmark | 5.4 | (0.4) | a | a | a | a | a | a | a | 4.6 | (0.4) | a | a | a | a |
| Finland | 5.3 | (0.3) | a | a | a | a | a | a | a | 2.4 | (0.2) | a | a | a | a |
| France | 23.8 | (1.0) | 9.1 | (1.8) | **14.7** | (1.9) | **11.3** | **0.83** | (0.22) | 9.6 | (0.6) | 5.0 | (1.2) | **4.6** | (1.3) |
| Germany | 21.7 | (0.6) | 13.0 | (5.1) | 8.6 | (5.2) | 7.4 | 0.52 | (0.45) | 7.5 | (0.4) | 1.5 | (1.4) | **5.9** | (1.5) |
| Greece | 48.1 | (1.3) | 23.5 | (1.6) | **24.7** | (2.0) | **17.8** | **0.77** | (0.12) | 49.3 | (1.4) | 24.2 | (2.1) | **25.1** | (2.6) |
| Hungary | 39.3 | (1.6) | 27.3 | (1.3) | **12.0** | (2.0) | 1.3 | 0.06 | (0.10) | 12.6 | (0.9) | 9.4 | (0.9) | **3.2** | (1.3) |
| Iceland | 14.7 | (0.6) | c | c | c | c | c | c | c | 6.7 | (0.5) | c | c | c | c |
| Ireland | 21.5 | (0.7) | 18.2 | (5.4) | 3.3 | (5.5) | -0.5 | -0.03 | (0.40) | 9.7 | (0.5) | 12.5 | (3.5) | -2.8 | (3.6) |
| Italy | 44.1 | (0.8) | 31.7 | (0.8) | **12.4** | (1.1) | 1.2 | 0.05 | (0.07) | 13.4 | (0.5) | 14.7 | (0.7) | -1.3 | (0.9) |
| Japan | 10.9 | (0.8) | 5.0 | (0.7) | **5.9** | (1.1) | **3.1** | **0.44** | (0.19) | 9.8 | (0.7) | 4.2 | (0.8) | **5.7** | (1.0) |
| Korea | 35.2 | (0.9) | 18.1 | (1.7) | **17.0** | (1.9) | **10.8** | **0.55** | (0.13) | 35.9 | (1.1) | 15.6 | (1.2) | **20.2** | (1.6) |
| Luxembourg | 23.5 | (0.7) | 20.8 | (1.8) | 2.7 | (1.9) | 2.3 | 0.14 | (0.11) | 7.5 | (0.5) | 4.4 | (0.9) | **3.0** | (1.0) |
| Mexico | 19.0 | (0.9) | 15.6 | (0.6) | **3.4** | (1.2) | **3.3** | 0.24 | (0.08) | 17.1 | (0.9) | 14.2 | (0.8) | **3.0** | (1.3) |
| Netherlands | 7.8 | (0.5) | 6.4 | (0.8) | 1.4 | (0.9) | -0.9 | -0.14 | (0.16) | 2.6 | (0.4) | 5.9 | (0.9) | **-3.3** | (1.0) |
| New Zealand | 17.2 | (0.6) | a | a | a | a | a | a | a | 9.9 | (0.5) | a | a | a | a |
| Norway | 5.3 | (0.4) | a | a | a | a | a | a | a | 4.9 | (0.4) | a | a | a | a |
| Poland | 19.3 | (0.8) | a | a | a | a | a | a | a | 10.7 | (0.6) | a | a | a | a |
| Portugal | 27.2 | (1.0) | 23.1 | (2.2) | 4.1 | (2.5) | 3.9 | 0.21 | (0.14) | 14.7 | (0.8) | 14.1 | (1.7) | 0.6 | (1.8) |
| Slovak Republic | 28.8 | (1.5) | 21.3 | (1.2) | **7.5** | (1.9) | **3.4** | **0.19** | (0.09) | 12.1 | (0.8) | 10.0 | (0.8) | 2.1 | (1.2) |
| Spain | 28.6 | (0.8) | a | a | a | a | a | a | a | 26.1 | (0.7) | a | a | a | a |
| Sweden | 7.5 | (0.5) | c | c | c | c | c | c | c | 5.8 | (0.4) | c | c | c | c |
| Switzerland | 20.0 | (0.5) | 18.3 | (2.7) | 1.7 | (2.7) | 1.1 | 0.07 | (0.16) | 6.2 | (0.4) | 8.0 | (2.3) | -1.8 | (2.3) |
| Turkey | 16.4 | (1.0) | 9.2 | (0.8) | **7.2** | (1.2) | **4.7** | **0.45** | (0.13) | 12.8 | (0.8) | 8.3 | (0.8) | **4.6** | (1.1) |
| United Kingdom | 17.4 | (0.5) | a | a | a | a | a | a | a | 7.5 | (0.5) | a | a | a | a |
| United States | 17.4 | (0.8) | a | a | a | a | a | a | a | 12.5 | (0.9) | a | a | a | a |
| **OECD average** | **20.8** | **(0.2)** | **16.5** | **(0.5)** | **8.2** | **(0.5)** | **4.6** | **0.30** | **(0.04)** | **11.8** | **(0.1)** | **9.6** | **(0.3)** | **3.8** | **(0.4)** |
| Argentina | 31.2 | (1.3) | 31.8 | (6.3) | -0.6 | (6.4) | -4.0 | -0.18 | (0.25) | 19.1 | (0.9) | 22.7 | (4.8) | -3.6 | (5.0) |
| Azerbaijan | 30.5 | (1.1) | 51.4 | (9.6) | **-21.0** | (9.6) | **-26.5** | **-1.11** | (0.45) | 40.7 | (1.1) | 55.6 | (10.9) | -15.0 | (11.1) |
| Brazil | 19.7 | (0.6) | a | a | a | a | a | a | a | 17.9 | (0.5) | a | a | a | a |
| Bulgaria | 26.9 | (1.3) | 26.8 | (1.2) | 0.1 | (1.7) | -2.3 | -0.12 | (0.09) | 16.9 | (1.2) | 18.3 | (1.6) | -1.4 | (2.0) |
| Chile | 13.5 | (0.8) | 5.4 | (2.0) | **8.1** | (2.0) | 6.0 | 0.75 | (0.41) | 9.5 | (0.5) | 5.9 | (2.3) | 3.5 | (2.3) |
| Colombia | 26.4 | (0.9) | 20.6 | (2.1) | **5.8** | (2.5) | **6.3** | **0.36** | (0.16) | 18.4 | (0.8) | 15.0 | (1.9) | 3.4 | (2.0) |
| Croatia | 34.0 | (1.7) | 25.5 | (0.9) | **8.5** | (1.8) | -1.0 | -0.05 | (0.12) | 7.3 | (0.7) | 10.7 | (0.7) | **-3.4** | (0.9) |
| Estonia | 17.3 | (0.7) | a | a | a | a | a | a | a | 8.1 | (0.5) | a | a | a | a |
| Hong Kong-China | 24.6 | (1.4) | 17.5 | (2.5) | **7.2** | (2.9) | -0.9 | -0.05 | (0.19) | 18.3 | (0.8) | 12.2 | (2.0) | **6.0** | (2.1) |
| Indonesia | 18.7 | (0.7) | 11.3 | (1.7) | **7.4** | (1.8) | **7.1** | **0.60** | (0.19) | 20.5 | (0.9) | 14.3 | (1.0) | **6.2** | (1.4) |
| Israel | 42.8 | (1.2) | 39.2 | (3.0) | 3.6 | (3.4) | -0.1 | -0.00 | (0.12) | 19.8 | (0.9) | 22.4 | (1.8) | -2.6 | (2.0) |
| Jordan | 34.4 | (0.8) | a | a | a | a | a | a | a | 25.2 | (0.8) | a | a | a | a |
| Kyrgyzstan | 26.1 | (0.8) | 41.1 | (9.6) | -14.9 | (9.5) | -11.8 | -0.55 | (0.36) | 26.8 | (0.9) | 34.6 | (7.1) | -7.8 | (7.1) |
| Latvia | 32.2 | (1.2) | 34.0 | (4.4) | -1.8 | (4.4) | 2.1 | 0.10 | (0.20) | 14.0 | (0.5) | 16.0 | (3.9) | -2.0 | (4.0) |
| Liechtenstein | 14.0 | (1.8) | a | a | a | a | a | a | a | 2.8 | (1.0) | a | a | a | a |
| Lithuania | 17.8 | (0.8) | c | c | c | c | c | c | c | 7.0 | (0.4) | c | c | c | c |
| Macao-China | 22.0 | (0.7) | 0.00 | (2.6) | **11.7** | (2.7) | **10.5** | **0.78** | (0.30) | 20.6 | (0.7) | 18.2 | (3.8) | 2.5 | (3.9) |
| Montenegro | 42.6 | (1.5) | 35.0 | (1.0) | **7.6** | (1.9) | **-4.7** | **-0.20** | (0.10) | 16.7 | (0.9) | 22.6 | (0.9) | **-5.9** | (1.3) |
| Qatar | 36.2 | (0.7) | a | a | a | a | a | a | a | 25.4 | (0.6) | a | a | a | a |
| Romania | 26.6 | (1.5) | 32.1 | (2.7) | -5.5 | (3.1) | -10.8 | -0.51 | (0.16) | 16.8 | (0.9) | 29.4 | (3.1) | **-12.6** | (3.2) |
| Russian Federation | 22.9 | (0.9) | 13.6 | (1.6) | **9.3** | (1.8) | **8.2** | **0.57** | (0.15) | 13.1 | (0.9) | 9.0 | (1.1) | **4.1** | (1.3) |
| Serbia | 46.0 | (2.3) | 35.8 | (1.2) | **10.2** | (2.6) | -3.1 | -0.13 | (0.14) | 13.1 | (1.3) | 12.8 | (0.6) | 0.3 | (1.4) |
| Slovenia | 28.6 | (1.0) | 24.9 | (0.9) | **3.8** | (1.4) | 0.3 | 0.02 | (0.10) | 5.6 | (0.7) | 7.5 | (0.4) | **-1.9** | (0.8) |
| Chinese Taipei | 24.6 | (0.7) | 22.1 | (0.8) | **2.4** | (1.1) | 1.4 | 0.08 | (0.08) | 23.7 | (0.6) | 23.5 | (0.9) | 0.2 | (1.0) |
| Thailand | 20.5 | (0.8) | 20.3 | (2.6) | 0.2 | (2.7) | -0.1 | -0.01 | (0.16) | 24.2 | (0.9) | 23.2 | (2.6) | 1.0 | (2.7) |
| Tunisia | 30.8 | (1.4) | a | a | a | a | a | a | a | 28.3 | (1.1) | a | a | a | a |
| Uruguay | 31.2 | (0.8) | 13.4 | (1.6) | **17.8** | (1.8) | **15.6** | **0.94** | (0.17) | 21.9 | (0.8) | 14.4 | (2.5) | **7.6** | (2.6) |

*Note:* Values that are statistically significant at the 5% level (p < 0.05) are indicated in bold.

© OECD 2011 Quality Time for Students: Learning In and Out of School

Table 3.19 Percentage of students by different types of out-of-school-time lessons, by academic and vocational orientation of schools
[Part 3/5]

| | | Proportion of students participating in out-of-school lessons with non-school teachers | | | | | | | | | | | If students' ESCS was equal to the national average ESCS, and schools' average ESCS was equal to the national average of schools' average ESCS | | |
| | | Large group lessons | | | | | | At least one of these types of out-of-school lessons | | | | | | | | |
| | | Academic schools | | Vocational schools | | Difference (academic-vocational) | | Academic schools | | Vocational schools | | Difference (academic-vocational) | | Difference (academic-vocational) | Increase in the logit of participating in out-of-school-time lessons by being in an academic school | |
| | | % | S.E. | % | S.E. | Dif. | S.E. | % | S.E. | % | S.E. | Dif. | S.E. | Dif. in % | Logistic regression coefficient | S.E. |
|---|---|---|---|---|---|---|---|---|---|---|---|---|---|---|---|---|
| OECD | Australia | 6.9 | (0.3) | 10.1 | (1.0) | -3.2 | (1.1) | 23.5 | (0.6) | 20.2 | (1.2) | 3.2 | (1.2) | 1.5 | 0.09 | (0.08) |
| | Austria | 3.4 | (0.8) | 7.3 | (0.5) | -3.9 | (0.9) | 31.3 | (1.9) | 21.2 | (0.8) | 10.1 | (1.9) | 10.0 | 0.52 | (0.15) |
| | Belgium | 3.0 | (0.3) | 5.8 | (0.6) | -2.8 | (0.6) | 26.4 | (0.9) | 18.1 | (0.8) | 8.3 | (1.2) | 7.1 | 0.42 | (0.08) |
| | Canada | 7.1 | (0.3) | a | a | a | a | 22.8 | (0.6) | a | a | a | a | a | a | a |
| | Czech Republic | 6.1 | (0.6) | 5.1 | (0.9) | 1.0 | (1.0) | 23.7 | (1.0) | 19.1 | (1.4) | 4.6 | (1.8) | 2.9 | 0.18 | (0.11) |
| | Denmark | 3.9 | (0.4) | a | a | a | a | 10.4 | (0.7) | a | a | a | a | a | a | a |
| | Finland | 3.7 | (0.3) | a | a | a | a | 8.5 | (0.4) | a | a | a | a | a | a | a |
| | France | 5.2 | (0.5) | 2.5 | (0.7) | 2.6 | (0.9) | 27.9 | (1.1) | 12.2 | (2.1) | 15.7 | (2.2) | 12.8 | 0.80 | (0.20) |
| | Germany | 3.9 | (0.4) | 0.0 | (0.0) | 3.9 | (0.4) | 27.6 | (0.6) | 14.6 | (4.4) | 13.1 | (4.5) | 12.3 | 0.75 | (0.35) |
| | Greece | 18.3 | (1.0) | 20.3 | (2.4) | -2.0 | (2.6) | 75.3 | (1.1) | 41.0 | (2.5) | 34.3 | (2.8) | 24.2 | 1.07 | (0.14) |
| | Hungary | 10.6 | (1.0) | 7.4 | (0.7) | 3.2 | (1.2) | 45.6 | (1.5) | 32.8 | (1.5) | 12.8 | (2.1) | 6.7 | 0.29 | (0.10) |
| | Iceland | 5.1 | (0.4) | c | c | c | c | 19.8 | (0.7) | c | c | c | c | c | c | c |
| | Ireland | 6.6 | (0.5) | 9.0 | (3.8) | -2.4 | (3.9) | 29.0 | (0.8) | 23.6 | (5.3) | 5.4 | (5.3) | 1.2 | 0.06 | (0.33) |
| | Italy | 7.1 | (0.5) | 10.5 | (0.5) | -3.4 | (0.7) | 50.9 | (0.9) | 41.9 | (0.9) | 9.0 | (1.2) | 1.6 | 0.06 | (0.07) |
| | Japan | 8.5 | (0.8) | 7.3 | (0.9) | 1.2 | (1.2) | 22.9 | (1.3) | 11.9 | (1.3) | 11.0 | (1.8) | 3.9 | 0.27 | (0.16) |
| | Korea | 30.3 | (1.0) | 15.6 | (1.2) | 14.7 | (1.6) | 65.3 | (1.1) | 32.5 | (2.2) | 32.8 | (2.5) | 15.3 | 0.62 | (0.13) |
| | Luxembourg | 6.0 | (0.7) | 2.5 | (0.6) | 3.5 | (0.7) | 28.6 | (0.7) | 23.4 | (2.0) | 5.2 | (2.1) | 5.5 | 0.29 | (0.11) |
| | Mexico | 17.1 | (0.9) | 14.2 | (0.5) | 2.9 | (1.1) | 32.1 | (1.2) | 26.9 | (0.8) | 5.2 | (1.6) | 5.2 | 0.25 | (0.08) |
| | Netherlands | 2.6 | (0.3) | 6.3 | (0.9) | -3.8 | (1.0) | 10.6 | (0.6) | 12.3 | (1.3) | -1.7 | (1.4) | -2.2 | -0.22 | (0.14) |
| | New Zealand | 6.9 | (0.4) | a | a | a | a | 23.9 | (0.7) | a | a | a | a | a | a | a |
| | Norway | 5.0 | (0.4) | a | a | a | a | 9.9 | (0.6) | a | a | a | a | a | a | a |
| | Poland | 10.0 | (0.5) | a | a | a | a | 28.9 | (0.9) | a | a | a | a | a | a | a |
| | Portugal | 8.5 | (0.6) | 6.3 | (1.5) | 2.3 | (1.5) | 35.8 | (1.2) | 32.0 | (2.6) | 3.7 | (3.0) | 3.4 | 0.15 | (0.14) |
| | Slovak Republic | 9.0 | (0.9) | 5.3 | (0.6) | 3.8 | (1.1) | 33.8 | (1.5) | 24.5 | (1.2) | 9.3 | (1.9) | 5.9 | 0.29 | (0.09) |
| | Spain | 10.5 | (0.5) | a | a | a | a | 43.4 | (0.8) | a | a | a | a | a | a | a |
| | Sweden | 7.1 | (0.4) | m | m | m | m | 13.2 | (0.6) | c | c | c | c | c | c | c |
| | Switzerland | 4.9 | (0.3) | 3.3 | (1.3) | 1.6 | (1.4) | 24.8 | (0.6) | 22.7 | (3.6) | 2.1 | (3.6) | 1.7 | 0.10 | (0.20) |
| | Turkey | 17.9 | (1.5) | 10.9 | (1.1) | 7.0 | (1.8) | 31.7 | (1.7) | 19.0 | (1.3) | 12.6 | (2.2) | 6.6 | 0.36 | (0.11) |
| | United Kingdom | 7.4 | (0.4) | a | a | a | a | 24.1 | (0.7) | a | a | a | a | a | a | a |
| | United States | 11.6 | (0.8) | a | a | a | a | 25.2 | (1.1) | a | a | a | a | a | a | a |
| | **OECD average** | 8.5 | (0.1) | 7.9 | (0.3) | 1.4 | (0.3) | 29.2 | (0.2) | 23.7 | (0.5) | 10.4 | (0.6) | 6.7 | 0.33 | (0.04) |
| Partners | Argentina | 12.8 | (0.8) | 25.9 | (7.1) | -13.1 | (7.2) | 39.7 | (1.2) | 47.6 | (4.7) | -7.8 | (5.0) | -10.4 | -0.42 | (0.25) |
| | Azerbaijan | 38.9 | (1.1) | 40.8 | (11.9) | -1.9 | (11.9) | 62.6 | (1.0) | 75.7 | (8.1) | -13.1 | (8.1) | -14.5 | -0.70 | (0.52) |
| | Brazil | 15.4 | (0.5) | a | a | a | a | 33.1 | (0.7) | a | a | a | a | a | a | a |
| | Bulgaria | 15.1 | (1.2) | 18.8 | (1.7) | -3.7 | (2.0) | 38.3 | (1.5) | 37.8 | (1.4) | 0.4 | (2.0) | -1.0 | -0.04 | (0.09) |
| | Chile | 8.3 | (0.5) | 9.5 | (2.5) | -1.3 | (2.4) | 21.7 | (0.9) | 12.7 | (2.4) | 8.9 | (2.3) | 7.8 | 0.56 | (0.21) |
| | Colombia | 16.6 | (0.8) | 15.7 | (1.8) | 0.9 | (2.0) | 37.6 | (1.0) | 32.3 | (1.7) | 5.3 | (2.1) | 6.2 | 0.28 | (0.09) |
| | Croatia | 4.5 | (0.6) | 9.1 | (0.6) | -4.6 | (0.8) | 38.9 | (1.7) | 32.1 | (1.0) | 6.9 | (1.9) | -1.4 | -0.06 | (0.10) |
| | Estonia | 7.3 | (0.5) | a | a | a | a | 23.4 | (0.7) | a | a | a | a | a | a | a |
| | Hong Kong-China | 30.8 | (1.2) | 20.0 | (2.6) | 10.9 | (2.8) | 53.4 | (1.3) | 34.7 | (3.9) | 18.7 | (4.2) | 6.9 | 0.27 | (0.18) |
| | Indonesia | 19.0 | (0.9) | 10.3 | (1.2) | 8.7 | (1.3) | 36.0 | (1.0) | 24.5 | (2.1) | 11.5 | (2.4) | 11.9 | 0.58 | (0.11) |
| | Israel | 14.7 | (0.8) | 18.5 | (2.4) | -3.8 | (2.4) | 53.3 | (1.4) | 50.0 | (2.9) | 3.4 | (3.2) | 1.4 | 0.06 | (0.12) |
| | Jordan | 21.9 | (0.8) | a | a | a | a | 48.0 | (0.9) | a | a | a | a | a | a | a |
| | Kyrgyzstan | 31.7 | (1.0) | 34.5 | (7.0) | -2.8 | (7.1) | 48.4 | (1.0) | 56.3 | (8.7) | -7.9 | (8.7) | -9.7 | -0.39 | (0.37) |
| | Latvia | 17.3 | (0.7) | 10.9 | (2.8) | 6.4 | (3.1) | 42.3 | (1.1) | 42.7 | (5.1) | -0.5 | (5.1) | 3.7 | 0.15 | (0.21) |
| | Liechtenstein | 2.4 | (0.8) | a | a | a | a | 16.1 | (2.0) | a | a | a | a | a | a | a |
| | Lithuania | 6.6 | (0.5) | c | c | c | c | 23.4 | (0.8) | c | c | c | c | c | c | c |
| | Macao-China | 19.5 | (0.7) | 11.6 | (2.7) | 7.9 | (2.9) | 39.3 | (0.8) | 24.3 | (3.9) | 15.0 | (4.0) | 13.0 | 0.60 | (0.22) |
| | Montenegro | 12.0 | (0.9) | 20.1 | (0.8) | -8.1 | (1.2) | 49.0 | (1.4) | 46.7 | (0.9) | 2.2 | (1.7) | -7.5 | -0.30 | (0.10) |
| | Qatar | 22.8 | (0.5) | a | a | a | a | 48.5 | (0.7) | a | a | a | a | a | a | a |
| | Romania | 10.8 | (1.0) | 30.8 | (2.0) | -20.1 | (2.2) | 35.2 | (1.3) | 49.2 | (2.4) | -13.9 | (2.7) | -16.0 | -0.66 | (0.13) |
| | Russian Federation | 13.1 | (0.7) | 10.5 | (1.5) | 2.6 | (1.6) | 32.8 | (1.2) | 21.5 | (2.3) | 11.3 | (2.7) | 10.4 | 0.53 | (0.16) |
| | Serbia | 4.3 | (0.7) | 10.3 | (0.7) | -6.1 | (0.9) | 50.0 | (2.4) | 40.9 | (1.1) | 9.1 | (2.6) | -1.9 | -0.08 | (0.13) |
| | Slovenia | 3.0 | (0.3) | 7.1 | (0.4) | -4.1 | (0.6) | 32.9 | (1.1) | 29.6 | (0.9) | 3.3 | (1.5) | 2.5 | 0.12 | (0.09) |
| | Chinese Taipei | 46.5 | (1.2) | 29.1 | (1.0) | 17.4 | (1.5) | 64.2 | (0.8) | 43.6 | (0.9) | 20.6 | (1.2) | 15.0 | 0.61 | (0.05) |
| | Thailand | 32.0 | (1.3) | 27.0 | (2.6) | 5.0 | (2.9) | 45.5 | (1.3) | 36.9 | (3.6) | 8.6 | (3.8) | 8.1 | 0.33 | (0.15) |
| | Tunisia | 19.3 | (0.9) | a | a | a | a | 44.9 | (1.4) | a | a | a | a | a | a | a |
| | Uruguay | 11.9 | (0.6) | 13.1 | (2.1) | -1.2 | (2.2) | 39.4 | (1.0) | 23.3 | (2.1) | 16.1 | (2.3) | 13.8 | 0.65 | (0.14) |

Note: Values that are statistically significant at the 5% level (p < 0.05) are indicated in bold.

Table 3.19 **Percentage of students by different types of out-of-school-time lessons,**
[Part 4/5] **by academic and vocational orientation of schools**

| | Proportion of students participating in out-of-school lessons with school teachers | | | | | | | | | | | | | |
| | One-to-one lessons | | | | | | | | | Small group lessons | | | | | |
| | Academic schools | | Vocational schools | | Difference (academic-vocational) | | If students' ESCS was equal to the national average ESCS, and schools' average ESCS was equal to the national average of schools' average ESCS | | | Academic schools | | Vocational schools | | Difference (academic-vocational) | |
| | | | | | | | Difference (academic-vocational) | Increase in the logit of participating in out-of-school-time lessons by being in an academic school | | | | | | | |
| | % | S.E. | % | S.E. | Dif. | S.E. | Dif. in % | Logistic regression coefficient | S.E. | % | S.E. | % | S.E. | Dif. | S.E. |
| **OECD** | | | | | | | | | | | | | | | |
| Australia | 6.4 | (0.3) | 9.8 | (1.1) | **-3.5** | (1.1) | **-3.2** | **-0.44** | (0.13) | 6.8 | (0.4) | 11.1 | (1.3) | **-4.3** | (1.3) |
| Austria | 4.7 | (0.9) | 5.7 | (0.5) | -1.0 | (1.0) | 1.9 | 0.38 | (0.22) | 13.4 | (1.4) | 13.0 | (0.9) | 0.4 | (1.6) |
| Belgium | 6.6 | (0.5) | 8.0 | (0.7) | -1.4 | (0.9) | -0.2 | -0.02 | (0.15) | 7.3 | (0.6) | 8.5 | (0.7) | -1.2 | (1.0) |
| Canada | 12.3 | (0.4) | a | a | a | a | a | a | a | 10.5 | (0.4) | a | a | a | a |
| Czech Republic | 15.0 | (0.9) | 13.2 | (1.2) | 1.8 | (1.5) | **3.6** | **0.31** | (0.12) | 12.2 | (0.8) | 9.1 | (1.1) | **3.1** | (1.4) |
| Denmark | 5.3 | (0.4) | a | a | a | a | a | a | a | 8.0 | (0.5) | a | a | a | a |
| Finland | 8.1 | (0.5) | a | a | a | a | a | a | a | 9.4 | (0.5) | a | a | a | a |
| France | 7.2 | (0.6) | 5.4 | (1.0) | 1.8 | (1.2) | **2.6** | **0.51** | (0.24) | 18.3 | (0.8) | 14.3 | (1.2) | **4.0** | (1.3) |
| Germany | 5.9 | (0.5) | 1.5 | (1.1) | **4.5** | (1.3) | 4.5 | 1.62 | (0.98) | 7.8 | (0.6) | 6.2 | (1.8) | 1.5 | (1.9) |
| Greece | 10.1 | (0.7) | 24.5 | (3.1) | **-14.4** | (3.2) | **-10.9** | **-0.86** | (0.20) | 13.8 | (0.9) | 20.9 | (2.3) | **-7.1** | (2.5) |
| Hungary | 18.0 | (1.2) | 12.1 | (0.9) | **5.9** | (1.6) | **7.8** | **0.62** | (0.13) | 15.5 | (1.1) | 10.7 | (1.0) | **4.8** | (1.4) |
| Iceland | 10.4 | (0.5) | c | c | c | c | c | c | c | 14.5 | (0.6) | c | c | c | c |
| Ireland | 7.0 | (0.5) | 11.2 | (4.6) | -4.3 | (4.6) | -2.7 | -0.38 | (0.51) | 8.9 | (0.6) | 13.3 | (4.3) | -4.4 | (4.4) |
| Italy | a | a | a | a | a | a | a | a | a | 35.5 | (1.2) | 37.0 | (1.1) | -1.4 | (1.6) |
| Japan | 3.4 | (0.3) | 4.7 | (0.6) | **-1.3** | (0.7) | -0.2 | -0.05 | (0.22) | 5.6 | (0.3) | 9.7 | (1.0) | **-4.1** | (1.1) |
| Korea | 9.3 | (0.5) | 10.2 | (1.1) | -0.9 | (1.2) | -0.8 | -0.09 | (0.17) | 16.6 | (0.8) | 17.0 | (1.0) | -0.4 | (1.3) |
| Luxembourg | 14.3 | (0.5) | 10.6 | (1.4) | **3.7** | (1.5) | **4.7** | **0.45** | (0.17) | 15.0 | (0.6) | 12.0 | (1.3) | **3.0** | (1.4) |
| Mexico | 19.5 | (1.1) | 12.8 | (0.5) | **6.7** | (1.3) | **5.6** | **0.44** | (0.08) | 19.7 | (0.9) | 13.2 | (0.6) | **6.6** | (1.1) |
| Netherlands | 6.4 | (0.6) | 10.2 | (0.9) | **-3.8** | (1.1) | -1.5 | -0.22 | (0.17) | 7.5 | (0.6) | 11.5 | (0.9) | **-3.9** | (1.0) |
| New Zealand | 9.1 | (0.8) | a | a | a | a | a | a | a | 9.7 | (0.6) | a | a | a | a |
| Norway | 8.5 | (0.5) | a | a | a | a | a | a | a | 11.9 | (0.6) | a | a | a | a |
| Poland | 14.7 | (0.6) | a | a | a | a | a | a | a | 23.1 | (0.8) | a | a | a | a |
| Portugal | 22.8 | (1.0) | 16.7 | (2.0) | **6.0** | (2.2) | **5.5** | **0.36** | (0.16) | 32.8 | (1.2) | 25.9 | (2.3) | **6.9** | (2.5) |
| Slovak Republic | 41.9 | (2.0) | 15.4 | (1.0) | **26.6** | (2.2) | **31.7** | **1.67** | (0.14) | 23.2 | (1.4) | 11.4 | (0.9) | **11.8** | (1.6) |
| Spain | 8.5 | (0.5) | a | a | a | a | a | a | a | 10.8 | (0.4) | a | a | a | a |
| Sweden | 8.8 | (0.6) | c | c | c | c | c | c | c | 14.3 | (0.6) | c | c | c | c |
| Switzerland | 7.0 | (0.3) | 3.5 | (1.4) | **3.5** | (1.4) | 3.5 | 0.74 | (0.44) | 10.6 | (0.4) | 3.3 | (0.9) | **7.3** | (0.9) |
| Turkey | 7.6 | (0.9) | 7.7 | (0.6) | -0.1 | (1.1) | 1.0 | 0.15 | (0.20) | 9.4 | (0.8) | 9.2 | (0.8) | 0.1 | (1.1) |
| United Kingdom | 11.3 | (0.4) | a | a | a | a | a | a | a | 17.7 | (0.6) | a | a | a | a |
| United States | 22.4 | (1.0) | a | a | a | a | a | a | a | 19.1 | (0.9) | a | a | a | a |
| **OECD average** | **11.5** | **(0.1)** | **10.2** | **(0.4)** | **1.7** | **(0.4)** | **2.3** | **0.29** | **(0.08)** | **14.3** | **(0.1)** | **13.5** | **(0.4)** | **1.2** | **(0.4)** |
| **Partners** | | | | | | | | | | | | | | | |
| Argentina | 10.6 | (0.9) | 12.1 | (5.1) | -1.5 | (5.1) | 0.3 | 0.03 | (0.52) | 12.4 | (1.0) | 18.4 | (5.8) | -6.0 | (5.9) |
| Azerbaijan | 38.9 | (1.3) | 43.8 | (8.7) | -4.9 | (8.7) | -6.4 | -0.26 | (0.37) | 37.1 | (1.3) | 47.9 | (13.1) | -10.8 | (13.1) |
| Brazil | 13.6 | (0.6) | a | a | a | a | a | a | a | 23.5 | (0.8) | a | a | a | a |
| Bulgaria | 20.9 | (1.9) | 23.2 | (2.1) | -2.3 | (2.9) | 0.0 | 0.00 | (0.14) | 17.2 | (1.2) | 21.5 | (2.0) | -4.3 | (2.4) |
| Chile | 8.4 | (0.5) | 2.7 | (0.9) | **5.7** | (1.1) | **6.0** | **1.35** | (0.38) | 16.3 | (0.8) | 13.5 | (3.1) | 2.7 | (3.1) |
| Colombia | 15.8 | (1.2) | 11.2 | (1.9) | **4.6** | (1.9) | 3.9 | 0.35 | (0.20) | 21.1 | (1.2) | 15.0 | (2.8) | **6.2** | (2.9) |
| Croatia | 9.0 | (0.9) | 14.8 | (0.6) | **-5.9** | (1.0) | -0.6 | -0.06 | (0.18) | 7.5 | (1.1) | 12.6 | (0.7) | **-5.0** | (1.3) |
| Estonia | 18.4 | (0.9) | a | a | a | a | a | a | a | 13.7 | (0.7) | a | a | a | a |
| Hong Kong-China | 5.5 | (0.5) | 11.1 | (1.0) | **-5.6** | (1.1) | **-2.6** | **-0.42** | (0.18) | 16.4 | (0.9) | 23.8 | (1.6) | **-7.4** | (1.7) |
| Indonesia | 36.6 | (1.8) | 7.3 | (1.4) | **29.3** | (1.9) | **28.0** | **1.96** | (0.16) | 30.0 | (1.3) | 9.5 | (2.8) | **20.5** | (2.5) |
| Israel | 19.7 | (1.0) | 25.8 | (3.6) | -6.1 | (3.8) | -3.8 | -0.23 | (0.19) | 19.6 | (0.9) | 26.8 | (2.8) | **-7.2** | (2.9) |
| Jordan | 27.4 | (1.0) | a | a | a | a | a | a | a | 31.7 | (0.9) | a | a | a | a |
| Kyrgyzstan | 64.1 | (1.1) | 45.9 | (6.4) | **18.3** | (6.2) | 1.6 | 0.07 | (0.22) | 44.3 | (1.1) | 32.3 | (7.3) | 12.0 | (7.2) |
| Latvia | 35.0 | (1.2) | 25.3 | (4.0) | **9.7** | (4.4) | **7.8** | **0.37** | (0.25) | 25.8 | (1.1) | 19.7 | (3.1) | 6.1 | (3.3) |
| Liechtenstein | 5.8 | (1.2) | a | a | a | a | a | a | a | 7.9 | (1.3) | a | a | a | a |
| Lithuania | 12.0 | (0.6) | c | c | c | c | c | c | c | 17.6 | (0.8) | c | c | c | c |
| Macao-China | 14.2 | (0.6) | 20.1 | (4.6) | -5.9 | (4.6) | -3.7 | -0.27 | (0.31) | 22.7 | (0.7) | 24.2 | (4.2) | -1.5 | (4.2) |
| Montenegro | 17.6 | (1.0) | 28.7 | (0.7) | **-11.1** | (1.3) | **-4.9** | **-0.27** | (0.12) | 11.4 | (0.8) | 20.8 | (0.8) | **-9.4** | (1.1) |
| Qatar | 33.9 | (0.6) | a | a | a | a | a | a | a | 29.1 | (0.5) | a | a | a | a |
| Romania | 22.2 | (1.1) | 42.2 | (3.0) | **-19.9** | (3.3) | **-16.4** | **-0.78** | (0.18) | 20.8 | (1.2) | 36.1 | (2.1) | **-15.3** | (2.4) |
| Russian Federation | 31.5 | (1.0) | 26.1 | (1.8) | **5.4** | (2.2) | **6.1** | **0.30** | (0.12) | 33.0 | (1.3) | 22.3 | (2.1) | **10.6** | (2.3) |
| Serbia | 6.8 | (1.0) | 11.6 | (0.8) | **-4.8** | (1.2) | -2.5 | -0.30 | (0.21) | 9.0 | (1.2) | 13.4 | (0.8) | **-4.4** | (1.5) |
| Slovenia | 7.6 | (0.7) | 10.1 | (0.4) | **-2.5** | (0.9) | 2.2 | 0.28 | (0.15) | 9.1 | (0.8) | 8.7 | (0.5) | 0.4 | (0.9) |
| Chinese Taipei | 11.4 | (0.6) | 19.8 | (1.2) | **-8.4** | (1.4) | **-4.6** | **-0.38** | (0.11) | 18.7 | (0.7) | 30.3 | (1.4) | **-11.5** | (1.6) |
| Thailand | 20.9 | (0.7) | 21.9 | (1.9) | -1.0 | (2.1) | -0.8 | -0.05 | (0.12) | 26.6 | (0.9) | 28.5 | (2.9) | -2.0 | (3.0) |
| Tunisia | 42.6 | (1.3) | a | a | a | a | a | a | a | 32.8 | (1.2) | a | a | a | a |
| Uruguay | 9.1 | (0.6) | 13.2 | (4.5) | -4.1 | (4.6) | -3.9 | -0.41 | (0.44) | 8.9 | (0.6) | 9.6 | (1.8) | -0.7 | (1.9) |

*Note:* Values that are statistically significant at the 5% level (p < 0.05) are indicated in bold.

© OECD 2011 Quality Time for Students: Learning In and Out of School

**Table 3.19** Percentage of students by different types of out-of-school-time lessons,
[Part 5/5] by academic and vocational orientation of schools

| | | Proportion of students participating in out-of-school lessons with school teachers | | | | | | | | | | | | |
| | | Large group lessons | | | | | At least one of these types of out-of-school lessons | | | | | | | |
| | | | | | | | | | | | | | If students' ESCS was equal to the national average ESCS, and schools' average ESCS was equal to the national average of schools' average ESCS | | |
| | | Academic schools | | Vocational schools | | Difference (academic-vocational) | | Academic schools | | Vocational schools | | Difference (academic-vocational) | | Difference (academic-vocational) | Increase in the logit of participating in out-of-school-time lessons by being in an academic school | |
| | | % | S.E. | % | S.E. | Dif. | S.E. | % | S.E. | % | S.E. | Dif. | S.E. | Dif. in % | Logistic regression coefficient | S.E. |
|---|---|---|---|---|---|---|---|---|---|---|---|---|---|---|---|---|
| OECD | Australia | 7.8 | (0.3) | 11.2 | (1.0) | **-3.3** | (1.0) | 13.6 | (0.5) | 18.4 | (1.6) | **-4.8** | (1.6) | **-4.4** | **-0.34** | (0.11) |
| | Austria | 17.5 | (1.9) | 14.9 | (1.1) | 2.6 | (2.3) | 26.1 | (2.2) | 22.2 | (1.3) | 3.9 | (2.6) | **10.0** | **0.53** | (0.17) |
| | Belgium | 4.3 | (0.4) | 8.0 | (0.6) | **-3.6** | (0.8) | 12.8 | (0.7) | 15.9 | (0.9) | **-3.1** | (1.3) | -0.5 | -0.04 | (0.12) |
| | Canada | 11.3 | (0.4) | a | a | a | a | 21.3 | (0.6) | a | a | a | a | a | a | a |
| | Czech Republic | 14.4 | (0.8) | 12.0 | (1.4) | 2.4 | (1.6) | 25.1 | (1.1) | 20.6 | (1.9) | **4.4** | (2.2) | **7.3** | **0.42** | (0.14) |
| | Denmark | 8.0 | (0.5) | a | a | a | a | 14.1 | (0.7) | a | a | a | a | a | a | a |
| | Finland | 12.1 | (0.6) | a | a | a | a | 18.2 | (0.7) | a | a | a | a | a | a | a |
| | France | 10.6 | (0.6) | 7.8 | (1.3) | **2.8** | (1.3) | 24.5 | (0.9) | 18.5 | (1.7) | **6.0** | (1.9) | **6.6** | **0.40** | (0.13) |
| | Germany | 10.4 | (0.6) | 7.0 | (4.8) | 3.4 | (4.9) | 17.8 | (0.7) | 12.7 | (6.6) | 5.1 | (6.7) | 7.1 | 0.60 | (0.63) |
| | Greece | 8.0 | (0.6) | 20.2 | (2.6) | **-12.2** | (2.7) | 19.9 | (1.0) | 35.8 | (3.2) | **-16.0** | (3.3) | **-10.8** | **-0.58** | (0.16) |
| | Hungary | 18.6 | (1.4) | 13.8 | (0.9) | **4.8** | (1.6) | 35.2 | (1.9) | 25.0 | (1.3) | **10.2** | (2.3) | **14.0** | **0.67** | (0.12) |
| | Iceland | 14.1 | (0.6) | c | c | c | c | 27.0 | (0.7) | c | c | c | c | c | c | c |
| | Ireland | 9.8 | (0.6) | 13.7 | (4.6) | -3.9 | (4.8) | 16.9 | (0.8) | 22.3 | (5.7) | -5.4 | (5.9) | -2.4 | -0.17 | (0.36) |
| | Italy | 26.2 | (1.0) | 25.5 | (0.8) | 0.7 | (1.2) | 45.3 | (1.5) | 46.1 | (1.0) | -0.8 | (1.8) | -3.9 | -0.16 | (0.09) |
| | Japan | 29.2 | (1.4) | 34.4 | (2.3) | -5.2 | (2.6) | 33.3 | (1.4) | 40.0 | (2.2) | **-6.7** | (2.6) | -2.5 | -0.11 | (0.12) |
| | Korea | 37.4 | (1.5) | 32.3 | (2.4) | 5.1 | (2.8) | 51.9 | (1.3) | 45.0 | (2.7) | **6.9** | (3.0) | **9.3** | **0.37** | (0.16) |
| | Luxembourg | 10.6 | (0.5) | 4.8 | (0.8) | **5.8** | (0.9) | 26.1 | (0.6) | 20.2 | (1.7) | **5.9** | (1.8) | **7.7** | **0.45** | (0.11) |
| | Mexico | 26.0 | (1.1) | 19.1 | (0.7) | **7.0** | (1.3) | 36.2 | (1.2) | 27.3 | (0.9) | **8.9** | (1.5) | **8.2** | **0.38** | (0.07) |
| | Netherlands | 6.7 | (0.6) | 8.4 | (1.0) | -1.7 | (1.1) | 14.1 | (1.0) | 19.1 | (1.2) | **-5.0** | (1.3) | -0.5 | -0.03 | (0.11) |
| | New Zealand | 9.1 | (0.6) | a | a | a | a | 17.7 | (0.9) | a | a | a | a | a | a | a |
| | Norway | 17.2 | (0.7) | a | a | a | a | 23.8 | (0.8) | a | a | a | a | a | a | a |
| | Poland | 26.7 | (0.9) | a | a | a | a | 41.2 | (1.0) | a | a | a | a | a | a | a |
| | Portugal | 24.9 | (1.2) | 16.9 | (2.1) | **8.0** | (2.3) | 49.1 | (1.4) | 39.8 | (2.9) | **9.3** | (3.1) | **8.8** | **0.36** | (0.14) |
| | Slovak Republic | 34.3 | (1.7) | 10.5 | (1.1) | **23.9** | (1.9) | 51.9 | (2.0) | 21.4 | (1.3) | **30.6** | (2.3) | **37.3** | **1.71** | (0.15) |
| | Spain | 9.8 | (0.5) | a | a | a | a | 18.6 | (0.6) | a | a | a | a | a | a | a |
| | Sweden | 20.9 | (0.7) | c | c | c | c | 26.5 | (0.8) | c | c | c | c | c | c | c |
| | Switzerland | 14.6 | (0.7) | 6.8 | (1.2) | **7.8** | (1.6) | 23.3 | (0.7) | 11.4 | (1.2) | **11.9** | (1.5) | **11.9** | **0.88** | (0.13) |
| | Turkey | 13.3 | (1.0) | 12.0 | (1.0) | 1.3 | (1.4) | 20.3 | (1.3) | 19.0 | (1.2) | 1.3 | (1.8) | **4.2** | **0.27** | (0.12) |
| | United Kingdom | 19.5 | (0.7) | a | a | a | a | 31.8 | (0.9) | a | a | a | a | a | a | a |
| | United States | 18.1 | (1.0) | a | a | a | a | 32.4 | (1.2) | a | a | a | a | a | a | a |
| | **OECD average** | **16.4** | **(0.2)** | **14.7** | **(0.5)** | **2.4** | **(0.5)** | **27.2** | **(0.2)** | **25.3** | **(0.6)** | **3.3** | **(0.7)** | **5.5** | **0.30** | **(0.05)** |
| Partners | Argentina | 11.1 | (1.0) | 19.1 | (9.7) | -8.0 | (9.7) | 19.9 | (1.4) | 31.0 | (9.5) | -11.1 | (9.6) | -6.7 | -0.38 | (0.45) |
| | Azerbaijan | 48.5 | (1.4) | 42.9 | (8.9) | 5.6 | (9.0) | 67.6 | (1.4) | 71.0 | (6.3) | -3.4 | (6.4) | -4.1 | -0.19 | (0.34) |
| | Brazil | 20.4 | (0.7) | a | a | a | a | 34.3 | (0.9) | a | a | a | a | a | a | a |
| | Bulgaria | 21.9 | (1.6) | 23.8 | (1.9) | -1.8 | (2.4) | 34.5 | (2.1) | 35.3 | (2.4) | -0.8 | (3.2) | 2.7 | 0.12 | (0.12) |
| | Chile | 17.9 | (0.8) | 10.5 | (2.9) | **7.4** | (3.1) | 27.5 | (1.1) | 17.6 | (3.5) | **9.8** | (3.7) | **11.4** | **0.69** | (0.26) |
| | Colombia | 19.8 | (1.1) | 17.2 | (2.5) | 2.6 | (2.6) | 30.1 | (1.4) | 25.8 | (2.3) | 4.3 | (2.3) | 3.2 | 0.16 | (0.12) |
| | Croatia | 6.3 | (1.2) | 14.2 | (0.8) | **-7.9** | (1.4) | 16.0 | (1.7) | 24.1 | (0.9) | **-8.1** | (1.9) | -1.3 | -0.08 | (0.19) |
| | Estonia | 18.6 | (0.7) | a | a | a | a | 32.1 | (1.0) | a | a | a | a | a | a | a |
| | Hong Kong-China | 41.7 | (1.4) | 46.0 | (5.0) | -4.4 | (5.3) | 48.0 | (1.4) | 56.1 | (4.4) | -8.0 | (4.7) | 1.8 | 0.07 | (0.20) |
| | Indonesia | 40.1 | (1.7) | 9.8 | (1.4) | **30.3** | (1.9) | 58.8 | (1.9) | 17.9 | (3.5) | **41.0** | (3.4) | **41.4** | **1.90** | (0.17) |
| | Israel | 19.1 | (0.8) | 25.3 | (2.9) | **-6.2** | (3.1) | 33.9 | (1.1) | 41.6 | (3.5) | **-7.7** | (3.8) | -4.3 | -0.19 | (0.14) |
| | Jordan | 40.9 | (0.9) | a | a | a | a | 56.6 | (1.1) | a | a | a | a | a | a | a |
| | Kyrgyzstan | 53.0 | (1.2) | 46.6 | (4.9) | 6.4 | (4.9) | 78.8 | (1.1) | 62.5 | (7.7) | **16.3** | (7.5) | -0.6 | -0.04 | (0.33) |
| | Latvia | 29.2 | (1.2) | 22.9 | (3.9) | 6.3 | (4.0) | 50.8 | (1.3) | 42.8 | (5.3) | 8.0 | (5.5) | 5.4 | 0.22 | (0.24) |
| | Liechtenstein | 10.6 | (1.6) | a | a | a | a | 16.7 | (1.9) | a | a | a | a | a | a | a |
| | Lithuania | 19.3 | (0.8) | c | c | c | c | 34.4 | (1.0) | c | c | c | c | c | c | c |
| | Macao-China | 34.9 | (0.7) | 38.7 | (6.5) | -3.8 | (6.5) | 46.8 | (0.8) | 46.3 | (5.6) | 0.5 | (5.6) | 6.3 | 0.25 | (0.23) |
| | Montenegro | 13.6 | (1.0) | 25.6 | (0.9) | **-12.1** | (1.3) | 26.4 | (1.3) | 38.7 | (0.9) | **-12.3** | (1.5) | -2.4 | -0.11 | (0.09) |
| | Qatar | 29.5 | (0.6) | a | a | a | a | 45.3 | (0.6) | a | a | a | a | a | a | a |
| | Romania | 16.4 | (1.5) | 39.8 | (1.9) | **-23.3** | (2.5) | 34.4 | (1.6) | 58.6 | (2.2) | **-24.2** | (2.7) | **-16.3** | **-0.67** | (0.16) |
| | Russian Federation | 37.3 | (1.4) | 32.8 | (2.8) | 4.4 | (2.8) | 59.3 | (1.4) | 46.7 | (2.6) | **12.6** | (2.8) | **13.7** | **0.55** | (0.12) |
| | Serbia | 8.5 | (1.2) | 16.9 | (1.0) | **-8.4** | (1.6) | 18.4 | (1.7) | 25.6 | (1.1) | **-7.2** | (2.1) | 0.0 | 0.00 | (0.15) |
| | Slovenia | 9.6 | (0.7) | 13.7 | (0.6) | **-4.2** | (0.9) | 19.3 | (1.0) | 21.0 | (0.7) | -1.8 | (1.3) | 6.8 | **0.43** | (0.11) |
| | Chinese Taipei | 31.4 | (0.8) | 41.8 | (1.0) | **-10.3** | (1.2) | 40.6 | (1.0) | 53.1 | (1.4) | **-12.4** | (1.7) | -5.2 | -0.21 | (0.09) |
| | Thailand | 39.8 | (1.3) | 34.8 | (3.0) | 4.9 | (3.3) | 48.6 | (1.2) | 40.4 | (3.2) | **8.2** | (3.5) | **8.1** | **0.33** | (0.14) |
| | Tunisia | 30.5 | (0.9) | a | a | a | a | 54.0 | (1.2) | a | a | a | a | a | a | a |
| | Uruguay | 8.3 | (0.6) | 11.4 | (1.9) | -3.0 | (2.0) | 16.0 | (0.8) | 25.8 | (4.9) | **-9.8** | (5.0) | -8.5 | -0.54 | (0.29) |

*Note:* Values that are statistically significant at the 5% level (p < 0.05) are indicated in bold.

### Table 3.20 Percentage of students by different types of out-of-school-time lessons, by school location
[Part 1/5]

| | Proportion of students participating in out-of-school-time lessons | | | | | |
| | Rural (fewer than 100 000 people) | | City (over 100 000 people) | | Difference (rural-city) | |
| | % | S.E. | % | S.E. | Dif. | S.E. |
|---|---|---|---|---|---|---|
| Australia | 27.4 | (1.1) | 33.7 | (0.8) | **-6.2** | (1.4) |
| Austria | 35.7 | (1.4) | 37.4 | (2.2) | -1.7 | (2.6) |
| Belgium | 29.0 | (0.8) | 34.5 | (1.4) | **-5.4** | (1.7) |
| Canada | 33.5 | (0.9) | 38.8 | (1.1) | **-5.3** | (1.3) |
| Czech Republic | 37.4 | (1.1) | 36.3 | (2.0) | 1.1 | (2.3) |
| Denmark | 20.0 | (0.8) | 21.2 | (3.1) | -1.2 | (3.3) |
| Finland | 23.1 | (0.7) | 24.7 | (1.6) | -1.6 | (1.7) |
| France | a | a | 41.6 | (0.9) | a | a |
| Germany | 36.0 | (1.0) | 40.0 | (1.9) | -4.0 | (2.4) |
| Greece | 77.1 | (1.4) | 75.9 | (2.0) | 1.2 | (2.7) |
| Hungary | 53.4 | (1.5) | 55.5 | (2.0) | -2.1 | (2.7) |
| Iceland | 39.3 | (1.0) | 43.7 | (1.2) | **-4.5** | (1.5) |
| Ireland | 37.8 | (1.2) | 39.5 | (1.6) | -1.6 | (2.1) |
| Italy | 65.4 | (0.8) | 69.2 | (1.3) | **-3.8** | (1.6) |
| Japan | 43.1 | (1.9) | 47.0 | (1.7) | -3.8 | (2.4) |
| Korea | 70.6 | (2.7) | 80.7 | (1.0) | **-10.1** | (3.0) |
| Luxembourg | 43.5 | (0.7) | 46.9 | (2.6) | -3.3 | (2.7) |
| Mexico | 52.0 | (1.3) | 43.4 | (1.1) | **8.7** | (1.8) |
| Netherlands | 22.6 | (1.0) | 20.6 | (1.2) | 2.0 | (1.5) |
| New Zealand | 29.7 | (1.6) | 37.2 | (1.0) | **-7.5** | (2.0) |
| Norway | 27.1 | (0.9) | 30.1 | (1.6) | -3.1 | (1.8) |
| Poland | 55.1 | (1.1) | 59.5 | (2.1) | -4.3 | (2.4) |
| Portugal | 68.0 | (1.2) | 71.3 | (2.7) | -3.3 | (3.3) |
| Slovak Republic | 56.7 | (1.3) | 49.4 | (4.7) | 7.3 | (5.2) |
| Spain | 54.7 | (1.0) | 52.5 | (1.2) | 2.2 | (1.6) |
| Sweden | 31.7 | (1.0) | 33.1 | (1.7) | -1.4 | (2.0) |
| Switzerland | 39.3 | (0.8) | 43.2 | (1.5) | **-3.9** | (1.7) |
| Turkey | 35.9 | (1.7) | 37.9 | (1.7) | -2.0 | (2.5) |
| United Kingdom | 43.8 | (1.0) | 48.9 | (1.8) | **-5.1** | (1.9) |
| United States | 37.9 | (1.1) | 50.5 | (2.7) | **-12.6** | (2.9) |
| **OECD average** | 42.3 | (0.2) | 44.8 | (0.4) | **-2.6** | (0.4) |
| Argentina | 49.6 | (1.7) | 47.2 | (1.7) | 2.4 | (2.3) |
| Azerbaijan | 78.6 | (1.4) | 82.6 | (1.5) | -4.1 | (2.1) |
| Brazil | 49.1 | (1.1) | 47.4 | (1.4) | 1.7 | (1.7) |
| Bulgaria | 54.9 | (1.9) | 52.7 | (1.6) | 2.3 | (2.5) |
| Chile | 37.6 | (2.0) | 39.0 | (1.4) | -1.4 | (2.5) |
| Colombia | 54.0 | (1.4) | 47.6 | (1.5) | **6.4** | (2.1) |
| Croatia | 44.7 | (1.3) | 46.8 | (1.2) | -2.1 | (1.7) |
| Estonia | 44.5 | (1.2) | 50.0 | (1.6) | **-5.5** | (2.1) |
| Hong Kong-China | a | a | 75.4 | (0.9) | a | a |
| Indonesia | 68.7 | (1.9) | 51.7 | (5.1) | **17.0** | (5.1) |
| Israel | 63.8 | (1.5) | 64.8 | (1.7) | -1.0 | (2.4) |
| Jordan | 73.5 | (1.1) | 71.2 | (1.5) | 2.3 | (1.8) |
| Kyrgyzstan | 87.1 | (1.1) | 75.2 | (2.7) | **11.9** | (3.0) |
| Latvia | 72.8 | (1.4) | 68.7 | (1.4) | **4.1** | (2.0) |
| Liechtenstein | 28.2 | (2.4) | a | a | a | a |
| Lithuania | 48.0 | (1.3) | 50.1 | (1.7) | -2.1 | (2.1) |
| Macao-China | 65.3 | (1.5) | 61.7 | (0.9) | 3.6 | (1.9) |
| Montenegro | 60.9 | (0.8) | 64.4 | (1.4) | **-3.5** | (1.6) |
| Qatar | 63.9 | (0.7) | 61.5 | (1.3) | 2.4 | (1.5) |
| Romania | 60.6 | (1.5) | 53.1 | (2.7) | 7.5 | (3.4) |
| Russian Federation | 73.5 | (1.9) | 63.5 | (1.4) | **10.0** | (2.1) |
| Serbia | 52.4 | (1.4) | 56.1 | (1.6) | -3.8 | (2.2) |
| Slovenia | 41.2 | (0.8) | 42.4 | (1.2) | -1.3 | (1.5) |
| Chinese Taipei | 73.5 | (1.2) | 75.8 | (0.8) | -2.3 | (1.7) |
| Thailand | 62.1 | (1.5) | 67.5 | (2.5) | -5.4 | (3.2) |
| Tunisia | 69.6 | (1.2) | 74.9 | (2.8) | -5.3 | (3.2) |
| Uruguay | 43.9 | (1.6) | 46.0 | (1.3) | -2.1 | (2.2) |

*Note:* Values that are statistically significant at the 5% level (p < 0.05) are indicated in bold.

© OECD 2011 Quality Time for Students: Learning In and Out of School

**Table 3.20** [Part 2/5] **Percentage of students by different types of out-of-school-time lessons, by school location**

| | | Proportion of students participating in out-of-school lessons with non-school teachers | | | | | | | | | | | | |
| | | One-to-one lessons | | | | | | | | | Small group lessons | | | | |
| | | | | | | | | If students' ESCS was equal to the national average ESCS, and schools' average ESCS was equal to the national average of schools' average ESCS | | | | | | | |
| | | Rural (fewer than 100 000 people) | | City (over 100 000 people) | | Difference (rural-city) | | Difference (rural-city) | Increase in the logit of participating in out-of-school-time lessons by being in rural area | | Rural (fewer than 100 000 people) | | City (over 100 000 people) | | Difference (rural-city) | |
| | | % | S.E. | % | S.E. | Dif. | S.E. | Dif. in % | Logistic regression coefficient | S.E. | % | S.E. | % | S.E. | Dif. | S.E. |
|---|---|---|---|---|---|---|---|---|---|---|---|---|---|---|---|---|
| OECD | Australia | 12.8 | (0.7) | 19.0 | (0.6) | **-6.2** | (1.0) | -3.8 | **-0.29** | (0.08) | 7.2 | (0.6) | 8.7 | (0.5) | -1.4 | (0.7) |
| | Austria | 15.3 | (0.9) | 19.6 | (1.5) | **-4.2** | (1.7) | -2.0 | -0.15 | (0.14) | 7.1 | (0.6) | 9.1 | (1.2) | -2.0 | (1.3) |
| | Belgium | 16.9 | (0.8) | 20.5 | (1.5) | **-3.5** | (1.8) | -3.6 | **-0.25** | (0.09) | 7.0 | (0.4) | 8.4 | (1.0) | -1.4 | (1.1) |
| | Canada | 14.2 | (0.6) | 19.3 | (0.8) | **-5.1** | (1.0) | -3.5 | **-0.26** | (0.07) | 7.3 | (0.4) | 9.9 | (0.6) | **-2.7** | (0.7) |
| | Czech Republic | 14.4 | (0.7) | 21.2 | (2.1) | **-6.8** | (2.3) | -3.5 | -0.26 | (0.16) | 7.9 | (0.7) | 8.2 | (1.3) | -0.4 | (1.2) |
| | Denmark | 4.9 | (0.4) | 8.3 | (2.0) | -3.4 | (2.1) | -3.1 | -0.52 | (0.31) | 4.5 | (0.4) | 6.3 | (1.8) | -1.8 | (1.8) |
| | Finland | 5.1 | (0.4) | 6.4 | (0.8) | -1.4 | (0.9) | -1.1 | -0.22 | (0.17) | 2.2 | (0.2) | 3.2 | (0.8) | -1.0 | (0.8) |
| | France | a | a | 22.3 | (0.9) | a | a | a | a | a | a | a | 9.2 | (0.5) | a | a |
| | Germany | 20.9 | (0.9) | 24.0 | (1.6) | -3.1 | (2.1) | -2.8 | -0.16 | (0.12) | 6.8 | (0.4) | 9.3 | (1.0) | **-2.5** | (1.1) |
| | Greece | 45.4 | (1.5) | 43.9 | (2.4) | 1.4 | (3.1) | **9.1** | **0.37** | (0.10) | 48.9 | (1.8) | 40.7 | (2.0) | **8.2** | (2.9) |
| | Hungary | 31.1 | (1.4) | 34.6 | (1.9) | -3.5 | (2.5) | **4.4** | **0.21** | (0.09) | 10.9 | (0.9) | 10.9 | (1.0) | -0.0 | (1.4) |
| | Iceland | 12.3 | (0.6) | 20.2 | (1.1) | **-8.0** | (1.1) | **-4.6** | **-0.37** | (0.09) | 6.2 | (0.5) | 8.2 | (0.8) | **-2.0** | (0.9) |
| | Ireland | 21.7 | (0.8) | 20.9 | (1.3) | 0.7 | (1.5) | 3.3 | **0.21** | (0.08) | 9.3 | (0.6) | 10.9 | (1.1) | -1.6 | (1.2) |
| | Italy | 35.6 | (0.7) | 41.6 | (1.1) | **-6.0** | (1.4) | 0.4 | 0.02 | (0.06) | 14.5 | (0.5) | 13.1 | (1.2) | 1.4 | (1.4) |
| | Japan | 7.0 | (0.7) | 10.8 | (0.9) | **-3.8** | (1.1) | -1.3 | -0.17 | (0.13) | 6.7 | (0.9) | 9.4 | (0.8) | **-2.7** | (1.2) |
| | Korea | 23.4 | (2.2) | 32.7 | (0.9) | **-9.3** | (2.3) | -0.5 | -0.03 | (0.15) | 21.1 | (1.5) | 33.1 | (1.1) | **-12.0** | (1.9) |
| | Luxembourg | 23.2 | (0.7) | 22.4 | (2.4) | 0.7 | (2.5) | 1.0 | 0.05 | (0.14) | 7.0 | (0.5) | 7.8 | (1.4) | -0.8 | (1.3) |
| | Mexico | 17.0 | (1.1) | 18.8 | (0.8) | -1.8 | (1.4) | **2.5** | **0.17** | (0.09) | 17.0 | (1.0) | 15.4 | (0.9) | 1.6 | (1.4) |
| | Netherlands | 6.8 | (0.5) | 9.1 | (1.0) | -2.2 | (1.2) | -1.6 | -0.24 | (0.14) | 3.6 | (0.5) | 3.5 | (0.7) | 0.1 | (0.8) |
| | New Zealand | 11.8 | (0.7) | 21.8 | (1.0) | **-10.0** | (1.2) | **-7.5** | **-0.56** | (0.09) | 7.4 | (0.7) | 12.0 | (0.6) | **-4.6** | (0.9) |
| | Norway | 4.9 | (0.4) | 9.2 | (1.2) | **-4.3** | (1.2) | **-4.1** | **-0.67** | (0.18) | 4.6 | (0.4) | 7.0 | (1.1) | -2.4 | (1.2) |
| | Poland | 17.2 | (0.9) | 26.0 | (1.6) | **-8.7** | (1.9) | 2.1 | 0.15 | (0.12) | 9.6 | (0.7) | 13.9 | (1.5) | **-4.3** | (1.6) |
| | Portugal | 24.6 | (0.9) | 33.6 | (3.6) | **-9.0** | (3.8) | 0.2 | 0.01 | (0.15) | 14.8 | (0.8) | 14.1 | (1.9) | 0.7 | (2.2) |
| | Slovak Republic | 25.2 | (1.1) | 27.6 | (3.5) | -2.4 | (3.7) | 4.1 | 0.23 | (0.18) | 11.5 | (0.6) | 9.2 | (1.0) | 2.3 | (1.2) |
| | Spain | 29.3 | (0.9) | 27.6 | (1.2) | 1.8 | (1.4) | **4.6** | **0.23** | (0.07) | 29.6 | (0.9) | 20.8 | (1.0) | **8.8** | (1.3) |
| | Sweden | 6.6 | (0.5) | 10.0 | (0.9) | **-3.4** | (1.0) | -3.2 | **-0.43** | (0.13) | 5.4 | (0.4) | 7.1 | (0.9) | -1.7 | (1.0) |
| | Switzerland | 18.3 | (0.6) | 29.0 | (1.4) | **-10.7** | (1.6) | **-7.0** | **-0.41** | (0.09) | 6.2 | (0.5) | 6.0 | (0.6) | 0.2 | (0.8) |
| | Turkey | 12.4 | (1.0) | 14.5 | (1.0) | -2.1 | (1.4) | 0.9 | 0.09 | (0.09) | 10.4 | (0.7) | 11.5 | (0.8) | -1.0 | (1.0) |
| | United Kingdom | 16.6 | (0.6) | 19.3 | (1.1) | **-2.7** | (1.2) | **-4.2** | **-0.29** | (0.08) | 6.4 | (0.5) | 9.6 | (1.1) | **-3.2** | (1.2) |
| | United States | 14.7 | (0.7) | 22.1 | (1.8) | **-7.4** | (2.0) | **-7.2** | **-0.49** | (0.11) | 10.0 | (0.6) | 17.0 | (2.0) | **-7.0** | (2.1) |
| | **OECD average** | 17.6 | (0.2) | 21.9 | (0.3) | **-4.3** | (0.4) | **-1.9** | **-0.13** | (0.02) | 10.7 | (0.1) | 11.8 | (0.2) | **-1.1** | (0.3) |
| Partners | Argentina | 30.4 | (1.7) | 32.4 | (2.0) | -2.0 | (2.6) | 3.0 | 0.14 | (0.10) | 19.5 | (1.3) | 18.7 | (1.4) | 0.8 | (1.9) |
| | Azerbaijan | 28.7 | (1.4) | 37.6 | (1.4) | **-8.9** | (1.9) | 0.2 | 0.01 | (0.09) | 41.1 | (1.3) | 39.7 | (1.9) | 1.4 | (2.5) |
| | Brazil | 17.8 | (0.7) | 22.2 | (1.0) | **-4.3** | (1.3) | -0.5 | -0.03 | (0.08) | 17.5 | (0.7) | 18.4 | (0.9) | -0.9 | (1.1) |
| | Bulgaria | 24.4 | (1.1) | 31.4 | (1.4) | **-7.0** | (1.8) | -2.4 | -0.12 | (0.10) | 18.0 | (1.4) | 16.9 | (1.0) | 1.1 | (1.7) |
| | Chile | 11.1 | (1.4) | 14.8 | (0.8) | **-3.7** | (1.6) | 0.7 | 0.07 | (0.14) | 9.8 | (0.9) | 9.3 | (0.7) | 0.6 | (1.2) |
| | Colombia | 24.3 | (0.9) | 26.6 | (1.3) | -2.3 | (1.7) | 2.7 | 0.14 | (0.10) | 18.5 | (1.3) | 17.1 | (1.1) | 1.3 | (1.8) |
| | Croatia | 25.6 | (1.2) | 32.0 | (1.2) | **-6.4** | (1.7) | -1.9 | -0.09 | (0.10) | 10.1 | (0.7) | 9.1 | (0.8) | 1.1 | (1.0) |
| | Estonia | 13.3 | (0.8) | 27.4 | (1.5) | **-14.2** | (1.8) | **-13.6** | **-0.88** | (0.15) | 7.2 | (0.5) | 10.6 | (1.1) | **-3.4** | (1.2) |
| | Hong Kong-China | a | a | 24.1 | (1.3) | a | a | a | a | a | a | a | 17.8 | (0.8) | a | a |
| | Indonesia | 16.5 | (0.7) | 21.3 | (3.9) | -4.8 | (4.0) | 0.1 | 0.01 | (0.23) | 19.4 | (0.9) | 19.2 | (1.3) | 0.2 | (1.4) |
| | Israel | 39.4 | (1.7) | 44.8 | (1.8) | **-5.4** | (2.7) | -4.7 | -0.19 | (0.11) | 21.0 | (1.2) | 18.8 | (1.4) | 2.2 | (2.0) |
| | Jordan | 32.6 | (1.0) | 37.0 | (1.3) | **-4.5** | (1.7) | **-3.7** | **-0.16** | (0.08) | 27.2 | (1.2) | 22.3 | (1.1) | **4.9** | (1.7) |
| | Kyrgyzstan | 26.1 | (0.8) | 27.6 | (2.5) | -1.5 | (2.6) | 1.9 | 0.10 | (0.13) | 27.8 | (1.0) | 23.1 | (1.9) | **4.7** | (2.2) |
| | Latvia | 29.5 | (1.4) | 37.8 | (1.8) | **-8.3** | (2.1) | -1.7 | -0.08 | (0.09) | 13.6 | (0.7) | 15.2 | (1.0) | -1.7 | (1.3) |
| | Liechtenstein | 14.7 | (1.9) | a | a | a | a | a | a | a | 2.6 | (1.0) | a | a | a | a |
| | Lithuania | 13.4 | (0.9) | 24.8 | (1.4) | **-11.4** | (1.6) | -2.7 | -0.20 | (0.14) | 6.4 | (0.5) | 7.9 | (0.9) | -1.5 | (1.0) |
| | Macao-China | 23.4 | (1.5) | 21.5 | (0.8) | 1.9 | (1.8) | 2.5 | 0.14 | (0.10) | 22.6 | (1.5) | 20.2 | (0.8) | 2.4 | (1.6) |
| | Montenegro | 34.3 | (0.9) | 43.5 | (1.7) | **-9.2** | (1.9) | **-7.4** | **-0.31** | (0.09) | 20.8 | (0.7) | 20.6 | (1.3) | 0.2 | (1.5) |
| | Qatar | 36.5 | (0.7) | 35.3 | (1.3) | 1.2 | (1.5) | 2.0 | 0.09 | (0.07) | 25.6 | (0.7) | 24.1 | (1.3) | 1.5 | (1.5) |
| | Romania | 26.5 | (1.4) | 29.3 | (2.5) | -2.8 | (2.9) | -0.8 | -0.04 | (0.17) | 21.4 | (1.3) | 18.2 | (2.1) | 3.2 | (2.5) |
| | Russian Federation | 21.2 | (1.2) | 22.5 | (1.3) | -1.4 | (1.9) | **3.3** | **0.20** | (0.09) | 13.0 | (1.1) | 11.9 | (0.8) | 1.0 | (1.1) |
| | Serbia | 34.5 | (1.5) | 44.6 | (1.7) | **-10.1** | (2.3) | -4.7 | **-0.20** | (0.10) | 14.0 | (0.8) | 11.2 | (0.7) | **2.7** | (1.1) |
| | Slovenia | 24.7 | (0.7) | 30.2 | (1.3) | **-5.4** | (1.5) | **-4.4** | **-0.22** | (0.07) | 6.8 | (0.5) | 6.1 | (0.6) | 0.7 | (0.8) |
| | Chinese Taipei | 22.9 | (0.9) | 24.2 | (0.8) | -1.3 | (1.4) | -0.3 | -0.02 | (0.08) | 24.8 | (1.3) | 23.0 | (0.7) | 1.8 | (1.7) |
| | Thailand | 19.9 | (0.8) | 22.3 | (1.4) | -2.4 | (1.6) | 0.0 | 0.00 | (0.10) | 24.1 | (0.9) | 23.9 | (1.7) | 0.2 | (1.8) |
| | Tunisia | 27.6 | (1.2) | 46.0 | (3.7) | **-18.4** | (4.0) | **-8.3** | **-0.38** | (0.15) | 26.4 | (1.0) | 38.4 | (2.9) | **-12.0** | (3.2) |
| | Uruguay | 27.8 | (1.3) | 31.2 | (1.3) | -3.4 | (2.0) | 1.4 | 0.07 | (0.10) | 20.4 | (1.1) | 22.2 | (1.1) | -1.8 | (1.7) |

*Note:* Values that are statistically significant at the 5% level (p < 0.05) are indicated in bold.

**Table 3.20** [Part 3/5] **Percentage of students by different types of out-of-school-time lessons, by school location**

| | Proportion of students participating in out-of-school lessons with non-school teachers | | | | | | | | | | |
| | Large group lessons | | | | | | At least one of these types of out-of-school lessons | | | | | | If students' ESCS was equal to the national average ESCS, and schools' average ESCS was equal to the national average of schools' average ESCS | | |
| | Rural (fewer than 100 000 people) | | City (over 100 000 people) | | Difference (rural-city) | | Rural (fewer than 100 000 people) | | City (over 100 000 people) | | Difference (rural-city) | | Difference (rural-city) | Increase in the logit of participating in out-of-school-time lessons by being in rural area | |
| | % | S.E. | % | S.E. | Dif. | S.E. | % | S.E. | % | S.E. | Dif. | S.E. | Dif. in % | Logistic regression coefficient | S.E. |
|---|---|---|---|---|---|---|---|---|---|---|---|---|---|---|---|
| Australia | 6.0 | (0.4) | 8.1 | (0.4) | **-2.1** | (0.5) | 17.9 | (0.8) | 26.5 | (0.8) | **-8.6** | (1.2) | **-7.0** | **-0.41** | (0.08) |
| Austria | 6.4 | (0.5) | 5.6 | (1.2) | 0.8 | (1.4) | 22.5 | (0.9) | 27.7 | (1.9) | **-5.2** | (2.1) | -4.2 | -0.23 | (0.13) |
| Belgium | 4.1 | (0.4) | 4.9 | (0.9) | -0.8 | (1.0) | 21.5 | (0.8) | 25.4 | (1.4) | **-4.0** | (1.8) | -4.2 | **-0.24** | (0.09) |
| Canada | 6.5 | (0.4) | 7.9 | (0.6) | **-1.4** | (0.6) | 19.9 | (0.7) | 26.7 | (1.1) | **-6.9** | (1.3) | -5.2 | **-0.30** | (0.07) |
| Czech Republic | 5.7 | (0.6) | 5.5 | (1.1) | 0.2 | (1.3) | 20.4 | (0.9) | 26.7 | (2.0) | **-6.3** | (2.3) | -3.0 | -0.18 | (0.14) |
| Denmark | 3.9 | (0.5) | 2.1 | (0.7) | **1.7** | (0.9) | 10.0 | (0.7) | 12.4 | (2.8) | -2.4 | (2.9) | -2.5 | -0.25 | (0.27) |
| Finland | 3.6 | (0.3) | 4.0 | (0.5) | -0.4 | (0.6) | 8.0 | (0.4) | 10.7 | (1.2) | **-2.7** | (1.3) | -2.3 | -0.28 | (0.14) |
| France | a | a | 4.9 | (0.4) | a | a | a | a | 26.4 | (1.0) | a | a | a | a | a |
| Germany | 3.2 | (0.5) | 5.9 | (0.9) | **-2.7** | (1.0) | 26.4 | (0.8) | 30.8 | (1.6) | **-4.4** | (1.9) | -3.9 | **-0.19** | (0.10) |
| Greece | 19.7 | (1.3) | 16.7 | (1.3) | 3.0 | (1.8) | 71.3 | (1.6) | 70.4 | (2.3) | 0.9 | (3.1) | 9.4 | 0.46 | (0.12) |
| Hungary | 9.5 | (0.8) | 7.8 | (0.9) | 1.7 | (1.3) | 37.5 | (1.5) | 39.5 | (1.8) | -1.9 | (2.6) | 4.0 | 0.17 | (0.10) |
| Iceland | 5.6 | (0.5) | 4.4 | (0.6) | 1.2 | (0.7) | 18.1 | (0.7) | 24.4 | (1.2) | **-6.3** | (1.2) | -3.3 | **-0.21** | (0.08) |
| Ireland | 5.5 | (0.4) | 10.4 | (1.2) | **-4.9** | (1.3) | 28.1 | (0.9) | 31.7 | (1.7) | -3.6 | (1.9) | -1.3 | -0.06 | (0.09) |
| Italy | 9.5 | (0.5) | 7.6 | (0.8) | **1.9** | (1.0) | 44.7 | (0.7) | 49.2 | (1.4) | **-4.5** | (1.6) | -0.3 | -0.01 | (0.07) |
| Japan | 7.1 | (0.8) | 8.8 | (0.8) | -1.7 | (1.0) | 16.2 | (1.3) | 22.4 | (1.4) | **-6.2** | (1.9) | -1.2 | -0.08 | (0.12) |
| Korea | 12.4 | (1.4) | 29.5 | (0.9) | **-17.1** | (1.6) | 37.3 | (2.1) | 61.5 | (1.2) | **-24.2** | (2.3) | -5.3 | -0.22 | (0.16) |
| Luxembourg | 5.3 | (0.3) | 7.7 | (1.2) | **-2.4** | (1.2) | 28.1 | (0.7) | 26.9 | (2.5) | 1.1 | (2.6) | 0.9 | 0.05 | (0.13) |
| Mexico | 18.5 | (1.1) | 13.8 | (0.7) | **4.7** | (1.4) | 30.8 | (1.3) | 30.1 | (1.1) | 0.7 | (1.8) | **3.8** | **0.18** | (0.09) |
| Netherlands | 3.5 | (0.4) | 4.2 | (0.8) | -0.8 | (0.9) | 10.3 | (0.7) | 13.6 | (1.1) | **-3.3** | (1.3) | -3.2 | **-0.31** | (0.12) |
| New Zealand | 5.8 | (0.6) | 7.9 | (0.6) | **-2.1** | (0.9) | 17.2 | (0.9) | 29.6 | (0.9) | **-12.4** | (1.4) | **-11.6** | **-0.66** | (0.09) |
| Norway | 5.0 | (0.4) | 5.6 | (0.8) | -0.7 | (1.0) | 9.2 | (0.6) | 15.1 | (1.2) | **-5.9** | (1.3) | **-5.7** | **-0.55** | (0.12) |
| Poland | 9.2 | (0.5) | 12.5 | (1.1) | **-3.3** | (1.2) | 25.7 | (1.0) | 39.4 | (2.0) | **-13.7** | (2.3) | -0.9 | -0.04 | (0.11) |
| Portugal | 8.3 | (0.7) | 8.0 | (0.9) | 0.3 | (1.2) | 33.2 | (1.0) | 42.4 | (3.9) | **-9.2** | (4.3) | 1.0 | 0.04 | (0.15) |
| Slovak Republic | 7.5 | (0.6) | 6.1 | (1.2) | 1.4 | (1.3) | 29.2 | (1.1) | 32.5 | (4.1) | -3.3 | (4.3) | 2.8 | 0.14 | (0.19) |
| Spain | 11.4 | (0.7) | 9.0 | (0.6) | **2.4** | (0.9) | 44.8 | (1.0) | 41.4 | (1.3) | **3.4** | (1.5) | **7.2** | **0.29** | (0.07) |
| Sweden | 6.4 | (0.4) | 9.4 | (1.0) | **-3.0** | (1.0) | 12.0 | (0.6) | 17.3 | (1.3) | **-5.3** | (1.4) | **-5.3** | **-0.43** | (0.11) |
| Switzerland | 4.8 | (0.3) | 4.0 | (0.7) | 0.8 | (0.8) | 23.2 | (0.7) | 32.7 | (1.5) | **-9.5** | (1.8) | **-7.2** | **-0.37** | (0.09) |
| Turkey | 13.6 | (1.4) | 16.4 | (1.5) | -2.9 | (2.1) | 24.0 | (1.5) | 29.1 | (1.8) | **-5.1** | (2.5) | 2.0 | 0.11 | (0.10) |
| United Kingdom | 6.2 | (0.4) | 9.6 | (1.0) | **-3.5** | (1.1) | 22.5 | (0.7) | 27.5 | (1.5) | **-5.0** | (1.5) | **-6.0** | **-0.32** | (0.08) |
| United States | 9.2 | (0.6) | 15.8 | (2.0) | **-6.6** | (2.1) | 21.2 | (0.8) | 32.5 | (2.5) | **-11.3** | (2.6) | **-11.0** | **-0.57** | (0.11) |
| **OECD average** | 7.7 | (0.1) | 8.8 | (0.2) | **-1.2** | (0.2) | 25.2 | (0.2) | 30.7 | (0.3) | **-5.7** | (0.4) | **-2.8** | **-0.15** | (0.02) |
| Argentina | 13.6 | (1.0) | 12.1 | (1.2) | 1.6 | (1.6) | 40.0 | (1.6) | 39.8 | (1.8) | 0.2 | (2.4) | 4.1 | 0.17 | (0.09) |
| Azerbaijan | 40.1 | (1.4) | 35.0 | (1.8) | **5.1** | (2.5) | 61.9 | (1.3) | 65.4 | (1.8) | -3.5 | (2.3) | 0.2 | 0.01 | (0.13) |
| Brazil | 15.3 | (0.7) | 15.7 | (0.9) | -0.3 | (1.1) | 32.1 | (0.8) | 34.3 | (1.2) | -2.2 | (1.5) | 0.8 | 0.03 | (0.07) |
| Bulgaria | 19.0 | (1.4) | 12.6 | (1.4) | **6.4** | (1.9) | 36.0 | (1.5) | 41.5 | (1.5) | **-5.6** | (2.2) | -2.8 | -0.12 | (0.11) |
| Chile | 9.5 | (1.0) | 7.6 | (0.6) | 1.9 | (1.3) | 20.5 | (1.5) | 22.2 | (1.0) | -1.7 | (1.8) | 1.7 | 0.10 | (0.11) |
| Colombia | 17.4 | (0.9) | 15.2 | (1.1) | 2.2 | (1.4) | 36.1 | (1.0) | 37.4 | (1.4) | -1.3 | (1.8) | 2.8 | 0.12 | (0.10) |
| Croatia | 8.3 | (0.6) | 6.9 | (0.7) | 1.4 | (0.9) | 31.9 | (1.2) | 37.7 | (1.1) | **-5.8** | (1.6) | -2.0 | -0.09 | (0.09) |
| Estonia | 6.6 | (0.6) | 9.3 | (0.8) | **-2.7** | (1.0) | 19.1 | (0.9) | 34.4 | (1.8) | **-15.3** | (2.2) | **-14.7** | **-0.77** | (0.15) |
| Hong Kong-China | a | a | 30.1 | (1.1) | a | a | a | a | 52.1 | (1.2) | a | a | a | a | a |
| Indonesia | 17.3 | (0.9) | 17.7 | (2.4) | -0.4 | (2.4) | 32.9 | (1.0) | 38.7 | (3.3) | -5.9 | (3.5) | -0.5 | -0.02 | (0.14) |
| Israel | 16.4 | (1.0) | 14.3 | (1.4) | 2.1 | (1.8) | 50.7 | (1.8) | 54.6 | (2.1) | -3.8 | (2.8) | -2.9 | -0.12 | (0.11) |
| Jordan | 24.7 | (1.2) | 17.8 | (1.1) | **6.9** | (1.7) | 48.3 | (1.2) | 47.6 | (1.3) | 0.7 | (1.9) | -0.5 | -0.02 | (0.09) |
| Kyrgyzstan | 32.8 | (1.1) | 25.4 | (2.6) | **7.4** | (2.8) | 49.1 | (1.1) | 44.9 | (2.5) | 4.2 | (2.7) | 4.2 | 0.17 | (0.11) |
| Latvia | 18.0 | (1.0) | 15.2 | (1.2) | 2.9 | (1.5) | 39.7 | (1.3) | 47.6 | (1.9) | **-7.9** | (2.1) | -1.1 | -0.05 | (0.08) |
| Liechtenstein | 2.3 | (0.8) | a | a | a | a | 16.9 | (2.2) | a | a | a | a | a | a | a |
| Lithuania | 6.9 | (0.6) | 6.2 | (0.8) | 0.7 | (1.0) | 19.5 | (1.0) | 29.7 | (1.5) | **-10.2** | (1.8) | -2.2 | -0.13 | (0.12) |
| Macao-China | 21.9 | (1.5) | 18.9 | (0.8) | 2.9 | (1.7) | 40.3 | (1.7) | 38.9 | (0.9) | 1.4 | (2.0) | 2.1 | 0.09 | (0.08) |
| Montenegro | 17.1 | (0.8) | 18.1 | (1.3) | -0.9 | (1.5) | 44.6 | (0.9) | 53.0 | (1.6) | **-8.4** | (1.9) | **-7.3** | **-0.29** | (0.08) |
| Qatar | 22.8 | (0.7) | 21.6 | (1.2) | 1.2 | (1.4) | 48.7 | (0.8) | 47.4 | (1.4) | 1.2 | (1.5) | -0.6 | -0.02 | (0.06) |
| Romania | 17.6 | (1.1) | 13.3 | (2.2) | 4.3 | (2.6) | 38.7 | (1.5) | 38.3 | (2.3) | 0.4 | (2.9) | -0.9 | -0.04 | (0.15) |
| Russian Federation | 13.1 | (0.8) | 12.2 | (0.8) | 0.9 | (1.1) | 30.7 | (1.6) | 32.3 | (1.6) | -1.5 | (2.3) | 2.7 | 0.12 | (0.08) |
| Serbia | 9.9 | (0.7) | 7.0 | (0.8) | **2.8** | (1.1) | 40.2 | (1.5) | 48.1 | (1.6) | **-7.9** | (2.3) | -3.1 | -0.12 | (0.09) |
| Slovenia | 5.5 | (0.4) | 4.2 | (0.6) | 1.3 | (0.7) | 29.8 | (0.7) | 33.7 | (1.3) | **-3.9** | (1.6) | **-3.4** | **-0.16** | (0.07) |
| Chinese Taipei | 33.7 | (1.3) | 43.9 | (1.2) | **-10.2** | (1.9) | 50.5 | (1.6) | 60.3 | (1.1) | **-9.7** | (2.2) | -2.9 | -0.12 | (0.08) |
| Thailand | 29.5 | (1.0) | 36.5 | (3.0) | **-6.9** | (3.1) | 42.0 | (1.3) | 50.8 | (3.0) | **-8.8** | (3.3) | 0.4 | 0.02 | (0.11) |
| Tunisia | 19.5 | (1.0) | 18.2 | (2.2) | 1.3 | (2.5) | 42.6 | (1.2) | 56.1 | (3.7) | **-13.5** | (3.9) | -9.3 | **-0.37** | (0.16) |
| Uruguay | 11.7 | (0.9) | 12.4 | (0.8) | -0.7 | (1.2) | 36.0 | (1.5) | 40.0 | (1.3) | -4.0 | (2.1) | 0.7 | 0.03 | (0.08) |

*Note:* Values that are statistically significant at the 5% level (p < 0.05) are indicated in bold.

© OECD 2011 Quality Time for Students: Learning In and Out of School

## Table 3.20 Percentage of students by different types of out-of-school-time lessons, by school location
[Part 4/5]

| | Proportion of students participating in out-of-school lessons with school teachers | | | | | | | | | | | | | |
| --- | --- | --- | --- | --- | --- | --- | --- | --- | --- | --- | --- | --- | --- |
| | One-to-one lessons | | | | | | | | Small group lessons | | | | |
| | | | | | | | If students' ESCS was equal to the national average ESCS, and schools' average ESCS was equal to the national average of schools' average ESCS | | | | | | |
| | Rural (fewer than 100 000 people) | | City (over 100 000 people) | | Difference (rural-city) | | Difference (rural-city) | Increase in the logit of participating in out-of-school-time lessons by being in rural area | | Rural (fewer than 100 000 people) | | City (over 100 000 people) | | Difference (rural-city) | |
| | % | S.E. | % | S.E. | Dif. | S.E. | Dif. in % | Logistic regression coefficient | S.E. | % | S.E. | % | S.E. | Dif. | S.E. |
| **OECD** | | | | | | | | | | | | | | | |
| Australia | 7.9 | (0.6) | 6.0 | (0.4) | **1.9** | (0.7) | **1.4** | **0.23** | (0.11) | 8.4 | (0.7) | 6.5 | (0.4) | **1.9** | (0.8) |
| Austria | 6.0 | (0.6) | 4.2 | (0.8) | 1.8 | (1.0) | 1.2 | 0.29 | (0.17) | 14.0 | (1.1) | 11.2 | (1.4) | 2.8 | (1.8) |
| Belgium | 6.8 | (0.4) | 8.2 | (1.1) | -1.4 | (1.1) | -1.3 | -0.19 | (0.15) | 7.3 | (0.5) | 9.9 | (1.3) | -2.5 | (1.4) |
| Canada | 12.5 | (0.5) | 12.2 | (0.7) | 0.4 | (0.9) | -0.1 | -0.01 | (0.09) | 10.8 | (0.5) | 9.9 | (0.7) | 0.9 | (0.8) |
| Czech Republic | 15.1 | (0.8) | 10.1 | (1.4) | **5.1** | (1.6) | 0.8 | 0.07 | (0.20) | 11.9 | (0.8) | 7.4 | (0.9) | **4.5** | (1.1) |
| Denmark | 4.9 | (0.4) | 6.4 | (1.6) | -1.5 | (1.7) | -1.9 | -0.39 | (0.28) | 7.7 | (0.5) | 8.3 | (1.5) | -0.6 | (1.7) |
| Finland | 8.7 | (0.7) | 5.9 | (0.8) | **2.8** | (1.1) | 2.3 | 0.34 | (0.18) | 9.7 | (0.6) | 8.6 | (0.8) | 1.1 | (1.0) |
| France | a | a | 7.0 | (0.6) | a | a | 0.0 | 0.00 | (0.00) | a | a | 17.9 | (0.7) | a | a |
| Germany | 5.1 | (0.4) | 7.3 | (1.4) | -2.2 | (1.5) | -2.1 | -0.38 | (0.22) | 7.1 | (0.7) | 9.6 | (1.4) | -2.5 | (1.7) |
| Greece | 14.3 | (1.1) | 8.3 | (0.9) | **5.9** | (1.6) | **4.3** | **0.44** | (0.16) | 15.8 | (1.1) | 13.2 | (1.2) | 2.6 | (1.6) |
| Hungary | 14.2 | (0.9) | 15.5 | (1.4) | -1.3 | (1.7) | -2.1 | -0.16 | (0.13) | 12.9 | (1.1) | 12.7 | (1.0) | 0.2 | (1.5) |
| Iceland | 10.8 | (0.6) | 10.2 | (0.8) | 0.6 | (1.0) | 0.2 | 0.02 | (0.12) | 15.1 | (0.7) | 13.3 | (1.0) | 1.8 | (1.1) |
| Ireland | 7.1 | (0.7) | 6.8 | (0.7) | 0.3 | (1.0) | -0.7 | -0.11 | (0.15) | 8.8 | (0.7) | 9.5 | (1.1) | -0.6 | (1.4) |
| Italy | a | a | a | a | a | a | a | a | a | 35.8 | (0.9) | 37.3 | (1.4) | -1.5 | (1.6) |
| Japan | 3.7 | (0.6) | 3.8 | (0.4) | -0.1 | (0.7) | -0.7 | -0.20 | (0.20) | 6.7 | (0.7) | 6.6 | (0.5) | 0.2 | (0.9) |
| Korea | 8.4 | (1.1) | 9.7 | (0.5) | -1.3 | (1.3) | -2.0 | -0.25 | (0.18) | 16.3 | (1.4) | 16.8 | (0.7) | -0.5 | (1.6) |
| Luxembourg | 13.5 | (0.5) | 17.1 | (2.0) | -3.6 | (2.1) | **-4.2** | **-0.33** | (0.16) | 14.2 | (0.5) | 18.3 | (1.8) | **-4.1** | (1.9) |
| Mexico | 22.6 | (1.4) | 12.1 | (0.6) | **10.5** | (1.6) | 1.9 | 0.14 | (0.09) | 23.2 | (1.0) | 12.1 | (0.6) | **11.2** | (1.2) |
| Netherlands | 7.9 | (0.6) | 6.4 | (1.0) | 1.5 | (1.1) | 1.1 | 0.17 | (0.17) | 9.5 | (0.7) | 6.4 | (0.9) | **3.0** | (1.1) |
| New Zealand | 10.4 | (1.4) | 8.0 | (0.8) | 2.4 | (1.7) | 1.5 | 0.19 | (0.26) | 9.7 | (1.0) | 9.7 | (0.9) | -0.0 | (1.4) |
| Norway | 8.3 | (0.5) | 10.3 | (1.1) | -2.0 | (1.3) | **-3.0** | **-0.35** | (0.15) | 12.0 | (0.6) | 11.6 | (1.5) | 0.4 | (1.7) |
| Poland | 15.3 | (0.7) | 12.8 | (1.2) | 2.5 | (1.4) | 0.8 | 0.06 | (0.14) | 24.0 | (0.9) | 20.4 | (1.5) | **3.6** | (1.7) |
| Portugal | 22.1 | (1.1) | 21.5 | (1.7) | 0.6 | (1.9) | **-4.7** | **-0.27** | (0.11) | 32.3 | (1.3) | 30.3 | (2.2) | 2.0 | (2.5) |
| Slovak Republic | 32.2 | (1.4) | 19.5 | (3.1) | **12.8** | (3.6) | **9.6** | **0.49** | (0.25) | 19.1 | (1.1) | 11.4 | (1.9) | **7.7** | (2.1) |
| Spain | 8.3 | (0.5) | 9.0 | (0.8) | -0.7 | (0.9) | -1.4 | -0.19 | (0.12) | 10.9 | (0.5) | 10.7 | (0.8) | 0.2 | (1.0) |
| Sweden | 8.7 | (0.7) | 9.0 | (1.0) | -0.3 | (1.2) | -0.2 | -0.02 | (0.14) | 14.5 | (0.6) | 13.6 | (1.5) | 0.9 | (1.7) |
| Switzerland | 6.7 | (0.4) | 6.3 | (0.8) | 0.4 | (0.9) | -0.4 | -0.07 | (0.15) | 10.3 | (0.4) | 9.2 | (1.0) | 1.1 | (1.1) |
| Turkey | 8.4 | (1.0) | 6.8 | (0.6) | 1.5 | (1.2) | 0.2 | 0.03 | (0.14) | 11.4 | (0.9) | 7.2 | (0.6) | **4.2** | (1.1) |
| United Kingdom | 9.9 | (0.4) | 13.5 | (1.0) | **-3.6** | (1.0) | **-2.4** | **-0.24** | (0.09) | 17.3 | (0.9) | 18.1 | (1.2) | -0.8 | (1.6) |
| United States | 19.7 | (1.0) | 27.4 | (2.4) | **-7.7** | (2.7) | **-7.5** | **-0.42** | (0.12) | 16.9 | (1.0) | 22.9 | (1.9) | **-6.0** | (2.1) |
| **OECD average** | 11.4 | (0.2) | 10.4 | (0.2) | **0.9** | (0.3) | -0.3 | -0.04 | (0.03) | 14.3 | (0.2) | 13.4 | (0.2) | **1.1** | (0.3) |
| **Partners** | | | | | | | | | | | | | | | |
| Argentina | 11.7 | (1.4) | 9.0 | (1.1) | 2.7 | (1.9) | 1.1 | 0.12 | (0.21) | 15.3 | (1.4) | 8.4 | (1.3) | **6.9** | (2.0) |
| Azerbaijan | 39.0 | (1.6) | 38.8 | (1.6) | 0.2 | (2.3) | 3.8 | 0.16 | (0.11) | 36.9 | (1.5) | 38.4 | (1.9) | -1.5 | (2.4) |
| Brazil | 14.0 | (0.8) | 12.7 | (0.8) | 1.3 | (1.1) | 0.7 | 0.06 | (0.10) | 25.5 | (1.0) | 20.9 | (1.1) | **4.6** | (1.4) |
| Bulgaria | 26.7 | (1.9) | 13.5 | (1.6) | **13.2** | (2.4) | 4.4 | 0.28 | (0.15) | 22.7 | (1.5) | 12.8 | (1.2) | **9.9** | (1.9) |
| Chile | 9.6 | (0.8) | 7.6 | (0.6) | 2.0 | (1.1) | 0.7 | 0.09 | (0.14) | 18.0 | (1.2) | 15.1 | (1.1) | 2.9 | (1.6) |
| Colombia | 19.2 | (1.8) | 10.1 | (1.1) | **9.1** | (2.1) | **5.8** | **0.48** | (0.24) | 25.1 | (1.8) | 14.5 | (1.6) | **10.6** | (2.4) |
| Croatia | 15.2 | (0.7) | 9.7 | (0.8) | **5.5** | (1.1) | 2.4 | 0.22 | (0.12) | 12.4 | (0.7) | 9.0 | (0.8) | **3.4** | (1.0) |
| Estonia | 18.6 | (1.0) | 18.1 | (1.9) | 0.5 | (2.2) | **-5.1** | **-0.33** | (0.17) | 15.0 | (0.9) | 10.6 | (1.1) | **4.4** | (1.5) |
| Hong Kong-China | a | a | 5.9 | (0.4) | a | a | a | a | a | a | a | 16.9 | (0.7) | a | a |
| Indonesia | 35.5 | (1.9) | 13.3 | (3.0) | **22.2** | (3.1) | **13.8** | **0.74** | (0.27) | 29.4 | (1.4) | 13.3 | (3.5) | **16.1** | (3.3) |
| Israel | 22.6 | (1.4) | 18.3 | (1.9) | 4.4 | (2.4) | 3.7 | 0.24 | (0.16) | 22.5 | (1.3) | 19.1 | (1.6) | 3.4 | (2.1) |
| Jordan | 29.8 | (1.5) | 23.8 | (1.5) | **6.0** | (2.3) | 2.4 | 0.12 | (0.13) | 34.6 | (1.3) | 27.2 | (1.3) | **7.4** | (1.9) |
| Kyrgyzstan | 67.5 | (1.1) | 43.5 | (3.8) | **24.0** | (4.1) | **13.0** | **0.55** | (0.20) | 46.5 | (1.3) | 30.4 | (2.4) | **16.1** | (2.7) |
| Latvia | 39.2 | (1.5) | 25.4 | (1.7) | **13.8** | (2.2) | **7.1** | **0.33** | (0.13) | 28.6 | (1.3) | 19.4 | (1.7) | **9.1** | (2.0) |
| Liechtenstein | 5.9 | (1.3) | a | a | a | a | a | a | a | 7.8 | (1.3) | a | a | a | a |
| Lithuania | 11.9 | (0.7) | 12.0 | (1.1) | -0.1 | (1.2) | -1.3 | -0.13 | (0.15) | 19.7 | (1.0) | 14.3 | (1.3) | **5.4** | (1.6) |
| Macao-China | 14.5 | (1.1) | 14.2 | (0.7) | 0.3 | (1.3) | -0.4 | -0.03 | (0.11) | 27.4 | (1.3) | 21.8 | (0.8) | **5.7** | (1.5) |
| Montenegro | 27.1 | (0.8) | 21.4 | (1.5) | **5.7** | (1.7) | 3.7 | 0.21 | (0.08) | 18.9 | (0.7) | 15.6 | (1.1) | **3.3** | (1.4) |
| Qatar | 33.6 | (0.7) | 32.6 | (1.2) | 1.0 | (1.4) | **-4.4** | **-0.20** | (0.07) | 28.5 | (0.6) | 29.6 | (1.3) | -1.1 | (1.5) |
| Romania | 29.8 | (1.3) | 24.1 | (2.5) | 5.7 | (2.9) | 0.1 | 0.00 | (0.17) | 27.5 | (1.6) | 21.3 | (1.7) | **6.1** | (2.5) |
| Russian Federation | 33.5 | (1.3) | 26.8 | (1.1) | **6.8** | (1.7) | **4.7** | **0.22** | (0.08) | 35.4 | (1.5) | 25.9 | (1.4) | **9.6** | (2.0) |
| Serbia | 11.9 | (1.0) | 7.9 | (0.9) | **4.0** | (1.4) | 2.3 | 0.27 | (0.17) | 14.2 | (0.9) | 9.3 | (0.9) | **4.9** | (1.3) |
| Slovenia | 9.8 | (0.6) | 7.2 | (0.6) | **2.6** | (0.9) | 1.3 | 0.17 | (0.12) | 9.6 | (0.6) | 7.7 | (0.7) | **2.0** | (0.9) |
| Chinese Taipei | 17.1 | (1.2) | 13.0 | (0.9) | **4.2** | (1.4) | 0.8 | 0.04 | (0.13) | 27.7 | (1.5) | 20.2 | (1.0) | **7.5** | (2.1) |
| Thailand | 22.5 | (0.9) | 16.9 | (1.5) | **5.5** | (1.9) | 2.0 | 0.13 | (0.12) | 28.5 | (1.2) | 22.2 | (1.6) | **6.3** | (2.1) |
| Tunisia | 43.7 | (1.5) | 37.4 | (3.9) | 6.3 | (4.3) | 5.8 | 0.24 | (0.21) | 34.5 | (1.3) | 24.3 | (2.7) | **10.2** | (3.0) |
| Uruguay | 10.2 | (1.2) | 8.7 | (0.7) | 1.5 | (1.5) | 1.3 | 0.15 | (0.19) | 10.1 | (0.8) | 7.5 | (0.8) | **2.6** | (1.1) |

*Note*: Values that are statistically significant at the 5% level (p < 0.05) are indicated in bold.

## Table 3.20 Percentage of students by different types of out-of-school-time lessons, by school location
[Part 5/5]

| | Proportion of students participating in out-of-school lessons with school teachers | | | | | | | | | | | | |
|---|---|---|---|---|---|---|---|---|---|---|---|---|---|
| | Large group lessons | | | | | | At least one of these types of out-of-school lessons | | | | | | |
| | | | | | | | | | | | | | If students' ESCS was equal to the national average ESCS, and schools' average ESCS was equal to the national average of schools' average ESCS | |
| | Rural (fewer than 100 000 people) | | City (over 100 000 people) | | Difference (rural-city) | | Rural (fewer than 100 000 people) | | City (over 100 000 people) | | Difference (rural-city) | | Difference (rural-city) | Increase in the logit of participating in out-of-school-time lessons by being in rural area |
| | % | S.E. | % | S.E. | Dif. | S.E. | % | S.E. | % | S.E. | Dif. | S.E. | Dif. in % | Logistic regression coefficient | S.E. |
| **OECD** Australia | 9.6 | (0.6) | 7.3 | (0.4) | **2.3** | (0.7) | 15.9 | (1.0) | 12.9 | (0.6) | **3.1** | (1.1) | 2.3 | 0.19 | (0.08) |
| Austria | 16.6 | (1.2) | 13.6 | (1.4) | 3.1 | (2.0) | 24.9 | (1.5) | 20.0 | (1.9) | **4.9** | (2.5) | 4.0 | 0.23 | (0.13) |
| Belgium | 5.9 | (0.3) | 6.4 | (0.9) | -0.5 | (1.0) | 13.6 | (0.5) | 16.3 | (1.6) | -2.6 | (1.7) | -2.4 | -0.19 | (0.09) |
| Canada | 11.7 | (0.6) | 10.6 | (0.6) | 1.1 | (0.7) | 21.8 | (0.7) | 20.6 | (0.9) | 1.1 | (1.0) | 0.2 | 0.01 | (0.07) |
| Czech Republic | 14.5 | (0.9) | 7.9 | (1.5) | **6.6** | (1.7) | 24.9 | (1.2) | 16.0 | (1.8) | **8.9** | (2.1) | 4.0 | 0.24 | (0.14) |
| Denmark | 8.2 | (0.6) | 5.2 | (1.2) | **3.0** | (1.4) | 13.8 | (0.8) | 12.5 | (2.1) | 1.3 | (2.4) | 1.1 | 0.10 | (0.27) |
| Finland | 12.0 | (0.6) | 12.8 | (1.1) | -0.8 | (1.3) | 18.3 | (0.8) | 17.9 | (1.3) | 0.4 | (1.5) | -1.2 | -0.08 | (0.14) |
| France | a | a | 10.4 | (0.5) | a | a | a | a | 23.9 | (0.8) | a | a | a | a | a |
| Germany | 9.9 | (0.8) | 11.4 | (1.5) | -1.5 | (1.8) | 16.6 | (0.9) | 19.5 | (2.1) | -2.8 | (2.5) | -2.8 | -0.19 | (0.10) |
| Greece | 10.8 | (1.0) | 7.8 | (1.2) | **3.0** | (1.4) | 23.7 | (1.4) | 19.6 | (1.5) | **4.2** | (2.1) | 1.1 | 0.06 | (0.12) |
| Hungary | 16.0 | (1.0) | 15.6 | (1.2) | 0.4 | (1.6) | 29.3 | (1.5) | 29.6 | (1.8) | -0.3 | (2.4) | -1.4 | -0.07 | (0.10) |
| Iceland | 13.2 | (0.7) | 16.0 | (1.0) | **-2.8** | (1.1) | 27.4 | (0.9) | 26.6 | (1.1) | 0.9 | (1.3) | 1.9 | 0.10 | (0.08) |
| Ireland | 10.1 | (0.7) | 9.4 | (1.3) | 0.7 | (1.6) | 17.4 | (1.0) | 15.7 | (1.5) | 1.7 | (1.9) | -0.7 | -0.05 | (0.09) |
| Italy | 25.6 | (0.8) | 26.4 | (1.2) | -0.8 | (1.5) | 45.0 | (0.9) | 47.5 | (1.7) | -2.5 | (1.8) | -1.8 | -0.07 | (0.07) |
| Japan | 31.1 | (2.0) | 30.1 | (1.5) | 1.0 | (2.4) | 35.5 | (1.9) | 34.6 | (1.6) | 0.9 | (2.5) | -2.0 | -0.09 | (0.12) |
| Korea | 42.0 | (3.3) | 35.2 | (1.5) | 6.9 | (3.6) | 54.3 | (2.9) | 49.7 | (1.3) | 4.6 | (3.2) | 6.8 | 0.27 | **(0.16)** |
| Luxembourg | 9.8 | (0.5) | 11.0 | (1.3) | -1.2 | (1.3) | 24.9 | (0.6) | 29.6 | (2.1) | **-4.6** | (2.1) | **-5.6** | **-0.28** | **(0.13)** |
| Mexico | 31.4 | (1.2) | 16.2 | (0.6) | **15.2** | (1.4) | 41.8 | (1.4) | 24.8 | (0.9) | **17.0** | (1.7) | 3.1 | 0.14 | **(0.09)** |
| Netherlands | 7.7 | (0.6) | 5.6 | (0.7) | **2.2** | (0.9) | 16.8 | (1.0) | 11.8 | (1.2) | **5.0** | (1.5) | 4.6 | 0.38 | (0.12) |
| New Zealand | 9.1 | (0.8) | 9.1 | (0.7) | -0.0 | (1.1) | 19.3 | (1.7) | 16.4 | (1.1) | 2.9 | (2.1) | 1.5 | 0.11 | (0.09) |
| Norway | 17.7 | (0.8) | 15.1 | (1.5) | 2.5 | (1.7) | 24.1 | (0.9) | 22.6 | (1.5) | 1.5 | (1.8) | -0.3 | -0.02 | (0.12) |
| Poland | 28.0 | (1.1) | 22.5 | (1.4) | **5.5** | (1.8) | 42.9 | (1.2) | 35.9 | (1.9) | **7.0** | (2.2) | 0.6 | 0.02 | (0.11) |
| Portugal | 25.2 | (1.3) | 19.0 | (2.0) | **6.3** | (2.5) | 48.7 | (1.5) | 44.6 | (3.0) | 4.0 | (3.5) | -6.6 | -0.26 | (0.15) |
| Slovak Republic | 25.1 | (1.3) | 15.9 | (3.2) | **9.2** | (3.7) | 40.4 | (1.5) | 26.9 | (4.0) | **13.5** | (4.5) | 10.2 | 0.45 | (0.19) |
| Spain | 9.9 | (0.6) | 9.6 | (0.8) | 0.3 | (1.0) | 18.4 | (0.8) | 19.0 | (1.1) | -0.6 | (1.4) | -2.5 | -0.16 | (0.07) |
| Sweden | 21.4 | (0.8) | 19.3 | (1.0) | 2.0 | (1.2) | 27.1 | (0.9) | 24.6 | (1.5) | 2.6 | (1.7) | 0.8 | 0.04 | (0.11) |
| Switzerland | 14.9 | (0.7) | 9.2 | (1.2) | **5.7** | (1.5) | 23.2 | (0.8) | 18.1 | (1.6) | **5.2** | (2.0) | 2.1 | 0.13 | (0.09) |
| Turkey | 14.9 | (1.2) | 10.7 | (0.9) | **4.1** | (1.5) | 22.6 | (1.5) | 16.9 | (1.2) | **5.7** | (2.0) | 3.3 | 0.21 | (0.10) |
| United Kingdom | 18.4 | (0.9) | 21.4 | (1.5) | -3.0 | (1.9) | 30.5 | (1.2) | 33.5 | (1.7) | -3.0 | (2.2) | -0.2 | -0.01 | **(0.08)** |
| United States | 16.0 | (0.9) | 21.8 | (2.4) | -5.8 | (2.6) | 29.1 | (1.2) | 38.3 | (2.7) | **-9.2** | (3.0) | **-8.9** | **-0.40** | (0.11) |
| **OECD average** | 16.8 | (0.2) | 14.4 | (0.2) | **2.2** | (0.3) | 27.3 | (0.2) | 24.9 | (0.3) | **2.4** | (0.4) | 0.5 | 0.03 | (0.02) |
| **Partners** Argentina | 13.4 | (1.4) | 8.0 | (1.2) | **5.4** | (1.9) | 23.2 | (1.9) | 15.5 | (1.8) | **7.7** | (2.7) | 3.8 | 0.25 | **(0.09)** |
| Azerbaijan | 49.2 | (1.6) | 45.5 | (2.8) | 3.7 | (3.3) | 67.5 | (1.7) | 67.9 | (2.1) | -0.4 | (2.8) | 1.0 | 0.04 | **(0.13)** |
| Brazil | 21.5 | (1.0) | 18.7 | (1.1) | 2.8 | (1.5) | 36.6 | (1.1) | 30.9 | (1.2) | **5.7** | (1.5) | **4.1** | **0.19** | (0.07) |
| Bulgaria | 26.8 | (1.6) | 15.5 | (1.5) | **11.3** | (2.2) | 40.2 | (2.2) | 25.3 | (1.6) | **14.9** | (2.7) | **7.0** | **0.31** | (0.11) |
| Chile | 18.9 | (1.2) | 17.0 | (1.0) | 1.9 | (1.7) | 29.1 | (1.7) | 26.2 | (1.4) | 2.9 | (2.3) | -1.1 | -0.06 | (0.11) |
| Colombia | 24.3 | (1.4) | 13.7 | (1.4) | **10.5** | (1.9) | 36.1 | (1.7) | 21.8 | (1.7) | **14.4** | (2.4) | 6.7 | 0.33 | (0.10) |
| Croatia | 13.3 | (0.8) | 9.7 | (1.0) | **3.6** | (1.3) | 24.4 | (1.1) | 17.3 | (1.3) | **7.1** | (1.7) | 3.0 | 0.18 | (0.09) |
| Estonia | 20.6 | (0.9) | 13.6 | (1.2) | **7.0** | (1.5) | 33.9 | (1.3) | 27.6 | (2.1) | **6.3** | (2.6) | -1.6 | -0.07 | **(0.15)** |
| Hong Kong-China | a | a | 42.0 | (1.3) | a | a | a | a | 48.6 | (1.3) | a | a | a | a | a |
| Indonesia | 38.8 | (1.8) | 16.4 | (3.2) | **22.4** | (3.4) | 57.4 | (2.1) | 25.4 | (5.2) | **32.0** | (5.2) | 23.5 | 0.97 | (0.14) |
| Israel | 21.4 | (1.1) | 19.0 | (1.5) | 2.4 | (1.9) | 37.9 | (1.6) | 32.0 | (1.8) | **5.9** | (2.5) | 5.3 | 0.23 | (0.11) |
| Jordan | 43.2 | (1.2) | 37.4 | (1.5) | **5.8** | (1.9) | 59.2 | (1.4) | 52.7 | (1.9) | **6.4** | (2.3) | 2.5 | 0.10 | **(0.09)** |
| Kyrgyzstan | 55.9 | (1.4) | 37.0 | (3.2) | **18.9** | (3.7) | 82.0 | (1.2) | 60.2 | (4.1) | **21.8** | (4.4) | 9.2 | 0.52 | (0.11) |
| Latvia | 33.0 | (1.6) | 21.0 | (1.4) | **12.0** | (2.1) | 55.4 | (1.7) | 40.5 | (1.4) | **14.9** | (2.4) | 7.2 | 0.29 | (0.08) |
| Liechtenstein | 10.1 | (1.6) | a | a | a | a | 16.6 | (2.0) | a | a | a | a | a | a | a |
| Lithuania | 20.9 | (1.0) | 17.0 | (1.4) | **4.0** | (1.8) | 37.3 | (1.2) | 29.8 | (1.8) | **7.6** | (2.1) | 3.9 | 0.17 | **(0.12)** |
| Macao-China | 35.8 | (1.6) | 34.8 | (0.8) | 1.0 | (1.7) | 49.4 | (1.5) | 46.2 | (0.9) | 3.2 | (1.8) | 1.6 | 0.07 | **(0.08)** |
| Montenegro | 23.8 | (0.7) | 17.7 | (1.3) | **6.1** | (1.4) | 37.3 | (0.9) | 29.7 | (1.3) | **7.6** | (1.5) | 5.2 | 0.24 | (0.08) |
| Qatar | 29.2 | (0.7) | 28.6 | (1.3) | 0.6 | (1.5) | 44.9 | (0.7) | 44.4 | (1.4) | 0.5 | (1.6) | -4.8 | -0.19 | **(0.06)** |
| Romania | 27.0 | (1.6) | 16.8 | (2.6) | **10.2** | (3.2) | 46.1 | (1.8) | 34.1 | (2.7) | **12.0** | (3.5) | 3.0 | 0.12 | (0.15) |
| Russian Federation | 42.4 | (1.8) | 28.1 | (1.4) | **14.3** | (2.4) | 63.1 | (1.7) | 49.7 | (1.5) | **13.4** | (2.3) | 11.5 | 0.47 | **(0.08)** |
| Serbia | 15.8 | (1.0) | 12.9 | (1.2) | 2.9 | (1.5) | 26.2 | (1.2) | 19.7 | (1.3) | **6.5** | (1.8) | 2.7 | 0.15 | **(0.09)** |
| Slovenia | 12.8 | (0.6) | 9.7 | (0.7) | **3.2** | (0.9) | 22.3 | (0.7) | 16.6 | (1.0) | **5.7** | (1.2) | 4.0 | **0.26** | **(0.07)** |
| Chinese Taipei | 40.9 | (1.4) | 32.0 | (1.1) | **8.9** | (2.0) | 52.4 | (1.6) | 41.2 | (1.3) | **11.2** | (2.3) | 4.9 | 0.20 | (0.08) |
| Thailand | 39.9 | (1.5) | 36.5 | (1.7) | 3.4 | (2.4) | 48.4 | (1.5) | 44.4 | (1.7) | 4.0 | (2.5) | **7.2** | **0.29** | (0.11) |
| Tunisia | 31.7 | (1.1) | 24.6 | (2.8) | **7.1** | (3.2) | 55.2 | (1.4) | 48.7 | (3.8) | 6.5 | (4.2) | 1.5 | 0.06 | (0.16) |
| Uruguay | 8.5 | (0.8) | 9.0 | (0.7) | -0.6 | (1.0) | 17.9 | (1.4) | 16.2 | (1.0) | 1.7 | (1.8) | 0.1 | 0.01 | (0.08) |

*Note:* Values that are statistically significant at the 5% level (p < 0.05) are indicated in bold.

© OECD 2011 Quality Time for Students: Learning In and Out of School

## Table 4.1a Performance in science, mathematics and reading and learning time in science, in mathematics and on the language of instruction
[Part 1/2]

| | | | | | | | Mean learning hours per week | | | | | | | | | | | |
| | Performance | | | | | | Science | | | | | | Mathematics | | | | | |
| | Science | | Mathematics | | Reading | | Regular school lessons | | Out-of-school-time lessons | | Individual study | | Regular school lessons | | Out-of-school-time lessons | | Individual study | |
| | Mean | S.E. | Mean | S.E. | Mean | S.E. | Mean | S.E. | Mean | S.E. | Mean | S.E. | Mean | S.E. | Mean | S.E. | Mean | S.E. |
|---|---|---|---|---|---|---|---|---|---|---|---|---|---|---|---|---|---|---|
| Australia | 527 | (2.3) | 520 | (2.2) | 513 | (2.1) | 3.24 | (0.0) | 0.36 | (0.0) | 1.17 | (0.0) | 4.10 | (0.0) | 0.75 | (0.0) | 1.79 | (0.0) |
| Austria | 511 | (3.9) | 505 | (3.7) | 490 | (4.1) | 2.47 | (0.1) | 0.21 | (0.0) | 1.28 | (0.0) | 3.22 | (0.0) | 0.51 | (0.0) | 2.13 | (0.0) |
| Belgium | 510 | (2.5) | 520 | (3.0) | 501 | (3.0) | 2.63 | (0.0) | 0.32 | (0.0) | 1.25 | (0.0) | 3.58 | (0.0) | 0.55 | (0.0) | 1.79 | (0.0) |
| Canada | 534 | (2.0) | 527 | (2.0) | 527 | (2.4) | 4.00 | (0.0) | 0.55 | (0.0) | 1.55 | (0.0) | 4.50 | (0.0) | 0.94 | (0.0) | 1.97 | (0.0) |
| Czech Republic | 513 | (3.5) | 510 | (3.6) | 483 | (4.2) | 2.93 | (0.1) | 0.54 | (0.0) | 1.00 | (0.0) | 4.00 | (0.0) | 0.76 | (0.0) | 1.32 | (0.0) |
| Denmark | 496 | (3.1) | 513 | (2.6) | 494 | (3.2) | 3.21 | (0.0) | 0.77 | (0.0) | 1.09 | (0.0) | 4.44 | (0.0) | 1.36 | (0.0) | 1.74 | (0.0) |
| Finland | 563 | (2.0) | 548 | (2.3) | 547 | (2.1) | 3.13 | (0.0) | 0.32 | (0.0) | 1.07 | (0.0) | 3.45 | (0.0) | 0.37 | (0.0) | 1.20 | (0.0) |
| France | 495 | (3.4) | 496 | (3.2) | 488 | (4.1) | 2.85 | (0.1) | 0.55 | (0.0) | 1.31 | (0.0) | 3.84 | (0.0) | 0.93 | (0.0) | 1.74 | (0.0) |
| Germany | 516 | (3.8) | 504 | (3.9) | 495 | (4.4) | 3.06 | (0.0) | 0.51 | (0.0) | 1.71 | (0.0) | 3.88 | (0.0) | 0.82 | (0.0) | 2.27 | (0.0) |
| Greece | 473 | (3.2) | 459 | (3.0) | 460 | (4.0) | 3.18 | (0.1) | 1.99 | (0.0) | 1.85 | (0.0) | 3.45 | (0.0) | 2.23 | (0.1) | 2.01 | (0.0) |
| Hungary | 504 | (2.7) | 491 | (2.9) | 482 | (3.3) | 2.51 | (0.0) | 1.00 | (0.0) | 1.60 | (0.0) | 3.29 | (0.0) | 1.29 | (0.0) | 1.84 | (0.0) |
| Iceland | 491 | (1.6) | 506 | (1.8) | 484 | (1.9) | 2.97 | (0.0) | 0.29 | (0.0) | 1.16 | (0.0) | 4.74 | (0.0) | 0.72 | (0.0) | 1.71 | (0.0) |
| Ireland | 508 | (3.2) | 501 | (2.8) | 517 | (3.5) | 2.54 | (0.0) | 0.32 | (0.0) | 1.20 | (0.0) | 3.66 | (0.0) | 0.72 | (0.0) | 1.76 | (0.0) |
| Italy | 475 | (2.0) | 462 | (2.3) | 469 | (2.4) | 2.91 | (0.1) | 0.58 | (0.0) | 2.10 | (0.0) | 3.74 | (0.0) | 0.89 | (0.0) | 2.48 | (0.0) |
| Japan | 531 | (3.4) | 523 | (3.3) | 498 | (3.6) | 2.70 | (0.1) | 0.26 | (0.0) | 0.69 | (0.0) | 4.24 | (0.1) | 0.71 | (0.0) | 1.48 | (0.1) |
| Korea | 522 | (3.4) | 547 | (3.8) | 556 | (3.8) | 3.58 | (0.1) | 1.02 | (0.0) | 1.22 | (0.1) | 4.70 | (0.0) | 2.28 | (0.0) | 2.31 | (0.1) |
| Luxembourg | 486 | (1.1) | 490 | (1.1) | 479 | (1.3) | 2.33 | (0.0) | 0.50 | (0.0) | 1.25 | (0.0) | 3.86 | (0.0) | 0.83 | (0.0) | 1.71 | (0.0) |
| Mexico | 410 | (2.7) | 406 | (2.9) | 410 | (3.1) | 3.15 | (0.0) | 1.01 | (0.0) | 2.12 | (0.0) | 3.94 | (0.0) | 1.18 | (0.0) | 2.26 | (0.0) |
| Netherlands | 525 | (2.7) | 531 | (2.6) | 507 | (2.9) | 2.17 | (0.0) | 0.54 | (0.0) | 1.21 | (0.0) | 2.87 | (0.0) | 0.69 | (0.0) | 1.47 | (0.0) |
| New Zealand | 530 | (2.7) | 522 | (2.4) | 521 | (3.0) | 4.06 | (0.0) | 0.41 | (0.0) | 1.28 | (0.0) | 4.38 | (0.0) | 0.68 | (0.0) | 1.59 | (0.0) |
| Norway | 487 | (3.1) | 490 | (2.6) | 484 | (3.2) | 2.64 | (0.0) | 0.93 | (0.0) | 1.23 | (0.0) | 3.39 | (0.0) | 1.05 | (0.0) | 1.40 | (0.0) |
| Poland | 498 | (2.3) | 495 | (2.4) | 508 | (2.8) | 2.72 | (0.0) | 0.62 | (0.0) | 2.02 | (0.0) | 4.36 | (0.0) | 0.78 | (0.0) | 2.09 | (0.0) |
| Portugal | 474 | (3.0) | 466 | (3.1) | 472 | (3.6) | 3.21 | (0.0) | 0.63 | (0.0) | 2.09 | (0.0) | 3.61 | (0.0) | 0.81 | (0.0) | 1.96 | (0.0) |
| Slovak Republic | 488 | (2.6) | 492 | (2.8) | 466 | (3.1) | 2.46 | (0.1) | 0.65 | (0.0) | 1.39 | (0.0) | 3.29 | (0.1) | 0.88 | (0.0) | 1.69 | (0.0) |
| Spain | 488 | (2.6) | 480 | (2.3) | 461 | (2.2) | 3.12 | (0.0) | 0.68 | (0.0) | 1.74 | (0.0) | 3.42 | (0.0) | 0.99 | (0.0) | 1.96 | (0.0) |
| Sweden | 503 | (2.4) | 502 | (2.4) | 507 | (3.4) | 2.81 | (0.0) | 0.50 | (0.0) | 1.15 | (0.0) | 3.09 | (0.0) | 0.61 | (0.0) | 1.18 | (0.0) |
| Switzerland | 512 | (3.2) | 530 | (3.2) | 499 | (3.1) | 2.36 | (0.0) | 0.39 | (0.0) | 1.12 | (0.0) | 3.86 | (0.0) | 0.70 | (0.0) | 1.69 | (0.0) |
| Turkey | 424 | (3.8) | 424 | (4.9) | 447 | (4.2) | 2.86 | (0.0) | 1.35 | (0.1) | 1.64 | (0.0) | 3.82 | (0.1) | 2.08 | (0.0) | 2.31 | (0.0) |
| United Kingdom | 515 | (2.3) | 495 | (2.1) | 495 | (2.3) | 4.25 | (0.0) | 0.48 | (0.0) | 1.45 | (0.0) | 3.78 | (0.0) | 0.63 | (0.0) | 1.49 | (0.0) |
| United States | 489 | (4.2) | 474 | (4.0) | m | m | 3.51 | (0.1) | 0.78 | (0.0) | 1.68 | (0.0) | 3.77 | (0.0) | 1.15 | (0.0) | 2.05 | (0.0) |
| **OECD average** | 500 | (0.5) | 498 | (0.5) | 492 | (0.6) | 2.99 | (0.0) | 0.64 | (0.0) | 1.42 | (0.0) | 3.81 | (0.0) | 0.96 | (0.0) | 1.81 | (0.0) |
| Argentina | 391 | (6.1) | 381 | (6.2) | 374 | (7.2) | 2.26 | (0.1) | 0.49 | (0.0) | 1.59 | (0.0) | 2.95 | (0.1) | 0.78 | (0.0) | 1.82 | (0.0) |
| Azerbaijan | 382 | (2.8) | 476 | (2.3) | 353 | (3.1) | 2.84 | (0.1) | 1.36 | (0.0) | 2.64 | (0.0) | 3.79 | (0.1) | 1.70 | (0.0) | 2.95 | (0.1) |
| Brazil | 390 | (2.8) | 370 | (2.9) | 393 | (3.7) | 2.21 | (0.0) | 0.79 | (0.0) | 1.70 | (0.0) | 3.15 | (0.0) | 1.21 | (0.0) | 1.80 | (0.0) |
| Bulgaria | 434 | (6.1) | 413 | (6.1) | 402 | (6.9) | 2.63 | (0.1) | 0.98 | (0.0) | 2.00 | (0.1) | 2.98 | (0.1) | 1.14 | (0.0) | 2.08 | (0.1) |
| Chile | 438 | (4.3) | 411 | (4.6) | 442 | (5.0) | 2.33 | (0.1) | 0.83 | (0.0) | 1.52 | (0.0) | 3.49 | (0.1) | 0.99 | (0.0) | 1.60 | (0.0) |
| Colombia | 388 | (3.4) | 370 | (3.8) | 385 | (5.1) | 3.50 | (0.1) | 0.95 | (0.0) | 1.83 | (0.0) | 4.21 | (0.1) | 1.23 | (0.0) | 1.93 | (0.0) |
| Croatia | 493 | (2.4) | 467 | (2.4) | 477 | (2.8) | 2.02 | (0.0) | 0.43 | (0.0) | 1.46 | (0.0) | 3.05 | (0.0) | 0.77 | (0.0) | 1.80 | (0.0) |
| Estonia | 531 | (2.5) | 515 | (2.7) | 501 | (2.9) | 3.27 | (0.0) | 0.76 | (0.0) | 1.54 | (0.0) | 4.19 | (0.0) | 0.99 | (0.0) | 1.96 | (0.0) |
| Hong Kong-China | 542 | (2.5) | 547 | (2.7) | 536 | (2.4) | 3.14 | (0.1) | 0.88 | (0.0) | 1.44 | (0.0) | 5.23 | (0.0) | 1.39 | (0.0) | 2.24 | (0.0) |
| Indonesia | 393 | (5.7) | 391 | (5.6) | 393 | (5.9) | 3.23 | (0.0) | 1.04 | (0.0) | 1.78 | (0.0) | 4.09 | (0.1) | 1.36 | (0.0) | 1.99 | (0.0) |
| Israel | 454 | (3.7) | 442 | (4.3) | 439 | (4.6) | 2.43 | (0.1) | 0.98 | (0.0) | 1.35 | (0.0) | 4.12 | (0.0) | 2.15 | (0.0) | 2.33 | (0.1) |
| Jordan | 422 | (2.8) | 384 | (3.3) | 401 | (3.3) | 3.25 | (0.1) | 1.52 | (0.0) | 2.65 | (0.0) | 3.48 | (0.0) | 1.82 | (0.0) | 2.69 | (0.0) |
| Kyrgyzstan | 322 | (2.9) | 311 | (3.4) | 285 | (3.5) | 2.09 | (0.1) | 1.36 | (0.0) | 2.14 | (0.0) | 2.88 | (0.1) | 1.55 | (0.0) | 2.22 | (0.0) |
| Latvia | 490 | (3.0) | 486 | (3.0) | 479 | (3.7) | 2.86 | (0.1) | 0.65 | (0.0) | 1.80 | (0.0) | 4.49 | (0.0) | 1.20 | (0.0) | 2.44 | (0.0) |
| Liechtenstein | 522 | (4.1) | 525 | (4.2) | 510 | (3.9) | 2.57 | (0.1) | 0.52 | (0.1) | 1.20 | (0.1) | 3.98 | (0.1) | 0.58 | (0.0) | 1.49 | (0.1) |
| Lithuania | 488 | (2.8) | 486 | (2.9) | 470 | (3.0) | 2.69 | (0.0) | 0.57 | (0.0) | 1.69 | (0.0) | 3.50 | (0.0) | 0.74 | (0.0) | 1.78 | (0.0) |
| Macao-China | 511 | (1.1) | 525 | (1.3) | 492 | (1.1) | 3.74 | (0.0) | 1.00 | (0.0) | 1.37 | (0.0) | 5.41 | (0.0) | 1.20 | (0.0) | 2.07 | (0.0) |
| Montenegro | 412 | (1.1) | 399 | (1.4) | 392 | (1.2) | 2.83 | (0.0) | 1.05 | (0.0) | 2.20 | (0.0) | 3.09 | (0.0) | 0.93 | (0.0) | 2.03 | (0.0) |
| Qatar | 349 | (0.9) | 318 | (1.0) | 312 | (1.2) | 2.66 | (0.0) | 1.48 | (0.0) | 2.04 | (0.0) | 3.11 | (0.0) | 1.85 | (0.0) | 2.22 | (0.0) |
| Romania | 418 | (4.2) | 415 | (4.2) | 396 | (4.7) | 2.26 | (0.1) | 1.03 | (0.0) | 1.61 | (0.0) | 3.01 | (0.1) | 1.50 | (0.0) | 2.16 | (0.0) |
| Russian Federation | 479 | (3.7) | 476 | (3.9) | 440 | (4.3) | 3.73 | (0.1) | 1.12 | (0.0) | 2.87 | (0.1) | 3.63 | (0.1) | 1.13 | (0.0) | 2.23 | (0.0) |
| Serbia | 436 | (3.0) | 435 | (3.5) | 401 | (3.5) | 2.86 | (0.1) | 0.78 | (0.0) | 1.71 | (0.0) | 3.27 | (0.0) | 0.97 | (0.0) | 1.82 | (0.0) |
| Slovenia | 519 | (1.1) | 504 | (1.0) | 494 | (1.0) | 2.82 | (0.0) | 0.72 | (0.0) | 1.53 | (0.0) | 3.33 | (0.0) | 1.02 | (0.0) | 1.92 | (0.0) |
| Chinese Taipei | 532 | (3.6) | 549 | (4.1) | 496 | (3.4) | 2.89 | (0.1) | 0.78 | (0.0) | 1.24 | (0.0) | 4.26 | (0.1) | 1.53 | (0.0) | 1.88 | (0.0) |
| Thailand | 421 | (2.1) | 417 | (2.3) | 417 | (2.6) | 3.81 | (0.0) | 0.91 | (0.0) | 1.80 | (0.0) | 3.77 | (0.0) | 0.92 | (0.0) | 1.81 | (0.0) |
| Tunisia | 386 | (3.0) | 365 | (4.0) | 380 | (4.0) | 2.62 | (0.0) | 1.93 | (0.0) | 2.61 | (0.0) | 3.39 | (0.0) | 2.42 | (0.0) | 2.57 | (0.0) |
| Uruguay | 428 | (2.7) | 427 | (2.6) | 413 | (3.4) | 2.40 | (0.0) | 0.61 | (0.0) | 1.32 | (0.0) | 3.31 | (0.0) | 0.84 | (0.0) | 1.57 | (0.0) |

**Table 4.1a** Performance in science, mathematics and reading and learning time in science,
[Part 2/2] in mathematics and on the language of instruction

| | Mean learning hours per week | | | | | | Percentage of total learning time allocated to regular school lessons, by subject | | | | | |
| | Regular school lessons | | Language of instruction | | | | Science | | Mathematics | | Language of instruction | |
| | | | Out-of-school-time lessons | | Individual study | | | | | | | |
| | Mean | S.E. | Mean | S.E. | Mean | S.E. | % | S.E. | % | S.E. | % | S.E. |
|---|---|---|---|---|---|---|---|---|---|---|---|---|
| **OECD** Australia | 4.06 | (0.0) | 0.66 | (0.0) | 1.71 | (0.0) | 70.9 | (0.3) | 65.8 | (0.3) | 67.1 | (0.3) |
| Austria | 2.87 | (0.0) | 0.24 | (0.0) | 1.55 | (0.0) | 64.1 | (0.6) | 58.5 | (0.5) | 65.5 | (0.4) |
| Belgium | 3.49 | (0.0) | 0.46 | (0.0) | 1.35 | (0.0) | 63.5 | (0.4) | 63.1 | (0.3) | 67.3 | (0.3) |
| Canada | 4.43 | (0.0) | 0.86 | (0.0) | 1.74 | (0.0) | 66.3 | (0.4) | 63.3 | (0.3) | 65.6 | (0.3) |
| Czech Republic | 3.72 | (0.0) | 0.61 | (0.0) | 1.16 | (0.0) | 68.7 | (0.6) | 70.3 | (0.4) | 71.6 | (0.4) |
| Denmark | 5.50 | (0.0) | 1.68 | (0.0) | 2.16 | (0.0) | 66.7 | (0.5) | 62.3 | (0.3) | 62.2 | (0.3) |
| Finland | 3.13 | (0.0) | 0.36 | (0.0) | 1.13 | (0.0) | 70.9 | (0.4) | 71.1 | (0.3) | 70.7 | (0.4) |
| France | 4.01 | (0.0) | 0.77 | (0.0) | 1.51 | (0.0) | 62.9 | (0.5) | 62.6 | (0.3) | 67.0 | (0.4) |
| Germany | 3.66 | (0.0) | 0.61 | (0.0) | 1.89 | (0.0) | 58.0 | (0.5) | 58.4 | (0.3) | 62.3 | (0.4) |
| Greece | 3.18 | (0.0) | 1.63 | (0.0) | 1.94 | (0.0) | 48.3 | (0.6) | 49.4 | (0.5) | 51.0 | (0.5) |
| Hungary | 3.18 | (0.0) | 1.31 | (0.0) | 1.86 | (0.0) | 51.5 | (0.5) | 54.3 | (0.4) | 53.2 | (0.4) |
| Iceland | 4.52 | (0.0) | 0.46 | (0.0) | 1.54 | (0.0) | 70.1 | (0.4) | 69.4 | (0.3) | 71.8 | (0.3) |
| Ireland | 3.55 | (0.0) | 0.63 | (0.0) | 1.75 | (0.0) | 66.2 | (0.4) | 63.6 | (0.4) | 64.3 | (0.4) |
| Italy | 4.62 | (0.0) | 0.79 | (0.0) | 2.95 | (0.0) | 54.0 | (0.3) | 55.0 | (0.2) | 57.2 | (0.2) |
| Japan | 3.82 | (0.0) | 0.43 | (0.0) | 0.94 | (0.0) | 78.4 | (0.4) | 71.7 | (0.5) | 78.1 | (0.5) |
| Korea | 4.48 | (0.0) | 1.45 | (0.0) | 1.40 | (0.0) | 67.4 | (0.6) | 57.0 | (0.5) | 66.4 | (0.5) |
| Luxembourg | 3.50 | (0.0) | 0.60 | (0.0) | 1.38 | (0.0) | 59.8 | (0.4) | 63.3 | (0.3) | 67.3 | (0.3) |
| Mexico | 3.73 | (0.0) | 1.10 | (0.0) | 2.06 | (0.0) | 48.5 | (0.4) | 54.5 | (0.4) | 55.1 | (0.4) |
| Netherlands | 2.92 | (0.0) | 0.64 | (0.0) | 1.33 | (0.0) | 56.4 | (0.6) | 60.0 | (0.4) | 63.0 | (0.4) |
| New Zealand | 4.39 | (0.0) | 0.65 | (0.0) | 1.57 | (0.0) | 73.1 | (0.4) | 69.6 | (0.4) | 70.2 | (0.4) |
| Norway | 3.60 | (0.0) | 1.16 | (0.0) | 1.44 | (0.0) | 59.6 | (0.5) | 62.2 | (0.4) | 62.2 | (0.5) |
| Poland | 4.64 | (0.0) | 0.70 | (0.0) | 2.22 | (0.0) | 53.2 | (0.4) | 62.5 | (0.3) | 63.5 | (0.3) |
| Portugal | 3.27 | (0.0) | 0.57 | (0.0) | 1.79 | (0.0) | 54.6 | (0.5) | 58.9 | (0.4) | 61.0 | (0.4) |
| Slovak Republic | 3.12 | (0.1) | 0.89 | (0.0) | 1.74 | (0.0) | 58.7 | (0.6) | 60.6 | (0.5) | 59.0 | (0.5) |
| Spain | 3.60 | (0.0) | 0.58 | (0.0) | 1.89 | (0.0) | 58.9 | (0.3) | 57.7 | (0.3) | 62.7 | (0.3) |
| Sweden | 3.12 | (0.0) | 0.68 | (0.0) | 1.26 | (0.0) | 66.7 | (0.6) | 68.1 | (0.5) | 66.7 | (0.5) |
| Switzerland | 3.65 | (0.0) | 0.49 | (0.0) | 1.40 | (0.0) | 62.1 | (0.4) | 63.6 | (0.4) | 67.5 | (0.4) |
| Turkey | 3.99 | (0.1) | 1.81 | (0.0) | 2.18 | (0.0) | 51.2 | (0.5) | 50.8 | (0.4) | 54.7 | (0.6) |
| United Kingdom | 3.89 | (0.0) | 0.59 | (0.0) | 1.59 | (0.0) | 70.7 | (0.3) | 67.1 | (0.3) | 67.6 | (0.3) |
| United States | 3.64 | (0.0) | 1.11 | (0.0) | 1.87 | (0.0) | 58.5 | (0.5) | 55.4 | (0.5) | 55.8 | (0.6) |
| **OECD average** | 3.78 | (0.0) | 0.82 | (0.0) | 1.68 | (0.0) | 62.0 | (0.1) | 61.7 | (0.1) | 63.9 | (0.1) |
| **Partners** Argentina | 2.39 | (0.1) | 0.43 | (0.0) | 1.64 | (0.0) | 53.1 | (0.8) | 55.0 | (0.6) | 55.2 | (0.6) |
| Azerbaijan | 3.69 | (0.0) | 1.80 | (0.0) | 3.10 | (0.0) | 43.1 | (0.6) | 47.1 | (0.5) | 44.9 | (0.6) |
| Brazil | 3.10 | (0.0) | 1.18 | (0.0) | 1.74 | (0.0) | 50.3 | (0.4) | 54.4 | (0.5) | 54.4 | (0.4) |
| Bulgaria | 2.91 | (0.0) | 1.09 | (0.0) | 2.05 | (0.1) | 48.8 | (0.7) | 51.2 | (0.5) | 51.8 | (0.5) |
| Chile | 3.45 | (0.1) | 1.00 | (0.0) | 1.56 | (0.0) | 49.0 | (0.6) | 56.8 | (0.5) | 57.4 | (0.6) |
| Colombia | 3.92 | (0.1) | 1.15 | (0.0) | 1.84 | (0.0) | 58.9 | (0.6) | 60.7 | (0.6) | 60.2 | (0.6) |
| Croatia | 3.33 | (0.0) | 0.39 | (0.0) | 1.58 | (0.0) | 54.5 | (0.5) | 58.3 | (0.5) | 66.8 | (0.4) |
| Estonia | 3.48 | (0.0) | 0.88 | (0.0) | 1.62 | (0.0) | 61.5 | (0.5) | 62.2 | (0.4) | 61.8 | (0.5) |
| Hong Kong-China | 5.19 | (0.0) | 0.81 | (0.0) | 1.64 | (0.0) | 61.0 | (0.5) | 62.6 | (0.4) | 70.9 | (0.4) |
| Indonesia | 3.64 | (0.1) | 1.25 | (0.0) | 1.80 | (0.0) | 54.6 | (1.0) | 57.2 | (0.6) | 56.3 | (0.7) |
| Israel | 3.03 | (0.0) | 1.33 | (0.0) | 1.66 | (0.0) | 54.4 | (0.7) | 51.4 | (0.6) | 54.0 | (0.5) |
| Jordan | 3.56 | (0.1) | 1.77 | (0.0) | 2.59 | (0.0) | 42.9 | (0.6) | 43.2 | (0.5) | 44.2 | (0.6) |
| Kyrgyzstan | 2.74 | (0.1) | 1.70 | (0.0) | 2.34 | (0.0) | 35.4 | (0.6) | 42.0 | (0.5) | 39.9 | (0.5) |
| Latvia | 3.69 | (0.0) | 0.88 | (0.0) | 2.01 | (0.0) | 56.1 | (0.5) | 58.2 | (0.3) | 59.2 | (0.4) |
| Liechtenstein | 3.66 | (0.1) | 0.32 | (0.0) | 1.24 | (0.1) | 61.8 | (1.4) | 66.7 | (1.2) | 69.8 | (1.2) |
| Lithuania | 3.66 | (0.0) | 0.66 | (0.0) | 1.82 | (0.0) | 57.1 | (0.5) | 60.7 | (0.4) | 62.3 | (0.4) |
| Macao-China | 5.32 | (0.0) | 1.06 | (0.0) | 1.49 | (0.0) | 64.7 | (0.4) | 66.2 | (0.4) | 71.4 | (0.3) |
| Montenegro | 2.93 | (0.0) | 0.75 | (0.0) | 1.99 | (0.0) | 46.8 | (0.4) | 52.5 | (0.4) | 53.0 | (0.4) |
| Qatar | 2.90 | (0.0) | 1.59 | (0.0) | 2.04 | (0.0) | 40.7 | (0.3) | 43.3 | (0.3) | 44.7 | (0.3) |
| Romania | 3.30 | (0.1) | 1.52 | (0.0) | 2.19 | (0.0) | 48.1 | (0.6) | 49.5 | (0.6) | 50.6 | (0.6) |
| Russian Federation | 2.04 | (0.0) | 0.82 | (0.0) | 1.55 | (0.0) | 48.6 | (0.5) | 53.9 | (0.5) | 48.2 | (0.6) |
| Serbia | 3.17 | (0.0) | 0.93 | (0.0) | 1.70 | (0.0) | 56.8 | (0.5) | 59.3 | (0.5) | 60.2 | (0.5) |
| Slovenia | 3.25 | (0.0) | 0.73 | (0.0) | 1.48 | (0.0) | 55.7 | (0.4) | 55.6 | (0.3) | 60.9 | (0.4) |
| Chinese Taipei | 4.37 | (0.1) | 0.69 | (0.0) | 1.77 | (0.0) | 63.7 | (0.4) | 59.7 | (0.4) | 66.1 | (0.4) |
| Thailand | 3.10 | (0.0) | 0.56 | (0.0) | 1.71 | (0.0) | 63.9 | (0.4) | 63.4 | (0.4) | 62.5 | (0.4) |
| Tunisia | 3.14 | (0.1) | 1.78 | (0.0) | 2.12 | (0.0) | 37.3 | (0.4) | 41.7 | (0.4) | 45.6 | (0.7) |
| Uruguay | 2.74 | (0.0) | 0.65 | (0.0) | 1.35 | (0.0) | 56.2 | (0.5) | 60.8 | (0.4) | 60.8 | (0.5) |

© OECD 2011 Quality Time for Students: Learning In and Out of School

### Table 4.1b  Cross-country relationship between absolute learning time and performance, by subject

|  | Science | Mathematics | Reading |
|---|---|---|---|
| Intercept | 304 | 110 | 182 |
| Learning time in regular school lessons | 87 | 138 | 112 |
| Learning time in regular school lessons (squared) | -10 | -11 | -9 |
| Explained variance in student performance | 0.07 | 0.25 | 0.25 |
| Intercept | 573 ** | 607 ** | 503 ** |
| Learning time in out-of-school-time lessons | -167 ** | -192 * | -22 |
| Learning time in out-of-school-time lessons (squared) | 40 | 51 | -22 |
| Explained variance in student performance | 0.41 | 0.23 | 0.29 |
| Intercept | 704 ** | 715 ** | 675 ** |
| Learning time in individual study | -208 * | -196 | -167 |
| Learning time in individual study (squared) | 37 | 34 | 24 |
| Explained variance in student performance | 0.42 | 0.14 | 0.28 |

*Note:* Values that are statistically significant are indicated by * at the 5% level (p < 0.05) or by ** at the 10% level (p < 0.10).

### Table 4.1c  Cross-country relationship between relative learning time and performance, by subject

|  | Science | Mathematics | Reading |
|---|---|---|---|
| Intercept | -74 | -255 | -277 |
| Percentage of total learning time allocated to regular school lessons | 15 ** | 19 * | 19 ** |
| Percentage of total learning time allocated to regular school lessons (squared) | -0.09 * | -0.12 | -0.12 * |
| Explained variance in student performance | 0.63 | 0.54 | 0.68 |
| Intercept | 552 ** | 573 ** | 480 ** |
| Percentage of total learning time allocated to out-of-school-time lessons | -5 | -8 | 4 |
| Percentage of total learning time allocated to out-of-school-time lessons (squared) | -0.04 | 0.03 | -0.38 |
| Explained variance in student performance | 0.44 | 0.35 | 0.45 |
| Intercept | 444 ** | 776 ** | 496 ** |
| Percentage of total learning time allocated to individual study | 9 | -14 | 6 |
| Percentage of total learning time allocated to individual study (squared) | -0.26 | 0.11 | -0.26 |
| Explained variance in student performance | 0.40 | 0.31 | 0.46 |

*Note:* Values that are statistically significant are indicated by * at the 5% level (p < 0.05) or by ** at the 10% level (p < 0.10).

[Part 1/2]
## Table 4.2a Performance in science, by learning time in regular school lessons in science

| | Science performance for students who do not spend any time in regular school lessons in science | | Difference in science performance between students who spend the following learning hours per week in regular school lessons in science and students who do not spend any time in regular school lessons in science | | | | | | | | | | | | | | | |
|---|---|---|---|---|---|---|---|---|---|---|---|---|---|---|---|---|---|---|
| | | | | | | | | | | | Accounting for socio-economic background of students and schools | | | | | | | |
| | | | Less than 2 hours per week | | 2 hours or more but less than 4 hours per week | | 4 hours or more but less than 6 hours per week | | 6 hours or more per week | | Less than 2 hours per week | | 2 hours or more but less than 4 hours per week | | 4 hours or more but less than 6 hours per week | | 6 hours or more per week | |
| | Mean score | S.E. | Dif. | S.E. | Dif. | S.E. | Dif. | S.E. | Dif. | S.E. | Dif. | S.E. | Dif. | S.E. | Dif. | S.E. | Dif. | S.E. |
| **OECD** | | | | | | | | | | | | | | | | | | |
| Australia | 484 | (3.0) | **-18.1** | (4.4) | **50.0** | (3.7) | **70.7** | (3.8) | **101.3** | (6.0) | **-19.8** | (3.9) | **37.7** | (3.1) | **52.1** | (3.2) | **81.9** | (5.3) |
| Austria | 464 | (4.9) | **23.6** | (5.4) | **60.7** | (5.3) | **108.2** | (6.9) | **110.5** | (8.5) | **11.7** | (4.3) | **32.3** | (4.5) | **60.4** | (5.6) | **66.5** | (9.4) |
| Belgium | 436 | (4.3) | **63.8** | (4.8) | **102.3** | (5.2) | **124.1** | (5.9) | **142.4** | (6.3) | **43.0** | (4.2) | **56.9** | (4.4) | **73.1** | (4.6) | **96.3** | (5.9) |
| Canada | 492 | (4.0) | 1.7 | (4.7) | **43.4** | (4.7) | **61.9** | (4.4) | **74.7** | (4.0) | -0.5 | (4.3) | **36.0** | (4.1) | **50.2** | (4.0) | **59.4** | (3.9) |
| Czech Republic | 478 | (6.6) | 7.3 | (7.8) | **28.3** | (7.6) | **88.1** | (7.2) | **123.7** | (7.2) | 2.3 | (6.6) | **20.3** | (6.2) | **64.3** | (6.1) | **78.5** | (6.5) |
| Denmark | 421 | (12.6) | **30.8** | (12.8) | **83.6** | (12.0) | **97.7** | (12.7) | **107.6** | (17.9) | 22.7 | (11.9) | **68.0** | (11.1) | **78.3** | (11.5) | **77.7** | (14.8) |
| Finland | 497 | (7.6) | **30.6** | (8.3) | **69.3** | (8.1) | **95.8** | (7.9) | **115.5** | (11.1) | **27.2** | (8.0) | **61.4** | (7.8) | **84.5** | (7.3) | **102.2** | (10.5) |
| France | 408 | (6.7) | **41.9** | (6.5) | **101.0** | (6.9) | **161.7** | (7.5) | **180.2** | (8.6) | **28.5** | (6.6) | **63.1** | (6.4) | **100.2** | (7.4) | **112.9** | (7.8) |
| Germany | 456 | (7.3) | **32.9** | (7.0) | **70.7** | (7.5) | **105.3** | (7.7) | **136.0** | (7.5) | **12.1** | (6.0) | **32.9** | (5.9) | **53.3** | (6.2) | **69.9** | (7.7) |
| Greece | 387 | (5.4) | **47.0** | (5.5) | **94.6** | (5.7) | **129.1** | (6.8) | **140.6** | (8.1) | **39.1** | (5.2) | **73.5** | (5.4) | **97.6** | (6.7) | **99.0** | (7.2) |
| Hungary | 487 | (7.7) | -13.6 | (7.9) | **23.7** | (7.9) | **70.3** | (8.9) | **105.4** | (9.8) | 3.8 | (6.0) | **20.8** | (6.3) | **46.8** | (7.0) | **62.8** | (7.8) |
| Iceland | 418 | (9.9) | **43.4** | (11.2) | **86.7** | (10.3) | **91.1** | (11.0) | **92.1** | (16.5) | **43.9** | (10.8) | **82.9** | (10.0) | **82.0** | (10.6) | **80.4** | (16.2) |
| Ireland | 458 | (5.8) | **36.3** | (5.9) | **74.1** | (6.3) | **55.4** | (7.0) | **84.0** | (14.5) | **27.2** | (4.9) | **57.4** | (4.6) | **43.7** | (5.6) | **69.9** | (12.8) |
| Italy | 456 | (10.2) | -11.0 | (10.3) | **25.6** | (11.0) | **49.8** | (10.8) | **65.3** | (11.3) | **12.7** | (5.4) | **35.5** | (5.6) | **51.8** | (6.1) | **76.7** | (6.5) |
| Japan | 476 | (14.6) | 24.2 | (15.1) | **63.5** | (14.4) | **96.5** | (15.6) | **108.0** | (19.6) | 20.9 | (13.3) | **43.7** | (12.2) | **52.8** | (13.7) | **54.0** | (16.6) |
| Korea | 460 | (12.1) | 2.5 | (10.1) | **60.7** | (11.7) | **81.9** | (12.1) | **104.2** | (29.5) | -0.9 | (10.9) | **47.4** | (11.4) | **56.0** | (11.8) | **66.2** | (15.7) |
| Luxembourg | 437 | (4.1) | **37.3** | (5.0) | **64.8** | (4.7) | **94.4** | (5.0) | **96.5** | (7.3) | 22.2 | (4.1) | **42.9** | (4.0) | **63.6** | (4.2) | **71.1** | (7.0) |
| Mexico | 420 | (2.8) | **-30.5** | (3.4) | 1.1 | (3.1) | **13.1** | (3.6) | -3.8 | (3.7) | **-22.4** | (2.9) | -1.3 | (2.8) | **8.5** | (3.0) | -4.6 | (3.1) |
| Netherlands | 490 | (4.0) | **17.1** | (4.8) | **54.2** | (4.1) | **88.8** | (5.4) | **129.5** | (7.3) | **8.2** | (3.4) | **28.0** | (3.6) | **48.0** | (4.9) | **77.0** | (6.3) |
| New Zealand | 458 | (6.9) | **-20.9** | (9.4) | **58.7** | (7.8) | **99.5** | (7.4) | **134.0** | (8.4) | -14.3 | (7.6) | **46.4** | (6.7) | **81.3** | (6.2) | **104.9** | (7.6) |
| Norway | 411 | (8.8) | **54.1** | (9.2) | **94.2** | (9.1) | **92.6** | (10.2) | 24.6 | (18.9) | **50.3** | (9.0) | **86.2** | (8.8) | **79.4** | (9.5) | 14.5 | (18.4) |
| Poland | 450 | (7.1) | **21.3** | (7.4) | **58.0** | (7.5) | **84.9** | (7.8) | **93.1** | (11.2) | **24.1** | (6.8) | **54.2** | (6.8) | **76.0** | (7.4) | **81.0** | (10.5) |
| Portugal | 482 | (5.4) | **-61.1** | (4.9) | **-21.3** | (5.5) | **36.7** | (5.9) | **47.6** | (5.5) | **-36.2** | (5.3) | -6.3 | (5.3) | **39.3** | (5.2) | **46.9** | (5.0) |
| Slovak Republic | 430 | (5.1) | **36.5** | (4.8) | **78.8** | (5.8) | **107.8** | (6.4) | **145.2** | (6.7) | **23.9** | (4.6) | **54.8** | (5.6) | **73.4** | (6.1) | **87.0** | (6.2) |
| Spain | 461 | (4.0) | **-18.5** | (5.1) | **31.6** | (4.7) | **58.5** | (4.3) | **97.8** | (5.4) | **-15.8** | (4.6) | **26.4** | (4.2) | **46.6** | (4.0) | **77.2** | (5.4) |
| Sweden | 425 | (14.5) | **45.1** | (14.7) | **93.3** | (14.3) | **88.8** | (13.1) | **85.9** | (18.4) | **26.0** | (11.5) | **70.9** | (11.2) | **65.6** | (11.2) | **49.9** | (15.9) |
| Switzerland | 449 | (4.4) | **41.8** | (3.8) | **78.9** | (4.5) | **119.9** | (5.4) | **147.1** | (7.4) | **33.1** | (3.8) | **59.7** | (4.3) | **86.4** | (5.2) | **93.4** | (6.3) |
| Turkey | 401 | (2.6) | **-19.3** | (3.8) | **12.8** | (3.8) | **58.7** | (7.3) | **95.0** | (8.5) | **-8.8** | (4.1) | **17.8** | (3.6) | **42.0** | (4.9) | **63.9** | (4.1) |
| United Kingdom | 415 | (9.1) | 8.3 | (9.1) | **75.0** | (8.7) | **125.3** | (9.3) | **157.1** | (10.0) | 6.9 | (8.9) | **64.8** | (8.7) | **103.2** | (9.3) | **125.5** | (9.6) |
| United States | 435 | (7.2) | 6.9 | (6.7) | **50.3** | (7.8) | **98.8** | (7.5) | **91.2** | (9.2) | 2.2 | (5.8) | **32.6** | (6.9) | **69.5** | (6.0) | **67.1** | (8.2) |
| **OECD average** | 448 | (7.7) | 15.4 | (8.0) | **59.0** | (7.9) | **88.5** | (8.3) | **104.4** | (11.9) | 12.4 | (7.1) | **44.9** | (6.9) | **64.3** | (7.3) | **73.6** | (9.9) |
| **Partners** | | | | | | | | | | | | | | | | | | |
| Argentina | 352 | (6.9) | **30.8** | (5.8) | **64.9** | (7.5) | **95.5** | (8.5) | **117.7** | (12.3) | **21.1** | (5.8) | **41.6** | (6.9) | **63.2** | (8.3) | **81.2** | (11.9) |
| Azerbaijan | 358 | (4.4) | **19.3** | (4.5) | **33.2** | (5.0) | **44.3** | (6.2) | **43.8** | (5.2) | **17.1** | (4.7) | **31.1** | (5.0) | **39.4** | (6.1) | **41.0** | (5.5) |
| Brazil | 347 | (5.0) | **25.6** | (5.5) | **61.2** | (5.4) | **112.5** | (8.2) | **132.5** | (14.1) | **21.0** | (5.1) | **44.4** | (4.9) | **72.8** | (7.0) | **86.9** | (9.4) |
| Bulgaria | 373 | (5.7) | **41.7** | (5.7) | **88.1** | (7.2) | **122.0** | (9.9) | **123.0** | (10.3) | **25.5** | (4.6) | **47.5** | (5.8) | **66.2** | (5.9) | **74.1** | (8.7) |
| Chile | 392 | (4.2) | **30.5** | (4.8) | **57.1** | (5.2) | **97.7** | (5.6) | **118.4** | (7.5) | **19.1** | (4.1) | **34.3** | (4.2) | **58.4** | (4.8) | **66.4** | (6.0) |
| Colombia | 371 | (8.1) | **-4.5** | (8.4) | **16.4** | (8.1) | **33.7** | (8.3) | **56.5** | (9.4) | 4.0 | (8.1) | **20.9** | (8.1) | **31.5** | (8.3) | **42.3** | (9.0) |
| Croatia | 447 | (3.0) | **56.0** | (4.1) | **60.6** | (3.9) | **91.4** | (6.8) | **84.8** | (9.6) | **32.9** | (3.8) | **35.3** | (3.8) | **53.7** | (5.7) | **52.1** | (8.3) |
| Estonia | 460 | (9.8) | **40.8** | (9.1) | **66.7** | (10.4) | **107.2** | (10.0) | **117.5** | (9.7) | **41.3** | (8.6) | **63.5** | (9.7) | **99.2** | (9.5) | **108.8** | (9.4) |
| Hong Kong-China | 522 | (3.0) | **-41.2** | (5.2) | -0.7 | (6.5) | **41.5** | (4.6) | **78.2** | (3.9) | **-33.9** | (4.6) | -2.4 | (6.3) | **33.4** | (4.6) | **67.4** | (3.8) |
| Indonesia | 377 | (5.9) | **-19.1** | (5.6) | **13.2** | (6.6) | **47.5** | (9.2) | **62.5** | (9.3) | -12.3 | (7.1) | 15.4 | (8.3) | **34.2** | (10.2) | **38.6** | (8.2) |
| Israel | 424 | (5.8) | **19.0** | (6.2) | **54.5** | (6.2) | **92.2** | (6.3) | **99.1** | (9.7) | **21.6** | (5.3) | **51.0** | (5.1) | **83.6** | (5.8) | **89.1** | (8.3) |
| Jordan | 375 | (4.3) | **24.9** | (5.1) | **56.8** | (4.8) | **79.0** | (6.3) | **93.3** | (6.3) | **21.6** | (4.6) | **47.6** | (4.4) | **65.5** | (5.1) | **79.2** | (5.5) |
| Kyrgyzstan | 304 | (3.2) | **20.7** | (3.5) | **48.4** | (4.5) | **63.6** | (6.0) | **60.0** | (10.4) | **15.2** | (3.4) | **38.7** | (4.3) | **44.1** | (5.1) | **50.3** | (5.6) |
| Latvia | 438 | (6.9) | **30.8** | (7.4) | **54.3** | (7.7) | **88.7** | (7.9) | **100.4** | (8.0) | **24.8** | (6.9) | **47.4** | (7.3) | **76.9** | (6.8) | **83.7** | (6.9) |
| Liechtenstein[2] | 493 | (7.6) | c | c | **34.0** | (10.2) | **76.9** | (19.6) | c | c | c | c | **23.8** | (9.3) | **43.4** | (14.3) | c | c |
| Lithuania | 412 | (8.4) | **53.2** | (8.9) | **85.5** | (9.0) | **121.1** | (9.1) | **102.7** | (9.7) | **41.2** | (8.5) | **68.4** | (8.0) | **94.8** | (8.0) | **85.0** | (9.3) |
| Macao-China | 496 | (2.8) | **-30.3** | (4.2) | 2.2 | (3.7) | **26.0** | (4.1) | **60.5** | (3.6) | **-23.9** | (4.2) | **7.8** | (3.9) | **30.5** | (4.3) | **63.4** | (3.6) |
| Montenegro | 370 | (3.6) | **23.7** | (4.2) | **60.1** | (4.1) | **77.5** | (4.6) | **77.3** | (6.1) | **19.4** | (4.1) | **46.1** | (4.1) | **60.2** | (4.6) | **61.4** | (5.2) |
| Qatar | 315 | (2.5) | **14.4** | (3.6) | **48.1** | (3.2) | **90.7** | (4.5) | **98.4** | (5.3) | **15.8** | (3.6) | **43.7** | (3.2) | **80.1** | (4.6) | **88.3** | (5.2) |
| Romania | 376 | (5.5) | **29.0** | (5.2) | **66.6** | (6.1) | **80.1** | (7.1) | **86.0** | (9.4) | **19.7** | (5.3) | **44.5** | (5.8) | **53.4** | (5.9) | **54.6** | (6.4) |
| Russian Federation | 429 | (6.5) | **22.1** | (5.9) | **47.6** | (6.5) | **74.9** | (6.7) | **83.5** | (7.4) | **17.5** | (5.2) | **35.9** | (5.9) | **60.6** | (6.0) | **71.4** | (6.9) |
| Serbia | 385 | (5.1) | **29.1** | (5.3) | **60.6** | (5.5) | **93.5** | (6.4) | **98.4** | (6.7) | **21.0** | (4.8) | **39.7** | (5.0) | **64.0** | (6.1) | **63.1** | (6.3) |
| Slovenia | 459 | (4.2) | **30.4** | (5.2) | **68.2** | (4.9) | **114.5** | (6.2) | **132.7** | (5.9) | 9.3 | (5.2) | **26.5** | (4.8) | **50.5** | (5.5) | **62.3** | (5.6) |
| Chinese Taipei | 470 | (7.8) | **24.3** | (6.7) | **87.2** | (7.2) | **96.6** | (8.1) | **108.1** | (8.0) | **12.9** | (5.7) | **52.7** | (5.8) | **61.8** | (5.8) | **68.0** | (6.0) |
| Thailand[1] | 423 | (1.1) | a | a | **41.8** | (1.3) | **86.4** | (1.5) | **83.8** | (2.1) | a | a | **37.2** | (1.1) | **63.3** | (1.2) | **64.1** | (1.8) |
| Tunisia | 342 | (4.7) | **33.4** | (5.2) | **50.3** | (5.5) | **89.1** | (7.3) | **93.4** | (8.6) | **29.3** | (5.3) | **42.9** | (5.7) | **71.7** | (6.6) | **71.2** | (6.6) |
| Uruguay | 401 | (4.4) | **19.9** | (5.0) | **42.9** | (5.4) | **62.6** | (6.1) | **99.7** | (6.7) | **10.8** | (4.8) | **24.0** | (5.3) | **39.9** | (5.5) | **58.0** | (6.1) |

1. As there are no students who do not spend any time in regular school lessons in science, the first column presents science performance for students who spend less than 2 hours per week in regular school lessons in science. Differences are computed based on students who spend less than 2 hours per week in regular school lessons in science.
2. As there are less than 30 students who do not spend any time in regular school lessons in science, the first column presents science performance for students who spend less than 2 hours per week in regular school lessons in science. Differences are computed based on students who spend less than 2 hours per week in regular school lessons in science.

*Note*: Values that are statistically significant at the 5% level ($p < 0.05$) are indicated in bold.

244

© OECD 2011 Quality Time for Students: Learning In and Out of School

[Part 2/2]

## Table 4.2a Performance in science, by learning time in regular school lessons in science

| | Difference in science performance between students who spend the following learning hours per week in regular school lessons in science and students who do not spend any time in regular school lessons in science | | | | | | | | Percentage of students, by lower and upper secondary schools | | | | | | | | | | | |
|---|---|---|---|---|---|---|---|---|---|---|---|---|---|---|---|---|---|---|---|---|
| | Accounting for socio-economic background of students and schools as well as learning time in out-of-school-time lessons and individual study in science | | | | | | | | No time | | | | Less than 2 hours per week | | | | 2 hours or more per week | | | |
| | Less than 2 hours per week | | 2 hours or more but less than 4 hours per week | | 4 hours or more but less than 6 hours per week | | 6 hours or more per week | | Lower secondary school | | Upper secondary school | | Lower secondary school | | Upper secondary school | | Lower secondary school | | Upper secondary school | |
| | Dif. | S.E. | Dif. | S.E. | Dif. | S.E. | Dif. | S.E. | % | S.E. | % | S.E. | % | S.E. | % | S.E. | % | S.E. | % | S.E. |
| **OECD** | | | | | | | | | | | | | | | | | | | | |
| Australia | **-28.8** | (4.3) | **20.5** | (3.7) | **32.2** | (3.8) | **60.8** | (6.0) | 47.3 | (2.0) | 52.7 | (2.0) | 87.1 | (1.2) | 12.9 | (1.2) | 85.2 | (0.6) | 14.8 | (0.6) |
| Austria | **19.8** | (4.6) | **40.6** | (4.4) | **70.5** | (5.6) | **80.3** | (9.2) | 4.3 | (1.4) | 95.7 | (1.4) | 9.3 | (1.2) | 90.7 | (1.2) | 5.1 | (0.7) | 94.9 | (0.7) |
| Belgium | **36.9** | (4.6) | **49.2** | (5.0) | **67.0** | (5.5) | **90.4** | (6.6) | 3.6 | (0.8) | 96.4 | (0.8) | 4.2 | (0.6) | 95.8 | (0.6) | 3.6 | (0.4) | 96.4 | (0.4) |
| Canada | 3.2 | (4.6) | **38.2** | (4.7) | **51.2** | (4.5) | **59.9** | (4.6) | 28.6 | (1.8) | 71.4 | (1.8) | 22.9 | (1.2) | 77.1 | (1.2) | 11.5 | (0.7) | 88.5 | (0.7) |
| Czech Republic | 4.1 | (6.9) | **23.4** | (6.6) | **71.0** | (6.5) | **86.4** | (6.8) | 24.0 | (2.9) | 76.0 | (2.9) | 55.8 | (2.3) | 44.2 | (2.3) | 49.2 | (1.9) | 50.8 | (1.9) |
| Denmark | 18.1 | (12.1) | **62.5** | (11.3) | **73.1** | (11.6) | **77.4** | (14.9) | 97.4 | (2.6) | 2.6 | (2.6) | 99.7 | (0.4) | 0.3 | (0.4) | 98.7 | (0.4) | 1.3 | (0.4) |
| Finland | **24.0** | (8.0) | **54.3** | (7.9) | **75.5** | (7.7) | **94.3** | (10.3) | 100.0 | (0.0) | a | a | 100.0 | (0.0) | a | a | 100.0 | (0.0) | c | c |
| France | **24.9** | (6.6) | **57.8** | (6.7) | **92.7** | (7.7) | **106.5** | (8.3) | 53.0 | (5.4) | 47.0 | (5.4) | 68.3 | (1.8) | 31.7 | (1.8) | 23.3 | (1.2) | 76.7 | (1.2) |
| Germany | **12.6** | (5.7) | **33.9** | (5.9) | **54.8** | (6.1) | **74.4** | (7.5) | 86.9 | (4.5) | 13.1 | (4.5) | 97.3 | (0.8) | 2.7 | (0.8) | 98.5 | (0.3) | 1.5 | (0.3) |
| Greece | **39.7** | (5.3) | **73.8** | (5.5) | **97.7** | (6.8) | **100.2** | (7.5) | 19.1 | (3.0) | 80.9 | (3.0) | 9.1 | (1.8) | 90.9 | (1.8) | 5.7 | (0.8) | 94.3 | (0.8) |
| Hungary | 6.7 | (6.7) | **26.7** | (7.0) | **54.8** | (7.6) | **72.9** | (8.4) | 7.9 | (1.9) | 92.1 | (1.9) | 10.7 | (1.4) | 89.3 | (1.4) | 5.5 | (0.9) | 94.5 | (0.9) |
| Iceland | **34.1** | (11.3) | **67.8** | (10.5) | **70.6** | (11.3) | **76.1** | (15.7) | 96.6 | (1.7) | 3.4 | (1.7) | 100.0 | (0.0) | a | a | 99.4 | (0.1) | 0.6 | (0.1) |
| Ireland | **23.7** | (5.9) | **50.3** | (6.0) | **38.5** | (6.9) | **69.4** | (13.3) | 47.4 | (3.0) | 52.6 | (3.0) | 49.4 | (2.4) | 50.6 | (2.4) | 68.0 | (1.0) | 32.0 | (1.0) |
| Italy | **10.9** | (5.2) | **31.7** | (5.3) | **51.6** | (6.0) | **74.6** | (6.8) | 3.1 | (1.1) | 96.9 | (1.1) | 2.8 | (0.8) | 97.2 | (0.8) | 1.0 | (0.3) | 99.0 | (0.3) |
| Japan | 16.0 | (12.9) | **38.3** | (11.8) | **47.0** | (13.1) | **52.4** | (15.7) | a | a | 100.0 | (0.0) | a | a | 100.0 | (0.0) | a | a | 100.0 | (0.0) |
| Korea | -9.9 | (11.3) | **35.1** | (11.5) | **39.6** | (11.8) | **48.6** | (14.3) | 2.1 | (1.7) | 97.9 | (1.7) | 3.0 | (1.8) | 97.0 | (1.8) | 2.0 | (0.6) | 98.0 | (0.6) |
| Luxembourg | **25.8** | (4.4) | **46.1** | (3.9) | **68.4** | (4.5) | **82.6** | (7.2) | 64.2 | (2.0) | 35.8 | (2.0) | 79.0 | (0.8) | 21.0 | (0.8) | 51.5 | (0.7) | 48.5 | (0.7) |
| Mexico | **-18.5** | (3.8) | 3.2 | (3.8) | **13.3** | (4.0) | 1.2 | (4.3) | 29.9 | (1.9) | 70.1 | (1.9) | 53.2 | (2.3) | 46.8 | (2.3) | 42.8 | (2.4) | 57.2 | (2.4) |
| Netherlands | **15.2** | (3.9) | **34.5** | (4.5) | **56.5** | (5.7) | **83.5** | (6.8) | 77.9 | (1.8) | 22.1 | (1.8) | 79.0 | (1.7) | 21.0 | (1.7) | 66.2 | (1.3) | 33.8 | (1.3) |
| New Zealand | **-22.2** | (8.1) | **33.7** | (7.0) | **62.2** | (6.5) | **88.1** | (8.0) | 4.4 | (1.4) | 95.6 | (1.4) | 13.2 | (2.0) | 86.8 | (2.0) | 5.6 | (0.3) | 94.4 | (0.3) |
| Norway | **45.4** | (8.9) | **78.8** | (8.9) | **82.5** | (10.1) | **32.5** | (22.4) | 100.0 | (0.0) | a | a | 99.8 | (0.2) | 0.2 | (0.2) | 99.4 | (0.4) | 0.6 | (0.4) |
| Poland | **20.9** | (6.8) | **53.6** | (6.8) | **77.0** | (7.3) | **88.5** | (10.3) | 100.0 | (0.0) | a | a | 99.8 | (0.0) | 0.2 | (0.0) | 99.3 | (0.1) | 0.7 | (0.1) |
| Portugal | **-34.8** | (6.5) | -4.6 | (7.0) | **40.9** | (6.5) | **52.4** | (6.9) | 16.7 | (2.4) | 83.3 | (2.4) | 88.7 | (1.2) | 11.3 | (1.2) | 41.7 | (1.5) | 58.3 | (1.5) |
| Slovak Republic | **21.9** | (4.7) | **53.3** | (5.7) | **73.0** | (6.2) | **88.7** | (6.5) | 17.4 | (3.0) | 82.6 | (3.0) | 45.0 | (2.9) | 55.0 | (2.9) | 35.1 | (2.3) | 64.9 | (2.3) |
| Spain | **-19.9** | (5.0) | **15.9** | (4.7) | **34.8** | (4.8) | **63.8** | (5.9) | 99.9 | (0.1) | 0.1 | (0.1) | 100.0 | (0.0) | a | a | 100.0 | (0.0) | c | c |
| Sweden | **28.6** | (11.1) | **66.5** | (10.7) | **67.7** | (10.7) | **58.9** | (14.5) | 83.9 | (5.2) | 16.1 | (5.2) | 97.0 | (0.6) | 3.0 | (0.6) | 98.5 | (0.3) | 1.5 | (0.3) |
| Switzerland | **29.2** | (4.1) | **54.5** | (4.6) | **82.9** | (5.5) | **93.8** | (6.0) | 81.1 | (2.8) | 18.9 | (2.8) | 90.8 | (1.7) | 9.2 | (1.7) | 77.3 | (1.3) | 22.7 | (1.3) |
| Turkey | **-13.7** | (4.3) | **11.2** | (4.0) | **33.2** | (5.5) | **52.3** | (4.7) | 2.1 | (0.4) | 97.9 | (0.4) | 5.1 | (1.5) | 94.9 | (1.5) | 6.3 | (2.0) | 93.7 | (2.0) |
| United Kingdom | -7.1 | (9.7) | **46.6** | (9.1) | **81.2** | (9.9) | **103.4** | (10.4) | 1.2 | (0.7) | 98.8 | (0.7) | 1.3 | (0.5) | 98.7 | (0.5) | 0.3 | (0.1) | 99.7 | (0.1) |
| United States | 1.4 | (6.6) | **33.1** | (7.5) | **66.9** | (6.5) | **65.8** | (8.9) | 20.4 | (3.9) | 79.6 | (3.9) | 18.6 | (3.8) | 81.4 | (3.8) | 8.3 | (0.8) | 91.7 | (0.8) |
| **OECD average** | **10.3** | (7.3) | **41.0** | (7.2) | **60.9** | (7.6) | **72.7** | (10.2) | 45.5 | (2.5) | 62.2 | (2.6) | 54.8 | (1.6) | 52.2 | (1.6) | 47.9 | (1.1) | 53.7 | (1.0) |
| **Partners** | | | | | | | | | | | | | | | | | | | | |
| Argentina | **16.9** | (5.4) | **35.5** | (6.0) | **57.9** | (7.5) | **76.9** | (12.4) | 42.7 | (3.8) | 57.3 | (3.8) | 32.7 | (2.3) | 67.3 | (2.3) | 22.2 | (2.0) | 77.8 | (2.0) |
| Azerbaijan | **15.7** | (4.8) | **28.5** | (5.1) | **36.2** | (6.3) | **35.4** | (6.0) | 54.1 | (3.4) | 45.9 | (3.4) | 53.5 | (2.1) | 46.5 | (2.1) | 63.1 | (1.9) | 36.9 | (1.9) |
| Brazil | **19.0** | (5.3) | **43.4** | (5.2) | **75.1** | (7.0) | **91.0** | (9.1) | 37.5 | (3.0) | 62.5 | (3.0) | 34.3 | (2.0) | 65.7 | (2.0) | 30.2 | (1.9) | 69.8 | (1.9) |
| Bulgaria | **29.7** | (4.5) | **52.8** | (6.1) | **70.7** | (6.2) | **80.6** | (9.1) | 12.1 | (2.4) | 87.9 | (2.4) | 7.9 | (1.2) | 92.1 | (1.2) | 4.3 | (0.8) | 95.7 | (0.8) |
| Chile | **22.4** | (4.4) | **40.4** | (4.3) | **65.3** | (5.3) | **76.1** | (6.4) | 13.0 | (2.4) | 87.0 | (2.4) | 2.7 | (0.6) | 97.3 | (0.6) | 1.7 | (0.4) | 98.3 | (0.4) |
| Colombia | 1.0 | (8.4) | **17.8** | (8.2) | **28.1** | (8.5) | **40.9** | (9.9) | 34.4 | (4.8) | 65.6 | (4.8) | 44.1 | (2.4) | 55.9 | (2.4) | 39.0 | (2.0) | 61.0 | (2.0) |
| Croatia | **35.6** | (4.4) | **37.8** | (4.6) | **57.2** | (5.9) | **55.0** | (8.4) | 0.8 | (0.6) | 99.2 | (0.6) | 0.3 | (0.3) | 99.7 | (0.3) | 0.2 | (0.2) | 99.8 | (0.2) |
| Estonia | **42.1** | (8.4) | **63.6** | (9.2) | **99.3** | (9.0) | **109.2** | (8.8) | 99.4 | (0.6) | 0.6 | (0.6) | 99.1 | (0.2) | 0.9 | (0.2) | 97.9 | (0.2) | 2.1 | (0.2) |
| Hong Kong-China | **-41.3** | (6.3) | -12.5 | (8.1) | **22.9** | (7.9) | **56.0** | (7.0) | 18.2 | (1.3) | 81.8 | (1.3) | 71.8 | (2.7) | 28.2 | (2.7) | 41.3 | (1.2) | 58.7 | (1.2) |
| Indonesia | **-15.4** | (7.5) | 12.0 | (8.5) | **31.6** | (10.7) | **36.8** | (9.0) | 18.5 | (3.7) | 81.5 | (3.7) | 68.9 | (4.3) | 31.1 | (4.3) | 50.0 | (4.2) | 50.0 | (4.2) |
| Israel | **26.9** | (5.3) | **61.1** | (5.5) | **100.6** | (7.0) | **110.9** | (8.6) | 8.1 | (1.3) | 91.9 | (1.3) | 15.5 | (1.5) | 84.5 | (1.5) | 14.5 | (1.6) | 85.5 | (1.6) |
| Jordan | **18.7** | (4.5) | **44.1** | (4.4) | **60.6** | (5.4) | **75.1** | (5.5) | 100.0 | (0.0) | a | a | 100.0 | (0.0) | a | a | 100.0 | (0.0) | a | a |
| Kyrgyzstan | **15.1** | (3.3) | **38.7** | (4.6) | **43.9** | (5.6) | **50.8** | (6.7) | 77.6 | (2.0) | 22.4 | (2.0) | 74.9 | (1.6) | 25.1 | (1.6) | 72.7 | (1.8) | 27.3 | (1.8) |
| Latvia | **20.9** | (6.8) | **44.4** | (7.4) | **76.9** | (7.0) | **86.9** | (7.0) | 98.4 | (0.7) | 1.6 | (0.7) | 97.5 | (0.6) | 2.5 | (0.6) | 96.1 | (0.5) | 3.9 | (0.5) |
| Liechtenstein[2] | c | c | **25.4** | (9.6) | **46.8** | (14.7) | c | c | c | c | c | c | 92.8 | (1.3) | 7.2 | (1.3) | 87.5 | (1.0) | 12.5 | (1.0) |
| Lithuania | **37.9** | (8.6) | **65.8** | (8.2) | **92.4** | (8.1) | **86.7** | (8.8) | 100.0 | (0.0) | a | a | 100.0 | (0.0) | a | a | 100.0 | (0.0) | 0.0 | (0.0) |
| Macao-China | **-28.1** | (4.5) | 2.9 | (4.3) | **24.4** | (4.9) | **54.7** | (4.7) | 29.9 | (1.5) | 70.1 | (1.5) | 80.6 | (1.5) | 19.4 | (1.5) | 64.4 | (0.4) | 35.6 | (0.4) |
| Montenegro | **21.9** | (4.2) | **47.9** | (4.3) | **61.2** | (4.7) | **65.3** | (5.8) | 1.1 | (0.5) | 98.9 | (0.5) | 0.4 | (0.3) | 99.6 | (0.3) | 0.1 | (0.1) | 99.9 | (0.1) |
| Qatar | **17.3** | (3.6) | **45.7** | (3.4) | **79.4** | (4.2) | **87.6** | (5.1) | 23.9 | (1.2) | 76.1 | (1.2) | 30.0 | (0.8) | 70.0 | (0.8) | 17.1 | (0.5) | 82.9 | (0.5) |
| Romania | **18.5** | (5.8) | **45.5** | (6.5) | **55.9** | (6.7) | **59.1** | (8.0) | 100.0 | (0.0) | a | a | 100.0 | (0.0) | a | a | 100.0 | (0.0) | a | a |
| Russian Federation | **14.7** | (4.9) | **30.7** | (5.8) | **53.3** | (5.8) | **63.5** | (6.6) | 44.2 | (4.5) | 55.8 | (4.5) | 45.3 | (3.5) | 54.7 | (3.5) | 33.8 | (1.8) | 66.2 | (1.8) |
| Serbia | **20.3** | (4.9) | **38.4** | (5.3) | **63.1** | (6.1) | **62.5** | (6.7) | 1.7 | (0.7) | 98.3 | (0.7) | 2.3 | (0.8) | 97.7 | (0.8) | 1.7 | (0.7) | 98.3 | (0.7) |
| Slovenia | **13.0** | (5.0) | **32.9** | (4.9) | **57.4** | (5.4) | **67.9** | (5.8) | 9.0 | (3.0) | 91.0 | (3.0) | 5.6 | (1.1) | 94.4 | (1.1) | 1.6 | (0.4) | 98.4 | (0.4) |
| Chinese Taipei | 6.0 | (5.9) | **39.6** | (5.9) | **45.4** | (5.9) | **46.3** | (6.2) | 12.4 | (1.5) | 87.6 | (1.5) | 24.1 | (1.8) | 75.9 | (1.8) | 40.2 | (1.3) | 59.8 | (1.3) |
| Thailand[1] | a | a | **38.1** | (1.1) | **65.6** | (1.2) | **70.8** | (1.9) | a | a | a | a | a | a | 100.0 | (0.0) | 34.2 | (1.2) | 65.8 | (1.2) |
| Tunisia | **27.3** | (5.3) | **39.7** | (5.6) | **67.4** | (6.7) | **67.0** | (6.8) | 76.7 | (2.6) | 23.3 | (2.6) | 56.2 | (2.1) | 43.8 | (2.1) | 37.4 | (1.8) | 62.6 | (1.8) |
| Uruguay | **12.8** | (5.1) | **26.3** | (5.6) | **43.5** | (6.3) | **60.7** | (6.2) | 44.9 | (2.8) | 55.1 | (2.8) | 34.4 | (1.6) | 65.6 | (1.6) | 27.5 | (1.9) | 72.5 | (1.9) |

1. As there are no students who do not spend any time in regular school lessons in science, the first column presents science performance for students who spend less than 2 hours per week in regular school lessons in science. Dfferences are computed based on students who spend less than 2 hours per week in regular school lessons in science.
2. As there are less than 30 students who do not spend any time in regular school lessons in science, the first column presents science performance for students who spend less than 2 hours per week in regular school lessons in science. Differences are computed based on students who spend less than 2 hours per week in regular school lessons in science.

*Note*: Values that are statistically significant at the 5% level ($p < 0.05$) are indicated in bold.

[Part 1/2]
## Table 4.2b Performance in mathematics, by learning time in regular school lessons in mathematics

| | Mathematics performance for students who do not spend any time in regular school lessons in mathematics | | Difference in mathematics performance between students who spend the following learning hours per week in regular school lessons in mathematics and students who do not spend any time in regular school lessons in mathematics | | | | | | | |
| | | | Less than 2 hours per week | | 2 hours or more but less than 4 hours per week | | 4 hours or more but less than 6 hours per week | | 6 hours or more per week | |
| | Mean score | S.E. | Dif. | S.E. | Dif. | S.E. | Dif. | S.E. | Dif. | S.E. |
|---|---|---|---|---|---|---|---|---|---|---|
| Australia | 464 | (6.8) | -13.4 | (7.4) | 55.8 | (7.3) | 70.7 | (7.1) | 79.2 | (7.4) |
| Austria | 480 | (9.6) | -9.6 | (9.6) | 42.3 | (10.1) | 27.3 | (9.7) | -2.1 | (12.4) |
| Belgium | 442 | (8.2) | 35.8 | (7.7) | 71.1 | (8.1) | 125.6 | (8.3) | 121.7 | (9.2) |
| Canada | 496 | (6.1) | -14.4 | (5.9) | 32.6 | (5.9) | 45.5 | (6.3) | 46.7 | (5.8) |
| Czech Republic | 438 | (17.1) | 18.4 | (16.4) | 88.9 | (17.0) | 84.5 | (17.5) | 79.3 | (16.9) |
| Denmark[2] | 449 | (8.2) | c | c | 70.7 | (7.6) | 70.0 | (8.1) | 60.7 | (9.1) |
| Finland | 503 | (14.6) | -4.3 | (14.8) | 50.6 | (14.5) | 54.0 | (15.1) | 61.0 | (17.1) |
| France | 414 | (11.5) | 11.9 | (12.5) | 77.1 | (12.3) | 108.3 | (12.0) | 75.2 | (18.4) |
| Germany | 457 | (17.5) | 13.4 | (12.7) | 77.9 | (17.7) | 53.6 | (17.5) | 5.9 | (15.8) |
| Greece | 389 | (8.8) | 27.0 | (9.1) | 73.7 | (9.6) | 96.9 | (10.0) | 97.3 | (10.5) |
| Hungary | 436 | (8.3) | 11.0 | (8.2) | 70.0 | (8.8) | 75.3 | (9.0) | 63.2 | (13.9) |
| Iceland | 442 | (7.4) | c | c | 72.4 | (7.8) | 73.9 | (7.4) | 48.9 | (8.7) |
| Ireland[2] | 439 | (11.7) | 25.5 | (11.6) | 81.8 | (11.6) | 65.5 | (11.8) | 30.7 | (12.5) |
| Italy | 390 | (7.1) | 26.6 | (8.3) | 68.4 | (6.8) | 99.3 | (7.4) | 81.6 | (8.6) |
| Japan[2] | 442 | (9.5) | c | c | 49.1 | (9.0) | 108.7 | (9.2) | 130.4 | (10.7) |
| Korea | 419 | (13.4) | 32.2 | (14.1) | 101.3 | (13.3) | 141.9 | (13.1) | 158.7 | (16.3) |
| Luxembourg | 424 | (9.3) | 28.1 | (10.8) | 69.5 | (9.7) | 83.9 | (9.6) | 34.3 | (11.7) |
| Mexico | 348 | (7.6) | 23.8 | (7.2) | 55.6 | (7.4) | 92.0 | (7.6) | 71.2 | (7.5) |
| Netherlands | 471 | (5.8) | 29.7 | (5.7) | 82.2 | (5.4) | 74.1 | (5.9) | 29.6 | (11.5) |
| New Zealand | 463 | (11.4) | -22.0 | (12.5) | 45.2 | (11.5) | 79.9 | (11.7) | 49.7 | (12.5) |
| Norway | 402 | (9.0) | 43.5 | (10.0) | 99.0 | (8.9) | 107.7 | (9.4) | 56.7 | (12.7) |
| Poland | 442 | (8.5) | 2.5 | (9.1) | 56.5 | (8.8) | 66.5 | (8.5) | 59.5 | (9.3) |
| Portugal | 455 | (6.0) | -58.1 | (6.4) | 1.4 | (6.8) | 45.9 | (6.4) | 48.4 | (8.1) |
| Slovak Republic | 431 | (13.1) | 32.2 | (14.5) | 80.9 | (13.6) | 65.6 | (13.4) | 60.1 | (20.3) |
| Spain | 412 | (7.9) | 5.3 | (9.0) | 76.7 | (8.1) | 92.4 | (8.4) | 40.0 | (9.9) |
| Sweden | 408 | (13.5) | 60.1 | (14.7) | 106.8 | (13.4) | 85.3 | (13.3) | 60.6 | (18.7) |
| Switzerland | 504 | (9.0) | -4.7 | (10.5) | 37.6 | (9.5) | 32.3 | (9.9) | -2.0 | (9.9) |
| Turkey | 375 | (5.5) | -3.4 | (6.5) | 27.7 | (6.9) | 80.1 | (8.2) | 91.1 | (10.8) |
| United Kingdom | 430 | (12.5) | -8.7 | (12.3) | 73.2 | (12.3) | 73.6 | (12.6) | 77.4 | (14.1) |
| United States | 431 | (8.3) | 0.1 | (8.2) | 35.0 | (9.3) | 80.3 | (8.2) | 61.3 | (7.9) |
| **OECD average** | **436** | **(10.5)** | **10.7** | **(10.6)** | **64.4** | **(10.7)** | **78.1** | **(10.8)** | **60.6** | **(12.8)** |
| Argentina | 341 | (8.8) | 10.4 | (8.4) | 57.0 | (9.2) | 91.0 | (9.3) | 69.1 | (11.1) |
| Azerbaijan | 454 | (3.5) | 13.2 | (3.8) | 26.0 | (3.9) | 30.1 | (4.0) | 29.6 | (3.6) |
| Brazil | 300 | (8.9) | 29.5 | (7.8) | 85.0 | (9.2) | 109.2 | (9.5) | 106.4 | (11.1) |
| Bulgaria | 361 | (7.0) | 21.3 | (6.3) | 74.2 | (7.2) | 91.5 | (10.3) | 101.4 | (14.5) |
| Chile | 360 | (5.3) | 18.8 | (5.4) | 44.5 | (6.0) | 83.4 | (7.5) | 97.8 | (7.1) |
| Colombia | 297 | (11.9) | 24.7 | (12.7) | 70.9 | (11.7) | 87.9 | (11.7) | 110.9 | (12.6) |
| Croatia | 443 | (7.2) | -6.7 | (7.9) | 27.8 | (7.6) | 51.5 | (8.0) | 7.4 | (15.8) |
| Estonia | 446 | (13.1) | 34.9 | (12.0) | 63.5 | (12.3) | 81.6 | (13.3) | 71.9 | (12.8) |
| Hong Kong-China | 426 | (10.3) | 32.4 | (12.9) | 102.1 | (11.5) | 129.5 | (11.3) | 141.8 | (10.2) |
| Indonesia | 298 | (11.4) | 36.7 | (11.1) | 87.3 | (12.2) | 118.8 | (12.1) | 111.9 | (13.8) |
| Israel | 418 | (15.7) | -19.6 | (14.8) | 17.1 | (15.5) | 59.3 | (15.1) | 46.8 | (15.7) |
| Jordan | 341 | (5.4) | 18.5 | (5.3) | 47.9 | (6.0) | 76.9 | (6.2) | 72.2 | (6.8) |
| Kyrgyzstan | 280 | (3.8) | 18.8 | (3.6) | 51.0 | (5.0) | 78.6 | (5.4) | 81.5 | (6.5) |
| Latvia | 419 | (14.4) | 10.3 | (15.4) | 61.8 | (13.9) | 75.7 | (14.3) | 85.5 | (15.1) |
| Liechtenstein[2] | 487 | (13.7) | c | c | 68.7 | (15.5) | 36.2 | (15.1) | c | c |
| Lithuania | 405 | (7.7) | 27.4 | (7.9) | 95.6 | (8.6) | 108.7 | (8.2) | 97.2 | (8.9) |
| Macao-China | 446 | (11.1) | 4.4 | (12.1) | 56.4 | (12.6) | 86.2 | (11.3) | 92.3 | (11.4) |
| Montenegro | 370 | (5.2) | 7.6 | (6.2) | 50.5 | (6.2) | 54.3 | (6.3) | 41.0 | (6.9) |
| Qatar | 284 | (4.0) | 13.3 | (4.4) | 35.6 | (5.5) | 78.5 | (4.8) | 73.9 | (5.7) |
| Romania | 362 | (8.3) | 23.8 | (9.0) | 59.4 | (8.5) | 89.6 | (9.5) | 65.5 | (13.9) |
| Russian Federation | 400 | (9.1) | 35.2 | (9.2) | 72.5 | (8.8) | 100.1 | (9.3) | 117.2 | (11.0) |
| Serbia | 384 | (7.3) | 30.8 | (8.2) | 54.0 | (7.7) | 78.3 | (7.6) | 60.8 | (10.5) |
| Slovenia | 477 | (6.6) | -9.1 | (7.1) | 29.5 | (7.2) | 58.8 | (6.6) | 27.0 | (9.1) |
| Chinese Taipei | 437 | (8.5) | 25.8 | (6.9) | 87.8 | (8.3) | 151.4 | (8.6) | 160.5 | (9.5) |
| Thailand[1] | 396 | (1.6) | a | a | 57.2 | (1.5) | 91.6 | (1.6) | 80.9 | (2.4) |
| Tunisia | 323 | (5.2) | 5.5 | (5.8) | 50.2 | (7.4) | 77.7 | (6.8) | 52.5 | (6.6) |
| Uruguay | 353 | (7.1) | 24.3 | (8.1) | 99.3 | (8.0) | 97.5 | (7.7) | 94.8 | (11.2) |

1. As there are no students who do not spend any time in regular school lessons in mathematics, the first column presents mathematics performance for students who spend less than 2 hours per week in regular school lessons in mathematics. Differences are computed based on students who spend less than 2 hours per week in regular school lessons in mathematics.
2. As there are less than 30 students who do not spend any time in regular school lessons in mathematics, the first column presents mathematics performance for students who spend less than 2 hours per week in regular school lessons in mathematics. Differences are computed based on students who spend less than 2 hours per week in regular school lessons in mathematics. Denmark, Iceland, and Japan were not included when calculating the OECD average.
Note: Values that are statistically significant at the 5% level (p < 0.05) are indicated in bold.

© OECD 2011 Quality Time for Students: Learning In and Out of School

[Part 2/2]
## Table 4.2b Performance in mathematics, by learning time in regular school lessons in mathematics

| | Difference in mathematics performance between students who spend the following learning hours per week in regular school lessons in mathematics and students who do not spend any time in regular school lessons in mathematics | | | | | | | | | | | | | | | |
| | Accounting for socio-economic background of students and schools | | | | | | | | Accounting for socio-economic background of students and schools as well as learning time in out-of-school-time lessons and individual study in mathematics | | | | | | | |
| | Less than 2 hours per week | | 2 hours or more but less than 4 hours per week | | 4 hours or more but less than 6 hours per week | | 6 hours or more per week | | Less than 2 hours per week | | 2 hours or more but less than 4 hours per week | | 4 hours or more but less than 6 hours per week | | 6 hours or more per week | |
| | Dif. | S.E. | Dif. | S.E. | Dif. | S.E. | Dif. | S.E. | Dif. | S.E. | Dif. | S.E. | Dif. | S.E. | Dif. | S.E. |
|---|---|---|---|---|---|---|---|---|---|---|---|---|---|---|---|---|
| **OECD** | | | | | | | | | | | | | | | | |
| Australia | -4.2 | (6.7) | **52.6** | (6.6) | **60.8** | (6.1) | **68.6** | (6.5) | -10.1 | (7.2) | **38.6** | (7.0) | **45.0** | (6.7) | **53.0** | (6.9) |
| Austria | -3.1 | (8.8) | **19.7** | (9.3) | 11.9 | (8.9) | -0.0 | (11.7) | 1.5 | (9.6) | **29.9** | (10.0) | **28.7** | (9.5) | **30.9** | (10.7) |
| Belgium | **19.2** | (6.5) | **38.9** | (6.4) | **71.1** | (6.3) | **73.2** | (8.8) | **15.3** | (7.2) | **33.2** | (7.1) | **64.8** | (7.0) | **75.7** | (9.5) |
| Canada | **-14.7** | (5.7) | **28.1** | (5.4) | **38.3** | (6.0) | **37.0** | (5.7) | -5.6 | (5.8) | **38.2** | (5.7) | **45.9** | (6.2) | **45.7** | (5.9) |
| Czech Republic | 11.9 | (16.1) | **53.0** | (15.5) | **57.2** | (16.1) | **51.2** | (16.0) | 15.3 | (15.9) | **56.8** | (15.6) | **64.0** | (16.2) | **62.4** | (16.1) |
| Denmark[2] | c | c | **59.9** | (7.2) | **57.4** | (7.7) | **49.2** | (8.3) | c | c | **58.4** | (7.3) | **58.0** | (7.7) | **55.6** | (8.2) |
| Finland | -1.8 | (12.7) | **45.2** | (12.5) | **47.9** | (13.1) | **56.4** | (15.2) | -3.1 | (12.7) | **37.4** | (12.4) | **40.5** | (13.1) | **50.6** | (15.6) |
| France | 3.8 | (10.7) | **40.8** | (10.5) | **54.9** | (10.0) | **36.3** | (15.0) | 4.3 | (10.9) | **38.5** | (10.5) | **51.5** | (10.1) | **38.7** | (14.6) |
| Germany | -0.5 | (10.4) | **23.9** | (10.0) | 16.0 | (10.6) | -3.6 | (10.2) | 3.8 | (9.9) | **25.2** | (10.0) | 19.9 | (10.5) | 11.2 | (10.9) |
| Greece | **25.1** | (8.1) | **55.8** | (8.2) | **71.9** | (8.7) | **72.8** | (9.0) | **22.9** | (8.5) | **51.3** | (8.5) | **66.1** | (9.2) | **64.7** | (9.7) |
| Hungary | 3.5 | (7.8) | **32.5** | (8.4) | **38.4** | (8.3) | **30.8** | (10.9) | 8.1 | (7.9) | **38.5** | (8.6) | **46.7** | (8.7) | **48.6** | (11.6) |
| Iceland | c | c | **67.7** | (7.8) | **68.5** | (7.3) | **45.6** | (8.5) | c | c | **54.3** | (8.1) | **55.5** | (7.7) | **39.5** | (9.0) |
| Ireland[2] | **20.1** | (11.2) | **65.4** | (10.8) | **49.5** | (11.1) | 21.8 | (11.7) | **22.0** | (10.7) | **63.7** | (10.2) | **49.4** | (10.5) | **27.6** | (11.2) |
| Italy | **16.4** | (7.3) | **39.9** | (6.0) | **69.2** | (6.9) | **57.6** | (7.8) | **18.1** | (7.5) | **42.4** | (6.2) | **71.6** | (7.0) | **67.5** | (8.2) |
| Japan[2] | c | c | **32.1** | (8.3) | **61.7** | (8.7) | **74.7** | (10.2) | c | c | **30.7** | (8.1) | **58.8** | (8.5) | **72.1** | (9.7) |
| Korea | **32.3** | (15.8) | **86.6** | (14.6) | **112.9** | (14.0) | **123.1** | (14.0) | 18.5 | (15.1) | **67.9** | (13.4) | **85.8** | (12.7) | **90.1** | (12.8) |
| Luxembourg | **19.5** | (10.4) | **47.3** | (9.4) | **50.6** | (9.1) | 14.1 | (11.1) | **26.4** | (10.0) | **49.8** | (9.0) | **54.1** | (9.0) | **29.0** | (10.9) |
| Mexico | **22.9** | (6.4) | **48.3** | (6.3) | **71.6** | (6.0) | **55.8** | (6.1) | **21.3** | (6.6) | **46.6** | (6.7) | **68.8** | (6.3) | **55.8** | (6.6) |
| Netherlands | 8.0 | (5.5) | **41.8** | (5.5) | **40.8** | (5.1) | 10.1 | (9.8) | **17.7** | (5.9) | **47.5** | (5.6) | **47.6** | (5.4) | **40.2** | (9.6) |
| New Zealand | -16.1 | (11.6) | **31.7** | (11.3) | **61.4** | (11.5) | **35.1** | (11.5) | -15.0 | (11.8) | **25.8** | (11.7) | **49.6** | (12.0) | **33.7** | (12.3) |
| Norway | **38.1** | (10.2) | **89.2** | (9.2) | **94.9** | (9.4) | **48.3** | (12.9) | **38.1** | (11.2) | **84.2** | (10.2) | **92.2** | (10.5) | **60.2** | (13.0) |
| Poland | 6.0 | (9.1) | **52.6** | (8.7) | **60.4** | (8.0) | **51.3** | (8.8) | 6.7 | (9.0) | **51.5** | (8.7) | **59.0** | (8.0) | **52.7** | (8.8) |
| Portugal | **-33.7** | (6.2) | **14.1** | (6.6) | **44.9** | (5.9) | **43.5** | (7.7) | **-39.2** | (8.6) | 5.3 | (8.9) | **37.0** | (8.5) | **38.7** | (10.9) |
| Slovak Republic | **25.5** | (10.1) | **51.3** | (9.8) | **44.6** | (9.8) | **32.1** | (13.3) | **24.1** | (10.0) | **50.6** | (9.5) | **45.7** | (9.7) | **37.0** | (13.5) |
| Spain | 5.3 | (8.4) | **67.7** | (7.6) | **75.9** | (7.8) | **30.7** | (9.1) | 1.9 | (9.0) | **57.4** | (8.0) | **65.6** | (8.4) | **27.7** | (9.5) |
| Sweden | **44.3** | (13.8) | **90.8** | (12.4) | **71.7** | (12.4) | **40.0** | (16.6) | **44.4** | (14.5) | **85.1** | (13.3) | **75.7** | (12.9) | **44.4** | (17.9) |
| Switzerland | -10.5 | (9.8) | 13.8 | (9.6) | 14.2 | (10.1) | -10.4 | (9.6) | -2.9 | (9.8) | **22.9** | (9.4) | **23.7** | (10.0) | 6.2 | (9.8) |
| Turkey | 5.7 | (7.5) | **33.9** | (6.8) | **58.6** | (6.5) | **65.6** | (9.5) | -3.3 | (7.7) | **23.1** | (7.0) | **44.2** | (6.8) | **46.8** | (7.6) |
| United Kingdom | -8.6 | (11.2) | **54.4** | (10.6) | **52.6** | (10.6) | **57.4** | (11.4) | -15.7 | (12.2) | **39.1** | (11.9) | **37.7** | (11.8) | **47.0** | (12.9) |
| United States | -1.9 | (7.3) | **23.0** | (8.0) | **56.0** | (7.0) | **45.7** | (7.0) | 4.9 | (7.5) | **33.7** | (8.1) | **63.1** | (7.2) | **57.6** | (7.6) |
| **OECD average** | **7.9** | (9.9) | **46.0** | (9.5) | **55.5** | (9.5) | **42.4** | (11.0) | **8.2** | (10.1) | **43.9** | (9.7) | **53.5** | (9.7) | **46.1** | (11.3) |
| **Partners** | | | | | | | | | | | | | | | | |
| Argentina | 10.1 | (9.1) | **41.4** | (9.9) | **62.6** | (10.0) | **42.5** | (13.7) | 8.6 | (8.3) | **39.2** | (8.9) | **59.5** | (9.2) | **42.6** | (13.1) |
| Azerbaijan | **12.7** | (3.9) | **25.5** | (4.1) | **29.6** | (4.1) | **28.8** | (3.8) | **9.8** | (3.9) | **21.7** | (4.2) | **26.3** | (4.3) | **26.0** | (3.9) |
| Brazil | **22.6** | (7.5) | **61.2** | (8.0) | **76.5** | (7.6) | **80.5** | (8.8) | **19.6** | (7.6) | **58.3** | (8.1) | **74.0** | (7.7) | **80.8** | (8.8) |
| Bulgaria | **20.5** | (6.1) | **47.2** | (6.4) | **58.6** | (8.1) | **66.3** | (9.5) | **17.8** | (6.6) | **44.9** | (6.9) | **59.2** | (8.8) | **69.1** | (11.0) |
| Chile | **15.7** | (4.3) | **32.1** | (4.4) | **56.8** | (5.4) | **60.7** | (4.7) | **16.9** | (4.3) | **35.2** | (4.6) | **59.4** | (5.4) | **65.2** | (4.7) |
| Colombia | 22.6 | (13.0) | **61.2** | (11.3) | **72.3** | (10.9) | **83.7** | (11.4) | 20.9 | (12.7) | **57.2** | (11.2) | **67.8** | (10.4) | **79.6** | (11.2) |
| Croatia | 0.2 | (7.4) | **21.0** | (6.7) | **29.8** | (7.5) | 8.2 | (13.1) | 1.7 | (7.3) | **21.5** | (6.8) | **32.4** | (7.6) | 21.1 | (13.0) |
| Estonia | **29.6** | (12.3) | **53.2** | (12.8) | **68.2** | (12.8) | **59.3** | (12.7) | **29.3** | (11.7) | **52.7** | (12.2) | **67.9** | (12.0) | **65.7** | (11.7) |
| Hong Kong-China | **29.6** | (12.9) | **84.8** | (12.1) | **107.8** | (11.8) | **120.5** | (10.7) | 19.5 | (14.2) | **69.3** | (13.3) | **90.2** | (12.6) | **100.9** | (11.7) |
| Indonesia | **28.6** | (11.8) | **69.1** | (11.2) | **92.2** | (11.3) | **98.9** | (13.1) | 21.8 | (11.6) | **61.0** | (11.1) | **83.8** | (11.1) | **90.6** | (13.0) |
| Israel | -11.9 | (14.7) | 11.5 | (15.4) | **43.6** | (15.3) | **34.4** | (15.3) | -4.6 | (13.8) | 26.7 | (14.9) | **60.5** | (14.9) | **57.3** | (15.6) |
| Jordan | **16.2** | (4.8) | **35.1** | (5.2) | **62.2** | (4.9) | **56.0** | (5.5) | **11.9** | (4.6) | **30.0** | (5.2) | **57.3** | (5.0) | **52.4** | (5.6) |
| Kyrgyzstan | **12.3** | (3.1) | **35.4** | (3.6) | **55.7** | (4.3) | **57.9** | (5.2) | **11.0** | (3.3) | **34.2** | (3.9) | **54.9** | (4.6) | **60.4** | (5.5) |
| Latvia | 13.1 | (15.6) | **59.5** | (14.1) | **69.3** | (14.4) | **77.1** | (15.2) | 10.0 | (16.0) | **55.5** | (14.6) | **68.2** | (14.7) | **80.2** | (15.3) |
| Liechtenstein[2] | c | c | 10.9 | (14.7) | 1.5 | (13.8) | c | c | c | c | 13.0 | (15.7) | 1.6 | (13.9) | c | c |
| Lithuania | **17.9** | (7.2) | **72.6** | (7.6) | **81.2** | (7.4) | **67.5** | (8.3) | **16.3** | (7.3) | **68.1** | (7.8) | **75.9** | (7.8) | **64.6** | (8.5) |
| Macao-China | 5.7 | (12.0) | **56.4** | (12.6) | **84.0** | (11.5) | **88.4** | (11.5) | 0.1 | (12.5) | **50.0** | (12.8) | **74.3** | (11.9) | **77.2** | (11.8) |
| Montenegro | 11.2 | (5.9) | **44.5** | (6.0) | **44.8** | (6.2) | **36.7** | (6.7) | 9.3 | (5.9) | **38.7** | (6.0) | **39.4** | (6.5) | **31.7** | (6.6) |
| Qatar | **10.8** | (4.3) | **27.0** | (5.2) | **59.8** | (4.8) | **54.8** | (5.6) | 7.6 | (4.8) | **25.3** | (6.0) | **61.3** | (5.3) | **56.6** | (6.8) |
| Romania | **19.6** | (8.4) | **40.4** | (8.2) | **57.6** | (9.3) | **43.7** | (11.6) | **17.5** | (7.9) | **37.1** | (7.8) | **54.0** | (8.9) | **43.5** | (11.8) |
| Russian Federation | **29.7** | (9.5) | **59.9** | (9.3) | **84.5** | (9.6) | **95.5** | (11.2) | **25.5** | (9.9) | **53.5** | (9.6) | **76.7** | (10.0) | **88.1** | (11.8) |
| Serbia | **22.4** | (8.3) | **37.5** | (7.6) | **45.3** | (7.7) | **35.9** | (9.7) | **17.3** | (8.4) | **32.3** | (7.6) | **41.6** | (8.0) | **39.3** | (10.3) |
| Slovenia | -11.1 | (6.3) | 7.0 | (6.7) | 8.9 | (6.3) | -8.2 | (8.4) | -3.8 | (6.3) | **16.6** | (6.6) | **20.6** | (6.5) | 16.0 | (9.0) |
| Chinese Taipei | **24.1** | (6.7) | **74.0** | (7.1) | **110.1** | (6.7) | **111.7** | (7.7) | 10.4 | (6.9) | **50.4** | (7.2) | **80.6** | (7.1) | **79.1** | (8.0) |
| Thailand[1] | a | a | **48.5** | (1.2) | **72.0** | (1.4) | **67.4** | (1.9) | a | a | **46.6** | (1.2) | **70.8** | (1.4) | **69.5** | (1.9) |
| Tunisia | 5.9 | (5.9) | **35.4** | (5.7) | **55.4** | (5.7) | **37.9** | (5.7) | 3.6 | (6.1) | **33.1** | (6.0) | **52.5** | (5.9) | **35.8** | (6.2) |
| Uruguay | **22.4** | (7.4) | **72.0** | (6.7) | **69.2** | (6.8) | **65.9** | (9.4) | **25.0** | (7.8) | **72.8** | (7.1) | **69.3** | (7.3) | **68.9** | (10.1) |

1. As there are no students who do not spend any time in regular school lessons in mathematics, the first column presents mathematics performance for students who spend less than 2 hours per week in regular school lessons in mathematics. Differences are computed based on students who spend less than 2 hours per week in regular school lessons in mathematics.
2. As there are less than 30 students who do not spend any time in regular school lessons in mathematics, the first column presents mathematics performance for students who spend less than 2 hours per week in regular school lessons in mathematics. Differences are computed based on students who spend less than 2 hours per week in regular school lessons in mathematics. Denmark, Iceland, and Japan were not included when calculating the OECD average.
*Note:* Values that are statistically significant at the 5% level (p < 0.05) are indicated in bold.

### Table 4.2c  Performance in reading, by learning time in regular school lessons on the language of instruction
[Part 1/2]

| | Reading performance for students who do not spend any time in regular school lessons on the language of instruction | | Difference in reading performance between students who spend the following learning hours per week in regular school lessons on the language of instruction and students who do not spend any time in regular school lessons on the language of instruction | | | | | | | |
| | | | Less than 2 hours per week | | 2 hours or more but less than 4 hours per week | | 4 hours or more but less than 6 hours per week | | 6 hours or more per week | |
| | Mean score | S.E. | Dif. | S.E. | Dif. | S.E. | Dif. | S.E. | Dif. | S.E. |
|---|---|---|---|---|---|---|---|---|---|---|
| **OECD** | | | | | | | | | | |
| Australia | 420 | (10.1) | 19.8 | (10.1) | **95.1** | (10.1) | **110.4** | (10.3) | **99.4** | (10.9) |
| Austria | 453 | (11.1) | 12.2 | (11.3) | **63.2** | (10.7) | 8.5 | (13.3) | **-50.2** | (15.0) |
| Belgium | 433 | (14.8) | **48.0** | (12.6) | **83.5** | (14.9) | **96.5** | (15.0) | 14.6 | (18.5) |
| Canada | 502 | (5.5) | **-26.2** | (6.5) | **27.5** | (6.1) | **39.7** | (5.6) | **45.4** | (5.7) |
| Czech Republic | 401 | (15.1) | **38.9** | (17.1) | **104.8** | (15.3) | **87.0** | (15.9) | **62.0** | (17.7) |
| Denmark[2] | 409 | (10.6) | c | c | **71.8** | (12.0) | **94.8** | (10.4) | **92.3** | (10.7) |
| Finland | 500 | (12.5) | 7.5 | (13.8) | **55.0** | (13.2) | **55.5** | (13.2) | **53.3** | (17.5) |
| France | 387 | (14.4) | 24.0 | (13.3) | **91.4** | (14.0) | **128.7** | (14.1) | **95.9** | (20.0) |
| Germany | 455 | (16.3) | 16.7 | (13.4) | **77.8** | (16.3) | **48.3** | (15.9) | 9.5 | (15.0) |
| Greece | 368 | (9.8) | **54.5** | (9.0) | **109.0** | (9.5) | **122.7** | (10.4) | **121.2** | (10.7) |
| Hungary | 390 | (14.5) | **42.1** | (14.2) | **102.0** | (14.1) | **131.8** | (14.9) | **103.1** | (18.3) |
| Iceland[2] | 410 | (7.7) | c | c | **79.6** | (8.2) | **88.0** | (7.7) | **71.0** | (9.3) |
| Ireland | 456 | (15.4) | 23.8 | (14.9) | **83.4** | (14.9) | **65.6** | (14.8) | 23.8 | (15.1) |
| Italy | 379 | (9.7) | **27.0** | (10.0) | **81.0** | (9.4) | **116.6** | (9.5) | **99.4** | (10.4) |
| Japan[2] | 419 | (8.8) | c | c | **67.2** | (7.3) | **106.7** | (8.8) | **119.7** | (13.5) |
| Korea | 425 | (19.0) | **45.6** | (16.9) | **115.1** | (18.9) | **145.3** | (18.8) | **153.8** | (19.1) |
| Luxembourg | 438 | (7.7) | -12.8 | (9.2) | **48.5** | (8.1) | **65.9** | (7.9) | 19.2 | (11.8) |
| Mexico | 367 | (7.8) | 8.3 | (7.1) | **54.1** | (8.0) | **80.2** | (8.2) | **44.6** | (8.3) |
| Netherlands | 470 | (12.6) | 19.4 | (12.2) | **55.5** | (11.5) | **34.9** | (12.8) | **-58.6** | (19.4) |
| New Zealand | 414 | (17.7) | 13.7 | (19.6) | **88.5** | (18.1) | **132.9** | (17.8) | **94.3** | (18.7) |
| Norway | 367 | (15.0) | **60.2** | (14.2) | **129.1** | (14.8) | **148.0** | (15.0) | **116.9** | (17.7) |
| Poland | 410 | (9.8) | **29.7** | (10.4) | **80.4** | (10.5) | **114.7** | (9.7) | **108.8** | (10.1) |
| Portugal | 413 | (13.8) | -11.6 | (13.6) | **77.1** | (12.9) | **73.1** | (13.2) | **82.4** | (14.8) |
| Slovak Republic | 374 | (21.2) | **72.9** | (20.5) | **116.2** | (21.3) | **83.8** | (22.4) | **96.0** | (26.1) |
| Spain | 384 | (7.9) | 13.6 | (8.5) | **86.8** | (8.1) | **99.4** | (8.0) | **51.2** | (11.8) |
| Sweden | 432 | (19.0) | **43.0** | (20.2) | **90.7** | (19.0) | **64.8** | (19.4) | 29.3 | (21.5) |
| Switzerland | 485 | (12.6) | **-30.3** | (12.1) | **27.5** | (12.8) | **26.2** | (12.5) | -19.5 | (13.7) |
| Turkey | 392 | (13.0) | 10.2 | (12.5) | **47.3** | (12.7) | **83.1** | (13.1) | **64.5** | (14.1) |
| United Kingdom | 412 | (19.4) | 0.0 | (18.4) | **92.0** | (19.1) | **95.9** | (19.7) | **89.9** | (20.2) |
| United States | m | m | m | m | m | m | m | m | m | m |
| **OECD average** | 420 | (13.9) | 21.2 | (13.7) | **80.1** | (13.8) | **86.9** | (14.1) | **59.6** | (16.1) |
| **Partners** | | | | | | | | | | |
| Argentina | 329 | (12.4) | **31.0** | (13.2) | **81.0** | (12.8) | **86.9** | (12.0) | **60.8** | (20.9) |
| Azerbaijan | 321 | (6.8) | **20.6** | (7.0) | **41.2** | (7.0) | **48.4** | (6.3) | **48.2** | (7.4) |
| Brazil | 341 | (7.5) | 18.0 | (11.2) | **73.4** | (7.9) | **87.8** | (8.9) | **72.5** | (9.4) |
| Bulgaria | 327 | (9.7) | **41.0** | (8.7) | **108.5** | (10.7) | **111.0** | (10.1) | **96.8** | (11.9) |
| Chile | 398 | (8.6) | 8.4 | (8.1) | **42.5** | (8.4) | **82.3** | (9.1) | **84.5** | (9.4) |
| Colombia | 317 | (12.7) | 10.1 | (12.4) | **71.3** | (12.1) | **95.3** | (12.2) | **72.3** | (13.9) |
| Croatia | 440 | (10.5) | 9.5 | (9.6) | **39.6** | (9.6) | **61.1** | (10.5) | -12.2 | (14.7) |
| Estonia | 430 | (14.5) | **34.1** | (15.0) | **74.8** | (14.4) | **90.0** | (14.9) | **72.2** | (14.9) |
| Hong Kong-China | 461 | (16.5) | -5.2 | (15.4) | **67.1** | (16.8) | **90.4** | (15.6) | **83.1** | (17.0) |
| Indonesia | 303 | (13.0) | **54.1** | (12.0) | **97.4** | (13.7) | **110.0** | (12.2) | **86.9** | (13.5) |
| Israel | 410 | (9.2) | 10.4 | (9.8) | **55.6** | (8.8) | **67.3** | (9.7) | **53.0** | (10.8) |
| Jordan | 348 | (7.8) | **32.3** | (7.5) | **54.2** | (7.8) | **86.8** | (8.3) | **87.2** | (8.2) |
| Kyrgyzstan | 237 | (4.5) | **37.7** | (5.3) | **79.4** | (6.5) | **105.2** | (8.1) | **89.0** | (6.2) |
| Latvia | 418 | (16.8) | 28.7 | (15.8) | **62.6** | (15.8) | **76.6** | (16.2) | **72.6** | (19.5) |
| Liechtenstein[2] | 466 | (12.7) | c | c | **76.6** | (16.3) | **43.6** | (13.6) | c | c |
| Lithuania | 395 | (14.0) | 19.6 | (13.4) | **81.3** | (13.7) | **104.7** | (14.2) | **91.9** | (15.1) |
| Macao-China | 417 | (17.5) | 13.8 | (19.0) | **69.0** | (18.0) | **82.1** | (17.3) | **85.1** | (18.2) |
| Montenegro | 356 | (4.0) | **10.3** | (4.8) | **61.0** | (5.3) | **76.1** | (4.8) | **40.4** | (6.3) |
| Qatar | 270 | (4.7) | **28.9** | (5.5) | **47.9** | (5.5) | **95.9** | (6.2) | **92.0** | (7.6) |
| Romania | 302 | (7.9) | **41.8** | (8.0) | **107.1** | (8.7) | **129.4** | (8.9) | **98.5** | (12.4) |
| Russian Federation | 392 | (11.6) | **57.4** | (11.2) | **46.1** | (11.2) | **44.7** | (13.4) | 30.0 | (14.8) |
| Serbia | 349 | (7.2) | **28.1** | (7.1) | **55.4** | (7.0) | **84.5** | (7.5) | **45.0** | (10.8) |
| Slovenia | 446 | (6.2) | 10.2 | (6.9) | **50.8** | (6.6) | **85.7** | (6.4) | **66.5** | (9.3) |
| Chinese Taipei | 413 | (10.1) | 14.1 | (9.0) | **64.9** | (9.6) | **110.7** | (9.9) | **114.8** | (10.1) |
| Thailand[1] | 400 | (2.2) | a | a | **52.6** | (2.1) | **81.0** | (2.3) | **57.9** | (2.6) |
| Tunisia | 347 | (9.1) | 5.2 | (7.6) | **37.4** | (8.2) | **77.1** | (8.4) | **34.3** | (9.9) |
| Uruguay | 364 | (9.2) | 17.7 | (9.9) | **89.2** | (9.6) | **70.3** | (9.6) | 21.5 | (14.5) |

1. As there are no students who do not spend any time in regular school lessons on the language of instruction, the first column presents language of instruction performance for students who spend less than 2 hours per week in regular school lessons on the language of instruction. Differences are computed based on students who spend less than 2 hours per week in regular school lessons on the language of instruction.

2. As there are less than 30 students who do not spend any time in regular school lessons on the language of instruction, the first column presents language of instruction performance for students who spend less than 2 hours per week in regular school lessons on the language of instruction. Differences are computed based on students who spend less than 2 hours per week in regular school lessons on the language of instruction. Denmark, Iceland, and Japan were not included when calculating the OECD average.

Note: Values that are statistically significant at the 5% level (p < 0.05) are indicated in bold.

© OECD 2011  Quality Time for Students: Learning In and Out of School

### Table 4.2c [Part 2/2] Performance in reading, by learning time in regular school lessons on the language of instruction

Difference in reading performance between students who spend the following learning hours per week in regular school lessons on the language of instruction and students who do not spend any time in regular school lessons on the language of instruction

| | | Accounting for socio-economic background of students and schools | | | | | | | | Accounting for socio-economic background of students and schools as well as learning time in out-of-school-time lessons and individual study on the language of instruction | | | | | | | |
|---|---|---|---|---|---|---|---|---|---|---|---|---|---|---|---|---|---|
| | | Less than 2 hours per week | | 2 hours or more but less than 4 hours per week | | 4 hours or more but less than 6 hours per week | | 6 hours or more per week | | Less than 2 hours per week | | 2 hours or more but less than 4 hours per week | | 4 hours or more but less than 6 hours per week | | 6 hours or more per week | |
| | | Dif. | S.E. | Dif. | S.E. | Dif. | S.E. | Dif. | S.E. | Dif. | S.E. | Dif. | S.E. | Dif. | S.E. | Dif. | S.E. |
| **OECD** | Australia | 15.0 | (10.8) | 77.6 | (10.6) | 87.1 | (10.7) | 78.5 | (11.2) | 14.0 | (11.0) | 66.8 | (10.8) | 74.5 | (10.9) | 73.1 | (11.5) |
| | Austria | 8.7 | (10.1) | 35.0 | (10.2) | 3.8 | (11.2) | -35.0 | (14.4) | 14.4 | (10.2) | 43.3 | (10.4) | 19.1 | (11.8) | 0.1 | (14.4) |
| | Belgium | 33.8 | (10.6) | 54.7 | (11.9) | 56.6 | (12.1) | 13.6 | (16.3) | 30.3 | (9.8) | 46.9 | (10.4) | 49.2 | (10.7) | 17.1 | (16.1) |
| | Canada | -19.7 | (6.0) | 25.1 | (5.4) | 35.8 | (5.0) | 38.7 | (5.4) | -14.4 | (6.7) | 28.4 | (6.0) | 35.7 | (5.7) | 39.6 | (6.0) |
| | Czech Republic | 55.4 | (14.4) | 93.2 | (13.0) | 90.2 | (13.3) | 69.4 | (14.2) | 47.9 | (14.8) | 84.8 | (13.2) | 81.4 | (13.5) | 65.9 | (14.5) |
| | Denmark[2] | c | c | 61.4 | (11.5) | 81.6 | (10.9) | 80.5 | (10.9) | c | c | 56.9 | (11.4) | 75.5 | (10.7) | 75.1 | (10.9) |
| | Finland | 4.7 | (12.8) | 47.3 | (12.1) | 48.0 | (11.8) | 46.3 | (15.1) | -2.0 | (12.5) | 32.4 | (11.9) | 31.2 | (11.7) | 29.8 | (15.0) |
| | France | 26.8 | (13.8) | 65.1 | (14.9) | 87.1 | (14.7) | 68.8 | (17.9) | 23.6 | (14.1) | 59.5 | (15.1) | 78.7 | (15.1) | 66.3 | (18.4) |
| | Germany | 12.3 | (9.6) | 39.0 | (9.2) | 32.9 | (8.8) | 23.3 | (10.2) | 14.4 | (9.6) | 36.6 | (8.8) | 32.0 | (8.6) | 37.5 | (9.8) |
| | Greece | 51.3 | (8.0) | 91.0 | (8.3) | 101.6 | (9.0) | 100.9 | (9.2) | 51.0 | (8.4) | 90.7 | (8.7) | 103.0 | (9.5) | 102.8 | (9.7) |
| | Hungary | 32.1 | (9.8) | 66.9 | (9.6) | 83.4 | (10.0) | 66.2 | (12.7) | 33.0 | (9.8) | 69.6 | (9.3) | 88.6 | (9.5) | 80.4 | (12.5) |
| | Iceland[2] | c | c | 74.3 | (8.2) | 83.8 | (7.8) | 68.1 | (9.3) | c | c | 57.3 | (8.1) | 65.3 | (7.5) | 56.9 | (8.9) |
| | Ireland | 21.3 | (13.3) | 68.5 | (13.6) | 54.3 | (13.7) | 18.6 | (14.1) | 21.2 | (12.7) | 61.7 | (13.0) | 50.6 | (13.3) | 26.9 | (13.7) |
| | Italy | 22.5 | (9.3) | 54.2 | (8.3) | 80.1 | (8.7) | 70.2 | (9.1) | 17.2 | (8.7) | 48.7 | (7.9) | 69.0 | (8.4) | 60.3 | (9.0) |
| | Japan[2] | c | c | 40.4 | (7.6) | 54.3 | (8.6) | 57.0 | (12.6) | c | c | 37.8 | (7.6) | 51.0 | (8.5) | 53.4 | (12.2) |
| | Korea | 48.3 | (18.1) | 101.5 | (19.8) | 122.8 | (19.9) | 128.1 | (19.7) | 35.8 | (17.9) | 88.7 | (19.4) | 106.4 | (19.5) | 111.5 | (19.6) |
| | Luxembourg | -7.5 | (7.3) | 39.9 | (6.2) | 42.9 | (6.1) | 17.6 | (9.7) | 0.8 | (7.2) | 36.7 | (6.5) | 42.3 | (6.2) | 34.5 | (9.9) |
| | Mexico | 11.8 | (6.8) | 45.1 | (7.1) | 61.8 | (6.6) | 36.7 | (7.1) | 7.0 | (7.0) | 40.1 | (7.7) | 55.6 | (7.1) | 34.7 | (7.6) |
| | Netherlands | -1.3 | (8.2) | 22.3 | (7.1) | 24.6 | (8.3) | -42.2 | (17.2) | -1.2 | (8.3) | 16.5 | (7.4) | 20.9 | (8.6) | -38.5 | (16.5) |
| | New Zealand | 20.6 | (17.7) | 75.5 | (15.9) | 112.8 | (15.7) | 80.5 | (16.8) | 23.2 | (17.5) | 71.7 | (15.8) | 102.3 | (15.7) | 88.3 | (17.2) |
| | Norway | 57.7 | (13.9) | 121.7 | (14.1) | 137.2 | (14.0) | 104.9 | (17.5) | 55.5 | (13.5) | 114.1 | (13.5) | 129.4 | (13.7) | 112.3 | (17.6) |
| | Poland | 27.9 | (10.9) | 74.7 | (10.6) | 104.2 | (9.8) | 94.5 | (10.4) | 26.5 | (10.7) | 70.5 | (10.5) | 96.6 | (9.8) | 89.5 | (10.3) |
| | Portugal | -8.9 | (12.7) | 61.5 | (11.7) | 57.0 | (12.2) | 64.2 | (13.8) | -3.7 | (12.5) | 56.3 | (11.6) | 54.1 | (11.9) | 66.8 | (13.6) |
| | Slovak Republic | 56.8 | (13.2) | 80.0 | (13.2) | 61.7 | (13.9) | 69.3 | (19.1) | 48.9 | (14.3) | 68.7 | (14.6) | 50.3 | (15.3) | 54.8 | (19.3) |
| | Spain | 11.8 | (8.4) | 76.8 | (7.8) | 88.3 | (7.5) | 46.7 | (11.5) | 7.8 | (8.7) | 60.2 | (8.2) | 68.4 | (8.0) | 36.6 | (10.7) |
| | Sweden | 32.6 | (18.0) | 78.3 | (17.0) | 53.4 | (17.9) | 9.2 | (22.2) | 30.6 | (18.3) | 71.0 | (17.3) | 52.1 | (18.3) | 24.3 | (22.1) |
| | Switzerland | -24.5 | (10.1) | 15.7 | (11.0) | 14.1 | (10.5) | -25.5 | (11.4) | -19.8 | (9.7) | 13.2 | (10.7) | 11.4 | (10.1) | -14.7 | (11.2) |
| | Turkey | 9.0 | (11.2) | 36.1 | (11.5) | 56.0 | (12.2) | 47.5 | (12.2) | 7.6 | (11.6) | 34.0 | (11.7) | 54.0 | (12.1) | 46.3 | (12.1) |
| | United Kingdom | 1.0 | (18.8) | 73.8 | (19.1) | b | (19.0) | 71.1 | (18.5) | -5.5 | (18.4) | 57.6 | (18.3) | 59.0 | (18.5) | 62.2 | (18.2) |
| | United States | m | m | m | m | m | m | m | m | m | m | m | m | m | m | m | m |
| | **OECD average** | 19.2 | (12.2) | 62.3 | (12.1) | 67.9 | (12.2) | 48.5 | (14.3) | 17.8 | (12.2) | 56.5 | (12.0) | 62.1 | (12.2) | 50.3 | (14.3) |
| **Partners** | Argentina | 26.7 | (14.6) | 60.1 | (14.0) | 63.8 | (13.7) | 26.5 | (19.7) | 21.2 | (14.4) | 50.0 | (13.8) | 57.6 | (13.4) | 28.9 | (21.5) |
| | Azerbaijan | 19.0 | (7.0) | 38.4 | (7.0) | 42.6 | (6.8) | 40.3 | (7.4) | 20.0 | (7.4) | 39.2 | (7.5) | 43.5 | (7.5) | 43.4 | (8.6) |
| | Brazil | 17.7 | (9.5) | 57.0 | (7.9) | 67.4 | (8.9) | 58.5 | (8.9) | 11.9 | (9.4) | 51.9 | (8.0) | 64.5 | (9.0) | 60.8 | (9.4) |
| | Bulgaria | 25.3 | (7.8) | 59.7 | (8.4) | 69.8 | (8.9) | 60.1 | (11.1) | 21.7 | (8.0) | 54.9 | (8.5) | 67.6 | (9.3) | 62.3 | (11.8) |
| | Chile | 12.2 | (7.1) | 34.7 | (7.3) | 60.4 | (7.6) | 57.2 | (7.5) | 16.0 | (7.3) | 40.7 | (7.4) | 65.3 | (7.6) | 65.0 | (7.7) |
| | Colombia | 6.4 | (12.8) | 54.7 | (12.7) | 72.8 | (12.4) | 52.4 | (13.8) | 8.1 | (12.9) | 55.1 | (12.7) | 73.6 | (12.5) | 57.7 | (14.6) |
| | Croatia | 16.6 | (8.7) | 38.1 | (8.4) | 45.7 | (9.2) | 5.8 | (11.8) | 16.5 | (8.3) | 31.1 | (7.9) | 38.3 | (8.5) | 9.9 | (12.6) |
| | Hong Kong-China | -4.3 | (13.9) | 54.2 | (14.5) | 76.0 | (13.3) | 72.0 | (14.9) | -7.6 | (13.0) | 51.6 | (13.8) | 71.1 | (12.7) | 67.9 | (14.0) |
| | Indonesia | 50.7 | (10.5) | 81.3 | (11.5) | 90.1 | (11.1) | 87.3 | (12.2) | 44.6 | (10.6) | 74.7 | (11.3) | 85.0 | (10.9) | 84.5 | (12.1) |
| | Israel | 13.3 | (9.4) | 47.8 | (8.4) | 56.5 | (9.4) | 47.6 | (10.8) | 25.3 | (9.3) | 63.2 | (8.1) | 77.3 | (9.1) | 81.6 | (11.4) |
| | Jordan | 31.1 | (7.3) | 48.4 | (7.2) | 75.1 | (7.3) | 80.1 | (7.4) | 27.7 | (7.8) | 48.5 | (7.8) | 72.1 | (8.2) | 80.8 | (8.1) |
| | Kyrgyzstan | 24.3 | (5.2) | 57.7 | (6.3) | 79.7 | (6.7) | 68.8 | (6.3) | 22.0 | (5.0) | 54.2 | (5.9) | 73.3 | (6.6) | 66.0 | (5.8) |
| | Latvia | 29.5 | (14.3) | 54.0 | (14.5) | 72.7 | (14.7) | 68.8 | (16.2) | 13.1 | (15.1) | 43.3 | (15.2) | 58.5 | (15.3) | 60.4 | (17.0) |
| | Liechtenstein[2] | c | c | 11.5 | (11.5) | 6.3 | (10.4) | c | c | c | c | 20.0 | (11.5) | 8.0 | (10.4) | c | c |
| | Lithuania | 16.7 | (12.3) | 68.2 | (12.3) | 86.6 | (12.5) | 77.5 | (13.2) | 10.2 | (12.1) | 58.2 | (12.0) | 72.2 | (12.5) | 67.5 | (13.1) |
| | Macao-China | 16.2 | (18.2) | 68.2 | (17.4) | 82.4 | (16.8) | 84.2 | (17.5) | 11.8 | (18.2) | 64.5 | (17.3) | 76.8 | (16.7) | 80.4 | (17.4) |
| | Montenegro | 9.6 | (4.8) | 48.0 | (5.0) | 57.2 | (4.5) | 28.1 | (5.7) | 10.8 | (5.3) | 43.7 | (5.5) | 50.2 | (5.4) | 27.2 | (6.9) |
| | Qatar | 30.2 | (5.4) | 43.2 | (5.2) | 87.2 | (5.9) | 84.8 | (7.5) | 28.4 | (6.0) | 45.7 | (5.9) | 92.7 | (6.1) | 95.3 | (8.1) |
| | Romania | 31.9 | (8.7) | 77.6 | (9.3) | 92.0 | (9.4) | 73.0 | (12.4) | 27.9 | (8.8) | 69.2 | (9.5) | 80.0 | (9.8) | 60.0 | (14.0) |
| | Russian Federation | 46.4 | (10.6) | 34.8 | (10.4) | 32.3 | (11.6) | 20.8 | (13.6) | 42.7 | (9.6) | 32.6 | (9.7) | 33.2 | (11.3) | 22.1 | (12.9) |
| | Serbia | 22.6 | (6.4) | 41.5 | (6.6) | 48.4 | (6.9) | 26.5 | (9.5) | 17.4 | (6.3) | 35.3 | (6.5) | 43.3 | (7.0) | 25.8 | (9.8) |
| | Slovenia | 12.3 | (7.6) | 37.9 | (7.4) | 55.1 | (6.7) | 43.6 | (8.5) | 14.0 | (7.3) | 39.2 | (7.2) | 55.8 | (6.7) | 48.3 | (8.5) |
| | Chinese Taipei | 9.9 | (8.7) | 51.7 | (8.9) | 77.3 | (9.2) | 75.2 | (9.7) | 4.7 | (8.7) | 42.4 | (8.5) | 64.7 | (9.0) | 61.9 | (9.3) |
| | Thailand[1] | a | a | 46.1 | (1.7) | 67.0 | (1.7) | 53.2 | (2.0) | a | a | 44.5 | (1.6) | 67.3 | (1.7) | 59.9 | (1.9) |
| | Tunisia | 17.6 | (6.1) | 43.6 | (7.2) | 74.9 | (7.2) | 51.1 | (8.6) | 18.7 | (6.3) | 46.5 | (7.3) | 77.9 | (7.2) | 59.5 | (8.9) |
| | Uruguay | 19.6 | (9.1) | 65.5 | (8.9) | 72.8 | (8.6) | 35.8 | (12.1) | 19.6 | (9.6) | 61.6 | (9.6) | 60.7 | (9.2) | 35.3 | (13.0) |

1. As there are no students who do not spend any time in regular school lessons on the language of instruction, the first column presents language of instruction performance for students who spend less than 2 hours per week in regular school lessons on the language of instruction. Differences are computed based on students who spend less than 2 hours per week in regular school lessons on the language of instruction.

2. As there are less than 30 students who do not spend any time in regular school lessons on the language of instruction, the first column presents language of instruction performance for students who spend less than 2 hours per week in regular school lessons on the language of instruction. Differences are computed based on students who spend less than 2 hours per week in regular school lessons on the language of instruction. Denmark, Iceland, and Japan were not included when calculating the OECD average.

*Note:* Values that are statistically significant at the 5% level (p < 0.05) are indicated in bold.

## Table 4.3 Percentage of students who think it is very important to do well in each subject, by learning time in regular school lessons

| | | Science | | | | | | | | Mathematics | | | | | | | | Language of instruction | | | | | | | |
|---|---|---|---|---|---|---|---|---|---|---|---|---|---|---|---|---|---|---|---|---|---|---|---|---|---|
| | | All students | | Students who spend less than 6 hours in school regular lessons | | Students who spend 6 hours or more in school regular lessons | | Difference (less than 6 hours - 6 hours or more) | | All students | | Students who spend less than 6 hours in school regular lessons | | Students who spend 6 hours or more in school regular lessons | | Difference (less than 6 hours - 6 hours or more) | | All students | | Students who spend less than 6 hours in school regular lessons | | Students who spend 6 hours or more in school regular lessons | | Difference (less than 6 hours - 6 hours or more) | |
| | | % | S.E. | % | S.E. | % | S.E. | Dif. | S.E. | % | S.E. | % | S.E. | % | S.E. | Dif. | S.E. | % | S.E. | % | S.E. | % | S.E. | Dif. | S.E. |
| OECD | Australia | 31.2 | (0.6) | 29.2 | (0.6) | 58.6 | (1.8) | **-29.4** | (1.9) | 62.6 | (0.7) | 61.6 | (0.7) | 74.5 | (1.5) | **-12.9** | (1.4) | 64.9 | (0.6) | 64.4 | (0.6) | 73.5 | (1.7) | **-9.1** | (1.8) |
| | Austria | 21.6 | (0.9) | 20.4 | (0.9) | 37.7 | (3.0) | **-17.3** | (3.3) | 58.8 | (0.9) | 58.3 | (0.9) | 80.7 | (2.5) | **-22.3** | (2.6) | 55.2 | (1.4) | 55.1 | (1.4) | 77.5 | (6.6) | **-22.3** | (6.5) |
| | Belgium | 19.5 | (0.6) | 17.3 | (0.6) | 46.3 | (2.1) | **-29.0** | (2.2) | 47.0 | (0.8) | 46.7 | (0.8) | 60.3 | (3.2) | **-13.6** | (3.3) | 37.9 | (0.8) | 37.6 | (0.9) | 60.5 | (5.2) | **-22.9** | (5.3) |
| | Canada | 40.4 | (0.6) | 37.1 | (0.7) | 54.4 | (1.6) | **-17.3** | (1.7) | 67.6 | (0.5) | 66.3 | (0.7) | 72.2 | (1.0) | **-5.9** | (1.3) | 54.9 | (0.6) | 53.0 | (0.6) | 61.8 | (1.0) | **-8.8** | (1.1) |
| | Czech Republic | 15.0 | (0.9) | 12.9 | (0.9) | 26.7 | (1.6) | **-13.8** | (1.9) | 49.4 | (1.1) | 48.4 | (1.2) | 64.4 | (3.1) | **-16.1** | (3.2) | 47.7 | (0.9) | 47.4 | (1.0) | 57.8 | (4.9) | -10.3 | (5.3) |
| | Denmark | 23.2 | (0.8) | 22.6 | (0.7) | 44.7 | (6.3) | **-22.1** | (6.3) | 63.3 | (1.0) | 62.0 | (1.1) | 74.1 | (2.4) | **-12.0** | (2.7) | 68.4 | (0.8) | 66.0 | (1.0) | 72.0 | (1.1) | **-6.1** | (1.5) |
| | Finland | 11.9 | (0.6) | 11.4 | (0.6) | 24.1 | (3.6) | **-12.7** | (3.6) | 32.6 | (0.7) | 32.6 | (0.7) | 37.3 | (5.4) | -4.7 | (5.3) | 27.5 | (0.9) | 27.4 | (0.9) | 46.3 | (4.7) | **-18.9** | (4.8) |
| | France | 25.5 | (1.0) | 22.3 | (0.9) | 61.2 | (2.5) | **-38.9** | (2.5) | 51.8 | (1.0) | 51.5 | (1.0) | 64.2 | (4.8) | **-12.7** | (4.9) | 45.6 | (0.9) | 45.1 | (0.9) | 59.6 | (4.1) | **-14.5** | (4.1) |
| | Germany | 26.5 | (0.8) | 25.1 | (0.8) | 38.9 | (2.5) | **-13.9** | (2.3) | 67.1 | (0.9) | 66.3 | (0.9) | 78.2 | (3.1) | **-11.9** | (3.1) | 58.1 | (0.9) | 57.5 | (0.8) | 74.6 | (3.1) | **-17.1** | (3.2) |
| | Greece | 34.2 | (0.9) | 31.9 | (0.9) | 60.1 | (2.4) | **-28.2** | (2.4) | 52.5 | (1.0) | 51.1 | (1.0) | 75.4 | (2.3) | **-24.3** | (2.2) | 47.4 | (1.0) | 45.5 | (1.0) | 67.2 | (2.1) | **-21.7** | (2.1) |
| | Hungary | 16.4 | (0.7) | 15.3 | (0.6) | 36.6 | (3.5) | **-21.3** | (3.4) | 30.9 | (1.0) | 30.0 | (0.9) | 54.0 | (4.6) | **-24.0** | (4.5) | 35.2 | (1.0) | 34.0 | (1.1) | 71.6 | (3.9) | **-37.6** | (4.0) |
| | Iceland | 35.7 | (0.8) | 35.0 | (0.8) | 68.8 | (5.4) | **-33.8** | (5.5) | 80.7 | (0.7) | 79.9 | (0.8) | 86.2 | (1.2) | **-6.3** | (1.5) | 64.8 | (0.7) | 64.1 | (0.8) | 71.2 | (1.7) | **-7.1** | (1.8) |
| | Ireland | 30.3 | (0.8) | 29.9 | (0.8) | 52.1 | (6.0) | **-22.1** | (6.0) | 72.9 | (0.7) | 73.1 | (0.8) | 75.0 | (2.5) | -1.9 | (2.6) | 62.8 | (1.0) | 62.0 | (1.0) | 76.2 | (2.6) | **-14.2** | (2.7) |
| | Italy | 28.4 | (0.8) | 26.8 | (0.8) | 40.2 | (1.9) | **-13.3** | (1.9) | 49.8 | (0.7) | 48.9 | (0.8) | 64.9 | (2.0) | **-16.1** | (2.1) | 58.5 | (0.8) | 56.3 | (0.9) | 66.0 | (1.2) | **-9.7** | (1.5) |
| | Japan | 24.8 | (0.7) | 24.6 | (0.7) | 36.7 | (5.0) | **-12.1** | (4.9) | 51.3 | (1.1) | 48.8 | (1.1) | 67.0 | (1.9) | **-18.3** | (2.2) | 49.5 | (0.7) | 48.9 | (0.8) | 60.6 | (2.7) | **-11.7** | (2.7) |
| | Korea | 24.6 | (1.0) | 23.8 | (0.8) | 44.0 | (10.3) | -20.2 | (10.4) | 58.4 | (1.0) | 57.2 | (1.0) | 67.4 | (2.0) | **-10.2** | (2.0) | 55.2 | (1.0) | 54.2 | (1.1) | 65.6 | (2.4) | **-11.4** | (2.7) |
| | Luxembourg | 27.6 | (0.7) | 25.9 | (0.7) | 60.3 | (3.4) | **-34.3** | (3.3) | 52.0 | (0.7) | 51.2 | (0.7) | 68.9 | (3.8) | **-17.6** | (3.8) | 51.1 | (0.7) | 51.0 | (0.8) | 58.1 | (3.7) | -7.1 | (3.9) |
| | Mexico | 41.6 | (0.9) | 40.5 | (1.0) | 46.7 | (1.4) | **-6.3** | (1.5) | 78.5 | (0.6) | 77.4 | (0.7) | 84.1 | (1.1) | **-6.7** | (1.3) | 67.9 | (0.8) | 66.6 | (0.8) | 74.6 | (1.8) | **-8.0** | (1.7) |
| | Netherlands | 23.3 | (0.7) | 21.3 | (0.7) | 51.0 | (3.4) | **-29.7** | (3.3) | 40.8 | (0.9) | 40.7 | (1.0) | 59.5 | (6.8) | **-18.8** | (7.0) | 38.0 | (0.9) | 37.5 | (0.9) | 62.0 | (7.8) | **-24.5** | (7.6) |
| | New Zealand | 33.6 | (0.9) | 31.4 | (0.9) | 57.7 | (2.7) | **-26.3** | (2.9) | 65.6 | (0.7) | 65.4 | (0.8) | 72.9 | (2.7) | **-7.5** | (2.8) | 61.9 | (0.7) | 61.3 | (0.8) | 72.9 | (2.7) | **-11.6** | (3.0) |
| | Norway | 28.6 | (0.8) | 28.4 | (0.9) | 45.1 | (7.5) | **-16.7** | (7.6) | 56.4 | (1.0) | 56.6 | (1.0) | 61.6 | (4.6) | -5.0 | (4.4) | 41.7 | (1.0) | 41.8 | (1.0) | 43.5 | (2.6) | -1.7 | (2.9) |
| | Poland | 23.6 | (0.7) | 22.5 | (0.7) | 50.3 | (4.1) | **-27.8** | (4.2) | 36.1 | (0.8) | 35.0 | (0.8) | 44.7 | (1.9) | **-9.7** | (1.9) | 42.2 | (0.7) | 40.7 | (0.8) | 49.1 | (1.5) | **-8.4** | (1.7) |
| | Portugal | 38.4 | (1.0) | 32.1 | (1.1) | 62.0 | (1.8) | **-29.9** | (2.1) | 54.9 | (1.0) | 53.4 | (1.1) | 70.5 | (2.3) | **-17.0** | (2.5) | 43.4 | (1.1) | 42.9 | (1.1) | 50.6 | (3.8) | **-7.7** | (3.7) |
| | Slovak Republic | 16.7 | (0.7) | 15.0 | (0.7) | 32.6 | (2.5) | **-17.6** | (2.5) | 47.4 | (1.2) | 47.1 | (1.2) | 60.2 | (5.0) | **-13.0** | (5.0) | 53.9 | (1.0) | 53.9 | (1.0) | 69.8 | (5.7) | **-15.8** | (5.8) |
| | Spain | 36.4 | (0.8) | 33.2 | (0.8) | 63.1 | (1.8) | **-29.9** | (2.1) | 55.8 | (0.7) | 56.1 | (0.7) | 61.9 | (4.2) | -5.8 | (4.3) | 47.7 | (0.6) | 47.8 | (0.7) | 58.4 | (3.6) | **-10.6** | (3.7) |
| | Sweden | 27.0 | (0.8) | 26.7 | (0.8) | 56.5 | (6.1) | **-29.8** | (6.1) | 58.8 | (0.9) | 58.9 | (0.9) | 62.5 | (7.4) | -3.5 | (7.4) | 61.5 | (1.1) | 61.2 | (1.1) | 79.1 | (5.1) | **-17.9** | (4.6) |
| | Switzerland | 16.9 | (0.6) | 15.6 | (0.5) | 38.6 | (2.8) | **-23.0** | (2.7) | 60.6 | (0.9) | 59.9 | (0.9) | 68.1 | (2.3) | **-8.2** | (2.4) | 52.6 | (0.8) | 51.7 | (0.8) | 71.2 | (2.7) | **-19.5** | (2.8) |
| | Turkey | 44.1 | (1.1) | 39.5 | (1.2) | 65.3 | (1.8) | **-25.9** | (2.2) | 69.8 | (1.0) | 68.3 | (1.0) | 85.1 | (2.2) | **-16.7** | (2.3) | 64.6 | (1.3) | 62.6 | (1.4) | 80.7 | (2.2) | **-18.2** | (2.3) |
| | United Kingdom | 41.3 | (0.8) | 39.3 | (0.8) | 55.9 | (2.2) | **-16.7** | (2.2) | 66.4 | (0.9) | 66.0 | (0.9) | 78.9 | (2.3) | **-12.9** | (2.5) | 67.7 | (0.8) | 67.6 | (0.8) | 74.4 | (2.6) | **-6.8** | (2.6) |
| | United States | 43.0 | (0.6) | 41.3 | (0.7) | 56.5 | (1.9) | **-15.3** | (2.0) | 68.7 | (0.9) | 67.7 | (0.9) | 76.1 | (1.7) | **-8.4** | (1.7) | 60.2 | (0.9) | 59.6 | (1.0) | 67.3 | (1.9) | **-7.7** | (1.8) |
| | **OECD average** | 28.4 | (0.1) | 26.6 | (0.1) | 49.1 | (0.7) | **-22.5** | (0.7) | 57.0 | (0.2) | 56.2 | (0.2) | 68.4 | (0.6) | **-12.1** | (0.6) | 52.9 | (0.2) | 52.1 | (0.2) | 65.8 | (0.7) | **-13.6** | (0.7) |
| Partners | Argentina | 41.9 | (1.1) | 40.9 | (1.1) | 55.5 | (5.5) | **-14.5** | (5.6) | 61.0 | (1.1) | 60.9 | (1.1) | 75.0 | (4.0) | **-14.0** | (4.3) | 49.3 | (1.1) | 49.5 | (1.2) | 46.9 | (6.9) | 2.7 | (7.1) |
| | Azerbaijan | 54.3 | (1.2) | 52.4 | (1.2) | 64.4 | (3.1) | **-12.0** | (3.2) | 50.2 | (1.2) | 46.8 | (1.3) | 60.3 | (1.9) | **-13.6** | (1.8) | 69.6 | (1.2) | 67.9 | (1.3) | 79.6 | (1.7) | **-11.7** | (1.8) |
| | Brazil | 41.4 | (0.7) | 40.5 | (0.7) | 60.4 | (4.6) | **-19.9** | (4.6) | 64.2 | (0.8) | 63.4 | (0.9) | 74.3 | (2.2) | **-10.9** | (2.3) | 71.1 | (0.7) | 70.4 | (0.8) | 79.4 | (1.8) | **-9.0** | (1.9) |
| | Bulgaria | 31.9 | (1.0) | 29.7 | (1.0) | 47.2 | (2.5) | **-17.5** | (2.6) | 58.2 | (1.4) | 57.0 | (1.5) | 77.1 | (2.4) | **-20.2** | (2.5) | 61.3 | (1.3) | 60.9 | (1.4) | 78.4 | (2.8) | **-17.5** | (2.8) |
| | Chile | 47.0 | (1.1) | 45.7 | (1.1) | 65.3 | (3.3) | **-19.5** | (3.2) | 77.1 | (0.7) | 76.3 | (0.8) | 83.1 | (1.3) | **-6.7** | (1.4) | 72.1 | (1.1) | 71.5 | (1.2) | 77.9 | (1.3) | **-6.4** | (1.5) |
| | Colombia | 53.4 | (1.2) | 51.4 | (1.2) | 70.0 | (3.8) | **-18.6** | (4.1) | 70.4 | (0.8) | 69.0 | (0.9) | 77.9 | (2.2) | **-8.9** | (2.4) | 63.3 | (1.3) | 62.2 | (1.5) | 73.7 | (3.2) | **-11.4** | (3.3) |
| | Croatia | 18.7 | (0.8) | 18.3 | (0.8) | 39.2 | (4.9) | **-20.9** | (4.9) | 37.0 | (1.0) | 36.8 | (0.9) | 51.9 | (6.8) | **-15.1** | (6.7) | 42.0 | (1.1) | 41.9 | (1.1) | 47.7 | (5.4) | -5.7 | (5.6) |
| | Estonia | 24.1 | (0.8) | 23.2 | (0.9) | 30.7 | (2.2) | **-7.4** | (2.4) | 58.6 | (1.0) | 58.2 | (1.0) | 65.0 | (2.3) | **-6.8** | (2.3) | 54.6 | (0.9) | 54.5 | (0.9) | 58.9 | (3.9) | -4.4 | (4.0) |
| | Hong Kong-China | 34.6 | (0.9) | 23.7 | (1.1) | 60.0 | (1.6) | **-36.3** | (2.1) | 55.9 | (1.3) | 52.2 | (1.6) | 60.8 | (1.4) | **-8.6** | (1.8) | 52.8 | (1.0) | 49.9 | (1.5) | 57.2 | (1.5) | **-7.3** | (2.3) |
| | Indonesia | 43.1 | (1.4) | 40.9 | (1.4) | 58.3 | (2.4) | **-17.5** | (2.5) | 60.1 | (0.9) | 58.8 | (1.0) | 67.0 | (2.2) | **-8.2** | (2.3) | 58.2 | (1.0) | 56.9 | (1.1) | 68.5 | (2.1) | **-11.6** | (2.4) |
| | Israel | 34.6 | (0.9) | 32.0 | (1.0) | 61.7 | (3.4) | **-29.7** | (3.5) | 68.7 | (1.1) | 67.1 | (1.2) | 83.0 | (1.3) | **-15.9** | (1.4) | 50.3 | (1.1) | 48.7 | (1.1) | 63.2 | (3.2) | **-14.5** | (3.2) |
| | Jordan | 59.3 | (0.8) | 57.1 | (0.9) | 70.9 | (1.9) | **-13.8** | (2.0) | 58.1 | (1.0) | 55.6 | (1.1) | 71.6 | (1.8) | **-15.9** | (1.8) | 52.9 | (1.0) | 51.2 | (1.1) | 61.2 | (1.7) | **-10.0** | (1.9) |
| | Kyrgyzstan | 49.4 | (0.9) | 47.3 | (1.0) | 57.8 | (3.1) | **-10.5** | (3.3) | 61.9 | (0.9) | 59.8 | (0.9) | 72.4 | (1.8) | **-12.6** | (1.9) | 64.8 | (0.7) | 63.2 | (0.7) | 73.4 | (2.3) | **-10.3** | (2.4) |
| | Latvia | 15.4 | (0.7) | 13.9 | (0.7) | 31.1 | (2.1) | **-17.1** | (2.1) | 61.0 | (0.9) | 60.1 | (1.0) | 66.6 | (1.9) | **-6.6** | (2.1) | 52.2 | (1.0) | 51.9 | (1.0) | 60.8 | (3.0) | **-8.9** | (3.1) |
| | Liechtenstein | 20.0 | (1.8) | 19.1 | (2.0) | 31.4 | (9.6) | -12.3 | (10.7) | 54.8 | (2.6) | 53.2 | (2.6) | 71.6 | (8.9) | **-18.4** | (8.7) | 45.6 | (2.4) | 44.7 | (2.5) | 53.7 | (15.3) | -9.0 | (15.7) |
| | Lithuania | 32.7 | (0.8) | 32.0 | (0.8) | 47.6 | (3.6) | **-15.6** | (3.8) | 61.8 | (0.9) | 61.3 | (0.9) | 70.1 | (2.8) | **-8.8** | (2.8) | 63.1 | (1.1) | 62.2 | (1.2) | 73.2 | (2.5) | **-11.0** | (2.8) |
| | Macao-China | 26.4 | (0.9) | 21.4 | (1.0) | 40.3 | (1.9) | **-18.9** | (2.1) | 39.1 | (0.9) | 35.8 | (1.2) | 43.1 | (1.4) | **-7.2** | (1.8) | 60.1 | (1.1) | 56.2 | (1.5) | 65.3 | (1.6) | **-9.1** | (2.2) |
| | Montenegro | 33.4 | (0.8) | 31.3 | (0.9) | 47.7 | (2.4) | **-16.3** | (2.8) | 37.4 | (0.7) | 35.8 | (0.8) | 49.0 | (2.4) | **-13.2** | (2.5) | 56.3 | (0.7) | 54.9 | (0.8) | 70.6 | (2.3) | **-15.7** | (2.5) |
| | Qatar | 51.7 | (0.6) | 50.2 | (0.6) | 64.0 | (1.8) | **-13.8** | (1.8) | 49.2 | (0.7) | 47.8 | (0.7) | 62.1 | (2.0) | **-14.3** | (2.0) | 46.5 | (0.7) | 45.3 | (0.7) | 55.7 | (2.2) | **-10.4** | (2.3) |
| | Romania | 24.9 | (0.7) | 23.7 | (0.8) | 36.7 | (2.2) | **-13.0** | (2.6) | 55.3 | (1.5) | 53.8 | (1.7) | 77.7 | (3.1) | **-23.9** | (3.5) | 63.3 | (1.1) | 62.5 | (1.2) | 80.0 | (3.2) | **-17.5** | (3.5) |
| | Russian Federation | 22.5 | (0.7) | 21.4 | (0.8) | 26.2 | (1.5) | **-4.7** | (1.8) | 53.8 | (1.1) | 52.6 | (1.2) | 65.3 | (2.5) | **-12.7** | (2.5) | 54.3 | (0.9) | 54.1 | (0.9) | 64.9 | (5.4) | -10.8 | (5.7) |
| | Serbia | 21.8 | (0.8) | 20.1 | (0.8) | 34.3 | (2.5) | **-14.2** | (2.5) | 33.0 | (0.9) | 32.5 | (0.9) | 46.1 | (3.8) | **-13.6** | (3.8) | 45.7 | (0.9) | 45.3 | (0.9) | 58.0 | (3.2) | **-12.7** | (3.5) |
| | Slovenia | 21.5 | (0.6) | 19.9 | (0.6) | 32.7 | (2.5) | **-12.8** | (2.6) | 45.8 | (0.8) | 45.8 | (0.9) | 53.8 | (4.2) | -8.0 | (4.3) | 44.8 | (0.8) | 44.7 | (0.8) | 55.6 | (4.7) | **-10.9** | (4.7) |
| | Chinese Taipei | 27.4 | (0.6) | 25.8 | (0.6) | 48.1 | (2.4) | **-22.3** | (2.6) | 44.7 | (0.9) | 42.3 | (1.0) | 55.7 | (1.3) | **-13.5** | (1.5) | 47.1 | (0.6) | 46.3 | (0.7) | 51.6 | (1.3) | **-5.3** | (1.5) |
| | Thailand | 60.9 | (0.9) | 57.0 | (1.0) | 82.7 | (1.6) | **-25.7** | (1.8) | 69.0 | (0.8) | 67.6 | (0.8) | 84.9 | (1.9) | **-17.3** | (2.2) | 55.2 | (1.0) | 55.1 | (1.0) | 61.8 | (7.2) | -6.7 | (7.3) |
| | Tunisia | 60.3 | (1.1) | 58.7 | (1.1) | 74.8 | (2.4) | **-16.1** | (2.5) | 58.2 | (1.0) | 56.6 | (1.1) | 75.4 | (2.4) | **-18.8** | (2.8) | 46.0 | (1.3) | 44.2 | (1.3) | 69.0 | (2.8) | **-24.9** | (2.8) |
| | Uruguay | 37.0 | (0.9) | 35.7 | (1.0) | 53.7 | (2.6) | **-18.0** | (2.6) | 59.1 | (0.9) | 58.3 | (0.9) | 74.3 | (3.6) | **-16.0** | (3.6) | 46.0 | (0.9) | 45.6 | (0.9) | 67.1 | (5.7) | **-21.5** | (5.7) |

*Note*: Values that are statistically significant at the 5% level ($p < 0.05$) are indicated in bold.

250

© OECD 2011 Quality Time for Students: Learning In and Out of School

**Table 4.4** Percentage of students who take optional science courses, by learning time in regular lessons in science

| | | No time | | Less than 2 hours per week | | 2 hours or more but less than 4 hours per week | | 4 hours or more but less than 6 hours per week | | 6 hours or more per week | | Difference (4 to 6 hours - 6 hours or more) | |
|---|---|---|---|---|---|---|---|---|---|---|---|---|---|
| | | % | S.E. | % | S.E. | % | S.E. | % | S.E. | % | S.E. | Dif. | S.E. |
| OECD | Australia | 61.3 | (2.9) | 44.3 | (2.1) | 37.7 | (1.6) | 35.5 | (1.7) | 61.7 | (2.2) | -26.2 | (2.1) |
| | Austria | 25.4 | (2.4) | 22.5 | (1.3) | 16.6 | (1.3) | 11.1 | (1.5) | 21.4 | (3.9) | -10.3 | (3.8) |
| | Belgium | 18.9 | (2.2) | 19.3 | (1.0) | 13.5 | (0.9) | 58.8 | (1.8) | 50.0 | (2.7) | 8.8 | (3.2) |
| | Canada | 19.6 | (1.7) | 27.6 | (1.6) | 23.2 | (1.1) | 26.4 | (1.0) | 30.8 | (1.1) | -4.4 | (1.4) |
| | Czech Republic | 17.9 | (2.9) | 24.6 | (1.9) | 22.0 | (1.7) | 14.2 | (1.8) | 12.7 | (1.7) | 1.5 | (2.1) |
| | Denmark | 35.1 | (5.5) | 30.0 | (2.3) | 19.7 | (1.0) | 20.0 | (1.3) | 38.1 | (6.8) | -18.1 | (6.9) |
| | Finland | 13.6 | (3.0) | 13.2 | (1.2) | 10.6 | (1.0) | 12.0 | (1.4) | 20.0 | (3.5) | -7.9 | (3.0) |
| | France | 15.1 | (1.9) | 9.2 | (1.0) | 7.3 | (0.7) | 6.4 | (1.1) | 10.7 | (2.0) | -4.3 | (2.2) |
| | Germany | 30.7 | (2.5) | 25.8 | (1.6) | 25.5 | (1.7) | 27.8 | (1.9) | 36.8 | (2.8) | -9.0 | (2.9) |
| | Greece | 61.8 | (3.1) | 49.9 | (2.3) | 35.4 | (1.5) | 30.7 | (1.4) | 46.7 | (2.8) | -16.0 | (2.8) |
| | Hungary | 19.1 | (3.5) | 15.8 | (1.2) | 15.0 | (1.1) | 13.4 | (1.5) | 27.3 | (4.0) | -13.9 | (4.0) |
| | Iceland | 33.1 | (5.9) | 27.7 | (1.5) | 34.1 | (0.9) | 52.0 | (1.9) | 69.2 | (5.2) | -17.1 | (5.3) |
| | Ireland | 68.1 | (3.6) | 62.2 | (2.4) | 49.3 | (2.0) | 55.5 | (2.4) | 77.9 | (4.2) | -22.4 | (4.4) |
| | Italy | a | a | a | a | a | a | a | a | a | a | a | a |
| | Japan | 40.0 | (6.6) | 21.1 | (1.7) | 20.2 | (1.2) | 24.7 | (2.4) | 36.5 | (9.1) | -11.8 | (9.0) |
| | Korea | 80.7 | (6.9) | 73.7 | (3.1) | 67.0 | (2.2) | 69.7 | (2.2) | 83.3 | (5.4) | -13.6 | (5.7) |
| | Luxembourg | 26.6 | (2.4) | 25.2 | (1.1) | 24.5 | (1.2) | 20.3 | (1.9) | 21.9 | (2.6) | -1.6 | (3.0) |
| | Mexico | 59.5 | (1.7) | 69.9 | (1.6) | 61.8 | (1.8) | 59.5 | (1.8) | 65.2 | (2.1) | -5.7 | (2.8) |
| | Netherlands | 45.2 | (2.9) | 42.9 | (1.7) | 42.5 | (1.6) | 43.3 | (2.2) | 59.6 | (3.4) | -16.3 | (3.6) |
| | New Zealand | 60.8 | (4.2) | 59.4 | (3.0) | 41.5 | (2.4) | 42.1 | (2.0) | 77.3 | (2.5) | -35.2 | (2.5) |
| | Norway | a | a | a | a | a | a | a | a | a | a | a | a |
| | Poland | a | a | a | a | a | a | a | a | a | a | a | a |
| | Portugal | 49.1 | (4.2) | 41.7 | (2.2) | 36.8 | (1.9) | 52.2 | (2.2) | 55.7 | (2.3) | -3.6 | (2.7) |
| | Slovak Republic | 20.8 | (1.8) | 16.9 | (0.9) | 15.4 | (1.3) | 14.9 | (1.8) | 12.7 | (2.0) | 2.2 | (2.4) |
| | Spain | 54.0 | (2.8) | 43.1 | (1.5) | 50.0 | (1.3) | 55.4 | (2.1) | 70.3 | (2.4) | -14.8 | (2.9) |
| | Sweden | 36.2 | (8.1) | 17.6 | (2.2) | 10.8 | (0.8) | 14.1 | (2.2) | 48.7 | (8.7) | -34.6 | (9.0) |
| | Switzerland | 33.4 | (1.8) | 24.3 | (1.0) | 19.8 | (1.2) | 18.2 | (1.7) | 14.9 | (2.6) | 3.4 | (3.4) |
| | Turkey | 60.5 | (2.9) | 58.4 | (2.5) | 44.3 | (1.8) | 33.7 | (3.5) | 39.6 | (2.7) | -5.9 | (3.8) |
| | United Kingdom | 68.8 | (5.5) | 69.2 | (3.4) | 74.2 | (1.8) | 70.7 | (1.9) | 79.2 | (2.3) | -8.6 | (3.0) |
| | United States | 47.6 | (3.4) | 46.2 | (1.9) | 45.2 | (2.2) | 34.7 | (1.7) | 45.8 | (2.1) | -11.1 | (2.4) |
| | **OECD average** | 40.8 | (0.8) | 36.4 | (0.4) | 32.0 | (0.3) | 34.0 | (0.4) | 45.0 | (0.8) | -11.0 | (0.8) |
| Partners | Argentina | 66.3 | (3.6) | 59.9 | (2.8) | 52.5 | (3.2) | 54.9 | (5.4) | 63.1 | (7.1) | -8.2 | (9.1) |
| | Azerbaijan | 73.1 | (2.6) | 64.5 | (2.3) | 57.0 | (2.6) | 61.5 | (3.3) | 62.1 | (3.5) | -0.6 | (4.0) |
| | Brazil | 69.6 | (5.1) | 68.8 | (2.6) | 64.2 | (2.7) | 46.1 | (7.0) | 48.0 | (6.3) | -1.9 | (8.7) |
| | Bulgaria | 48.6 | (3.2) | 40.9 | (1.8) | 31.3 | (1.7) | 28.3 | (2.5) | 29.6 | (2.7) | -1.3 | (3.1) |
| | Chile | 47.5 | (3.1) | 39.1 | (2.0) | 32.9 | (2.3) | 29.7 | (2.5) | 31.0 | (2.5) | -1.3 | (2.9) |
| | Colombia | 76.4 | (5.7) | 82.3 | (2.6) | 73.8 | (2.3) | 74.4 | (3.9) | 78.6 | (9.5) | -4.3 | (8.1) |
| | Croatia | 13.2 | (2.2) | 7.7 | (0.9) | 7.8 | (0.7) | 8.2 | (1.4) | 13.9 | (3.5) | -5.7 | (4.0) |
| | Estonia | 46.8 | (5.8) | 34.4 | (2.0) | 27.3 | (1.5) | 18.5 | (1.4) | 17.6 | (2.0) | 0.9 | (2.2) |
| | Hong Kong-China | 50.0 | (4.0) | 47.1 | (3.3) | 32.4 | (2.4) | 31.1 | (2.5) | 35.1 | (1.8) | -4.0 | (3.1) |
| | Indonesia | 79.7 | (3.1) | 72.9 | (1.4) | 66.5 | (1.3) | 66.6 | (2.9) | 69.1 | (2.6) | -2.4 | (3.0) |
| | Israel | 62.8 | (2.6) | 50.6 | (2.2) | 54.7 | (1.7) | 63.5 | (3.0) | 72.5 | (3.0) | -9.0 | (3.9) |
| | Jordan | 68.9 | (2.8) | 59.0 | (2.1) | 47.7 | (1.9) | 32.7 | (2.3) | 35.3 | (2.6) | -2.6 | (3.1) |
| | Kyrgyzstan | 74.9 | (1.7) | 73.3 | (1.3) | 71.4 | (1.8) | 66.7 | (2.7) | 67.8 | (4.7) | -1.1 | (4.8) |
| | Latvia | 49.0 | (3.3) | 40.1 | (1.5) | 34.7 | (1.6) | 28.4 | (2.1) | 26.7 | (2.5) | 1.8 | (3.1) |
| | Liechtenstein | 63.7 | (15.3) | 28.1 | (4.2) | 31.7 | (3.5) | 21.8 | (7.9) | 13.4 | (8.3) | 8.4 | (11.4) |
| | Lithuania | 40.3 | (5.5) | 24.9 | (1.4) | 19.5 | (1.3) | 14.5 | (1.5) | 19.5 | (3.2) | -5.0 | (3.5) |
| | Macao-China | 68.6 | (3.6) | 60.7 | (2.8) | 48.9 | (1.7) | 46.4 | (2.2) | 45.1 | (2.0) | 1.3 | (3.0) |
| | Montenegro | 61.0 | (2.8) | 53.5 | (1.5) | 39.1 | (1.6) | 34.2 | (1.8) | 36.0 | (2.7) | -1.8 | (3.4) |
| | Qatar | 78.3 | (1.8) | 71.7 | (1.2) | 56.6 | (1.4) | 52.1 | (1.9) | 51.1 | (2.1) | 1.0 | (2.5) |
| | Romania | 68.7 | (2.9) | 63.0 | (2.1) | 61.2 | (3.2) | 59.8 | (4.5) | 66.1 | (2.9) | -6.3 | (5.9) |
| | Russian Federation | 4.0 | (1.4) | 3.2 | (0.9) | 2.4 | (0.7) | 1.3 | (0.3) | 1.9 | (1.1) | -0.6 | (1.0) |
| | Serbia | a | a | a | a | a | a | a | a | a | a | a | a |
| | Slovenia | 20.0 | (1.8) | 17.4 | (0.9) | 13.7 | (1.0) | 10.7 | (1.3) | 10.5 | (1.5) | 0.2 | (1.9) |
| | Chinese Taipei | 34.0 | (3.8) | 34.3 | (1.8) | 27.9 | (1.0) | 17.8 | (1.3) | 17.7 | (2.0) | 0.2 | (1.9) |
| | Thailand | a | a | 77.3 | (5.9) | 68.2 | (1.2) | 65.5 | (1.9) | 68.9 | (2.1) | -3.4 | (2.3) |
| | Tunisia | 85.3 | (2.1) | 74.9 | (1.3) | 73.0 | (1.5) | 72.3 | (3.1) | 70.1 | (2.9) | 2.2 | (3.5) |
| | Uruguay | 36.9 | (3.2) | 27.9 | (1.9) | 21.8 | (1.6) | 22.4 | (2.8) | 18.0 | (2.7) | 4.5 | (4.0) |

*Note:* Values that are statistically significant at the 5% level (p < 0.05) are indicated in bold.

### Table 4.5a — Relationship between performance in science and learning time in regular school lessons in science, by students' perception of how important it is to do well in science

| | Time spent in regular school lessons in science (1) | | Time spent in regular school lessons in science (squared) (2) | | Students who think it is very important to do well in science (1=very important 0=not very important) (3) | | Differential effect of time spent in regular school lessons in science for students who think it is very important to do well in science (1) * (3) | | PISA index of economic, social and cultural status of students (1 unit increase) (4) | | School average of PISA index of economic, social and cultural status of students (1 unit increase) (5) | | Intercept | |
|---|---|---|---|---|---|---|---|---|---|---|---|---|---|---|
| | Change in score | S.E. | Change in score | S.E. | Change in score | S.E. | Change in score | S.E. | Change in score | S.E. | Change in score | S.E. | Mean | S.E. |
| **Australia** | **24.5** | (1.9) | **-2.0** | (0.3) | **22.6** | (6.0) | **3.9** | (1.4) | **43.6** | (4.6) | **23.1** | (1.5) | 452.5 | (3.3) |
| Austria | **16.1** | (2.5) | -1.0 | (0.4) | -4.6 | (6.9) | **5.0** | (1.9) | **98.7** | (7.0) | **9.3** | (1.8) | 456.9 | (3.9) |
| Belgium | **20.3** | (2.0) | **-1.6** | (0.3) | -3.6 | (7.3) | 3.0 | (1.7) | **86.8** | (5.2) | **14.1** | (1.2) | 461.7 | (3.6) |
| Canada | **16.4** | (2.0) | **-1.3** | (0.3) | **12.2** | (6.1) | **3.8** | (1.2) | **33.7** | (4.4) | **18.7** | (1.4) | 470.2 | (4.0) |
| Czech Republic | **7.7** | (2.6) | 0.5 | (0.4) | **-25.1** | (7.7) | **6.5** | (1.5) | **85.4** | (7.5) | **17.1** | (1.6) | 483.3 | (4.3) |
| Denmark | **35.6** | (3.8) | **-3.8** | (0.6) | 16.0 | (8.6) | 1.7 | (2.3) | **36.8** | (7.4) | **28.1** | (1.9) | 408.0 | (6.9) |
| Finland | **23.2** | (3.0) | **-1.6** | (0.4) | **37.4** | (9.5) | 2.2 | (2.2) | 7.3 | (5.8) | **23.9** | (1.5) | 499.1 | (5.1) |
| France | **24.9** | (2.5) | **-1.9** | (0.3) | -1.1 | (7.5) | **7.3** | (1.7) | **72.5** | (4.8) | **13.8** | (1.7) | 453.5 | (4.8) |
| Germany | **11.5** | (2.2) | -0.4 | (0.3) | 8.8 | (6.1) | 1.5 | (1.6) | **93.3** | (5.9) | **12.7** | (1.4) | 457.3 | (4.4) |
| Greece | **29.7** | (2.5) | **-2.8** | (0.3) | -5.4 | (5.0) | **6.5** | (1.2) | **48.2** | (4.9) | **10.6** | (1.5) | 424.7 | (4.8) |
| Hungary | **7.5** | (2.4) | 0.2 | (0.4) | -6.6 | (6.2) | **3.5** | (1.6) | **78.8** | (4.5) | **5.2** | (1.5) | 491.8 | (4.2) |
| Iceland | **35.4** | (4.2) | **-5.0** | (0.7) | **21.2** | (8.8) | **7.1** | (2.3) | -0.7 | (4.9) | **23.5** | (1.9) | 411.0 | (7.3) |
| Ireland | **27.8** | (2.8) | **-3.5** | (0.5) | **23.9** | (6.8) | 2.6 | (2.3) | **41.3** | (5.8) | **22.0** | (2.0) | 465.2 | (4.7) |
| Italy | **17.6** | (1.8) | -1.0 | (0.3) | **-14.1** | (4.7) | **3.6** | (1.2) | **78.5** | (5.2) | **6.3** | (1.0) | 444.3 | (3.9) |
| Japan | **18.2** | (3.8) | -1.8 | (0.6) | **15.6** | (7.2) | 2.8 | (2.1) | **115.5** | (9.2) | 4.5 | (2.2) | 496.6 | (6.8) |
| Korea | **25.4** | (5.4) | **-2.5** | (0.7) | 6.9 | (9.7) | 3.1 | (2.4) | **72.4** | (7.7) | **7.5** | (1.8) | 466.0 | (11.2) |
| Luxembourg | **17.7** | (1.9) | **-1.7** | (0.3) | -7.2 | (5.5) | **5.8** | (1.5) | **67.0** | (2.4) | **22.0** | (1.4) | 451.6 | (2.7) |
| Mexico | **4.9** | (1.3) | **-0.6** | (0.2) | -3.2 | (3.0) | 2.6 | (0.7) | **35.7** | (2.2) | **6.3** | (0.8) | 445.8 | (3.0) |
| Netherlands | **11.1** | (2.1) | -0.1 | (0.3) | 0.5 | (6.4) | 2.6 | (1.7) | **104.9** | (6.2) | **9.6** | (1.7) | 471.3 | (3.5) |
| New Zealand | **34.5** | (2.8) | **-2.5** | (0.4) | -4.1 | (10.7) | **6.6** | (2.1) | **41.3** | (5.9) | **32.5** | (1.6) | 428.6 | (5.2) |
| Norway | **44.6** | (3.5) | **-6.6** | (0.6) | **18.8** | (9.3) | 1.6 | (3.0) | **29.2** | (7.3) | **25.7** | (2.0) | 400.5 | (6.4) |
| Poland | **23.5** | (2.4) | **-2.1** | (0.4) | -0.4 | (6.7) | **5.2** | (1.9) | **15.1** | (5.1) | **32.2** | (1.6) | 467.3 | (4.0) |
| Portugal | **19.9** | (3.0) | -1.2 | (0.4) | 1.1 | (7.9) | **6.9** | (1.6) | **27.0** | (3.4) | **11.0** | (1.4) | 437.0 | (5.1) |
| Slovak Republic | **22.0** | (2.5) | **-1.6** | (0.3) | -10.8 | (6.5) | **3.9** | (1.6) | **60.5** | (5.0) | **17.4** | (1.8) | 464.0 | (3.8) |
| Spain | **10.9** | (1.6) | -0.3 | (0.2) | 2.3 | (5.1) | **6.7** | (1.2) | **16.7** | (2.7) | **17.9** | (1.3) | 462.9 | (3.2) |
| Sweden | **41.4** | (3.6) | **-5.5** | (0.6) | **25.0** | (9.8) | 2.3 | (3.1) | **29.6** | (6.5) | **27.7** | (2.4) | 420.4 | (6.7) |
| Switzerland | **26.3** | (2.5) | **-2.1** | (0.4) | **16.9** | (6.9) | 1.2 | (1.7) | **63.5** | (5.7) | **21.5** | (1.6) | 460.3 | (3.8) |
| Turkey | **4.6** | (1.7) | 0.5 | (0.3) | -0.2 | (4.2) | 2.1 | (1.0) | **54.4** | (4.5) | **7.0** | (1.2) | 480.3 | (6.8) |
| United Kingdom | **31.7** | (3.4) | **-2.0** | (0.4) | -7.6 | (6.8) | **5.9** | (1.3) | **56.3** | (5.0) | **26.4** | (1.9) | 404.0 | (7.8) |
| United States | **21.6** | (2.5) | **-1.6** | (0.4) | 5.6 | (6.0) | 3.1 | (1.3) | **47.6** | (6.4) | **26.7** | (1.8) | 426.5 | (4.4) |
| **OECD average** | **21.9** | (0.5) | **-1.9** | (0.1) | **4.7** | (1.3) | **4.0** | (0.3) | **54.7** | (1.0) | **17.5** | (0.3) | 452.1 | (1.0) |
| **Argentina** | **13.9** | (3.2) | -0.8 | (0.5) | **-14.7** | (7.3) | 4.4 | (2.5) | **48.2** | (5.9) | **12.1** | (1.8) | 415.3 | (6.9) |
| Azerbaijan | **13.1** | (2.5) | -1.0 | (0.3) | -1.1 | (4.0) | -1.4 | (1.1) | **11.0** | (4.9) | **6.5** | (1.0) | 371.7 | (4.3) |
| Brazil | **13.6** | (2.1) | -0.5 | (0.4) | **-12.1** | (4.9) | **4.1** | (1.8) | **41.8** | (3.3) | **6.7** | (1.4) | 424.4 | (4.6) |
| Bulgaria | **18.2** | (2.6) | **-1.4** | (0.4) | **-12.9** | (4.9) | **3.2** | (1.5) | **71.0** | (6.0) | **12.0** | (1.6) | 426.3 | (5.0) |
| Chile | **12.6** | (1.8) | **-0.7** | (0.3) | -3.4 | (3.7) | 2.1 | (1.3) | **42.8** | (3.3) | **9.1** | (1.4) | 453.0 | (4.0) |
| Colombia | **7.0** | (3.1) | -0.4 | (0.4) | **-14.8** | (7.8) | **3.9** | (1.7) | **26.1** | (3.3) | **10.9** | (1.8) | 412.2 | (6.1) |
| Croatia | **14.9** | (2.3) | **-1.5** | (0.4) | 3.8 | (6.9) | 2.5 | (2.1) | **71.7** | (6.4) | **13.2** | (1.5) | 483.3 | (3.6) |
| Estonia | **18.3** | (3.0) | -0.9 | (0.4) | -5.7 | (6.5) | **5.2** | (1.6) | **37.2** | (7.1) | **19.1** | (1.9) | 475.3 | (5.1) |
| Hong Kong-China | **-7.8** | (2.8) | **2.1** | (0.4) | **15.8** | (8.6) | 2.6 | (1.5) | **52.4** | (6.4) | 3.2 | (1.8) | 564.4 | (6.4) |
| Indonesia | **12.0** | (3.9) | -0.7 | (0.4) | **-12.1** | (4.7) | 1.9 | (1.2) | **42.9** | (5.2) | 1.1 | (1.0) | 434.5 | (8.4) |
| Israel | **22.1** | (2.4) | **-1.8** | (0.4) | 8.3 | (7.0) | **4.6** | (2.0) | **66.6** | (8.7) | **20.5** | (2.5) | 403.1 | (4.5) |
| Jordan | **15.9** | (2.2) | **-1.2** | (0.3) | -2.6 | (3.9) | **4.6** | (1.1) | **23.1** | (4.6) | **16.1** | (1.2) | 409.8 | (4.6) |
| Kyrgyzstan | **16.2** | (2.3) | **-1.4** | (0.3) | **-11.1** | (3.1) | 0.1 | (1.1) | **69.7** | (5.8) | **4.8** | (1.5) | 366.5 | (4.7) |
| Latvia | **18.0** | (2.9) | -1.0 | (0.4) | 0.8 | (7.3) | 1.6 | (1.7) | **27.8** | (6.6) | **19.0** | (2.1) | 452.0 | (4.2) |
| Liechtenstein | **16.5** | (7.2) | -0.9 | (1.1) | -13.5 | (24.3) | 8.7 | (7.0) | **141.2** | (10.3) | 14.7 | (5.4) | 456.6 | (11.7) |
| Lithuania | **24.4** | (2.8) | **-2.2** | (0.4) | 2.5 | (5.1) | **3.4** | (1.6) | **44.8** | (5.6) | **21.5** | (1.5) | 440.8 | (4.0) |
| Macao-China | **12.6** | (2.4) | 0.4 | (0.3) | **15.6** | (9.6) | 0.4 | (1.9) | **26.5** | (3.4) | **5.0** | (1.9) | 473.7 | (4.5) |
| Montenegro | **19.9** | (2.1) | **-1.8** | (0.3) | **-14.3** | (4.0) | 3.0 | (1.1) | **64.7** | (3.6) | **6.7** | (1.5) | 386.2 | (2.8) |
| Qatar | **18.8** | (1.7) | **-1.4** | (0.3) | 0.6 | (3.3) | **4.2** | (1.0) | **41.9** | (2.4) | -1.1 | (1.4) | 306.6 | (2.5) |
| Romania | **18.7** | (2.7) | **-1.9** | (0.4) | **-14.2** | (5.5) | **6.4** | (1.6) | **53.8** | (6.2) | **11.1** | (2.6) | 418.9 | (5.4) |
| Russian Federation | **13.2** | (2.4) | -0.6 | (0.3) | -12.4 | (6.5) | **3.6** | (1.5) | **41.7** | (6.8) | **19.0** | (1.8) | 450.2 | (4.4) |
| Serbia | **17.8** | (2.0) | **-1.3** | (0.3) | -4.8 | (5.4) | 2.3 | (1.5) | **63.2** | (5.0) | **9.8** | (1.3) | 412.8 | (3.7) |
| Slovenia | **11.0** | (2.3) | -0.3 | (0.3) | 6.8 | (4.9) | 1.3 | (1.4) | **108.2** | (6.6) | **7.4** | (1.8) | 477.2 | (3.3) |
| Chinese Taipei | **23.3** | (2.4) | **-2.2** | (0.3) | **13.0** | (4.5) | 3.1 | (1.3) | **94.1** | (6.0) | **9.3** | (1.5) | 521.2 | (5.0) |
| Thailand | **-4.2** | (6.0) | 1.9 | (0.7) | 2.5 | (5.1) | 3.1 | (1.3) | **32.0** | (2.4) | **6.4** | (1.2) | 451.1 | (12.4) |
| Tunisia | **13.6** | (2.8) | **-1.1** | (0.4) | 6.0 | (5.1) | **4.0** | (1.4) | **33.9** | (4.0) | 2.1 | (1.3) | 399.3 | (6.8) |
| Uruguay | **7.9** | (2.6) | -0.3 | (0.4) | -7.7 | (4.9) | **3.8** | (1.4) | **42.3** | (3.5) | **11.9** | (1.5) | 446.4 | (3.7) |

*Note*: Values that are statistically significant at the 5% level (p < 0.05) are indicated in bold.

© OECD 2011 Quality Time for Students: Learning In and Out of School

### Table 4.5b Relationship between performance in science and learning time in regular school lessons in science, by students' perception of how important it is to do well in science in academic and vocational schools

| | All students | | | | | | Students from academic schools | | | | | | Students from vocational schools | | | | | |
|---|---|---|---|---|---|---|---|---|---|---|---|---|---|---|---|---|---|---|
| | Time spent in regular school lessons in science | | Students who think it is very important to do well in science (1=very important 0=not very important) | | Differential effect of time spent in regular school lessons in science for students who think it is very important to do well in science | | Time spent in regular school lessons in science | | Students who think it is very important to do well in science (1=very important 0=not very important) | | Differential effect of time spent in regular school lessons in science for students who think it is very important to do well in science | | Time spent in regular school lessons in science | | Students who think it is very important to do well in science (1=very important 0=not very important) | | Differential effect of time spent in regular school lessons in science for students who think it is very important to do well in science | |
| | (1) | | (2) | | (1) * (2) | | (3) | | (4) | | (3) * (4) | | (5) | | (6) | | (5) * (6) | |
| | Change in score | S.E. | Change in score | S.E. | Change in score | S.E. | Change in score | S.E. | Change in score | S.E. | Change in score | S.E. | Change in score | S.E. | Change in score | S.E. | Change in score | S.E. |
| **OECD** | | | | | | | | | | | | | | | | | | |
| Australia | **24.5** | (1.9) | **22.6** | (6.0) | **3.9** | (1.4) | **24.5** | (2.2) | **23.2** | (5.7) | **3.9** | (1.4) | **23.6** | (6.8) | 16.1 | (32.0) | 3.3 | (6.5) |
| Austria | **16.1** | (2.5) | -4.6 | (6.9) | **5.0** | (1.9) | **13.6** | (4.2) | -10.7 | (14.1) | **8.6** | (3.4) | **16.4** | (2.6) | 3.0 | (6.6) | 1.8 | (2.1) |
| Belgium | **20.3** | (2.0) | -3.6 | (7.3) | 3.0 | (1.7) | **7.0** | (2.7) | 10.4 | (10.0) | 0.0 | (2.1) | **22.5** | (3.6) | **-27.0** | (9.6) | **7.1** | (2.7) |
| Canada | **16.4** | (2.0) | **12.2** | (6.1) | **3.8** | (1.2) | **16.4** | (2.0) | **12.2** | (6.1) | **3.8** | (1.2) | a | a | a | a | a | a |
| Czech Republic | **7.7** | (2.6) | **-25.1** | (7.7) | **6.5** | (1.5) | **13.0** | (3.2) | -11.0 | (7.8) | **4.6** | (1.4) | **10.1** | (4.1) | -23.6 | (13.4) | 5.6 | (3.4) |
| Denmark | **35.6** | (3.8) | 16.0 | (8.6) | 1.7 | (2.3) | **35.6** | (3.8) | 16.0 | (8.6) | 1.7 | (2.3) | a | a | a | a | a | a |
| Finland | **23.2** | (3.0) | **37.4** | (9.5) | 2.2 | (2.2) | **23.2** | (3.0) | **37.4** | (9.5) | 2.2 | (2.2) | a | a | a | a | a | a |
| France | **24.9** | (2.5) | -1.1 | (7.5) | **7.3** | (1.7) | **29.4** | (2.6) | 0.8 | (8.1) | **7.0** | (1.9) | 8.0 | (4.9) | -2.7 | (18.7) | -4.1 | (8.1) |
| Germany | **11.5** | (2.2) | 8.8 | (6.1) | 1.5 | (1.6) | **13.5** | (2.2) | 8.6 | (6.2) | 1.6 | (1.5) | c | c | c | c | c | c |
| Greece | **29.7** | (2.5) | -5.4 | (5.0) | **6.5** | (1.2) | **26.9** | (2.9) | -3.6 | (6.8) | **5.9** | (1.5) | **25.7** | (4.6) | -13.5 | (7.8) | 4.4 | (3.8) |
| Hungary | **7.5** | (2.4) | -6.6 | (6.2) | **3.5** | (1.6) | **10.9** | (4.0) | -4.8 | (9.5) | **4.9** | (2.4) | 4.7 | (3.0) | -0.0 | (8.2) | -1.9 | (2.5) |
| Iceland | **35.4** | (4.2) | **21.2** | (8.8) | **7.1** | (2.3) | **35.8** | (4.2) | **20.0** | (8.7) | **7.4** | (2.3) | c | c | c | c | c | c |
| Ireland | **27.8** | (2.8) | **23.9** | (6.8) | 2.6 | (2.3) | **27.0** | (2.8) | **25.0** | (6.7) | 2.4 | (2.3) | c | c | c | c | c | c |
| Italy | **17.6** | (1.8) | **-14.1** | (4.7) | **3.6** | (1.2) | **24.2** | (3.8) | 3.8 | (8.5) | 1.1 | (2.0) | **13.4** | (1.7) | **-26.1** | (5.9) | **5.0** | (1.5) |
| Japan | **18.2** | (3.8) | **15.6** | (7.2) | 2.8 | (2.1) | **22.4** | (4.7) | **19.1** | (8.7) | 2.5 | (2.5) | 12.6 | (8.6) | 18.8 | (12.0) | -3.9 | (4.7) |
| Korea | **25.4** | (5.4) | 6.9 | (9.7) | 3.1 | (2.4) | **29.5** | (9.1) | 11.4 | (13.2) | 2.3 | (3.3) | **15.3** | (6.3) | -10.9 | (15.0) | 5.0 | (4.2) |
| Luxembourg | **17.7** | (1.9) | -7.2 | (5.5) | **5.8** | (1.5) | **26.6** | (2.3) | -2.4 | (5.8) | **3.7** | (1.8) | **14.3** | (5.0) | 19.9 | (16.2) | -1.9 | (3.2) |
| Mexico | **4.9** | (1.3) | -3.2 | (3.0) | **2.6** | (0.7) | **9.9** | (1.5) | -1.4 | (4.0) | **2.3** | (0.9) | -2.2 | (1.6) | -3.9 | (3.6) | **2.7** | (0.8) |
| Netherlands | **11.1** | (2.1) | 0.5 | (6.4) | 2.6 | (1.7) | **5.9** | (2.1) | 1.4 | (7.6) | 2.2 | (1.8) | **10.7** | (4.7) | -3.7 | (8.1) | 1.8 | (4.1) |
| New Zealand | **34.5** | (2.8) | -4.1 | (10.7) | **6.6** | (2.3) | **34.5** | (2.8) | -4.1 | (10.7) | **6.6** | (2.1) | a | a | a | a | a | a |
| Norway | **44.6** | (3.5) | **18.8** | (9.3) | 1.6 | (3.0) | **44.6** | (3.5) | **18.8** | (9.3) | 1.6 | (3.0) | a | a | a | a | a | a |
| Poland | **23.5** | (2.4) | -0.4 | (6.7) | **5.2** | (1.9) | **23.5** | (2.4) | -0.4 | (6.7) | **5.2** | (1.9) | a | a | a | a | a | a |
| Portugal | **19.9** | (3.0) | 1.1 | (7.9) | **6.9** | (1.6) | **18.7** | (3.3) | 3.5 | (8.1) | **7.3** | (1.7) | **26.5** | (6.5) | -24.7 | (19.5) | 6.4 | (4.2) |
| Slovak Republic | **22.0** | (2.5) | -10.8 | (6.5) | **3.9** | (1.6) | **28.6** | (3.3) | -6.5 | (8.4) | 3.8 | (2.0) | **21.6** | (4.1) | -0.9 | (9.7) | -1.2 | (2.4) |
| Spain | **10.9** | (1.6) | 2.3 | (5.1) | **6.7** | (1.2) | **10.9** | (1.6) | 2.3 | (5.1) | **6.7** | (1.2) | a | a | a | a | a | a |
| Sweden | **41.4** | (3.6) | **25.0** | (9.8) | 2.3 | (3.1) | **42.6** | (3.5) | **26.0** | (9.7) | 2.1 | (3.1) | c | c | c | c | c | c |
| Switzerland | **26.3** | (2.5) | **16.9** | (6.9) | 1.2 | (1.7) | **28.5** | (2.7) | **20.0** | (6.7) | 0.3 | (1.6) | **12.9** | c | c | c | c | c |
| Turkey | **4.6** | (1.7) | -0.2 | (4.2) | **2.1** | (1.0) | **8.9** | (2.1) | -3.7 | (6.5) | 2.4 | (1.4) | -0.5 | (2.5) | 0.6 | (5.5) | 1.8 | (1.7) |
| United Kingdom | **31.7** | (3.4) | -7.6 | (6.8) | **5.9** | (1.3) | **31.7** | (3.4) | -7.6 | (6.8) | **5.9** | (1.3) | a | a | a | a | a | a |
| United States | **21.6** | (2.5) | 5.6 | (6.0) | **3.1** | (1.3) | **21.6** | (2.5) | 5.6 | (6.0) | **3.1** | (1.3) | a | a | a | a | a | a |
| **OECD average** | **21.9** | (0.5) | **4.7** | (1.3) | **4.0** | (0.3) | **23.0** | (0.6) | **7.0** | (1.5) | **3.8** | (0.4) | **13.9** | (1.2) | -4.9 | (3.5) | **2.0** | (1.0) |
| **Partners** | | | | | | | | | | | | | | | | | | |
| Argentina | **13.9** | (3.2) | **-14.7** | (7.3) | 4.4 | (2.5) | **15.0** | (3.3) | **-15.6** | (7.6) | 4.5 | (2.6) | -24.6 | (24.1) | 1.1 | (25.8) | 9.4 | (9.6) |
| Azerbaijan | **13.1** | (2.5) | -1.1 | (4.0) | -1.4 | (1.1) | **12.9** | (2.5) | -1.9 | (3.9) | -1.2 | (1.1) | c | c | c | c | c | c |
| Brazil | **13.6** | (2.1) | **-12.1** | (4.9) | **4.1** | (1.8) | **13.6** | (2.1) | **-12.1** | (4.9) | **4.1** | (1.8) | a | a | a | a | a | a |
| Bulgaria | **18.2** | (2.6) | **-12.9** | (4.9) | **3.2** | (1.5) | **20.6** | (3.8) | **-14.2** | (6.7) | 3.7 | (2.0) | **16.7** | (3.9) | -11.0 | (7.9) | 2.3 | (2.2) |
| Chile | **12.6** | (1.8) | -3.4 | (3.7) | 2.1 | (1.3) | **14.7** | (1.8) | -1.4 | (3.8) | 1.5 | (1.3) | -3.4 | (16.0) | -3.2 | (22.4) | 21.0 | (11.1) |
| Colombia | **7.0** | (3.1) | -14.8 | (7.8) | **3.9** | (1.7) | **10.3** | (2.8) | **-15.9** | (7.4) | **4.2** | (1.8) | -1.0 | (8.3) | 7.2 | (17.3) | -0.7 | (4.1) |
| Croatia | **14.9** | (2.3) | 3.8 | (6.9) | 2.5 | (2.1) | -2.7 | (5.9) | 2.8 | (17.2) | 3.3 | (4.7) | **18.7** | (2.8) | -2.8 | (7.2) | 3.5 | (2.5) |
| Estonia | **18.3** | (3.0) | -5.7 | (6.5) | **5.2** | (1.6) | **18.3** | (3.0) | -5.7 | (6.5) | **5.2** | (1.6) | a | a | a | a | a | a |
| Hong Kong-China | **-7.8** | (2.8) | 15.8 | (8.6) | 2.6 | (1.5) | **-7.8** | (2.9) | 15.8 | (9.4) | 2.5 | (1.6) | -3.0 | (5.4) | 32.3 | (18.6) | 1.6 | (3.4) |
| Indonesia | **12.0** | (3.9) | **-12.1** | (4.7) | 1.9 | (1.2) | **17.3** | (2.5) | **-8.8** | (4.2) | **2.7** | (1.0) | **15.8** | (5.9) | 2.9 | (9.1) | -3.8 | (2.7) |
| Israel | **22.1** | (2.4) | 8.3 | (7.0) | **4.6** | (2.0) | **22.1** | (2.4) | 14.0 | (8.0) | 2.9 | (2.1) | **19.4** | (7.4) | -13.8 | (11.8) | **12.2** | (4.5) |
| Jordan | **15.9** | (2.2) | -2.6 | (3.9) | **4.6** | (1.1) | **15.9** | (2.2) | -2.6 | (3.9) | **4.6** | (1.1) | a | a | a | a | a | a |
| Kyrgyzstan | **16.2** | (2.3) | **-11.1** | (3.1) | 0.1 | (1.1) | **15.9** | (2.3) | **-11.3** | (3.2) | 0.1 | (1.1) | 14.9 | (10.1) | 0.6 | (16.6) | 3.3 | (4.6) |
| Latvia | **18.0** | (2.9) | 0.8 | (7.3) | 1.6 | (1.7) | **18.3** | (3.0) | 1.3 | (7.5) | 1.2 | (1.7) | 16.9 | (9.9) | 53.4 | (39.7) | -4.6 | (7.1) |
| Liechtenstein | **16.5** | (7.2) | -13.5 | (24.3) | 8.7 | (7.0) | **16.5** | (7.2) | -13.5 | (24.3) | 8.7 | (7.0) | a | a | a | a | a | a |
| Lithuania | **24.4** | (2.8) | 2.5 | (5.1) | 3.4 | (1.6) | **23.9** | (2.7) | 2.0 | (5.1) | 3.5 | (1.5) | c | c | c | c | c | c |
| Macao-China | **12.6** | (2.4) | 15.6 | (9.6) | 0.4 | (1.9) | **12.8** | (2.4) | 15.3 | (9.6) | 0.5 | (1.8) | c | c | c | c | c | c |
| Montenegro | **19.9** | (2.1) | **-14.3** | (4.0) | 3.0 | (1.1) | **14.5** | (3.8) | -14.7 | (9.3) | 3.5 | (2.1) | **20.5** | (2.7) | **-17.1** | (4.8) | 2.7 | (1.4) |
| Qatar | **18.8** | (1.7) | 0.6 | (3.3) | **4.2** | (1.0) | **18.8** | (1.7) | 0.6 | (3.3) | **4.2** | (1.0) | a | a | a | a | a | a |
| Romania | **18.7** | (2.7) | **-14.2** | (5.5) | **6.4** | (1.6) | **15.6** | (2.7) | -11.1 | (7.9) | 5.4 | (2.0) | 7.3 | (3.1) | -9.1 | (6.8) | 5.8 | (3.0) |
| Russian Federation | **13.2** | (2.4) | -12.4 | (6.5) | 3.6 | (1.5) | **14.5** | (2.6) | **-16.7** | (6.9) | 4.2 | (1.7) | 3.4 | (4.9) | 9.5 | (14.3) | 1.1 | (3.7) |
| Serbia | **17.8** | (2.0) | -4.8 | (5.4) | 2.3 | (1.5) | **11.9** | (4.8) | 9.6 | (12.9) | 1.2 | (3.1) | **19.7** | (2.2) | -6.3 | (6.1) | 1.2 | (1.9) |
| Slovenia | **11.0** | (2.3) | 6.8 | (4.9) | 1.3 | (1.4) | **17.0** | (4.0) | **32.6** | (8.4) | -1.7 | (1.9) | **7.3** | (2.7) | -4.7 | (6.1) | -0.4 | (2.2) |
| Chinese Taipei | **23.3** | (2.4) | **13.0** | (4.5) | 3.1 | (1.3) | **32.3** | (2.3) | **19.6** | (6.2) | 2.0 | (1.6) | **10.3** | (4.2) | 6.4 | (6.3) | 0.9 | (2.2) |
| Thailand | -4.2 | (6.0) | 2.5 | (5.1) | 3.1 | (1.3) | 16.5 | (6.8) | 1.9 | (5.9) | 3.3 | (1.4) | 8.8 | (9.7) | 5.6 | (12.2) | 1.3 | (4.8) |
| Tunisia | **13.6** | (2.8) | 6.0 | (5.1) | **4.0** | (1.4) | **13.6** | (2.8) | 6.0 | (5.1) | **4.0** | (1.4) | a | a | a | a | a | a |
| Uruguay | **7.9** | (2.6) | -7.7 | (4.9) | 3.8 | (1.4) | **10.5** | (2.8) | -6.3 | (5.3) | 3.6 | (1.4) | -3.1 | (9.1) | -2.8 | (21.5) | -1.5 | (7.2) |

*Note:* Values that are statistically significant at the 5% level (p < 0.05) are indicated in bold.

253

[Part 1/2]
## Table 4.6a  Performance in science, by learning time in out-of-school-time lessons in science

| | Science performance for students who do not spend any time in out-of-school-time lessons in science | | Difference in science performance between students who spend the following learning hours per week in out-of-school-time lessons in science and students who do not spend any time in out-of-school-time lessons in science | | | | | | | |
| | | | Less than 2 hours per week | | 2 hours or more but less than 4 hours per week | | 4 hours or more but less than 6 hours per week | | 6 hours or more per week | |
| | Mean score | S.E. | Dif. | S.E. | Dif. | S.E. | Dif. | S.E. | Dif. | S.E. |
|---|---|---|---|---|---|---|---|---|---|---|
| **OECD** | | | | | | | | | | |
| Australia | 534 | (2.2) | **-14.0** | (2.4) | **-29.4** | (5.2) | **-32.4** | (12.6) | c | c |
| Austria | 522 | (3.7) | **-61.6** | (5.6) | **-79.1** | (10.3) | **-139.9** | (17.8) | c | c |
| Belgium | 525 | (2.1) | **-25.9** | (3.5) | **-44.0** | (5.9) | **-51.0** | (15.3) | c | c |
| Canada | 547 | (1.9) | **-23.4** | (2.9) | **-34.5** | (4.4) | **-35.7** | (9.4) | -42.0 | (23.4) |
| Czech Republic | 520 | (3.6) | 3.0 | (3.8) | -12.0 | (7.1) | -9.4 | (12.9) | c | c |
| Denmark | 498 | (4.1) | 1.3 | (4.2) | -4.1 | (5.6) | 4.5 | (11.6) | c | c |
| Finland | 573 | (2.0) | **-31.5** | (3.0) | **-45.5** | (8.9) | c | c | c | c |
| France | 507 | (3.8) | **-17.7** | (4.2) | -3.3 | (6.4) | **-46.3** | (18.1) | c | c |
| Germany | 539 | (3.2) | **-38.0** | (3.4) | **-63.9** | (6.3) | **-76.5** | (10.8) | c | c |
| Greece | 464 | (4.8) | -4.0 | (5.0) | **25.5** | (4.9) | **38.5** | (6.1) | **36.0** | (9.9) |
| Hungary | 515 | (3.0) | **-14.1** | (3.3) | **-21.6** | (4.9) | -14.8 | (8.3) | c | c |
| Iceland | 500 | (1.9) | **-25.2** | (5.1) | **-49.9** | (8.3) | c | c | c | c |
| Ireland | 517 | (3.3) | **-24.7** | (4.0) | **-34.2** | (7.2) | c | c | c | c |
| Italy | 488 | (2.0) | **-28.9** | (3.0) | **-40.0** | (4.0) | **-35.4** | (7.2) | **-49.6** | (11.1) |
| Japan | 537 | (3.3) | **-16.6** | (4.9) | **-71.3** | (8.2) | c | c | c | c |
| Korea | 508 | (4.5) | **21.7** | (4.8) | **42.6** | (5.6) | **49.7** | (9.1) | 40.4 | (46.6) |
| Luxembourg | 503 | (1.4) | **-40.8** | (3.6) | **-57.4** | (6.3) | **-77.1** | (11.8) | c | c |
| Mexico | 426 | (2.7) | **-20.8** | (2.7) | **-24.8** | (3.6) | **-36.4** | (6.8) | **-82.1** | (11.3) |
| Netherlands | 539 | (3.1) | **-25.0** | (4.3) | **-48.0** | (7.1) | **-26.3** | (14.1) | c | c |
| New Zealand | 542 | (2.6) | **-21.7** | (4.1) | **-43.9** | (8.6) | **-66.5** | (20.9) | c | c |
| Norway | 507 | (3.0) | **-17.1** | (3.1) | **-40.4** | (5.0) | **-51.9** | (11.9) | c | c |
| Poland | 504 | (2.7) | **-8.1** | (3.1) | **-24.6** | (6.4) | -21.6 | (16.6) | c | c |
| Portugal | 485 | (3.1) | **-31.3** | (3.8) | **-13.5** | (6.1) | -15.4 | (9.8) | c | c |
| Slovak Republic | 481 | (3.2) | **24.7** | (4.1) | **43.2** | (5.5) | **48.4** | (12.5) | 21.4 | (17.7) |
| Spain | 502 | (2.6) | **-33.7** | (3.1) | **-31.4** | (4.2) | **-33.3** | (11.1) | **-52.5** | (16.8) |
| Sweden | 521 | (2.6) | **-34.0** | (3.2) | **-61.2** | (7.1) | c | c | c | c |
| Switzerland | 521 | (3.2) | **-26.8** | (4.0) | **-42.1** | (7.2) | **-47.0** | (23.8) | c | c |
| Turkey | 409 | (2.8) | **11.7** | (4.1) | **36.6** | (6.6) | **72.0** | (9.3) | **80.4** | (10.9) |
| United Kingdom | 523 | (2.6) | **-10.7** | (3.5) | **-31.9** | (5.5) | **-48.5** | (15.7) | **-50.6** | (25.2) |
| United States | 505 | (4.2) | **-22.0** | (3.5) | **-36.7** | (6.5) | **-47.8** | (10.0) | **-72.8** | (21.1) |
| **OECD average** | 509 | (3.1) | **-18.5** | (3.8) | **-28.0** | (6.5) | **-28.0** | (13.3) | -17.1 | (22.0) |
| **Partners** | | | | | | | | | | |
| Argentina | 412 | (5.4) | **-43.5** | (6.7) | **-40.3** | (8.1) | **-44.6** | (15.0) | c | c |
| Azerbaijan | 388 | (3.0) | -1.7 | (2.9) | -5.8 | (3.8) | 2.1 | (4.8) | **12.9** | (6.3) |
| Brazil | 391 | (3.0) | **8.0** | (3.8) | 4.2 | (5.6) | 10.7 | (12.0) | 4.9 | (28.3) |
| Bulgaria | 454 | (5.7) | **-21.7** | (4.5) | **-29.7** | (6.0) | **-22.2** | (9.8) | **-49.3** | (21.5) |
| Chile | 447 | (4.5) | **-15.9** | (3.7) | -10.2 | (5.2) | -6.6 | (10.1) | -38.0 | (20.0) |
| Colombia | 393 | (3.7) | -3.3 | (3.1) | 9.3 | (4.8) | -11.2 | (9.3) | c | c |
| Croatia | 500 | (2.6) | **-14.1** | (3.8) | **-35.2** | (5.9) | **-26.2** | (11.3) | c | c |
| Estonia | 549 | (2.7) | **-28.7** | (2.7) | **-53.2** | (4.3) | **-45.8** | (11.4) | c | c |
| Hong Kong-China | 535 | (2.7) | **13.1** | (4.1) | **25.4** | (5.7) | **33.2** | (7.8) | **54.3** | (9.9) |
| Indonesia | 389 | (6.8) | 5.4 | (3.2) | **17.3** | (7.7) | **28.5** | (11.4) | 1.7 | (13.4) |
| Israel | 475 | (4.2) | **-13.0** | (4.7) | **-22.9** | (6.0) | **-35.6** | (10.9) | -23.3 | (21.5) |
| Jordan | 433 | (2.8) | **-8.8** | (3.1) | -8.7 | (4.5) | -2.5 | (6.4) | **-24.3** | (10.1) |
| Kyrgyzstan | 347 | (4.7) | **-17.7** | (4.3) | **-26.2** | (5.0) | **-30.5** | (6.7) | **-35.9** | (9.1) |
| Latvia | 498 | (3.0) | **-16.1** | (3.8) | **-22.1** | (4.6) | -7.7 | (11.4) | c | c |
| Liechtenstein | 541 | (6.0) | **-44.5** | (12.5) | c | c | c | c | a | a |
| Lithuania | 501 | (3.4) | **-26.5** | (4.4) | **-48.3** | (5.5) | **-57.0** | (10.1) | c | c |
| Macao-China | 514 | (1.7) | -2.2 | (3.2) | **-13.0** | (4.7) | **-14.1** | (6.9) | **16.9** | (8.6) |
| Montenegro | 429 | (1.7) | **-22.9** | (3.1) | **-25.1** | (4.7) | **-28.6** | (7.1) | **-49.5** | (9.5) |
| Qatar | 378 | (2.2) | **-35.5** | (3.0) | **-29.3** | (3.2) | **-12.5** | (5.6) | -15.2 | (10.1) |
| Romania | 420 | (4.4) | 3.4 | (3.5) | -3.1 | (5.3) | -2.2 | (9.6) | -39.5 | (20.9) |
| Russian Federation | 486 | (3.7) | **-8.8** | (3.2) | -6.8 | (4.8) | 1.8 | (7.9) | -1.0 | (15.2) |
| Serbia | 443 | (3.2) | **-8.4** | (2.7) | -5.9 | (4.4) | 1.5 | (12.4) | **-56.6** | (15.4) |
| Slovenia | 533 | (2.0) | **-20.7** | (4.1) | **-33.1** | (5.9) | -19.1 | (12.0) | **-40.3** | (20.4) |
| Chinese Taipei | 533 | (3.9) | **-17.7** | (3.9) | **35.5** | (4.0) | **46.1** | (7.9) | **46.3** | (11.8) |
| Thailand | 419 | (2.0) | **-10.9** | (3.5) | **16.9** | (6.5) | **38.8** | (10.0) | **82.7** | (12.8) |
| Tunisia | 376 | (3.6) | **8.5** | (3.9) | **22.9** | (4.1) | **31.5** | (5.9) | **36.0** | (9.4) |
| Uruguay | 444 | (2.8) | **-22.2** | (4.2) | **-23.4** | (6.0) | -13.3 | (12.0) | c | c |

*Note*: Values that are statistically significant at the 5% level (p < 0.05) are indicated in bold.

© OECD 2011  Quality Time for Students: Learning In and Out of School

[Part 2/2]
## Table 4.6a Performance in science, by learning time in out-of-school-time lessons in science

Difference in science performance between students who spend the following learning hours per week in out-of-school-time lessons in science and students who do not spend any time in out-of-school-time lessons in science

| | Accounting for socio-economic background of students and schools | | | | | | | | Accounting for socio-economic background of students and schools as well as learning time in regular school lessons and individual study in science | | | | | | | |
|---|---|---|---|---|---|---|---|---|---|---|---|---|---|---|---|---|
| | Less than 2 hours per week | | 2 hours or more but less than 4 hours per week | | 4 hours or more but less than 6 hours per week | | 6 hours or more per week | | Less than 2 hours per week | | 2 hours or more but less than 4 hours per week | | 4 hours or more but less than 6 hours per week | | 6 hours or more per week | |
| | Dif. | S.E. | Dif. | S.E. | Dif. | S.E. | Dif. | S.E. | Dif. | S.E. | Dif. | S.E. | Dif. | S.E. | Dif. | S.E. |
| **OECD** | | | | | | | | | | | | | | | | |
| Australia | -15.6 | (2.2) | -29.4 | (4.7) | -36.2 | (11.8) | c | c | -25.3 | (2.4) | -56.4 | (5.0) | -74.6 | (12.3) | c | c |
| Austria | -38.1 | (4.3) | -62.1 | (8.5) | -112.3 | (15.1) | c | c | -34.9 | (4.3) | -61.4 | (8.5) | -114.9 | (13.7) | c | c |
| Belgium | -16.8 | (2.9) | -31.0 | (5.0) | -38.0 | (10.8) | c | c | -25.6 | (2.7) | -40.8 | (4.6) | -52.6 | (11.5) | c | c |
| Canada | -23.4 | (2.6) | -36.2 | (4.1) | -37.3 | (9.1) | -38.7 | (23.9) | -25.4 | (2.6) | -45.6 | (4.2) | -52.4 | (10.0) | -58.9 | (24.2) |
| Czech Republic | 0.9 | (3.8) | -15.2 | (6.3) | -20.2 | (13.6) | c | c | -5.4 | (3.4) | -26.3 | (6.2) | -39.0 | (11.9) | c | c |
| Denmark | -0.6 | (3.6) | -5.8 | (5.1) | -2.2 | (12.2) | c | c | -7.6 | (3.3) | -12.4 | (5.9) | -8.3 | (13.1) | c | c |
| Finland | -30.6 | (2.9) | -43.4 | (9.0) | c | c | c | c | -32.0 | (2.8) | -47.7 | (8.6) | c | c | c | c |
| France | -11.4 | (3.3) | -13.5 | (5.2) | -39.8 | (13.7) | c | c | -15.3 | (2.9) | -27.8 | (4.8) | -67.1 | (12.4) | c | c |
| Germany | -28.9 | (3.2) | -46.0 | (5.4) | -60.0 | (10.5) | c | c | -29.0 | (3.0) | -46.0 | (4.8) | -66.6 | (11.0) | c | c |
| Greece | -8.4 | (4.0) | 9.4 | (4.1) | 18.0 | (5.3) | 21.8 | (8.3) | -8.8 | (3.7) | -5.3 | (4.0) | -4.1 | (5.2) | 0.9 | (8.4) |
| Hungary | -2.1 | (2.7) | -9.2 | (3.6) | -3.0 | (6.2) | c | c | -5.8 | (2.8) | -18.5 | (3.5) | -20.0 | (6.1) | c | c |
| Iceland | -26.2 | (4.8) | -57.8 | (8.2) | c | c | c | c | -27.3 | (4.6) | -61.0 | (8.4) | c | c | c | c |
| Ireland | -25.0 | (3.8) | -36.4 | (7.1) | c | c | c | c | -36.0 | (3.9) | -51.5 | (7.4) | c | c | c | c |
| Italy | -22.2 | (2.7) | -32.4 | (3.7) | -29.7 | (6.6) | -40.2 | (10.5) | -23.1 | (2.6) | -39.1 | (3.4) | -41.5 | (7.0) | -56.2 | (12.3) |
| Japan | -13.7 | (3.9) | -56.5 | (7.7) | c | c | c | c | -21.0 | (3.8) | -65.8 | (7.9) | c | c | c | c |
| Korea | 6.7 | (3.9) | 16.5 | (4.6) | 17.2 | (7.1) | -9.0 | (27.3) | -2.2 | (3.8) | 1.7 | (4.5) | -2.6 | (7.0) | -38.3 | (20.2) |
| Luxembourg | -32.0 | (3.0) | -47.0 | (5.4) | -48.0 | (10.4) | c | c | -33.7 | (3.0) | -52.6 | (5.5) | -64.0 | (11.7) | c | c |
| Mexico | -13.7 | (2.1) | -15.8 | (3.2) | -25.7 | (4.7) | -54.7 | (10.0) | -14.4 | (2.0) | -19.4 | (3.1) | -32.1 | (4.3) | -55.0 | (9.5) |
| Netherlands | -12.4 | (2.9) | -30.8 | (5.4) | -32.1 | (11.4) | c | c | -17.9 | (2.9) | -44.6 | (5.5) | -51.0 | (11.6) | c | c |
| New Zealand | -25.7 | (3.2) | -42.6 | (7.1) | -65.5 | (15.6) | c | c | -29.9 | (3.3) | -59.9 | (6.4) | -90.2 | (17.0) | c | c |
| Norway | -16.7 | (2.8) | -41.6 | (4.6) | -51.0 | (11.5) | c | c | -24.5 | (2.9) | -50.0 | (5.9) | -54.6 | (11.8) | c | c |
| Poland | -9.0 | (2.9) | -27.4 | (5.5) | -23.6 | (13.9) | c | c | -9.8 | (2.8) | -34.1 | (5.4) | -39.7 | (14.5) | c | c |
| Portugal | -22.7 | (3.3) | -13.6 | (5.4) | -16.6 | (8.8) | c | c | -23.5 | (3.1) | -27.5 | (4.8) | -37.7 | (8.8) | c | c |
| Slovak Republic | 13.1 | (3.6) | 16.8 | (5.3) | 24.0 | (11.3) | -1.3 | (12.5) | 3.5 | (3.4) | -4.5 | (5.4) | 3.0 | (11.0) | -9.6 | (11.0) |
| Spain | -32.9 | (2.7) | -33.2 | (3.8) | -35.9 | (8.9) | -47.2 | (13.8) | -27.6 | (2.7) | -38.4 | (3.7) | -45.3 | (7.9) | -56.1 | (12.0) |
| Sweden | -32.8 | (3.0) | -56.7 | (6.5) | c | c | c | c | -36.9 | (3.1) | -58.2 | (7.0) | c | c | c | c |
| Switzerland | -20.0 | (3.3) | -29.7 | (6.5) | -40.1 | (19.6) | c | c | -23.2 | (3.2) | -37.4 | (6.1) | -49.2 | (19.2) | c | c |
| Turkey | 10.0 | (3.1) | 21.2 | (4.4) | 42.8 | (4.5) | 52.7 | (6.7) | 2.9 | (3.3) | 2.8 | (4.7) | 14.1 | (4.7) | 16.7 | (7.2) |
| United Kingdom | -7.9 | (3.2) | -26.8 | (4.5) | -42.1 | (15.2) | -37.8 | (24.7) | -13.5 | (2.9) | -39.5 | (4.7) | -68.8 | (13.5) | -96.1 | (28.8) |
| United States | -19.0 | (3.1) | -28.5 | (5.1) | -41.3 | (9.6) | -59.3 | (16.9) | -18.6 | (3.2) | -39.3 | (4.9) | -57.8 | (11.0) | -73.8 | (16.4) |
| **OECD average** | **-15.9** | **(3.3)** | **-26.8** | **(5.7)** | **-27.9** | **(11.3)** | **-21.4** | **(17.0)** | **-19.7** | **(3.2)** | **-36.9** | **(5.7)** | **-44.7** | **(11.3)** | **-42.6** | **(16.5)** |
| **Partners** | | | | | | | | | | | | | | | | |
| Argentina | -35.4 | (5.8) | -29.6 | (7.8) | -38.4 | (12.9) | c | c | -37.5 | (5.7) | -36.6 | (7.5) | -58.1 | (12.7) | c | c |
| Azerbaijan | 0.9 | (2.7) | -3.7 | (3.4) | 2.7 | (4.8) | 10.9 | (6.0) | 1.6 | (2.8) | -7.5 | (3.6) | -5.1 | (5.0) | -3.6 | (6.2) |
| Brazil | 0.4 | (3.3) | -6.5 | (4.6) | 10.0 | (11.2) | 11.7 | (20.6) | -3.0 | (3.2) | -15.9 | (4.4) | -8.9 | (11.1) | -14.8 | (18.5) |
| Bulgaria | -15.0 | (3.0) | -25.6 | (4.9) | -20.8 | (6.9) | -34.3 | (15.5) | -20.4 | (3.6) | -42.2 | (4.8) | -47.1 | (7.9) | -58.0 | (17.3) |
| Chile | -10.1 | (2.9) | -10.7 | (4.0) | -11.5 | (8.1) | -32.3 | (16.1) | -16.1 | (2.7) | -28.0 | (3.9) | -37.9 | (8.0) | -56.5 | (16.9) |
| Colombia | 0.7 | (3.4) | 9.9 | (4.6) | -6.3 | (7.3) | c | c | -2.4 | (3.1) | 4.7 | (4.6) | -13.5 | (7.9) | c | c |
| Croatia | -19.3 | (3.4) | -37.5 | (4.9) | -35.7 | (9.5) | c | c | -28.5 | (3.3) | -51.8 | (4.8) | -53.8 | (9.5) | c | c |
| Estonia | -25.9 | (2.8) | -49.5 | (4.0) | -43.8 | (10.8) | c | c | -25.5 | (2.5) | -50.6 | (3.6) | -58.3 | (10.9) | c | c |
| Hong Kong-China | 11.6 | (3.8) | 16.7 | (5.0) | 23.5 | (8.2) | 40.9 | (10.1) | -10.7 | (3.9) | -22.2 | (4.8) | -30.9 | (8.2) | -23.7 | (10.6) |
| Indonesia | 1.6 | (2.6) | 1.9 | (4.1) | 11.2 | (4.0) | -5.7 | (10.1) | -1.1 | (2.5) | -2.1 | (4.2) | 3.6 | (7.6) | -13.7 | (9.2) |
| Israel | -5.5 | (4.3) | -8.1 | (5.4) | -12.4 | (9.7) | -26.1 | (18.9) | -15.9 | (4.8) | -26.3 | (5.8) | -39.8 | (9.2) | -44.4 | (21.6) |
| Jordan | -10.9 | (3.0) | -11.0 | (3.8) | -6.2 | (5.9) | -23.8 | (9.8) | -9.6 | (3.1) | -14.9 | (3.7) | -22.5 | (5.4) | -40.2 | (9.4) |
| Kyrgyzstan | -10.6 | (3.2) | -14.3 | (4.1) | -17.3 | (6.2) | -22.0 | (8.8) | -16.5 | (3.5) | -26.9 | (4.4) | -39.2 | (6.9) | -39.1 | (9.1) |
| Latvia | -12.2 | (3.6) | -19.2 | (4.1) | -11.1 | (11.6) | c | c | -17.9 | (3.3) | -25.8 | (3.9) | -20.3 | (11.2) | c | c |
| Liechtenstein | -6.3 | (11.4) | c | c | c | c | a | a | -11.7 | (11.6) | c | c | c | c | a | a |
| Lithuania | -19.7 | (3.9) | -36.4 | (4.8) | -44.8 | (9.9) | c | c | -18.9 | (3.6) | -43.8 | (5.0) | -61.4 | (9.8) | c | c |
| Macao-China | -0.6 | (3.2) | -11.0 | (4.7) | -11.5 | (6.8) | 17.5 | (8.3) | -7.0 | (3.0) | -24.1 | (4.3) | -38.5 | (6.7) | -15.7 | (7.7) |
| Montenegro | -17.9 | (2.7) | -21.7 | (4.3) | -26.0 | (6.2) | -36.9 | (7.9) | -21.8 | (2.7) | -35.2 | (4.3) | -49.6 | (6.1) | -65.5 | (8.6) |
| Qatar | -30.2 | (2.8) | -25.9 | (3.1) | -13.9 | (4.9) | -14.3 | (9.4) | -27.4 | (2.8) | -36.0 | (3.3) | -39.4 | (5.1) | -44.6 | (10.0) |
| Romania | -0.7 | (3.7) | -6.5 | (4.3) | -4.0 | (8.0) | -25.5 | (12.2) | -11.2 | (3.5) | -24.3 | (4.5) | -27.7 | (8.1) | -56.5 | (14.8) |
| Russian Federation | -5.8 | (2.7) | -5.0 | (5.0) | -0.3 | (7.0) | 0.3 | (14.8) | -7.5 | (2.9) | -12.9 | (4.7) | -10.0 | (7.0) | -6.2 | (15.4) |
| Serbia | -7.3 | (2.4) | -9.2 | (4.1) | 0.8 | (10.5) | -32.6 | (12.1) | -13.3 | (2.4) | -23.2 | (3.6) | -22.5 | (10.7) | -62.7 | (14.0) |
| Slovenia | -12.6 | (2.9) | -26.9 | (4.0) | -14.0 | (10.1) | -34.1 | (20.9) | -13.6 | (2.9) | -34.5 | (4.2) | -27.9 | (10.7) | -39.3 | (22.3) |
| Chinese Taipei | -15.7 | (3.0) | 18.9 | (3.4) | 21.0 | (7.3) | 20.8 | (11.0) | -24.9 | (2.8) | -4.3 | (3.0) | -6.7 | (6.7) | -8.6 | (10.6) |
| Thailand | -16.5 | (3.2) | -3.4 | (3.7) | 4.7 | (7.0) | 31.5 | (10.1) | -20.3 | (2.8) | -20.7 | (3.5) | -25.7 | (5.9) | -12.1 | (9.2) |
| Tunisia | 7.3 | (3.6) | 17.2 | (3.5) | 22.0 | (4.7) | 30.2 | (7.6) | 1.5 | (3.4) | 5.0 | (3.8) | 4.0 | (4.8) | 8.4 | (7.4) |
| Uruguay | -16.6 | (3.4) | -21.3 | (5.6) | -14.0 | (10.1) | c | c | -19.5 | (3.5) | -34.2 | (5.2) | -35.3 | (9.1) | c | c |

*Note*: Values that are statistically significant at the 5% level (p < 0.05) are indicated in bold.

[Part 1/2]
## Table 4.6b  Performance in mathematics, by learning time in out-of-school-time lessons in mathematics

| | Mathematics performance for students who do not spend any time in out-of-school-time lessons in mathematics | | Difference in mathematics performance between students who spend the following learning hours per week in out-of-school-time lessons in mathematics and students who do not spend any time in out-of-school-time lessons in mathematics | | | | | | | |
| | | | Less than 2 hours per week | | 2 hours or more but less than 4 hours per week | | 4 hours or more but less than 6 hours per week | | 6 hours or more per week | |
| | Mean score | S.E. | Dif. | S.E. | Dif. | S.E. | Dif. | S.E. | Dif. | S.E. |
|---|---|---|---|---|---|---|---|---|---|---|
| Australia | 533 | (2.1) | -23.2 | (2.3) | -30.5 | (4.2) | -47.9 | (6.2) | -34.9 | (8.9) |
| Austria | 521 | (3.9) | -37.4 | (4.4) | -56.1 | (7.2) | -79.7 | (11.3) | -109.1 | (19.5) |
| Belgium | 546 | (2.4) | -42.5 | (3.4) | -58.5 | (5.7) | -84.4 | (8.3) | -67.7 | (16.5) |
| Canada | 547 | (2.1) | -27.9 | (2.5) | -41.4 | (3.0) | -47.5 | (4.6) | -51.5 | (10.3) |
| Czech Republic | 527 | (4.2) | -18.2 | (3.5) | -36.0 | (6.7) | -49.0 | (11.5) | -35.9 | (15.9) |
| Denmark | 534 | (3.8) | -20.3 | (3.8) | -34.0 | (4.5) | -49.3 | (7.0) | -44.9 | (17.9) |
| Finland | 559 | (2.3) | -33.2 | (2.8) | -52.9 | (7.1) | c | c | c | c |
| France | 521 | (3.8) | -38.1 | (3.5) | -41.1 | (4.2) | -61.4 | (10.3) | c | c |
| Germany | 536 | (3.6) | -46.8 | (3.5) | -66.8 | (4.4) | -80.6 | (7.8) | -108.3 | (15.2) |
| Greece | 441 | (4.5) | 6.4 | (4.8) | 36.4 | (4.9) | 37.8 | (6.0) | 41.0 | (8.0) |
| Hungary | 510 | (3.9) | -21.2 | (4.0) | -28.6 | (4.8) | -44.2 | (7.9) | -50.4 | (14.8) |
| Iceland | 526 | (2.3) | -40.5 | (3.2) | -55.3 | (5.4) | -89.4 | (11.0) | c | c |
| Ireland | 518 | (3.0) | -27.3 | (2.7) | -45.5 | (5.0) | -66.6 | (9.3) | -76.4 | (16.2) |
| Italy | 477 | (2.1) | -19.0 | (2.6) | -35.9 | (4.0) | -55.7 | (5.5) | -64.8 | (7.6) |
| Japan | 523 | (3.6) | 4.2 | (4.7) | 1.2 | (6.3) | -9.8 | (9.5) | 3.7 | (16.2) |
| Korea | 504 | (5.0) | 35.6 | (5.5) | 65.9 | (5.5) | 77.5 | (6.4) | 92.2 | (10.8) |
| Luxembourg | 515 | (1.6) | -38.9 | (3.2) | -58.5 | (4.1) | -106.8 | (7.9) | -114.2 | (17.8) |
| Mexico | 423 | (3.1) | -22.0 | (3.5) | -18.6 | (3.9) | -38.8 | (6.1) | -40.6 | (9.8) |
| Netherlands | 553 | (2.9) | -33.5 | (2.9) | -50.8 | (5.3) | -59.0 | (10.2) | c | c |
| New Zealand | 541 | (2.5) | -34.2 | (3.4) | -48.7 | (6.3) | -60.9 | (9.0) | -80.9 | (17.2) |
| Norway | 510 | (3.1) | -15.6 | (3.4) | -40.7 | (4.8) | -43.9 | (10.2) | -92.4 | (19.0) |
| Poland | 507 | (2.9) | -14.6 | (3.1) | -29.0 | (4.5) | -38.6 | (10.2) | -14.9 | (17.1) |
| Portugal | 479 | (2.7) | -23.2 | (3.7) | -16.6 | (4.8) | -14.5 | (9.2) | c | c |
| Slovak Republic | 491 | (3.6) | 10.7 | (4.7) | 14.3 | (6.3) | -9.6 | (10.6) | c | c |
| Spain | 497 | (2.6) | -30.1 | (2.6) | -35.4 | (3.4) | -36.0 | (5.0) | -60.4 | (12.7) |
| Sweden | 524 | (2.3) | -41.7 | (3.5) | -59.8 | (5.8) | -93.2 | (11.0) | c | c |
| Switzerland | 551 | (3.4) | -37.8 | (3.4) | -58.8 | (5.6) | -111.3 | (10.2) | -117.5 | (12.8) |
| Turkey | 403 | (4.2) | 7.9 | (3.8) | 43.0 | (5.0) | 46.7 | (6.3) | 72.5 | (9.3) |
| United Kingdom | 509 | (2.5) | -22.3 | (3.1) | -38.9 | (4.5) | -52.9 | (9.2) | -61.3 | (22.2) |
| United States | 501 | (4.5) | -36.9 | (4.0) | -47.0 | (4.3) | -61.9 | (7.5) | -65.4 | (9.0) |
| OECD average | 511 | (3.3) | -22.7 | (3.6) | -30.8 | (5.2) | -45.9 | (8.7) | -47.0 | (14.7) |
| Argentina | 402 | (6.1) | -22.7 | (4.5) | -43.1 | (8.2) | -31.6 | (14.5) | -9.9 | (13.5) |
| Azerbaijan | 475 | (2.6) | 4.3 | (2.4) | 3.9 | (2.8) | 2.7 | (3.6) | 2.8 | (3.9) |
| Brazil | 376 | (3.7) | -3.8 | (4.7) | 1.3 | (5.3) | 11.0 | (7.2) | -12.2 | (15.1) |
| Bulgaria | 429 | (6.0) | -18.5 | (4.4) | -9.2 | (5.1) | -17.7 | (10.1) | -9.8 | (14.3) |
| Chile | 421 | (5.3) | -13.9 | (3.7) | -8.1 | (4.9) | -15.4 | (7.8) | -23.0 | (13.1) |
| Colombia | 378 | (4.0) | -7.9 | (4.3) | 0.6 | (4.2) | -6.2 | (9.2) | 20.5 | (13.3) |
| Croatia | 481 | (2.6) | -24.6 | (2.9) | -41.5 | (3.5) | -40.0 | (9.6) | -75.4 | (16.7) |
| Estonia | 532 | (3.2) | -21.8 | (3.1) | -40.5 | (4.0) | -63.9 | (7.1) | -67.5 | (12.5) |
| Hong Kong-China | 554 | (4.0) | -8.8 | (4.4) | -5.9 | (4.9) | -20.6 | (7.8) | -14.8 | (11.3) |
| Indonesia | 386 | (6.1) | 5.5 | (3.1) | 15.2 | (6.5) | 11.0 | (7.9) | 7.4 | (13.0) |
| Israel | 475 | (5.4) | -24.1 | (5.7) | -31.2 | (5.8) | -43.3 | (6.3) | -26.8 | (9.5) |
| Jordan | 392 | (3.7) | -6.6 | (3.2) | -4.7 | (4.1) | -0.4 | (4.8) | -0.8 | (6.7) |
| Kyrgyzstan | 335 | (5.1) | -16.9 | (4.6) | -21.7 | (5.5) | -22.5 | (6.9) | -18.0 | (9.5) |
| Latvia | 498 | (4.3) | -14.1 | (4.3) | -20.8 | (6.3) | -23.1 | (6.9) | -30.7 | (18.6) |
| Liechtenstein | 540 | (5.9) | -33.3 | (12.0) | c | c | c | c | a | a |
| Lithuania | 496 | (3.5) | -8.3 | (3.8) | -33.2 | (6.0) | -54.9 | (9.5) | c | c |
| Macao-China | 533 | (2.1) | -9.9 | (3.6) | -14.5 | (5.9) | -21.3 | (7.4) | -17.2 | (9.1) |
| Montenegro | 415 | (1.9) | -24.7 | (4.0) | -23.1 | (4.7) | -30.5 | (7.4) | -30.4 | (11.0) |
| Qatar | 347 | (3.0) | -33.9 | (4.1) | -22.0 | (4.2) | -32.6 | (5.7) | -64.2 | (6.5) |
| Romania | 416 | (5.4) | -3.2 | (5.2) | 7.0 | (5.8) | -2.1 | (7.9) | -2.9 | (12.4) |
| Russian Federation | 473 | (4.4) | 6.9 | (3.3) | 9.3 | (5.3) | 16.9 | (9.0) | 2.5 | (14.1) |
| Serbia | 443 | (3.7) | -6.6 | (3.3) | -5.2 | (4.4) | -8.1 | (8.4) | -44.3 | (12.6) |
| Slovenia | 532 | (1.9) | -37.1 | (3.7) | -55.5 | (4.0) | -68.5 | (7.6) | -84.0 | (13.3) |
| Chinese Taipei | 532 | (4.8) | -18.6 | (4.6) | 64.3 | (5.0) | 58.6 | (6.2) | 57.7 | (10.9) |
| Thailand | 415 | (2.6) | -10.0 | (3.5) | 20.9 | (5.3) | 35.5 | (9.0) | 29.2 | (16.3) |
| Tunisia | 352 | (4.2) | 7.5 | (4.5) | 31.6 | (5.9) | 24.3 | (5.5) | 29.9 | (5.9) |
| Uruguay | 443 | (3.2) | -22.9 | (3.7) | -25.1 | (7.0) | -13.2 | (8.1) | -25.8 | (19.5) |

*Note*: Values that are statistically significant at the 5% level (p < 0.05) are indicated in bold.

© OECD 2011  Quality Time for Students: Learning In and Out of School

[Part 2/2]
## Table 4.6b Performance in mathematics, by learning time in out-of-school-time lessons in mathematics

Difference in mathematics performance between students who spend the following learning hours per week in out-of-school-time lessons in mathematics and students who do not spend any time in out-of-school-time lessons in mathematics

| | Accounting for socio-economic background of students and schools | | | | | | | | Accounting for socio-economic background of students and schools as well as learning time in regular school lessons and individual study in mathematics | | | | | | | |
|---|---|---|---|---|---|---|---|---|---|---|---|---|---|---|---|---|
| | Less than 2 hours per week | | 2 hours or more but less than 4 hours per week | | 4 hours or more but less than 6 hours per week | | 6 hours or more per week | | Less than 2 hours per week | | 2 hours or more but less than 4 hours per week | | 4 hours or more but less than 6 hours per week | | 6 hours or more per week | |
| | Dif. | S.E. | Dif. | S.E. | Dif. | S.E. | Dif. | S.E. | Dif. | S.E. | Dif. | S.E. | Dif. | S.E. | Dif. | S.E. |
| **OECD** | | | | | | | | | | | | | | | | |
| Australia | **-22.7** | (2.1) | **-28.9** | (4.0) | **-45.9** | (5.8) | **-24.6** | (9.0) | **-22.0** | (2.1) | **-41.5** | (3.9) | **-69.8** | (6.0) | **-52.4** | (9.4) |
| Austria | **-36.3** | (3.9) | **-59.1** | (5.9) | **-67.0** | (9.4) | **-94.6** | (15.9) | **-35.9** | (3.9) | **-55.8** | (6.0) | **-58.8** | (9.6) | **-74.2** | (16.7) |
| Belgium | **-34.0** | (2.7) | **-51.6** | (4.6) | **-68.8** | (7.9) | **-50.6** | (12.5) | **-35.0** | (2.7) | **-57.0** | (4.7) | **-73.6** | (8.1) | **-66.1** | (12.3) |
| Canada | **-26.4** | (2.3) | **-40.9** | (2.7) | **-48.7** | (4.4) | **-52.6** | (10.0) | **-23.9** | (2.3) | **-45.3** | (3.1) | **-55.1** | (5.0) | **-55.0** | (9.7) |
| Czech Republic | **-16.0** | (3.4) | **-30.3** | (6.8) | **-37.7** | (10.8) | -22.9 | (14.2) | **-17.7** | (3.3) | **-30.5** | (6.7) | **-29.5** | (10.4) | -5.6 | (17.4) |
| Denmark | **-16.3** | (3.4) | **-30.6** | (4.0) | **-43.9** | (6.7) | -33.8 | (15.9) | **-17.5** | (3.6) | **-31.6** | (4.0) | **-36.8** | (7.8) | -22.5 | (17.1) |
| Finland | **-30.8** | (2.7) | **-51.3** | (6.6) | c | c | c | c | **-29.4** | (2.8) | **-52.0** | (7.1) | c | c | c | c |
| France | **-23.1** | (2.7) | **-33.6** | (3.9) | **-49.1** | (9.0) | c | c | **-25.1** | (2.5) | **-41.8** | (3.8) | **-61.3** | (9.1) | c | c |
| Germany | **-32.0** | (2.6) | **-47.4** | (4.4) | **-48.4** | (6.7) | **-68.2** | (13.4) | **-32.0** | (2.6) | **-47.2** | (4.3) | **-43.7** | (6.8) | **-58.7** | (14.0) |
| Greece | -2.5 | (4.3) | **12.5** | (3.6) | **15.6** | (4.8) | **23.8** | (6.8) | -6.0 | (4.3) | 2.5 | (3.8) | 2.5 | (4.8) | 6.2 | (7.1) |
| Hungary | **-15.4** | (2.7) | **-20.8** | (3.3) | **-28.2** | (5.6) | **-34.1** | (11.9) | **-17.7** | (2.8) | **-29.4** | (3.3) | **-41.2** | (7.0) | **-45.2** | (12.6) |
| Iceland | **-40.5** | (3.0) | **-58.7** | (4.9) | **-94.1** | (11.1) | **-84.5** | (18.2) | **-38.1** | (3.0) | **-55.2** | (5.1) | **-85.2** | (12.2) | **-73.8** | (18.9) |
| Ireland | **-27.0** | (2.4) | **-43.1** | (5.0) | **-64.3** | (8.9) | **-65.9** | (14.7) | **-26.7** | (2.3) | **-46.4** | (5.2) | **-66.6** | (8.7) | **-57.0** | (19.1) |
| Italy | **-19.1** | (2.3) | **-38.5** | (3.6) | **-52.3** | (5.0) | **-59.4** | (7.1) | **-16.7** | (2.1) | **-41.1** | (3.4) | **-60.3** | (5.2) | **-72.0** | (7.8) |
| Japan | -5.2 | (3.9) | **-14.4** | (4.5) | **-33.5** | (7.4) | **-36.6** | (16.2) | -8.8 | (3.5) | **-22.7** | (4.2) | **-51.4** | (8.0) | **-58.8** | (15.3) |
| Korea | **19.4** | (4.7) | **36.1** | (4.4) | **40.1** | (5.0) | **44.1** | (6.5) | **9.4** | (4.7) | **14.5** | (3.9) | **12.0** | (4.8) | **10.7** | (6.2) |
| Luxembourg | **-32.8** | (2.7) | **-51.2** | (3.6) | **-81.9** | (6.0) | **-93.0** | (15.3) | **-32.5** | (2.7) | **-50.7** | (3.6) | **-75.0** | (6.8) | **-74.7** | (15.8) |
| Mexico | **-14.4** | (2.5) | **-10.2** | (3.1) | **-24.1** | (5.3) | **-21.5** | (8.1) | **-12.8** | (2.4) | **-13.6** | (3.0) | **-31.0** | (5.3) | **-26.3** | (7.5) |
| Netherlands | **-21.3** | (2.3) | **-34.5** | (4.3) | **-46.5** | (8.3) | c | c | **-23.3** | (2.5) | **-41.2** | (4.5) | **-45.6** | (8.3) | c | c |
| New Zealand | **-32.7** | (3.0) | **-49.1** | (5.3) | **-57.6** | (8.2) | **-59.9** | (15.6) | **-31.8** | (3.1) | **-54.7** | (5.5) | **-72.8** | (8.4) | **-77.3** | (17.5) |
| Norway | **-16.9** | (3.1) | **-41.3** | (4.2) | **-50.5** | (9.5) | **-89.8** | (17.9) | **-26.5** | (3.1) | **-55.3** | (4.9) | **-62.2** | (10.3) | **-89.1** | (18.2) |
| Poland | **-12.4** | (2.8) | **-30.1** | (4.5) | **-40.3** | (9.7) | -24.5 | (14.6) | **-12.0** | (2.7) | **-32.6** | (4.3) | **-45.4** | (9.8) | **-35.1** | (14.5) |
| Portugal | **-17.1** | (3.0) | **-23.3** | (4.3) | **-20.6** | (8.5) | c | c | **-18.3** | (2.8) | **-30.1** | (4.4) | **-41.6** | (8.4) | c | c |
| Slovak Republic | 2.6 | (3.6) | -2.5 | (5.4) | **-28.5** | (9.5) | c | c | -0.0 | (3.4) | -4.9 | (5.2) | **-29.6** | (9.4) | c | c |
| Spain | **-30.8** | (2.3) | **-36.3** | (2.9) | **-35.0** | (5.1) | **-58.0** | (11.7) | **-25.3** | (2.1) | **-39.1** | (2.8) | **-39.9** | (4.6) | **-53.8** | (10.3) |
| Sweden | **-38.5** | (3.3) | **-57.1** | (4.9) | **-92.9** | (12.5) | c | c | **-37.5** | (3.5) | **-51.5** | (5.3) | **-79.5** | (13.3) | c | c |
| Switzerland | **-27.5** | (2.9) | **-43.7** | (4.8) | **-88.5** | (9.8) | **-90.7** | (13.2) | **-26.9** | (2.9) | **-41.5** | (4.6) | **-76.1** | (9.1) | **-66.5** | (13.9) |
| Turkey | 4.9 | (3.5) | **23.3** | (3.6) | **28.5** | (4.8) | **44.0** | (6.2) | -3.5 | (4.1) | 6.3 | (4.4) | 3.8 | (5.3) | **19.7** | (6.8) |
| United Kingdom | **-19.0** | (2.9) | **-30.9** | (4.2) | **-45.9** | (9.3) | -26.3 | (22.0) | **-20.3** | (2.8) | **-38.0** | (4.5) | **-62.3** | (9.3) | **-50.4** | (22.3) |
| United States | **-27.4** | (2.9) | **-38.5** | (3.7) | **-46.4** | (6.3) | **-49.5** | (7.9) | **-24.2** | (2.9) | **-46.3** | (4.1) | **-61.9** | (7.2) | **-58.3** | (10.9) |
| **OECD average** | **-20.4** | (3.1) | **-30.9** | (4.5) | **-43.3** | (8.0) | **-42.9** | (13.4) | **-21.3** | (3.1) | **-35.8** | (4.6) | **-49.6** | (8.2) | **-47.3** | (14.1) |
| **Partners** | | | | | | | | | | | | | | | | |
| Argentina | **-26.5** | (3.7) | **-41.7** | (5.9) | -25.5 | (13.5) | -14.9 | (12.9) | **-24.2** | (3.7) | **-42.0** | (5.3) | -35.6 | (13.0) | -16.2 | (14.0) |
| Azerbaijan | 4.4 | (2.4) | 3.8 | (2.8) | 2.6 | (3.6) | 2.0 | (4.0) | 3.6 | (2.5) | 0.5 | (2.8) | -4.9 | (3.6) | -5.2 | (4.2) |
| Brazil | **-7.3** | (3.5) | -6.2 | (4.4) | 1.1 | (5.9) | -6.1 | (13.7) | **-7.4** | (3.3) | **-11.0** | (4.7) | -8.5 | (7.1) | -15.5 | (14.1) |
| Bulgaria | **-10.1** | (3.5) | **-11.6** | (3.8) | **-18.1** | (4.8) | -6.6 | (12.7) | **-12.8** | (3.4) | **-24.2** | (3.8) | **-39.5** | (9.9) | **-38.4** | (14.3) |
| Chile | **-9.0** | (2.6) | -4.5 | (3.5) | **-13.6** | (6.6) | **-21.0** | (10.4) | **-12.6** | (2.4) | **-15.3** | (3.4) | **-28.4** | (6.6) | **-40.6** | (11.4) |
| Colombia | -3.5 | (3.8) | 3.8 | (4.7) | -0.8 | (8.7) | 26.7 | (15.1) | -6.9 | (3.7) | -7.2 | (4.3) | -15.9 | (8.3) | 8.0 | (16.6) |
| Croatia | **-27.0** | (2.2) | **-42.7** | (3.2) | **-54.2** | (7.7) | **-79.7** | (14.7) | **-27.0** | (2.2) | **-46.2** | (3.2) | **-58.8** | (7.8) | **-84.9** | (15.2) |
| Estonia | **-16.8** | (2.9) | **-38.3** | (4.0) | **-59.8** | (5.5) | **-65.2** | (12.4) | **-19.0** | (2.9) | **-43.2** | (3.8) | **-64.7** | (6.3) | **-68.2** | (12.1) |
| Hong Kong-China | **-8.9** | (3.9) | **-13.4** | (4.1) | **-28.1** | (7.6) | -13.4 | (10.7) | **-11.9** | (3.6) | **-24.2** | (4.0) | **-50.9** | (7.9) | **-47.7** | (11.1) |
| Indonesia | 1.4 | (3.1) | 7.1 | (5.0) | 7.2 | (6.1) | 6.8 | (10.8) | -0.4 | (3.0) | -0.4 | (4.5) | -5.4 | (5.8) | -3.1 | (9.4) |
| Israel | **-26.7** | (5.0) | **-33.6** | (5.3) | **-39.0** | (6.3) | **-34.0** | (9.1) | **-28.3** | (4.8) | **-37.5** | (5.5) | **-45.8** | (6.5) | **-48.0** | (10.5) |
| Jordan | -7.2 | (3.0) | -5.0 | (3.5) | -4.3 | (4.6) | -6.3 | (6.6) | -4.6 | (3.0) | **-8.6** | (3.3) | **-16.0** | (4.8) | **-23.1** | (7.2) |
| Kyrgyzstan | **-10.7** | (3.8) | **-14.5** | (4.7) | **-12.0** | (5.7) | -11.8 | (8.8) | **-16.3** | (3.5) | **-27.5** | (4.4) | **-37.9** | (6.1) | **-37.3** | (9.0) |
| Latvia | **-13.7** | (3.8) | **-21.8** | (5.0) | **-29.8** | (6.4) | **-41.2** | (16.2) | **-13.8** | (3.6) | **-22.9** | (5.2) | **-26.3** | (6.3) | -30.9 | (16.4) |
| Liechtenstein | 3.6 | (9.4) | c | c | c | c | a | a | -0.0 | (10.3) | c | c | c | c | a | a |
| Lithuania | **-7.8** | (3.4) | **-36.8** | (4.7) | **-41.4** | (8.4) | c | c | **-8.0** | (3.3) | **-41.4** | (4.8) | **-53.4** | (8.9) | c | c |
| Macao-China | **-9.7** | (3.6) | **-18.7** | (5.8) | **-24.2** | (7.4) | **-20.5** | (8.7) | **-8.2** | (3.3) | **-24.6** | (5.5) | **-35.8** | (7.6) | **-35.1** | (9.0) |
| Montenegro | **-22.8** | (3.5) | **-24.0** | (3.8) | **-34.4** | (6.6) | **-35.0** | (8.4) | **-21.5** | (3.4) | **-31.3** | (3.8) | **-44.2** | (6.5) | **-43.8** | (8.4) |
| Qatar | **-26.0** | (3.7) | **-18.6** | (3.7) | **-27.6** | (5.2) | **-48.2** | (6.1) | **-23.7** | (3.8) | **-27.2** | (3.7) | **-42.8** | (4.9) | **-72.8** | (6.4) |
| Romania | -1.8 | (4.6) | 1.8 | (6.3) | -7.7 | (6.0) | -4.7 | (9.3) | -6.2 | (3.9) | **-13.8** | (6.7) | **-27.3** | (6.8) | **-31.4** | (9.6) |
| Russian Federation | 6.4 | (3.3) | 4.0 | (5.1) | 14.1 | (8.5) | -0.5 | (12.4) | 3.5 | (3.1) | -5.2 | (4.9) | 1.6 | (8.7) | -19.8 | (14.7) |
| Serbia | **-10.4** | (2.9) | **-11.2** | (3.9) | -13.2 | (7.9) | **-33.1** | (11.0) | **-14.1** | (3.0) | **-16.6** | (4.1) | **-21.7** | (7.9) | **-38.9** | (11.6) |
| Slovenia | **-23.0** | (2.7) | **-39.3** | (3.5) | **-55.4** | (6.5) | **-53.2** | (10.5) | **-23.4** | (2.9) | **-43.0** | (3.4) | **-59.5** | (6.5) | **-56.2** | (12.8) |
| Chinese Taipei | **-15.1** | (3.7) | **28.4** | (3.8) | **26.1** | (5.5) | **26.1** | (9.8) | **-16.8** | (3.4) | **6.7** | (2.8) | -2.8 | (4.9) | -6.0 | (10.1) |
| Thailand | **-15.4** | (2.9) | -3.3 | (4.2) | **13.3** | (6.3) | 2.6 | (13.7) | **-17.8** | (2.6) | **-16.1** | (4.2) | -10.1 | (5.9) | **-32.1** | (12.2) |
| Tunisia | 4.6 | (4.1) | **14.1** | (4.3) | **11.4** | (4.9) | **17.0** | (5.3) | -6.6 | (4.0) | -3.4 | (4.7) | -7.1 | (5.1) | -3.4 | (5.6) |
| Uruguay | **-21.7** | (3.2) | **-26.3** | (5.9) | -17.0 | (7.8) | -19.4 | (18.4) | **-19.7** | (3.0) | **-31.4** | (6.2) | **-28.5** | (8.9) | -33.7 | (19.1) |

*Note:* Values that are statistically significant at the 5% level (p < 0.05) are indicated in bold.

### Table 4.6c Performance in reading, by learning time in out-of-school-time lessons on the language of instruction
[Part 1/2]

| | Reading performance for students who do not spend any time in out-of-school-time lessons on the language of instruction | | Difference in reading performance between students who spend the following learning hours per week in out-of-school-time lessons on the language of instruction and students who do not spend any time in out-of-school-time lessons on the language of instruction | | | | | | | |
| | | | Less than 2 hours per week | | 2 hours or more but less than 4 hours per week | | 4 hours or more but less than 6 hours per week | | 6 hours or more per week | |
| | Mean score | S.E. | Dif. | S.E. | Dif. | S.E. | Dif. | S.E. | Dif. | S.E. |
|---|---|---|---|---|---|---|---|---|---|---|
| **OECD** | | | | | | | | | | |
| Australia | 532 | (2.0) | **-39.4** | (2.3) | **-53.3** | (3.8) | **-73.1** | (6.0) | **-93.6** | (11.5) |
| Austria | 506 | (3.6) | **-76.2** | (8.0) | **-116.7** | (13.8) | **-101.2** | (13.5) | c | c |
| Belgium | 527 | (2.4) | **-56.5** | (3.4) | **-72.1** | (5.9) | **-111.7** | (21.2) | **-113.8** | (22.3) |
| Canada | 549 | (2.2) | **-39.3** | (2.6) | **-46.6** | (3.8) | **-55.1** | (6.1) | **-33.1** | (9.2) |
| Czech Republic | 497 | (4.3) | **-16.7** | (3.8) | **-26.1** | (8.5) | -33.8 | (18.8) | -24.1 | (26.0) |
| Denmark | 517 | (4.6) | **-25.3** | (4.6) | **-29.1** | (4.3) | **-28.0** | (6.5) | -11.0 | (11.9) |
| Finland | 556 | (2.2) | **-31.6** | (3.6) | **-43.6** | (7.8) | c | c | c | c |
| France | 513 | (4.1) | **-45.1** | (4.2) | **-43.3** | (5.2) | **-62.4** | (15.0) | c | c |
| Germany | 532 | (3.3) | **-61.6** | (4.9) | **-89.3** | (5.8) | **-101.3** | (9.3) | **-141.4** | (22.4) |
| Greece | 466 | (4.5) | **-15.8** | (4.6) | 4.5 | (4.8) | 1.3 | (6.1) | 8.8 | (9.3) |
| Hungary | 508 | (4.1) | **-34.6** | (4.2) | **-38.8** | (5.0) | **-40.8** | (8.2) | **-29.0** | (13.4) |
| Iceland | 502 | (2.1) | **-38.6** | (4.1) | **-76.0** | (7.9) | **-99.5** | (14.0) | c | c |
| Ireland | 538 | (3.5) | **-47.6** | (3.9) | **-64.8** | (6.1) | **-98.1** | (9.9) | **-92.5** | (15.0) |
| Italy | 491 | (2.3) | **-53.0** | (4.2) | **-67.1** | (5.4) | **-78.5** | (6.5) | **-69.1** | (10.1) |
| Japan | 505 | (3.5) | **-14.2** | (5.2) | **-47.0** | (8.8) | **-69.7** | (13.5) | c | c |
| Korea | 535 | (5.5) | **25.7** | (4.9) | **44.5** | (5.8) | **47.0** | (6.9) | **33.1** | (12.9) |
| Luxembourg | 506 | (1.5) | **-57.8** | (3.5) | **-91.7** | (5.9) | **-142.7** | (11.0) | **-138.5** | (14.9) |
| Mexico | 432 | (3.0) | **-26.0** | (3.2) | **-36.1** | (4.1) | **-44.7** | (9.8) | **-98.3** | (19.9) |
| Netherlands | 537 | (2.7) | **-51.2** | (4.1) | **-75.5** | (6.0) | **-97.9** | (10.5) | c | c |
| New Zealand | 546 | (2.5) | **-51.0** | (4.4) | **-67.4** | (6.1) | **-105.0** | (11.3) | **-96.8** | (16.8) |
| Norway | 508 | (3.5) | **-18.1** | (3.8) | **-37.9** | (5.5) | **-32.7** | (11.8) | **-68.0** | (16.1) |
| Poland | 520 | (3.2) | **-17.6** | (3.6) | **-38.0** | (7.2) | **-60.6** | (12.3) | **-62.1** | (21.5) |
| Portugal | 499 | (3.2) | **-66.4** | (4.8) | **-78.4** | (7.7) | **-81.8** | (10.0) | c | c |
| Slovak Republic | 460 | (4.3) | **22.0** | (4.6) | **18.3** | (7.3) | -4.6 | (14.8) | c | c |
| Spain | 481 | (2.1) | **-56.0** | (3.4) | **-70.0** | (4.9) | **-66.6** | (6.4) | **-107.8** | (15.6) |
| Sweden | 529 | (3.7) | **-40.9** | (3.5) | **-48.2** | (6.1) | **-67.2** | (14.3) | **-92.5** | (15.1) |
| Switzerland | 520 | (2.9) | **-57.1** | (4.1) | **-85.6** | (8.0) | **-102.9** | (10.8) | **-133.1** | (17.4) |
| Turkey | 458 | (5.9) | **-11.6** | (4.9) | -9.6 | (5.2) | -11.3 | (9.2) | -8.9 | (9.5) |
| United Kingdom | 514 | (2.4) | **-37.0** | (3.6) | **-57.8** | (5.8) | **-75.6** | (10.9) | **-86.2** | (25.3) |
| United States | m | m | m | m | m | m | m | m | m | m |
| **OECD average** | 510 | (3.4) | **-35.8** | (4.3) | **-49.7** | (6.6) | **-64.2** | (11.5) | **-69.4** | (16.8) |
| **Partners** | | | | | | | | | | |
| Argentina | 404 | (6.5) | **-67.5** | (7.9) | **-94.2** | (12.1) | **-108.8** | (22.1) | c | c |
| Azerbaijan | 367 | (4.2) | **-12.3** | (4.3) | **-12.4** | (4.8) | -8.5 | (4.8) | -10.3 | (7.2) |
| Brazil | 406 | (4.6) | -6.7 | (3.9) | **-16.9** | (5.1) | **-25.9** | (11.3) | -26.0 | (18.3) |
| Bulgaria | 432 | (7.1) | **-40.2** | (5.6) | **-44.4** | (9.1) | **-36.0** | (10.2) | **-39.1** | (19.0) |
| Chile | 467 | (5.6) | **-34.3** | (4.4) | **-43.4** | (5.0) | **-53.7** | (9.6) | **-63.0** | (18.7) |
| Colombia | 406 | (5.1) | **-25.4** | (4.9) | **-32.5** | (5.5) | **-30.5** | (12.4) | -30.1 | (18.3) |
| Croatia | 492 | (2.4) | **-50.8** | (4.7) | **-75.8** | (6.3) | **-78.9** | (12.0) | c | c |
| Estonia | 521 | (2.9) | **-33.0** | (2.9) | **-49.6** | (5.1) | **-60.3** | (8.7) | c | c |
| Hong Kong-China | 548 | (2.9) | **-20.0** | (3.9) | **-36.6** | (5.7) | **-44.0** | (8.5) | **-41.1** | (14.7) |
| Indonesia | 403 | (7.0) | **-8.9** | (2.9) | **-18.3** | (4.8) | **-27.5** | (8.3) | **-45.1** | (12.9) |
| Israel | 479 | (4.9) | **-33.5** | (5.5) | **-51.3** | (6.2) | **-90.5** | (8.5) | **-65.4** | (14.1) |
| Jordan | 425 | (4.0) | **-24.5** | (3.6) | **-24.1** | (4.2) | **-31.7** | (5.6) | **-40.9** | (8.0) |
| Kyrgyzstan | 315 | (6.2) | **-23.3** | (5.4) | **-25.0** | (6.7) | -14.3 | (7.7) | **-32.4** | (9.3) |
| Latvia | 498 | (4.5) | **-29.0** | (4.1) | **-38.9** | (5.1) | **-62.4** | (11.7) | c | c |
| Liechtenstein | 525 | (4.6) | **-42.6** | (15.3) | c | c | c | c | a | a |
| Lithuania | 487 | (3.5) | **-30.1** | (4.7) | **-57.6** | (6.3) | **-55.0** | (9.1) | **-82.1** | (17.1) |
| Macao-China | 505 | (1.7) | **-15.9** | (3.0) | **-34.6** | (4.9) | **-47.4** | (6.9) | **-35.6** | (9.0) |
| Montenegro | 409 | (1.7) | **-34.6** | (3.9) | **-37.4** | (5.2) | **-22.1** | (8.4) | **-54.1** | (11.6) |
| Qatar | 356 | (2.9) | **-48.3** | (4.1) | **-47.5** | (4.7) | **-58.3** | (6.3) | **-90.7** | (10.0) |
| Romania | 404 | (5.8) | **-10.9** | (4.9) | -8.3 | (6.2) | 0.8 | (9.1) | 8.2 | (11.2) |
| Russian Federation | 450 | (4.3) | **-11.0** | (3.1) | **-25.5** | (5.6) | **-38.6** | (13.2) | -12.4 | (19.3) |
| Serbia | 417 | (3.7) | **-26.2** | (3.4) | **-31.6** | (4.9) | **-27.9** | (8.6) | **-47.2** | (13.3) |
| Slovenia | 518 | (1.5) | **-39.6** | (2.7) | **-57.5** | (4.2) | **-55.6** | (11.5) | c | c |
| Chinese Taipei | 509 | (3.5) | **-37.1** | (4.0) | **-13.4** | (3.8) | **-26.0** | (9.2) | -16.9 | (13.1) |
| Thailand | 430 | (2.7) | **-35.7** | (2.9) | **-54.3** | (5.7) | **-74.1** | (8.9) | c | c |
| Tunisia | 409 | (6.7) | **-25.0** | (6.0) | **-38.9** | (7.4) | **-37.5** | (8.3) | **-39.2** | (10.8) |
| Uruguay | 435 | (3.5) | **-35.9** | (4.9) | **-34.4** | (8.9) | -20.0 | (17.9) | **-68.3** | (27.9) |

*Note:* Values that are statistically significant at the 5% level (p < 0.05) are indicated in bold.

© OECD 2011 Quality Time for Students: Learning In and Out of School

## Table 4.6c [Part 2/2] Performance in reading, by learning time in out-of-school-time lessons on the language of instruction

Difference in reading performance between students who spend the following learning hours per week in out-of-school-time lessons on the language of instruction and students who do not spend any time in out-of-school-time lessons on the language of instruction

| | Accounting for socio-economic background of students and schools | | | | | | | | Accounting for socio-economic background of students and schools as well as learning time in regular school lessons and individual study on the language of instruction | | | | | | | |
|---|---|---|---|---|---|---|---|---|---|---|---|---|---|---|---|---|
| | Less than 2 hours per week | | 2 hours or more but less than 4 hours per week | | 4 hours or more but less than 6 hours per week | | 6 hours or more per week | | Less than 2 hours per week | | 2 hours or more but less than 4 hours per week | | 4 hours or more but less than 6 hours per week | | 6 hours or more per week | |
| | Dif. | S.E. | Dif. | S.E. | Dif. | S.E. | Dif. | S.E. | Dif. | S.E. | Dif. | S.E. | Dif. | S.E. | Dif. | S.E. |
| **OECD** | | | | | | | | | | | | | | | | |
| Australia | **-35.3** | (2.1) | **-47.9** | (3.5) | **-68.2** | (5.9) | **-84.9** | (10.8) | **-32.6** | (2.2) | **-56.6** | (3.7) | **-83.8** | (6.1) | **-95.1** | (12.2) |
| Austria | **-48.0** | (6.9) | **-80.5** | (13.3) | **-53.5** | (13.4) | c | c | **-45.9** | (7.0) | **-70.6** | (13.6) | **-37.3** | (13.8) | c | c |
| Belgium | **-36.1** | (3.0) | **-49.5** | (4.7) | **-87.2** | (18.4) | **-78.9** | (21.6) | **-36.9** | (3.0) | **-51.3** | (5.0) | **-79.0** | (18.9) | **-65.7** | (22.4) |
| Canada | **-33.8** | (2.3) | **-44.1** | (3.0) | **-53.5** | (5.3) | **-41.7** | (8.8) | **-30.8** | (2.4) | **-51.3** | (3.7) | **-70.3** | (6.3) | **-49.3** | (10.9) |
| Czech Republic | **-9.9** | (3.3) | **-16.2** | (7.6) | -22.8 | (16.7) | -21.2 | (23.3) | **-13.3** | (3.3) | **-20.8** | (7.6) | -15.5 | (16.0) | 16.2 | (25.6) |
| Denmark | **-21.6** | (4.2) | **-25.2** | (3.9) | **-24.6** | (5.8) | -8.8 | (12.5) | **-18.4** | (3.9) | **-31.0** | (3.8) | **-31.9** | (6.4) | -14.7 | (12.7) |
| Finland | **-28.9** | (3.4) | **-41.0** | (7.7) | c | c | c | c | **-29.8** | (3.4) | **-55.1** | (7.6) | c | c | c | c |
| France | **-21.0** | (3.6) | **-20.6** | (4.7) | **-33.3** | (11.3) | c | c | **-20.3** | (3.4) | **-33.6** | (4.9) | **-55.3** | (10.9) | c | c |
| Germany | **-37.7** | (4.0) | **-50.4** | (4.8) | **-62.1** | (7.7) | **-81.1** | (14.5) | **-36.9** | (4.0) | **-52.7** | (5.0) | **-61.5** | (8.3) | **-70.1** | (13.9) |
| Greece | **-15.9** | (3.9) | -1.5 | (4.4) | 0.6 | (9.0) | 4.9 | (9.0) | **-14.9** | (3.7) | **-11.4** | (4.0) | **-15.9** | (6.1) | -6.8 | (9.4) |
| Hungary | **-18.1** | (3.4) | **-22.0** | (3.5) | **-31.3** | (7.0) | -13.9 | (10.1) | **-18.8** | (3.6) | **-35.8** | (3.4) | **-47.9** | (6.8) | -22.4 | (12.1) |
| Iceland | **-39.1** | (3.9) | **-79.9** | (7.6) | **-101.6** | (13.2) | c | c | **-34.3** | (3.9) | **-75.8** | (7.2) | **-85.4** | (14.1) | c | c |
| Ireland | **-39.6** | (4.0) | **-56.1** | (5.7) | **-89.9** | (9.1) | **-83.6** | (13.3) | **-36.4** | (3.8) | **-57.4** | (5.9) | **-90.3** | (9.8) | **-73.8** | (15.2) |
| Italy | **-34.7** | (3.1) | **-51.5** | (4.8) | **-60.9** | (6.0) | **-51.8** | (8.6) | **-26.4** | (3.1) | **-49.4** | (4.7) | **-65.7** | (6.0) | **-52.2** | (9.0) |
| Japan | **-14.9** | (4.4) | **-36.1** | (6.6) | **-70.3** | (12.4) | c | c | **-19.8** | (4.4) | **-45.2** | (7.2) | **-84.9** | (13.8) | c | c |
| Korea | 11.8 | (3.9) | **24.0** | (4.3) | **19.9** | (6.4) | 9.5 | (11.6) | 6.0 | (3.7) | **11.6** | (3.9) | 3.2 | (6.0) | -6.8 | (12.2) |
| Luxembourg | **-42.2** | (3.2) | **-65.9** | (5.5) | **-108.6** | (9.8) | **-106.6** | (12.6) | **-39.8** | (3.2) | **-65.3** | (5.7) | **-103.9** | (11.1) | **-98.3** | (12.6) |
| Mexico | **-15.0** | (2.2) | **-20.8** | (3.6) | **-26.0** | (8.7) | **-73.4** | (17.4) | **-14.3** | (2.1) | **-23.4** | (3.3) | **-33.1** | (9.3) | **-72.5** | (17.3) |
| Netherlands | **-30.1** | (3.0) | **-45.4** | (4.8) | **-58.6** | (11.2) | c | c | **-30.2** | (3.1) | **-47.5** | (5.0) | **-54.5** | (11.5) | c | c |
| New Zealand | **-44.9** | (3.7) | **-61.0** | (5.6) | **-96.3** | (10.1) | **-89.9** | (14.9) | **-39.4** | (3.7) | **-65.6** | (5.8) | **-108.0** | (11.1) | **-99.5** | (19.7) |
| Norway | **-17.2** | (3.6) | **-36.5** | (5.3) | **-36.1** | (11.6) | **-74.7** | (15.9) | **-25.6** | (3.4) | **-54.6** | (5.1) | **-50.4** | (12.6) | **-70.7** | (18.3) |
| Poland | **-13.5** | (3.8) | **-33.2** | (6.8) | **-57.8** | (11.4) | **-60.8** | (17.8) | **-12.5** | (3.7) | **-34.8** | (6.5) | **-69.5** | (11.8) | **-69.7** | (18.3) |
| Portugal | **-47.5** | (3.5) | **-63.4** | (6.6) | **-71.2** | (9.4) | c | c | **-41.1** | (3.4) | **-62.0** | (6.5) | **-80.1** | (9.4) | c | c |
| Slovak Republic | **13.7** | (3.5) | **12.0** | (5.8) | -5.4 | (11.6) | c | c | **6.9** | (3.3) | -1.0 | (6.0) | -14.0 | (12.5) | c | c |
| Spain | **-49.5** | (3.1) | **-60.7** | (4.5) | **-57.7** | (6.3) | **-95.8** | (14.4) | **-37.3** | (3.0) | **-60.2** | (4.3) | **-64.5** | (6.0) | **-83.7** | (12.7) |
| Sweden | **-35.9** | (3.6) | **-44.3** | (5.3) | **-68.7** | (14.8) | **-94.7** | (18.0) | **-38.6** | (3.3) | **-46.8** | (6.1) | **-66.1** | (14.8) | **-68.8** | (15.4) |
| Switzerland | **-41.8** | (3.6) | **-66.9** | (6.7) | **-80.1** | (10.3) | **-111.8** | (14.2) | **-38.1** | (3.3) | **-63.0** | (6.5) | **-64.4** | (9.0) | **-80.4** | (17.0) |
| Turkey | -6.4 | (3.5) | -1.9 | (4.2) | 2.5 | (11.0) | 0.2 | (7.8) | -6.1 | (3.4) | -8.8 | (4.4) | -11.6 | (7.3) | -9.9 | (8.1) |
| United Kingdom | **-29.2** | (3.2) | **-47.4** | (6.0) | **-60.0** | (9.3) | -64.6 | (24.5) | **-30.1** | (3.1) | **-60.2** | (6.3) | **-80.6** | (9.3) | **-91.9** | (28.1) |
| United States | m | m | m | m | m | m | m | m | m | m | m | m | m | m | m | m |
| **OECD average** | **-27.0** | (3.6) | **-39.1** | (5.9) | **-52.2** | (10.4) | **-58.3** | (15.1) | **-26.1** | (3.6) | **-44.1** | (5.9) | **-57.9** | (10.7) | **-56.5** | (16.2) |
| **Partners** | | | | | | | | | | | | | | | | |
| Argentina | **-54.9** | (7.3) | **-70.9** | (11.8) | **-97.8** | (18.8) | c | c | **-50.2** | (7.2) | **-70.7** | (11.5) | **-104.2** | (18.0) | c | c |
| Azerbaijan | -7.6 | (4.2) | **-10.4** | (4.1) | **-9.7** | (4.6) | -10.4 | (7.1) | -5.8 | (4.4) | **-12.5** | (4.1) | **-17.1** | (4.6) | **-19.6** | (7.2) |
| Brazil | **-6.7** | (3.1) | **-15.3** | (4.1) | **-18.3** | (9.3) | -15.7 | (15.5) | -4.8 | (2.9) | **-17.6** | (4.6) | **-21.9** | (9.4) | -13.1 | (15.5) |
| Bulgaria | **-20.7** | (3.9) | **-33.1** | (5.9) | **-25.1** | (9.0) | **-36.0** | (14.7) | **-23.9** | (3.9) | **-48.4** | (5.9) | **-55.0** | (9.3) | **-72.7** | (15.1) |
| Chile | **-17.9** | (3.3) | **-24.9** | (4.0) | **-36.0** | (8.6) | **-43.7** | (15.6) | **-17.7** | (3.2) | **-36.5** | (4.3) | **-59.9** | (9.7) | **-59.3** | (19.0) |
| Colombia | **-15.2** | (4.8) | **-20.0** | (4.9) | -22.6 | (12.1) | -26.3 | (17.2) | **-16.2** | (4.5) | **-22.8** | (5.7) | **-27.3** | (11.9) | -24.1 | (19.1) |
| Croatia | **-39.1** | (4.0) | **-64.0** | (6.7) | **-62.1** | (10.6) | c | c | **-37.5** | (3.9) | **-68.1** | (6.7) | **-70.1** | (11.0) | c | c |
| Estonia | **-28.4** | (2.7) | **-42.0** | (4.1) | **-53.8** | (8.5) | c | c | **-28.7** | (2.7) | **-47.6** | (4.8) | **-62.7** | (8.7) | c | c |
| Hong Kong-China | **-12.0** | (4.2) | **-25.4** | (5.4) | **-34.6** | (9.0) | **-29.2** | (14.5) | **-9.9** | (4.0) | **-30.8** | (5.6) | **-51.6** | (9.3) | **-43.9** | (14.3) |
| Indonesia | -6.8 | (3.0) | **-9.9** | (3.9) | **-13.1** | (6.5) | **-33.9** | (12.1) | **-9.4** | (3.0) | **-13.4** | (3.7) | **-20.2** | (5.6) | **-34.9** | (13.1) |
| Israel | **-30.2** | (5.4) | **-42.0** | (5.7) | **-75.2** | (8.7) | **-58.6** | (13.8) | **-36.6** | (5.2) | **-52.5** | (5.3) | **-86.0** | (8.7) | **-60.3** | (15.1) |
| Jordan | **-21.3** | (3.4) | **-18.6** | (3.9) | **-26.3** | (6.0) | **-32.1** | (7.9) | **-16.3** | (3.5) | **-19.4** | (4.1) | **-35.2** | (6.4) | **-49.1** | (7.3) |
| Kyrgyzstan | **-11.6** | (4.5) | -12.9 | (6.2) | -2.4 | (7.6) | -13.8 | (8.2) | **-14.5** | (4.6) | **-29.7** | (6.2) | **-33.5** | (8.2) | **-42.5** | (9.8) |
| Latvia | **-20.3** | (3.5) | **-32.1** | (5.1) | **-52.9** | (10.0) | c | c | **-21.2** | (3.5) | **-35.0** | (4.8) | **-52.7** | (10.8) | c | c |
| Liechtenstein | -4.6 | (10.6) | c | c | c | c | a | a | -2.8 | (11.8) | c | c | c | c | a | a |
| Lithuania | **-21.9** | (3.9) | **-47.4** | (5.7) | **-42.9** | (8.5) | **-63.8** | (17.3) | **-16.0** | (3.6) | **-50.3** | (5.8) | **-56.9** | (9.4) | **-80.0** | (21.2) |
| Macao-China | **-15.2** | (3.0) | **-35.1** | (4.8) | **-47.3** | (7.0) | **-37.4** | (9.1) | **-14.0** | (2.9) | **-36.9** | (4.8) | **-50.5** | (6.8) | **-41.0** | (9.5) |
| Montenegro | **-26.7** | (3.7) | **-29.9** | (5.1) | **-19.3** | (7.5) | **-49.0** | (11.0) | **-24.8** | (3.7) | **-41.9** | (5.3) | **-35.4** | (7.6) | **-48.2** | (12.7) |
| Qatar | **-42.0** | (3.8) | **-39.3** | (4.4) | **-50.6** | (6.4) | **-76.5** | (10.0) | **-42.4** | (3.9) | **-50.3** | (4.4) | **-68.1** | (6.5) | **-95.8** | (10.6) |
| Romania | -7.4 | (3.7) | -5.1 | (5.4) | 1.5 | (9.9) | **19.5** | (9.9) | -7.8 | (3.7) | **-19.2** | (5.6) | **-24.8** | (8.4) | -12.1 | (11.3) |
| Russian Federation | **-6.7** | (2.9) | **-20.9** | (5.6) | **-32.7** | (12.1) | -3.9 | (20.0) | **-7.1** | (3.0) | **-18.9** | (5.6) | **-25.6** | (11.2) | 17.4 | (18.5) |
| Serbia | **-17.3** | (3.2) | **-24.6** | (3.8) | **-21.4** | (8.1) | **-31.3** | (12.4) | **-20.0** | (3.1) | **-32.5** | (4.0) | **-32.8** | (8.9) | **-40.0** | (14.2) |
| Slovenia | **-20.5** | (2.2) | **-33.4** | (3.7) | **-18.3** | (7.8) | c | c | **-20.4** | (2.2) | **-40.9** | (3.5) | **-37.8** | (7.9) | c | c |
| Chinese Taipei | **-22.9** | (3.0) | **-9.8** | (3.5) | **-21.0** | (9.0) | -11.8 | (11.5) | **-16.2** | (2.9) | **-17.9** | (3.0) | **-35.8** | (8.4) | **-27.2** | (11.9) |
| Thailand | **-26.6** | (3.1) | **-41.8** | (5.4) | **-53.7** | (7.8) | c | c | **-30.6** | (3.1) | **-51.0** | (6.0) | **-67.0** | (7.9) | c | c |
| Tunisia | -8.1 | (4.4) | **-13.9** | (4.6) | -10.5 | (5.9) | -12.8 | (8.6) | **-15.0** | (4.0) | **-26.8** | (4.5) | **-28.9** | (6.4) | **-34.6** | (9.8) |
| Uruguay | **-20.8** | (4.4) | **-19.7** | (8.1) | -9.0 | (15.7) | -31.0 | (23.3) | **-20.7** | (4.3) | **-31.5** | (8.6) | -21.0 | (16.0) | -45.5 | (30.1) |

*Note:* Values that are statistically significant at the 5% level (p < 0.05) are indicated in bold.

259

[Part 1/3]

## Table 4.7 Students' latent performance, by different types of out-of-school-time lessons[1]

| | | Direct effects of the following types of out-of-school-time lessons on students' latent performance[2] | | | | | | | | | | | | | | | | | | | |
|---|---|---|---|---|---|---|---|---|---|---|---|---|---|---|---|---|---|---|---|---|---|
| | | Group lessons with school teacher | | Group lessons with non-school teachers | | Group lessons with both school and non-school teachers | | One-to-one lessons with non-school teacher | | Both one-to-one and group lessons with school teachers | | Both one-to-one and group lessons with non-school teachers | | Both one-to-one and group lessons with both school and non-school teachers | | Other types of out-of-school-time lessons | | Student's PISA index of economic, social and cultural status | | School average index of economic, social and cultural status | |
| | | Change in score | S.E. | Change in score | S.E. | Change in score | S.E. | Change in score | S.E. | Change in score | S.E. | Change in score | S.E. | Change in score | S.E. | Change in score | S.E. | Change in score | S.E. | Change in score | S.E. |
| OECD | Australia | **-10.7** | (4.6) | **21.7** | (5.5) | **-44.0** | (8.8) | 4.9 | (3.0) | **-37.1** | (7.4) | -8.6 | (5.3) | **-71.4** | (5.9) | **-17.8** | (4.9) | **22.7** | (1.1) | **44.6** | (3.9) |
| | Austria | **-12.6** | (4.5) | **-37.7** | (6.1) | **-56.8** | (7.1) | **-25.0** | (4.8) | **-33.2** | (9.9) | **-33.8** | (12.0) | **-58.8** | (5.2) | **-44.6** | (13.2) | **8.7** | (1.3) | **93.1** | (4.6) |
| | Belgium | **-30.6** | (4.8) | 10.6 | (5.7) | **-78.3** | (10.5) | **-16.6** | (3.4) | **-35.5** | (8.1) | **-32.0** | (6.1) | **-73.3** | (6.8) | **-37.8** | (5.7) | **15.3** | (1.1) | **97.5** | (5.2) |
| | Canada | **-9.9** | (3.9) | 4.2 | (5.6) | **-51.7** | (8.6) | **-14.6** | (3.3) | **-46.4** | (4.6) | **-20.8** | (4.9) | **-73.7** | (4.7) | **-28.7** | (4.1) | **20.3** | (1.0) | **35.7** | (4.2) |
| | Czech Republic | **-11.6** | (5.8) | 11.3 | (8.2) | **-50.0** | (13.4) | **-13.1** | (3.5) | **-44.5** | (6.9) | **-17.8** | (7.0) | **-76.9** | (6.0) | **-33.5** | (6.3) | **14.2** | (1.2) | **89.3** | (5.7) |
| | Denmark | **-22.8** | (5.3) | 5.9 | (8.2) | **-58.9** | (14.8) | -15.8 | (8.3) | **-72.2** | (8.3) | **-40.3** | (10.9) | **-82.8** | (9.5) | **-67.6** | (10.9) | **26.4** | (1.4) | **36.1** | (5.9) |
| | Finland | **-47.0** | (4.6) | -0.7 | (9.1) | **-45.5** | (17.8) | **-15.9** | (7.6) | **-49.3** | (6.2) | **27.9** | (12.9) | **-77.5** | (8.6) | **-24.3** | (7.9) | **23.6** | (1.2) | **10.6** | (4.5) |
| | France | -2.2 | (3.9) | -6.2 | (7.8) | **-43.0** | (13.7) | **-23.2** | (3.9) | **-20.7** | (10.1) | **-20.9** | (5.2) | **-41.3** | (5.9) | **-36.1** | (7.9) | **16.3** | (1.4) | **93.8** | (4.7) |
| | Germany | 5.3 | (4.6) | -3.3 | (5.1) | **-50.2** | (8.8) | **-17.3** | (3.4) | **-58.9** | (12.9) | **-30.6** | (8.4) | **-54.2** | (7.5) | **-30.1** | (6.6) | **12.7** | (1.1) | **110.8** | (4.9) |
| | Greece | 1.0 | (9.4) | **36.7** | (4.7) | 15.6 | (8.1) | **12.6** | (5.2) | **-38.1** | (8.3) | **20.1** | (4.7) | **-32.5** | (4.7) | -17.9 | (12.1) | **15.5** | (1.5) | **56.3** | (5.0) |
| | Hungary | 5.7 | (4.7) | -12.2 | (9.8) | **-24.4** | (8.7) | **-6.8** | (3.1) | -6.3 | (5.5) | **-9.2** | (4.7) | **-23.9** | (3.8) | **-17.4** | (5.9) | **6.9** | (1.2) | **83.8** | (4.5) |
| | Iceland | -4.8 | (5.1) | 16.0 | (9.6) | -4.7 | (10.8) | **-41.5** | (5.0) | **-60.3** | (7.0) | **-35.5** | (8.8) | **-76.3** | (9.7) | **-47.9** | (10.2) | **24.8** | (1.2) | 3.3 | (6.5) |
| | Ireland | **-20.5** | (5.6) | **10.8** | (5.4) | **-37.2** | (15.4) | **-11.8** | (3.4) | **-86.3** | (9.0) | **-27.4** | (6.1) | **-73.4** | (7.2) | **-57.3** | (8.4) | **26.0** | (1.5) | **36.9** | (4.6) |
| | Italy | **6.7** | (2.7) | **-15.5** | (5.2) | **-39.5** | (4.3) | **-14.8** | (2.8) | **a** | a | **-43.1** | (4.6) | **-19.2** | (2.7) | **a** | a | **8.2** | (1.0) | **86.1** | (5.0) |
| | Japan | **-18.3** | (3.5) | 4.8 | (5.6) | **-30.8** | (5.5) | **-18.2** | (5.7) | **-45.1** | (10.6) | 4.9 | (7.9) | **-51.5** | (6.8) | **-29.5** | (11.2) | **3.7** | (1.2) | **95.7** | (7.3) |
| | Korea | **28.0** | (4.5) | **28.1** | (4.8) | **27.2** | (5.0) | **15.5** | (5.4) | 0.6 | (9.7) | **13.9** | (5.3) | **18.6** | (5.0) | -3.3 | (10.3) | **6.6** | (1.4) | **68.1** | (6.5) |
| | Luxembourg | **-13.6** | (5.1) | -3.3 | (8.4) | **-71.7** | (14.8) | **-18.1** | (3.8) | **-45.3** | (6.4) | **-31.7** | (7.8) | **-76.0** | (6.6) | **-20.9** | (6.6) | **25.6** | (2.2) | **77.8** | (5.1) |
| | Mexico | **-14.8** | (3.3) | 3.5 | (4.4) | **-43.2** | (3.9) | **-17.1** | (6.1) | **-38.0** | (4.2) | **-10.9** | (3.0) | **-53.5** | (3.3) | **-47.6** | (6.5) | **7.7** | (0.8) | **46.5** | (3.2) |
| | Netherlands | 7.3 | (7.0) | -16.3 | (9.3) | **-65.5** | (11.2) | **-18.3** | (5.7) | **-28.3** | (7.1) | **-33.2** | (9.7) | **-48.2** | (8.3) | **-20.1** | (6.5) | **8.6** | (1.0) | **111.7** | (6.2) |
| | New Zealand | -2.5 | (6.9) | 5.4 | (7.3) | **-58.7** | (11.0) | **-9.1** | (4.6) | **-47.3** | (8.9) | **-27.4** | (8.5) | **-81.4** | (7.5) | **-22.8** | (10.5) | **33.3** | (1.5) | **46.1** | (4.3) |
| | Norway | **-32.5** | (4.0) | **-35.2** | (16.3) | **-59.5** | (9.0) | **-23.3** | (10.8) | **-92.1** | (7.1) | **-32.2** | (13.3) | **-100.8** | (5.8) | **-73.1** | (11.4) | **20.8** | (1.3) | **27.2** | (6.0) |
| | Poland | **11.6** | (3.1) | **21.0** | (5.7) | **-25.2** | (6.9) | -5.9 | (4.5) | **-34.7** | (5.2) | 3.8 | (7.1) | **-45.2** | (4.3) | **-39.0** | (7.3) | **31.7** | (1.3) | **16.1** | (4.5) |
| | Portugal | **-15.5** | (3.7) | 6.5 | (5.4) | **-49.4** | (13.5) | -4.3 | (4.3) | **-45.5** | (4.3) | -5.1 | (5.3) | **-64.1** | (6.1) | **-29.2** | (6.3) | **22.4** | (1.5) | **38.4** | (4.7) |
| | Slovak Republic | 6.9 | (7.1) | -3.2 | (8.5) | **-40.5** | (15.8) | **-19.7** | (5.2) | 4.0 | (5.3) | -6.9 | (4.3) | **-29.6** | (5.1) | **-32.4** | (6.4) | **19.3** | (1.7) | **65.5** | (7.8) |
| | Spain | **-34.7** | (3.8) | **13.8** | (3.0) | **-87.6** | (8.3) | **-18.5** | (3.3) | **-76.7** | (5.2) | **-11.0** | (3.0) | **-82.1** | (4.2) | **-53.8** | (7.6) | **23.6** | (1.2) | **25.9** | (3.1) |
| | Sweden | **-53.0** | (3.7) | -10.7 | (17.1) | **-71.6** | (7.5) | -10.3 | (8.3) | **-91.3** | (6.1) | -12.2 | (11.0) | **-111.0** | (5.1) | **-71.7** | (11.5) | **22.1** | (2.0) | **25.7** | (6.0) |
| | Switzerland | 4.7 | (3.8) | -5.8 | (6.8) | **-74.2** | (11.1) | **-19.4** | (3.0) | **-66.8** | (9.2) | **-38.7** | (6.5) | **-76.4** | (8.7) | **-53.8** | (7.8) | **22.1** | (1.3) | **73.1** | (5.9) |
| | Turkey | **10.6** | (5.0) | **40.6** | (5.6) | **-17.6** | (7.1) | 6.4 | (5.1) | -5.1 | (5.5) | **26.2** | (5.5) | **-19.5** | (5.3) | -11.0 | (8.1) | **8.3** | (1.1) | **71.1** | (6.0) |
| | United Kingdom | **23.0** | (3.9) | 1.0 | (6.3) | **-38.1** | (7.9) | -3.9 | (4.3) | **-13.5** | (6.3) | **-26.1** | (9.4) | **-46.3** | (5.3) | **-18.8** | (6.3) | **25.4** | (1.4) | **62.2** | (5.1) |
| | United States | -7.1 | (5.9) | -6.3 | (8.4) | **-60.2** | (9.0) | 0.6 | (6.6) | **-38.2** | (5.5) | **-21.6** | (7.9) | **-80.2** | (4.7) | **-23.8** | (5.4) | **29.2** | (1.6) | **41.5** | (5.7) |
| | OECD average | **-8.5** | (0.9) | **2.9** | (1.4) | **-44.5** | (1.9) | **-12.1** | (1.0) | **-43.2** | (1.4) | **-16.0** | (1.4) | **-59.4** | (1.1) | **-34.9** | (1.6) | **18.4** | (0.2) | **59.0** | (1.0) |
| Partners | Argentina | **-26.5** | (11.9) | **18.5** | (7.5) | **-56.4** | (11.0) | -2.8 | (4.8) | **-37.0** | (8.1) | -8.1 | (6.2) | **-58.8** | (8.3) | **-44.2** | (11.8) | **14.3** | (1.9) | **68.6** | (7.8) |
| | Azerbaijan | 1.6 | (3.7) | **17.3** | (5.8) | 5.9 | (3.8) | 9.6 | (6.5) | 2.6 | (4.2) | **10.9** | (5.3) | **-6.5** | (2.7) | 7.5 | (4.3) | **7.4** | (0.8) | **12.4** | (5.6) |
| | Brazil | **-18.2** | (3.5) | 3.0 | (4.8) | **-34.2** | (4.6) | 0.5 | (4.2) | **-49.0** | (5.5) | **-13.5** | (5.4) | **-38.2** | (3.8) | **-21.2** | (7.1) | **11.4** | (1.2) | **61.4** | (4.1) |
| | Bulgaria | **19.6** | (5.7) | **27.4** | (6.0) | **-20.6** | (8.5) | **-10.5** | (4.5) | **-37.3** | (6.3) | **-18.2** | (6.1) | **-58.7** | (4.6) | **-19.3** | (7.6) | **13.3** | (1.7) | **79.9** | (6.0) |
| | Chile | -4.1 | (3.7) | -2.8 | (7.1) | **-29.1** | (5.6) | **-23.5** | (4.4) | **-26.8** | (6.1) | -14.0 | (7.6) | **-48.0** | (4.9) | **-23.4** | (10.0) | **13.9** | (1.3) | **58.8** | (3.9) |
| | Colombia | **-18.6** | (4.0) | 0.8 | (5.1) | **-47.1** | (9.4) | **-17.1** | (5.2) | **-42.7** | (5.7) | -3.8 | (3.9) | **-47.4** | (5.0) | **-38.7** | (9.6) | **13.8** | (1.3) | **37.9** | (4.6) |
| | Croatia | **-13.2** | (6.0) | -2.6 | (5.0) | **-60.4** | (10.1) | **-13.3** | (3.6) | **-38.4** | (6.8) | **-23.3** | (4.3) | **-62.2** | (5.7) | **-21.4** | (5.6) | **12.4** | (1.3) | **70.0** | (6.6) |
| | Estonia | **-24.3** | (4.6) | **15.3** | (5.4) | **-61.5** | (11.0) | **-25.5** | (6.1) | **-34.9** | (5.4) | **-29.3** | (6.1) | **-67.1** | (4.6) | **-38.5** | (5.8) | **18.6** | (1.4) | **35.4** | (6.5) |
| | Hong Kong-China | 6.8 | (4.1) | **20.6** | (5.3) | **14.4** | (5.4) | **-14.6** | (6.3) | **-45.6** | (16.4) | -8.5 | (6.1) | **-28.6** | (4.6) | **-58.8** | (14.8) | **9.1** | (1.5) | **62.1** | (7.0) |
| | Indonesia | -8.0 | (5.1) | 2.2 | (3.7) | **-21.3** | (6.8) | -6.0 | (6.7) | **-19.0** | (5.9) | -7.6 | (6.1) | **-37.6** | (5.6) | **-13.1** | (5.7) | **2.8** | (0.8) | **49.5** | (5.1) |
| | Israel | -12.4 | (8.2) | 17.7 | (9.1) | **-25.9** | (10.8) | 4.6 | (5.6) | **-38.5** | (7.3) | 7.6 | (6.8) | **-55.3** | (5.4) | -17.6 | (9.3) | **21.3** | (2.1) | **51.1** | (8.3) |
| | Jordan | 3.7 | (3.6) | -3.3 | (5.1) | **-27.9** | (7.0) | -6.5 | (5.3) | **-35.2** | (5.1) | **-14.1** | (5.1) | **-43.7** | (3.7) | **-45.7** | (7.3) | **22.6** | (1.5) | **33.4** | (5.8) |
| | Kyrgyzstan | **24.8** | (6.0) | **20.0** | (5.7) | 2.9 | (6.0) | **29.9** | (7.3) | **15.9** | (4.9) | **30.7** | (6.7) | **-9.8** | (4.7) | 1.8 | (5.4) | **6.9** | (1.1) | **65.0** | (5.1) |
| | Latvia | 7.9 | (4.7) | **18.7** | (6.0) | **-28.0** | (10.1) | **-13.8** | (4.2) | -6.3 | (5.6) | **-10.9** | (5.6) | **-36.7** | (4.5) | **-24.8** | (5.9) | **21.3** | (1.6) | **32.0** | (6.4) |
| | Lithuania | **16.0** | (3.9) | 5.2 | (7.5) | **-27.8** | (9.9) | -7.6 | (4.5) | **-21.6** | (5.8) | -6.3 | (7.4) | **-46.9** | (5.6) | **-21.9** | (6.9) | **23.2** | (1.3) | **47.6** | (5.1) |
| | Macao-China | 3.8 | (3.0) | **-10.2** | (4.9) | **-29.5** | (5.4) | **-39.0** | (7.6) | **-47.3** | (7.1) | **-30.4** | (7.0) | **-60.0** | (4.5) | **-57.0** | (8.0) | **7.2** | (2.0) | **25.1** | (9.8) |
| | Montenegro | -6.2 | (5.8) | -10.9 | (8.1) | **-41.2** | (9.4) | -4.0 | (5.6) | **-35.6** | (5.8) | **-17.9** | (5.5) | **-54.8** | (3.6) | **-30.1** | (5.8) | **10.7** | (1.6) | **60.7** | (11.9) |
| | Qatar | -7.5 | (10.6) | 15.9 | (13.0) | **-45.8** | (5.8) | -6.1 | (6.4) | **-40.0** | (5.1) | -11.8 | (6.8) | **-51.7** | (4.8) | **-30.9** | (6.1) | **2.6** | (1.2) | **41.4** | (10.5) |
| | Romania | **-13.4** | (6.4) | **-17.3** | (5.6) | **-39.6** | (8.1) | **-7.4** | (3.8) | **-29.8** | (5.3) | -4.6 | (7.3) | **-46.9** | (4.9) | **-14.3** | (5.6) | **13.3** | (2.0) | **54.5** | (5.9) |
| | Russian Federation | **16.5** | (4.0) | 16.0 | (8.5) | -4.2 | (7.7) | -2.8 | (6.0) | -3.3 | (4.7) | -6.6 | (6.0) | **-16.5** | (4.7) | **-15.5** | (5.3) | **18.0** | (1.4) | **38.9** | (5.3) |
| | Serbia | **-19.2** | (5.0) | 3.0 | (9.8) | **-40.1** | (9.9) | **-11.4** | (2.9) | **-50.5** | (7.3) | **-15.8** | (3.9) | **-46.5** | (3.9) | **-25.4** | (6.0) | **11.8** | (1.2) | **72.3** | (4.6) |
| | Slovenia | -7.0 | (5.5) | -5.6 | (7.3) | **-60.3** | (19.8) | **-20.3** | (3.0) | **-21.6** | (8.7) | **-26.5** | (6.9) | **-47.9** | (4.6) | **-35.4** | (5.4) | **6.2** | (1.1) | **112.5** | (5.6) |
| | Chinese Taipei | **8.4** | (3.4) | **35.6** | (3.5) | 5.1 | (4.3) | -5.5 | (4.6) | **-32.0** | (5.2) | -0.9 | (3.8) | **-23.9** | (3.3) | **-35.6** | (8.0) | **9.7** | (1.3) | **86.0** | (5.6) |
| | Thailand | -5.8 | (3.4) | -0.1 | (3.5) | **-12.9** | (3.9) | -8.0 | (9.1) | **-18.5** | (4.5) | 1.9 | (6.8) | **-42.4** | (3.1) | **-29.2** | (7.3) | **10.2** | (1.3) | **44.2** | (2.8) |
| | Tunisia | 3.9 | (5.0) | -13.7 | (10.1) | **-22.6** | (6.2) | **-14.2** | (5.9) | **-8.9** | (4.0) | 1.2 | (4.4) | **-38.8** | (4.2) | -7.8 | (5.7) | **8.7** | (1.2) | **51.8** | (5.8) |
| | Uruguay | 3.3 | (8.5) | **16.8** | (6.0) | -26.5 | (14.5) | -3.8 | (4.0) | -8.9 | (8.4) | 4.1 | (3.7) | **-46.6** | (5.3) | **-47.6** | (10.2) | **17.9** | (1.4) | **57.5** | (3.6) |

1. This table is based on the structural equation model in Box 4.1.
2. Direct effects are the relationship between two variables while holding other variables constant in the model.
3. Logit is positive when the probability of attending this type of out-of-school-time lesson is higher for socio-economically advantaged students than socio-economically disadvantaged students. Logit is negative when the probability of attending this type of out-of-school-time lesson is higher for socio-economically disadvantaged students than socio-economically advantaged students.
4. Logit is positive when the probability of attending this type of out-of-school-time lesson is higher for students in socio-economically advantaged schools than students in socio-economically disadvantaged schools. Logit is negative when the probability of attending this type of out-of-school-time lesson is higher for students in socio-economically disadvantaged schools than students in socio-economically advantaged schools.
5. The metric of the variable of students' latent performance is set by fixing the factor loading of students' performance in science to 1.

*Note*: Values that are statistically significant at the 5% level ($p < 0.05$) are indicated in bold.

260

© OECD 2011 Quality Time for Students: Learning In and Out of School

[Part 2/3]

## Table 4.7 Students' latent performance, by different types of out-of-school-time lessons[1]

| | Direct effects of student's and school's PISA index of economic, social and cultural status on the following types of out-of-school-time lessons[2] | | | | | | | | | | | | | | | | | | | |
|---|---|---|---|---|---|---|---|---|---|---|---|---|---|---|---|---|---|---|---|---|
| | Group lessons with school teacher | | | | Group lesson with non-school teacher | | | | Group lesson with both school and non-school teachers | | | | One-to-one lesson with non-school teacher | | | | Both one-to-one and group lessons with school teachers | | | |
| | Student's PISA index of economic, social and cultural status | | School average PISA index of economic, social and cultural status | | Student's PISA index of economic, social and cultural status | | School average PISA index of economic, social and cultural status | | Student's PISA index of economic, social and cultural status | | School average PISA index of economic, social and cultural status | | Student's PISA index of economic, social and cultural status | | School average PISA index of economic, social and cultural status | | Student's PISA index of economic, social and cultural status | | School average PISA index of economic, social and cultural status | |
| | Logit[3] | S.E. | Logit[4] | S.E. | Logit | S.E. | Logit | S.E. | Logit | S.E. | Logit | S.E. | Logit | S.E. | Logit | S.E. | Logit | S.E. | Logit | S.E. |
| **OECD** | | | | | | | | | | | | | | | | | | | | |
| Australia | 0.05 | (0.05) | -0.23 | (0.12) | -0.02 | (0.05) | 0.13 | (0.19) | 0.14 | (0.12) | **-0.48** | (0.23) | **0.32** | (0.04) | **0.55** | (0.09) | 0.01 | (0.08) | -0.33 | (0.19) |
| Austria | **-0.12** | (0.06) | **0.29** | (0.15) | **-0.31** | (0.15) | 0.28 | (0.20) | **-0.29** | (0.11) | -0.35 | (0.21) | **0.22** | (0.06) | **0.97** | (0.15) | 0.21 | (0.16) | **-1.06** | (0.22) |
| Belgium | -0.07 | (0.07) | -0.17 | (0.15) | 0.03 | (0.10) | 0.13 | (0.17) | -0.24 | (0.18) | **-0.87** | (0.29) | **0.34** | (0.05) | **0.43** | (0.10) | -0.09 | (0.10) | -0.31 | (0.23) |
| Canada | 0.05 | (0.05) | **-0.42** | (0.11) | -0.02 | (0.07) | **0.59** | (0.15) | 0.05 | (0.11) | -0.37 | (0.24) | **0.37** | (0.05) | **0.37** | (0.11) | -0.02 | (0.07) | **-0.38** | (0.16) |
| Czech Republic | **-0.18** | (0.09) | 0.13 | (0.15) | **0.30** | (0.11) | **0.66** | (0.19) | -0.04 | (0.16) | -0.32 | (0.33) | **0.43** | (0.07) | **0.58** | (0.11) | 0.00 | (0.08) | **-0.66** | (0.20) |
| Denmark | -0.01 | (0.06) | 0.09 | (0.18) | 0.02 | (0.09) | -0.07 | (0.29) | 0.02 | (0.20) | 0.16 | (0.38) | -0.05 | (0.11) | **0.91** | (0.30) | **-0.42** | (0.13) | -0.41 | (0.31) |
| Finland | **-0.14** | (0.05) | -0.16 | (0.18) | 0.15 | (0.13) | 0.34 | (0.31) | -0.34 | (0.22) | 0.42 | (0.54) | **0.41** | (0.11) | -0.01 | (0.24) | -0.10 | (0.07) | -0.18 | (0.27) |
| France | **-0.13** | (0.05) | 0.19 | (0.10) | -0.13 | (0.18) | -0.12 | (0.28) | -0.19 | (0.17) | **-0.84** | (0.31) | **0.40** | (0.06) | **0.69** | (0.11) | **-0.35** | (0.09) | -0.24 | (0.22) |
| Germany | -0.03 | (0.06) | -0.12 | (0.14) | 0.12 | (0.10) | **0.39** | (0.17) | 0.22 | (0.15) | **-1.30** | (0.43) | **0.10** | (0.05) | **0.61** | (0.11) | 0.10 | (0.17) | -0.16 | (0.36) |
| Greece | -0.19 | (0.11) | -0.25 | (0.20) | **-0.10** | (0.05) | **0.47** | (0.15) | **-0.32** | (0.10) | -0.01 | (0.20) | **0.26** | (0.06) | **0.88** | (0.12) | -0.19 | (0.13) | **-0.45** | (0.20) |
| Hungary | **-0.18** | (0.07) | -0.01 | (0.13) | -0.04 | (0.13) | -0.21 | (0.20) | -0.22 | (0.16) | **-0.71** | (0.22) | **0.36** | (0.05) | **0.38** | (0.11) | -0.05 | (0.09) | -0.22 | (0.22) |
| Iceland | **-0.11** | (0.05) | 0.24 | (0.23) | **0.32** | (0.11) | **-0.71** | (0.32) | 0.11 | (0.18) | -0.34 | (0.54) | 0.16 | (0.09) | **0.81** | (0.29) | **-0.23** | (0.09) | 0.09 | (0.32) |
| Ireland | -0.10 | (0.07) | **-0.71** | (0.17) | **0.23** | (0.08) | **0.38** | (0.15) | -0.08 | (0.16) | **-0.93** | (0.30) | **0.26** | (0.05) | **0.30** | (0.11) | 0.03 | (0.14) | **-1.09** | (0.30) |
| Italy | **-0.15** | (0.03) | 0.00 | (0.07) | -0.13 | (0.07) | -0.17 | (0.13) | -0.05 | (0.06) | **-0.80** | (0.11) | **0.28** | (0.03) | **0.41** | (0.07) | a | a | a | a |
| Japan | 0.04 | (0.04) | **-0.47** | (0.11) | 0.12 | (0.07) | **1.47** | (0.18) | -0.03 | (0.08) | 0.08 | (0.20) | **0.24** | (0.09) | **1.06** | (0.19) | 0.28 | (0.17) | **-0.76** | (0.27) |
| Korea | **-0.14** | (0.05) | **-0.53** | (0.12) | 0.04 | (0.05) | **0.75** | (0.13) | 0.09 | (0.06) | **0.57** | (0.12) | **0.30** | (0.07) | -0.09 | (0.15) | **-0.44** | (0.10) | 0.04 | (0.22) |
| Luxembourg | **-0.16** | (0.08) | -0.06 | (0.23) | **-0.28** | (0.14) | **0.75** | (0.24) | 0.15 | (0.26) | **-1.51** | (0.45) | **0.28** | (0.05) | 0.26 | (0.14) | -0.16 | (0.09) | -0.42 | (0.25) |
| Mexico | **-0.13** | (0.05) | **-0.44** | (0.09) | **0.28** | (0.07) | **0.33** | (0.10) | 0.18 | (0.09) | **-0.57** | (0.15) | **0.41** | (0.09) | **0.66** | (0.14) | -0.15 | (0.09) | **-0.40** | (0.13) |
| Netherlands | -0.03 | (0.08) | -0.09 | (0.19) | -0.14 | (0.13) | 0.08 | (0.32) | -0.23 | (0.16) | **-1.23** | (0.43) | **0.41** | (0.09) | **0.80** | (0.19) | 0.05 | (0.11) | **-0.52** | (0.21) |
| New Zealand | 0.04 | (0.08) | -0.03 | (0.21) | 0.16 | (0.10) | 0.18 | (0.19) | -0.27 | (0.14) | **-1.09** | (0.33) | **0.28** | (0.06) | **0.88** | (0.16) | -0.05 | (0.10) | 0.37 | (0.38) |
| Norway | **-0.14** | (0.04) | -0.16 | (0.11) | -0.15 | (0.17) | **1.02** | (0.39) | -0.14 | (0.14) | 0.18 | (0.29) | **0.36** | (0.12) | **0.72** | (0.35) | **-0.35** | (0.08) | 0.03 | (0.21) |
| Poland | **-0.13** | (0.04) | **-0.57** | (0.11) | **0.49** | (0.08) | **0.54** | (0.14) | -0.07 | (0.10) | 0.24 | (0.18) | **0.61** | (0.06) | **0.59** | (0.11) | **-0.22** | (0.07) | -0.30 | (0.15) |
| Portugal | **-0.20** | (0.06) | **-0.39** | (0.11) | **0.48** | (0.11) | 0.19 | (0.15) | 0.09 | (0.16) | -0.34 | (0.30) | **0.41** | (0.06) | **0.57** | (0.13) | **-0.15** | (0.07) | **-0.38** | (0.14) |
| Slovak Republic | **-0.24** | (0.09) | 0.23 | (0.17) | -0.09 | (0.14) | **0.63** | (0.24) | 0.18 | (0.26) | -0.47 | (0.37) | **0.25** | (0.06) | **0.63** | (0.13) | -0.09 | (0.06) | -0.31 | (0.16) |
| Spain | **-0.38** | (0.06) | -0.07 | (0.12) | **0.23** | (0.05) | 0.07 | (0.11) | **-0.50** | (0.14) | 0.07 | (0.20) | **0.23** | (0.05) | **0.51** | (0.10) | **-0.26** | (0.09) | -0.32 | (0.24) |
| Sweden | **-0.23** | (0.04) | **-0.42** | (0.13) | 0.19 | (0.17) | **0.59** | (0.29) | -0.19 | (0.12) | -0.44 | (0.28) | **0.62** | (0.13) | -0.18 | (0.28) | **-0.37** | (0.09) | 0.18 | (0.33) |
| Switzerland | 0.04 | (0.05) | **-0.66** | (0.15) | 0.12 | (0.09) | -0.32 | (0.19) | **-0.32** | (0.12) | -0.51 | (0.28) | **0.15** | (0.05) | **0.68** | (0.10) | **-0.29** | (0.12) | -0.41 | (0.24) |
| Turkey | 0.03 | (0.06) | -0.25 | (0.18) | **0.23** | (0.07) | **1.10** | (0.14) | -0.02 | (0.12) | **-0.64** | (0.28) | **0.52** | (0.11) | **0.42** | (0.15) | -0.15 | (0.11) | -0.22 | (0.29) |
| United Kingdom | 0.08 | (0.04) | **-0.45** | (0.10) | 0.01 | (0.10) | 0.02 | (0.21) | 0.06 | (0.10) | **-0.70** | (0.22) | **0.26** | (0.05) | **0.57** | (0.12) | -0.09 | (0.07) | **-0.49** | (0.18) |
| United States | -0.10 | (0.08) | -0.17 | (0.15) | **0.31** | (0.11) | -0.08 | (0.24) | -0.09 | (0.12) | **-0.61** | (0.22) | **0.48** | (0.09) | 0.11 | (0.17) | -0.11 | (0.07) | -0.13 | (0.15) |
| OECD average | **-0.10** | (0.01) | -0.19 | (0.03) | **0.08** | (0.02) | **0.31** | (0.04) | -0.08 | (0.03) | **-0.46** | (0.06) | **0.32** | (0.01) | **0.53** | (0.03) | **-0.13** | (0.02) | **-0.33** | (0.04) |
| **Partners** | | | | | | | | | | | | | | | | | | | | |
| Argentina | **-0.22** | (0.10) | **-0.78** | (0.28) | 0.17 | (0.11) | -0.09 | (0.23) | -0.16 | (0.21) | **-0.80** | (0.34) | **0.16** | (0.07) | **0.74** | (0.11) | 0.19 | (0.14) | **-0.67** | (0.17) |
| Azerbaijan | -0.03 | (0.07) | -0.05 | (0.14) | **-0.17** | (0.08) | -0.13 | (0.20) | -0.07 | (0.06) | -0.11 | (0.13) | **0.27** | (0.11) | **1.06** | (0.16) | **0.21** | (0.08) | -0.14 | (0.20) |
| Brazil | **-0.16** | (0.06) | -0.05 | (0.11) | 0.13 | (0.09) | 0.15 | (0.12) | 0.18 | (0.10) | **-0.62** | (0.13) | **0.36** | (0.10) | **0.52** | (0.14) | 0.11 | (0.10) | -0.26 | (0.21) |
| Bulgaria | -0.01 | (0.08) | 0.16 | (0.14) | **0.31** | (0.12) | **0.53** | (0.21) | -0.01 | (0.18) | -0.28 | (0.19) | **0.17** | (0.08) | **0.89** | (0.13) | -0.02 | (0.11) | **-0.69** | (0.17) |
| Chile | **-0.22** | (0.07) | 0.01 | (0.12) | 0.09 | (0.15) | 0.16 | (0.19) | -0.13 | (0.14) | **-0.77** | (0.17) | **0.41** | (0.11) | **0.67** | (0.13) | 0.09 | (0.13) | -0.21 | (0.19) |
| Colombia | -0.12 | (0.10) | **-0.58** | (0.15) | **0.35** | (0.10) | -0.02 | (0.12) | -0.09 | (0.14) | **-0.52** | (0.23) | **0.26** | (0.08) | **0.41** | (0.12) | -0.15 | (0.16) | -0.39 | (0.33) |
| Croatia | 0.01 | (0.08) | -0.11 | (0.19) | 0.16 | (0.11) | 0.34 | (0.22) | -0.13 | (0.18) | **-0.91** | (0.38) | **0.24** | (0.05) | **0.72** | (0.12) | 0.03 | (0.09) | **-0.76** | (0.21) |
| Estonia | -0.11 | (0.06) | **-0.48** | (0.18) | **0.29** | (0.10) | 0.50 | (0.32) | 0.20 | (0.12) | -0.48 | (0.41) | **0.14** | (0.06) | **0.68** | (0.20) | -0.01 | (0.07) | **-0.81** | (0.18) |
| Hong Kong-China | **-0.20** | (0.04) | **-0.79** | (0.12) | 0.07 | (0.05) | **0.72** | (0.13) | **0.20** | (0.05) | **-0.50** | (0.15) | **0.35** | (0.07) | **0.44** | (0.13) | -0.08 | (0.11) | **-0.72** | (0.37) |
| Indonesia | **-0.13** | (0.06) | -0.08 | (0.15) | 0.22 | (0.12) | **0.48** | (0.14) | **0.16** | (0.07) | -0.07 | (0.13) | **0.33** | (0.11) | **0.72** | (0.19) | 0.02 | (0.05) | **-0.80** | (0.17) |
| Israel | **-0.25** | (0.07) | -0.25 | (0.17) | -0.03 | (0.13) | -0.11 | (0.22) | -0.27 | (0.15) | **-0.59** | (0.20) | **0.36** | (0.05) | **1.03** | (0.14) | -0.12 | (0.09) | **-0.61** | (0.20) |
| Jordan | -0.09 | (0.05) | 0.04 | (0.11) | -0.03 | (0.11) | -0.04 | (0.17) | -0.07 | (0.07) | **-0.43** | (0.16) | **0.29** | (0.08) | **0.54** | (0.18) | 0.10 | (0.07) | -0.21 | (0.15) |
| Kyrgyzstan | -0.01 | (0.07) | **0.37** | (0.15) | -0.20 | (0.12) | **1.01** | (0.20) | -0.04 | (0.09) | -0.28 | (0.18) | -0.10 | (0.13) | **1.44** | (0.23) | **0.15** | (0.05) | **-0.40** | (0.12) |
| Latvia | **-0.19** | (0.07) | **-0.36** | (0.18) | 0.02 | (0.11) | **0.53** | (0.21) | -0.16 | (0.11) | 0.35 | (0.25) | **0.20** | (0.06) | **0.96** | (0.16) | **-0.21** | (0.06) | **-1.15** | (0.17) |
| Lithuania | -0.07 | (0.05) | **-0.50** | (0.13) | -0.02 | (0.10) | 0.34 | (0.19) | -0.12 | (0.12) | -0.45 | (0.28) | **0.40** | (0.06) | **0.87** | (0.13) | **0.16** | (0.07) | **-0.44** | (0.18) |
| Macao-China | -0.05 | (0.03) | -0.08 | (0.21) | **0.28** | (0.08) | 0.21 | (0.14) | -0.06 | (0.05) | -0.33 | (0.24) | **0.42** | (0.10) | 0.31 | (0.20) | -0.05 | (0.06) | -0.45 | (0.26) |
| Montenegro | **-0.19** | (0.07) | **-0.61** | (0.19) | 0.07 | (0.10) | 0.42 | (0.28) | **-0.31** | (0.15) | **-0.66** | (0.33) | **0.32** | (0.05) | **1.03** | (0.19) | -0.09 | (0.09) | **-0.77** | (0.29) |
| Qatar | -0.12 | (0.06) | 0.36 | (0.25) | -0.03 | (0.10) | -0.03 | (0.22) | -0.20 | (0.12) | -0.27 | (0.23) | **0.25** | (0.06) | **0.68** | (0.18) | 0.00 | (0.06) | **-0.40** | (0.14) |
| Romania | -0.21 | (0.13) | -0.36 | (0.20) | 0.23 | (0.13) | -0.17 | (0.21) | -0.07 | (0.13) | **-0.78** | (0.20) | **0.21** | (0.08) | **0.65** | (0.13) | 0.13 | (0.09) | **-0.48** | (0.17) |
| Russian Federation | **-0.14** | (0.04) | -0.02 | (0.11) | 0.02 | (0.09) | 0.38 | (0.33) | 0.01 | (0.09) | -0.14 | (0.19) | **0.36** | (0.07) | **0.82** | (0.21) | -0.06 | (0.05) | **-0.73** | (0.14) |
| Serbia | **-0.17** | (0.07) | **-0.46** | (0.19) | 0.24 | (0.13) | 0.45 | (0.25) | -0.15 | (0.14) | **-1.28** | (0.29) | **0.19** | (0.04) | **0.61** | (0.09) | 0.14 | (0.11) | **-1.02** | (0.21) |
| Slovenia | 0.01 | (0.08) | -0.32 | (0.19) | 0.14 | (0.15) | 0.50 | (0.32) | -0.03 | (0.14) | -0.45 | (0.33) | -0.01 | (0.04) | **0.55** | (0.13) | **-0.34** | (0.13) | 0.04 | (0.28) |
| Chinese Taipei | **-0.16** | (0.04) | **-0.39** | (0.09) | **0.18** | (0.04) | **1.14** | (0.13) | 0.04 | (0.05) | **-0.22** | (0.09) | **0.24** | (0.09) | **0.59** | (0.19) | **-0.28** | (0.06) | **-0.76** | (0.16) |
| Thailand | -0.06 | (0.07) | 0.20 | (0.13) | -0.01 | (0.06) | **0.48** | (0.10) | 0.04 | (0.07) | **0.55** | (0.12) | **0.46** | (0.15) | 0.07 | (0.24) | 0.10 | (0.09) | **-0.37** | (0.14) |
| Tunisia | -0.12 | (0.09) | **-0.66** | (0.18) | -0.12 | (0.12) | 0.07 | (0.23) | -0.12 | (0.12) | **-0.49** | (0.24) | **0.22** | (0.11) | **0.38** | (0.18) | **0.27** | (0.05) | **-0.25** | (0.10) |
| Uruguay | -0.02 | (0.10) | -0.41 | (0.23) | **0.33** | (0.10) | 0.16 | (0.15) | 0.14 | (0.21) | **-1.27** | (0.32) | **0.21** | (0.08) | **0.37** | (0.11) | -0.03 | (0.13) | 0.11 | (0.17) |

1. This table is based on the structural equation model in Box 4.1.
2. Direct effects are the relationship between two variables while holding other variables constant in the model.
3. Logit is positive when the probability of attending this type of out-of-school-time lesson is higher for socio-economically advantaged students than socio-economically disadvantaged students. Logit is negative when the probability of attending this type of out-of-school-time lesson is higher for socio-economically disadvantaged students than socio-economically advantaged students.
4. Logit is positive when the probability of attending this type of out-of-school-time lesson is higher for students in socio-economically advantaged schools than students in socio-economically disadvantaged schools. Logit is negative when the probability of attending this type of out-of-school-time lesson is higher for students in socio-economically disadvantaged schools than students in socio-economically advantaged schools.
5. The metric of the variable of students' latent performance is set by fixing the factor loading of students' performance in science to 1.

*Note*: Values that are statistically significant at the 5% level ($p < 0.05$) are indicated in bold.

 © OECD 2011

[Part 3/3]

## Table 4.7 Students' latent performance, by different types of out-of-school-time lessons[1]

| | | Direct effects of student's and school's PISA index of economic, social and cultural status on the following types of out-of-school-time lessons[2] | | | | | | | | | | | | Students' latent performance[5] | | | | | |
|---|---|---|---|---|---|---|---|---|---|---|---|---|---|---|---|---|---|---|---|
| | | Both one-to-one and group lessons with non-school teachers | | | | Both one-to-one and group lessons with both school and non-school teachers | | | | Both one-to-one and group lessons with both school and non-school teachers | | | | | | | | | |
| | | Student's PISA index of economic, social and cultural status[3] | | School average PISA index of economic, social and cultural status[4] | | Student's PISA index of economic, social and cultural status[3] | | School average PISA index of economic, social and cultural status[4] | | Student's PISA index of economic, social and cultural status[3] | | School average PISA index of economic, social and cultural status[4] | | Performance in science | | Performance in mathematics | | Performance in reading | |
| | | Logit | S.E. | Logit | S.E. | Logit | S.E. | Logit | S.E. | Logit | S.E. | Logit | S.E. | Factor loading | S.E. | Factor loading | S.E. | Factor loading | S.E. |
| OECD | Australia | 0.08 | (0.06) | 0.06 | (0.15) | 0.02 | (0.07) | **-0.37** | (0.15) | **0.28** | (0.08) | 0.15 | (0.16) | 1.00 | (0.00) | 0.84 | (0.01) | 0.89 | (0.01) |
| | Austria | **0.41** | (0.17) | -0.03 | (0.36) | 0.09 | (0.08) | **-0.41** | (0.18) | -0.08 | (0.21) | 0.06 | (0.37) | 1.00 | (0.00) | 0.93 | (0.02) | 0.99 | (0.03) |
| | Belgium | **0.22** | (0.10) | -0.13 | (0.19) | 0.12 | (0.08) | **-0.59** | (0.19) | **0.24** | (0.10) | 0.04 | (0.18) | 1.00 | (0.00) | 1.02 | (0.03) | 1.03 | (0.02) |
| | Canada | 0.16 | (0.09) | **0.38** | (0.19) | 0.03 | (0.05) | -0.19 | (0.12) | **0.15** | (0.07) | 0.02 | (0.16) | 1.00 | (0.00) | 0.85 | (0.01) | 0.94 | (0.01) |
| | Czech Republic | **0.23** | (0.10) | 0.30 | (0.20) | **-0.35** | (0.13) | -0.61 | (0.46) | **-0.47** | (0.12) | 0.42 | (0.41) | 1.00 | (0.00) | 0.85 | (0.01) | 0.85 | (0.01) |
| | Denmark | -0.11 | (0.19) | -0.25 | (0.39) | -0.05 | (0.11) | -0.33 | (0.33) | 0.06 | (0.13) | -0.55 | (0.42) | 1.00 | (0.00) | 0.87 | (0.01) | 0.81 | (0.01) |
| | Finland | **0.46** | (0.18) | 0.56 | (0.55) | 0.09 | (0.08) | -0.27 | (0.18) | 0.27 | (0.14) | -0.20 | (0.29) | 1.00 | (0.00) | 0.87 | (0.02) | 0.91 | (0.02) |
| | France | -0.04 | (0.10) | 0.28 | (0.17) | **0.28** | (0.10) | **-0.86** | (0.18) | 0.11 | (0.13) | -0.15 | (0.20) | 1.00 | (0.00) | 0.96 | (0.02) | 1.03 | (0.03) |
| | Germany | **0.33** | (0.14) | **-0.58** | (0.22) | **0.11** | (0.05) | **-0.64** | (0.12) | 0.23 | (0.13) | 0.07 | (0.37) | 1.00 | (0.00) | 0.87 | (0.02) | 0.97 | (0.03) |
| | Greece | **0.23** | (0.05) | 0.12 | (0.13) | **0.20** | (0.07) | -0.05 | (0.16) | 0.04 | (0.10) | 0.26 | (0.16) | 1.00 | (0.00) | 0.99 | (0.02) | 0.98 | (0.03) |
| | Hungary | 0.03 | (0.08) | **0.51** | (0.13) | -0.08 | (0.09) | **0.89** | (0.33) | -0.14 | (0.10) | -0.47 | (0.28) | 1.00 | (0.00) | 0.86 | (0.01) | 0.93 | (0.01) |
| | Iceland | **0.31** | (0.08) | **0.67** | (0.30) | **0.30** | (0.09) | **-1.09** | (0.25) | 0.02 | (0.13) | 0.02 | (0.26) | 1.00 | (0.00) | 0.83 | (0.01) | 0.92 | (0.01) |
| | Ireland | **0.48** | (0.08) | 0.12 | (0.16) | **0.25** | (0.03) | **0.33** | (0.06) | a | a | a | a | 1.00 | (0.00) | 0.92 | (0.02) | 0.96 | (0.02) |
| | Italy | **0.25** | (0.06) | -0.12 | (0.11) | **0.17** | (0.09) | 0.14 | (0.16) | -0.19 | (0.16) | -0.18 | (0.38) | 1.00 | (0.00) | 0.85 | (0.02) | 0.95 | (0.02) |
| | Japan | 0.23 | (0.15) | **1.50** | (0.41) | **0.23** | (0.05) | **0.26** | (0.08) | 0.18 | (0.13) | -0.58 | (0.30) | 1.00 | (0.00) | 0.97 | (0.02) | 0.92 | (0.02) |
| | Korea | **0.30** | (0.06) | **0.57** | (0.14) | -0.09 | (0.05) | **-0.78** | (0.21) | **0.23** | (0.08) | 0.00 | (0.20) | 1.00 | (0.00) | 0.90 | (0.02) | 0.96 | (0.02) |
| | Luxembourg | **-0.23** | (0.09) | -0.19 | (0.37) | **0.15** | (0.05) | **-0.92** | (0.11) | 0.01 | (0.10) | -0.24 | (0.17) | 1.00 | (0.00) | 1.02 | (0.03) | 1.08 | (0.03) |
| | Mexico | **0.35** | (0.06) | **0.36** | (0.09) | 0.18 | (0.12) | **-1.15** | (0.26) | 0.10 | (0.13) | 0.01 | (0.27) | 1.00 | (0.00) | 0.90 | (0.02) | 0.96 | (0.03) |
| | Netherlands | **0.50** | (0.22) | -0.41 | (0.45) | -0.00 | (0.10) | **-0.53** | (0.26) | 0.04 | (0.09) | -0.13 | (0.30) | 1.00 | (0.00) | 0.79 | (0.01) | 0.88 | (0.01) |
| | New Zealand | **0.23** | (0.09) | 0.40 | (0.27) | -0.05 | (0.09) | -0.39 | (0.21) | 0.02 | (0.14) | 0.11 | (0.39) | 1.00 | (0.00) | 0.89 | (0.02) | 0.97 | (0.01) |
| | Norway | 0.17 | (0.20) | 0.55 | (0.42) | **0.17** | (0.06) | -0.02 | (0.11) | 0.10 | (0.12) | 0.01 | (0.19) | 1.00 | (0.00) | 0.89 | (0.01) | 0.98 | (0.01) |
| | Poland | **0.62** | (0.08) | **0.58** | (0.15) | 0.09 | (0.07) | **-0.39** | (0.15) | -0.15 | (0.10) | -0.02 | (0.18) | 1.00 | (0.00) | 0.97 | (0.02) | 1.02 | (0.02) |
| | Portugal | **0.31** | (0.08) | 0.03 | (0.14) | **0.33** | (0.07) | **-0.33** | (0.14) | 0.14 | (0.11) | 0.21 | (0.17) | 1.00 | (0.00) | 0.94 | (0.02) | 1.01 | (0.02) |
| | Slovak Republic | **0.26** | (0.07) | **0.32** | (0.13) | 0.08 | (0.07) | -0.09 | (0.13) | -0.20 | (0.12) | **0.43** | (0.20) | 1.00 | (0.00) | 0.92 | (0.01) | 0.86 | (0.01) |
| | Spain | **0.26** | (0.04) | **-0.35** | (0.09) | -0.12 | (0.08) | **-0.56** | (0.22) | -0.08 | (0.16) | -0.14 | (0.44) | 1.00 | (0.00) | 0.89 | (0.01) | 0.93 | (0.02) |
| | Sweden | **0.29** | (0.12) | -0.01 | (0.46) | -0.06 | (0.07) | **-0.58** | (0.20) | -0.02 | (0.09) | 0.26 | (0.21) | 1.00 | (0.00) | 0.92 | (0.01) | 0.87 | (0.01) |
| | Switzerland | **0.20** | (0.10) | 0.31 | (0.23) | **0.27** | (0.08) | **-0.59** | (0.17) | **0.46** | (0.12) | **-0.69** | (0.31) | 1.00 | (0.00) | 1.03 | (0.03) | 0.98 | (0.04) |
| | Turkey | **0.42** | (0.09) | **0.43** | (0.15) | 0.10 | (0.06) | **-0.70** | (0.14) | **0.18** | (0.09) | -0.19 | (0.17) | 1.00 | (0.00) | 0.78 | (0.01) | 0.87 | (0.01) |
| | United Kingdom | 0.16 | (0.10) | -0.10 | (0.23) | -0.06 | (0.05) | **-0.95** | (0.19) | 0.12 | (0.07) | 0.04 | (0.13) | 1.00 | (0.00) | 0.86 | (0.02) | m | m |
| | United States | 0.06 | (0.10) | **-0.44** | (0.18) | **0.22** | (0.09) | **-0.62** | (0.15) | **0.46** | (0.15) | -0.45 | (0.32) | 1.00 | (0.00) | 0.92 | (0.03) | 1.13 | (0.03) |
| | OECD average | **0.24** | (0.02) | **0.18** | (0.05) | **0.09** | (0.01) | **-0.41** | (0.04) | **0.07** | (0.02) | -0.07 | (0.05) | 1.00 | (0.00) | 0.90 | (0.00) | 0.95 | (0.00) |
| Partners | Argentina | **0.18** | (0.08) | **0.40** | (0.13) | **0.21** | (0.04) | -0.02 | (0.10) | 0.11 | (0.11) | **0.41** | (0.16) | 1.00 | (0.00) | 0.52 | (0.03) | 0.84 | (0.07) |
| | Azerbaijan | **0.28** | (0.12) | 0.39 | (0.20) | **0.36** | (0.05) | **-0.31** | (0.09) | **0.39** | (0.15) | -0.32 | (0.21) | 1.00 | (0.00) | 1.01 | (0.03) | 1.00 | (0.04) |
| | Brazil | **0.22** | (0.08) | **0.39** | (0.14) | **0.14** | (0.06) | **-0.71** | (0.11) | -0.10 | (0.11) | -0.16 | (0.17) | 1.00 | (0.00) | 0.87 | (0.02) | 1.01 | (0.03) |
| | Bulgaria | **0.24** | (0.09) | **0.37** | (0.16) | **0.27** | (0.10) | **-0.41** | (0.17) | 0.20 | (0.19) | -0.02 | (0.25) | 1.00 | (0.00) | 0.94 | (0.02) | 0.98 | (0.03) |
| | Chile | **0.44** | (0.16) | 0.16 | (0.23) | 0.09 | (0.07) | **-0.50** | (0.17) | 0.00 | (0.11) | -0.24 | (0.18) | 1.00 | (0.00) | 1.00 | (0.02) | 1.03 | (0.03) |
| | Colombia | **0.40** | (0.08) | 0.19 | (0.13) | 0.01 | (0.09) | **-0.58** | (0.12) | **0.33** | (0.16) | **-0.67** | (0.33) | 1.00 | (0.00) | 1.03 | (0.04) | 1.13 | (0.05) |
| | Croatia | **0.15** | (0.07) | 0.12 | (0.17) | 0.02 | (0.06) | **-0.91** | (0.24) | 0.07 | (0.10) | -0.23 | (0.19) | 1.00 | (0.00) | 0.90 | (0.01) | 0.95 | (0.02) |
| | Estonia | **0.40** | (0.08) | 0.01 | (0.18) | -0.06 | (0.07) | -0.23 | (0.18) | -0.06 | (0.08) | **-0.41** | (0.19) | 1.00 | (0.00) | 0.93 | (0.01) | 0.93 | (0.02) |
| | Hong Kong-China | **0.39** | (0.08) | **0.76** | (0.14) | **0.38** | (0.05) | -0.18 | (0.12) | **0.41** | (0.14) | **-0.79** | (0.38) | 1.00 | (0.00) | 0.98 | (0.02) | 0.80 | (0.02) |
| | Indonesia | **0.65** | (0.09) | **0.28** | (0.14) | **0.36** | (0.05) | **-0.86** | (0.13) | -0.03 | (0.08) | **-0.88** | (0.18) | 1.00 | (0.00) | 1.15 | (0.02) | 1.06 | (0.02) |
| | Israel | 0.10 | (0.09) | **0.38** | (0.17) | 0.07 | (0.05) | **-0.69** | (0.13) | 0.09 | (0.09) | 0.36 | (0.22) | 1.00 | (0.00) | 0.90 | (0.03) | 0.99 | (0.02) |
| | Jordan | 0.04 | (0.07) | 0.09 | (0.16) | **0.18** | (0.04) | **-0.53** | (0.10) | -0.01 | (0.11) | 0.24 | (0.25) | 1.00 | (0.00) | 0.87 | (0.02) | 0.95 | (0.02) |
| | Kyrgyzstan | **0.37** | (0.15) | **1.04** | (0.18) | **0.08** | (0.03) | **-0.46** | (0.11) | **-0.13** | (0.06) | -0.17 | (0.13) | 1.00 | (0.00) | 1.05 | (0.03) | 1.17 | (0.03) |
| | Latvia | **0.36** | (0.08) | **0.43** | (0.16) | **0.25** | (0.05) | **-0.44** | (0.14) | 0.07 | (0.09) | -0.11 | (0.16) | 1.00 | (0.00) | 0.89 | (0.02) | 0.95 | (0.02) |
| | Lithuania | **0.51** | (0.11) | 0.34 | (0.19) | **0.22** | (0.08) | -0.05 | (0.15) | **0.47** | (0.10) | -0.19 | (0.18) | 1.00 | (0.00) | 0.92 | (0.01) | 0.93 | (0.02) |
| | Macao-China | **0.25** | (0.08) | 0.02 | (0.17) | -0.02 | (0.05) | -0.17 | (0.14) | 0.02 | (0.12) | -0.05 | (0.41) | 1.00 | (0.00) | 0.97 | (0.03) | 0.82 | (0.02) |
| | Montenegro | **0.31** | (0.05) | 0.09 | (0.20) | 0.11 | (0.06) | **-0.80** | (0.14) | 0.12 | (0.08) | **-0.32** | (0.16) | 1.00 | (0.00) | 0.94 | (0.02) | 1.03 | (0.03) |
| | Qatar | 0.04 | (0.06) | -0.22 | (0.17) | **0.19** | (0.04) | **-0.76** | (0.13) | 0.06 | (0.09) | -0.18 | (0.17) | 1.00 | (0.00) | 0.97 | (0.03) | 1.24 | (0.03) |
| | Romania | **0.24** | (0.10) | 0.30 | (0.18) | **0.16** | (0.07) | **-0.84** | (0.13) | **0.24** | (0.10) | -0.07 | (0.20) | 1.00 | (0.00) | 0.97 | (0.03) | 0.97 | (0.03) |
| | Russian Federation | **0.27** | (0.08) | 0.07 | (0.18) | **0.18** | (0.04) | -0.15 | (0.12) | **0.23** | (0.07) | **0.45** | (0.15) | 1.00 | (0.00) | 0.88 | (0.02) | 0.87 | (0.02) |
| | Serbia | **0.32** | (0.07) | 0.16 | (0.13) | 0.04 | (0.06) | **-0.41** | (0.14) | **0.32** | (0.11) | -0.18 | (0.25) | 1.00 | (0.00) | 1.01 | (0.02) | 0.99 | (0.02) |
| | Slovenia | 0.10 | (0.13) | 0.18 | (0.22) | **0.17** | (0.07) | **-0.75** | (0.18) | -0.03 | (0.10) | -0.29 | (0.27) | 1.00 | (0.00) | 0.85 | (0.02) | 0.81 | (0.02) |
| | Chinese Taipei | **0.17** | (0.06) | **0.29** | (0.12) | **0.08** | (0.04) | **-0.41** | (0.09) | -0.03 | (0.13) | **-0.83** | (0.21) | 1.00 | (0.00) | 1.04 | (0.02) | 0.83 | (0.01) |
| | Thailand | **0.47** | (0.13) | **0.60** | (0.18) | **0.35** | (0.05) | **-0.53** | (0.09) | -0.07 | (0.16) | -0.15 | (0.26) | 1.00 | (0.00) | 0.98 | (0.02) | 0.95 | (0.02) |
| | Tunisia | 0.15 | (0.09) | **0.83** | (0.14) | **0.23** | (0.04) | **-0.40** | (0.10) | -0.04 | (0.09) | 0.32 | (0.16) | 1.00 | (0.00) | 1.06 | (0.02) | 1.09 | (0.03) |
| | Uruguay | **0.33** | (0.06) | **0.24** | (0.10) | **0.36** | (0.09) | **-0.46** | (0.14) | 0.14 | (0.24) | -0.27 | (0.43) | 1.00 | (0.00) | 0.96 | (0.02) | 1.12 | (0.03) |

1. This table is based on the structural equation model in Box 4.1.
2. Direct effects are the relationship between two variables while holding other variables constant in the model.
3. Logit is positive when the probability of attending this type of out-of-school-time lesson is higher for socio-economically advantaged students than socio-economically disadvantaged students. Logit is negative when the probability of attending this type of out-of-school-time lesson is higher for socio-economically disadvantaged students than socio-economically advantaged students.
4. Logit is positive when the probability of attending this type of out-of-school-time lesson is higher for students in socio-economically advantaged schools than students in socio-economically disadvantaged schools. Logit is negative when the probability of attending this type of out-of-school-time lesson is higher for students in socio-economically disadvantaged schools than students in socio-economically advantaged schools.
5. The metric of the variable of students' latent performance is set by fixing the factor loading of students' performance in science to 1.

*Note*: Values that are statistically significant at the 5% level ($p < 0.05$) are indicated in bold.

262

© OECD 2011 Quality Time for Students: Learning In and Out of School

[Part 1/2]
## Table 4.8a  Performance in science, by learning time in individual study in science

| | Science performance for students who do not spend any time in individual study in science | | Difference in science performance between students who spend the following learning hours per week in individual study in science and students who do not spend any time in individual study in science | | | | | | | |
| | | | Less than 2 hours per week | | 2 hours or more but less than 4 hours per week | | 4 hours or more but less than 6 hours per week | | 6 hours or more per week | |
| | Mean score | S.E. | Dif. | S.E. | Dif. | S.E. | Dif. | S.E. | Dif. | S.E. |
|---|---|---|---|---|---|---|---|---|---|---|
| **OECD** Australia | 489 | (2.1) | **51.4** | (2.2) | **71.8** | (3.8) | **79.1** | (6.5) | **98.2** | (10.9) |
| Austria | 505 | (4.3) | **20.7** | (4.3) | -2.9 | (6.2) | -3.9 | (9.5) | **-25.8** | (12.3) |
| Belgium | 463 | (3.3) | **72.9** | (4.0) | **80.3** | (4.6) | **68.8** | (7.9) | **57.6** | (17.3) |
| Canada | 513 | (3.0) | **28.1** | (3.1) | **39.0** | (3.4) | **38.2** | (6.3) | **40.8** | (9.1) |
| Czech Republic | 506 | (4.0) | **24.8** | (3.3) | **16.9** | (6.4) | 1.2 | (10.6) | -7.1 | (27.5) |
| Denmark | 474 | (4.7) | **33.9** | (4.2) | **19.1** | (6.5) | 25.4 | (13.8) | c | c |
| Finland | 537 | (2.9) | **35.5** | (3.0) | **30.8** | (5.2) | **33.0** | (12.2) | c | c |
| France | 445 | (4.7) | **63.8** | (4.7) | **97.7** | (6.1) | **88.7** | (11.8) | **92.3** | (24.8) |
| Germany | 483 | (6.3) | **52.7** | (5.8) | **47.1** | (6.2) | **25.4** | (7.3) | 16.7 | (10.4) |
| Greece | 452 | (4.2) | **22.3** | (4.5) | **35.1** | (4.9) | **43.6** | (6.8) | **32.1** | (11.0) |
| Hungary | 495 | (4.5) | **9.3** | (4.4) | **19.6** | (5.4) | **23.7** | (7.8) | **30.0** | (15.2) |
| Iceland | 466 | (3.9) | **36.9** | (4.6) | **33.6** | (6.9) | 14.7 | (13.7) | c | c |
| Ireland | 481 | (4.3) | **41.3** | (4.0) | **49.0** | (5.5) | **31.5** | (8.5) | 22.3 | (14.3) |
| Italy | 457 | (7.2) | 14.2 | (7.4) | **32.1** | (7.9) | **39.7** | (8.2) | **41.0** | (8.8) |
| Japan | 512 | (3.9) | **39.4** | (4.0) | **26.2** | (9.0) | **61.5** | (16.9) | c | c |
| Korea | 486 | (5.5) | **45.7** | (4.8) | **65.5** | (6.2) | **82.8** | (11.0) | **92.1** | (38.8) |
| Luxembourg | 473 | (2.6) | **26.1** | (3.4) | **11.2** | (5.1) | 0.5 | (8.7) | -1.7 | (12.8) |
| Mexico | 420 | (4.6) | **-9.6** | (4.0) | -0.8 | (4.9) | -4.9 | (5.3) | -10.3 | (6.6) |
| Netherlands | 503 | (3.9) | **36.2** | (3.3) | **41.2** | (4.9) | **39.4** | (9.3) | c | c |
| New Zealand | 484 | (3.9) | **62.0** | (4.5) | **81.6** | (5.6) | **80.4** | (11.8) | **94.3** | (16.6) |
| Norway | 468 | (4.1) | **35.8** | (4.1) | **19.2** | (5.9) | 1.5 | (11.0) | c | c |
| Poland | 474 | (5.4) | **26.8** | (5.1) | **27.8** | (5.8) | **30.9** | (6.7) | **44.2** | (8.6) |
| Portugal | 473 | (5.5) | **-9.5** | (4.8) | **18.4** | (5.5) | **19.7** | (6.6) | 16.8 | (9.7) |
| Slovak Republic | 465 | (3.8) | **30.6** | (4.1) | **50.0** | (5.4) | **55.5** | (8.5) | **44.4** | (11.9) |
| Spain | 459 | (3.3) | **28.5** | (3.5) | **53.0** | (3.6) | **68.0** | (4.4) | **39.5** | (11.3) |
| Sweden | 482 | (4.7) | **32.7** | (5.4) | **22.5** | (5.9) | -1.6 | (11.7) | c | c |
| Switzerland | 478 | (3.6) | **51.4** | (3.5) | **45.9** | (5.8) | 0.3 | (10.3) | -23.8 | (19.9) |
| Turkey | 403 | (2.5) | **19.8** | (4.5) | **38.6** | (5.2) | **65.6** | (9.5) | **74.8** | (10.8) |
| United Kingdom | 450 | (4.6) | **70.3** | (4.5) | **103.9** | (5.4) | **85.4** | (9.4) | **96.0** | (14.7) |
| United States | 456 | (6.5) | **35.2** | (5.7) | **56.1** | (5.3) | **54.0** | (7.7) | **60.0** | (11.9) |
| **OECD average** | 475 | (4.4) | **34.3** | (4.4) | **41.0** | (5.7) | **38.3** | (9.7) | **40.2** | (16.2) |
| **Partners** Argentina | 370 | (8.2) | **32.2** | (6.6) | **46.1** | (7.1) | **57.7** | (9.4) | **52.8** | (14.0) |
| Azerbaijan | 372 | (4.3) | **10.1** | (3.8) | **16.9** | (3.9) | **22.7** | (4.3) | **30.7** | (5.1) |
| Brazil | 373 | (3.9) | **26.3** | (4.0) | **26.4** | (4.8) | **23.2** | (5.4) | 18.0 | (9.2) |
| Bulgaria | 406 | (5.1) | **28.6** | (5.6) | **54.9** | (7.2) | **67.5** | (9.2) | **65.9** | (12.0) |
| Chile | 419 | (5.5) | **23.1** | (4.8) | **31.7** | (6.9) | **36.1** | (8.2) | 1.3 | (12.4) |
| Colombia | 379 | (4.9) | **14.3** | (4.8) | **19.7** | (4.7) | **18.7** | (8.3) | -5.5 | (12.2) |
| Croatia | 468 | (2.9) | **33.7** | (3.8) | **48.9** | (4.1) | **46.8** | (5.5) | **41.8** | (10.8) |
| Estonia | 514 | (3.6) | **22.9** | (3.2) | **25.7** | (4.4) | **29.5** | (6.4) | -3.8 | (16.4) |
| Hong Kong-China | 517 | (2.7) | **24.9** | (3.9) | **58.2** | (4.1) | **74.4** | (7.0) | **89.5** | (7.7) |
| Indonesia | 380 | (5.7) | **14.7** | (4.8) | **21.1** | (4.5) | **19.0** | (7.0) | 3.7 | (10.9) |
| Israel | 465 | (4.6) | **15.2** | (5.1) | **-15.0** | (5.7) | **-25.5** | (9.2) | -16.4 | (15.3) |
| Jordan | 384 | (3.9) | **38.0** | (4.9) | **50.1** | (4.7) | **55.9** | (6.1) | **58.8** | (7.0) |
| Kyrgyzstan | 316 | (3.9) | **16.2** | (3.9) | **23.6** | (4.2) | **27.1** | (5.7) | **18.9** | (5.3) |
| Latvia | 464 | (4.8) | **32.8** | (4.4) | **31.1** | (5.6) | **28.1** | (7.0) | 20.8 | (13.0) |
| Liechtenstein | 479 | (11.1) | **61.6** | (12.5) | 44.5 | (27.5) | c | c | c | c |
| Lithuania | 460 | (4.2) | **32.1** | (4.5) | **41.8** | (5.1) | **30.5** | (6.8) | **35.5** | (11.2) |
| Macao-China | 492 | (2.0) | **19.8** | (3.0) | **41.3** | (3.9) | **53.4** | (5.6) | **62.3** | (9.0) |
| Montenegro | 387 | (3.6) | **22.0** | (4.3) | **39.8** | (4.5) | **47.1** | (5.4) | **56.5** | (7.1) |
| Qatar | 332 | (2.6) | **18.5** | (3.3) | **32.3** | (3.8) | **37.5** | (5.1) | **63.3** | (8.4) |
| Romania | 398 | (4.3) | **25.0** | (5.2) | **35.6** | (4.8) | **32.1** | (8.1) | **54.5** | (11.6) |
| Russian Federation | 442 | (6.3) | **27.0** | (5.3) | **48.2** | (6.2) | **60.8** | (6.0) | **56.5** | (5.9) |
| Serbia | 412 | (3.7) | **28.7** | (3.9) | **44.8** | (4.7) | **53.9** | (6.5) | **53.3** | (6.7) |
| Slovenia | 497 | (3.1) | **26.9** | (3.5) | **38.6** | (4.9) | **48.6** | (8.3) | 4.3 | (11.2) |
| Chinese Taipei | 491 | (4.7) | **54.9** | (3.6) | **80.5** | (5.6) | **97.1** | (6.3) | **119.9** | (11.0) |
| Thailand | 397 | (4.3) | **17.8** | (3.6) | **38.0** | (5.0) | **53.8** | (7.4) | **67.4** | (8.7) |
| Tunisia | 354 | (5.3) | **34.6** | (5.7) | **40.6** | (6.4) | **48.4** | (6.2) | **42.4** | (7.6) |
| Uruguay | 415 | (4.2) | **23.7** | (4.6) | **34.2** | (5.7) | **42.4** | (8.8) | 14.8 | (19.6) |

*Note:* Values that are statistically significant at the 5% level (p < 0.05) are indicated in bold.

[Part 2/2]
## Table 4.8a Performance in science, by learning time in individual study in science

| | Difference in science performance between students who spend the following learning hours per week in individual study in science and students who do not spend any time in individual study in science | | | | | | | | | | | | | | | |
| | Accounting for socio-economic background of students and schools | | | | | | | | Accounting for socio-economic background of students and schools as well as learning time in regular school lessons and out-of-school-time lessons in science | | | | | | | |
| | Less than 2 hours per week | | 2 hours or more but less than 4 hours per week | | 4 hours or more but less than 6 hours per week | | 6 hours or more per week | | Less than 2 hours per week | | 2 hours or more but less than 4 hours per week | | 4 hours or more but less than 6 hours per week | | 6 hours or more per week | |
| | Dif. | S.E. | Dif. | S.E. | Dif. | S.E. | Dif. | S.E. | Dif. | S.E. | Dif. | S.E. | Dif. | S.E. | Dif. | S.E. |
|---|---|---|---|---|---|---|---|---|---|---|---|---|---|---|---|---|
| Australia | 37.0 | (2.0) | 50.5 | (3.2) | 59.7 | (5.9) | 69.6 | (10.2) | 32.1 | (2.5) | 45.9 | (4.0) | 55.0 | (6.9) | 56.8 | (10.1) |
| Austria | 7.8 | (3.1) | -6.0 | (4.8) | -7.0 | (7.3) | -11.4 | (8.8) | -2.7 | (3.0) | -17.0 | (4.5) | -16.8 | (6.5) | -22.8 | (9.7) |
| Belgium | 39.4 | (3.3) | 38.7 | (3.9) | 33.2 | (6.5) | 28.1 | (12.2) | 20.2 | (3.3) | 13.9 | (4.0) | 11.0 | (6.2) | 7.8 | (9.2) |
| Canada | 18.0 | (3.0) | 21.4 | (3.4) | 21.8 | (6.0) | 19.9 | (9.0) | 10.8 | (3.6) | 12.8 | (4.2) | 13.3 | (6.0) | 13.5 | (9.8) |
| Czech Republic | 14.4 | (3.5) | 2.0 | (6.0) | -5.4 | (8.7) | -15.7 | (22.7) | 3.3 | (3.7) | -14.3 | (5.3) | -19.0 | (8.7) | -28.4 | (20.1) |
| Denmark | 24.7 | (4.3) | 10.2 | (5.8) | 11.2 | (11.5) | c | c | 17.3 | (4.2) | 2.4 | (5.9) | 1.7 | (11.8) | c | c |
| Finland | 30.0 | (2.8) | 23.4 | (4.7) | 28.3 | (11.6) | c | c | 22.7 | (3.1) | 17.4 | (4.5) | 15.4 | (12.0) | c | c |
| France | 31.8 | (3.8) | 47.3 | (5.0) | 33.1 | (8.7) | 45.1 | (14.9) | 19.7 | (3.6) | 25.1 | (4.5) | 9.9 | (7.9) | 21.5 | (14.4) |
| Germany | 24.5 | (4.6) | 16.8 | (5.1) | 1.4 | (6.0) | 3.3 | (9.4) | 18.4 | (4.6) | 9.0 | (4.9) | -1.6 | (6.1) | -1.3 | (9.0) |
| Greece | 14.0 | (4.2) | 19.7 | (4.2) | 19.8 | (5.9) | 17.3 | (9.9) | 4.2 | (4.0) | 1.9 | (3.7) | -1.2 | (5.8) | -12.1 | (9.5) |
| Hungary | 7.2 | (4.0) | 9.6 | (4.5) | 11.7 | (6.6) | 13.2 | (11.0) | -1.2 | (3.6) | -3.2 | (4.1) | -7.7 | (6.0) | -11.5 | (11.4) |
| Iceland | 33.1 | (4.5) | 26.3 | (6.9) | 4.9 | (12.4) | c | c | 23.3 | (4.4) | 19.3 | (6.6) | 14.2 | (12.8) | c | c |
| Ireland | 31.7 | (3.2) | 35.2 | (4.8) | 15.7 | (7.3) | 10.8 | (12.8) | 19.3 | (4.2) | 26.8 | (5.9) | 13.7 | (7.6) | -3.6 | (13.7) |
| Italy | 24.4 | (3.5) | 31.0 | (4.3) | 32.9 | (4.8) | 35.7 | (5.9) | 11.2 | (3.1) | 11.5 | (3.7) | 10.3 | (4.3) | 5.1 | (6.1) |
| Japan | 21.5 | (3.9) | 9.4 | (7.5) | 33.4 | (15.7) | c | c | 22.0 | (3.7) | 16.8 | (7.4) | 39.9 | (13.6) | c | c |
| Korea | 30.3 | (3.4) | 39.6 | (4.2) | 51.7 | (7.7) | 49.2 | (19.0) | 25.2 | (3.4) | 32.2 | (4.2) | 45.2 | (7.8) | 48.2 | (18.1) |
| Luxembourg | 12.1 | (2.9) | 3.8 | (4.7) | -5.4 | (7.6) | -9.0 | (11.8) | 7.5 | (3.1) | 3.7 | (4.8) | -5.4 | (7.6) | -3.9 | (11.1) |
| Mexico | -6.9 | (3.1) | -1.3 | (3.8) | -3.0 | (4.2) | -3.4 | (5.3) | 0.1 | (4.4) | 5.0 | (5.0) | 3.8 | (5.6) | 4.6 | (6.6) |
| Netherlands | 16.0 | (2.8) | 18.8 | (4.6) | 17.7 | (6.8) | c | c | 4.1 | (3.8) | 5.2 | (5.7) | -0.4 | (7.1) | c | c |
| New Zealand | 44.2 | (3.9) | 52.3 | (5.4) | 48.8 | (10.9) | 68.5 | (14.9) | 32.8 | (3.9) | 42.6 | (5.3) | 45.5 | (10.5) | 66.4 | (15.8) |
| Norway | 30.6 | (3.7) | 10.6 | (5.3) | -8.2 | (10.3) | c | c | 30.1 | (3.6) | 21.9 | (6.0) | 11.6 | (11.5) | c | c |
| Poland | 22.1 | (4.7) | 23.1 | (5.1) | 24.7 | (6.2) | 33.0 | (8.1) | 13.7 | (4.6) | 6.4 | (5.0) | 3.5 | (6.1) | 11.2 | (8.4) |
| Portugal | 4.3 | (4.2) | 23.4 | (4.7) | 20.3 | (5.7) | 17.5 | (8.8) | 7.1 | (5.8) | 11.0 | (6.6) | 2.7 | (7.0) | -2.6 | (9.2) |
| Slovak Republic | 19.0 | (4.1) | 24.5 | (5.3) | 25.1 | (8.1) | 12.0 | (9.9) | 5.0 | (4.1) | -1.4 | (5.4) | -6.5 | (9.1) | -16.8 | (9.4) |
| Spain | 21.1 | (3.1) | 41.0 | (3.2) | 51.5 | (4.2) | 27.7 | (10.1) | 18.4 | (3.6) | 28.5 | (3.6) | 30.5 | (4.8) | 4.8 | (8.2) |
| Sweden | 27.7 | (5.1) | 15.0 | (5.5) | -20.2 | (11.8) | c | c | 24.8 | (4.9) | 19.8 | (5.7) | 1.6 | (10.1) | c | c |
| Switzerland | 37.8 | (3.0) | 26.7 | (4.6) | -8.0 | (9.5) | -14.4 | (18.7) | 21.4 | (3.1) | 7.6 | (4.4) | -21.7 | (7.8) | 19.4 | (19.6) |
| Turkey | 17.3 | (3.5) | 29.9 | (3.7) | 41.8 | (4.7) | 50.5 | (6.2) | 6.1 | (3.5) | 6.1 | (4.1) | 9.1 | (5.0) | 13.4 | (5.9) |
| United Kingdom | 53.2 | (4.4) | 71.3 | (5.0) | 56.2 | (8.0) | 68.0 | (13.0) | 42.3 | (4.7) | 57.0 | (5.5) | 52.7 | (8.0) | 67.1 | (14.3) |
| United States | 19.9 | (4.0) | 30.2 | (4.6) | 25.5 | (6.5) | 28.6 | (9.9) | 14.7 | (4.4) | 21.4 | (5.2) | 16.4 | (6.7) | 22.0 | (9.3) |
| **OECD average** | **23.6** | **(3.7)** | **24.8** | **(4.9)** | **20.4** | **(8.4)** | **23.7** | **(12.2)** | **15.8** | **(3.9)** | **14.5** | **(5.1)** | **10.9** | **(8.3)** | **9.6** | **(11.9)** |
| Argentina | 20.2 | (6.3) | 30.1 | (7.0) | 38.1 | (8.2) | 32.0 | (12.3) | 15.0 | (5.9) | 21.4 | (6.6) | 20.0 | (8.1) | 14.5 | (11.5) |
| Azerbaijan | 11.6 | (3.5) | 18.0 | (3.5) | 23.0 | (4.1) | 30.8 | (4.8) | 5.9 | (3.9) | 9.5 | (4.0) | 11.2 | (4.5) | 18.7 | (5.3) |
| Brazil | 15.1 | (3.8) | 13.6 | (4.8) | 9.9 | (5.1) | 11.7 | (8.6) | 10.1 | (3.9) | 5.4 | (4.7) | -3.3 | (5.1) | 0.5 | (8.7) |
| Bulgaria | 7.8 | (4.9) | 19.0 | (5.3) | 25.5 | (6.5) | 23.7 | (7.2) | 3.2 | (4.8) | 11.9 | (5.2) | 15.5 | (6.5) | 10.8 | (7.2) |
| Chile | 12.0 | (3.6) | 17.3 | (5.2) | 11.1 | (6.4) | 4.6 | (10.5) | 6.0 | (3.6) | 8.4 | (4.9) | 3.1 | (6.4) | -5.7 | (11.5) |
| Colombia | 15.4 | (4.6) | 17.7 | (5.0) | 14.7 | (7.1) | 5.6 | (12.1) | 11.3 | (4.5) | 10.5 | (4.7) | 6.7 | (6.8) | -3.5 | (11.1) |
| Croatia | 19.8 | (3.2) | 27.7 | (3.4) | 25.1 | (5.3) | 19.5 | (9.5) | 4.4 | (3.2) | 14.4 | (3.7) | 11.1 | (4.9) | 7.9 | (8.7) |
| Estonia | 17.6 | (3.3) | 18.2 | (4.3) | 20.0 | (6.2) | -8.6 | (14.3) | 13.8 | (3.0) | 10.7 | (3.7) | 12.2 | (5.7) | -4.8 | (14.6) |
| Hong Kong-China | 20.9 | (3.8) | 43.6 | (3.7) | 60.0 | (6.8) | 70.5 | (8.9) | 19.0 | (5.9) | 26.8 | (6.5) | 31.1 | (9.0) | 39.2 | (10.3) |
| Indonesia | 15.6 | (5.7) | 16.7 | (4.4) | 11.9 | (5.3) | 3.5 | (9.6) | 7.2 | (4.0) | 3.6 | (3.5) | -2.3 | (5.0) | -8.1 | (9.1) |
| Israel | 17.5 | (4.4) | -1.6 | (5.5) | -4.3 | (8.7) | -6.4 | (13.4) | -0.3 | (5.1) | -18.8 | (6.2) | -28.4 | (9.1) | -30.2 | (13.4) |
| Jordan | 29.4 | (4.5) | 39.5 | (4.6) | 45.4 | (5.8) | 48.2 | (6.7) | 19.2 | (4.6) | 24.7 | (4.7) | 29.8 | (6.2) | 26.8 | (6.8) |
| Kyrgyzstan | 16.5 | (2.9) | 25.6 | (3.7) | 31.7 | (4.7) | 25.9 | (4.9) | 11.4 | (3.1) | 20.2 | (4.0) | 23.2 | (5.3) | 20.1 | (5.0) |
| Latvia | 30.4 | (4.2) | 26.9 | (4.7) | 21.5 | (5.7) | 16.0 | (11.0) | 18.0 | (4.3) | 8.1 | (4.7) | 2.1 | (5.7) | -8.8 | (11.4) |
| Liechtenstein | 26.9 | (9.7) | 18.3 | (19.5) | c | c | c | c | 27.6 | (9.8) | 13.1 | (19.2) | c | c | c | c |
| Lithuania | 21.2 | (3.9) | 27.7 | (3.8) | 16.4 | (6.1) | 26.6 | (10.5) | 13.6 | (3.8) | 13.6 | (3.8) | 5.1 | (6.5) | 13.4 | (9.7) |
| Macao-China | 20.0 | (3.0) | 38.6 | (3.9) | 48.8 | (5.6) | 57.0 | (8.6) | 13.5 | (3.1) | 22.9 | (4.6) | 27.6 | (6.0) | 28.1 | (8.5) |
| Montenegro | 18.1 | (3.9) | 31.0 | (4.2) | 36.1 | (4.9) | 48.5 | (6.5) | 8.8 | (4.1) | 17.8 | (4.6) | 20.2 | (5.6) | 29.7 | (6.8) |
| Qatar | 16.7 | (3.1) | 28.3 | (3.6) | 32.9 | (4.8) | 57.1 | (8.0) | 9.4 | (3.1) | 17.0 | (3.8) | 13.6 | (4.4) | 24.8 | (8.0) |
| Romania | 17.3 | (4.3) | 19.6 | (4.3) | 17.0 | (5.7) | 38.6 | (10.5) | 10.5 | (4.7) | 9.4 | (4.7) | 7.2 | (6.4) | 26.9 | (9.2) |
| Russian Federation | 19.6 | (4.8) | 36.8 | (5.6) | 47.6 | (6.2) | 45.4 | (5.4) | 11.6 | (4.6) | 19.4 | (5.5) | 22.6 | (5.2) | 17.9 | (5.1) |
| Serbia | 17.1 | (3.6) | 23.9 | (4.5) | 25.1 | (5.5) | 35.6 | (6.1) | 11.6 | (3.8) | 14.6 | (4.8) | 11.8 | (5.4) | 22.3 | (6.5) |
| Slovenia | 5.9 | (3.5) | 8.2 | (3.8) | 17.8 | (8.1) | -11.4 | (11.0) | 1.3 | (3.5) | -0.8 | (3.8) | 7.0 | (7.8) | -16.3 | (12.3) |
| Chinese Taipei | 32.5 | (2.9) | 50.2 | (4.1) | 57.9 | (4.9) | 77.2 | (9.4) | 26.8 | (2.8) | 34.9 | (4.1) | 41.2 | (4.9) | 58.6 | (9.8) |
| Thailand | 18.9 | (3.9) | 33.9 | (4.4) | 46.0 | (5.9) | 57.2 | (8.2) | 17.9 | (3.8) | 26.2 | (4.3) | 32.8 | (6.0) | 33.7 | (7.6) |
| Tunisia | 25.0 | (5.7) | 29.6 | (6.0) | 36.2 | (5.2) | 31.6 | (7.0) | 15.8 | (5.4) | 15.0 | (5.9) | 16.5 | (5.4) | 8.3 | (6.9) |
| Uruguay | 9.5 | (4.3) | 17.7 | (5.6) | 20.3 | (8.5) | 0.4 | (14.7) | 5.0 | (4.9) | 12.6 | (6.2) | 11.6 | (9.3) | -3.5 | (15.2) |

*Note:* Values that are statistically significant at the 5% level (p < 0.05) are indicated in bold.

© OECD 2011 Quality Time for Students: Learning In and Out of School

[Part 1/2]
## Table 4.8b Performance in mathematics, by learning time in individual study in mathematics

| | Mathematics performance for students who do not spend any time in individual study in mathematics | | Difference in mathematics performance between students who spend the following learning hours per week in individual study in mathematics and students who do not spend any time in individual study in mathematics | | | | | | | |
| | | | Less than 2 hours per week | | 2 hours or more but less than 4 hours per week | | 4 hours or more but less than 6 hours per week | | 6 hours or more per week | |
| | Mean score | S.E. | Dif. | S.E. | Dif. | S.E. | Dif. | S.E. | Dif. | S.E. |
|---|---|---|---|---|---|---|---|---|---|---|
| Australia | 482 | (2.9) | **38.2** | (2.8) | **58.1** | (3.2) | **60.9** | (4.4) | **59.7** | (7.4) |
| Austria | 498 | (7.7) | **21.7** | (6.6) | 9.3 | (6.8) | -8.8 | (8.4) | **-48.4** | (10.5) |
| Belgium | 477 | (4.8) | **51.8** | (5.2) | **80.2** | (5.4) | **62.0** | (6.9) | **51.4** | (12.6) |
| Canada | 521 | (3.2) | **9.7** | (3.2) | **14.1** | (3.5) | **12.3** | (4.5) | 8.1 | (6.2) |
| Czech Republic | 511 | (4.9) | **13.3** | (4.9) | -2.0 | (6.2) | **-31.6** | (10.1) | **-31.0** | (13.3) |
| Denmark | 498 | (4.8) | **23.4** | (4.9) | **15.5** | (4.9) | -3.3 | (6.7) | -15.2 | (13.0) |
| Finland | 530 | (4.1) | **24.8** | (4.1) | **18.1** | (4.7) | 11.5 | (12.3) | c | c |
| France | 451 | (5.4) | **45.9** | (5.2) | **73.7** | (6.2) | **61.0** | (9.4) | **41.1** | (18.4) |
| Germany | 476 | (12.1) | **43.1** | (11.6) | **44.8** | (11.6) | 16.8 | (13.4) | -0.9 | (11.7) |
| Greece | 435 | (3.8) | **23.0** | (4.3) | **43.4** | (4.6) | **38.7** | (5.6) | **38.1** | (8.9) |
| Hungary | 474 | (5.0) | **19.1** | (4.6) | **30.8** | (6.1) | **22.8** | (9.2) | -8.9 | (14.6) |
| Iceland | 499 | (5.0) | **14.3** | (5.0) | 7.0 | (5.0) | -9.6 | (8.5) | **-28.2** | (13.3) |
| Ireland | 488 | (5.3) | **15.5** | (4.9) | **26.6** | (4.7) | **20.6** | (7.5) | -15.1 | (9.6) |
| Italy | 425 | (4.2) | **29.9** | (4.2) | **51.2** | (5.1) | **51.9** | (5.9) | **48.8** | (7.0) |
| Japan | 486 | (4.5) | **38.9** | (4.0) | **67.6** | (5.0) | **80.1** | (7.6) | **87.2** | (11.1) |
| Korea | 483 | (5.5) | **49.0** | (4.5) | **91.2** | (6.2) | **110.5** | (7.9) | **129.4** | (13.8) |
| Luxembourg | 482 | (4.0) | **17.0** | (4.9) | **10.1** | (5.0) | -13.1 | (8.1) | **-41.4** | (10.5) |
| Mexico | 391 | (5.9) | **16.1** | (5.5) | **30.5** | (6.0) | **19.8** | (6.6) | 9.1 | (7.3) |
| Netherlands | 505 | (5.2) | **36.6** | (4.5) | **44.8** | (5.9) | **26.2** | (8.9) | -27.7 | (20.5) |
| New Zealand | 492 | (3.9) | **35.1** | (4.0) | **51.3** | (5.6) | **46.8** | (7.2) | 25.3 | (15.8) |
| Norway | 468 | (4.4) | **35.4** | (4.6) | **34.0** | (5.5) | 13.7 | (9.8) | -10.9 | (21.7) |
| Poland | 478 | (5.0) | **18.4** | (4.7) | **27.7** | (5.3) | **15.7** | (6.8) | **37.6** | (8.5) |
| Portugal | 443 | (4.7) | **22.4** | (5.2) | **43.7** | (4.9) | **35.4** | (7.5) | 19.5 | (10.4) |
| Slovak Republic | 478 | (5.4) | **21.5** | (5.9) | **24.0** | (6.4) | 15.9 | (8.4) | **32.6** | (12.1) |
| Spain | 444 | (4.4) | **39.2** | (4.2) | **50.8** | (4.6) | **49.9** | (5.8) | **24.9** | (9.4) |
| Sweden | 505 | (3.9) | 4.0 | (3.6) | **-12.9** | (5.7) | **-38.5** | (12.3) | -26.1 | (17.9) |
| Switzerland | 533 | (5.7) | 5.2 | (4.4) | -8.5 | (5.7) | **-39.9** | (8.1) | **-71.9** | (15.4) |
| Turkey | 385 | (4.6) | **33.4** | (5.6) | **54.5** | (6.4) | **69.5** | (9.0) | **78.9** | (10.8) |
| United Kingdom | 450 | (4.7) | **49.8** | (4.8) | **64.6** | (4.6) | **50.1** | (10.4) | **49.5** | (16.3) |
| United States | 458 | (5.4) | **12.3** | (4.6) | **36.0** | (5.2) | **24.5** | (5.9) | 13.7 | (8.6) |
| **OECD average** | **475** | **(5.3)** | **26.9** | **(5.1)** | **36.0** | **(5.7)** | **25.7** | **(8.4)** | 14.8 | (12.9) |
| Argentina | 369 | (9.3) | **21.7** | (7.6) | **37.0** | (8.3) | **22.3** | (10.6) | 8.9 | (14.3) |
| Azerbaijan | 462 | (2.7) | **13.3** | (3.3) | **18.4** | (3.3) | **20.0** | (3.3) | **19.7** | (3.0) |
| Brazil | 349 | (5.5) | **28.7** | (4.7) | **34.2** | (6.4) | **31.6** | (7.8) | **29.1** | (9.4) |
| Bulgaria | 386 | (6.1) | **26.6** | (4.8) | **51.2** | (6.2) | **58.2** | (8.5) | **66.6** | (11.0) |
| Chile | 392 | (5.4) | **24.7** | (4.1) | **32.4** | (5.5) | **26.2** | (7.7) | 14.8 | (9.5) |
| Colombia | 352 | (6.1) | **20.7** | (5.9) | **35.2** | (6.3) | **32.5** | (7.0) | **28.8** | (10.4) |
| Croatia | 462 | (3.3) | 4.2 | (3.5) | **13.3** | (3.8) | **21.4** | (5.3) | 0.0 | (10.8) |
| Estonia | 497 | (5.3) | **21.9** | (5.3) | **27.9** | (5.2) | **12.9** | (5.7) | 5.0 | (7.0) |
| Hong Kong-China | 489 | (7.7) | **52.8** | (8.7) | **77.7** | (8.0) | **85.2** | (9.3) | **95.8** | (9.3) |
| Indonesia | 348 | (7.2) | **42.5** | (6.6) | **56.2** | (6.9) | **41.8** | (7.1) | **31.3** | (9.2) |
| Israel | 464 | (6.6) | -6.2 | (6.7) | **-19.4** | (6.1) | **-23.8** | (8.6) | -11.3 | (9.0) |
| Jordan | 350 | (5.2) | **34.5** | (5.4) | **46.6** | (5.2) | **44.0** | (6.2) | **51.1** | (6.7) |
| Kyrgyzstan | 297 | (5.1) | **26.8** | (4.2) | **32.5** | (5.8) | **41.0** | (6.5) | **26.1** | (5.6) |
| Latvia | 467 | (8.5) | **22.0** | (7.8) | **29.5** | (7.9) | 14.3 | (9.9) | -2.2 | (9.5) |
| Liechtenstein | 489 | (19.4) | **44.1** | (21.2) | 31.4 | (21.7) | c | c | c | c |
| Lithuania | 450 | (3.8) | **39.5** | (3.9) | **55.8** | (4.7) | **54.1** | (6.8) | **46.3** | (10.5) |
| Macao-China | 494 | (3.7) | **26.3** | (4.8) | **49.2** | (5.0) | **48.8** | (6.9) | **59.0** | (7.7) |
| Montenegro | 380 | (4.3) | **20.3** | (4.7) | **38.3** | (5.4) | **39.9** | (6.9) | **37.5** | (8.4) |
| Qatar | 296 | (3.7) | **25.1** | (4.3) | **39.0** | (4.3) | **37.9** | (5.5) | **39.1** | (8.4) |
| Romania | 391 | (5.6) | **17.2** | (5.1) | **40.6** | (6.4) | 33.8 | (7.6) | **52.4** | (8.9) |
| Russian Federation | 439 | (7.8) | **30.3** | (6.5) | **50.6** | (7.1) | **60.2** | (8.9) | **65.1** | (10.3) |
| Serbia | 414 | (4.6) | **27.6** | (4.3) | **33.1** | (4.9) | **38.2** | (6.2) | **24.4** | (9.4) |
| Slovenia | 490 | (4.7) | **15.4** | (5.3) | **25.6** | (6.1) | **25.1** | (7.2) | -2.3 | (8.7) |
| Chinese Taipei | 474 | (5.6) | **67.8** | (3.9) | **119.7** | (5.8) | **134.2** | (7.2) | **144.9** | (7.6) |
| Thailand | 391 | (6.0) | **18.8** | (5.9) | **41.5** | (6.5) | **49.9** | (7.4) | **81.8** | (9.2) |
| Tunisia | 335 | (4.9) | **34.7** | (5.1) | **44.9** | (6.2) | **41.3** | (6.7) | **40.0** | (7.8) |
| Uruguay | 410 | (4.8) | **23.9** | (5.2) | **35.6** | (6.3) | **35.8** | (7.8) | 8.0 | (13.8) |

*Note*: Values that are statistically significant at the 5% level (p < 0.05) are indicated in bold.

[Part 2/2]
## Table 4.8b  Performance in mathematics, by learning time in individual study in mathematics

Difference in mathematics performance between students who spend the following learning hours per week in individual study in mathematics and students who do not spend any time in individual study in mathematics

| | Accounting for socio-economic background of students and schools | | | | | | | | Accounting for socio-economic background of students and schools as well as learning time in regular school lessons and out-of-school-time lessons in mathematics | | | | | | | |
|---|---|---|---|---|---|---|---|---|---|---|---|---|---|---|---|---|
| | Less than 2 hours per week | | 2 hours or more but less than 4 hours per week | | 4 hours or more but less than 6 hours per week | | 6 hours or more per week | | Less than 2 hours per week | | 2 hours or more but less than 4 hours per week | | 4 hours or more but less than 6 hours per week | | 6 hours or more per week | |
| | Dif. | S.E. | Dif. | S.E. | Dif. | S.E. | Dif. | S.E. | Dif. | S.E. | Dif. | S.E. | Dif. | S.E. | Dif. | S.E. |
| **OECD** Australia | **27.7** | (2.6) | **38.3** | (2.9) | **40.8** | (4.0) | **41.8** | (6.8) | **26.9** | (2.8) | **40.3** | (3.1) | **51.0** | (4.2) | **52.8** | (6.6) |
| Austria | 8.4 | (6.1) | -5.5 | (6.8) | **-20.3** | (7.0) | **-50.4** | (10.5) | 3.8 | (6.4) | -9.2 | (7.0) | **-19.6** | (7.5) | **-46.9** | (10.8) |
| Belgium | **28.2** | (3.8) | **34.9** | (4.2) | **14.2** | (4.9) | 11.7 | (9.1) | **21.5** | (4.2) | **22.1** | (4.6) | 9.3 | (6.3) | 6.4 | (7.8) |
| Canada | 3.6 | (3.1) | 2.8 | (3.6) | -0.0 | (4.5) | -6.1 | (5.9) | 5.1 | (3.2) | 6.0 | (3.9) | 6.2 | (4.8) | 1.1 | (6.6) |
| Czech Republic | 4.9 | (3.9) | -8.5 | (5.0) | **-29.6** | (9.2) | **-27.5** | (11.0) | **7.7** | (3.8) | -3.5 | (5.0) | **-21.3** | (9.8) | **-28.3** | (12.0) |
| Denmark | **16.9** | (4.7) | 8.4 | (4.7) | -12.2 | (6.4) | -18.8 | (12.7) | **14.6** | (4.9) | **10.6** | (4.8) | -3.4 | (7.8) | -12.3 | (14.8) |
| Finland | **19.0** | (3.9) | **10.7** | (4.5) | 3.0 | (11.3) | c | c | **18.1** | (3.7) | **15.1** | (4.7) | 18.9 | (11.3) | c | c |
| France | **20.6** | (5.1) | **26.7** | (5.4) | **18.7** | (6.8) | 7.3 | (11.8) | **23.1** | (4.9) | **31.2** | (5.3) | **28.8** | (6.8) | **27.1** | (12.0) |
| Germany | **16.2** | (6.5) | **12.5** | (5.8) | -2.9 | (6.7) | -10.7 | (7.5) | **20.5** | (6.3) | **18.5** | (5.8) | 10.4 | (6.7) | 7.3 | (7.9) |
| Greece | **17.0** | (3.6) | **27.3** | (3.5) | **20.5** | (5.0) | **27.8** | (7.4) | **10.2** | (3.5) | **14.6** | (3.6) | 5.9 | (5.2) | 13.9 | (7.8) |
| Hungary | 2.0 | (3.9) | **8.2** | (4.2) | 2.0 | (6.9) | -10.9 | (9.3) | 5.2 | (4.1) | **10.7** | (4.5) | 6.8 | (7.6) | -3.6 | (9.4) |
| Iceland | **12.0** | (4.7) | 1.7 | (4.7) | -13.6 | (8.4) | **-24.3** | (12.0) | **14.0** | (4.5) | 8.4 | (4.7) | 3.8 | (8.3) | -0.3 | (11.7) |
| Ireland | 7.6 | (4.0) | **13.0** | (4.1) | 10.0 | (6.7) | **-21.9** | (9.4) | **7.7** | (3.8) | **16.7** | (4.0) | **24.4** | (6.0) | 12.7 | (10.2) |
| Italy | **13.5** | (4.3) | **21.2** | (5.0) | **21.0** | (5.5) | **17.6** | (6.1) | 6.4 | (4.2) | 8.3 | (4.9) | 8.1 | (5.4) | 6.0 | (6.3) |
| Japan | **17.9** | (3.4) | **28.6** | (4.7) | **32.3** | (6.8) | **31.3** | (9.9) | **16.9** | (3.3) | **25.5** | (4.2) | **29.0** | (6.3) | **29.4** | (10.0) |
| Korea | **32.0** | (3.9) | **59.9** | (5.1) | **72.1** | (5.2) | **83.9** | (7.1) | **19.9** | (3.9) | **42.0** | (4.7) | **52.8** | (5.3) | **66.2** | (6.7) |
| Luxembourg | **8.4** | (4.2) | -0.1 | (4.4) | **-21.9** | (7.3) | **-38.7** | (9.6) | **8.9** | (3.9) | 5.9 | (4.2) | -6.1 | (7.1) | -12.6 | (9.5) |
| Mexico | **15.2** | (4.6) | **26.3** | (4.5) | **19.0** | (5.2) | **16.6** | (6.5) | 8.1 | (4.7) | **15.7** | (4.7) | 10.6 | (5.5) | 7.4 | (7.1) |
| Netherlands | **12.2** | (5.7) | **12.3** | (4.5) | -4.1 | (7.8) | **-38.5** | (14.6) | 4.9 | (4.2) | 7.6 | (4.6) | -1.3 | (7.8) | **-31.8** | (15.2) |
| New Zealand | **22.5** | (3.8) | **29.4** | (5.2) | **24.6** | (6.4) | 17.4 | (14.1) | **26.1** | (3.9) | **38.9** | (5.2) | **46.0** | (6.4) | **52.4** | (14.9) |
| Norway | **30.4** | (4.3) | **25.0** | (5.2) | 2.5 | (8.7) | -20.2 | (18.7) | **31.1** | (4.6) | **36.4** | (5.8) | **24.0** | (8.5) | 17.1 | (18.5) |
| Poland | **15.9** | (4.4) | **22.6** | (4.8) | **14.4** | (6.7) | **29.1** | (7.3) | **9.3** | (4.2) | **12.7** | (4.7) | 6.3 | (6.3) | **25.5** | (7.2) |
| Portugal | **23.5** | (4.9) | **36.0** | (4.6) | **26.1** | (7.0) | 15.8 | (8.4) | **22.1** | (6.2) | **26.9** | (6.1) | 17.6 | (9.0) | 6.9 | (9.1) |
| Slovak Republic | 10.0 | (5.5) | 6.5 | (4.7) | -6.4 | (7.9) | 9.0 | (10.2) | 7.0 | (5.1) | 2.9 | (5.8) | -7.4 | (7.7) | 16.1 | (9.5) |
| Spain | **29.3** | (4.1) | **39.5** | (4.4) | **35.7** | (5.3) | 16.8 | (8.6) | **24.4** | (4.2) | **31.0** | (4.1) | **28.2** | (5.3) | **17.9** | (8.8) |
| Sweden | 0.3 | (3.5) | **-17.5** | (5.4) | **-50.1** | (10.8) | -26.0 | (15.8) | 5.3 | (3.5) | 1.7 | (5.8) | -10.1 | (10.2) | 8.1 | (18.5) |
| Switzerland | 3.4 | (3.8) | -7.4 | (4.7) | **-32.9** | (6.7) | **-57.8** | (14.1) | 2.3 | (4.1) | -5.4 | (5.0) | **-19.3** | (6.8) | **-32.3** | (14.7) |
| Turkey | **27.4** | (4.6) | **37.7** | (4.9) | **50.2** | (6.1) | **55.4** | (7.0) | **13.9** | (4.8) | **14.5** | (5.5) | **21.8** | (6.9) | **20.6** | (7.3) |
| United Kingdom | **35.4** | (4.1) | **39.4** | (5.3) | **31.7** | (6.9) | **34.8** | (13.4) | **35.8** | (4.2) | **45.4** | (4.1) | **48.6** | (6.4) | **56.3** | (14.4) |
| United States | 3.8 | (3.8) | **16.6** | (4.2) | 9.2 | (5.4) | -1.9 | (7.4) | 6.4 | (3.8) | **14.8** | (4.6) | 8.5 | (6.1) | 1.4 | (7.9) |
| **OECD average** | **16.2** | (4.3) | **18.2** | (4.8) | 8.5 | (7.0) | 2.2 | (10.6) | **14.2** | (4.4) | **16.9** | (4.9) | 12.6 | (7.2) | 9.8 | (11.0) |
| **Partners** Argentina | **16.0** | (8.0) | **24.7** | (9.2) | **22.7** | (9.2) | 11.5 | (12.6) | 9.2 | (6.7) | 12.5 | (8.2) | 10.0 | (8.5) | 0.7 | (12.4) |
| Azerbaijan | **13.2** | (3.3) | **18.3** | (3.3) | **19.7** | (3.4) | **19.1** | (3.2) | **8.3** | (3.3) | **10.3** | (3.2) | **10.8** | (3.5) | **10.2** | (3.2) |
| Brazil | **16.8** | (4.3) | **18.1** | (4.8) | **19.1** | (6.2) | 13.4 | (8.3) | **12.5** | (4.5) | 8.7 | (5.0) | 7.3 | (6.4) | -1.4 | (8.8) |
| Bulgaria | **15.1** | (4.5) | **23.2** | (4.7) | **25.0** | (6.2) | **30.6** | (8.1) | **11.9** | (4.9) | **13.5** | (4.9) | **15.4** | (6.4) | **18.4** | (8.2) |
| Chile | **14.1** | (3.4) | **18.8** | (3.5) | **11.8** | (5.9) | 13.1 | (8.6) | **8.6** | (3.3) | **10.2** | (3.7) | 1.9 | (5.5) | 3.8 | (8.7) |
| Colombia | **22.2** | (5.0) | **32.4** | (5.7) | **30.8** | (7.4) | **32.3** | (8.6) | **18.3** | (4.3) | **25.9** | (5.4) | **25.4** | (7.0) | **24.2** | (8.9) |
| Croatia | **7.2** | (3.4) | **8.8** | (3.8) | 8.2 | (5.2) | -2.5 | (7.5) | **7.6** | (3.4) | **9.6** | (4.0) | **12.6** | (5.2) | 6.3 | (7.5) |
| Estonia | **16.8** | (4.6) | **20.0** | (4.6) | 5.1 | (5.7) | -4.5 | (7.0) | **14.5** | (4.5) | **17.9** | (4.4) | 9.0 | (4.9) | 3.7 | (6.5) |
| Hong Kong-China | **36.0** | (6.9) | **53.6** | (5.7) | **61.0** | (7.4) | **73.8** | (8.3) | **28.8** | (7.2) | **44.4** | (6.3) | **53.6** | (7.2) | **62.2** | (8.4) |
| Indonesia | **35.4** | (5.5) | **44.2** | (5.7) | **37.8** | (6.8) | **30.7** | (8.4) | **21.2** | (4.8) | **25.2** | (5.3) | **19.8** | (5.6) | **15.3** | (6.9) |
| Israel | -7.8 | (6.0) | **-17.9** | (6.2) | **-19.7** | (8.3) | -14.8 | (8.8) | -4.6 | (5.7) | **-15.0** | (6.2) | **-16.8** | (8.5) | -7.7 | (10.2) |
| Jordan | **28.1** | (4.7) | **36.3** | (4.4) | **33.8** | (5.0) | **41.5** | (6.0) | **18.5** | (4.5) | **21.9** | (4.3) | **18.2** | (5.0) | **24.8** | (6.1) |
| Kyrgyzstan | **21.4** | (3.9) | **26.8** | (4.8) | **35.6** | (5.4) | **32.3** | (4.9) | **15.9** | (3.9) | **19.2** | (4.9) | **24.9** | (5.8) | **20.0** | (4.7) |
| Latvia | **18.9** | (6.2) | **22.2** | (6.4) | 6.5 | (8.3) | -6.9 | (9.0) | **12.2** | (6.1) | 12.1 | (6.4) | -4.8 | (8.2) | **-19.4** | (8.7) |
| Liechtenstein | 21.3 | (16.0) | 17.1 | (17.4) | c | c | c | c | 17.8 | (16.8) | 16.6 | (18.0) | c | c | c | c |
| Lithuania | **26.5** | (3.5) | **36.2** | (4.1) | **35.4** | (6.2) | **31.0** | (9.3) | **15.5** | (3.6) | **21.3** | (4.3) | **25.4** | (6.0) | **20.3** | (8.3) |
| Macao-China | **23.0** | (4.9) | **41.1** | (5.0) | **38.4** | (6.9) | **48.0** | (7.8) | **23.8** | (4.7) | **37.6** | (5.0) | **38.9** | (6.5) | **46.1** | (7.8) |
| Montenegro | **20.3** | (4.4) | **33.1** | (5.2) | **36.4** | (6.4) | **36.1** | (7.7) | **15.6** | (4.3) | **22.9** | (5.2) | **30.0** | (6.4) | **30.8** | (7.4) |
| Qatar | **20.6** | (3.9) | **30.9** | (4.2) | **31.0** | (5.3) | **31.4** | (7.7) | **18.3** | (4.3) | **23.4** | (4.5) | **19.0** | (5.6) | **23.2** | (7.6) |
| Romania | **13.4** | (5.5) | **25.9** | (6.6) | **23.8** | (8.3) | **31.0** | (6.3) | 9.2 | (5.1) | **18.1** | (6.6) | **19.0** | (9.2) | **28.9** | (7.2) |
| Russian Federation | **18.8** | (6.0) | **35.3** | (6.8) | **43.2** | (8.0) | **49.6** | (10.6) | 6.9 | (5.6) | **14.8** | (6.3) | **16.0** | (7.1) | 17.6 | (10.7) |
| Serbia | **16.6** | (3.8) | **16.4** | (4.4) | **16.7** | (5.4) | 2.8 | (7.5) | **17.8** | (4.0) | **16.2** | (4.8) | **17.4** | (6.1) | 7.1 | (8.1) |
| Slovenia | 4.3 | (4.1) | -1.3 | (4.4) | -3.3 | (5.9) | **-15.2** | (7.6) | **8.1** | (4.1) | 6.4 | (4.6) | 8.4 | (6.2) | 2.4 | (8.5) |
| Chinese Taipei | **46.5** | (3.1) | **77.3** | (3.7) | **82.1** | (4.7) | **92.1** | (6.1) | **37.0** | (2.9) | **53.7** | (3.6) | **57.2** | (4.9) | **67.9** | (6.1) |
| Thailand | **17.8** | (5.5) | **35.0** | (6.0) | **39.9** | (7.0) | **66.1** | (9.0) | **17.0** | (5.2) | **26.5** | (5.4) | **24.3** | (6.5) | **41.1** | (8.3) |
| Tunisia | **25.5** | (4.6) | **31.5** | (4.9) | **28.7** | (5.5) | **29.7** | (6.7) | **20.0** | (4.4) | **19.5** | (5.1) | **15.1** | (5.6) | **17.2** | (6.8) |
| Uruguay | **10.1** | (4.9) | **15.0** | (5.5) | 14.9 | (8.0) | 14.5 | (13.5) | 5.7 | (5.1) | 9.6 | (5.6) | 14.1 | (8.7) | 11.2 | (14.6) |

*Note*: Values that are statistically significant at the 5% level (p < 0.05) are indicated in bold.

© OECP 2011 Quality Time for Students: Learning In and Out of School

## Table 4.8c Performance in reading, by learning time in individual study on the language of instruction
[Part 1/2]

| | | Reading performance for students who do not spend any time in individual study on the language of instruction | | Difference in reading performance between students who spend the following learning hours per week in individual study on the language of instruction and students who do not spend any time in individual study on the language of instruction | | | | | | | |
| | | | | Less than 2 hours per week | | 2 hours or more but less than 4 hours per week | | 4 hours or more but less than 6 hours per week | | 6 hours or more per week | |
| | | Mean score | S.E. | Dif. | S.E. | Dif. | S.E. | Dif. | S.E. | Dif. | S.E. |
|---|---|---|---|---|---|---|---|---|---|---|---|
| OECD | Australia | 475 | (3.1) | **43.3** | (2.9) | **54.9** | (3.6) | **41.2** | (5.2) | **24.9** | (8.8) |
| | Austria | 493 | (5.3) | 14.8 | (5.3) | -14.3 | (6.9) | **-45.9** | (10.5) | **-105.2** | (15.3) |
| | Belgium | 470 | (6.2) | **51.9** | (6.0) | **42.4** | (6.2) | -3.2 | (13.2) | -4.8 | (16.6) |
| | Canada | 514 | (3.0) | **16.9** | (3.0) | **26.6** | (3.8) | **28.1** | (5.5) | **14.0** | (7.3) |
| | Czech Republic | 473 | (6.4) | **27.4** | (5.6) | 13.4 | (6.9) | -13.2 | (16.7) | -7.5 | (26.6) |
| | Denmark | 465 | (6.8) | **28.6** | (7.1) | **43.0** | (6.8) | **31.3** | (8.3) | **30.9** | (11.5) |
| | Finland | 520 | (4.0) | **33.0** | (3.8) | **39.8** | (6.3) | **29.9** | (12.3) | **51.1** | (19.1) |
| | France | 454 | (6.3) | **37.8** | (5.5) | **62.4** | (6.1) | **58.0** | (10.1) | 33.5 | (28.4) |
| | Germany | 497 | (7.2) | **21.0** | (6.2) | 13.4 | (7.4) | -12.4 | (9.1) | **-47.4** | (9.8) |
| | Greece | 444 | (5.4) | **19.7** | (4.9) | **25.0** | (4.9) | **29.6** | (6.2) | **28.6** | (9.3) |
| | Hungary | 453 | (6.6) | **31.4** | (6.4) | **43.1** | (7.3) | **41.2** | (8.8) | 16.2 | (14.1) |
| | Iceland | 460 | (5.2) | **35.9** | (5.4) | **30.2** | (5.9) | -10.3 | (10.3) | -24.7 | (21.2) |
| | Ireland | 509 | (5.5) | **11.9** | (5.1) | **22.3** | (5.9) | 3.1 | (6.9) | **-23.6** | (10.4) |
| | Italy | 416 | (6.8) | **43.7** | (6.1) | **63.9** | (6.7) | **70.0** | (7.2) | c | c |
| | Japan | 473 | (4.6) | **40.4** | (4.0) | **39.6** | (6.4) | **49.6** | (14.1) | **74.3** | (21.4) |
| | Korea | 518 | (6.0) | **44.9** | (4.9) | **63.1** | (5.8) | **68.3** | (8.1) | **74.2** | (12.5) |
| | Luxembourg | 477 | (3.9) | **16.1** | (4.2) | -5.8 | (5.4) | **-54.5** | (8.8) | **-58.2** | (15.1) |
| | Mexico | 392 | (7.0) | **23.8** | (6.3) | **30.5** | (7.0) | **19.3** | (7.9) | 6.7 | (9.5) |
| | Netherlands | 494 | (6.3) | **28.7** | (5.5) | 10.3 | (6.0) | **-32.0** | (11.0) | -4.0 | (20.4) |
| | New Zealand | 492 | (5.1) | **42.1** | (5.1) | **41.7** | (6.6) | 18.4 | (9.9) | 9.1 | (12.6) |
| | Norway | 456 | (5.1) | **45.6** | (5.5) | **44.0** | (7.0) | **30.3** | (10.2) | -22.0 | (12.7) |
| | Poland | 474 | (6.0) | **32.0** | (5.9) | **45.1** | (6.3) | **47.3** | (6.6) | **39.0** | (10.3) |
| | Portugal | 443 | (8.8) | **36.7** | (7.0) | **32.1** | (8.1) | **29.5** | (9.9) | 7.3 | (18.1) |
| | Slovak Republic | 431 | (5.3) | **43.1** | (5.3) | **52.5** | (6.1) | **49.5** | (8.5) | **50.4** | (13.2) |
| | Spain | 424 | (4.0) | **42.4** | (4.2) | **49.4** | (4.5) | **48.4** | (6.0) | **34.5** | (9.7) |
| | Sweden | 493 | (6.1) | **25.2** | (5.7) | **16.9** | (5.9) | 1.3 | (10.6) | -29.1 | (25.6) |
| | Switzerland | 493 | (5.0) | **14.7** | (4.5) | -0.8 | (5.6) | **-46.3** | (10.4) | **-80.8** | (15.6) |
| | Turkey | 450 | (9.7) | 1.7 | (6.9) | -0.5 | (9.1) | 3.1 | (9.8) | -3.8 | (13.2) |
| | United Kingdom | 447 | (5.3) | **52.5** | (5.2) | **73.5** | (6.1) | **53.7** | (10.9) | **58.4** | (23.0) |
| | United States | m | m | m | m | m | m | m | m | m | m |
| | **OECD average** | 469 | (5.9) | **31.3** | (5.4) | **33.0** | (6.3) | 18.4 | (9.8) | 5.1 | (16.4) |
| Partners | Argentina | 362 | (12.0) | **25.4** | (9.5) | **37.3** | (10.6) | 27.0 | (19.0) | -43.3 | (17.0) |
| | Azerbaijan | 347 | (6.0) | 8.0 | (4.8) | **12.9** | (5.3) | **18.4** | (5.5) | **19.2** | (5.6) |
| | Brazil | 379 | (6.7) | **28.5** | (5.0) | **28.2** | (7.4) | -3.9 | (8.8) | -13.7 | (14.0) |
| | Bulgaria | 363 | (7.7) | **43.0** | (6.9) | **67.7** | (7.5) | **70.6** | (10.1) | **74.3** | (13.8) |
| | Chile | 440 | (6.8) | 7.6 | (5.3) | **13.3** | (6.1) | 4.2 | (8.4) | -19.8 | (14.1) |
| | Colombia | 376 | (6.9) | **17.1** | (6.6) | **19.2** | (6.2) | 12.4 | (10.9) | -8.3 | (18.4) |
| | Croatia | 472 | (4.1) | **8.0** | (3.6) | **11.9** | (4.9) | **19.4** | (7.1) | -22.6 | (13.1) |
| | Estonia | 476 | (4.2) | **31.9** | (4.7) | **36.6** | (4.9) | 12.4 | (7.7) | 11.3 | (11.7) |
| | Hong Kong-China | 517 | (6.4) | **23.9** | (6.6) | **25.6** | (6.8) | **28.3** | (7.5) | 10.0 | (12.4) |
| | Indonesia | 359 | (12.1) | **38.9** | (9.8) | **36.8** | (10.9) | 22.6 | (13.4) | -0.0 | (15.5) |
| | Israel | 455 | (5.5) | 9.6 | (5.1) | -14.7 | (7.2) | **-35.5** | (8.5) | **-39.0** | (12.0) |
| | Jordan | 375 | (6.9) | **35.2** | (6.9) | **36.7** | (6.9) | **32.4** | (7.2) | **27.8** | (8.7) |
| | Kyrgyzstan | 258 | (4.5) | **40.0** | (4.9) | **47.8** | (6.8) | **51.7** | (6.2) | **62.6** | (6.5) |
| | Latvia | 451 | (12.3) | **35.7** | (10.6) | **31.8** | (12.0) | 21.2 | (12.9) | 22.2 | (16.2) |
| | Liechtenstein | 498 | (15.9) | 24.1 | (18.4) | -15.8 | (22.9) | c | c | c | c |
| | Lithuania | 433 | (4.4) | **40.5** | (4.6) | **57.5** | (5.8) | **48.4** | (7.0) | **35.8** | (11.7) |
| | Macao-China | 480 | (2.8) | **20.4** | (3.5) | **13.8** | (4.5) | 4.8 | (6.7) | -10.7 | (12.8) |
| | Montenegro | 365 | (4.5) | **30.2** | (5.2) | **47.0** | (5.6) | **58.1** | (7.5) | **23.1** | (8.0) |
| | Qatar | 296 | (4.5) | **30.0** | (4.9) | **31.8** | (5.0) | **28.8** | (8.1) | -6.7 | (8.7) |
| | Romania | 352 | (7.7) | **37.5** | (6.3) | **60.9** | (6.8) | **75.8** | (7.7) | **74.0** | (8.2) |
| | Russian Federation | 424 | (7.6) | **24.1** | (6.9) | 14.3 | (7.1) | 13.8 | (8.7) | -18.5 | (20.1) |
| | Serbia | 380 | (4.5) | **29.9** | (4.1) | **30.0** | (4.9) | **29.9** | (6.2) | **24.8** | (9.3) |
| | Slovenia | 481 | (3.6) | **19.8** | (4.2) | **24.9** | (4.9) | 13.6 | (7.4) | 1.0 | (12.4) |
| | Chinese Taipei | 446 | (5.1) | **49.8** | (3.6) | **76.7** | (4.7) | **78.0** | (7.3) | **74.3** | (7.3) |
| | Thailand | 407 | (5.1) | **12.2** | (4.7) | 9.7 | (6.0) | 10.8 | (7.5) | 3.0 | (9.5) |
| | Tunisia | 378 | (6.2) | **15.6** | (5.6) | -0.7 | (6.0) | 0.5 | (8.0) | 1.1 | (8.5) |
| | Uruguay | 395 | (6.4) | **32.6** | (6.3) | **44.2** | (7.4) | 25.2 | (16.3) | 17.2 | (18.7) |

*Note*: Values that are statistically significant at the 5% level (p < 0.05) are indicated in bold.

### Table 4.8c Performance in reading, by learning time in individual study on the language of instruction
[Part 2/2]

| | Difference in reading performance between students who spend the following learning hours per week in individual study on the language of instruction and students who do not spend any time in individual study on the language of instruction | | | | | | | | | | | | | | | |
| --- | --- | --- | --- | --- | --- | --- | --- | --- | --- | --- | --- | --- | --- | --- | --- | --- |
| | Accounting for socio-economic background of students and schools | | | | | | | | Accounting for socio-economic background of students and schools as well as learning time in regular school lessons and out-of-school-time lessons on the language of instruction | | | | | | | |
| | Less than 2 hours per week | | 2 hours or more but less than 4 hours per week | | 4 hours or more but less than 6 hours per week | | 6 hours or more per week | | Less than 2 hours per week | | 2 hours or more but less than 4 hours per week | | 4 hours or more but less than 6 hours per week | | 6 hours or more per week | |
| | Dif. | S.E. | Dif. | S.E. | Dif. | S.E. | Dif. | S.E. | Dif. | S.E. | Dif. | S.E. | Dif. | S.E. | Dif. | S.E. |
| **OECD** | | | | | | | | | | | | | | | | |
| Australia | 29.9 | (3.0) | 35.1 | (3.3) | 23.0 | (5.0) | 9.3 | (8.2) | 31.1 | (3.0) | 40.2 | (3.3) | 43.2 | (5.2) | 35.7 | (8.2) |
| Austria | 4.5 | (4.1) | -17.0 | (5.0) | -31.4 | (7.5) | -70.3 | (14.5) | 2.0 | (4.2) | -14.8 | (5.3) | -21.1 | (7.9) | -53.3 | (14.2) |
| Belgium | 25.9 | (5.0) | 17.7 | (5.4) | -17.2 | (10.1) | -10.4 | (17.4) | 24.7 | (4.3) | 20.7 | (5.1) | -2.5 | (10.9) | 23.9 | (18.0) |
| Canada | 10.1 | (2.7) | 12.8 | (3.8) | 13.9 | (4.7) | -1.0 | (7.4) | 15.2 | (2.7) | 20.0 | (4.1) | 29.2 | (5.0) | 10.8 | (8.5) |
| Czech Republic | 23.9 | (4.3) | 15.9 | (6.2) | -4.0 | (15.1) | -19.6 | (17.8) | 25.2 | (4.5) | 19.5 | (5.8) | 2.6 | (15.2) | -25.3 | (20.4) |
| Denmark | 24.0 | (6.7) | 34.7 | (6.7) | 25.6 | (7.7) | 31.0 | (11.6) | 22.9 | (6.7) | 35.6 | (6.8) | 28.7 | (8.6) | 30.7 | (12.1) |
| Finland | 29.7 | (3.6) | 35.5 | (5.9) | 24.8 | (12.1) | 47.9 | (18.3) | 30.1 | (3.5) | 44.4 | (5.4) | 42.0 | (12.0) | 71.2 | (16.2) |
| France | 22.7 | (4.7) | 33.8 | (4.9) | 33.4 | (8.5) | 4.4 | (24.5) | 24.4 | (4.6) | 36.6 | (5.0) | 44.8 | (8.2) | 27.4 | (21.9) |
| Germany | 15.9 | (5.4) | 13.3 | (5.8) | -2.2 | (6.8) | -24.4 | (10.4) | 18.2 | (5.8) | 18.3 | (6.2) | 12.0 | (7.2) | -12.6 | (10.4) |
| Greece | 15.4 | (4.1) | 17.5 | (4.4) | 22.2 | (5.1) | 19.7 | (8.3) | 7.5 | (4.4) | 2.4 | (4.5) | 3.8 | (6.1) | -2.7 | (8.8) |
| Hungary | 16.7 | (5.1) | 23.6 | (6.0) | 20.2 | (7.3) | 10.3 | (10.5) | 11.7 | (5.1) | 17.2 | (5.7) | 13.0 | (6.6) | 0.6 | (10.4) |
| Iceland | 33.6 | (5.3) | 27.0 | (5.9) | -8.2 | (10.3) | -22.4 | (19.7) | 31.1 | (5.1) | 29.0 | (5.6) | 10.1 | (9.0) | 10.7 | (19.5) |
| Ireland | 7.7 | (4.7) | 14.4 | (5.6) | -4.6 | (6.2) | -23.5 | (10.1) | 9.5 | (4.6) | 20.0 | (5.6) | 19.1 | (6.5) | 15.2 | (9.1) |
| Italy | 28.1 | (6.9) | 34.8 | (7.2) | 33.8 | (7.7) | c | c | 24.9 | (4.6) | 26.7 | (6.4) | 27.4 | (6.5) | c | c |
| Japan | 22.5 | (4.0) | 17.7 | (5.5) | 15.5 | (12.2) | 33.1 | (20.0) | 24.9 | (4.1) | 25.0 | (5.7) | 33.3 | (11.6) | 41.0 | (16.8) |
| Korea | 29.4 | (3.9) | 38.3 | (4.3) | 40.8 | (6.0) | 39.5 | (9.6) | 21.1 | (3.7) | 26.6 | (4.2) | 28.8 | (6.1) | 31.5 | (9.5) |
| Luxembourg | 12.4 | (3.7) | 1.1 | (4.5) | -33.0 | (7.7) | -40.0 | (14.0) | 14.0 | (3.8) | 12.1 | (4.8) | -2.7 | (8.2) | -8.6 | (14.9) |
| Mexico | 22.8 | (5.6) | 28.6 | (6.3) | 20.9 | (7.2) | 16.3 | (8.1) | 16.4 | (6.7) | 20.4 | (7.7) | 17.1 | (8.6) | 14.7 | (10.0) |
| Netherlands | 15.3 | (4.1) | 8.1 | (4.7) | -12.9 | (9.7) | -2.9 | (13.3) | 20.7 | (4.4) | 21.0 | (5.1) | 10.7 | (9.6) | 26.5 | (13.7) |
| New Zealand | 26.2 | (4.9) | 21.1 | (6.1) | 1.8 | (9.2) | -9.4 | (10.7) | 30.6 | (4.7) | 34.3 | (5.7) | 36.3 | (8.5) | 46.4 | (12.4) |
| Norway | 40.5 | (5.1) | 35.3 | (6.6) | 16.0 | (9.5) | -29.1 | (12.7) | 37.0 | (5.1) | 41.3 | (6.6) | 29.8 | (9.2) | 5.3 | (17.6) |
| Poland | 28.7 | (5.2) | 40.4 | (5.6) | 42.6 | (6.2) | 37.2 | (9.2) | 20.1 | (5.2) | 27.2 | (5.5) | 33.5 | (6.1) | 32.8 | (9.3) |
| Portugal | 32.5 | (6.3) | 29.7 | (6.7) | 26.7 | (8.5) | 16.5 | (13.5) | 27.5 | (5.8) | 24.8 | (6.1) | 32.3 | (7.9) | 17.2 | (12.6) |
| Slovak Republic | 30.7 | (4.6) | 40.2 | (5.4) | 37.1 | (7.6) | 41.1 | (11.7) | 26.0 | (4.6) | 35.3 | (6.0) | 35.5 | (8.4) | 43.5 | (11.8) |
| Spain | 33.9 | (3.8) | 41.3 | (4.0) | 40.6 | (5.9) | 28.1 | (9.1) | 27.8 | (3.9) | 32.8 | (4.0) | 34.5 | (5.4) | 28.4 | (8.1) |
| Sweden | 22.0 | (5.9) | 10.8 | (5.9) | -7.2 | (9.7) | -43.6 | (23.8) | 28.6 | (5.9) | 29.2 | (6.6) | 27.0 | (8.3) | 5.4 | (21.1) |
| Switzerland | 14.9 | (4.3) | 2.3 | (4.7) | -36.0 | (9.9) | -58.9 | (13.8) | 15.9 | (4.1) | 13.4 | (4.7) | -8.1 | (8.2) | -17.0 | (14.9) |
| Turkey | 10.5 | (4.8) | 14.4 | (5.6) | 21.1 | (6.7) | 14.3 | (10.1) | 8.7 | (4.7) | 10.6 | (5.4) | 14.9 | (6.1) | 8.1 | (10.2) |
| United Kingdom | 37.1 | (4.8) | 46.4 | (5.3) | 34.3 | (9.6) | 38.3 | (18.7) | 39.2 | (4.5) | 55.5 | (5.3) | 57.8 | (8.7) | 66.9 | (19.1) |
| United States | m | m | m | m | m | m | m | m | m | m | m | m | m | m | m | m |
| **OECD average** | **23.0** | **(4.8)** | **23.3** | **(5.5)** | **11.6** | **(8.6)** | **1.1** | **(14.3)** | **22.0** | **(4.8)** | **25.0** | **(5.5)** | **21.9** | **(8.4)** | **16.9** | **(14.2)** |
| **Partners** | | | | | | | | | | | | | | | | |
| Argentina | 20.5 | (7.0) | 27.9 | (9.9) | 24.8 | (13.9) | -36.3 | (16.1) | 15.4 | (7.1) | 20.4 | (10.2) | 24.0 | (14.6) | -20.1 | (16.0) |
| Azerbaijan | 9.9 | (4.3) | 14.4 | (4.8) | 16.7 | (5.4) | 18.6 | (5.8) | 2.3 | (4.9) | 3.7 | (5.2) | 5.5 | (6.2) | 7.7 | (6.5) |
| Brazil | 18.8 | (4.1) | 19.6 | (5.5) | -5.5 | (6.9) | -11.5 | (11.7) | 15.1 | (4.0) | 12.7 | (5.1) | -10.6 | (7.6) | -17.1 | (11.0) |
| Bulgaria | 23.6 | (5.6) | 30.9 | (5.9) | 34.0 | (8.3) | 39.8 | (9.8) | 22.8 | (5.7) | 28.2 | (6.2) | 35.2 | (8.4) | 45.2 | (10.4) |
| Chile | 10.4 | (4.9) | 15.5 | (5.6) | 12.3 | (8.2) | -6.9 | (12.5) | 10.1 | (5.0) | 18.6 | (5.7) | 20.7 | (9.2) | 1.2 | (13.5) |
| Colombia | 12.8 | (6.1) | 12.9 | (5.9) | 7.2 | (11.2) | -3.9 | (17.7) | 13.6 | (5.7) | 13.5 | (6.7) | 13.4 | (11.2) | 1.5 | (18.4) |
| Croatia | 12.7 | (3.3) | 13.5 | (3.9) | 15.5 | (5.5) | -16.7 | (10.6) | 11.0 | (3.3) | 16.6 | (3.8) | 23.4 | (5.5) | 0.6 | (10.1) |
| Estonia | 28.7 | (5.2) | 34.2 | (5.5) | 14.6 | (7.7) | 11.3 | (11.4) | 28.1 | (4.9) | 34.4 | (5.4) | 20.7 | (8.2) | 30.4 | (11.6) |
| Hong Kong-China | 16.8 | (5.6) | 19.3 | (5.7) | 24.5 | (6.5) | 12.1 | (11.8) | 17.3 | (5.2) | 20.9 | (5.6) | 31.8 | (6.2) | 19.4 | (10.6) |
| Indonesia | 32.2 | (7.9) | 29.5 | (8.7) | 25.7 | (10.0) | 12.2 | (14.7) | 23.5 | (7.0) | 20.3 | (7.4) | 20.6 | (9.0) | 5.6 | (12.6) |
| Israel | 8.5 | (4.9) | -9.2 | (7.6) | -26.1 | (8.1) | -34.8 | (12.7) | 7.1 | (5.1) | -3.1 | (7.5) | -11.5 | (9.4) | -25.4 | (15.1) |
| Jordan | 32.3 | (6.2) | 34.6 | (6.1) | 33.3 | (6.6) | 31.5 | (7.9) | 23.8 | (6.5) | 22.1 | (6.3) | 21.2 | (7.1) | 16.4 | (8.2) |
| Kyrgyzstan | 27.5 | (5.0) | 38.3 | (6.5) | 43.3 | (6.3) | 61.4 | (6.9) | 15.8 | (5.1) | 23.6 | (6.9) | 26.5 | (6.5) | 43.0 | (7.6) |
| Latvia | 34.9 | (7.5) | 30.6 | (8.5) | 21.1 | (9.4) | 18.7 | (12.1) | 30.8 | (7.5) | 26.8 | (8.5) | 17.2 | (9.5) | 17.6 | (12.8) |
| Liechtenstein | 12.9 | (15.7) | -14.9 | (18.5) | c | c | c | c | 12.9 | (15.7) | -6.8 | (19.6) | c | c | c | c |
| Lithuania | 27.5 | (4.4) | 43.0 | (5.5) | 35.1 | (6.5) | 28.8 | (10.2) | 21.0 | (4.6) | 31.4 | (5.6) | 30.2 | (7.0) | 31.5 | (12.0) |
| Macao-China | 17.8 | (3.5) | 9.7 | (4.5) | -1.1 | (6.7) | -16.3 | (13.2) | 20.2 | (3.6) | 15.8 | (4.7) | 13.7 | (7.0) | 0.5 | (10.8) |
| Montenegro | 21.8 | (4.6) | 33.4 | (4.7) | 44.8 | (6.8) | 19.1 | (7.6) | 11.7 | (4.5) | 19.4 | (5.7) | 29.7 | (7.3) | 17.2 | (9.2) |
| Qatar | 26.7 | (4.7) | 29.4 | (4.9) | 28.8 | (7.8) | -2.7 | (8.4) | 26.5 | (5.2) | 26.9 | (5.1) | 17.6 | (8.3) | -6.2 | (8.8) |
| Romania | 30.9 | (5.4) | 46.9 | (5.8) | 62.6 | (6.7) | 58.9 | (7.6) | 21.2 | (5.8) | 33.7 | (6.5) | 50.3 | (7.8) | 47.5 | (8.6) |
| Russian Federation | 13.5 | (6.1) | 5.7 | (5.8) | 7.3 | (8.8) | -31.8 | (17.8) | 7.1 | (5.8) | 5.0 | (5.4) | 10.0 | (8.7) | -26.9 | (17.8) |
| Serbia | 18.3 | (3.5) | 18.9 | (4.1) | 13.3 | (5.7) | 12.0 | (7.7) | 21.7 | (3.5) | 24.8 | (4.2) | 22.2 | (6.4) | 30.2 | (8.6) |
| Slovenia | 13.9 | (3.4) | 15.9 | (3.7) | 18.7 | (6.5) | 5.2 | (10.6) | 13.9 | (3.6) | 17.3 | (3.8) | 17.6 | (7.4) | 3.9 | (9.4) |
| Chinese Taipei | 31.0 | (3.3) | 46.4 | (3.9) | 49.5 | (6.2) | 46.2 | (7.0) | 29.9 | (3.1) | 38.6 | (3.7) | 42.9 | (6.1) | 39.9 | (7.5) |
| Thailand | 18.0 | (3.9) | 20.8 | (4.4) | 25.5 | (5.9) | 22.5 | (9.4) | 22.6 | (3.7) | 28.8 | (4.5) | 39.0 | (5.5) | 32.4 | (8.9) |
| Tunisia | 20.8 | (4.6) | 14.5 | (5.2) | 19.7 | (7.0) | 20.3 | (7.0) | 14.2 | (4.6) | 9.3 | (5.1) | 15.0 | (6.8) | 15.8 | (7.9) |
| Uruguay | 20.9 | (5.6) | 33.1 | (6.6) | 21.5 | (14.8) | 22.4 | (16.8) | 11.5 | (6.1) | 21.3 | (7.3) | 16.5 | (14.8) | 31.1 | (23.3) |

*Note:* Values that are statistically significant at the 5% level (p < 0.05) are indicated in bold.

© OECD 2011 Quality Time for Students: Learning In and Out of School

# ORGANISATION FOR ECONOMIC CO-OPERATION AND DEVELOPMENT

The OECD is a unique forum where governments work together to address the economic, social and environmental challenges of globalisation. The OECD is also at the forefront of efforts to understand and to help governments respond to new developments and concerns, such as corporate governance, the information economy and the challenges of an ageing population. The Organisation provides a setting where governments can compare policy experiences, seek answers to common problems, identify good practice and work to co-ordinate domestic and international policies.

The OECD member countries are: Australia, Austria, Belgium, Canada, Chile, the Czech Republic, Denmark, Estonia, Finland, France, Germany, Greece, Hungary, Iceland, Ireland, Israel, Italy, Japan, Korea, Luxembourg, Mexico, the Netherlands, New Zealand, Norway, Poland, Portugal, the Slovak Republic, Slovenia, Spain, Sweden, Switzerland, Turkey, the United Kingdom and the United States. The European Commission takes part in the work of the OECD.

OECD Publishing disseminates widely the results of the Organisation's statistics gathering and research on economic, social and environmental issues, as well as the conventions, guidelines and standards agreed by its members.

OECD PUBLISHING, 2, rue André-Pascal, 75775 PARIS CEDEX 16
(98 2010 05 1 P) ISBN 978-92-64-08754-5 – No. 57485 2011

3  2044  118  365  782